PRINCIPLES OF
ECONOMICS

SECOND EDITION

ROBERT H. FRANK
Cornell University

BEN S. BERNANKE
Princeton University

Boston   Burr Ridge, IL   Dubuque, IA   Madison, WI   New York   San Francisco   St. Louis
Bangkok   Bogotá   Caracas   Kuala Lumpur   Lisbon   London   Madrid   Mexico City
Milan   Montreal   New Delhi   Santiago   Seoul   Singapore   Sydney   Taipei   Toronto

The McGraw·Hill Companies

 Irwin

PRINCIPLES OF ECONOMICS

Published by McGraw-Hill/Irwin, a business unit of The McGraw-Hill Companies, Inc., 1221
Avenue of the Americas, New York, NY, 10020. Copyright © 2004, 2001 by The McGraw-Hill
Companies, Inc. All rights reserved. No part of this publication may be reproduced or
distributed in any form or by any means, or stored in a database or retrieval system, without the
prior written consent of The McGraw-Hill Companies, Inc., including, but not limited to, in any
network or other electronic storage or transmission, or broadcast for distance learning.
Some ancillaries, including electronic and print components, may not be available to customers
outside the United States.

This book is printed on acid-free paper.

domestic   3 4 5 6 7 8 9 0 DOW/DOW 0 9 8 7 6 5 4 3
international   2 3 4 5 6 7 8 9 0 DOW/DOW 0 9 8 7 6 5 4 3

ISBN   0-07-250330-0

Cover: Leaded glass window designed by Frank Lloyd Wright for the Dave Thomas House,
Springfield, Illinois, circa 1904, 61 cm x 97.5 cm

Photo: Doug Carr, Springfield, Illinois

Design of book: The images in the design of this book are based on elements of the architecture
of Frank Lloyd Wright, specifically from the leaded glass windows seen in many of his houses.
Wright's design was rooted in nature and based on simplicity and harmony. His windows use
elemental geometry to abstract natural forms, complementing and framing the natural world
outside. This concept of seeing the world through an elegantly structured framework ties in
nicely to the idea of framing one's view of the world through the window of economics.

The typeface used for some of the elements was taken from the Arts and Crafts movement. The
typeface, as well as the color palette, bring in the feeling of that movement in a way that
complements the geometric elements of Wright's windows. The Economic Naturalist icon is
visually set apart from the more geometric elements but is a representation of the inspirational
force behind all of Wright's work.

Publisher: *Gary Burke*
Executive sponsoring editor: *Paul Shensa*
Senior developmental editor: *ThomasThompson*
Marketing manager: *Martin D. Quinn*
Senior producer, Media technology: *Melissa Kansa*
Senior project manager: *Kimberly D. Hooker*
Manager, new book production: *Melonie Salvati*
Lead designer: *Matthew Baldwin*
Photo research coordinator: *Judy Kausal*
Photo researcher: *Robin Sand*
Lead supplement producer: *Becky Szura*
Senior digital content specialist: *Brian Nacik*
Typeface: *10/12 Sabon Roman*
Compositor: *GTS Graphics, Inc.*
Printer: *R. R. Donnelley, Willard*

Library of Congress Cataloging-in-Publication Data

Frank, Robert H.
    Principles of economics / Robert H. Frank, Ben S. Bernanke.—2nd ed.
       p. cm.
    Various multi-media instructional aids, including web sites, are available to supplement
the text.
    Includes index.
    ISBN 0-07-250330-0 (alk. paper)—ISBN 0-07-121459-3 (international : alk. paper)
    1. Economics. I. Bernanke, Ben. II. Title.
    HB171.5.F734 2004
    330--dc21
                                                           2003041272
INTERNATIONAL EDITION ISBN 0-07-121459-3

www.mhhe.com

DEDICATION

For Ellen

For Anna

R. H. F.

B. S. B.

ROBERT H. FRANK

Professor Frank received his B.S. from Georgia Tech in 1966, then taught math and science for two years as a Peace Corps volunteer in rural Nepal. He received his M.A. in statistics and his Ph.D. in economics in 1972 from the University of California at Berkeley. He is the H. J. Louis Professor of Economics at the Johnson Graduate School of Management at Cornell University, where he has taught since 1972. During a leave of absence from Cornell he served as chief economist for the Civil Aeronautics Board (1978–1980), a Fellow at the Center for Advanced Study in the Behavioral Sciences (1992–1993), and Professor of American Civilization at l'École des Hautes Études en Sciences Sociales in Paris (2000–2001).

Professor Frank is the author of a best-selling intermediate economics textbook—*Microeconomics and Behavior,* Fifth Edition (McGraw-Hill/Irwin, 2003). He has published on a variety of subjects, including price and wage discrimination, public utility pricing, the measurement of unemployment spell lengths, and the distributional consequences of direct foreign investment. His research has focused on rivalry and cooperation in economic and social behavior. His books on these themes include *Choosing the Right Pond: Human Behavior and the Quest for Status* (Oxford University Press, 1985) and *Passions Within Reason: The Strategic Role of the Emotions* (W.W. Norton, 1988). He and Philip Cook are coauthors of *The Winner-Take-All Society* (The Free Press, 1995), which received a Critic's Choice Award and appeared on both the *New York Times* Notable Books list and *Business Week* Ten Best list for 1995. His most recent general-interest publication, *Luxury Fever* (The Free Press, 1999), was named to the Knight-Ridder Best Books list for 1999. He was awarded an Andrew W. Mellon Professorship (1987–1990), a Kenan Enterprise Award (1993), and a Merrill Scholars Program Outstanding Educator Citation (1991). Professor Frank's introductory microeconomics course has graduated more than 6,000 enthusiastic economic naturalists over the years.

BEN S. BERNANKE

Professor Bernanke received his B.A. in economics from Harvard University in 1975 and his Ph.D. in economics from MIT in 1979. He taught at the Stanford Graduate School of Business from 1979 to 1985 and moved to Princeton University in 1985, where he is the Howard Harrison and Gabrielle Snyder Beck Professor of Economics and Public Affairs, and where he served as Chairman of the Economics Department. He has consulted for the Board of Governors of the European Central Bank and other central banks, and he served on a U.S. State Department Committee that advises the Israeli government on economic policy. He is a member of the American Academy of Arts and Sciences, Fellow of the Econometrics Society, and a Research Associate for the National Bureau of Economic Research. He has been a visiting scholar at the Federal Reserve System in Boston, Philadelphia, and New York. And in August 2002, he was named to the Board of Governors of the Federal Reserve.

Professor Bernanke's intermediate textbook, with Andrew Abel, *Macroeconomics,* Fourth Edition (Addison-Wesley, 2001), is a best seller in its field. He has written more than 50 scholarly publications in macroeconomics, macroeconomic history, and finance. He has done significant research on the causes of the Great Depression, the role of financial markets and institutions in the business cycle, and measuring the effects of monetary policy on the economy. His two most recent books, both published by Princeton University Press, are *Inflation Targeting: Lessons from the International Experience* (with coauthors) and *Essays on the Great Depression.* He is the editor of the *American Economic Review* and has been the coeditor of the *NBER Macroeconomics Annual* and of *Economics Letters.* He has served as associate editor for the *Journal of Financial Intermediation,* the *Quarterly Journal of Economics,* the *Journal of Money, Credit, and Banking,* and the *Review of Economics and Statistics.* Professor Bernanke has taught principles of economics at both Stanford and Princeton.

PREFACE

In recent years, innovative texts in mathematics, science, foreign languages, and other fields have achieved dramatic pedagogical gains by abandoning the traditional encyclopedic approach in favor of attempting to teach a short list of core principles in depth. The enthusiastic reactions of users of the first edition of this book confirm that this less-is-more approach affords similar gains in introductory economics. Although recent editions of a few other texts have paid lip service to this new approach, ours is by consensus the most carefully thought out and well-executed text in this mold. Avoiding excessive reliance on formal mathematical derivations, it presents concepts intuitively through examples drawn from familiar contexts. It relies throughout on a well-articulated short list of core principles, which it reinforces repeatedly by illustrating and applying each in numerous contexts. It asks students periodically to apply these principles to answer related questions, exercises, and problems.

The text encourages students to become "economic naturalists," people who employ basic economic principles to understand and explain what they observe in the world around them. An economic naturalist understands, for example, that infant safety seats are required in cars but not in airplanes because the marginal cost of space to accommodate these seats is typically zero in cars but often hundreds of dollars in airplanes. Such examples engage students' interest while teaching them to see each feature of their economic landscape as the reflection of an implicit or explicit cost-benefit calculation.

Our second edition has incorporated several significant pedagogical improvements. Based on extensive reviewer feedback, it offers (1) even more streamlined coverage of the cost-benefit approach in the introductory chapter; (2) exercises that are more closely tied to the examples; (3) for important or difficult concepts, expanded narrative explanations that are more accessible to average students; and (4) expanded coverage of several key topics (see below). The result is a revision that is even more clutter-free, engaging, and pedagogically effective than its predecessor.

FEATURES

- **Core Principles Emphasized:** A few core principles do most of the work in economics. By focusing almost exclusively on these principles, the text ensures that students leave the course with a deep mastery of them. In contrast, traditional encyclopedic texts so overwhelm students with detail that they often leave the course with little useful working knowledge at all.

- **Economic Naturalism Introduced in Micro:** Our ultimate goal is to produce "economic naturalists"—people who see each human action as the result of an implicit or explicit cost-benefit calculation. The economic naturalist sees mundane details of ordinary existence in a new light and becomes actively engaged in the attempt to understand them. Some representative examples:

  - Why do auto manufacturers no longer make cars without heaters?

  - Why are whales, but not chickens, threatened with extinction?

  - Why do movie theaters give student discounts on the price of admission but not on the price of popcorn?

ECONOMIC
NATURALIST

- **Economic Naturalism Expanded in Macro:** This feature, arguably more applied here than in microeconomics, still involves an explicit or implicit cost-benefit calculation. In macro the economic naturalist might ask the following:

  - Why was the United States able to experience rapid growth and low inflation in the latter part of the 1990s?

  - What caused the 2001 recession in the United States?

  - How did the Fed react to recession and the terror attacks in 2001?

- **Active Learning Stressed:** The only way to learn to hit an overhead smash in tennis or to speak a foreign language is through repeated practice. The same is true for learning economics. Accordingly, we consistently introduce new ideas in the context of simple examples and then follow them with applications showing how they work in familiar settings. At frequent intervals, we pose exercises that both test and reinforce the understanding of these ideas. The end-of-chapter questions and problems are carefully crafted to help students internalize and extend core concepts. Experience with our first edition confirms that our text really does prepare students to apply basic economic principles to solve economic puzzles drawn from the real world.

- **Modern Microeconomics:** Economic surplus, introduced in Chapter 1 and applied repeatedly thereafter, is more fully developed here than in any other text. This concept underlies the argument for economic efficiency as an important social goal. Rather than speak of trade-offs between efficiency and other goals, we stress that maximizing economic surplus facilitates the achievement of *all* goals. *Common decision pitfalls* identified by 2002 Nobel Laureate Daniel Kahneman and others—such as the tendency to ignore implicit costs, the tendency not to ignore sunk costs, and the tendency to confuse average and marginal costs and benefits—are introduced early in Chapter 1. The book devotes a chapter to the economics of information, making available in intuitively accessible form key insights that earned the 2001 Nobel Prize in economics for George Akerlof, Joseph Stiglitz, and Michael Spence.

- **Modern Macroeconomics:** Recent developments have renewed interest in cyclical fluctuations without challenging the importance of such long-run issues as growth, productivity, the evolution of real wages, and capital formation. Our treatment of these issues is organized as follows:

  - A five-chapter treatment of long-run issues prior to an analysis of short-run fluctuations, followed by a modern treatment of short-term fluctuations and stabilization policy, emphasizing the important distinction between short- and long-run behavior of the economy.

  - Consistent with both media reporting and recent research on the central bank reaction function, we treat the interest rate rather than the money supply as the primary instrument of Fed policy.

  - The analysis of aggregate demand and aggregate supply relates output to inflation, rather than to the price level, sidestepping the necessity of a separate derivation of the link between the output gap and inflation.

  - This book places a heavy emphasis on globalization, starting with an analysis of its effects on real wage inequality and progressing to such issues as the benefits of trade, the causes and effects of protectionism, the role of capital flows in domestic capital formation, the link between exchange rates and monetary policy, and the sources of speculative attacks on currencies.

- **Web site:** The site was developed by Scott Simkins of North Carolina A & T State University, an expert in the growing field of economics education on the World Wide Web. The ambitious web site contains a host of features that will enhance the principles classroom, including dynamic graphs, e-mail updates, microeconomic experiments, current news articles, information about the text, an eLearning session, and more.

IMPROVEMENTS

- **Introductory Material Shortened and Refined:** The material from the first edition's Chapters 1 and 2 has been reworked and condensed into one chapter in an effort to launch these important concepts as clearly and efficiently as possible. From the very beginning, the focus is on how rational people make choices among alternative courses of action.

- **Separate Chapter on Elasticity Added:** The material covered in this chapter (Chapter 4) was covered in parts of two separate chapters in the first edition (Chapters 5 and 6). The new combined chapter streamlines the presentation by making use of definitions and formulas common to both the supply and demand sides. The chapter also adds several new applications and graphical summaries of key relationships.

- **Cost Curve Coverage Added:** Responding to reviewer feedback, we added an introduction to average total cost and average variable cost curves in Chapter 6. To make the presentation as simple and uncluttered as possible, no single diagram ever portrays more than three cost curves at once, and most employ only two. While this treatment remains faithful to our belief that full-blown coverage of production functions and cost curves is ill-advised at the principles level, it also provides substantially greater teaching flexibility. For example, it enables instructors to portray profits and losses graphically (Chapters 6, 8, and 9) and to discuss a firm's shutdown condition in diagrammatic terms (Chapter 6). It also facilitates an enriched discussion of the invisible hand process by which profit and loss signals drive resource allocation in competitive markets (Chapter 8).

- **Strategic Theory Accessible:** Chapter 10, "Thinking Strategically," includes many examples of how simple elements of game theory can be used not only to illuminate the interactions among oligopolists and other imperfectly competitive firms, but also to shed light on common patterns of human social interaction. This chapter

  - Opens with an account of how the producers of a Robert DeNiro film lost several hundred thousand dollars by shooting most of the film before negotiating with the singer who was slated to appear in the final scene.

  - Introduces the important Nash Equilibrium concept through a series of intuitively accessible examples.

  - Includes an extended discussion of the important prisoner's dilemma and strategies that have been developed for solving it.

  - Deals with ultimatum bargaining games and unselfish human behavior.

- **More Streamlined Discussion of Labor Markets and Income Redistribution:** Chapter 13 now contains material from the chapters on "Labor Markets" (13) and "Income Redistribution" (16) in the first edition. The new chapter is half the combined length of the earlier chapters, accomplished in part by eliminating examples, in part by trimming topic coverage. Sections on monopsony and comparable worth from the original Chapter 13 and sections on utilitarianism, tax policy and occupational choice, progressive consumption taxation, and redistribution and cost-benefit analysis from the original Chapter 16 have been omitted.

■ **Early Chapter on International Trade:** The first edition had a brief section on international trade at the end of Chapter 3 on comparative advantage. This material has been expanded to an entire chapter (16) on trade. Because international trade involves important micro principles and policy issues, students will benefit greatly from this expanded coverage earlier in the book.

■ **Long-Run Coverage Expanded:** Chapter 23 of the first edition dealt with financial markets, money, and the Fed; capital flows was dealt with as part of a later, international chapter. Because of the importance of these topics, we expanded the material into two long-run chapters in this edition. These chapters are now titled "Money, Prices, and the Federal Reserve" (23) and "Financial Markets and International Capital Flows" (24).

■ **Short-Run Coverage More Accessible:** Economic concepts are more streamlined, providing a smoother flow of economic reasoning for students. There are new Economic Naturalists (ENs) that help students better understand how policymakers react to changes in economic conditions. These ENs allow students to bridge the gap between theory and practice more effectively. There is a complete graphical/verbal discussion of the key economic concepts in each chapter for instructors and students who find this material most accessible in a nonmathematical presentation. But for those instructors who wish to reinforce specific concepts with a more formal mathematical approach, chapter appendixes provide a full algebraic treatment of the corresponding chapter concepts.

Students are provided with a clear, consistent framework for understanding modern economic theory and policymaking. They systematically develop a powerful model for understanding a wide range of short-run issues that are relevant in today's economy. Updated examples in each chapter are both topical and effective at illustrating key points. Each chapter provides students with examples and hands-on exercises to promote practice with key concepts and the workings of the short-run model. This hands-on approach to learning helps students better understand how economic policy affects interest rates, inflation, unemployment, exchange rates, and output and gets students more engaged in the learning process. Chapter-by-chapter benefits include the following:

■ The development of the Keynesian cross in Chapter 26 places more emphasis on graphs and verbal explanations, with an optional mathematical treatment in the appendix. The new presentation makes it easier for students to understand the basic economic concepts underlying the short-run model.

■ Chapter 27 continues to focus on the Federal Reserve's use of the interest rate as the primary policy tool, allowing students to more easily relate economic concepts to real-world macroeconomic policy decisions reported in the news.

■ The *AD-AS* model is developed systematically in Chapter 28 (based on concepts introduced in Chapters 26 and 27) using a graphical/verbal approach, allowing students to better understand the link among economic theory, real-world macroeconomic behavior, and macroeconomic policy-making. Again, an algebraic treatment of material in this chapter is provided in the appendix.

■ **Modern International Finance:** Chapter 29 focuses on a particularly important variable in international economics, the exchange rate. The exchange rate plays a key role in determining patterns of trade. Moreover, the type of exchange rate systems a country adopts has important implications for the effectiveness of its macroeconomic policies.

THE CHALLENGE

The world is a more competitive place now than it was when we started teaching in the 1970s. In arena after arena, business as usual is no longer good enough. Baseball players used to drink beer and go fishing during the off-season, but they now lift weights and ride exercise bicycles. Assistant professors used to work on their houses on weekends, but the current crop can be found most weekends at the office. The competition for student attention has grown similarly more intense. There are many tempting courses in the typical college curriculum, and even more tempting diversions outside the classroom. Students are freer than ever to pick and choose. Yet many of us seem to operate under the illusion that most freshmen arrive with a burning desire to become economics majors. And many of us do not yet seem to have recognized that students' cognitive abilities and powers of concentration are scarce resources. To hold our ground we must become not only more selective in what we teach, but also more effective as advocates for our discipline. We must persuade students that we offer something of value.

A well-conceived and well-executed introductory course in economics can teach our students more about society and human behavior in a single term than virtually any other course in the university. This course can and should be an intellectual adventure of the first order. Not all students who take the kind of course we envisioned when writing this book will go on to become economics majors of course. But many will, and even those who do not will leave with a sense of admiration for the power of economic ideas.

A salesperson knows that he or she often gets only one chance to make a good first impression on a potential customer. Analogously, the principles course is often our only shot at persuading students to appreciate the value of economics. By trying to teach them everything we know—rather than teaching them the most important things we know—we too often squander this opportunity.

SUPPLEMENTS

We continue to believe that an ancillary package is most useful if each element in it is part of a well-considered whole, and here, as with the first edition, we've tried hard to coordinate all the elements. We have also worked hard to improve each element within the package—for example, the PowerPoints are more extensive and more sophisticated, the Instructor's Manual now provides more help than before, the Test Banks are larger and the questions more closely tied to the textbook, the Study Guide sends students to the web site more often, the web site itself is more extensive and more accessible, and the DiscoverEcon Tutorial Software is more student-friendly than ever and now allows instructors e-submission capability and easy syllabus linking. Finally, we listened to you about what, in the first edition, needed work and tried to make it better.

FOR THE INSTRUCTOR

Instructor's Manual: Prepared by Margaret Ray at Mary Washington College, this manual will be extremely useful for all teachers, but especially for those new to the job. In addition to such general topics as Using the Web Site, Economic Education Resources, Innovative Ideas, and Tips for Teaching, there is, for each chapter, An Overview, An Outline, Core Principles, Important Concepts, Teaching Objectives, Web Site Applications, In-Class Activities, More Economic Naturalists, Answers to Textbook Problems, Sample Homework, and a Sample Reading Quiz.

Test Banks: Prepared by Sheryl Ball at Virginia Polytechnic Institute (micro) and Nancy Jianakoplos at Colorado State University (macro), each manual contains nearly 3,000 multiple-choice questions categorized by Teaching Objective (from the Study Guide); Learning Level (knowledge, comprehension, application, analysis); Type (graph, calculation, word problem); and Source (textbook, Study Guide, Web, unique).

Computerized Test Banks: The print test banks are also available in the latest Diploma test-generating software—micro and macro, ensuring maximum flexibility in test preparation, including the reconfiguring of graphing exercises. This Brownstone program is the gold standard of testing programs. It is available in both a Windows and Macintosh format.

PowerPoints: Prepared by Steve Smith and Jeff Caldwell at Rose State, these slides—micro and macro—contain all of the illustrations in the textbook, along with a detailed, chapter-by-chapter review of the important ideas presented in the textbook. These teachers have done PowerPoints for many books at both the principles and intermediate level.

Overhead Transparencies: These more than 280, four-color acetates contain all the illustrations presented in the textbook. They are available in micro and macro packages.

Instructor's CD-ROM: This remarkable Windows software program, which contains the complete Instructor's Manual, Computerized Test Banks, Power-Points, and a full set of lecture notes for principles of microeconomics (prepared by Bob Frank for his successful introductory course at Cornell University) and macroeconomics (prepared by Scott Simkins at North Carolina A&T State University) also allows the instructor to create presentations from any of the materials on the CD or from additional material that can be imported.

Online Learning Center (www.mhhe.com/economics/frankbernanke2): For teachers there are, among other things, an online newsletter called "The Teaching Exchange"; the Instructor's Manual; the PowerPoints; Economics on the Web, an annotated set of URLs/links to sites of interest to economists; a graphing library; a description of what's on the student site; and some Optional Material from the book.

FOR THE STUDENT

Study Guide: Written by Jack Mogab and Bruce McClung at Southwest Texas State University, this book provides the following elements for each chapter: a Pretest; a Learning Objective Grid; a Key Point Review with Learning Tips; some Self-Tests (Key Term Matching, Multiple Choice, Problems) with answers; and an extension of the guide to the web site, where students may practice with graphing.

Online Learning Center (www.mhhe.com/economics/frankbernanke2): For students there are such useful and exciting features for the book as a whole as Interpreting the News—articles and summaries of relevant articles with analysis and discussion questions; a Math Tutor—help for those whose math skills are rusty; e-mail Updates—periodic sending of information/study tips; the Glossary from the textbook; and Economics on the Web—annotated URLs useful for economics students. Additionally, for each chapter there is an Electronic Learning Session that opens with a brief recap of the chapter, is then followed by a test with answers and analysis; and is followed by a set of study sessions based on Economic Naturalist Exercises; Graphing Exercises; PowerPoints; and Key Terms; and which is finally followed by a second quiz, with answers and analysis.

DiscoverEcon Software: Created by Gerald Nelson of the University of Illinois, DiscoverEcon is the best-selling academic economics software available. This widely class-tested software is Windows-based and text-specific. The software is available either in a standard CD format or via the Web by using a unique student pass code packaged free with each new book. Features contained in every chapter include

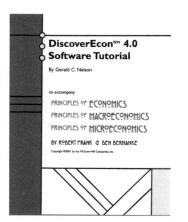

> Multiple-choice test questions: The user chooses the number of questions in the test; the software selects randomly from the question bank for the chapter.

> Chapter Review Questions and Problems: All end-of-chapter materials are included in the software. Students can enter answers, with graphs where needed, and send them to their instructors.

> Match the terms: This exercise challenges the student to match randomly selected key glossary terms with their appropriate glossary explanation.

In addition, you will find

> New ensubmission capability: Instructors may now set up their courses for ensubmission so that all exercise results for each student can be viewed and downloaded to other Windows applications (Web-based version only). In the web version, essay answers can be graded, with comments, and returned to students.

> Easy syllabus linking: For those instructors using a course management system, specific "pages" in DiscoverEcon can be linked to specific parts of the course web site. This makes navigation and therefore self-assessment easier than ever for both student and instructor.

> The opportunity to experiment with graphs, those seen in the classroom and the textbook: The software includes movies (graphs are drawn step-by-step with explanatory text appearing as the graph is constructed), interactive graphs (students change a parameter and see how the graph changes), and interactive exercises (students interpret a graph based on concepts presented) in the text and in the software.

Business Week Edition: Your students can subscribe to 15 weeks of *Business Week* for a specially priced rate. Students will receive a pass code card shrink-wrapped with their new text. The card directs students to a web site where they enter the code and then gain access to *Business Week*'s registration page to enter address info and set up their print and online subscription as well.

Wall Street Journal Edition: Your students can subscribe to the *Wall Street Journal* for 15 weeks at a specially priced rate. Students will receive a "How to Use the *WSJ*" handbook plus a pass code card shrink-wrapped with the text. The card directs students to a web site where they enter the code and then gain access to the *WSJ* registration page to enter address information and set up their print and online subscription, and also set up their subscription to Dow Jones Interactive online for the 15-week period.

ACKNOWLEDGMENTS

We are greatly indebted to Professor Scott Simkins at North Carolina A&T State University for a number of important contributions to the book, most especially providing Examples and Exercises in the short-run chapters. Our thanks go to our publisher, Gary Burke, for his unwavering faith in our project over the past several years. Without his support and encouragement, we never could have produced this book. Tom Thompson, our development editor, was enormously helpful as he guided us with intelligence, patience, and tact through three major revisions of the original manuscript, and further extensive revisions for the second edition. We also thank Paul Shensa, the sponsoring editor, and Marty Quinn, the marketing manager, whose considerable experience, insightful suggestions, and extensive knowledge of the marketplace were of incalculable help. We are especially grateful to Betty Morgan, our superb manuscript editor. And we are also grateful to the production team, whose professionalism was outstanding: Kimberly Hooker, Project Manager; Melonie Salvati, Production Supervisor; Becky Szura, Supplements Coordinator, and Melissa Kansa, Media Tech Producer.

Finally, our sincere thanks to the following teachers and colleagues, whose thorough reviews and thoughtful suggestions led to innumerable substantive improvements to both editions:

Ehsan Ahmed
James Madison University

Ercument Aksoy
Los Angeles Valley College

Richard Anderson
Texas A&M University

Michael Balch
University of Iowa

Daniel Berkowitz
University of Pittsburgh

Guatam Bhattacharya
University of Kansas

Scott Bierman
Carleton College

Bruce Blonigen
University of Oregon

Beth Bogan
Princeton University

George Borts
Brown University

Isaac Brannon
University of
Wisconsin–Oshkosh

Nancy Brooks
University of Vermont

Bruce Brown
California Polytechnic
Institute–Pomona

Douglas Brown
Georgetown University

Marie Bussings-Burk
Southern Indiana University

David Carr
University of Colorado

Edward Castranova
California State
University–Fullerton

Tom Cate
Northern Kentucky University

Jack Chambless
Valencia Community College

James Cover
University of Alabama

John D'Amico
Hilbert College

Carl Davidson
Michigan State University

Robert Deckle
University of Southern California

Lynn Pierson Doti
Chapman College

Donald Dutkowsky
Syracuse University

David Eaton
Murray State University

Nancy Fox
Saint Joseph's College

John Francis
University of
Wisconsin–Oshkosh

Roger Franz
San Diego State University

Susan Gale
New York University

Johah Gelbach
University of Maryland

Linda Ghent
East Carolina University

Kirk Gifford
Ricks College

Robert Gillette
University of Kentucky

Stephen Gohman
University of Louisville

John Graham
Rutgers University–Newark

Refet Gurkaynak
Princeton University

Galina Hale
University of
California–Berkeley

Russell Hardy
New Mexico State University

Mehdi Haririan
Bloomsburg University

Joseph Haslag
University of Missouri

Susan Hayes
Sonoma State University

Bruce Herrick
Washington and Lee University

William Hogan
University of
Massachusetts–Dartmouth

Mary Jean Horney
Furman University

Frederick Inaba
Washington State University

Nancy Jianakoplos
Colorado State University

Robert Johnson
University of San Diego

Rogear Kaufman
Smith College

Elizabeth Kelley
University of
Wisconsin–Madison

Herbert Kiesling
Indiana University

Bruce Kingma
State University of New
York–Albany

Faik Koray
Louisiana State University

Maria Kula
Roger Williams University

Leonard Lardaro
University of Rhode Island

Mary Lesser
Iona College

Anthony Lima
California State
University–Hayward

Bruce Linster
U.S. Air Force Academy

Tom Love
North Central University

Steven McCafferty
The Ohio State University

Edward McNertney
Texas Christian University

William Merrill
Iowa State University

Paul Nelson
Northeast Louisiana State
University

Neil Niman
University of New Hampshire

Norman Obst
Michigan State University

Frank O'Connor
Eastern Kentucky University

Charles Okeke
Community College of Southern
Nevada

Duane Oyen
University of Wisconsin–Eau
Claire

Theodore Palivos
Louisiana State University

Jan Palmer
Ohio University

Hong Park
Saginaw Valley State University

Michael Potepan
San Francisco State University

Rahim Quazi
University of Georgia

Steve Robinson
University of North
Carolina–Wilmington

Christina Romer
University of California–Berkeley

David Romer
University of California–Berkeley

Greg Rose
Sacramento City College

Jeffrey Rous
University of North Texas

Daniel Rubenson
Southern Oregon University

Richard Salvucci
Trinity University

Edward Scahill
University of Scranton

Neil Skaggs
Illinois State University

Dennis Starleaf
Iowa State University

Pamela Schmitt
U.S. Naval Academy

Esther-Mirjam Sent
University of Notre Dame

John Solow
University of Iowa

Martin Spechler
Indiana University/Purdue
University–Indianapolis

Michael Stroup
Stephen F. Austin University

Helen Tauchen
University of North
Carolina–Chapel Hill

Philip Taylor
Wesleyan University (Georgia)

Jennifer Tessendorf
Hobart & William Smith College

Nora Underwood
University of California–Davis

Kay Unger
University of Montana

Norm Van Cott
Ball State University

Stephan Weiler
Colorado State University

Charles Weise
Gettysburg College

Jeffrey Weiss
City University of New
York–Baruch College

Richard Winkelman
Arizona State University

Mark Wohar
University of Nebraska–Omaha

Louise Wolitz
University of Texas–Austin

Darrel Young
University of Texas–Austin

Zenon Zygmont
Western Oregon University

BRIEF CONTENTS

CONTENTS

Chapter 3   **Supply and Demand: An Introduction**   57

Chapter 28   Inflation and Aggregate Supply   737

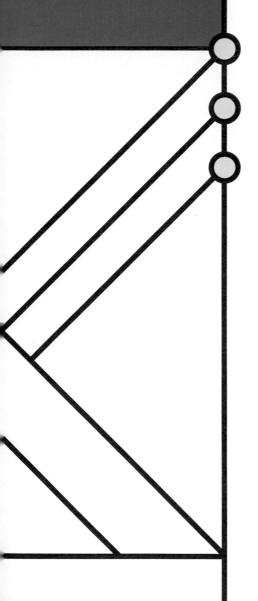

PART

1

INTRODUCTION

As you begin the study of economics, perhaps the most important thing to realize is that economics is not a collection of settled facts, to be copied down and memorized. Mark Twain said that nothing is older than yesterday's newspaper, and the same can be said of yesterday's economic statistics. Indeed, the only prediction about the economy that can be made with confidence is that there will continue to be large, and largely unpredictable, changes.

If economics is not a set of durable facts, then what is it? Fundamentally, it is a way of thinking about the world. Over many years economists have developed some simple but widely applicable principles that are useful for understanding almost any economic situation, from the relatively simple economic decisions that individuals make every day to the workings of highly complex markets, such as international financial markets. The principal objective of this book, and of this course, is to help you learn these principles and how to apply them to a variety of economic questions and issues.

The three chapters of Part I lay out the basic economic principles that will be used throughout the book. Chapter 1 introduces the notion of scarcity—the unavoidable fact that, although our needs and wants are boundless, the resources available to satisfy them are limited. The chapter goes on to show that deciding whether to take an action by comparing the cost and benefit of the action is a useful approach for dealing with the inevitable trade-offs that scarcity creates. Chapter 1 then discusses several important decision pitfalls and concludes by introducing the concept of *economic naturalism*. Chapter 2 goes beyond individual decision making to consider trade, among both individuals and countries. An important reason for trade is that it permits people (or countries) to specialize in the production of particular goods and services, which in turn enhances productivity and raises standards of living. Finally, Chapter 3 presents an overview of the concepts of supply and demand, perhaps the most basic and familiar tools used by economists.

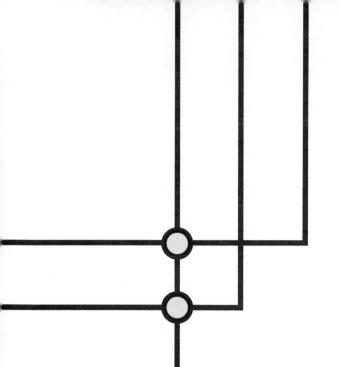

THINKING LIKE AN ECONOMIST

■

How many students are in your introductory economics class? Some classes have just 20 or so; others average 35, 100, or 200 students. At some schools, introductory economics classes may have as many as 2,000 students. What size is best?

If cost were no object, the best size for an introductory economics course—or any other course, for that matter—might be a single student. Think about it: the whole course, all term long, with just you and your professor! Everything could be custom-tailored to your own background and ability, allowing you to cover the material at just the right pace. The tutorial format would also promote close communication and personal trust between you and your professor. And your grade would depend more heavily on what you actually learned than on your luck when taking multiple-choice exams. We may even suppose, for the sake of discussion, that studies by educational psychologists prove definitively that students learn best in the tutorial format.

Why, then, do so many universities continue to schedule introductory classes with hundreds of students? The simple reason is that costs *do* matter. They matter not just to the university administrators who must build classrooms and pay faculty salaries, but also to *you*. The direct cost of providing you with your own personal introductory economics course—most notably, the professor's salary and the expense of providing a classroom in which to meet—might easily top $20,000. *Someone* has to pay these costs. In private universities, a large share of the cost would be recovered directly from higher tuition payments; in state universities, the burden would be split between higher tuition payments and higher tax payments. But in either case, the course would be unaffordable for many, if not most, students.

With a larger class size, of course, the cost per student goes down. For example, in a class of 300 students, the cost of an introductory economics course might come to as little as $100 per student. But a class that large would

Are small classes "better" than large ones?

economics the study of how people make choices under conditions of scarcity and of the results of those choices for society

surely compromise the quality of the learning environment. Compared to the custom tutorial format, however, it would be dramatically more affordable.

In choosing what size introductory economics course to offer, then, university administrators confront a classic economic trade-off. In making the class larger, they lower the quality of instruction—a bad thing—but at the same time, they reduce costs, and hence the tuition students must pay—a good thing.

ECONOMICS: STUDYING CHOICE IN A WORLD OF SCARCITY

Even in rich societies like the United States, *scarcity* is a fundamental fact of life. There is never enough time, money, or energy to do everything we want to do or have everything we would like to have. **Economics** is the study of how people make choices under conditions of scarcity, and of the results of those choices for society.

In the class-size example just discussed, a motivated economics student might definitely prefer to be in a class of 20 rather than a class of 100, everything else being equal. But other things, of course, are not equal. Students can enjoy the benefits of having smaller classes, but only at the price of having less money for other activities. The student's choice inevitably will come down to the relative importance of competing activities.

That such trade-offs are widespread and important is one of the core principles of economics. We call it the **scarcity principle**, because the simple fact of scarcity makes trade-offs necessary. Another name for the scarcity principle is the **no-free-lunch principle** (which comes from the observation that even lunches that are given to you are never really free—somebody, somehow, always has to pay for them).

The Scarcity Principle (also called the No-Free-Lunch Principle): Although we have boundless needs and wants, the resources available to us are limited. So having more of one good thing usually means having less of another.

Inherent in the idea of a trade-off is the fact that choice involves compromise between competing interests. Economists resolve such trade-offs by using *cost-benefit analysis,* which is based on the disarmingly simple principle that an action should be taken if, and only if, its benefits exceed its costs. We call this statement the **cost-benefit principle**, and it, too, is one of the core principles of economics:

The Cost-Benefit Principle: An individual (or a firm, or a society) should take an action if, and only if, the extra benefits from taking the action are at least as great as the extra costs.

With the cost-benefit principle in mind, let's think about our class-size question again. Imagine that classrooms come in only two sizes—100-seat lecture halls and 20-seat classrooms—and that your university currently offers introductory economics courses to classes of 100 students. Question: Should administrators reduce the class size to 20 students? Answer: Reduce if, and only if, the value of the improvement in instruction outweighs its additional cost.

This rule sounds simple, but to apply it we need some way to measure the relevant costs and benefits—a task that is often difficult in practice. If we make a few simplifying assumptions, however, we can see how the analysis might work. On the cost side, the primary expense of reducing class size from 100 to 20 is that we will now need five professors instead of just one. We'll also need five smaller classrooms rather than a single big one, and this too may add slightly to the expense of the move. For the sake of discussion, suppose that the cost with a class size of 20 turns out to be $1,000 per student more than the cost per student when the class size is 100. Should administrators switch to the smaller class size? If they apply the cost-benefit principle, they will realize that *the reduction in class size makes sense only if the value of attending the smaller class is at least $1,000 per student greater than the value of attending the larger class.*

Would you (or your family) be willing to pay an extra $1,000 for a smaller economics class? If not, and if other students feel the same way, then sticking with the larger class size makes sense. But if you and others would be willing to pay the extra tuition, then reducing the class size to 20 makes good economic sense.

Notice that the "best" class size, from an economic point of view, will generally not be the same as the "best" size from the point of view of an educational psychologist. The difference arises because the economic definition of "best" takes into account both the benefits *and* the costs of different class sizes. The psychologist ignores costs and looks only at the learning benefits of different class sizes.

In practice, of course, different people will feel differently about the value of smaller classes. People with high incomes, for example, tend to be willing to pay more for the advantage, which helps to explain why average class size is smaller, and tuition higher, at private schools whose students come predominantly from high-income families.

The cost-benefit framework for thinking about the class-size problem also suggests a possible reason for the gradual increase in average class size that has been taking place in American colleges and universities. During the last 15 years, professors' salaries have risen sharply, making smaller classes more costly. During the same period, median family income—and hence the willingness to pay for smaller classes—has remained roughly constant. When the cost of offering smaller classes goes up but willingness to pay for smaller classes does not, universities shift to larger class sizes.

Scarcity and the trade-offs that result also apply to resources other than money. Bill Gates is the richest man on Earth. His wealth was once estimated at over $100 billion—more than the combined wealth of the poorest 40 percent of Americans. Gates has enough money to buy more houses, cars, vacations, and other consumer goods than he could possibly use. Yet Gates, like the rest of us, has only 24 hours each day and a limited amount of energy. So even he confronts trade-offs, in that any activity he pursues—whether it be building his business empire or redecorating his mansion—uses up time and energy that he could otherwise spend on other things. Indeed, someone once calculated that the value of Gates's time is so great that pausing to pick up a $100 bill from the sidewalk simply wouldn't be worth his while.

If Bill Gates saw a $100 bill lying on the sidewalk, would it be worth his time to pick it up?

APPLYING THE COST-BENEFIT PRINCIPLE

In studying choice under scarcity, we'll usually begin with the premise that people are **rational**, which means they have well-defined goals and try to fulfill them as best they can. The cost-benefit principle illustrated in the class-size example is a fundamental tool for the study of how rational people make choices.

As in the class-size example, often the only real difficulty in applying the cost-benefit rule is to come up with reasonable measures of the relevant benefits and costs. Only in rare instances will exact dollar measures be conveniently available. But the cost-benefit framework can lend structure to your thinking even when no relevant market data are available.

To illustrate how we proceed in such cases, the following example asks you to decide whether to perform an action whose cost is described only in vague, qualitative terms.

rational person someone with well-defined goals who tries to fulfill those goals as best he or she can

EXAMPLE 1.1

Should you walk downtown to save $10 on a $25 computer game?

Imagine you are about to buy a $25 computer game at the nearby campus store when a friend tells you that the same game is on sale at a downtown store for only $15. If the downtown store is a 30-minute walk away, where should you buy the game?

The cost-benefit principle tells us that you should buy it downtown if the benefit of doing so exceeds the cost. The benefit of taking any action is the dollar value of everything you gain by taking it. Here, the benefit of buying downtown is exactly $10, since that is the amount you will save on the purchase price of the game. The cost of taking any action is the dollar value of everything you give up by taking it. Here, the cost of buying downtown is the dollar value you assign to the time and trouble it takes to make the trip. But how do we estimate that dollar value?

One way is to perform the following hypothetical auction. Imagine that a stranger has offered to pay you to do an errand that involves the same walk downtown (perhaps to drop off a letter for her at the post office). If she offered you a payment of, say, $1,000, would you accept? If so, we know that your cost of walking downtown and back must be less than $1,000. Now imagine her offer being reduced in small increments until you finally refuse the last offer. For example, if you would agree to walk downtown and back for $9.00 but not for $8.99, then your cost of making the trip is $9.00. In this case, you should buy the game downtown, because the $10 you'll save (your benefit) is greater than your $9.00 cost of making the trip.

But suppose, alternatively, that your cost of making the trip had been greater than $10. In that case, your best bet would have been to buy the game from the nearby campus store. Confronted with this choice, different people may choose differently, depending on how costly they think it is to make the trip downtown. But although there is no uniquely correct choice, most people who are asked what they would do in this situation say they would buy the game downtown.

ECONOMIC SURPLUS

economic surplus the economic surplus from taking any action is the benefit of taking that action minus its cost

Suppose again that in Example 1.1 your "cost" of making the trip downtown was $9. Compared to the alternative of buying the game at the campus store, buying it downtown resulted in an **economic surplus** of $1, the difference between the benefit of making the trip and its cost. In general, your goal as an economic decision maker is to choose those actions that generate the largest possible economic surplus. This means taking all actions that yield a positive total economic surplus, which is just another way of restating the cost-benefit principle.

Note that the fact that your best choice was to buy the game downtown doesn't imply that you *enjoy* making the trip, any more than choosing a large class means that you prefer large classes to small ones. It simply means that the trip is less unpleasant than the prospect of paying $10 extra for the game. Once again, you've faced a trade-off—in this case, the choice between a cheaper game and the free time gained by avoiding the trip.

OPPORTUNITY COST

opportunity cost the opportunity cost of an activity is the value of the next-best alternative that must be forgone in order to undertake the activity

Of course your mental auction could have produced a different outcome. Suppose, for example, that the time required for the trip is the only time you have left to study for a difficult test the next day. Or suppose you are watching one of your favorite movies on cable, or that you are tired and would love a short nap. In such cases, we say that the **opportunity cost** of making the trip—that is, the value of what you must sacrifice to walk downtown and back—is high, and you are more likely to decide against making the trip.

In this example, if watching the last hour of the cable TV movie is the most valuable opportunity that conflicts with the trip downtown, the opportunity cost of making the trip is the dollar value you place on pursuing that opportunity— that is, the largest amount you'd be willing to pay to avoid missing the end of the movie. Note that the opportunity cost of making the trip is not the combined value of *all* possible activities you could have pursued, but only the value of your *best* alternative—the one you would have chosen had you not made the trip.

Throughout the text we will pose exercises like the one that follows. You'll find that pausing to answer them will help you to master key concepts in economics. Because doing these exercises isn't very costly (indeed, many students report that they are actually fun), the cost-benefit principle indicates that it's well worth your while to do them.

EXERCISE 1.1

You would again save $10 by buying the game downtown rather than at the campus store, but your cost of making the trip is now $12, not $9. How much economic surplus would you get from buying the game downtown? Where should you buy it?

THE ROLE OF ECONOMIC MODELS

Economists use the cost-benefit principle as an abstract model of how an idealized rational individual would choose among competing alternatives. (By "abstract model" we mean a simplified description that captures the essential elements of a situation and allows us to analyze them in a logical way.) A computer model of a complex phenomenon like climate change, which must ignore many details and includes only the major forces at work, is an example of an abstract model.

Noneconomists are sometimes harshly critical of the economist's cost-benefit model on the grounds that people in the real world never conduct hypothetical mental auctions before deciding whether to make trips downtown. But this criticism betrays a fundamental misunderstanding of how abstract models can help to explain and predict human behavior. Economists know perfectly well that people don't conduct hypothetical mental auctions when they make simple decisions. All the cost-benefit principle really says is that a rational decision is one that is explicitly or implicitly based on a weighing of costs and benefits.

Most of us make sensible decisions most of the time, without being consciously aware that we are weighing costs and benefits, just as most people ride a bike without being consciously aware of what keeps them from falling. Through trial and error, we gradually learn what kinds of choices tend to work best in different contexts, just as bicycle riders internalize the relevant laws of physics, usually without being conscious of them.

Even so, learning the explicit principles of cost-benefit analysis can help us make better decisions, just as knowing about physics can help in learning to ride a bicycle. For instance, when a young economist was teaching his oldest son to ride a bike, he followed the time-honored tradition of running alongside the bike and holding onto his son, then giving him a push and hoping for the best. After several hours and painfully skinned elbows and knees, his son finally got it. A year later, someone pointed out that the trick to riding a bike is to turn slightly in whichever direction the bike is leaning. Of course! The economist passed this information along to his second son, who learned to ride almost instantly. Just as knowing a little physics can help you learn to ride a bike, knowing a little economics can help you make better decisions.

RECAP   COST-BENEFIT ANALYSIS

Scarcity is a basic fact of economic life. Because of it, having more of one good thing almost always means having less of another (the *scarcity principle*). The cost-benefit principle holds that an individual (or a firm, or a society) should take an action if, and only if, the extra benefit from taking the action is at least as great as the extra cost. The benefit of taking any action minus the cost of taking the action is called the *economic surplus* from that action. Hence the cost-benefit principle suggests that we take only those actions that create additional economic surplus.

FOUR IMPORTANT DECISION PITFALLS*

Rational people will apply the cost-benefit principle most of the time, although probably in an intuitive and approximate way, rather than through explicit and precise calculation. Knowing that rational people tend to compare costs and benefits enables economists to predict their likely behavior. As noted earlier, for example, we can predict that students from wealthy families are more likely than others to attend colleges that offer small classes. (Again, while the cost of small classes is the same for all families, the benefit of small classes, as measured by what people are willing to pay for them, tends to be higher for wealthier families.)

PITFALL 1: MEASURING COSTS AND BENEFITS AS PROPORTIONS RATHER THAN ABSOLUTE DOLLAR AMOUNTS

As the next example makes clear, the cost-benefit principle proves helpful in another way. The example demonstrates that people aren't born with an infallible instinct for weighing the relevant costs and benefits of many daily decisions. Indeed, one of the rewards of studying economics is that it can improve the quality of your decisions.

EXAMPLE 1.2   **Should you walk downtown to save $10 on a $2,020 laptop computer?**

You are about to buy a $2,020 laptop computer at the nearby campus store when a friend tells you that the same computer is on sale at a downtown store for only $2,010. If the downtown store is half an hour's walk away, where should you buy the computer?

Assuming that the laptop is light enough to carry without effort, the structure of this example is exactly the same as that of Example 1.1—the only difference being that the price of the laptop is dramatically higher than the price of the computer game. As before, the benefit of buying downtown is the dollar amount you'll save, namely, $10. And since it's exactly the same trip, its cost must also be the same as before. So if you are perfectly rational, you should make the same decision in both cases. Yet when real people are asked what they would do in these situations, the overwhelming majority say they would walk downtown to buy the game but would buy the laptop at the campus store. When asked to explain, most of them say something like "The trip was worth it for the game because you save 40 percent, but not worth it for the laptop because you save only $10 out of $2,020."

This is faulty reasoning. The benefit of the trip downtown is not the *proportion* you save on the original price. Rather, it is the *absolute dollar amount*

---

*The examples in this section are inspired by the pioneering research of Daniel Kahneman and the late Amos Tversky. Kahneman was awarded the 2002 Nobel Prize in economics for his efforts to integrate insights from psychology into economics.

you save. Since the benefit of walking downtown to buy the laptop is $10—exactly the same as for the computer game—and since the cost of the trip must also be the same in both cases, the economic surplus from making both trips must be exactly the same. And that means that a rational decision maker would make the same decision in both cases. Yet, as noted, most people choose differently.

EXERCISE 1.2

Which is more valuable, saving $100 on a $2,000 plane ticket to Tokyo or saving $90 on a $200 plane ticket to Chicago?

The pattern of faulty reasoning in the decision just discussed is one of several decision pitfalls to which people are often prone. In the discussion that follows, we will identify three additional decision pitfalls. In some cases, people ignore costs or benefits that they ought to take into account, while on other occasions they are influenced by costs or benefits that are irrelevant.

PITFALL 2: IGNORING OPPORTUNITY COSTS

Sherlock Holmes, Arthur Conan Doyle's legendary detective, was successful because he saw details that most others overlooked. In *Silver Blaze*, Holmes is called on to investigate the theft of an expensive racehorse from its stable. A Scotland Yard inspector assigned to the case asks Holmes whether some particular aspect of the crime requires further study. "Yes," Holmes replies, and describes "the curious incident of the dog in the nighttime." "The dog did nothing in the nighttime," responds the puzzled inspector. But as Holmes realized, that was precisely the problem. The watchdog's failure to bark when Silver Blaze was stolen meant that the watchdog knew the thief. This clue ultimately proved the key to unraveling the mystery.

Just as we often don't notice when a dog fails to bark, many of us tend to overlook the implicit value of activities that fail to happen. As discussed earlier, however, intelligent decisions require taking the value of forgone opportunities properly into account.

The opportunity cost of an activity, once again, is the value of the next-best alternative that must be forgone in order to engage in that activity. If buying a computer game downtown means not watching the last hour of a movie, then the value to you of watching the end of that movie is an opportunity cost of the trip. Many people make bad decisions because they tend to ignore the value of such forgone opportunities. To avoid overlooking opportunity costs, economists often translate questions like "Should I walk downtown?" into ones like "Should I walk downtown or watch the end of the movie?"

Opportunity costs are like dogs that fail to bark in the night.

Should you use your frequent-flyer coupon to fly to Fort Lauderdale for spring break?

EXAMPLE 1.3

With spring break only a week away, you are still undecided about whether to go to Fort Lauderdale with a group of classmates at the University of Iowa. The round-trip airfare from Cedar Rapids is $500, but you have a frequent-flyer coupon you could use to pay for the trip. All other relevant costs for the vacation week at the beach total exactly $1,000. The most you would be willing to pay for the Fort Lauderdale vacation is $1,350. That amount is your benefit of taking the vacation. Your only alternative use for your frequent-flyer coupon is for your plane trip to Boston the weekend after spring break to attend your brother's wedding. (Your coupon expires shortly thereafter.) If the Cedar Rapids–Boston round-trip airfare is $400, should you use your frequent-flyer coupon to fly to Fort Lauderdale for spring break?

The cost-benefit principle tells us that you should go to Fort Lauderdale if the benefits of the trip exceed its costs. If not for the complication of the frequent-flyer

Is your flight to Fort Lauderdale "free" if you travel on a frequent-flyer coupon?

coupon, solving this problem would be a straightforward matter of comparing your benefit from the week at the beach to the sum of all relevant costs. And since your airfare and other costs would add up to $1,500, or $150 more than your benefit from the trip, you would not go to Fort Lauderdale.

But what about the possibility of using your frequent-flyer coupon to make the trip? Using it for that purpose might make the flight to Fort Lauderdale seem free, suggesting you would reap an economic surplus of $350 by making the trip. But doing so would also mean you would have to fork over $400 for your airfare to Boston. So the opportunity cost of using your coupon to go to Fort Lauderdale is really $400. If you use it for that purpose, the trip still ends up being a loser, because the cost of the vacation, $1,400, exceeds the benefit by $50. In cases like these, you are much more likely to decide sensibly if you ask yourself, "Should I use my frequent-flyer coupon for this trip or save it for an upcoming trip?"

We cannot emphasize strongly enough that the key to using the concept of opportunity cost correctly lies in recognizing precisely what taking a given action prevents us from doing. The following exercise illustrates this point by modifying the details of Example 1.3 slightly.

EXERCISE 1.3

Same as Example 1.3, except that now your frequent-flyer coupon expires in a week, so your only chance to use it will be for the Fort Lauderdale trip. Should you use your coupon?

PITFALL 3: FAILURE TO IGNORE SUNK COSTS

The opportunity cost pitfall is one in which people ignore costs they ought to take into account. In another common pitfall, the reverse is true: People are influenced by costs they ought to ignore. *The only costs that should influence a decision about whether to take an action are those that we can avoid by not taking the action.* As a practical matter, however, many decision makers appear to be influenced by **sunk costs**—costs that are beyond recovery at the moment a decision is made. For example, money spent on a nontransferable, nonrefundable airline ticket is a sunk cost.

sunk cost a cost that is beyond recovery at the moment a decision must be made

Because sunk costs must be borne *whether or not an action is taken,* they are irrelevant to the decision of whether to take the action. The sunk-cost pitfall (the mistake of being influenced by sunk costs) is illustrated clearly in the following example.

EXAMPLE 1.4 | **How much should you eat at an all-you-can-eat restaurant?**

Sangam, an Indian restaurant in Philadelphia, offers an all-you-can-eat lunch buffet for $5. Customers pay $5 at the door, and no matter how many times they refill their plates, there is no additional charge. One day, as a goodwill gesture, the owner of the restaurant tells 20 randomly selected guests that their lunch is on the house. The remaining guests pay the usual price. If all diners are rational, will there be any difference in the average quantity of food consumed by people in these two groups?

Having eaten their first helping, diners in each group confront the following question: "Should I go back for another helping?" For rational diners, if the benefit of doing so exceeds the cost, the answer is yes; otherwise it is no. Note that at the moment of decision about a second helping, the $5 charge for the lunch is a sunk cost. Those who paid it have no way to recover it. Thus, for both groups, the (extra) cost of another helping is exactly zero. And since the people who received the free lunch were chosen at random, there is no reason to suppose that their appetites or incomes are different from those of other diners. The benefit of another helping thus should be the same, on average, for people in both groups. And since their respective costs and benefits of an additional helping are the same, the two groups should eat the same number of helpings, on average.

Psychologists and economists have experimental evidence, however, that people in such groups do *not* eat similar amounts.[1] In particular, those for whom the luncheon charge is not waived tend to eat substantially more than those for whom the charge is waived. People in the former group seem somehow determined to "get their money's worth." Their implicit goal is apparently to minimize the average cost per bite of the food they eat. Yet minimizing average cost is not a particularly sensible objective. It brings to mind the man who drove his car on the highway at night, even though he had nowhere to go, because he wanted to boost his average fuel economy. The irony is that diners who are determined to get their money's worth usually end up eating too much, as evidenced later by their regrets about having gone back for their last helpings.

The fact that the cost-benefit criterion failed the test of prediction in this example does nothing to invalidate its advice about what people *should* do. If you are letting sunk costs influence your decisions, you can do better by changing your behavior.

PITFALL 4: FAILURE TO UNDERSTAND THE AVERAGE–MARGINAL DISTINCTION

Often we are confronted with the choice of whether or not to engage in an activity (for example, whether or not to shop downtown). But in many situations, the issue is not whether to pursue the activity at all, but rather the *extent* to which it should be pursued. We can apply the cost-benefit principle in such situations by repeatedly asking the question "Should I increase the level at which I am currently pursuing the activity?"

In attempting to answer this question, the focus should always be on the benefit and cost of an *additional* unit of activity. To emphasize this focus, economists refer to the cost of an additional unit of activity as the **marginal cost** of the activity. Similarly, the benefit of an additional unit of the activity is the **marginal benefit** of the activity.

When the problem is to discover the proper level at which to pursue an activity, the cost-benefit rule is to keep increasing the level as long as marginal benefit of the activity exceeds its marginal cost. As the following example illustrates, however, people often fail to apply this rule correctly.

marginal cost the increase in total cost that results from carrying out one additional unit of an activity

marginal benefit the increase in total benefit that results from carrying out one additional unit of an activity

Should NASA expand the space shuttle program from four launches per year to five?

EXAMPLE 1.5

Professor Kösten Banifoot, a prominent supporter of the National Aeronautics and Space Administration's (NASA) space shuttle program, estimated that the gains from the program are currently $24 billion per year (an average of $6 billion per launch) and that its costs are currently $20 billion per year (an average of $5 billion per launch). On the basis of these estimates, Professor Banifoot testified before Congress that NASA should definitely expand the space shuttle program. Should Congress follow his advice?

To discover whether expanding the program makes economic sense, we must compare the marginal cost of a launch to its marginal benefit. The professor's estimates, however, tell us only the **average cost** and **average benefit** of the program—which are, respectively, the total cost of the program divided by the

average cost the total cost of undertaking n units of an activity divided by n

average benefit the total benefit of undertaking n units of an activity divided by n

[1]See, for example, Richard Thaler, "Toward a Positive Theory of Consumer Choice," *Journal of Economic Behavior and Organization*, **1**, no. 1, 1980.

number of launches and the total benefit divided by the number of launches. Knowing the average benefit and average cost per launch for all shuttles launched thus far is simply not useful for deciding whether to expand the program. Of course, the average cost of the launches undertaken so far *might* be the same as the cost of adding another launch. But it might also be either higher or lower than the marginal cost of a launch. The same statement holds true regarding average and marginal benefits.

Suppose, for the sake of discussion, that the benefit of an additional launch is in fact the same as the average benefit per launch thus far, $6 billion. Should NASA add another launch? Not if the cost of adding the fifth launch would be more than $6 billion. And the fact that the average cost per launch is only $5 billion simply does not tell us anything about the marginal cost of the fifth launch.

Suppose, for example, that the relationship between the number of shuttles launched and the total cost of the program is as described in Table 1.1. The average cost per launch (third column) when there are four launches would then be $20 billion/4 = $5 billion per launch, just as Professor Banifoot testified. But note in the second column of the table that adding a fifth launch would raise costs from $20 billion to $32 billion, making the marginal cost of the fifth launch $12 billion. So if the benefit of an additional launch is $6 billion, increasing the number of launches from four to five would make absolutely no economic sense.

TABLE 1.1
How Total Cost Varies with the Number of Launches

Number of launches	Total cost ($ billions)	Average cost ($ billion/launch)
0	0	0
1	3	3
2	7	3.5
3	12	4
4	20	5
5	32	6.4

The following example illustrates how to apply the cost-benefit principle correctly in this case.

EXAMPLE 1.6

How many space shuttles should NASA launch?

NASA must decide how many space shuttles to launch. The benefit of each launch is estimated to be $6 billion, and the total cost of the program again depends on the number of launches in the manner shown in Table 1.1. How many shuttles should NASA launch?

NASA should continue to launch shuttles as long as the marginal benefit of the program exceeds its marginal cost. In this example, the marginal benefit is constant at $6 billion per launch, regardless of the number of shuttles launched. NASA should thus keep launching shuttles as long as the marginal cost per launch is less than or equal to $6 billion.

Applying the definition of marginal cost to the total cost entries in the second column of Table 1.1 yields the marginal cost values in the third column of Table 1.2. (Because marginal cost is the change in total cost that results when we change the number of launches by one, we place each marginal cost entry midway

TABLE 1.2
How Marginal Cost Varies with the Number of Launches

Number of launches	Total cost ($ billion)	Marginal cost ($ billion/launch)
0	0	
		3
1	3	
		4
2	7	
		5
3	12	
		8
4	20	
		12
5	32	

between the rows showing the corresponding total cost entries.) Thus, for example, the marginal cost of increasing the number of launches from one to two is $4 billion, the difference between the $7 billion total cost of two launches and the $3 billion total cost of one launch.

As we see from a comparison of the $6 billion marginal benefit per launch with the marginal cost entries in the third column of Table 1.2, the first three launches satisfy the cost-benefit test, but the fourth and fifth launches do not. NASA should thus launch three space shuttles.

EXERCISE 1.4

If the marginal benefit of each launch had been not $6 billion but $9 billion, how many shuttles should NASA have launched?

The cost-benefit framework emphasizes that the only relevant costs and benefits in deciding whether to pursue an activity further are *marginal* costs and benefits— measures that correspond to the *increment* of activity under consideration. In many contexts, however, people seem more inclined to compare the *average* cost and benefit of the activity. As Example 1.5 made clear, increasing the level of an activity may not be justified, even though its average benefit at the current level is significantly greater than its average cost.

Here's an exercise that further illustrates the importance of the average–marginal distinction.

EXERCISE 1.5

Should a basketball team's best player take all the team's shots?
A professional basketball team has a new assistant coach. The assistant notices that one player scores on a higher percentage of his shots than other players. Based on this information, the assistant suggests to the head coach that the star player should take *all* the shots. That way, the assistant reasons, the team will score more points and win more games.

On hearing this suggestion, the head coach fires his assistant for incompetence. What was wrong with the assistant's idea?

The preceding examples make the point that people *sometimes* choose irrationally. We must stress that our purpose in discussing these examples was not to suggest that people *generally* make irrational choices. On the contrary, most people appear to choose sensibly most of the time, especially when their decisions are important or familiar ones. The economist's focus on rational choice thus offers not only useful advice about making better decisions, but also a basis for predicting and explaining human behavior. We used the cost-benefit approach in this way when discussing how rising faculty salaries have led to larger class sizes. And as we will see, similar reasoning helps to explain human behavior in virtually every other domain.

RECAP   **FOUR IMPORTANT DECISION PITFALLS**

1. **The pitfall of measuring costs or benefits proportionally.** Many decision makers treat a change in cost or benefit as insignificant if it constitutes only a small proportion of the original amount. Absolute dollar amounts, not proportions, should be employed to measure costs and benefits.

2. **The pitfall of ignoring opportunity costs.** When performing a cost-benefit analysis of an action, it is important to account for all relevant *opportunity costs,* defined as the values of the most highly valued alternatives that must be forgone in order to carry out the action. A resource (such as a frequent-flyer coupon) may have a high opportunity cost, even if you originally got it "for free," if its best alternative use has high value. The identical resource may have a low opportunity cost, however, if it has no good alternative uses.

3. **The pitfall of not ignoring sunk costs.** When deciding whether to perform an action, it is important to ignore sunk costs—those costs that cannot be avoided even if the action is not taken. Even though a ticket to a concert may have cost you $100, if you have already bought it and cannot sell it to anyone else, the $100 is a sunk cost and should not influence your decision about whether to go to the concert.

4. **The pitfall of using average instead of marginal costs and benefits.** Decision makers often have ready information about the total cost and benefit of an activity, and from these it is simple to compute the activity's average cost and benefit. A common mistake is to conclude that an activity should be increased if its average benefit exceeds its average cost. The cost-benefit principle tells us that the level of an activity should be increased if, and only if, its *marginal* benefit exceeds its *marginal* cost.

Some costs and benefits, especially marginal costs and benefits and opportunity costs, are important for decision making, while others, like sunk costs and average costs and benefits, are essentially irrelevant. This conclusion is implicit in our original statement of the cost-benefit principle (an action should be taken if, and only if, the extra benefits of taking it exceed the extra costs). Yet so important are the pitfalls of using proportions instead of absolute dollar amounts, of ignoring opportunity costs, of taking sunk costs into account, and of confusing average and marginal costs and benefits that we enumerate these pitfalls separately as one of the core ideas for repeated emphasis.

The Not-All-Costs-and-Benefits-Matter-Equally Principle: Some costs and benefits (for example, opportunity costs and marginal costs and benefits) matter in making decisions, whereas others (for example, sunk costs and average costs and benefits) don't.

ECONOMICS: MICRO AND MACRO

By convention, we use the term **microeconomics** to describe the study of individual choices and of group behavior in individual markets. **Macroeconomics,** by contrast, is the study of the performance of national economies and of the policies that governments use to try to improve that performance. Macroeconomics tries to understand the determinants of such things as the national unemployment rate, the overall price level, and the total value of national output.

Our focus in this chapter is on issues that confront the individual decision maker, whether that individual confronts a personal decision, a family decision, a business decision, a government policy decision, or indeed any other type of decision. Further on, we'll consider economic models of groups of individuals, such as all buyers or all sellers in a specific market. Later still we will turn to broader economic issues and measures.

No matter which of these levels is our focus, however, our thinking will be shaped by the fact that although economic needs and wants are effectively unlimited, the material and human resources that can be used to satisfy them are finite. Clear thinking about economic problems must therefore always take into account the idea of trade-offs—the idea that having more of one good thing usually means having less of another. Our economy and our society are shaped to a substantial degree by the choices people have made when faced with trade-offs.

microeconomics the study of individual choice under scarcity and its implications for the behavior of prices and quantities in individual markets

macroeconomics the study of the performance of national economies and the policies that governments use to try to improve that performance

THE APPROACH OF THIS TEXT

Choosing the number of students to register in each class is just one of many important decisions in planning an introductory economics course. Another decision, to which the scarcity principle applies just as strongly, concerns which of many different topics to include on the course syllabus. There is a virtually inexhaustible set of topics and issues that might be covered in an introductory course, but only limited time in which to cover them. There is no free lunch. Covering some topics inevitably means omitting others.

All textbook authors are necessarily forced to pick and choose. A textbook that covered *all* the issues ever written about in economics would take up more than a whole floor of your campus library. It is our firm view that most introductory textbooks try to cover far too much. One reason that each of us was drawn to the study of economics was that a relatively short list of the discipline's core ideas can explain a great deal of the behavior and events we see in the world around us. So rather than cover a large number of ideas at a superficial level, our strategy is to focus on this short list of core ideas, returning to each entry again and again, in many different contexts. This strategy will enable you to internalize these ideas remarkably well in the brief span of a single course. And the benefit of learning a small number of important ideas well will far outweigh the cost of having to ignore a host of other, less important ideas.

So far, we've already encountered three core ideas: the scarcity principle, the cost-benefit principle, and the principle that not all costs and benefits matter equally. As these core ideas reemerge in the course of our discussions, we'll call your attention to them. And shortly after a *new* core idea appears, we'll highlight it by formally restating it.

A second important element in the philosophy of this text is our belief in the importance of active learning. In the same way that you can learn Spanish only by speaking and writing it, or tennis only by playing the game, you can learn economics only by *doing* economics. And because we want you to learn how to do economics, rather than just to read or listen passively as the authors or your instructor does economics, we will make every effort to encourage you to stay actively involved.

For example, instead of just telling you about an idea, we will usually first motivate the idea by showing you how it works in the context of a specific example. Often, these examples will be followed by exercises for you to try, as well as applications that show the relevance of the idea to real life. Try working the exercises *before* looking up the answers (which are at the back of the corresponding chapter).

Think critically about the applications: Do you see how they illustrate the point being made? Do they give you new insight into the issue? Work the problems at the end of the chapters, and take extra care with those relating to points that you do not fully understand. Apply economic principles to the world around you. (We'll say more about this when we discuss economic naturalism below.) Finally, when you come across an idea or example that you find interesting, tell a friend about it. You'll be surprised to discover how much the mere act of explaining it helps you understand and remember the underlying principle. The more actively you can become engaged in the learning process, the more effective your learning will be.

ECONOMIC NATURALISM

With the rudiments of the cost-benefit framework under your belt, you are now in a position to become an "economic naturalist," someone who uses insights from economics to help make sense of observations from everyday life. People who have studied biology are able to observe and marvel at many details of nature that would otherwise have escaped their notice. For example, on a walk in the woods in early April the novice may see only trees whereas the biology student notices many different species of trees and understands why some are already into leaf while others still lie dormant. Likewise, the novice may notice that in some animal species males are much larger than females, but the biology student knows that pattern occurs only in species in which males take several mates. Natural selection favors larger males in those species because their greater size helps them prevail in the often bloody contests among males for access to females. By contrast, males tend to be roughly the same size as females in monogamous species, in which there is much less fighting for mates.

In similar fashion, learning a few simple economic principles enables us to see the mundane details of ordinary human existence in a new light. Whereas the uninitiated often fail even to notice these details, the economic naturalist not only sees them, but becomes actively engaged in the attempt to understand them. Let's consider a few examples of questions economic naturalists might pose for themselves.

Why do many hardware manufacturers include more than $1,000 worth of "free" software with a computer selling for only slightly more than that?

The software industry is different from many others in the sense that its customers care a great deal about product compatibility. When you and your classmates are working on a project together, for example, your task will be much simpler if you all use the same word-processing program. Likewise, an executive's life will be easier at tax time if her financial software is the same as her accountant's.

The implication is that the benefit of owning and using any given software program increases with the number of other people who use that same product. This unusual relationship gives the producers of the most popular programs an enormous advantage and often makes it hard for new programs to break into the market.

Recognizing this pattern, the Intuit Corporation offered computer makers free copies of *Quicken*, its personal financial-management software. Computer makers, for their part, were only too happy to include the program, since it made their new computers more attractive to buyers. *Quicken* soon became the standard for personal financial-management programs. By giving away free copies of the program, Intuit "primed the pump," creating an enormous demand for upgrades of *Quicken* and for more advanced versions of related software. Thus *TurboTax* and *Macintax,* Intuit's personal income-tax software, have become the standards for tax-preparation programs.

Inspired by this success story, other software developers have jumped onto the bandwagon. Most hardware now comes bundled with a host of free software programs. Some software developers are even rumored to *pay* computer makers to include their programs!

The free-software example illustrates a case in which the *benefit* of a product depends on the number of other people who own that product. As the next example demonstrates, the *cost* of a product may also depend on the number of others who own it.

Why don't auto manufacturers make cars without heaters?

Virtually every new car sold in the United States today has a heater. But not every car has a CD player. Why this difference?

One might be tempted to answer that although everyone *needs* a heater, people can get along without CD players. Yet heaters are of little use in places like Hawaii and southern California. What is more, cars produced as recently as the 1950s did *not* all have heaters. (The classified ad that led one young economic naturalist to his first car, a 1955 Pontiac, boasted that the vehicle had a radio, heater, and whitewall tires.)

Although heaters cost extra money to manufacture and are not useful in all parts of the country, they do not cost *much* money and are useful on at least a few days each year in most parts of the country. As time passed and people's incomes grew, manufacturers found that people were ordering fewer and fewer cars without heaters. At some point it actually became cheaper to put heaters in *all* cars, rather than bear the administrative expense of making some cars with heaters and others without. No doubt a few buyers would still order a car without a heater if they could save some money in the process. But catering to these customers is just no longer worth it.

Similar reasoning explains why certain cars today cannot be purchased without a CD player. Buyers of the 2003 BMW 745i, for example, got a CD player whether they wanted one or not. Most buyers of this car, which sells for approximately $75,000, have high incomes, so the overwhelming majority of them would have chosen to order a CD player had it been sold as an option. Because of the savings made possible when all cars are produced with the same equipment, it would have actually cost BMW more to supply cars for the few who would want them without CD players.

Buyers of the least-expensive makes of car have much lower incomes on average than BMW 745i buyers. Accordingly, most of them have more pressing alternative uses for their money than to buy CD players for their cars, and this explains why most inexpensive makes continue to offer CD players only as options.

ECONOMIC NATURALIST 1.2

The insights afforded by the preceding example suggest an answer to the following strange question:

Why do the keypad buttons on drive-up automatic teller machines have Braille dots?

Braille dots on elevator buttons and on the keypads of walk-up automatic teller machines enable blind people to participate more fully in the normal flow of daily activity. But even though blind people can do many remarkable things, they cannot drive automobiles on public roads. Why, then, do the manufacturers of automatic teller machines install Braille dots on the machines at drive-up locations?

The answer to this riddle is that once the keypad molds have been manufactured, the cost of producing buttons with Braille dots is no higher than the cost of producing smooth buttons. Making both would require separate sets of molds and two different types of inventory. If the patrons of drive-up machines found buttons with Braille dots harder to use, there might be a reason to incur these extra costs. But since the dots pose no difficulty for sighted users, the best and cheapest solution is to produce only keypads with dots.

The preceding example was suggested by Cornell student Bill Tjoa, in response to the following assignment:

EXERCISE 1.6

In 500 words or less, use cost-benefit analysis to explain some pattern of events or behavior you have observed in your own environment.

There is probably no more useful step you can take in your study of economics than to perform several versions of the assignment in Exercise 1.6. Students who do so almost invariably become lifelong economic naturalists. Their mastery of economic concepts not only does not decay with the passage of time; it actually grows stronger. We urge you, in the strongest possible terms, to make this investment!

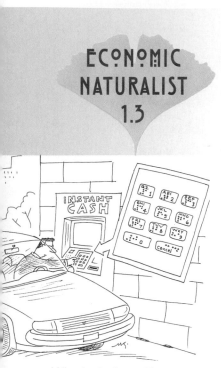

ECONOMIC NATURALIST 1.3

Why do the keypad buttons on drive-up automatic teller machines have Braille dots?

■ SUMMARY ■

- Economics is the study of how people make choices under conditions of scarcity and of the results of those choices for society. Economic analysis of human behavior begins with the assumption that people are rational—that they have well-defined goals and try to achieve them as best they can. In trying to achieve their goals, people normally face trade-offs: Because material and human resources are limited, having more of one good thing means making do with less of some other good thing.

- Our focus in this chapter has been on how rational people make choices among alternative courses of action. Our basic tool for analyzing these decisions is cost-benefit analysis. The cost-benefit principle says that a person should take an action if, and only if, the benefit of that action is at least as great as its cost. The benefit of an action is defined as the largest dollar amount the person would be willing to pay in order to take the action. The cost of an action is defined as the dollar value of everything the person must give up in order to take the action.

- Often the question is not whether to pursue an activity but rather how many units of it to pursue. In these cases, the rational person pursues additional units as long as the marginal benefit of the activity (the benefit from pursuing an additional unit of it) exceeds its marginal cost (the cost of pursuing an additional unit of it).

- In using the cost-benefit framework, we need not presume that people choose rationally all the time. Indeed, we identified four common pitfalls that plague decision makers in all walks of life: a tendency to treat small proportional changes as insignificant, a tendency to ignore opportunity costs, a tendency not to ignore sunk costs, and a tendency to confuse average and marginal costs and benefits.

- Microeconomics is the study of individual choices and of group behavior in individual markets, while macroeconomics is the study of the performance of national economies and of the policies that governments use to try to improve economic performance.

▪ CORE PRINCIPLES ▪

 The Scarcity Principle (also called the **No-Free-Lunch Principle**)
Although we have boundless needs and wants, the resources available to us are limited. So having more of one good thing usually means having less of another.

 The Cost-Benefit Principle
An individual (or a firm, or a society) should take an action if, and only if, the extra benefits from taking the action are at least as great as the extra costs.

 The Not-All-Costs-and-Benefits-Matter-Equally Principle
Some costs and benefits (for example, opportunity costs and marginal costs and benefits) matter in making decisions, whereas others (for example, sunk costs and average costs and benefits) don't.

▪ KEY TERMS ▪

---

average benefit (11)
average cost (11)
economics (4)
economic surplus (6)

macroeconomics (15)
marginal benefit (11)
marginal cost (11)
microeconomics (15)

opportunity cost (6)
rational person (5)
sunk cost (10)

▪ REVIEW QUESTIONS ▪

---

1. A friend of yours on the tennis team says "Private tennis lessons are definitely better than group lessons." Explain what you think he means by this statement. Then use the cost-benefit principle to explain why private lessons are not necessarily the best choice for everyone.

2. True or false: Your willingness to drive downtown to save $30 on a new appliance should depend on what fraction of the total selling price $30 is. Explain.

3. Why might someone who is trying to decide whether to see a movie be more likely to focus on the $9 ticket price than on the $20 she would fail to earn by not babysitting?

4. Many people think of their air travel as being free when they use frequent-flyer coupons. Explain why these people are likely to make wasteful travel decisions.

5. Is the nonrefundable tuition payment you made to your university this semester a sunk cost? How would your answer differ if your university were to offer a full tuition refund to any student who dropped out of school during the first two months of the semester?

▪ PROBLEMS ▪

---

1. The most you would be willing to pay for having a freshly washed car before going out on a date is $6. The smallest amount for which you would be willing to wash someone else's car is $3.50. You are going out this evening, and your car is dirty. How much economic surplus would you receive from washing it?

2. To earn extra money in the summer, you grow tomatoes and sell them at the farmers' market for 30 cents per pound. By adding compost to your garden, you can increase your yield as shown in the table on page 20. If compost costs 50 cents per pound and your goal is to make as much money as possible, how many pounds of compost should you add?

Pounds of compost	Pounds of tomatoes
0	100
1	120
2	125
3	128
4	130
5	131
6	131.5

3. Residents of your city are charged a fixed weekly fee of $6 for garbage collection. They are allowed to put out as many cans as they wish. The average household disposes of three cans of garbage per week under this plan. Now suppose that your city changes to a "tag" system. Each can of refuse to be collected must have a tag affixed to it. The tags cost $2 each and are not reusable. What effect do you think the introduction of the tag system will have on the total quantity of garbage collected in your city? Explain briefly.

4. Once a week, Smith purchases a six-pack of cola and puts it in his refrigerator for his two children. He invariably discovers that all six cans are gone on the first day. Jones also purchases a six-pack of cola once a week for his two children, but unlike Smith, he tells them that each may drink no more than three cans. If the children use cost-benefit analysis each time they decide whether to drink a can of cola, explain why the cola lasts much longer at Jones's house than at Smith's.

5. Tom is a mushroom farmer. He invests all his spare cash in additional mushrooms, which grow on otherwise useless land behind his barn. The mushrooms double in weight during their first year, after which time they are harvested and sold at a constant price per pound. Tom's friend Dick asks Tom for a loan of $200, which he promises to repay after 1 year. How much interest will Dick have to pay Tom in order for Tom to recover his opportunity cost of making the loan? Explain briefly.

6. Suppose that in the last few seconds you devoted to question 1 on your physics exam you earned 4 extra points, while in the last few seconds you devoted to question 2 you earned 10 extra points. You earned a total of 48 and 12 points, respectively, on the two questions, and the total time you spent on each was the same. If you could take the exam again, how—if at all—should you reallocate your time between these questions?

7. Martha and Sarah have the same preferences and incomes. Just as Martha arrived at the theater to see a play, she discovered that she had lost the $10 ticket she had purchased earlier. Sarah also just arrived at the theater planning to buy a ticket to see the same play when she discovered that she had lost a $10 bill from her wallet. If both Martha and Sarah are rational and both still have enough money to pay for a ticket, is one of them more likely than the other to go ahead and see the play anyway?

8.* You and your friend Joe have identical tastes. At 2 P.M., you go to the local Ticketmaster outlet and buy a $30 ticket to a basketball game to be played that night in Syracuse, 50 miles north of your home in Ithaca. Joe plans to attend the same game, but because he cannot get to the Ticketmaster outlet, he plans to buy his ticket at the game. Tickets sold at the game cost only $25, because they carry no Ticketmaster surcharge. (Many people nonetheless pay the higher price at Ticketmaster, to be sure of getting good seats.) At 4 P.M., an unexpected snowstorm begins, making the prospect of the drive to Syracuse much less attractive than before (but assuring the availability of good seats). If both you and Joe are rational, is one of you more likely to attend the game than the other?

9.* For each long-distance call anywhere in the continental United States, a new phone service will charge users 30 cents per minute for the first 2 minutes and 2 cents per

*Problems marked with an asterisk (*) are more difficult.

minute for additional minutes in each call. Tom's current phone service charges 10 cents per minute for all calls, and his calls are never shorter than 7 minutes. If Tom's dorm switches to the new phone service, what will happen to the average length of his calls?

10.*The meal plan at university A lets students eat as much as they like for a fixed fee of $500 per semester. The average student there eats 250 pounds of food per semester. University B charges $500 for a book of meal tickets that entitles the student to eat 250 pounds of food per semester. If the student eats more than 250 pounds, he or she pays $2 for each additional pound; if the student eats less, he or she gets a $2 per pound refund. If students are rational, at which university will average food consumption be higher? Explain briefly.

■ ANSWERS TO IN-CHAPTER EXERCISES ■

1.1   The benefit of buying the game downtown is again $10 but the cost is now $12, so your economic surplus from buying it downtown would be $10 − $12 = −$2. Since your economic surplus from making the trip would be negative, you should buy at the campus store.

1.2   Saving $100 is $10 more valuable than saving $90, even though the percentage savings is much greater in the case of the Chicago ticket.

1.3   Since you now have no alternative use for your coupon, the opportunity cost of using it to pay for the Fort Lauderdale trip is zero. That means your economic surplus from the trip will be $1,350 − $1,000 = $350 > 0, so you should use your coupon and go to Fort Lauderdale.

1.4   The marginal benefit of the fourth launch is $9 billion, which exceeds its marginal cost of $8 billion, so the fourth launch should be added. But the fifth launch should not, since its marginal cost ($12 billion) exceeds its marginal benefit ($9 billion).

1.5   If the star player takes one more shot, some other player must take one less. The fact that the star player's *average* success rate is higher than the other player's does not mean that the probability of making his *next* shot (the marginal benefit of having him shoot once more) is higher than the probability of another player making his next shot. Indeed, if the best player took all his team's shots, the other team would focus its defensive effort entirely on him, in which case letting others shoot would definitely pay.

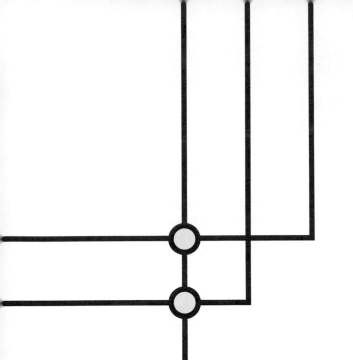

WORKING WITH EQUATIONS, GRAPHS, AND TABLES

■

Although many of the examples and most of the end-of-chapter problems in this book are quantitative, none requires mathematical skills beyond rudimentary high school algebra and geometry. In this brief appendix we review some of the skills you'll need for dealing with these examples and problems.

One important skill is to be able to read simple verbal descriptions and translate the information they provide into the relevant equations or graphs. You'll also need to be able to translate information given in tabular form into an equation or graph, and sometimes you'll need to translate graphical information into a table or equation. The following examples illustrate all the tools you'll need.

USING A VERBAL DESCRIPTION TO CONSTRUCT AN EQUATION

We begin with an example that shows how to construct a long-distance telephone billing equation from a verbal description of the billing plan.

EXAMPLE A.1

Your long-distance telephone plan charges you $5 per month plus 10 cents per minute for long-distance calls. Write an equation that describes your monthly telephone bill.

equation a mathematical expression that describes the relationship between two or more variables

variable a quantity that is free to take a range of different values

dependent variable a variable in an equation whose value is determined by the value taken by another variable in the equation

independent variable a variable in an equation whose value determines the value taken by another variable in the equation

constant (or parameter) a quantity that is fixed in value

An **equation** is a simple mathematical expression that describes the relationship between two or more **variables**, or quantities that are free to assume different values in some range. The most common type of equation we'll work with contains two types of variable: **dependent variable** and **independent variable**. In this example, the dependent variable is the dollar amount of your monthly telephone bill, and the independent variable is the variable on which your bill depends, namely, the volume of long-distance calls you make during the month. Your bill also depends on the $5 monthly fee and the 10 cents per minute charge. But in this example, those amounts are **constants**, not variables. A constant, also called a **parameter**, is a quantity in an equation that is fixed in value, not free to vary. As the terms suggest, the dependent variable describes an outcome that depends on the value taken by the independent variable.

Once you've identified the dependent variable and the independent variable, choose simple symbols to represent them. In algebra courses, X is typically used to represent the independent variable and Y the dependent variable. Many people find it easier to remember what the variables stand for, however, if they choose symbols that are linked in some straightforward way to the quantities that the variables represent. Thus, in this example, we might use B to represent your monthly *bill* in dollars and T to represent the total *time* in minutes you spent during the month on long-distance calls.

Having identified the relevant variables and chosen symbols to represent them, you are now in a position to write the equation that links them:

$$B = 5 + 0.10T, \tag{A.1}$$

where B is your monthly long-distance bill in dollars and T is your monthly total long-distance calling time in minutes. The fixed monthly fee (5) and the charge per minute (0.10) are parameters in this equation. Note the importance of being clear about the units of measure. Because B represents the monthly bill in dollars, we must also express the fixed monthly fee and the per-minute charge in dollars, which is why the latter number appears in Equation A.1 as 0.10 rather than 10. Equation A.1 follows the normal convention in which the dependent variable appears by itself on the left-hand side while the independent variable or variables and constants appear on the right-hand side.

Once we have the equation for the monthly bill, we can use it to calculate how much you'll owe as a function of your monthly volume of long-distance calls. For example, if you make 32 minutes of calls, you can calculate your monthly bill by simply substituting 32 minutes for T in Equation A.1:

$$B = 5 + 0.10(32) = 8.20. \tag{A.2}$$

Your monthly bill when you make 32 minutes of calls is thus equal to $8.20.

EXERCISE A.1

Under the monthly billing plan described in Example A.1, how much would you owe for a month during which you made 45 minutes of long-distance calls?

GRAPHING THE EQUATION OF A STRAIGHT LINE

The next example shows how to portray the billing plan described in Example A.1 as a graph.

Construct a graph that portrays the monthly long-distance telephone billing plan described in Example A.1, putting your telephone charges, in dollars per month, on the vertical axis, and your total volume of calls, in minutes per month, on the horizontal axis.

The first step in responding to this instruction is the one we just took, namely, to translate the verbal description of the billing plan into an equation. When graphing an equation, the normal convention is to use the vertical axis to represent the dependent variable and the horizontal axis to represent the independent variable. In Figure A.1, we therefore put B on the vertical axis and T on the horizontal axis. One way to construct the graph shown in the figure is to begin by plotting the monthly bill values that correspond to several different total amounts of long-distance calls. For example, someone who makes 10 minutes of calls during the month would have a bill of $B = 5 + 0.10(10) = \$6$. Thus, in Figure A.1 the value of 10 minutes per month on the horizontal axis corresponds to a bill of \$6 per month on the vertical axis (point A). Someone who makes 30 minutes of long-distance calls during the month will have a monthly bill of $B = 5 + 0.10(30) = \$8$, so the value of 30 minutes per month on the horizontal axis corresponds to \$8 per month on the vertical axis (point C). Similarly, someone who makes 70 minutes of long-distance calls during the month will have a monthly bill of $B = 5 + 0.10(70) = \$12$, so the value of 70 minutes on the horizontal axis corresponds to \$12 on the vertical axis (point D). The line joining these points is the graph of the monthly billing Equation A.1.

As shown in Figure A.1, the graph of the equation $B = 5 + 0.10T$ is a straight line. The parameter 5 is the **vertical intercept** of the line—the value of B when $T = 0$, or the point at which the line intersects the vertical axis. The parameter 0.10 is the **slope** of the line, which is the ratio of the **rise** of the line to the corresponding **run.** The ratio rise/run is simply the vertical distance between any two points on the line divided by the horizontal distance between those points. For example, if we choose points A and C in Figure A.1, the rise is $8 - 6 = 2$ and the corresponding run is $30 - 10 = 20$, so rise/run $= 2/20 = 0.10$. More generally, for the graph of any equation $Y = a + bX$, the parameter a is the vertical intercept and the parameter b is the slope.

EXAMPLE A.2

vertical intercept in a straight line, the value taken by the dependent variable when the independent variable equals zero

slope in a straight line, the ratio of the vertical distance the straight line travels between any two points *(rise)* to the corresponding horizontal distance *(run)*

FIGURE A.1
The Monthly Telephone Bill in Example A.1.
The graph of the equation $B = 5 + 0.10T$ is the straight line shown. Its vertical intercept is 5, and its slope is 0.10.

DERIVING THE EQUATION OF A STRAIGHT LINE FROM ITS GRAPH

The next example shows how to derive the equation for a straight line from a graph of the line.

EXAMPLE A.3

Figure A.2 shows the graph of the monthly billing plan for a new long-distance plan. What is the equation for this graph? How much is the fixed monthly fee under this plan? How much is the charge per minute?

FIGURE A.2

Another Monthly Long-Distance Plan.

The vertical distance between points A and C is $12 - 8 = 4$ units, and the horizontal distance between points A and C is $40 - 20 = 20$, so the slope of the line is $4/20 = 1/5 = 0.20$. The vertical intercept (the value of B when $T = 0$) is 4. So the equation for the billing plan shown is $B = 4 + 0.20T$.

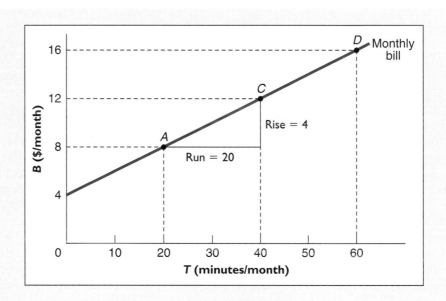

The slope of the line shown is the rise between any two points divided by the corresponding run. For points A and C, rise $= 12 - 8 = 4$, and run $= 40 - 20 = 20$, so the slope equals rise/run $= 4/20 = 1/5 = 0.20$. And since the horizontal intercept of the line is 4, its equation must be given by

$$B = 4 + 0.20T. \qquad (A.3)$$

Under this plan, the fixed monthly fee is the value of the bill when $T = 0$, which is $4. The charge per minute is the slope of the billing line, 0.20, or 20 cents per minute.

EXERCISE A.2

Write the equation for the billing plan shown in the accompanying graph. How much is its fixed monthly fee? Its charge per minute?

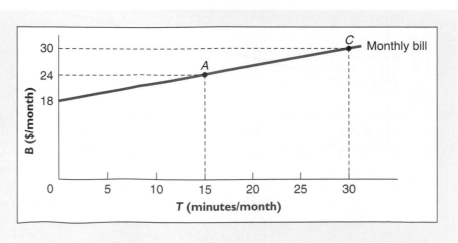

CHANGES IN THE VERTICAL INTERCEPT AND SLOPE

Examples A.4 and A.5 and Exercises A.3 and A.4 provide practice in seeing how a line shifts with a change in its vertical intercept or slope.

EXAMPLE A.4

Show how the billing plan whose graph is in Figure A.2 would change if the monthly fixed fee were increased from \$4 to \$8.

An increase in the monthly fixed fee from \$4 to \$8 would increase the vertical intercept of the billing plan by \$4 but would leave its slope unchanged. An increase in the fixed fee thus leads to a parallel upward shift in the billing plan by \$4, as shown in Figure A.3. For any given number of minutes of long-distance calls, the monthly charge on the new bill will be \$4 higher than on the

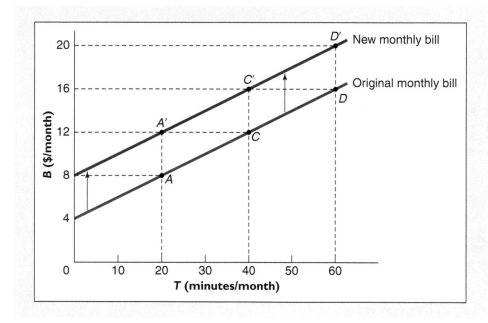

FIGURE A.3
The Effect of an Increase in the Vertical Intercept.
An increase in the vertical intercept of a straight line produces an upward parallel shift in the line.

old bill. Thus 20 minutes of calls per month costs \$8 under the original plan (point A) but \$12 under the new plan (point A'). And 40 minutes costs \$12 under the original plan (point C), \$16 under the new plan (point C'); and 60 minutes costs \$16 under the original plan (point D), \$20 under the new plan (point D').

EXERCISE A.3

Show how the billing plan whose graph is in Figure A.2 would change if the monthly fixed fee were reduced from \$4 to \$2.

EXAMPLE A.5

Show how the billing plan whose graph is in Figure A.2 would change if the charge per minute were increased from 20 cents to 40 cents.

Because the monthly fixed fee is unchanged, the vertical intercept of the new billing plan continues to be 4. But the slope of the new plan, shown in Figure A.4, is 0.40, or twice the slope of the original plan. More generally, in the equation $Y = a + bX$, an increase in b makes the slope of the graph of the equation steeper.

FIGURE A.4

The Effect of an Increase in the Charge per Minute.

Because the fixed monthly fee continues to be $4, the vertical intercept of the new plan is the same as that of the original plan. With the new charge per minute of 40 cents, the slope of the billing plan rises from 0.20 to 0.40.

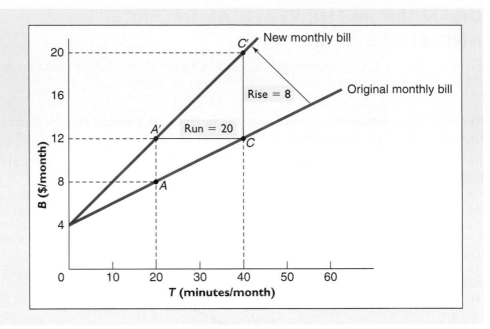

EXERCISE A.4

Show how the billing plan whose graph is in Figure A.2 would change if the charge per minute were reduced from 20 cents to 10 cents.

Exercise A.4 illustrates the general rule that in an equation $Y = a + bX$, a reduction in b makes the slope of the graph of the equation less steep.

CONSTRUCTING EQUATIONS AND GRAPHS FROM TABLES

Example A.6 and Exercise A.5 show how to transform tabular information into an equation or graph.

EXAMPLE A.6

Table A.1 shows four points from a monthly long-distance telephone billing equation. If all points on this billing equation lie on a straight line, find the vertical intercept of the equation and graph it. What is the monthly fixed fee? What is the charge per minute? Calculate the total bill for a month with 1 hour of long-distance calls.

TABLE A.1
Points on a Long-Distance Billing Plan

Long-distance bill ($/month)	Total long-distance calls (minutes/month)
10.50	10
11.00	20
11.50	30
12.00	40

One approach to this problem is simply to plot any two points from the table on a graph. Since we are told that the billing equation is a straight line, that line must be the one that passes through any two of its points. Thus, in Figure A.5 we use

FIGURE A.5
Plotting the Monthly Billing Equation from a Sample of Points.
Point A is taken from row 2, Table A.1, and point C from row 4. The monthly billing plan is the straight line that passes through these points.

A to denote the point from Table A.1 for which a monthly bill of $11 corresponds to 20 minutes per month of calls (second row) and C to denote the point for which a monthly bill of $12 corresponds to 40 minutes per month of calls (fourth row). The straight line passing through these points is the graph of the billing equation.

Unless you have a steady hand, however, or use extremely large graph paper, the method of extending a line between two points on the billing plan is unlikely to be very accurate. An alternative approach is to calculate the equation for the billing plan directly. Since the equation is a straight line, we know that it takes the general form $B = f + sT$, where f is the fixed monthly fee and s is the slope. Our goal is to calculate the vertical intercept f and the slope s. From the same two points we plotted earlier, A and C, we can calculate the slope of the billing plan as $s = \text{rise/run} = 1/20 = 0.05$.

So all that remains is to calculate f, the fixed monthly fee. At point C on the billing plan, the total monthly bill is $12 for 40 minutes, so we can substitute $B = 12$, $s = 0.05$, and $T = 40$ into the general equation $B = f + sT$ to obtain

$$12 = f + 0.05(40), \tag{A.4}$$

or

$$12 = f + 2, \tag{A.5}$$

which solves for $f = 10$. So the monthly billing equation must be

$$B = 10 + 0.05T. \tag{A.6}$$

For this billing equation, the fixed fee is $10 per month, the calling charge is 5 cents per minute ($0.05/minute), and the total bill for a month with 1 hour of long-distance calls is $B = 10 + 0.05(60) = \$13$, just as shown in Figure A.5.

EXERCISE A.5

The following table shows four points from a monthly long-distance telephone billing plan.

Long-distance bill ($/month)	Total long-distance calls (minutes/month)
20.00	10
30.00	20
40.00	30
50.00	40

> If all points on this billing plan lie on a straight line, find the vertical intercept of the corresponding equation without graphing it. What is the monthly fixed fee? What is the charge per minute? How much would the charges be for 1 hour of long-distance calls per month?

▪ KEY TERMS ▪

constant (24)
dependent variable (24)
equation (24)
independent variable (24)

parameter (24)
rise (25)
run (25)
slope (25)

variable (24)
vertical intercept (25)

▪ ANSWERS TO IN-APPENDIX EXERCISES ▪

A.1 To calculate your monthly bill for 45 minutes of calls, substitute 45 minutes for T in equation A.1 to get $B = 5 + 0.10(45) = \$9.50$.

A.2 Calculating the slope using points A and C, we have rise $= 30 - 24 = 6$ and run $= 30 - 15 = 15$, so rise/run $= 6/15 = 2/5 = 0.40$. And since the horizontal intercept of the line is 18, its equation is $B = 18 + 0.40T$. Under this plan, the fixed monthly fee is $18, and the charge per minute is the slope of the billing line, 0.40, or 40 cents per minute.

A.3 A $2 reduction in the monthly fixed fee would produce a downward parallel shift in the billing plan by $2.

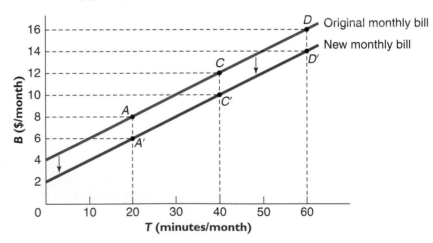

A.4 With an unchanged monthly fixed fee, the vertical intercept of the new billing plan continues to be 4. The slope of the new plan is 0.10, half the slope of the original plan.

A.5 Let the billing equation be $B = f + sT$, where f is the fixed monthly fee and s is the slope. From the first two points in the table, calculate the slope s = rise/run = $10/10 = 1.0$. To calculate f, we can use the information in row 1 of the table to write the billing equation as $20 = f + 1.0(10)$ and solve for $f = 10$. So the monthly billing equation must be $B = 10 + 1.0T$. For this billing equation, the fixed fee is $10 per month, the calling charge is $1 per minute, and the total bill for a month with 1 hour of long-distance calls is $B = 10 + 1.0(60) = \$70$.

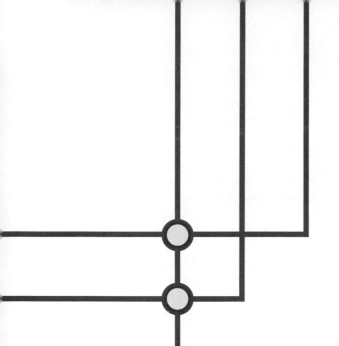

COMPARATIVE ADVANTAGE: THE BASIS FOR EXCHANGE

■

During a stint as a Peace Corps volunteer in rural Nepal, a young economic naturalist employed a cook named Birkhaman, who came from a remote Himalayan village in neighboring Bhutan. Although Birkhaman had virtually no formal education, he was spectacularly resourceful. His primary duties, to prepare food and maintain the kitchen, he performed extremely well. But he also had other skills. He could thatch a roof, butcher a goat, and repair shoes. An able tinsmith and a good carpenter, he could sew and fix a broken alarm clock, as well as plaster walls. And he was a local authority on home remedies.

Birkhaman's range of skills was broad even in Nepal, where the least skilled villager could perform a wide range of services that most Americans hire others to perform. Why this difference in skills and employment?

One might be tempted to answer that the Nepalese are simply too poor to hire others to perform these services. Nepal is indeed a poor country, whose income per person is less than one one-hundredth that of the United States. Few Nepalese have spare cash to spend on outside services. But as reasonable as this poverty explanation may seem, the reverse is actually the case. The Nepalese do not perform their own services because they are poor; rather, they are poor largely *because* they perform their own services.

The alternative to a system in which everyone is a jack of all trades is one in which people *specialize* in particular goods and services, then satisfy their needs by trading among themselves. Economic systems based on specialization and the exchange of goods and services are generally far more productive than those with less specialization. Our task in this chapter is to investigate why

Did this man perform most of his own services because he was poor, or was he poor because he performed most of his own services?

this is so. In doing so we will explore why people choose to exchange goods and services in the first place, rather than having each person produce his or her own food, cars, clothing, shelter, and the like.

As this chapter will show, the reason that specialization is so productive is the existence of what economists call *comparative advantage*. Roughly, a person has a comparative advantage at producing a particular good or service, say, haircuts, if that person is *relatively* more efficient at producing haircuts than at producing other goods or services. We will see that we can all have more of *every* good and service if each of us specializes in the activities at which we have a comparative advantage.

This chapter will also introduce the *production possibilities curve,* which is a graphical method of describing the combinations of goods and services that an economy can produce. The development of this tool will allow us to see much more precisely how specialization enhances the productive capacity of even the simplest economy.

EXCHANGE AND OPPORTUNITY COST

The scarcity principle (see Chapter 1) reminds us that the opportunity cost of spending more time on any one activity is having less time available to spend on others. As the following example makes clear, this principle helps explain why everyone can do better by concentrating on those activities at which he or she performs best relative to others.

EXAMPLE 2.1

Should a top lawyer prepare his own will?

absolute advantage one person has an absolute advantage over another if he or she takes fewer hours to perform a task than the other person

comparative advantage one person has a comparative advantage over another if his or her opportunity cost of performing a task is lower than the other person's opportunity cost

Should Johnnie Cochran write his own will?

Attorney Johnnie Cochran gained national attention as the leader of the legal team that, against all odds, won O. J. Simpson's acquittal of the charge of murdering his former wife and her friend in 1994. By consensus, Cochran is one of the most able attorneys in the country. For example, when the *California Lawyer* magazine asked leading California attorneys whom they would hire if they were charged with a serious felony, Cochran's was the name most often mentioned. But although Cochran devotes virtually all of his working hours to high-profile litigation, he is also competent to perform a much broader range of legal services. Suppose, for example, that he could prepare his own will in two hours, only half as long as it would take any other attorney. Does that mean that Cochran should prepare his own will?

On the strength of his talent as a litigator, Cochran earns several million dollars a year, which means that the opportunity cost of any time he spends preparing his will would be more than $1,000 per hour. Attorneys who specialize in property law typically earn far less than that amount. Cochran would have little difficulty engaging a competent property lawyer who could prepare his will for him for less than $800. So even though Cochran's considerable skills would enable him to perform this task more quickly than another attorney, it would not be in his interest to prepare his own will.

In the preceding example, economists would say that Cochran has an **absolute advantage** at preparing his will but a **comparative advantage** at trial work. He has an absolute advantage at preparing his will because he can perform that task in less time than a property lawyer could. Even so, the property lawyer has a comparative advantage at preparing wills because his opportunity cost of performing that task is lower than Cochran's.

The point of Example 2.1 is not that people whose time is valuable should never perform their own services. That example made the implicit assumption that Cochran would have been equally happy to spend an hour preparing his will or preparing for a trial. But suppose he was tired of trial preparation and felt it might be enjoyable to refresh his knowledge of property law. Preparing his own will might then have made perfect sense! But unless he expected to gain special satisfaction from performing that task, he would almost certainly do better to hire a property lawyer. The property lawyer would also benefit, or else she wouldn't have offered to prepare wills for the stated price.

THE PRINCIPLE OF COMPARATIVE ADVANTAGE

One of the most important insights of modern economics is that when two people (or two nations) have different opportunity costs of performing various tasks, they can always increase the total value of available goods and services by trading with one another. The following simple example captures the logic behind this insight.

Should Paula update her own web page?

EXAMPLE 2.2

Consider a small community in which Paula is the only professional bicycle mechanic and Beth is the only professional HTML programmer. Paula also happens to be an even better HTML programmer than Beth. If the amount of time each of them takes to perform these tasks is as shown in Table 2.1, and if each regards the two tasks as equally pleasant (or unpleasant), does the fact that Paula can program faster than Beth imply that Paula should update her own web page?

The entries in the table show that Paula has an absolute advantage over Beth in both activities. While Paula, the mechanic, needs only 20 minutes to update a web page, Beth, the programmer, needs 30 minutes. Paula's advantage over Beth is even greater when the task is fixing bikes: She can complete a repair in only 10 minutes, compared to Beth's 30 minutes.

TABLE 2.1
Productivity Information for Paula and Beth

	Time to update a web page	Time to complete a bicycle repair
Paula	20 minutes	10 minutes
Beth	30 minutes	30 minutes

But the fact that Paula is a better programmer than Beth does *not* imply that Paula should update her own web page. As with the lawyer who litigates instead of preparing his own will, Beth has a comparative advantage over Paula at programming: She is *relatively* more productive at programming than Paula. Similarly, Paula has a comparative advantage in bicycle repair. (Remember that a person has a comparative advantage at a given task if his or her opportunity cost of performing that task is lower than another person's.)

What is Beth's opportunity cost of updating a web page? Since she takes 30 minutes to update each page—the same amount of time she takes to fix a bicycle—her opportunity cost of updating a web page is one bicycle repair. In other words, by taking the time to update a web page, Beth is effectively giving up the opportunity to do one bicycle repair. Paula, in contrast, can complete two bicycle repairs in the time she takes to update a single web page. For her, the opportunity cost of updating a web page is two bicycle repairs. Paula's opportunity cost of programming, measured in terms of bicycle repairs forgone, is twice as high as Beth's. Thus Beth has a comparative advantage at programming.

The interesting and important implication of the opportunity cost comparison summarized in Table 2.2 is that the total number of bicycle repairs and web updates accomplished if Paula and Beth both spend part of their time at each activity will always be smaller than the number accomplished if each specializes in the activity in which she has a comparative advantage. Suppose, for example, that people in their community demand a total of 16 web page updates per day.

TABLE 2.2
Opportunity Costs for Paula and Beth

	Opportunity cost of updating a web page	Opportunity cost of a bicycle repair
Paula	2 bicycle repairs	0.5 web page updates
Beth	1 bicycle repair	1 web page update

If Paula spent half her time updating web pages and the other half repairing bicycles, an eight-hour workday would yield 12 web page updates and 24 bicycle repairs. To complete the remaining 4 updates, Beth would have to spend two hours programming, which would leave her six hours to repair bicycles. And since she takes 30 minutes to do each repair, she would have time to complete 12 of them. So when the two women try to be jacks-of-all-trades, they end up completing a total of 16 web page updates and 36 bicycle repairs.

Consider what would have happened had each woman specialized in her activity of comparative advantage. Beth could have updated 16 web pages on her own, and Paula could have performed 48 bicycle repairs. Specialization would have created an additional 12 bicycle repairs out of thin air.

"We're a natural, Rachel. I handle intellectual property, and you're a content-provider."

When computing the opportunity cost of one good in terms of another, we must pay close attention to the form in which the productivity information is presented. In the preceding example, we were told how many minutes each person needed to perform each task. Alternatively, we might be told how many units of each task each person can perform in an hour. Work through the following exercise to see how to proceed when information is presented in this alternative format.

EXERCISE 2.1

Should Barb update her own web page?

Consider a small community in which **Barb** is the only professional bicycle mechanic and **Pat** is the only professional HTML programmer. If their productivity rates at the two tasks are as shown in the table, and if each regards the two tasks as equally pleasant (or unpleasant), does the fact that Barb can program faster than Pat imply that Barb should update her own web page?

	Productivity in programming	Productivity in bicycle repair
Pat	2 web page updates per hour	1 repair per hour
Barb	3 web page updates per hour	3 repairs per hour

The principle illustrated by the preceding examples is so important that we state it formally as one of the core principles of the course:

The Principle of Comparative Advantage: Everyone does best when each person (or each country) concentrates on the activities for which his or her opportunity cost is lowest.

Indeed, the gains made possible from specialization based on comparative advantage constitute the rationale for market exchange. They explain why each person does not devote 10 percent of his or her time to producing cars, 5 percent to growing food, 25 percent to building housing, 0.0001 percent to performing brain surgery, and so on. By concentrating on those tasks at which we are relatively most productive, together we can produce vastly more than if we all tried to be self-sufficient.

This insight brings us back to Birkhaman the cook. Though Birkhaman's versatility was marvelous, he was neither as good a doctor as someone who has been trained in medical school, nor as good a repairman as someone who spends each day fixing things. If a number of people with Birkhaman's native talents had joined together, each of them specializing in one or two tasks, together they would have enjoyed more and better goods and services than each could possibly have produced independently. Although there is much to admire in the resourcefulness of people who have learned through necessity to rely on their own skills, that path is no route to economic prosperity.

Specialization and its effects provide ample grist for the economic naturalist. Here's an example from the world of sports.

Where have all the .400 hitters gone?

In baseball, a .400 hitter is a player who averages at least four hits every 10 times he comes to bat. Though never common in professional baseball, .400 hitters used to appear relatively frequently. Early in the twentieth century, for example, a player known as Wee Willie Keeler batted .432, meaning that he got a hit in over 43 percent of his times at bat. But since Ted Williams of the Boston Red Sox batted .406 in 1941, there has not been a single .400 hitter in the major leagues. Why not?

Some baseball buffs argue that the disappearance of the .400 hitter means today's baseball players are not as good as yesterday's. But that claim does not withstand close examination. We can document, for example, that today's players are bigger, stronger, and faster than those of Willie Keeler's day. (Wee Willie himself was just a little over 5 feet, 4 inches, and he weighed only 140 pounds.)

ECONOMIC NATURALIST 2.1

Why has no major league baseball player batted .400 since Ted Williams did it more than half a century ago?

Bill James, a leading analyst of baseball history, argues that the .400 hitter has disappeared because the quality of play in the major leagues has *improved*, not declined. In particular, pitching and fielding standards are higher, which makes batting .400 more difficult.

Why has the quality of play in baseball improved? Although there are many reasons, including better nutrition, training, and equipment, specialization has also played an important role.[1] At one time, pitchers were expected to pitch for the entire game. Now pitching staffs include pitchers who specialize in starting the game ("starters"), others who specialize in pitching two or three innings in the middle of the game ("middle relievers"), and still others who specialize in pitching only the last inning ("closers"). Each of these roles requires different skills and tactics. Pitchers may also specialize in facing left-handed or right-handed batters, in striking batters out, or in getting batters to hit balls on the ground. Similarly, few fielders today play multiple defensive positions; most specialize in only one. Some players specialize in defense (to the detriment of their hitting skills); these "defensive specialists" can be brought in late in the game to protect a lead. Even in managing and coaching, specialization has increased markedly. Relief pitchers now have their own coaches, and statistical specialists use computers to discover the weaknesses of opposing hitters. The net result of these increases in specialization is that even the weakest of today's teams play highly competent defensive baseball. With no "weaklings" to pick on, hitting .400 over an entire season has become a near-impossible task.

SOURCES OF COMPARATIVE ADVANTAGE

At the individual level, comparative advantage often appears to be the result of inborn talent. For instance, some people seem to be naturally gifted at programming computers while others seem to have a special knack for fixing bikes. But comparative advantage is more often the result of education, training, or experience. Thus we usually leave the design of kitchens to people with architectural training, the drafting of contracts to people who have studied law, and the teaching of physics to people with advanced degrees in that field.

At the national level, comparative advantage may derive from differences in natural resources or from differences in society or culture. The United States, which has a disproportionate share of the world's leading research universities, has a comparative advantage in the design of electronic computing hardware and software. Canada, which has one of the world's highest per-capita endowments of farm and forest land, has a comparative advantage in the production of agricultural products. Topography and climate explain why Colorado specializes in the skiing industry while Hawaii specializes as an ocean resort.

Seemingly noneconomic factors can also give rise to comparative advantage. For instance, the emergence of English as the de facto world language gives English-speaking countries a comparative advantage over non–English-speaking nations in the production of books, movies, and popular music. Even a country's institutions may affect the likelihood that it will achieve comparative advantage in a particular pursuit. For example, cultures that encourage entrepreneurship will tend to have a comparative advantage in the introduction of new products, whereas those that promote high standards of care and craftsmanship will tend to have a comparative advantage in the production of high-quality variants of established products.

[1]For an interesting discussion of specialization and the decline of the .400 hitter from the perspective of an evolutionary biologist, see Stephen Jay Gould, *Full House,* New York: Three Rivers Press, 1996, Part 3.

Televisions and videocassette recorders were developed and first produced in the United States, but today the U.S. accounts for only a minuscule share total world production of these products. Why did the United States fail to retain its lead in these markets?

That televisions and VCRs were developed in the United States is explained in part by the country's comparative advantage in technological research, which in turn was supported by the country's outstanding system of higher education. Other contributing factors were high expenditures on the development of electronic components for the military and a culture that actively encourages entrepreneurship. As for the production of these products, America enjoyed an early advantage partly because the product designs were themselves evolving rapidly at first, which favored production facilities located in close proximity to the product designers. Early production techniques also relied intensively on skilled labor, which is abundant in the United States. In time, however, product designs stabilized and many of the more complex manufacturing operations were automated. Both of these changes gradually led to greater reliance on relatively less skilled production workers. And at that point, factories located in high-wage countries like the United States could no longer compete with those located in low-wage areas overseas.

RECAP   EXCHANGE AND OPPORTUNITY COST

Gains from exchange are possible if trading partners have comparative advantages in producing different goods and services. You have a comparative advantage in producing, say, web pages, if your opportunity cost of producing a web page—measured in terms of other production opportunities forgone—is smaller than the corresponding opportunity costs of your trading partners. Maximum production is achieved if each person specializes in producing the good or service in which he or she has the lowest opportunity cost (the principle of comparative advantage). Comparative advantage makes specialization worthwhile even if one trading partner is more productive than others, in absolute terms, in every activity.

COMPARATIVE ADVANTAGE AND PRODUCTION POSSIBILITIES

Comparative advantage and specialization allow an economy to produce more than if each person tries to produce a little of everything. In this section we gain further insight into the advantages of specialization by introducing a graph that can be used to describe the various combinations of goods and services that an economy can produce.

THE PRODUCTION POSSIBILITIES CURVE

We begin with a hypothetical economy in which only two goods are produced, coffee and pine nuts. It is a small island economy, and "production" consists either of picking coffee beans that grow on small bushes on the island's central valley floor or of picking pine nuts that grow on trees on the steep hillsides overlooking the valley. The more time workers spend picking coffee, the less time they have available for picking nuts. So if people want to drink more coffee, they must make do with a smaller amount of nuts.

If we know how productive workers are at each activity, we can summarize the various combinations of coffee and nuts they can pick each day. This menu of possibilities is known as the **production possibilities curve**.

production possibilities curve a graph that describes the maximum amount of one good that can be produced for every possible level of production of the other good

To keep matters simple, we begin with an example in which the economy has only a single worker who can divide her time between the two activities.

EXAMPLE 2.3

What is the production possibilities curve for an economy in which Susan is the only worker?

Consider a society consisting only of Susan, who allocates her production time between coffee and nuts. She is short and has nimble fingers, two qualities that make her more productive at picking coffee than at picking nuts. She can pick 2 pounds of nuts or 4 pounds of coffee in an hour. If she works a total of 6 hours per day, describe her production possibilities curve—the graph that displays, for each level of nut production, the maximum amount of coffee that Susan can pick.

The vertical axis in Figure 2.1 shows Susan's daily production of coffee, and the horizontal axis shows her daily production of nuts. Let's begin by looking at two extreme allocations of her time. First, suppose she employs her entire work-day (6 hours) picking coffee. In that case, since she can pick 4 pounds of coffee per hour, she would pick 24 pounds per day of coffee and zero pounds of nuts. That combination of coffee and nut production is represented by point A in Figure 2.1. It is the vertical intercept of Susan's production possibilities curve.

Now suppose, instead, that Susan devotes all her time to picking nuts. Since she can pick 2 pounds of nuts per hour, her total daily production would be 12 pounds of nuts. That combination is represented by point D in Figure 2.1, the horizontal intercept of Susan's production possibilities curve. Because Susan's production of each good is exactly proportional to the amount of time she devotes to that good, the remaining points along her production possibilities curve will lie on the straight line that joins A and D.

For example, suppose that Susan devotes 4 hours each day to picking coffee and 2 hours to picking nuts. She will then end up with (4 hours/day) × (4 pounds/hour) = 16 pounds of coffee per day and (2 hours/day) × (2 pounds/hour) = 4 pounds of nuts. This is the point labeled B in Figure 2.1. Alternatively, if she devotes 2 hours to coffee and 4 to nuts, she will get (2 hours/day) × (4 pounds/hour) = 8 pounds of coffee per day and (4 hours/day) × (2 pounds/hour) = 8 pounds of nuts. This alternative combination is represented by point C in Figure 2.1.

Since Susan's production possibilities curve (PPC) is a straight line, its slope is constant. The absolute value of the slope of Susan's PPC is the ratio of its vertical

FIGURE 2.1
Susan's Production Possibilities.
For the production relationships given, the production possibilities curve is a straight line.

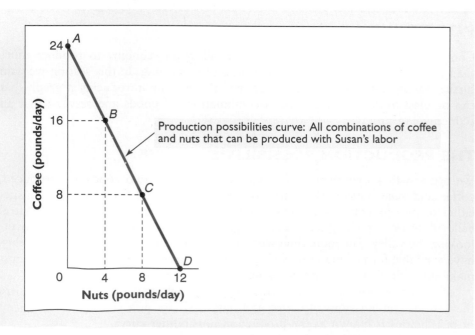

Production possibilities curve: All combinations of coffee and nuts that can be produced with Susan's labor

intercept to its horizontal intercept: (24 pounds of coffee/day)/(12 pounds of nuts/day) = (2 pounds of coffee)/(1 pound of nuts). (Be sure to keep track of the units of measure on each axis when computing this ratio.) *This ratio means that Susan's opportunity cost of an additional pound of nuts is 2 pounds of coffee.*

Note that Susan's opportunity cost (OC) of nuts can also be expressed as the following simple formula:

$$OC_{nuts} = \frac{\text{loss in coffee}}{\text{gain in nuts}}, \qquad (2.1)$$

where "loss in coffee" means the amount of coffee given up, and "gain in nuts" means the corresponding increase in nuts. Likewise, Susan's opportunity cost of coffee is expressed by this formula:

$$OC_{coffee} = \frac{\text{loss in nuts}}{\text{gain in coffee}}. \qquad (2.2)$$

To say that Susan's opportunity cost of an additional pound of nuts is 2 pounds of coffee is thus equivalent to saying that her opportunity cost of a pound of coffee is 1/2 pound of nuts.

The downward slope of the production possibilities curve shown in Figure 2.1 illustrates the scarcity principle—the idea that because our resources are limited, having more of one good thing generally means having to settle for less of another (see Chapter 1). Susan can have an additional pound of coffee if she wishes, but only if she is willing to give up half a pound of nuts. If Susan is the only person in the economy, her opportunity cost of producing a good becomes, in effect, its price. Thus the price she has to pay for an additional pound of coffee is half a pound of nuts; or the price she has to pay for an additional pound of nuts is 2 pounds of coffee.

Any point that lies either along the production possibilities curve or within it is said to be an **attainable point,** meaning that it can be produced with currently available resources. In Figure 2.2, for example, points *A, B, C, D,* and *E* are attainable points. Points that lie outside the production possibilities curve

attainable point any combination of goods that can be produced using currently available resources

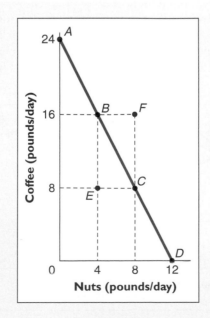

FIGURE 2.2
Attainable and Efficient Points on Susan's Production Possibilities Curve.
Points that lie either along the production possibilities curve (for example, A, B, C, and D) or within it (for example, E) are said to be attainable. Points that lie outside the production possibilities curve (for example, F) are unattainable. Points that lie along the curve are said to be efficient, while those that lie within the curve are said to be inefficient.

unattainable point any combination of goods that cannot be produced using currently available resources

are said to be **unattainable**, meaning that they cannot be produced using currently available resources. In Figure 2.2, *F* is an unattainable point because Susan cannot pick 16 pounds of coffee per day *and* 8 pounds of nuts. Points that lie within the curve are said to be **inefficient**, in the sense that existing resources would allow for production of more of at least one good without sacrificing the production of any other good. At *E*, for example, Susan is picking only 8 pounds of coffee per day and 4 pounds of nuts, which means that she could increase her coffee harvest by 8 pounds per day without giving up any nuts (by moving from *E* to *B*). Alternatively, Susan could pick as many as 4 additional pounds of nuts each day without giving up any coffee (by moving from *E* to *C*). An **efficient** point is one that lies along the production possibilities curve. At any such point, more of one good can be produced only by producing less of the other.

inefficient point any combination of goods for which currently available resources enable an increase in the production of one good without a reduction in the production of the other

efficient point any combination of goods for which currently available resources do not allow an increase in the production of one good without a reduction in the production of the other

EXERCISE 2.2

For the PPC shown in Figure 2.2, state whether the following points are attainable and/or efficient:

a. **20 pounds per day of coffee, 4 pounds per day of nuts.**

b. **12 pounds per day of coffee, 6 pounds per day of nuts.**

c. **4 pounds per day of coffee, 8 pounds per day of nuts.**

HOW INDIVIDUAL PRODUCTIVITY AFFECTS THE SLOPE AND POSITION OF THE PPC

To see how the slope and position of the production possibilities curve depend on an individual's productivity, let's compare Susan's PPC to that of Tom, who is less productive at picking coffee but more productive at picking nuts.

EXAMPLE 2.4

How do changes in productivity affect the opportunity cost of nuts?

Tom is tall and an agile climber, qualities that make him especially well suited for picking nuts that grow on hillside trees. He can pick 4 pounds of nuts or 2 pounds of coffee per hour. If Tom were the only person in the economy, describe the economy's production possibilities curve.

We can construct Tom's PPC the same way we did Susan's. Note first that if Tom devotes an entire workday (6 hours) to coffee picking, he ends up with (6 hours/day) × (2 pounds/hour) = 12 pounds of coffee per day and zero pounds of nuts. So the vertical intercept of Tom's PPC is *A* in Figure 2.3. If instead he

FIGURE 2.3
Tom's Production Possibilities Curve.
Tom's opportunity cost of producing one pound of nuts is only half a pound of coffee.

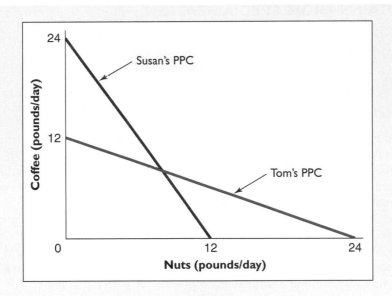

FIGURE 2.4
Individual Production Possibilities Curves Compared.
Tom is less productive in coffee than Susan, but more productive in nuts.

devotes all his time to picking nuts, he gets (6 hours/day) × (4 pounds/hour) = 24 pounds of nuts per day and no coffee. That means the horizontal intercept of his PPC is *D* in Figure 2.3. Because Tom's production of each good is proportional to the amount of time he devotes to it, the remaining points on his PPC will lie along the straight line that joins these two extreme points.

For example, if he devotes 4 hours each day to picking coffee and 2 hours to picking nuts, he will end up with (4 hours/day) × (2 pounds/hour) = 8 pounds of coffee per day and (2 hours/day) × (4 pounds/hour) = 8 pounds of nuts per day. This is the point labeled *B* in Figure 2.3. Alternatively, if he devotes 2 hours to coffee and 4 to nuts, he will get (2 hours/day) × (2 pounds/hour) = 4 pounds of coffee per day and (4 hours/day) × (4 pounds/hour) = 16 pounds of nuts. This alternative combination is represented by point *C* in Figure 2.3.

How does Tom's PPC compare with Susan's? Note in Figure 2.4 that because Tom is absolutely less productive than Susan at picking coffee, the vertical intercept of his PPC lies closer to the origin than Susan's. By the same token, because Susan is absolutely less productive than Tom at picking nuts, the horizontal intercept of her PPC lies closer to the origin than Tom's. For Tom, the opportunity cost of an additional pound of nuts is 1/2 pound of coffee, which is one-fourth Susan's opportunity cost of nuts. This difference in opportunity costs shows up as a difference in the slopes of their PPCs: the absolute value of the slope of Tom's PPC is 1/2, whereas Susan's is 2.

In this example, Tom has both an absolute advantage and a comparative advantage over Susan in picking nuts. Susan, for her part, has both an absolute advantage and a comparative advantage over Tom in picking coffee.

We cannot emphasize strongly enough that the principle of comparative advantage is a relative concept—one that makes sense only when the productivities of two or more people (or countries) are being compared. To cement this idea, work through the following exercise.

EXERCISE 2.3

Suppose Susan can pick 2 pounds of coffee per hour or 4 pounds of nuts per hour; Tom can pick 1 pound of coffee per hour and 1 pound of nuts per hour. What is Susan's opportunity cost of picking a pound of nuts? What is Tom's opportunity cost of picking a pound of nuts? Where does Susan's comparative advantage now lie?

THE GAINS FROM SPECIALIZATION

Earlier we saw that a comparative advantage arising from disparities in individual opportunity costs creates gains for everyone (see Examples 2.1 and 2.2). The following example shows how the same point can be illustrated using production possibility curves.

EXAMPLE 2.5

How costly is failure to specialize?

Suppose that in Example 2.4 Susan and Tom had divided their time so that each person's output consisted of half nuts and half coffee. How much of each good would Tom and Susan have been able to consume? How much could they have consumed if each had specialized in the activity for which he or she enjoyed a comparative advantage?

Since Tom can pick twice as many pounds of nuts in an hour as pounds of coffee, to pick equal quantities of each, he must spend 2 hours picking coffee for every hour he devotes to picking nuts. And since he works a 6-hour day, that means spending 2 hours picking nuts and 4 hours picking coffee. Dividing his time in this way, he will end up with 8 pounds of coffee per day and 8 pounds of nuts. Similarly, since Susan can pick twice as many pounds of coffee in an hour as pounds of nuts, to pick equal quantities of each, she must spend 2 hours picking nuts for every hour she devotes to picking coffee. And since she too works a 6-hour day, that means spending 2 hours picking coffee and 4 hours picking nuts. So, like Tom, she will end up with 8 pounds of coffee per day and 8 pounds of nuts. (See Figure 2.5.) Their combined daily production will thus be 16 pounds of each good. By contrast, had they each specialized in their respective activities of comparative advantage, their combined daily production would have been 24 pounds of each good.

If they exchange coffee and nuts with one another, each can consume a combination of the two goods that would have been unattainable if exchange had not been possible. For example, Susan can give Tom 12 pounds of coffee in exchange for 12 pounds of nuts, enabling each to consume 4 pounds per day more of each good than when each produced and consumed alone. Note that point *E* in Figure 2.5, which has 12 pounds per day of each good, lies beyond each person's PPC, yet is easily attainable with specialization and exchange.

FIGURE 2.5
Production without Specialization.
When Tom and Susan divide their time so that each produces the same number of pounds of coffee and nuts, they can consume a total of 16 pounds of coffee and 16 pounds of nuts each day.

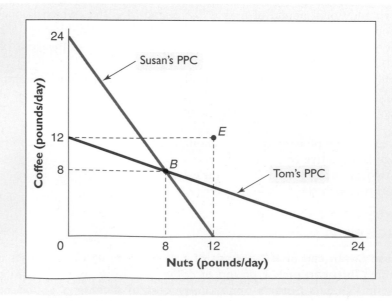

As the following exercise illustrates, the gains from specialization grow larger as the difference in opportunity costs increases.

EXERCISE 2.4

How do differences in opportunity cost affect the gains from specialization? Susan can pick 5 pounds of coffee or 1 pound of nuts in an hour. Tom can pick 1 pound of coffee or 5 pounds of nuts in an hour. Assuming they again work 6-hour days and want to consume coffee and nuts in equal quantities, by how much will specialization increase their consumption compared to the alternative in which each produced only for his or her own consumption?

Although the gains from specialization and exchange grow with increases in the differences in opportunity costs among trading partners, these differences alone still seem insufficient to account for the enormous differences in living standards between rich and poor countries. Average income in the 20 richest countries in the year 2000, for example, was over $27,000 per person, compared to only $211 per person in the 20 poorest countries.[1] Although we will say more later about specialization's role in explaining these differences, we first discuss how to construct the PPC for an entire economy and examine how factors other than specialization might cause it to shift outward over time.

A PRODUCTION POSSIBILITIES CURVE FOR A MANY-PERSON ECONOMY

Although most actual economies consist of millions of workers, the process of constructing a production possibilities curve for an economy of that size is really no different from the process for a one-person economy. Consider again an economy in which the only two goods are coffee and nuts, with coffee again on the vertical axis and nuts on the horizontal axis. The vertical intercept of the economy's PPC is the total amount of coffee that could be picked if all available workers worked full-time picking coffee. Thus the maximum attainable amount of coffee production is shown for the hypothetical economy in Figure 2.6 as 100,000 pounds per day (an amount chosen arbitrarily, for illustrative purposes). The horizontal intercept of the PPC is the amount of nuts that could be picked if all available workers worked full-time picking nuts, shown for this same economy as 80,000 pounds per day (also an amount chosen arbitrarily). But note that the PPC shown in the diagram is not a straight line—as in the earlier examples involving only a single worker—but rather a curve that is bowed out from the origin.

We'll say more in a moment about the reasons for this shape. But first note that a bow-shaped PPC means that the opportunity cost of producing nuts increases as the economy produces more of them. Notice, for example, that when the economy moves from *A,* where it is producing only coffee, to *B,* it gets 20,000 pounds of nuts per day by giving up only 5,000 pounds per day of coffee. When nut production is increased still further, however—for example, by moving from *B* to *C*—the economy again gives up 5,000 pounds per day of coffee yet this time gets only 10,000 additional pounds of nuts. This

---

[1]High-income countries: Australia, Austria, Belgium, Canada, China, Hong Kong, Denmark, Finland, France, Germany, Iceland, Ireland, Japan, Luxembourg, Netherlands, Norway, Singapore, Sweden, Switzerland, United Kingdom, and United States. Low-income countries: Burkina Faso, Burundi, Central African Republic, Chad, Ethiopia, Ghana, Guinea-Bisau, Kenya, Madagascar, Malawi, Mali, Mozambique, Myanmar, Nepal, Niger, Nigeria, Rwanda, Sierra Leone, Tanzania, and Uganda. (Source: Global Policy Forum, http://www.globalpolicy.org/).

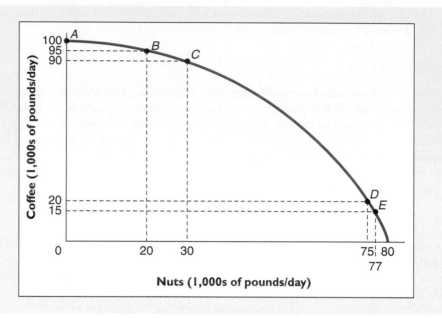

FIGURE 2.6
Production Possibilities Curve for a Large Economy.
For an economy with millions of workers, the PPC typically has a gentle outward bow shape.

pattern of increasing opportunity cost persists over the entire length of the PPC. For example, note that in moving from *D* to *E,* the economy again gives up 5,000 pounds per day of coffee but now gains only 2,000 pounds a day of nuts. Note, finally, that the same pattern of increasing opportunity cost applies to coffee. Thus, as more coffee is produced, the opportunity cost of producing additional coffee—as measured by the amount of nuts that must be sacrificed—also rises.

Why is the PPC for the multiperson economy bow-shaped? The answer lies in the fact that some resources are relatively well suited for picking nuts while others are relatively well suited for picking coffee. If the economy is initially producing only coffee and wants to begin producing some nuts, which workers will it reassign? Recall Susan and Tom, the two workers discussed in Example 2.5, in which Tom's comparative advantage was picking nuts and Susan's comparative advantage was picking coffee. If both workers were currently picking coffee and you wanted to reassign one of them to pick nuts instead, whom would you send? Tom would be the clear choice, because his departure would cost the economy only half as much coffee as Susan's and would augment nut production by twice as much.

The principle is the same in any large multiperson economy, except that the range of opportunity cost differences across workers is even greater than in the earlier two-worker example (Example 2.5). As we keep reassigning workers from coffee production to nut production, sooner or later we must withdraw even coffee specialists like Susan from coffee production. Indeed, we must eventually reassign others whose opportunity cost of producing nuts is far higher than hers.

The shape of the production possibilities curve shown in Figure 2.6 illustrates the general principle that when resources have different opportunity costs, we should always exploit the resource with the lowest opportunity cost first. We call this the *low-hanging-fruit principle,* in honor of the fruit picker's rule of picking the most accessible fruit first:

The Principle of Increasing Opportunity Cost (also called "The Low-Hanging-Fruit Principle"): In expanding the production of any good, first employ those resources with the lowest opportunity cost, and only afterward turn to resources with higher opportunity costs.

A Note on the Logic of the Fruit Picker's Rule

Why should a fruit picker harvest the low-hanging fruit first? This rule makes sense for several reasons. For one, the low-hanging fruit is easier (and hence cheaper) to pick, and if he planned on picking only a limited amount of fruit to begin with, he would clearly come out ahead by avoiding the less accessible fruit on the higher branches. But even if he planned on picking all the fruit on the tree, he would do better to start with the lower branches first, because this would enable him to enjoy the revenue from the sale of the fruit sooner.

The fruit picker's job can be likened to the task confronting a new CEO who has been hired to reform an inefficient, ailing company. The CEO has limited time and attention, so it makes sense to focus first on problems that are relatively easy to correct and whose elimination will provide the biggest improvements in performance—the low-hanging fruit. Later on, the CEO can worry about the many smaller improvements needed to raise the company from very good to excellent.

Again, the important message of the low-hanging-fruit principle is to be sure to take advantage of your most favorable opportunities first.

 RECAP   **COMPARATIVE ADVANTAGE AND PRODUCTION POSSIBILITIES**

For an economy that produces two goods, the production possibilities curve describes the maximum amount of one good that can be produced for every possible level of production of the other good. Attainable points are those that lie on or within the curve, and efficient points are those that lie along the curve. The slope of the production possibilities curve tells us the opportunity cost of producing an additional unit of the good measured along the horizontal axis. The principle of increasing opportunity cost, or the low-hanging-fruit principle, tells us that the slope of the production possibilities curve becomes steeper as we move downward to the right. The greater the differences among individual opportunity costs, the more bow-shaped the production possibilities curve will be, and the more bow-shaped the production possibilities curve, the greater will be the potential gains from specialization.

FACTORS THAT SHIFT THE ECONOMY'S PRODUCTION POSSIBILITIES CURVE

As its name implies, the production possibilities curve provides a summary of the production options open to any society. At any given moment, the PPC confronts society with a trade-off. The only way people can produce and consume more nuts is to produce and consume less coffee. In the long run, however, it is often possible to increase production of all goods. This is what is meant when people speak of economic growth. As shown in Figure 2.7, economic growth is an outward shift in the economy's production possibilities curve. It can result from increases in the amount of productive resources available or from improvements in knowledge or technology that render existing resources more productive.

What causes the quantity of productive resources to grow in an economy? One factor is investment in new factories and equipment. When workers have more and better equipment to work with, their productivity increases, often dramatically. This is surely an important factor behind the differences in living standards between rich and poor countries. According to one study, for example, the value of capital investment per worker in the United States is about $30,000, while in Nepal the corresponding figure is less than $1,000.[1]

Such large differences in capital per worker don't occur all at once. They are a consequence of decades, even centuries, of differences in rates of savings and

[1]Alan Heston and Robert Summers, "The Penn World Table (Mark 5): An Expanded Set of International Comparisons, 1950–1988," *Quarterly Journal of Economics*, May 1991, pp. 327–368.

FIGURE 2.7

Economic Growth: An Outward Shift in the Economy's PPC.

Increases in productive resources (such as labor and capital equipment) or improvements in knowledge and technology cause the PPC to shift outward. They are the main factors that drive economic growth.

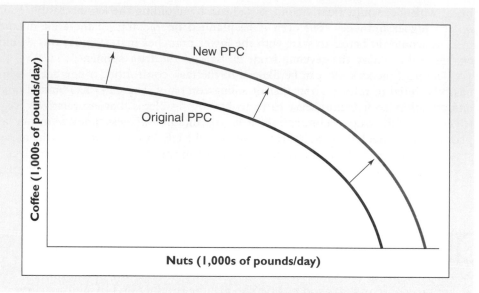

investment. Over time, even small differences in rates of investment can translate into extremely large differences in the amount of capital equipment available to each worker. Differences of this sort are often self-reinforcing: Not only do higher rates of saving and investment cause incomes to grow, but the resulting higher income levels also make it easier devote additional resources to savings and investment. Over time, then, even small initial productivity advantages from specialization can translate into very large income gaps.

Population growth also causes an economy's PPC curve to shift outward and thus is often listed as one of the sources of economic growth. But because population growth also generates more mouths to feed, it cannot by itself raise a country's standard of living. Indeed it may even cause a decline in the standard of living if existing population densities have already begun to put pressure on available land, water, and other scarce resources.

Perhaps the most important source of economic growth is improvements in knowledge and technology. As economists have long recognized, such improvements often lead to higher output through increased specialization. Improvements in technology often occur spontaneously, but more frequently they are directly or indirectly the result of increases in education.

Earlier we discussed a two-person example in which individual differences in opportunity cost led to a threefold gain from specialization (Exercise 2.4). Real-world gains from specialization often are far more spectacular than those in the example. One reason is that specialization not only capitalizes on preexisting differences in individual skills but also deepens those skills through practice and experience. Moreover, it eliminates many of the switching and start-up costs people incur when they move back and forth among numerous tasks. These gains apply not only to people but also to the tools and equipment they use. Breaking a task down into simple steps, each of which can be performed by a different machine, greatly multiplies the productivity of individual workers.

Even in simple settings, these factors can combine to increase productivity hundreds- or even thousands-fold. Adam Smith, the Scottish philosopher who is remembered today as the founder of modern economics, was the first to recognize the enormity of the gains made possible by the division and specialization of labor. Consider, for instance, his description of work in an eighteenth-century Scottish pin factory:

> One man draws out the wire, another straightens it, a third cuts it,
> a fourth points it, a fifth grinds it at the top for receiving the head;
> to make the head requires two or three distinct operations . . . I have

seen a small manufactory of this kind where only ten men were employed ... [who] could, when they exerted themselves, make among them about twelve pounds of pins in a day. There are in a pound upwards of four thousand pins of middling size. Those ten persons, therefore, could make among them upwards of forty-eight thousand pins in a day. Each person, therefore, making a tenth part of forty-eight thousand pins, might be considered as making four thousand eight hundred pins in a day. But if they had all wrought separately and independently, and without any of them having been educated to this peculiar business, they certainly could not each of them have made twenty, perhaps not one pin in a day.[1]

The gains in productivity that result from specialization are indeed often prodigious. They constitute the single most important explanation for why societies that don't rely heavily on specialization and exchange are rapidly becoming relics.

WHY HAVE SOME COUNTRIES BEEN SLOW TO SPECIALIZE?

You may be asking yourself, "If specialization is such a great thing, why don't people in poor countries like Nepal just specialize?" If so, you are in good company. Adam Smith spent many years attempting to answer precisely the same question. In the end, his explanation was that population density is an important precondition for specialization. Smith, ever the economic naturalist, observed that work tended to be far more specialized in the large cities of England in the eighteenth century than in the rural highlands of Scotland:

> In the lone houses and very small villages which are scattered about in so desert a country as the Highlands of Scotland, every farmer must be butcher, baker and brewer for his own family.... A country carpenter ... is not only a carpenter, but a joiner, a cabinet maker, and even a carver in wood, as well as a wheelwright, a ploughwright, a cart and waggon maker.[2]

In contrast, each of these same tasks was performed by a different specialist in the large English and Scottish cities of Smith's day. Scottish highlanders also would have specialized had they been able to, but the markets in which they participated were simply too small and fragmented. Of course, high population density by itself provides no guarantee that specialization will result in rapid economic growth. But especially before the arrival of modern shipping and electronic communications technology, low population density was a definite obstacle to gains from specialization.

Nepal remains one of the most remote and isolated countries on the planet. As recently as the mid-1960s, its average population density was less than 30 people per square mile (as compared, for example, to more than 1,000 people per square mile in New Jersey). Specialization was further limited by Nepal's rugged terrain. Exchanging goods and services with residents of other villages was difficult, because the nearest village in most cases could be reached only after trekking several hours, or even days, over treacherous Himalayan trails. More than any other factor, this extreme isolation accounts for Nepal's longstanding failure to benefit from widespread specialization.

Population density is by no means the only important factor that influences the degree of specialization. Specialization may be severely impeded, for example, by laws and customs that limit people's freedom to transact freely with one another. The communist governments of North Korea and the former East Germany restricted exchange severely, which helps explain why those countries achieved

---

[1]Adam Smith, *The Wealth of Nations,* New York: Everyman's Library, 1910 (1776), book 1.
[2]*The Wealth of Nations,* book 1, chapter 3.

far less specialization than South Korea and the former West Germany, whose governments were far more supportive of exchange.

CAN WE HAVE TOO MUCH SPECIALIZATION?

Of course, the mere fact that specialization boosts productivity does not mean that more specialization is always better than less, for specialization also entails costs. For example, most people appear to enjoy variety in the work they do, yet variety tends to be one of the first casualties as workplace tasks become ever more narrowly specialized.

Indeed, one of Karl Marx's central themes was that the fragmentation of workplace tasks often exacts a heavy psychological toll on workers. Thus, he wrote,

> All means for the development of production ... mutilate the laborer into a fragment of a man, degrade him to the level of an appendage of a machine, destroy every remnant of charm in his work and turn it into hated toil.[1]

Charlie Chaplin's 1936 film, *Modern Times,* paints a vivid portrait of the psychological costs of repetitive factory work. As an assembly worker, Chaplin's only task, all day every day, is to tighten the nuts on two bolts as they pass before him on the assembly line. Finally he snaps and staggers from the factory, wrenches in hand, tightening every nutlike protuberance he encounters.

Do the extra goods made possible by specialization simply come at too high a price? We must certainly acknowledge at least the *potential* for specialization to proceed too far. Yet specialization need not entail rigidly segmented, mind-numbingly repetitive work. And it is important to recognize that *failure* to specialize entails costs as well. Those who don't specialize must accept low wages or work extremely long hours.

When all is said and done, we can expect to meet life's financial obligations in the shortest time—thereby freeing up more time to do whatever else we wish—if

Can specialization proceed too far?

---

[1]Karl Marx, *Das Kapital,* New York: Modern Library, pp. 708, 709.

we concentrate at least a significant proportion of our efforts on those tasks for which we have a comparative advantage.

COMPARATIVE ADVANTAGE AND INTERNATIONAL TRADE

The same logic that leads the individuals in an economy to specialize and exchange of goods with one another also leads nations to specialize and trade among themselves. As with individuals, each nation can benefit from exchange, even though one may be generally more productive than the other in absolute terms.

If trade between nations is so beneficial, why are free-trade agreements so controversial?

One of the most heated issues in the 1996 presidential campaign was President Clinton's support for the North American Free Trade Agreement (NAFTA), a treaty to sharply reduce trade barriers between the United States and its immediate neighbors north and south. The treaty attracted fierce opposition from third-party candidate Ross Perot, who insisted that it would mean unemployment for millions of American workers. If exchange is so beneficial, why does anyone oppose it?

The answer is that while reducing barriers to international trade increases the total value of all goods and services produced in each nation, it does not guarantee that each individual citizen will do better. One specific concern regarding NAFTA was that it would help Mexico to exploit a comparative advantage in the production of goods made by unskilled labor. Although U.S. consumers would benefit from reduced prices for such goods, many Americans feared that unskilled workers in the United States would lose their jobs to workers in Mexico.

In the end, NAFTA was enacted over the vociferous opposition of American labor unions. So far, however, studies have failed to detect significant job losses among unskilled workers in the United States.

We will look at international trade in much more detail in Chapter 16.

ECONOMIC NATURALIST 2.3

 RECAP COMPARATIVE ADVANTAGE AND INTERNATIONAL TRADE

Nations, like individuals, can benefit from exchange, even though one trading partner may be more productive than the other in absolute terms. The greater the difference between domestic opportunity costs and world opportunity costs, the more a nation benefits from exchange with other nations. But expansions of exchange do not guarantee that each individual citizen will do better. In particular, unskilled workers in high-wage countries may be hurt in the short run by the reduction of barriers to trade with low-wage nations.

■ SUMMARY ■

- One person has an *absolute* advantage over another in the production of a good if she can produce more of that good than the other person. One person has a *comparative* advantage over another in the production of a good if she is

relatively more efficient than the other person at producing that good, meaning that her opportunity cost of producing it is lower than her counterpart's. Specialization based on comparative advantage is the basis for economic exchange. When each person specializes in the task at which he or she is relatively most efficient, the economic pie is maximized, making possible the largest slice for everyone.

- At the individual level, comparative advantage may spring from differences in talent or ability or from differences in education, training, and experience. At the national level, sources of comparative advantage include these innate and learned differences, as well as differences in language, culture, institutions, climate, natural resources, and a host of other factors.

- The production possibilities curve is a simple device for summarizing the possible combinations of output that a society can produce if it employs its resources efficiently. In a simple economy that produces only coffee and nuts, the PPC shows the maximum quantity of coffee production (vertical axis) possible at each level of nut production (horizontal axis). The slope of the PPC at any point represents the opportunity cost of nuts at that point, expressed in pounds of coffee.

- All production possibilities curves slope downward because of the scarcity principle, which states that the only way a

consumer can get more of one good is to settle for less of another. In economies whose workers have different opportunity costs of producing each good, the slope of the PPC becomes steeper as consumers move downward along the curve. This change in slope illustrates the principle of increasing opportunity cost (or the low-hanging-fruit principle), which states that in expanding the production of any good, a society should first employ those resources that are relatively efficient at producing that good, only afterward turning to those that are less efficient.

- Factors that cause a country's PPC to shift outward over time include investment in new factories and equipment, population growth, and improvements in knowledge and technology.

- The same logic that prompts individuals to specialize in their production and exchange goods with one another also leads nations to specialize and trade with one another. On both levels, each trading partner can benefit from an exchange, even though one may be more productive than the other, in absolute terms, for each good. For both individuals and nations, the benefits of exchange tend to be larger the larger are the differences between the trading partners' opportunity costs.

■ CORE PRINCIPLES ■

The Principle of Comparative Advantage
Everyone does best when each person (or each country) concentrates on the activities for which his or her opportunity cost is lowest.

The Principle of Increasing Opportunity Cost (also called "The Low-Hanging-Fruit Principle")
In expanding the production of any good, first employ those resources with the lowest opportunity cost, and only afterward turn to resources with higher opportunity costs.

■ KEY TERMS ■

absolute advantage (34)
attainable point (41)
comparative advantage (34)

efficient point (42)
inefficient point (42)

production possibilities curve (39)
unattainable point (42)

■ REVIEW QUESTIONS ■

1. Explain what "having a comparative advantage" at producing a particular good or service means. What does "having an absolute advantage" at producing a good or service mean?

2. How will a reduction in the number of hours worked each day affect an economy's production possibilities curve?

3. How will technological innovations that boost labor productivity affect an economy's production possibilities curve?

4. Why does saying that people are poor because they do not specialize make more sense than saying that people perform their own services because they are poor?

5. What factors have helped the United States to become the world's leading exporter of movies, books, and popular music?

▪ PROBLEMS ▪

1. Ted can wax 4 cars per day or wash 12 cars. Tom can wax 3 cars per day or wash 6. What is each man's opportunity cost of washing a car? Who has a comparative advantage in washing cars?

2. Ted can wax a car in 20 minutes or wash a car in 60 minutes. Tom can wax a car in 15 minutes or wash a car in 30 minutes. What is each man's opportunity cost of washing a car? Who has a comparative advantage in washing cars?

3. Toby can produce 5 gallons of apple cider or 2.5 ounces of feta cheese per hour. Kyle can produce 3 gallons of apple cider or 1.5 ounces of feta cheese per hour. Can Toby and Kyle benefit from specialization and trade? Explain.

4. Nancy and Bill are auto mechanics. Nancy takes 4 hours to replace a clutch and 2 hours to replace a set of brakes. Bill takes 6 hours to replace a clutch and 2 hours to replace a set of brakes. State whether anyone has an absolute advantage at either task and, for each task, identify who has a comparative advantage.

5. Consider a society consisting only of Helen, who allocates her time between sewing dresses and baking bread. Each hour she devotes to sewing dresses yields 4 dresses, and each hour she devotes to baking bread yields 8 loaves of bread. If Helen works a total of 8 hours per day, graph her production possibilities curve.

6. Refer to the preceding question. Which of the points listed below is efficient? Which is attainable?
   a. 28 dresses per day, 16 loaves per day.
   b. 16 dresses per day, 32 loaves per day.
   c. 18 dresses per day, 24 loaves per day.

7. Suppose that in Problem 5 a sewing machine is introduced that enables Helen to sew 8 dresses per hour rather than only 4. Show how this development shifts her production possibilities curve.

8. Refer to the preceding question to explain what is meant by the following statement: "An increase in productivity with respect to any one good increases our options for producing and consuming all other goods."

9. Susan can pick 4 pounds of coffee in an hour or 2 pounds of nuts. Tom can pick 2 pounds of coffee in an hour or 4 pounds of nuts. Each works 6 hours per day.
   a. What is the maximum number of pounds of coffee the two can pick in a day?
   b. What is the maximum number of pounds of nuts the two can pick in a day?
   c. If Susan and Tom were picking the maximum number of pounds of coffee when they decided that they would like to begin picking 4 pounds of nuts per day, who would pick the nuts, and how many pounds of coffee would they still be able to pick?
   d. Now suppose Susan and Tom were picking the maximum number of pounds of nuts when they decided that they would like to begin picking 8 pounds of coffee per day. Who would pick the coffee, and how many pounds of nuts would they still be able to pick?
   e. Would it be possible for Susan and Tom to pick a total of 26 pounds of nuts and 20 pounds of coffee each day? If so, how much of each good should each person pick?

10.*Refer to the two-person economy described in the preceding problem.
   a. Is the point (30 pounds of coffee per day, 12 pounds of nuts per day) an attainable point? Is it an efficient point? What about the point (24 pounds of coffee per day, 24 pounds of nuts per day)?
   b. On a graph with pounds of coffee per day on the vertical axis and pounds of nuts per day on the horizontal axis, show all the points you identified in Problem 9, parts a–e, and Problem 10a. Connect these points with straight lines. Is the result the PPC for the economy consisting of Susan and Tom?

*Problems marked with an asterisk (*) are more difficult.

c. Suppose that Susan and Tom could buy or sell coffee and nuts in the world market at a price of $2 per pound for coffee and $2 per pound for nuts. If each person specialized completely in the good for which he or she had a comparative advantage, how much could they earn by selling all their produce?

d. At the prices just described, what is the maximum amount of coffee Susan and Tom could buy in the world market? The maximum amount of nuts? Would it be possible for them to consume 40 pounds of nuts and 8 pounds of coffee each day?

e. In light of their ability to buy and sell in world markets at the stated prices, show on the same graph all combinations of the two goods it would be possible for them to consume.

■ ANSWERS TO IN-CHAPTER EXERCISES ■

2.1

	Productivity in programming	**Productivity in bicycle repair**
Pat	2 web page updates per hour	1 repair per hour
Barb	3 web page updates per hour	3 repairs per hour

The entries in the table tell us that Barb has an absolute advantage over Pat in both activities. While Barb, the mechanic, can update 3 web pages per hour, Pat, the programmer, can update only 2. Barb's absolute advantage over Pat is even greater in the task of fixing bikes—3 repairs per hour versus Pat's 1.

But as in Example 2.2, the fact that Barb is a better programmer than Pat does not imply that Barb should update her own web page. Barb's opportunity cost of updating a web page is 1 bicycle repair, whereas Pat must give up only half a repair to update a web page. Pat has a comparative advantage over Barb at programming, and Barb has a comparative advantage over Pat at bicycle repair.

2.2 In the accompanying graph, A (20 pounds per day of coffee, 4 pounds per day of nuts) is unattainable; B (12 pounds per day of coffee, 6 pounds per day of nuts) is both attainable and efficient; and C (4 pounds per day of coffee, 8 pounds per day of nuts) is both attainable and inefficient.

2.3 Susan's opportunity cost of picking a pound of nuts is now 1/2 pound of coffee, and Tom's opportunity cost of picking a pound of nuts is now only 1 pound of coffee. So Tom has a comparative advantage at picking coffee, and Susan has a comparative advantage at picking nuts.

2.4 Since Tom can pick five times as many pounds of nuts in an hour as pounds of coffee, to pick equal quantities of each, he must spend 5 hours picking coffee for every hour he devotes to picking nuts. And since he works a 6-hour day, that means spending 5 hours picking coffee and 1 hour picking nuts. Dividing his time in this way, he will end up with 5 pounds of each good. Similarly, if she is to pick equal quantities of each good, Susan must spend 5 hours picking nuts and 1 hour picking coffee. So she too picks 5 pounds of each good if she divides her 6-hour day in this way. Their combined daily production will thus be 10 pounds of each good. By working together and specializing, however, they can produce and consume a total of 30 pounds per day of each good.

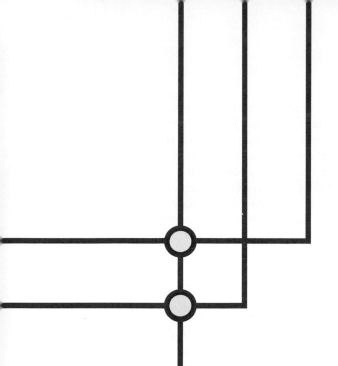

CHAPTER 3

SUPPLY AND DEMAND: AN INTRODUCTION

■

T he stock of foodstuffs on hand at any moment in New York City's grocery stores, restaurants, and private kitchens is sufficient to feed the area's 10 million residents for at most a week or so. Since most of these residents have nutritionally adequate and highly varied diets, and since almost no food is produced within the city proper, provisioning New York requires that millions of pounds of food and drink be delivered to locations throughout the city each day.

No doubt many New Yorkers, buying groceries at their favorite local markets or eating at their favorite Italian restaurants, give little or no thought to the nearly miraculous coordination of people and resources that is required to feed city residents on a daily basis. But near-miraculous it is, nevertheless. Even if the supplying of New York City consisted only of transporting a fixed collection of foods to a given list of destinations each day, it would be quite an impressive operation, requiring at least a small (and well-managed) army to carry out.

Yet the entire process is astonishingly more complex than that. For example, the system must somehow ensure that not only *enough* food is delivered to satisfy New Yorkers' discriminating palates, but also the *right kinds* of food. There mustn't be too much pheasant and not enough smoked eel; or too much bacon and not enough eggs; or too much caviar and not enough canned tuna; and so on. Similar judgments must be made *within* each category of food and drink: There must be the right amount of Swiss cheese, and the right amounts of provolone, gorgonzola, and feta.

But even this doesn't begin to describe the complexity of the decisions and actions required to provide our nation's largest city with its daily bread.

Someone has to decide where each particular type of food gets produced, and how, and by whom. Someone must decide how much of each type of food gets delivered to *each* of the tens of thousands of restaurants and grocery stores in the city. Someone must determine whether the deliveries should be made in big trucks or small ones, arrange that the trucks be in the right place at the right time, and ensure that gasoline and qualified drivers be available.

Thousands of individuals must decide what role, if any, they will play in this collective effort. Some people—just the right number—must choose to drive food-delivery trucks rather than trucks that deliver lumber. Others must become the mechanics who fix these trucks rather than carpenters who build houses. Others must become farmers rather than architects or bricklayers. Still others must become chefs in upscale restaurants, or flip burgers at McDonald's, instead of becoming plumbers or electricians.

Yet despite the almost incomprehensible number and complexity of the tasks involved, somehow the supplying of New York City manages to get done remarkably smoothly. Oh, a grocery store will occasionally run out of flank steak, or a diner will sometimes be told that someone else has just ordered the last serving of roast duck. But if episodes like these stick in memory, it is only because they are rare. For the most part, New York's food delivery system—like that of every other city in the country—functions so seamlessly that it attracts virtually no notice.

The situation is strikingly different in New York City's rental housing market. According to one recent estimate, the city needs between 20,000 and 40,000 new housing units each year merely to keep up with population growth and to replace existing housing that is deteriorated beyond repair. The actual rate of new construction in the city, however, is only 6,000 units per year. As a result, America's most densely populated city has been experiencing a protracted housing shortage. Yet, paradoxically, in the midst of this shortage, apartment houses are being demolished; and in the vacant lots left behind, people from the neighborhoods are planting flower gardens!

New York City is experiencing not only a growing shortage of rental housing, but also chronically strained relations between landlords and tenants. In one all-too-typical case, for example, a photographer living in a loft on the Lower East Side waged an eight-year court battle with his landlord that generated literally thousands of pages of legal documents. "Once we put up a doorbell for ourselves," the photographer recalled, "and [the landlord] pulled it out, so we pulled out the wires to his doorbell."[1] The landlord, for his part, accused the photographer of obstructing his efforts to renovate the apartment. According to the landlord, the tenant preferred for the apartment to remain in substandard condition, since that gave him an excuse to withhold rent payments.

Same city, two strikingly different patterns: In the food industry, goods and services are available in wide variety, and people (at least those with adequate income) are generally satisfied with what they receive and the choices available to them. In contrast, in the rental housing industry, chronic shortages and chronic dissatisfaction are rife among both buyers and sellers. Why this difference?

The brief answer is that New York City relies on a complex system of administrative rent regulations to allocate housing units but leaves the allocation of food essentially in the hands of market forces—the forces of supply and demand. Although intuition might suggest otherwise, both theory and experience suggest that the seemingly chaotic and unplanned outcomes of market forces can in most cases do a better job of allocating economic resources than can (for example) a government agency, even if the agency has the best of intentions.

Why does New York City's food distribution system work so much better than its housing market?

---

[1] Quoted by John Tierney, "The Rentocracy: At the Intersection of Supply and Demand," *New York Times Magazine,* May 4, 1997, p. 39.

In this chapter we'll explore how markets allocate food, housing, and other goods and services, usually with remarkable efficiency despite the complexity of the tasks. To be sure, markets are by no means perfect, and our stress on their virtues is to some extent an attempt to counteract what most economists view as an underappreciation by the general public of their remarkable strengths. But in the course of our discussion we'll see why markets function so smoothly most of the time, and why bureaucratic rules and regulations rarely work as well in solving complex economic problems.

To convey an understanding of how markets work is a major goal of this course, and in this chapter we provide only a brief introduction and overview. As the course proceeds we will discuss the economic role of markets in considerably more detail, paying attention to some of the problems of markets as well as their strengths.

WHAT, HOW, AND FOR WHOM? CENTRAL PLANNING VERSUS THE MARKET

No city, state, or society—regardless of how it is organized—can escape the need to answer certain basic economic questions. For example, how much of our limited time and other resources should we devote to building housing, how much to the production of food, and how much to providing other goods and services? What techniques should we use to produce each good? Who should be assigned to each specific task? And how should the resulting goods and services be distributed among people?

In the thousands of different societies for which records are available, issues like these have been decided in essentially one of two ways. One approach is for all economic decisions to be made centrally, by an individual or small number of individuals on behalf of a larger group. For example, in many agrarian societies throughout history, families or other small groups consumed only those goods and services that they produced for themselves, and a single clan or family leader made most important production and distribution decisions. On an immensely larger scale, the economic organization of the former Soviet Union (and other communist countries) was also largely centralized. In so-called centrally planned communist nations, a central bureaucratic committee established production targets for the country's farms and factories, developed a master plan for how to achieve the targets (including detailed instructions concerning who was to produce what), and set up guidelines for the distribution and use of the goods and services produced.

Neither form of centralized economic organization is much in evidence today. When implemented on a small scale, as in a self-sufficient family enterprise, centralized decision making is certainly feasible. For the reasons discussed in the preceding chapter, however, the jack-of-all-trades approach was doomed once it became clear how dramatically people could improve their living standards by specialization—that is, by having each individual focus his or her efforts on a relatively narrow range of tasks. And with the fall of the Soviet Union and its satellite nations in the late 1980s, there are now only three communist economies left in the world: Cuba, North Korea, and China. The first two of these appear to be on their last legs, economically speaking, and China has by now largely abandoned any attempt to control production and distribution decisions from the center. The major remaining examples of centralized allocation and control now reside in the bureaucratic agencies that administer programs like New York City's rent controls—programs that are themselves becoming increasingly rare.

At the beginning of the twenty-first century we are therefore left, for the most part, with the second major form of economic system, one in which production and distribution decisions are left to individuals interacting in private markets. In the so-called capitalist, or free-market economies, people decide for themselves which careers to pursue and which products to produce or buy. In fact, there are no *pure* free-market economies today. Modern industrial countries are more properly described as "mixed economies," meaning that goods and services are allocated by a combination of free markets, regulation, and other forms of collective control. Still, it makes sense to refer to such systems as free-market economies, because people are for the most part free to start businesses, to shut them down, or to sell them. And within broad limits, the distribution of goods and services is determined by individual preferences backed by individual purchasing power, which in most cases comes from the income people earn in the labor market.

In country after country, markets have replaced centralized control for the simple reason that they tend to assign production tasks and consumption benefits much more effectively. The popular press, and the conventional wisdom, often asserts that economists disagree about important issues. (As someone once quipped, "If you lay all the economists in the world end to end, they still wouldn't reach a conclusion.") The fact is, however, that there is overwhelming agreement among economists about a broad range of issues, with the great majority accepting the efficacy of markets as means for allocating society's scarce resources. For example, a recent survey found that more than 90 percent of American professional economists believe that rent regulations like the ones implemented by New York City do more harm than good. That the stated aim of these regulations—to make rental housing more affordable for middle- and low-income families—is clearly benign was not enough to prevent them from wreaking havoc on New York City's housing market. To see why, we must explore how goods and services are allocated in private markets, and why nonmarket means of allocating goods and services often do not produce the expected results.

BUYERS AND SELLERS IN MARKETS

market the market for any good consists of all buyers or sellers of that good

Beginning with some simple concepts and definitions, we will explore how the interactions among buyers and sellers in markets determine the prices and quantities of the various goods and services traded in those markets. We begin by defining a market: The **market** for any good consists of all the buyers and sellers of that good. So, for example, the market for pizza on a given day in a given place is just the set of people (or other economic actors, like firms) potentially able to buy or sell pizza at that time and location.

In the market for pizza, sellers comprise the individuals and companies that either do sell—or might, under the right circumstances, sell—pizza. Similarly, buyers in this market include all individuals who buy—or might buy—pizza.

In most parts of the country a decent pizza—or some other life-sustaining meal—can still be had for less than $8. Where does the market price of pizza come from? Looking beyond pizza to the vast array of other goods that are bought and sold every day, we may ask, "Why are some goods cheap and others expensive?" Aristotle had no idea. Nor did Plato, or Copernicus, or Newton. On reflection, it is astonishing that, for almost the entire span of human history, not even the most intelligent and creative minds on Earth had any real inkling of how to answer that seemingly simple question. Even Adam Smith, the Scottish moral philosopher whose *Wealth of Nations* launched the discipline of economics in 1776, suffered confusion on this issue.

Smith and other early economists (including Karl Marx) thought that the market price of a good was determined by its cost of production. But although costs surely do affect prices, they cannot explain why one of Pablo Picasso's paintings sells for so much more than one of Jackson Pollock's.

Stanley Jevons and other nineteenth-century economists tried to explain price by focusing on the value people derived from consuming different goods and services. It certainly seems plausible that people will pay a lot for a good they value highly. Yet willingness to pay cannot be the whole story, either. Deprive a person in the desert of water, for example, and he will be dead in a matter of hours, and yet water sells for less than a penny a gallon. By contrast, human beings can get along perfectly well without gold, and yet gold sells for more than $250 an ounce.

Cost of production? Value to the user? Which is it? The answer, which seems obvious to today's economists, is that both matter. Writing in the late nineteenth century, the British economist Alfred Marshall was among the first to show clearly how costs and value interact to determine both the prevailing market price for a good and the amount of it that is bought and sold. Our task in the pages ahead will be to explore Marshall's insights and gain some practice in applying them. As a first step, we introduce the two main components of Marshall's pathbreaking analysis: the demand curve and the supply curve.

THE DEMAND CURVE

In the market for pizza, the **demand curve** for pizza is a simple schedule or graph that tells us how many slices people would be willing to buy at different prices. By convention, economists usually put price on the vertical axis of the demand curve and quantity on the horizontal axis.

A fundamental property of the demand curve is that it is downward-sloping with respect to price. For example, the demand curve for pizza tells us that as the price of pizza falls, buyers will buy more slices. Thus the daily demand curve for pizza in Chicago on a given day might look like the curve seen in Figure 3.1. (Although economists usually refer to demand and supply "curves," we often draw them as straight lines in examples.)

The demand curve in Figure 3.1 tells us that when the price of pizza is low—say $2 per slice—buyers will want to buy 16,000 slices per day, whereas they will want to buy only 12,000 slices at a price of $3, and only 8,000 at a price of $4. The demand curve for pizza—as for any other good—slopes downward for multiple reasons. Some of these reasons have to do with the individual consumer's reactions to price changes. Thus, as pizza becomes more expensive, a consumer may switch to chicken sandwiches, hamburgers, or other foods that substitute for pizza. This is called the **substitution effect** of a price change. In addition, a price increase reduces the quantity demanded because it reduces purchasing power: A consumer simply can't afford to buy as many slices of pizza at higher prices as at lower prices. This is called the **income effect** of a price change.

Why do Pablo Picasso's paintings sell for so much more than Jackson Pollock's?

demand curve a schedule or graph showing the quantity of a good that buyers wish to buy at each price

substitution effect the change in the quantity demanded of a good that results because buyers switch to substitutes when the price of the good changes

income effect the change in the quantity demanded of a good that results because a change in the price of a good changes the buyer's purchasing power

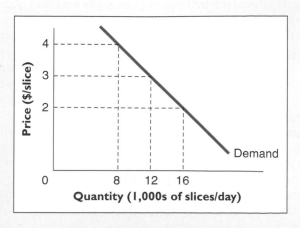

FIGURE 3.1
The Daily Demand Curve for Pizza in Chicago.
The demand curve for any good is a downward-sloping function of its price.

buyer's reservation price the largest dollar amount the buyer would be willing to pay for a good

Another reason that the demand curve slopes downward is that consumers differ in terms of how much they are willing to pay for the good. The cost-benefit principle tells us that a given person will buy the good if the benefit he expects to receive from it exceeds its cost. The benefit is the **buyer's reservation price,** the highest dollar amount he would be willing to pay for the good. The cost of the good is the actual amount that the buyer actually must pay for it, which is the market price of the good. In most markets, different buyers have different reservation prices. Thus when the good sells for a high price, it will satisfy the cost-benefit test for fewer buyers than when it sells for a lower prices.

To put this same point another way, the fact that the demand curve for a good is downward-sloping reflects the fact that the reservation price of the marginal buyer declines as the quantity of the good bought increases. Here the marginal buyer is the person who purchases the last unit of the good that is sold. If buyers are currently purchasing 12,000 slices of pizza a day in Figure 3.1, for example, the reservation price for the buyer of the 12,000th slice must be $3. (If someone had been willing to pay more than that, the quantity demanded at a price of $3 would have been more than 12,000 to begin with.) By similar reasoning, when the quantity sold is 16,000 slices per day, the marginal buyer's reservation price must be only $2.

We defined the demand curve for any good as a schedule telling how much of it consumers wish to purchase at various prices. This is called the *horizontal interpretation* of the demand curve. Using the horizontal interpretation, we start with price on the vertical axis and read the corresponding quantity demanded on the horizontal axis. Thus, at a price of $4 per slice, the demand curve in Figure 3.1 tells us that the quantity of pizza demanded will be 8,000 slices per day.

The demand curve can also be interpreted in a second way, which is to start with quantity on the horizontal axis and then read the marginal buyer's reservation price on the vertical axis. Thus, when the quantity of pizza sold is 8,000 slices per day, the demand curve in Figure 3.1 tells us that the marginal buyer's reservation price is $4 per slice. This second way of reading the demand curve is called the *vertical interpretation*.

EXERCISE 3.1

In Figure 3.1, what is the marginal buyer's reservation price when the quantity of pizza sold is 10,000 slices per day? For the same demand curve, what will be the quantity of pizza demanded at a price of $2.50 per slice?

THE SUPPLY CURVE

supply curve a curve or schedule showing the quantity of a good that sellers wish to sell at each price

In the market for pizza, the **supply curve** is a simple schedule or graph that tells us, for each possible price, the total number of slices that all pizza vendors would be willing to sell at that price. What does the supply curve of pizza look like? The answer to this question is based on the logical assumption that suppliers should be willing to sell additional slices as long as the price they receive is sufficient to cover their opportunity costs of supplying them. Thus, if what someone could earn by selling a slice of pizza is insufficient to compensate her for what she could have earned if she had spent her time and invested her money in some other way, she will not sell that slice. Otherwise, she will.

Just as buyers differ with respect to the amounts they are willing to pay for pizza, sellers also differ with respect to their opportunity costs of supplying pizza. For those with limited education and work experience, the opportunity cost of selling pizza is relatively low (because such individuals typically do not have a lot of high-paying alternatives). For others the opportunity cost of selling pizza is of moderate value, and for still others—like rock stars and professional athletes—it is prohibitively high. In part because of these differences in opportunity cost among people, the daily supply curve of pizza will be *upward-sloping* with respect

FIGURE 3.2
The Daily Supply Curve of Pizza in Chicago.
At higher prices, sellers generally offer more units for sale.

to price. As an illustration, see Figure 3.2, which shows a hypothetical supply curve for pizza in the Chicago market on a given day.

The fact that the supply curve slopes upward may be seen as a consequence of the low-hanging-fruit principle, discussed in the preceding chapter. This principle tells us that as we expand the production of pizza, we turn first to those whose opportunity costs of producing pizza are lowest, and only then to others with higher opportunity costs.

Like the demand curve, the supply curve can be interpreted either horizontally or vertically. Under the horizontal interpretation, we begin with a price, then go over to the supply curve to read the quantity that sellers wish to sell at that price on the horizontal axis. For instance, at a price of $2 per slice, sellers in Figure 3.2 wish to sell 8,000 slices per day.

Under the vertical interpretation, we begin with a quantity, then go up to the supply curve to read the corresponding marginal cost on the vertical axis. Thus, if sellers in Figure 3.2 are currently supplying 12,000 slices per day, the opportunity cost of the marginal seller is $3 per slice. In other words, the supply curve tells us that the marginal cost of producing the 12,000th slice of pizza is $3. (If someone could produce a 12,001st slice for less than $3, she would have an incentive to supply it, so the quantity of pizza supplied at $3 per slice would not have been 12,000 slices per day to begin with.) By similar reasoning, when the quantity of pizza supplied is 16,000 slices per day, the marginal cost of producing another slice must be $4. The **seller's reservation price** for selling an additional unit of a good is her marginal cost of producing that good. It is the smallest dollar amount for which she would not be financially worse off if she sold an additional unit.

seller's reservation price the smallest dollar amount for which a seller would be willing to sell an additional unit, generally equal to marginal cost

EXERCISE 3.2

In Figure 3.2, what is the marginal cost of a slice of pizza when the quantity of pizza sold is 10,000 slices per day? For the same supply curve, what will be the quantity of pizza supplied at a price of $3.50 per slice?

 RECAP   **DEMAND AND SUPPLY CURVES**

The *market* for a good consists of the actual and potential buyers and sellers of that good. For any given price, the *demand curve* shows the quantity that demanders would be willing to buy, and the *supply curve* shows the quantity that suppliers of the good would be willing to sell. Suppliers are willing to sell more at higher prices (supply curves slope upward) and demanders are willing to buy less at higher prices (demand curves slope downward).

MARKET EQUILIBRIUM

equilibrium a system is in
equilibrium when there is no
tendency for it to change

The concept of **equilibrium** is employed in both the physical and social sciences, and it is of central importance in economic analysis. In general, a system is in equilibrium when all forces at work within the system are canceled by others, resulting in a stable, balanced, or unchanging situation. In physics, for example, a ball hanging from a spring is said to be in equilibrium when the spring has stretched sufficiently that the upward force it exerts on the ball is exactly counterbalanced by the downward force of gravity. In economics, a market is said to be in equilibrium when no participant in the market has any reason to alter his or her behavior, so that there is no tendency for production or prices in that market to change.

equilibrium price and
equilibrium quantity the
values of price and quantity for
which quantity supplied and
quantity demanded are equal

If we want to determine the final position of a ball hanging from a spring, we need to find the point at which the forces of gravity and spring tension are balanced and the system is in equilibrium. Similarly, if we want to find the price at which a good will sell (which we will call the **equilibrium price**) and the quantity of it that will be sold (the **equilibrium quantity**), we need to find the equilibrium in the market for that good. The basic tools for finding the equilibrium in a market for a good are the supply and demand curves for that good. For reasons that we will explain, the equilibrium price and equilibrium quantity of a good are the price and quantity at which the supply and demand curves for the good intersect. For the hypothetical supply and demand curves shown earlier for the pizza market in Chicago, the equilibrium price will therefore be $3 per slice, and the equilibrium quantity of pizza sold will be 12,000 slices per day, as shown in Figure 3.3.

In Figure 3.3, note that at the equilibrium price of $3 per slice, both sellers and buyers are "satisfied" in the following sense: Buyers are buying exactly the quantity of pizza they wish to buy at that price (12,000 slices per day) and sellers are selling exactly the quantity of pizza they wish to sell (also 12,000 slices per day). And since they are satisfied in this sense, neither buyers nor sellers face any incentives to change their behavior.

market equilibrium occurs in a
market when all buyers and
sellers are satisfied with their
respective quantities at the
market price

Note the limited sense of the term "satisfied" in the definition of **market equilibrium.** It doesn't mean that sellers would not be pleased to receive a price higher than the equilibrium price. Rather, it means only that they're able to sell all they wish to sell at that price. Similarly, to say that buyers are satisfied at the equilibrium price doesn't mean that they would not be happy to pay less than the equilibrium price. Rather, it means only that they're able to buy exactly as many units of the good as they wish to at the equilibrium price.

Note also that if the price of pizza in our Chicago market were anything other than $3 per slice, either buyers or sellers would frustrated. Suppose, for example, that the price of pizza were $4 per slice, as shown in Figure 3.4. At that price, buyers wish to buy only 8,000 slices per day, but sellers wish to sell 16,000.

FIGURE 3.3
**The Equilibrium Price
and Quantity of Pizza
in Chicago.**
The equilibrium quantity and
price of a product are the
values that correspond to
the intersection of the supply
and demand curves for that
product.

FIGURE 3.4
Excess Supply.
When price exceeds the equilibrium price, there is excess supply, or surplus, the difference between quantity supplied and quantity demanded.

And since no one can force someone to buy a slice of pizza against her wishes, this means that buyers will buy only the 8,000 slices they wish to buy. So when the price exceeds the equilibrium price, it is sellers who end up being frustrated. At a price of $4 in this example, they are left with an **excess supply** of 8,000 slices per day.

Conversely, suppose that the price of pizza in our Chicago market were less than the equilibrium price—say, $2 per slice. As shown in Figure 3.5, buyers want to buy 16,000 slices per day at that price, whereas sellers want to sell only 8,000. And since sellers cannot be forced to sell pizza against their wishes, this time it is the buyers who end up being frustrated. At a price of $2 per slice in this example, they experience an **excess demand** of 8,000 slices per day.

An extraordinary feature of private markets for goods and services is their automatic tendency to gravitate toward their respective equilibrium prices and quantities. The mechanisms by which this happens are implicit in our definitions of excess supply and excess demand. Suppose, for example, that the price of pizza in our hypothetical market was $4 per slice, leading to excess supply as shown in Figure 3.4. Because sellers are frustrated in the sense of wanting to sell more pizza than buyers wish to buy, sellers have an incentive to take whatever steps they can to increase their sales. The simplest strategy available to them is to cut their price slightly. Thus, if one seller reduced his price from $4 to, say, $3.95 per slice, he would attract many of the buyers who had been paying $4 per slice for pizza supplied by other sellers. Those sellers, in order to recover their lost business, would

excess supply the amount by which quantity supplied exceeds quantity demanded when the price of a good exceeds the equilibrium price

excess demand the amount by which quantity demanded exceeds quantity supplied when the price of a good lies below the equilibrium price

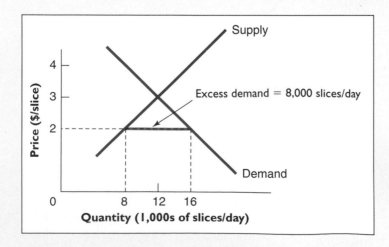

FIGURE 3.5
Excess Demand.
When price lies below the equilibrium price, there is excess demand, the difference between quantity demanded and quantity supplied.

then have an incentive to match the price cut. But notice that if all sellers lowered their prices to $3.95 per slice, there would still be considerable excess supply. So sellers would face continuing incentives to cut their prices. This pressure to cut prices will not go away until price falls all the way to $3 per slice.

Conversely, suppose that price starts out less than the equilibrium price—say, $2 per slice. This time it is buyers who are frustrated. A person who can't get all the pizza he wants at a price of $2 per slice has an incentive to offer a higher price, hoping to obtain pizza that would otherwise have been sold to other buyers. And sellers, for their part, will be only too happy to post higher prices as long as queues of frustrated buyers remain.

The upshot is that price has a tendency to gravitate to its equilibrium level under conditions of either excess supply or excess demand. And when price reaches its equilibrium level, both buyers and sellers are satisfied in the technical sense of being able to buy or sell precisely the amounts of their choosing.

EXAMPLE 3.1

Samples of points on the demand and supply curves of a pizza market are provided in Table 3.1. Graph the demand and supply curves for this market, and find its equilibrium price and quantity.

TABLE 3.1
Points along the Demand and Supply Curves of a Pizza Market

Demand for Pizza		Supply of Pizza	
Price ($/slice)	Quantity demanded (1,000 of slices/day)	Price ($/slice)	Quantity Supplied (1,000 of slices/day)
1	8	1	2
2	6	2	4
3	4	3	6
4	2	4	8

The points in the table are plotted in Figure 3.6. and then joined to indicate the supply and demand curves for this market. These curves intersect to yield an equilibrium price of $2.50 per slice and an equilibrium quantity of 5,000 slices per day.

FIGURE 3.6
Graphing Supply and Demand and Finding the Equilibrium Price and Quantity.
To graph the demand and supply curve, plot the relevant points given in the table and then join them with a line. The equilibrium price and quantity occur at the intersection of these curves.

We emphasize that market equilibrium does not necessarily produce an ideal outcome for all market participants. Thus, in the example just considered, market participants are satisfied with the amount of pizza they buy and sell at a price of $2.50 per slice, but for a poor buyer this may signify little more than that he *can't* buy additional pizza without sacrificing other more highly valued purchases.

Indeed, buyers with extremely low incomes often have difficulty purchasing even basic goods and services, which has prompted governments in almost every society to attempt to ease the burdens of the poor. Yet the laws of supply and demand cannot simply be repealed by an act of the legislature. In the next section we will see that when legislators attempt to prevent markets from reaching their equilibrium prices and quantities, they often do more harm than good.

RENT CONTROLS RECONSIDERED

Consider again the market for rental housing units in New York City, and suppose that the demand and supply curves for one-bedroom apartments are as shown in Figure 3.7. This market, left alone, would reach an equilibrium monthly rent of $1,600, at which 2 million one-bedroom apartments would be rented. Both landlords and tenants would be satisfied, in the sense that they would not wish to rent either more or fewer units at that price.

This would not necessarily mean, of course, that all is well and good. Many potential tenants, for example, might simply be unable to afford a rent of $1,600 per month and thus be forced to remain homeless (or to move out of the city to a cheaper location). Suppose that, acting purely out of benign motives, legislators made it unlawful for landlords to charge more than $800 per month for one-bedroom apartments. Their stated aim in enacting this law was that no person should have to remain homeless because decent housing was unaffordable.

But note in Figure 3.8 that when rents for one-bedroom apartments are prevented from rising above $800 per month, landlords are willing to supply only 1 million apartments per month, 1 million fewer than at the equilibrium monthly rent of $1,600. Note also that at the controlled rent of $800 per month, tenants want to rent 3 million one-bedroom apartments per month. (For example, many people who would have decided to live in New Jersey rather than pay $1,600 a month in New York will now choose to live in the city.) So when rents are prevented from rising above $800 per month, we see an excess demand for one-bedroom apartments of 2 million units each month. Put another way, the rent controls result in a housing shortage of 2 million units

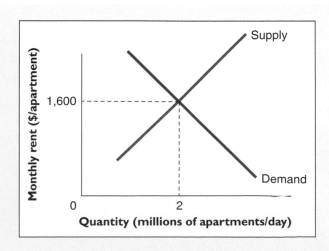

FIGURE 3.7
An Unregulated Housing Market.
For the supply and demand curves shown, the equilibrium monthly rent is $1,600, and 2 million apartments will be rented at that price.

FIGURE 3.8
Rent Controls.
When rents are prohibited from rising to the equilibrium level, the result is excess demand in the housing market.

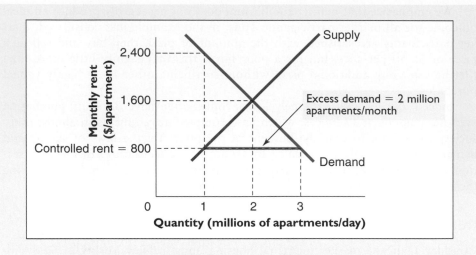

each month. What is more, the number of apartments actually available *declines* by 1 million units per month.

If the housing market were completely unregulated, the immediate response to such a high level of excess demand would be for rents to rise sharply. But here the law prevents them from rising above $800. Many other ways exist, however, in which the pressures of excess demand can make themselves felt. For instance, owners will quickly learn that they are free to spend less on maintaining the quality of their rental units. After all, if there are scores of renters knocking at the door of each vacant apartment, a landlord has considerable room to maneuver. Leaking pipes, peeling paint, broken furnaces, and other problems are less likely to receive prompt attention—or, indeed, any attention at all—when rents are set well below market-clearing levels.

Nor are reduced availability of apartments and poorer maintenance of existing apartments the only difficulties. With an offering of only 1 million apartments per month, we see in Figure 3.8 that there are renters who would be willing to pay as much as $2,400 per month for an apartment. This pressure almost always finds ways, legal or illegal, of expressing itself. In New York City, for example, it is not uncommon to see "finder's fees" or "key deposits" as high as several thousand dollars. Owners who cannot charge a market-clearing rent for their apartments also have the option of converting them to condominiums or co-ops, which enables them to sell their assets for prices much closer to their true economic value.

Even when rent-controlled apartment owners do not hike their prices in these various ways, serious misallocations result. For instance, ill-suited roommates often remain together despite their constant bickering, because each is reluctant to reenter the housing market. Or a widow might steadfastly remain in her seven-room apartment even after her children have left home, because it is much cheaper than alternative dwellings not covered by rent control. It would be much better for all concerned if she relinquished that space to a larger family that valued it more highly. But under rent controls, she has no economic incentive to do so.

There is also another more insidious cost of rent controls. In markets without rent controls, landlords cannot discriminate against potential tenants on the basis of race, religion, sexual orientation, physical disability, or national origin without suffering an economic penalty. Refusal to rent to members of specific groups would reduce the demand for their apartments, which would mean having to accept lower rents. When rents are artificially pegged below their equilibrium level, however, the resulting excess demand for apartments enables landlords to engage in discrimination with no further economic penalty.

"If you leave me, you know, you'll
never see this kind of rent again"

Rent controls are not the only instance in which governments have attempted to repeal the law of supply and demand in the interest of helping the poor. During the late 1970s, for example, the federal government tried to hold the price of gasoline below its equilibrium level out of concern that high gasoline prices imposed unacceptable hardships on low-income drivers. As with controls in the rental housing market, unintended consequences of price controls in the gasoline market made the policy an extremely costly way of trying to aid the poor. For example, gasoline shortages resulted in long lines at the pumps, a waste not only of valuable time, but also of gasoline as cars sat idling for extended periods.

In their opposition to rent controls and similar measures, are economists revealing a total lack of concern for the poor? Although this claim is sometimes made by those who don't understand the issues, or who stand to benefit in some way from government regulations, there is little justification for it. *Economists simply realize that there are much more effective ways to help poor people than to try to give them apartments and other goods at artificially low prices.*

One straightforward approach would be to give the poor additional income and let them decide for themselves how to spend it. True, there are also practical difficulties involved in transferring additional purchasing power into the hands of the poor—most importantly, the difficulty of targeting cash to the genuinely needy without weakening others' incentives to fend for themselves. But there are practical ways to overcome this difficulty. For example, for far less than the waste caused by price controls, the government could afford generous subsidies to the wages of the working poor and could sponsor public-service employment for those who are unable to find jobs in the private sector.

Regulations that peg prices below equilibrium levels have far-reaching effects on market outcomes. The following exercise asks you to consider what happens when a price control is established at a level above the equilibrium price.

EXERCISE 3.3

In the rental housing market whose demand and supply curves are shown below, what will be the effect of a law that prevents rents from rising above $1,200 per month?

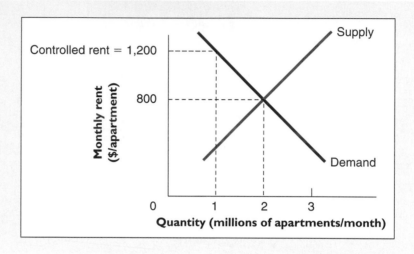

PIZZA PRICE CONTROLS?

The sources of the contrast between the rent-controlled housing market and the largely unregulated food markets in New York City can be seen more vividly by trying to imagine what would happen if concern for the poor led the city's leaders to implement price controls on pizza. Suppose, for example, that the supply and demand curves for pizza are as shown in Figure 3.9, and that the city imposes a **price ceiling** of $2 per slice, making it unlawful to charge more than that amount. At $2 per slice, buyers want to buy 16,000 slices per day, but sellers want to sell only 8,000.

At a price of $2 per slice, every pizza restaurant in the city will have long queues of buyers trying unsuccessfully to purchase pizza. Frustrated buyers will

price ceiling a maximum allowable price, specified by law

FIGURE 3.9
Price Controls in the Pizza Market.
A price ceiling below the equilibrium price of pizza would result in excess demand for pizza.

behave rudely to clerks, who will respond in kind. Friends of restaurant managers will begin to get preferential treatment. Devious pricing strategies will begin to emerge (such as the $2 slice of pizza sold in combination with a $5 cup of Coke). Pizza will be made from poorer-quality ingredients. Rumors will begin to circulate about sources of black-market pizza. And so on.

The very idea of not being able to buy a pizza seems absurd, yet precisely such things happen routinely in markets in which prices are held below the equilibrium levels. For example, prior to the collapse of communist governments, it was considered normal in those countries for people to stand in line for hours to buy basic goods, while the politically connected had first choice of those goods that were available.

 RECAP   **MARKET EQUILIBRIUM**

Market equilibrium, the situation in which all buyers and sellers are satisfied with their respective quantities at the market price, occurs at the intersection of the supply and demand curves. The corresponding price and quantity are called the *equilibrium price* and the *equilibrium quantity.*

Unless prevented by regulation, prices and quantities are driven toward their equilibrium values by the actions of buyers and sellers. If the price is initially too high, so that there is excess supply, frustrated sellers will cut their price in order to sell more. If the price is initially too low, so that there is excess demand, competition among buyers drives the price upward. This process continues until equilibrium is reached.

PREDICTING AND EXPLAINING CHANGES IN PRICES AND QUANTITIES

If we know how the factors that govern supply and demand curves are changing, we can make informed predictions about how prices and the corresponding quantities will change. But when describing changing circumstances in the marketplace, we must take care to recognize some important terminological distinctions. For example, we must distinguish between the meanings of the seemingly similar expressions **change in the quantity demanded** and **change in demand**. When we speak of a "change in the quantity demanded," this means the change in the quantity that people wish to buy that occurs in response to a change in price. For instance, Figure 3.10(a) depicts an increase in the quantity demanded that occurs

change in the quantity demanded a movement along the demand curve that occurs in response to a change in price

change in demand a shift of the entire demand curve

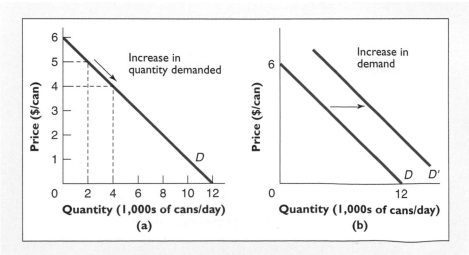

FIGURE 3.10
An Increase in the Quantity Demanded vs. an Increase in Demand.
(a) An increase in quantity demanded describes a downward movement along the demand curve as price falls. (b) An increase in demand describes an outward shift of the demand curve.

in response to a reduction in the price of tuna. When the price falls from $5 to $4 per can, the quantity demanded rises from 2,000 to 4,000 cans per day. By contrast, when we speak of a "change in demand," this means a *shift in the entire demand curve*. For example, Figure 3.10(b) depicts an increase in demand, meaning that at every price the quantity demanded is higher than before. In summary, a "change in the quantity demanded" refers to a movement *along* the demand curve, and a "change in demand" means a *shift* of the entire curve.

A similar terminological distinction applies on the supply side of the market. A **change in supply** means a shift in the entire supply curve, whereas a **change in the quantity supplied** refers to a movement along the supply curve.

Alfred Marshall's supply and demand model is one of the most useful tools of the economic naturalist. Once we understand the forces that govern the placements of supply and demand curves, we are suddenly in a position to make sense of a host of interesting observations in the world around us.

> *change in supply* a shift of the entire supply curve
>
> *change in the quantity supplied* a movement along the supply curve that occurs in response to a change in price

SHIFTS IN DEMAND

To get a better feel for how the supply and demand model enables us to predict and explain price and quantity movements, it is helpful to begin with a few simple examples. The first one illustrates a shift in demand that results from events outside the particular market itself.

EXAMPLE 3.2

What will happen to the equilibrium price and quantity of tennis balls if court rental fees decline?

Let the initial supply and demand curves for tennis balls be as shown by the curves S and D in Figure 3.11, where the resulting equilibrium price and quantity are $1 per ball and 40 million balls per month, respectively. Tennis courts and tennis balls are what economists call **complements,** goods that are more valuable when used in combination than when used alone. Tennis balls, for example, would be of little value if there were no tennis courts on which to play. (Tennis balls would still have *some* value even without courts—for example, to the parents who pitch them to their children for batting practice.) As tennis courts become cheaper to use, people will respond by playing more tennis, and this will increase their demand for tennis balls. A decline in court-rental fees will thus shift the demand curve for tennis balls rightward to D'. (A "rightward shift" of a demand curve can also be described as an "upward shift." These distinctions correspond, respectively, to the horizontal and vertical interpretations of the demand curve.)

> *complements* two goods are complements in consumption if an increase in the price of one causes a leftward shift in the demand curve for the other (or if a decrease causes a rightward shift)

FIGURE 3.11

The Effect on the Market for Tennis Balls of a Decline in Court Rental Fees.

When the price of a complement falls, demand shifts right, causing equilibrium price and quantity to rise.

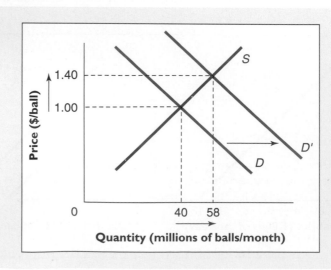

Note in Figure 3.11 that for the illustrative demand shift shown, the new equilibrium price of tennis balls, $1.40, is higher than the original price, and the new equilibrium quantity, 58 million balls per month, is higher than the original quantity.

What will happen to the equilibrium price and quantity of overnight letter delivery service as the price of Internet access falls?

Suppose the initial supply and demand curves for overnight letter deliveries are as shown by the curves S and D in Figure 3.12, and that the resulting equilibrium price and quantity are denoted P and Q. E-mail messages and overnight letters are examples of what economists call **substitutes**, meaning that, in many applications at least, the two serve similar functions for people. (Many noneconomists would call them substitutes, too. Economists don't *always* choose obscure terms for important concepts!) When two goods or services are substitutes, a decrease in the price of one will cause a leftward shift in the demand curve for the other. (A "leftward shift" in a demand curve can also be described as a "downward shift.") Diagrammatically, the demand curve for overnight delivery service shifts from D to D' in Figure 3.12.

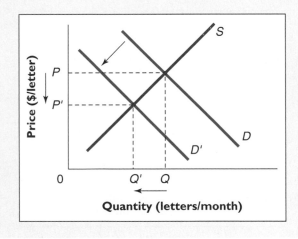

As the figure shows, both the new equilibrium price, P', and the new equilibrium quantity, Q', are lower than the initial values, P and Q. Cheaper Internet access probably won't put Federal Express and UPS out of business, but it will definitely cost them many customers.

To summarize, economists define goods as substitutes if an increase in the price of one causes a rightward shift in the demand curve for the other. By contrast, goods are complements if an increase in the price of one causes a leftward shift in the demand curve for the other.

The concepts of substitutes and complements enable you to answer questions like the one posed in the following exercise.

EXERCISE 3.4

How will a decline in airfares affect intercity bus fares and the price of hotel rooms in resort communities?

Demand curves are shifted not just by changes in the prices of substitutes and complements but also by other factors that change the amounts that people are willing to pay for a given good or service. One of the most important such factors is income.

EXAMPLE 3.3

substitutes two goods are substitutes in consumption if an increase in the price of one causes a rightward shift in the demand curve for the other. (or if a decrease causes a leftward shift)

FIGURE 3.12
The Effect on the Market for Overnight Letter Delivery of a Decline in the Price of Internet Access.
When the price of a substitute falls, demand shifts left, causing equilibrium price and quantity to fall.

When the federal government implements a large pay increase for its employees, why do rents for apartments located near Washington Metro stations go up relative to rents for apartments located far away from Metro stations?

For the citizens of Washington, D.C., a substantial proportion of whom are government employees, it is more convenient to live in an apartment located one block from the nearest subway station than to live in one that is 20 blocks away. Conveniently located apartments thus command relatively high rents. Suppose the initial demand and supply curves for such apartments are as shown in Figure 3.13. Following a federal pay raise, some government employees who live in less convenient apartments will be willing and able to use part of their extra income to bid for more conveniently located apartments, and those who already live in such apartments will be willing and able to pay more to keep them. The effect of the pay raise is thus to shift the demand curve for conveniently located apartments to the right, as indicated by the demand curve labeled D' in Figure 3.13. As a result, both the equilibrium price and quantity of such apartments, P' and Q', will be higher than before.

FIGURE 3.13
The Effect of a Federal Pay Raise on the Rent for Conveniently Located Apartments in Washington, D.C.
An increase in income shifts demand for a normal good to the right, causing equilibrium price and quantity to rise.

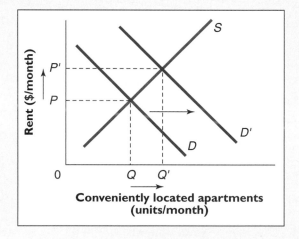

It might seem natural to ask how there could be an increase in the number of conveniently located apartments, which might appear to be fixed by the constraints of geography. But one must never underestimate the ingenuity of sellers when they confront an opportunity to make money by supplying more of something that people want. For example, if rents rose sufficiently, some landlords might respond by converting warehouse space to residential use. Or perhaps people with cars who do not place high value on living near a subway station might sell their apartments to landlords, thereby freeing them for people eager to rent them. (Note that these responses constitute movements along the supply curve of conveniently located apartments, as opposed to shifts in that supply curve.)

When incomes increase, the demand curves for most goods will behave like the demand curve for conveniently located apartments, and in recognition of that fact, economists have chosen to call such goods **normal goods.**

Not all goods are normal goods, however. In fact, the demand curves for some goods actually shift leftward when income goes up, and such goods are called **inferior goods.**

When would having more money tend to make you want to buy less of something? In general, this will happen in the case of goods for which there exist attractive substitutes that sell for only slightly higher prices. Apartments in an unsafe, inconveniently located neighborhood are an example. Most residents would choose to move out of such neighborhoods as soon as they could afford

normal good one whose demand curve shifts rightward when the incomes of buyers increase and leftward when the incomes of buyers decrease

inferior good one whose demand curve shifts leftward when the incomes of buyers increase and rightward when the incomes of buyers decrease to, which means that an increase in income would cause the demand for such apartments to shift leftward.

EXERCISE 3.5

How will a large pay increase for federal employees affect the rents for apartments located far away from Washington Metro stations?

Ground beef with high fat content is another example of an inferior good. For health reasons, most people prefer grades of meat with low fat content, and when they do buy high-fat meats it is usually a sign of budgetary pressure. When people in this situation receive higher incomes, they usually switch quickly to leaner grades of meat.

Preferences, or tastes, are another important factor that determines whether a given good will meet the cost-benefit test. Steven Spielberg's film *Jurassic Park* appeared to kindle a powerful, if previously latent, preference among children for toy dinosaurs. When this film was first released, the demand for such toys shifted sharply to the right. And the same children who couldn't find enough dinosaur toys suddenly seemed to lose interest in toy designs involving horses and other present-day animals, whose respective demand curves shifted sharply to the left.

Expectations about the future are another factor that may cause demand curves to shift. If Apple Macintosh users hear a credible rumor, for example, that a cheaper or significantly upgraded model will be introduced next month, the demand curve for the current model is likely to shift leftward.

SHIFTS IN THE SUPPLY CURVE

The preceding examples involved changes that gave rise to shifts in demand curves. Next, we'll look at what happens when supply curves shift. Because the supply curve is based on costs of production, anything that changes production costs will shift the supply curve, and will hence result in a new equilibrium quantity and price.

What will happen to the equilibrium price and quantity of skateboards if the price of fiberglass, a substance used for making skateboards, rises?

EXAMPLE 3.4

Suppose the initial supply and demand curves for skateboards are as shown by the curves *S* and *D* in Figure 3.14, resulting in an equilibrium price and quantity of $60 per skateboard and 1,000 skateboards per month, respectively. Since fiberglass is one of the ingredients used to produce skateboards, the effect of an increase in the price of fiberglass is to raise the marginal cost of producing skateboards.

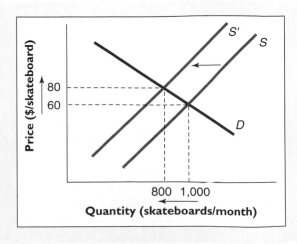

FIGURE 3.14
The Effect on the Skateboard Market of an Increase in the Price of Fiberglass.
When input prices rise, supply shifts left, causing equilibrium price to rise and equilibrium quantity to fall.

How will this affect the supply curve of skateboards? Recall that the supply curve is upward-sloping because when the price of skateboards is low, only those potential sellers whose marginal cost of making skateboards is low can sell boards profitably, whereas at higher prices, those with higher marginal costs can also enter the market profitably (again, the low-hanging-fruit principle). So if the cost of one of the ingredients used to produce skateboards rises, the number of potential sellers who can profitably sell skateboards at any given price will fall. And this, in turn, implies a leftward shift in the supply curve for skateboards. Note that a "leftward shift" in a supply curve can also be viewed as an "upward shift" in the same curve. The first corresponds to the horizontal interpretation of the supply curve, while the second corresponds to the vertical interpretation. We will use these expressions to mean exactly the same thing. The new supply curve (after the price of fiberglass rises) is the curve labeled S' in Figure 3.14.

Does an increase in the cost of fiberglass have any effect on the demand curve for skateboards? The demand curve tells us how many skateboards buyers wish to purchase at each price. Any given buyer is willing to purchase a skateboard if his reservation price for it exceeds its market price. And since each buyer's reservation price, which is based on the benefits of owning a skateboard, does not depend on the price of fiberglass, there should be no shift in the demand curve for skateboards.

In Figure 3.14, we can now see what happens when the supply curve shifts leftward and the demand curve remains unchanged. For the illustrative supply curve shown, the new equilibrium price of skateboards, $80, is higher than the original price, and the new equilibrium quantity, 800 per month, is lower than the original quantity. (These new equilibrium values are merely illustrative. There is insufficient information provided in the example to determine their exact values.) People who don't place a value of at least $80 on owning a skateboard will choose to spend their money on something else.

The effects on equilibrium price and quantity run in the opposite direction whenever marginal costs of production decline, as illustrated in the next example.

EXAMPLE 3.5

What will happen to the equilibrium price and quantity of new houses if the wage rate of carpenters falls?

Suppose the initial supply and demand curves for new houses are as shown by the curves S and D in Figure 3.15, resulting in an equilibrium price of $120,000 per house and an equilibrium quantity of 40 houses per month. A decline in the wage rate of carpenters reduces the marginal cost of making new houses, and this means that, for any given price of houses, more builders can profitably serve

FIGURE 3.15

The Effect on the Market for New Houses of a Decline in Carpenters' Wage Rates.

When input prices fall, supply shifts right, causing equilibrium price to fall and equilibrium quantity to rise.

the market than before. Diagrammatically, this means a rightward shift in the supply curve of houses, from S to S'. (A "rightward shift" in the supply curve can also be described as a "downward shift.")

Does a decrease in the wage rate of carpenters have any effect on the demand curve for houses? The demand curve tells us how many houses buyers wish to purchase at each price. Because carpenters are now earning less than before, the maximum amount that they are willing to pay for houses may fall, which would imply a leftward shift in the demand curve for houses. But because carpenters make up only a tiny fraction of all potential home buyers, we may assume that this shift is negligible. Thus a reduction in carpenters' wages produces a significant rightward shift in the supply curve of houses, but no appreciable shift in the demand curve.

We see from Figure 3.15 that the new equilibrium price, $90,000 per house, is lower than the original price, and the new equilibrium quantity, 50 houses per month, is higher than the original quantity.

Both of the preceding examples involved changes in the cost of an ingredient, or input, in the production of the good in question—fiberglass in the production of skateboards and carpenters' labor in the production of houses. As the following example illustrates, supply curves also shift when technology changes.

Why do major term papers go through so many more revisions today than in the 1970s?

Students in the dark days before word processors were in widespread use could not make even minor revisions in their term papers without having to retype their entire manuscripts from scratch. The availability of word-processing technology has of course radically changed the picture. Instead of having to retype the entire draft, now only the changes need be entered.

In Figure 3.16, the curves labeled S and D depict the supply and demand curves for revisions in the days before word processing, and the curve S' depicts the supply curve for revisions today. As the diagram shows, the result is not only a sharp decline in the price per revision, but also a corresponding increase in the equilibrium number of revisions.

ECONOMIC NATURALIST 3.2

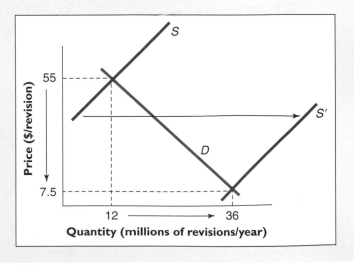

FIGURE 3.16
The Effect of Technical Change on the Market for Term-Paper Revisions.
When a new technology reduces the cost of production, supply shifts right, causing equilibrium price to fall and equilibrium quantity to rise.

Note that in the preceding discussion we implicitly assumed that students purchased typing services in a market. In fact, however, many students type their own term papers. Does that make a difference? Even if no money actually changes hands, students pay a price when they revise their term papers—namely, the opportunity cost of the time it takes to perform that task. Because technology has radically reduced that cost, we would expect to see a large increase in the number of term-paper revisions even if most students type their own work.

Changes in input prices and technology are two of the most important factors that give rise to shifts in supply curves. In the case of agricultural commodities, weather may be another important factor, with favorable conditions shifting the supply curves of such products to the right, and unfavorable conditions shifting them to the left. (Weather may also affect the supply curves of non-agricultural products through its effects on the national transportation system.) Expectations of future price changes may also shift current supply curves, as when the expectation of poor crops from a current drought causes suppliers to withhold supplies from existing stocks in the hope of selling at higher prices in the future. Changes in the number of sellers in the market can also cause supply curves to shift.

FOUR SIMPLE RULES

For supply and demand curves that have the conventional slopes (upward-sloping for supply curves, downward-sloping for demand curves), the preceding examples illustrate the four basic rules that govern how shifts in supply and demand affect equilibrium prices and quantities. These rules are summarized in Figure 3.17.

FIGURE 3.17
Four Rules Governing the Effects of Supply and Demand Shifts.

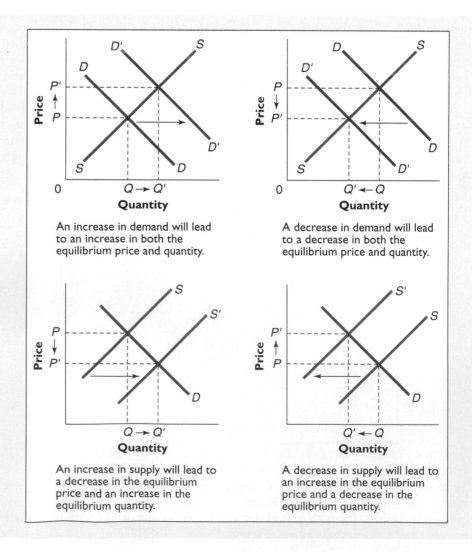

An increase in demand will lead to an increase in both the equilibrium price and quantity.

A decrease in demand will lead to a decrease in both the equilibrium price and quantity.

An increase in supply will lead to a decrease in the equilibrium price and an increase in the equilibrium quantity.

A decrease in supply will lead to an increase in the equilibrium price and a decrease in the equilibrium quantity.

RECAP   **FACTORS THAT SHIFT SUPPLY AND DEMAND**

Factors that cause an increase (rightward or upward shift) in demand:

1. A decrease in the price of complements to the good or service.

2. An increase in the price of substitutes for the good or service.

3. An increase in income (for a normal good).

4. An increased preference by demanders for the good or service.

5. An increase in the population of potential buyers.

6. An expectation of higher prices in the future.

When these factors move in the opposite direction, demand will shift left.

Factors that cause an increase (rightward or downward shift) in supply:

1. A decrease in the cost of materials, labor, or other inputs used in the production of the good or service.

2. An improvement in technology that reduces the cost of producing the good or service.

3. A improvement in the weather (especially for agricultural products).

4. An increase in the number of suppliers.

5. An expectation of lower prices in the future.

When these factors move in the opposite direction, supply will shift left.

The qualitative rules summarized in Figure 3.17 hold for supply or demand shifts of any magnitude, provided the curves have their conventional slopes. But as the next example demonstrates, when both supply and demand curves shift at the same time, the direction in which equilibrium price or quantity changes will depend on the relative magnitudes of the shifts.

How do shifts in *both* demand and supply affect equilibrium quantities and prices?

EXAMPLE 3.6

What will happen to the equilibrium price and quantity in the corn tortilla chip market if both of the following events occur: (1) researchers prove that the oils in which tortilla chips are fried are harmful to human health; and (2) the price of corn harvesting equipment falls?

The conclusion regarding the health effects of the oils will shift the demand for tortilla chips to the left, because many people who once bought chips in the belief that they were healthful will now switch to other foods. The decline in the price of harvesting equipment will shift the supply of chips to the right, because additional farmers will now find it profitable to enter the corn market. In Figures 3.18(a) and 3.18(b), the original supply and demand curves are denoted by S and D, while the new curves are denoted by S' and D'. Note that in both panels, the shifts lead to a decline in the equilibrium price of chips.

But note also that the effect of the shifts on equilibrium quantity cannot be determined without knowing their relative magnitudes. Taken separately, the demand shift causes a decline in equilibrium quantity, whereas the supply shift causes an increase in equilibrium quantity. The net effect of the two shifts thus depends on which of the individual effects is larger. In Figure 3.18(a), the demand shift dominates, so equilibrium quantity declines. In Figure 3.18(b), the supply shift dominates, so equilibrium quantity goes up.

FIGURE 3.18
The Effects of Simultaneous Shifts in Supply and Demand.
When demand shifts left and supply shifts right, equilibrium price falls, but equilibrium quantity may either rise (b) or fall (a).

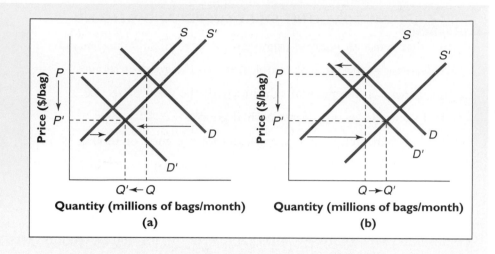

(a)   (b)

The following exercise asks you to consider a simple variation on the problem posed in Example 3.6.

EXERCISE 3.6

What will happen to the equilibrium price and quantity in the corn tortilla chip market if both of the following events occur: (1) researchers discover that a vitamin found in corn helps protect against cancer and heart disease; and (2) a swarm of locusts destroys part of the corn crop?

ECONOMIC NATURALIST 3.3

Why do the prices of some goods, like airline tickets to Europe, go up during the months of heaviest consumption, while others, like sweet corn, go down?

Seasonal price movements for airline tickets are primarily the result of seasonal variations in demand. Thus ticket prices to Europe are highest during the summer months because the demand for tickets is highest during those months, as shown in Figure 3.19(a), where the w and s subscripts denote winter and summer values, respectively.

By contrast, seasonal price movements for sweet corn are primarily the result of seasonal variations in supply. The price of sweet corn is lowest in the summer months because its supply is highest during those months, as seen in Figure 3.19(b).

FIGURE 3.19
Seasonal Variation in the Air Travel and Corn Markets.
(a) Prices are highest during the period of heaviest consumption when heavy consumption is the result of high demand. (b) Prices are lowest during the period of heaviest consumption when heavy consumption is the result of high supply.

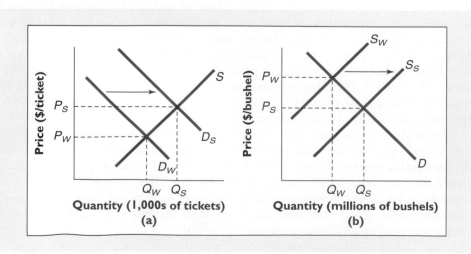

(a)   (b)

MARKETS AND SOCIAL WELFARE

Markets represent a highly effective system of allocating resources. When a market for a good is in equilibrium, the equilibrium price conveys important information to potential suppliers about the value that potential demanders place on that good. At the same time, the equilibrium price informs potential demanders about the opportunity cost of supplying the good. This rapid, two-way transmission of information is the reason that markets can coordinate an activity as complex as supplying New York City with food and drink, even though no one person or organization oversees the process.

But are the prices and quantities determined in market equilibrium socially optimal, in the sense of maximizing total economic surplus? That is, does equilibrium in unregulated markets always maximize the difference between the total benefits and total costs experienced by market participants? As we will see, the answer is "it depends": A market that is out of equilibrium, such as the rent-controlled New York housing market, always creates opportunities for individuals to arrange transactions that will increase their individual economic surplus. As we will see, however, a market for a good that is in equilibrium makes the largest possible contribution to total economic surplus only when its supply and demand curves fully reflect the costs and benefits associated with the production and consumption of that good.

CASH ON THE TABLE

In economics we assume that all exchange is purely voluntary. This means that a transaction cannot take place unless the buyer's reservation price for the good exceeds the seller's reservation price. When that condition is met and a transaction takes place, both parties receive an economic surplus. The **buyer's surplus** from the transaction is the difference between his reservation price and the price he actually pays. The **seller's surplus** is the difference between the price she receives and her reservation price. The **total surplus** from the transaction is the sum of the buyer's surplus and the seller's surplus. It is also equal to the difference between the buyer's reservation price and the seller's reservation price.

buyer's surplus the difference between the buyer's reservation price and the price he or she actually pays

Suppose there is a potential buyer whose reservation price for an additional slice of pizza is $4 and a potential seller whose reservation price is only $2. If this buyer purchases a slice of pizza from this seller for $3, the total surplus generated by this exchange is $4 − $2 = $2, of which $4 − $3 = $1 is the buyer's surplus and $3 − $2 = $1 is the seller's surplus.

seller's surplus the difference between the price received by the seller and his or her reservation price

A regulation that prevents the price of a good from reaching its equilibrium level unnecessarily prevents exchanges of this sort from taking place, and in the process reduces total economic surplus. Consider again the effect of price controls imposed in the market for pizza. The demand curve in Figure 3.20 tells us that if a price ceiling of $2 per slice were imposed, only 8,000 slices of pizza per day would be sold. At that quantity, the vertical interpretations of the supply and demand curves tell us that a buyer would be willing to pay as much as $4 for an additional slice and that a seller would be willing to sell one for as little $2. The difference—$2 per slice—is the additional economic surplus that would result if an additional slice were produced and sold. As noted earlier, an extra slice sold at a price of $3 would result in an additional $1 of economic surplus for both buyer and seller.

total surplus the difference between the buyer's reservation price and the seller's reservation price

When a market is out of equilibrium, it is always possible to identify mutually beneficial exchanges of this sort. When people have failed to take advantage of all mutually beneficial exchanges, we often say that there is **"cash on the table"**— the economist's metaphor for unexploited opportunities. When the price in a market is below the equilibrium price, there is cash on the table, because the reservation price of sellers (marginal cost) will always be lower than the reservation price of buyers. In the absence of a law preventing buyers paying more than $2

cash on the table economic metaphor for unexploited gains from exchange

FIGURE 3.20
Price Controls in the Pizza Market.
A price ceiling below the equilibrium price of pizza would result in excess demand for pizza.

per slice, restaurant owners would quickly raise their prices and expand their production until the equilibrium price of $3 per slice was reached. At that price, buyers would be able to get precisely the 12,000 slices of pizza they want to buy each day. All mutually beneficial opportunities for exchange would have been exploited, leaving no more cash on the table.

Buyers and sellers in the marketplace have an uncanny ability to detect the presence of cash on the table. It is almost as if unexploited opportunities gave off some exotic scent triggering neurochemical explosions in the olfactory centers of their brains. The desire to scrape cash off the table and into their pockets is what drives sellers in each of New York City's thousands of individual food markets to work diligently to meet their customers' demands. That they succeed to a far higher degree than participants in the city's rent-controlled housing market is plainly evident. Whatever flaws it might have, the market system moves with considerably greater speed and agility than any centralized allocation mechanisms yet devised. But as we emphasize in the following section, this does not mean that markets *always* lead to the greatest good for all.

SMART FOR ONE, DUMB FOR ALL

socially optimal quantity the quantity of a good that results in the maximum possible economic surplus from producing and consuming the good

The **socially optimal quantity** of any good is the quantity that maximizes the total economic surplus that results from producing and consuming the good. From the cost-benefit principle, we know that we should keep expanding production of the good as long as its marginal benefit is at least as great as its marginal cost. This means that the socially optimal quantity is that level for which the marginal cost and marginal benefit of the good are the same.

When the quantity of a good is less than the socially optimal quantity, boosting its production will increase total economic surplus. By the same token, when the quantity of a good exceeds the socially optimal quantity, reducing its production will increase total economic surplus. **Economic efficiency,** or **efficiency,** occurs when all goods and services in the economy are produced and consumed at their respective socially optimal levels.

efficiency (also called **economic efficiency**) occurs when all goods and services are produced and consumed at their respective socially optimal levels

Efficiency is an important social goal. Failure to achieve efficiency means that total economic surplus is smaller than it could have been. Movements toward efficiency make the total economic pie larger, making it possible for everyone to have a larger slice. The importance of efficiency will be a recurring theme as we move forward, and we state it here as one of the core principles:

The Efficiency Principle: Efficiency is an important social goal, because when the economic pie grows larger, everyone can have a larger slice.

Is the market equilibrium quantity of a good efficient? That is, does it maximize the total economic surplus received by participants in the market for that good? When the private market for a given good is in equilibrium, we can say that the cost *to the seller* of producing an additional unit of the good is the same as the benefit *to the buyer* of having an additional unit. If all costs of producing the good are borne directly by sellers, and if all benefits from the good accrue directly to buyers, it follows that the market equilibrium quantity of the good will equate the marginal cost and marginal benefit of the good. And this means that the equilibrium quantity also maximizes total economic surplus.

But sometimes the production of a good entails costs that fall on people other than those who sell the good. This will be true, for instance, for goods whose production generates significant levels of environmental pollution (a topic we will explore in much greater detail in Chapter 11). As extra units of these goods are produced, the extra pollution harms other people besides sellers. In the market equilibrium for such goods, the benefit *to buyers* of the last good produced is, as before, equal to the cost incurred by sellers to produce that good. But since producing that good also imposed pollution costs on others, we know that the *full* marginal cost of the last unit produced—the seller's private marginal cost plus the marginal pollution cost borne by others—must be higher than the benefit of the last unit produced. So in this case the market equilibrium quantity of the good will be larger than the socially optimal quantity. Total economic surplus would be higher if output of the good were lower. Yet neither sellers nor buyers have any incentive to alter their behavior.

Another possibility is that people other than those who buy a good may receive significant benefits from it. For instance, when someone purchases a vaccination against measles from her doctor, she not only protects herself against measles, but she also makes it less likely that others will catch this disease. From the perspective of society as a whole, we should keep increasing the number of vaccinations until their marginal cost equals their marginal benefit. The marginal benefit of a vaccination is the value of the protection it provides the person vaccinated *plus* the value of the protection it provides all others. Private consumers, however, will choose to be vaccinated only if the marginal benefit *to them* exceeds the price of the vaccination. In this case, then, the market equilibrium quantity of vaccinations will be smaller than the quantity that maximizes total economic surplus. Again, however, individuals would have no incentive to alter their behavior.

Situations like the ones just discussed provide examples of behaviors that we may call "smart for one but dumb for all." In each case, the individual actors are behaving rationally. They are pursuing their goals as best they can, and yet there remain unexploited opportunities for gain from the point of view of the whole society. The difficulty is that these opportunities cannot be exploited by individuals acting alone. In subsequent chapters we will see how people can often organize collectively to exploit such opportunities. For now, we simply summarize this discussion in the form of the following core principle:

The Equilibrium Principle (also called the "no-cash-on-the-table" principle): A market in equilibrium leaves no unexploited opportunities for individuals, but may not exploit all gains achievable through collective action.

 RECAP   MARKETS AND SOCIAL WELFARE

When the supply and demand curves for a good reflect all significant costs and benefits associated with the production and consumption of that good, the market equilibrium will result in the largest possible economic surplus. But if people other than buyers benefit from the good, or if people other than sellers bear costs because of it, market equilibrium need not result in the largest possible economic surplus.

▪ SUMMARY ▪

- Eighteenth-century economists tried to explain differences in the prices of goods by focusing on differences in their cost of production. But this approach cannot explain why a conveniently located house sells for more than one that is less conveniently located. Early nineteenth-century economists tried to explain price differences by focusing on differences in what buyers were willing to pay. But this approach cannot explain why the price of a lifesaving appendectomy is less than that of a surgical facelift.

- Alfred Marshall's model of supply and demand explains why neither cost of production nor value to the purchaser (as measured by willingness to pay) is, by itself, sufficient to explain why some goods are cheap and others are expensive. To explain variations in price, we must examine the interaction of cost and willingness to pay. As we've seen in this chapter, goods differ in price because of differences in their respective supply and demand curves.

- The demand curve is a downward-sloping line that tells what quantity buyers will demand at any given price. The supply curve is an upward-sloping line that tells what quantity sellers will offer at any given price. Market equilibrium occurs when the quantity buyers demand at the market price is exactly the same as the quantity that sellers offer. The equilibrium price-quantity pair is the one at which the demand and supply curves intersect. In equilibrium, market price measures both the value of the last unit sold to buyers and the cost of the resources required to produce it.

- When the price of a good lies above its equilibrium value, there is an excess supply of that good. Excess supply motivates sellers to cut their prices, and price continues to fall until the equilibrium price is reached. When price lies below its equilibrium value, there is excess demand. With excess demand, frustrated buyers are motivated to offer higher prices, and the upward pressure on prices persists until equilibrium is reached. A remarkable feature of the market system is that, relying only on the tendency of people to respond in self-interested ways to market price signals, it somehow manages to coordinate the actions of literally billions of buyers and sellers worldwide. When excess demand or excess supply occurs, it tends to be small and brief, except in markets where regulations prevent full adjustment of prices.

- The efficiency of markets in allocating resources does not eliminate social concerns about how goods and services are distributed among different people. For example, we often lament the fact many buyers enter the market with too little income to buy even the most basic goods and services. Concern for the well-being of the poor has motivated many governments to intervene in a variety of ways to alter the outcomes of market forces. Sometimes these interventions take the form of laws that peg prices below their equilibrium levels. Such laws almost invariably generate harmful, if unintended, consequences. Programs like rent-control laws, for example, lead to severe housing shortages, black marketeering, and a rapid deterioration of the relationship between landlords and tenants.

- If the difficulty is that the poor have too little money, the best solution is to discover ways of boosting their incomes directly. The law of supply and demand cannot be repealed by the legislature. But legislatures do have the capacity to alter the underlying forces that govern the shape and position of supply and demand schedules.

- The basic supply and demand model is a primary tool of the economic naturalist. Changes in the equilibrium price of a good, and in the amount of it traded in the marketplace, can be predicted on the basis of shifts in its supply or demand curves. The following four rules hold for any good with a downward-sloping demand curve and an upward-sloping supply curve:

  - An increase in demand will lead to an increase in equilibrium price and quantity.
  - A reduction in demand will lead to a reduction in equilibrium price and quantity.
  - An increase in supply will lead to a reduction in equilibrium price and an increase in equilibrium quantity.
  - A decrease in supply will lead to an increase in equilibrium price and a reduction in equilibrium quantity.

- Incomes, tastes, population, expectations, and the prices of substitutes and complements are among the factors that shift demand schedules. Supply schedules, in turn, are primarily governed by such factors as technology, input prices, expectations, the number of sellers, and, especially for agricultural products, the weather.

- When the supply and demand curves for a good reflect all significant costs and benefits associated with the production and consumption of that good, the market equilibrium price will guide people to produce and consume the quantity of the good that results in the largest possible economic surplus. This conclusion, however, does not apply if others, beside buyers, benefit from the good (as when someone benefits from his neighbor's purchase of a vaccination against measles), or if others besides sellers bear costs because of the good (as when its production generates pollution). In such cases, market equilibrium does not result in the greatest gain for all.

▪ CORE PRINCIPLES ▪

The Efficiency Principle
Efficiency is an important social goal, because when the economic pie grows larger, everyone can have a larger slice.

The Equilibrium Principle
A market in equilibrium leaves no unexploited opportunities for individuals, but may not exploit all gains achievable through collective action.

▪ KEY TERMS ▪

buyer's reservation price (62)
buyer's surplus (81)
cash on the table (81)
change in demand (71)
change in quantity demanded (71)
change in quantity supplied (72)
change in supply (72)
complements (72)
demand curve (61)
efficiency (82)

equilibrium (64)
equilibrium price (64)
equilibrium quantity (64)
excess demand (65)
excess supply (65)
income effect (61)
inferior good (74)
market (60)
market equilibrium (64)

normal good (74)
price ceiling (70)
seller's reservation price (63)
seller's surplus (81)
socially optimal quantity (82)
substitutes (73)
substitution effect (61)
supply curve (62)
total surplus (81)

▪ REVIEW QUESTIONS ▪

1. Why isn't knowing the cost of producing a good sufficient to predict its market price?

2. Distinguish between the meaning of the expressions "change in demand" and "change in the quantity demanded."

3. Last year a government official proposed that gasoline price controls be imposed to protect the poor from rising gasoline prices. What evidence could you consult to discover whether this proposal was enacted?

4. Explain the distinction between the horizontal and vertical interpretations of the demand curve.

5. Give an example of behavior you have observed that could be described as "smart for one but dumb for all."

▪ PROBLEMS ▪

1. State whether the following pairs of goods are complements or substitutes. (If you think pair is ambiguous in this respect, explain why.)
   a. Tennis courts and squash courts.
   b. Squash racquets and squash balls.
   c. Ice cream and chocolate.
   d. Cloth diapers and paper diapers.

2. How would each of the following affect the U.S. market supply curve for corn?
   a. A new and improved crop rotation technique is discovered.
   b. The price of fertilizer falls.
   c. The government offers new tax breaks to farmers.
   d. A tornado sweeps through Iowa.

3. Indicate how you think each of the following would shift demand in the indicated market:
   a. Incomes of buyers in the market for Adirondack vacations increase.
   b. Buyers in the market for pizza read a study linking hamburger consumption to heart disease.
   c. Buyers in the market for CDs learn of an increase in the price of audiocassettes (a substitute for CDs).
   d. Buyers in the market for CDs learn of an increase in the price of CDs.

4. An Arizona student claims to have spotted a UFO over the desert outside of Tucson. How will his claim affect the *supply* (not the quantity supplied) of binoculars in Tucson stores?

5. What will happen to the equilibrium price and quantity of oranges if the wage paid to orange pickers rises?

6. How will an increase in the birth rate affect the equilibrium price of land?

7. What will happen to the equilibrium price and quantity of fish if fish oils are found to help prevent heart disease?

8. What will happen to the equilibrium price and quantity of beef if the price of chickenfeed increases?

9. Use supply and demand analysis to explain why hotel room rental rates near your campus during parents' weekend and graduation weekend might differ from the rates charged during the rest of the year.

10. How will a new law mandating an increase in required levels of automobile insurance affect the equilibrium price and quantity in the market for new automobiles?

11. Suppose the current issue of the *New York Times* reports an outbreak of mad cow disease in Nebraska, as well as the discovery of a new breed of chickens that gain more weight than existing breeds that consume the same amount of food. How will these developments affect the equilibrium price and quantity of chicken sold in the United States?

12. What will happen to the equilibrium quantity and price of potatoes if population increases and a new, higher yielding variety of potato plant is developed?

13. What will happen to the equilibrium price and quantity of apples if apples are discovered to help prevent colds and a fungus kills 10 percent of existing apple trees?

14. What will happen to the equilibrium quantity and price of corn if the price of butter (a complement) increases and the price of fertilizer decreases?

15. Twenty-five years ago, tofu was available only from small businesses operating in predominantly Asian sections of large cities. Today tofu has become popular as a high-protein health food and is widely available in supermarkets throughout the United States. At the same time, tofu production has evolved to become factory-based using modern food-processing technologies. Draw a diagram with demand and supply curves depicting the market for tofu 25 years ago and the market for tofu today. Given the information above, what does the demand-supply model predict about changes in the volume of tofu sold in the United States between then and now? What does it predict about changes in the price of tofu?

■ ANSWERS TO IN-CHAPTER EXERCISES ■

3.1 At a quantity of 10,000 slices per day, the marginal buyer's reservation price is $3.50 per slice. At a price of $2.50 per slice, the quantity demanded will be 14,000 slices per day.

3.2 At a quantity of 10,000 slices per day, the marginal cost of pizza is $2.50 per slice. At a price of $3.50 per slice, the quantity supplied will be 14,000 slices per day.

3.3 Since landlords are permitted to charge less than the maximum rent established by rent-control laws, a law that sets the maximum rent at $1,200 will have no effect on the rents actually charged in this market, which will settle at the equilibrium value of $800 per month.

3.4 Travel by air and travel by intercity bus are substitutes, so a decline in airfares will shift the demand for bus travel to the left, resulting in lower bus fares and fewer bus trips taken. Travel by air and the use of resort hotels are complements, so a decline in airfares will shift the demand for resort hotel rooms to the right, resulting in higher hotel rates and an increase in the number of rooms rented.

3.5 Apartments located far from Washington Metro stations are an inferior good. A pay increase for federal workers will thus shift the demand curve for such apartments downward, which will lead to a reduction in their equilibrium rent.

3.6 The vitamin discovery shifts the demand for chips to the right, and the crop losses shift the supply of chips to the left. Both shifts result in an increase in the equilibrium price of chips. But depending on the relative magnitude of the shifts, the equilibrium quantity of chips may either rise (left panel) or fall (right panel).

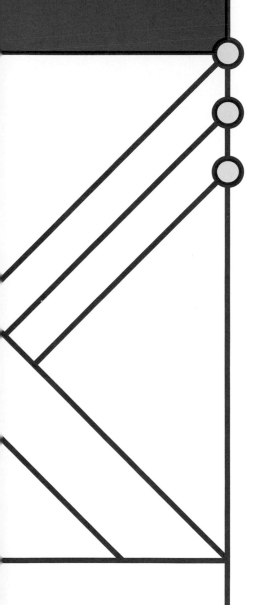

PART

2

COMPETITION AND THE INVISIBLE HAND

■

Having grasped the basic core principles of economics, you are now in a position to sharpen your understanding of how consumers and firms behave. In Part 2 our focus will be on how things work in an idealized, perfectly competitive economy in which consumers are perfectly informed and no firm has market power.

We begin in Chapter 4 by exploring the concept of elasticity, which describes the sensitivity of demand and supply to variations in prices, incomes, and other economic factors. In our review of supply and demand in Part 1, we asked you simply to assume the law of demand, which says that demand curves are downward-sloping. In Chapter 5 we will see that this law is a simple consequence of the fact that people spend their limited incomes in rational ways. In Chapter 6 our focus will shift to the seller's side of the market, where our task will be to see why upward-sloping supply curves are a consequence of production decisions taken by firms whose goal is to maximize profit.

Our agenda in Chapter 7 is to develop more carefully and fully the concept of economic surplus introduced in Part 1 and to investigate the conditions under which unregulated markets generate the largest possible economic surplus. We will also explore why attempts to interfere with market outcomes often lead to unintended and undesired consequences.

Finally, in Chapter 8 we will investigate the economic forces by which the invisible hand of the marketplace guides profit-seeking firms and satisfaction-seeking consumers in ways that, to a surprising degree, serve society's ends. These forces encourage aggressive cost cutting by firms, even though the resulting gains will eventually take the form of lower prices rather than higher profits. We will also see why misunderstanding of competitive forces often results in costly errors, both in everyday decision making and in government policy.

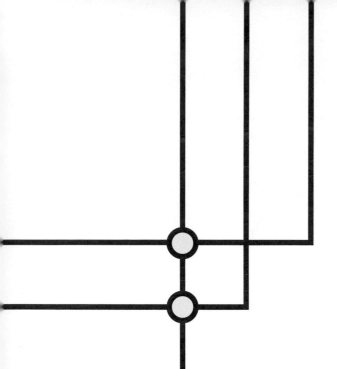

ELASTICITY

■

Many illicit drug users commit crimes to finance their addiction. The connection between drugs and crime has led to calls for more vigorous efforts to stop the smuggling of illicit drugs. But can such efforts reduce the likelihood that your laptop computer will be stolen in the next month? If attempts to reduce the supply of illicit drugs are successful, their effect will be to increase the market price of drugs. (From our basic supply and demand analysis, we can see that this increase in price is caused by a leftward shift in the supply curve for drugs.) The law of demand tells us that drug users will respond by consuming a smaller quantity of drugs. But the amount of crime drug users commit depends not on the *quantity* of drugs they consume, but rather on their *total expenditure* on drugs. Depending on the specific characteristics of the demand curve for illicit drugs, a price increase might reduce total expenditure on drugs, but it could also raise total expenditure.

Suppose, for example, that extra border patrols shift the supply curve in the market for illicit drugs to the left, as shown in Figure 4.1. As a result, the equilibrium quantity of drugs would fall from 50,000 to 40,000 ounces per day, and the price of drugs would rise from $50 to $80 per ounce. The total amount spent on drugs, which was $2,500,000 per day (50,000 ounces/day × $50/ounce), would rise to $3,200,000 per day (40,000 ounces/day × $80/ounce). In this case, then, efforts to stem the supply of drugs would actually increase the likelihood of your laptop being stolen.

Other benefits from stemming the flow of illicit drugs might still outweigh the resulting increase in crime. But knowing that the policy might increase drug-related crime would clearly be useful to law-enforcement authorities.

Our task in this chapter will be to introduce the concept of elasticity, a measure of the extent to which quantity demanded and quantity supplied

FIGURE 4.1
The Effect of Extra Border Patrols on the Market for Illicit Drugs.
Extra patrols shift supply leftward and reduce the quantity demanded, but they may actually increase the total amount spent on drugs.

Could reducing the supply of illegal drugs cause an increase in drug-related burglaries?

respond to variations in price, income, and other factors. In the preceding chapter, we saw how shifts in supply and demand curves enabled us to predict the direction of change in the equilibrium values of price and quantity. An understanding of price elasticity will enable us to make even more precise statements about the effects of such changes. In the illicit-drug example just considered, the decrease in supply led to an increase in total spending. In many other cases, a decrease in supply will lead to a reduction in total spending. Why this difference? The underlying phenomenon that explains this pattern, we will see, is price elasticity of demand. We will explore why some goods have higher price elasticity of demand than others and the implications of that fact for how total spending responds to changes in prices. We will also discuss price elasticity of supply and examine the factors that explain why it takes different values for different goods.

PRICE ELASTICITY OF DEMAND

When the price of a good or service rises, the quantity demanded falls. But to predict the effect of the price increase on total expenditure, we must also know how much quantity falls. The quantity demanded of some goods, such as salt, is not very sensitive to changes in price. Indeed, even if the price of salt were to double, or to fall by half, most people would alter their consumption of it hardly at all. For other goods, however, the quantity demanded is extremely responsive to changes in price. For example, when a luxury tax was imposed on yachts in the early 1990s, purchases of yachts plummeted sharply.

PRICE ELASTICITY DEFINED

price elasticity of demand
percentage change in quantity demanded that results from a 1 percent change in price

The **price elasticity of demand** for a good is a measure of the responsiveness of the quantity demanded of that good to changes in its price. Formally, the price elasticity of demand for a good is defined as the percentage change in the quantity demanded that results from a 1 percent change in its price. For example, if the price of beef falls by 1 percent and the quantity demanded rises by 2 percent, then the price elasticity of demand for beef has a value of −2.

Although the definition just given refers to the response of quantity demanded to a 1 percent change in price, it can also be adapted to other variations in price, provided they are relatively small. In such cases, we calculate the price elasticity of demand as the percentage change in quantity demanded divided by the corresponding percentage change in price. Thus, if a 2 percent reduction in the price of pork led to a 6 percent increase in the quantity of pork demanded, the price elasticity of demand for pork would be

$$\frac{\text{Percentage change in quality demanded}}{\text{Percentage change in price}} = \frac{6 \text{ percent}}{-2 \text{ percent}} = -3. \qquad (4.1)$$

Strictly speaking, the price elasticity of demand will always be negative (or zero), because price changes are always in the opposite direction from changes in quantity demanded. So for convenience, we can drop the negative sign and speak of price elasticities in terms of absolute value. The demand for a good is said to be **elastic** with respect to price if the absolute value of its price elasticity is greater than 1. It is said to be **inelastic** if the absolute value of its price elasticity is less than 1. Finally, demand is said to be **unit elastic** if the absolute value of its price elasticity is equal to 1. (See Figure 4.2.)

elastic demand is elastic with respect to price if price elasticity of demand is greater than 1

inelastic demand is inelastic with respect to price if price elasticity of demand is less than 1

unit elastic demand is unit elastic with respect to price if price elasticity of demand equals 1

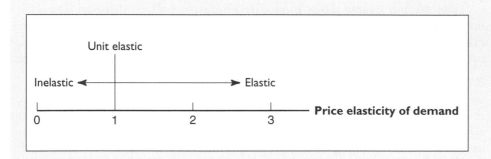

FIGURE 4.2
Elastic and Inelastic Demand.
Demand for a good is called elastic, unit elastic, or inelastic with respect to price if the price elasticity is greater than 1, equal to 1, or less than 1, respectively.

EXAMPLE 4.1

What is the elasticity of demand for pizza?

When the price of pizza is $1 per slice, buyers wish to purchase 400 slices per day, but when price falls to $0.97 per slice, the quantity demanded rises to 404 slices per day. At the original price, what is the price elasticity of demand for pizza? Is the demand for pizza elastic with respect to price?

In response to a 3 percent reduction in the price of pizza, the quantity demanded increases by 1 percent. The price elasticity of demand for pizza is thus (1 percent)/(3 percent) = 1/3. So when the initial price of pizza is $1, the demand for pizza is not elastic with respect to price; it is inelastic.

EXERCISE 4.1

What is the elasticity of demand for season ski passes?

When the price of a season ski pass is $400, buyers wish to purchase 10,000 passes per year, but when price falls to $380, the quantity demanded rises to 12,000 passes per year. At the original price, what is the price elasticity of demand for ski passes? Is the demand for ski passes elastic with respect to price?

DETERMINANTS OF PRICE ELASTICITY OF DEMAND

What factors determine the price elasticity of demand for a good or service? To answer this question, recall that before a rational consumer buys any product, the product must first pass the cost-benefit test. For instance, consider a good (such as a dorm refrigerator) that you buy only one unit of (if you buy it at all). Suppose that, at the current price, you have decided to buy it. Now imagine that the price goes up by 10 percent. Will a price increase of this magnitude be likely to make you change your mind? The answer will depend on factors like the following.

Substitution Possibilities

When the price of a product you want to buy goes up significantly, you are likely to ask yourself, "Is there some other good that can do roughly the same job, but

If the price of salt were to double, would you use less of it?

for less money?" If the answer is yes, then you can escape the effect of the price increase by simply switching to the substitute product. But if the answer is no, you are more likely to stick with your current purchase.

These observations suggest that the price elasticity of demand will tend to be higher for products for which close substitutes are readily available. Salt, for example, has no close substitutes, which is one reason that the demand for it is highly inelastic. Note, however, that while the quantity of salt people demand is highly insensitive to price, the same cannot be said of the demand for any *specific brand* of salt. After all, despite what salt manufacturers say about the special advantages of their own labels, consumers tend to regard one brand of salt as a virtually perfect substitute for another. Thus, if Morton were to raise the price of its salt significantly, many people would simply switch to some other brand.

The vaccine against rabies is another product for which there are essentially no attractive substitutes. A person who is bitten by a rabid animal and does not take the vaccine faces a certain and painful death. So most people in that position would pay any price they could afford rather than do without the vaccine.

Budget Share

Suppose the price of key rings suddenly were to double. How would that affect the number of key rings you buy? If you're like most people, it would have no effect at all. Think about it—a doubling of the price of a 25-cent item that you buy only every few years is simply nothing to worry about. By contrast, if the price of the new car you were about to buy suddenly doubled, you would definitely want to check out possible substitutes, such as a used car or a smaller new model. You might also consider holding on to your current car a little longer. The larger the share of your budget an item accounts for, the greater is your incentive to look for substitutes when the price of the item rises. Big-ticket items therefore tend to have higher price elasticities of demand.

Time

Home appliances come in a variety of models, some more energy-efficient than others. As a general rule, the more efficient an appliance is, the higher its price. If you were about to buy a new air conditioner and electric rates suddenly rose sharply, it would be in your interest to buy a more efficient machine than you had originally planned. But suppose you had already bought the machine before you learned of the rate increase. In all likelihood, it would not pay you discard the machine right away and replace it with a more efficient model. Rather, you would wait until the machine wore out, or until you moved, before making the switch.

As this example illustrates, substitution of one product or service for another takes time. Some substitutions occur in the immediate aftermath of a price increase, but many others take place years or even decades later. For this reason, the price elasticity of demand for any good or service will be higher in the long run than in the short run.

 RECAP **FACTORS THAT INFLUENCE PRICE ELASTICITY**

The price elasticity of demand for a good or service tends to be larger when substitutes for the good are more readily available, when the good's share in the consumer's budget is larger, and when consumers have more time to adjust to a change in price.

SOME REPRESENTATIVE ELASTICITY ESTIMATES

As the entries in Table 4.1 show, the price elasticities of demand for different products often differ substantially—in this sample, ranging from a high of 2.8 for green peas to a low of 0.18 for theater and opera tickets. This variability is explained in part by the determinants of elasticity just discussed. Patrons of theater and opera, for example, tend to have high incomes, implying that the shares of their budgets devoted to these items are likely to be small. What is more, theater and opera patrons are often highly knowledgeable and enthusiastic about these art forms; for many of them, there are simply no acceptable substitute forms of entertainment.

TABLE 4.1
Price Elasticity Estimates for Selected Products

Good or service	Price elasticity
Green peas	2.80
Restaurant meals	1.63
Automobiles	1.35
Electricity	1.20
Beer	1.19
Movies	0.87
Air travel (foreign)	0.77
Shoes	0.70
Coffee	0.25
Theater, opera	0.18

SOURCE: These short-run elasticity estimates are taken from the following sources: Ronald Fisher, *State and Local Public Finance*, Chicago: Irwin, 1996; H. S. Houthakker and Lester Taylor, *Consumer Demand in the United States: Analyses and Projections*, 2nd ed., Cambridge, MA: Harvard University Press, 1970; L. Taylor, "The Demand for Electricity: A Survey," *Bell Journal of Economics*, Spring 1975; K. Elzinga, "The Beer Industry," in *The Structure of American Industry*, Walter Adams, ed., New York: Macmillan, 1977.

Why is the price elasticity of demand more than 14 times larger for green peas than for theater and opera performances? The answer cannot be that income effects loom any larger for green peas than for theater tickets. Even though the average consumer of green peas earns much less than the average theater or opera patron, the share of a typical family's budget devoted to green peas is surely very small. What differentiates green peas from theater and opera performances is that there are so many more close substitutes for peas than for opera and theater. The lowly green pea, which is mostly found in the canned goods or frozen foods sections of supermarkets, just does not seem to have inspired a loyal consumer following.

USING PRICE ELASTICITY OF DEMAND

An understanding of the factors that govern price elasticity of demand is necessary not only to make sense of consumer behavior, but also to design effective public policy. Consider, for example, the debate about how taxes affect smoking among teenagers.

Will a higher tax on cigarettes curb teenage smoking?

Consultants hired by the tobacco industry have testified in Congress against higher cigarette taxes aimed at curbing teenage smoking. The main reason teenagers smoke is that their friends smoke, these consultants testified, and they concluded that higher taxes would have little effect. Does the consultants' testimony make economic sense?

The consultants are almost certainly right that peer influence is the most important determinant of teen smoking. But that does not imply that a higher tax

ECONOMIC NATURALIST 4.1

on cigarettes would have little impact on adolescent smoking rates. Because most teenagers have little money to spend at their own discretion, cigarettes constitute a significant share of a typical teenage smoker's budget. The price elasticity of demand is thus likely to be far from negligible. For at least some teenage smokers, a higher tax would make smoking unaffordable. And even among those who could afford the higher prices, at least some others would choose to spend their money on other things rather than pay the higher prices.

Given that the tax would affect at least *some* teenage smokers, the consultants' argument begins to unravel. If the tax deters even a small number of smokers directly through its effect on the price of cigarettes, it will also deter others indirectly, by reducing the number of peer role models who smoke. And those who refrain because of these indirect effects will in turn no longer influence others to smoke, and so on. So even if the direct effect of higher cigarette taxes on teen smoking is small, the cumulative effects may be extremely large. The mere fact that peer pressure may be the primary determinant of teen smoking therefore does not imply that higher cigarette taxes will have no significant impact on the number of teens who smoke.

Why was the luxury tax on yachts such a disaster?

ECONOMIC NATURALIST 4.2

Under the Omnibus Budget Reconciliation Act of 1990, Congress imposed a luxury tax on yachts costing more than $100,000, along with similar taxes on a handful of other luxury goods. Before these taxes were imposed, the Joint Committee on Taxation estimated that they would yield more than $31 million in revenue in 1991. But in fact their yield was little more than half that amount, $16.6 million. Several years later, the Joint Economic Committee estimated that the tax on yachts had led to a loss of 7,600 jobs in the U.S. boating industry. Taking account of lost income taxes and increased unemployment benefits, the U.S. government actually came out $7.6 million behind in fiscal 1991 as a result of its luxury taxes—almost $39 million worse than the initial projection. What went wrong?

The 1990 law imposed no luxury taxes on yachts built and purchased outside the United States. What Congress failed to consider was that such yachts are almost perfect substitutes for yachts built and purchased in the United States. And, no surprise, when prices on domestic yachts went up because of the tax, yacht buyers switched in droves to foreign models. A tax imposed on a good with high elasticity of demand stimulates large rearrangements of consumption but yields little revenue. Had Congress done the economic analysis properly, it would have predicted that this particular tax would be a big loser. Facing angry protests from unemployed New England shipbuilders, Congress repealed the luxury tax on yachts in 1993.

Why did the luxury tax on yachts backfire?

A GRAPHICAL INTERPRETATION OF PRICE ELASTICITY

For small changes in price, price elasticity of demand is the proportion by which quantity demanded changes divided by the corresponding proportion by which price changes. This formulation enables us to construct a simple expression for the price elasticity of demand for a good using only minimal information about its demand curve.

To illustrate, suppose we let P represent the current price of the good and Q the quantity demanded at that price. Similarly, let ΔP represent a small change in the current price and ΔQ the resulting change in quantity demanded. (See Figure 4.3.) The expression $\Delta P/P$ will then stand for the proportion by which price changes when P changes by ΔP; and $\Delta Q/Q$ will stand for the corresponding

FIGURE 4.3
A Graphical Interpretation of Price Elasticity of Demand.
Price elasticity of demand at any point along a straight-line demand curve is the ratio of price to quantity at that point times the reciprocal of the slope of the demand curve.

proportion by which quantity changes. The formula for price elasticity may then be written as

$$\text{Price elasticity} = \epsilon = \frac{\Delta Q/Q}{\Delta P/P}. \tag{4.2}$$

Suppose, for example, that 20 units were sold at the original price of 100, and that when price rose to 105, quantity demanded fell to 15 units. Neglecting the negative sign of the quantity change, we would then have $\Delta Q/Q = 5/20$ and $\Delta P/P = 5/100$, which yields $\epsilon = (5/20)/(5/100) = 5$.

One attractive feature of this formula is that it has a straightforward graphical interpretation. Thus, if we want to calculate the price elasticity of demand at point A on the demand curve shown in Figure 4.3, we can begin by rewriting the right-hand side of equation (4.2) as $(P/Q) \times (\Delta Q/\Delta P)$. And since the slope of the demand curve is equal to $\Delta P/\Delta Q$, $\Delta Q/\Delta P$ is the reciprocal of that slope: $\Delta Q/\Delta P = 1/\text{slope}$. So the price elasticity of demand at point A, denoted ϵ_A, has the following simple formula:

$$\epsilon_A = \frac{P}{Q} \times \frac{1}{\text{slope}}. \tag{4.3}$$

To demonstrate how convenient this graphical interpretation of elasticity can be, suppose we want to find the price elasticity of demand at point A on the demand curve in Figure 4.4. The slope of this demand curve is the ratio of its vertical intercept to its horizontal intercept: $20/5 = 4$. So $1/\text{slope} = 1/4$. (Actually, the slope is -4, but we again ignore the minus sign for convenience, since price elasticity of

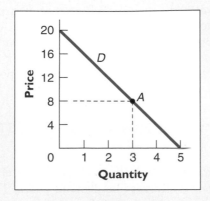

FIGURE 4.4
Calculating Price Elasticity of Demand.
The price elasticity of demand at A is given by $(P/Q) \times (1/\text{slope}) = (8/3) \times (1/4) = 2/3$.

demand always has the same sign.) The ratio P/Q at point A is 8/3, so the price elasticity at point A is equal to $(P/Q) \times (1/\text{slope}) = (8/3) \times (1/4) = 2/3$. This means that when the price of the good is 8, a 3 percent reduction in price will lead to a 2 percent increase in quantity demanded.

EXERCISE 4.2

What is the price elasticity of demand when $P = 4$ on the demand curve in Figure 4.4?

EXAMPLE 4.2

For the demand curves D_1 and D_2 shown in Figure 4.5, calculate the price elasticity of demand when $P = 4$. What is the price elasticity of demand on D_2 when $P = 1$?

FIGURE 4.5

Price Elasticity and the Steepness of the Demand Curve.

When price and quantity are the same, price elasticity of demand is always greater for the less steep of two demand curves.

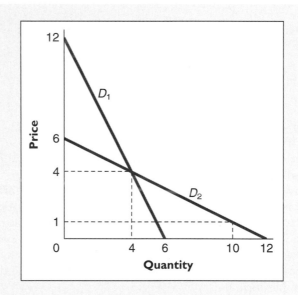

These elasticities can be calculated easily using the formula $\epsilon = (P/Q) \times (1/\text{slope})$. The slope of D_1 is the ratio of its vertical intercept to its horizontal intercept: $12/6 = 2$. So $(1/\text{slope})$ is 1/2 for D_1. Similarly, the slope of D_2 is the ratio of its vertical intercept to its horizontal intercept: $6/12 = 1/2$. So the reciprocal of the slope of D_2 is 2. For both demand curves, $Q = 4$ when $P = 4$, so $(P/Q) = 4/4 = 1$ for each. Thus the price elasticity of demand when $P = 4$ is $(1) \times (1/2) = 1/2$ for D_1 and $(1) \times (2) = 2$ for D_2. When $P = 1$, $Q = 10$ on D_2, so $(P/Q) = 1/10$. Thus price elasticity of demand $= (1/10) \times (2) = 1/5$ when $P = 1$ on D_2.

Example 4.2 illustrates the general rule that if two demand curves have a point in common, the steeper curve must be the less elastic of the two with respect to price at that point. But note carefully that this does not mean that the steeper curve is less elastic at *every* point. Thus we saw that at $P = 1$, price elasticity of demand on D_2 was only 1/5, or less than half the corresponding elasticity on the steeper D_1 at $P = 4$.

PRICE ELASTICITY CHANGES ALONG A STRAIGHT-LINE DEMAND CURVE

As a glance at our elasticity formula makes clear, price elasticity has a different value at every point along a straight-line demand curve. The slope of a straight-line demand curve is constant, which means that 1/slope is also constant. But the

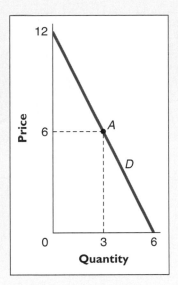

FIGURE 4.6
Elasticity at the Midpoint of a Straight-Line Demand Curve.
The price elasticity of demand at the midpoint of any straight-line demand curve always takes the value 1.

price-quantity ratio, P/Q, declines as we move down the demand curve. The elasticity of demand thus declines steadily as we move downward along a straight-line demand curve.

Since price elasticity is the percentage change in quantity demanded divided by the corresponding percentage change in price, this pattern makes sense. After all, a price movement of a given absolute size is small in percentage terms when it occurs near the top of the demand curve, where price is high, but large in percentage terms when it occurs near the bottom of the demand curve, where price is low. Likewise, a quantity movement of a given absolute value is large in percentage terms when it occurs near the top of the demand curve, where quantity is low, and small in percentage terms when it occurs near the bottom of the curve, where quantity is high.

The graphical interpretation of elasticity also makes it easy to see why the price elasticity of demand at the midpoint of any straight-line demand curve must always be 1. Consider, for example, the price elasticity of demand at point A on the demand curve D shown in Figure 4.6. At that point, the ratio P/Q is equal to $6/3 = 2$. The slope of this demand curve is the ratio of its vertical intercept to its horizontal intercept, $12/6 = 2$. So $(1/\text{slope}) = 1/2$ (again, we neglect the negative sign for simplicity). Inserting these values into the graphical elasticity formula yields $\epsilon_A = (P/Q) \times (1/\text{slope}) = (2) \times (1/2) = 1$.

This result holds not just for the particular demand curve shown, but also for any other straight-line demand curve.[1] A glance at the formula also tells us that since P/Q declines as we move downward along a straight-line demand curve, price elasticity of demand must be less than 1 at any point below the midpoint. By the same token, price elasticity must be greater than 1 for any point above the midpoint. Figure 4.7 summarizes these findings by denoting the elastic, inelastic, and unit elastic portions of any straight-line demand curve.

TWO SPECIAL CASES

There are actually two important exceptions to the general rule that elasticity declines along straight-line demand curves. Note that the horizontal demand

---

[1]To see why, note that at the midpoint of any such curve, P is exactly half the vertical intercept of the demand curve and Q is exactly half the horizontal intercept. Since the ratio of the vertical intercept to the horizontal intercept is the slope of the demand curve, the ratio (P/Q) must also be equal to the slope of the demand curve. And this means that $(1/\text{slope})$ will always be equal to (Q/P). Thus the product $(P/Q) \times (1/\text{slope}) = (P/Q) \times (Q/P)$ will always be exactly 1 at the midpoint of any straight-line demand curve.

FIGURE 4.7

Price Elasticity Regions along a Straight-Line Demand Curve.

Demand is elastic on the top half, unit elastic at the midpoint, and inelastic on the bottom half of a straight-line demand curve.

FIGURE 4.8

Perfectly Elastic and Perfectly Inelastic Demand Curves.

The horizontal demand curve (a) is perfectly elastic, or infinitely elastic, at every point. Even the slightest increase in price leads consumers to desert the product in favor of substitutes. The vertical demand curve (b) is perfectly inelastic at every point. Consumers do not, or cannot, switch to substitutes even in the face of large increases in price.

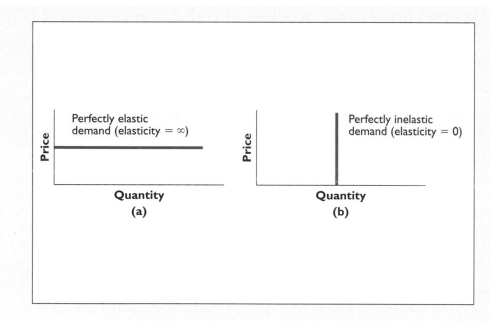

perfectly elastic demand
demand is perfectly elastic with respect to price if price elasticity of demand is infinite

perfectly inelastic demand
demand is perfectly inelastic with respect to price if price elasticity of demand is zero

curve in Figure 4.8(a) has a slope of zero, which means that the reciprocal of its slope is infinite. Price elasticity of demand is thus infinite at every point along a horizontal demand curve. Such demand curves are said to be **perfectly elastic**.

In contrast, the demand curve in Figure 4.8(b) is vertical, which means that its slope is infinite. The reciprocal of its slope is thus equal to zero. Price elasticity of demand is thus exactly zero at every point along the curve. For this reason, vertical demand curves are said to be **perfectly inelastic**.

THE MIDPOINT FORMULA

Suppose you encounter a question like the following on a standardized test in economics:

> At a price of 3, quantity demanded of a good is 6, while at a price of 4, quantity demanded is 4. What is the price elasticity of demand for this good?

Let's attempt to answer this question by using the formula $\epsilon = (\Delta Q/Q)/(\Delta P/P)$. In Figure 4.9 we first plot the two price–quantity pairs given in the question and then draw the straight-line demand curve that connects them. From the graph, it is clear that $\Delta P = 1$ and $\Delta Q = 2$. But what values do we use for P and Q? If we use $P = 4$ and $Q = 4$ (point A), we get an elasticity of 2. But if we use $P = 3$ and

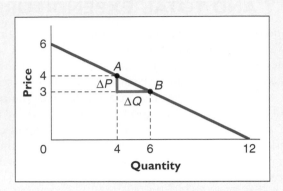

FIGURE 4.9
Two Points on a Demand Curve.

$Q = 6$ (point B), we get an elasticity of 1. Thus, if we reckon price and quantity changes as proportions of their values at point A we get one answer, but if we compute them as proportions of their values at point B we get another. Neither of these answers is incorrect. The fact that they differ is merely a reflection of the fact that the elasticity of demand differs at every point along a straight-line demand curve.

Strictly speaking, the original question ("What is the price elasticity of demand for this good?") was not well posed. To have elicited a uniquely correct answer, it should have been "What is the price elasticity of demand at point A?" or "What is the price elasticity of demand at point B?" Economists have nonetheless developed a convention, which we call the *midpoint formula,* for answering ambiguous questions like the one originally posed. If the two points in question are (Q_A, P_A) and (Q_B, P_B), this formula is given by

$$\epsilon = \frac{\Delta Q / [(Q_A + Q_B)/2]}{\Delta P / [(P_A + P_B)/2]}. \tag{4.4}$$

The midpoint formula thus sidesteps the question of which price–quantity pair to use by using averages of the new and old values. The formula reduces to

$$\epsilon = \frac{\Delta Q / (Q_A + Q_B)}{\Delta P / (P_A + P_B)}. \tag{4.5}$$

For the two points shown in Figure 4.9, the midpoint formula yields $\epsilon = [2/(4 + 6)]/[1/(4 + 3)] = 1.4$, which lies between the values for price elasticity at A and B.

We will not employ the midpoint formula again in this text. Hereafter, all questions concerning elasticity will employ the measure discussed earlier, which is called *point elasticity.*

RECAP   **CALCULATING PRICE ELASTICITY OF DEMAND**

The price elasticity of demand for a good is the percentage change in the quantity demanded that results from a 1 percent change in its price. Mathematically, the elasticity of demand at a point along a demand curve is equal to $(P/Q) \times (1/\text{slope})$, where P and Q represent price and quantity and $(1/\text{slope})$ is the reciprocal of the slope of the demand curve at that point. Demand is elastic with respect to price if the absolute value of its price elasticity exceeds 1; inelastic if price elasticity is less than 1; and unit elastic if price elasticity is equal to 1.

ELASTICITY AND TOTAL EXPENDITURE

Sellers of goods and services will often have a strong interest in being able to answer questions like "Will consumers spend more on my product if I sell more units at a lower price or fewer units at a higher price?" As it turns out, the answer to this question depends critically on the price elasticity of demand. To see why, let us first examine how the total amount spent on a good varies with the price of the good.

The total daily expenditure on a good is simply the daily number of units bought times the price for which it sells. The market demand curve for a good tells us the quantity that will be sold at each price. We can thus use the information on the demand curve to show how the total amount spent on a good will vary with its price.

To illustrate, let's calculate how much moviegoers will spend on tickets each day if the demand curve is as shown in Figure 4.10 and the price is $2 per ticket (a). The demand curve tells us that at a price of $2 per ticket, 500 tickets per day will be sold, so total expenditure at that price will be $1,000 per day. If tickets sell not for $2 but for $4 apiece, 400 tickets will be sold each day (b), so total expenditure at the higher price will be $1,600 per day.

FIGURE 4.10
The Demand Curve for Movie Tickets.
An increase in price from $2 to $4 per ticket increases total expenditure on tickets.

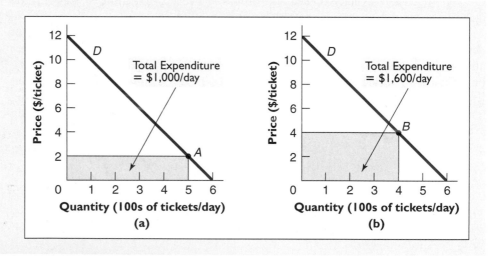

Note that the total amount consumers spend on a product each day must equal the total amount sellers of the product receive. That is to say, the terms **total expenditure** and **total revenue** are simply two sides of the same coin:

> **Total Expenditure = Total Revenue:** The dollar amount that consumers spend on a product $(P \times Q)$ is equal to the dollar amount that sellers receive.

It might seem that an increase in the market price of a product should always result in an increase in the total revenue received by sellers. But although that happened in the case we just saw, it needn't always be so. The law of demand tells us that when the price of a good rises, people will buy less of it. The two factors that govern total revenue—price and quantity—will thus always move in opposite directions. When price goes up and quantity goes down, the product of the two may go either up or down.

Note, for example, that for the demand curve shown in Figure 4.11 (which is the same as the one in Figure 4.10), a rise in price from $8 per ticket (a) to $10 per ticket (b) will cause total expenditure on tickets to go down. Thus people will spend $1,600 per day on tickets at a price of $8, but only $1,000 per day at a price of $10.

The general rule illustrated by Figures 4.10 and 4.11 is that a price increase will produce an increase in total revenue whenever it is greater, in percentage

FIGURE 4.11
The Demand Curve for
Movie Tickets.
An increase in price from $8
to $10 per ticket results in a
fall in total expenditure on
tickets.

terms, than the corresponding percentage reduction in quantity demanded. Although the two price increases (from $2 to $4 and from $8 to $10) were of the same absolute value—$2 in each case—they are much different when expressed as a percentage of the original price. An increase from $2 to $4 represents a 100 percent increase in price, whereas an increase from $8 to $10 represents only a 25 percent increase in price. And although the quantity reductions caused by the two price increases were also equal in absolute terms, they too are very different when expressed as percentages of the quantities originally sold. Thus, although the decline in quantity demanded was 100 tickets per day in each case, it was just a 20 percent reduction in the first case (from 500 units to 400 in Figure 4.10) but a 50 percent reduction in the second (from 200 units to 100 in Figure 4.11). In the second case, the negative effect on total expenditure of the 50 percent quantity reduction outweighed the positive effect of the 25 percent price increase. The reverse happened in the first case: the 100 percent increase in price (from $2 to $4) outweighed the 20 percent reduction in quantity (from 5 units to 4 units).

The following example provides further insight into the relationship between total revenue and price.

For the demand curve shown in Figure 4.12, draw a separate graph showing how total expenditure varies with the price of movie tickets.

EXAMPLE 4.3

FIGURE 4.12
The Demand Curve for
Movie Tickets.

The first step in constructing this graph is to calculate total expenditure for a sample of price points on the demand curve and record the results, as in Table 4.2. The next step is to plot total expenditure at each of the price points on a graph, as in Figure 4.13. Finally, sketch the curve by joining these points. (If greater accuracy is required, you can use a larger sample of points than the one shown in Table 4.2.)

TABLE 4.2
Total Expenditure as a Function of Price

Price ($/ticket)	Total expenditure ($/day)
12	0
10	1,000
8	1,600
6	1,800
4	1,600
2	1,000
0	0

FIGURE 4.13
Total Expenditure as a Function of Price.
For a good whose demand curve is a straight line, total expenditure reaches a maximum at the price corresponding to the midpoint of the demand curve.

Note in Figure 4.13 that as the price per ticket increases from 0 to $6, total expenditure increases. But as the price rises from $6 to $12, total expenditure decreases. Total expenditure reaches a maximum of $1,800 per day at a price of $6.

The pattern observed in Example 4.3 holds true in general. For a straight-line demand curve, total expenditure is highest at the price that lies on the midpoint of the demand curve.

Bearing in mind these observations about how expenditure varies with price, let's return to the question of how the effect of a price change on total expenditure depends on the price elasticity of demand. Suppose, for example, that the business manager of a rock band knows he can sell 5,000 tickets to the band's weekly summer concerts if he sets the price at $20 per ticket. If the elasticity of demand for tickets is equal to 3, will total ticket revenue go up or down in response to a 10 percent increase in the price of tickets?

Total revenue from tickets sold is currently ($20/ticket) × (5,000 tickets/ week) = $100,000 per week. The fact that the price elasticity of demand for tickets is 3 implies that a 10 percent increase in price will produce a 30 percent reduction in the number of tickets sold, which means that quantity will fall to 3,500 tickets per week. Total expenditure on tickets will therefore fall to (3,500 tickets/week) × ($22/ticket) = $77,000 per week, which is significantly less than the current spending total.

What would have happened to total expenditure if the band manager had *reduced* ticket prices by 10 percent, from $20 to $18? Again assuming a price elasticity of 3, the result would have been a 30 percent increase in tickets sold— from 5,000 per week to 6,500 per week. The resulting total expenditure would have been ($18/ticket) × (6,500 tickets/week) = $117,000 per week, significantly more than the current total.

These examples illustrate the following important rule about how price changes affect total expenditure for an elastically demanded good:

> When price elasticity is greater than 1, changes in price and changes in total expenditure always move in opposite directions.

Let's look at the intuition behind this rule. Total expenditure is the product of price and quantity. For an elastically demanded product, the percentage change in quantity will be larger than the corresponding percentage change in price. Thus the change in quantity will more than offset the change in revenue per unit sold.

Now let's see how total spending responds to a price increase when demand is *inelastic* with respect to price. Consider a case like the one just considered except that the elasticity of demand for tickets is not 3 but 0.5. How will total expenditure respond to a 10 percent increase in ticket prices? This time the number of tickets sold will fall by only 5 percent to 4,750 tickets per week, which means that total expenditure on tickets will rise to (4,750 tickets/week) × ($22/ticket) = $104,500 per week, or $4,500 per week more than the current expenditure level.

In contrast, a 10 percent price reduction (from $20 to $18 per ticket) when price elasticity is 0.5 would cause the number to tickets sold to grow by only 5 percent, from 5,000 per week to 5,250 per week, resulting in total expenditure of ($18/ticket) × (5,250 tickets/week) = $94,500 per week, significantly less than the current total.

As these examples illustrate, the effect of price changes on total expenditure when demand is inelastic is precisely the opposite of what it was when demand was elastic:

> For a product whose price elasticity of demand is less than 1, price changes and total expenditure changes always move in the same direction.

Again, the intuition behind this rule is straightforward. For a product whose demand is inelastic with respect to price, the percentage change in quantity demanded will be smaller than the corresponding percentage change in price. The change in revenue per unit sold (price) will thus more than offset the change in the number of units sold.

The relationship between elasticity and the effect of a price change on total revenue are summarized in Table 4.3, where the symbol ϵ is used to denote elasticity.

Recall that in the example with which we began this chapter, an increase in the price of drugs led to an increase in the total amount spent on drugs. That will happen whenever the demand for drugs is inelastic with respect to price, as it was in that example. Had the demand for drugs instead been elastic with respect to price, the drug supply interruption would have led to a reduction in total expenditure on drugs.

INCOME ELASTICITY AND CROSS-PRICE ELASTICITY OF DEMAND

The elasticity of demand for a good can be defined not only with respect to its own price but also with respect to the prices of substitutes or complements, or even to income. For example, the elasticity of demand for peanuts with respect to the

TABLE 4.3
Elasticity and the Effect of a Price Change on Total Expenditure

If demand is...	A price increase will...	A price reduction will...
elastic ($\epsilon > 1$)	reduce total expenditure $P \times Q = PQ$	increase total expenditure $P \times Q = PQ$
inelastic ($\epsilon < 1$)	increase total expenditure $P \times Q = PQ$	reduce total expenditure $P \times Q = PQ$

cross-price elasticity of demand the percentage by which quantity demanded of the first good changes in response to a 1 percent change in the price of the second

income elasticity of demand the percentage by which quantity demanded changes in response to a 1 percent change in income

price of cashews—also known as the **cross-price elasticity of demand** for peanuts with respect to cashew prices—is the percentage by which the quantity of peanuts demanded changes in response to a 1 percent change in the price of cashews. The **income elasticity of demand** for peanuts is the percentage by which the quantity demanded of peanuts changes in response to a 1 percent change in income.

Unlike the elasticity of demand for a good with respect to its own price, these other elasticities may be either positive or negative, so it is important to note their algebraic signs carefully. The income elasticity of demand for inferior goods, for example, is negative, whereas the income elasticity of demand for normal goods is positive. When the cross-price elasticity of demand for two goods is positive— as in the peanuts/cashews example—the two goods are substitutes. When it is negative, the two goods are complements. The elasticity of demand for tennis racquets with respect to court rental fees, for example, is less than zero.

EXERCISE 4.3

If a 10 percent increase in income causes the number of students who choose to attend private universities to go up by 5 percent, what is the income elasticity of demand for private universities?

◯ RECAP   CROSS-PRICE AND INCOME ELASTICITIES

When the elasticity of demand for one good with respect to the price of another good is positive, the two goods are substitutes; when this cross-price elasticity of demand is negative, the two goods are complements. A normal good has positive income elasticity of demand and an inferior good has negative income elasticity of demand.

THE PRICE ELASTICITY OF SUPPLY

price elasticity of supply the percentage change in quantity supplied that occurs in response to a 1 percent change in price

On the buyer's side of the market, we use price elasticity of demand to measure the responsiveness of quantity demanded to changes in price. On the seller's side of the market, the analogous measure is **price elasticity of supply**. It is defined as the percentage change in quantity supplied that occurs in response to a 1 percent change in price. For example, if a 1 percent increase in the price of peanuts leads to a 2 percent increase in the quantity supplied, the price elasticity of supply of peanuts would be 2.

The mathematical formula for price elasticity of supply at any point is the same as the corresponding expression for price elasticity of demand:

$$\text{Price elasticity of supply} = \frac{\Delta Q/Q}{\Delta P/P}. \tag{4.6}$$

where P and Q are the price and quantity at that point, ΔP is a small change in the initial price, and ΔQ the resulting change in quantity.

As with the corresponding expression for price elasticity of demand, Equation 4.6 can be rewritten as $(P/Q) \times (\Delta Q/\Delta P)$. And since $(\Delta Q/\Delta P)$ is the reciprocal of the slope of the supply curve, the right-hand side of Equation 4.6 is equal to $(P/Q) \times (1/\text{slope})$—the same expression we saw for price elasticity of demand. Price and quantity are always positive, as is the slope of the typical supply curve, which implies that price elasticity of supply will be a positive number at every point.

Consider the supply curve shown in Figure 4.14. The slope of this supply curve is 1/3, so the reciprocal of this slope is 3. Using the formula, this means that the price elasticity of supply at A is $(4/12) \times (3) = 1$. The corresponding expression at B, $(5/15) \times (3)$, yields exactly the same value. Indeed, because the ratio P/Q is the same at every point along the supply curve shown, price elasticity of supply will be exactly 1 at every point along this curve. Note the contrast between this result and our earlier finding that price elasticity of demand declines as we move downward along any straight-line demand curve.

FIGURE 4.14
Calculating the Price Elasticity of Supply Graphically.
Price elasticity of supply is $(P/Q) \times (1/\text{slope})$, which at A is $(4/12) \times (12/4) = 1$, exactly the same as at B. The price elasticity of supply is equal to 1 at any point along a straight-line supply curve that passes through the origin.

Why price elasticity equals 1 at every point in this illustration is explained by one special property: The supply curve was a straight line through the origin. For movements along any such line, both price and quantity always change in exactly the same proportion.

Elasticity is not constant, however, along straight-line supply curves like the one in Figure 4.15, which does not pass through the origin. Although the slope of this supply curve is equal to 1 at every point, the ratio P/Q declines as we move to the right along the curve. Elasticity at A is equal to $(4/2) \times (1) = 2$ and declines to $(5/3) \times (1) = 5/3$ at B.

EXERCISE 4.4

For the supply curve shown in Figure 4.15, calculate the elasticity of supply when $P = 3$.

FIGURE 4.15

A Supply Curve for which Price Elasticity Declines as Quantity Rises.
For the supply curve shown, (1/slope) is the same at every point, but the ratio P/Q declines as Q increases. So elasticity = $(P/Q) \times$ (1/slope) declines as quantity increases.

On the buyer's side of the market, two important polar cases were demand curves with infinite price elasticity and zero price elasticity. As the next two examples illustrate, analogous polar cases exist on the seller's side of the market.

EXAMPLE 4.4

What is the elasticity of supply of land within the borough limits of Manhattan?

Land in Manhattan sells in the market for a price, just like aluminum or corn or automobiles or any other product. And the demand for land in Manhattan is a downward-sloping function of its price. For all practical purposes, however, its supply is completely fixed. No matter whether its price is high or low, the same amount of it is available in the market. The supply curve of such a good is vertical, and its price elasticity is zero at every price. Supply curves like the one shown in Figure 4.16 are said to be **perfectly inelastic**.

perfectly inelastic supply
supply is perfectly inelastic with respect to price if elasticity is zero

FIGURE 4.16

A Perfectly Inelastic Supply Curve.
Price elasticity of supply is zero at every point along a vertical supply curve.

EXAMPLE 4.5

What is the elasticity of supply of lemonade?

Suppose that the ingredients required to bring a cup of lemonade to market and their respective costs are as follows:

Paper cup	2.0 cents
Lemon	3.8 cents
Sugar	2.0 cents
Water	0.2 cents
Ice	1.0 cents
Labor (30 seconds @ $6/hour)	5.0 cents

If these proportions remain the same no matter how many cups of lemonade are made, and the inputs can be purchased in any quantities at the stated prices, draw the supply curve of lemonade and compute its price elasticity.

Since each cup of lemonade costs exactly 14¢ to make, no matter how many cups are made, the marginal cost of lemonade is constant at 14¢ per cup. And since each point on a supply curve is equal to marginal cost (see Chapter 3), this means that the supply curve of lemonade is not upward-sloping but is instead a horizontal line at 14¢ per cup (Figure 4.17). The price elasticity of supply of lemonade is infinite.

FIGURE 4.17
A Perfectly Elastic Supply Curve.
The elasticity of supply is infinite at every point along a horizontal supply curve.

Whenever additional units of a good can be produced by using the same combination of inputs, purchased at the same prices, as have been used so far, the supply curve of that good will be horizontal. Such supply curves are said to be **perfectly elastic**.

perfectly elastic supply supply is perfectly elastic with respect to price if elasticity of supply is infinite

DETERMINANTS OF SUPPLY ELASTICITY

The two preceding examples suggest some of the factors that govern the elasticity of supply of a good or service. The lemonade case was one whose production process was essentially like a cooking recipe. For such cases, we can exactly double our output by doubling each ingredient. If the price of each ingredient remains fixed, the marginal cost of production for such goods will be constant—and hence their horizontal supply curves.

The Manhattan land example is a contrast in the extreme. The inputs that were used to produce land in Manhattan—even if we knew what they were— could not be duplicated at any price.

The key to predicting how elastic the supply of a good will be with respect to price is to know the terms on which additional units of the inputs involved in producing that good can be acquired. In general, the more easily additional units of these inputs can be acquired, the higher price elasticity of supply will be. The following factors (among others) govern the ease with which additional inputs can be acquired by a producer.

Flexibility of Inputs
To the extent that production of a good requires inputs that are also useful for the production of other goods, it is relatively easy to lure additional inputs away from their current uses, making supply of that good relatively elastic with respect to price. Thus the fact that lemonade production requires labor with only minimal skills means that a large pool of workers could shift from other activities to lemonade production if a profitable opportunity arose. Brain surgery, by contrast, requires elaborately trained and specialized labor, which means that even a large price increase would not increase available supplies, except in the very long run.

Mobility of Inputs

If inputs can be easily transported from one site to another, an increase in the price of a product in one market will enable a producer in that market to summon inputs from other markets. For example, the supply of agricultural products is made more elastic with respect to price by the fact that thousands of farm workers are willing to migrate northward during the growing season. The supply of entertainment is similarly made more elastic by the willingness of entertainers to hit the road. Circus performers, lounge singers, comedians, and even exotic dancers often spend a substantial fraction of their time away from home. For instance, according to a 1996 *New York Times* article, the top exotic dancers "basically follow the action, so the same entertainers who worked the Indianapolis 500 now head to Atlanta for the Olympics."

For most goods, the price elasticity of supply increases each time a new highway is built; or when the telecommunications network improves, or indeed when any other development makes it easier to find and transport inputs from one place to another.

Ability to Produce Substitute Inputs

The inputs required to produce finished diamond gemstones include raw diamond crystal, skilled labor, and elaborate cutting and polishing machinery. In time, the number of people with the requisite skills can be increased, as can the amount of specialized machinery. The number of raw diamond crystals buried in the earth is probably fixed in the same way that Manhattan land is fixed, but unlike Manhattan land, rising prices will encourage miners to spend the effort required to find a larger proportion of those crystals. Still, the supply of natural gemstone diamonds tends to be relatively inelastic because of the difficulty of augmenting the number of diamond crystals.

The day is close at hand, however, when gemstone makers will be able to produce synthetic diamond crystals that are indistinguishable from real ones. Indeed, there are already synthetic crystals that fool even highly experienced jewelers. The introduction of a perfect synthetic substitute for natural diamond crystals would increase the price elasticity of supply of diamonds (or, at any rate, the price elasticity of supply of gemstones that look and feel just like diamonds).

Time

Because it takes time for producers to switch from one activity another, and because it takes time to build new machines and factories and train additional skilled workers, the price elasticity of supply will be higher for most goods in the long run than in the short run. In the short run, a manufacturer's inability to augment existing stocks of equipment and skilled labor may make it impossible to expand output beyond a certain limit. But if a shortage of managers was the bottleneck, new MBAs can be graduated in only two years. Or if a shortage of legal staff is the problem, new lawyers can be trained in three years. In the long run, firms can always buy new equipment, build new factories, and hire additional skilled workers.

The conditions that gave rise to the perfectly elastic supply curve for lemonade in the example we discussed earlier are also satisfied for many other products in the long run. If a product can be copied (in the sense that any company can acquire the design and other technological information required to produce it), and if the inputs needed for its production are used in roughly fixed proportions and are available at fixed market prices, then the long-run supply curve for that product will be horizontal. But many products do not satisfy these conditions, and their supply curves remain steeply upward-sloping, even in the very long run.

"In six more weeks, these M.B.A.s will be ready for market."

Why are gasoline prices so much more volatile than car prices?

Automobile price changes in the United States usually occur just once a year, when manufacturers announce an increase of only a few percentage points. In contrast, gasoline prices often fluctuate wildly from day to day. As shown in Figure 4.18, for example, the highest daily gasoline prices in California's two largest cities were three times higher than the lowest daily prices during a recent year. Why this enormous difference in volatility?

With respect to price volatility, at least two important features distinguish the gasoline market from the market for cars. One is that the short-run price elasticity of demand for gasoline is much smaller than the corresponding elasticity for

ECONOMIC NATURALIST 4.3

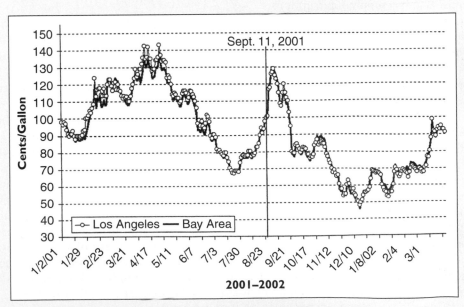

FIGURE 4.18
Gasoline Prices in Two California Cities.

SOURCE: Oil Price Information Service (http://www.opisnet.com).

FIGURE 4.19

Greater Volatility in Gasoline Prices than in Car Prices.

Gasoline prices are more volatile prices because supply shifts are larger and more frequent in the gasoline market (a) than in the car market (b), and also because supply and demand are less elastic in the short run in the gasoline market.

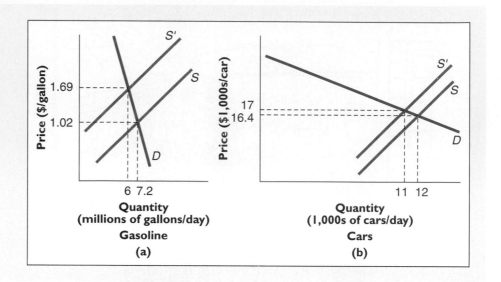

cars. The other is that supply shifts are much more pronounced and frequent in the gasoline market than in the car market. (See Figure 4.19.)

Why are the two markets different in these ways? Consider first the difference in price elasticities of demand. The quantity of gasoline we demand depends largely on the kinds of cars we own and the amounts we drive them. In the short run, car ownership and commuting patterns are almost completely fixed, so even if the price of gasoline were to change sharply, the quantity we demand would not change by much. In contrast, if there were a sudden dramatic change in the price of cars, we could always postpone or accelerate our next car purchases.

To see why the supply curve in the gasoline market experiences larger and more frequent shifts than the supply curve in the car market, we need only examine the relative stability of the inputs employed by sellers in these two markets. Most of the inputs used in producing cars—steel, glass, rubber, plastics, electronic, components, labor, and others—are reliably available to car makers. In contrast, the key input used in making gasoline—crude oil—is subject to profound and unpredictable supply interruptions.

This is so in part because much of the world's supply of crude oil is controlled by OPEC, a group of oil-exporting countries that has sharply curtailed its oil shipments to the United States on several previous occasions. Even in the absence of formal OPEC action, however, large supply curtailments often occur in the oil market—for example, whenever producers fear that political instability might engulf the major oil-producing countries of the Middle East.

Note in Figure 4.18 the sharp spike in gasoline prices that occurred just after the terrorist attacks on the World Trade Center and Pentagon on September 11, 2001. Because many believed that the aim of these attacks was to provoke large-scale war between Muslim societies and the West, fears of an impending oil supply interruption were perfectly rational. And such fears alone can trigger a temporary supply interruption, even if war is avoided. The prospect of war creates the expectation of oil supply cutbacks that would cause higher prices in the future, which leads producers to withdraw some of their oil from current markets (in order to sell it at higher prices later). But once the fear of war recedes, the supply curve of gasoline reverts with equal speed to its earlier position. Given the low short-run price elasticity of demand for gasoline, that's all it takes to generate the considerable price volatility we see in this market.

Price volatility is also common in markets in which demand curves fluctuate sharply and supply curves are highly inelastic. One such market was California's unregulated market for wholesale electricity during the summer of 2000. The supply of electrical generating capacity was essentially fixed in the short run. And because air conditioning accounts for a large share of demand, several spells of unusually warm weather caused demand to shift sharply to the right. Price at one point reached more than four times its highest level from the previous summer.

UNIQUE AND ESSENTIAL INPUTS: THE ULTIMATE SUPPLY BOTTLENECK

Fans of professional basketball are an enthusiastic bunch. Directly through their purchases of tickets and indirectly through their support of television advertisers, they spend literally billions of dollars each year on the sport. But these dollars are not distributed evenly across all teams. A disproportionate share of all revenues and product endorsement fees accrue to the people associated with consistently winning teams, and at the top of this pyramid generally stands the National Basketball Association's championship team.

Consider the task of trying to produce a championship team in the NBA. What are the inputs you would need? Talented players, a shrewd and dedicated coach and assistants, trainers, physicians, an arena, practice facilities, means for transporting players to away games, a marketing staff, and so on. And whereas some of these inputs can be acquired at reasonable prices in the marketplace, many others cannot. Indeed, the most important input of all—highly talented players—is in extremely limited supply. *This is so because the very definition of talented player is inescapably relative—simply put, such a player is one who is better than most others.*

Given the huge payoff that accrues to the NBA championship team, it is no surprise that the bidding for the most talented players has become so intense. If there were a long list of 7-foot, 3-inch, 325-pound centers, the Los Angeles Lakers wouldn't have had to pay Shaquille O'Neal $120 million over a seven-year contract. But, of course, the supply of such players is extremely limited. There are many hungry organizations that would like nothing better than to claim the NBA championship each year, yet no matter how much each is willing to spend, only one can succeed. The supply of NBA championship teams is perfectly inelastic with respect to price even in the very long run.

Sports champions are by no means the only important product whose supply elasticity is constrained by the inability to reproduce unique and essential inputs. In the movie industry, for example, although the supply of movies starring Jim Carrey is not perfectly inelastic, there are only so many films he can make each year. Because his films consistently generate huge box office revenues, scores of film producers want to sign him for their projects. But because there isn't enough of him to go around, his salary per film is more than $20 million.

In the long run, unique and essential inputs are the only truly significant supply bottleneck. If it were not for the inability to duplicate the services of such inputs, most goods and services would have extremely high price elasticities of supply in the long run.

■ SUMMARY ■

- The price elasticity of demand is a measure of how strongly buyers respond to changes in price. It is the percentage change in quantity demanded that occurs in response to a 1 percent change in price. The demand for a good is called elastic with respect to price if its price elasticity is more than 1; inelastic if its price elasticity is less than 1; and unit elastic if its price elasticity is equal to 1.

- Goods such as salt, which occupy only a small share of the typical consumer's budget and have few or no good substi-

tutes, tend to have low price elasticity of demand. Goods like new cars of a particular make and model, which occupy large budget shares and have many attractive substitutes, tend to have high price elasticity of demand. Price elasticity of demand is higher in the long run than in the short run because people often need time to adjust to price changes.

- The price elasticity of demand at a point along a demand curve can also be expressed as the formula $\epsilon = (\Delta Q/Q)/(\Delta P/P)$. Here, P and Q represent price and quantity at that point, and ΔQ and ΔP represent small changes in price and quantity. For straight-line demand curves, this formula can also be expressed as $\epsilon = (P/Q) \times (1/\text{slope})$. These formulations tell us that price elasticity declines in absolute terms as we move down a straight-line demand curve.

• A cut in price will increase total spending on a good if demand is elastic but reduce it if demand is inelastic. An increase in price will increase total spending on a good if demand is inelastic but reduce it if demand is elastic. Total expenditure on a good reaches a maximum when price elasticity of demand is equal to 1.

• Analogous formulas are used to define the elasticity of demand for a good with respect to income and the prices of other goods. In each case, elasticity is the percentage change in quantity demanded divided by the corresponding percentage change in income or price.

• Price elasticity of supply is defined as the percentage change in quantity supplied that occurs in response to a 1 percent change in price. The mathematical formula for the price elasticity of supply at any point is $(\Delta Q/Q)/(\Delta P/P)$, where P and Q are the price and quantity at that point, ΔP is a small change in the initial price, and ΔQ is the resulting change in quantity. This formula can also be expressed as $(P/Q) \times (1/\text{slope})$, where $(1/\text{slope})$ is the reciprocal of the slope of the supply curve.

• The price elasticity of supply of a good depends on how difficult or costly it is to acquire additional units of the inputs involved in producing that good. In general, the more easily additional units of these inputs can be acquired, the higher price elasticity of supply will be. It is easier to expand production of a product if the inputs used to produce that product are similar to inputs used to produce other products, if inputs are relatively mobile, or if an acceptable substitute for existing inputs can be developed. And like the price elasticity of demand, the price elasticity of supply is greater in the long run than in the short run.

▪ KEY TERMS ▪

cross-price elasticity of demand (106)
elastic (93)
income elasticity of demand (106)
inelastic (93)
perfectly elastic demand (100)

perfectly elastic supply (109)
perfectly inelastic demand (100)
perfectly inelastic supply (108)
price elasticity of demand (92)

price elasticity of supply (106)
total expenditure (102)
total revenue (102)
unit elastic (93)

▪ REVIEW QUESTIONS ▪

1. Why does a consumer's price elasticity of demand for a good depend on the fraction of the consumer's income spent on that good?

2. Why does the elasticity of demand for a good with respect to its own price decline as we move down along a straight-line demand curve?

3. Under what conditions will an increase in the price of a product lead to a reduction in total spending for that product?

4. Why do economists pay little attention to the algebraic sign of the elasticity of demand for a good with respect to its own price, yet pay careful attention to the algebraic sign of the elasticity of demand for a good with respect to another good's price?

5. Why is supply elasticity higher in the long run than in the short run?

▪ PROBLEMS ▪

1. On the accompanying demand curve, calculate the price elasticity of demand at points A, B, C, D, and E.

2. The schedule below shows the number of packs of bagels bought in Davis, California, each day at a variety of prices.

Price of bagels ($/pack)	Number of packs purchased per day
6	0
5	3,000
4	6,000
3	9,000
2	12,000
1	15,000
0	18,000

a. Graph the daily demand curve for packs of bagels in Davis.
b. Calculate the price elasticity of demand at the point on the demand curve at which the price of bagels is $3 per pack.
c. If all bagel shops increased the price of bagels from $3 per pack to $4 per pack, what would happen to total revenues?
d. Calculate the price elasticity of demand at a point on the demand curve where the price of bagels is $2 per pack.
e. If bagel shops increased the price of bagels from $2 per pack to $3 per pack, what would happen to total revenues?

3. Suppose, while rummaging through your uncle's closet, you found the original painting of *Dogs Playing Poker,* a valuable piece of art. You decided to set up a display in your uncle's garage. The demand curve to see this valuable piece of art is as shown in the diagram. What price should you charge if your goal is to maximize your revenues from tickets sold? On a graph, show the inelastic and elastic regions of the demand curve.

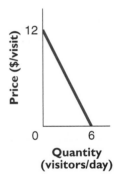

4. Is the demand for a particular brand of car, like a Chevrolet, likely to be more or less price-elastic than the demand for all cars? Explain.

5. Among the following groups—senior executives, junior executives, and students—which is likely to have the most and which is likely to have the least price-elastic demand for membership in the Association of Business Professionals?

6. A 2 percent increase in the price of milk causes a 4 percent reduction in the quantity demanded of chocolate syrup. What is the cross-price elasticity of demand for milk with respect to the price of chocolate syrup? Are the two goods complements or substitutes?

7. What are the respective price elasticities of supply at *A* and *B* on the supply curve shown in the accompanying figure?

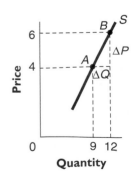

8. Suppose that the ingredients required to bring a slice of pizza to market and their respective costs are as listed in the table:

Paper plate	2 cents
Flour	8 cents
Tomato sauce	20 cents
Cheese	30 cents
Labor (3 minutes @ $12/hour)	60 cents

If these proportions remain the same no matter how many slices are made, and the inputs can be purchased in any quantities at the stated prices, draw the supply curve of pizza slices and compute its price elasticity.

9.* At point *A* on the demand curve shown, by what percentage will a 1 percent increase in the price of the product affect total expenditure on the product?

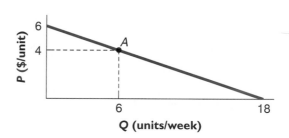

10.* In an attempt to induce citizens to conserve energy, the government enacted regulations requiring that all air conditioners be more efficient in their use of electricity. After this regulation was implemented, government officials were then surprised to discover that people used even more electricity than before. Using the concept of price elasticity, explain how this

*Problems marked with an asterisk (*) are more difficult.

■ ANSWERS TO IN-CHAPTER EXERCISES ■

4.1 In response to a 5 percent reduction in the price of ski passes, the quantity demanded increased by 20 percent. The price elasticity of demand for ski passes is thus (20 percent)/(5 percent) = 4, and that means that at the initial price of $400, the demand for ski passes is elastic with respect to price.

4.2 At point *A* in the accompanying diagram, $P/Q = 4/4 = 1$. The slope of this demand curve is 20/5 = 4, so $\epsilon = 1(1/\text{slope}) = 1/4$.

4.3 Income elasticity = percentage change in quantity demanded/percentage change in income = 5 percent/10 percent = 0.5.

4.4 For this supply curve, $Q = 1$ when $P = 3$, so elasticity of supply = $(P/Q) \times (1/\text{slope}) = (3) \times (1) = 3$.

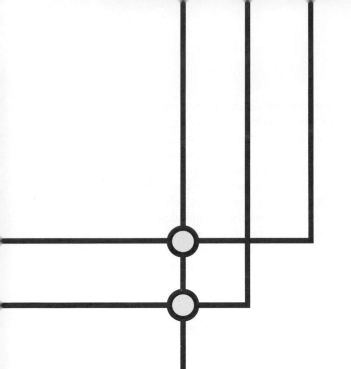

DEMAND: THE BENEFIT SIDE OF THE MARKET

■

On the northern border of a large university in the East, a creek widens to form a picturesque lake, fondly remembered by generations of alumni as a popular recreation spot. Over the years, the lake had gradually silted in, and by the late 1980s, even paddling a canoe across it had become impossible. A generous alumnus then sponsored an effort to restore the lake. Heavy dredging equipment hauled out load after load of mud, and months later the lake was finally silt-free.

To mark the occasion, the university held a ceremony. Bands played, the president spoke, a chorus sang, and distinguished visitors applauded the donor's generosity. Hundreds of faculty and students turned out for the festivities. Spotting a good opportunity to promote their product, the proprietors of a local ice cream store set up a temporary stand at the water's edge, with a large sign: "Free Ice Cream."

Word spread. Soon scores of people were lined up waiting to try Vanilla Almond Delight, Hazelnut Cream, and Fudge Faire. The ice cream was plentiful, and because it was free, everyone could obviously afford it—or so it seemed. In fact, many people who wanted ice cream that day never got any. The reason, of course, was that they found waiting in a long line too steep a price.

When a good or service is scarce, it must somehow be rationed among competing users. In most markets, monetary prices perform that task. But in the case of a stand offering free ice cream, waiting time becomes the effective rationing device. Having to stand in line is a cost, no less so than having to part with some money.

This example drives home the point that although the demand curve is usually described as a relationship between the quantity demanded of a good and its monetary price, the relationship is really a much more general one. At bottom, the demand curve is a relationship between the quantity demanded and *all* costs—monetary and nonmonetary—associated with acquiring a good.

Our task in this chapter will be to explore the demand side of the market in greater depth than was possible in Chapter 3. There we merely asked you to accept as an intuitively plausible claim that the quantity demanded of a good or service declines as its price rises. This relationship is known as the law of demand, and we will see how it emerges as a simple consequence of the assumption that people spend their limited incomes in rational ways. In the process, we will see more clearly the dual roles of income and substitution as factors that account for the law of demand. We will also see how to generate market demand curves by adding the demand curves for individual buyers horizontally. Finally, we will see how to use the demand curve to generate a measure of the total benefit that buyers reap from their participation in a market.

THE LAW OF DEMAND

With our discussion of the free ice cream offer in mind, let us restate the law of demand as follows:

Law of Demand: People do less of what they want to do as the cost of doing it rises.

By stating the law of demand this way, we can see it as a direct consequence of the cost-benefit principle, which says that an activity should be pursued if (and only if) its benefits are at least as great as its costs. Recall that we measure the benefit of an activity by the highest price we'd be willing to pay to pursue it—namely, our reservation price for the activity. When the cost of an activity rises, it is more likely to exceed our reservation price, and we are therefore less likely to pursue that activity.

The law of demand applies to BMWs, cheap key rings, and "free" ice cream, not to mention compact discs, manicures, medical care, and acid-free rain. It stresses that a "cost" is the sum of *all* the sacrifices—monetary and nonmonetary, implicit and explicit—we must make to engage in an activity.

THE ORIGINS OF DEMAND

How much are you willing to pay for the latest Alanis Morisette CD? The answer will clearly depend on how you feel about her music. To Morisette's diehard fans, buying the new release might seem absolutely essential; they'd pay a steep price indeed. But those who don't like Morisette's music may be unwilling to buy it at any price.

Wants (also called "preferences" or "tastes") are clearly an important determinant of a consumer's reservation price for a good. But that begs the question of where wants come from. Many tastes—such as the taste for water on a hot day or for a comfortable place to sleep at night—are largely biological in origin. But many others are heavily shaped by culture, and even basic cravings may be socially molded. For example, people raised in southern India develop a taste for hot curry dishes, while those raised in England generally prefer milder foods.

Tastes for some items may remain stable for many years, but tastes for others may be highly volatile. Although books about the *Titanic* disaster have been continuously available since the vessel sank in the spring of 1912, not until the appearance of James Cameron's blockbuster film did these books begin to sell in large quantities. In the spring of 1998, five of the 15 books on the *New York Times* paperback bestseller list were about the *Titanic* itself or one of the actors in the film. Yet none of these books, or any other book about the *Titanic*, made the bestseller list in 1999. Still, echoes of the film continued to reverberate in the marketplace. In the years since its release, for example, demand for ocean cruises has grown sharply, and several television networks have introduced shows set on cruise ships.

Peer influence provides another example of how social forces often influence demand. Indeed, it is often the most important single determinant of demand. For instance, if our goal is to predict whether a young man will purchase an illegal recreational drug, knowing how much income he has is not very helpful. Knowing the prices of whiskey and other legal substitutes for illicit drugs also tells us little. Although these factors do influence purchase decisions, by themselves they are weak predictors. But if we know that most of the young man's best friends are heavy drug users, there is a reasonably good chance that he will use drugs as well.

Another important way in which social forces shape demand is in the relatively common desire to consume goods and services that are recognized as the best of their kind. For instance, many people want to hear Luciano Pavorotti sing, not just because of the quality of his voice, but because he is widely regarded as the world's best—or at least the world's best known—tenor.

Consider, too, the decision of how much to spend on an interview suit. As the employment counselors never tire of reminding us, making a good first impression is extremely important when you go for a job interview. At the very least, that means showing up in a suit that looks good. But looking good is a relative concept. If everyone else shows up in a $200 suit, you'll look good if you show up in a $300 suit. But you won't look as good in that same $300 suit if everyone else shows up in suits costing $1,000. The amount you'll choose to spend on an interview suit, then, clearly depends on how much others in your circle are spending.

NEEDS VERSUS WANTS

In everyday language, we distinguish between goods and services people need and those they merely want. For example, we might say that someone wants a ski vacation in Utah, but what he really needs is a few days off from his daily routine; or that someone wants a house with a view, but what she really needs is shelter from the elements. Likewise, since people need protein to survive, we might say that a severely malnourished person needs more protein. But it would strike us as odd to say that anyone—even a malnourished person—needs more prime filet of beef, since health can be restored by consuming far less expensive sources of protein.

Economists like to emphasize that once we have achieved bare subsistence levels of consumption—the amount of food, shelter, and clothing required to maintain our health—we can abandon all reference to needs and speak only in terms of wants. This linguistic distinction helps us to think more clearly about the true nature of our choices.

For instance, someone who says "Californians don't have nearly as much water as they need" will tend to think differently about water shortages than someone who says "Californians don't have nearly as much water as they want when the price of water is low." The first person is likely to focus on regulations to prevent people from watering their lawns, or on projects to capture additional runoff from the Sierra Nevada mountains. The second person is more likely to focus on the low price of water in California. Whereas remedies of the first sort are often costly and extremely difficult to implement, raising the price of water is both simple and effective.

Why does California experience chronic water shortages?

Some might respond that the state must serve the needs of a large population with a relatively low average annual rainfall. Yet other states, like New Mexico, have even less rainfall per person and do not experience water shortages nearly as often as California. California's problem exists because local governments sell water at extremely low prices, which encourages Californians to use water in ways that make no sense for a state with low rainfall. For instance, rice, which is well suited for conditions in high-rainfall states like South Carolina, requires extensive irrigation in California. But because California farmers can obtain water so cheaply, they plant and flood hundreds of thousands of acres of rice paddies each spring in the Central Valley. Two thousand tons of water are needed to produce one ton of rice, but many other grains can be produced with only half that amount. If the price of California water were higher, farmers would simply switch to other grains.

Likewise, cheap water encourages homeowners in Los Angeles and San Diego to plant water-intensive lawns and shrubs, like the ones common in the East and Midwest. By contrast, residents of cities like Santa Fe, New Mexico, where water prices are high, choose native plantings that require little or no watering.

TRANSLATING WANTS INTO DEMAND

It's a simple fact of life that although our resources are finite, our appetites for good things are boundless. Even if we had unlimited bank accounts, we'd quickly run out of the time and energy needed to do all the things we wanted to do. Our challenge is to use our limited resources to fulfill our desires to the greatest possible degree. And that leaves us with this practical question: How should we allocate our incomes among the various goods and services that are available? To answer this question, it's helpful to begin by recognizing that the goods and services we buy are not ends in themselves, but rather means for satisfying our desires.

MEASURING WANTS: THE CONCEPT OF UTILITY

Economists use the concept of *utility* to represent the satisfaction people derive from their consumption activities. The assumption is that people try to allocate their incomes so as to maximize their satisfaction, a goal that is referred to as *utility maximization.*

Early economists imagined that the utility associated with different activities might someday be subject to precise measurement. The nineteenth-century British economist Jeremy Bentham, for example, wrote of a "utilometer," a device that could be used to measure the amount of utility provided by different consumption activities. Although no such device existed in Bentham's day, contemporary neuropsychologists now have equipment that can generate at least crude measures of satisfaction.

Figure 5.1, for example, shows a subject who is connected to an apparatus that measures the intensity of electrical waves emanating from his brain. University of Wisconsin psychologist Richard Davidson and his colleagues documented that subjects with relatively heavy brain wave measures emanating from the left prefrontal cortex tend to be happier (as assessed by a variety of other measures) than subjects with relatively heavy brain wave measures emanating from the right prefrontal cortex.

Jeremy Bentham would have been thrilled to learn that a device like the one pictured in Figure 5.1 might exist some day. His ideal utilometer would measure utility in utils, much as a thermometer measures temperature in degrees Fahrenheit or Celsius. It would assign a numerical utility value to every activity—watching a movie, eating a cheeseburger, and so on. Unfortunately, even sophisticated devices like the one shown in Figure 5.1 are far from capable of such fine-grained assessments.

Photo courtesy of Richard J. Davidson

FIGURE 5.1
Can Utility Be Measured Electronically?
Scientists have shown that higher levels of electrical activity on the brain's left side are strongly associated with higher levels of satisfaction.

For Bentham's intellectual enterprise, however, the absence of a real utilometer was of no practical significance. Even without such a machine, he could continue to envision the consumer as someone whose goal was to maximize the total utility she obtained from the goods she consumed. Bentham's "utility maximization model," we will see, affords important insights about how a rational consumer ought to spend her income. To explore how the model works, we begin with an unusually simple problem, the one facing a consumer who reaches the front of the line at a free ice cream stand. How many cones of ice cream should this person, whom we'll call Sarah, ask for? Table 5.1 shows the relationship between the total number of ice cream cones Sarah eats per hour and the total utility, measured in utils per hour, she derives from them. Note that the measurements in the table are stated in terms of cones per hour and utils per hour. Why "per hour"? Because without an explicit time dimension, we would have no idea whether a given quantity was a lot or a little. Five ice cream cones in a lifetime isn't much, but five in an hour would be more than most of us would care to eat.

As the entries in Table 5.1 show, Sarah's total utility increases with each cone she eats, up to the fifth cone. Eating 5 cones per hour makes her happier than eating 4, which makes her happier than eating 3, and so on. But beyond 5 cones per hour, consuming more ice cream actually makes Sarah less happy. Thus the sixth cone reduces her total utility from 150 utils per hour to 140 utils per hour.

We can display the utility information in Table 5.1 graphically, as in Figure 5.2. Note in the graph that the more cones per hour Sarah eats, the more utils she

TABLE 5.1
Sarah's Total Utility from Ice Cream Consumption

Cone quantity (cones/hour)	Total utility (utils/hour)
0	0
1	50
2	90
3	120
4	140
5	150
6	140

FIGURE 5.2
Sarah's Total Utility from Ice Cream Consumption.
For most goods, utility rises at a diminishing rate with additional consumption.

gets—but again only up to the fifth cone. Once she moves beyond 5, her total utility begins to decline. Sarah's happiness reaches a maximum of 150 utils when she eats 5 cones per hour. At that point she has no incentive to eat the sixth cone, even though it's absolutely free. Eating it would actually make her worse off.

Table 5.1 and Figure 5.2 illustrate another important aspect of the relationship between utility and consumption—namely, that the additional utility from additional units of consumption declines as total consumption increases. Thus, whereas 1 cone per hour is a *lot* better—by 50 utils—than zero, 5 cones per hour is just a *little* better than 4 (just 10 utils' worth).

marginal utility the additional utility gained from consuming an additional unit of a good

The term **marginal utility** denotes the amount by which total utility changes when consumption changes by one unit. In Table 5.2, the third column shows the marginal utility values that correspond to changes in Sarah's level of ice cream consumption. For example, the second entry in that column represents the increase in total utility (measured in utils per cone) when Sarah's consumption rises from 1 cone per hour to 2. Note that the marginal utility entries in the third column are placed midway between the rows of the preceding columns. We do this to indicate that marginal utility corresponds to the movement from one

TABLE 5.2
Sarah's Total and Marginal Utility from Ice Cream Consumption

Cone quantity (cones/hour)	Total utility (utils/hour)	Marginal utility (utils/cone)
0	0	—
		50
1	50	
		40
2	90	
		30
3	120	
		20
4	140	
		10
5	150	
		−10
6	140	

Marginal utility

$$= \frac{\text{change in utility}}{\text{change in consumption}}$$

$$= \frac{90 \text{ utils} - 50 \text{ utils}}{2 \text{ cones} - 1 \text{ cone}}$$

$$= 40 \text{ utils/cone}$$

consumption quantity to the next. Thus we would say that the marginal utility of moving from 1 to 2 cones per hour is 40 utils per cone.

Because marginal utility is the change in utility that occurs as we move from one quantity to another, when we graph marginal utility we normally adopt the convention of plotting each specific marginal utility value halfway between the two quantities to which it corresponds. Thus, in Figure 5.3, we plot the marginal utility value of 40 utils per cone midway between 1 cone per hour and 2 cones per hour, and so on. (In this example, the marginal utility graph is a downward-sloping straight line for the region shown, but this need not always be the case.)

The tendency for marginal utility to decline as consumption increases beyond some point is called the **law of diminishing marginal utility.** It holds not just for Sarah's consumption of ice cream in this illustration, but also for most other goods for most consumers. If we have one brownie or one Ferrari, we're happier than we are with none; if we have two, we'll be even happier—but not twice as happy—and so on. Though this pattern is called a law, there are exceptions. Indeed, some consumption activities even seem to exhibit *increasing* marginal utility. For example, an unfamiliar song may seem irritating the first time you hear it, then gradually become more tolerable the next few times you hear it. Before long, you may discover that you *like* the song, and you may even find yourself singing it in the shower. Notwithstanding such exceptions, the law of diminishing marginal utility is a plausible characterization of the relationship between utility and consumption for many goods. Unless otherwise stated, we'll assume that it holds for the various goods we discuss.

What will Sarah do when she gets to the front of the line? At that point, the opportunity cost of the time she spent waiting is a sunk cost, and is hence irrelevant to her decision about how many cones to order. And since there is no monetary charge for the cones, the cost of ordering an additional one is zero. According to the cost-benefit principle, Sarah should therefore continue to order cones as long as the marginal benefit (here, the marginal utility she gets from an additional cone) is greater than or equal to zero. As we can see from the entries in Table 5.2, marginal utility is positive up to and including the fifth cone but becomes negative after 5 cones. Thus, as noted earlier, Sarah should order 5 cones.

In this highly simplified example, Sarah's utility-maximization problem is just like the one she'd confront if she were deciding how much water to drink from a public fountain. (Solution: Keep drinking until the marginal utility of water declines to zero.)

law of diminishing marginal utility the tendency for the additional utility gained from consuming an additional unit of a good to diminish as consumption increases beyond some point

**FIGURE 5.3
Diminishing Marginal Utility.**
The more cones Sarah consumes each hour, the smaller her marginal utility will be. For Sarah, consumption of ice cream cones satisfies the law of diminishing marginal utility.

ALLOCATING A FIXED INCOME BETWEEN TWO GOODS

Most of us confront considerably more complex purchase decisions than the one Sarah faced. For one thing, we generally must make decisions not just about a single good but about many. Another complication is that the cost of consuming additional units of each good will rarely be zero.

To see how to proceed in more complex cases, let's suppose Sarah must decide how to spend a fixed sum of money on two different goods, each with a positive price. Should she spend all of it on one of the goods, or part of it on each? The law of diminishing marginal utility suggests that spending it all on a single good isn't a good strategy. Rather than devote more and more money to the purchase of a good we already consume in large quantities (and whose marginal utility is therefore relatively low), we generally do better to spend that money on other goods we don't have much of, whose marginal utility will likely be higher.

The simplest way to illustrate how economists think about the spending decisions of a utility-maximizing consumer is to work through an example like the following:

EXAMPLE 5.1

Is Sarah maximizing her utility from consuming chocolate and vanilla ice cream (I)?

Chocolate ice cream sells sell for $2 per pint and vanilla sells for $1. Sarah has a budget of $400 per year to spend on ice cream, and her marginal utility from consuming each type varies with the amount consumed as shown in Figure 5.4. If she is currently buying 200 pints of vanilla and 100 pints of chocolate each year, is she maximizing her utility?

FIGURE 5.4
Marginal Utility Curves for Two Flavors of Ice Cream (I).
At Sarah's current consumption levels, her marginal utility of chocolate ice cream is 25 percent higher than her marginal utility of vanilla. But chocolate is twice as expensive as vanilla.

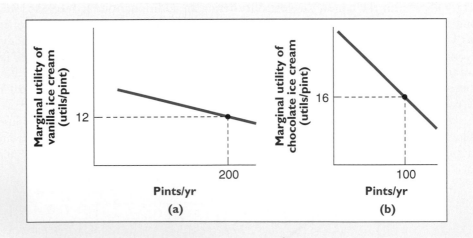

Note first that with 200 pints per year of vanilla and 100 pints of chocolate, Sarah is spending $200 per year on each type of ice cream, for a total expenditure of $400 per year on ice cream, exactly the amount in her budget. By spending her money in this fashion, is she getting as much utility as possible? Note in Figure 5.4(b) that her marginal utility from chocolate ice cream is 16 utils per pint. Since chocolate costs $2 per pint, her current spending on chocolate is yielding additional utility at the rate of (16 utils/pint)/($2/pint) = 8 utils per dollar. Similarly, note in Figure 5.4(a) that Sarah's marginal utility for vanilla is 12 utils per pint. And since vanilla costs only $1 per pint, her current spending on vanilla is yielding (12 utils/pint)/($1/pint) = 12 utils per dollar. In other words, at her current rates of consumption of the two flavors, her spending yields higher marginal utility per dollar for vanilla than for chocolate. And this means that Sarah cannot possibly be maximizing her total utility.

To see why, note that if she spent $2 less on chocolate (that is, if she bought one pint less than before), she would lose about 16 utils;[1] but with the same $2, she could buy two additional pints of vanilla, which would boost her utility by about 24 utils,[2] for a net gain of about 8 utils. Under Sarah's current budget allocation, she is thus spending too little on vanilla and too much on chocolate.

In the next example, we'll see what happens if Sarah spends $100 per year less on chocolate and $100 per year more on vanilla.

Is Sarah maximizing her utility from consuming chocolate and vanilla ice cream (II)?

EXAMPLE 5.2

Sarah's total ice cream budget and the prices of the two flavors are the same as in Example 5.1. If her marginal utility from consuming each type varies with the amount consumed as shown in Figure 5.5 and if she is currently buying 300 pints of vanilla and 50 pints of chocolate each year, is she maximizing her utility?

Note first that the direction of Sarah's rearrangement of her spending makes sense in light of Example 5.1, in which we saw that she was spending too much on chocolate and too little on vanilla. Spending $100 less on chocolate ice cream causes

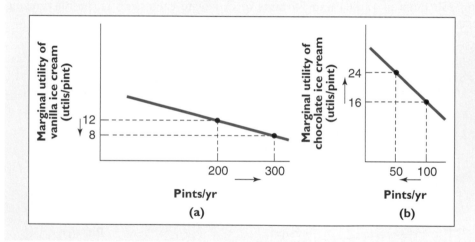

FIGURE 5.5
Marginal Utility Curves for Two Flavors of Ice Cream (II).
When Sarah increases her consumption of vanilla (a), her marginal utility of vanilla falls. Conversely, when she reduces her consumption of chocolate (b), her marginal utility of chocolate rises.

her marginal utility from that flavor to rise from 16 to 24 utils per pint [Figure 5.5(b)]. By the same token, spending $100 more on vanilla ice cream causes her marginal utility from that flavor to fall from 12 to 8 utils per pint [Figure 5.5(a)]. Both movements are a simple consequence of the law of diminishing marginal utility.

Since chocolate still costs $2 per pint, her spending on chocolate now yields additional utility at the rate of (24 utils/pint)/($2/pint) = 12 utils per dollar. Similarly, since vanilla still costs $1 per pint, her spending on vanilla now yields additional utility at the rate of only (8 utils/pint)/($1/pint) = 8 utils per dollar. So at her new rates of consumption of the two flavors, her spending yields higher marginal utility per dollar for chocolate than for vanilla—precisely the opposite of the ordering we saw in Example 5.1.

Sarah has thus made too big an adjustment in her effort to remedy her original consumption imbalance. Starting from the new combination of flavors (300 pints per year of vanilla and 50 pints per year of chocolate), for example, if she then bought two fewer pints of vanilla (which would reduce her utility by about 16 utils) and used the $2 she saved to buy an additional pint of chocolate (which would

[1]The actual reduction would be slightly larger than 16 utils, because her marginal utility of chocolate rises slightly as she consumes less of it.
[2]The actual increase will be slightly smaller than 24 utils, because her marginal utility of vanilla falls slightly as she buys more of it.

boost her utility by about 24 utils), she would experience a net gain of about 8 utils. So again, her current combination of the two flavors fails to maximize her total utility. This time, she is spending too little on chocolate and too much on vanilla.

EXERCISE 5.1

In Example 5.1, verify that the stated combination of flavors in Example 5.2 costs exactly the amount that Sarah has budgeted for ice cream.

optimal combination of goods the affordable combination that yields the highest total utility

What is Sarah's **optimal combination** the two flavors? In other words, among all the combinations of vanilla and chocolate ice cream that Sarah can afford, which one provides the maximum possible total utility? The following example illustrates the condition that this optimal combination must satisfy.

EXAMPLE 5.3

Is Sarah maximizing her utility from consuming chocolate and vanilla ice cream (III)?

Sarah's total ice cream budget and the prices of the two flavors are again as in Examples 5.1 and 5.2. If her marginal utility from consuming each type varies with the amounts consumed as shown in Figure 5.6 and if she is currently buying 250 pints of vanilla and 75 pints of chocolate each year, is she maximizing her utility?

FIGURE 5.6
Marginal Utility Curves for Two Flavors of Ice Cream (III).
At her current consumption levels, marginal utility per dollar is exactly the same for each flavor.

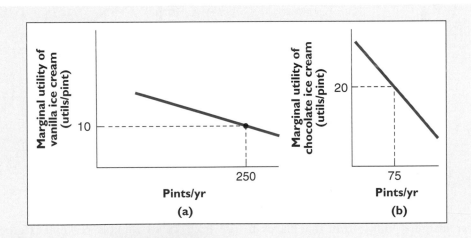

As you can easily verify, the combination of 250 pints per year of vanilla and 75 pints per year of chocolate again costs a total of $400, exactly the amount of Sarah's ice cream budget. Her marginal utility from chocolate is now 20 utils per pint [Figure 5.6(b)], and since chocolate still costs $2 per pint, her spending on chocolate now yields additional utility at the rate of (20 utils/pint)/($2/pint) = 10 utils per dollar. Sarah's marginal utility for vanilla is now 10 utils per pint [Figure 5.6(a)], and since vanilla still costs $1 per pint, her last dollar spent on vanilla now also yields (10 utils/pint)/($1/pint) = 10 utils per dollar. So at her new rates of consumption of the two flavors, her spending yields precisely the same marginal utility per dollar for each flavor. Thus, if she spent a little less on chocolate and a little more on vanilla (or vice versa), her total utility would not change at all. For example, if she bought two more pints of vanilla (which would increase her utility by 20 utils) and one fewer pint of chocolate (which would reduce her utility by 20 utils), both her total expenditure on ice cream and her total utility would remain the same as before. *When her marginal utility per dollar is the same for each flavor, it is impossible for Sarah to rearrange her spending to increase total utility.* So 250 pints of vanilla and 75 pints of chocolate per year is the optimal combination of the two flavors.

THE RATIONAL SPENDING RULE

Example 5.3 illustrates the **rational spending rule** for solving the problem of how to allocate a fixed budget across different goods. The optimal, or utility-maximizing, combination must satisfy this rule.

The Rational Spending Rule: Spending should be allocated across goods so that the marginal utility per dollar is the same for each good.

The rational spending rule can be expressed in the form of a simple formula. If we use MU_C to denote marginal utility from chocolate ice cream consumption (again measured in utils per pint), and P_C to denote the price of chocolate (measured in dollars per pint), then the ratio MU_C/P_C will represent the marginal utility per dollar spent on chocolate, measured in utils per dollar. Similarly, if we use MU_V to denote the marginal utility from vanilla ice cream consumption and P_V to denote the price of vanilla, then MU_V/P_V will represent the marginal utility per dollar spent on vanilla. The marginal utility per dollar will be exactly the same for the two types—and hence total utility will be maximized—when the following simple equation for the rational spending rule for two goods is satisfied:

$$MU_C/P_C = MU_V/P_V.$$

The rational spending rule is easily generalized to apply to spending decisions regarding large numbers of goods. In its most general form, it says that the ratio of marginal utility to price must be the same for each good the consumer buys. If the ratio were higher for one good than for another, the consumer could always increase her total utility by buying more of the first good and less of the second.

Strictly speaking, the rational spending rule applies to goods that are perfectly divisible, such as milk or gasoline. Many other goods, such as bus rides and television sets, can be consumed only in whole-number amounts. In such cases, it may not be possible to satisfy the rational spending rule exactly. For example, when you buy one television set, your marginal utility per dollar spent on televisions may be somewhat higher than the corresponding ratio for other goods, yet if you bought a second set the reverse might well be true. Your best alternative in such cases is to allocate each additional dollar you spend to the good for which your marginal utility per dollar is highest.[1]

Notice that we have not chosen to classify the rational spending rule as one of the core principles of economics. We omit it from this list not because the rule is unimportant, but because it follows directly from the cost-benefit principle. And as we noted earlier, there is considerable advantage in keeping the list of core principles as small as possible. (If we included 200 principles on this list, there's a good chance you wouldn't remember any of them a few years from now.)

INCOME AND SUBSTITUTION EFFECTS REVISITED

In Chapter 3, we saw that the quantity of a good that consumers wish to purchase depends on its own price, the prices of substitutes and complements, and on consumer incomes. We also saw that when the price of a good changes, the quantity of it demanded changes for two reasons—the substitution effect and the income effect. The substitution effect refers to the fact that when the price of a good goes up, substitutes for that good become relatively more attractive, causing some consumers to abandon the good for its substitutes.

The income effect refers to the fact a price change makes the consumer either poorer or richer in real terms. Consider, for instance, the effect of a change in the price of one of the ice cream flavors in Example 5.3. At the original prices ($2 per

[1]See Problems 6 and 10 at the end of the chapter for examples.

pint for chocolate, $1 per pint for vanilla), Sarah's $400 annual ice cream budget would have enabled her to buy at most 200 pints per year of chocolate or 400 pints per year of vanilla. If the price of vanilla rose to $2 per pint, that would reduce not only the maximum amount of vanilla she could afford (from 400 to 200 pints per year) but also the maximum amount of chocolate she could afford in combination with any given amount of vanilla. For example, at the original price of $1 per pint for vanilla, Sarah could afford to buy 150 pints of chocolate while buying 100 pints of vanilla; but when the price of vanilla rises to $2, she can buy only 100 pints of chocolate while buying 100 pints of vanilla. As noted in Chapter 3, a reduction in real income shifts the demand curves for normal goods to the left.

The rational spending rule helps us see more clearly why a change in the price of one good affects demands for other goods. The rule requires that the ratio of marginal utility to price be the same for all goods. This means that if the price of one good goes up, the ratio of its current marginal utility to its new price will be lower than for other goods. Consumers can then increase their total utility by devoting smaller proportions of their incomes to that good and larger proportions to others.

EXAMPLE 5.4   **How should Sarah respond to a reduction in the price of chocolate ice cream?**

Sarah's total ice cream budget is again $400 per year and prices of the two flavors are again $2 per pint for chocolate and $1 per pint for vanilla. Her marginal utility from consuming each type varies with the amounts consumed as shown in Figure 5.7. She is currently buying 250 pints of vanilla and 75 pints of chocolate each year, which is the optimal combination for her at these prices (see Example 5.3). How should she reallocate her spending among the two flavors if the price of chocolate ice cream falls to $1 per pint?

FIGURE 5.7
Marginal Utility Curves for Two Flavors of Ice Cream (IV).
At the current combination of flavors, marginal utility per dollar is the same for each flavor. When the price of chocolate falls, marginal utility per dollar becomes higher for chocolate than for vanilla. To redress this imbalance, Sarah should buy more chocolate and less vanilla.

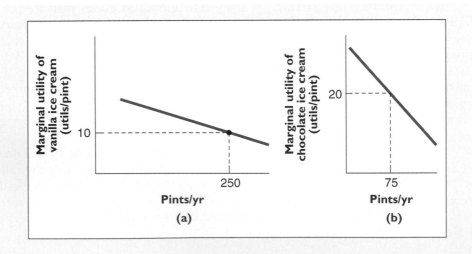

Because the quantities shown in Figure 5.7 constitute the optimal combination of the two flavors for Sarah at the original prices, they must exactly satisfy the rational spending rule:

$$MU_C/P_C = (20 \text{ utils/pint})/\$2/\text{pint} = 10 \text{ utils/dollar}$$
$$= MU_V/P_V = (10 \text{ utils/pint})/(\$1/\text{pint}).$$

When the price of chocolate falls to $1 per pint, the original quantities will no longer satisfy the rational spending rule, because the marginal utility per dollar for chocolate will suddenly be twice what it was before:

$$MU_C/P_C = (20 \text{ utils/pint})/\$1/\text{pint} = 20 \text{ utils/dollar}$$
$$> MU_V/P_V = 10 \text{ utils/dollar}.$$

To redress this imbalance, Sarah must rearrange her spending on the two flavors in such a way as to increase the marginal utility per dollar for vanilla relative to the marginal utility per dollar for chocolate. And as we see in Figure 5.7, that will happen if she buys a larger quantity than before of chocolate and a smaller quantity than before of vanilla.

EXERCISE 5.2

John spends all of his income on two goods, food and shelter. The price of food is $5 per pound and the price of shelter is $10 per square yard. At his current consumption levels, his marginal utilities for the two goods are 20 utils per pound and 30 utils per square yard, respectively. Is John maximizing his utility? If not, how should he reallocate his spending?

In Chapter 1 we saw that people often make bad decisions because they fail to appreciate the distinction between average and marginal costs and benefits. As the following example illustrates, this pitfall also arises when people attempt to apply the economist's model of utility maximization.

Should Eric consume more apples?

EXAMPLE 5.5

Eric gets a total of 1,000 utils per week from his consumption of apples and a total of 400 utils per week from his consumption of oranges. The price of apples is $2 each, the price of oranges is $1 each, and he consumes 50 apples and 50 oranges each week. True or false: Eric should consume more apples and fewer oranges.

Eric spends $100 per week on apples and $50 on oranges. He thus averages (1,000 utils/week)/($100/week) = 10 utils per dollar from his consumption of apples and (400 utils/week)/($50/week) = 8 utils per dollar from his consumption of oranges. Many might be tempted to respond that because Eric's average utility per dollar for apples is higher than for oranges, he should consume more apples. But knowing only his *average* utility per dollar for each good simply does not enable us to say whether his current combination is optimal. To make that determination, we need to compare Eric's *marginal* utility per dollar for each good. The information given simply doesn't permit us to make that comparison.

RECAP   **TRANSLATING WANTS INTO DEMAND**

The scarcity principle challenges us to allocate our incomes among the various goods that are available so as to fulfill our desires to the greatest possible degree. The optimal combination of goods is the affordable combination that yields the highest total utility. For goods that are perfectly divisible, the rational spending rule tells us that the optimal combination is one for which the marginal utility per dollar is the same for each good. If this condition were not satisfied, the consumer could increase her utility by spending less on goods for which the marginal utility per dollar was lower and more on goods for which her marginal utility was higher.

APPLYING THE RATIONAL SPENDING RULE

The real payoff from learning the law of demand and the rational spending rule lies not in working through hypothetical examples, but in using these abstract concepts to make sense of the world around you. To encourage you in your efforts to become an economic naturalist, we turn now to a sequence of examples in this vein.

SUBSTITUTION AT WORK

In the first of these examples, we focus on the role of substitution. When the price of a good or service goes up, rational consumers generally turn to less expensive substitutes. Can't meet the payments on a new car? Then buy a used one, or rent an apartment on a bus or subway line. French restaurants too pricey? Then go out for Chinese, or eat at home more often. National Football League tickets too high? Watch the game on television, or read a book. Can't afford a book? Check one out of the library, or download some reading matter from the Internet. Once you begin to see substitution at work, you will be amazed by the number and richness of the examples that confront you every day.

ECONOMIC NATURALIST 5.2

Why do the wealthy in Manhattan live in smaller houses than the wealthy in Seattle?

Microsoft cofounder Bill Gates lives in a 45,000-square-foot house in Seattle, Washington. His house is large even by the standards of Seattle, many of whose wealthy residents live in houses with more than 10,000 square feet of floor space. By contrast, persons of similar wealth in Manhattan rarely live in houses larger than 5,000 square feet. Why this difference?

For people trying to decide how large a house to buy, the most obvious difference between Manhattan and Seattle is the huge difference in housing prices. The cost of land alone is several times higher in Manhattan than in Seattle, and construction costs are also much higher. Although plenty of New Yorkers could *afford* to build a 45,000-square-foot mansion, Manhattan housing prices are so high that they simply choose to live in smaller houses and spend what they save in other ways—on lavish summer homes in eastern Long Island, for instance. New Yorkers also eat out and go to the theater more often than their wealthy counterparts in other U.S. cities.

Would Bill Gates build a 45,000-square-foot house if he lived in Manhattan?

An especially vivid illustration of substitution occurred during the late 1970s, when fuel shortages brought on by interruptions in the supply of oil from the Middle East led to sharp increases in the price of gasoline and other fuels. In a variety of ways—some straightforward, others remarkably ingenious—consumers changed their behavior to economize on the use of energy. They formed car pools, switched to public transportation, bought four-cylinder cars, moved closer to work, took fewer trips, turned down their thermostats, installed insulation, storm windows, and solar heaters, and bought more efficient appliances. Many people even moved farther south to escape high winter heating bills.

As the next example points out, consumers not only abandon a good in favor of substitutes when it gets more expensive, but they also return to that good when prices return to their original levels.

ECONOMIC NATURALIST 5.3

Why did people turn to four-cylinder cars in the 1970s, only to shift back to six- and eight-cylinder cars in the 1990s?

In 1973, the price of gasoline was 38 cents per gallon. The following year the price shot up to 52 cents per gallon in the wake of a major disruption of oil supplies. A second disruption in 1979 drove the 1980 price to $1.19 per gallon. These sharp increases in the price of gasoline led to big increases in the demand for cars with four-cylinder engines, which delivered much better fuel economy than the six- and eight-cylinder cars most people had owned. After 1980, however, fuel supplies stabilized, and prices rose only slowly, reaching $1.40 per gallon by 1999. Yet despite the continued rise in the price of gasoline, the switch to smaller engines did not continue. By the late 1980s, the proportion of cars sold with six- and eight-cylinder engines began rising again. Why this reversal?

The key to explaining these patterns is to focus on changes in the **real price** of gasoline. When someone decides how big an automobile engine to choose, what matters is not the **nominal price** of gasoline, but the price of gasoline *relative* to all other goods. After all, for a consumer faced with a decision of whether to spend $1.40 for a gallon of gasoline, the important question is how much utility she could get from other things she could purchase with the same money. Even though the price of gasoline has continued to rise slowly in nominal, or dollar, terms since 1981, it has declined sharply relative to the price of other goods. Indeed, in terms of real purchasing power, the 1999 price was actually slightly lower than the 1973 price. (That is, in 1999 $1.40 bought slightly more goods and services than 38 cents bought in 1973.) It is this decline in the real price of gasoline that accounts for the reversal of the trend toward smaller engines.

A sharp decline in the real price of gasoline also helps account for the explosive growth in sport utility vehicles in the 1990s. Almost 4 million SUVs were sold in the United States in 2001, up from only 750,000 in 1990. Some of them—like the Ford Excursion—weigh more than 7,500 pounds (three times as much as a Honda Civic) and get less than 10 miles per gallon on city streets. Vehicles like these would have been dismal failures during the 1970s, but they're by far the hottest sellers in the current cheap-energy environment.

> *real price* the dollar price of a good relative to the average dollar price of all other goods
>
> *nominal price* the absolute price of a good in dollar terms

"We motored over to say hi!"

Here's another closely related example of the influence of price on spending decisions.

Why are automobile engines smaller in England than in the United States?

In England, the most popular model of BMW's 5-series car is the 516i, whereas in the United States it is the 525i. The engine in the 516i is 40 percent smaller than the engine in the 525i. Why this difference?

In both countries, BMWs appeal to professionals with roughly similar incomes, so the difference cannot be explained by differences in purchasing power. Rather, it is the direct result of the heavy tax the British levy on gasoline. With tax, a gallon of gasoline sells for almost $6 in England—more than four times the price in the United States. This difference encourages the British to choose smaller, more fuel-efficient engines.

ECONOMIC NATURALIST 5.4

THE IMPORTANCE OF INCOME DIFFERENCES

The most obvious difference between the rich and the poor is that the rich have higher incomes. To explain why the wealthy generally buy larger houses than the poor, we need not assume that the wealthy feel more strongly about housing than the poor. A much simpler explanation is that the total utility from housing, as with most other goods, increases with the amount that one consumes.

As the next example illustrates, income influences the demand not only for housing and other goods, but also for quality of service.

Why are waiting lines longer in poorer neighborhoods?

As part of a recent promotional campaign, a Baskin-Robbins retailer offered free ice cream at two of its franchise stores. The first was located in a high-income neighborhood, the second in a low-income neighborhood. Why was the queue for free ice cream longer in the low-income neighborhood?

Residents of both neighborhoods must decide whether to stand in line for free ice cream or go to some other store and avoid the line by paying the usual price. If we make the plausible assumption that people with higher incomes are more willing than others to pay to avoid standing in line, we should expect to see shorter lines in the high-income neighborhood.

Similar reasoning helps explain why lines are shorter in grocery stores that cater to high-income consumers. Keeping lines short at *any* grocery store means hiring more clerks, which means charging higher prices. High-income consumers are more likely than others to be willing to pay for shorter lines.

 RECAP   **APPLYING THE RATIONAL SPENDING RULE**

Application of the rational spending rule highlights the important roles of income and substitution in explaining differences in consumption patterns—among individuals, among communities, and across time. The rule also highlights the fact that real, as opposed to nominal, prices and income are what matter. The demand for a good falls when the real price of a substitute falls or the real price of a complement rises.

INDIVIDUAL AND MARKET DEMAND CURVES

If we know what each individual's demand curve for a good looks like, how can we use that information to construct the market demand curve for the good? We must add the individual demand curves together, a process that is straightforward but requires care.

HORIZONTAL ADDITION

Suppose that there only two buyers—Smith and Jones—in the market for canned tuna, and that their demand curves are as shown in Figure 5.8(a) and (b). To construct the market demand curve for canned tuna, we simply announce a sequence of prices and then add the quantity demanded by each buyer at each price. For example, at a price of $4 per can, Smith demands 6 cans per week (a) and Jones demands 2 cans per week (b), for a market demand of 8 cans per week (c).

The process of adding individual demand curves to get the market demand curve is known as *horizontal addition*, a term used to emphasize that we are adding quantities, which are measured on the horizontal axes of individual demand curves.

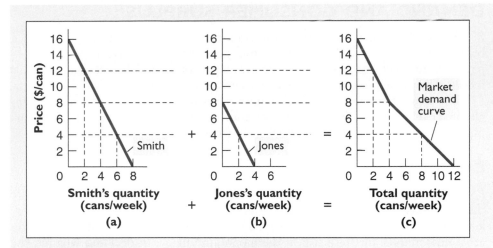

FIGURE 5.8
Individual and Market Demand Curves for Canned Tuna.
The quantity demanded at any price on the market demand curve (c) is the sum of the individual quantities demanded at that price, (a) and (b).

EXERCISE 5.3

The buyers' side of the market for movie tickets consists of two consumers whose demands are as shown in the diagram below. Graph the market demand curve for this market.

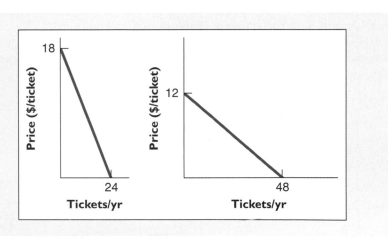

Figure 5.9 illustrates the special case in which each of 1,000 consumers in the market has the same demand curve (a). To get the market demand curve (b) in this case, we simply multiply each quantity on the representative individual demand curve by 1,000.

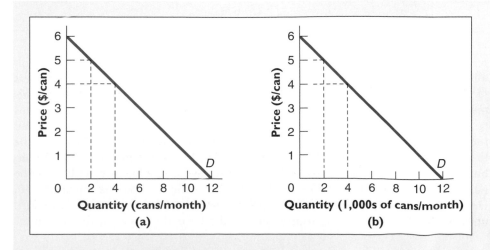

FIGURE 5.9
The Individual and Market Demand Curves When All Buyers Have Identical Demand Curves.
When individual demand curves are identical, we get the market demand curve (b) by multiplying each quantity on the individual demand curve (a) by the number of consumers in the market.

DEMAND AND CONSUMER SURPLUS

In Chapter 1 we first encountered the concept of economic surplus, which in a buyer's case is the difference between the most she would have been willing to pay for a product and the amount she actually pays for it. The economic surplus received by buyers is often referred to a **consumer surplus**.

The term consumer surplus sometimes refers to the surplus received by a single buyer in a transaction. On other occasions it is used to denote the total surplus received by all buyers in a market or collection of markets.

consumer surplus the difference between a buyer's reservation price for a product and the price actually paid

CALCULATING ECONOMIC SURPLUS

For performing cost-benefit analysis it is often important to be able to measure the total consumer surplus received by all buyers who participate in a given market. For example, a road linking a mountain village and a port city would create a new market for fresh fish in the mountain village; in deciding whether the road should be built, analysts would want to count as one of its benefits the gains that would be reaped by buyers in this new market.

To illustrate how economists actually measure consumer surplus, we'll consider a hypothetical market for a good with 11 potential buyers, each of whom can buy a maximum of one unit of the good each day. The first potential buyer's reservation price for the product is $11; the second buyer's reservation price is $10; the third buyer's reservation price is $9; and so on. The demand curve for this market will have the staircase shape shown in Figure 5.10. We can think of this curve as the digital counterpart of traditional analog demand curves. (If the units shown on the horizontal axis were fine enough, this digital curve would be visually indistinguishable from its analog counterparts.)

FIGURE 5.10

A Market with a "Digital" Demand Curve.

When a product can be sold only in whole-number amounts, its demand curve has the stair-step shape shown.

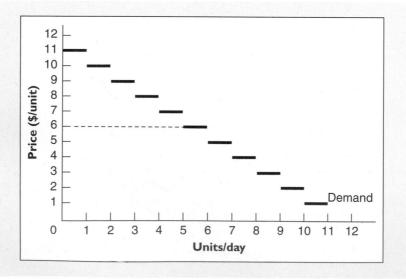

Suppose the good whose demand curve is shown in Figure 5.10 were available at a price of $6 per unit. How much total consumer surplus would buyers in this market reap? At a price of $6, six units per day would be sold in this market. The buyer of the sixth unit would receive no economic surplus, since his reservation price for that unit was exactly $6, the same as its selling price. But the first five buyers would reap a surplus for their purchases. The buyer of the first unit, for example, would have been willing to pay as much as $11 for it, but since she would pay only $6, she would receive a surplus of exactly $5. The buyer of the second unit, who would have been willing to pay as much as $10, would receive a surplus of $4. The surplus would be $3 for the buyer of the third unit, $2 for the buyer of the fourth unit, and $1 for the buyer of the fifth unit.

If we add all the buyers' surpluses together, we get a total of $15 of consumer surplus each day. That surplus corresponds to the shaded area shown in Figure 5.11.

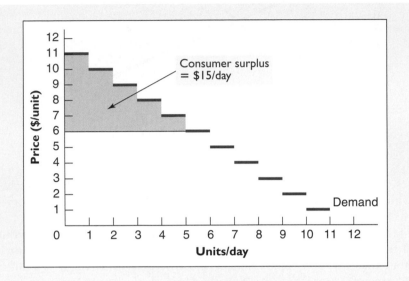

FIGURE 5.11
Consumer Surplus.
Consumer surplus (shaded region) is the cumulative difference between the most that buyers are willing to pay for each unit and the price they actually pay.

EXERCISE 5.4

Calculate consumer surplus for a demand curve like the one just described except that the buyers' reservation prices for each unit are $2 higher than before.

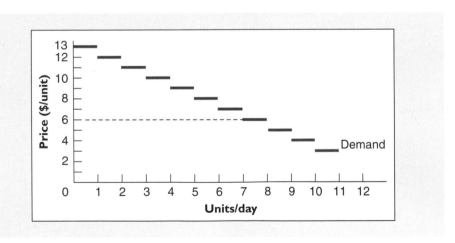

Now suppose we want to calculate consumer surplus in a market with a conventional straight-line demand curve. As the following example illustrates, this task is a simple extension of the method used for digital demand curves.

How much do buyers benefit from their participation in the market for milk?   **EXAMPLE 5.6**

Consider the market for milk whose demand and supply curves are shown in Figure 5.12, which has an equilibrium price of $2 per gallon and an equilibrium quantity of 4,000 gallons per day. How much consumer surplus do the buyers in this market reap?

In Figure 5.12, note first that, as in Figure 5.11, the last unit exchanged each day generates no consumer surplus at all. Note also that for all milk sold up to 4,000 gallons per day, buyers receive consumer surplus, just as in Figure 5.11.

FIGURE 5.12
Supply and Demand in the Market for Milk.
For the supply and demand curves shown, the equilibrium price of milk is $2 per gallon and the equilibrium quantity is 4,000 gallons per day.

For these buyers, consumer surplus is the cumulative difference between the most they would be willing to pay for milk (as measured on the demand curve) and the price they actually pay.

Total consumer surplus received by buyers in the milk market is thus the shaded triangle between the demand curve and the market price in Figure 5.13. Note that this area is a right triangle whose vertical arm is $h = \$1$/gallon and whose horizontal arm is $b = 4{,}000$ gallons/day. And since the area of any triangle is equal to $(1/2)bh$, consumer surplus in this market is equal to

$$(1/2)(4{,}000 \text{ gallons/day})(\$1/\text{gallon}) = \$2{,}000/\text{day}.$$

FIGURE 5.13
Consumer Surplus in the Market for Milk.
Consumer surplus it the area of the shaded triangle ($2,000/day).

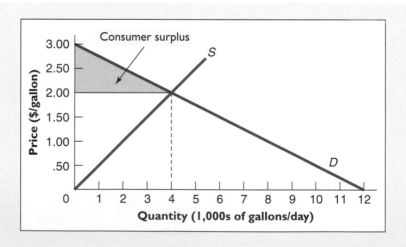

A useful way of thinking about consumer surplus is to ask what is the highest price consumers would pay, in the aggregate, for the right to continue participating in this milk market. The answer is $2,000 per day, since that is the amount by which their combined benefits exceed their combined costs.

As discussed in Chapter 3, the demand curve for a good can be interpreted either horizontally or vertically. The horizontal interpretation tells us, for each price, the total quantity that consumers wish to buy at that price. The vertical interpretation tells us, for each quantity, the most a buyer would be willing to pay for the good at that quantity. For the purpose of computing consumer surplus, we rely on the vertical interpretation of the demand curve. The value on the vertical axis that corresponds to each point along the demand curve corresponds to the marginal buyer's reservation price for the good. Consumer surplus is the cumulative sum of the differences between these reservation prices and the market price. It is the area bounded above by the demand curve and bounded below by the market price.

▪ SUMMARY ▪

- The rational consumer allocates income among different goods so that the marginal utility gained from the last dollar spent on each good is the same. This rational spending rule gives rise to the law of demand, which states that people do less of what they want to do as the cost of doing it rises. Here, "cost" refers to the sum of all monetary and nonmonetary sacrifices—explicit and implicit—that must be made in order to engage in the activity.

- The ability to substitute one good for another is an important factor behind the law of demand. Because virtually every good or service has at least some substitutes, economists prefer to speak in terms of wants rather than needs. We face choices, and describing our demands as needs is misleading because it suggests we have no options.

- For normal goods, the income effect is a second important reason that demand curves slope downward. When the price of such a good falls, not only does it become more attractive relative to its substitutes, but the consumer also acquires more real purchasing power, and this, too, augments the quantity demanded.

- The demand curve is a schedule that shows the amounts of a good people want to buy at various prices. Demand curves can be used to summarize the price-quantity relationship for a single individual, but more commonly we employ them to summarize that relationship for an entire market. At any quantity along a demand curve, the corresponding price represents the amount by which the consumer (or consumers) would benefit from having an additional unit of the product. For this reason, the demand curve is sometimes described as a summary of the benefit side of the market.

- Consumer surplus is a quantitative measure of the amount by which buyers benefit as a result of their ability to purchase goods at the market price. It is the area between the demand curve and the market price.

▪ KEY TERMS ▪

consumer surplus (134)
law of demand (118)
law of diminishing marginal
    utility (123)

marginal utility (122)
nominal price (131)
optimal combination of
    goods (126)

rational spending rule (127)
real price (131)

▪ REVIEW QUESTIONS ▪

1. Why do economists prefer to speak of demands arising out of "wants" rather than "needs"?

2. Explain why economists consider the concept of utility useful, even if psychologists cannot measure it precisely.

3. Why does the law of diminishing marginal utility encourage people to spread their spending across many different types of goods?

4. Explain why a good or service that is offered at a monetary price of zero is unlikely to be a truly "free" good from an economic perspective.

5. Give an example of a good that you have consumed for which your marginal utility increased with the amount of it you consumed.

▪ PROBLEMS ▪

1. In which type of restaurant do you expect the service to be more prompt and courteous: an expensive gourmet restaurant or an inexpensive diner? Explain.

2. You are having lunch at an all-you-can-eat buffet. If you are rational, what should be your marginal utility from the last morsel of food you swallow?

3. Martha's current marginal utility from consuming orange juice is 75 utils per ounce and her marginal utility from consuming coffee is 50 utils per ounce. If orange juice costs 25 cents per ounce and coffee costs 20 cents per ounce, is Martha maximizing her total utility from the two beverages? If so, explain how you know. If not, how should she rearrange her spending?

4. Toby's current marginal utility from consuming peanuts is 100 utils per ounce and his marginal utility from consuming cashews is 200 utils per ounce. If peanuts cost 10 cents per ounce and cashews cost 25 cents per ounce, is Toby maximizing his total utility from the kinds of nuts? If so, explain how you know. If not, how should he rearrange his spending?

5. Sue gets a total of 20 utils per week from her consumption of pizza and a total of 40 utils per week from her consumption of yogurt. The price of pizza is $1 per slice, the price of yogurt is $1 per cup, and she consumes 10 slices of pizza and 20 cups of yogurt each week. True or false: Sue is consuming the optimal combination of pizza and yogurt.

6. Ann lives in Princeton and commutes by train each day to her job in New York City (20 round trips per month). When the price of a round trip goes up from $10 to $20, she responds by consuming exactly the same number of trips as before, while spending $200 per month less on restaurant meals.
   a. Does the fact that her quantity of train travel is completely unresponsive to the price increase imply that Ann is not a rational consumer?
   b. Explain why an increase in train travel might affect the amount she spends on restaurant meals.

7. For the demand curve shown, find the total amount of consumer surplus that results in the gasoline market if gasoline sells for $2 per gallon.

8. Tom has a weekly allowance of $24, all of which he spends on pizza and movie rentals, whose prices are $6 per slice and $3 per rental, respectively. If slices of pizza and movie rentals are available only in whole-number amounts, list all possible combinations of the two goods that Tom can purchase each week with his allowance.

9.* Refer to problem 8. Tom's total utility is the sum of the utility he derives from pizza and movie rentals. If these utilities vary with the amounts consumed as shown in the table, and pizzas and movie rentals are again consumable only in whole-number amounts, how many pizzas and how many movie rentals should Tom consume each week?

Pizzas/week	Utils/week from pizza	Movie rentals/ week	Utils/week from rentals
0	0	0	0
1	20	1	40
2	38	2	46
3	54	3	50
4	68	4	54
5	80	5	56
6	90	6	57
7	98	7	57
8	104	8	57

*Problems marked with an asterisk (*) are more difficult.

10.* The buyers' side of the market for amusement park tickets consists of two consumers whose demands are as shown in the diagram below.
 a. Graph the market demand curve for this market.
 b. Calculate the total consumer surplus in the amusement park market if tickets sell for $12 each.

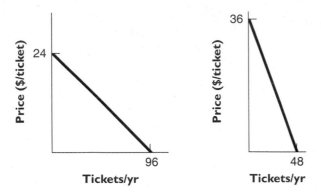

■ ANSWERS TO IN-CHAPTER EXERCISES ■

5.1 The combination of 300 pints per year of vanilla ($300) and 50 pints of chocolate ($100) costs a total of $400, which is exactly equal to Sarah's ice cream budget.

5.2 The rational spending rule requires $MU_F/P_F = MU_C/P_C$ where MU_F and MU_C are John's marginal utilities from food and clothing and P_F and P_C are the prices of food and clothing, respectively. At John's original combination, $MU_F/P_F = 4$ utils per dollar and $MU_C/P_C = 3$ utils per dollar. John should thus spend more of his income on food and less on clothing.

5.3 Adding the two individual demand curves, (a) and (b), horizontally yields the market demand curve (c):

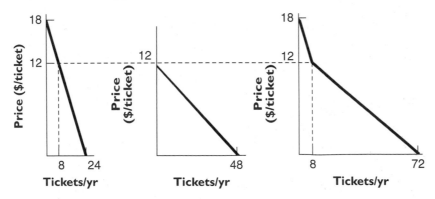

5.4 Consumer surplus is now the new shaded area, $28 per day.

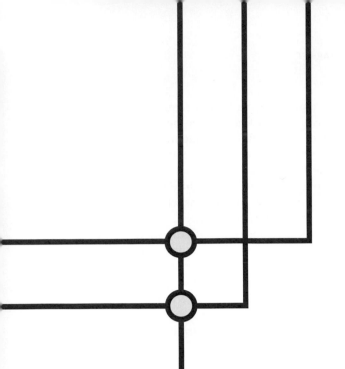

PERFECTLY COMPETITIVE SUPPLY: THE COST SIDE OF THE MARKET

■

Cars that took more than 50 hours to assemble in the 1970s are now built in less than 8 hours. Similar productivity growth has occurred in many other manufacturing industries. Yet in many service industries, productivity has grown only slowly, if at all. For example, the London Philharmonic Orchestra performs Beethoven's Fifth Symphony with no fewer musicians today than it did in 1850. And it still takes a barber about half an hour to cut someone's hair, just as it always has.

Given the spectacular growth in manufacturing workers' productivity, it is no surprise that their real wages have risen more than fivefold during the last century. But why have real wages for service workers risen just as much? If barbers and musicians are no more productive than they were at the turn of the century, why are they now paid five times as much?

An answer is suggested by the observation that the opportunity cost of pursuing any given occupation is the most one could have earned in some other occupation. Most people who become barbers or musicians could instead have chosen jobs in manufacturing. If workers in service industries were not paid roughly as much as they could have earned in other occupations, many of them would not have been willing to work in service industries in the first place.

The trajectories of wages in manufacturing and service industries illustrate the intimate link between the prices at which goods and services are offered for

Why are barbers paid five times as much now as in 1900, even though they can't cut hair any faster than they could then?

sale in the market and the opportunity cost of the resources required to produce them. Whereas our focus in the preceding chapter was on the buyer's side of the market, our focus here will be on sellers. Earlier, we saw that the demand curve is a schedule that tells how many units buyers wish to purchase at different prices. Our task here is to gain insight into the factors that shape the supply curve, the schedule that tells how many units suppliers wish to sell at different prices.

Although the demand side and the supply side of the market are different in several ways, many of these differences are superficial. Indeed, the behavior of both buyers and sellers is in an important sense fundamentally the same. After all, the two groups confront essentially similar questions—in the buyer's case, "Should I buy another unit?" and in the seller's, "Should I sell another unit?" What is more, buyers and sellers use the same criterion for answering these questions. Thus a rational consumer will buy another unit if its benefit exceeds its cost; and a rational seller will sell another unit if the cost of making it is less than the extra revenue he can get from selling it (the familiar cost-benefit principle again).

THINKING ABOUT SUPPLY: THE IMPORTANCE OF OPPORTUNITY COST

Do you live in a state that requires refundable soft drink container deposits? If so, you've probably noticed that some people always redeem their own containers while other people pass up this opportunity, leaving their used containers to be recycled by others. The recycling of used containers is a service, and its production obeys the same logic that applies to the production of other goods and services. As the following sequence of recycling examples makes clear, the supply curve for a good or service is rooted in the individual's choice of whether to produce it.

EXAMPLE 6.1

How much time should Harry spend recycling soft drink containers?

Harry is trying to decide how to divide his time between his job as a dishwasher in the dining hall, which pays $6 an hour for as many hours as he chooses to work, and gathering soft drink containers to redeem for deposit, in which case his pay depends on both the deposit per container and the number of containers he finds. Earnings aside, Harry is indifferent between the two tasks, and the number of containers he will find depends, as shown in the table below, on the number of hours per day he searches:

Search time (hours/day)	Total number of containers found	Additional number of containers found
0	0	
		600
1	600	
		400
2	1,000	
		300
3	1,300	
		200
4	1,500	
		100
5	1,600	

If the containers may be redeemed for 2 cents each, how many hours should Harry spend searching for containers?

For each additional hour Harry spends searching for soft drink containers, he loses the $6 he could have earned as a dishwasher. This is his hourly opportunity cost of searching for soft drink containers. His benefit from each hour spent searching for containers is the number of additional containers he finds (shown in column 3 of the table) times the deposit he collects per container. Since he can redeem each container for 2 cents, his first hour spent collecting containers will yield earnings of 600($0.02) = $12, or $6 more than he could have earned as a dishwasher.

By the cost-benefit principle, then, Harry should spend his first hour of work each day searching for soft drink containers rather than washing dishes. A second hour searching for containers will yield 400 additional containers, for additional earnings of $8, so it too satisfies the cost-benefit test. A third hour spent searching yields 300 additional containers, for 300($0.02) = $6 of additional earnings. Since this is exactly what Harry could have earned washing dishes, he is indifferent between spending his third hour of work each day on one task or the other. For the sake of discussion, however, we'll assume that he resolves ties in favor of searching for containers, in which case he will spend three hours each day searching for containers.

What is the lowest redemption price that would induce Harry to spend at least one hour per day recycling? Since he will find 600 containers in his first hour of search, a one-cent deposit on each container would enable him to match his $6 per hour opportunity cost. More generally, if the redemption price is p, and the next hour spent searching yields ΔQ additional containers, then Harry's additional earnings from searching the additional hour will be $p(\Delta Q)$. This means that the smallest redemption price that will lead Harry to search another hour must satisfy the equation

$$p(\Delta Q) = \$6. \tag{6.1}$$

How high would the redemption price of containers have to be to induce Harry to search for a second hour? Since he can find $\Delta Q = 400$ additional containers if he searches for a second hour, the smallest redemption price that will lead him to do so must satisfy $p(400) = \$6$, which solves for $p = 1.5$ cents.

EXERCISE 6.1

In Example 6.1, calculate the smallest container redemption prices that will lead Harry to search a third, fourth, and fifth hour.

By searching for soft drink containers, Harry becomes, in effect, a supplier of container-recycling services. In Exercise 6.1, we saw that Harry's reservation prices for his third, fourth, and fifth hours of container search are 2, 3, and 6 cents, respectively. Having calculated these reservation prices, we can now plot his supply curve of container-recycling services. This curve, which plots the redemption price per container on the vertical axis and the number of containers recycled each day on the horizontal axis, is shown in Figure 6.1. Harry's individual supply curve of container-recycling services tells us the number of containers he is willing to recycle at various redemption prices.

Like those we saw in Chapter 3, the supply curve shown in Figure 6.1 is upward-sloping. There are exceptions to this general rule, but sellers of most goods will offer higher quantities at higher prices than at lower prices.

The relationship between the individual and market supply curves for a product is analogous to the relationship between the individual and market demand curves. The quantity that corresponds to a given price on the market demand curve is the sum of the quantities demanded at that price by all individual buyers in the market. Likewise, the quantity that corresponds to any given price on the market supply curve is the sum of the quantities supplied at that price by all individual sellers in the market.

Suppose, for example, that the supply side of the recycling-services market consists only of Harry and his identical twin, Barry, whose individual supply curve is

FIGURE 6.1

An Individual Supply Curve for Recycling Services.

When the deposit price increases, it becomes attractive to abandon alternative pursuits to spend more time searching for soft drink containers.

the same as Harry's. To generate the market supply curve, we first put the individual supply curves side by side, as shown in Figure 6.2(a) and (b). We then announce a price, and for that price add the individual quantities supplied to obtain the total quantity supplied in the market. Thus, at a price of 3 cents per container, both Harry and Barry wish to recycle 1,500 cans per day, so the total market supply at that price is 3,000 cans per day. Proceeding in like manner for a sequence of prices, we generate the market supply curve for recycling services shown in Figure 6.2(c). This is the same process of horizontal summation by which we generated market demand curves from individual demand curves in Chapter 5.

FIGURE 6.2

The Market Supply Curve for Recycling Services.

To generate the market supply curve (c) from the individual supply curves (a) and (b), we add the individual supply curves horizontally.

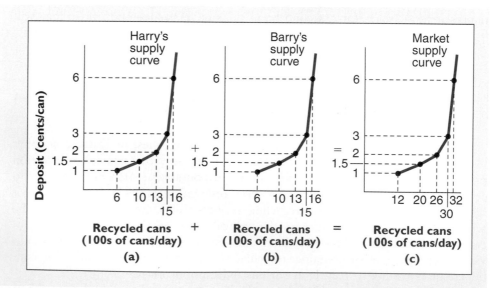

Alternatively, if there were many suppliers with individual supply curves identical to Harry's, we could generate the market supply curve by simply multiplying each quantity value on the individual supply curve by the number of suppliers. For instance, Figure 6.3 shows the supply curve for a market in which there are 1,000 suppliers with individual supply curves like Harry's.

Why do individual supply curves tend to be upward-sloping? One explanation is suggested by the principle of increasing opportunity cost, or low-hanging-fruit principle. Container recyclers should always look first for the containers that are easiest to find—such as those in plain view in readily accessible locations. As the redemption price rises, it will pay to incur the additional cost of searching farther from the beaten path.

If all individuals have identical upward-sloping supply curves, the market supply curve will be upward-sloping as well. But there is an important additional reason for the positive slope of market supply curves: Individual suppliers generally differ with respect to their opportunity costs of supplying the product. (The principle of increasing opportunity cost applies not only to each individual searcher, but also *across* individuals.) Thus, whereas people facing unattractive employment opportunities in other occupations may be willing to recycle soft drink containers even when the redemption price is low, those with more attractive options will recycle only if the redemption price is relatively high.

In summary, then, the upward slope of the supply schedule reflects the fact that costs tend to rise when producers expand production, partly because each individual exploits her most attractive opportunities first, but also because different potential sellers face different opportunity costs.

PROFIT-MAXIMIZING FIRMS IN PERFECTLY COMPETITIVE MARKETS

To explore the nature of the supply curve of a product more fully, we must say more about the goals of the organizations that supply the product and the kind of economic environment in which they operate. In virtually every economy, goods and services are produced by a variety of organizations that pursue a host of different motives. The Red Cross supplies blood because its organizers and donors want to help people in need; the local government fixes potholes because the mayor was elected on a promise to do so; karaoke singers perform because they like public attention; and car-wash employees are driven primarily by the hope of making enough money to pay their rent.

PROFIT MAXIMIZATION

Notwithstanding this rich variety of motives, *most* goods and services that are offered for sale in a market economy are sold by private firms whose main reason for existing is to earn **profit** for their owners. A firm's profit is the difference between the total revenue it receives from the sale of its product and all costs it incurs in producing it.

A **profit-maximizing firm** is one whose primary goal is to maximize the amount of profit it earns. The supply curves that economists use in standard supply and demand theory are based on the assumption that goods are sold by

profit the total revenue a firm receives from the sale of its product minus all costs— explicit and implicit—incurred in producing it

profit-maximizing firm a firm whose primary goal is to maximize the difference between its total revenues and total costs *perfectly competitive market* a market in which no individual supplier has significant influence on the market price of the product

price taker a firm that has no influence over the price at which it sells its product

profit-maximizing firms in **perfectly competitive markets,** which are markets in which individual firms have no influence over the market prices of the products they sell. Because of their inability to influence market price, perfectly competitive firms are often described as **price takers.**

The following four conditions are often taken to be characteristic of markets that are perfectly competitive:

1. **All firms sell the same standardized product.** Although this condition is almost never literally satisfied, it holds as a rough approximation for many markets. Thus the markets for concrete building blocks of a given size, or for apples of a given variety, may be described in this way. This condition implies that buyers are willing to switch from one seller to another if by so doing they can obtain a lower price.

2. **The market has many buyers and sellers, each of which buys or sells only a small fraction of the total quantity exchanged.** This condition implies that individual buyers and sellers will be price takers, regarding the market price of the product as a fixed number beyond their control. For example, a single farmer's decision to plant fewer acres of wheat would have no appreciable impact on the market price of wheat, just as an individual consumer's decision to become a vegetarian would have no perceptible effect on the price of beef.

3. **Productive resources are mobile.** This condition implies that if a potential seller identifies a profitable business opportunity in a market, he or she will be able to obtain the labor, capital, and other productive resources necessary to enter that market. By the same token, sellers who are dissatisfied with the opportunities they confront in a given market are free to leave that market and employ their resources elsewhere.

4. **Buyers and sellers are well informed.** This condition implies that buyers and sellers are aware of the relevant opportunities available to them. If that were not so, buyers would be unable to seek out sellers who charge the lowest prices, and sellers would have no means of deploying their resources in the markets in which they would earn the most.

The market for wheat closely approximates a perfectly competitive market. The market for operating systems for desktop computers, however, does not. More than 90 percent of desktop operating systems are sold by Microsoft, giving the company enough influence in that market to have significant control over the price it charges. For example, if it were to raise the price of its latest edition of Windows by, say, 20 percent, some consumers might switch to Macintosh or Linux, and others might postpone their next upgrade; but many—perhaps even most—would continue with their plans to buy.

By contrast, if an individual wheat farmer were to charge even just 10 cents more than the current market price for a bushel of wheat, he wouldn't be able to sell any of his wheat at all. And since he can sell as much wheat as he wishes at the market price, he has no motive to charge less.

THE DEMAND CURVE FACING A PERFECTLY COMPETITIVE FIRM

From the perspective of individual firm in a perfectly competitive market, what does the demand curve for its product look like? Since it can sell as much or as little as it wishes at the prevailing market price, the demand curve for its product is perfectly elastic at the market price. Figure 6.4(a) shows the market demand and supply curves intersecting to determine a market price of P_0. Figure 6.4(b) shows the product demand curve, D_i, as seen by any individual firm in this market, a horizontal line at the price market price level P_0.

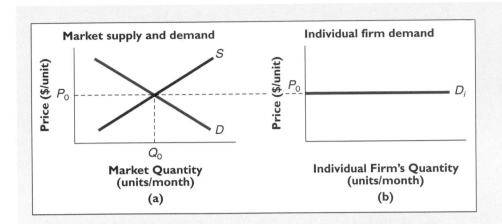

FIGURE 6.4
The Demand Curve Facing a Perfectly Competitive Firm.
The market demand and supply curves intersect to determine the market price of the product (a). The individual firm's demand curve, D_i (b), is a horizontal line at the market price.

Many of the conclusions of the standard supply and demand model also hold for **imperfectly competitive firms**—those firms, like Microsoft, that have at least some ability to vary their own prices. But certain other conclusions do not, as we shall see when we examine the behavior of such firms more closely in Chapter 9.

Since a perfectly competitive firm has no control over the market price of its product, it needn't worry about choosing the level at which to set that price. As we've seen, the equilibrium market price in a competitive market comes from the intersection of the industry supply and demand curves. The challenge confronting the perfectly competitive firm is to choose its output level so that it makes as much profit as it can at that price. As we investigate how the competitive firm responds to this challenge, we'll see once again the pivotal role of our core principle that some costs are more important than others.

imperfectly competitive firm a firm that has at least some control over the market price of its product

PRODUCTION IN THE SHORT RUN

To gain a deeper understanding of the origins of the supply curve, it is helpful to consider a perfectly competitive firm confronting the decision of how much to produce. The firm in question is a small company that makes glass bottles. To keep things simple, suppose that the silica required for making bottles is available free of charge from a nearby desert, and that the only costs incurred by the firm are the wages it pays its employees and the lease payment on its bottle-making machine. The employees and the machine are the firm's only two **factors of production**—inputs used to produce goods and services. In more complex examples, factors of production might also include land, structures, entrepreneurship, and possibly others, but for the moment we consider only labor and capital.

When we refer to the **short run**, we mean a period of time during which at least some of the firm's factors of production cannot be varied. For our bottle maker, we will assume that the number of employees can be varied on short notice but that the capacity of its bottle-making machine can be altered only with significant delay. For this firm, then, the short run is simply that period of time during which the firm cannot alter the capacity of its bottle-making machine. By contrast, when we speak of the **long run**, we refer to a time period of sufficient length that all the firm's factors of production are variable.

Table 6.1 shows how the company's bottle production depends on the number of hours its employees spend on the job each day. The output–employment relationship described in Table 6.1 exhibits a pattern that is common to many such relationships. Each time we add an additional unit of labor, output grows, but beyond some point the additional output that results from each additional unit of labor begins to diminish. Note in the right column, for example, that output gains begin to diminish with the third employee. Economists refer to this pattern as the

factor of production an input used in the production of a good or service

short run a period of time sufficiently short that at least some of the firm's factors of production are fixed

long run a period of time of sufficient length that all the firm's factors of production are variable

TABLE 6.1
Employment and Output for a Glass Bottle Maker

Total number of employees per day	Total number of bottles per day
0	0
1	80
2	200
3	260
4	300
5	330
6	350
7	362

law of diminishing returns a property of the relationship between the amount of a good or service produced and the amount of a variable factor required to produce it; it says that when some factors of production are fixed, increased production of the good eventually requires ever-larger increases in the variable factor

fixed factor of production an input whose quantity cannot be altered in the short run

variable factor of production an input whose quantity can be altered in the short run

fixed cost the sum of all payments made to the firm's fixed factors of production

law of diminishing returns, and it always refers to situations in which at least some factors of production are fixed. Here, the **fixed factor** is the bottle-making machine, and the **variable factor** is labor. In the context of this example, the law of diminishing returns says simply that successive increases in the labor input eventually yield smaller and smaller increments in bottle output. (Strictly speaking, the law ought to be called the law of *eventually* diminishing returns, because output may initially grow at an increasing rate with additional units of the variable factor.)

Typically, returns from additional units of the variable input eventually diminish because of some form of congestion. For instance, in an office with three secretaries and only a single desktop computer, we would not expect to get three times as many letters typed per hour as in an office with only one secretary, because only one person can use a computer at a time.

SOME IMPORTANT COST CONCEPTS

For the bottle-making firm described in Table 6.1, suppose the lease payment for the company's bottle-making machine is $40 per day, which must be paid whether the company makes any bottles or not. This payment is both a **fixed cost** (since it does not depend on the number of bottles per day the firm makes) and, for the duration of the lease, a sunk cost. The first two columns of Table 6.2

TABLE 6.2
Fixed, Variable, and Total Costs of Bottle Production

Employees per day	Bottles per day	Fixed cost ($/day)	Variable cost ($/day)	Total cost ($/day)	Marginal cost ($/bottle)
0	0	40	0	40	
					0.15
1	80	40	12	52	
					0.10
2	200	40	24	64	
					0.20
3	260	40	36	76	
					0.33
4	300	40	48	88	
					0.40
5	330	40	60	100	
					0.60
6	350	40	72	112	
					1.00
7	362	40	84	124	

reproduce the employment and output entries from Table 6.1, and the firm's fixed cost appears in column 3.

The company's payment to its employees is called **variable cost,** because unlike fixed cost, it varies with the number of bottles the company produces. The variable cost of producing 200 bottles per day, for example, is shown in column 4 of Table 6.2 as $24 per day. Column 5 shows the firm's **total cost,** which is the sum of its fixed and variable costs. Column 6, finally, shows the firm's **marginal cost,** a measure of how its total cost changes when its output changes. Specifically, marginal cost is defined as the change in total cost divided by the corresponding change in output. Note, for example, that when the firm expands production from 80 to 200 bottles per day, its total cost goes up by $12, which gives rise to the marginal cost entry of ($12/day)/(120 bottles/day) = $0.10 per bottle. To emphasize that marginal cost refers to the change in total cost when quantity changes, we place the marginal cost entries between the corresponding quantity rows of the table.

variable cost the sum of all payments made to the firm's variable factors of production

total cost the sum of all payments made to the firm's fixed and variable factors of production

marginal cost as output changes from one level to another, the change in total cost divided by the corresponding change in output

CHOOSING OUTPUT TO MAXIMIZE PROFIT

In the following examples and exercises, we'll explore how the company's decision about how many bottles to produce depends on the price of bottles, the wage, and the cost of capital.

If bottles sell for 35 cents each, how many bottles should the company described in Table 6.2 produce each day?

EXAMPLE 6.2

To answer this question, we need simply apply the cost-benefit principle to the question "Should the firm expand its level of output?" If its goal is to maximize its profit, the answer to this question will be to expand as long as the marginal benefit from expanding is at least as great as the marginal cost. Since the perfectly competitive firm can sell as many bottles as it wishes at the market price of $0.35 per bottle, its marginal benefit from selling an additional bottle is $0.35. If we compare this marginal benefit with the marginal cost entries shown in column 6 of Table 6.2, we see that the firm should keep expanding until it reaches 300 bottles per day (4 employees per day). To expand beyond that level it would have to hire a fifth employee, and the resulting marginal cost ($0.40 per bottle) would exceed the marginal benefit.

To confirm that the cost-benefit principle thus applied identifies the profit-maximizing number of bottles to produce, we can calculate profit levels directly, as in Table 6.3. Column 3 of this table reports the firm's revenue from the sale of bottles, which is calculated as the product of the number of bottles produced

TABLE 6.3
Output, Revenue, Costs, and Profit

Employees per day	Output (bottles/day)	Total revenue ($/day)	Total cost ($/day)	Profit ($/day)
0	0	0	40	−40
1	80	28	52	−24
2	200	70	64	6
3	260	91	76	15
4	300	105	88	17
5	330	115.50	100	15.50
6	350	122.50	112	10.50
7	362	126.70	124	2.70

per day and the price of $0.35 per bottle. Note, for example, that in the third row of that column total revenue is (200 bottles/day)($0.35/bottle) = $70 per day. Column 5 reports the firm's total daily profit, which is just the difference between its total revenue (column 3) and its total cost (column 4). Note that the largest profit entry in column 5, $17 per day, occurs at an output of 300 bottles per day, just as suggested by our earlier application of the cost-benefit principle.

As the following exercise demonstrates, an increase in the price of the product gives rise to an increase in the profit-maximizing level of output.

EXERCISE 6.2

Same as Example 6.2, except now bottles sell for 62 cents each.

The following exercise illustrates that a fall in the wage rate leads to a decline in marginal cost, which also causes an increase in the profit-maximizing level of output.

EXERCISE 6.3

Same as Example 6.2, except now employees receive a wage of $6 per day.

Suppose that in Example 6.2 the firm's fixed cost had been not $40 per day but $45 per day. How, if at all, would that have affected the firm's profit-maximizing level of output? The answer is "not at all." Each entry in the profit column of Table 6.3 would have been $5 per day smaller than before, but the maximum profit entry still would have been 300 bottles per day.

The observation that the profit-maximizing quantity does not depend on fixed costs is not an idiosyncrasy of this example. That it holds true in general is an immediate consequence of the cost-benefit principle, which says that a firm should increase its output if, and only if, the *marginal* benefit exceeds the *marginal* cost. Neither the marginal benefit of expanding (which is the market price of bottles) nor the marginal cost of expanding is affected by a change in the firm's fixed cost.

When the law of diminishing returns applies (that is, when some factors of production are fixed), marginal cost goes up as the firm expands production beyond some point. Under these circumstances, the firm's best option is to keep expanding output as long as marginal cost is less than price.

Note in Example 6.2 that if the company's fixed cost had been any more than $57 per day, it would have made a loss at *every* possible level of output. As long as it still had to pay its fixed cost, however, its best bet would have been to continue producing 300 bottles per day. It is better, after all, to experience a smaller loss than a larger one. If a firm in that situation expected conditions to remain the same, though, it would want to get out of the bottle business as soon as its equipment lease expired.

A NOTE ON THE FIRM'S SHUTDOWN CONDITION

It might seem that a firm that can sell as much output as it wishes at a constant market price would *always* do best in the short run by producing and selling the output level for which price equals marginal cost. But there are exceptions to this rule. Suppose, for example, that the market price of the firm's product falls so low that its revenue from sales is smaller than its variable cost at all possible levels of output. The firm should then cease production for the time being. By shutting down, it will suffer a loss equal to its fixed costs. But by remaining open, it would suffer an even larger loss.

More formally, if P denotes the market price of the product and Q denotes the number of units produced and sold, then $P \times Q$ is the firm's total revenue from sales, and if we use VC to denote the firm's variable cost, the rule is that the firm should shut down in the short run if $P \times Q$ is less than VC for every level of Q:

Short-run shutdown condition: $P \times Q < VC$ for all levels of Q.

EXERCISE 6.4

In Example 6.2, suppose bottles sold not for $0.35 but only $0.10. Calculate the profit corresponding to each level of output, as in Table 6.3, and verify that the firm's best option is to cease operations in the short run.

AVERAGE VARIABLE COST AND AVERAGE TOTAL COST

Suppose that the firm is unable to cover its variable cost at any level of output—that is, suppose that $P \times Q < VC$ for all levels of Q. It must then also be true that $P < VC/Q$ for all levels of Q, since we obtain the second inequality by simply dividing both sides of the first one by Q. VC/Q is the firm's **average variable cost**—its variable cost divided by its output. The firm's short-run shutdown condition may thus be restated a second way: Discontinue operations in the short run if the product price is less than the minimum value of its average variable cost (AVC). Thus

average variable cost (AVC) variable cost divided by total output

Short-run shutdown condition (alternate version): $P < $ minimum value of AVC.

As we'll see in the next section, this version of the shutdown condition often enables us to tell at a glance whether the firm should continue operations.

A related cost concept that facilitates assessment of the firm's profitability is **average total cost** (ATC), which is total cost (TC) divided by output (Q): $ATC = TC/Q$. The firm's profit, again, is the difference between its total revenue ($P \times Q$) and its total cost. And since total cost is equal to average total cost times quantity, the firm's profit is also equal to $(P \times Q) - (ATC \times Q)$. A firm is said to be **profitable** if its revenue ($P \times Q$) exceeds its total cost ($ATC \times Q$). A firm can thus be profitable only if the price of its product price (P) exceeds its ATC for some level of output.

average total cost (ATC) total cost divided by total output

profitable firm a firm whose total revenue exceeds its total cost

Keeping track of all these cost concepts may seem tedious. In the next section, however, we will see that the payoff from doing so is that they enable us to recast the profit-maximization decision in a simple graphical framework.

A GRAPHICAL APPROACH TO PROFIT MAXIMIZATION

For the bottle-making firm we have been discussing, average variable cost and average total cost values are shown in columns 4 and 6 of Table 6.4. Using the entries in this table, we plot the firm's average total cost, average variable cost, and marginal cost curves in Figure 6.5. (Because marginal cost corresponds to the change in total cost as we move between two output levels, each marginal cost value in Table 6.4 is plotted at an output level midway between those in the adjacent rows.)

We call your attention to several features of the cost curves in Figure 6.5. Note, for example, that the upward-sloping portion of the marginal cost curve (MC) corresponds to the region of diminishing returns discussed earlier. Thus, as the firm moves beyond two employees per day (200 bottles per day), the increments to total output become smaller with each additional employee, which means that the cost of producing additional bottles (MC) must be increasing in this region.

TABLE 6.4

Average Variable Cost and Average Total Cost of Bottle Production

Employees per day	Bottles per day	Variable cost ($/day)	Average variable cost ($/unit of output)	Total cost ($/day)	Average total cost ($/unit of output)	Marginal cost ($/bottle)
0	0	0		40		
						0.15
1	80	12	0.15	52	0.65	
						0.10
2	200	24	0.12	64	0.32	
						0.20
3	260	36	0.138	76	0.292	
						0.33
4	300	48	0.16	88	0.293	
						0.40
5	330	60	0.182	100	0.303	
						0.60
6	350	72	0.206	112	0.32	
						1.00
7	362	84	0.232	124	0.343	

FIGURE 6.5

The Marginal, Average Variable, and Average Total Cost Curves for a Bottle Manufacturer.
The MC curve cuts both the AVC and ATC curves at their minimum points. The upward-sloping portion of the marginal cost curve corresponds to the region of diminishing returns.

Note also that the definition of marginal cost implies that the marginal cost curve must intersect both the average variable cost curve (*AVC*) and the average total cost curve (*ATC*) at their respective minimum points. To see why, consider the logic that explains what happens to the average weight of children in a third-grade class when a new student joins the class. If the new (marginal) student is lighter than the previous average weight for the class, average weight will fall, but if the new student is heavier than the previous average, average weight will rise. By the same token, when marginal cost is below average total cost or average variable cost, the corresponding average cost must be falling, and vice versa. And this ensures that the marginal cost curve must pass through the minimum points of both average cost curves.

Seeing the bottle maker's *AVC* curve displayed graphically makes the question posed in Exercise 6.4 much easier to answer. The question, recall, was whether the firm should shut down in the short run if the price of bottle was only $0.10. A glance at Figure 6.5 reveals that the firm should indeed shut down, because this price lies below the minimum value of its *AVC* curve, making it impossible for the firm to cover its variable costs at any output level.

PRICE = MARGINAL COST: THE MAXIMUM-PROFIT CONDITION

In Example 6.2, we implicitly assumed that the bottle maker could employ workers only in whole-number amounts. Under these conditions, we saw that the profit-maximizing output level was one for which marginal cost was somewhat less than price (because adding yet another employee would have pushed marginal cost higher than price). In the next example, we will see that when output and employment can be varied continuously, the maximum-profit condition is that price be equal to marginal cost.

For the bottle maker whose cost curves are shown in Figure 6.6, find the profit-maximizing output level if bottles sell for $0.20 each. How much profit will this firm earn? What is the lowest price at which this firm would continue to operate in the short run?

EXAMPLE 6.3

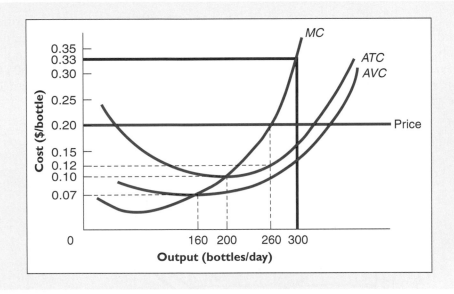

FIGURE 6.6
Price = Marginal Cost: The Perfectly Competitive Firm's Profit-Maximizing Supply Rule.
If price is greater than marginal cost, the firm can increase its profit by expanding production and sales. If price is less than marginal cost, the firm can increase its profit by producing and selling less output.

The cost-benefit principle tells us that this firm should continue to expand as long as price is at least as great as marginal cost. In Figure 6.6 we see that we see that if the firm follows this rule, it will produce 260 bottles per day, the quantity at which price and marginal cost are equal. To gain further confidence that 260 must be the profit-maximizing quantity when the price is $0.20 per bottle, first suppose that the firm had sold some amount less than that—say, only 200 bottles per day. Its benefit from expanding output by one bottle would then be the bottle's market price, here 20 cents. The cost of expanding output by one bottle is equal (by definition) to the firm's marginal cost, which at 200 bottles per day is only 10 cents (see Figure 6.6). So by selling the 201st bottle for 20 cents and producing it for an extra cost of only 10 cents, the firm will increase its profit by 20 − 10 = 10 cents per day. In a similar way, we can show that for *any* quantity less than the level at which price equals marginal cost, the seller can boost profit by expanding production.

Conversely, suppose that the firm was currently selling more than 260 bottles per day—say, 300—at a price of 20 cents each. In Figure 6.6 we see that marginal cost at an output of 300 is 33 cents per bottle. If the firm then contracted its output by one bottle per day, it would cut its costs by 33 cents while losing only 20 cents in revenue. As a result, its profit would grow by 13 cents per day. The same argument can be made regarding any quantity larger than 260, so if the firm is currently selling an output at which price is less than marginal cost, it can always do better by producing and selling fewer bottles.

We have thus established that if the firm sold fewer than 260 bottles per day, it could earn more profit by expanding; and if it sold more than 260, it could earn more by contracting. It follows that at a market price of 20 cents per bottle, the seller maximizes its profit by selling 260 units per week, the quantity for which price and marginal cost are exactly the same.

At that quantity the firm will collect total revenue of $P \times Q = (\$0.20/\text{bottle})$ (260 bottles/day) = \$52 per day. Note in Figure 6.6 that at 260 bottles per day the firm's average total cost is $ATC = \$0.12$ per bottle, which means that its total cost is $ATC \times Q = (\$0.12/\text{bottle})$(260 bottles/day) = \$31.20 per day. The firm's profit is the difference between its total revenue and its total cost, or \$20.80 per day. Note, finally, that the minimum value of the firm's AVC curve is \$0.07. So if the price of bottles fell below 7 cents each, the firm would shut down in the short run.

Another attractive feature of the graphical method of finding the profit-maximizing output level is that it permits us to calculate the firm's profit graphically. Thus, for the firm in the preceding example, daily profit is simply the difference between price and ATC times the number of units sold: ($\$0.20/\text{bottle} - \$0.12/\text{bottle}$)(260 bottles/day) = \$20.80 per day, which is the area of the shaded rectangle in Figure 6.7.

FIGURE 6.7
Measuring Profit Graphically.
Profit is equal to $(P - ATC) \times Q$, which is equal to the area of the shaded rectangle.

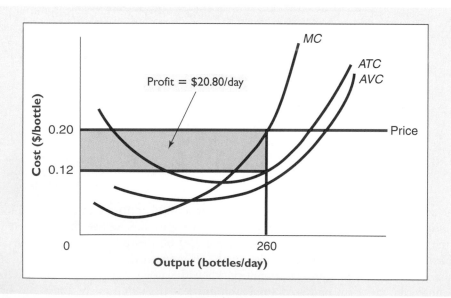

Not all firms are as fortunate as the one shown in Figure 6.7. Suppose, for example, that the price of bottles had been not 20 cents but only 8 cents. Since that price is greater than the minimum value of AVC (see Figure 6.8), the firm should continue to operate in the short run by producing the level of output for which price equals marginal cost (180 bottles per day). But because price is less than ATC at that level of output, the firm will now experience a loss, or negative profit, on its operations. This profit is calculated as $(P - ATC) \times Q = (\$0.08/\text{bottle} - \$0.10/\text{bottle}) \times (180 \text{ bottles/day}) = -\$3.60$ per day, which is equal to the area of the shaded rectangle in Figure 6.8.

In Chapter 8, we will see how firms move resources in response to the incentives implicit in profits and losses. But such movements occur in the long run, and our focus here is on production decisions in the short run.

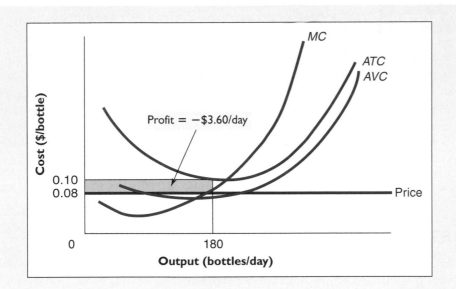

FIGURE 6.8
A Negative Profit.
When price is less than *ATC* at the profit-maximizing quantity, the firm experiences a loss, which is equal to the area of the shaded rectangle.

THE "LAW" OF SUPPLY

The law of demand tells us that consumers buy less of a product when its price rises. If there were an analogous law of supply, it would say that producers offer more of a product for sale when its price rises. Is there such a law? We know that supply curves are essentially marginal cost curves, and that because of the law of diminishing returns, marginal cost curves are upward-sloping in the short run. And so there is indeed a law of supply that applies as stated in the short run.

In the long run, however, the law of diminishing returns does not apply. (Recall that it holds only if at least some factors of production are fixed.) Because firms can vary the amounts of *all* factors of production they use in the long run, they can often double their production by simply doubling the amount of each input they use. In such cases costs would be exactly proportional to output, and the firm's marginal cost curve in the long run would be horizontal, not upward-sloping. So for now we'll say only that the "law" of supply holds as stated in the short run but not necessarily in the long run. For both the long run and the short run, however, *the perfectly competitive firm's supply curve is its marginal cost curve.*[1]

Every quantity of output along the market supply curve represents the summation of all the quantities individual sellers offer at the corresponding price. So the correspondence between price and marginal cost exists for the market supply curve as well as for the individual supply curves that lie behind it. That is, *for every price–quantity pair along the market supply curve, price will be equal to each seller's marginal cost of production.*

This is why we sometimes say that the supply curve represents the cost side of the market, whereas the demand curve represents the benefit side of the market. At every point along a market demand curve, price represents what buyers would be willing to pay for an additional unit of the product—and this, in turn, is how we measure the amount by which they would benefit by having an additional unit of the product. Likewise, at every point along a market supply curve, price measures what it would cost producers to expand production by one unit.

---

[1]Again, this rule holds subject to the provision that total revenue exceed variable production cost at the output level for which price equals marginal cost.

RECAP **THE COMPETITIVE FIRM'S SUPPLY CURVE**

The perfectly competitive firm faces a horizontal demand curve for its product, meaning that it can sell any quantity it wishes at the market price. In the short run, the firm's goal is to choose the level of output that maximizes its profits. It will accomplish this by choosing the output level for which its marginal cost is equal to the market price of its product, provided that price exceeds average variable cost. The perfectly competitive firm's supply curve is the portion of its marginal cost curve that lies above its average variable cost curve. At the profit-maximizing quantity, the firm's profit is the product of that quantity and the difference between price and average total cost.

DETERMINANTS OF SUPPLY REVISITED

What factors give rise to changes in supply? (Again, remember that a "change in supply" refers to a shift in the entire supply curve, as opposed to a movement along the curve, which we call a "change in the quantity supplied.") A seller will offer more units if the benefit of selling extra output goes up relative to the cost of producing it. And since the benefit of selling output in a perfectly competitive market is a fixed market price that is beyond the seller's control, our search for factors that influence supply naturally focuses on the cost side of the calculation. The preceding examples suggest why the following factors, among others, will affect the likelihood that a product will satisfy the cost-benefit test for a given supplier.

TECHNOLOGY

Perhaps the most important determinant of production cost is technology. Improvements in technology make it possible to produce additional units of output at lower cost. This shifts each individual supply curve downward (or, equivalently, outward) and hence shifts the market supply curve downward as well. Over time, the introduction of more sophisticated machinery has resulted in dramatic increases in the number of goods produced per hour of effort expended. Every such development gives rise to an outward shift in the market supply curve.

But how do we know technological change will reduce the cost of producing goods and services? Might not new equipment be so expensive that producers who used it would have higher costs than those who relied on earlier designs? If so, then rational producers simply would not use the new equipment. The only technological changes that rational producers will adopt are those that will reduce their cost of production.

INPUT PRICES

Whereas technological change generally (although not always) leads to gradual shifts in supply, changes in the prices of important inputs can give rise to large supply shifts literally overnight. As discussed in Chapter 4, for example, the price of crude oil, which is the most important input in the production of gasoline, often fluctuates sharply, and the resulting shifts in supply cause gasoline prices to exhibit corresponding fluctuations.

Similarly, when wage rates rise, the marginal cost of any business that employs labor also rises, shifting supply curves to the left (or, equivalently, upward). When interest rates fall, the opportunity cost of capital equipment also falls, causing supply to shift to the right.

THE NUMBER OF SUPPLIERS

Just as demand curves shift to the right when population grows, supply curves also shift to the right as the number of individual suppliers grows. For example, if container recyclers die or retire at a higher rate than new recyclers enter the industry, the supply curve for recycling services will shift to the left. Conversely, if a rise in the unemployment rate leads more people to recycle soft drink containers (by reducing the opportunity cost of time spent recycling), the supply curve of recycling services will shift to the right.

EXPECTATIONS

Expectations about future price movements can affect how much sellers choose to offer in the current market. Suppose, for example, that recyclers expect the future price of aluminum to be much higher than the current price because of growing use of aluminum components in cars. The rational recycler would then have an incentive to withhold aluminum from the market at today's lower price, thereby to have more available to sell at the higher future price. Conversely, if recyclers expected next year's price of aluminum to be lower than this year's, their incentive would be to offer more aluminum for sale in today's market.

CHANGES IN PRICES OF OTHER PRODUCTS

Apart from technological change, perhaps the most important determinant of supply is variation in the prices of other goods and services that sellers might produce. Prospectors, for example, search for those precious metals for which the surplus of benefits over costs is greatest. When the price of silver rises, many stop looking for gold and start looking for silver. Conversely, when the price of platinum falls, many platinum prospectors shift their attention to gold.

RECAP   THE DETERMINANTS OF SUPPLY

Among the relevant factors causing supply curves to shift are new technologies, changes in input prices, changes in the number of sellers, expectations of future price changes, and changes in the prices of other products that firms might produce.

APPLYING THE THEORY OF SUPPLY

Whether the activity is producing new soft drink containers or recycling used ones, or indeed any other production activity at all, the same logic governs all supply decisions in perfectly competitive markets (and in any other setting in which sellers can sell as much as they wish to at a constant price): Keep expanding output until marginal cost is equal to the price of the product. This logic helps us understand why recycling efforts are more intensive for some products than others.

When recycling is left to private market forces, why are many more aluminum beverage containers recycled than glass ones?

In both cases, recyclers gather containers until their marginal costs are equal to the containers' respective redemption prices. When recycling is left to market forces, the redemption price for a container is based on what companies can sell it (or the materials in it) for. Aluminum containers can be easily processed into scrap aluminum, which commands a high price, and this leads profit-seeking companies to offer a high redemption price for aluminum cans. By contrast, the

**ECONOMIC
NATURALIST
6.1**

glass from which glass containers are made has only limited resale value, primarily because the raw materials required to make new glass are so cheap. This difference leads profit-seeking companies to offer much lower redemption prices for glass containers than for aluminum ones.

The high redemption prices for aluminum cans induce many people to track these cans down, whereas the low redemption prices for glass containers leads most people to ignore them. If recycling is left completely to market forces, then, we would expect to see aluminum soft drink containers quickly recycled, whereas glass containers would increasingly litter the landscape. This is in fact the pattern we do see in states without recycling laws. (More on how these laws work in a moment.) This pattern is a simple consequence of the fact that the supply curves of container-recycling services are upward-sloping.

The acquisition of valuable raw materials is only one of two important benefits from recycling. The second is that, by removing litter, recycling makes the environment more pleasant for everyone. As the next example suggests, this second benefit might easily justify the cost of recycling substantial numbers of glass containers.

EXAMPLE 6.4

What is the socially optimal amount of recycling of glass containers?

Suppose that the 60,000 citizens of Burlington, Vermont, would collectively be willing to pay 6 cents for each glass container removed from their local environment. If the local market supply curve of glass container–recycling services is as shown in Figure 6.9, what is the socially optimal level of glass container recycling?

FIGURE 6.9
The Supply Curve of Container Recycling Services for Burlington, Vermont.

Suppose the citizens of Burlington authorize their city government to collect tax money to finance litter removal. If the benefit of each glass container removed, as measured by what residents are collectively willing to pay, is 6 cents, the government should offer to pay 6 cents for each glass container recycled. To maximize the total economic surplus from recycling, we should recycle that number of containers for which the marginal cost of recycling is equal to the 6-cent marginal benefit. Given the market supply curve shown, the optimal quantity is 16,000 containers per day, and that is how many will be redeemed when the government offers 6 cents per container.

Although 16,000 containers per day will be removed from the environment in the preceding example, others will remain. After all, some are discarded in remote locations, and a redemption price of 6 cents per container is simply not high enough to induce people to track them all down.

So why not offer an even higher price, and get rid of *all* glass container litter? For the example given, the reason is that the marginal cost of removing the 16,001st glass container each day is greater than the benefit of removing it. Total economic surplus is largest when we remove litter only up to the point that the marginal benefit of litter removal is equal to its marginal cost, which occurs when 16,000 containers per day are recycled. To proceed past that point is actually wasteful.

Many people become upset when they first hear economists say that the socially optimal amount of litter is greater than zero. In the minds of these people, the optimal amount of litter is *exactly* zero. But this position completely ignores the scarcity principle. Granted, there would be benefits from reducing litter further, but there would also be costs. Spending more on litter removal therefore means spending less on other useful things. No one would insist that the optimal amount of dirt in his own home is zero. (If someone does make this claim, ask him why he doesn't stay home all day vacuuming the dust that is accumulating in his absence.) If it doesn't pay to remove all the dust from your house, it doesn't pay to remove all the bottles from the environment. Precisely the same logic applies in each case.

Is the socially optimal quantity of litter zero?

If 16,000 containers per day is the optimal amount of litter removal, can we expect the individual spending decisions of private citizens to result in that amount of litter removal? Unfortunately we cannot. The problem is that anyone who paid for litter removal individually would bear the full cost of those services while reaping only a tiny fraction of the benefit. In the previous example, the 60,000 citizens of Burlington reaped a total benefit of 6 cents per container removed, which means a benefit of only (6/60,000) = 0.0001 cent per person! Someone who paid 6 cents for someone else to remove a container would thus be incurring a cost 60,000 times greater than his share of the resulting benefit.

Note that the incentive problem here is similar to the one discussed in Chapter 3 for the person deciding whether to be vaccinated against an illness. The problem was that the incentive to be vaccinated was too weak, because even though the patient bears the full cost of the vaccination, many of the resulting benefits accrue to others. Thus an important part of the extra benefit from any one person being vaccinated is that others also become less likely to contract the illness.

In the case of glass container litter, in short, we have an example in which private market forces do not produce the best attainable outcome for society as a whole. Even people who carelessly toss containers on the ground, rather than recycle them, are often offended by the unsightly landscape to which their own actions contribute. Indeed, this is why they often support laws mandating adequate redemption prices for glass containers.

Activities that generate litter are a good illustration of the equilibrium principle described in Chapter 3 (also called, for reasons this example makes clear, the smart-for-one, dumb-for-all principle). People who litter do so not because they don't care about the environment, but because their private incentives make littering misleadingly attractive. Recycling requires some effort, after all, yet no individual's recycling efforts have a noticeable effect on the quality of the environment. The soft-drink-container deposit laws enacted by numerous states were a simple way to bring individual interests more closely into balance with the interests of society as a whole. The vast majority of container litter disappeared almost literally overnight in states that enacted these laws.

EXERCISE 6.5

If the supply curve of glass container–recycling services is as shown in the diagram, and each of the city's 60,000 citizens would be willing to pay 0.00005 cents for each glass container removed from the landscape, at what level should the city government set the redemption price for glass containers, and how many will be recycled each day?

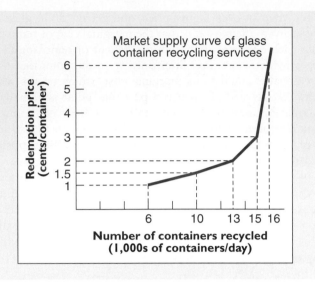

SUPPLY AND PRODUCER SURPLUS

producer surplus the amount by which price exceeds the seller's reservation price

The economic surplus received by a buyer is called consumer surplus. The analogous construct for a seller is **producer surplus,** the difference between the price a seller actually receives for the product and the lowest price for which she would have been willing to sell it (her reservation price, which in general will be her marginal cost).

As in the case of consumer surplus, the term producer surplus sometimes refers to the surplus received by a single seller in a transaction, while on other occasions it describes the total surplus received by all sellers in a market or collection of markets.

CALCULATING PRODUCER SURPLUS

In the preceding chapter we saw that consumer surplus in a market is the area bounded above by the demand curve and bounded below by the market price. Producer surplus in a market is calculated in an analogous way. As the following example illustrates, it is the area bounded above by the market price and bounded below by the market supply curve.

EXAMPLE 6.5

How much do sellers benefit from their participation in the market for milk?

Consider the market for milk whose demand and supply curves are shown in Figure 6.10, which has an equilibrium price of $2 per gallon and an equilibrium

FIGURE 6.10

Supply and Demand in the Market for Milk.

For the supply and demand curves shown, the equilibrium price of milk is $2 per gallon and the equilibrium quantity is 4,000 gallons per day.

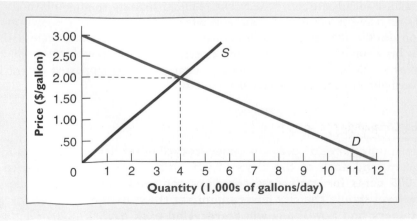

quantity of 4,000 gallons per day. How much producer surplus do the sellers in this market reap?

In Figure 6.10, note first that for all milk sold up to 4,000 gallons per day, sellers receive a surplus equal to the difference between the market price of $2 per gallon and their reservation price as given by the supply curve. Total producer surplus received by buyers in the milk market is thus the shaded triangle between the supply curve and the market price in Figure 6.11. Note that this area is a right triangle whose vertical arm is $b = \$2$/gallon and whose horizontal arm is $b = 4,000$ gallons/day. And since the area of any triangle is equal to $(1/2)bh$, producer surplus in this market is equal to

$$(1/2)(4,000 \text{ gallons/day})(\$2/\text{gallon}) = \$4,000/\text{day}.$$

FIGURE 6.11
Producer Surplus in the Market for Milk.
Producer surplus is the area of the shaded triangle ($4,000/day).

Producer surplus in this example may be thought of as the highest price sellers would pay, in the aggregate, for the right to continue participating in the milk market. It is $4,000 per day, since that is the amount by which their combined benefits exceed their combined costs.

As discussed in Chapter 3, the supply curve for a good can be interpreted either horizontally or vertically. The horizontal interpretation tells us, for each price, the total quantity that producers wish to sell at that price. The vertical interpretation tells us, for each quantity, the smallest amount a seller would be willing to accept for the good. For the purpose of computing producer surplus, we rely on the vertical interpretation of the supply curve. The value on the vertical axis that corresponds to each point along the supply curve corresponds to the marginal seller's reservation price for the good, which is the marginal cost of producing it. Producer surplus is the cumulative sum of the differences between the market price and these reservation prices. It is the area bounded above by market price and bounded below by the supply curve.

■ SUMMARY ■

- The supply curve for a good or service is a schedule that for any price tells us the quantity that sellers wish to supply at that price. The prices at which goods and services are offered for sale in the market depend, in turn, on the opportunity cost of the resources required to produce them.

- Supply curves tend to be upward-sloping, at least in the short run, in part because of the low-hanging-fruit principle. In general, rational producers will always take advantage of

their best opportunities first, moving on to more difficult or costly opportunities only after their best ones have been exhausted. Reinforcing this tendency is the law of diminishing returns, which says that when some factors of production are held fixed, the amount of additional variable factors required to produce successive increments in output grows larger.

- For perfectly competitive markets—or, more generally, for markets in which individual sellers can sell whatever quantity they wish at constant price—the seller's best option is to sell that quantity of output for which price equals marginal cost, provided price exceeds the minimum value of average variable cost. The supply curve for the seller thus coincides with the portion of his marginal cost curve that exceeds average variable cost. This is why we sometimes say the supply curve represents the cost side of the market (in contrast to the demand curve, which represents the benefit side of the market).

- An important terminological distinction from the demand side of the market also applies on the supply side of the market. A "change in supply" means a shift in the entire supply curve, whereas a "change in the quantity supplied" means a movement along the supply curve. The factors that cause supply curves to shift include technology, input prices, the number of sellers, expectations of future price changes, and the prices of other products that firms might produce.

- Producer surplus is a measure of the economic surplus reaped by a seller or sellers in a market. It is the cumulative sum of the differences between the market price and their reservation prices, which is the area bounded above by market price and bounded below by the supply curve.

■ KEY TERMS ■

average total cost (*ATC*) (151)	long run (147)	profitable firm (151)
average variable cost (*AVC*) (151)	marginal cost (149)	profit-maximizing firm (145)
factor of production (147)	perfectly competitive market (146)	short run (147)
fixed cost (148)	price taker (146)	total cost (149)
fixed factor of production (148)	producer surplus (160)	variable cost (149)
imperfectly competitive firm (147)	profit (145)	variable factor of production (148)
law of diminishing returns (148)		

■ REVIEW QUESTIONS ■

1. Explain why you would expect supply curves to slope upward on the basis of the principle of increasing opportunity cost.

2. Which do you think is more likely to be a fixed factor of production for an ice cream producer during the next two months, its factory building or its workers who operate the machines? Explain.

3. Economists often stress that congestion helps account for the law of diminishing returns. With this in mind, explain why it would be impossible to feed all the people on Earth with food grown in a single flowerpot, even if unlimited water, labor, seed, fertilizer, sunlight, and other inputs were available.

4. True or false: The perfectly competitive firm should *always* produce the output level for which price equals marginal cost.

5. Why do we use the vertical interpretation of the supply curve when we measure producer surplus?

■ PROBLEMS ■

1. Zoe is trying to decide how to divide her time between her job as a wedding photographer, which pays $27 per hour for as many hours as she chooses to work, and as a fossil collector, in which her pay depends both on the price of fossils and the number of them she finds. Earnings aside, Zoe is indifferent between the two tasks, and the number of fossils she can find depends on the number of hours a day she searches, as shown in the table below:

Hours per day	Total fossils per day
1	5
2	9
3	12
4	14
5	15

a. Derive a table with price in dollar increments from $0 to $30 in the first column and the quantity of fossils Zoe is willing to supply per day at that price in the second.

b. Plot these points in a graph with price on the vertical axis and quantity per day on the horizontal. What is this curve called?

2. A price-taking firm makes air conditioners. The market price of one of their new air conditioners is $120. Its total cost information is given in the table below:

Air conditioners per day	Total cost ($ per day)
1	100
2	150
3	220
4	310
5	405
6	510
7	650
8	800

How many air conditioners should the firm produce per day if its goal is to maximize its profit?

3. The Paducah Slugger Company makes baseball bats out of lumber supplied to it by Acme Sporting Goods, which pays Paducah $10 for each finished bat. Paducah's only factors of production are lathe operators and a small building with a lathe. The number of bats per day it produces depends on the number of employee-hours per day, as shown in the table below.

Number of bats per day	Number of employee-hours per day
0	0
5	1
10	2
15	4
20	7
25	11
30	16
35	22

a. If the wage is $15 per hour and Paducah's daily fixed cost for the lathe and building is $60, what is the profit-maximizing quantity of bats?

b. What would be the profit-maximizing number of bats if the firm's fixed cost were not $60 per day but only $30?

4. In the preceding question, how would Paducah's profit-maximizing level of output be affected if the government imposed a tax of $10 per day on the company? (Hint: Think of this tax as equivalent to a $10 increase in fixed cost.) What would Paducah's profit-maximizing level of output be if the government imposed a tax of $2 per bat? (Hint: Think of this tax as a $2 per bat increase in the firm's marginal cost.) Why do these two taxes have such different effects?

5. The supply curves for the only two firms in a competitive industry are given by $P = 2Q_1$ and $P = 2 + Q_2$, where Q_1 is the output of firm 1 and Q_2 is the output of firm 2. What is the market supply curve for this industry? (Hint: Graph the two curves side by side, then add their respective quantities at a sample of different prices.)

6. Calculate daily producer surplus for the market for pizza whose demand and supply curves are shown in the graph.

7. For the pizza seller whose marginal, average variable, and average total cost curves are shown in the accompanying diagram, what is the profit-maximizing level of output and how much profit will this producer earn if the price of pizza is $2.50 per slice?

8. For the pizza seller whose marginal, average variable, and average total cost curves are shown in the accompanying diagram, what is the profit-maximizing level of output and how much profit will this producer earn if the price of pizza is $0.80 per slice?

9.* For the pizza seller whose marginal, average variable, and average total cost curves are shown in the accompanying diagram, what is the profit-maximizing level of output and how much profit will this producer earn if the price of pizza is $0.50 per slice?

10.* For the pizza seller whose marginal, average variable, and average total cost curves are shown in the accompanying diagram (who is the same seller as in problem 9), what is the profit-maximizing level of output and how much profit will this producer earn if the price of pizza is $1.18 per slice?

▪ ANSWERS TO IN-CHAPTER EXERCISES ▪

6.1 Since Harry will find 300 containers if he searches a third hour, we find his reservation price for searching a second hour by solving $p(300) = \$6$ for $p = 2$ cents. His reservation prices for additional hours of search are calculated in an analogous way.

Fourth hour: $p(200) = \$6$, so $p = 3$ cents.

Fifth hour: $p(100) = \$6$, so $p = 6$ cents.

6.2 If bottles sell for 62 cents each, the firm should continue to expand up to and including the sixth employee (350 bottles per day).

6.3 The relevant costs are now as shown in the table on the next page. With each variable and marginal cost entry half what it was in Example 6.2, the firm should now hire six employees and produce 350 bottles per day.

*Problems marked with an asterisk (*) are more difficult.

Employees per day	Bottles per day	Fixed cost ($/day)	Variable cost ($/day)	Total cost ($/day)	Marginal cost ($/bottle)
0	0	40	0	40	
					0.075
1	80	40	6	46	
					0.05
2	200	40	12	52	
					0.10
3	260	40	18	58	
					0.167
4	300	40	24	64	
					0.20
5	330	40	30	70	
					0.30
6	350	40	36	76	
					0.50
7	362	40	42	82	

6.4 Because the firm makes its smallest loss when it hires zero employees, it should shut down in the short run.

Employees per day	Output (bottles/day)	Total revenue ($/day)	Total cost ($/day)	Profit ($/day)
0	0	0	40	−40
1	80	8	52	−44
2	200	20	64	−44
3	260	26	76	−50
4	300	30	88	−58
5	330	33	100	−67
6	350	35	112	−77
7	362	36.20	124	−87.80

6.5 The fact that each of the city's 60,000 residents is willing to pay 0.00005 cents for each bottle removed means that the collective benefit of each bottle removed is (60,000)(0.00005) = 3 cents. So the city should set the redemption price at 3 cents, and from the supply curve we see that 15,000 bottles per day will be recycled at that price.

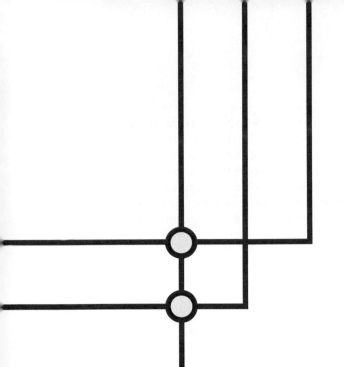

CHAPTER

7

EFFICIENCY AND EXCHANGE

■

Armando Lopez sat watching one of the national political conventions on television one August night as one orator after another extolled the virtues of the free enterprise system. "The greatest engine of progress mankind has ever witnessed," one of the speakers called it. "A rising tide that will lift all boats," said another.

Lopez, however, was skeptical, for though he had worked hard and played by society's rules, his standard of living had been deteriorating rather than improving. Downsized from his draftsman's position at an aircraft plant the year before, Lopez was working as a janitor for a local office-cleaning company, the best job he had been able to find after months of searching. He could not afford to repair the leaky roof and faulty plumbing at his house in East Los Angeles. Indeed, his two older children had dropped out of college because he could no longer afford their tuition bills. Though his commute to work was only six miles each way, freeway congestion made it a 90-minute trip most mornings. His wife's recurrent asthma attacks, triggered by local air pollution, had recently worsened. Without health insurance, the family's medical bills had been mounting rapidly. And there had been four deaths from drive-by shootings in their neighborhood in the last year.

Given the stark contrast between his own experience and the lofty claims of the orators he was listening to, Lopez's skepticism about the virtues of the free enterprise system was understandable. Yet informed students of the market system understand that it could never have been expected to prevent Lopez's problems in the first place. *In certain domains*—indeed, in very broad domains—markets are every bit as remarkable as their strongest proponents assert. Yet there are many problems they simply cannot be expected to solve. For example, private markets cannot by themselves guarantee an income distribution that most people regard as fair. Nor can they ensure clean air, uncongested highways, or safe neighborhoods for all.

Yet markets do enable society to produce sufficient resources to meet all these goals and more. In virtually all successful societies, however, markets are supplemented by active political coordination in at least some instances. We will almost always achieve our goals more effectively if we know what tasks private markets can do well, and then allow them to perform those tasks. Unfortunately, the discovery that markets cannot solve *every* problem seems to have led some critics to conclude that markets cannot solve *any* problems. This misperception is a dangerous one, because it has prompted attempts to prevent markets from doing even those tasks for which they are ideally suited.

Our task in this chapter will be to explore why many tasks are best left to the market. We will explore the conditions under which unregulated markets generate the largest possible economic surplus. We will also discuss why attempts to interfere with market outcomes often lead to unintended and undesired consequences. We will see why public utilities can more efficiently serve their customers if they set prices in a way that closely mimics the market. And we will also discuss why the economic burden of a tax does not always fall most heavily on the parties from whom it is directly collected.

MARKET EQUILIBRIUM AND EFFICIENCY

As noted in Chapter 3, the mere fact that markets coordinate the production of a large and complex list of goods and services is reason enough to marvel at them. But economists make an even stronger claim—namely, that markets not only produce these goods, but also produce them as efficiently as possible.

efficient (or Pareto efficient) a situation is efficient if no change is possible that will help some people without harming others

The term **efficient**, as economists use it, has a narrow technical meaning. When we say that market equilibrium is efficient, we mean simply this: *If price and quantity take anything other than their equilibrium values, a transaction that will make at least some people better off without harming others can always be found.* This conception of efficiency is also known as **Pareto efficiency**, after Vilfredo Pareto, the nineteenth-century Italian economist who introduced it.

Why is market equilibrium efficient in this sense? The answer is that it is always possible to construct an exchange that helps some without harming others whenever a market is out of equilibrium. Suppose, for example, that the supply and demand curves for milk are as shown in Figure 7.1, and that the current price of milk is $1 per gallon. At that price, sellers offer only 2,000 gallons of milk a day. At that quantity, the marginal buyer values an extra gallon of milk at $2. This is the price that corresponds to 2,000 gallons a day on the demand curve, which represents what the marginal buyer is willing to pay for an additional gallon (another application of the vertical interpretation of the demand curve). We also know that the cost of producing an extra gallon of milk is only $1. This is the price that corresponds to 2,000 gallons a day on the supply curve,

FIGURE 7.1

A Market in Which Price Is Below the Equilibrium Level.

In this market, milk is currently selling for $1 per gallon, $0.50 below the equilibrium price of $1.50 per gallon.

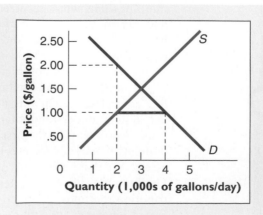

which equals marginal cost (another application of the vertical interpretation of the supply curve).

Furthermore, a price of $1 per gallon leads to excess demand of 2,000 gallons per day, which means that many frustrated buyers cannot buy as much milk as they want at the going price. Now suppose a supplier sells an extra gallon of milk to the most eager of these buyers for $1.25, as in Figure 7.2. Since the extra gallon cost only $1 to produce, the seller is $0.25 better off than before. And since the most eager buyer values the extra gallon at $2, that buyer is $0.75 better off than before. In sum, the transaction creates an extra $1 of economic surplus out of thin air!

FIGURE 7.2

How Excess Demand Creates an Opportunity for a Surplus-Enhancing Transaction.

At a market price of $1 per gallon, the most intensely dissatisfied buyer is willing to pay $2 for an additional gallon, which a seller can produce at a cost of only $1. If this buyer pays the seller $1.25 for the extra gallon, the buyer gains an economic surplus of $0.75 and the seller gains an economic surplus of $0.25.

Note that none of the other buyers or sellers is harmed by this transaction. Thus milk selling for only $1 per gallon cannot be efficient. As the following exercise illustrates, there was nothing special about the price of $1 per gallon. Indeed, if milk sells for *any* price below $1.50 per gallon (the market equilibrium price), we can design a similar transaction, which means that selling milk for any price less than $1.50 per gallon cannot be efficient.

EXERCISE 7.1

In Figure 7.1, suppose that milk initially sells for 50 cents per gallon. Describe a transaction that will create additional economic surplus for both buyer and seller without causing harm to anyone else.

What is more, it is always possible to describe a transaction that will create additional surplus for both buyer and seller whenever the price lies above the market equilibrium level. Suppose, for example, that the current price is $2 per gallon in the milk market shown in Figure 7.1. At that price, we have excess supply of 2,000 gallons per day (see Figure 7.3). Suppose the most dissatisfied producer sells a gallon of milk for $1.75 to the buyer who values it most highly. This buyer, who would have been willing to pay $2, will be $0.25 better off than before. Likewise the producer, who would have been willing to sell milk for as little as $1 per gallon (the marginal cost of production at 2,000 gallons per day), will be $0.75 better off than before. As when the price was $1 per gallon, the new transaction creates $1 of additional economic surplus without harming any other buyer or seller. Since we could design a similar surplus-enhancing transaction at any price above the equilibrium level, selling milk for more than $1.50 per gallon cannot be efficient.

FIGURE 7.3
How Excess Supply Creates an Opportunity for a Surplus-Enhancing Transaction.
At a market price of $2 per gallon, dissatisfied sellers can produce an additional gallon of milk at a cost of only $1, which is $1 less than a buyer would be willing to pay for it. If the buyer pays the seller $1.75 for an extra gallon, the buyer gains an economic surplus of $0.25 and the seller gains an economic surplus of $0.75.

The vertical interpretations of the supply and demand curves thus make it clear why only the equilibrium price in a market can be efficient. When the price is either higher or lower than the equilibrium price, the quantity exchanged in the market will always be lower than the equilibrium quantity. If the price is below equilibrium, the quantity sold will be the amount that sellers offer. If the price is above equilibrium, the quantity sold will be the amount that buyers wish to buy. In either case, the vertical value on the demand curve at the quantity exchanged, which is the value of an extra unit to buyers, must be larger than the vertical value on the supply curve, which is the marginal cost of producing that unit.

So the market equilibrium price is the *only* price at which buyers and sellers cannot design a surplus-enhancing transaction. The market equilibrium price leads, in other words, to the largest possible total economic surplus. In this specific, limited sense, free markets are said to produce and distribute goods and services efficiently.

Actually, to claim that market equilibrium is always efficient even in this limited sense is an overstatement. The claim holds only if buyers and sellers are well informed, if markets are perfectly competitive, and if the demand and supply curves satisfy certain other restrictions. For example, market equilibrium will not be efficient if the individual marginal cost curves that add up to the market supply curve fail to include all relevant costs of producing the product. Thus, as we saw in Chapter 3, the true cost of expanding output will be higher than indicated by the market supply curve if production generates pollution that harms others. The equilibrium output will then be inefficiently large and the equilibrium price inefficiently low.

Likewise, market equilibrium will not be efficient if the individual demand curves that make up the market demand curve do not capture all the relevant benefits of buying additional units of the product. For instance, if a homeowner's willingness to pay for ornamental shrubs is based only on the enjoyment she herself gains from them, and not on any benefits that may accrue to her neighbors, the market demand curve for shrubs will understate their value to the neighborhood. The equilibrium quantity of ornamental shrubs will be inefficiently small, and the market price for shrubs will be inefficiently low.

We will take up such market imperfections in greater detail in later chapters. For now, we will confine our attention to perfectly competitive markets whose demand curves capture all relevant benefits and whose supply curves capture all relevant costs. For such goods, market equilibrium will always be efficient in the limited sense described earlier.

EFFICIENCY IS NOT THE ONLY GOAL

The fact that market equilibrium maximizes economic surplus is an attractive feature, to be sure. Bear in mind, however, that "efficient" does not mean the same thing as "good." For example, the market for milk may be in equilibrium at a price of $1.50 per gallon, yet many poor families may be unable to afford milk for their children at that price. Still others may not even have a place for their children to sleep.

Efficiency is a concept that that is based on predetermined attributes of buyers and sellers—their incomes, tastes, abilities, knowledge, and so on. Through the combined effects of individual cost-benefit decisions, these attributes give rise to the supply and demand curves for each good produced in an economy. If we are concerned about inequality in the distribution of attributes like income, we should not be surprised to discover that markets do not always yield outcomes we like.

Most of us could agree, for example, that the world would be a better one if all people had enough income to feed their families adequately. The claim that equilibrium in the market for milk is efficient means simply that *taking people's incomes as given,* the resulting allocation of milk cannot be altered so as to help some people without at the same time harming others.

To this a critic of the market system might respond: So what? As such critics rightly point out, imposing costs on others may be justified if doing so will help those with sufficiently important unmet demands. For example, most people would prefer to fund homeless shelters with their tax dollars rather than let the homeless freeze to death. Arguing in these terms, American policymakers responded to rapid increases in the price of oil in the late 1970s by imposing price controls on home heating oil. And many of us might agree that if the alternative had been to take no action at all, price controls might have been justified in the name of social justice.

But the economist's concept of market efficiency makes clear that there *must* be a better alternative policy. Price controls on oil prevent the market from reaching equilibrium, and as we've seen, that means forgoing transactions that would benefit some people without harming others.

WHY EFFICIENCY SHOULD BE THE FIRST GOAL

Efficiency is important not because it is a desirable end in itself, but because it enables us to achieve all our other goals to the fullest possible extent. Whenever a market is out of equilibrium, it is always possible to generate additional economic surplus. To gain additional economic surplus is to gain more of the resources we need to do the things we want to do. Whenever any market is out of equilibrium, there is waste, and waste is always bad thing.

 RECAP   **EQUILIBRIUM AND EFFICIENCY**

When a market is not in equilibrium—because price is either above the equilibrium level or below it—the quantity exchanged is always less than the equilibrium level. At such a quantity, a transaction can always be made in which both buyer and seller benefit from the exchange of an additional unit of output. A market in equilibrium is said to be efficient, or Pareto efficient, meaning that no reallocation is possible that will benefit some people without harming others.

Total economic surplus in a market is maximized when exchange occurs at the equilibrium price. But the fact that equilibrium is "efficient" in this sense does not mean that it is "good." All markets can be in equilibrium, yet many people may lack sufficient income to buy even basic goods and services. Still, permitting markets to reach equilibrium is important, because when economic surplus is maximized, it is possible to pursue every goal more fully.

THE COST OF PREVENTING PRICE ADJUSTMENTS

PRICE CEILINGS

During 1979, an interruption in oil supplies from the Middle East caused the price of home heating oil to rise by more than 100 percent. Concern about the hardship this sudden price increase would impose on poor families in northern states led the government to impose a price ceiling in the market for home heating oil. This price ceiling prohibited sellers from charging more than a specified amount for heating oil.

The following example illustrates why imposing a price ceiling on heating oil, though well intended, was a bad idea.

EXAMPLE 7.1

How much waste does a price ceiling on heating oil cause?

Suppose the demand and supply curves for home heating oil are as shown in Figure 7.4, in which the equilibrium price is $1.40 per gallon. And suppose that at that price, many poor families cannot heat their homes adequately. Out of concern for the poor, legislators pass a law setting the maximum price at $1 per gallon. How much lost economic surplus does this policy cost society?

FIGURE 7.4
Economic Surplus in an Unregulated Market for Home Heating Oil.
For the supply and demand curves shown, the equilibrium price of home heating oil is $1.40 per gallon, and the equilibrium quantity is 3,000 gallons per day. Consumer surplus is the area of the upper shaded triangle ($900 per day). Producer surplus is the area of the lower shaded triangle (also $900 per day).

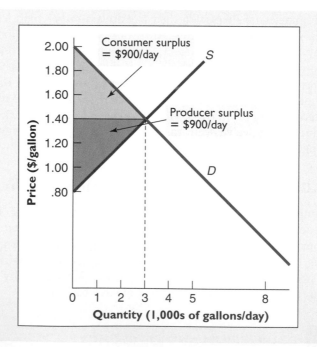

First, let's calculate total economic surplus without price controls. If this market is not regulated, 3,000 gallons per day will be sold at a price of $1.40 per gallon. In Figure 7.4, the economic surplus received by buyers is the area of the upper shaded triangle. Since the height of this triangle is $0.60 per gallon, and its base is 3,000 gallons per day, its area is equal to (1/2)(3,000 gallons/day)($0.60/gallon) = $900 per day. The economic surplus received by producers is the area of the lower shaded triangle. Since this triangle also has an area of $900 per day, total economic surplus in this market will be $1,800 per day.

If the price of heating oil is prevented from rising above $1 per gallon, only 1,000 gallons per day will be sold, and the total economic surplus will be reduced by the area of the lined triangle shown in Figure 7.5. Since the height of this triangle is $0.80 per gallon, and its base is 2,000 gallons per day, its area is (1/2)(2,000 gallons/day)($0.80/gallon) = $800 per day. Producer surplus falls from

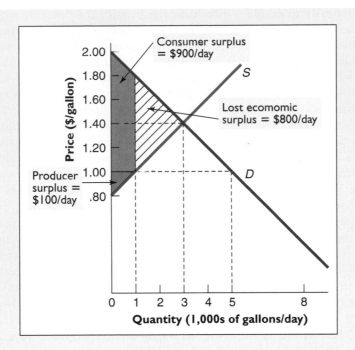

FIGURE 7.5

The Waste Caused by Price Controls.

By limiting output in the home heating oil market to 1,000 gallons per day, price controls cause a loss in economic surplus of $800 per day (area of the lined triangle).

$900 per day in the unregulated market to the area of the lower shaded triangle, or (1/2)(1,000 gallons/day)($0.20/gallon) = $100 per day, which is a loss of $800 per day. Thus the loss in total economic surplus is equal to the loss in producer surplus, which means that the new consumer surplus must be the same as the original consumer surplus. To verify this, note that consumer surplus with the price ceiling is the area of the upper shaded figure, which is again $900 per day. (Hint: To compute this area, first split the figure into a rectangle and a triangle.) By preventing the home heating oil market from reaching equilibrium, price controls waste $800 of producer surplus per day without creating any additional surplus for consumers!

EXERCISE 7.2

In Example 7.1, by how much would total economic surplus have been reduced if the price ceiling had been set not at $1 but at $1.20 per gallon?

For several reasons the reduction in total economic surplus shown in Figure 7.5 is a conservative estimate of the waste caused by attempts to hold price below its equilibrium level. For one thing, the analysis assumes that each of the 1,000 gallons per day that are sold in this market will end up in the hands of the consumers who value them most—in the diagram, those whose reservation prices are above $1.80 per gallon. But since any buyer whose reservation price is above $1 per gallon will want to buy at the ceiling price, much of the oil actually sold is likely to go to buyers whose reservation prices are below $1.80. Suppose, for example, that a buyer whose reservation price was $1.50 per gallon made it into the line outside a heating oil supplier just ahead of a buyer whose reservation price was $1.90 per gallon. If each buyer had a 20-gallon tank to fill, and if the first buyer got the last of the day's available oil, then total surplus would be smaller by $8 that day than if the oil had gone to the second buyer.

A second reason that the reduction in surplus shown in Figure 7.5 is likely to be an underestimate is that shortages typically prompt buyers to take costly actions to enhance their chances of being served. For example, if the heating oil distributor begins selling its available supplies at 6:00 A.M., many buyers may arrive several hours early to ensure a place near the front of the line. Yet when all buyers incur the cost of arriving earlier, no one gets any more oil than before.

Notwithstanding the fact that price ceilings reduce total economic surplus, their defenders might argue that controls are justified because they enable at least some low-income families to buy heating oil at affordable prices. Yes, but the same objective could have been accomplished in a much less costly way—namely, by giving the poor more income with which to buy heating oil.

It may seem natural to wonder whether the poor, who have limited political power, can really hope to receive income transfers that would enable them to heat their homes. On reflection, the answer to this question would seem to be yes, *if the alternative is to impose price controls that would be even more costly than the income transfers.* After all, the price ceiling as implemented ends up costing heating oil sellers $800 per day in lost economic surplus. So they ought to be willing to pay some amount less than $800 a day in additional taxes in order to escape the burden of controls. The additional tax revenue could finance income transfers that would be far more beneficial to the poor than price controls.

This point is so important, and so often misunderstood by voters and policymakers, that we will emphasize it by putting it another way. Think of the economic surplus from a market as a pie to be divided among the various market participants. Figure 7.6(a) represents the $1,000 per day of total economic surplus available to participants in the home heating oil market when the government limits the price of oil to $1 per gallon. We divided this pie into two slices, labeled *R* and *P*, to denote the surpluses received by rich and poor participants. Figure 7.6(b) represents the $1,800 per day of total economic surplus available when the price of home heating oil is free to reach its equilibrium level. This pie is divided among rich and poor participants in the same proportion as the pie in the left panel.

The important point to notice is this: *Because the pie on the right side is larger, both rich and poor participants in the home heating oil market can get a bigger slice of the pie than they would have had under price controls.* Rather than tinker with the market price of oil, it is in everyone's interest to simply transfer additional income to the poor.

FIGURE 7.6

When the Pie Is Larger, Everyone Can Have a Bigger Slice.
Any policy that reduces total economic surplus is a missed opportunity to make everyone better off.

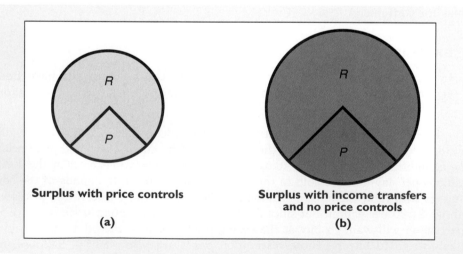

Surplus with price controls

(a)

Surplus with income transfers and no price controls

(b)

Supporters of price controls may object that income transfers to the poor might weaken people's incentive to work, and thus might prove extremely costly in the long run. Difficult issues do indeed arise in the design of programs for transferring income to the poor—issues we will consider in some detail in later chapters. But for now, suffice it to say that ways exist to transfer income without undermining work incentives significantly. One such method is the "earned-income tax credit," a program that supplements the wages of low-income workers. Given such programs, transferring income to the poor will always be more efficient than trying to boost their living standard through price controls.

PRICE SUBSIDIES

Sometimes governments try to assist low-income consumers by subsidizing the prices of "essential" goods and services. France and Russia, for example, have taken this approach at various points by subsidizing the price of bread. But as the following example illustrates, such subsidies are like price ceilings in that they reduce total economic surplus.

By how much do subsidies reduce total economic surplus in the market for bread?

A small island nation imports bread for its population at the world price of $2 per loaf. If the domestic demand curve for bread is as shown in Figure 7.7, by how much will total economic surplus decline in this market if the government provides a $1 per loaf subsidy?

EXAMPLE 7.2

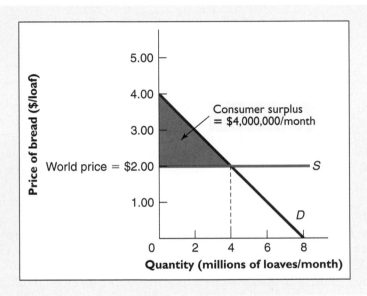

FIGURE 7.7
Economic Surplus in a Bread Market without Subsidy.
For the demand curve shown, consumer surplus (area of the shaded triangle) is $4,000,000. This amount is equal to total economic surplus in the domestic bread market, since no bread is produced domestically.

With no subsidy, the equilibrium price of bread in this market would be the world price of $2 per loaf, and the equilibrium quantity would be 4,000,000 loaves per month. The shaded triangle in Figure 7.7 represents consumer economic surplus for buyers in the domestic bread market. The height of this triangle is $2 per loaf, and its base is 4,000,000 loaves per month, so its area is equal to (1/2)(4,000,000 loaves/month)($2/loaf) = $4,000,000 per month. Because the country can import as much bread as it wishes at the world price of $2 per loaf, supply is perfectly elastic in this market. Because the marginal cost of each loaf of bread to sellers is exactly the same as the price buyers pay, producer surplus in this market is zero. So total economic surplus is exactly equal to consumer surplus, which, again, is $4,000,000 per month.

Now suppose that the government administers its $1 per loaf subsidy program by purchasing bread in the world market at $2 per loaf and reselling it in the domestic market for only $1 per loaf. At the new lower price buyers will now consume not 4,000,000 loaves per month but 6,000,000. Consumer surplus for buyers in the bread market is now the area of the larger shaded triangle in Figure 7.8: (1/2)($3/loaf) (6,000,000 loaves/month) = $9,000,000 per month, or $5,000,000 per month more than before. The catch is that the subsidy wasn't free. Its cost, which must be borne by taxpayers, is ($1/loaf)(6,000,000 loaves/month) = $6,000,000 per month. So even though consumer surplus in the bread market is larger than before, the net effect of the subsidy program is actually to reduce total economic surplus by $1,000,000 per month.

FIGURE 7.8

The Reduction in Economic Surplus from a Subsidy.

Since the marginal cost of bread is $2 per loaf, total economic surplus is maximized at 4,000,000 loaves per month, the quantity for which the marginal buyer's reservation price is equal to marginal cost. The reduction in economic surplus from consuming an additional 2,000,000 loaves per month is $1,000,000 per month, the area of the smaller shaded triangle.

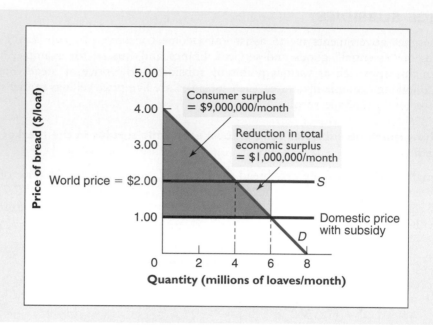

Another way to see why the subsidy reduces total economic surplus by that amount is to note that total economic surplus is maximized at 4,000,000 loaves per month, the quantity for which the marginal buyer's reservation price is equal to marginal cost, and that the subsidy induces additional consumption of 2,000,000 loaves per month. Each additional loaf has a marginal cost of $2 but is worth less than that to the buyer (as indicated by the fact that the vertical coordinate of the demand curve lies below $2 for consumption beyond 4,000,000). As monthly consumption expands from 4,000,000 to 6,000,000 loaves per month, the cumulative difference between the marginal cost of bread and its value to buyers is the area of the smaller shaded triangle in Figure 7.8, which is $1,000,000 per month.

This reduction in economic surplus constitutes pure waste—no different, from the perspective of participants in this market, than if someone had siphoned that much cash out of their bank accounts each month and thrown it into a bonfire.

EXERCISE 7.3

How much total economic surplus would have been lost if the bread subsidy been set at $0.50 per loaf instead of $1.00?

Compared to a bread subsidy, a much better policy would be to give low-income people some additional income and then let them bid for bread on the open market. Subsidy advocates who complain that taxpayers would be unwilling to give low-income people income transfers must be asked to explain why people would be willing to tolerate subsidies, which are so much *more* costly than income transfers. Logically, if voters are willing to support subsidies, they should be even more eager to support income transfers to low-income persons.

This is not to say that the poor reap no benefit at all from bread subsidies. Since they get to buy bread at lower prices and since the subsidy program is financed by taxes collected primarily from middle- and upper-income families, poor families probably come out ahead on balance. *The point is that for the same expense, we could do much more to help the poor.* Their problem is that they have too little income. The simplest and best solution is not to try to peg the prices of the goods they and others buy below equilibrium levels, but rather to give them some additional money.

FIRST-COME, FIRST-SERVED POLICIES

Governments are not the only institutions that attempt to promote social goals by preventing markets from reaching equilibrium. Some universities, for example, attempt to protect access by low-income students to concerts and sporting events by selling a limited number of tickets below the market-clearing price on a first-come, first-served basis.

The commercial airline industry was an early proponent of the use of the first-come, first-served allocation method, which it employed to ration seats on overbooked flights. Throughout the industry's history, most airlines have routinely accepted more reservations for their flights than there are seats on those flights. Most of the time, this practice causes no difficulty, because many reservation holders don't show up to claim their seats. Indeed, if airlines did not overbook their flights, most flights would take off with many more empty seats, forcing airlines to charge higher ticket prices to cover their costs.

The only real difficulty is that every so often, more people actually do show up for a flight than there are seats on the plane. Until the late 1970s, airlines dealt with this problem by boarding passengers on a first-come, first-served basis. For example, if 120 people showed up for a flight with 110 seats, the last 10 to arrive were "bumped," or forced to wait for the next available flight.

The bumped passengers often complained bitterly, and no wonder, since many of them ended up missing important business meetings or family events. As the following example illustrates, there was fortunately a simple solution to this problem.

Why does no one complain any longer about being bumped from an overbooked flight?

In 1978, airlines abandoned their first-come, first-served policy in favor of a new procedure. Since then, their practice has been to solicit volunteers to give up their seats on oversold flights in return for a cash payment or free ticket. Now, the only people who give up their seats are those who volunteer to do so in return for compensation. And hence the complete disappearance of complaints about being bumped from overbooked flights.

Which of the two policies—first-come, first-served or compensation for volunteers—is more efficient? The difficulty with the first-come, first-served policy is that it gives little weight to the interests of passengers with pressing reasons for arriving at their destination on time. Such passengers can sometimes avoid losing their seats by showing up early, but passengers coming in on connecting flights often cannot control when they arrive. And the cost of showing up early is likely to be highest for precisely those people who place the highest value on not missing a flight (such as business executives, whose opportunity cost of waiting in airports is high).

For the sake of illustration, suppose that 37 people show up for a flight with only 33 seats. One way or another, four people will have to wait for another flight. Suppose we ask each of them "What is the most you would be willing to pay to fly now rather than wait?" Typically, different passengers will have different reservation prices for avoiding the wait. Suppose that the person who is most willing to pay would pay up to $60 rather than miss the flight; that the person second-most willing to pay would pay up to $59; that the person third-most willing to pay would pay up to $58; and so on. In that case, the person with the smallest reservation price for avoiding the wait would have a reservation price of $24. For the entire group of 37 passengers, the average reservation price for avoiding the wait would be ($60 + $59 + $58 + · · · + $24)/37 = $42.

Given the difficulty of controlling airport arrival times, the passengers who get bumped under the first-come, first-served policy are not likely to differ systematically from others with respect to their reservation price for not missing the flight. On average, then, the total cost imposed on the four bumped passengers

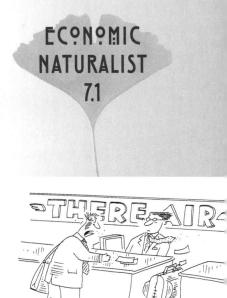

ECONOMIC NATURALIST 7.1

Why are passenger complaints about overbooked flights a thing of the past?

would be four times the average reservation price of $42, or $168. As far as those four passengers are concerned, that total is a pure loss of consumer surplus.

How does this cost compare with the cost imposed on bumped passengers when the airline compensates volunteers? Suppose the airline solicits volunteers by conducting an informal auction, increasing its cash compensation offer by $1 increments until it has the desired number of volunteers. As the incentive to stay behind rises, more people will volunteer; those whose reservation prices are the lowest will volunteer first. In this example, offers below $24 would generate no volunteers. An offer of $24 would generate one volunteer; an offer of $25 would generate two volunteers; and so on. A compensation payment of $27 would generate the necessary four volunteers.

What is the net cost of the compensation policy? While the airline pays out (4)($27) = $108 in compensation payments, not all that amount represents lost economic surplus. Thus the passenger whose reservation price for missing the flight is $24 receives a net gain in economic surplus of $3—the difference between the $27 compensation payment and her $24 reservation price. Similarly, those whose reservation prices were $25 and $26 receive a net gain of $2 and $1, respectively. The cost of the cash compensation policy net of these gains is thus $108 − $6 = $102, or $66 less than under the first-come, first-served policy.

The compensation policy is more efficient than the first-come, first-served policy because it establishes a market for a scarce resource that would otherwise be allocated by nonmarket means. Figure 7.9 shows the supply and demand curves for seats under the compensation policy. In this market, the equilibrium price of not having to wait is $27. People who choose not to volunteer at that price incur an opportunity cost of $27 in order not to miss the flight. The four people who do volunteer accept $27 as ample compensation—indeed, more than ample for three of them.

FIGURE 7.9
Equilibrium in the Market for Seats on Oversold Flights.
The demand curve for remaining on the flight is generated by plotting the reservation prices in descending order. The equilibrium compensation payment for volunteers who give up their seats is $27—the price at which 4 passengers volunteer to wait and the remaining 33 choose not to wait.

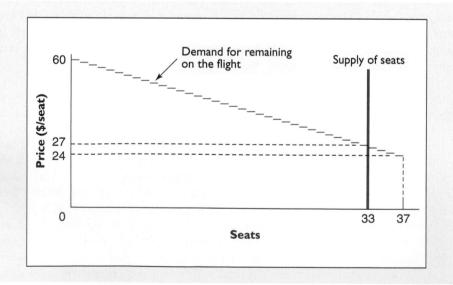

An interesting footnote to this example is that the airlines' policy change evoked a fierce protest from the Aviation Consumer Action Project (ACAP), a group that portrayed itself as a watchdog for the interests of airline passengers. ACAP's concern was that the shift to a system of compensation payments would mean that poor people would most often end up waiting for the next flight. This was a curious objection, for several reasons. Although the people who volunteer to wait in return for a compensation payment probably have lower incomes, on average, than those who don't volunteer, the income distributions of the two groups overlap considerably. Many financially comfortable persons with no pressing appointments will gladly volunteer to wait, while many people with lower incomes will choose not to. But more important, the previous policy of first-come, first-served was manifestly less attractive to the poor than the new policy. After all, passengers give up their seats under the volunteer policy only when they find the payment offered sufficient to compensate for the inconvenience of waiting. We may suspect that few poor persons would be grateful if ACAP had succeeded in persuading the government to block the switch to compensation payments.

How should a tennis pro handle the overbooking problem?

EXAMPLE 7.3

Anticipating a high proportion of no-shows, a tennis pro routinely books five people for each of his group lesson slots, even though he is able to teach only three people at a time. One day, all five people show up for their lessons at 10 A.M., the first lesson slot of the morning. Their respective arrival times and the maximum amounts each would be willing to pay to avoid postponing his or her lesson are as given in the table.

Player	Arrival time	Reservation price
Ann	9:50 A.M.	$ 4
Bill	9:52 A.M.	3
Carrie	9:55 A.M.	6
Dana	9:56 A.M.	10
Earl	9:59 A.M.	3

If the tennis pro accommodates the players on a first-come, first-served basis, by how much will total economic surplus be smaller than if he had offered cash compensation to induce two volunteers to reschedule? Which system is more efficient?

The result of using a first-come, first-served policy will be that Dana and Earl, the last two to arrive, will have to postpone their lessons. Since the cost of waiting is $10 for Dana and $3 for Earl, the total cost of the first-come, first-served policy is $13.

Suppose that the pro had instead offered cash compensation payments to elicit volunteers. If he offered a payment of $3, both Bill and Earl would be willing to wait. The total cost of the cash compensation policy would therefore be only $6, or $7 less than under the first-come, first-served policy. So the cash compensation policy is more efficient.

You might feel tempted to ask why the tennis pro would bother to offer cash compensation when he has the option of saving the $6 by continuing with his current policy of first-come, first-served. Or you might wonder why an airline would bother to offer cash compensation to elicit volunteers to wait for the next flight. But we know that it is possible for *everyone* to do better under an efficient policy than under an inefficient one. (When the pie is bigger, everyone can have a larger slice.) The following exercise asks you to design such a transaction for the tennis-lesson example.

EXERCISE 7.4

Describe a set of cash transfers in Example 7.3 that would make each of the five students and the tennis pro better off than under the first-come, first-served policy. (Hint: Imagine that the tennis pro tells his students that he will stick with first-come, first served unless they agree to contribute to the compensation pool as he requests.)

In practice, transactions like the one called for in Exercise 7.4 would be cumbersome to administer. Typically, the seller is in a position to solve such problems more easily by offering cash payments to elicit volunteers, and then financing those cash payments by charging slightly higher prices. Buyers, for their part, are willing to pay the higher prices because they value the seller's promise not to cancel their reservations without compensation.

 RECAP   **THE COST OF BLOCKING PRICE ADJUSTMENTS**

In an effort to increase the economic welfare of disadvantaged consumers, governments often implement policies that attempt to prevent markets from reaching equilibrium. Price ceilings and subsidies attempt to make housing and other basic goods more affordable for poor families. Private organizations also implement policies that prevent markets from reaching equilibrium, such as allocation on a first-come, first-served basis. Such policies always reduce total economic surplus relative to the alternative of letting prices seek their equilibrium levels. It is always possible to design alternative policies under which rich and poor alike fare better.

MARGINAL COST PRICING OF PUBLIC SERVICES

The largest possible total economic surplus is achieved in private markets when goods are exchanged at equilibrium prices, where the value of the last unit to the buyer is exactly equal to the seller's marginal cost of producing it. Suppose the government has decided to become the provider of a good or service, such as water or electricity. If the government's goal is to maximize the resulting total economic surplus, how much should it charge its customers? The theory of market exchange, normally applied to perfectly competitive firms that can sell any quantity they choose at a constant market price, helps to answer this question. Consider the following example, in which a local government supplies water to its residents.

EXAMPLE 7.4   **What is the marginal cost of water in Gainesville?**

The municipal water supply company in Gainesville, Florida, has three potential sources of water: an underground spring, a nearby lake, and the Atlantic Ocean. The spring can supply up to 1 million gallons per day at a cost of 0.2 cents per gallon. The lake can supply an additional 2 million gallons per day at a cost of 0.8 cents per gallon. Additional water must be distilled from the ocean

FIGURE 7.10
The Marginal Cost Curve for Water.
The current marginal cost of water is the cost of producing an extra gallon by means of the most expensive production source currently in use.

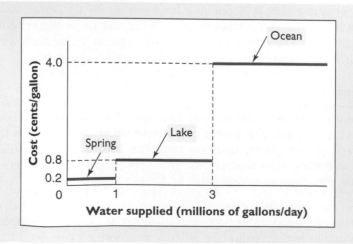

at a cost of 4.0 cents per gallon. Draw the marginal cost curve for water in Gainesville.

The low-hanging-fruit principle tells us that the city will use the cheapest source of water first (the spring). Only when the quantity demanded exceeds the spring's capacity will the city turn to the next least expensive source, the lake; and only when the lake's capacity is exhausted will the city supply water from the ocean. The marginal cost curve will thus be as shown in Figure 7.10.

As the next example illustrates, total economic surplus is maximized when the government charges each customer exactly the marginal cost of the water he or she consumes.

How much should the government charge for water?

EXAMPLE 7.5

In the preceding example, suppose that if the price of water were 4.0 cents per gallon, citizens of Gainesville would consume 4 million gallons per day. Given the marginal cost curve shown in Figure 7.10, how much should the city charge a citizen whose water comes from the underground spring? How much should it charge someone whose water comes from the lake?

The citizens of Gainesville will enjoy the largest possible economic surplus if the price they pay for water exactly equals the marginal cost of providing it. Since the total amount of water demanded at 4.0 cents per gallon exceeds 3 million gallons per day, the city will have to supply at least some households with water distilled from the Atlantic Ocean, at a cost of 4.0 cents per gallon. At 4 million gallons per day, the marginal cost of water is thus 4.0 cents per gallon, and *this is true no matter where the water comes from.* As long as the city must get *some* of its water from the ocean, the marginal cost of water taken from the underground spring is also 4.0 cents per gallon. Water taken from the lake has a marginal cost of 4.0 cents per gallon as well.

This statement might seem to contradict the claim that water drawn from the spring costs only 0.2 cents per gallon, water drawn from the lake, only 0.8 cents per gallon. But there is no contradiction. To see why, ask yourself how much the city would save if a family that currently gets its water from the spring were to reduce its consumption by 1 gallon per day. The cutback would enable the city to divert that gallon of spring water to some other household that currently gets its water from the ocean, which in turn would reduce consumption of ocean water by 1 gallon. So if a family currently served by the spring were to reduce its daily consumption by 1 gallon, the cost savings would be exactly 4.0 cents. And that, by definition, is the marginal cost of water.

To encourage the efficient use of water, the city should charge every household 4.0 cents per gallon for all the water it consumes. Charging any household less than that would encourage households to use water whose marginal benefit is less than its marginal cost. For example, suppose the city charged households who get their water from the spring only 0.2 cents per gallon. Those households would then expand their use of water until the benefit they received from the last gallon used equaled 0.2 cents. Because that gallon could have been used to serve someone who is currently using water distilled from the ocean, for whom the value of the marginal gallon is 4 cents, its use would entail a loss in economic surplus of 3.8 cents.

EXERCISE 7.5

Suppose that at a price of 0.8 cents per gallon of water, the citizens of Gainesville would consume a total of only 2 million gallons per day. If the marginal cost of water is as shown in Figure 7.10, how much should the city charge for water? Should that same charge apply to people who get their water from the spring?

RECAP   **MARGINAL COST PRICING OF PUBLIC SERVICES**

When a good is provided by a public utility from several sources, the marginal cost of serving a customer is the cost associated with the least efficient source in use. A public utility should set price equal to marginal cost if its goal is to maximizes economic surplus.

TAXES AND EFFICIENCY

WHO PAYS A TAX IMPOSED ON SELLERS OF A GOOD?

Politicians of all stripes seem loath to propose new taxes. But when additional public revenue must be raised, most seem to feel more comfortable proposing taxes paid by sellers than taxes paid by consumers. When pressed to explain why, many respond that businesses can more easily afford to pay extra taxes. Yet the burden of a tax collected from the sellers of a good need not fall exclusively on sellers. Suppose, for example, that a tax of $1 per pound is collected from potato farmers in the market whose demand and supply curves are shown as D and S in Figure 7.11.

FIGURE 7.11

The Effect of a Tax on the Equilibrium Quantity and Price of Potatoes.

With no tax, 3 million pounds of potatoes are sold each month at a price of $3 per pound. With a tax of $1 per pound collected from sellers, consumers end up paying $3.50 per pound (including tax), while sellers receive only $2.50 per pound (net of tax). Equilibrium quantity falls from 3 million pounds per month to 2.5 million.

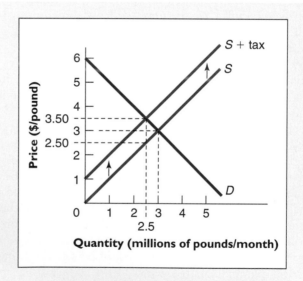

In this market the initial equilibrium price and quantity are $3 per pound and 3 million pounds per month, respectively. From the farmers' perspective, the imposition of a tax of $1 per pound is essentially the same as a $1 increase in the marginal cost of producing each pound of potatoes, and hence the tax results in an upward shift in the supply curve by $1 per pound.

As shown in Figure 7.11, the new equilibrium price (including the tax) will be $3.50, and the new equilibrium quantity will be 2.5 million pounds per month. The net price per pound received by producers is one dollar less than the price paid by the consumer, or $2.50. Even though the tax was collected entirely from potato sellers, the burden of the tax fell on both buyers and sellers—on buyers, because they pay $0.50 per pound more than before the tax; and on sellers, because they receive $0.50 per pound less than before the tax.

The burden of the tax need not fall equally on buyers and sellers, as in the illustration just discussed. Indeed, as the following example illustrates, a tax levied on sellers may end up being paid entirely by buyers.

How will a tax on cars affect their prices in the long run?

Suppose that, given sufficient time, all the inputs required to produce cars can be acquired in unlimited quantities at fixed market prices. If the inputs required to produce each car cost $20,000, how will the long-run equilibrium price of auto-mobiles be affected if a tax of $100 per car is levied on manufacturers?

The fact that all the inputs needed to build cars can be acquired at constant prices suggests that the long-run marginal cost of making cars is constant—or, in other words, that the long-run supply curve of cars is horizontal at $20,000 per car. A tax of $100 per car effectively raises marginal cost by $100 per car, and thus shifts the supply curve upward by exactly $100. If the demand curve for cars is as shown by curve *D* in Figure 7.12, the effect is to raise the equilibrium price of cars by exactly $100, to $20,100. The equilibrium quantity of cars falls from 2 million per month to 1.9 million.

ECONOMIC
NATURALIST
7.2

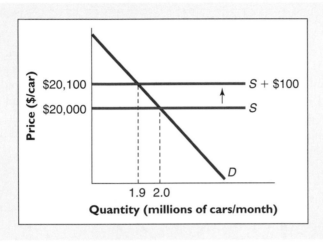

FIGURE 7.12
The Effect of a Tax on Sellers of a Good with Infinite Price Elasticity of Supply.
When the supply curve for a good is perfectly elastic, the burden of a tax collected from sellers falls entirely on buyers.

Although the long-run supply curve shown in Figure 7.12 is in one sense an extreme case (since its price elasticity is infinite), it is by no means an unrepresentative one. For as we discussed in Chapter 4, the long-run supply curve will tend to be horizontal when it is possible to acquire more of all the necessary inputs at constant prices. As a first approximation, this can be accomplished for many—perhaps even most—goods and services in a typical economy.

For goods with perfectly elastic supply curves, the entire burden of any tax is borne by the buyer.[1] That is, the increase in the equilibrium price is exactly equal to the tax. For this empirically relevant case, then, there is special irony in the common political practice of justifying taxes on business by saying that businesses have greater ability to pay than consumers.

HOW A TAX COLLECTED FROM A SELLER AFFECTS ECONOMIC SURPLUS

We saw earlier that perfectly competitive markets distribute goods and services efficiently if demand curves reflect all relevant benefits and supply curves reflect all relevant costs. If a tax is imposed on sellers in such a market, will the new market equilibrium still be efficient? Consider again the potato market discussed earlier, whose supply and demand curves are reproduced in Figure 7.13. In the absence of a tax, 3 million pounds of potatoes a month would be sold in this market at a price of $3 per pound, and the resulting total economic surplus would be $9 million per month (the area of the shaded triangle).

[1]In the example given, the tax was collected from sellers. If you go on to take intermediate microeconomics, you will see that the same conclusions apply when a tax is collected from buyers.

FIGURE 7.13

The Market for Potatoes without Taxes.

Without taxes, total surplus in the potato market equals the area of the shaded triangle, $9 million per month.

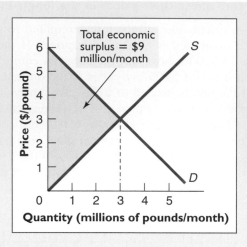

FIGURE 7.14

The Effect of a $1 per Pound Tax on Potatoes.

A $1 per pound tax on potatoes would cause an upward shift in the supply curve by $1. The sum of producer and consumer surplus would shrink to the area of the shaded triangle, $6.25 million per month.

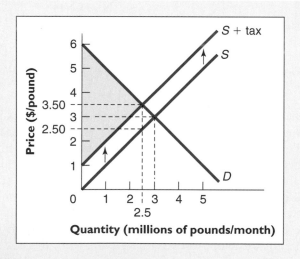

With a tax of $1 per pound collected from potato sellers, the new equilibrium price of potatoes would be $3.50 per pound (of which sellers receive $2.50, net of tax), and only 2.5 millions pounds of potatoes would be sold each month (see Figure 7.14). The total economic surplus reaped by buyers and sellers in the potato market would be the area of the shaded triangle shown in Figure 7.14, which is $6.25 million per month—or $2.75 million less than before.

This drop in surplus may sound like an enormous loss. But it is a misleading figure, because it fails to take account of the value of the additional tax revenue collected, which is equal to $2.5 million per month ($1 per pound on 2.5 million pounds of potatoes). If the government needs to collect no more than a given total amount of tax revenue in order to pay for the services it provides, then the potato tax revenue should enable it to reduce other taxes by $2.5 million per month. So although buyers and sellers lose $2.75 million per month in economic surplus from their participation in the potato market, they also enjoy a $2.5 million reduction in the other taxes they pay. On balance, then, the net reduction in total economic surplus is only $0.25 million.

Graphically, the loss in total economic surplus caused by the imposition of the tax can be shown as the small shaded triangle in Figure 7.15. This loss in surplus is often described as the **deadweight loss** from the tax.

Still, a loss in economic surplus, however small, is something people would prefer to avoid, and taxes like the one just described undoubtedly reduce economic surplus in the markets on which they are imposed. As Federal Reserve

deadweight loss the reduction in total economic surplus that results from the adoption of a policy

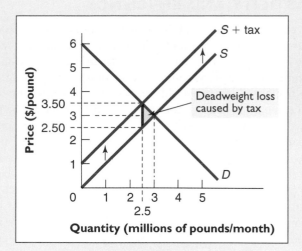

FIGURE 7.15
The Deadweight Loss Caused by a Tax.
For the market shown, the loss in economic surplus caused by a tax of $1 per pound of potatoes equals the area of the small shaded triangle, or $250,000 per month.

Board chairman Alan Greenspan remarked, "All taxes are a drag on economic growth. It's only a question of degree."[1]

A tax reduces economic surplus because it distorts the basic cost-benefit criterion that would ordinarily guide efficient decisions about production and consumption. In the example just considered, the cost-benefit principle tells us that we should expand potato production up to the point at which the benefit of the last pound of potatoes consumed (as measured by what buyers are willing to pay for it) equals the cost of producing it (as measured by the producer's marginal cost). That condition was satisfied in the potato market before the tax, but it is not satisfied once the tax is imposed. In Figure 7.15, for example, note that when potato consumption is 2.5 million pounds per month, the value of an additional pound of potatoes to consumers is $3.50, whereas the cost to producers is only $2.50, not including the tax. (The cost to producers, including the tax, is $3.50 per pound, but again we note that this tax is not a cost to society as a whole because it offsets other taxes that would otherwise have to be collected.)

Is a tax on potatoes necessarily "bad"? (When economists say that a policy, such as a tax, is "bad," they mean that it lowers total economic surplus.) To answer this question, we must first identify the best alternative to taxing potatoes. You may be tempted to say "Don't tax anything at all!" On a moment's reflection, however, you will realize that this is surely not the best option. After all, a country that taxed nothing could not pay for even the most minimal public services, such as road maintenance, fire protection, and national defense. And a country without at least minimal defense capability could not hope to maintain its independence for long. (We will consider why we often empower government to provide public goods in Chapter 15.) On balance, if taxing potatoes were the best way to avoid doing without highly valued public services, then a small deadweight loss in the potato market would be a small price indeed.

So the real question is whether there are other things we could tax that would be better than taxing potatoes. The problem with a tax on any activity is that if market incentives encourage people to pursue the "right" amount of the activity (that is, the surplus-maximizing amount), then a tax will encourage them to pursue too little of it. As economists have long recognized, this observation suggests that taxes will cause smaller deadweight losses if they are imposed on goods for which the equilibrium quantity is not highly sensitive to changes in production costs.

[1]*The Wall Street Journal*, March 26, 1997, p. A1.

TAXES, ELASTICITY, AND EFFICIENCY

Suppose the government put a tax of 50 cents per pound on table salt. How would this affect the amount of salt you and others use? In Chapter 4 we saw that the demand for salt is highly inelastic with respect to price, because salt has few substitutes and occupies only a minuscule share in most family budgets. Because the imposition of a tax on table salt would not result in a significant reduction in the amount of it consumed, the deadweight loss from this tax would be relatively small. More generally, the deadweight loss from a per-unit tax imposed on the seller of a good will be smaller the smaller is the price elasticity of demand for the good.

Figure 7.16 illustrates how the deadweight loss from a tax declines as the demand for a good becomes less elastic with respect to price. In both (a) and (b), the original supply and demand curves yield an equilibrium price of $2 per unit and an equilibrium quantity of 24 units per day. The deadweight loss from a tax of $1 per unit imposed on the good shown in Figure 7.16(a) is the area of the shaded triangle in (a), which is $2.50 per day. The demand curve in Figure 7.16(b), D_2, is less elastic at the equilibrium price of $2 than the demand curve in (a), D_1 [this follows from the fact that P/Q is the same in both cases, whereas 1/slope is smaller in (b)]. The deadweight loss from the same $1 per unit tax imposed on the good in Figure 7.16(b) is the area of the shaded triangle in (b), which is only $1.50 per day.

FIGURE 7.16

Elasticity of Demand and the Deadweight Loss from a Tax.

At the equilibrium price and quantity, price elasticity of demand is smaller for the good shown in (b) than for the good shown in (a). The area of the deadweight loss triangle in (b), $1.50 per day, is smaller than the area of the deadweight loss triangle in (a), $2.50 per day.

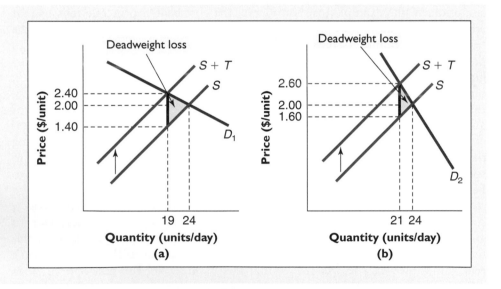

The reduction in equilibrium quantity that results from a tax on a good will also be smaller the smaller is the elasticity of supply of the good. In Figure 7.17, for example, the original supply and demand curves for the markets portrayed in each part yield an equilibrium price of $2 per unit and an equilibrium quantity of 72 units per day. The deadweight loss from a tax of $1 per unit imposed on the good shown in Figure 7.17(a) is the area of the shaded triangle in (a), which is $7.50 per day. The supply curve in Figure 7.17(b), S_2, is less elastic at the equilibrium price than the supply curve in the (a), S_1 [again because P/Q is the same in both cases, whereas 1/slope is smaller in (b)]. The deadweight loss from the same $1 per unit tax imposed on the good in Figure 7.17(b) is the area of the shaded triangle in (b), which is only $4.50 per day.

The deadweight loss from a tax imposed on a good whose supply curve is perfectly inelastic will be zero. This explains why many economists continue to favor the tax advocated by Henry George in the nineteenth century. George proposed that all taxes on labor and goods be abolished and replaced by a single tax on land. Such a tax, he argued, would cause no significant loss in economic surplus because the supply of land is almost perfectly inelastic.

FIGURE 7.17

Elasticity of Supply and the Deadweight Loss from a Tax.

At the equilibrium price and quantity, price elasticity of supply is smaller for the good shown in (b) than for the good shown in (a). The area of the deadweight loss triangle in (b), $4.50 per day, is smaller than the area of the deadweight loss triangle in (a), $7.50 per day.

TAXES, EXTERNAL COSTS, AND EFFICIENCY

Even more attractive than taxing land, from an efficiency standpoint, is taxing activities that people tend to pursue to excess. We have mentioned activities that generate environmental pollution as one example; in later chapters we will discuss others. Whereas a tax on land does not reduce economic surplus, a tax on pollution can actually increase total economic surplus. Taxes on activities that cause harm to others kill two birds with one stone: They generate revenue to pay for useful public services and at the same time discourage people from pursuing the harmful activities. The notion that taxes always and everywhere constitute an obstacle to efficiency simply does not withstand careful scrutiny.

RECAP   TAXES AND EFFICIENCY

A tax levied on the seller of a product has the same effect on equilibrium quantity and price as a rise in marginal cost equal to the amount of the tax. The burden of a tax imposed on sellers will generally be shared among both buyers and sellers. In the extreme case of a good whose elasticity of supply is infinite, the entire burden of the tax is borne by buyers.

A tax imposed on a product whose supply and demand curves embody all relevant costs and benefits associated with its production and use will result in a deadweight loss—a reduction in total economic surplus in the market for the taxed good. Such taxes may nonetheless be justified if the value of the public services financed by the tax outweighs this deadweight loss. In general, the deadweight loss from a tax on a good will be smaller the smaller are the good's price elasticities of supply and demand. Taxes on activities that generate harm to others may produce a net gain in economic surplus, even apart from the value of public services they finance.

▪ SUMMARY ▪

- When the supply and demand curves for a product capture all the relevant costs and benefits of producing that product, then market equilibrium for that product will be efficient. In such a market, if price and quantity do not equal their equilibrium values, a transaction can be found that will make at least some people better off without harming others.

- Total economic surplus is a measure of the amount by which participants in a market benefit by participating in it. It is the sum of total consumer surplus and total producer surplus in the market. One of the attractive properties of market equilibrium is that it maximizes the value of total economic surplus.

- Efficiency should not be equated with social justice. If we believe that the distribution of income among people is unjust, we won't like the results produced by the intersection of the supply and demand curves based on that income distribution, even though those results are efficient.

- Even so, we should always strive for efficiency because it enables us to achieve all our other goals to the fullest possible extent. Whenever a market is out of equilibrium, the economic pie can be made larger. And with a larger pie, everyone can have a larger slice.

- Regulations or policies that prevent markets from reaching equilibrium—such as price ceilings, price subsidies, and first-come, first-served allocation schemes—are often defended on the grounds that they help the poor. But such schemes reduce economic surplus, meaning that we can find alternatives under which both rich and poor would be better off. The main difficulty of the poor is that they have too little income. Rather than trying to control the prices of the goods they buy, we could do better by enacting policies that raise the incomes of the poor and then letting prices seek their equilibrium levels. Those who complain that the poor lack the political power to obtain such income transfers must explain why the poor have the power to impose regulations that are far more costly than income transfers.

- Even when a good is provided by a public utility rather than a private firm, the theory of competitive supply has important implications for how to provide the good most efficiently. The general rule is that a public utility maximizes economic surplus by charging its customers the marginal cost of the goods it provides.

- Critics often complain that taxes make the economy less efficient. A tax will indeed reduce economic surplus if the supply and demand curves in the market for the taxed good reflect all the relevant costs and benefits of its production and consumption. But this decline in surplus may be more than offset by the increase in economic surplus made possible by public goods financed with the proceeds of the tax. The best taxes are imposed on activities that would otherwise be pursued to excess, such as activities that generate environmental pollution. Such taxes not only do not reduce economic surplus; they actually increase it.

▪ KEY TERMS ▪

deadweight loss (184)   efficiency (or Pareto efficiency) (168)

▪ REVIEW QUESTIONS ▪

1. Why do economists emphasize efficiency as an important goal of public policy?

2. You are a senator considering how to vote on a policy that would increase the economic surplus of workers by $100 million per year but reduce the economic surplus of retirees by $1 million per year. What additional measure might you combine with the policy to ensure that the overall result is a better outcome for everyone?

3. Why does the loss in total economic surplus directly experienced by participants in the market for a good that is taxed overstate the overall loss in economic surplus that results from the tax?

4. Why is compensating volunteers to relinquish their seats on overbooked flights more efficient than a policy of first-come, first-served?

5. Why do price ceilings reduce economic surplus?

▪ PROBLEMS ▪

1. Suppose the weekly demand and supply curves for used DVDs in Lincoln, Nebraska, are as shown in the diagram. Calculate
   a. The weekly consumer surplus.
   b. The weekly producer surplus.
   c. The maximum weekly amount that producers and consumers in Lincoln would be willing to pay to be able to buy and sell used DVDs in any given week.

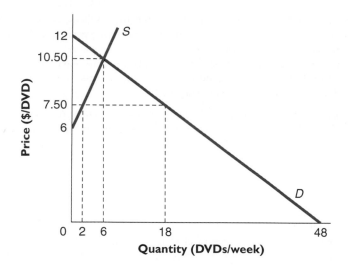

2. Refer to Problem 1. Suppose a coalition of students from Lincoln High School succeeds in persuading the local government to impose a price ceiling of $7.50 on used DVDs, on the grounds that local suppliers are taking advantage of teenagers by charging exorbitant prices.
  a. Calculate the weekly shortage of used DVDs that will result from this policy.
  b. Calculate the total economic surplus lost every week as a result of the price ceiling.

3. The Kubak crystal caves are renowned for their stalactites and stalagmites. The warden of the caves offers a tour each afternoon at 2 P.M. sharp. The caves can be shown to only four people per day without disturbing their fragile ecology. Occasionally, however, more than four people want to see the caves on the same day. The following table lists the people who wanted to see the caves on September 24, 2003, together with their respective times of arrival and reservation prices for taking the tour that day.

	Arrival time	Reservation price ($)
Herman	1:48	20
Jon	1:50	14
Kate	1:53	30
Jack	1:56	15
Penny	1:57	40
Fran	1:59	12
Faith	2:00	17

  a. If the tour is "free" and the warden operates it on a first-come, first-served basis, what will the total consumer surplus be for the four people who get to go on the tour on that day?
  b. Suppose the warden solicits volunteers to postpone their tour by offering increasing amounts of cash compensation until only four people still wish to see the caves that day. If he gives each volunteer the same compensation payment, how much money will he have to offer to generate the required number of volunteers? What is the total economic surplus under this policy?
  c. Why is the compensation policy more efficient than the first-come, first-served policy?
  d. Describe a way of financing the warden's compensation payments that will make everyone, including the warden, either better off or no worse off than under the first-come, first-served approach.

4. Suppose the weekly demand for a certain good, in thousands of units, is given by the equation $P = 8 - Q$, and the weekly supply of the good is given by the equation $P = 2 + Q$, where P is the price in dollars.
  a. Calculate the total weekly economic surplus generated at the market equilibrium.

b. Suppose a per-unit tax of $2, to be collected from sellers, is imposed in this market. Calculate the direct loss in economic surplus experienced by participants in this market as a result of the tax.

c. How much government revenue will this tax generate each week? If the revenue is used to offset other taxes paid by participants in this market, what will be their net reduction in total economic surplus?

5. Is a company's producer surplus the same as its profit? (Hint: A company's total cost is equal to the sum of all marginal costs incurred in producing its output, plus any fixed costs.)

6. In Charlotte, North Carolina, citizens can get their electric power from two sources: a hydroelectric generator and a coal-fired steam generator. The hydroelectric generator can supply up to 100 units of power per day at a constant marginal cost of 1 cent per unit. The steam generator can supply any additional power that is needed at a constant marginal cost of 10 cents per unit. When electricity costs 10 cents per unit, residents of Charlotte demand 200 units per day.

a. Draw the marginal cost curve of electric power production in Charlotte.

b. How much should the city charge for electric power? Explain. Should it charge the same price for a family whose power comes from the hydroelectric generator as it does for a family whose power comes from the steam generator?

7. The municipal water works of Cortland draws water from two sources, an underground spring and a nearby lake. Water from the spring costs 2 cents per 100 gallons to deliver, and the spring has a capacity of 1 million gallons per day. Water from the lake costs 4 cents per 100 gallons to deliver and is available in unlimited quantities. The demand for water in the summer months in Cortland is $P = 20 - 0.001Q$, where P is the price of water in cents per 100 gallons, and Q is quantity demanded in hundreds of gallons per day. The demand curve for water in the winter months is $P = 10 - 0.001Q$. If the water works wants to encourage efficient water use, how much should it charge for water in the summer months? In the winter months?

8.* Phil's demand curve for visits to the Gannett walk-in medical clinic is given by $P = 48 - 8Q$, where P is the price per visit in dollars and Q is the number of visits per semester. The marginal cost of providing medical services at Gannett is $24 per visit. Phil has a choice between two health policies, A and B. Both policies cover all the costs of any serious illness from which Phil might suffer. Policy A also covers the cost of visits to the walk-in clinic, whereas policy B does not. Thus if Phil chooses policy B, he must pay $24 per visit to the walk-in clinic.

a. If the premiums the insurance company charges for policies A and B must cover their respective costs, by how much will the two premiums differ, and what will be the difference in Phil's total expenditure for medical care under the two policies?

b. Which policy will Phil choose?

c. What is the most Phil would be willing to pay for the right to continue buying that policy?

9.* The government of Islandia, a small island nation, imports heating oil at a price of $2 per gallon and makes it available to citizens at a price of $1 per gallon. If Islandians' demand curve for heating oil is given by $P = 6 - Q$, where P is the price per gallon in dollars and Q is the quantity in millions of gallons per year, how much economic surplus is lost as a result of the government's policy?

10.* Refer to Problem 9. Suppose each of the 1 million Islandian households has the same demand curve for heating oil.

a. What is the household demand curve?

b. How much consumer surplus would each household lose if it had to pay $2 per gallon instead of $1 per gallon for heating oil, assuming there were no other changes in the household budget?

c. With the money saved by not subsidizing oil, by how much could the Islandian government afford to cut each family's annual taxes?

d. If the government abandoned its oil subsidy and implemented the tax cut, by how much would each family be better off?

e. How does the resulting total gain for the 1 million families compare with your calculation of the lost surplus in the Problem 9?

*Problems marked with an asterisk (*) are more difficult.

■ ANSWERS TO IN-CHAPTER EXERCISES ■

7.1 At a price of 50 cents per gallon, there is excess demand of 4,000 gallons per day. Suppose a seller produces an extra gallon of milk (marginal cost = 50 cents) and sells it to the buyer who values it most (reservation price = $2.50) for $1.50. Both buyer and seller will gain additional economic surplus of $1, and no other buyers or sellers will be hurt by the transaction.

7.2 As shown in the accompanying diagram, the new loss in total economic surplus is $200 per day.

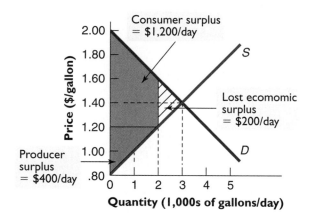

7.3 With a $0.50 per loaf subsidy, the new domestic price becomes $1.50 per loaf. The new lost surplus is the area of the small shaded triangle in the diagram: (1/2)($0.50/ loaf)(1,000,000 loaves/month) = $250,000 per month.

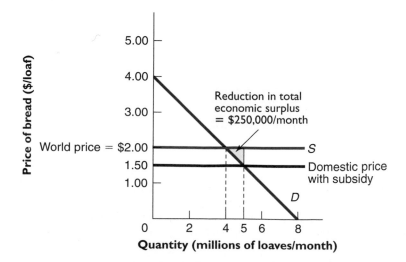

7.4 Under first-come, first-served, Dana will have to postpone his lesson. Since Dana would be willing to pay up to $10 to avoid postponing it, he will be better off if the pro asks for a contribution of, say, $8, and then lets him take Bill's place at the scheduled time. The pro could then give $4 to Bill, which would make him $1 better off than if he had not postponed his lesson. The remaining $4 of Dana's payment could be distributed by giving $1 each to Ann, Carrie, Earl, and the tennis pro.

Player	Arrival time	Reservation price ($)
Ann	9:50 A.M.	4
Bill	9:52 A.M.	3
Carrie	9:55 A.M.	6
Dana	9:56 A.M.	10
Earl	9:59 A.M.	3

7.5 At a consumption level of 2 million gallons per day, the marginal source of water is the lake, which has a marginal cost of 0.8 cents per gallon. The city should charge everyone 0.8 cents per gallon, including those who get their water from the spring.

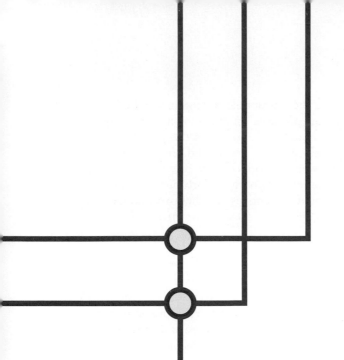

CHAPTER

8

THE QUEST FOR PROFIT AND THE INVISIBLE HAND

■

The market for ethnic cuisine in Ithaca, New York, offered few choices in the early 1970s: the city had one Japanese, two Greek, four Italian, and three Chinese restaurants. But now, some 30 years later and with essentially the same population, Ithaca has one Sri Lankan, two Indian, one Spanish, five Thai, two Korean, two Vietnamese, four Mexican, three Greek, seven Italian, two Japanese, and nine Chinese restaurants. In at least some of the city's other markets, however, the range of available choices has narrowed. For example, several companies provided telephone answering service in 1972, but only one does so today.

Rare indeed is the marketplace in which the identities of the buyers and sellers remain static for extended periods. New businesses enter, established ones leave. There are more body-piercing studios in Ithaca now and fewer watch-repair shops; more marketing consultants and fewer intercity bus companies; and more appliances in stainless steel or black finishes, fewer in avocado or coppertone.

Driving these changes is the businessowner's quest for profit. Businesses migrate to industries and locations in which profit opportunities abound and desert those whose prospects appear bleak. In perhaps the most widely quoted passage from his landmark treatise, *The Wealth of Nations,* Adam Smith wrote,

> It is not from the benevolence of the butcher, the brewer, or the baker that we expect our dinner, but from their regard of their own interest. We address ourselves not to their humanity, but to their self-love, and never talk to them of our necessities, but of their advantage.

Why do most American cities now have more tattoo parlors and fewer watch repair shops than in 1972?

Smith went on to argue that although the entrepreneur "intends only his own gain," he is "led by an invisible hand to promote an end which was no part of his intention." As Smith saw it, even though self-interest is the prime mover of economic activity, the end result is an allocation of goods and services that serves society's collective interests remarkably well. If producers are offering "too much" of one product and "not enough" of another, profit opportunities immediately alert entrepreneurs to that fact and provide incentives for them to take remedial action. All the while, the system exerts relentless pressure on producers to hold the price of each good close to its cost of production, and indeed to reduce that cost in any ways possible.

Our task in this chapter is to gain deeper insight into the nature of the forces that guide the invisible hand. What exactly does "profit" mean? How is it measured, and how does the quest for it serve society's ends? And if competition holds price close to the cost of production, why do so many entrepreneurs become fabulously wealthy? We will also discuss cases in which misunderstanding of Smith's theory results in costly errors, both in everyday decision making and in the realm of government policy.

THE CENTRAL ROLE OF ECONOMIC PROFIT

The economic theory of business behavior is built on the assumption that the firm's goal is to maximize its profit. So we must be clear at the outset about what, exactly, profit means.

THREE TYPES OF PROFIT

explicit costs the actual payments a firm makes to its factors of production and other suppliers

accounting profit the difference between a firm's total revenue and its explicit cost

implicit costs the opportunity costs of the resources supplied by the firm's owners

economic profit (or excess profit) the difference between a firm's total revenue and the sum of its explicit and implicit costs

The economist's understanding of profit is different from the accountant's, and the distinction between the two is important to understanding how the invisible hand works. Accountants define the annual profit of a business as the difference between the revenue it takes in and its **explicit costs** for the year, which are the actual payments the firm makes to its factors of production and other suppliers. Profit thus defined is called **accounting profit**.

Accounting profit = total revenue − explicit costs.

Accounting profit is the most familiar profit concept in everyday discourse. It is the one that companies use, for example, when they provide statements about their profits in press releases or annual reports.

Economists, by contrast, define profit as the difference between the firm's total revenue and not just its explicit costs, but also its **implicit costs,** which are the opportunity costs of all the resources supplied by the firm's owners. Profit thus defined is called **economic profit,** or **excess profit.**

Economic profit = total revenue − explicit costs − implicit costs.

To illustrate the difference between accounting profit and economic profit, consider a firm with $400,000 in total annual revenue whose only explicit costs are workers' salaries totaling $250,000 per year. The owners of this firm have supplied machines and other capital equipment with a total resale value of $1 million. This firm's accounting profit, then, is the difference between its total revenue of $400,000 per year and its explicit costs of $250,000 per year, or $150,000 per year.

To calculate the firm's economic profit, we must first calculate the opportunity cost of the resources supplied by the firm's owners. Suppose the current annual interest rate on savings accounts is 10 percent. Had owners not invested in capital equipment, they could have earned an additional $100,000 per year interest by depositing their $1 million in a savings account. So the firm's economic profit is $400,000 per year − $250,000 per year − $100,000 per year = $50,000 per year.

Note that this economic profit is smaller than the accounting profit by exactly the amount of the firm's implicit costs—the $100,000 per year opportunity cost of the resources supplied by the firm's owners. This difference between a business's accounting profit and its economic profit is called its **normal profit**. Normal profit is simply the opportunity cost of the resources supplied to a business by its owners.

Figure 8.1 illustrates the difference between accounting and economic profit. Figure 8.1(a) represents a firm's total revenues, while (b) and (c) show how these revenues are apportioned among the various cost and profit categories.

normal profit the opportunity cost of the resources supplied by a firm's owners, equal to accounting profit minus economic profit

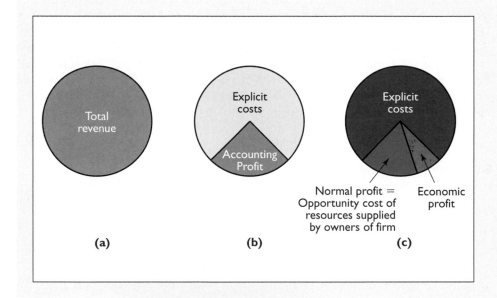

FIGURE 8.1
The Difference between Accounting Profit and Economic Profit.
Accounting profit (b) is the difference between total revenue and explicit costs. Normal profit (c) is the opportunity cost of all resources supplied by firm's owners. Economic profit (c) is the difference between total revenue and all costs, explicit and implicit (also equal to the difference between accounting profit and normal profit).

"All I know, Harrison, is that I've been on the board forty years and have yet to see an excess profit."

The following examples illustrate why the distinction between accounting and economic profit is so important.

EXAMPLE 8.1

Should Pudge Buffet stay in the farming business?

Pudge Buffet is a corn farmer who lives near Lincoln, Nebraska. His payments for land and equipment rental and for other supplies come to $10,000 per year. The only input he supplies is his own labor, and he considers farming just as attractive as his only other employment opportunity, managing a retail store at a salary of $11,000 per year. Apart from the matter of pay, Pudge is indifferent between farming and being a manager. Corn sells for a constant price per bushel in an international market too large to be affected by changes in one farmer's corn production. Pudge's revenue from corn sales is $22,000 per year. What is his accounting profit? His economic profit? His normal profit? Should he remain a corn farmer?

As shown in Table 8.1, Pudge's accounting profit is $12,000 per year, the difference between his $22,000 annual revenue and his $10,000 yearly payment for land, equipment, and supplies. His economic profit is that amount less the opportunity cost of his labor. Since the latter is the $11,000 per year he could have earned as a store manager, he is making an economic profit of $1,000 per year. Finally, his normal profit is the $11,000 opportunity cost of the only resource he supplies, namely, his labor. Since Pudge likes the two jobs equally well, he will be better off by $1,000 per year if he remains in farming.

TABLE 8.1
Revenue, Cost, and Profit Summary for Example 8.1

Total revenue ($/year)	Explicit costs ($/year)	Implicit costs ($/year)	Accounting profit (= total revenue − explicit costs) ($/year)	Economic profit (= total revenue − explicit costs − implicit costs) ($/year)	Normal profit (= implicit costs) ($/year)
22,000	10,000	11,000	12,000	1,000	11,000

EXERCISE 8.1

In Example 8.1, how will Pudge's economic profit change if his annual revenue from corn production is not $22,000, but $20,000? Should he continue to farm?

If you worked through this exercise, you saw that Pudge now has an economic profit of −$1,000 per year. A negative economic profit is also called an **economic loss**. If Pudge expects to sustain an economic loss indefinitely, his best bet would be to abandon farming in favor of managing a retail store.

You might think that if Pudge could just save enough money to buy his own land and equipment, his best option would be to remain a farmer. But as the following example illustrates, that impression is based on a failure to perceive the difference between accounting profit and economic profit.

economic loss an economic profit that is less than zero

EXAMPLE 8.2

Does owning one's own land make a difference?

Refer to Exercise 8.1. Suppose Pudge's Uncle Warren, who owns the farmland Pudge has been renting, dies and leaves Pudge that parcel of land. If the land could be rented to some other farmer for $6,000 per year, should Pudge remain in farming?

As shown in Table 8.2, if Pudge continues to farms his own land, his accounting profit will be $16,000 per year, or $6,000 more than in Exercise 8.1. But his economic profit will still be the same as before—that is, −$1,000 per year—because Pudge must deduct the $6,000 per year opportunity cost of farming his

TABLE 8.2
Revenue, Cost, and Profit Summary for Example 8.2

Total revenue ($/year)	Explicit costs ($/year)	Implicit costs ($/year)	Accounting profit (= total revenue − explicit costs) ($/year)	Economic profit (= total revenue − explicit costs − implicit costs) ($/year)	Normal profit (= implicit costs) ($/year)
20,000	4,000	17,000	16,000	−1,000	17,000

own land, even though he no longer must make an explicit payment to his uncle for it. The normal profit from owning and operating his farm will be $17,000 per year—the opportunity cost of the land and labor he provides. But since Pudge earns an accounting profit of only $16,000, he will again do better to abandon farming for the managerial job.

Pudge obviously would be wealthier as an owner than he was as a renter. But the question of whether to remain a farmer is answered the same way whether Pudge rents his farmland or owns it. He should stay in farming only if that is the option that yields the highest economic profit.

 RECAP   **THE CENTRAL ROLE OF ECONOMIC PROFIT**

A firm's accounting profit is the difference between its revenue and the sum of all explicit costs it incurs. Economic profit is the difference between the firm's revenue and *all* costs it incurs—both explicit and implicit. Normal profit is the opportunity cost of the resources supplied by the owners of the firm. When a firm's accounting profit is exactly equal to the opportunity cost of the inputs supplied by the firm's owners, the firm's economic profit is zero. For a firm to remain in business in the long run, it must earn an economic profit greater than or equal to zero.

THE INVISIBLE HAND THEORY

TWO FUNCTIONS OF PRICE

In the free enterprise system, market prices serve two important and distinct functions. The first, the **rationing function of price,** is to distribute scarce goods among potential claimants, ensuring that those who get them are the ones who value them most. Thus, if three people want the only antique clock for sale at an auction, the clock goes home with the person who bids the most for it. The second function, the **allocative function of price,** is to direct productive resources to different sectors of the economy. Resources leave markets in which price cannot cover the cost of production and enter those in which price exceeds the cost of production.

Both the allocative and rationing functions of price underlie Adam Smith's celebrated theory of the **invisible hand** of the market. Recall that Smith thought the market system channels the selfish interests of individual buyers and sellers so as to promote the greatest good for society. The carrot of economic profit and the stick of economic loss, he argued, were the only forces necessary to ensure not only that existing supplies in any market would be allocated efficiently, but also that resources would be allocated across markets to produce the most efficient possible mix of goods and services.

rationing function of price to distribute scarce goods to those consumers who value them most highly

allocative function of price to direct resources away from overcrowded markets and toward markets that are underserved

invisible hand theory Adam Smith's theory that the actions of independent, self-interested buyers and sellers will often result in the most efficient allocation of resources

RESPONSES TO PROFITS AND LOSSES

To get a feel for how the invisible hand works, we begin by looking at how market forces respond to economic profits and losses. If a firm is to remain in business in the long run, it must cover all its costs, both explicit and implicit. A firm's normal profit is just a cost of doing business. Thus the owner of a firm that earns no more than a normal profit has managed only to recover the opportunity cost of the resources invested in the firm. By contrast, the owner of a firm that makes a positive economic profit earns more than the opportunity cost of the invested resources; she earns a normal profit and then some.

Naturally, everyone would be delighted to earn more than a normal profit, and no one wants to earn less. The result is that those markets in which firms are earning an economic profit tend to attract additional resources, whereas markets in which firms are experiencing economic losses tend to lose resources.

To see how this happens, we'll examine the workings of the market for corn whose short-run supply and demand curves are shown in Figure 8.2(a). Figure 8.2(b) depicts the marginal and average total cost curves for a representative farm. The equilibrium price of $2 per bushel is determined by the supply–demand intersection in (a). The representative farm whose MC and ATC curves are shown in (b) then maximizes its profit by producing the quantity for which price equals marginal cost, 130,000 bushels of corn per year.

FIGURE 8.2

Economic Profit in the Short Run in the Corn Market.

At an equilibrium price of $2 per bushel (a), the typical farm earns an economic profit of $104,000 per year (b).

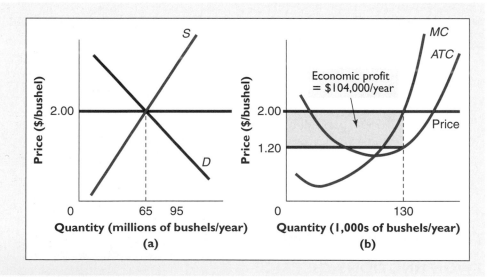

Recall from Chapter 6 that average total cost at any output level is the sum of all costs divided by output. The difference between price and *ATC* is thus equal to the average amount of economic profit earned per unit sold. In Figure 8.2(b), that difference is $0.80 per unit. With 130,000 bushels per year sold, the representative farm thus earns an economic profit of $104,000 per year.

The existence of positive economic profit in the corn market means that producers in that market are earning more than their opportunity cost of farming. For simplicity, we assume that the inputs required to enter the corn market—land, labor, equipment, and the like—are available at constant prices and that anyone is free to enter this market if he or she chooses. The key point is that since price exceeds the opportunity cost of the resources required to enter the market, others *will* want to enter. And as they add their corn production to the amount already on offer, supply shifts to the right, causing the market equilibrium price to fall, as shown in Figure 8.3(a). At the new price of $1.50 per bushel, the representative farm now earns much less economic profit than before, only $50,400 per year [Figure 8.3(b)].

For simplicity, we assume that all farms employ the same standard production method, so that their *ATC* curves are identical. Entry will then continue until

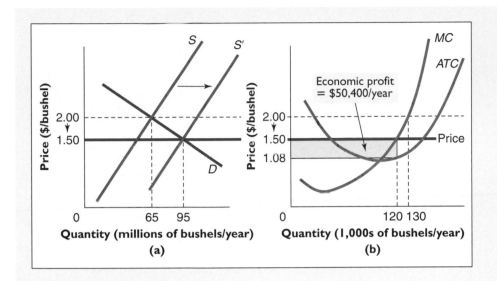

FIGURE 8.3
The Effect of Entry on Price and Economic Profit.
At the original price of $2 per bushel, existing farmers earned economic profit, prompting new farmers to enter. With entry, supply shifts right [from S to S' in (a)] and equilibrium price falls, as does economic profit (b).

price falls all the way to the minimum value of *ATC*. (At any price higher than that, economic profit would still be positive, and entry would continue, driving price still lower.) Recall from Chapter 6 that the short-run marginal cost curve intersects the *ATC* curve at the minimum point of the *ATC* curve. This means that once price reaches the minimum value of *ATC*, the profit-maximizing rule of setting price equal to marginal cost results in a quantity for which price and *ATC* are the same. And when that happens, economic profit for the representative farm will be exactly zero, as shown in Figure 8.4(b).

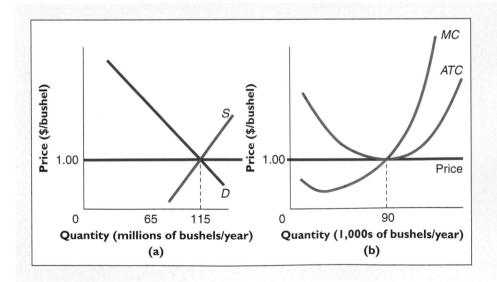

FIGURE 8.4
Equilibrium when Entry Ceases.
Further entry ceases once price falls to the minimum value of *ATC*. At that point all firms earn a normal economic profit. Equivalently, each earns an economic profit of zero.

In the adjustment process just considered, the initial equilibrium price had been above the minimum value of *ATC*, giving rise to positive economic profits. Suppose instead that the market demand curve for corn had intersected the short-run supply curve at a price below the minimum value each firm's *ATC* curve, as shown in Figure 8.5(a). As long as this price is above the minimum value of average variable cost,[1] each farm will supply that quantity of corn for which price equals marginal cost, shown as 70,000 bushels per year in Figure 8.5(b). Note, however, that at that quantity, the farm's average total cost is $1.05 per bushel, or $0.30 more than the price for which it sells each bushel. As shown in (b), the farm thus sustains an economic loss of $21,000 per year.

[1]This qualification refers to the firm's shutdown condition, discussed in Chapter 6.

FIGURE 8.5

A Short-Run Economic Loss in the Corn Market.
When price is below the minimum value of *ATC* (a), each farm sustains an economic loss (b).

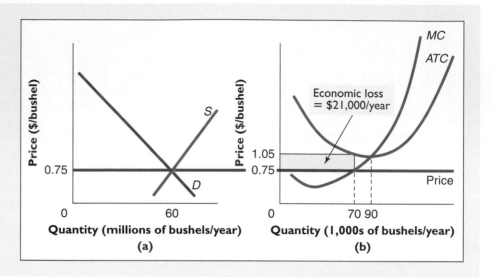

If the demand curve that led to the low price and resulting economic losses in Figure 8.5 is expected to persist, farmers will begin to abandon farming for other activities that promise better returns. This means that the supply curve for corn will shift to the left, resulting in higher prices and smaller losses. Exit from corn farming will continue, in fact, until price has again risen to $1 per bushel, at which point there will be no incentive for further exit. Once again we see a stable equilibrium in which price is $1 per bushel, as shown in Figure 8.6.

FIGURE 8.6

Equilibrium when Exit Ceases.
Further exit ceases once price rises to the minimum value of *ATC*. At that point all firms earn a normal economic profit. Equivalently, each earns an economic profit of zero.

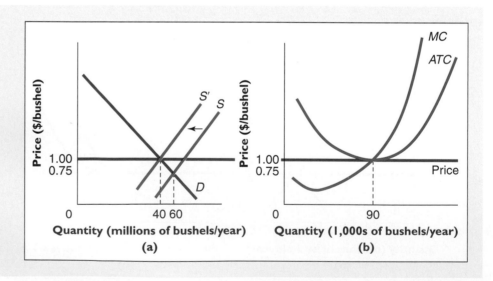

Given our simplifying assumptions that all corn farms employ a standardized production method and that inputs can be purchased in any quantities at fixed prices, the price of corn cannot remain above $1 per bushel (the minimum point on the *ATC* curve) in the long run. Any higher price would stimulate additional entry until price again fell to that level. Further, the price of corn cannot remain below $1 per bushel in the long run, because any lower price would stimulate exit until the price of corn again rose to $1 per bushel.

The fact that firms are free to enter or leave an industry at any time ensures that in the long run all firms in the industry will to tend earn zero economic profit. Their *goal* is not to earn zero profit. Rather, the zero-profit tendency is a consequence of the price movements associated with entry and exit. As the equilibrium principle—also called the no-cash-on-the-table principle (see Chapter 3)—

predicts, when people confront an opportunity for gain, they are almost always quick to exploit it.

What does the long-run supply curve look like in the corn market just discussed? This question is equivalent to asking "What is the marginal cost of producing additional bushels of corn in the long run?" In general, adjustment in the long run may entail not just entry and exit of standardized firms, but also the ability of firms to alter the mix of capital equipment and other fixed inputs they employ. Explicit consideration of this additional step would complicate the analysis considerably but would not alter the basic logic of the simpler account we present here, which assumes that all firms operate with the same standard mix of fixed inputs in the short run. Under this assumption, the long-run adjustment process consists exclusively of the entry and exit of firms that use a single standardized production method.

The fact that a new firm could enter or leave this corn market at any time means that corn production can always be augmented or reduced in the long run at a cost of $1 per bushel. And this, in turn, means that the long-run supply curve of corn will be a horizontal line at a price equal to the minimum value of the ATC curve, $1 per bushel. Since the long-run marginal cost (LMC) of producing corn is constant, so is the long-run average cost (LAC) and it, too, is $1 per bushel, as shown in Figure 8.7(a). Figure 8.7(b) shows the MC and ATC curves of a representative corn farm. At a price of $1 per bushel, this corn market is said to be in long-run equilibrium. The representative farm produces 90,000 bushels of corn each year, the quantity for which price equals its marginal cost. And since price is exactly equal to ATC, this farm also earns an economic profit of zero.

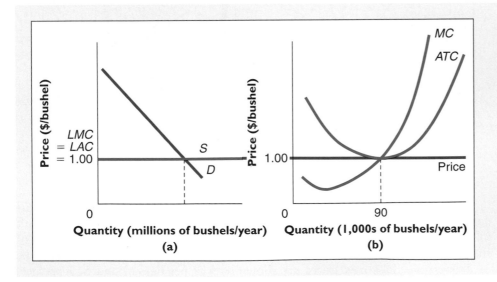

FIGURE 8.7

Long-Run Equilibrium in a Corn Market with Constant Long-Run Average Cost.
When each producer has the same ATC curve, the industry can supply as much or as little output as buyers wish to buy at a price equal to the minimum value of ATC (a). At that price, the representative producer (b) earns zero economic profit.

These observations call attention to two attractive features of the invisible hand theory. One is that the market outcome is efficient in the long run. Note, for example, that when the corn market is in long-run equilibrium, the value to buyers of the last unit of corn sold is $1 per bushel, which is exactly the same as the long-run marginal cost of producing it. Thus there is no possible rearrangement of resources that would make some participants in this market better off without causing harm to some others. If farmers were to expand production, for example, the added costs incurred would exceed the added benefits; and if they were to contract production, the cost savings would be less than the benefits forgone.

A second attractive feature of long-run competitive equilibrium is the market outcome can be described as fair, in the sense that the price buyers must pay is no higher than the cost incurred by suppliers. That cost includes a normal profit, the opportunity cost of the resources supplied by owners of the firm.

We must emphasize that Smith's invisible hand theory does not mean that market allocation of resources is optimal in every way. It simply means that markets are efficient in the limited technical sense discussed in the preceding chapter. Thus, if the current allocation differs from the market-equilibrium allocation, the invisible hand theory implies that we can reallocate resources in a way that makes some people better off without harming others.

The following example affords additional insight into how Smith's invisible hand works in practice.

EXAMPLE 8.3

What happens in a city with "too many" hair stylists and "too few" aerobics instructors?

At the initial equilibrium quantities and prices in the markets for haircuts and aerobics classes shown in Figure 8.8, all suppliers are currently earning zero economic profit. Now suppose that styles suddenly change in favor of longer hair and increased physical fitness. If the long-run marginal cost of altering current production levels is constant in both markets, describe how prices and quantities will change in each market, both in the short run and the long run. Are the new equilibrium quantities socially optimal?

FIGURE 8.8
Initial Equilibrium in the Markets for (a) Haircuts and (b) Aerobics Classes.
MC_H and ATC_H are the marginal cost and average total cost curves for a representative hair stylist, and MC_A and ATC_A are the marginal cost and average total cost curves for a representative aerobics instructor. Both markets are initially in long-run equilibrium, with sellers in each market earning zero economic profit.

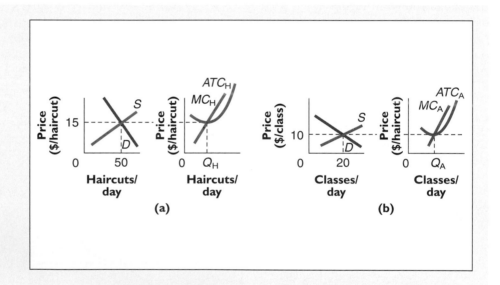

The shift to longer hair styles means a leftward shift in the demand for haircuts, while the increased emphasis on physical fitness implies a rightward shift in the demand curve for aerobics classes, as seen in Figure 8.9. As a result of these demand shifts, the new short-run equilibrium prices change. For the sake of illustration, these new prices are shown as $12 per haircut and $15 per aerobics class.

Because each producer was earning zero economic profit at the original equilibrium prices, hair stylists will experience economic losses and aerobics instructors will experience economic profits at the new prices, as seen in Figure 8.10.

Because the short-run equilibrium price of haircuts results in economic losses for hair stylists, some hair stylists will begin to leave that market in search of more favorable opportunities elsewhere. As a result, the short-run supply curve of haircuts will shift leftward, resulting in a higher equilibrium price. Exit of hair stylists will continue until the price of haircuts rises sufficiently to cover the long-run opportunity cost of providing them, which by assumption is $15.

By the same token, because the short-run equilibrium price of aerobics classes results in economic profits for instructors, outsiders will begin to enter that market, causing the short-run supply curve of classes to shift rightward.

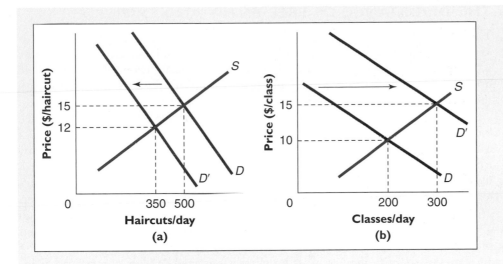

FIGURE 8.9
The Short-Run Effect of Demand Shifts in Two Markets.
The decline in demand for haircuts causes the price of haircuts to fall from $15 to $12 in the short run (a), while the increase in demand for aerobics classes causes the price of classes to rise from $10 to $15 in the short run (b).

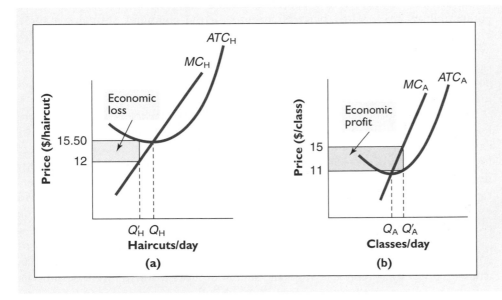

FIGURE 8.10
Economic Profit and Loss in the Short Run.
The assumed demand shifts result in an economic loss for the representative hair stylist (a) and an economic profits for the representative aerobics instructor (b).

New instructors will continue to enter until the price of classes falls to the long-run opportunity cost of providing them. By assumption, that cost is $10. Once all adjustments have taken place, there will be fewer haircuts and more aerobics classes than before. But because marginal costs in both markets were assumed constant in the long run, the prices of the two goods will again be at their original levels.

It bears mention that those stylists who leave the hair-cutting market will not necessarily be the same people who enter the aerobics teaching market. Indeed, given the sheer number of occupations a former hair stylist might choose to pursue, the likelihood of such a switch is low. Movements of resources will typically involve several indirect steps. Thus a former hair stylist might become a secretary, and a former postal worker might become an aerobics instructor.

We also note that the invisible hand theory says nothing about how long these adjustments might take. In some markets, especially labor markets, the required movements might take months or even years. But if the supply and demand curves remain stable, the markets will eventually reach equilibrium prices and quantities. And the new prices and quantities will be socially optimal in the same sense as before. Because the value to buyers of the last unit sold will be the same as the marginal cost of producing it, no additional transactions will be possible that benefit some without harming others.

THE IMPORTANCE OF FREE ENTRY AND EXIT

The allocative function of price cannot operate unless firms can enter new markets and leave existing ones at will. If new firms could not enter a market in which existing firms were making a large economic profit, economic profit would not tend to fall to zero over time, and price would not tend to gravitate toward the marginal cost of production.

barrier to entry any force that prevents firms from entering a new market

Forces that inhibit firms from entering new markets are sometimes called **barriers to entry.** In the book publishing market, for example, the publisher of a book enjoys copyright protection granted by the government. Copyright law forbids other publishers from producing and selling their own editions of protected works. This barrier allows the price of a popular book to remain significantly above its cost of production for an extended period, all the while generating an economic profit for its publisher. (A copyright provides no *guarantee* of a profit, and indeed most new books actually generate an economic loss for their publishers.)

Barriers to entry may result from practical as well as legal constraints. Some economists, for example, have argued that the compelling advantages of product compatibility have created barriers to entry in the computer software market. Since more than 90 percent of new desktop computers come with Microsoft's Windows software already installed, rival companies have difficulty selling other operating systems that may prevent users from exchanging files with friends and colleagues. This fact, more than any other, explains Microsoft's spectacular profit history.

No less important than the freedom to enter a market is the freedom to leave. When the airline industry was regulated by the federal government, air carriers were often required to serve specific markets, even though they were losing money in them. When firms discover that a market, once entered, is difficult or impossible to leave, they become reluctant to enter new markets. Barriers to exit thus become barriers to entry. Without reasonably free entry and exit, then, the implications of Adam Smith's invisible hand theory cannot be expected to hold.

All things considered, however, producers enjoy a high degree of freedom of entry in most U.S. markets. Because free entry is one of the defining characteristics of perfectly competitive markets, unless otherwise stated, we'll assume its existence.

RECAP   **THE INVISIBLE HAND THEORY**

In market economies, the allocative and rationing functions of prices guide resources to their most highly valued uses. Prices influence how much of each type of good gets produced (the allocative function). Firms enter industries in which prices are sufficiently high to sustain an economic profit and leave those in which low prices result in an economic loss. Prices also direct existing supplies of goods to the buyers who value them most (the rationing function).

Industries in which firms earn a positive economic profit tend to attract new firms, shifting industry supply to the right. Firms tend to leave industries in which they sustain an economic loss, shifting supply curves to the left. In each case, the supply movements continue until economic profit reaches zero. In long-run equilibrium, the value of the last unit produced to buyers is equal to its marginal cost of production, leaving no possibility for additional mutually beneficial transactions.

ECONOMIC RENT VERSUS ECONOMIC PROFIT

Microsoft chairman Bill Gates is the wealthiest man on the planet, largely because the problem of compatibility prevents rival suppliers from competing effectively in the many software markets dominated by his company. Yet numerous people have become fabulously rich even in markets with no conspicuous barriers to entry. If market forces push economic profit toward zero, how can that happen?

The answer to this question hinges on the distinction between economic profit and **economic rent.** Most people think of rent as the payment they make to a landlord or the supplier of a dorm refrigerator, but the term *economic rent* has a different meaning. Economic rent is that portion of the payment for an input that is above the supplier's reservation price for that input. Suppose, for example, that a landowner's reservation price for an acre of land is $100 per year. That is, suppose he would be willing to lease it to a farmer as long as he received an annual payment of at least $100, but for less that amount he would rather leave it fallow. If a farmer gives him an annual payment not of $100 but of $1,000, the landowner's economic rent from that payment will be $900 per year.

economic rent that part of the payment for a factor of production that exceeds the owner's reservation price

Economic profit is like economic rent in that it, too, may be seen as the difference between what someone is paid (the businessowner's total revenue) and her reservation price for remaining in business (the sum of all her costs, explicit and implicit). But whereas competition pushes economic profit toward zero, it has no such effect on the economic rent for inputs that cannot be replicated easily. For example, although the lease payments for land may remain substantially above the landowner's reservation price, year in and year out, new land cannot come onto the market to reduce or eliminate the economic rent through competition. There is, after all, only so much land to be had.

As the following example illustrates, economic rent can accrue to people as well as land.

How much economic rent will a talented chef get?

EXAMPLE 8.4

A community has 100 restaurants, 99 of which employ chefs of normal ability at a salary of $30,000 per year, the same as the amount they could earn in other occupations that are equally attractive to them. But the 100th restaurant has an unusually talented chef. Because of her reputation, diners are willing to pay 50 percent more for the meals she cooks than for those prepared by ordinary chefs. Owners of the 99 restaurants with ordinary chefs each collect $300,000 per year in revenue, which is just enough to ensure that each earns exactly a normal profit. If the talented chef's opportunities outside the restaurant industry are the same as those of ordinary chefs, how much will she be paid by her employer at equilibrium? How much of her pay will be economic rent? How much economic profit will her employer earn?

Because diners are willing to pay 50 percent more for meals cooked by the talented chef, the owner who hires her will take in total receipts not of $300,000 per year but of $450,000. In the long run, competition should assure that the talented chef's total pay each year will be $180,000 per year, the sum of the $30,000 that ordinary chefs get and the $150,000 in extra revenues for which she is solely responsible. Since the talented chef's reservation price is the amount she could earn outside the restaurant industry—by assumption, $30,000 per year, the same as for ordinary chefs—her economic rent is $150,000 per year. The economic profit of the owner who hires her will be exactly zero.

Since the talented chef's opportunities outside the restaurant industry are no better than an ordinary chef's, why is it necessary to pay the talented chef so much? Suppose her employer were to pay her only $60,000, which they both would consider a generous salary, since it is twice what ordinary chefs earn. The employer would then earn an economic profit of $120,000 per year, since his annual revenue would be $150,000 more than that of ordinary restaurants, but his costs would be only $30,000 more.

But this economic profit would create an opportunity for the owner of some other restaurant to bid the talented chef away. For example, if the owner of a competing restaurant were to hire the talented chef at a salary of $70,000, the chef would be $10,000 per year better off, and the rival owner would earn an economic profit of $110,000 per year, rather than his current economic profit of zero. Furthermore, if the talented chef is the sole reason that a restaurant earns a positive economic profit, the bidding for that chef should continue as long as any economic profit remains. Some other owner will pay her $80,000, still another $90,000, and so on. Equilibrium will be reached only when the talented chef's salary has been bid up to the point that no further economic profit remains—in Example 8.4, at an annual paycheck of $180,000.

This bidding process assumes, of course, that the reason for the chef's superior performance is that she possesses some personal talent that cannot be copied. If instead it were the result of, say, training at a culinary institute in France, then her privileged position would erode over time, as other chefs sought similar training.

RECAP **ECONOMIC RENT VERSUS ECONOMIC PROFIT**

Economic rent is the amount by which the payment to a factor of production exceeds the supplier's reservation price. Unlike economic profit, which is driven toward zero by competition, economic rent may persist for extended periods, especially in the case of factors with special talents that cannot easily be duplicated.

THE INVISIBLE HAND IN ACTION

To help develop your intuition about how the invisible hand works, we will examine how it helps us gain insight into patterns we observe in a wide variety of different contexts. In each case, the key idea we want you to focus on is that opportunities for private gain seldom remain unexploited for very long. Perhaps more than any other, this idea encapsulates the essence of that distinctive mindset known as "thinking like an economist."

THE INVISIBLE HAND AT THE SUPERMARKET AND ON THE FREEWAY

Why do you seldom see one supermarket checkout line that is substantially shorter than all the others?

As the following example illustrates, the no-cash-on-the-table principle refers not just to opportunities to earn economic profits in cash, but also to any other opportunity to achieve a more desirable outcome.

ECONOMIC NATURALIST 8.1

Why do supermarket checkout lines all tend to be roughly the same length?

Pay careful attention the next few times you go grocery shopping, and you'll notice that the lines at all the checkout stations tend to be roughly the same length. Suppose you saw one line that was significantly shorter than the others as you wheeled your cart toward the checkout area. Which line would you choose? The shorter one, of course; and because most shoppers would do the same, the short line seldom remains shorter for long.

EXERCISE 8.2

Use the no-cash-on-the-table principle to explain why all lanes on a crowded, multilane freeway move at about the same speed.

THE INVISIBLE HAND AND COST-SAVING INNOVATIONS

When economists speak of perfectly competitive firms, they have in mind businesses whose contribution to total market output is too small to have a perceptible impact on market price. As explained in Chapter 6, such firms are often called price takers: They take the market price of their product as given and then produce that quantity of output for which marginal cost equals that price.

This characterization of the competitive firm gives the impression that the firm is essentially a passive actor in the marketplace. Yet for most firms, that is anything but the case. As the next example illustrates, even those firms that cannot hope to influence the market prices of their products have very powerful incentives to develop and introduce cost-saving innovations.

How do cost-saving innovations affect economic profit in the short run? In the long run?

EXAMPLE 8.5

Forty merchant marine companies operate supertankers that carry oil from the Middle East to the United States. The cost per trip, including a normal profit, is $500,000. An engineer at one of these companies develops a more efficient propeller design that results in fuel savings of $20,000 per trip. How will this innovation affect the company's accounting and economic profits? Will these changes persist in the long run?

In the short run, the reduction in a single firm's costs will have no impact on the market price of transoceanic shipping services. The firm with the more efficient propeller will thus earn an economic profit of $20,000 per trip (since its total revenue will be the same as before, while its total cost will now be $20,000 per trip lower). As other firms learn about the new design, however, they will begin to adopt it, causing their individual supply curves to shift downward (since the marginal cost per trip at these firms will drop by $20,000). The shift in these individual supply curves will cause the market supply curve to shift, which in turn will result in a lower market price for shipping and a decline in economic profit at the firm where the innovation originated. When all firms have adopted the new, efficient design, the long-run supply curve for the industry will have shifted downward by $20,000 per trip, and each company will again be earning only a normal profit. At that point, any firm that did *not* adopt the new propeller design would suffer an economic loss of $20,000 per trip.

The incentive to come up with cost-saving innovations in order to reap economic profit is one of the most powerful forces on the economic landscape. Its beauty, in terms of the invisible hand theory, is that competition among firms ensures that the resulting cost savings will be passed along to consumers in the long run.

THE INVISIBLE HAND IN REGULATED MARKETS

The carrot of economic profit and the stick of economic loss guide resource movements in regulated markets no less than in unregulated ones. Consider the taxi industry, which many cities regulate by licensing cabs. These licenses are often called medallions, because they are issued in the form of a metal shield that must be affixed to the hood of the cab, where enforcement officials can easily see it. Cities that regulate cabs in this fashion typically issue fewer medallions than the equilibrium number of taxicabs in similar markets that are not regulated. Officials then allow the medallions to be bought and sold in the marketplace. As the next example demonstrates, the issuance of taxi medallions alters the equilibrium quantity of taxicabs but does not change the fundamental rule that resources flow in response to profit and loss signals.

Why do New York City taxicab medallions sell for more than $250,000?

Because New York City issues far fewer taxi medallions than would-be taxi owners could employ profitably, the equilibrium passenger fare is higher than the direct cost of operating a taxicab. Suppose the cost of operating a cab full time—including car, fuel, maintenance, depreciation, and the opportunity cost of the driver's time, but excluding the purchase price of a medallion—is $40,000 per year, and a cab in full-time operation will collect $60,000 per year in fares. If the annual interest rate on savings accounts is 8 percent, how much will a medallion cost in equilibrium? Will the owner of a medallion earn an economic profit?

If the medallion were free and could not be sold to others, its owner would earn an economic profit of $20,000 per year—the difference between his $60,000 in fares and his $40,000 in operating cost. But the lure of this economic profit would induce outsiders to enter the taxi industry, which could be done by purchasing an owner's medallion.

How much would the entrant be willing to pay for a medallion? If one were available for, say, $100,000, would it be a good buy? Since $100,000 in the bank would earn only $8,000 per year in interest but would bring $20,000 in earnings if used to purchase a taxi medallion, the answer must be yes. In fact, when the annual interest rate is 8 percent, a rational buyer's reservation price for a stream of economic profits of $20,000 per year is the amount of money he would have to put in the bank to earn that much interest each year—$250,000. At any amount less than that, medallions would be underpriced.

Clearly, the owner of a $250,000 medallion has a valuable asset. The opportunity cost of using it to operate a taxi is forgone interest of $20,000 per year. So the medallion owner who takes in $60,000 in fares actually covers only the cost of the resources he has invested in his operation. His economic profit is zero. From the perspective of the medallion owner, the $20,000 difference between his fares and his explicit costs is an economic rent.

EXERCISE 8.3

How much would the medallion in the preceding example sell for if the annual interest rate were not 8 percent but 4 percent?

Another regulated market in which the invisible hand was very much in evidence was the regulated commercial airline industry. Until late 1978, airlines were heavily regulated by the Civil Aeronautics Board (CAB), an agency of the federal government. Carriers could not provide air service between two cities unless they were given explicit permission to do so. The CAB also prescribed the fares carriers could charge. The standard practice was to set fares well above the cost of providing service on most routes, and then require carriers to use some of the resulting economic profit to pay for service on sparsely traveled routes. But as the following example illustrates, the CAB failed to reckon with the invisible hand.

Why did major commercial airlines install piano bars on the upper decks of Boeing 747s in the 1970s?

At the high airfares the CAB established on the New York to Los Angeles and other popular transcontinental routes in the 1970s, any air carrier that managed to fill a flight with passengers would have earned tens of thousands of dollars in economic profit on that one flight alone. The invisible hand theory tells us that resources will flow into any market in which economic profit is positive and out of any market in which economic profit is negative, eventually driving economic profit to zero. But although an influx of resources will normally cause prices to fall in an unregulated market, the CAB's rules prevented fares from falling. The rules could not prohibit carriers from competing with one another in other ways, however. Because passengers care not only about fares, but also about the frequency of service, a carrier can steal business from rivals simply by adding another flight. Carriers did so, adding flights to their routes until economic profit disappeared. The CAB's goal of generating surplus revenue to pay for service on sparsely traveled routes was doomed from the start.

Adding insult to injury, the policy of setting high fares on heavily traveled routes was wasteful, insofar as it resulted in so many flights on such routes that each flight left with a substantial number of empty seats. Carrier executives quickly realized that they could fill many of those seats by offering service enhancements that would lure passengers away from other airlines. For instance, one carrier converted the upper deck of its 747s to a piano bar, and other airlines quickly followed suit. Others offered elaborate meals. Recognizing this difficulty, the CAB responded by trying to regulate the kinds of food carriers could serve, leading in one case to a protracted legal squabble over the definition of a sandwich.

The problem is not that the extra amenities carriers offered were of *no* value whatever to passengers. Piano bars and more frequent flights were obviously of value to many travelers. But for efficiency's sake, additional amenities should be offered only if their benefit exceeds their cost, and most passengers would not voluntarily have paid for the high level of amenities air carriers offered in the 1970s. Evidence for this claim comes from the operations of several intrastate airlines, which were exempt from federal regulation. Unregulated carriers in California provided service on the San Francisco to San Diego route for about half the fare charged by regulated carriers on the Washington to Boston route of the same distance. Though the California carriers were free to offer more frequent service and more elaborate in-flight amenities, passengers voted with their dollars to sacrifice those amenities for lower airfares.

THE INVISIBLE HAND IN ANTIPOVERTY PROGRAMS

As the next example shows, failure to understand the logic of the invisible hand can lead not only to inefficient government regulation, but also to antipoverty programs that are doomed to fail.

How will an irrigation project affect the incomes of poor farmers?

EXAMPLE 8.6

Suppose unskilled workers must choose between working in a textile mill at $8,000 per year and growing rice on a rented parcel of farmland. One worker can farm an 80-acre rice parcel, which rents for $5,000 a year. Such farms yield $16,000 per year in revenue, and the total nonlabor costs of bringing the crop to market are $3,000 per year. The net incomes of rice farmers are thus $8,000 per year—the same as those of textile workers. A state legislator has introduced a bill to fund an irrigation project that would double the output of rice on farms operated by tenant farmers. If the state's contribution to the total supply of rice is too small to affect the price, how will the project affect the incomes of tenant farmers over the long run?

The direct effect of the project will be to double rice yields, which means that each farmer will sell $32,000 worth of rice per year rather than $16,000. If nothing else changed, farmers' incomes would rise from $8,000 per year to $24,000 per year. But the no-cash-on-the-table principle tells us that farmers cannot sustain this income level. From the perspective of textile workers, there is cash on the table in farming. Seeing an opportunity to triple their incomes, many will want to switch to farming. But since the supply of land is fixed, farm rents will rise as textile workers begin bidding for them. They will continue to rise as long as farmers can earn more than textile workers. The long-run effect of the project, then, will be to raise the rent on rice farms, from $5,000 per year to $21,000 (since at the higher rent the incomes of rice farmers and textile workers will again be the same). Thus the irrigation project will increase the wealth of landowners but will have no long-run effect on the incomes of tenant farmers.

THE INVISIBLE HAND IN THE STOCK MARKET

One of the most competitive markets on the planet is the market for stocks and bonds on Wall Street in New York. And as we will see, public understanding of how the invisible hand works in this market is often no better than the state legislator's understanding of how the rice market works.

Calculating the Value of a Share of Stock

A share of stock in a company is a claim to a share of the current and future accounting profits of that company. Thus, if you own 1 percent of the total number of shares of a company's stock, you effectively own 1 percent of the company's annual accounting profit, both now and in the future. (We say "effectively" because companies generally do not distribute their accounting profit to shareholders each year; many reinvest their earnings in the company's operations. Such reinvestment benefits the stockholder by enlarging the company and increasing its future accounting profit.) The price of a share of stock depends not only on a company's accounting profit, however, but also on the market rate of interest, as the next example illustrates.

EXAMPLE 8.7

How much will a share of stock sell for?

Suppose we know with certainty that a company's accounting profit will be $1 million this year and every year. If the company has issued a total of 1,000 shares of stock, and the annual interest rate is 5 percent, at what price will each share sell?

Because there are 1,000 shares of stock, each share entitles its owner to one-thousandth of the company's annual accounting profit, or $1,000 per year. Owning this stock is like having a bank deposit that earns $1,000 per year in interest. To calculate the economic value of the stock, therefore, we need only ask how much an investor would need to deposit in the bank at 5 percent interest to generate an annual interest payment of $1,000. The answer is $20,000, and that is the price that each share will command in the stock market.

Calculating the Present Value of Future Costs and Benefits

Someone who is trying to estimate how much a business is worth must take account of the fact that earnings received in the future are less valuable than earnings received today. Consider a company whose only accounting profit, $14,400, will occur exactly two years from now. At all other times its accounting profit will be exactly zero. How much is ownership of this company worth?

time value of money the fact that a given dollar amount today is equivalent to a larger dollar amount in the future, because the money can be invested in an interest-bearing account in the meantime

To answer this question, we need to employ the concept of the **time value of money**—the fact that money deposited in an interest-bearing account today will grow in value over time.

present value for an annual interest rate r, the present value (PV) of a payment (M) to be received T years from now is the amount that would have to be deposited today at interest rate r to generate a balance of M after T years: $PV = M/(1 + r)^T$

Our goal is to compute what economists call the **present value** of a $14,400 payment to be received in two years. We can think of this present value as the amount that would have to be deposited in an interest-bearing bank account today to generate a balance of $14,400 two years from today. Let PV denote present value and r the market rate of interest, measured as a fraction. (For example, an annual interest rate of 10 percent would correspond to $r = 0.10$.) If we put $100 in an account today at 10 percent annual interest, we will have $100(1.10) = 110 in the account after one year. If we leave $100 in the same account for two years, we will have $100(1.10)(1.10) = $100(1.10)^2 = 121. More generally, if we put PV in the bank today at the interest rate r, we will have $PV(1 + r)$ one year from now and $PV(1 + r)^2$ two years from now. So to find the present value of a $14,400 payment to be received two years from now we simply solve the equation $14,400 = PV(1 + r)^2$ and get $PV = $14,400/(1 + r)^2$. If the interest rate is 20 percent, then $PV = $14,400/(1.2)^2 = $10,000$. To verify this answer, note that $10,000 deposited at 20 percent interest today would grow to $10,000(1 + 0.2) = $12,000$ by the end of one year, and that amount left on deposit for a second year would grow to $12,000(1 + 0.2) = $14,400$.

More generally, when the interest rate is r, the present value of a payment M to be received T years from now is given by the equation

$$PV = \frac{M}{(1 + r)^T}. \qquad (8.1)$$

EXERCISE 8.4

What is the present value of a payment of $1,728 to be received three years from now if the annual interest rate is 20 percent?

The Efficient Markets Hypothesis

In practice, of course, no one knows with certainty what a company's future profits will be. So the current price of a share of stock will depend not on the actual amount of future profits, but on investors' estimates of them. These estimates incorporate information about current profits, prospects for the company's industry, the state of the economy, demographic trends, and a host of other factors. As this information changes, investors' estimates of future profits change with it, along with the prices of a share of stock.

How fast does new information affect the price of a stock? With blazing speed, according to the **efficient markets hypothesis.** The theory says that the current price of a stock incorporates all available information relevant to the company's earnings. The plausibility of this theory is evident if we think for a moment about what might happen if it were false. Suppose, for example, that at 9:00 A.M. on Monday, October 14, some investors acquire new information to the effect that the company in Example 8.7 will realize accounting profits not of $1 million per year, but of $2 million. This information implies that the new equilibrium price for each share of its stock should be $40,000. Now suppose that the price were to remain at its current level ($20,000) for 24 hours before rising gradually to $40,000 over the next two weeks. If so, an investor privy to this information could double her wealth in two weeks without working hard, taking any risk, or even being lucky. All she would have to do is invest all her wealth in the stock at today's price of $20,000 per share.

We may safely assume that there is no shortage of investors who would be delighted to double their wealth without having to work hard or take risks. But in the example just described, they would have to buy shares of the stock within 24 hours of learning of the new profit projections. As eager investors rushed to buy the stock, its price would rise quickly, so that those who waited until the end of the day to buy would miss much of the opportunity for gain. To get the full advantage of the new information, they would have to make their purchases earlier in the day. As more and more investors rushed to buy shares, the window of opportunity would grow narrower and narrower. In the end, the duration of the opportunity to profit from the new information may be just a few minutes long.

In practice, of course, new information often takes time to interpret, and different investors may have different beliefs about exactly what it means. Early information may signal an impending change that is far from certain. As time passes, events may confirm or contradict the implications of the earlier information. The usual pattern is for information to emerge in bits and pieces, and for stock prices to adjust in small increments as each new bit of information emerges. But this does not mean that the price of a stock adjusts gradually to new information. Rather, it means that new information usually emerges gradually. And as each piece of new information emerges, the market reacts almost instantly.

For example, when a Florida jury awarded a lung cancer patient $750,000 in damages in July 1996, the price of tobacco stocks plummeted roughly 20 percent *within minutes.* The award broke a long series of legal precedents in which tobacco companies were not held liable for the illnesses suffered by smokers. When the verdict was announced, no one knew whether it would be reversed on

efficient markets hypothesis
the theory that the current price of stock in a corporation reflects all relevant information about its current and future earnings prospects

appeal or whether it would influence future verdicts in such cases. Yet investors who had been monitoring the case carefully knew instantly that massive new financial liabilities had become much more likely.

Despite such persuasive evidence in favor of the efficient markets hypothesis, many investors seem to believe that information about the next sure investment bonanza is as close as their broker's latest newsletter. Securities salespersons in New York routinely call investors to offer the latest tips on how to invest their money. The difficulty is that by the time information reaches investors in this way, days, weeks, or even months will have gone by, and the information will have already been incorporated into any stock prices for which it might have been relevant.

The *Wall Street Journal* publishes a feature in which a group of leading investment advisers predict which stocks will increase most in price during the coming months. The *Journal* then compares the forecasts with the performance of a randomly selected set of stocks. The usual finding is that the randomly selected portfolios perform little differently from those chosen by the "experts." Some of the experts do better than average, others worse. This pattern is consistent with the economist's theory that the invisible hand moves with unusual speed to eliminate profit opportunities in financial markets.

Why isn't a stock portfolio consisting of America's "best-managed companies" a good investment?

Each year *Fortune* magazine asks executives at the nation's largest companies to list those U.S. firms, excluding their own, that are managed most efficiently. Imagine that you see the results of this survey and immediately purchase 100 shares of stock in each of the top 10 companies on the list. How well might you expect those stocks to perform relative to a randomly selected portfolio?

A stock is said to "perform well" if its price rises more rapidly than the prices of other stocks. Changes in the price of a company's stock depend not on investors' current beliefs about the company's accounting profit, but on changes in those beliefs. Suppose, for the sake of argument, that the "best-managed" companies had higher accounting profits than other companies at the time of the *Fortune* survey. Because the prices you paid for their stocks would have reflected those higher earnings, there would be no reason to expect their prices to rise more rapidly than those of other stocks.

But won't the accounting profits of a well-managed company be likely to grow more rapidly than those of other companies? Perhaps, but even if so, beliefs to that effect would also be reflected in current stock prices. Indeed, the stocks of many software, biotechnology, and Internet commerce companies sell at high prices years before they ever post their first dollar of accounting profit.

An understanding of the invisible hand theory might even lead us to question whether a "well-managed" company will have higher accounting profit than other companies. After all, if an unusually competent manager were known to be the reason a company consistently posted a positive economic profit, other companies could be expected to bid for the manager's services, causing her salary to rise. And the market for the manager's services will not reach equilibrium until her salary has captured all the gains for which her talent is responsible.

We must stress that our point in the preceding example is *not* that good management doesn't matter. Good management is obviously better than bad management, for it increases total economic surplus. The point is that the reward for good performance tends to be captured by those who provide that performance. And that is a good thing, insofar as it provides powerful incentives for everyone to perform well.

RECAP   **THE INVISIBLE HAND IN ACTION**

Because individuals and firms are generally eager to improve their position, opportunities for gain seldom remain unexploited for long. Early adopters of cost-saving innovations enjoy temporary economic profits. But as additional firms adopt the innovations, the resulting downward supply shift causes price to fall. In the long run, economic profit returns to zero, and all cost savings are passed on to consumers.

The quest for advantage guides resources not only in perfectly competitive markets, but also in heavily regulated markets. Firms can almost always find ways to expand sales in markets in which the regulated price permits an economic profit or withdraw service from markets in which the regulated price results in an economic loss.

An understanding of invisible hand theory is also important for the design of antipoverty programs. An irrigation program that makes land more productive, for example, will raise the incomes of tenant farmers only temporarily. In the long run, the gains from such projects tend to be captured as higher rents to landowners.

The efficient markets hypothesis says that the price of a firm's stock at any moment reflects all available information that is relevant for predicting the firm's future earnings. This hypothesis identifies several common beliefs as false—among them that stocks in well-managed companies perform better than stocks in poorly managed ones and that ordinary investors can make large financial gains by trading stocks on the basis of information reported in the news media.

THE DISTINCTION BETWEEN AN EQUILIBRIUM AND A SOCIAL OPTIMUM

The equilibrium, or no-cash-on-the-table, principle tells us that when a market reaches equilibrium, no further opportunities for gain are available to individuals. This principle implies that the market prices of resources that people own will eventually reflect their economic value. (As we will see in later chapters, the same cannot be said of resources that are not owned by anyone, such as fish in international waters.)

The no-cash-on-the-table principle is sometimes misunderstood to mean that there are *never* any valuable opportunities to exploit. For example, the story is told of two economists on their way to lunch when they spot what appears to be a $100 bill lying on the sidewalk. When the younger economist stoops to pick up the bill, his older colleague restrains him, saying "That can't be a $100 dollar bill." "Why not?" asks the younger colleague. "If it were, someone would have picked it up by now," the older economist replies.

The no-cash-on-the-table principle means not that there *never* are any unexploited opportunities, but that there are none when the market is *in equilibrium*. Occasionally a $100 bill does lie on the sidewalk, and the person who first spots it and picks it up gains a windfall. Likewise, when a company's earnings prospects improve, *somebody* must be the first to recognize the opportunity, and that person can make a lot of money by purchasing the stock quickly.

Still, the no-cash-on-the-table principle is important. It tells us, in effect, that there are only three ways to earn a big payoff: to work especially hard; to have some unusual skill, talent, or training; or simply to be lucky. The person who finds a big bill on the sidewalk is lucky, as are many of the investors whose stocks perform better than average. Other investors whose stocks do well achieve their gains through hard work or special talent. For example, the legendary investor Warren Buffett, whose portfolio has grown in value at almost three times the stock market average for the last 40 years, spends long hours studying annual financial reports and has a remarkably keen eye for the telling detail. Thousands of others work just as hard yet fail to beat the market averages.

It is important to stress, however, that a market being in equilibrium implies only that no additional opportunities are available *to individuals*. It does not imply that the resulting allocation is necessarily best from the point of view of society as a whole.

SMART FOR ONE, DUMB FOR ALL

Adam Smith's profound insight was that the individual pursuit of self-interest often promotes the broader interests of society. But unlike some of his modern disciples, Smith was under no illusion that this is *always* the case. Note, for example, Smith's elaboration on his description of the entrepreneur led by the invisible hand "to promote an end which was no part of his intention":

> Nor is it *always* the worse for society that it was no part of it. By pursuing his own interest he *frequently* promotes that of society more effectively than when he really intends to promote it. (Emphasis added.)

As Smith was well aware, the individual pursuit of self-interest often does not coincide with society's interest. In Chapter 3 we cited activities that generate environmental pollution as an example of conflicting economic interests, noting that behavior in those circumstances may be described as smart for one, but dumb for all. As the following example suggests, extremely high levels of investment in earnings forecasts can also be smart for one, dumb for all.

Are there "too many" smart people working as corporate earnings forecasters?

Stock analysts use complex mathematical models to forecast corporate earnings. The more analysts invest in the development of these models, the more accurate the models become. Thus the analyst whose model produces a reliable forecast sooner than others can reap a windfall by buying stocks whose prices are about to rise. Given the speed with which stock prices respond to new information, however, the results of even the second-fastest forecasting model may come too late to be of much use. Individual stock analysts thus face a powerful incentive to invest more and more money in their models, in the hope of generating the fastest forecast. Does this incentive result in the socially optimal level of investment in forecast models?

Beyond some point, increased speed of forecasting is of little benefit to society as a whole, whose interests suffer little when the price of a stock moves to its proper level a few hours more slowly. If *all* stock analysts spent less money on their forecasting models, *someone's* model would still produce the winning forecast, and the resources that might otherwise be devoted to fine-tuning the models could be put to more valued uses. Yet if any one individual spends less, he can be sure the winning forecast will not be his.

The invisible hand went awry in the situation just described because the benefit of an investment to the individual who made it was larger than the benefit of that investment to society as a whole. In later chapters we will discuss a broad class of investments with this property. In general, the efficacy of the invisible hand depends on the extent to which the individual costs and benefits of actions taken in the marketplace coincide with the respective costs and benefits of those actions to society. These exceptions notwithstanding, some of the most powerful forces at work in competitive markets clearly promote society's interests.

> ⬤ **RECAP** **EQUILIBRIUM VERSUS SOCIAL OPTIMUM**
>
> A market in equilibrium is one in which no additional opportunities for gain remain available to individual buyers or sellers. The no-cash-on-the table principle describes powerful forces that help push markets toward equilibrium. But even if all markets are in equilibrium, the resulting allocation of resources need not be socially optimal. Equilibrium will not be socially optimal when the costs or benefits to individual participants in the market differ from those experienced by society as a whole.

▪ SUMMARY ▪

- Accounting profit is the difference between a firm's revenue and its explicit expenses. It differs from economic profit, which is the difference between revenue and the sum of the firm's explicit and implicit costs. Normal profit is the difference between accounting profit and economic profit. It is the opportunity cost of the resources supplied to a business by its owners.

- The quest for economic profit is the invisible hand that drives resource allocation in market economies. Markets in which businesses earn an economic profit tend to attract additional resources, whereas markets in which businesses experience an economic loss tend to lose resources. If new firms enter a market with economic profits, that market's supply curve shifts to the right, causing a reduction in the price of the product. Prices will continue to fall until economic profits are eliminated. By contrast, the departure of firms from markets with economic losses causes the supply curve in such markets to shift left, increasing the price of the product. Prices will continue to rise until economic losses are eliminated. In the long run, market forces drive economic profits and losses toward zero.

- When market supply and demand curves reflect the underlying costs and benefits to society of the production of a good or service, the quest for economic profit ensures not only that existing supplies are allocated efficiently among individual buyers, but also that resources are allocated across markets in the most efficient way possible. In any allocation other than the one generated by the market, resources could be rearranged to benefit some people without harming others.

- Economic rent is the portion of the payment for an input that exceeds the reservation price for that input. If a professional baseball player who is willing to play for as little as $100,000 per year is paid $15 million, he earns an economic rent of $14,900,000 per year. Whereas the invisible hand drives economic profit toward zero over the long run, economic rent can persist indefinitely, because replicating the services of players like Derek Jeter is impossible. Talented individuals who are responsible for the superior performance of a business will tend to capture the resulting financial gains as economic rents.

- Failure to understand the logic of Adam Smith's invisible hand often compromises the design of regulatory programs. For instance, when regulation prevents firms from lowering prices to capture business from rivals, firms generally find other ways in which to compete. Thus, if airline regulators set passenger fares above cost, air carriers will try to capture additional business by offering extra amenities and more frequent service. Likewise, many antipoverty programs have been compromised by failure to consider how incentives change people's behavior.

- A share of stock in a company is a claim to a share of the current and future accounting profits of that company. The price of a share of stock depends not only on its accounting profits, but on the market rate of interest, since the interest rate affects the present value of future costs and benefits. When the annual interest rate is r, the present value (PV) of a payment M to be received (or paid) T years from now is the amount that would have to be deposited in an account today at interest rate r to generate a balance of M after T years: $PV = M/(1 + r)^T$.

- According to the efficient markets hypothesis, the market price of a stock incorporates all currently available information that is relevant to that company's earnings. If this hypothesis were untrue, people could earn large sums of money without working hard, having talent, or being lucky.

- The no-cash-on-the-table principle implies that if someone owns a valuable resource, the market price of that resource will fully reflect its economic value. The implication of this principle is not that lucrative opportunities never exist, but rather that such opportunities cannot exist when markets are in equilibrium.

- The benefit of an investment to an individual sometimes differs from its benefit to society as a whole. Such conflicting incentives may give rise to behavior that is smart for one but dumb for all. Despite such exceptions, the invisible hand of the market works remarkably well much of the time. One of the market system's most important contributions to social well-being is the pressure it creates to adopt cost-saving innovations. Competition among firms ensures that the resulting cost savings get passed along to consumers in the long run.

▪ KEY TERMS ▪

accounting profit (194)
allocative function of price (197)
barrier to entry (204)
economic loss (196)
economic profit (194)

economic rent (205)
efficient markets hypothesis (211)
explicit costs (194)
implicit costs (194)
invisible hand theory (197)

normal profit (195)
present value (210)
rationing function of price (197)
time value of money (210)

▪ REVIEW QUESTIONS ▪

1. Why do most cities in the United States now have more radios but fewer radio repair shops than they did in 1960?

2. How can a businessowner who earns $10 million per year from his business credibly claim to earn zero economic profit?

3. Why do market forces drive economic profit but not economic rent toward zero?

4. Why did airlines that once were regulated by the government generally fail to earn an economic profit, even on routes with relatively high fares?

5. Why is a payment of $10,000 to be received one year from now more valuable than a payment of $10,000 to be received two years from now?

▪ PROBLEMS ▪

1. True or False: Explain why the following statements are true or false:
   a. The economic maxim "There's no cash on the table" means that there are never any unexploited economic opportunities.
   b. Firms in competitive environments make no accounting profit when the market is in long-run equilibrium.
   c. Firms that can introduce cost-saving innovations can make an economic profit in the short run.

2. Explain why new software firms that give away their software products at a short-run economic loss are nonetheless able to sell their stock at positive prices.

3. John Jones owns and manages a café in Collegetown whose annual revenue is $5,000. Annual expenses are as follows:

Labor	$2,000
Food and drink	500
Electricity	100
Vehicle lease	150
Rent	500
Interest on loan for equipment	1,000

    a. Calculate John's annual accounting profit.

    b. John could earn $1,000 per year as a recycler of aluminum cans. However, he prefers to run the café. In fact, he would be willing to pay up to $275 per year to run the café rather than to recycle. Is the café making an economic profit? Should John stay in the café business? Explain.

    c. Suppose the café's revenues and expenses remain the same, but recyclers' earnings rise to $1,100 per year. Is the café still making an economic profit? Explain.

    d. Suppose John had not had to get a $10,000 loan at an annual interest rate of 10 percent to buy equipment, but instead had invested $10,000 of his own money in equipment. How would your answer to parts a and b change?

    c. If John can earn $1,000 a year as a recycler, and he likes recycling just as well as running the café, how much additional revenue would the café have to collect each year to earn a normal profit?

4. The city of New Orleans has 200 advertising companies, 199 of which employ designers of normal ability at a salary of $100,000 a year. Paying this salary, each of the 199 firms makes a normal profit on $500,000 in revenue. However, the 200th company employs Janus Jacobs, an unusually talented designer. This company collects $1,000,000 in revenues because of Jacobs's talent.

    a. How much will Jacobs earn? What proportion of his annual salary will be economic rent?

    b. Why won't the advertising company for which Jacobs works be able to earn an economic profit?

5. Explain carefully why, in the absence of a patent, a technical innovation invented and pioneered in one tofu factory will cause the supply curve for the entire tofu industry to shift to the right. What will finally halt the rightward shift?

6. The government of the Republic of Self-Reliance has decided to limit imports of machine tools, to encourage development of locally made machine tools. To do so, the government offers to sell a small number of machine-tool import licenses. To operate a machine-tool import business costs $30,000, excluding the cost of the import license. An importer of machine tools can expect to earn $50,000 per year. If the annual interest rate is 10 percent, for how much will the government be able to auction the import licenses? Will the owner of a license earn an economic profit?

7. Unskilled workers in a poor cotton-growing region must choose between working in a factory for $6,000 a year or being a tenant cotton farmer. One farmer can work a 120-acre farm, which rents for $10,000 a year. Such farms yield $20,000 worth of cotton each year. The total nonlabor cost of producing and marketing the cotton is $4,000 a year. A local politician whose motto is "working people come first" has promised that if he is elected, his administration will fund a fertilizer, irrigation, and marketing scheme that will triple cotton yields on tenant farms at no charge to tenant farmers.

    a. If the market price of cotton would be unaffected by this policy and no new jobs would be created in the cotton-growing industry, how would the project affect the incomes of tenant farmers in the short run? In the long run?

    b. Who would reap the benefit of the scheme in the long run? How much would they gain each year?

8. You have a friend who is a potter. He holds a permanent patent on an indestructible teacup whose sale generates $30,000 a year more revenue than production costs. If the annual interest rate is 20 percent, what is the market value of his patent?

9. You have an opportunity to buy an apple orchard that produces $25,000 per year in total revenue. To run the orchard, you would have to give up your current job, which pays $10,000 per year. If you would find both jobs equally satisfying, and the annual interest rate is 10 percent, what is the highest price you would be willing to pay for the orchard?

10. Louisa, a renowned chef, owns one of the 1,000 spaghetti restaurants in Sicily. Each restaurant serves 100 plates of spaghetti a night at $5 per plate. Louisa knows she can develop a new sauce at the same cost as the current sauce, which would be so tasty that all 100,000 spaghetti eaters would buy her spaghetti at $10 per plate. There

are two problems: developing the new sauce would require some experimental cost; and the other spaghetti producers could figure out the recipe after one day.

a. What is the highest experimental cost Louisa would be willing to incur?

b. How would your answer change if Louisa could enforce a year-long patent on her new sauce? (Assume that the interest rate is zero.)

▪ ANSWERS TO IN-CHAPTER EXERCISES ▪

8.1 As shown in the table below, Pudge's accounting profit is now $10,000, the difference between his $20,000 annual revenue and his $10,000 per year payment for land, equipment, and supplies. His economic profit is that amount minus the opportunity cost of his labor—again, the $11,000 per year he could have earned as a store manager. So Pudge is now earning a negative economic profit, −$1,000 per year. As before, his normal profit is the $11,000 per year opportunity cost of his labor. Although an accountant would say Pudge is making an annual profit of $10,000, that amount is less than a normal profit for his activity. An economist would therefore say that he is making an economic loss of $1,000 per year. Since Pudge likes the two jobs equally well, he will be better off by $1,000 per year if he leaves farming to become a manager.

Total revenue ($/year)	Explicit costs ($/year)	Implicit costs ($/year)	Accounting profit (= total revenue − explicit costs) ($/year)	Economic profit (= total revenue − explicit costs − implicit costs) ($/year)	Normal profit (= implicit costs) ($/year)
20,000	10,000	11,000	10,000	−1,000	11,000

8.2 If each lane did not move at about the same pace, any driver in a slower lane could reduce his travel time by simply switching to a faster one. People will exploit these opportunities until each lane moves at about the same pace.

8.3 If the taxi medallion were available for free, it would still command an economic profit of $20,000 per year. So its value is still the answer to the question "How much would you need to put in the bank to generate interest earnings of $20,000 per year?" When the interest rate is 4 percent a year, the answer is $500,000, or twice what the medallion was worth at an interest rate of 8 percent.

8.4 $PV = \$1,728/(1.2)^3 = \$1,000$.

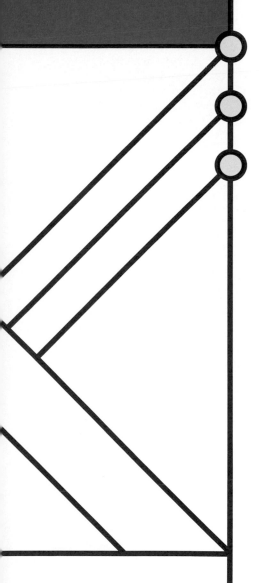

PART

3

MARKET IMPERFECTIONS

■

We now abandon Adam Smith's frictionless world to investigate what happens when people and firms interact in markets plagued by a variety of imperfections. Not surprisingly, the invisible hand that served society so well in the perfectly competitive world often goes astray in this new environment.

Our focus in Chapter 9 will be on how markets served by only one or a small number of firms differ from those served by perfectly competitive firms. We will see that although monopolies often escape the pressures that constrain the profits of their perfectly competitive counterparts, the two types of firm also have many important similarities.

In Chapter 10 we will investigate how the allocation of resources is affected when activities generate costs of benefits that accrue to people not directly involved in those activities. We will see that if parties cannot easily negotiate with one another, the self-serving actions of individuals usually will not lead to efficient outcomes.

In Chapters 1 to 10 economic decision makers confronted an environment that was essentially fixed. In Chapter 11, however, we will discuss cases in which people can expect their actions to alter the behavior of others, as when a firm's decision to advertise or launch a new product induces a rival to follow suit. Interdependencies of this sort are the rule rather than the exception, and we will explore how to take them into account using simple theories of games.

Although the invisible hand theory assumes that buyers and sellers are perfectly informed about all relevant options, this assumption is almost never satisfied in practice. In Chapter 12 we will explore how basic economic principles can help imperfectly informed individuals and firms make the best use of the limited information they possess.

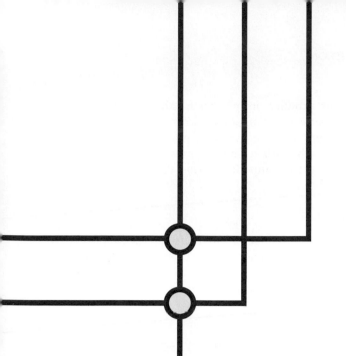

MONOPOLY AND OTHER FORMS OF IMPERFECT COMPETITION

■

Some years ago, schoolchildren around the country became obsessed with the game of Magic. To play, you need a deck of Magic Cards, available only from the creators of the game. But unlike ordinary playing cards, which can be bought in most stores for only a dollar or two, a deck of Magic Cards sells for upward of $10. And since Magic Cards cost no more to manufacture than ordinary playing cards, their producer earns an enormous economic profit.

In a normal competitive market, entrepreneurs would see this economic profit as cash on the table. It would entice them to offer Magic Cards at slightly lower prices so that eventually the cards would sell for roughly their cost of production, just as ordinary playing cards do. But Magic Cards have been on the market for years now, and that hasn't happened. The reason is that the cards are copyrighted, which means the government has granted the creators of the game an exclusive license to sell them.

The holder of a copyright is an example of an **imperfectly competitive firm,** or **price setter,** that is, a firm with at least some latitude to set its own price. The competitive firm, by contrast, is a price taker, a firm with no influence over the price of its product.

Our focus in this chapter will be on the ways in which markets served by imperfectly competitive firms differ from those served by perfectly competitive firms. One salient difference is the imperfectly competitive firm's ability, under certain circumstances, to charge more than its cost of production. But if the producer of Magic Cards could charge any price it wished, why does it charge only $10? Why not $100, or even $1,000? We'll see that even though such a

Why do Magic Cards sell for 10 times as much as ordinary playing cards, even though they cost no more to produce?

price setter or imperfectly competitive firm a firm with at least some latitude to set its own price

pure monopoly the only supplier of a unique product with no close substitutes

oligopolist a firm that produces a product for which only a few rival firms produce close substitutes

monopolistically competitive firm one of a large number of firms that produce slightly differentiated products that are reasonably close substitutes for one another

company may be the only seller of its product, its pricing freedom is far from absolute. We'll also see how some imperfectly competitive firms manage to earn an economic profit, even in the long run, and even without government protections like copyright. And we'll explore why Adam Smith's invisible hand is less in evidence in a world served by imperfectly competitive firms.

IMPERFECT COMPETITION

The perfectly competitive market is an ideal; the actual markets we encounter in everyday life differ from the ideal in varying degrees. In a classification scheme whose arbitrariness most economists would feel hard-pressed to defend, economics texts usually distinguish among three types of imperfectly competitive market structures.

DIFFERENT FORMS OF IMPERFECT COMPETITION

Farthest from the perfectly competitive ideal is the **pure monopoly,** a market in which a single firm is the lone seller of a unique product. The producer of Magic Cards is a pure monopolist, as are many providers of electric power. If the residents of Miami don't buy their electricity from the Florida Power and Light Company, they simply do without.

Somewhat closer to the perfectly competitive ideal is **oligopoly,** the market structure in which only a few firms sell a given product. Examples include the market for long-distance telephone service, in which firms like AT&T, Sprint, and MCI are the principal providers. Closer still to perfect competition is the industry structure known as **monopolistic competition,** which typically consists of a relatively large number of firms that sell the same product with slight differentiations. Examples of this structure include local gasoline stations, which differ not so much in the gas they sell as in their physical locations.

As we'll see in the next section, the essential characteristic that differentiates imperfectly competitive firms from perfectly competitive firms is the same in each of the three cases. So for convenience, we'll use the term *monopolist* to refer to any of the three types of imperfectly competitive firms.

THE ESSENTIAL DIFFERENCE BETWEEN PERFECTLY AND IMPERFECTLY COMPETITIVE FIRMS

In advanced economics courses, professors generally devote much attention to the analysis of subtle differences in the behavior of different types of imperfectly competitive firms. Far more important for our purposes, however, will be to focus on the single, common feature that differentiates all imperfectly competitive firms from their perfectly competitive counterparts—namely, that *whereas the perfectly competitive firm faces a perfectly elastic demand curve for its product, the imperfectly competitive firm faces a downward-sloping demand curve.*

In the perfectly competitive industry, the supply and demand curves intersect to determine an equilibrium market price. At that price, the perfectly competitive firm can sell as many units as it wishes. It has no incentive to charge more than the market price, because it won't sell anything if it does so. Nor does it have any incentive to charge less than the market price, because it can sell as many units as it wants to at the market price. The perfectly competitive firm's demand curve is thus a horizontal line at the market price, as we saw in Chapter 6.

By contrast, if a local gasoline retailer—an imperfect competitor—charges a few pennies more than its rivals for a gallon of gas, some of its customers may desert it. But others will remain, perhaps because they are willing to pay a little extra to continue stopping at their most convenient location. An imperfectly competitive firm thus faces a negatively sloped demand curve. Figure 9.1 summarizes this contrast between the demand curves facing perfectly competitive and imperfectly competitive firms.

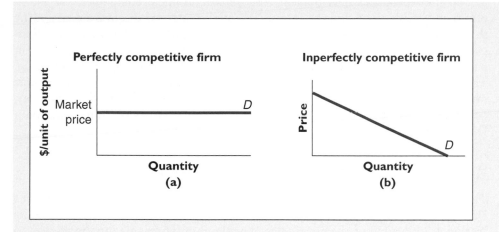

FIGURE 9.1
The Demand Curves Facing Perfectly and Imperfectly Competitive Firms.
(a) The demand curve confronting a perfectly competitive firm is perfectly elastic at the market price.
(b) The demand curve confronting an imperfectly competitive firm is downward-sloping.

RECAP   **IMPERFECT COMPETITION**

Perfect competition is an ideal case, at best only approximated in actual industries. Economists study three other types of market structure that differ in varying degrees from perfect competition: monopoly, an industry with only one seller of a unique product; oligopoly, an industry with only a few sellers; and monopolistic competition, an industry in which many firms sell products that are close, but imperfect, substitutes for one another. The demand curve confronting a perfectly competitive firm is perfectly elastic at the market price, while the demand curve confronting an imperfectly competitive firm is downward-sloping.

If the Sunoco station at State and Meadow Streets raised its gasoline prices by 3 cents per gallon, would all its customers shop elsewhere?

FIVE SOURCES OF MARKET POWER

Firms that confront downward-sloping demand curves are sometimes said to enjoy **market power,** a term that refers to their ability to set the prices of their products. A common misconception is that a firm with market power can sell any quantity at any price it wishes. It cannot. All it can do is pick a price–quantity combination along its demand curve. If the firm chooses to raise its price, it must settle for reduced sales.

Why do some firms have market power while others do not? Since market power often carries with it the ability to charge a price above the cost of production, such power tends to arise from factors that limit competition. In practice, the following five factors often confer such power: exclusive control over inputs, patents and copyrights, government licenses or franchises, economies of scale, and network economies.

market power a firm's ability to raise the price of a good without losing all its sales

EXCLUSIVE CONTROL OVER IMPORTANT INPUTS

If a single firm controls an input essential to the production of a given product, that firm will have market power. For example, to the extent that some tenants are willing to pay a premium for office space in the country's tallest building, the Sears Tower, the owner of that building has market power.

PATENTS AND COPYRIGHTS

Patents give the inventors or developers of new products the exclusive right to sell those products for a specified period of time. By insulating sellers from competition for an interval, patents enable innovators to charge higher prices to recoup their product's development costs. Pharmaceutical companies, for example, spend millions of dollars on research in the hope of discovering new drug therapies for serious illnesses. The drugs they discover are insulated from competition for an interval—currently 17 years in the United States—by government patents. For the life of the patent, only the patent holder may legally sell the drug. This protection enables the patent holder to set a price above the marginal cost of production to recoup the cost of the research on the drug. In the same way, copyrights protect the authors of movies, software, music, books, and other published works.

GOVERNMENT LICENSES OR FRANCHISES

The Yosemite Concession Services Corporation has an exclusive license from the U.S. government to run the lodging and concession operations at Yosemite National Park. One of the government's goals in granting this monopoly was to preserve the wilderness character of the area to the greatest degree possible. And indeed, the inns and cabins offered by the Yosemite Concession Services Company blend nicely with the valley's scenery. No garish neon signs mar the national park as they do in places where rivals compete for the tourist's dollars.

ECONOMIES OF SCALE (NATURAL MONOPOLIES)

constant returns to scale a production process is said to have constant returns to scale if, when all inputs are changed by a given proportion, output changes by the same proportion

When a firm doubles all its factors of production, what happens to its output? If output exactly doubles, the firm's production process is said to exhibit **constant returns to scale.** If output more than doubles, the production process is said to exhibit **increasing returns to scale,** or **economies of scale.** When production is subject to economies of scale, the average cost of production declines as the number of units produced increases. For example, in the generation of electricity, the use of larger generators lowers the unit cost of production. The markets for such products tend to be served by a single seller, or perhaps only a few sellers, because having a large number of sellers would result in significantly higher costs. A monopoly that results from economies of scale is called a **natural monopoly.**

increasing returns to scale a production process is said to have increasing returns to scale if, when all inputs are changed by a given proportion, output changes by more than that proportion; also called *economies of scale*

NETWORK ECONOMIES

natural monopoly a monopoly that results from economies of scale

Although most of us don't care what brand of dental floss others use, many products do become much more valuable to us as more people use them. In the case of home recorders, for instance, the VHS format's defeat of the competing Beta format was explained not by its superior picture quality—indeed, on most important technical dimensions, Beta was regarded by experts as superior to VHS. Rather, VHS won simply because it managed to gain a slight sales edge on the initial version of Beta, which could not record programs longer than one hour. Although Beta later corrected this deficiency, the VHS lead proved insuperable. Once the fraction of consumers owning VHS passed a critical threshold, the reasons for choosing it became compelling—variety and availability of tape rental, access to repair facilities, the capability to exchange tapes with friends, and so on.

A similar network economy helped to account for the dominant position of Microsoft's Windows operating system, which, as noted earlier, is currently installed in more than 90 percent of all personal computers. Because Microsoft's initial sales advantage gave software developers a strong incentive to write for the

Windows format, the inventory of available software in the Windows format is now vastly larger than that for any competing operating system. And although general-purpose software like word processors and spreadsheets continues to be available for multiple operating systems, specialized professional software and games usually appear first—and often only—in the Windows format. This software gap and the desire to achieve compatibility for file sharing gave people a good reason for choosing Windows, even if, as in the case of many Apple Macintosh users, they believed a competing system was otherwise superior.

By far the most important and enduring of these sources of market power are economies of scale and network economies. Lured by economic profit, firms almost always find substitutes for exclusive inputs. Thus, real estate developer Donald Trump has proposed a building taller than the Sears Tower, to be built on the west side of Manhattan. Likewise, firms can often evade patent laws by making slight changes in design of products. Patent protection is only temporary, in any case. Finally, governments grant very few franchises each year. But economies of scale are both widespread and enduring.

Firmly entrenched network economies can be as persistent a source of natural monopoly as economies of scale. Indeed, network economies are essentially similar to economies of scale. When network economies are of value to the consumer, a product's quality increases as the number of users increases, so we can say that any given quality level can be produced at lower cost as sales volume increases. Thus network economies may be viewed as just another form of economies of scale in production, and that's how we'll treat them here.

 RECAP   **FIVE SOURCES OF MARKET POWER**

A firm's power to raise its price without losing its entire market stems from exclusive control of important inputs, patents and copyrights, government licenses, economies of scale, or network economies. By far the most important and enduring of these are economies of scale and network economies.

ECONOMIES OF SCALE AND THE IMPORTANCE OF FIXED COSTS

As we saw in Chapter 6, variable costs are those that vary with the level of output produced, while fixed costs are independent of output. Strictly speaking, there are no fixed costs in the long run, because all inputs can be varied. But as a practical matter, start-up costs often loom large for the duration of a product's useful life. Most of the costs involved in the production of computer software, for example, are fixed costs of this sort, one-time costs incurred in writing and testing the software. Once those tasks are done, additional copies of the software can be produced at a very low marginal cost. A good such as software, whose production entails large fixed costs and low variable costs, will be subject to significant economies of scale. Because by definition fixed costs don't increase as output increases, the average total cost of production for such goods will decline sharply as output increases.

To illustrate, consider a production process for which total cost is given by the equation $TC = F + MQ$, where F is fixed cost, M is marginal cost (assumed constant in this illustration), and Q is the level of output produced. For the production process with this simple total cost function, variable cost is simply MQ, the product of marginal cost and quantity. Average total cost, TC/Q, is equal to $F/Q + M$. As Q increases, average cost declines steadily, because the fixed costs are spread out over more and more units of output.

Figure 9.2 shows the total production cost [part (a)] and average total cost [part (b)] for a firm with the total cost curve $TC = F + MQ$ and the corresponding average total cost curve $ATC = F/Q + M$. The average total cost curve [part (b)] shows the decline in per-unit cost as output grows. Though average total cost is always higher than marginal cost for this firm, the difference between the two diminishes as output grows. At extremely high levels of output, average total cost becomes very close to marginal cost (M). Because the firm is spreading out its fixed cost over an extremely large volume of output, fixed cost per unit becomes almost insignificant.

FIGURE 9.2

Total and Average Total Costs for a Production Process with Economies of Scale.

For a firm whose total cost curve of producing Q units of output per year is $TC = F + MQ$, total cost (a) rises at a constant rate as output grows, while average total cost (b) declines. Average total cost is always higher than marginal cost for this firm, but the difference becomes less significant at high output levels.

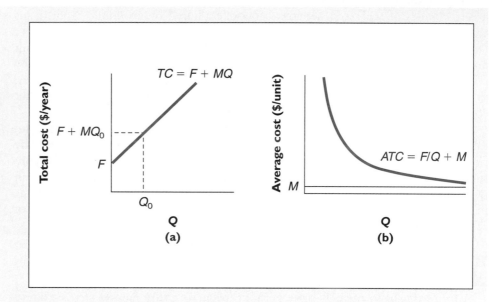

As Examples 9.1 and 9.2 illustrate, the importance of economies of scale depends on how large fixed cost is in relation to marginal cost.

EXAMPLE 9.1

Two video game producers, Nintendo and Playstation, each have fixed costs of $200,000 and marginal costs of $0.80 per game. If Nintendo produces 1 million units per year and Playstation produces 1.2 million, how much lower will Playstation's average total production cost be?

Table 9.1 summarizes the relevant cost categories for the two firms. Note in the bottom row that Playstation enjoys only a 3-cent average cost advantage over Nintendo. Even though Nintendo produces 20 percent fewer copies of its video game than Playstation, it does not suffer a significant cost disadvantage because fixed cost is a relatively small part of total production cost.

TABLE 9.1
Costs for Two Computer Game Producers (1)

	Nintendo	Playstation
Annual production	1,000,000	1,200,000
Fixed cost	$200,000	$200,000
Variable cost	$800,000	$960,000
Total cost	$1,000,000	$1,160,000
Average total cost per game	$1.00	$0.97

But note how the picture changes when fixed cost looms large relative to marginal cost.

Two video game producers, Nintendo and Playstation, each have fixed costs of $10,000,000 and marginal costs of $0.20 per video game. If Nintendo produces 1 million units per per year and Playstation produces 1.2 million, how much lower will Playstation's average total cost be?

EXAMPLE 9.2

TABLE 9.2
Costs for Two Computer Game Producers (2)

	Nintendo	Playstation
Annual production	1,000,000	1,200,000
Fixed cost	$10,000,000	$10,000,000
Variable cost	$200,000	$240,000
Total cost	$10,200,000	$10,240,000
Average total cost per game	$10.20	$8.53

The relevant cost categories for the two firms are now summarized in Table 9.2. The bottom row shows that Playstation enjoys a $1.67 average total cost advantage over Nintendo, substantially larger than in Example 9.1.

If the video games the two firms produce are essentially similar, the fact that Playstation can charge significantly lower prices and still cover its costs should enable it to attract customers away from Nintendo. As more and more of the market goes to Playstation, its cost advantage will become self-reinforcing. Table 9.3 shows how a shift of 500,000 units from Nintendo to Playstation would cause Nintendo's average total cost to rise to $20.20 per unit, while Playstation's average total cost would fall to $6.08 per unit. The fact that a firm could not long survive at such a severe disadvantage explains why the video game market is served now by only a small number of firms.

TABLE 9.3
Costs for Two Computer Game Producers (3)

	Nintendo	Playstation
Annual production	500,000	1,700,000
Fixed cost	$10,000,000	$10,000,000
Variable cost	$100,000	$340,000
Total cost	$10,100,000	$10,340,000
Average total cost per game	$20.20	$6.08

EXERCISE 9.1

How big will Playstation's unit cost advantage be if it sells 2,000,000 units per year, while Nintendo sells only 300,000?

An important worldwide economic trend during recent decades is that an increasing share of the value embodied in the goods and services we buy stems from fixed investment in research and development. For example, in 1984 some 80 percent of the cost of a computer was in its hardware (which has relatively high marginal cost); the remaining 20 percent was in its software. But by 1990 those proportions were reversed. Fixed cost now accounts for about 85 percent of total costs in the computer software industry, whose products are included in a growing share of ordinary manufactured goods.

Why does Intel sell the overwhelming majority of all microprocessors used in personal computers?

The fixed investment required to produce a new leading-edge microprocessor such as the Intel Pentium chip currently runs upward of $2 billion. But once the chip has been designed and the manufacturing facility built, the marginal cost of producing each chip is only pennies. This cost pattern explains why Intel currently sells more than 80 percent of all microprocessors.

As fixed cost becomes more and more important, the perfectly competitive pattern of many small firms, each producing only a small share of its industry's total output, becomes less common. For this reason, we must develop a clear sense of how the behavior of firms with market power differs from that of the perfectly competitive firm.

> **RECAP**   **ECONOMIES OF SCALE AND THE IMPORTANCE OF FIXED COSTS**
>
> Research, design, engineering, and other fixed costs account for an increasingly large share of all costs required to bring products successfully to market. For products with large fixed costs, marginal cost is lower, often substantially, than average total cost, and average total cost declines, often sharply, as output grows. This cost pattern explains why many industries are dominated by either a single firm or a small number of firms.

PROFIT MAXIMIZATION FOR THE MONOPOLIST

Regardless of whether a firm is a price taker or a price setter, economists assume that its basic goal is to maximize its profit. Another commonality is that the operational decision confronting both types of firm is to select the output level that results in the greatest possible difference between total revenue and total cost. But there are some important differences in how the two types of firm carry out this decision.

For both the perfectly competitive firm and the monopolist, the marginal benefit of expanding output is the additional revenue the firm will receive if it sells one additional unit of output. In both cases, this marginal benefit is called the firm's **marginal revenue.** For the perfectly competitive firm, marginal revenue is exactly equal to the market price of the product.

marginal revenue the change in a firm's total revenue that results from a one-unit change in output

MARGINAL REVENUE FOR THE MONOPOLIST

The logic of profit maximization is precisely the same for the monopolist as for the perfectly competitive firm. In both cases, the firm keeps expanding output as long as the benefit of doing so exceeds the cost. The calculation of marginal cost is also precisely the same for the monopolist as for the perfectly competitive firm. *The only significant difference between the two cases concerns the calculation of marginal revenue.*

As we have seen, marginal revenue for a competitive firm is simply the market price. If that price is $6, then the marginal benefit of selling an extra unit is exactly $6. *To a monopolist, in contrast, the marginal benefit of selling an additional unit is strictly less than the market price.* As the following discussion will make clear, the reason is that while the perfectly competitive firm can sell as many units as it wishes at the market price, the monopolist can sell an additional unit only if it cuts the price—and it must do so not just for the additional unit but for the units it is currently selling.

Suppose, for example, that a monopolist with the demand curve shown in Figure 9.3 is currently selling 2 units of output at a price of $6 per unit. What would be its marginal revenue from selling an additional unit?

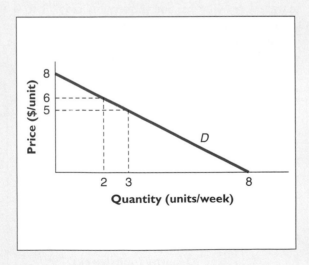

FIGURE 9.3
The Monopolist's Benefit from Selling an Additional Unit.
The monopolist shown receives $12 per week in total revenue by selling 2 units per week at a price of $6 each. This monopolist could earn $15 per week by selling 3 units per week at a price of $5 each. In that case, the benefit from selling the third unit would be $15 − $12 = $3, less than its selling price of $5.

This monopolist's total revenue from the sale of 2 units per week is ($6 per unit) (2 units per week) = $12 per week. Its total revenue from the sale of 3 units per week would be $15 per week. The difference—$3 per week—is the marginal revenue from the sale of the third unit each week. Note that this amount is not only smaller than the original price ($6) but smaller than the new price ($5) as well.

EXERCISE 9.2

Calculate marginal revenue for the monopolist in Figure 9.3 as it expands output from 3 to 4 units per week, and then from 4 to 5 units per week.

For the monopolist whose demand curve is shown in Figure 9.3, a sequence of increases in output—from 2 to 3, from 3 to 4, and from 4 to 5—will yield marginal revenue of $3, $1, and −$1, respectively. We can display these results in tabular form, as in Table 9.4.

TABLE 9.4
Marginal Revenue for a Monopolist ($ per unit)

Quantity	Marginal revenue
2	
	3
3	
	1
4	
	−1
5	

Note in the table that the marginal revenue values are displayed between the two quantity figures to which they correspond. For example, when the firm expanded its output from 2 units per week to 3, its marginal revenue was $3 per unit. Strictly speaking, this marginal revenue corresponds to neither quantity but to the movement between those quantities, hence its placement in the table. Likewise, in moving from 3 to 4 units per week, the firm earned marginal revenue of $1 per unit so that figure is placed midway between the quantities of 3 and 4, and so on.

To graph marginal revenue as a function of quantity, we would plot the marginal revenue for the movement from 2 to 3 units of output per week ($3) at a quantity value of 2.5, because 2.5 lies midway between 2 and 3. Similarly, we would plot the marginal revenue for the movement from 3 to 4 units per week ($1) at a quantity of 3.5 units per week, and the marginal revenue for the movement from 4 to 5 units per week (−$1) at a quantity of 4.5. The resulting marginal revenue curve *MR*, is shown in Figure 9.4.

FIGURE 9.4
Marginal Revenue in Graphical Form.
Because a monopolist must cut price to sell an extra unit, not only for the extra unit sold but also for all existing units, marginal revenue from the sale of the extra unit is less than its selling price.

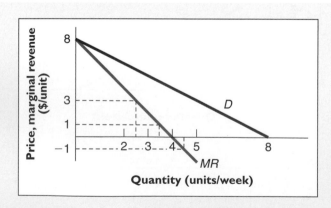

More generally, consider a monopolist with a straight-line demand curve whose vertical intercept is *a* and whose horizontal intercept is Q_0, as shown in Figure 9.5. This monopolist's marginal revenue curve will also have a vertical intercept of *a*, and it will be twice as steep as the demand curve. Thus its horizontal intercept will be not Q_0, but $Q_0/2$, as shown in Figure 9.5.

Marginal revenue curves can also be expressed algebraically. If the formula for the monopolist's demand curve is $P = a - bQ$, then the formula for its marginal revenue curve will be $MR = a - 2bQ$. If you have had calculus, this relationship

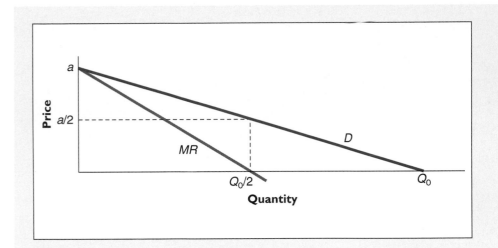

FIGURE 9.5
The Marginal Revenue Curve for a Monopolist with a Straight-Line Demand Curve.
For a monopolist with the demand curve shown, the corresponding marginal revenue curve has the same vertical intercept as the demand curve, and a horizontal intercept only half as large as that of the demand curve.

is easy to derive,[1] but even without calculus you can verify it by working through a few numerical examples. First translate the formula for the demand curve into a diagram, and then construct the corresponding marginal revenue curve graphically. Reading from the graph, write the formula for that marginal revenue curve.

THE MONOPOLIST'S PROFIT-MAXIMIZING DECISION RULE

Having derived the monopolist's marginal revenue curve, we are now in a position to describe how the monopolist chooses the output level that maximizes profit. As in the case of the perfectly competitive firm, the cost-benefit principle says that the monopolist should continue to expand output as long as the gain from doing so exceeds the cost. At the current level of output, the benefit from expanding output is the marginal revenue value that corresponds to that output level. The cost of expanding output is the marginal cost at that level of output. Whenever marginal revenue exceeds marginal cost, the firm should expand. Conversely, whenever marginal revenue falls short of marginal cost, the firm should reduce its output. *Profit is maximized at the level of output for which marginal revenue precisely equals marginal cost.*

When the monopolist's profit-maximizing rule is stated in this way, we can see that the perfectly competitive firm's rule is actually a special case of the monopolist's rule. When the perfectly competitive firm expands output by one unit, its marginal revenue exactly equals the product's market price (because the perfectly competitive firm can expand sales by a unit without having to cut the price of existing units). So when the perfectly competitive firm equates price with marginal cost, it is also equating marginal revenue with marginal cost.

What is the monopolist's profit-maximizing output level?

EXAMPLE 9.3

Consider a monopolist with the demand and marginal cost curves shown in Figure 9.6. If this firm is currently producing 12 units per week, should it expand or contract production? What is the profit-maximizing level of output?

In Figure 9.7, we begin by constructing the marginal revenue curve that corresponds to the monopolist's demand curve. It has the same vertical intercept as the demand curve, and its horizontal intercept is half as large. Note that the monopolist's marginal revenue at 12 units per week is zero, which is clearly less than its marginal cost of $3 per unit. This monopolist will therefore earn a higher

---

[1]For those who have had an introductory course in calculus, marginal revenue can be expressed as the derivative of total revenue with respect to output. If $P = a - bQ$, then total revenue will be given by $TR = PQ = aQ - bQ^2$, which means that $MR = dTR/dQ = a - 2bQ$.

FIGURE 9.6

The Demand and Marginal Cost Curves for a Monopolist.

At the current output level of 12 units per week, price equals marginal cost. Since the monopolist's price is always greater than marginal revenue, marginal revenue must be less than marginal cost, which means this monopolist should produce less.

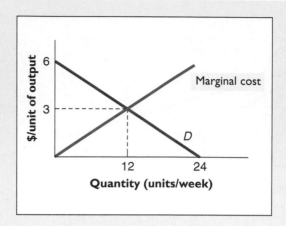

FIGURE 9.7

The Monopolist's Profit-Maximizing Output Level.

This monopolist maximizes profit by selling 8 units per week, the output level at which marginal revenue equals marginal cost. The profit-maximizing price is $4 per unit, the price that corresponds to the profit-maximizing quantity on the demand curve.

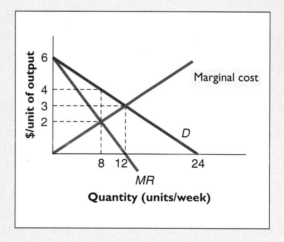

profit by contracting production until marginal revenue equals marginal cost, which occurs at an output level of 8 units per week. At this profit-maximizing output level the firm will charge $4 per unit, the price that corresponds to 8 units per week on the demand curve.

EXERCISE 9.3

Find the profit-maximizing price and level of output for a monopolist with the demand curve $P = 12 - Q$ and the marginal cost curve $MC = 2Q$, where P is the price of the product in dollars per unit and Q is output in units per week.

BEING A MONOPOLIST DOESN'T GUARANTEE AN ECONOMIC PROFIT

The fact that the profit-maximizing price for a monopolist will always be greater than marginal cost provides no assurance that the monopolist will earn an economic profit. Consider, for example, the long-distance telephone service provider whose demand, marginal revenue, marginal cost, and average total cost curves are shown in Figure 9.8(a). This monopolist maximizes its daily profit by selling 20 million minutes per day of calls at a price of $0.10 per minute. At that quantity, $MR = MC$, yet price is $0.02 per minute less than the company's average total cost of $0.12 per minute. As a result, the company sustains an economic loss of $0.02 per minute on all calls provided, or a total loss of ($0.02 per minute)(20,000,000 minutes per day) = $400,000 per day.

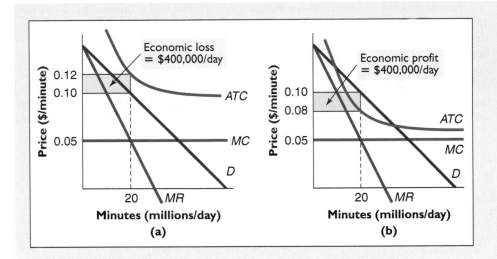

FIGURE 9.8

Even a Monopolist May Suffer an Economic Loss. The monopolist in (a) maximizes its profit by selling 20 million minutes per day of calls but suffers an economic loss of **$400,000** per day in the process. Because the profit-maximizing price of the monopolist in (b) exceeds *ATC*, this monopolist earns an economic profit.

The monopolist in Figure 9.8(a) suffered a loss because its profit-maximizing price was lower than its *ATC*. If the monopolist's profit-maximizing price exceeds its average total cost, however, the company will of course earn an economic profit. Consider, for example, the long-distance provider shown in Figure 9.8(b). This firm has the same demand, marginal revenue, and marginal cost curves as the firm shown in Figure 9.8(a). But because the firm in part (b) has lower fixed costs, its *ATC* curve is lower at every level of output than the *ATC* curve in (a). At the profit-maximizing price of $0.10 per minute, the firm in Figure 9.8(b) earns an economic profit of $0.02 per minute, for a total economic profit of $400,000 per day.

RECAP   **PROFIT MAXIMIZATION FOR THE MONOPOLIST**

Both the perfectly competitive firm and the monopolist maximize profit by choosing the output level at which marginal revenue equals marginal cost. But whereas marginal revenue equals market price for the perfectly competitive firm, it is always less than market price for the monopolist. A monopolist will earn an economic profit only if price exceeds average total cost at the profit-maximizing level of output.

WHY THE INVISIBLE HAND BREAKS DOWN UNDER MONOPOLY

In our discussion of equilibrium in perfectly competitive markets in Chapters 7 and 8, we saw conditions under which the self-serving pursuits of consumers and firms were consistent with the broader interests of society as a whole. Let's explore whether the same conclusion holds true for the case of imperfectly competitive firms.

Consider the monopolist in Example 9.3. Is this firm's profit-maximizing output level efficient from society's point of view? For any given level of output, the corresponding price on the demand curve indicates the amount buyers would be willing to pay for an additional unit of output. When the monopolist is producing 8 units per week, the marginal benefit to society of an additional unit of output is thus $4 (see Figure 9.7). And since the marginal cost of an additional unit at that output level is only $2 (again, see Figure 9.7), society would gain a net benefit of $2 per unit if the monopolist were to expand production by one unit above the profit-maximizing level. Because this economic surplus is not realized, the profit-maximizing monopolist is socially inefficient.

Recall that the existence of inefficiency means that the economic pie is smaller than it might be. If that is so, why doesn't the monopolist simply expand production? The answer is that the monopolist would gladly do so, if only there were some way to maintain the price of existing units and cut the price of only the extra units. As a practical matter, however, that is not always possible.

Consider again the monopolist in Example 9.3, whose demand and marginal cost curves are reproduced in Figure 9.9. For the market served by this monopolist, what is the socially efficient level of output?

FIGURE 9.9

The Demand and Marginal Cost Curves for a Monopolist.

The socially optimal output level is 12 units per week, the quantity for which the marginal benefit *to the public* is exactly the same as marginal cost.

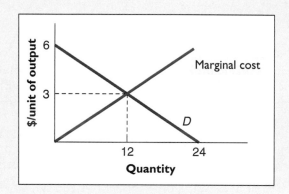

At any output level, the cost to society of an additional unit of output is the same as the cost to the monopolist, namely, the amount shown on the monopolist's marginal cost curve. The marginal benefit *to society* (not to the monopolist) of an extra unit of output is simply the amount people are willing to pay for it, which is the amount shown on the monopolist's demand curve. To achieve social efficiency, the monopolist should expand production until the marginal benefit to society equals the marginal cost, which in this case occurs at a level of 12 units per week. Social efficiency is thus achieved at the output level at which the market demand curve intersects the monopolist's marginal cost curve.

The fact that marginal revenue is less than price for the monopolist results in a deadweight loss. For the monopolist just discussed, the size of this deadweight loss is equal to the area of the pale blue triangle in Figure 9.10, which is (1/2)($2 per unit)(4 units per week) = $4 per week. That is the amount by which total economic surplus is reduced because the monopolist produces too little.

FIGURE 9.10

The Deadweight Loss from Monopoly.

A loss in economic surplus results because the profit-maximizing level of output (8 units per week) is less than the socially optimal level of output (12 units per week). This deadweight loss is the area of the pale blue triangle, $4 per week.

For a monopolist, profit maximization occurs when marginal cost equals marginal revenue. Since the monopolist's marginal revenue is always less than price, the monopolist's profit-maximizing output level is always below the socially efficient level. Under perfect competition, by contrast, profit maximization occurs when marginal cost equals the market price—the same criterion that must be satisfied for social efficiency. This difference explains why the invisible hand of the market is less evident in monopoly markets than in perfectly competitive markets.

If perfect competition is socially efficient and monopoly is not, why isn't monopoly against the law? The nation's legislators have in fact tried to limit the extent of monopoly through the antitrust laws. But even the most enthusiastic proponents of those laws recognize the limited utility of the legislative approach, since the alternatives to monopoly often entail problems of their own.

Suppose, for example, that a monopoly results from a patent that prevents all but one firm from manufacturing some highly valued product. Would society be better off without patents? Probably not, because eliminating such protection would discourage innovation. Virtually all successful industrial nations grant some form of patent protection, which gives firms a chance to recover the research and development costs without which new products would seldom reach the market.

Or suppose that the market in question is a natural monopoly—one that, because of economies of scale, is most cheaply served by a single firm. Would society do better to require this market to be served by many small firms, each with significantly higher average costs of production? Such a requirement would merely replace one form of inefficiency with another.

In short, we live in an imperfect world. Monopoly is socially inefficient, and that, needless to say, is bad. But the alternatives to monopoly aren't perfect, either.

 RECAP   **WHY THE MONOPOLIST PRODUCES "TOO LITTLE" OUTPUT**

The monopolist maximizes profit at the output level for which marginal revenue equals marginal cost. Because its profit-maximizing price exceeds marginal revenue, and hence also marginal cost, the benefit to society of the last unit produced (the market price) must be greater than the cost of the last unit produced (the marginal cost). So the output level for an industry served by a profit-maximizing monopolist is smaller than the socially optimal level of output.

USING DISCOUNTS TO EXPAND THE MARKET

The source of inefficiency in monopoly markets is the fact that the benefit to the monopolist of expanding output is less than the corresponding benefit to society. From the monopolist's point of view, the price reduction the firm must grant existing buyers to expand output is a loss. But from the point of view of those buyers, each dollar of price reduction is a gain—one dollar more in their pockets.

Note the tension in this situation, which is similar to the tension that exists in all other situations in which the economic pie is smaller than it might otherwise be. As the efficiency principle reminds us, when the economic pie grows larger, everyone can have a larger slice. To say that monopoly is inefficient means that steps could be taken to make some people better off without harming others. If people have a healthy regard for their own self-interest, why doesn't someone take those steps? Why, for example, doesn't the monopolist from the earlier examples sell 8 units of output at a price of $4, and then once those buyers are out the door, cut the price for more price-sensitive buyers?

PRICE DISCRIMINATION DEFINED

Sometimes the monopolist does precisely that. Charging different buyers different prices for the same good or service is a practice known as **price discrimination**.

price discrimination the practice of charging different buyers different prices for essentially the same good or service

Examples of price discrimination include senior citizens' and children's discounts on movie tickets, supersaver discounts on air travel, and rebate coupons on retail merchandise.

Attempts at price discrimination seem to work effectively in some markets, but not in others. Buyers are not stupid, after all; if the monopolist periodically offered a 50 percent discount on the $8 list price, those who were paying $8 might anticipate the next price cut and postpone their purchases to take advantage of it. In some markets, however, buyers may not know, or simply may not take the trouble to find out, how the price they pay compares to the prices paid by other buyers. Alternatively, the monopolist may be in a position to prevent some groups from buying at the discount prices made available to others. In such cases, the monopolist can price-discriminate effectively.

Why do many movie theaters offer discount tickets to students?

ECONOMIC NATURALIST 9.2

Whenever a firm offers a discount, the goal is to target that discount to buyers who would not purchase the product without it. People with low incomes generally have lower reservation prices for movie tickets than people with high incomes. Because students generally have lower disposable incomes than working adults, theater owners can expand their audiences by charging lower prices to students than to adults. Student discounts are one practical way of doing so. Offering student discounts also entails no risk of some people buying the product at a low price and then reselling it to others at a higher price.

HOW PRICE DISCRIMINATION AFFECTS OUTPUT

In Examples 9.4 to 9.6 we will see how the ability to price-discriminate affects the monopolist's profit-maximizing level of output. First we will consider a baseline case in which the monopolist must charge the same price to every buyer.

EXAMPLE 9.4

How many manuscripts should Carla edit?

Carla supplements her income as a teaching assistant by editing term papers for undergraduates. There are eight students per week for whom she might edit, each with a reservation price as given in the following table.

Student	Reservation price
A	$40
B	38
C	36
D	34
E	32
F	30
G	28
H	26

Carla is a profit maximizer. If the opportunity cost of her time to edit each paper is $29 and she must charge the same price to each student, how many papers should she edit? How much economic profit will she make? How much accounting profit?

Table 9.5 summarizes Carla's total and marginal revenue at various output levels. To generate the amounts in the total revenue column, we simply multiplied the corresponding reservation price by the number of students whose reservation prices were at least that high. For example, to edit 4 papers per week (for

TABLE 9.5
Total and Marginal Revenue from Editing

Student	Reservation price ($ per paper)	Total revenue ($ per week)	Marginal revenue ($ per paper)
A	40	40	40
			36
B	38	76	
			32
C	36	108	
			28
D	34	136.	
			24
E	32	160	
			20
F	30	180	
			16
G	28	196	
			12
H	26	208	

students A, B, C, and D), Carla must charge a price no higher than D's reservation price ($34). So her total revenue when she edits 4 papers per week is (4)($34) = $136 per week. Carla should keep expanding the number of students she serves as long as her marginal revenue exceeds the opportunity cost of her time. Marginal revenue, or the difference in total revenue that results from adding another student, is shown in the last column of Table 9.5.

Note that if Carla were editing 2 papers per week, her marginal revenue from editing a third paper would be $32. Since that amount exceeds her $29 opportunity cost, she should take on the third paper. But since the marginal revenue of taking on a fourth paper would be only $28, Carla should stop at 3 papers per week. The total opportunity cost of the time required to edit the 3 papers is (3)($29) = $87, so Carla's economic profit is $108 − $87 = $21 per week. Since Carla incurs no explicit costs, her accounting profit will be $108 per week.

What is the socially efficient number of papers for Carla to edit?

EXAMPLE 9.5

Again, suppose that Carla's opportunity cost of editing is $29 per paper and that she could edit as many as 8 papers per week for students whose reservation prices are again as listed in the following table.

Student	Reservation price
A	$40
B	38
C	36
D	34
E	32
F	30
G	28
H	26

What is the socially efficient number of papers for Carla to edit? If she must charge the same price to each student, what will her economic and accounting profits be if she edits the socially efficient number of papers?

Students *A* to *F* are willing to pay more than Carla's opportunity cost, so serving these students is socially efficient. But students *G* and *H* are unwilling to pay at least $29 for Carla's services. The socially efficient outcome, therefore, is for Carla to edit 6 papers per week. To attract that number, she must charge a price no higher than $30 per paper. Her total revenue will be (6)($30) = $180 per week, slightly more than her total opportunity cost of (6)($29) = $174 per week. Her economic profit will thus be only $6 per week. Again, because Carla incurs no explicit costs, her accounting profit will be the same as her total revenue, $180 per week.

EXAMPLE 9.6

If Carla can price-discriminate, how many papers should she edit?

Suppose Carla is a shrewd judge of human nature. After a moment's conversation with a student, she can discern that student's reservation price. The reservation prices of her potential customers are again as given in the following table. If Carla confronts the same market as before, but can charge students their respective reservation prices, how many papers should she edit, and how much economic and accounting profit will she make?

Student	Reservation price
A	$40
B	38
C	36
D	34
E	32
F	30
G	28
H	26

Carla will edit papers for students *A* to *F* and charge each exactly his or her reservation price. Because students *G* and *H* have reservation prices below $29, Carla will not edit their papers. Carla's total revenue will be $40 + $38 + $36 + $34 + $32 + $30 = $210 per week, which is also her accounting profit. Her total opportunity cost of editing 6 papers is (6)($29) = $174 per week, so her economic profit will be $210 − $174 = $36 per week, $30 per week more than when she was constrained to charge each customer the same price.

perfectly discriminating monopolist a firm that charges each buyer exactly his or her reservation price

A monopolist who can charge each buyer exactly his or her reservation price is called a **perfectly discriminating monopolist.** Notice that when Carla was discriminating among customers in this way, her profit-maximizing level of output was exactly the same as the socially efficient level of output: 6 papers per week. With a perfectly discriminating monopoly, there is no loss of efficiency. All buyers who are willing to pay a price high enough to cover marginal cost will be served.

Note that although total economic surplus is maximized by a perfectly discriminating monopolist, consumers would have little reason to celebrate if they found themselves dealing with such a firm. After all, consumer surplus is exactly zero for the perfectly discriminating monopolist. In this instance, total economic surplus and producer surplus are one and the same.

In practice, of course, perfect price discrimination can never occur, because no seller knows each and every buyer's precise reservation price. But even if some sellers did know, practical difficulties would stand in the way of their charging a separate price to each buyer. For example, in many markets the seller could not prevent buyers who bought at low prices from reselling to other buyers at higher prices, capturing some of the seller's business in the process. Despite these difficulties, price discrimination is widespread. But it is generally *imperfect price discrimination*, that is, price discrimination in which at least some buyers are charged less than their reservation prices.

THE HURDLE METHOD OF PRICE DISCRIMINATION

The profit-maximizing seller's goal is to charge each buyer the highest price that buyer is willing to pay. Two primary obstacles prevent sellers from achieving this goal. First, sellers don't know exactly how much each buyer is willing to pay. And second, they need some means of excluding those who are willing to pay a high price from buying at a low price. These are formidable problems, which no seller can hope to solve completely.

One common method by which sellers achieve a crude solution to both problems is to require buyers to overcome some obstacle to be eligible for a discount price. This method is called the **hurdle method of price discrimination.** For example, the seller might sell a product at a standard list price and offer a rebate to any buyer who takes the trouble to mail in a rebate coupon.

The hurdle method solves both the seller's problems, provided that buyers with low reservation prices are more willing than others to jump the hurdle. Because the decision to jump the hurdle is subject to the cost-benefit test, such a link seems to exist. As noted earlier, buyers with low incomes are more likely than others to have low reservation prices (at least in the case of normal goods). Because of the low opportunity cost of their time, they are more likely than others to take the trouble to send in rebate coupons. Rebate coupons thus target a discount toward those buyers whose reservation prices are low and who therefore might not buy the product otherwise.

A **perfect hurdle** is one that separates buyers precisely according to their reservation prices, and in the process imposes no cost on those who jump the hurdle. With a perfect hurdle, the highest reservation price among buyers who jump the hurdle will be lower than the lowest reservation price among buyers who choose not to jump the hurdle. In practice, perfect hurdles do not exist. Some buyers will always jump the hurdle, even though their reservation prices are high. And hurdles will always exclude at least some buyers with low reservation prices. Even so, many commonly used hurdles do a remarkably good job of targeting discounts to buyers with low reservation prices. In the examples that follow, we will assume for convenience that the seller is using a perfect hurdle.

How much should Carla charge for editing if she uses a perfect hurdle?

Suppose Carla again has the opportunity to edit as many as 8 papers per week for the students whose reservation prices are as given in the following table. This time she can offer a rebate coupon that gives a discount to any student who takes the trouble to mail it back to her. Suppose further that students whose reservation prices are at least $36 never mail in the rebate coupons, while those whose reservation prices are below $36 always do so.

hurdle method of price discrimination the practice by which a seller offers a discount to all buyers who overcome some obstacle

perfect hurdle a threshold that completely segregates buyers whose reservation prices lie above it from others whose reservation prices lie below it, imposing no cost on those who jump the hurdle

EXAMPLE 9.7

Student	Reservation price
A	$40
B	38
C	36
D	34
E	32
F	30
G	28
H	26

If Carla's opportunity cost of editing each paper is again $29, what should her list price be, and what amount should she offer as a rebate? Will her economic profit be larger or smaller than when she lacked the discount option (Example 9.4)?

The rebate coupon allows Carla to divide her original market into two submarkets in which she can charge two different prices. The first submarket consists of students A, B, and C, whose reservation prices are at least $36 and who therefore will not bother to mail in a rebate coupon. The second submarket consists of students D to H, whose lower reservation prices indicate a willingness to use rebate coupons.

In each submarket, Carla must charge the same price to every buyer, just like an ordinary monopolist. She should therefore keep expanding output in each submarket as long as marginal revenue in that market exceeds her marginal cost. The relevant data for the two submarkets are displayed in Table 9.6.

On the basis of the entries in the marginal revenue column for the list price submarket, we see that Carla should serve all three students (A, B, and C), since marginal revenue for each exceeds $29. Her profit-maximizing price in the list price submarket is $36, the highest price she can charge in that market and still sell her services to students A, B, and C. For the discount price submarket, marginal revenue exceeds $29 only for the first two students (D and E). So the profit-maximizing price in this submarket is $32, the highest price Carla can charge and still sell her services to D and E. (A discount price of $32 means that students who mail in the coupon will receive a rebate of $4 on the $36 list price.)

Note that the rebate offer enables Carla to serve a total of five students per week, compared to only three without the offer (see Example 9.4). Carla's combined total revenue for the two markets is (3)($36) + 2($32) = $172 per week. Since her opportunity cost is $29 per paper, or a total of (5)($29) = $145 per week, her economic profit is $172 per week − $145 per week = $27 per week, $6 more than when she did not offer the rebate.

TABLE 9.6
Price Discrimination with a Perfect Hurdle

Student	Reservation price ($ per paper)	Total revenue ($ per week)	Marginal revenue ($ per paper)
List Price Submarket			
A	40	40	40
B	38	76	36
C	36	108	32
Discount Price Submarket			
D	34	34	34
E	32	64	30
F	30	90	26
G	28	112	22
H	26	130	18

EXERCISE 9.4

Refer to Example 9.7. How much should Carla charge in each submarket if she knows that only those students whose reservation prices are below $34 will use rebate coupons?

IS PRICE DISCRIMINATION A BAD THING?

We are so conditioned to think of discrimination as bad that we may be tempted to conclude that price discrimination must run counter to the public interest. In Example 9.7, however, both consumer and producer surplus were actually enhanced by the monopolist's use of the hurdle method of price discrimination. To show this, we compare consumer and producer surplus when Carla employs the hurdle method (Example 9.7) to the corresponding values when she charges the same price to all buyers (Example 9.4).

When Carla had to charge the same price to every customer, she edited only the papers of students A, B, and C, each of whom paid a price of $36. We can tell at a glance that the total surplus must be larger under the hurdle method, because not only are students A, B, and C served at the same price ($36), but also students E and F are now served at a price of $32.

To confirm this intuition, we can calculate the exact amount of the surplus. For any student who hires Carla to edit her paper, consumer surplus is the difference between her reservation price and the price actually paid. In both the single price and discount price examples, student A's consumer surplus is thus $40 − $36 = $4; student B's consumer surplus is $38 − $36 = $2; and student C's consumer surplus is $36 − $36 = 0. Total consumer surplus in the list price submarket is thus $4 + $2 = $6 per week, which is the same as total consumer surplus in Example 9.4. But now the discount price submarket generates additional consumer surplus. Specifically, student D receives $2 per week of consumer surplus, since this student's reservation price of $34 is $2 more than the discount price of $32. So total consumer surplus is now $6 + $2 = $8 per week, or $2 per week more than before.

Carla's producer surplus also increases under the hurdle method. For each paper she edits, her producer surplus is the price she charges minus her reservation price ($29). In the single-price case, Carla's surplus was (3)($36 − $29) = $21 per week. When she offers a rebate coupon, she earns the same producer surplus as before from students A, B, and C, and additional (2)($32 − $29) = $6 per week from students D and E. Total producer surplus with the discount is thus $21 + $6 = $27 per week. Adding that amount to the total consumer surplus of $8 per week, we get a total economic surplus of $35 per week with the rebate coupons, $8 per week more than without the rebate.

Note, however, that even with the rebate, the final outcome is not socially efficient, because Carla does not serve student F, even though this student's reservation price of $30 exceeds her opportunity cost of $29. But though the hurdle method is not perfectly efficient, it is still more efficient than charging a single price to all buyers.

EXAMPLES OF PRICE DISCRIMINATION

Once you grasp the principle behind the hurdle method of price discrimination, you will begin to see examples of it all around you. Next time you visit a grocery, hardware, or appliance store, for instance, notice how many different product promotions include cash rebates. Temporary sales are another illustration of the hurdle method. Most of the time, stores sell most of their merchandise at the "regular" price but periodically offer special sales at a significant discount. The hurdle in this instance is taking the trouble to find out when and where the sales occur and then going to the store during that period. This technique works because buyers who care most about price (mainly, those with low reservation prices) are more likely to monitor advertisements carefully and buy only during sale periods.

To give another example, book publishers typically launch a new book in hardcover form at a price from $20 to $30, and a year later they bring out a paperback edition priced between $5 and $15. In this instance, the hurdle involves having to wait the extra year and accepting a slight reduction in the quality of the finished product. People who are strongly concerned about price end up waiting for the paperback edition, while those with high reservation prices usually spring for the hardback.

Or take the example of automobile producers, who typically offer several different models with different trim and accessories. Although GM's actual cost of producing a Cadillac may be only $2,000 more than its cost of producing a Chevrolet, the Cadillac's selling price may be $10,000 to $15,000 higher than the Chevrolet's. Buyers with low reservation prices purchase the Chevrolet, while those with high reservation prices are more likely to choose the Cadillac.

Commercial air carriers have perfected the hurdle method to an extent matched by almost no other seller. Their supersaver fares are often less than half their regular coach fares. To be eligible for these discounts, travelers must purchase their tickets 7 to 21 days in advance, and their journey must include a Saturday night stayover. Vacation travelers can more easily satisfy these restrictions than business travelers, whose schedules often change at the last moment and whose trips seldom involve Saturday stayovers. And—no surprise—the business traveler's reservation price tends to be much higher than the vacation traveler's.

Many sellers employ not just one hurdle but several by offering deeper discounts to buyers who jump successively more difficult hurdles. For example, movie producers release their major films to first-run theaters at premium prices, then several months later to neighborhood theaters at a few dollars less. Still later they make the films available on pay-per-view cable channels, then release them on video, and finally permit them to be shown on network television. Each successive hurdle involves waiting a little longer, and in the case of the televised versions, accepting lower quality. These hurdles are remarkably effective in segregating moviegoers according to their reservation prices.

Recall that the efficiency loss from single-price monopoly occurs because to the monopolist the benefit of expanding output is smaller than the benefit to society as a whole. The hurdle method of price discrimination reduces this loss by giving the monopolist a practical means of cutting prices for price-sensitive buyers only. In general, the more finely the monopolist can partition a market using the hurdle method, the smaller the efficiency loss. Hurdles are not perfect, however, and some degree of efficiency will inevitably be lost.

Why might an appliance retailer instruct its clerks to hammer dents into the sides of its stoves and refrigerators?

The Sears "Scratch 'n' Dent Sale" is another example of how retailers use quality differentials to segregate buyers according to their reservation prices. Many Sears stores hold an annual sale in which they display appliances with minor scratches and blemishes in the parking lot at deep discounts. People who don't care much about price are unlikely to turn out for these events, but those with very low reservation prices often get up early to be first in line. Indeed, these sales have proven so popular that it might even be in a retailer's interest to put dents in some of its sale items deliberately.

Would a profit-maximizing appliance retailer ever deliberately damage its own merchandise?

ECONOMIC NATURALIST 9.3

RECAP   USING DISCOUNTS TO EXPAND THE MARKET

A price-discriminating monopolist is one who charges different prices to different buyers for essentially the same good or service. A common method of price discrimination is the hurdle method, which involves granting a discount to buyers who jump over a hurdle, such as mailing in a rebate coupon. An effective hurdle is one that is more easily cleared by buyers with low reservation prices than by buyers with high reservation prices. Such a hurdle enables the monopolist to expand output and thereby reduce the deadweight loss from monopoly pricing.

PUBLIC POLICY TOWARD NATURAL MONOPOLY

Monopoly is problematic not only because of the loss in efficiency associated with restricted output but also because the monopolist earns an economic profit at the buyer's expense. Many people are understandably uncomfortable about having to purchase from the sole provider of any good or service. For this reason, voters in many societies have empowered government to adopt policies aimed at controlling natural monopolists.

There are several ways to achieve this aim. A government may assume ownership and control of a natural monopoly, or it may merely attempt to regulate the prices it charges. In some cases government solicits competitive bids from private firms to produce natural monopoly services. In still other cases, governments attempt to dissolve natural monopolies into smaller entities that compete with one another. But many of these policies create economic problems of their own. In each case, the practical challenge is to come up with the solution that yields the greatest surplus of benefits over costs. Natural monopoly may be inefficient and unfair, but, as noted earlier, the alternatives to natural monopoly are far from perfect.

STATE OWNERSHIP AND MANAGEMENT

Natural monopoly is inefficient because the monopolist's profit-maximizing price is greater than its marginal cost. But even if the natural monopolist *wanted* to set price equal to marginal cost, it could not do so and hope to remain in business. After all, the defining feature of a natural monopoly is economies of scale in production, which means that marginal cost will always be less than average total cost. Setting price equal to marginal cost would fail to cover average total cost, which implies an economic loss.

Consider the case of a local cable television company. Once an area has been wired for cable television, the marginal cost of adding an additional subscriber is very low. For the sake of efficiency, all subscribers should pay a price equal to that marginal cost. Yet a cable company that priced in this manner would never be able to recover the fixed cost of setting up the network. This same problem applies not just to cable television companies but to all other natural monopolies. Even if such firms wanted to set price equal to marginal cost (which, of course, they do not, since they will earn more by setting marginal revenue equal to marginal cost), they cannot do so without suffering an economic loss.

One way to attack the efficiency and fairness problems is for the government to take over the industry, set price equal to marginal cost, and then absorb the resulting losses out of general tax revenues. This approach has been followed with good results in the state-owned electric utility industry in France, whose efficient pricing methods have set the standard for electricity pricing worldwide.

But state ownership and efficient management do not always go hand in hand. Granted, the state-owned natural monopoly is free to charge marginal cost, while the private natural monopoly is not. Yet private natural monopolies often face a much stronger incentive to cut costs than their government-owned counterparts. When the private monopolist figures out a way to cut $1 from the cost of production, its profit goes up by $1. But when the government manager of a state-owned monopoly cuts $1 from the cost of production, the government typically cuts the monopoly's budget by $1. Think back to your last visit to the Department of Motor Vehicles. Did it strike you as an efficiently managed organization?

Whether the efficiency that is gained by being able to set price equal to marginal cost outweighs the inefficiency that results from a weakened incentive to cut costs is an empirical question.

STATE REGULATION OF PRIVATE MONOPOLIES

In the United States, the most common method of curbing monopoly profits is for government merely to regulate the natural monopoly rather than own it. Most states, for example, take this approach with electric utilities, natural gas providers, local telephone companies, and cable television companies. The standard procedure in these cases is called **cost-plus regulation:** Government regulators gather data on the monopolist's explicit costs of production and then permit the monopolist to set prices that cover those costs, plus a markup to assure a normal return on the firm's investment.

cost-plus regulation a method of regulation under which the regulated firm is permitted to charge a price equal to its explicit costs of production plus a markup to cover the opportunity cost of resources provided by the firm's owners

While it may sound reasonable, cost-plus regulation has several pitfalls. First, it generates costly administrative proceedings in which regulators and firms quarrel over which of the firm's expenditures can properly be included in the costs it is allowed to recover. This question is difficult to answer even in theory. Consider a firm like Pacific Telesis, whose local telephone service is subject to cost-plus regulation but whose other products and services are unregulated. Many Pacific Telesis employees, from the president on down, are involved in both regulated and unregulated activities. How should their salaries be allocated between the two? The company has a strong incentive to argue for greater allocation to the regulated activities, which allows it to capture more revenue from captive customers in the local telephone market.

A second problem with cost-plus regulation is that it blunts the firm's incentive to adopt cost-saving innovations, for when it does, regulators require the firm to cut its rates. The firm gets to keep its cost savings in the current period, which is a stronger incentive to cut costs than the one facing a government-owned monopoly. But the incentive to cut costs would be stronger still if the firm could retain its cost savings indefinitely. Furthermore, in cases in which regulators set rates by allowing the monopolist to add a fixed markup to costs incurred, the regulated monopolist may actually have an incentive to *increase* costs rather than reduce them. Outrageous though the thought may be, the monopolist may earn a higher profit by installing gold-plated faucets in the company rest rooms.

Finally, cost-plus regulation does not solve the natural monopolist's basic problem, the inability to set price equal to marginal cost without losing money. Although these are all serious problems, governments seem to be in no hurry to abandon cost-plus regulation.

EXCLUSIVE CONTRACTING FOR NATURAL MONOPOLY

One of the most promising methods for dealing with natural monopoly is for the government to invite private firms to bid for the natural monopolist's market. The government specifies in detail the service it wants—cable television, fire protection, garbage collection—and firms submit bids describing how much they will charge for the service. The low bidder wins the contract.

The incentive to cut costs under such an arrangement is every bit as powerful as that facing ordinary competitive firms. Competition among bidders should also eliminate any concerns about the fairness of monopoly profits. And if the government is willing to provide a cash subsidy to the winning bidder, exclusive contracting even allows the monopolist to set price equal to marginal cost.

Contracting has been employed with good results in municipal fire protection and garbage collection. Communities that employ private companies to provide these services often spend only half as much as adjacent communities served by municipal fire and sanitation departments.

Despite these attractive features, however, exclusive contracting is not without problems, especially when the service to be provided is complex or requires a large fixed investment in capital equipment. In such cases, contract specifications may be so detailed and complicated that they become tantamount to regulating the firm directly. And in cases involving a large fixed investment—electric power generation and distribution, for example—officials face the question of how to transfer the assets if a new firm wins the contract. The winning firm naturally wants to acquire the assets as cheaply as possible, but the retiring firm is entitled to a fair price for them. What, in such cases, is a fair price?

Fire protection and garbage collection are simple enough that the costs of contracting out these functions is not prohibitive. But in other cases, such costs might easily outweigh any savings made possible by exclusive contracting.

VIGOROUS ENFORCEMENT OF ANTITRUST LAWS

The nineteenth century witnessed the accumulation of massive private fortunes, the likes of which had never been seen in the industrialized world. Public sentiment ran high against the so-called robber barons of the period—the Carnegies, Rockefellers, Mellons, and others. In 1890, Congress passed the Sherman Act, which declared illegal any conspiracy "to monopolize, or attempt to monopolize . . . any part of the trade or commerce among the several States." And in 1914, Congress passed the Clayton Act, whose aim was to prevent corporations from acquiring shares in a competitor if the transaction would "substantially lessen competition or create a monopoly."

Antitrust laws have helped to prevent the formation of cartels, or coalitions of firms that collude to raise prices above competitive levels. But they have also caused some harm. For example, federal antitrust officials spent more than a decade trying to break up the IBM Corporation in the belief that it had achieved an unhealthy dominance in the computer industry. That view was proved comically wrong by IBM's subsequent failure to foresee and profit from the rise of the personal computer. By breaking up large companies and discouraging mergers between companies in the same industry, antitrust laws may help to promote competition, but they may also prevent companies from achieving economies of scale.

A final possibility is simply to ignore the problem of natural monopoly: to let the monopolist choose the quantity to produce and sell it at whatever price the market will bear. The obvious objections to this policy are the two we began with, namely, that a natural monopoly is not only inefficient but also unfair. But just as the hurdle method of price discrimination mitigates efficiency losses, it also lessens the concern about taking unfair advantage of buyers.

Consider first the source of the natural monopolist's economic profit. This firm, recall, is one with economies of scale, which means that its average production cost declines as output increases. Efficiency requires that price be set at marginal cost, but because the natural monopolist's marginal cost is lower than its average cost, it cannot charge all buyers the marginal cost without suffering an economic loss.

The depth and prevalence of discount pricing suggests that whatever economic profit a natural monopolist earns generally will not come out of the discount buyer's pocket. Although discount prices are higher than the monopolist's marginal cost of production, in most cases they are lower than the average cost. Thus the monopolist's economic profit, if any, must come from buyers who pay list price. And since those buyers have the option, in most cases, of jumping a hurdle and paying a discount price, their contribution, if not completely voluntary, is at least not strongly coerced.

So much for the source of the monopolist's economic profit. What about its disposition? Who gets it? A large chunk—some 35 percent, in many cases—goes to the federal government via the corporate income tax. The remainder is paid out to shareholders, some of whom are wealthy and some of whom are not. These shareholder profits are also taxed by state and even local governments. In the end, two-thirds or more of a monopolist's economic profit may fund services provided by governments of various levels.

Both the source of the monopolist's economic profit (the list price buyer) and the disposition of that profit (largely, to fund public services) cast doubt on the claim that monopoly profit constitutes a social injustice on any grand scale. Nevertheless, the hurdle method of differential pricing cannot completely eliminate the fairness and efficiency problems that result from monopoly pricing. In the end, then, we are left with a choice among imperfect alternatives. As the cost-benefit principle emphasizes, the best choice is the one for which the balance of benefits over costs is largest. But which choice that is will depend on the circumstances at hand.

RECAP   PUBLIC POLICY TOWARD NATURAL MONOPOLY

The natural monopolist sets price above marginal cost, resulting in too little output from society's point of view (the efficiency problem). The natural monopolist may also earn an economic profit at buyers' expense (the fairness problem). Policies for dealing with the efficiency and fairness problems include state ownership and management, state regulation, exclusive contracting, and vigorous enforcement of antitrust laws. Each of these remedies entails problems of its own.

■ SUMMARY ■

- Our concern in this chapter was the conduct and performance of the imperfectly competitive firm, a firm that has at least some latitude to set its own price. Economists often distinguish among three different types of imperfectly competitive firms: the pure monopolist, the lone seller of a product in a given market; the oligopolist, one of only a few sellers of a given product; and the monopolistic competitor, one of a relatively large number of firms that sell similar though slightly differentiated products.

- Although advanced courses in economics devote much attention to differences in behavior among these three types of firm, our focus was on the common feature that differentiates them from perfectly competitive firms. Whereas the perfectly competitive firm faces an infinitely elastic demand curve for its product, the imperfectly competitive firm faces a downward-sloping demand curve. For convenience, we use the term *monopolist* to refer to any of the three types of imperfectly competitive firms.

- Monopolists are sometimes said to enjoy market power, a term that refers to their power to set the price of their product. Market power stems from exclusive control over important inputs, from economies of scale, from patents and government licenses or franchises, and from network economies. The most important and enduring of these five sources of market power are economies of scale and network economies.

- Unlike the perfectly competitive firm, for which marginal revenue exactly equals market price, the monopolist realizes a marginal revenue that is always less than its price. This shortfall reflects the fact that to sell more output, the monopolist must cut the price not only to additional buyers but to existing buyers as well. For the monopolist with a

straight-line demand curve, the marginal revenue curve has the same vertical intercept and a horizontal intercept that is half as large as the intercept for the demand curve.

- Whereas the perfectly competitive firm maximizes profit by producing at the level at which marginal cost equals the market price, the monopolist maximizes profit by equating marginal cost with marginal revenue, which is significantly lower than the market price. The result is an output level that is best for the monopolist but smaller than the level that would be best for society as a whole. At the profit-maximizing level of output, the benefit of an extra unit of output (the market price) is greater than its cost (the marginal cost). At the socially efficient level of output, where the monopolist's marginal cost curve intersects the demand curve, the benefit and cost of an extra unit are the same.

- Both the monopolist and its potential customers can do better if the monopolist can grant discounts to price-sensitive buyers. The extreme example is the perfectly discriminating monopolist, who charges each buyer exactly his or her reservation price. Such producers are socially efficient, because they sell to every buyer whose reservation price is at least as high as the marginal cost.

- One common method of targeting discounts toward price-sensitive buyers is the hurdle method of price discrimination, in which the buyer becomes eligible for a discount only after overcoming some obstacle, such as mailing in a rebate coupon. This technique works well because those buyers who care most about price are more likely than others to jump the hurdle. While the hurdle method reduces the efficiency loss associated with single-price monopoly, it does not completely eliminate it.

• The various policies that governments employ to mitigate concerns about fairness and efficiency losses arising from natural monopoly include state ownership and management of natural monopolies, state regulation, private contracting, and vigorous enforcement of antitrust laws. Each of these remedies entails costs as well as benefits. In some cases, a combination of policies will produce a better outcome than simply allowing natural monopolists to do as they please. But in other cases, a hands-off policy may be the best available option.

■ KEY TERMS ■

constant returns to scale (224)
cost-plus regulation (244)
economies of scale (224)
hurdle method of price discrimination (239)
imperfectly competitive firm (221)
increasing returns to scale (224)

marginal revenue (229)
market power (223)
monopolistically competitive firm (222)
natural monopoly (224)
oligopolist (222)

perfect hurdle (239)
perfectly discriminating monopolist (238)
price discrimination (235)
price setter (222)
pure monopoly (222)

■ REVIEW QUESTIONS ■

1. What important characteristic do all three types of imperfectly competitive firm share?

2. True or false: A firm with market power can sell whatever quantity it wishes at whatever price it chooses.

3. Why do most successful industrial societies offer patents and copyright protection, even though these protections enable sellers to charge higher prices?

4. Why is marginal revenue always less than price for a monopolist but equal to price for a perfectly competitive firm?

5. True or false: Because a natural monopolist charges a price greater than marginal cost, it necessarily earns a positive economic profit.

■ PROBLEMS ■

1. Two car manufacturers, Saab and Volvo, have fixed costs of $1 billion and marginal costs of $10,000 per car. If Saab produces 50,000 cars per year and Volvo produces 200,000, calculate the average production cost for each company. On the basis of these costs, which company's market share do you think will grow in relative terms?

2. State whether the following statements are true or false, and explain why.
   a. In a perfectly competitive industry the industry demand curve is horizontal, whereas for a monopoly it is downward-sloping.
   b. Perfectly competitive firms have no control over the price they charge for their product.
   c. For a natural monopoly, average cost declines as the number of units produced increases over the relevant output range.

3. A single-price profit-maximizing monopolist:
   a. Causes excess demand, or shortages, by selling too few units of a good or service.
   b. Chooses the output level at which marginal revenue begins to increase.
   c. Always charges a price above the marginal cost of production.
   d. Also maximizes marginal revenue.
   e. None of the above statements is true.

4. If a monopolist could perfectly price-discriminate:
   a. The marginal revenue curve and the demand curve would coincide.
   b. The marginal revenue curve and the marginal cost curve would coincide.
   c. Every consumer would pay a different price.
   d. Marginal revenue would become negative at some output level.
   e. The resulting pattern of exchange would still be socially inefficient.

5. Explain why price discrimination and the existence of slightly different variants of the same product tend to go hand in hand. Give an example from your own experience.

6. What is the socially desirable price for a natural monopoly to charge? Why will a natural monopoly that attempts to charge the socially desirable price invariably suffer an economic loss?

7. TotsPoses, Inc., a profit-maximizing business, is the only photography business in town that specializes in portraits of small children. George, who owns and runs TotsPoses, expects to encounter an average of eight customers per day, each with a reservation price shown in the following table.

Customer	Reservation price ($ per photo)
A	50
B	46
C	42
D	38
E	34
F	30
G	26
H	22

a. If the total cost of each photoportrait is $12, how much should George charge if he must charge a single price to all customers? At this price, how many portraits will George produce each day? What will be his economic profit?
b. How much consumer surplus is generated each day at this price?
c. What is the socially efficient number of portraits?
d. George is very experienced in the business and knows the reservation price of each of his customers. If he is allowed to charge any price he likes to any consumer, how many portraits will he produce each day, and what will his economic profit be?
e. In this case, how much consumer surplus is generated each day?
f. Suppose George is permitted to charge two prices. He knows that customers with a reservation price above $30 never bother with coupons, whereas those with a reservation price of $30 or less always use them. At what level should George set the list price of a portrait? At what level should he set the discount price? How many photoportraits will he sell at each price?
g. In this case, what is George's economic profit, and how much consumer surplus is generated each day?

8. Suppose that the University of Michigan Cinema is a local monopoly whose demand curve for adult tickets on Saturday night is $P = 12 - 2Q$, where P is the price of a ticket in dollars and Q is the number of tickets sold in hundreds. The demand for children's tickets on Sunday afternoon is $P = 8 - 3Q$, and for adult tickets on Sunday afternoon, $P = 10 - 4Q$. On both Saturday night and Sunday afternoon, the marginal cost of an additional patron, child or adult, is $2.
a. What is the marginal revenue curve in each of the three submarkets?
b. What price should the cinema charge in each of the three markets if its goal is to maximize profit?

9. Suppose you are a monopolist in the market for a specific video game. Your demand curve is given by $P = 80 - Q/2$, and your marginal cost curve is $MC = Q$. Your fixed costs equal $400.
a. Graph the demand and marginal cost curve.
b. Derive and graph the marginal revenue curve.
c. Calculate and indicate on the graph the equilibrium price and quantity.
d. What is your profit?
e. What is the level of consumer surplus?

10. Beth is a second-grader who sells lemonade on a street corner in your neighborhood. Each cup of lemonade costs Beth 20 cents to produce; she has no fixed costs. The

reservation prices for the 10 people who walk by Beth's lemonade stand each day are listed in the following table.

Person	A	B	C	D	E	F	G	H	I	J
Reservation price	$1.00	$0.90	$0.80	$0.70	$0.60	$0.50	$0.40	$0.30	$0.20	$0.10

Beth knows the distribution of reservation prices (that is, she knows that one person is willing to pay $1, another $0.90, and so on), but she does not know any specific individual's reservation price.

a. Calculate the marginal revenue of selling an additional cup of lemonade. (Start by figuring out the price Beth would charge if she produced only one cup of lemonade, and calculate the total revenue; then find the price Beth would charge if she sold two cups of lemonade; and so on.)

b. What is Beth's profit-maximizing price?

c. At that price, what are Beth's economic profit and total consumer surplus?

d. What price should Beth charge if she wants to maximize total economic surplus?

e. Now suppose Beth can tell the reservation price of each person. What price would she charge each person if she wanted to maximize profit? Compare her profit to the total surplus calculated in part d.

■ ANSWERS TO IN-CHAPTER EXERCISES ■

9.1 The relevant cost figures are as shown in the following table, which shows that the Playstation's unit-cost advantage is now $50.20 − $5.20 = $45.00.

	Nintendo	**Playstation**
Annual production	200,000	2,000,000
Fixed cost	$10,000,000	$10,000,000
Variable cost	$40,000	$400,000
Total cost	$10,040,000	$10,400,000
Average total cost per game	$50.20	$5.20

9.2 When the monopolist expands from 3 to 4 units per week, total revenue rises from $15 to $16 per week, which means that the marginal revenue from the sale of the fourth unit is only $1 per week. When the monopolist expands from 4 to 5 units per week, total revenue drops from $16 to 15 per week, which means that the marginal revenue from the sale of the fifth unit is actually negative, or −$1 per week.

9.3 For the demand curve $P = 12 − Q$, the corresponding marginal revenue curve is $MR = 12 − 2Q$. Equating MR and MC, we solve the equation $12 − 2Q = 2Q$ for $Q = 3$. Substituting $Q = 3$ into the demand equation, we solve for the profit-maximizing price, $P = 12 − 3 = 9$.

9.4 As the marginal revenue column in the following table shows, Carla should again serve students *A*, *B*, and *C* in the list price submarket (at a price of $36), and only student *E* in the discount submarket (at a price of $32).

Student	Reservation price ($ per paper)	Total revenue ($ per week)	Marginal revenue ($ per paper)
List Price Submarket			
			40
A	40	40	
			36
B	38	76	
			32
C	36	108	
			28
D	34	136	
Discount Price Submarket			
			32
E	32	32	
			28
F	30	60	
			24
G	28	84	
			20
H	26	104	

THINKING STRATEGICALLY

■

At a Christmas Eve dinner party in 1997, actor Robert DeNiro pulled singer Tony Bennett aside for a moment. "Hey Tony—there's a film I want you in," DeNiro said. He was referring to the project that became the 1999 Warner Brothers hit comedy *Analyze This,* in which the troubled head of a crime family, played by DeNiro, seeks the counsel of a psychotherapist, played by Billy Crystal. In the script, both the mob boss and his therapist are big fans of Bennett's music.

Bennett heard nothing further about the project for almost a year. Then his son and financial manager, Danny Bennett, got a phone call from Warner Brothers, in which the studio offered Tony $15,000 to sing "Got the World on a String" in the movie's final scene. As Danny described the conversation, ". . . they made a fatal mistake. They told me they had already shot the film. So I'm like: 'Hey, they shot the whole film around Tony being the end gag and they're offering me $15,000?'"[1]

Warner Brothers wound up paying $200,000 for Bennett's performance.

In business negotiations, as in life, timing can be everything. If executives at Warner Brothers had thought the problem through carefully, they would have negotiated with Bennett *before* shooting the movie. At that point Bennett would have realized that the script could be rewritten if he asked too high a fee. By waiting, studio executives left themselves with no other option than to pay Bennett's price.

The payoff to many actions depends not only on the actions themselves but also on when they are taken and how they relate to actions taken by others. In previous chapters, economic decision makers confronted an environment that was essentially fixed. This chapter will focus on cases in which people must

---

[1]As quoted by Geraldine Fabrikant, "Talking Money with Tony Bennett," *The New York Times,* May 2, 1999, Money & Business, p. 1.

consider the effect of their behavior on others. For example, an imperfectly competitive firm will want to weigh the likely responses of rivals when deciding whether to cut prices or to increase the advertising budget. Interdependencies of this sort are the rule rather than the exception in economic and social life. To make sense of the world we live in, then, we must take these interdependencies into account.

THE THEORY OF GAMES

In chess, tennis, or any other game, the payoff to a given move depends on what your opponent does in response. In choosing your move, therefore, you must anticipate your opponent's responses, how you might respond, and what further moves your own response might elicit. To analyze such situations, in which the payoffs to different actors depend on the actions their opponents take, economists and other behavioral scientists have devised the mathematical theory of games.

THE THREE ELEMENTS OF A GAME

basic elements of a game the players, the strategies available to each player, and the payoffs each player receives for each possible combination of strategies

Any game has three **basic elements:** the players, the list of possible actions (or strategies) each player can choose from, and the payoffs the players receive for each combination of strategies. How these elements combine to form the basis of a theory of behavior will become clear in the context of the following illustrative examples.

EXAMPLE 10.1

Should United Airlines spend more money on advertising?

Suppose that United Airlines and American are the only air carriers that serve the Chicago–St. Louis market. Each currently earns an economic profit of $6,000 per flight on this route. If United increases its advertising spending in this market by $1,000 per flight and American spends no more on advertising than it does now, United's profit will rise to $8,000 per flight and American's will fall to $2,000. If both spend $1,000 more on advertising, each will earn an economic profit of $5,500 per flight. These payoffs are symmetric, so if United stands pat while American increases its spending by $1,000, United's economic profit will fall to $2,000 per flight and American's will rise to $8,000. If each must decide independently whether to increase spending on advertising, what should United do?

Think of this situation as a game. What are its three elements? The players are the two airlines, each of which must choose one of two strategies: to raise spending by $1,000 or to leave it the same. The payoffs are the economic profits that correspond to the four possible scenarios resulting from their choices. One way to summarize the relevant information about this game is to display the players, strategies, and payoffs in the form of a simple table called a **payoff matrix** (see Table 10.1).

payoff matrix a table that describes the payoffs in a game for each possible combination of strategies

Confronted with the payoff matrix in Table 10.1, what should United Airlines do? The essence of strategic thinking is to begin by looking at the situation from the other party's point of view. Suppose American assumes that United will raise its spending on advertising (the top row in Table 10.1). In that case, American's best bet would be to follow suit (the left column in Table 10.1). Why is the left column American's best response when United chooses the top row? American's economic profits, given in the upper left cell of Table 10.1, will be $5,500 as compared to only $2,000 if it keeps spending level (see the upper right cell).

Alternatively, suppose American assumes that United will keep its ad spending level (that is, United will choose the bottom row in Table 10.1). In that case, American would still do better to increase spending, because it would earn $8,000 (the lower left cell) as compared to only $6,000 if it keeps spending level (lower right cell). In this particular game, no matter which strategy United chooses, American will earn a higher economic profit by increasing its spending on advertising. And since this game is perfectly symmetric, a similar conclusion holds for United: No matter which strategy American chooses, United will do better by increasing its spending on ads.

TABLE 10.1
The Payoff Matrix for an Advertising Game

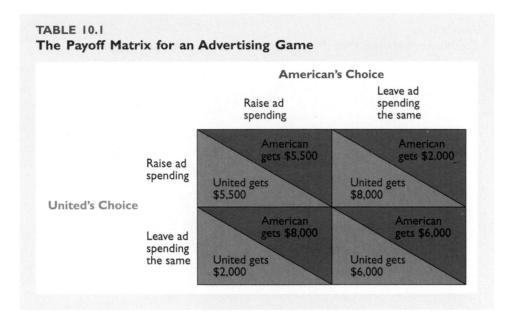

When one player has a strategy that yields a higher payoff no matter which choice the other player makes, that player is said to have a **dominant strategy.** Not all games involve dominant strategies, but both players in this game have one, and that is to increase spending on ads. For both players, to leave ad spending the same is a **dominated strategy**—one that leads to a lower payoff than an alternative choice, regardless of the other player's choice.

Notice, however, that when each player chooses the dominant strategy, the resulting payoffs are smaller than if each had left spending unchanged. When United and American increase their spending on ads, each earns only $5,500 in economic profits as compared to the $6,000 each would have earned without the increase. (We'll say more below about this apparent paradox.)

dominant strategy one that yields a higher payoff no matter what the other players in a game choose

dominated strategy any other strategy available to a player who has a dominant strategy

NASH EQUILIBRIUM

A game is said to be in equilibrium if each player's strategy is the best he or she can choose, given the other players' chosen strategies. This definition of equilibrium is sometimes called a **Nash equilibrium,** after the Nobel laureate John Nash, who developed the concept in the early 1950s. When a game is in equilibrium, no player has any incentive to deviate from his or her current strategy.

If each player in a game has a dominant strategy, as in Example 10.1, equilibrium occurs when each player follows that strategy. But even in games in which not every player has a dominant strategy, we can often identify an equilibrium outcome. Consider, for instance, the following variation on the advertising game in Example 10.1.

Nash equilibrium any combination of strategies in which each player's strategy is his or her best choice, given the other players' strategies

Should American spend more money on advertising?

EXAMPLE 10.2

Suppose United Airlines and American are the only carriers that serve the Chicago–St. Louis market. Their payoff matrix for advertising decisions is shown in Table 10.2. Does United have a dominant strategy? Does American? If each firm does the best it can, given the incentives facing the other, what will be the outcome of this game?

In this game, no matter what United does, American will do better to raise its ad spending, so raising the advertising budget is a dominant strategy for American. United, however, does not have a dominant strategy. If American raises its spending, United will do better to stand pat; if American stands pat, however, United will do better to spend more. But even though United does not have a dominant strategy, we can still predict what is likely to happen in this game. After all, United's managers know what the payoff matrix is, so they can predict that

TABLE 10.2
Equilibrium When One Player Lacks a Dominant Strategy

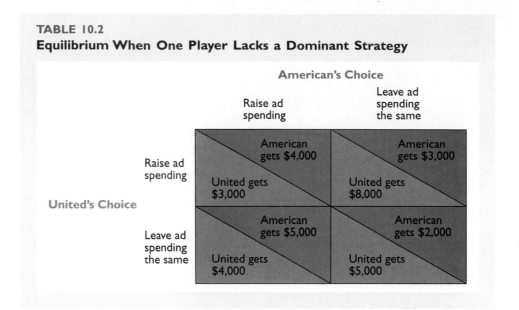

American will spend more on ads (since that is American's dominant strategy). Thus the best strategy for United, given the prediction that American will spend more on ads, is to keep its own spending level. If both players do the best they can, taking account of the incentives each faces, this game will end in the lower left cell of the payoff matrix: American will raise its spending on ads and United will not. (Note that when both players are positioned in the lower left cell, neither has any incentive to change its strategy.)

Note that the choices corresponding to the lower left cell in Table 10.2 satisfy the definition of a Nash equilibrium. If United found itself in that cell, its alternative would be to raise its ad spending, a move that would reduce its payoff from $4,000 to $3,000. So United has no incentive to abandon the lower left cell. Similarly, if American found itself in the lower left cell of Table 10.2, its alternative would be to leave ad spending the same, a move that would reduce its payoff from $5,000 to $2,000. So American also has no incentive to abandon the lower left cell. And that means that the lower left cell of Table 10.2 is a Nash equilibrium—a combination of strategies for which each player's choice is the best available option, given the choice made by the other player.

EXERCISE 10.1

What should United and American do if their payoff matrix is modified as follows?

THE THEORY OF GAMES

The three elements of any game are the players, the list of strategies from which they can choose, and the payoffs to each combination of strategies. Players in some games have a dominant strategy, one that yields a higher payoff regardless of the strategies chosen by other players.

Equilibrium in a game occurs when each player's strategy choice yields the highest payoff available, given the strategies chosen by other players. Such a combination of strategies is called a Nash equilibrium.

THE PRISONER'S DILEMMA

The game in Example 10.1 belongs to an important class of games called the **prisoner's dilemma**. In the prisoner's dilemma, when each player chooses his dominant strategy, the result is unattractive to the group of players as a whole.

THE ORIGINAL PRISONER'S DILEMMA

Example 10.3 recounts the original scenario from which the prisoner's dilemma drew its name.

Should the prisoners confess?

Two prisoners, Horace and Jasper, are being held in separate cells for a serious crime that they did in fact commit. The prosecutor, however, has only enough hard evidence to convict them of a minor offense, for which the penalty is a year in jail. Each prisoner is told that if one confesses while the other remains silent, the confessor will go scot-free and the other will spend 20 years in prison. If both confess, they will get an intermediate sentence of 5 years. (These payoffs are summarized in Table 10.3.) The two prisoners are not allowed to communicate with one another. Do they have a dominant strategy? If so, what is it?

prisoner's dilemma a game in which each player has a dominant strategy, and when each plays it, the resulting payoffs are smaller than if each had played a dominated strategy

EXAMPLE 10.3

TABLE 10.3
The Payoff Matrix for a Prisoner's Dilemma

In this game, the dominant strategy for each prisoner is to confess. No matter what Jasper does, Horace will get a lighter sentence by speaking out. If Jasper confesses, Horace will get 5 years (upper left cell) instead of 20 (lower left cell). If Jasper remains silent, Horace will go free (upper right cell) instead of spending a year in jail (lower right cell). Because the payoffs are perfectly symmetric, Jasper will also do better to confess, no matter what Horace does. The difficulty is that when each follows his dominant strategy and confesses, both will do worse than if each had shown restraint. When both confess, they each get 5 years (upper left cell) instead of the 1 year they would have gotten by remaining silent (lower right cell). Hence the name of this game, the prisoner's dilemma.

EXERCISE 10.2

GM and Chrysler must both decide whether to invest in a new process. Games 1 and 2 below show how their profits depend on the decisions they might make. Which of these games is a prisoner's dilemma?

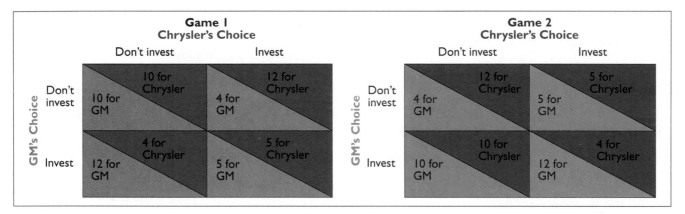

The prisoner's dilemma is one of the most powerful metaphors in all of human behavioral science. Countless social and economic interactions have payoff structures analogous to the one confronted by the two prisoners. Some of those interactions occur between only two players, as in the examples just discussed; many others involve larger groups. But regardless of the number of players involved, the common thread is one of conflict between the narrow self-interest of individuals and the broader interests of larger communities.

PRISONER'S DILEMMAS CONFRONTING IMPERFECTLY COMPETITIVE FIRMS

cartel a coalition of firms that agrees to restrict output for the purpose of earning an economic profit

A **cartel** is any coalition of firms that conspires to restrict production for the purpose of earning an economic profit. As we will see in the next example, the problem confronting oligopolists who are trying to form a cartel is a classic illustration of the prisoner's dilemma.

Why are cartel agreements notoriously unstable?

Consider a market for bottled water served by only two firms, Aquapure and Mountain Spring. Each firm can draw water free of charge from a mineral spring located on its own land. Customers supply their own bottles. Rather than compete with one another, the two firms decide to collude by selling water at the price a profit-maximizing pure monopolist would charge. Under their agreement (which constitutes a cartel), each firm would produce and sell half the quantity of water demanded by the market at the monopoly price (see Figure 10.1). The agreement is not legally enforceable, however, which means that each firm has the option of charging less than the agreed price. If one firm sells water for less than the other firm, it will capture the entire quantity demanded by the market at the lower price.

Why is this agreement likely to collapse?

Since the marginal cost of mineral water is zero, the profit-maximizing quantity for a monopolist with the demand curve shown in Figure 10.1 is 1,000 bottles per day, the quantity for which marginal revenue equals marginal cost. At that quantity, the monopoly price is $1 per bottle. If the firms abide by their agreement,

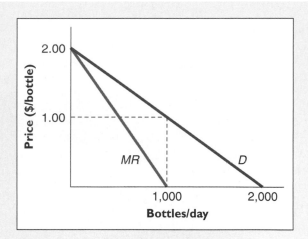

FIGURE 10.1
The Market Demand for Mineral Water.
Faced with the demand curve shown, a monopolist with zero marginal cost would produce 1,000 bottles per day (the quantity at which marginal revenue equals zero) and sell them at a price of $1.00 per bottle.

each will sell half the market total, or 500 bottles per day at a price of $1 per bottle, for an economic profit of $500 per day.

But suppose Aquapure reduced its price to $0.90 per bottle. By underselling Mineral Spring, it would capture the entire quantity demanded by the market, which as shown in Figure 10.2 is 1,100 bottles per day. Aquapure's economic profit would rise from $500 per day to ($0.90 per bottle)(1,100 bottles per day) = $990

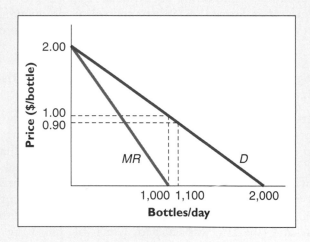

FIGURE 10.2
The Temptation to Violate a Cartel Agreement.
By cutting its price from $1 per bottle to $0.90 per bottle, Aquapure can sell the entire market quantity demanded at that price, 1,100 bottles per day, rather than half the monopoly quantity of 1,000 bottles per day.

per day, almost twice as much as before. In the process, Mountain Spring's economic profit would fall from $500 per day to zero. Rather than see its economic profit disappear, Mountain Spring would match Aquapure's price cut, recapturing its original 50 percent share of the market. But when each firm charges $0.90 per bottle and sells 550 bottles per day, each earns an economic profit of ($0.90 per bottle)(550 bottles per day) = $495 per day, or $5 per day less than before.

Suppose we view the cartel agreement as an economic game in which the two available strategies are to sell for $1 per bottle or to sell for $0.90 per bottle. The payoffs are the economic profits that result from these strategies. Table 10.4 shows the payoff matrix for this game. Each firm's dominant strategy is to sell at the lower price, yet in following that strategy, each earns a lower profit than if each had sold at the higher price.

The game does not end with both firms charging $0.90 per bottle. Each firm knows that if it cuts the price a little further, it can recapture the entire market, and in the process earn a substantially higher economic profit. At every step the rival firm will match any price cut, until the price falls all the way to the marginal cost—in this example, zero.

TABLE 10.4
The Payoff Matrix for a Cartel Agreement

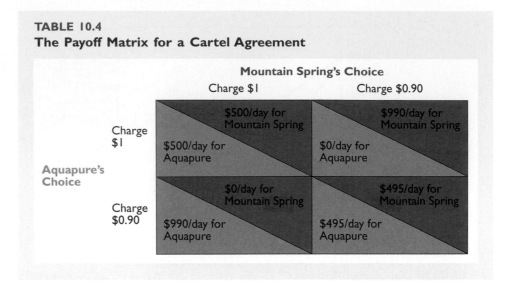

Cartel agreements confront participants with the economic incentives inherent in the prisoner's dilemma, which explains why such agreements have historically been so unstable. Usually a cartel involves not just two firms, but several, an arrangement that can make retaliation against price cutters extremely difficult. In many cases, discovering which parties have broken the agreement is difficult. For example, the Organization of Petroleum Exporting Countries (OPEC), a cartel of oil producers formed in 1960 to control oil production, has no practical way to prevent member countries from secretly pumping oil offshore in the dead of night.

How did Congress unwittingly solve the television advertising dilemma confronting cigarette producers?

In 1970, Congress enacted a law making cigarette advertising on television illegal after January 1, 1971. As evidenced by the steadily declining proportion of Americans who smoke, this law seems to have achieved its stated purpose of protecting citizens against a proven health hazard. But the law also had an unintended effect, which was to increase the economic profit of cigarette makers, at least in the short run. In the year before the law's passage, manufacturers spent more than $300 million on advertising, about $60 million more than they spent during the year after the law was enacted. Much of the saving in advertising expenditures in 1971 was reflected in higher cigarette profits at year-end. But if eliminating television advertising made companies more profitable, why didn't the manufacturers eliminate the ads on their own?

When an imperfectly competitive firm advertises its product, its demand curve shifts rightward, for two reasons. First, people who have never used that type of product learn about it, and some buy it. Second, people who consume a different brand of the product may switch brands. The first effect boosts sales industrywide; the second merely redistributes existing sales.

Although advertising produces both effects in the cigarette industry, its primary effect is brand switching. Thus the decision of whether to advertise confronts the individual firm with a prisoner's dilemma. Table 10.5 shows the payoffs facing a pair of cigarette producers trying to decide whether to advertise. If both firms advertise on TV (upper left cell), each earns a profit of only $10 million per year as compared to a profit of $20 million per year for each if neither advertises (lower right cell). Clearly, both will benefit if neither advertises.

Yet note the powerful incentive that confronts each firm. RJR sees that if Philip Morris doesn't advertise, RJR can earn higher profits by advertising ($35 million per year) than by not advertising ($20 million per year). RJR also sees that if Philip

TABLE 10.5
Cigarette Advertising as a Prisoner's Dilemma

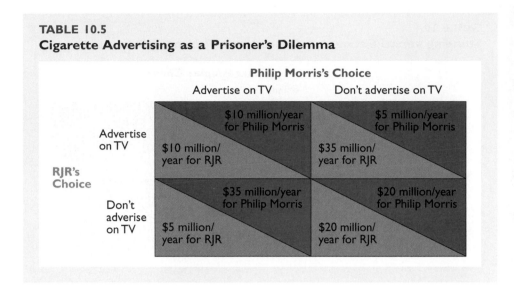

Morris does advertise, RJR will again earn more by advertising ($10 million per year) than by not advertising ($5 million per year). Thus RJR's dominant strategy is to advertise. And because the payoffs are symmetric, Philip Morris's dominant strategy is also to advertise. So when each firm behaves rationally from its own point of view, the two together do worse than if they had both shown restraint. The congressional ad ban forced cigarette manufacturers to do what they could not have accomplished on their own.

PRISONER'S DILEMMAS IN EVERYDAY LIFE

As the following examples make clear, the prisoner's dilemma helps the economic naturalist to make sense of human behavior not only in the world of business, but in other domains of life as well.

Why do people often stand at concerts, even though they can see just as well when everyone sits?

A few years ago, an economic naturalist went with friends to hear Diana Ross sing. They bought good seats, some 20 rows from the stage. But before Ross had finished her first song, several people in front of them rose to their feet, presumably to get a better view. In doing so, they blocked the line of sight for others behind them, forcing those people to stand to see better. Before long, the entire crowd was standing. Then a few people in the front rows climbed atop their seats, blocking the views of those behind them and forcing them to stand on their seats too. The seats had fold-up bottoms, so from time to time someone who stood too close to the pivot point would tumble as the seat popped into its vertical position. All things considered, the outcome was far less satisfactory than if everyone had remained seated. Why this pattern of self-defeating behavior?

To understand what happened at the concert, note that standing is self-defeating only when viewed from the group's perspective. From the individual's perspective, however, standing passes the cost-benefit test. No matter what others do, an individual gets a better view by standing than by sitting. Suppose for the sake of discussion that you and other members of the audience would be willing to pay $2 to avoid standing and $3 to get a better view (or avoid having a worse one). In this multiperson prisoner's dilemma, you are one player and the rest of the audience is the other. The two strategies are to stand or to sit. Suppose everyone is seated to begin with. The payoffs you and others face will depend on the combination of strategies that you and others choose, as shown Table 10.6.

ECONOMIC
NATURALIST
10.3

TABLE 10.6
Standing versus Sitting at a Concert as a Prisoner's Dilemma

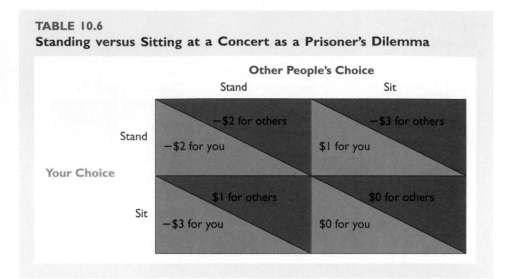

		Other People's Choice	
		Stand	Sit
Your Choice	Stand	−$2 for others / −$2 for you	−$3 for others / $1 for you
	Sit	$1 for others / −$3 for you	$0 for others / $0 for you

Since standing is tiring and the view is no better when everyone stands than when everyone sits, why do people often stand at concerts?

ECONOMIC NATURALIST 10.4

The payoff of 0 in the lower right cell of the payoff matrix reflects the fact that when everyone remains seated, everyone is just as well off as before. Your payoff of −$3 in the lower left cell reflects the fact that if you sit while others stand, you will have a worse view. Your payoff of −$2 in upper left cell reflects the fact that when you and others stand, you must endure the $2 cost of standing, even though you don't get a better view. Finally, your $1 payoff in the upper right cell represents the difference between your $3 benefit and your $2 cost of standing when you stand while others sit.

These payoffs mean that your dominant strategy is to stand. If others stand, you will get −$2 by standing, which is better than the −$3 you will get by sitting. If others sit, you will get $1 by standing, which is better than the $0 you will get by sitting. Since this game is symmetric, the dominant strategy for others is also to stand. Yet when everyone stands, everyone gets a payoff of −$2, which is $2 worse than if everyone had remained seated. As in all prisoner's dilemmas, the choice that is more attractive from the perspective of the individual turns out to be less attractive from the perspective of the group.

Why do people shout at parties?

Whenever large numbers of people gather for conversation in a closed space, the ambient noise level rises sharply. After attending such gatherings, people often complain of sore throats and hoarse voices. If everyone spoke at a normal volume at parties, the overall noise level would be lower, and people would hear just as well. So why do people shout?

Again the problem involves the difference between individual incentives and group incentives. Suppose everyone starts by speaking at a normal level. But because of the crowded conditions, conversation partners have difficulty hearing one another, even when no one is shouting. The natural solution, from the point of view of the individual, is to simply raise one's voice a bit. But that is also the natural solution for everyone else. And when everyone speaks more loudly, the ambient noise level rises, so no one hears any better than before.

No matter what others do, the individual will do better by speaking more loudly. Doing so is a dominant strategy for everyone, in fact. Yet when everyone follows the dominant strategy, the result is worse (no one can hear well) than if everyone had continued to speak normally. While shouting is wasteful, individuals acting alone have no better option. If anyone were to speak softly while others shout, that person wouldn't be heard. No one wants to go home with raw vocal cords, but people apparently prefer that cost to the alternative of not being heard at all.

TIT-FOR-TAT AND THE REPEATED PRISONER'S DILEMMA

When all players cooperate in a prisoner's dilemma, each gets a higher payoff than when all defect. So people who confront prisoner's dilemmas will be on the lookout for ways to create incentives for mutual cooperation. What they need is some way to penalize players who defect. When players interact with one another only once, this turns out to be difficult to achieve. But when they expect to interact repeatedly, new possibilities emerge.

A **repeated prisoner's dilemma** is a standard prisoner's dilemma that confronts the same players not just once but many times. Experimental research on repeated prisoner's dilemmas in the 1960s identified a simple strategy that proves remarkably effective at limiting defection. The strategy is called **tit-for-tat,** and here is how it works: The first time you interact with someone, you cooperate. In each subsequent interaction you simply do what that person did in the previous interaction. Thus, if your partner defected on your first interaction, you would then defect on your next interaction with her. If she then cooperates, your move next time will be to cooperate as well.

On the basis of elaborate computer simulations, University of Michigan political scientist Robert Axelrod showed that tit-for-tat was a remarkably effective strategy, even when pitted against a host of ingenious counterstrategies that had been designed for the explicit purpose of trying to exploit it. The success of tit-for-tat requires a reasonably stable set of players, each of whom can remember what other players have done in previous interactions. It also requires that players have a significant stake in what happens in the future, for it is the fear of retaliation that deters people from defecting.

Since rival firms in the same industry interact with one another repeatedly, it might seem that the tit-for-tat strategy would ensure widespread collusion to raise prices. And yet, as noted earlier, cartel agreements are notoriously unsuccessful. One difficulty is that tit-for-tat's effectiveness depends on there being only two players in the game. In competitive and monopolistically competitive industries there are generally many firms, and even in oligopolies there are often several. When there are more than two firms, and one defects now, how do the cooperators selectively punish the defector later? By cutting price? That will penalize everyone, not just the defector. Even if there are only two firms in an industry, these firms realize that other firms may enter their industry. So the would-be cartel members have to worry not only about each other, but also about the entire list of firms that might decide to compete with them. Each firm may see this as an impossible task and decide to defect now, hoping to reap at least some economic profit in the short run. What seems clear, in any event, is that the practical problems involved in implementing tit-for-tat have made it difficult to hold cartel agreements together for long.

repeated prisoner's dilemma a standard prisoner's dilemma that confronts the same players repeatedly

tit-for-tat a strategy for the repeated prisoner's dilemma in which players cooperate on the first move, then mimic their partner's last move on each successive move

RECAP   **THE PRISONER'S DILEMMA**

The prisoner's dilemma is a game in which each player has a dominant strategy, and in which the payoff to each player when each chooses that strategy is smaller than if each had chosen a dominated strategy. Incentives analogous to those found in the prisoner's dilemmas help to explain a broad range of behavior in business and everyday life—among them, excessive spending on advertising, cartel instability, standing at concerts, and shouting at parties. Cooperation in repeated prisoner's dilemmas can often be sustained by the tit-for-tat strategy, in which players cooperate on the first move and mimic their partner's previous move thereafter.

GAMES IN WHICH TIMING MATTERS

In the games discussed so far, players were assumed to choose their strategies simultaneously, and which player moved first didn't particularly matter. For example, in the prisoner's dilemma, players would follow their dominant strategies even if they knew in advance what strategies their opponents had chosen. But in other situations, such as the negotiations between Warner Brothers and Tony Bennett described at the beginning of this chapter, timing is of the essence.

THE ULTIMATUM BARGAINING GAME

The following example illustrates another game in which timing plays a crucial role.

EXAMPLE 10.4   **Should Michael accept Tom's offer?**

Tom and Michael are subjects in an experiment. The experimenter begins by giving $100 to Tom, who must then propose how to divide the money between himself and Michael. Tom can propose any division he chooses, provided the proposed amounts are whole dollars and he offers Michael at least $1. Suppose Tom proposes $X for himself and $(100 − X) for Michael, where X is a whole number no larger than 99. Michael must then say whether he accepts the proposal. If he does, each will get the proposed amount. But if Michael rejects the proposal, each player will get zero, and the $100 will revert to the experimenter. If Tom and Michael know they will play this game only once, and each wants to make as much money for himself as possible, what should Tom propose?

A payoff matrix is not a useful way to summarize the information in this game, because it says nothing about the timing of each player's move. For games in which timing matters, a **decision tree,** or **game tree,** is more useful. This type of diagram describes the possible moves in the sequence in which they may occur and lists the final payoffs for each possible combination of moves.

The decision tree for the game in Example 10.4 is shown in Figure 10.3. At *A,* Tom begins the game by making his proposal. At *B,* Michael responds to Tom's proposal. If he accepts (the top branch of the tree), Tom will get $X and Michael will get $(100 − X). If he refuses (the bottom branch of the tree), both will get nothing.

decision tree (or game tree) a diagram that describes the possible moves in a game in sequence and lists the payoffs that correspond to each possible combination of moves

FIGURE 10.3
Decision Tree for Example 10.4.
This decision tree shows the possible moves and payoffs for the game in Example 10.4 in the sequence in which they may occur.

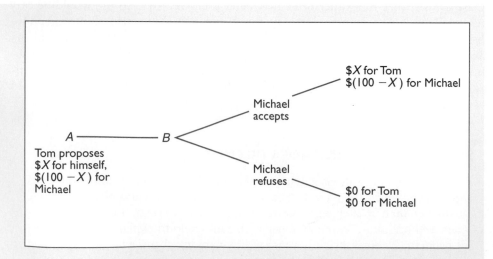

In thinking strategically about this game, the key for Tom is to put himself in Michael's shoes and imagine how he might react to various proposals. Because he knows Michael's goal is to make as much money as possible, he knows that Michael will accept his offer no matter how small, because the alternative is to reject it and get nothing. For instance, suppose Tom proposes $99 for himself and only $1 for Michael (see Figure 10.4). At *B*, Michael's best option is to accept the offer. This is a Nash equilibrium, because neither player has any incentive to deviate from the strategy he chose.

This type of game has been called the **ultimatum bargaining game,** because of the power of the first player to confront the second player with a take-it-or-leave-it offer. Michael could refuse a one-sided offer from Tom, but doing so would make him worse off than if he accepted it.

ultimatum bargaining game
one in which the first player has the power to confront the second player with a take-it-or-leave-it offer

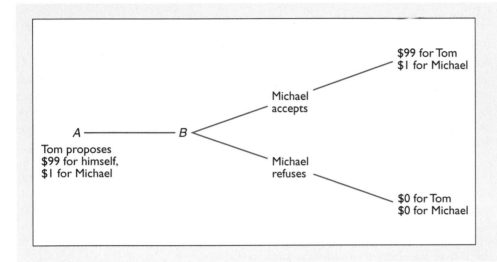

FIGURE 10.4

Tom's Best Strategy in an Ultimatum Bargaining Game.

Because Tom can predict that Michael will accept any positive offer, Tom's income-maximizing strategy at *A* is to offer Michael the smallest positive amount possible, $1.

Example 10.5 illustrates the importance of the timing of moves in determining the outcome of the ultimatum bargaining game.

What should Michael's acceptance threshold be?

EXAMPLE 10.5

Suppose we change the rules of the ultimatum bargaining game slightly so that Michael has the right to specify *in advance* the smallest offer he will accept. Once Michael announces this number, he is bound by it. If Tom's task is again to propose a division of the $100, what amount should Michael specify?

This seemingly minor change in the rules completely alters the game. Once Michael announces that $Y is the smallest offer he will accept, his active role in the game is over. If Y is $60 and Tom proposes $X for himself and $(100 − X) for Michael, his offer will be rejected automatically if X exceeds 40. The decision tree for this game is shown in Figure 10.5.

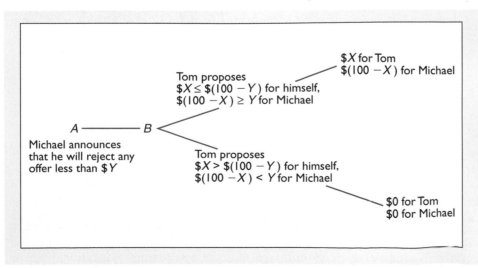

FIGURE 10.5

The Ultimatum Bargaining Game with an Acceptance Threshold.

If Michael can commit himself to a minimum acceptable offer threshold at *A*, he will fare dramatically better than in the standard ultimatum bargaining game.

When Michael announces that Y is the smallest offer he will accept, the best Tom can do is to propose $(100 − Y)$ for himself and Y for Michael. If he proposes any amount less than Y for Michael, both will get nothing at all. Since this reasoning holds for any value of Y less than 100, Michael's best bet is to announce an acceptance threshold of $99—the largest whole number that is less than $100. The equilibrium outcome of the game will then be $99 for Michael and only $1 for Tom, exactly the opposite of the outcome when Tom had the first move.

CREDIBLE THREATS AND PROMISES

credible threat a threat to take an action that is in the threatener's interest to carry out

Why couldn't Michael have threatened to refuse a one-sided offer in the original version of the game? While nothing prevented him from doing so, such a threat would not have been credible. In the language of game theory, a **credible threat** is one that is in the threatener's interest to carry out when the time comes to act. The problem in the original version of the game is that Michael would have no reason to carry out his threat to reject a one-sided offer in the event he actually received one. Once Tom announced such an offer, refusing it would not pass the cost-benefit test.

The concept of a credible threat figured prominently in the negotiations between Warner Brothers managers and Tony Bennett over the matter of Mr. Bennett's fee for performing in *Analyze This*. Once most of the film had been shot, managers knew they couldn't threaten credibly to refuse Mr. Bennett's salary demand, because at that point adapting the film to another singer would have been prohibitively costly. In contrast, a similar threat made before production of the movie had begun would have been credible.

"Listen to me, John. Tell them this is our final offer. Let 'em know we'll take an option at twenty-five million over five years—not a penny more, not a minute longer! If they balk, stall them for time and get back to me."

Here is another example in which one person suffers as a result of the inability to make a credible threat.

EXAMPLE 10.6

Is it safe to steal Veronica's briefcase?

When Veronica travels out of town on business, she usually brings along an expensive briefcase. A stranger takes a liking to her briefcase and assumes that because Veronica is an economist, she must be a self-interested, rational person.

If the cost to Veronica of pressing charges in the event her briefcase is stolen exceeds the value of the briefcase, can the stranger safely steal it?

Provided the thief's assumptions about Veronica are correct, he can get away with his crime. To press charges once her briefcase has been stolen, Veronica must call the police and will probably miss her flight home. Months later, she will have to return to testify at the thief's trial, and she may have to endure hostile cross-examination by the thief's attorney. Since these costs clearly exceed the value of the briefcase, a rational, self-interested person would simply write off the briefcase. But if Veronica could somehow have made a credible threat to press charges in the event her briefcase was stolen, she could have deterred the thief. The problem is that the thief knows the cost of retaliation will exceed the benefit, so the threat is not credible.

Just as in some games credible threats are impossible to make, in others **credible promises** are impossible. A credible promise is one that is in the interests of the promiser to keep when the time comes to act. In Example 10.7, both players suffer because of their inability to make a credible promise.

credible promise a promise to take an action that is in the promiser's interest to keep

EXAMPLE 10.7

Will the kidnapper release his victim?

A kidnapper who has seized a hostage for ransom suddenly changes his mind. He wants to set his victim free but is afraid that the victim will go to the police. Although the victim promises not to do so, both realize that he will have no incentive to keep his promise once he is free. The victim also realizes that the kidnapper would still pose a threat to him, out of fear that the victim may change his mind and go to the police. So if only to protect himself from the possibility of further harm, the victim has a powerful incentive to go to the police once he is free. Finally, if the victim goes to the police, the kidnapper will be caught and executed. The kidnapper desperately wants to set his victim free, but he prefers survival to execution. What will the kidnapper do?

The decision tree for this situation is shown in Figure 10.6. At *A*, the victim promises not to go to the police. He knows his life depends on the credibility of his promise, and at the moment he makes it, he sincerely means to keep it.

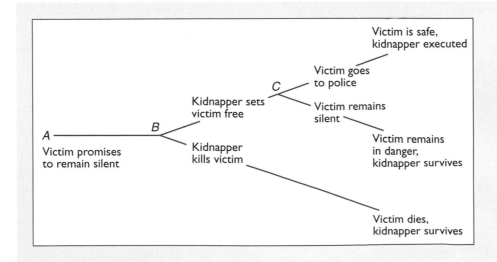

FIGURE 10.6

Decision Tree for the Kidnapper Game.
Both the kidnapper and the victim want to see the victim freed, but because the victim's promise to remain silent is not credible, the kidnapper kills him.

At *B* the kidnapper must decide what to do. If he sets his victim free (top branch at *B*), they reach *C*, where the victim must decide whether to go to the police. If the victim keeps his promise to remain silent (bottom branch at *C*), the kidnapper survives as a continuing threat to the victim. But if the victim goes to the police (top branch at *C*), the kidnapper will be caught and executed, and the victim will be safe. Since the victim prefers the second outcome, he will go to the police if freed. *And since the kidnapper can anticipate what will happen if the game reaches C, he cannot let the game reach that point.* His only hope of survival is to choose the bottom branch at *B*. The irony is that both he and the victim strongly prefer the alternative in which he sets the victim free and the victim remains silent.

Here is another instance in which both parties suffer because of the inability to make a credible promise.

EXAMPLE 10.8

Should the businessowner open a remote office?

The owner of a thriving business wants to start up an office in a distant city. If she hires someone to manage the new office, she can afford to pay a weekly salary of $1,000—a premium of $500 over what the manager would otherwise be able to earn—and still earn a weekly economic profit of $1,000 for herself. The owner's concern is that she will not be able to monitor the manager's behavior. The owner knows that by managing the remote office dishonestly, the manager can boost his take-home pay to $1,500 while causing the owner an economic loss of $500 per week. If the owner believes that all managers are selfish income maximizers, will she open the new office?

The decision tree for the remote office game is shown in Figure 10.7. At *A*, the managerial candidate promises to manage honestly, which brings the owner to *B*, where she must decide whether to open the new office. If she opens it, they reach *C*, where the manager must decide whether to manage honestly. If the manager's only goal is to make as much money as he can, he will manage dishonestly (bottom branch at *C*), since that way he will earn $500 more than by managing honestly (top branch at *C*).

FIGURE 10.7
Decision Tree for the Remote Office Game.
The best outcome is for the manager to open the office at *B* and for the manager to manage the office honestly at *C*. But if the manager is purely self-interested and the owner knows it, this path will not be an equilibrium outcome.

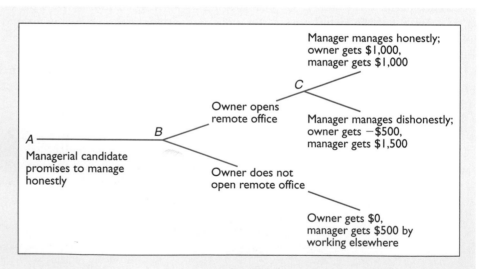

So if the owner opens the new office, she will end up with an economic loss of $500. If she had not opened the office (bottom branch at *B*), she would have realized an economic profit of zero. Since zero is better than −$500, the owner will choose not to open the remote office. In the end, the opportunity cost of the manager's inability to make a credible promise is $1,500: the manager's forgone $500 salary premium and the owner's forgone $1,000 return.

EXERCISE 10.3

Smith and Jones are playing a game in which Smith has the first move at A in the following decision tree. Once Smith has chosen either the top or bottom branch at A, Jones, who can see what Smith has chosen, must

choose the top or bottom branch at B or C. If the payoffs at the end of each branch are as shown, what is the equilibrium outcome of this game? If before Smith chose, Jones could make a credible commitment to choose either the top or bottom branch when his turn came, what would he do?

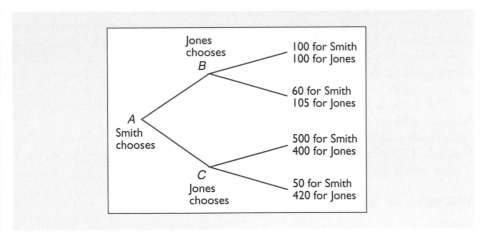

COMMITMENT PROBLEMS

Games like the one in Exercise 10.3, as well as the prisoner's dilemma, the cartel game, the ultimatum bargaining game, the kidnapper game, and the remote office game, confront players with a **commitment problem**, a situation in which they have difficulty achieving the desired outcome because they cannot make credible threats or promises. If both players in the prisoner's dilemma (Example 10.3) could make a binding promise to remain silent, both would be assured of a shorter sentence. Hence the logic of the underworld code of *omerta*, under which the family of anyone who provides evidence against a fellow mob member is killed. A similar logic explains the adoption of military arms control agreements, in which opponents sign an enforceable pledge to curtail weapons spending.

commitment problem a situation in which people cannot achieve their goals because of an inability to make credible threats or promises

The commitment problem in the kidnapper game (Example 10.7) could be solved if the victim could find some way of committing himself to remain silent once released. The economist Thomas Schelling suggests the following way out of the dilemma: "If the victim has committed an act whose disclosure could lead to blackmail, he may confess it; if not, he might commit one in the presence of his captor, to create a bond that will ensure his silence."[1] (Perhaps the victim could allow the kidnapper to photograph him in the process of some unspeakable act.) The blackmailable act serves as a **commitment device**, something that provides the victim with an incentive to keep his promise. Doing so will be unpleasant for him once he is freed, but clearly less so than not being able to make a credible promise.

commitment device a way of changing incentives so as to make otherwise empty threats or promises credible

Businessowners seem well aware of commitment problems in the workplace and have adopted a variety of commitment devices to solve them. Consider, for example, the problem confronting the owner of a restaurant. She wants her table staff to provide good service so that customers will enjoy their meals and come back in the future. And since good service is valuable to her, she would be willing to pay waiters extra for it. For their part, waiters would be willing to provide good service in return for the extra pay. The problem is that the owner cannot always monitor whether the waiters do provide good service. Her concern is that, having been paid extra for it, the waiters may slack off when she isn't looking. Unless the owner can find some way to solve this problem, she will not pay extra,

[1]Thomas Schelling, *The Strategy of Conflict,* Cambridge, Mass.: Harvard University Press, 1960, pp. 43, 44.

Will leaving a tip at an out-of-town restaurant affect the quality of service you receive?

the waiters will not provide good service, and she, they, and the diners will suffer. A better outcome for all concerned would be for the waiters to find some way to commit themselves to good service.

Restaurateurs in many countries have tried to solve this commitment problem by encouraging diners to leave tips at the end of their meals. The attraction of this solution is that the diner is *always* in a good position to monitor service quality. The diner should be happy to reward good service with a generous tip, since doing so will help to ensure good service in the future. And the waiter has a strong incentive to provide good service, because he knows that the size of his tip may depend on it.

The various commitment devices just discussed—the underworld code of *omerta,* military arms control agreements, the tip for the waiter—all work because they change the material incentives facing the decision makers. But as Example 10.9 illustrates, changing incentives in precisely the desired way is not always practical.

EXAMPLE 10.9

Will Sylvester leave a tip when dining on the road?

Sylvester has just finished a $100 steak dinner at a restaurant on Interstate 81, some 500 miles from home. The waiter provided good service. If Sylvester cares only about himself, will he leave a tip?

Once the waiter has provided good service, there is no way for him to take it back if the diner fails to leave a tip. In restaurants patronized by local diners, failure to tip is not a problem, because the waiter can simply provide poor service the next time a nontipper comes in. But the waiter lacks that leverage with out-of-town diners. Having already received good service, Sylvester must choose between paying $100 or $115 for his meal. If he is an essentially selfish person, the former choice may be a compelling one.

> **RECAP** **GAMES IN WHICH TIMING MATTERS**
>
> The outcomes in many games depend on the timing of each player's move. For such games, the payoffs are best summarized by a decision tree rather than a payoff matrix.
>
> The inability to make credible threats and promises often prevents people from achieving desired outcomes in many games. Games with this property are said to confront players with commitment problems. Such problems can sometimes be solved by employing commitment devices—ways of changing incentives to facilitate making credible threats or promises.

THE STRATEGIC ROLE OF PREFERENCES

In all the games we have discussed so far, players were assumed to care only about obtaining the best possible outcome for themselves. Thus each player's goal was to get the highest monetary payoff, the shortest jail sentence, the best chance of survival, and so on. The irony, in most of these games, is that players do not attain the best outcomes. Better outcomes can sometimes be achieved by altering the material incentives selfish players face, but not always.

If altering the relevant material incentives is not possible, commitment problems can sometimes be solved by altering people's psychological incentives. As Example 10.10 illustrates, in a society in which people are strongly conditioned to develop moral sentiments—feelings of guilt when they harm others, feelings of sympathy for their trading partners, feelings of outrage when they are treated unjustly—commitment problems arise less often than in more narrowly self-interested societies.

In a moral society, will the businessowner open a remote office?

EXAMPLE 10.10

Consider again the owner of the thriving business who is trying to decide whether to open an office in a distant city (Example 10.8). Suppose the society in which she lives is one in which all citizens have been strongly conditioned to behave honestly. Will she open the remote office?

Suppose, for instance, that the managerial candidate would suffer guilt pangs if he embezzled money from the owner. Most people would be reluctant to assign a monetary value to guilty feelings. But for the sake of discussion, let's suppose that those feelings are so unpleasant that the manager would be willing to pay at least $10,000 to avoid them. On this assumption, the manager's payoff if he manages dishonestly will not be $1,500 but $1,500 − $10,000 = −$8,500. The new decision tree is shown in Figure 10.8.

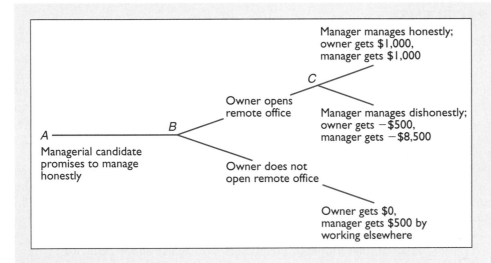

FIGURE 10.8
The Remote Office Game with an Honest Manager.
If the owner can identify a managerial candidate who would choose to manage honestly at *C*, she will hire that candidate at *B* and open the remote office.

In this case, the best choice for the owner at *B* will be to open the remote office, because she knows that at *C* the manager's best choice will be to manage honestly. The irony, of course, is that the honest manager in this example ends up richer than the selfish manager in Example 10.8, who earned only a normal salary.

ARE PEOPLE FUNDAMENTALLY SELFISH?

As Example 10.10 suggests, the assumption that people are self-interested in the narrow sense of the term does not always capture the full range of motives that govern choice in strategic settings. Think, for example, about the last time you had a meal at an out-of-town restaurant. Did you leave a tip? If so, your behavior was quite normal. Researchers have found that tipping rates in restaurants patronized mostly by out-of-town diners are essentially the same as in restaurants patronized mostly by local diners.

Reflect also on how you would behave in some of the other games we have discussed. In the ultimatum game, what would you do if your partner proposed $99 for himself and only $1 for you? Would you reject the offer? If so, you are not alone. Two findings of extensive laboratory studies of the ultimatum bargaining game challenge the assumption that most players are narrowly self-interested. First, the most common proposal by the first player in this game is not a 99–1 split, but a 50–50 split. And second, on the few occasions when the first player does propose a highly one-sided split, the second player almost always rejects it. Subjects who reject the offer often mention the satisfaction they experienced at having penalized the first player for an "unfair" offer.

Indeed, there are many exceptions to the outcomes predicted on the basis of the assumption that people are self-interested in the most narrow sense of the term. People who have been treated unjustly often seek revenge even at ruinous cost to themselves. Every day people walk away from profitable transactions whose terms they believe to be "unfair." And the British spent vast sums to defend the desolate Falkland Islands, even though they had little empire left against which to deter future aggression. (The Argentine writer Jorge Luis Borges likened the Falklands war to two bald men fighting over a comb.) In these and countless other ways, people do not seem to be pursuing self-interest narrowly defined. And if motives beyond narrow self-interest are significant, we must take them into account in attempting to predict and explain human behavior.

PREFERENCES AS SOLUTIONS TO COMMITMENT PROBLEMS

Economists tend to view preferences as ends in themselves. Taking them as given, they calculate what actions will best serve those preferences. This approach to the study of behavior is widely used by other social scientists and by game theorists, military strategists, philosophers, and others. In its standard form, it assumes purely self-interested preferences for present and future consumption goods of various sorts, leisure pursuits, and so on. Concerns about fairness, guilt, honor, sympathy, and the like typically play no role.

Preferences clearly affect the choices people make in strategic interactions. Sympathy for one's trading partner can make a businessperson trustworthy even when material incentives favor cheating. A sense of justice can prompt a person to incur the costs of retaliation, even when incurring those costs will not undo the original injury. It can also induce people to reject one-sided offers, even when their wealth would be increased by accepting them.

Note, however, that although preferences can clearly shape behavior in these ways, that alone does not solve commitment problems. The solution to such problems requires not only that a person *have* certain preferences, but also that others have some way of *discerning* them. Unless the businessowner can identify the trustworthy employee, that employee cannot land a job whose pay is predicated on trust. Unless the predator can identify a potential victim whose character will motivate retaliation, that person is likely to become a victim. And unless a person's potential trading partners can identify him as someone predisposed to reject one-sided offers, he will not be able to deter such offers.

From among those whom we might engage in ventures requiring trust, can we identify reliable partners? If people could make *perfectly* accurate character judgments, they could always steer clear of dishonest persons. That people continue to be victimized at least occasionally by dishonest persons suggests that perfectly reliable character judgments are either impossible to make or prohibitively expensive.

Vigilance in the choice of trading partners is an essential element in solving (or avoiding) commitment problems, for if there is an advantage in being honest and being perceived as such, there is an even greater advantage in only *appearing* to be honest. After all, a liar who appears trustworthy will have better opportunities than one who glances about furtively, sweats profusely, and has difficulty making eye contact. Indeed, the liar will have the same opportunities as an honest person but will get higher payoffs because the liar will exploit them to the fullest.

In the end, the question of whether people can make reasonably accurate character judgments is an empirical one. Experimental studies have shown that even on the basis of brief encounters involving strangers, subjects are adept at predicting who will cooperate and who will defect in prisoner's dilemma games. For example, in one experiment in which only 26 percent of subjects defected, the accuracy rate of predicted defections was more than 56 percent. One might expect that predictions regarding those we know well would be even more accurate.

Do you know someone who would return an envelope containing $1,000 in cash to you if you lost it at a crowded concert? If so, then you accept the claim that personal character can help people to solve commitment problems. As long as honest individuals can identify at least some others who are honest and can interact selectively with them, honest individuals can prosper in a competitive environment.

RECAP **THE STRATEGIC ROLE OF PREFERENCES**

Most applications of the theory of games assume that players are self-interested in the narrow sense of the term. In practice, however, many choices, such as leaving tips in out-of-town restaurants, appear inconsistent with this assumption.

The fact that people seem driven by a more complex range of motives makes behavior more difficult to predict but also creates new ways of solving commitment problems. Psychological incentives can often serve as commitment devices when changing players' material incentives is impractical. For example, people who are able to identify honest trading partners and interact selectively with them are able to solve commitment problems that arise from lack of trust.

■ SUMMARY ■

- Economists use the mathematical theory of games to analyze situations in which the payoffs of one's actions depend on the actions taken by others. Games have three basic elements: the players; the list of possible actions, or strategies, from which each player can choose; and the payoffs the players receive for those strategies. The payoff matrix is the most useful way to summarize this information in games in which the timing of the players' moves is not decisive. In games in which the timing of moves does matter, a decision tree summarizes the information in a much more useful format.

- A dominant strategy is one that yields a higher payoff regardless of the strategy chosen by the other player. In some games, such as the prisoner's dilemma, each player has a dominant strategy. The equilibrium occurs in such games when each player chooses his or her dominant strategy. In other games, not all players have a dominant strategy.

- Although the equilibrium outcome of any game is any combination of choices in which each player does the best

he can, given the choices made by others, the result is often unattractive from the perspective of players as group. The prisoner's dilemma has this feature. The incentive structure of this game helps explain such disparate social dilemmas as excessive advertising, military arms races, and failure to reap the potential benefits of interactions requiring trust.

- Individuals can often resolve these dilemmas if they can make binding commitments to behave in certain ways. Some commitments, such as those involved in military arms control agreements, are achieved by altering the material incentives confronting the players. Other commitments can be achieved by relying on psychological incentives to counteract material payoffs. Moral sentiments like guilt, sympathy, and a sense of justice often foster better outcomes than can be achieved by narrowly self-interested players. For this type of commitment to work, the relevant moral sentiments must be discernible by one's potential trading partners.

■ KEY TERMS ■

basic elements of a game (252)
cartel (256)
commitment device (267)
commitment problem (267)
credible promise (265)
credible threat (264)

decision tree (262)
dominant strategy (253)
dominated strategy (253)
game tree (262)
Nash equilibrium (253)
payoff matrix (252)

prisoner's dilemma (255)
repeated prisoner's dilemma (261)
tit-for-tat (261)
ultimatum bargaining game (263)

▪ REVIEW QUESTIONS ▪

1. Explain why a military arms race is an example of a prisoner's dilemma.

2. Why did Warner Brothers make a mistake by waiting until the filming of *Analyze This* was almost finished before negotiating with Tony Bennett to perform in the final scene?

3. Suppose General Motors is trying to hire a small firm to manufacture the door handles for Pontiac sedans. The task requires an investment in expensive capital equipment that cannot be used for any other purpose. Why might the president of the small firm refuse to undertake this venture without a long-term contract fixing the price of the door handles?

4. Would you be irrational to refuse a one-sided offer in an ultimatum bargaining game if you knew that you would be playing that game many times with the same partner?

5. Describe the commitment problem that narrowly self-interested diners and waiters would confront at restaurants located on interstate highways. Given that in such restaurants tipping does seem to assure reasonably good service, do you think people are always selfish in the narrowest sense?

▪ PROBLEMS ▪

1. In studying for his economics final, Sam is concerned about only two things: his grade and the amount of time he spends studying. A good grade will give him a benefit of 20; an average grade, a benefit of 5; and a poor grade, a benefit of 0. By studying a lot, Sam will incur a cost of 10; by studying a little, a cost of 6. Moreover, if Sam studies a lot and all other students study a little, he will get a good grade and they will get poor ones. But if they study a lot and he studies a little, they will get good grades and he will get a poor one. Finally, if he and all other students study the same amount of time, everyone will get average grades. Other students share Sam's preferences regarding grades and study time.
   a. Model this situation as a two-person prisoner's dilemma in which the strategies are to study a little and to study a lot, and the players are Sam and all other students. Include the payoffs in the matrix.
   b. What is the equilibrium outcome in this game? From the students' perspective, is it the best outcome?

2. Consider the following "dating game," which has two players, *A* and *B*, and two strategies, to buy a movie ticket or a baseball ticket. The payoffs, given in points, are as shown in the following matrix. Note that the highest payoffs occur when both *A* and *B* attend the same event.

		B	
		Buy movie ticket	Buy baseball ticket
A	Buy movie ticket	2 for A 3 for B	0 for A 0 for B
	Buy baseball ticket	1 for A 1 for B	3 for A 2 for B

Assume that players *A* and *B* buy their tickets separately and simultaneously. Each must decide what to do knowing the available choices and payoffs but not what the other has actually chosen. Each player believes the other to be rational and self-interested.
   a. Does either player have a dominant strategy?
   b. How many potential equilibriums are there? (*Hint:* To see whether a given combination of strategies is an equilibrium, ask whether either player could get a higher payoff by changing his or her strategy.)

c. Is this game a prisoner's dilemma? Explain.

d. Suppose player A gets to buy his or her ticket first. Player B does not observe A's choice but knows that A chose first. Player A knows that player B knows he or she chose first. What is the equilibrium outcome?

e. Suppose the situation is similar to part d, except that player B chooses first. What is the equilibrium outcome?

3. Blackadder and Baldrick are rational, self-interested criminals imprisoned in separate cells in a dark medieval dungeon. They face the prisoner's dilemma displayed in the following matrix.

| | | **Blackadder** | |
		Confess	Deny
Baldrick	Confess	5 years for each	0 years for Baldrick 20 years for Blackadder
	Deny	0 years for Blackadder 20 years for Baldrick	1 year for each

Assume that Blackadder is willing to pay $1,000 for each year by which he can reduce his sentence below 20 years. A corrupt jailer tells Blackadder that before he decides whether to confess or deny the crime, she can tell him Baldrick's decision. How much is this information worth to Blackadder?

4. The owner of a thriving business wants to open a new office in a distant city. If he can hire someone who will manage the new office honestly, he can afford to pay that person a weekly salary of $2,000 ($1,000 more than the manager would be able to earn elsewhere) and still earn an economic profit of $800. The owner's concern is that he will not be able to monitor the manager's behavior and that the manager would therefore be in a position to embezzle money from the business. The owner knows that if the remote office is managed dishonestly, the manager can earn $3,100 while causing the owner an economic loss of $600 per week.

a. If the owner believes that all managers are narrowly self-interested income maximizers, will he open the new office?

b. Suppose the owner knows that a managerial candidate is a devoutly religious person who condemns dishonest behavior and who would be willing to pay up to $15,000 to avoid the guilt she would feel if she were dishonest. Will the owner open the remote office?

5. Imagine yourself sitting in your car in a campus parking lot that is currently full, waiting for someone to pull out so that you can park your car. Somebody pulls out, but at the same moment a driver who has just arrived overtakes you in an obvious attempt to park in the vacated spot before you can. Suppose this driver would be willing to pay up to $10 to park in that spot and up to $30 to avoid getting into an argument with you. (That is, the benefit of parking is $10, and the cost of an argument is $30.) At the same time the other driver guesses, accurately, that you too would be willing to pay up to $30 to avoid a confrontation and up to $10 to park in the vacant spot.

a. Model this situation as a two-stage decision tree in which the other driver's bid to take the space is the opening move and your strategies are (1) to protest and (2) not to protest. If you protest (initiate an argument), the rules of the game specify that the other driver has to let you take the space. Show the payoffs at the end of each branch of the tree.

b. What is the equilibrium outcome?

c. What would be the advantage of being able to communicate credibly to the other driver that your failure to protest would be a significant psychological cost to you?

6. Newfoundland's fishing industry has recently declined sharply due to overfishing, even though fishing companies were supposedly bound by a quota agreement. If all fishing companies had abided by the agreement, yields could have been maintained at high levels.

a. Model this situation as a prisoner's dilemma in which the players are Company A and Company B and the strategies are to keep the quota and break the quota. Include appropriate payoffs in the matrix. Explain why overfishing is inevitable in the absence of effective enforcement of the quota agreement.

b. Provide another environmental example of a prisoner's dilemma.

c. In many potential prisoner's dilemmas, a way out of the dilemma for a would-be cooperator is to make reliable character judgments about the trustworthiness of potential partners. Explain why this solution is not available in many situations involving degradation of the environment.

7. Consider the following game, called matching pennies, which you are playing with a friend. Each of you has a penny hidden in your hand, facing either heads up or tails up (you know which way the one in your hand is facing). On the count of "three" you simultaneously show your pennies to each other. If the face-up side of your coin matches the face-up side of your friend's coin, you get to keep the two pennies. If the faces do not match, your friend gets to keep the pennies.

a. Who are the players in this game? What are each player's strategies? Construct a payoff matrix for the game.

b. Is there a dominant strategy? If so, what?

c. Is there an equilibrium? If so, what?

8. Consider the following game. Harry has four quarters. He can offer Sally from one to four of them. If she accepts his offer, she keeps the quarters Harry offered her and Harry keeps the others. If Sally declines Harry's offer, they both get nothing ($0). They play the game only once, and each cares only about the amount of money he or she ends up with.

a. Who are the players? What are each player's strategies? Construct a decision tree for this ultimatum bargaining game.

b. Given their goal, what is the optimal choice for each player?

9. Two airplane manufacturers are considering the production of a new product, a 150-passenger jet. Both are deciding whether to enter the market and produce the new plane. The payoff matrix is as shown (payoff values are in millions of dollars).

		Airbus	
		Produce	Don't produce
Boeing	Produce	−5 for each	100 for Boeing 0 for Airbus
	Don't produce	0 for Boeing 100 for Airbus	0 for each

The implication of these payoffs is that the market demand is large enough to support only one manufacturer. If both firms enter, both will sustain a loss.

a. Identify two possible equilibrium outcomes in this game.

b. Consider the effect of a subsidy. Suppose the European Union decides to subsidize the European producer, Airbus, with a check for $25 million if it enters the market. Revise the payoff matrix to account for this subsidy. What is the new equilibrium outcome?

c. Compare the two outcomes (pre- and post-subsidy). What qualitative effect does the subsidy have?

10.* Jill and Jack both have two pails that can be used to carry water down from a hill. Each makes only one trip down the hill, and each pail of water can be sold for $5. Carrying the pails of water down requires considerable effort. Both Jill and Jack would be willing to pay $2 each to avoid carrying one bucket down the hill and an additional $3 to avoid carrying a second bucket down the hill.

a. Given market prices, how many pails of water will each child fetch from the top of the hill?

*Problems marked with an asterisk (*) are more difficult.

b. Jill and Jack's parents are worried that the two children don't cooperate enough with one another. Suppose they make Jill and Jack share their revenues from selling the water equally. Given that both are self-interested, construct the payoff matrix for the decisions Jill and Jack face regarding the number of pails of water each should carry. What is the equilibrium outcome?

■ ANSWERS TO IN-CHAPTER EXERCISES ■

10.1 No matter what American does, United will do better to raise ad spending. No matter what United does, American will do better to leave ad spending the same. So each player will play its dominant strategy: United will raise its ad spending, and American will leave its ad spending the same.

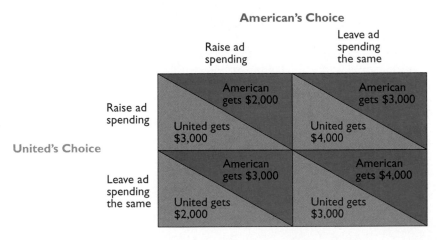

10.2 In game 1, no matter what Chrysler does, GM will do better to invest, and no matter what GM does, Chrysler will do better to invest. Each has a dominant strategy, but in following it, each does worse than if it had not invested. So game 1 is a prisoner's dilemma. In game 2, no matter what Chrysler does, GM again will do better to invest; but no matter what GM does, Chrysler will do better *not* to invest. Each has a dominant strategy, and in following it, each gets a payoff of 10—that is, 5 more than if each had played its dominated strategy. So game 2 is not a prisoner's dilemma.

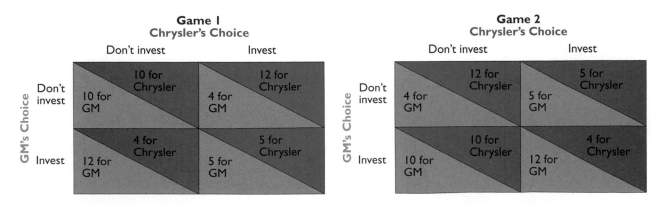

10.3 Smith assumes that Jones will choose the branch that maximizes his payoff, which is the bottom branch at either *B* or *C*. So Jones will choose the bottom branch when his turn comes, no matter what Smith chooses. Since Smith will do better (60) on the bottom branch at *B* than on the bottom branch at *C* (50), Smith will choose the top branch at *A*. So the equilibrium in this game is for Smith to choose the top branch at *A* and Jones to choose the bottom branch at *B*. Smith gets 60, and Jones gets 105. If Jones could make a credible commitment to choose the top branch no matter what, both would do better. Smith would choose the bottom branch at *A* and Jones would choose the top branch at *C*, giving Smith 500 and Jones 400.

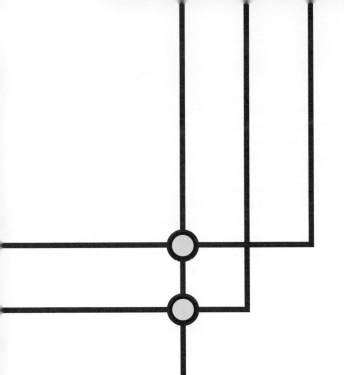

11

EXTERNALITIES
AND PROPERTY RIGHTS

■

A droll television ad for a British brand of pipe tobacco opens with a distinguished-looking gentleman sitting quietly on a park bench, smoking his pipe and reading a book of poetry. Before him lies a pond, unrippled except for a mother duck swimming peacefully with her ducklings. Suddenly a raucous group of teenage boys bursts onto the scene with a remote-controlled toy warship. Yelling and chortling, they launch their boat and maneuver it in aggressive pursuit of the terrified ducks.

Interrupted from his reverie, the gentleman looks up from his book and draws calmly on his pipe as he surveys the scene before him. He then reaches into his bag, pulls out a remote control of his own, and begins manipulating the joystick. The scene shifts underwater, where a miniature submarine rises from the depths of the pond. Once the boys' boat is in the sub's sights, the gentleman pushes a button on his remote control. Seconds later, the boat is blown to smithereens by a torpedo. The scene fades to a close-up of the tobacco company's label.

EXTERNAL COSTS AND BENEFITS

Many activities generate costs or benefits that accrue to people not directly involved in those activities. These effects are generally unintended. They are called **external costs** and **benefits**—**externalities,** for short. From the pipe smoker's point of view, the noise generated by the marauding boys was an external cost. And had others been disturbed by the boys' rowdiness, they may well have regarded the pipe smoker's retaliatory gesture as an external benefit.

external cost (or negative externality) a cost of an activity that falls on people other than those who pursue the activity

external benefit (or positive externality) a benefit of an activity received by people other than those who pursue the activity

externality an external cost or benefit of an activity

This chapter focuses on how externalities affect the allocation of resources. Adam Smith's theory of the invisible hand applies to an ideal marketplace in which externalities do not exist. In such situations, Smith argued, the self-interested actions of individuals would lead to socially efficient outcomes. We will see that when the parties affected by externalities can easily negotiate with one another, the invisible hand will still produce an efficient outcome.

But in many cases, such as the scene depicted in the tobacco ad, negotiation is impractical. In those cases, the self-serving actions of individuals simply will not lead to efficient outcomes. Because externalities are widespread, the attempt to forge solutions to the problems they cause is one of the most important rationales, not only for the existence of government but for a variety of other forms of collective action as well.

HOW EXTERNALITIES AFFECT RESOURCE ALLOCATION

The way in which externalities distort the allocation of resources can be seen clearly in the next several examples.

EXAMPLE 11.1

Does the honeybee keeper face the right incentives? (Part I)

Phoebe earns her living as a keeper of honeybees. Her neighbors on all sides grow apples. Because bees pollinate apple trees as they forage for nectar, the more hives Phoebe keeps, the larger the harvests will be in the surrounding orchards. If Phoebe takes only her own costs and benefits into account in deciding how many hives to keep, will she keep the socially optimal number of hives?

For the orchard owners, Phoebe's hives constitute an external benefit, or a positive externality. If she takes only her own personal costs and benefits into account, she will add hives only until the added revenue she gets from the last hive just equals the cost of adding it. But since the orchard owners also benefit from additional hives, the total benefit of adding another hive at that point will be greater than its cost. Phoebe, then, will keep too few hives.

As we will discuss later in the chapter, problems like the one just discussed have several possible solutions. One is for orchard owners to pay beekeepers for keeping additional hives. But such solutions often require complex negotiations between the affected parties. For the moment, we assume that such negotiations are not practical.

EXAMPLE 11.2

Does the honeybee keeper face the right incentives? (Part 2)

As in Example 11.1, Phoebe earns her living as a keeper of honeybees. But now her neighbors are not apple growers but an elementary school and a nursing home. The more hives Phoebe keeps, the more students and nursing home residents will be stung by bees. If Phoebe takes only her own costs and benefits into account in deciding how many hives to keep, will she keep the socially optimal number of hives?

For the students and nursing home residents, Phoebe's hives constitute an external cost, or a negative externality. If she considers only her own costs and benefits in deciding how many hives to keep, she will continue to add hives until the added revenue from the last hive is just enough to cover its cost. But since Phoebe's neighbors also incur costs when she adds a hive, the benefit of the last hive at that point will be smaller than its cost. Phoebe, in other words, will keep too many hives.

Every activity involves costs and benefits. When all the relevant costs and benefits of an activity accrue directly to the person who carries it out—that is, when the activity generates no externalities—the level of the activity that is best for the individual will be best for society as a whole. But when an activity generates externalities, be they positive or negative, individual self-interest does not produce the best allocation of resources. Individuals who consider only their own costs and benefits will tend to engage too much in activities that generate negative externalities and too little in activities that generate positive externalities. When an activity generates both positive and negative externalities, private and social interests will coincide only in the unlikely event that the opposing effects offset one another exactly.

THE GRAPHICAL PORTRAYAL OF EXTERNALITIES

The effects of externalities on resource allocation can be portrayed graphically. Consider first the case of negative externalities. Figure 11.1(a) depicts the supply (Private *MC*) and demand curves for a product whose production involves no external costs or benefits. We may imagine, for example, that the energy that powers the factories in this market comes from nonpolluting hydroelectric generators. The resulting equilibrium price and quantity in the market for this product will then be socially optimal, for the reasons discussed in Chapters 3 and 7: The value to buyers of the last unit of the product consumed will be exactly equal to the marginal cost of producing it ($1,300 per ton in each case), leaving no further possible gains from exchange.

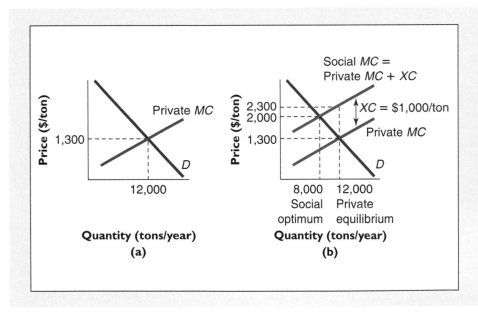

FIGURE 11.1
How External Costs Affect Resource Allocation.
When a market has no external costs or benefits (a), the resulting equilibrium quantity and price are socially optimal. By contrast, when production of a good is accompanied by an external cost (b), the market equilibrium price ($1,300 per ton) is too low, and the market equilibrium quantity (12,000 tons per year) is too high.

But now suppose that a protracted drought has eliminated hydroelectric power generation, forcing factories to rely instead on electric power produced by coal-burning generators. Now each ton of output produced is accompanied by an external pollution cost of *XC* = $1,000, as shown in Figure 11.1(b). Since the external pollution cost falls not on firm owners but on others who live downwind from their factories, Private *MC* is again the supply curve for this product, and its demand curve is again as before, so the equilibrium price and quantity will be exactly the same as in Figure 11.1(a), as determined by the intersection of the demand curve *(D)* and the supply curve (Private *MC*). But this time the private market equilibrium is not socially optimal. To see why, note that at $Q_{pvt} = 12,000$ tons per year, the value to consumers of the last unit of output produced was only $1,300 per ton, while the cost of producing that last unit (including the external cost) was $2,300 per ton. This means that society could gain additional economic surplus by producing fewer units of the product. Indeed, the same conclusion will continue to hold whenever the current output exceeds 8,000 tons per year, the output level at which the demand curve intersects Social *MC*. Social *MC*, the socially optimal supply curve of the product, is the result of adding the external cost, *XC*, to every value along Private *MC*. The socially optimal level of output of the good shown in Figure 11.1(b) is 8,000 tons per year, the level that exhausts all possibilities from exchange. For a good whose production generates external costs, the market equilibrium quantity will be higher than the socially optimal quantity.

What about a good whose production generates external benefits? In Figure 11.2, Private Demand is the demand curve for a product whose production generates an external benefit of *XB* per unit. The market equilibrium quantity of this good, Q_{pvt}, is the output level at which Private Demand intersects the supply curve of the product *(MC)*. This time market equilibrium quantity is smaller than the socially optimal level, denoted Q_{soc}. Q_{soc} is the output level at which *MC* intersects the socially optimal demand curve (Social Demand), which is obtained by adding the external benefit, *XB*, to every value along Private Demand. Note in the figure that in the case of positive externalities the private market equilibrium again fails to exhaust all possible gains from exchange. Thus at Q_{pvt} the marginal cost of producing an additional unit of output is only MB_{pvt}, which is smaller than the marginal benefit of an additional unit by the amount *XB*. For a good whose production generates external benefits, the market equilibrium quantity will be smaller than the socially optimal quantity.

FIGURE 11.2
A Good Whose Production Generates a Positive Externality for Consumers.
The market equilibrium quantity, Q_{pvt}, is smaller than the socially optimal quantity, Q_{soc}, because individual buyers are willing to pay only for the benefits they reap from directly consuming the product.

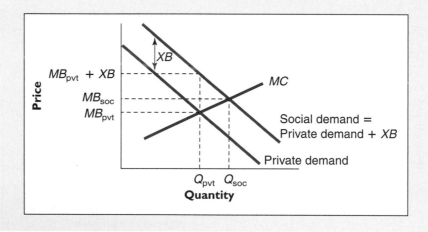

No matter whether externalities are positive or negative, they distort the allocation of resources in otherwise efficient markets. When externalities are present, the individual pursuit of self-interest will not result in the largest possible economic surplus. And when it does not, the outcome is by definition inefficient.

THE COASE THEOREM

To say that a situation is inefficient means that it can be rearranged in a way that would make at least some people better off without harming others. Such situations, we have seen, are a source of creative tension. The existence of inefficiency, after all, means that there is cash on the table, which usually triggers a race to see who can capture it. For example, we saw that because monopoly pricing results in an inefficiently low output level, the potential for gain gave monopolists an incentive to make discounts available to price-sensitive buyers. As the next examples illustrate, the inefficiencies that result from externalities create similar incentives for remedial action.

EXAMPLE 11.3   **Will Abercrombie dump toxins in the river? (Part I)**

Abercrombie's factory produces a toxic waste by-product. If Abercrombie dumps it in the river, he causes damage to Fitch, a fisherman located downstream. The toxins are short-lived and cause no damage to anyone other than Fitch. At a cost, Abercrombie can filter out the toxins, in which case Fitch will suffer no damage at all. The relevant gains and losses for the two individuals are listed in Table 11.1.

TABLE 11.1
Costs and Benefits of Eliminating Toxic Waste (Part 1)

	With filter	Without filter
Gains to Abercrombie	$100/day	$130/day
Gains to Fitch	$100/day	$50/day

If the law does not penalize Abercrombie for dumping toxins in the river, and if Abercrombie and Fitch cannot communicate with one another, will Abercrombie operate with or without a filter? Is that choice socially efficient?

Since Abercrombie earns $30 per day more without a filter than with one, his natural incentive is to operate without one. But the outcome when he does so is socially inefficient. Thus, when Abercrombie operates without a filter, the total daily gain to both parties is only $130 + $50 = $180, compared to $100 + $100 = $200 if Abercrombie had operated with a filter. The daily cost of the filter to Abercrombie is only $130 − $100 = $30, which is smaller than its daily benefit to Fitch of $100 − $50 = $50. The fact that Abercrombie does not install the filter implies a squandered daily surplus of $20.

Will Abercrombie dump toxins in the river? (Part 2)

Suppose the costs and benefits of using the filter are as in Example 11.3 except that Abercrombie and Fitch can now communicate with one another at no cost. Even though the law does not require him to do so, will Abercrombie use a filter?

This time, Abercrombie will use a filter. Recall from Chapter 7 the observation that when the economic pie grows larger, everyone can have a larger slice (the efficiency principle). Because use of a filter would result in the largest possible economic surplus, it would enable both Abercrombie and Fitch to have a larger net gain than before. Fitch thus has an incentive to *pay* Abercrombie to use a filter. For example, suppose Fitch offers Abercrombie $40 per day to compensate him for operating with a filter. Both Abercrombie and Fitch will then be exactly $10 per day better off than before, for a total daily net gain of $20.

EXAMPLE 11.4

EXERCISE 11.1

In Example 11.4, what is the largest whole-dollar amount by which Fitch could compensate Abercrombie for operating with a filter and still be better off than before?

Ronald Coase, a professor at the University of Chicago Law School, was the first to see clearly that if people can negotiate with one another at no cost over the right to perform activities that cause externalities, they will always arrive at an efficient solution. This insight, which is often called the **Coase theorem,** is a profoundly important idea, for which Coase (rhymes with "dose") was awarded the 1991 Nobel Prize in Economics.

Why, you might ask, should Fitch pay Abercrombie to filter out toxins that would not be there in the first place if not for Abercrombie's factory? The rhetorical force of this question is undeniable. Yet Coase points out that externalities are reciprocal in nature. The toxins do harm Fitch, to be sure, but preventing

Coase theorem if at no cost people can negotiate the purchase and sale of the right to perform activities that cause externalities, they can always arrive at efficient solutions to the problems caused by externalities

Abercrombie from emitting them would penalize Abercrombie, by exactly $30 per day. Why should Fitch necessarily have the right to harm Abercrombie? Indeed, as Example 11.5 illustrates, even if Fitch had that right, he would exercise it only if filtering the toxins proved the most efficient outcome.

EXAMPLE 11.5

Will Abercrombie dump toxins in the river? (Part 3)

Suppose the law says that Abercrombie may *not* dump toxins in the river unless he has Fitch's permission. If the relevant costs and benefits of filtering the toxins are as shown in Table 11.2, and if Abercrombie and Fitch can negotiate with one another at no cost, will Abercrombie filter the toxins?

TABLE 11.2
Costs and Benefits of Eliminating Toxic Waste (Part 3)

	With filter	Without filter
Gains to Abercrombie	$100/day	$150/day
Gains to Fitch	$100/day	$70/day

Note that this time the most efficient outcome is for Abercrombie to operate without a filter, for the total daily surplus in that case will be $220 as compared to only $200 with a filter. Under the law, however, Fitch has the right to insist that Abercrombie use a filter. We might expect him to exercise that right, since his own gain would rise from $70 to $100 per day if he did so. But because this outcome would be socially inefficient, we know that each party can do better.

Suppose, for example, that Abercrombie gives Fitch $40 per day in return for Fitch's permission to operate without a filter. Each would then have a net daily gain of $110, which is $10 better for each of them than if Fitch had insisted that Abercrombie use a filter. Abercrombie's pollution harms Fitch, sure enough. But failure to allow the pollution would have caused even greater harm to Abercrombie.

The Coase theorem tells us that regardless of whether the law holds polluters liable for damages, the affected parties will achieve efficient solutions to externalities if they can negotiate costlessly with one another. But note carefully that this does not imply that affected parties will be indifferent about whether the law holds polluters responsible for damages. If polluters are liable, they will end up with lower incomes and those who are injured by pollutants will end up with higher incomes than if the law does not hold polluters liable—even though the same efficient production methods are adopted in each case. When polluters are held liable, they must remove the pollution at their own expense. When they are not held liable, those who are injured by pollution must pay polluters to cut back.

Externalities are hardly rare and isolated occurrences. On the contrary, finding examples of actions that are altogether free of them is difficult. And because externalities can distort the allocation of resources, it is important to recognize them and deal intelligently with them. Consider the following example of an externality that arises because of shared living arrangements.

EXAMPLE 11.6

Will Ann and Betty share an apartment?

Ann and Betty can live together in a two-bedroom apartment for $600 per month, or separately in 2 one-bedroom apartments, each for $400 per month. If the rent paid were the same for both alternatives, the two women would be indifferent between living together or separately, except for one problem: Ann talks constantly on the telephone. Ann would pay up to $250 per month for this privilege. Betty, for her part, would pay up to $150 per month to have better access to the phone. If the two cannot install a second phone line, should they live together or separately?

Ann and Betty should live together only if the benefit of doing so exceeds the cost. The benefit of living together is the reduction in their rent. Since 2 one-bedroom apartments would cost a total of $800 per month, compared to $600 for a two-bedroom unit, their benefit from living together is $200 per month. Their cost of living together is the least costly accommodation they can make to Ann's objectionable telephone habits. Since Ann would be willing to pay up to $250 per month to avoid changing her behavior, the $200 rent saving is too small to persuade her to change. But Betty is willing to put up with Ann's behavior for a compensation payment of only $150 per month. Since that amount is smaller than the total saving in rent, the least costly solution to the problem is for Betty to live with Ann and simply put up with her behavior.

Table 11.3 summarizes the relevant costs and benefits of this shared living arrangement. The cost-benefit principle tells us that Ann and Betty should live together if and only if the benefit of living together exceeds the cost. The cost of the shared living arrangement is not the sum of all possible costs but the least costly accommodation to the problem (or problems) of shared living. Since the $200 per month saving in rent exceeds the least costly accommodation to the phone problem, Ann and Betty can reap a total gain in economic surplus of $50 per month by sharing their living quarters.

TABLE 11.3
The Gain in Surplus from Shared Living Arrangements

Benefits of Shared Living		
Total cost of separate apartments	**Total cost of shared apartment**	**Rent savings from sharing**
(2)($400/month) = $800/month	$600/month	$200/month

Costs of Shared Living			
Problem	**Ann's cost of solving problem**	**Betty's cost of solving problem**	**Least costly solution to the problem**
Ann's phone usage	Curtailed phone usage: $250/month	Tolerate phone usage: $150/month	Betty tolerates Ann's phone usage: $150/month

Gain in Surplus from Shared Living		
Rent savings ($200/month) −	Least costly accommodation to shared living problems ($150/month) =	Gain in surplus: $50/month

Some people might conclude that Ann and Betty should not live together, because if the two share the rent equally, Betty will end up paying $300 per month—which when added to the $150 cost of putting up with Ann's phone behavior comes to $50 more than the cost of living alone. As persuasive as that argument may sound, however, it is mistaken. The source of the error, as Example 11.7 makes clear, is the assumption that the two must share the rent equally.

EXAMPLE 11.7

What is the highest rent Betty would be willing to pay for the two-bedroom apartment?

In Example 11.6, what is the highest rent Betty would be willing to pay to share an apartment with Ann?

Betty's alternative is to live alone, which would mean paying $400 per month, her reservation price for a living arrangement with no phone problem. Since the most she would be willing to pay to avoid the phone problem is $150 per month, the highest monthly rent she would be willing to pay for the shared apartment is $400 − $150 = $250. If she pays that amount, Ann will have to pay the difference, namely, $350 per month, which is clearly a better alternative for Ann than paying $400 to live alone.

EXAMPLE 11.8

How much should Ann and Betty pay if they agree to split their economic surplus equally?

If Ann and Betty agree to live together and split the resulting gain in economic surplus equally, how much rent will each of them pay?

As we saw in Table 11.3, the total rent saving from the shared apartment is $200, and since the least costly solution to the phone problem is $150, the monthly gain in economic surplus is $50. We know that Ann's reservation price for living together is $400 per month and Betty's is $250 (see Example 11.7). So if the two women want to split the $50 monthly surplus equally, each should pay $25 less than her reservation price. Ann's monthly rent will thus be $375 and Betty's, $225. The result is that each is $25 per month better off than if she had lived alone.

EXERCISE 11.2

As in Example 11.6, Ann and Betty can live together in a two-bedroom apartment for $600 per month or separately in 2 one-bedroom apartments, each for $400 per month. Ann would pay up to $250 per month rather than moderate her telephone habits, and Betty would pay up to $150 per month to achieve reasonable access to the telephone. But Betty would also be willing to pay up to $60 per month to avoid the loss of privacy that comes with shared living space. Should the two women live together?

LEGAL REMEDIES FOR EXTERNALITIES

We have seen that efficient solutions to externalities can be found whenever the affected parties can negotiate with one another at no cost. But negotiation is not always practical. A motorist with a noisy muffler, for example, imposes costs on others, yet they cannot flag him down and offer him a compensation payment to fix his muffler. In recognition of this difficulty, most governments simply require that cars have working mufflers. Indeed, the explicit or implicit purpose of a large share—perhaps the lion's share—of laws is to solve problems caused by externalities. The goal of such laws is to help people achieve the solutions they might have reached had they been able to negotiate with one another.

When negotiation is costless, the task of adjustment generally falls on the party who can accomplish it at the lowest cost. For instance, in Example 11.6, Betty put up with Ann's annoying phone habits because doing so was less costly than asking Ann to change her habits. Many municipal noise ordinances also place the burden of adjustment on those who can accomplish it at lowest cost. Consider, for example, the restrictions on loud party music, which often take effect at a later hour on weekends than on weekdays. This pattern reflects both the fact that the gains from loud music tend to be larger on weekends and the fact that such music is more likely to disturb people on weekdays. By setting the noise curfew at different hours on different days of the week, the law places the burden on partygoers during the week and on sleepers during the weekend. Similar logic explains why noise ordinances allow motorists to honk their horns in most neighborhoods, but not in the immediate vicinity of a hospital.

As the following examples demonstrate, economic naturalists can hone their craft by focusing on laws whose purpose is to solve the problems caused by externalities.

What is the purpose of speed limits and other traffic laws?

A motorist driving a car at high speed endangers not just her own life and property but also the lives and property of others. Speed limits, no-passing zones, right-of-way rules, and a host of other traffic laws may be seen as reasoned attempts to limit the harm one party inflicts on another. Many jurisdictions even have laws requiring that motorists install snow tires on their cars by November 1. These laws promote not just safety but also the smooth flow of traffic: A single motorist who can't get up a snow-covered hill delays not only herself but also the motorists behind her.

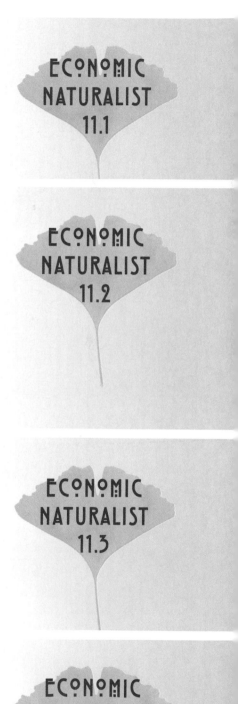

ECONOMIC NATURALIST 11.1

ECONOMIC NATURALIST 11.2

ECONOMIC NATURALIST 11.3

ECONOMIC NATURALIST 11.4

Why do most communities have zoning laws?

Most communities restrict the kinds of activities that take place in various parts of the city. Because many residents place a high value on living in an uncongested neighborhood, some cities have enacted zoning laws specifying minimum lot sizes. In places like Manhattan, where a shortage of land encourages developers to build very large and tall buildings, zoning laws limit both a building's height and the proportion of a lot it may occupy. Such restrictions recognize that the taller a building is, and the greater the proportion of its lot that it occupies, the more it blocks sunlight from reaching surrounding properties. The desire to control external costs also helps to explain why many cities establish separate zones for business and residential activity. Even within business districts, many cities limit certain kinds of commercial activity. For example, in an effort to revitalize the Times Square neighborhood, New York City enacted a zoning law banning adult bookstores and pornographic movie theaters from the area.

Why do many governments enact laws that limit the discharge of environmental pollutants?

Limitations on the discharge of pollutants into the environment are perhaps the clearest examples of laws aimed at solving problems caused by externalities. The details of these laws reflect the cost-benefit principle. The discharge of toxic wastes into rivers, for example, tends to be most strictly regulated on those waterways whose commercial fishing or recreational uses are most highly valued. On other waterways, the burden of adjustment is likely to fall more heavily on fishermen, recreational boaters, and swimmers. Similarly, air quality regulations tend to be strictest in the most heavily populated regions of the country, where the marginal benefit of pollution reduction is the greatest.

What is the purpose of free speech laws?

The First Amendment's protection of free speech and the pattern of exceptions to that protection are another illustration of how legal remedies are used to solve the problems caused by externalities. The First Amendment acknowledges the decisive value of open communication, as well as the practical difficulty of identifying and regulating acts of speech that cause more harm than good. Yet it does allow some important exceptions. For instance, it does not allow someone to yell "fire" in a crowded theater if there is no fire, nor does it allow someone to advocate the violent overthrow of the government. In those instances, the external benefits of free speech are far too small to justify the external costs.

Why does government subsidize the planting of trees on hillsides?

The laws discussed in the preceding examples are meant to regulate activities that generate negative externalities. But government also uses the law to encourage activities that generate positive externalities. The planting of trees on hillsides, for example, benefits not just the landowner but also his neighbors by limiting the danger of flooding. In recognition of this fact, many jurisdictions subsidize the planting of trees. Similarly, Congress budgets millions of dollars each year in support of basic research, an implicit acknowledgment of the positive externalities associated with the generation of new knowledge.

THE OPTIMAL AMOUNT OF NEGATIVE EXTERNALITIES IS NOT ZERO

Curbing pollution and other negative externalities entails both costs and benefits. As we saw in Chapter 6, the best policy is to curtail pollution until the cost of further abatement just equals the marginal benefit. In general, the marginal cost of abatement rises with the amount of pollution eliminated. (Following the low-hanging-fruit principle, polluters use the cheapest cleanup methods first and then turn to more expensive ones.) And the law of diminishing marginal utility suggests that beyond some point, the marginal benefit of pollution reduction tends to fall as more pollution is removed. As a result, the marginal cost and marginal benefit curves almost always intersect at less than the maximum amount of pollution reduction.

The intersection of the two curves marks instead the socially optimal level of pollution reduction. If pollution is curtailed by any less than that amount, society will gain more than it will lose by pushing the cleanup effort a little further. But if regulators push beyond the point at which the marginal cost and benefit curves intersect, society will incur costs that exceed the benefits. The existence of a socially optimal level of pollution reduction implies the existence of a socially optimal level of pollution, and that level will almost always be greater than zero.

As we saw in Chapter 6, because people have been conditioned to think of pollution as bad, many cringe when they hear the phrase "socially optimal level of pollution." How can any positive level of pollution be socially optimal? *But to speak of a socially optimal level of pollution is not the same as saying that pollution is good.* It is merely to recognize that society has an interest in cleaning up the environment, but only up to a certain point. The underlying idea is no different from the idea of an optimal level of dirt in an apartment. After all, even if you spent the whole day, every day, vacuuming your apartment, there would be *some* dirt left in it. And because you have better things to do than vacuum all day, you probably tolerate substantially more than the minimal amount of dirt. A dirty apartment is not good, nor is pollution in the air you breathe. But in both cases, the cleanup effort should be expanded only until the marginal benefit equals the marginal cost.

 RECAP   EXTERNAL COSTS AND BENEFITS

Externalities occur when the costs or benefits of an activity accrue to people other than those directly involved in the activity. The Coase theorem says that when affected parties can negotiate with one another without cost, activities will be pursued at efficient levels, even in the presence of positive or negative externalities. But when negotiation is prohibitively costly, inefficient behavior generally results. Activities that generate negative externalities are pursued to excess, while those that generate positive externalities are pursued too little. Laws and regulations are often adopted in an effort to alter inefficient behavior that results from externalities.

PROPERTY RIGHTS AND THE TRAGEDY OF THE COMMONS

People who grow up in the industrialized nations tend to take the institution of private property for granted. Our intuitive sense is that people have the right to own any property they acquire by lawful means and to do with that property much as they see fit. In reality, however, property laws are considerably more complex in terms of the rights they confer and the obligations they impose.

THE PROBLEM OF UNPRICED RESOURCES

To understand the laws that govern the use of property, we must begin by asking why societies created the institution of private property in the first place. The following examples, which show what happens to property that nobody owns, suggest an answer.

How many steers will villagers send onto the commons?

EXAMPLE 11.9

A village has five residents, each of whom has accumulated savings of $100. Each villager can use the money to buy a government bond that pays 13 percent interest per year or to buy a year-old steer, send it onto the commons to graze, and sell it after 1 year. The price the villager will get for the 2-year-old steer depends on the amount of weight it gains while grazing on the commons, which in turn depends on the number of steers sent onto the commons, as shown in Table 11.4.

The price of a 2-year-old steer declines with the number of steers grazing on the commons, because the more steers, the less grass available to each. The villagers make their investment decisions one at a time, and the results are public. If each villager decides how to invest individually, how many steers will be sent onto the commons, and what will be the village's total income?

TABLE 11.4
The Relationship between Herd Size and Steer Price

Number of steers on the commons	Price per 2-year-old steer ($)	Income per steer ($/year)
1	126	26
2	119	19
3	116	16
4	113	13
5	111	11

If a villager buys a $100 government bond, he will earn $13 of interest income at the end of 1 year. Thus he should send a steer onto the commons if and only if that steer will command a price of at least $113 as a 2-year-old. When each villager chooses in this self-interested way, we can expect four villagers to send a steer onto the commons. (Actually, the fourth villager would be indifferent between investing in a steer or buying a bond, since he would earn $13 either way. For the sake of discussion, we'll assume that in the case of a tie, people choose to be cattlemen.) The fifth villager, seeing that he would earn only $11 by sending a fifth steer onto the commons, will choose instead to buy a government bond. As a result of these decisions, the total village income will be $65 per year—$13 for the one bondholder and 4($13) = $52 for the four cattlemen.

Has Adam Smith's invisible hand produced the most efficient allocation of these villagers' resources? We can tell at a glance that it has not, since their total village income is only $65—precisely the same as it would have been had the possibility of cattle raising not existed. The source of the difficulty will become evident in Example 11.10.

EXAMPLE 11.10

What is the socially optimal number of steers to send onto the commons?

Suppose the five villagers in Example 11.9 confront the same investment opportunities as before, except that this time they are free to make their decisions as a group rather than individually. How many steers will they send onto the commons, and what will be their total village income?

This time the villagers' goal is to maximize the income received by the group as a whole. When decisions are made from this perspective, the criterion is to send a steer onto the commons only if its marginal contribution to village income is at least $13, the amount that could be earned from a government bond. As the entries in the last column of Table 11.5 indicate, the first steer clearly meets this criterion, since it contributes $26 to total village income. But the second steer does not. Sending that steer onto the commons raises the village's income from cattle raising from $26 to $38, a gain of just $12. The $100 required to buy the second steer would thus have been better invested in a government bond. Worse, the collective return from sending a third steer is only $10; from a fourth, only $4; and from a fifth, only $3.

TABLE 11.5
Marginal Income and the Socially Optimal Herd Size

Number of steers on the commons	Price per 2-year-old steer ($)	Income per steer ($/year)	Total cattle income ($/year)	Marginal income ($/year)
1	126	26	26	26
2	119	19	38	12
3	116	16	48	10
4	113	13	52	4
5	111	11	55	3

In sum, when investment decisions are made with the goal of maximizing total village income, the best choice is to buy four government bonds and send only a single steer onto the commons. The resulting village income will be $78: $26 from sending the single steer and $52 from the four government bonds. That amount is $13 more than the total income that resulted when villagers made their investment decisions individually. Once again, the reward from moving from an inefficient allocation to an efficient one is that the economic pie grows larger. And when the pie grows larger, everyone can get a larger slice. For instance, if the villagers agree to pool their income and share it equally, each will get $15.60, or $2.60 more than before.

EXERCISE 11.3

How would your answers to Examples 11.9 and 11.10 differ if the interest rate were not 13 percent but 11 percent per year?

Why do the villagers in Examples 11.9 and 11.10 do better when they make their investment decisions collectively? The answer is that when individuals decide alone, they ignore the fact that sending another steer onto the commons will cause existing steers to gain less weight. Their failure to consider this effect makes the return from sending another steer seem misleadingly high to them.

The grazing land on the commons is a valuable economic resource. When no one owns it, no one has any incentive to take the opportunity cost of using it into account. And when that happens, people will tend to use it until its marginal benefit is zero. This problem, and others similar to it, are known as the **tragedy of the commons**. The essential cause of the tragedy of the commons is the fact that one person's use of commonly held property imposes an external cost on others by making the property less valuable. The tragedy of the commons also provides a vivid illustration of the equilibrium principle (see Chapter 3). Each individual villager behaves rationally by sending an additional steer onto the commons, yet the overall outcome falls far short of the attainable ideal.

tragedy of the commons the tendency for a resource that has no price to be used until its marginal benefit falls to zero

THE EFFECT OF PRIVATE OWNERSHIP

As Example 11.11 illustrates, one solution to the tragedy of the commons is to place the village grazing land under private ownership.

How much will the right to control the village commons sell for?

EXAMPLE 11.11

Suppose the five villagers face the same investment opportunities as before, except that this time they decide to auction off the right to use the commons to the highest bidder. Assuming that villagers can borrow as well as lend at an annual interest rate of 13 percent, what price will the right to use the commons fetch? How will the owner of that property right use it, and what will be the resulting village income?

To answer these questions, simply ask yourself what you would do if you had complete control over how the grazing land were used. As we saw in Example 11.10, the most profitable way to use this land is to send only a single steer to graze on it. If you do so, you will earn a total of $26 per year. Since the opportunity cost of the $100 you spent on the single yearling steer is the $13 in interest you could have earned from a bond, your economic profit from sending a single steer onto the commons will be $13 per year, provided you can use the land for free. But you cannot; to finance your purchase of the property right, you must borrow money (since you used your $100 savings to buy a year-old steer).

What is the most you would be willing to pay for the right to use the commons? Since its use generates an income of $26 per year, or $13 more than the opportunity cost of your investment in the steer, the most you would pay is $100 (because that amount used to purchase a bond that pays 13 percent interest would also generate income of $13 per year). If the land were sold at auction, $100 is precisely the amount you would have to pay. Your annual earnings from the land would be exactly enough to pay the $13 interest on your loan and cover the opportunity cost of not having put your savings into a bond.

Note that when the right to use the land is auctioned to the highest bidder, the village achieves a more efficient allocation of its resources, because the owner has a strong incentive to take the opportunity cost of more intensive grazing fully into account. Total village income in this case will again be $78. If the annual interest on the $100 proceeds from selling the land rights is shared equally among the five villagers, each will again have an annual investment income of $15.60.

The logic of economic surplus maximization helps to explain why the most economically successful nations have all been ones with well-developed private property laws. Property that belongs to everyone belongs, in effect, to no one. Not only is its potential economic value never fully realized; it usually ends up being of no value at all.

Bear in mind, however, that in most countries the owners of private property are not free to do *precisely* as they wish with it. For example, local zoning laws may give the owner of a residential building lot the right to build a three-story house but not a six-story house. Here, too, the logic of economic surplus maximization applies, for a fully informed and rational legislature would define property rights so as to create the largest possible total economic surplus. In practice, of course, such ideal legislatures never really exist. Yet the essence of politics is the cutting of deals that make people better off. If a legislator could propose a change in the property laws that would enlarge the total economic surplus, she could also propose a scheme that would give each of her constituents a larger slice, thus enhancing her chances for reelection.

As an economic naturalist, challenge yourself to use this framework when thinking about the various restrictions you encounter in private property laws: zoning laws that constrain what you can build and what types of activities you can conduct on your land; traffic laws that constrain what you can do with your car; employment and environmental laws that constrain how you can operate your business. Your understanding of these and countless other laws will be enhanced by the insight that everyone can gain when the private property laws are defined so as to create the largest total economic surplus.

WHEN PRIVATE OWNERSHIP IS IMPRACTICAL

Do not be misled into thinking that the law provides an *ideal* resolution of all problems associated with externalities and the tragedy of the commons. Defining and enforcing efficient property rights entails costs, after all, and sometimes, as in the following examples, the costs outweigh the gains.

Why are shared milkshakes drunk too quickly?

Why do blackberries in public parks get picked too soon?

Wild blackberries grow profusely at the edge of a wooded area in a crowded city park. The blackberries will taste best if left to ripen fully, but they still taste reasonably good if picked and eaten a few days early. Will the blackberries be left to ripen fully?

Obviously, the costs of defining and enforcing the property rights to blackberries growing in a public park are larger than the potential gains, so the blackberries will remain common property. That means that whoever picks them first gets them. Even though everyone would benefit if people waited until the berries were fully ripe, everyone knows that those who wait are likely to end up with no berries at all. And that means that the berries will be eaten too soon.

Why are shared milkshakes consumed too quickly?

Sara and Susan are identical twins who have been given a chocolate milkshake to share. If each has a straw and each knows that the other is self-interested, will the twins consume the milkshake at an optimal rate?

Because drinking a milkshake too quickly chills the taste buds, the twins will enjoy their shake more if they drink it slowly. Yet each knows that the other will drink any part of the milkshake she doesn't finish herself. The result is that each will consume the shake at a faster rate than she would if she had half a shake all to herself.

Here are some further examples of the type of tragedy of the commons that is not easily solved by defining private ownership rights.

Harvesting timber on remote public land On remote public lands, enforcing restrictions against cutting down trees may be impractical. Each tree cutter knows that a tree that is not harvested this year will be bigger, and hence more valuable, next year. But he also knows that if he doesn't cut the tree down this year, someone else will. In contrast, private companies that grow trees on their own land have no incentive to harvest timber prematurely and a strong incentive to prevent outsiders from doing so.

Harvesting whales in international waters Each individual whaler knows that harvesting an extra whale reduces the breeding population, and hence the size of the future whale population. But the whaler also knows that any whale that is not harvested today will be taken by some other whaler. The solution would be to define and enforce property rights to whales. But the oceans are vast, and the behavior of whalers is hard to monitor. And even if their behavior could be monitored, the concept of national sovereignty would make the international enforcement of property rights problematic.

More generally, the animal species that are most severely threatened with extinction tend to be those that are economically valuable to humans but that are not privately owned by anyone. This is the situation confronting whales. Contrast it with the situation confronting chickens, which are also economically valuable to humans but which, unlike whales, are governed by traditional laws of private property. This difference explains why no one worries that Colonel Sanders might threaten the extinction of chickens.

Controlling multinational environmental pollution Each individual polluter may know that if he and all others pollute, the damage to the environment will be greater than the cost of not polluting. But if the environment is common property into which all are free to dump, each has a powerful incentive to pollute. If all polluters live under the jurisdiction of a single government, enforcing laws and regulations that limit the discharge of pollution may be practical. But if polluters come from many different countries, solutions are much more difficult to implement. Thus the Mediterranean Sea has long suffered serious pollution, because none of the many nations that border it has an economic incentive to consider the effects of its discharges on other countries.

As the world's population continues to grow, the absence of an effective system of international property rights will become an economic problem of increasing significance.

RECAP | PROPERTY RIGHTS AND THE TRAGEDY OF THE COMMONS

When a valuable resource has a price of zero, people will continue to exploit it as long as its marginal benefit remains positive. The tragedy of the commons describes situations in which valuable resources are squandered because users are not charged for them. In many cases, an efficient remedy for such waste is to define and enforce rights to the use of valuable property. But this solution is difficult to implement for resources such as the oceans and the atmosphere, because no single government has the authority to enforce property rights for these resources.

POSITIONAL EXTERNALITIES

Steffi Graf received more than $1.6 million in tournament winnings in 1992; her endorsement and exhibition earnings totaled several times that amount. By any reasonable measure, the quality of her play was outstanding, yet she consistently lost to archrival Monica Seles. But in April of 1993, Seles was stabbed in the back by a deranged fan and forced to withdraw from the tour. In the ensuing months, Graf's tournament winnings accumulated at almost double her 1992 pace, despite little change in the quality of her play.

PAYOFFS THAT DEPEND ON RELATIVE PERFORMANCE

In professional tennis and a host of other competitive situations, the rewards people receive typically depend not only on how they perform in absolute terms but also on how they perform relative to their closest rivals. In these situations, competitors have an incentive to take actions that will increase their odds of winning. For example, tennis players can increase their chances of winning by hiring personal fitness trainers and sports psychologists to travel with them on the tour. Yet the simple mathematics of competition tells us that the sum of all individual payoffs from such investments will be larger than the collective payoff. In any tennis match, for example, each contestant will get a sizable payoff from money spent on fitness trainers and sports psychologists, yet each match will have exactly one winner and one loser, no matter how much players spend. The overall gain to tennis spectators is likely to be small, and the overall gain to players as a group must be zero. To the extent that each contestant's payoff depends on his or her relative performance, then, the incentive to undertake such investments will be excessive, from a collective point of view.

Consider the following example.

Why do football players take anabolic steroids?

ECONOMIC NATURALIST 11.8

The offensive linemen of many National Football League teams currently average more than 330 pounds. In the 1970s, by contrast, offensive linemen in the league averaged barely 280 pounds, and the all-decade linemen of the 1940s averaged only 229 pounds. One reason that today's players are so much heavier is that players' salaries have escalated sharply over the last two decades, which has intensified competition for the positions. Size and strength are the two cardinal virtues of an offensive lineman, and other things being equal, the job will go to the larger and stronger of two rivals.

Size and strength, in turn, can be enhanced by the consumption of anabolic steroids. But if all players consume these substances, the rank ordering of players by size and strength—and hence the question of who lands the jobs—will be largely unaffected. And since the consumption of anabolic steroids entails potentially serious long-term health consequences, as a group football players are clearly worse off if they consume these drugs. So why do football players take steroids?

The problem here is that contestants for starting berths on the offensive line confront a prisoner's dilemma, like the ones analyzed in Chapter 10. Consider two closely matched rivals—Smith and Jones—who are competing for a single position. If neither takes steroids, each has a 50 percent chance of winning the job and a starting salary of $1 million per year. If both take steroids, each again has a 50 percent chance of winning the job. But if one takes steroids and the other doesn't, the first is sure to win the job. The loser ends up selling insurance for $30,000 per year. Neither likes the fact that the drugs may have adverse health consequences, but each would be willing to take that risk in return for a shot at the big salary. Given these choices, the two competitors face a payoff matrix like the one shown in Table 11.6.

TABLE 11.6
Payoff Matrix for Steroid Consumption

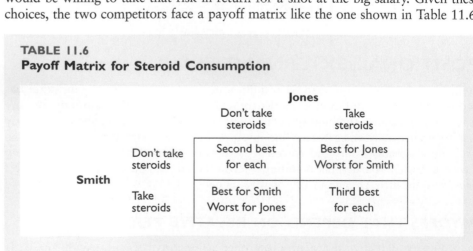

		Jones	
		Don't take steroids	Take steroids
Smith	Don't take steroids	Second best for each	Best for Jones Worst for Smith
	Take steroids	Best for Smith Worst for Jones	Third best for each

Clearly, the dominant strategy for both Smith and Jones is to take steroids. Yet when they do, each gets only the third-best outcome, whereas they could have gotten the second-best outcome by not taking the drugs. Hence the attraction of rules that forbid the consumption of anabolic steroids.

POSITIONAL ARMS RACES

The steroid problem is an example of a **positional externality.** Whenever the payoffs to one contestant depend at least in part on how he or she performs relative to a rival, any step that improves one side's relative position must necessarily worsen the other's. The standing-at-concerts example discussed in Chapter 10 (Economic Naturalist 10.3) is another instance of a positional externality. Just as the invisible hand of the market is weakened by the presence of standard externalities, it is also weakened by positional externalities.

positional externality occurs when an increase in one person's performance reduces the expected reward of another in situations in which reward depends on relative performance

*"I don't know why McGillicuddy is so pleased with
himself. We're <u>all</u> wee, darlin' men here."*

Here is another example of a positional externality.

Why do many grocery stores stay open all night, even in small towns?

Ithaca, New York, has seven large supermarkets, five of which are open 24 hours a day. The convenience of all-night shopping could be maintained at lower cost if all but one of the stores were to close during late-night hours. Why do many remain open?

Most people do the bulk of their shopping at a single store. If other relevant factors—price, location, merchandise quality, and so on—are essentially the same, people will choose the store with the most convenient hours. Suppose the two leading stores, Tops and Wegmans, currently close at midnight and are considering whether to stay open until 1 A.M. If one does so and the other doesn't, the store that is open longer will capture the lion's share of all business, not just from midnight to 1 A.M. but during other hours as well, because most people will do most of their shopping at the store with the most attractive offering. But suppose the benefit the public receives when each store stays open an extra hour—as measured by the higher prices people are willing to pay—is smaller than the cost to both stores of staying open the extra hour. Each store will then face a payoff matrix like the one shown in Table 11.7.

ECONOMIC
NATURALIST
11.9

TABLE 11.7
Payoff Matrix for Extended Shopping Hours

		Wegmans	
		Close at midnight	Close at 1:00 A.M.
Tops	Close at midnight	Second best for each	Best for Wegmans Worst for Tops
	Close at 1:00 A.M.	Best for Tops Worst for Wegmans	Third best for each

In this situation, the dominant strategy for each store is to remain open an extra hour, even though each would be better off if both closed at midnight. And of course, the rivalry does not stop there, for if both stay open until 1 A.M., each will see an opportunity to better its rival by staying open until 2. As long as the cost of staying open another hour is small relative to the gains received, all stores will stay open 24 hours a day. But though consumers do gain when stores remain open longer, beyond some point, the benefit to consumers is small relative to the costs borne by merchants. The problem is that for any individual merchant who fails to match a rival's hours, the costs will be even larger.

In such situations, the public might be well served by an amendment to the antitrust laws that permits stores to cooperate to limit their hours, perhaps through an agreement calling for each store to serve in rotation as the only all-night grocery. Local statutes that limit business hours might serve the same purpose. Such statutes, often called *blue laws,* remain on the books in many jurisdictions.

We have seen that positional externalities often lead contestants to engage in an escalating series of mutually offsetting investments in performance enhancement. We call such spending patterns **positional arms races.**

POSITIONAL ARMS CONTROL AGREEMENTS

Because positional arms races produce inefficient outcomes, people have an incentive to curtail them. Steps taken to reduce positional arms races, such as blue laws and rules against anabolic steroids, may therefore be thought of as **positional arms control agreements.**

Once you become aware of positional arms races, you will begin to see examples of them almost everywhere. You can hone your skills as an economic naturalist by asking these questions about every competitive situation you observe: What form do the investments in performance enhancement take? What steps have contestants taken to limit these investments? Sometimes positional arms control agreements are achieved by the imposition of formal rules or by the signing of legal contracts. Some examples of this type of agreement follow.

Campaign spending limits In the United States, presidential candidates routinely spend more than $100 million on advertising. Yet if both candidates double their spending on ads, each one's odds of winning will remain essentially the same. Recognition of this pattern led Congress to adopt strict spending limits for presidential candidates. (That those regulations have proved difficult to enforce does not call into question the logic behind the legislation.)

Roster limits Major League Baseball permits franchises to have only 25 players on the roster during the regular season. The National Football League sets its roster limit at 49; the National Basketball Association at 12. Why these limits? In their absence, any team could increase its chance of winning by simply

---

positional arms race a series of mutually offsetting investments in performance enhancement that is stimulated by a positional externality

positional arms control agreement an agreement in which contestants attempt to limit mutually offsetting investments in performance enhancement adding players. Inevitably, other teams would follow suit. On the plausible assumption that, beyond some point, larger rosters do not add much to the entertainment value for fans, roster limits are a sensible way to deliver sports entertainment at a more reasonable cost.

Arbitration agreements In the business world, contracting parties often sign a binding agreement that commits them to arbitration in the event of a dispute. By doing so, they sacrifice the option of pursuing their interests as fully as they might wish to later, but they also insulate themselves from costly legal battles. Other parties in the legal system may sometimes take steps to limit spending on litigation. For example, a federal judge in South Dakota recently announced—presumably to the approval of litigants—that he would read only the first 15 pages of any brief submitted to his court.

Mandatory starting dates for kindergarten A child who is a year or so older than most of her kindergarten classmates is likely to perform better, in relative terms, than if she had entered school with children her own age. And since most parents are aware that admission to prestigious universities and eligibility for top jobs upon graduation depend largely on *relative* academic performance, many are tempted to keep their children out of kindergarten a year longer than necessary. Yet there is no social advantage in holding *all* children back an extra year, since their relative performance would essentially be unaffected. In most jurisdictions, therefore, the law requires children who reach their fifth birthday before December 1 of a given year to start kindergarten the same year.

SOCIAL NORMS AS POSITIONAL ARMS CONTROL AGREEMENTS

In some cases, social norms may take the place of formal agreements to curtail positional arms races. Some familiar examples follow.

Nerd norms Some students care more—in the short run, at least—about the grades they get than how much they actually learn. When such students are graded on the curve—that is, on the basis of their performance relative to other students—a positional arms race ensues, because if all students were to double the amount of time they studied, the distribution of grades would remain essentially the same. Students who find themselves in this situation are often quick to embrace "nerd norms," which brand as social misfits those who "study too hard."

Fashion norms Social norms regarding dress and fashion often change quickly because of positional competitions. Consider, for instance, the person who wishes to be on the cutting edge of fashion. In some American social circles during the 1950s, that goal could be accomplished by having pierced ears. But as more and more people adopted the practice, it ceased to communicate avant-garde status. At the same time, those who wanted to make a conservative fashion statement gradually became freer to have their ears pierced.

For a period during the 1960s and 1970s, one could be on fashion's cutting edge by wearing two earrings in one earlobe. But by the 1990s multiple ear piercings had lost much of their social significance, the threshold of cutting-edge status having been raised to upward of a dozen piercings of each ear, or a smaller number of piercings of the nose, eyebrows, or other body parts. A similar escalation has taken place in the number, size, and placement of tattoos.

The increase in the required number of tattoos or body piercings has not changed the value of avant-garde fashion status to those who desire it. Being on the outer limits of fashion has much the same meaning now as it once did. So to the extent that there are costs associated with body piercings, tattoos, and other steps required to achieve avant-garde status, the current fashions are wasteful compared to earlier ones. In this sense, the erosion of social norms against tattoos and body piercings has produced a social loss. Of course, the costs

Is being on fashion's cutting edge more valuable now than in the 1950s?

Fabian Bimmer/Associated Press

associated with this loss are small in most cases. Yet since each body piercing entails a small risk of infection, the costs will continue to rise with the number of piercings. And once those costs reach a certain threshold, support may mobilize on behalf of social norms that discourage body mutilation.

Norms of taste Similar cycles occur with respect to behaviors considered to be in bad taste. In the 1950s, for example, prevailing norms prevented major national magazines from accepting ads that featured nude photographs. Naturally, advertisers had a powerful incentive to chip away at such norms in an effort to capture the reader's limited attention. And indeed, taboos against nude photographs have eroded in the same way as taboos against body mutilation.

Consider, for instance, the evolution of perfume ads. First came the nude silhouette; then, increasingly well-lighted and detailed nude photographs; and more recently, photographs of what appear to be group sex acts. Each innovation achieved just the desired effect: capturing the reader's instant and rapt attention. Inevitably, however, other advertisers followed suit, causing a shift in our sense of what is considered attention-grabbing. Photographs that once would have shocked readers now often draw little more than a bored glance.

Opinions differ, of course, about whether this change is an improvement. Many believe that the earlier, stricter norms were ill-advised, the legacy of a more prudish and repressive era. Yet even people who take that view are likely to believe that *some* kinds of photographic material ought not to be used in magazine advertisements. Obviously, what is acceptable will differ from person to person, and each person's threshold of discomfort will depend in part on current standards. But as advertisers continue to break new ground in their struggle to capture attention, the point may come when people begin to mobilize in favor of stricter standards of "public decency." Such a campaign would provide yet another example of a positional arms control agreement.

Norms against vanity Cosmetic and reconstructive surgery has produced dramatic benefits for many people, enabling badly disfigured accident victims to recover

"We're looking for the kind of bad taste that will grab—but not appall."

a normal appearance. It has also eliminated the extreme self-consciousness felt by people born with strikingly unusual features. Such surgery, however, is by no means confined to the conspicuously disfigured. Increasingly, "normal" people are seeking surgical improvements to their appearance. Some 2 million cosmetic "procedures" were done in 1991—six times the number just a decade earlier[1]—and demand has continued to grow steadily in the years since. Once a carefully guarded secret, these procedures are now offered as prizes in southern California charity raffles. And morticians have begun to complain that the noncombustible silicon implants used in breast and buttocks augmentation are clogging their crematoria.

In individual cases, cosmetic surgery may be just as beneficial as reconstructive surgery is for accident victims. Buoyed by the confidence of having a straight nose or a wrinkle-free complexion, patients sometimes go on to achieve much more than they ever thought possible. But the growing use of cosmetic surgery has also had an unintended side effect: It has altered the standards of normal appearance. A nose that once would have seemed only slightly larger than average may now seem jarringly big. The same person who once would have looked like an average 55-year-old may now look nearly 70. And someone who once would have tolerated slightly thinning hair or an average amount of cellulite may now feel compelled to undergo hair transplantation or liposuction. Because such procedures shift people's frame of reference, their payoffs to individuals are misleadingly large. From a social perspective, therefore, reliance on them is likely to be excessive.

Legal sanctions against cosmetic surgery are difficult to imagine. But some communities have embraced powerful social norms against cosmetic, surgery, heaping scorn and ridicule on the consumers of face-lifts and tummy tucks. In individual cases, such norms may seem cruel. Yet without them, many more people might feel compelled to bear the risk and expense of cosmetic surgery.

■ SUMMARY ■

- Externalities are the costs and benefits of activities that accrue to people who are not directly involved in those activities. When all parties affected by externalities can negotiate with one another at no cost, the invisible hand of the market will produce an efficient allocation of resources. According to the Coase theorem, the allocation of resources is efficient in such cases because the parties affected by externalities can compensate others for taking remedial action.

- Negotiation over externalities is often impractical, however. In these cases, the self-serving actions of individuals typically will not lead to an efficient outcome. The attempt to forge solutions to the problems caused by externalities is one of the most important rationales for collective action. Sometimes collective action takes the form of laws and government regulations that alter the incentives facing those who generate, or are affected by, externalities. Such remedies work best when they place the burden of accommodation on the parties who can accomplish it at the lowest cost. Traffic laws, zoning laws, environmental protection laws, and free speech laws are examples.

- Curbing pollution and other negative externalities entails costs as well as benefits. The optimal amount of pollution reduction is the amount for which the marginal benefit of further reduction just equals the marginal cost. In general,

this formula implies that the socially optimal level of pollution, or of any other negative externality, is greater than zero.

- When grazing land and other valuable resources are owned in common, no one has an incentive to take the opportunity cost of using those resources into account. This problem is known as the tragedy of the commons. Defining and enforcing private rights governing the use of valuable resources is often an effective solution to the tragedy of the commons. Not surprisingly, most economically successful nations have well-developed institutions of private property. Property that belongs to everyone belongs, in effect, to no one. Not only is its potential economic value never fully realized; it usually ends up having no value at all.

- The difficulty of enforcing property rights in certain situations explains a variety of inefficient outcomes, such as the excessive harvest of whales in international waters and the premature harvest of timber on remote public lands. The excessive pollution of seas that are bordered by many countries also results from a lack of enforceable property rights.

- Situations in which people's rewards depend on how well they perform in relation to their rivals give rise to positional externalities. In these situations, any step that improves one side's relative position necessarily worsens the other's.

[1]*The Economist,* January 11, 1992, p. 25.

Positional externalities tend to spawn positional arms races—escalating patterns of mutually offsetting investments in performance enhancement. Collective measures to curb positional arms races are known as positional arms control agreements. These collective actions may take the form of formal regulations or rules, such as rules against anabolic steroids in sports, campaign spending limits, and binding arbitration agreements. Informal social norms can also curtail positional arms races.

■ KEY TERMS ■

Coase theorem (281)
external benefit (278)
external cost (278)
externality (278)

negative externality (278)
positional arms control agreement (294)
positional arms race (294)

positional externality (293)
positive externality (278)
tragedy of the commons (289)

■ REVIEW QUESTIONS ■

1. What incentive problem explains why the freeways in cities like Los Angeles suffer from excessive congestion?

2. How would you explain to a friend why the optimal amount of freeway congestion is not zero?

3. If Congress could declare any activity that imposes external costs on others illegal, would such legislation be advisable?

4. Why does the Great Salt Lake, which is located wholly within the state of Utah, suffer lower levels of pollution than Lake Erie, which is bordered by several states and Canada?

5. Explain why the wearing of high-heeled shoes might be viewed as the result of a positional externality.

■ PROBLEMS ■

1. Determine whether the following statements are true or false, and briefly explain why:
   a. A given total emission reduction in a polluting industry will be achieved at the lowest possible total cost when the cost of the last unit of pollution curbed is equal for each firm in the industry.
   b. In an attempt to lower their costs of production, firms sometimes succeed merely in shifting costs to outsiders.

2. Phoebe keeps a bee farm next door to an apple orchard. She chooses her optimal number of beehives by selecting the honey output level at which her private marginal benefit from beekeeping equals her private marginal cost.
   a. Assume that Phoebe's private marginal benefit and marginal cost curves from beekeeping are normally shaped. Draw a diagram of them.
   b. Phoebe's bees help to pollinate the blossoms in the apple orchard, increasing the fruit yield. Show the social marginal benefit from Phoebe's beekeeping in your diagram.
   c. Phoebe's bees are Africanized killer bees that aggressively sting anyone who steps into their flight path. Phoebe, fortunately, is naturally immune to the bees' venom. Show the social marginal cost curve from Phoebe's beekeeping in your diagram.
   d. Indicate the socially optimal quantity of beehives on your diagram. Is it higher or lower than the privately optimal quantity? Explain.

3. Suppose the supply curve of boom box rentals in Golden Gate Park is given by $P = 5 + 0.1Q$, where P is the daily rent per unit in dollars and Q is the volume of units rented in hundreds per day. The demand curve for boom boxes is $20 - 0.2Q$. If each boom box imposes $3 per day in noise costs on others, by how much will the equilibrium number of boom boxes rented exceed the socially optimal number?

4. Refer to Problem 3. How would the imposition of a tax of $3 per unit on each daily boom box rental affect efficiency in this market?

5. Suppose the law says that Jones may *not* emit smoke from his factory unless he gets permission from Smith, who lives downwind. If the relevant costs and benefits of filtering the smoke from Jones's production process are as shown in the following table, and if Jones and Smith can negotiate with one another at no cost, will Jones emit smoke?

	Jones emits smoke	Jones does not emit smoke
Surplus for Jones	$200	$160
Surplus for Smith	400	420

6. John and Karl can live together in a two-bedroom apartment for $500 per month, or each can rent a single-bedroom apartment for $350 per month. Aside from the rent, the two would be indifferent between living together and living separately, except for one problem: John leaves dirty dishes in the sink every night. Karl would be willing to pay up to $175 per month to avoid John's dirty dishes. John, for his part, would be willing to pay up to $225 to be able to continue his sloppiness. Should John and Karl live together? If they do, will there be dirty dishes in the sink? Explain.

7. How, if at all, would your answer to Problem 6 differ if John would be willing to pay up to $30 per month to avoid giving up his privacy by sharing quarters with Karl?

8. Barton and Statler are neighbors in an apartment complex in downtown Manhattan. Barton is a concert pianist, and Statler is a poet working on an epic poem. Barton rehearses his concert pieces on the baby grand piano in his front room, which is directly above Statler's study. The following matrix shows the monthly payoffs to Barton and Statler when Barton's front room is and is not soundproofed. The soundproofing will be effective only if it is installed in Barton's apartment.

	Soundproofed	Not soundproofed
Gains to Barton	$100/month	$150/month
Gains to Statler	$120/month	$80/month

a. If Barton has the legal right to make any amount of noise he wants and he and Statler can negotiate with one another at no cost, will Barton install and maintain soundproofing? Explain. Is his choice socially efficient?

b. If Statler has the legal right to peace and quiet and can negotiate with Barton at no cost, will Barton install and maintain soundproofing? Explain. Is his choice socially efficient?

c. Does the attainment of an efficient outcome depend on whether Barton has the legal right to make noise, or Statler the legal right to peace and quiet?

9. Refer to Problem 8. Barton decides to buy a full-sized grand piano. The new payoff matrix is as follows:

	Soundproofed	Not soundproofed
Gains to Barton	$100/month	$150/month
Gains to Statler	$120/month	$60/month

a. If Statler has the legal right to peace and quiet and Barton and Statler can negotiate at no cost, will Barton install and maintain soundproofing? Explain. Is this outcome socially efficient?

b. Suppose that Barton has the legal right to make as much noise as he likes and that negotiating an agreement with Barton costs $15 per month. Will Barton install and maintain soundproofing? Explain. Is this outcome socially efficient?

c. Suppose Statler has the legal right to peace and quiet, and it costs $15 per month for Statler and Barton to negotiate any agreement. (Compensation for noise damage can be paid without incurring negotiation cost.) Will Barton install and maintain soundproofing? Is this outcome socially efficient?

d. Why does the attainment of a socially efficient outcome now depend on whether Barton has the legal right to make noise?

10.* A village has six residents, each of whom has accumulated savings of $100. Each villager can use this money either to buy a government bond that pays 15 percent interest per year or to buy a year-old llama, send it onto the commons to graze, and sell it after 1 year. The price the villager gets for the 2-year-old llama depends on the quality of the fleece it grows while grazing on the commons. That in turn depends on the animal's access to grazing, which depends on the number of llamas sent to the commons, as shown in the following table:

Number of llamas on the commons	Price per 2-year-old llama ($)
1	122
2	118
3	116
4	114
5	112
6	109

The villagers make their investment decisions one after another, and their decisions are public.

a. If each villager decides individually how to invest, how many llamas will be sent onto the commons, and what will be the resulting net village income?

b. What is the socially optimal number of llamas for this village? Why is that different from the actual number? What would net village income be if the socially optimal number of llamas were sent onto the commons?

c. The village committee votes to auction the right to graze llamas on the commons to the highest bidder. Assuming villagers can both borrow and lend at 15 percent annual interest, how much will the right sell for at auction? How will the new owner use the right, and what will be the resulting village income?

▪ ANSWERS TO IN-CHAPTER EXERCISES ▪

11.1 Since Fitch gains $50 per day when Abercrombie operates with a filter, he could pay Abercrombie as much as $49 per day and still come out ahead.

11.2 If the two were to live together, the most efficient way to resolve the telephone problem would be as before, for Betty to give up reasonable access to the phone. But on top of that cost, which is $150, Betty would also bear a $60 cost from the loss of her privacy. The total cost of their living together would thus be $210 per month. Since that amount is greater than the $200 saving in rent, the two should live separately.

11.3 The income figures from the different levels of investment in cattle would remain as before, as shown in the table. What is different is the opportunity cost of investing in each steer, which is now $11 per year instead of $13. The last column of the table shows that the socially optimal number of steers is now 2 instead of 1. And if individuals still favor holding cattle, all other things being equal, they will now send 5 steers onto the commons instead of 4, as shown in the middle column.

Number of steers on the commons	Price per 2-year-old steer ($)	Income per steer ($/year)	Total village income ($/year)	Marginal income ($/year)
1	126	26	26	
				26
2	119	19	38	
				12
3	116	16	48	
				10
4	113	13	52	
				4
5	111	11	55	
				3

*Problems marked with an asterisk (*) are more difficult.

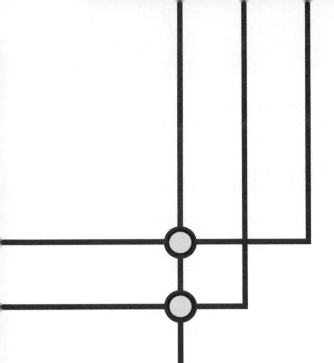

THE ECONOMICS
OF INFORMATION

■

Years ago, a naive young economist spent a week in Kashmir on a houseboat on scenic Dal Lake, outside the capital city of Srinagar. Kashmir is renowned for its woodcarvings, and one afternoon a man in a gondola stopped by to show the economist some of his wooden bowls. When the economist expressed interest in one of them, the woodcarver quoted a price of 200 rupees. The economist had lived in that part of Asia long enough to realize that the price was more than the woodcarver expected to get, so he made a counteroffer of 100 rupees.

The woodcarver appeared to take offense, saying that he couldn't possibly part with the bowl for less than 175 rupees. Suspecting that the woodcarver was merely feigning anger, the young economist held firm. The woodcarver appeared to become even angrier, but quickly retreated to 150 rupees. The economist politely restated his unwillingness to pay more than 100 rupees. The woodcarver then tried 125 rupees, and again the economist replied that 100 was his final offer. Finally, they struck a deal at 100 rupees, and with cash in hand, the woodcarver left in a huff.

Pleased with his purchase, the economist showed it to the houseboat's owner later that evening. "It's a lovely bowl," he agreed, and asked how much the economist had paid for it. The economist told him, expecting praise for his negotiating prowess. The host's failed attempt at suppressing a laugh was the economist's first clue that he had paid too much. When asked how much such a bowl would normally sell for, the houseboat owner was reluctant to respond. But the economist pressed him, and the host speculated that the seller had probably hoped for 30 rupees at most.

Adam Smith's invisible hand theory presumes that buyers are fully informed about the myriad ways in which they might spend their money—what goods and services are available, what prices they sell for, how long they last, how frequently they break down, and so on. But of course no one is ever really *fully* informed about anything. And sometimes, as in the transaction with the woodcarver, people are completely ignorant of even the most basic information. Still, life goes on, and most people muddle through somehow.

Consumers employ a variety of strategies for gathering information, some of which are better than others. They read *Consumer Reports,* talk to family and friends, visit stores, kick the tires on used cars, and so on. But one of the most important aspects of choosing intelligently without having complete information is having at least some idea of the extent of one's ignorance. Someone once said that there are two kinds of consumers in the world: those who don't know what they're doing and those who don't know that they don't know what they're doing. As in the case of the wooden bowl, the people in the second category are the ones who are most likely to choose foolishly.

Basic economic principles can help you in identifying those situations in which additional information is most likely to prove helpful. In this chapter, we will explore what those principles tell us about how much information to acquire and how to make the best use of limited information.

HOW THE MIDDLEMAN ADDS VALUE

One of the most common problems consumers confront is the need to choose among different versions of a product whose many complex features they do not fully understand. As Example 12.1 illustrates, in such cases consumers can sometimes rely on the knowledge of others.

EXAMPLE 12.1

How should a consumer decide which pair of skis to buy?

You need a new pair of skis, but the technology has changed considerably since you bought your last pair, and you don't know which of the current brands and models would be best for you. Skis R Us has the largest selection, so you go there and ask for advice. The salesperson appears to be well informed; after asking about your experience level and how aggressively you ski, he recommends the Salomon X-Scream 9. You buy a pair for $600, then head back to your apartment and show them to your roommate, who says that you could have bought them on the Internet for only $400. How do you feel about your purchase? Are the different prices charged by the two suppliers related to the services they offer? Were the extra services you got by shopping at Skis R Us worth the extra $200?

Internet retailers can sell for less because their costs are so much lower than those of full-service retail stores. Those stores, after all, must hire knowledgeable salespeople, put their merchandise on display, rent space in expensive shopping malls, and so on. Internet retailers and mail-order houses, by contrast, typically employ unskilled telephone clerks, and they store their merchandise in cheap warehouses. But if you are a consumer who doesn't know which is the right product for you, the extra expense of shopping at a specialty retailer is likely to be a good investment. Spending $600 on the right skis is smarter than spending $400 on the wrong ones.

Many people believe that wholesalers, retailers, and other agents who assist manufacturers in the sale of their products play a fundamentally different economic role from the one played by those who actually make the products. In this view, the production worker is the ultimate source of economic value added. Sales agents are often disparaged as mere middlemen, parasites on the efforts of others who do the real work.

MANKOFF

"On the one hand, eliminating the middleman would result in lower costs, increased sales, and greater consumer satisfaction; on the other hand, we're the middleman."

On a superficial level, this view might seem to be supported by the fact that many people go to great lengths to avoid paying for the services of sales agents. Many manufacturers cater to them by offering consumers a chance to "buy direct" and sidestep the middleman's commission. But on closer examination, we can see that the economic role of sales agents is essentially the same as that of production workers. Consider Example 12.2.

How does better information affect economic surplus?

EXAMPLE 12.2

Ellis has just inherited a rare Babe Ruth baseball card issued during the great slugger's rookie year. He'd like to keep the card but has reluctantly decided to sell it to pay some overdue bills. His reservation price for the card is $300, but he is hoping to get significantly more for it. He has two ways of selling it: He can place a classified ad in the local newspaper for $5, or he can list the card on eBay, the Internet auction service. If he sells the card on eBay, the fee will be 5 percent of the winning bid.

Because Ellis lives in a small town with few potential buyers of rare baseball cards, the local buyer with the highest reservation price is willing to pay $400 at most. If Ellis lists the card on eBay, however, a much larger number of potential buyers will see it. If the two eBay shoppers who are willing to pay the most for Ellis's card have reservation prices of $900 and $800, respectively, by how much will the total economic surplus be larger if Ellis sells his card on eBay? (For the sake of simplicity, assume that the eBay commission and the classified ad fee equal the respective costs of providing those services.)

In an eBay auction, each bidder reports his or her reservation price for an item. When the auction closes, the bidder with the highest reservation price wins, and the price he or she pays is the reservation price of the second highest bidder. So in this example, the Babe Ruth baseball card will sell for $800 if Ellis lists it on eBay. Net of the $40 eBay commission, Ellis will receive a payment of $760, or $460 more than his reservation price for the card. Ellis's economic surplus will thus be $460. The winning bidder's surplus will be $900 − $800 = $100, so the total surplus from selling the card on eBay will be $560.

If Ellis instead advertises the card in the local newspaper and sells it to the local buyer whose reservation price is $400, then Ellis's surplus (net of the newspaper's $5 fee) will be only $95, and the buyer's surplus will be $0. Thus total economic surplus will be $560 − $95 = $465 larger if Ellis sells the card on eBay than if he lists it in the local newspaper.

eBay provides a service by making information available to people who can make good use of it. A real increase in economic surplus results when an item ends up in the hands of someone who values it more highly than the person who otherwise would have bought it. That increase is just as valuable as the increase in surplus that results from manufacturing cars, growing corn, or any other productive activity.

 RECAP **HOW THE MIDDLEMAN ADDS VALUE**

In a world of incomplete information, sales agents and other middlemen add genuine economic value by increasing the extent to which goods and services find their way to the consumers who value them most. When a sales agent causes a good to be purchased by a person who values it by $20,000 more than the person who would have bought it in the absence of a sales agent, that agent augments total economic surplus by $20,000, an achievement on a par with the production of a $20,000 car.

THE OPTIMAL AMOUNT OF INFORMATION

 Without a doubt, having more information is better than having less. But information is generally costly to acquire. In most situations, the value of additional information will decline beyond some point. And because of the low-hanging-fruit principle, people tend to gather information from the cheapest sources first before turning to more costly ones. Typically, then, the marginal benefit of information will decline, and its marginal cost will rise, as the amount of information gathered increases.

THE COST-BENEFIT TEST

 Information gathering is an activity like any other. The cost-benefit principle tells us that a rational consumer will continue to gather information as long as its marginal benefit exceeds its marginal cost. Suppose, for the sake of discussion, that analysts had devised a scale that permits us to measure units of information, as on the horizontal axis of Figure 12.1. If the relevant marginal cost and marginal benefit curves are as shown in the diagram, a rational consumer will acquire I^* units of information, the amount for which the marginal benefit of information equals its marginal cost.

Another way to think about Figure 12.1 is that it shows the optimal level of ignorance. When the cost of acquiring information exceeds its benefits, acquiring

FIGURE 12.1
The Optimal Amount of Information.
For the marginal cost and benefit curves shown, the optimal amount of information is I^*. Beyond that point, information costs more to acquire than it is worth.

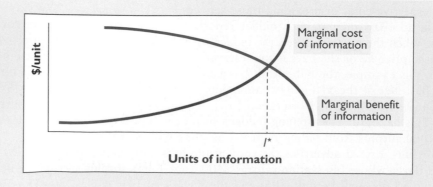

additional information simply does not pay. If information could be acquired free, decision makers would, of course, be glad to have it. But when the cost of acquiring the information exceeds the gain in value from the decision it will facilitate, people are better off to remain ignorant.

THE FREE-RIDER PROBLEM

Does the invisible hand assure that the optimal amount of advice will be made available to consumers in the marketplace? The next example suggests one reason that it might not.

Why is finding a knowledgeable salesclerk often difficult?

People can choose for themselves whether to bear the extra cost of retail shopping. Those who value advice and convenience can pay slightly higher prices, while those who know what they want can buy for less from a mail-order house. True or false: It follows that private incentives lead to the optimal amount of retail service.

The market would provide the optimal level of retail service except for one practical problem, namely, that consumers can make use of the services offered by retail stores without paying for them. After benefiting from the advice of informed salespersons and after inspecting the merchandise, the consumer can return home and buy the same item from an Internet retailer or mail-order house. Not all consumers do so, of course. But the fact that customers can benefit from the information provided by retail stores without paying for it is an example of the **free-rider problem,** an incentive problem that results in too little of a good or service being produced. Because retail stores have difficulty recovering the cost of providing information, private incentives are likely to yield less than the socially optimal level of retail service. So the statement above is false.

Why did Rivergate Books, the last bookstore in Lambertville, New Jersey, recently go out of business?

Small independent bookstores often manage to survive competition from large chains like Borders and Barnes and Noble by offering more personalized service. Janet Holbrooke, the proprietor of Rivergate Books, followed this strategy successfully for more than a decade before closing her doors in 1999. What finally led her to quit?

According to Mrs. Holbrooke, a retired English teacher, "When Barnes and Noble came in, a few people were curious, went to look, and bought some books. But they came back and said they wanted to be able to find things more easily and have clerks that had an idea of what their grandchildren might like to read, and we held our own."[1] Customers were also drawn in by special events, such as readings and book signings by authors. But during one of these events, Mrs. Holbrooke saw that her store's days were numbered:

> I found out that Gerald Stern, who won the National Book Award for poetry, was a Lambertville man, and I asked him if he would come in and do a reading. He gave a wonderful presentation, and we had a good turnout, but we sold very few books, and then I overheard one of the women who were presenting a book for his signature say that she had bought hers through Amazon.com. Here I thought we were bringing something special to the town. But if people are going to bring in books that they got from the Internet, then we don't have a chance.[2]

ECONOMIC NATURALIST 12.1

free-rider problem an incentive problem in which too little of a good or service is produced because nonpayers cannot be excluded from using it

ECONOMIC NATURALIST 12.2

---

[1]Quoted by Iver Peterson, "A Bookseller Quits Battle with Internet," *The New York Times,* June 27, 1999, p. 21.
[2]Ibid.

"In reply to your inquiry regarding the Burke garden hoe, please visit our Worldwide Web home page at: http://www.burke1903.com."

EXERCISE 12.1

Apart from its possible contribution to free-rider problems, how is increased access to the Internet likely to affect total economic surplus?

TWO GUIDELINES FOR RATIONAL SEARCH

In practice, of course, the exact value of additional information is difficult to know, so the amount of time and effort one should invest in acquiring it is not always obvious. But as Examples 12.3 and 12.4 suggest, the cost-benefit principle provides a strong conceptual framework for thinking about this problem.

EXAMPLE 12.3

Should a person living in Paris, Texas, spend more or less time searching for an apartment than someone living in Paris, France?

Suppose that rents for one-bedroom apartments in Paris, Texas, vary between $300 and $500 per month, with an average rent of $400 per month. Rents for similar one-bedroom apartments in Paris, France, vary between $2,000 and $3,000 per month, with an average rent of $2,500. In which city should a rational person expect to spend a longer time searching for an apartment?

In both cities, visiting additional apartments entails a cost, largely the opportunity cost of one's time. In both cities, the more apartments someone visits, the more likely it is that he or she will find one near the lower end of the rent distribution. But because rents are higher and are spread over a broader range in Paris, France, the expected saving from further time spent searching will be greater there than in Paris, Texas. And so a rational person will expect to spend more time searching for an apartment in France.

Example 12.3 illustrates the principle that spending additional search time is more likely to be worthwhile for expensive items than for cheap ones. For example, one should spend more time searching for a good price on a diamond engagement ring than for a good price on a stone made of cubic zirconium; more time searching for a low fare to Sydney, Australia, than for a low fare to Sidney, New York; and more time searching for a car than for a bicycle. By extension, hiring an agent—someone who can assist with a search—is more likely to be a good investment in searching for something expensive than for something cheap. For example, people typically engage real estate agents to help them find a house, but they seldom hire agents to help them buy a gallon of milk.

Who should expect to search longer for a good price on a used piano?

EXAMPLE 12.4

Both Tom and Tim are shopping for a used upright piano. To examine a piano listed in the classified ads, they must travel to the home of the piano's current owner. If Tom has a car and Tim does not and both are rational, which one should expect to examine fewer pianos before making his purchase?

The benefits of examining an additional piano are the same in both cases, namely, a better chance of finding a good instrument for a low price. But because it is more costly for Tim to examine pianos, he should expect to examine fewer of them than Tom.

Example 12.4 makes the point that when searching becomes more costly, we should expect to do less of it. And as a result, the prices we expect to pay will be higher when the cost of a search is higher.

THE GAMBLE INHERENT IN SEARCH

Suppose you are in the market for a one-bedroom apartment and have found one that rents for $400 per month. Should you rent it or search further in hopes of finding a cheaper apartment? Even in a large market with many vacant apartments, there is no guarantee that searching further will turn up a cheaper or better apartment. Searching further entails a cost, which might outweigh the gain. In general, someone who engages in further search must accept certain costs in return for unknown benefits. Thus further search invariably carries an element of risk.

In thinking about whether to take any gamble, a helpful first step is to compute its **expected value**—the average amount you would win (or lose) if you played that gamble an infinite number of times. To calculate the expected value of a gamble with more than one outcome, we first multiply each outcome by its corresponding probability of occurring, and then add. For example, suppose you win $1 if a coin flip comes up heads and lose $1 if it comes up tails. Since 1/2 is the probability of heads (and also the probability of tails), the expected value of this gamble is $(1/2)(\$1) + (1/2)(-\$1) = 0$. A gamble with an expected value of zero is called a **fair gamble**. If you played this gamble a large number of times, you wouldn't expect to make money, but you also wouldn't expect to lose money.

A **better-than-fair gamble** is one with a positive expected value. (For example, a coin flip in which you win $2 for heads and lose $1 for tails is a better-than-fair gamble.) A **risk-neutral** person is someone who would accept any gamble that is fair or better. A **risk-averse** person is someone who would refuse to take any fair gamble.

expected value of a gamble the sum of the possible outcomes of the gamble multiplied by their respective probabilities

fair gamble a gamble whose expected value is zero

better-than-fair gamble one whose expected value is positive

risk-neutral person someone who would accept any gamble that is fair or better

risk-averse person someone who would refuse any fair gamble

EXERCISE 12.2

Consider a gamble in which you win $4 if you flip a coin and it comes up heads and lose $2 if it comes up tails. What is the expected value of this gamble? Would a risk-neutral person accept it?

In Example 12.5 we apply these concepts to the decision of whether to search further for an apartment.

EXAMPLE 12.5

Should you search further for an apartment?

You have arrived in San Francisco for a 1-month summer visit and are searching for a one-bedroom sublet for the month. There are only two kinds of one-bedroom apartments in the neighborhood in which you wish to live, identical in every respect except that one rents for $400 and the other for $360. Of the vacant apartments in this neighborhood, 80 percent are of the first type and 20 percent are of the second type. The only way you can discover the rent for a vacant apartment is to visit it in person. The first apartment you visit is one that rents for $400. If you are risk-neutral and your opportunity cost of visiting an additional apartment is $6, should you visit another apartment or rent the one you've found?

If you visit one more apartment, you have a 20 percent chance of it being one that rents for $360 and an 80 percent chance of it being one that rents for $400. If the former, you'll save $40 in rent, but if the latter, you'll face the same rent as before. Since the cost of a visit is $6, visiting another apartment is a gamble with a 20 percent chance to win $40 − $6 = $34 and an 80 percent chance of losing $6 (which means "winning" −$6). The expected value of this gamble is thus (0.20)($34) + (0.80)(−$6) = $2. Visiting another apartment is a better-than-fair gamble, and since you are risk-neutral, you should take it.

EXERCISE 12.3

Refer to Example 12.5. Suppose you visit another apartment and discover it, too, is one that rents for $400. If you are risk-neutral, should you visit a third apartment?

THE COMMITMENT PROBLEM WHEN SEARCH IS COSTLY

When most people search for an apartment, they want a place to live not for just a month but for a year or more. Most landlords, for their part, are also looking for long-term tenants. Similarly, few people accept a full-time job in their chosen field unless they expect to hold the job for several years. Firms, too, generally prefer employees who will stay for extended periods. Finally, when most people search for mates, they are looking for someone with whom to settle down.

Because in all these cases search is costly, examining every possible option will never make sense. Apartment hunters don't visit every vacant apartment, nor do landlords interview every possible tenant. Job seekers don't visit every employer, nor do employers interview every job seeker. And not even the most determined searcher can manage to date every eligible mate. In these and other cases, people are rational to end their searches, even though they know a more attractive option surely exists out there somewhere.

But herein lies a difficulty. What happens when, by chance, a more attractive option comes along after the search has ceased? Few people would rent an apartment if they thought the landlord would kick them out the moment another tenant came along who was willing to pay higher rent. Few landlords would be willing to rent to a tenant if they expected her to move out the moment she discovers a cheaper apartment. Employers, job seekers, and people who are looking for mates would have similar reservations about entering relationships that could be terminated once a better option happened to come along.

This potential difficulty in maintaining stable matches between partners in ongoing relationships would not arise in a world of perfect information. In such a world, everyone would end up in the best possible relationship, so no one would be tempted to renege. But when information is costly and the search must be limited, there will always be the potential for existing relationships to dissolve.

In most contexts, people solve this problem not by conducting an exhaustive search (which is usually impossible, in any event) but by committing themselves to remain in a relationship once a mutual agreement has been reached to terminate the search. Thus landlords and tenants sign a lease that binds them to one another for a specified period, usually one year. Employees and firms enter into employment contracts, either formal or informal, under which each promises to honor his obligations to the other, except under extreme circumstances. And in most countries a marriage contract penalizes those who abandon their spouses. Entering into such commitments limits the freedom to pursue one's own interests. Yet most people freely accept such restrictions, because they know the alternative is failure to solve the search problem.

RECAP   THE OPTIMAL AMOUNT OF INFORMATION

Additional information creates value, but it is also costly to acquire. A rational consumer will continue to acquire information until its marginal benefit equals its marginal cost. Beyond that point, it is rational to remain uninformed.

Markets for information do not always function perfectly. Free-rider problems often hinder retailers' efforts to provide information to consumers.

Search inevitably entails an element of risk, because costs must be incurred without any assurance that search will prove fruitful. A rational consumer can minimize this risk by concentrating search efforts on goods for which the variation in price or quality is relatively high and on those for which the cost of search is relatively low.

ASYMMETRIC INFORMATION

One of the most common information problems occurs when the participants in a potential exchange are not equally well informed about the product or service that is offered for sale. For instance, the owner of a used car may know that the car is in excellent mechanical condition, but potential buyers cannot know that merely by inspecting it or taking it for a test drive. Economists use the term **asymmetric information** to describe situations in which buyers and sellers are not equally well informed about the characteristics of products or services. In these situations, sellers are typically much better informed than buyers, but sometimes the reverse will be true.

As Example 12.6 illustrates, the problem of asymmetric information can easily prevent exchanges that would benefit both parties.

asymmetric information situations in which buyers and sellers are not equally well informed about the characteristics of goods and services for sale in the marketplace

EXAMPLE 12.6

Will Jane sell her car to Tom?

Jane's 1998 Miata has 70,000 miles on the odometer, but most of these are highway miles driven during weekend trips to see her boyfriend in Toronto. (Highway driving causes less wear and tear on a car than city driving.) Moreover, Jane has maintained the car precisely according to the manufacturer's specifications. In short, she knows her car to be in excellent condition. Because she is about to start graduate school in Boston, however, Jane wants to sell the car. On average,

1998 Miatas sell for a price of $8,000, but because Jane knows her car to be in excellent condition, her reservation price for it is $10,000.

Tom wants to buy a used Miata. He would be willing to pay $13,000 for one that is in excellent condition but only $9,000 for one that is not in excellent condition. Tom has no way of telling whether Jane's Miata is in excellent condition. (He could hire a mechanic to examine the car, but doing so is expensive, and many problems cannot be detected even by a mechanic.) Will Tom buy Jane's car? Is this outcome efficient?

Because Jane's car looks no different from other 1998 Miatas, Tom will not pay $10,000 for it. After all, for only $8,000, he can buy some other 1998 Miata that is in just as good condition, as far as he can tell. Tom therefore will buy someone else's Miata, and Jane's will go unsold. This outcome is not efficient. If Tom had bought Jane's Miata for, say, $11,000, his surplus would have been $2,000 and Jane's another $1,000. Instead, Tom ends up buying a Miata that is in average condition (or worse), and his surplus is only $1,000. Jane gets no economic surplus at all.

THE LEMONS MODEL

We can't be sure, of course, that the Miata Tom ends up buying will be in worse condition than Jane's—since *someone* might have a car in perfect condition that must be sold even if the owner cannot get what it is really worth. Even so, the economic incentives created by asymmetric information suggest that most used cars that are put up for sale will be of lower-than-average quality. One reason is that people who mistreat their cars, or whose cars were never very good to begin with, are more likely than others to want to sell them. Buyers know from experience that cars for sale on the used car market are more likely to be "lemons" than cars that are not for sale. This realization causes them to lower their reservation prices for a used car.

But that's not the end of the story. Once used car prices have fallen, the owners of cars that are in good condition have an even stronger incentive to hold onto them. That causes the average quality of the cars offered for sale on the used car market to decline still further. Berkeley economist George Akerlof, a Nobel laureate, was the first to explain the logic behind this downward spiral.[1] Economists use the term **lemons model** to describe Akerlof's explanation of how asymmetric information affects the average quality of the used goods offered for sale.

lemons model George Akerlof's explanation of how asymmetric information tends to reduce the average quality of goods offered for sale

As Example 12.7 suggests, the lemons model has important practical implications for consumer choice.

EXAMPLE 12.7

Should you buy your aunt's car?

You want to buy a used Honda Accord. Your Aunt Germaine buys a new car every 4 years, and she has a 4-year-old Accord that she is about to trade in. You believe her report that the car is in good condition, and she is willing to sell it to you for $10,000, which is the current blue book value for 4-year-old Accords. (The blue book value of a car is the average price for which cars of that age and model sell in the used car market.) Should you buy your aunt's Honda?

Akerlof's lemons model tells us that cars for sale in the used car market will be of lower average quality than cars of the same vintage that are not for sale. If you believe your aunt's claim that her car is in good condition, then being able to buy it for its blue book value is definitely a good deal for you, since the blue

[1]George Akerlof, "The Market for Lemons," *Quarterly Journal of Economics*, 84:488–500, 1970.

book price is the equilibrium price for a car that is of lower quality than your aunt's.

Examples 12.8 and 12.9 illustrate the conditions under which asymmetric information about product quality results in a market in which *only* lemons are offered for sale.

How much will a naive buyer pay for a used car?

EXAMPLE 12.8

Consider a world with only two kinds of cars, good ones and lemons. An owner knows with certainty which type of car she has, but potential buyers cannot distinguish between the two types. Ten percent of all new cars produced are lemons. Good used cars are worth $10,000 to their owners, but lemons are worth only $6,000. Consider a naive consumer who believes that the used cars currently for sale have the same quality distribution as new cars (i.e., 90 percent good, 10 percent lemons). If this consumer is risk-neutral, how much would he be willing to pay for a used car?

Buying a car of unknown quality is a gamble, but a risk-neutral buyer would be willing to take the gamble provided it is fair. If the buyer can't tell the difference between a good car and a lemon, the probability that he will end up with a lemon is simply the proportion of lemons among the cars from which he chooses. The buyer believes he has a 90 percent chance of getting a good car and a 10 percent chance of getting a lemon. Given the prices he is willing to pay for the two types of car, his expected value of the car he buys will thus be 0.90($10,000) + 0.10($6,000) = $9,600. And since he is risk-neutral, that is his reservation price for a used car.

EXERCISE 12.4

How would your answer to the question posed in Example 12.8 differ if the proportion of new cars that are lemons had been not 10 percent but 20 percent?

Who will sell a used car for what the naive buyer is willing to pay?

EXAMPLE 12.9

Refer to Example 12.8. If you were the owner of a good used car, what would it be worth to you? Would you sell it to a naive buyer? What if you owned a lemon?

Since you know your car is good, it is worth $10,000 to you, by assumption. But since a naive buyer would be willing to pay only $9,600, neither you nor any other owner of a good car would be willing to sell to that buyer. If you had a lemon, of course, you would be happy to sell it to a naive buyer, since the $9,600 the buyer is willing to pay is $3,600 more than the lemon would be worth to you. So the only used cars for sale will be lemons. In time, buyers will revise their naively optimistic beliefs about the quality of the cars for sale on the used car market. In the end, all used cars will sell for a price of $6,000, and all will be lemons.

In practice, of course, the mere fact that a car is for sale does not guarantee that it is a lemon, because the owner of a good car will sometimes be forced to sell it, even at a price that does not reflect its condition. The logic of the lemons model explains this owner's frustration. The first thing sellers in this situation want a prospective buyer to know is the reason they are selling their cars. For example, classified ads often announce, "Just had a baby, must sell my 2002 Corvette" or "Transferred to Germany, must sell my 2003 Toyota Camry." Any time you pay the blue book price for a used car that is for sale for some reason unrelated to its condition, you are beating the market.

Why do new cars lose a significant fraction of their value as soon as they are driven from the showroom?

THE CREDIBILITY PROBLEM IN TRADING

Why can't someone with a high-quality used car simply *tell* the buyer about the car's condition? The difficulty is that buyers' and sellers' interests tend to conflict. Sellers of used cars, for example, have an economic incentive to overstate the quality of their products. Buyers, for their part, have an incentive to understate the amount they are willing to pay for used cars and other products (in the hope of bargaining for a lower price). Potential employees may be tempted to overstate their qualifications for a job. And people searching for mates have been known to engage in deception.

That is not to say that most people *consciously* misrepresent the truth in communicating with their potential trading partners. But people do tend to interpret ambiguous information in ways that promote their own interests. Thus, 92 percent of factory employees surveyed in one study rated themselves as more productive than the average factory worker. Psychologists call this phenomenon the "Lake Wobegon effect," after Garrison Keillor's mythical Minnesota homestead, where "all the children are above average."

Notwithstanding the natural tendency to exaggerate, the parties to a potential exchange can often gain if they can find some means to communicate their knowledge truthfully. In general, however, mere statements of relevant information will not suffice. People have long since learned to discount the used car salesman's inflated claims about the cars he is trying to unload. But as the next example illustrates, though communication between potential adversaries may be difficult, it is not impossible.

EXAMPLE 12.10

How can a used car seller signal high-quality credibly?

Jane knows her Miata to be in excellent condition, and Tom would be willing to pay considerably more than her reservation price if he could be confident of getting such a car. What kind of signal about the car's quality would Tom find credible?

Again, the potential conflict between Tom's and Jane's interests suggests that mere statements about the car's quality may not be persuasive. But suppose Jane offers a warranty, under which she agrees to remedy any defects the car develops over the next 6 months. Jane can afford to extend such an offer because she knows her car is unlikely to need expensive repairs. In contrast, the person who knows his car has a cracked engine block would never extend such an offer. The warranty is a credible signal that the car is in good condition. It enables Tom to buy the car with confidence, to both his and Jane's benefit.

THE COSTLY-TO-FAKE PRINCIPLE

costly-to-fake principle to communicate information credibly to a potential rival, a signal must be costly or difficult to fake

The preceding examples illustrate the **costly-to-fake principle**, which holds that if parties whose interests potentially conflict are to communicate credibly with one another, the signals they send must be costly or difficult to fake. If the seller of a defective car could offer an extensive warranty just as easily as the seller of a good car, a warranty offer would communicate nothing about the car's quality. But warranties entail costs that are significantly higher for defective cars than for good cars—hence their credibility as a signal of product quality.

To the extent that sellers have an incentive to portray a product in the most flattering light possible, their interests conflict with those of buyers, who want the most accurate assessment of product quality possible. Note that in the following example, the costly-to-fake principle applies to a producer's statement about the quality of a product.

Why do firms insert the phrase "As advertised on TV" when they advertise their products in magazines and newspapers?

Company *A* sponsors an expensive national television advertising campaign on behalf of its compact disc player, claiming it has the clearest sound and the best repair record of any CD player in the market. Company *B* makes similar claims in a sales brochure but does not advertise its product on television. If you had no additional information to go on, which company's claim would you find more credible? Why do you suppose Company *A* mentions its TV ads when it advertises its CD player in print media?

Accustomed as we are to discounting advertisers' inflated claims, the information given might seem to provide no real basis for a choice between the two products. On closer examination, however, we see that a company's decision to advertise its product on national television constitutes a credible signal about the product's quality. The cost of a national television campaign can run well into the millions of dollars, a sum a company would be foolish to spend on an inferior product.

For example, in 2002 Pepsi paid Britney Spears $8 million to appear in its two 30-second Super Bowl ads, and it paid more than $3.5 million to Fox TV for broadcasting those ads. National TV ads can attract the potential buyers' attention and persuade a small fraction of them to try a product. But these huge investments pay off only if the resulting initial sales generate other new business—either repeat sales to people who tried the product and liked it or sales to others who heard about the product from a friend.

Because ads cannot persuade buyers that a bad product is a good one, a company that spends millions of dollars advertising a bad product is wasting its money. An expensive national advertising campaign is therefore a credible signal that the producer *thinks* its product is a good one. Of course, the ads don't guarantee that a product *is* a winner, but in an uncertain world, they provide one more piece of information. Note, however, that the relevant information lies in the expenditure on the advertising campaign, not in what the ads themselves say.

These observations may explain why some companies mention their television ads in their print ads. Advertisers understand the costly-to-fake principle and hope that consumers will understand it as well.

As the next example illustrates, the costly-to-fake principle is also well known to many employers.

Why do many companies care so much about elite educational credentials?

Microsoft is looking for a hardworking, smart person for an entry-level managerial position in a new technical products division. Two candidates, Cooper and Duncan, seem alike in every respect but one: Cooper graduated with the highest honors from MIT, while Duncan graduated with a C+ average from Somerville College. Whom should Microsoft hire?

If you want to persuade prospective employers that you are both hardworking and intelligent, there is perhaps no more credible signal than to have graduated with distinction from a highly selective educational institution. Most people would like potential employers to think of them as hardworking and intelligent. But unless you actually have both those qualities, graduating with the highest honors from a school like MIT will be extremely difficult. The fact that Duncan graduated from a much less selective institution and earned only a C+ average is not proof positive that he is not diligent and talented, but companies are forced to play the percentages. In this case the odds strongly favor Cooper.

CONSPICUOUS CONSUMPTION AS A SIGNAL OF ABILITY

Some individuals of high ability are not highly paid. (Remember the best elementary school teacher you ever had.) And some people, such as the multibillionaire investor Warren Buffet, earn a lot, yet spend very little. But such cases run counter to general tendencies. In competitive markets, the people with the most ability tend to receive the highest salaries. And as suggested by the cost-benefit principle, the more someone earns, the more he or she is likely to spend on high-quality goods and services. As the following example suggests, these tendencies often lead us to infer a person's ability from the amount and quality of the goods he consumes.

Why do many clients seem to prefer lawyers who wear expensive suits?

You have been unjustly accused of a serious crime and are looking for an attorney. Your choice is between two lawyers who appear identical in all respects except for the things they buy. One of them wears a cheap polyester suit and arrives at the courthouse in a 10-year-old rust-eaten Dodge Colt. The other wears an impeccably tailored suit and drives a new BMW 745i. If this were the *only* information available to you at the time you chose, which lawyer would you hire?

The correlation between salary and the abilities buyers value most is particularly strong in the legal profession. A lawyer whose clients usually prevail in court will be much more in demand than one whose clients generally lose, and their fees will reflect the difference. The fact that one of the lawyers consumes much more than the other does not *prove* that he is the better lawyer, but if that is the only information you have, you can ill afford to ignore it.

If the less able lawyer loses business because of the suits he wears and the car he drives, why doesn't he simply buy better suits and a more expensive car? His choice is between saving for retirement or spending more on his car and clothing. In one sense, he cannot afford to buy a more expensive car, but in another sense, he cannot afford *not* to. If his current car is discouraging potential clients from hiring him, buying a better one may simply be a prudent investment. But because *all* lawyers have an incentive to make such investments, their effects tend to be mutually offsetting.

When all is said and done, the things people consume will continue to convey relevant information about their respective ability levels. The costly-to-fake principle tells us that the BMW 745i is an effective signal precisely because the lawyer of low ability cannot afford one, no matter how little he saves for retirement. Yet from a social perspective, the resulting spending pattern is inefficient, for the same reason that other positional arms races are inefficient (see Chapter 11). Society would be better off if everyone spent less and saved more for retirement.

The problem of conspicuous consumption as an ability signal does not arise with equal force in every environment. In small towns, where people tend to know one another well, a lawyer who tries to impress people by spending beyond her means is likely to succeed only in demonstrating how foolish she is. Thus the wardrobe a professional person "needs" in towns like Dubuque, Iowa, or Athens, Ohio, costs less than half as much as the wardrobe the same person would need in Manhattan or Los Angeles.

STATISTICAL DISCRIMINATION

In a competitive market with perfect information, the buyer of a service would pay the seller's cost of providing the service. In many markets, however—the market for fire insurance is one example—the seller does not know the exact cost of serving each individual buyer.

In such cases, the missing information has an economic value. If the seller can come up with even a rough estimate of the missing information, she can improve her position. As the following examples illustrate, firms often do so by imputing characteristics to individuals on the basis of the groups to which they belong.

Why do males under 25 years of age pay more than other drivers for auto insurance?

Gerald is 23 years old and is an extremely careful and competent driver. He has never had an accident, or even a moving traffic violation. His twin sister Geraldine has had two accidents, one of them serious, in the last 3 years and has accumulated three speeding tickets during that same period. Why does Gerald pay $1,600 per year for auto insurance, while Geraldine pays only $800?

The expected cost to an insurance company of insuring any given driver depends on the probability that the driver will be involved in an accident. No one knows what that probability is for any given driver, but insurance companies can estimate rather precisely the proportion of drivers in specific groups who will be involved in an accident in any given year. Males under 25 are much more likely than older males and females of any age to become involved in auto accidents. (Testosterone seems to have something to do with it.) Gerald pays more than his sister because even those males under 25 who have never had an accident are more likely to have one than females the same age who have had several accidents.

Of course, females who have had two accidents and accumulated several tickets in the last 3 years are more likely to have an accident than a female with a spotless driving record. The insurance company knows that and has increased Geraldine's premium accordingly. Yet it is still less than her brother's premium. That does not mean that Gerald is in fact more likely to have an accident than Geraldine. Indeed, given the twins' respective driving skills, Geraldine clearly poses the higher risk. But because insurance companies lack such detailed information, they are forced to set rates according to the information they possess.

To remain in business, an insurance company must collect enough money from premiums to cover the cost of the claims it pays out, plus whatever administrative expenses it incurs. Consider an insurance company that charges lower rates for young males with clean driving records than for females with blemished ones. Given that the former group is more likely to have accidents than the latter, the company cannot break even unless it charges females more, and males less, than the respective costs of insuring them. But if it does so, rival insurance companies will see cash on the table: They can offer females slightly lower rates and lure them away from the first company. The first company will end up with only young male policyholders and thus will suffer an economic loss at the low rates it charges. That is why, in equilibrium, young males with clean driving records pay higher insurance rates than young females with blemished records.

The insurance industry's policy of charging high rates to young male drivers is an example of **statistical discrimination**. Other examples include the common practice of paying higher salaries to people with college degrees than to people without them and the policy of favoring college applicants with high SAT scores. Statistical discrimination occurs whenever people or products are judged on the basis of the groups to which they belong.

Even though everyone *knows* that the characteristics of specific individuals can differ markedly from those of the group to which they belong, competition promotes statistical discrimination. For example, insurance companies know perfectly well that *some* young males are careful and competent drivers. But unless they can identify *which* males are the better drivers, competitive pressure forces them to act on their knowledge that as a group young males are more likely than others to generate insurance claims.

ECONOMIC NATURALIST 12.6

statistical discrimination the practice of making judgments about the quality of people, goods, or services based on the characteristics of the groups to which they belong

Similarly, employers know that many people with only a high school diploma are more productive than the average college graduate. But because employers usually cannot tell in advance who those people are, competitive pressure leads them to offer higher wages to college graduates, who are more productive, on average, than high school graduates. Universities, too, realize that many applicants with low SAT scores will earn higher grades than applicants with high scores. But if two applicants look equally promising except for their SAT scores, competition forces universities to favor the applicant with higher scores since, on average, that applicant will perform better than the other.

Statistical discrimination is the *result* of observable differences in group characteristics, not the cause of those differences. Young males, for example, do not generate more insurance claims because of statistical discrimination. Rather, statistical discrimination occurs because insurance companies know that young males generate more claims. Nor does statistical discrimination cause young males to pay insurance rates that are high in relation to the claims they generate. Among any group of young male drivers, some are careful and competent, and others are not. Statistical discrimination means the more able males will pay high rates relative to the volume of claims they generate, but it also means the less able male drivers will pay low rates relative to the claims they generate. On average, the group's rates will be appropriate to the claims its members generate.

Still, these observations do little to ease the frustration of the young male who knows himself to be a careful and competent driver, or the high school graduate who knows herself to be a highly productive employee. Competitive forces provide firms an incentive to identify such individuals and treat them more favorably whenever practical. When firms succeed in this effort, however, they have often discovered some other relevant information on group differences. For example, many insurance companies offer lower rates to young males who belong to the National Honor Society or make the dean's list at school. Members of those groups generate fewer claims, on average, than other young males. But even these groups include risky drivers, and the fact that companies offer discounts to their members means that all other young males must pay higher rates.

ADVERSE SELECTION

adverse selection the pattern in which insurance tends to be purchased disproportionately by those who are most costly for companies to insure

Although insurance companies routinely practice statistical discrimination, each individual within a group pays the same rate, even though individuals within the group often differ sharply in terms of their likelihood of filing claims. Within each group, buying insurance is thus most attractive to those individuals with the highest likelihood of filing claims. As a result, high-risk individuals are more likely to buy insurance than low-risk individuals, a pattern known as **adverse selection**. Adverse selection forces insurance companies to raise their premiums, which makes buying insurance even less attractive to low-risk individuals, which raises still further the average risk level of those who remain insured. In some cases, only those individuals faced with extreme risks may continue to find insurance an attractive purchase.

MORAL HAZARD

moral hazard the tendency of people to expend less effort protecting those goods that are insured against theft or damage

Moral hazard is another problem that makes buying insurance less attractive for the average person. This problem refers to the fact that some people take fewer precautions when they know they are insured. Someone whose car is insured, for example, may take less care to prevent it from being damaged or stolen. Driving cautiously and searching for safe parking spaces require effort, after all, and if the losses from failing to engage in these precautions are covered by insurance, some people will become less vigilant.

By offering policies with deductible provisions, insurance companies help many of their potential clients soften the consequences of problems like moral hazard and adverse selection. Under the terms of an automobile collision insurance policy with, say, a $1,000 deductible provision, the insurance company covers only those collision repair costs in excess of $1,000. For example, if you have an accident in which $3,000 in damage occurs to your car, the insurance company covers only $2,000, and you pay the remaining $1,000.

How does the availability of such policies mitigate the negative effects of adverse selection and moral hazard? Since the policies are cheaper for insurance companies to provide, they sell for lower prices. The lower prices represent a much better bargain, however, for those drivers who are least likely to file insurance claims, since those drivers are least likely to incur any uncovered repair costs. Policies with deductible provisions also confront careless drivers with more of the extra costs for which they are responsible, giving them additional incentives to take precautions.

These policies benefit insurance buyers in another way. Because the holder of a policy with a deductible provision will not file a claim at all if the damage to his car in an accident is less than the deductible threshold, insurance companies require fewer resources to process and investigate claims, savings that get passed along in the form of lower premiums.

RECAP   ASYMMETRIC INFORMATION

Asymmetric information describes situations in which not all parties to a potential exchange are equally well informed. In the typical case, the seller of a product will know more about its quality than the potential buyers. Such asymmetries often stand in the way of mutually beneficial exchange in the markets for high-quality goods, because buyers' inability to identify high quality makes them unwilling to pay a commensurate price.

Information asymmetries and other communication problems between potential exchange partners can often be solved through the use of signals that are costly or difficult to fake. Product warranties are such a signal, because the seller of a low-quality product would find them too costly to offer.

Buyers and sellers also respond to asymmetric information by attempting to judge the qualities of products and people on the basis of the groups to which they belong. A young male may know he is a good driver, but auto insurance companies must nonetheless charge him high rates because they know only that he is a member of a group that is frequently involved in accidents.

DISAPPEARING POLITICAL DISCOURSE

An intriguing illustration of statistical discrimination arises when a politician decides what to say about controversial public issues. Politicians have an interest in supporting the positions they genuinely believe in, but they also have an interest in winning reelection. As the next examples illustrate, the two motives often conflict, especially when a politician's statements about one subject convey information about her beliefs on other subjects.

Why do opponents of the death penalty often remain silent?

Quite apart from the question of whether execution of convicted criminals is morally legitimate, there are important practical arguments against capital punishment. For one thing, it is extremely expensive relative to the alternative of life without parole. Execution is costly because of judicial safeguards against execution of innocent persons. In each capital case prosecuted in the United States, these safeguards consume thousands of person-hours from attorneys and other

ECONOMIC
NATURALIST
12.7

officers of the court, at a cost that runs well into the millions of dollars.[1] Such efforts notwithstanding, the record is replete with examples of executed persons who are later shown to be innocent. Another argument against capital punishment is that many statistical studies find that it does not deter people from committing capital crimes. Though many political leaders in both parties find these and other arguments against capital punishment compelling, few politicians voice their opposition to capital punishment publicly. Why not?

A possible answer to this puzzle is suggested by the theory of statistical discrimination. Voters in both parties are concerned about crime and want to elect politicians who take the problem seriously. Suppose there are two kinds of politicians, some who in their heart of hearts take the crime issue seriously and others who merely pay lip service to it. Suppose also that voters classify politicians in a second way: those who publicly favor the death penalty or remain silent, and those who publicly oppose it. Some politicians will oppose the death penalty for the reasons just discussed, but others will oppose it because they are simply reluctant to punish criminals—perhaps because they believe that crime is ultimately more society's fault than the criminal's. (Politicians in the latter category are the ones voters think of as being "not serious about crime"; they are the ones most voters want to get rid of.) These two possible motives for opposing the death penalty suggest that the proportion of death penalty opponents who take the crime issue seriously, in the public's view, will be somewhat smaller than the corresponding proportion among proponents of the death penalty. For the sake of discussion, imagine that 95 percent of politicians who favor the death penalty and only 80 percent of politicians who oppose the death penalty are "serious about crime."

If you are a voter who cares about crime, how will your views about a politician be affected by hearing that he opposes the death penalty? If you knew nothing about that politician to begin with, your best guess on hearing his opposition to the death penalty would be that there is an 80 percent chance that he is serious about crime. Had he instead voiced support for the death penalty, your best guess would be that there is a 95 percent chance that he is serious about crime. And since voters are looking for politicians who are serious about crime, the mere act of speaking out against the death penalty will entail a small loss of political support even for those politicians who are extremely serious about crime.

Knowing this tendency on the part of voters, some politicians who are only marginally opposed to the death penalty may prefer to keep their views to themselves. As a result, the composition of the group that speaks out publicly against the death penalty will change slightly so that it is more heavily weighted with people reluctant to punish criminals in any way. Suppose, for example, that the proportion of death penalty opponents who are serious about crime falls from 80 to 60 percent. Now the political cost of speaking out against the death penalty rises, leading still more opponents to remain silent. Once the dust settles, very few opponents of capital punishment will risk stating their views publicly. In their desire to convince voters that they are tough on crime, some may even become outspoken proponents of the death penalty. In the end, public discourse will strongly favor capital punishment. But that is no reason to conclude that most leaders—or even most voters—genuinely favor it.

The economist Glen Loury was the first to call attention to the phenomenon described in the preceding example. We call it the problem of **disappearing political discourse**. Once you understand it, you will begin to notice examples not just in the political sphere but in everyday discourse as well.

disappearing political discourse the theory that people who support a position may remain silent, because speaking out would create a risk of being misunderstood

[1]See Philip J. Cook and Donna B. Slawson, "The Costs of Processing Murder Cases in North Carolina," The Sanford Institute of Public Policy, Duke University, Durham, N.C., 1993.

Why do proponents of legalized drugs remain silent?

That addictive drugs like heroine, cocaine, and methamphetamines cause enormous harm is not a matter of dispute. The clear intent of laws that ban commerce in these drugs is to prevent that harm. But the laws also entail costs. By making the drugs illegal, they substantially increase their price, leading many addicts to commit crimes to pay for drugs. The high incomes of illicit drug dealers also divert many people from legitimate careers and result in turf battles that often have devastating consequences for both participants and bystanders. If these drugs were legal, drug-related crime would vanish completely. Drug use would also rise, how significantly we do not know. In short, it is at least *conceivable* that legalizing addictive drugs might be sound public policy. Why, then, do virtually no politicians publicly favor such a policy?

Many politicians may simply believe that legalizing drugs is a bad idea. Theoretically, legalization could lead to such a steep rise in drug consumption that the cost of the policy might far outweigh its benefits. This concern, however, is not supported by experience in countries such as England and the Netherlands, which have tried limited forms of legalization. A second explanation is that politicians who favor legalization are reluctant to speak out for fear that others will misinterpret them. Suppose that some people favor legalization based on careful analysis of the costs and benefits, while other proponents are merely crazy. If the proportion of crazies is higher among supporters than among opponents of legalization, someone who speaks out in favor of legalization may cause those who do not know her to increase their estimate of the likelihood she is crazy. This possibility deters some proponents from speaking out, which raises the proportion of crazies among the remaining public supporters of legalization—and so on in a downward spiral, until most of the remaining public supporters really are crazy.

The disappearing political discourse problem helps to explain why the United States had difficulty reestablishing normal diplomatic relations with China, which were severed in the wake of the communist revolution. One could oppose communist expansionism and yet still favor normalized relations with China on the grounds that war is less likely when antagonists communicate openly. In the Cold War environment, however, American politicians were under enormous pressure to demonstrate their steadfast opposition to communism at every opportunity. Fearing that support for the normalization of relations with China would be misinterpreted as a sign of softness toward communism, many supporters of the policy remained silent. Not until Richard Nixon—whose anticommunist credentials no one could question—was elected president were diplomatic relations with China finally reopened.

The problem of disappearing discourse also helps explain the impoverished state of public debate on issues such as the reform of Social Security, Medicare, and other entitlement programs.

Why did the task of reestablishing normal diplomatic relations with China fall to President Richard Nixon, the lifelong communist basher?

▪ SUMMARY ▪

- Virtually every market exchange takes place on the basis of less than complete information. More information is beneficial both to buyers and to sellers, but information is costly to acquire. The rational individual therefore acquires information only up to the point at which its marginal benefit equals its marginal cost. Beyond that point one is rational to remain ignorant.

- Retailers and other sales agents are important sources of information. To the extent that they enable consumers to

find the right products and services, they add economic value. In that sense they are no less productive than the workers who manufacture goods or perform services directly. Unfortunately, the free-rider problem often prevents firms from offering useful product information.

- Several principles govern the rational search for information. Searching more intensively makes sense when the cost of a search is low, when quality is highly variable, or when prices vary widely. Further search is always a gamble. A risk-neutral person will search whenever the expected gains outweigh the expected costs. A rational search will always terminate before all possible options have been investigated. Thus in a search for a partner in an ongoing bilateral relationship, there is always the possibility that a better partner will turn up after the search is over. In most contexts, people deal with this problem by entering into contracts that commit them to their partners once they have mutually agreed to terminate the search.

- Many potentially beneficial transactions are prevented from taking place by asymmetric information—the fact that one party lacks information that the other has. For example, the owner of a used car knows whether it is in good condition, but potential buyers do not. Even though a buyer may be willing to pay more for a good car than the owner of such a car would require, the fact that the buyer cannot be sure he is getting a good car often discourages the sale. More generally, asymmetric information often prevents sellers from supplying the same quality level that consumers would be willing to pay for.

- Both buyers and sellers can often gain by finding ways of communicating what they know to one another. But because of the potential conflict between the interests of buyers and sellers, mere statements about the relevant information may not be credible. For a signal between potential trading partners to be credible, it must be costly to fake. For instance, the owner of a high-quality used car can credibly signal the car's quality by offering a warranty—an offer that the seller of a low-quality car could not afford to make.

- Firms and consumers often try to estimate missing information by making use of what they know about the groups to which people or things belong. For example, insurance firms estimate the risk of insuring individual young male drivers on the basis of the accident rates for young males as a group. This practice is known as statistical discrimination. Other examples include paying college graduates more than high school graduates and charging higher life insurance rates to 60-year-olds than to 20-year-olds. Statistical discrimination helps to explain the phenomenon of disappearing political discourse, which occurs when opponents of a practice such as the death penalty remain silent when the issue is discussed publicly.

■ KEY TERMS ■

adverse selection (316)
asymmetric information (309)
better-than-fair gamble (307)
costly-to-fake principle (312)
disappearing political discourse (318)

expected value of a gamble (307)
fair gamble (307)
free-rider problem (305)
lemons model (310)

moral hazard (316)
risk-averse person (307)
risk-neutral person (307)
statistical discrimination (315)

■ REVIEW QUESTIONS ■

1. Can it be rational for a consumer to buy a Chevrolet without having first taken test drives in competing models built by Ford, Chrysler, Honda, Toyota, and others?

2. Explain why a gallery owner who sells a painting might actually create more economic surplus than the artist who painted it.

3. Explain why used cars offered for sale are different, on average, from used cars not offered for sale.

4. Explain why the used-car market would be likely to function more efficiently in a community in which moral norms of honesty are strong than in a community in which such norms are weak.

5. Why might leasing a new Porsche be a good investment for an aspiring Hollywood film producer, even though he can't easily afford the monthly payments?

■ PROBLEMS ■

1. State whether the following are true or false, and briefly explain why:
   a. Companies spend billions of dollars advertising their products on network TV primarily because the texts of their advertisements persuade consumers that the advertised products are of high quality.
   b. You may not get the optimal level of advice from a retail shop when you go in to buy a lamp for your bike, because of the free-rider problem.
   c. If you need a lawyer, and all your legal expenses are covered by insurance, you should *always* choose the best-dressed lawyer with the most expensive car and the most ostentatiously furnished office.

d. The benefit of searching for a spouse is affected by the size of the community you live in.

2. Consumers know that some fraction x of all new cars produced and sold in the market are defective. The defective ones cannot be identified except by those who own them. Cars do not depreciate with use. Consumers are risk-neutral and value nondefective cars at $10,000 each. New cars sell for $5,000 and used ones for $2,500. What is the fraction x?

3. Carlos is risk-neutral and has an ancient farmhouse with great character for sale in Slaterville Springs. His reservation price for the house is $130,000. The only possible local buyer is Whitney, whose reservation price for the house is $150,000. The only other houses on the market are modern ranch houses that sell for $125,000, which is exactly equal to each potential buyer's reservation price for such a house. Suppose that if Carlos does not hire a realtor, Whitney will learn from her neighbor that Carlos's house is for sale and will buy it for $140,000. However, if Carlos hires a realtor, he knows that the realtor will put him in touch with an enthusiast for old farmhouses who is willing to pay up to $300,000 for the house. Carlos also knows that if he and this person negotiate, they will agree on a price of $250,000. If realtors charge a commission of 5 percent of the selling price and all realtors have opportunity costs of $2,000 for negotiating a sale, will Carlos hire a realtor? If so, how will total economic surplus be affected?

4. Ann and Barbara are computer programmers in Nashville who are planning to move to Seattle. Each owns a house that has just been appraised for $100,000. But whereas Ann's house is one of hundreds of highly similar houses in a large, well-known suburban development, Barbara's is the only one that was built from her architect's design. Who will benefit more by hiring a realtor to assist in selling her house, Ann or Barbara?

5. For each pair of occupations listed, identify the one for which the kind of car a person drives is more likely to be a good indication of how good she is at her job.
   a. Elementary school teacher, real estate agent
   b. Dentist, municipal government administrator
   c. Engineer in the private sector, engineer in the military

6. Brokers who sell stocks over the Internet can serve many more customers than those who transact business by mail or over the phone. How will the expansion of Internet access affect the average incomes of stockbrokers who continue to do business in the traditional way?

7. Whose income do you predict will be more affected by the expansion of Internet access:
   a. Stockbrokers or lawyers?
   b. Doctors or pharmacists?
   c. Bookstore owners or the owners of galleries that sell original oil paintings?

8. How will growing Internet access affect the number of film actors and musicians who have active fan clubs?

9. Fred, a retired accountant, and Jim, a government manager, are 63-year-old identical twins who collect antique pottery. Each has an annual income of $100,000 (Fred's from a pension, Jim's from salary). One buys most of his pottery at local auctions, and the other buys most of his from a local dealer. Which brother is more likely to buy at an auction, and does he pay more or less than his brother who buys from the local dealer?

10. Female heads of state (e.g., Israel's Golda Meir, India's Indira Gandhi, Britain's Margaret Thatcher) have often been described as more bellicose in foreign policy matters than the average male head of state. Using Loury's theory of disappearing discourse, suggest an explanation for this pattern.

■ ANSWERS TO IN-CHAPTER EXERCISES ■

12.1 Internet search is a cheap way to acquire information about many goods and services, so the effect of increased Internet access will be a downward shift in the supply curve of information. In equilibrium, people will acquire more information, and the goods and services they buy will more closely resemble those they would have chosen in an ideal world with perfect information. These effects will cause total economic surplus to grow. Some of these gains, however, might be offset if the Internet makes the free-rider problem more serious.

12.2 The probability of getting heads is 0.5, the same as the probability of getting tails. Thus the expected value of this gamble is $(0.5)(\$4) + (0.5)(-\$2) = \$1$. Since the gamble is better than fair, a risk-neutral person would accept it.

12.3 Since you still have a 20 percent chance of finding a cheaper apartment if you make another visit, the expected outcome of the gamble is again $2, and you should search again. The bad outcome of any previous search is a sunk cost and should not influence your decision about whether to search again.

12.4 The expected value of a new car will now be $0.8(\$10,000) + 0.2(\$6,000) = \$9,200$. Any risk-neutral consumer who believed that the quality distribution of used cars for sale was the same as the quality distribution of new cars off the assembly line would be willing to pay $9,200 for a used car.

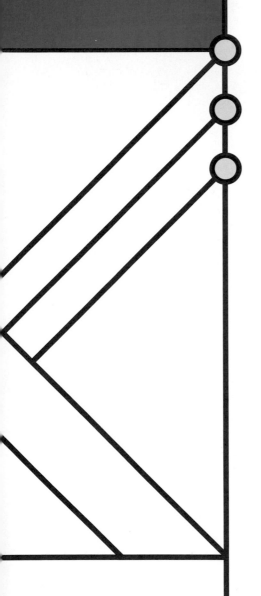

PART

4

ECONOMICS OF PUBLIC POLICY

■

Why do some people earn so much more money than others? No other single question in economics has stimulated nearly as much interest and discussion. Our aim in Chapter 13 will be to apply simple economic principles in an attempt to answer this question. We'll discuss the human capital model, which emphasizes the importance of differences in personal characteristics. But our focus will be on why people with similar personal characteristics often earn sharply different incomes. Among the factors we will consider are labor unions, winner-take-all markets, discrimination, and the effect of nonwage conditions of employment. In this chapter we will also explore whether income inequality is something society should be concerned about, and if so, whether practical remedies exist for it. We will see that government programs to redistribute income have costs as well as benefits.

In Chapter 14 we will explore economic policies for dealing with specific problems in the environmental, safety, and health domains, showing how careful application of basic economic principles can help society design policies that both expand the economic pie and make everyone's slice larger. The unifying thread running through the examples we will consider is the problem of scarcity. In each case, we will explore how the cost-benefit principle can help to resolve the resulting trade-offs.

In Chapter 15 we consider how big government should be, what sorts of goods and services it should provide, and how it should raise the revenue to pay for them. We will also investigate circumstances under which rational citizens might vest in government the power to constrain their behavior in various ways, and how such powers should be apportioned among local, state, and federal levels.

LABOR MARKETS, POVERTY, AND INCOME DISTRIBUTION

■

By only the slimmest of margins, Mary Lou Retton won the individual all-around gold medal in women's gymnastics at the Los Angeles Summer Olympic Games in 1984. In the years since, she has remained in the spotlight, continuing to earn millions of dollars from product endorsements and motivational speeches. In contrast, the silver medalist from 1984 has dropped completely from view. (Can you name her?) She is Ecaterina Szabo, one of the most talented Romanian gymnasts of her era, and although she came within a hairbreadth of beating Retton, wealth and international recognition were not to be hers.

Many physicians in Szabo's homeland are likewise every bit as talented and hardworking as physicians in the United States. But while American physicians earn an average annual income of almost $200,000, Romanian physicians earn so little that some of them supplement their incomes by cleaning the Bucharest apartments of expatriate Americans for just $10 a day.

Why do some people earn so much more than others? No other single question in economics has stimulated nearly as much interest and discussion. American citizenship, of course, is neither necessary nor sufficient for receiving high income. Many of the wealthiest people in the world come from extremely poor countries, and many Americans are homeless and malnourished.

Our aim in this chapter will be to employ simple economic principles in an attempt to explain why different people earn different salaries. We'll discuss the human capital model, which emphasizes the importance of differences in personal characteristics. But our focus will be on why people with similar personal characteristics often earn sharply different incomes. Among the factors we will

Why do small differences in performance sometimes translate into enormous differences in pay?

consider are labor unions, discrimination, the effect of nonwage conditions of employment, and winner-take-all markets. We will explore whether income inequality is something society should be concerned about, and if so, whether practical remedies for it exist. As we will see, government programs to redistribute income have costs as well as benefits. As always, policymakers must compare an imperfect status quo with the practical consequences of imperfect government remedies.

THE ECONOMIC VALUE OF WORK

In some respects, the sale of human labor is profoundly different from the sale of other goods and services. For example, although someone may legally relinquish all future rights to the use of her television set by selling it, the law does not permit people to sell themselves into slavery. The law does, however, permit employers to "rent" our services. And in many ways the rental market for labor services functions much like the market for most other goods and services. Each specific category of labor has a demand curve and a supply curve. These curves intersect to determine both the equilibrium wage and the equilibrium quantity of employment for each category of labor.

What is more, shifts in the relevant demand and supply curves produce changes analogous to those produced by shifts in the demand and supply curves for other goods and services. For instance, an increase in the demand for a specific category of labor will generally increase both the equilibrium wage and the equilibrium quantity of employment in that category. By the same token, an increase in the supply of labor to a given occupation will tend to increase the level of employment and lower the wage rate in that occupation.

As in our discussions of other markets, our strategy for investigating how the labor market works will be to go through a series of examples that shed light on different parts of the picture. In the first example, we focus on how the equilibrium principle helps us to understand how wages will differ among workers with different levels of productive ability.

EXAMPLE 13.1

How much will the potters earn?

Mackintosh Pottery Works is one of numerous identical companies that hire potters who mold clay into pots. These companies sell the pots for $1.10 each to a finishing company that glazes and fires them, and then sells them in the retail marketplace. Clay, which is available free of charge in unlimited quantities, is the only input used by the potters. Rennie and Laura are currently the only two potters who work for Mackintosh, whose only cost other than potters' salaries is a 10-cent handling cost for each pot it delivers to the finisher. Rennie delivers 100 pots per week and Laura delivers 120. If the labor market for potters is perfectly competitive, how much will each be paid?

We begin with the assumption that Rennie and Laura have decided to work full time as potters, so our focus is not on how much they will work but on how much they will be paid. After taking handling costs into account, the value of the pots that Rennie delivers is $100 per week, and that is the amount Mackintosh will pay him. To pay him less would risk having him bid away by a competitor. For example, if Mackintosh paid Rennie only $90 per week, the company would then enjoy an economic profit of $10 per week as a result of hiring him. Seeing this cash on the table, a rival firm could then offer Rennie $91, thus earning an additional economic profit of $9 per week by bidding him away from Mackintosh. So under the bidding pressure from rival employers, Mackintosh will have difficulty keeping Rennie if it pays him less than $100 per week. And the company would suffer an economic loss if it paid him more than $100 per week. Similarly, the value of the pots delivered each week by Laura is $120, and this will be her competitive equilibrium wage.

In the preceding example, the number of pots each potter delivered each week was that potter's **marginal physical product,** or **marginal product** (*MP*) for short. More generally, a worker's marginal product is the extra output the firm gets as a result of hiring that worker. When we multiply a worker's marginal product by the net price for which each unit of the product sells, we get that worker's **value of marginal product,** or *VMP.* (In the preceding example the "net price" of each pot was $1.00—the difference between the $1.10 sale price and the $0.10 handling charge.) The general rule in competitive labor markets is that *a worker's pay in long-run equilibrium will be equal to his or her VMP—the net contribution he or she makes to the employer's revenue.* Employers would be delighted to pay workers less than their respective VMPs, to be sure. But if labor markets are truly competitive, they cannot get away with doing so for long.

In Example 13.1, each worker's VMP was independent of the number of other workers employed by the firm. In such cases, we cannot predict how many workers a firm will hire. Mackintosh could break even with 2 potters, with 10, or even with 1,000 or more. In many other situations, however, we can predict exactly how many workers a firm will hire. Consider the following example.

marginal product of labor **(MP)** the additional output a firm gets by employing one additional unit of labor

value of marginal product of labor **(VMP)** the dollar value of the additional output a firm gets by employing one additional unit of labor

How many workers should Adirondack hire?

EXAMPLE 13.2

The Adirondack Woodworking Company hires workers in a competitive labor market at a wage of $350 per week to make kitchen cutting boards from scrap wood that is available free of charge. If the boards sell for $20 each and the company's weekly output varies with the number of workers hired as shown in Table 13.1, how many workers should Adirondack hire?

TABLE 13.1
**Employment and Productivity in a Woodworking Company
(when cutting boards sell for $20 each)**

Number of workers	Total number of cutting boards/week	MP (extra cutting boards/week)	VMP ($/week)
0	0		
		30	600
1	30		
		25	500
2	55		
		21	420
3	76		
		18	360
4	94		
		14	280
5	108		

In Example 13.1 our focus was on wage differences for employees whose productive abilities differed. In contrast, we assume here that all workers are equally productive and the firm faces a fixed market wage for each. The fact that the marginal product of labor declines with the number of workers hired is a consequence of the law of diminishing returns. (As discussed in Chapter 6, this law says that when a firm's capital or other productive inputs are held fixed in the short run, adding workers beyond some point results in ever smaller increases in output.) The third column of the table reports the marginal product for each additional worker, and the last column reports the value of each successive worker's marginal product—the number of cutting boards he or she adds times the selling price of $20. Adirondack should keep hiring as long as the next worker's *VMP* is at least $350 per week (the market wage). The first four workers have *VMPs* larger than $350, so Adirondack should hire them. But since hiring the fifth worker would add only $280 to weekly revenue, Adirondack should not hire that worker.

Note the similarity between the perfectly competitive firm's decision about how many workers to hire and the perfectly competitive firm's output decision we considered in Chapter 6. When labor is the only variable factor of production, the two decisions are essentially the same. Because of the unique correspondence between the firm's total output and the total number of workers it hires, deciding how many workers to hire is the same as deciding how much output to supply.

The worker's attractiveness to the employer depends not only on how many cutting boards he or she produces, but also on the price of cutting boards and on the wage rate. For example, because *VMP* rises when product price rises, an increase in product price will lead employers to hire more workers. Employers will also increase hiring when the wage rate falls.

EXERCISE 13.1

In Example 13.2, how many workers should Adirondack hire if the price of cutting boards rises to $26?

EXERCISE 13.2

In Example 13.2, how many workers should Adirondack hire if the wage rate falls to $275 per week?

RECAP   **THE ECONOMIC VALUE OF WORK**

In competitive labor markets, employers face pressure to pay each worker the value of his or her marginal product. When a firm can hire as many workers as it wishes at a given market wage, it should expand employment as long as the value of marginal product of labor exceeds the market wage.

THE EQUILIBRIUM WAGE AND EMPLOYMENT LEVELS

As we saw in Chapter 3, the equilibrium price and quantity in any competitive market occur at the intersection of the relevant supply and demand curves. The same is true in competitive markets for labor.

THE DEMAND CURVE FOR LABOR

An employer's reservation price for a worker is the most the employer could pay without suffering a decline in profit. As discussed, this reservation price for the employer in a perfectly competitive labor market is simply *VMP*, the value of the worker's marginal product. Because of the law of diminishing returns, we know that the marginal product of labor, and hence *VMP*, declines in the short run as the quantity of labor rises. The individual employer's demand curve for labor in any particular occupation—say, computer programmers—may thus be shown, as in Figure 13.1(a), as a downward-sloping function of the wage rate. Suppose firm 1 [part (a)] and firm 2 [part (b)] are the only two firms that employ programmers in a given community. The demand for programmers in that community will then be the horizontal sum of the individual firm demands [part (c)].

FIGURE 13.1
The Occupational Demand for Labor.
If firm 1 and firm 2 are the only firms that employ labor in a given occupation, we generate the demand curve for labor in that occupation by adding the individual demand curves horizontally.

THE SUPPLY CURVE OF LABOR

What does the supply curve of labor for a specific occupation look like? Will more labor be offered at high wage rates than at low wage rates? An equivalent way to pose the same question is to ask whether consumers will wish to consume less leisure at high wage rates than at low wage rates. By themselves, the principles of economic theory do not provide an answer to this question, because a change in the wage rate exerts two opposing effects on the quantity of leisure demanded. One is the substitution effect, which says that at a higher wage, leisure is more expensive, leading consumers to consume less of it. The second is the income effect, which says that at a higher wage, consumers have more purchasing power, leading them to consume more leisure. Which of these two opposing effects dominates is an empirical question.

For the economy as a whole during the past several centuries, the workweek has been declining and real wages have been rising. This pattern might seem to suggest that the supply curve of labor is downward-sloping, and for the economy as a whole it may be. There is also evidence that individual workers may sometimes work fewer hours when wage rates are high than when they are low. A study of taxicab drivers in New York City, for example, found that drivers quit earlier on rainy days (when the effective wage is high because of high demand for cab rides) than on sunny days (when the effective wage is lower).[1]

These observations notwithstanding, the supply of labor *to any particular occupation* is almost surely upward-sloping, because wage differences among occupations influence occupational choice. It is no accident, for example, that many more people are choosing jobs as computer programmers now than in 1970. Wages of programmers have risen sharply during the past several decades, which has led many people to forsake other career paths in favor of programming. Curve S in Figure 13.2 represents the supply curve of computer programmers. Its positive slope is typical of the supply curves for most individual occupations.

MARKET SHIFTS

As more tasks have become computerized in recent decades, the demand for programmers has grown, as shown by the shift from D_1 to D_2 in Figure 13.2. Equilibrium in the market for computer programmers occurs at the intersection of the

[1]L. Babcock, C. Camerer, G. Loewenstein, and R. Thaler, "Labor Supply of New York City Cab Drivers: One Day at a Time," *Quarterly Journal of Economics*, **111**: 408–441, 1997.

FIGURE 13.2
The Effect of an Increase in the Demand for Computer Programmers.
An increase in the demand for programmers from D_1 to D_2 results in an increase in the equilibrium level of employment (from L_1 to L_2) and an increase in the equilibrium wage (from W_1 to W_2).

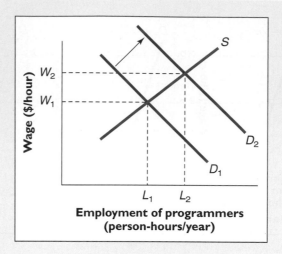

relevant supply and demand curves. The increase in demand has led to an increase in the equilibrium level of programmers from L_1 to L_2 and a rise in the equilibrium wage from W_1 to W_2.

As discussed in Chapter 8, the market for stocks and other financial assets reaches equilibrium very quickly in the wake of shifts in the underlying supply and demand curves. Labor markets, by contrast, are often much slower to adjust. When the demand for workers in a given profession increases, shortages may remain for months or even years, depending on how long it takes people to acquire the skills and training needed to enter the profession.

RECAP   **EQUILIBRIUM IN THE LABOR MARKET**

The demand for labor in a perfectly competitive labor market is the horizontal sum of each employer's *VMP* curve. The supply curve of labor for an individual labor market is upward-sloping, even though the supply curve of labor for the economy as a whole may be vertical or even downward-sloping. In each labor market, the demand and supply curves intersect to determine the equilibrium wage and level of employment.

EXPLAINING DIFFERENCES IN EARNINGS

The theory of competitive labor markets tells us that differences in pay reflect differences in the corresponding *VMP*s. Thus, in Example 13.1, Laura earned 20 percent more than Rennie because she made 20 percent more pots each week than he did. This difference in productivity may have resulted from an underlying difference in talent or training, or perhaps Laura simply worked harder than Rennie.

Yet often we see large salary differences even among people who appear equally talented and hardworking. Why, for example, do lawyers earn so much more than those plumbers who are just as smart as they are and work just as hard? And why do surgeons earn so much more than general practitioners? These wage differences might seem to violate the no-cash-on-the-table principle, which says that only differences in talent, luck, or hard work can account for long-run differences in earnings. For example, if plumbers could earn more by becoming lawyers, why don't they just switch occupations? Similarly, if general practitioners could boost their incomes by becoming surgeons, why didn't they become surgeons in the first place?

HUMAN CAPITAL THEORY

Answers to these questions are suggested by **human capital theory,** which holds that an individual's *VMP* is proportional to his or her stock of **human capital**— an amalgam of factors such as education, experience, training, intelligence, energy, work habits, trustworthiness, and initiative. According to this theory, some occupations pay better than others because they require larger stocks of human capital. For example, a general practitioner could become a surgeon, but only by extending her formal education by several more years. An even larger investment in additional education is required for a plumber to become a lawyer.

Differences in demand can result in some kinds of human capital being more valuable than others. Consider again the increase in demand for computer programmers that has been occurring for the past several decades. During that same time period, the demand for the services of tax accountants has fallen as more and more taxpayers have used tax-preparation software in lieu of hiring accountants to help them with their taxes. Both occupations require demanding technical training, but the training received by computer programmers now yields a higher return in the labor market.

human capital an amalgam of factors such as education, training, experience, intelligence, energy, work habits, trustworthiness, and initiative that affect the value of a worker's marginal product

human capital theory a theory of pay determination that says a worker's wage will be proportional to his or her stock of human capital

LABOR UNIONS

Two workers with the same amount of human capital may earn different wages if one of them belongs to a **labor union** and the other does not. A labor union is an organization through which workers attempt to bargain collectively with employers for better wages and working conditions.

Many economists believe that unions affect labor markets in much the same way that cartels affect product markets. To illustrate, consider a simple economy with two labor markets, neither of which is unionized initially. Suppose the total supply of labor to the two markets is fixed at $S_0 = 200$ workers per day, and that the demand curves are as shown by VMP_1 and VMP_2 in Figures 13.3(a) and (b).

labor union a group of workers who bargain collectively with employers for better wages and working conditions

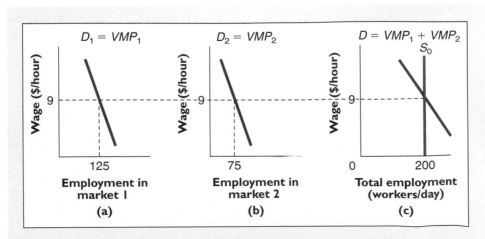

FIGURE 13.3

An Economy with Two Nonunionized Labor Markets.

Supply and demand intersect to determine a market wage of $9 per hour (c). At that wage, employers in market 1 hire 125 workers per day and employers in market 2 hire 75 workers per day. The *VMP* is $9 in each market.

The sum of the two demand curves, $VMP_1 + VMP_2$ [part (c)], intersects the supply curve to determine an equilibrium wage of $9 per hour. At that wage, firms in market 1 hire 125 workers per day [part (a)], and firms in market 2 hire 75 [part (b)].

Now suppose workers in market 1 form a union and refuse to work for less than $12 per hour. Because demand curves for labor are downward-sloping, employers of unionized workers reduce employment from 125 workers per day to 100 [Figure 13.4(a)]. The 25 displaced workers in the unionized market would of course be delighted to find other jobs in that market at $12 per hour. But they cannot, and so they are forced to seek employment in the nonunionized market. The result is an excess supply of 25 workers in the nonunion market at the original wage of $9 per hour. In time, wages in that market decline to $W_N = \$6$ per hour, the level at which 100 workers can find jobs in the nonunionized market [Figure 13.4(b)].

FIGURE 13.4

The Effect of a Union Wage Above the Equilibrium Wage.
When the unionized wage is pegged at $W_U = \$12$/hour (a), 25 workers are discharged. When these workers seek employment in the nonunionized market, the wage in that market falls to $W_N = \$6$/hour (b).

It might seem that the gains of the unionized workers are exactly offset by the losses of nonunionized workers. On closer inspection, however, we see that pegging the union wage above the equilibrium level actually reduces the value of total output. If labor were allocated efficiently between the two markets, its value of marginal product would have to be the same in each. Otherwise, the total value of output could be increased by moving workers from the low-VMP market to the high-VMP market. With the wage set initially at $9 per hour in both markets, the condition for efficient allocation was met, because labor's VMP was $9 per hour in both markets. But because the collective bargaining process drives wages (and hence VMPs) in the two markets apart, the value of total output is no longer maximized. To verify this claim, note that if a worker is taken out of the nonunionized market, the reduction in the value of output there will be only $6 per hour, which is less than the $12 per hour gain in the value of output when that same worker is added to the unionized market.

EXERCISE 13.3

In Figure 13.4, by how much would the value of total output be increased if the wage rate were $9 per hour in each market?

Wages paid to workers in a unionized firm are sometimes 50 percent or more above the wages paid to their nonunionized counterparts. To the alert economic naturalist, this difference prompts the following question:

If unionized firms have to pay more, how do they manage to survive in the face of competition from their nonunionized counterparts?

In fact, nonunionized firms sometimes do drive unionized firms out of business, as when the American textile industry moved to the South to escape the burden of high union wages in New England. Even so, unionized and nonunionized firms often manage to compete head-to-head for extended periods. If their costs are significantly higher, how do the unionized firms manage to survive?

The observed pay differential actually overstates the difference between the labor costs of the two types of firm. Because the higher union wage attracts an excess supply of workers, unionized employers can adopt more stringent hiring requirements than their nonunionized counterparts. As a result, unionized workers tend to be more experienced and skilled than nonunionized workers. Studies estimate that the union wage premium for workers with the same amount of human capital is only about 10 percent.

Another factor is that unions may actually boost the productivity of workers with any given amount of human capital, perhaps by improving communication between management and workers. Similarly, the implementation of formal grievance procedures, in combination with higher pay, may boost morale among unionized workers, leading to higher productivity. Labor turnover is also significantly lower in unionized firms, which reduces hiring and training costs. Studies suggest that union productivity may be sufficiently high to compensate for the premium in union wages. So even though wages are higher in unionized firms, these firms may not have significantly higher labor costs per unit of output than their nonunionized counterparts.

Only one in six American workers currently belongs to a labor union, about half the union membership rate during the 1950s. Because the union wage premium is small and applies to only a small fraction of the labor force, union membership in the United States is probably not an important explanation for why workers with similar qualifications often earn sharply different incomes.

COMPENSATING WAGE DIFFERENTIALS

If people are paid the value of what they produce, why do garbage collectors earn more than lifeguards? Picking up the trash is important, to be sure, but is it more valuable than saving the life of a drowning child? Similarly, we need not question the value of a timely plumbing repair to wonder why plumbers get paid more than fourth-grade teachers. Is replacing faucet washers really more valuable than educating children? As the next examples illustrate, the wage for a particular job depends not only on the value of what workers produce, but also on how attractive they find its working conditions.

Do tobacco company CEOs get paid extra for testifying that cigarette smoking does not cause cancer?

Why do some ad copy writers earn more than others?

You plan to pursue a career in advertising and have two job offers, one to write ad copy for the American Cancer Society, the other to write copy for Camel cigarette ads aimed at the youth market. Except for the subject matter of the ads, working conditions are identical in the two jobs. If each job paid $30,000 per year and offered the same prospects for advancement, which would you choose?

When this question was recently posed to a sample of graduating seniors at Cornell University almost 90 percent of them chose the American Cancer Society job. When asked how much more they would have to be paid to induce them to switch to the Camel cigarettes job, their median response was a premium of $15,000 per year. As this sample suggests, employers who offer jobs with less attractive working conditions cannot hope to fill them unless they also offer higher salaries.

compensating wage differential a difference in the wage rate—negative or positive—that reflects the attractiveness of a job's working conditions

Other things being equal, jobs with attractive working conditions will pay less than jobs with less attractive conditions. Wage differences associated with differences in working conditions are known as **compensating wage differentials**. Economists have identified compensating differentials for a host of different specific working conditions. Studies have found, for example, that safe jobs tend to pay less than otherwise similar jobs that entail greater risks to health and safety. Studies have also found that wages vary in accord with the attractiveness of the work schedule. For instance, working night shifts commands a wage premium, and teachers must accept lower wages in part because many of those with children value having hours that coincide with the school calendar.

DISCRIMINATION IN THE LABOR MARKET

Women and minorities continue to receive lower wage rates, on average, than white males with similar measures of human capital. This pattern poses a profound challenge to standard theories of competitive labor markets, which hold that competitive pressures will eliminate wage differentials not based on differences in productivity. Defenders of standard theories attribute the wage gap to unmeasured differences in human capital. Many critics of these theories reject the idea that labor markets are effectively competitive, and instead attribute the gap to various forms of discrimination.

Discrimination by Employers

Employer discrimination is the term used to describe wage differentials that arise from an arbitrary preference by an employer for one group of workers over another. An example occurs if two labor force groups, such as males and females, are equally productive, on average, yet some employers ("discriminators") prefer hiring males and are willing to pay higher wages to do so.

employer discrimination an arbitrary preference by an employer for one group of workers over another

Most consumers are not willing to pay more for a product produced by males than for an identical one produced by females (if indeed they even *know* which type of worker produced the product). If product price is unaffected by the composition of the workforce that produces the product, a firm's profit will be smaller the more males it employs, because males cost more yet are no more productive (on the assumption that discrimination is the cause of the wage gap). Thus the most profitable firms will be ones that employ only females.

Arbitrary wage gaps are an apparent violation of the no-cash-on-the-table principle. The initial wage differential provides an opportunity for employers who hire mostly females to grow at the expense of their rivals. Because such firms make an economic profit on the sale of each unit of output, their incentive is to expand as rapidly as they possibly can. And to do that, they would naturally want to continue hiring only the cheaper females.

But as profit-seeking firms continue to pursue this strategy, the supply of females at the lower wage rate will run out. The short-run solution is to offer females a slightly higher wage. But this strategy works only if other firms do not pursue it. Once they too start offering a higher wage, females will again be in short supply. The only stable outcome occurs when the wage of females reaches parity with the wage of males. The wage for both males and females will thus settle at the common value of their *VMP*.

Any employer who wants to voice a preference for hiring males must now do so by paying males a wage in excess of *VMP*. Employers can discriminate against females if they wish, but only if they are willing to pay premium wages to males out of their own profits. Not even the harshest critics of the competitive model seem willing to impute such behavior to the owners of capitalist enterprises.

Discrimination by Others

If employer discrimination is not the primary explanation of the wage gap, what is? In some instances, **customer discrimination** may provide a plausible explanation. For example, if people believe that juries and clients are less likely to take female or minority attorneys seriously, members of these groups will face a reduced incentive to attend law school, and law firms will face a reduced incentive to hire those who do.

Another possible source of persistent wage gaps is discrimination and socialization within the family. For example, families may provide less education for their female children, or they may socialize them to believe that lofty career ambitions are not appropriate.

customer discrimination the willingness of consumers to pay more for a product produced by members of a favored group, even if the quality of the product is unaffected

Other Sources of the Wage Gap

Part of the wage gap may be explained by compensating wage differentials that spring from differences in preferences for other nonwage elements of the compensation package. Jobs that involve exposure to physical risk, for example, command higher wages, and if men are relatively more willing to accept such risks, they will earn more than females with otherwise identical stocks of human capital. (The same difference would result if employers felt constrained by social norms not to assign female employees to risky jobs.)

Elements of human capital that are difficult to measure may also help to explain earnings differentials. For example, productivity is influenced not only by the quantity of education an individual has, which is easy to measure, but also by its quality, which is much harder to measure. Part of the black–white differential in wages may thus be due to the fact that schools in black neighborhoods have not been as good, on average, as those in white neighborhoods.

Differences in the courses people take in college appear to have similar implications for differences in productivity. For instance, students in math, engineering, or business—male or female—tend to earn significantly higher salaries than those who concentrate in the humanities. The fact that males are disproportionately represented in the former group gives rise to a male wage premium that is unrelated to employer discrimination.

"English lit—how about you?"

As economists have grown more sophisticated in their efforts to measure human capital and other factors that influence individual wage rates, unexplained wage differentials by sex and race have grown steadily smaller, and have even disappeared altogether in some studies.[1] Other studies, however, continue to find significant unexplained differentials by race and sex. Debate about discrimination in the workplace will continue until the causes of these differentials are more fully understood.

WINNER-TAKE-ALL MARKETS

Differences in human capital do much to explain observed differences in earnings. Yet earnings differentials have also grown sharply in many occupations within which the distribution of human capital among workers seems essentially unchanged. Consider the following example.

ECONOMIC NATURALIST 13.3

Why does Renée Fleming earn millions more than sopranos of only slightly lesser ability?

Although the best sopranos have always earned more than others with slightly lesser talents, the earnings gap is sharply larger now than it was in the nineteenth century. Today, top singers like Renée Fleming earn millions of dollars per year—hundreds or even thousands of times what sopranos only marginally less talented earn. Given that listeners in blind hearings often have difficulty identifying the most highly paid singers, why is this earnings differential so large?

The answer lies in a fundamental change in the way we consume most of our music. In the nineteenth century, virtually all professional musicians delivered their services in concert halls in front of live audiences. (In 1900, the state of Iowa alone had more than 1,300 concert halls!) Audiences of that day would have been delighted to listen to the world's best soprano, but no one singer could hope to perform in more than a tiny fraction of the world's concert halls. Today, in contrast, most of the music we hear comes in recorded form, which enables the best soprano to be literally everywhere at once. As soon as the master recording has been made, Renée Fleming's performance can be burned onto compact disks at the same low cost as for a slightly less talented singer's.

Tens of millions of buyers worldwide are willing to pay a few cents extra to hear the most talented performers. Recording companies would be delighted to hire those singers at modest salaries, for by so doing they would earn an enormous economic profit. But that would unleash bidding by rival recording companies for the best singers. Such bidding assures that the top singers will earn multimillion-dollar annual salaries (most of which constitute economic rents, as discussed in Chapter 8). Slightly less talented singers earn much less, because the recording industry simply does not need them.

winner-take-all labor market one in which small differences in human capital translate into large differences in pay

The market for sopranos is an example of a **winner-take-all market,** one in which small differences in ability or other dimensions of human capital translate into large differences in pay. Such markets have long been familiar in entertainment and professional sports. But as technology has enabled the most talented individuals to serve broader markets, the winner-take-all reward structure has become an increasingly important feature of modern economic life, permeating such diverse fields as law, journalism, consulting, medicine, investment banking, corporate management, publishing, design, fashion, even the hallowed halls of academe.

Contrary to what the name seems to imply, a winner-take-all market does not mean a market with literally only one winner. Indeed, hundreds of professional musicians earn multimillion-dollar annual salaries. Yet tens of thousands of others, many of them nearly as good, struggle to pay their bills.

[1] S. Polachek and M. Kim, "Panel Estimates of the Male–Female Earnings Functions," *Journal of Human Resources,* **29** (2): 406–428, 1994.

The fact that small differences in human capital often give rise to extremely large differences in pay might seem to contradict human capital theory. Note, however, that the winner-take-all reward pattern is completely consistent with the competitive labor market theory's claim that individuals are paid in accordance with the contributions they make to the employer's net revenue. The leverage of technology often amplifies small performance differentials into very large ones.

 RECAP   **EXPLAINING DIFFERENCES IN EARNINGS AMONG PEOPLE**

Earnings differ among people in part because of differences in their human capital, an amalgam of personal characteristics that affect productivity. But pay often differs substantially between two people with the same amount of human capital. This can happen for many reasons: one may belong to a labor union while the other does not; one may work in a job with less pleasant conditions; one may be the victim of discrimination; or one may work in an arena in which technology or other factors provide greater leverage to human capital.

RECENT TRENDS IN INEQUALITY

In the United States, as in most other market economies, most citizens receive most of their income from the sale of their own labor. An attractive feature of the free-market system is that it rewards initiative, effort, and risk taking. The harder, longer, and more effectively a person works, the more she will be paid.

Yet relying on the marketplace to distribute income also entails an important drawback: Those who do well often end up with vastly more money than they can spend, while those who fail often cannot afford even basic goods and services. Hundreds of thousands of American families are homeless, and still larger numbers go to bed hungry each night. Many distinguished philosophers have argued that such poverty in the midst of plenty is impossible to justify on moral grounds. It is thus troubling that income inequality has been growing rapidly in recent decades.

The period from the end of World War II until the early 1970s was one of balanced income growth in the United States. During that period, incomes grew at almost 3 percent a year for rich, middle-class, and poor Americans alike. In the ensuing years, however, the pattern of income growth has been dramatically different.

In the first row of Table 13.2, for example, notice that families in the bottom 20 percent of the income distribution saw their real incomes grow by less than

TABLE 13.2
Mean Income Received by Families in Each Income Quintile and by the Top 5 Percent of Families, 1980–2000 (2000 dollars)

Quintile	1980	1990	2000
Bottom 20 percent	$ 12,756	$ 12,625	$ 14,232
Second 20 percent	27,769	29,448	32,268
Middle 20 percent	41,950	45,352	50,925
Fourth 20 percent	58,200	65,222	74,918
Top 20 percent	97,991	121,212	155,527
Top 5 percent	139,302	190,187	272,349

SOURCE: U.S. Census Bureau (http://www.census.gov/hhes/income/histinc/f03.html).

12 percent from 1980 to 2000 (a growth rate of less than one-half of 1 percent per year). The third row of the table indicates that the real incomes of families in the middle quintile grew by less than 22 percent during the same 20-year period (a growth rate of less than 1 percent per year). In contrast, real incomes jumped more than 58 percent for families in the top quintile between 1980 and 2000, while those for families in the top 5 percent jumped by more than 95 percent. Even for these families, however, income growth rates were low relative to those of the immediate post–World War II decades.

The only people whose incomes have grown substantially faster than in that earlier period are those at the very pinnacle of the income ladder. Real earnings of the top 1 percent of U.S. earners, for example, have more than doubled since 1980, and those even higher up have taken home paychecks that might have seemed unimaginable just two decades ago. The CEOs of America's largest companies, who earned 42 times as much as the average worker in 1980, now earn more than 500 times as much. These executives now average roughly $20 million a year, and the highest paid among them earn considerably more.

It is important to emphasize that being near the bottom of the income distribution in one year does not necessarily mean being stranded there forever. On the contrary, people in the United States have always experienced a high degree of economic mobility by international standards. Many CEOs now earning multimillion-dollar paychecks, for example, were struggling young graduate students in 1980, and were hence among those classified in the bottom 20 percent of the income distribution for that year in Table 13.2. We must bear in mind, too, that not all economic mobility is upward. Many blue-collar workers, for instance, had higher real incomes in 1980 than they do today.

On balance, then, the entries in Table 13.2 tell an important story. In contrast to the economy a quarter-century ago, those near the top of the income ladder today are prospering as never before, while those further down have seen their living standards grow much more slowly.

 RECAP   **RECENT TRENDS IN INEQUALITY**

From 1945 until the mid-1970s, incomes grew at almost 3 percent a year for rich, middle-class, and poor families alike. In contrast, most of the income growth since the mid-1970s has been concentrated among top earners.

WHY IS INCOME INEQUALITY A MORAL PROBLEM?

John Rawls, a moral philosopher at Harvard University, constructed a cogent ethical critique of the marginal productivity system, one based heavily on the economic theory of choice itself.[1] In thinking about what constitutes a just distribution of income, Rawls asks us to imagine ourselves meeting to choose the rules for distributing income. The meeting takes place behind a "veil of ignorance," which conceals from participants any knowledge of what talents and abilities each has. Because no individual knows whether he is smart or dull, strong or weak, fast or slow, no one knows which rules of distribution would work to his own advantage.

Rawls argues that the rules people would choose in such a state of ignorance would necessarily be fair; and if the rules are fair, the income distribution to which they give rise will also be fair.

What sort of rules would people choose from behind a veil of ignorance? If the national income were a fixed amount, most people would probably give everyone

[1]John Rawls, *A Theory of Justice,* Cambridge, Mass.: Harvard University Press, 1971.

an equal share. That scenario is likely, Rawls argues, because most people are strongly risk-averse. Since an unequal income distribution would involve not only a chance of doing well but a chance of doing poorly, most people would prefer to eliminate the risk by choosing an equal distribution. Imagine, for example, that you and two friends have been told that an anonymous benefactor donated $300,000 to divide among you. How would you split it? If you are like most people, you would propose an equal division, or $100,000 for each of you.

Yet the attraction of equality is far from absolute. Indeed, the goal of absolute equality is quickly trumped by other concerns when we make the rules for distributing wealth in modern market economies. Wealth, after all, generally doesn't come from anonymous benefactors; we must produce it. In a large economy, if each person were guaranteed an equal amount of income, few would invest in education or the development of special talents; and as the next example illustrates, the incentive to work would be sharply reduced.

Does income sharing affect labor supply?

EXAMPLE 13.3

Sue is offered a job reshelving books in the University of Montana library from noon until 1 P.M. each Friday. Her reservation wage for this task is $10 per hour. If the library director offers Sue $100 per hour, how much economic surplus will she enjoy as a result of accepting the job? Now suppose the library director announces that the earnings from the job will be divided equally among the 400 students who live in Sue's dormitory. Will Sue still accept?

When the $100 per hour is paid directly to Sue, she accepts the job and enjoys an economic surplus of $100 − $10 = $90. If the $100 were divided equally among the 400 residents of Sue's dorm, however, each resident's share would be only 25 cents. Accepting the job would thus mean a negative surplus for Sue of $0.25 − $10 = −$9.75, so she will not accept the job.

EXERCISE 13.4

What is the largest dorm population for which Sue would accept the job on a pay-sharing basis?

In a country without rewards for hard work and risk taking, national income would be dramatically smaller than in a country with such rewards. Of course, material rewards for effort and risk taking necessarily lead to inequality. Rawls argues, however, that people would be willing to accept a certain degree of inequality as long as these rewards produced a sufficiently large increase in the total amount of output available for distribution.

But how much inequality would people accept? Much less than the amount produced by purely competitive markets, Rawls argues. The idea is that behind the veil of ignorance, each person would fear ending up in a disadvantaged position, so each would choose rules that would produce a more equal distribution of income than exists under the marginal productivity system. And since such choices *define* the just distribution of income, he argues, fairness requires at least some attempt to reduce the inequality produced by the market system.

RECAP WHY IS INCOME INEQUALITY A MORAL PROBLEM?

John Rawls argues that the degree of inequality typical of unregulated market systems is unfair because people would favor substantially less inequality if they chose distributional rules from behind a veil of ignorance.

METHODS OF INCOME REDISTRIBUTION

Although we as a society have an interest in limiting income inequality, programs for reducing it are often fraught with practical difficulties. The challenge is to find ways to raise the incomes of those who cannot fend for themselves, without at the same time undermining their incentive to work, and without using scarce resources to subsidize those who are not poor. Of course, some people simply cannot work, or cannot find work that pays enough to live on. In a world of perfect information, the government could make generous cash payments to those people, and withhold support from those who can fend for themselves. In practice, however, the two groups are often hard to distinguish from each other. And so we must choose among imperfect alternative measures.

WELFARE PAYMENTS AND IN-KIND TRANSFERS

in-kind transfer a payment made not in the form of cash, but in the form of a good or service

Cash transfers and in-kind transfers are at the forefront of antipoverty efforts around the globe. **In-kind transfers** are direct transfers of goods or services to low-income individuals or families, such as food stamps, public housing, subsidized school lunches, and Medicaid.

From the mid-1960s until 1996, the most important federal program of cash transfers was Aid to Families with Dependent Children (AFDC), which in most cases provided cash payments to poor single-parent households. Critics of this program charged that it created incentives that undermined family stability, because a poor mother was ineligible for AFDC payments in many states if her husband or other able-bodied adult male lived with her and her children. This provision confronted many long-term unemployed fathers with an agonizing choice. They could leave their families, making them eligible for public assistance; or they could remain, making them ineligible. Even many who deeply loved their families understandably chose to leave.

Personal Responsibility Act the 1996 federal law that transferred responsibility for welfare programs from the federal level to the state level and placed a five-year lifetime limit on payment of AFDC benefits to any given recipient

Concern about work incentives led Congress to pass the **Personal Responsibility Act** in 1996, abolishing the federal government's commitment to provide cash assistance to low-income families. The new law requires the federal government to make lump-sum cash grants to the states, which are then free to spend it on AFDC benefits or other income-support programs of their own design. For each welfare recipient, the new law also sets a five-year lifetime limit on receipt of benefits under the AFDC program.

Supporters of the Personal Responsibility Act argue that it has already reduced the nation's welfare rolls substantially, and that it will encourage greater self-reliance over the long run. Skeptics fear that denial of benefits may eventually impose severe hardships on poor children if overall economic conditions deteriorate even temporarily. Debate continues about the extent to which the observed rise in homelessness and malnutrition among the nation's poorest families during the economic downturn of 2001 was attributable to the Personal Responsibility Act. What is clear, however, is that abolition of a direct federal role in the nation's antipoverty effort does not eliminate the need to discover efficient ways of providing assistance to people in need.

MEANS-TESTED BENEFIT PROGRAMS

means-tested a benefit program whose benefit level declines as the recipient earns additional income

Many welfare programs, including AFDC, are **means-tested**, which means that the more income a family has, the smaller are the benefits it receives under these programs. The purpose of means testing is to avoid paying benefits to those who don't really need them. But because of the way welfare programs are administered, means testing often has a pernicious effect on work incentives.

Consider, for example, an unemployed participant in four welfare programs: food stamps, rent stamps, energy stamps, and day care stamps. Each program gives him $100 worth of stamps per month, which he is then free to spend on food, rent, energy, and day care. If he gets a job, his benefits in each program are reduced by 50 cents for each dollar he earns. Thus, if he accepts a job that pays $50 weekly, he will lose $25 in weekly benefits from each of the four welfare programs, for a total benefit reduction of $100 per week. Taking the job thus leaves him $50 per week worse off than before. Low-income persons need no formal training in economics to realize that seeking gainful employment does not pay under these circumstances.

What is more, means-tested programs of cash and in-kind transfers are extremely costly to administer. If the government were to eliminate all existing welfare and social service agencies that are involved in these programs, the resulting savings would be enough to lift every poor person out of poverty. One proposal to do precisely this is the negative income tax.

THE NEGATIVE INCOME TAX

Under the **negative income tax** (**NIT**), every man, woman, and child—rich or poor—would receive a substantial income tax credit, say $4,500 per year. A person who earns no income would receive this credit in cash. People who earn income would receive the same initial credit, and their income would continue to be taxed at some rate less than 100 percent.

negative income tax (NIT) a system under which the government would grant every citizen a cash payment each year, financed by an additional tax on earned income

The negative income tax would do much less than current programs to weaken work incentives because, unlike current programs, it would ensure that someone who earned an extra dollar would keep at least a portion of it. And because the program would be administered by the existing Internal Revenue Service, administrative costs would be far lower than under the current welfare system.

Despite these advantages, however, the negative income tax is by no means a perfect solution to the income-transfer problem. Although the incentive problem under the program would be less severe than under current welfare programs, it would remain a serious difficulty. To see why, note that if the negative income tax were the *sole* means of insulating people against poverty, the payment to people with no earned income would need to be at least as large as the government's official **poverty threshold.**

The poverty threshold is the annual income level below which a family is officially classified as "poor" by the government. The threshold is based on government estimates of the cost of the so-called economy food plan, the least costly of four nutritionally adequate food plans designed by the Department of Agriculture. The department's 1955 Household Food Consumption Survey found that families of three or more people spent approximately one-third of their after-tax income on food, so the government pegs the poverty threshold at three times the cost of the economy food plan. In 2001, that threshold was approximately $18,000 for a family of four.

poverty threshold the level of income below which the federal government classifies a family as poor

For a family of four living in a city, $18,000 a year is scarcely enough to make ends meet. But suppose a group of, say, eight families were to pool their negative tax payments and move to the mountains of northern New Mexico. With a total of $144,000 per year to spend, plus the fruits of their efforts at gardening and animal husbandry, such a group could live very nicely indeed.

Once a small number of experimental groups demonstrated the feasibility of quitting their jobs and living well on the negative income tax, others would surely follow suit. Two practical difficulties would ensue. First, as more and more people left their jobs to live at government expense, the program would eventually become prohibitively costly. And second, the political cost of the program would almost surely force supporters to abandon it long before that point. Reports of people living lives of leisure at taxpayers' expense would be sure to appear on the nightly news. People who work hard at their jobs all day long would wonder why their tax dollars were being used to support those who are capable of holding paying jobs, yet choose not to work. If the resulting political backlash did not completely eliminate the negative income tax program, it would force policymakers to cut back the payment, so that members of rural communes could no longer afford to live comfortably. And that would mean the payment would no longer support an urban family. This difficulty has led policymakers to focus on other ways to increase the incomes of the working poor.

MINIMUM WAGES

The United States and many other industrialized countries have sought to ease the burden of low-wage workers by enacting minimum wage legislation—laws that prohibit employers from paying workers less than a specified hourly wage. The federal minimum wage in the United States is currently set at $5.15 per hour, and several states have set minimum wage levels significantly higher. Washington State, for example, increased its minimum wage to $6.90 per hour in 2002.

How does a minimum wage affect the market for low-wage labor? In Figure 13.5, note that when the law prevents employers from paying less than W_{min}, employers hire fewer workers (a decline from L_0 to L_1). Unemployment results. The L_1 workers who keep their jobs earn more than before, but the $L_0 - L_1$ workers who lose their jobs earn nothing. Whether workers together earn more or less than before thus depends on the elasticity of demand for labor. If elasticity of demand is less than 1, workers as a group will earn more than before. If it is more than 1, workers as a group will earn less.

FIGURE 13.5
The Effect of Minimum Wage Legislation on Employment.
If minimum wage legislation requires employers to pay more than the equilibrium wage, the result will be a decline in employment for low-wage workers.

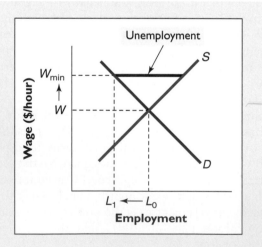

At one point, economists were almost unanimous in their opposition to minimum wage laws, arguing that those laws reduce total economic surplus, as do other regulations that prevent markets from reaching equilibrium. In recent years, however, some economists have softened their opposition to minimum wage laws, citing studies that have failed to show significant reductions in employment following increases in minimum wage levels. These studies may well imply that as a group low-income workers are better off with minimum wage laws than without them. But as we saw in Chapter 7, any policy that prevents a market from reaching equilibrium causes a reduction in total economic surplus—which means society ought to be able to find a more effective policy for helping low-wage workers.

THE EARNED-INCOME TAX CREDIT

One such policy is the **earned-income tax credit** (EITC), which gives low-wage workers a credit on their federal income tax each year. First proposed by President Richard Nixon, the EITC was enacted into law in 1975, and in the years since has drawn praise from both liberals and conservatives. The program is essentially a wage subsidy in the form of a credit against the amount a family owes in federal income taxes. For example, a family of four with total earned income of $13,000 in 2001 would have received an annual tax credit of about $4,000 under this program. That is, the program would have reduced the annual federal income tax payment of this family by roughly that amount. Families who earned less would have received a larger tax credit, and those who earned more would have received a smaller one. Families whose tax credit exceeds the amount of tax owed actually receive a check from the government for the difference. The EITC is thus essentially the same as a negative income tax, except that eligibility for the program is confined to people who work.

Like both the negative income tax and the minimum wage, the EITC puts extra income into the hands of workers who are employed at low wage levels. But unlike the minimum wage, the earned-income tax credit creates no incentive for employers to lay off low-wage workers.

The following examples illustrate how switching from a minimum wage to an earned-income tax credit can produce gains for both employers and workers.

earned-income tax credit *(EITC)* a policy under which low-income workers receive credits on their federal income tax

By how much will a minimum wage reduce total economic surplus?

Suppose the demand and supply curves for unskilled labor in the Tallahassee labor market are as shown in Figure 13.6. By how much will the imposition of a minimum wage at $7 per hour reduce total economic surplus? By how much do worker surplus and employer surplus change as a result of adopting the minimum wage?

In the absence of a minimum wage, the equilibrium wage for Tallahassee would be $5 per hour, and employment would be 5,000 person-hours per day. Both employers and workers would enjoy economic surplus equal to the area of the shaded triangles in Figure 13.6, $12,500 per day.

EXAMPLE 13.4

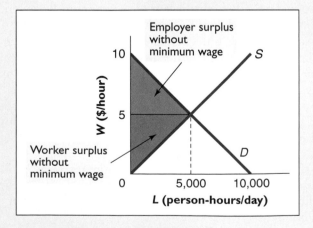

FIGURE 13.6
Worker and Employer Surplus in an Unregulated Labor Market.
For the demand and supply curves shown, worker surplus is the area of the lower shaded triangle, $12,500 per day, the same as employer surplus (upper shaded triangle).

With a minimum wage set at $7 per hour, employer surplus is the area of the cross-hatched triangle in Figure 13.7, $4,500 per day, and worker surplus is the area of the green shaded figure, $16,500 per day. The minimum wage thus reduces employer surplus by $8,000 per day and increases worker surplus by $4,000 per day. The net reduction in surplus is the area of the blue shaded triangle shown in Figure 13.7, $4,000 per day.

FIGURE 13.7

The Effect of a Minimum Wage on Economic Surplus.

A minimum wage of $7 per hour reduces employment in this market by 2,000 person-hours per day, for a reduction in total economic surplus of $4,000 per day (area of the blue shaded triangle). Employer surplus falls to $4,500 per day (area of cross-hatched triangle), while worker surplus rises to $16,500 per day (green shaded area).

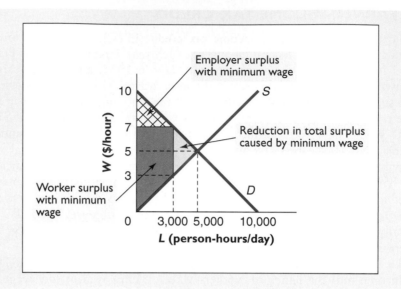

EXERCISE 13.5

In Example 13.4, by how much would total economic surplus have been reduced by the $7 minimum wage if labor demand in Tallahassee had been perfectly inelastic at 5,000 person-hours per day?

The following example illustrates the central message of the efficiency principle, which is that if the economic pie can be made larger, everyone can have a larger slice.

EXAMPLE 13.5

Refer to Example 13.4. How much would it cost the government each day to provide an earned-income tax credit under which workers as a group receive the same economic surplus as they do under the $7 per hour minimum wage? (Assume for simplicity that the earned-income tax credit has no effect on labor supply.)

With an earned-income tax credit in lieu of a minimum wage, employment will be 5,000 person-hours per day at $5 per hour, just as in the unregulated market. Since worker surplus in the unregulated market was $4,000 per day less than under the minimum wage, the government would have to offer a tax credit worth $0.80 per hour for each of the 5,000 person-hours of employment to restore worker surplus to the level obtained under the $7 minimum wage. With an EITC of that amount in effect, worker surplus would be the same as under the $7 minimum wage. If the EITC were financed by a $4,000 tax on employers, employer surplus would be $4,000 greater than under the $7 minimum wage.

We stress that our point is not that the minimum wage produces no gains for low-income workers, but rather that it is possible to provide even larger gains for these workers if we avoid policies that try to prevent labor markets from reaching equilibrium.

PUBLIC EMPLOYMENT FOR THE POOR

The main shortcoming of the EITC is that it does nothing for the unemployed poor. The negative income tax lacks that shortcoming but may substantially weaken work incentives. There is yet another method of transferring income to the poor that avoids both shortcomings. Government-sponsored jobs could pay wages to the unemployed poor for useful work. With public service employment, the specter of people living lives of leisure at public expense simply does not arise.

But public service employment has difficulties of its own. Evidence shows that if government jobs pay the same wages as private jobs, many people will leave their private jobs in favor of government jobs, apparently because they view government jobs as being more secure. Such a migration would make public service employment extremely expensive. Other worrisome possibilities are that such jobs might involve meaningless make-work tasks, and that they would prompt an expansion in government bureaucracy.

Acting alone, government-sponsored jobs for the poor, the EITC, or the negative income tax cannot solve the income-transfer problem. But a combination of these programs might do so.

A COMBINATION OF METHODS

Consider a negative income tax whose cash grant is far too small for anyone to live on, but that is supplemented if necessary by a public service job at below minimum wage. Keeping the wage in public service jobs well below the minimum wage would eliminate the risk of a large-scale exodus from private jobs. And while living well on either the negative income tax or the public service wage would be impossible, the two programs together could lift people out of poverty (see Figure 13.8).

To prevent an expansion of the bureaucracy, the government could solicit bids from private management companies to oversee the public service employment program. The fear that this program would inevitably become a make-work project is allayed by evidence that unskilled workers can, with proper supervision, perform many valuable tasks that would not otherwise be performed in the private sector. They can, for example, do landscaping and maintenance in public parks; provide transportation for the elderly and handicapped; fill potholes in city streets and replace burned-out street lamps; transplant seedlings in erosion control projects; remove graffiti from public places and paint government buildings; recycle newspapers and containers; staff day care centers; and so on.

Can unskilled workers perform useful public service jobs?

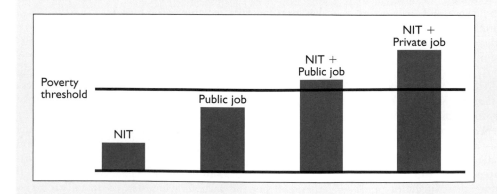

FIGURE 13.8
Income by Source in a Combination NIT–Jobs Program.
Together, a small negative income tax and a public job at below minimum wage would provide a family enough income to escape poverty, without weakening work incentives significantly.

This combination of a small negative income tax payment and public service employment at a subminimum wage would not be cheap. But the direct costs of existing welfare programs are also large, and the indirect costs, in the form of perverse work incentives and misguided attempts to control prices, are even larger. In economic terms, dealing intelligently with the income-transfer problem may in fact prove relatively inexpensive, once society recognizes the enormous opportunity cost of failing to deal intelligently with it.

RECAP　**METHODS OF INCOME REDISTRIBUTION**

Minimum wage laws reduce total economic surplus by contracting employment. The earned-income tax credit boosts the incomes of the working poor without that drawback, but neither policy provides benefits for those who are not employed.

Other instruments in the battle against poverty include in-kind transfers such as food stamps, subsidized school lunches, Medicaid, and public housing as well as cash transfers such as Aid to Families with Dependent Children. Because benefits under most of these programs are means-tested, beneficiaries often experience a net decline in income when they accept paid employment.

The negative income tax is an expanded version of the earned-income tax credit that includes those who are not employed. Combining this program with access to public service jobs would enable government to ensure adequate living standards for the poor without significantly undermining work incentives.

■ SUMMARY ■

- A worker's long-run equilibrium pay in a competitive labor market will be equal to the value of her marginal product (*VMP*)—the market value of whatever goods and services she produces for her employer. The law of diminishing returns says that when a firm's capital and other productive inputs are held fixed in the short run, adding workers beyond some point results in ever smaller increases in output. Firms that purchase labor in competitive labor markets face a constant wage, and they will hire labor up to the point at which *VMP* equals the market wage.

- Human capital theory says that an individual's *VMP* is proportional to his stock of human capital—an amalgam of education, experience, training, intelligence, and other factors that influence productivity. According to this theory, some occupations pay better than others simply because they require larger stocks of human capital.

- Wages often differ between individuals whose stocks of human capital appear nearly the same, as when one belongs to a labor union and the other does not. Compensating wage differentials—wage differences associated with differences in working conditions—are another important explanation for why individuals with similar human capital might earn different salaries. They help to explain why garbage collectors earn more than lifeguards and, more generally, why individuals with a given stock of human capital tend to earn more in jobs that have less attractive working conditions.

- Many firms pay members of certain groups—notably blacks and females—less than they pay white males who seem to have similar personal characteristics. If such wage gaps are the result of employer discrimination, their existence implies profit opportunities for firms that do not discriminate. Several other factors, including discrimination

by customers and institutions other than firms, may explain at least part of the observed wage gaps.

- Technologies that allow the most productive individuals to serve broader markets can translate even small differences in human capital into enormous differences in pay. Such technologies give rise to winner-take-all markets, which have long been common in sports and entertainment, and which are becoming common in other professions.

- Although incomes grew at almost 3 percent a year for all income classes during the three decades following World War II, the lion's share of income growth in the years since has been concentrated among top earners.

- Philosophers have argued that at least some income redistribution is justified in the name of fairness, because if people chose society's distributional rules without knowing their own personal circumstances, most would favor less inequality than would be produced by market outcomes.

- Policies and programs for reducing poverty include minimum wage laws, the earned-income tax credit, food stamps, subsidized school lunches, Medicaid, public housing, and Aid to Families with Dependent Children. Of these, all but the earned-income tax credit fail to maximize total economic surplus, either by interfering with work incentives or by preventing markets from reaching equilibrium.

- The negative income tax works much like the earned-income tax credit, except that it includes those who are not employed. A combination of a small negative income tax and access to public service jobs at subminimum wages could ensure adequate living standards for the poor without significantly undermining work incentives.

■ KEY TERMS ■

compensating wage differential (334)
customer discrimination (335)
earned-income tax credit (EITC) (343)
employer discrimination (334)
human capital (331)

human capital theory (331)
in-kind transfer (340)
labor union (331)
marginal product (*MP*) (327)
means-tested (340)

negative income tax (NIT) (341)
Personal Responsibility Act (340)
poverty threshold (341)
value of marginal product (*VMP*) (327)
winner-take-all market (336)

■ REVIEW QUESTIONS ■

1. Why is the supply curve of labor for any specific occupation likely to be upward-sloping, even if, for the economy as a whole, people work fewer hours when wage rates increase?

2. True or false: If the human capital possessed by two workers is nearly the same, their wage rates will be nearly the same. Explain.

3. How might recent changes in income inequality be related to the proliferation of technologies that enable the most productive individuals to serve broader markets?

4. Mention two self-interested reasons that a top earner might favor policies to redistribute income.

5. Why is exclusive reliance on the negative income tax unlikely to constitute a long-term solution to the poverty problem?

■ PROBLEMS ■

1. Mountain Breeze supplies air filters to the retail market and hires workers to assemble the components. An air filter sells for $26, and Mountain Breeze can buy the components for each filter for $1. Sandra and Bobby are two workers for Mountain Breeze. Sandra can assemble 60 air filters per month, and Bobby can assemble 70. If the labor market is perfectly competitive, how much will Sandra and Bobby be paid?

2. Stone, Inc., owns a clothing factory and hires workers in a competitive labor market to stitch cut denim fabric into jeans. The fabric required to make each pair of jeans costs $5. The company's weekly output of finished jeans varies with the number of workers hired, as shown in the following table:

Number of workers	Jeans (pairs/week)
0	0
1	25
2	45
3	60
4	72
5	80
6	85

a. If the jeans sell for $35 a pair, and the competitive market wage is $250 per week, how many workers should Stone hire? How many pairs of jeans will the company produce each week?

b. Suppose the Clothing Workers Union now sets a weekly minimum acceptable wage of $230 per week. All the workers Stone hires belong to the union. How does the minimum wage affect Stone's decision about how many workers to hire?

c. If the minimum wage set by the union had been $400 per week, how would the minimum wage affect Stone's decision about how many workers to hire?

d. If Stone again faces a market wage of $250 per week but the price of jeans rises to $45, how many workers will the company now hire?

3. Acme, Inc., supplies rocket ships to the retail market and hires workers to assemble the components. A rocket ship sells for $30,000, and Acme can buy the components for each rocket ship for $25,000. Wiley and Sam are two workers for Acme. Sam can assemble 1/5 of a rocket ship per month, and Wiley can assemble 1/10. If the labor market is perfectly competitive and rocket components are Acme's only other cost, how much will Sam and Wiley be paid?

4. Carolyn owns a soda factory and hires workers in a competitive labor market to bottle the soda. Her company's weekly output of bottled soda varies with the number of workers hired, as shown in the following table:

Number of workers	Cases/week
0	0
1	200
2	360
3	480
4	560
5	600

a. If each case sells for $10 more than the cost of the materials used in producing it and the competitive market wage is $1,000 per week, how many workers should Carolyn hire? How many cases will be produced per week?
b. Suppose the Soda Bottlers Union now sets a weekly minimum acceptable wage of $1,500 per week. All the workers Carolyn hires belong to the union. How does the minimum wage affect Carolyn's decision about how many workers to hire?
c. If the wage is again $1,000 per week but the price of soda rises to $15 per case, how many workers will Carolyn now hire?

5. Suppose the equilibrium wage for unskilled workers in New Jersey is $7 per hour. How will the wages and employment of unskilled workers in New Jersey change if the state legislature raises the minimum wage from $5.15 per hour to $6 per hour?

6. Jones, who is currently unemployed, is a participant in three means-tested welfare programs: food stamps, rent stamps, and day care stamps. Each program grants him $150 per month in stamps, which can be used like cash to purchase the good or service they cover.
a. If benefits in each program are reduced by 40 cents for each additional dollar Jones earns in the labor market, how will Jones's economic position change if he accepts a job paying $120 per week?
b. In light of your answer to part a, explain why means testing for welfare recipients has undesirable effects on work incentives.

7. Sue is offered a job reshelving books in the University of Montana library from noon until 1 P.M. each Friday. Her reservation wage for this task is $10 per hour.
a. If the library director offers Sue $100 per hour, how much economic surplus will she enjoy as a result of accepting the job?
b. Now suppose the library director announces that the earnings from the job will be divided equally among the 400 students who live in Sue's dormitory. Will Sue still accept?
c. Explain how your answers to parts a and b illustrate one of the incentive problems inherent in income redistribution programs.

8.* Suppose the demand and supply curves for unskilled labor in the Corvallis labor market are as shown in the accompanying figure. By how much will the imposition of a minimum wage at $12 per hour reduce total economic surplus? Calculate the amounts by which employer surplus and worker surplus change as a result of the minimum wage.

*Problems marked with an asterisk (*) are more difficult.

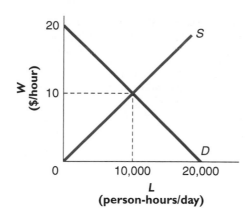

9.* Refer to Problem 8. How much would it cost the government each day to provide an earned-income tax credit under which workers as a group receive the same economic surplus as they do under the $12 per hour minimum wage? (Assume for simplicity that the earned-income tax credit has no effect on labor supply.)

10.* Suppose employers and workers are risk-neutral, and Congress is about to enact the $12 per hour minimum wage described in Problem 8. Congressional staff economists have urged legislators to consider adopting an earned-income tax credit instead. Suppose neither workers nor employers would support that proposal unless the expected value of each party's economic surplus would be at least as great as under the minimum wage. Describe an earned-income tax credit (and a tax that would raise enough money to pay for it) that would receive unanimous support from both workers and employers.

■ ANSWERS TO IN-CHAPTER EXERCISES ■

13.1 At a price of $26 per cutting board, the fifth worker has a *VMP* of $364 per week, so Adirondack should hire five workers.

13.2 Since the *VMP* of each worker exceeds $275, Adirondack should hire five workers.

13.3 When the wage rate is $9 per hour in each market, 25 fewer workers will be employed in the nonunionized market and 25 more in the unionized market. The loss in output from removing 25 workers from the nonunionized market is the sum of the *VMP*s of those workers, which is the shaded area in the right panel of the figure below. This area is $187.50 per hour. (*Hint:* To calculate this area, first break the figure into a rectangle and a triangle.) The gain in output from adding 25 workers to the unionized market is the shaded area in the left panel, which is $262.50 per hour. The net increase in output is thus $262.50 − $187.50 = $75 per hour.

*Problems marked with an asterisk (*) are more difficult.

13.4 Since Sue's reservation wage is $10 per hour, she must be paid at least that amount before she will accept the job. The largest dorm population for which she will accept is thus 10 residents, since her share in that case would be exactly $10 per hour.

13.5 With perfectly inelastic demand, employment would remain at 5,000 person-hours per day, so the minimum wage would cause no reduction in economic surplus.

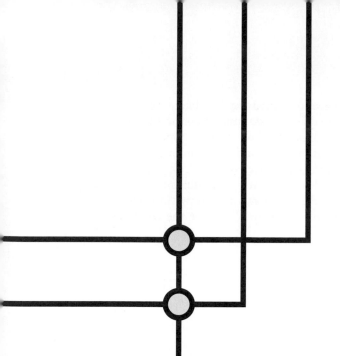

CHAPTER

14

THE ENVIRONMENT, HEALTH, AND SAFETY

■

In 1979, in the wake of the second major oil supply interruption in a decade, officials in the Carter administration met to discuss policies for reducing the risks to domestic security inherent in U.S. dependence on foreign oil. The proposal they ultimately put forward was a gasoline tax of 50 cents per gallon. Anticipating objections that the tax would impose an unacceptable hardship on the poor, policymakers proposed to return the revenues from the tax to the citizenry by reducing the payroll tax—the tax on wages that supports the Social Security system.

Proponents of the gasoline tax argued that in addition to reducing the nation's dependence on foreign oil, the tax would reduce air pollution and ease highway congestion. But critics ridiculed the proposal, charging that if the revenues from the tax were returned to the people, the quantity of gasoline demanded would remain essentially the same. Their argument tipped the debate, and officials never managed to implement the proposal.

But whatever the ultimate merits of the administration's proposal, there was no merit at all in the argument the critics used to attack it. True, the proposed tax rebate meant that people *could* have bought just as much gasoline as before the tax. Yet the tax would have given them a powerful incentive not to do so. As we saw in Chapter 5, consumers can change their behavior to escape the effects of a steep rise in the after-tax price of gasoline—by switching to cars with smaller, more fuel-efficient engines, forming carpools, and so on. Such changes free up money to spend on other goods and services, which become relatively more attractive because they are not taxed.

No society can hope to formulate and implement intelligent economic policies unless its citizens and leaders share an understanding of basic economic principles. Our aim in this chapter will be to explore how careful application of these principles can help us design policies that both expand the economic pie and make everyone's slice larger. We will explore the economics of health care delivery, environmental regulation, and public health and safety regulation. The unifying thread running through these issues is the problem of scarcity. In each case, we will explore how the cost-benefit principle can help to resolve the resulting trade-offs.

THE ECONOMICS OF HEALTH CARE DELIVERY

In the United States, real health care expenditures per capita have grown more rapidly than real income per capita for as long as the relevant data have been available. As a share of national income, health care costs have risen from only 4 percent in 1940 to roughly 14 percent today. Part of this increase is the result of costly new health care technologies and procedures. Diagnostic tests have grown more expensive and sophisticated, and procedures like coronary bypass surgery and organ transplantation have grown far more common. Yet a great deal of medical expenditure inflation has nothing to do with these high-tech developments. Rather, it is the result of fundamental changes in the way we pay for medical services.

The most important change has been the emergence of the so-called third-party payment system. Earlier in this century, many people insured themselves against catastrophic illness but purchased routine medical care out of their own pockets, just as they did food, clothing, and other consumer goods. But starting after World War II, and increasingly since the mid-1960s, people have come to depend on insurance for even routine medical services. Some of this insurance is provided privately by employers; some, by the government. In the latter category, Medicaid covers the medical expenses of the poor, and Medicare those of the elderly and disabled.

The spread of medical insurance, especially government-financed medical insurance, owes much to the belief that an inability to pay should not prevent people from receiving medical care they need. Indeed, medical insurance has surely done much to shelter people from financial hardship. The difficulty is that in its most common form, it has also spawned literally hundreds of billions of dollars of waste each year.

APPLYING THE COST-BENEFIT CRITERION

To understand the nature of this waste, we must recognize that although medical services differ from other services in many ways, they are in one fundamental respect the same: The cost-benefit test is the only sensible criterion for deciding which services ought to be performed. The fact that a medical procedure has *some* benefit does not, by itself, imply that the procedure should be performed. Rather, it should be performed only if its benefit, broadly construed, exceeds its cost.

The costs of medical procedures are relatively easy to measure, using the same methods applied to other goods and services. But the usual measure of the benefit of a good or service, a person's willingness to pay, may not be acceptable in the case of many medical services. For example, most of us would not conclude that a lifesaving appendectomy is unjustified merely because the person who needs it can afford to pay only half of its $2,000 cost. When someone lacks the resources to pay for what most of us would consider an essential medical service, society has at least some responsibility to help. Hence the proliferation of government-sponsored medical insurance.

Many other medical expenditures are not as pressing as an emergency appendectomy, however. Following such surgery, for example, the patient requires a period of recuperation in the hospital. How long should that period last—2 days? 5? 10? The cost-benefit principle is critically important to thinking intelligently about such questions. But as the following example illustrates, the third-party payment system has virtually eliminated cost-benefit thinking from the medical domain.

How long should David stay in the hospital?

EXAMPLE 14.1

To eliminate recurrent sore throats, David plans to have his tonsils removed. His surgeon tells him that the average hospital stay after this procedure is two days (some people stay only one day, while others stay three, four, or even five days). Hospital rooms cost $300 per day. If David's demand curve for days in the hospital is as shown in Figure 14.1, how many days will he stay if he must pay for his hospital room himself? How many days will he stay if his medical insurance fully covers the cost of his hospital room?

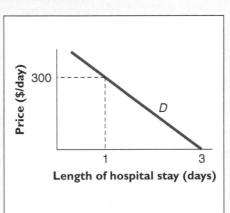

FIGURE 14.1

The Demand for Hospital Care.

The demand curve for postoperative hospital care is downward-sloping, just like any other demand curve. At higher prices, people choose shorter hospital stays, not because there is no benefit to a longer stay, but because they prefer to spend their money in other ways.

If David must pay for his hospital room himself, his best option will be to stay for just one day. But if the cost of his hospital room is completely covered by insurance, the marginal cost *to him* will be zero. In that case he will stay for three days.

EXERCISE 14.1

In Example 14.1, how long would David choose to stay in the hospital if his health insurance covered 50 percent of the cost of his hospital room?

Should we be concerned that people choose longer hospital stays when their expenses are fully insured? The cost-benefit principle tells us that a hospital stay should be extended another day only if the benefit of doing so would be at least as great as the cost of the resources required to extend the stay. But when hospital costs are fully covered by insurance, the decision maker sees a marginal cost of zero, when in fact the marginal cost is several hundred dollars. According to the cost-benefit criterion, then, full insurance coverage leads to wastefully long hospital stays. This is not to say that the additional days in the hospital do no good at all. Rather, their benefit is less than their cost. As the next example illustrates, a shorter hospital stay would increase total economic surplus.

How much waste does full insurance coverage cause?

EXAMPLE 14.2

Using the demand and cost information from Example 14.1, calculate how much waste results from full insurance coverage of David's hospital room.

If the marginal cost of an additional day in the hospital is $300, the supply curve of hospital room days in an open market would be horizontal at $300. If David had to pay that price, he would choose a one-day stay, which would result in the largest possible economic surplus. If he extends his stay past one day, cost continues to accumulate at the rate of $300 per day, but the benefit of additional care—as measured by his demand curve—falls below $300. If he stays three days, as he will if he has full insurance coverage, the two extra days cost society $600 but benefit David by only $300 (the area of the lower shaded triangle under David's demand curve in Figure 14.2). The amount by which the extra cost exceeds the extra benefit will thus be $300 (the area of the upper shaded triangle).

FIGURE 14.2
The Waste That Results from Full Insurance Coverage.
The area of the lower shaded triangle ($300) represents the benefit of extending the hospital stay from one day to three days. Since the cost of the extra two days is $600, the area of the upper shaded triangle ($300) represents the loss in economic surplus that results from the longer stay.

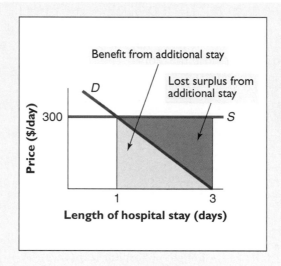

EXERCISE 14.2

In Example 14.2, how much waste would be caused by an insurance policy that reimbursed hospital room expenses at the rate of $150 per day?

DESIGNING A SOLUTION

In circumstances in which economic surplus has not been maximized, a transaction can always be found that will make both the patient *and* the insurance company better off. Suppose, for example, that the insurance company in Example 14.2 gives David a cash payment of $700 toward hospital expenses and lets him decide for himself how long to stay in the hospital. Confronted with a price of $300 per day, David would choose to stay only a single day. The $400 cash he would have left after paying his hospital bill is $100 more than enough to compensate him for the benefit he would lose by not staying an extra two days. (Again, that benefit is $300, the area of the lower shaded triangle in Figure 14.2.) A $700 cash payment would also leave his insurance company better off by $200 than if it had provided unlimited hospital coverage at no extra charge (since David would have stayed three days in that case, at a cost of $900 to his insurance company). And since no one else is harmed by this transaction, it represents a *Pareto improvement* over unlimited coverage, meaning a change that makes some people better off without harming others (see Chapter 7).

The amount of waste caused by full insurance coverage depends on the price elasticity of demand for medical services—the more elastic the demand, the greater the waste. Proponents of full coverage believe that the demand for medical services is almost completely inelastic with respect to price and that the resulting waste is therefore negligible. Critics of full coverage argue that the demand for medical services is actually quite sensitive to price and that the resulting waste is significant.

Who is right? One way to determine this is to examine whether people who lack full insurance coverage spend significantly less than those who have it. The economist W. G. Manning and several co-authors did so by performing an experiment in which they assigned subjects randomly to one of two different kinds of medical insurance policy.[1] The first group of subjects received **first-dollar coverage,** meaning that 100 percent of their medical expenses was covered by insurance. The second group got "$1,000-deductible" coverage, meaning that only expenses beyond the first $1,000 a year were covered. (For example, someone with $1,200 of medical bills would receive $1,200 from his insurance company if he belonged to the first group, but only $200 if he belonged to the second.) In effect, since most people incur less than $1,000 a year in medical expenses, most subjects in the second group effectively paid full price for their medical services, while subjects in the first group paid nothing. Manning and his colleagues found that *people with $1,000-deductible policies spent between 40 and 50 percent less on health care than subjects with first-dollar coverage. More important, there were no measurable differences in health outcomes between the two groups.*

Taken at face value, the results of the Manning study suggest that a large share of the inflation in medical expenditures since World War II has been caused by growth in first-dollar medical insurance. Why not simply abandon first-dollar coverage in favor of high deductibles? People would still be protected against financial catastrophe but would have a strong incentive to avoid medical services whose benefit does not exceed their cost.

Some would say that Medicaid and Medicare should not carry high deductibles because the resulting out-of-pocket payments would impose too great a burden on poor families. But as in other instances in which concern for the poor is offered in defense of an inefficient policy, an alternative can be designed that is better for rich and poor alike. For example, all health insurance could be written to include high deductibles, and the poor could be given an annual stipend to defray the initial medical expenses not covered by insurance. At year's end, any unspent stipend would be theirs to keep. Here again, concern for the well-being of the poor is simply no reason for not adopting the most efficient policy. As the efficiency principle reminds us, when the economic pie grows larger, it is possible for everyone to have a larger slice.

THE HMO REVOLUTION

During the 1990s, the high cost of conventional health insurance led many to people to switch to **health maintenance organizations (HMOs).** An HMO is a group of physicians that provides its patients with medical services in return for a fixed annual fee. As the next example illustrates, the incentive to provide any given medical service is weaker under the standard HMO contract than under conventional health insurance.

Why is a patient with a sore knee more likely to receive an MRI exam if he has conventional health insurance than if he belongs to a health maintenance organization?

When a patient visits his physician complaining of a sore knee, the physician has several options. After hearing the patient describe his symptoms and examining the knee manually, the physician may prescribe anti-inflammatory drugs and advise the patient to abstain from vigorous physical activity for a period; or she may advise the patient to undergo a magnetic resonance imaging (MRI) exam, a costly

first-dollar insurance coverage insurance that pays all expenses generated by the insured activity

health maintenance organization (HMO) a group of physicians that provides health services to individuals and families for a fixed annual fee

ECONOMIC NATURALIST 14.1

[1]W. G. Manning, J. P. Newhouse, E. B. Keeler, A. Liebowitz, and M. S. Marquis, "Health Insurance and the Demand for Medical Care," *American Economic Review,* 77: 251–277, June 1987.

diagnostic procedure that generates images of the inner workings of the injured joint. The physician in an HMO receives no additional revenue if she orders the MRI, because all services are covered by the patient's fixed annual fee. Under conventional health insurance, in contrast, the physician will be reimbursed at a fixed rate, usually well above her marginal cost, for each additional service performed.

"Well, Bob, it looks like a paper cut, but just to be sure, let's do lots of tests."

In many instances, the most prudent course of treatment is unambiguous, and in such cases physicians will make the same recommendation despite this striking difference in incentives. But in many other cases, it may not be obvious which decision is best. And in these cases, HMO physicians are less likely to order expensive tests.

People who switch to HMOs pay less for their health plans than those who stick with conventional health insurance, because the HMO contract provides a strong incentive for doctors not to prescribe nonessential services. Many people fear, however, that the very same incentive may sometimes result in their not receiving valuable care. These concerns have led to proposed legislation granting patients rights of appeal when they are denied care by an HMO.

PAYING FOR HEALTH INSURANCE

That access to medical care is extremely limited in many of the world's poorest nations is troubling, but perhaps not surprising. After all, citizens of those nations lack enough income to buy adequate food, shelter, and many other basic goods and services. What *is* surprising, however, is that despite the movement to less expensive HMO plans, some 40 million Americans had no health coverage of any kind in 2002. Politicians in both parties agree that something must be done to expand health coverage. But before an intelligent solution to this problem can be implemented, we must first understand why so many are without coverage in the first place.

In the richest country on Earth, why do so many people lack basic health insurance?

Although the incomes of most Americans are higher than ever, millions of American families continue to experience day-to-day financial distress. For example, at the height of the economic boom in 1998, one of every 68 families filed for bankruptcy, more than the number of families with children graduating from college that year. Under the circumstances, it is easy to see why many families in generally good health might be tempted to press their luck. After all, health coverage for a family of four with no preexisting medical conditions costs upwards of $5,000 a year, which is almost always far more than what such a family spends on medical services. The extra cash could help pay for a move into a better school district, for example, or at least keep creditors at bay.

As more people cancel their health coverage, going without insurance becomes more socially acceptable. Parents who didn't buy health insurance for their families were once viewed as irresponsible, but this stigma loses some of its sting as the number of uninsured grows. Making matters worse is the changing composition of the pool of the insured. As more healthy families forgo coverage, those left tend to be sicker and more costly to treat, forcing up premiums (an example of *adverse selection,* discussed in Chapter 12). In short, our health insurance system is in a long-term downward spiral. And as more people become uninsured, the problem will get worse, because the costs borne by those who remain insured will continue to escalate.

Government could eliminate the downward spiral by simply reimbursing each family up to $5,000 a year for health insurance. Government bureaucrats would not need to prescribe which doctors we see or micromanage any of the other details. They would simply process insurance receipts and send out reimbursement checks. This plan sounds expensive but would actually be less costly than the current system. The principal savings would come from delivering more cost-effective care to those who are now uninsured.

As it stands now, the untreated minor illnesses of the uninsured often develop into major illnesses, which are far more costly to treat. And when such illnesses befall the uninsured, we almost always treat them, often in costly emergency rooms. The resulting burden on hospitals leads to higher fees and increased government support—both of which now come largely out of the pockets of high-income taxpayers with health insurance.

The total budget needed to finance a $5,000 health insurance reimbursement for every American family—some $350 billion a year—would obviously require higher taxes. But for those whose employers currently provide health insurance, these taxes would be offset by an increase in salaries. After all, companies offer insurance not because they are charitable, but because they find doing so an effective way to compete for workers. Any company that did not offer higher salaries to previously insured workers would risk losing them to a company that did.

A universal reimbursement program would impose no net burden on taxpayers, because of both salary adjustments and reductions in the high cost of care for the uninsured. And by providing a powerful incentive for all families to buy insurance, it would reverse the current downward spiral.

Critics of health care reform may say that if some people want to save money by going without health insurance, that's their problem or their choice. Perhaps, but it's a problem for the rest of society as well, one that if left untended will grow steadily worse.

ECONOMIC NATURALIST 14.2

RECAP **THE ECONOMICS OF HEALTH CARE DELIVERY**

The rapid escalation in medical expenditures since World War II is attributable in large part to the spread of first-dollar insurance coverage, which encourages people to behave as if medical services were free of charge. Total economic surplus would be larger if we switched to insurance coverage with high deductibles, because such policies provide an incentive to use only those services whose benefit exceeds their cost.

The switch to HMOs addresses this problem, because the standard HMO contract provides a strong incentive for physicians not to prescribe nonessential services. Some voice concern, however, that HMO contracts may lead physicians to withhold services that satisfy the cost-benefit test.

Mounting insurance premiums have caused many people in good health to do without health coverage, resulting in higher premiums for those who remain insured. Government reimbursement for health coverage is one way to stop the downward spiral in health coverage.

USING PRICE INCENTIVES IN ENVIRONMENTAL REGULATION

As we saw in Chapter 11, goods whose production generates negative externalities, such as atmospheric pollution, tend to be overproduced whenever negotiation among private parties is costly. Suppose we decide, as a society, that the best attainable outcome would be to have half as much pollution as would occur under completely unregulated conditions. In that case, how should the cleanup effort be distributed among those firms that currently discharge pollution into the environment?

The most efficient—and hence best—distribution of effort is the one for which each polluter's marginal cost of abatement is exactly the same. To see why, imagine that under current arrangements, the cost to one firm of removing a ton of pollution from the air is larger than the cost to another firm. Society could then achieve the same total reduction in pollution at lower cost by having the first firm discharge 1 ton more into the air and the second firm 1 ton less.

Unfortunately, government regulators seldom have detailed information on how the cost of reducing pollution varies from one firm to another. Many pollution laws therefore require all polluters simply to cut back their emissions by the same proportion or to meet the same absolute emissions standards. If different polluters have different marginal costs of pollution abatement, however, these approaches will not be efficient.

TAXING POLLUTION

Fortunately, alternative policies can distribute the cleanup more efficiently, even if the government lacks detailed information about how much it costs different firms to curtail pollution. One method is to tax pollution and allow firms to decide for themselves how much pollution to emit. The following example illustrates the logic of this approach.

EXAMPLE 14.3

What is the least costly way to cut pollution by half?

Two firms, Sludge Oil and Northwest Lumber, each has access to five production processes, each of which has a different cost and produces a different amount of pollution. The daily costs of the processes and the number of tons of smoke emitted are as shown in Table 14.1. Pollution is currently unregulated, and negotiation between the firms and those who are harmed by pollution is impossible, which means that each firm uses process A, the least costly of the five. Each firm emits 4 tons of pollution per day, for a total of 8 tons of pollution day.

The government is considering two options for reducing total emissions by half. One is to require each firm to curtail its emissions by half. The other is to set a tax of $T per ton of smoke emitted each day. How large must T be to curtail emissions by half? What would be the total cost to society under each alternative?

TABLE 14.1
Costs and Emissions for Different Production Processes

Process (smoke)	A (4 tons/day)	B (3 tons/day)	C (2 tons/day)	D (1 ton/day)	E (0 tons/day)
Cost to Sludge Oil ($/day)	100	200	600	1,300	2,300
Cost to Northwest Lumber ($/day)	300	320	380	480	700

If each firm is required to cut pollution by half, each must switch from process A to process C. The result will be 2 tons per day of pollution for each firm. The cost of the switch for Sludge Oil will be $600 per day − $100 per day = $500 per day. The cost to Northwest Lumber will be $380 per day − $300 per day = $80 per day, for a total cost of $580 per day.

Consider now how each firm would react to a tax of $T per ton of pollution. If a firm can cut pollution by 1 ton per day, it will save $T per day in tax payments. Whenever the cost of cutting a ton of pollution is less than $T, then, each firm has an incentive to switch to a cleaner process. For example, if the tax were set at $40 per ton, Sludge Oil would stick with process A, because switching to process B would cost $100 per day extra but would save only $40 per day in taxes. Northwest Lumber, however, would switch to process B, because the $40 saving in taxes would be more than enough to cover the $20 cost of switching.

The problem is that a $40 per day tax on each ton of pollution results in a reduction of only 1 ton per day, 3 short of the 4-ton target. Suppose instead that the government imposed a tax of $101 per ton. Sludge Oil would then adopt process B, because the $100 extra daily cost of doing so would be less than the $101 saved in taxes. Northwest Lumber would adopt process D, because for every process up to and including C, the cost of switching to the next process would be less than the resulting tax saving.

Overall, then, a tax of $101 per ton would result in the desired pollution reduction of 4 tons per day. The total cost of the reduction would be only $280 per day ($100 per day for Sludge Oil and $180 per day for Northwest Lumber), or $300 per day less than when each firm was required to cut its pollution by half. (The taxes paid by the firms do not constitute a cost of pollution reduction, because the money can be used to reduce whatever taxes would otherwise need to be levied on citizens.)

EXERCISE 14.3

In Example 14.3, if the tax were $61 per ton of pollution emitted each day, which production processes would the two firms adopt?

The advantage of the tax approach is that it concentrates pollution reduction in the hands of the firms that can accomplish it at least cost. Requiring each firm to cut emissions by the same proportion ignores the fact that some firms can reduce pollution much more cheaply than others. Note that under the tax approach, the cost of the last ton of smoke removed is the same for each firm, so the efficiency condition is satisfied.

One problem with the tax approach is that unless the government has detailed knowledge about each firm's cost of reducing pollution, it cannot know how high to set the pollution tax. A tax that is too low will result in too much pollution, while a tax that is too high will result in too little. Of course, the government could start by setting a low tax rate and gradually increasing the rate until pollution is reduced to the target level. But because firms often incur substantial sunk costs when they switch from one process to another, that approach might be even more wasteful than requiring all firms to cut their emissions by the same proportion.

AUCTIONING POLLUTION PERMITS

Another alternative is to establish a target level for pollution and then auction off permits to emit that level. The virtues of this approach are illustrated in the following example.

EXAMPLE 14.4   **How much will pollution permits sell for?**

Two firms, Sludge Oil and Northwest Lumber, again have access to the production processes described earlier (which are reproduced in Table 14.2). The government's goal is to cut the current level of pollution, 8 tons per day, by half. To do so, the government auctions off four permits, each of which entitles the bearer to emit 1 ton of smoke per day. No smoke may be emitted without a permit. What price will the pollution permits fetch at auction, how many permits will each firm buy, and what will be the total cost of the resulting pollution reduction?

TABLE 14.2
Costs and Emissions for Different Production Processes

Process (smoke)	A (4 tons/day)	B (3 tons/day)	C (2 tons/day)	D (1 ton/day)	E (0 tons/day)
Cost to Sludge Oil ($/day)	100	200	600	1,300	2,300
Cost to Northwest Lumber ($/day)	300	320	380	480	700

If Sludge Oil has no permits, it must use process E, which costs $2,300 per day to operate. If it had one permit, it could use process D, which would save it $1,000 per day. Thus the most Sludge Oil would be willing to pay for a single 1-ton pollution permit is $1,000 per day. With a second permit, Sludge Oil could switch to process C and save another $700 per day; with a third permit, it could switch to process B and save another $400; and with a fourth permit, it could switch to process A and save another $100. Using similar reasoning, we can see that Northwest Lumber would pay up to $220 for one permit, up to $100 for a second, up to $60 for a third, and up to $20 for a fourth.

Suppose the government starts the auction at a price of $90. Sludge Oil will then demand four permits and Northwest Lumber will demand two, for a total demand of six permits. Since the government wishes to sell only four permits, it will keep raising the price until the two firms together demand a total of only four permits. Once the price reaches $101, Sludge Oil will demand three permits and Northwest Lumber will demand only one, for a total quantity demanded of four permits. Compared to the unregulated alternative, in which each firm used process A, the daily cost of the auction solution is $280: Sludge Oil spends $100 switching from process *A* to process *B,* and Northwest Lumber spends $180 switching from *A* to *D.* This total is $300 less than the cost of requiring each firm to reduce its emissions by half. (Again, the permit fees paid by the firms do not constitute a cost of cleanup, because the money can be used to reduce taxes that would otherwise have to be collected.)

The auction method has the same virtue as the tax method: It concentrates pollution reduction in the hands of those firms that can accomplish it at the lowest cost. But the auction method has other attractive features that the tax approach does not. First, it does not induce firms to commit themselves to costly investments that they will have to abandon if the cleanup falls short of the target level. And second, it allows private citizens a direct voice in determining where the emission level will be set. For example, any group that believes the pollution target is too lenient could raise money to buy permits at auction. By keeping those permits locked away in a safe, the group could ensure that they will not be used to emit pollution.

Several decades ago, when economists first proposed the auctioning of pollution permits, reactions of outrage were widely reported in the press. Most of those reactions amounted to the charge that the proposal would "permit rich firms to pollute to their hearts' content." Such an assertion betrays a total misunderstanding of the forces that generate pollution. Firms pollute not because they *want* to pollute, but because dirty production processes are cheaper than clean ones. Society's only real interest is in keeping the total amount of pollution from becoming excessive, not in *who* actually does the polluting. And in any event, the firms that do most of the polluting under an auction system will not be rich firms, but those for whom pollution reduction is most costly.

Economists have argued patiently against these misinformed objections to the auction system, and their efforts have finally borne fruit. The sale of pollution permits is now common in several parts of the United States, and there is growing interest in the approach in other countries.

 RECAP **USING PRICE INCENTIVES IN ENVIRONMENTAL REGULATION**

An efficient program for reducing pollution is one for which the marginal cost of abatement is the same for all polluters. Taxing pollution has this desirable property, as does the auction of pollution permits. The auction method has the advantage that regulators can achieve a desired abatement target without having detailed knowledge of the abatement technologies available to polluters.

WORKPLACE SAFETY REGULATION

Most industrialized countries have laws that attempt to limit the extent to which workers are exposed to health and safety risks on the job. These laws often are described as necessary to protect workers against exploitation by employers with market power. Given the working conditions we saw in the early stages of the industrial revolution, the idea that such exploitation pervades unregulated private markets has intuitive appeal. Witness Upton Sinclair's vivid account of life in the Chicago meat-packing factories at the turn of the twentieth century:

> Some worked at the stamping machines, and it was very seldom that
> one could work long there at the pace that was set, and not give
> out and forget himself, and have a part of his hand chopped off.
> There were the "hoisters," as they were called, whose task it was

to press the lever which lifted the dead cattle off the floor. They ran along a rafter, peering down through the damp and the steam; and as old Durham's architects had not built the killing room for the convenience of the hoisters, at every few feet they would have to stoop under a beam, say four feet above the one they ran on; which got them into the habit of stooping, so that in a few years they would be walking like chimpanzees. Worst of any, however, were the fertilizer men, and those who served in the cooking rooms. These people could not be shown to the visitors—for the odor of the fertilizer-man would scare any ordinary visitor at a hundred yards, and as for the other men, who worked in tank-rooms full of steam, and in which there were open vats near the level of the floor, their peculiar trouble was that they fell into the vats; and when they were fished out, there was never enough of them left to be worth exhibiting—sometimes they would be overlooked for days, till all but the bones of them had gone out to the world as Durham's Pure Leaf Lard.[1]

The miserable conditions of factory workers, juxtaposed with the often opulent lifestyle enjoyed by factory owners, seemed to affirm the idea that owners were exploiting workers. But if conditions in the factories were in fact too dangerous, how much safer should they have been?

Consider the question of whether to install a specific safety device—say, a guard rail on a lathe. Many people are reluctant to employ the cost-benefit principle to answer such a question. To them, safety is an absolute priority, so the guard rail should be installed regardless of its cost. Yet most of us do not make personal decisions about our own health and safety that way. No one you know, for example, gets the brakes on his car checked every day, even though doing so would reduce the likelihood of being killed in an accident. The reason, obviously, is that daily brake inspections would be very costly and would not reduce the probability of an accident significantly compared to annual or semiannual inspections.

The same logic can be applied to installing a guard rail on a lathe. If the amount one is willing to pay to reduce the likelihood of an accident exceeds the cost of the guard rail, it should be installed; otherwise, it should not be. And no matter how highly we value reducing the odds of an accident, we will almost surely settle for less than perfect safety. After all, to reduce the risk of an accident to nearly zero, one would have to enclose the lathe in a thick Plexiglas case and operate it with remote-controlled mechanical arms. Faced with the prohibitive cost of such an alternative, most of us would decide that the best approach is to add safety equipment whose benefit exceeds its cost and then use caution while operating the machine.

But will unregulated employers offer the level of workplace safety suggested by the cost-benefit principle? Most nations appear to have decided that they will not. As noted, virtually every industrial country now has comprehensive legislation mandating minimum safety standards in the workplace—laws usually described as safeguards against exploitation of workers.

Yet explaining safety regulation as an antidote for exploitation raises troubling questions. One difficulty stems from the economist's argument that competition for workers prods firms to provide the socially optimal level of amenities. For example, if an amenity—say, a guard rail on a lathe—costs $50 per month to install and maintain, and workers value it at $100 per month, then the firm must install the device or risk losing workers to a competitor that does. After all, if a competing firm were to pay workers $60 per month less than they currently

Is safety regulation needed to protect workers from exploitation?

[1]Upton Sinclair, *The Jungle*, New York: Doubleday, Page, and Co., 1906, p. 106.

earn, it could cover the cost of the device with $10 to spare, while providing a compensation package that is $40 per month more attractive than the first employer's.

To this argument, critics respond that in practice there is very little competition in the labor market. They argue that incomplete information, worker immobility, and other frictions create situations in which workers have little choice but to accept whatever conditions employers offer. But even if a firm were the *only* employer in the market, it would still have an incentive to install a $50 safety device that is worth $100 to the worker. Failure to do so would be to leave cash on the table.

Other defenders of regulation suggest that workers may not know about safety devices they lack. But that explanation, too, is troubling, because competing firms would have a strong incentive to call the devices to workers' attention. If the problem is that workers cannot move to the competing firm's location, then the firm can set up a branch near the exploited workers. Collusive agreements to restrain such competition should prove difficult to maintain, because each firm can increase its profit by cheating on the agreement.

In fact, worker mobility between firms is high, as is entry by new firms into existing markets; and as noted in Chapter 10, cartel agreements have always been notoriously unstable. Information may not be perfect, but if a new employer in town is offering a better deal, sooner or later word gets around.

Finally, if, despite these checks, some firms still manage to exploit their workers, we should expect those firms to earn a relatively high profit. But in fact we observe just the opposite. Year in and year out, firms that pay the *highest* wages are the most profitable. And so we are left with a puzzle. The fear of exploitation by employers with market power has led governments to adopt sweeping and costly safety regulations; yet the evidence suggests that exploitation cannot be a major problem. As the following example suggests, however, safety regulation might prove useful even in a perfectly competitive environment with complete information.

Will Don and Michael choose the optimal amount of safety?

EXAMPLE 14.5

Suppose Don and Michael are the only two members of a hypothetical community. They get satisfaction from three things—their income, safety on the job, and their position on the economic ladder. Suppose Don and Michael must both choose between two jobs, a safe job that pays $50 per week and a risky job that pays $80 per week. The value of safety to each is $40 per week. Having more income than one's neighbor is worth $40 per week to each; having less income than one's neighbor means a $40 per week reduction in satisfaction. (Having the same income as one's neighbor means no change in satisfaction.) Will Don and Michael make the best job choices possible in this situation?

Viewed in isolation, each person's decision should be to take the safe job. Granted, it pays $30 per week less than the risky job, but the extra safety it offers is worth $40 per week. So aside from the issue of relative income, the value of the safe job is $90 per week (its $50 salary plus $40 worth of safety), or $10 per week more than the risky job.

Once we incorporate concerns about relative income, however, the logic of the decision changes in a fundamental way. Now the attractiveness of each job depends on the job chosen by the other. The four possible combinations of choices and their corresponding levels of satisfaction are shown in Table 14.3. If each man chooses a safe job, he will get $50 of income, $40 worth of satisfaction from safety, and—because each will have the same income—zero satisfaction from relative income. So if each man chooses the safe job, each will get a total of $90 worth of satisfaction. If instead each man chooses the risky job, each will get $80 of income, zero satisfaction from safety, and because each has the same income as the other, zero satisfaction from relative income. If we compare the upper-left cell of the table to the lower-right cell, then, we can say unequivocally that Don and Michael would be happier if each took a safe job at lower income than if each chose a risky job with more income.

TABLE 14.3
The Effect of Concern about Relative Income on Worker Choices Regarding Safety

		Michael	
		Safe job @ $50/week	Risky job @ $80/week
Don	Safe job @ $50/week	$90 each	$50 for Don $120 for Michael
	Risky job @ $80/week	$120 for Don $50 for Michael	$80 each

But consider how the choice plays out once the two men recognize their interdependency. Suppose, for example, that Michael chooses the safe job. If Don then chooses the unsafe job, he ends up with a total of $120 of satisfaction—$80 in salary plus $40 from having more income than Michael. Michael, for his part, ends up with only $50 worth of satisfaction—$50 in salary plus $40 from safety, minus $40 from a having lower income than Don. Alternatively, suppose Michael chooses the risky job. Then Don will again do better to accept the risky job, for by doing so he gets $80 worth of satisfaction rather than $50.

In short, no matter which job Michael chooses, Don will get more satisfaction by choosing the risky job. Likewise, no matter which job Don chooses, Michael will do better by choosing the risky job. Yet when each follows his dominant strategy, they end up in the lower-right cell of the table, which provides only $80 per week of satisfaction to each—$10 less than if each had chosen the safe job. Thus their job-safety choice confronts them with a prisoner's dilemma (see Chapter 10). As in all such situations, when the players choose independently, they fail to make the most of their opportunities.

EXERCISE 14.4

How would your answer to the question posed in Example 14.5 have differed if the value of safety had been not $40 per week, but $20?

Example 14.5 suggests an alternative explanation for safety regulation, one that is not based on the need to protect workers from exploitation. If Don and Michael could choose collectively, they would pick the safe job and maximize their combined satisfaction. Thus each might support legislation that establishes safety standards in the workplace.

We stress that concern about relative income need not mean that people care only about having more or better goods than their neighbors. In our society, a person's relative income is important for reasons that everyone recognizes. For example, if you want to send your child to a good school, in most cases you must buy a house in a good school district. But who gets a house in a good school district? Those who have high relative income. Similarly, if everyone wants a house with a view, and only 10 percent of home sites have views, who gets them? The people in the top 10 percent of the income distribution, of course, and only those people. Many important outcomes in life depend on where a person stands on the economic ladder. And when people care about their relative income, rational, self-interested actions will not always lead to efficient outcomes in the labor market.

Regulation, however, does not always improve matters. The labor market may not be perfect, but government regulators aren't perfect either. Safety in the workplace is overseen by the Occupational Safety and Health Administration (OSHA), an agency that has drawn considerable criticism, much of it justified. Consider, for example, the following passage on safety requirements for ladders, taken verbatim from an early OSHA manual:

> The general slope of grain in flat steps of minimum dimension shall not be steeper than 1 in 12, except that for ladders under 10 feet in length the slope shall not be steeper than 1 in 10. The slope of grain in areas of local deviation shall not be steeper than 1 in 12 or 1 in 10 as specified above. For all ladders, cross grain not steeper than 1 in 10 are permitted in lieu of 1 in 12, provided the size is increased to afford at least 15 percent greater strength than for ladders built to minimum dimensions. Local deviations of grain associated with otherwise permissible irregularities are permitted.[1]

This befogged passage appears in a section devoted to ladders that is 30 pages long, two columns to the page. One can easily imagine the managers of a firm deciding that their best course of action is simply to abandon any activities requiring ladders.

As an alternative to OSHA-style prescriptive safety regulation, many economists favor programs that increase employers' financial incentives to reduce workplace injuries. The **workers' compensation** system provides a mechanism through which such a change might be achieved. Workers' compensation is a government insurance system that provides benefits to workers who are injured in the workplace. As currently administered, the program does not adjust each individual employer's premiums fully to reflect the claims generated by its workers. Employers with low injury rates thus pay premiums higher than needed to cover the claims generated by their workers, while those with high injury rates pay premiums too small to cover the claims generated by their workers.

workers' compensation a government insurance system that provides benefits to workers who are injured on the job.

Economists argue that revising insurance premiums to reflect the full social cost of the injuries sustained by each employer's workers would provide the optimal incentive to curtail injuries in the workplace. In effect, premiums set at this level would be an optimal tax on injuries, and this would be efficient for the same reason that a properly chosen tax on pollution is efficient. An injury tax set at the marginal cost of injury would encourage employers to adopt all safety measures whose benefits exceed their costs.

As in other domains, we are far more likely to achieve optimal safety levels in the workplace if we choose among policies on practical cost-benefit grounds rather than on the basis of slogans about the merits or flaws of the free market.

As the following example illustrates, costs and benefits play a pivotal role in decisions about whether the government chooses to constrain individual choice in the safety domain and if so, how.

Why does the government require safety seats for infants who travel in cars, but not for infants who travel in airplanes?

A mother cannot legally drive her six-month-old son to a nearby grocery store without first strapping him into a government-approved safety seat. Yet she can fly with him from Miami to Seattle with no restraining device at all. Why this difference?

ECONOMIC NATURALIST 14.3

---

[1]Quoted by Robert S. Smith, "Compensating Wage Differentials and Public Policy: A Review," *Industrial and Labor Relations Review,* **32**: 339–352, 1977.

In case of an accident—whether in a car or an airplane—an infant who is strapped into a safety seat is more likely to escape injury or death than one who is unrestrained. But the probability of being involved in a serious accident is hundreds of times higher when traveling by car than when traveling by air, so the benefit of having safety seats is greater for trips made by car. Using safety seats is also far more costly on plane trips than on car trips. Whereas most cars have plenty of extra room for a safety seat, parents might need to purchase an extra ticket to use one on an airplane. Most parents appear unwilling to pay $600 more per trip for a small increment in safety, for either themselves or their children.

> **RECAP   WORKPLACE SAFETY REGULATION**
>
> Most countries regulate safety in the workplace, a practice often defended as needed to protect workers from being exploited by employers with market power. Yet safety regulation might be attractive even in perfectly competitive labor markets, because the social payoff from investment in safety often exceeds the private payoff. An injury tax set at the marginal cost of injury would encourage optimal investment in workplace safety.

PUBLIC HEALTH AND SECURITY

Because public health and law enforcement officials are charged with protecting our health and safety, political leaders are often reluctant to discuss expenditures on public health and law enforcement in cost-benefit terms. But because we live in a world of scarcity, we cannot escape the fact that spending more in these areas means spending less on other things of value.

Illnesses, like accidents, are costly to prevent. The socially optimal expenditure on a health measure that reduces a specific illness is that amount for which the marginal benefit to society of the measure exactly equals its marginal cost. For example, in deciding how much to spend on vaccinating against a measles, a rational public health policy would expand the proportion of the population vaccinated until the marginal cost of an additional vaccination was exactly equal to the marginal value of the illnesses thus prevented.

As the following example illustrates, however, the decision of whether to become vaccinated looks very different from each individual's perspective.

ECONOMIC NATURALIST 14.4

Why do many states have laws requiring students to be vaccinated against childhood illnesses?

Proof of immunization against diphtheria, measles, poliomyelitis, and rubella is now universally required for entry into American public schools. Most states also require immunization against tetanus (49 states), pertussis (44 states), mumps (43 states), and hepatitis B (26 states). Why these requirements?

Being vaccinated against a childhood illness entails a small but potentially serious risk. The vaccine against pertussis (whooping cough), for example, is believed to cause some form of permanent brain damage in 1 out of every 110,000 children vaccinated. Contracting the disease itself also poses serious health risks, and in an environment in which infections were sufficiently likely to occur, individuals would have a compelling reason to bear the risk of being vaccinated in order to reduce the even larger risk from infection. The problem is that in an environment in which most children were vaccinated, infection rates would be low, making the risk of vaccination loom understandably large in the eyes of individual families. The ideal situation from the perspective of any individual family would be to remain unvaccinated in an environment in which all other families were vaccinated. But as more and more families decided to forgo vaccination, infection rates would mount. Eventually the vaccination rate would stabilize at the point at which the additional risk to the individual family of becoming vaccinated would be exactly equal to the risk from remaining unvaccinated. But this calculation ignores the fact that a decision to remain unvaccinated poses risk not just to the individual decision maker, but also to others who have decided to become vaccinated (since no vaccine affords 100 percent protection against infection).

Relegating the vaccination decision to individuals results in a suboptimally low vaccination rate, because individual decision makers fail to take adequate account of the cost that their becoming infected will impose on others. It is for this reason that most states require vaccinations against specific childhood illnesses.

Even these laws, however, allow parents to apply for exemptions on religious or philosophical grounds. Communities vary in the extent to which parents avail themselves of these exemptions. In Colorado, for example, Boulder County heads the list of parents who opt to exempt their children from taking the pertussis vaccine (with an exemption rate of 8.4 percent, more than four times the rate statewide). Not surprisingly, the incidence of whooping cough is much higher in Boulder (34.7 cases per year per 100,000 people) than in the state as a whole (9.4 cases per year per 100,000 people).[1]

Crimes, like childhood illnesses, are also costly to prevent. The socially optimal amount to spend on avoiding any specific type of crime is that amount for which the marginal benefit of reducing that crime exactly equals its marginal cost. As the next example illustrates, the cost-benefit principle helps to explain why society invests so much more heavily in preventing some crimes than in preventing others.

Why do more Secret Service agents guard the president than the vice president, and why do no Secret Service agents guard college professors?

ECONOMIC NATURALIST 14.5

When the president of the United States flies to Cleveland to give a speech, hundreds of federal agents are assigned to protect him against attack by an assassin. But when the vice president flies to Cleveland to give a speech, many fewer agents are assigned, and when a college professor goes to Cleveland for the same purpose, no agents are assigned at all. Why this difference?

According to the cost-benefit principle, the government should keep assigning agents in each case until the cost of an additional agent equals the value of the extra protection provided. In each of the three cases, the marginal cost of assigning agents is essentially the same. As shown in Figure 14.3, marginal cost (MC) is likely to be upward-sloping, because of the low-hanging-fruit principle, according to which the most effective agents should be assigned first.

The important difference among these three cases lies in the value of assigning additional agents. The marginal benefit of an agent assigned to the president [MB_P, part (a)] is much higher than the marginal benefit of an agent assigned to the vice president [MB_{VP}, part (b)], for at least two reasons. First, opponents of the government have a stronger motive to attack the president than the vice president, because the president's role is so much more important than the vice president's. Thus assigning an additional agent to the president is more likely to prevent an attack. And second, the benefit of preventing an attack against the president is much higher than that of preventing an attack against the vice president—again, because the president's role is so much more important. These observations imply that the optimal of number of agents to assign

Should college professors receive Secret Service protection when they give out-of-town lectures?

[1]Colorado Department of Public Health and Environment, *Vaccine Preventable Diseases in Colorado* (http://www.cdphe.state.co.us/de/Epidemiology/vaccinepreventable2000.pdf).

FIGURE 14.3

Differential Investment in Crime Prevention.

Because of differences in the marginal benefit of protection, more Secret Service agents are assigned to protect the president (a) than to protect the vice president (b), and none are assigned to protect an ordinary citizen (c).

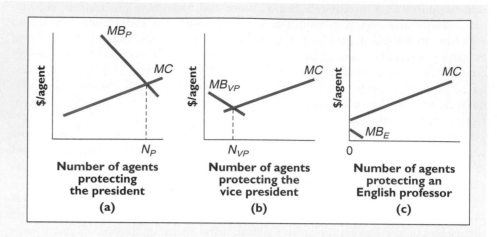

to the president [N_P, part (a)] is much greater than the optimal number of agents to assign to the vice president [N_{VP}, part (b)]. Finally, the optimal number of agents to assign to a traveling professor is zero [part (c)], because the marginal benefit of such an assignment (MB_E) is so small. After all, few people have any reason to attack a professor, and in the unlikely event of an attack, the consequences would be far less serious than if a prominent government leader were attacked.

Many critics of the cost-benefit approach complain that when applied in examples like the one just discussed, it gives short shrift to the dignity of human life. On closer inspection, however, this complaint is difficult to support. The recommendation to assign no Secret Service agents to protect a traveling college professor does not imply that the lives of ordinary citizens are not to be cherished. Rather, it simply acknowledges that even without Secret Service protection, not even a single traveling professor is likely to be assassinated in the course of the next 100 years. For the same money that we would spend to send agents on largely pointless assignments, we could install guard rails on dangerous mountain roads, purchase additional mobile coronary care units, or make any number of other investments that would save thousands of lives. The logic of the scarcity principle does not cease to apply whenever the choices we must make involve human health or safety.

RECAP   PUBLIC HEALTH AND SECURITY

The cost-benefit principle applies to public health and safety measures just as in other areas of public policy. Society's efforts to promote security should be expanded only to the point at which their marginal benefits equals their marginal costs.

■ SUMMARY ■

- Basic microeconomic principles can be applied to a variety of government policy questions. These principles help to show how different methods of paying for health care affect the efficiency with which medical services are delivered. In the case of health care, the gains from marginal cost pricing can often be achieved through insurance policies with large deductibles.

- An understanding of the forces that give rise to environmental pollution can help to identify those policy measures that will achieve a desired reduction in pollution at the lowest possible cost. Both the taxing of pollution and the sale of transferable pollution rights promote this goal. Each distributes the cost of the environmental cleanup effort so that the marginal cost of pollution abatement is the same for all polluters.

• A perennially controversial topic is the application of the cost-benefit principle to policies involving public health, safety, and security. Many critics feel that the use of cost-benefit analysis in this domain is not morally legitimate, because it involves putting a monetary price on human life. Yet the fundamental principle of scarcity applies to human health and safety, just as it does to other issues. Spending more on public health and safety necessarily means spending less on other things of value. Failure to weigh the relevant costs and benefits, then, means that society will be less likely to achieve its stated goals.

■ KEY TERMS ■

first-dollar insurance coverage (355)
health maintenance organization
(HMO) (355)

workers' compensation (365)

■ REVIEW QUESTIONS ■

1. Why is vaccination against many childhood illnesses a legal requirement for entry into public schools?

2. Why do economists believe that pollution taxes and effluent permits are a more efficient way to curb pollution than laws mandating across-the-board cutbacks?

3. Why is first-dollar health care coverage inefficient?

4. How would you explain to a skeptical bank manager why the socially optimal number of bank robberies is not zero?

5. Does it make sense for the Federal Aviation Administration to require more sophisticated and expensive safety equipment in large commercial passenger jets than in small private planes?

■ PROBLEMS ■

1. In the event he requires an appendectomy, David's demand for hospital accommodations is as shown in the diagram. David's current insurance policy fully covers the cost of hospital stays. The marginal cost of providing a hospital room is $150 per day. If David's only illness this year results in an appendectomy, how many days will he choose to stay in the hospital?

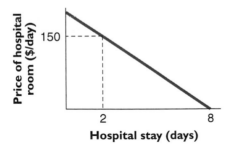

2. Refer to Problem 1. By how much would total economic surplus have been higher this year if David's hospital insurance covered only the cost of hospital stays that exceed $1,000 per illness?

3. Refer to Problems 1 and 2. Suppose David's employer adopts a new health care plan that pays 50 percent of all medical expenses up to $1,000 per illness, with full coverage thereafter. How will economic surplus under this plan compare with economic surplus with the policy in Problem 2?

4. In Los Angeles the demand for rhinoplasties (cosmetic surgical procedures that alter the appearance of the nose) is as shown in the diagram. The marginal cost of a rhinoplasty is $1,000 and the procedure is not currently covered by health insurance. By how much will total economic surplus change if the city council passes a law requiring employers to include full reimbursement for rhinoplasties in their employees' health coverage?

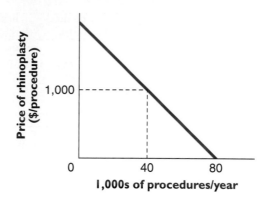

5. Refer to Problem 4. How would the change in total economic surplus be affected if the law instead required health insurance to pay only $500 per procedure?

6. Two firms, Sludge Oil and Northwest Lumber, have access to five production processes, each one of which has a different cost and gives off a different amount of pollution. The daily costs of the processes and the corresponding number of tons of smoke emitted are as shown in the following table:

Process (smoke)	A (4 tons/day)	B (3 tons/day)	C (2 tons/day)	D (1 ton/day)	E (0 tons/day)
Cost to Sludge Oil ($/day)	50	70	120	200	500
Cost to Northwest Lumber ($/day)	100	180	500	1,000	2,000

a. If pollution is unregulated, which process will each firm use, and what will be the daily smoke emission?

b. The City Council wants to curb smoke emissions by 50 percent. To accomplish this, it requires each firm to curb its emissions by 50 percent. What will be the total cost to society of this policy?

7. The City Council in the previous problem again wants to curb emissions by half. This time, it sets a tax of $T per day on each ton of smoke emitted. How large will T have to be to effect the desired reduction? What is the total cost to society of this policy?

8. Refer to Problem 7. Instead of taxing pollution, the city council decides to auction off four permits, each of which entitles the bearer to emit 1 ton of smoke per day. No smoke may be emitted without a permit. Suppose the government conducts the auction by starting at $1 and asking how many permits each firm wants to buy at that price. If the total is more than four, it then raises the price by $1, and asks again, and so on, until the total quantity of demanded permits falls to four. How much will each permit sell for in this auction? How many permits will each firm buy? What will be the total cost to society of this reduction in pollution?

9. Tom and Al are the only two members of a household. Each gets satisfaction from three things: his income, his safety at work, and his income relative to his roommate's income. Suppose Tom and Al must each choose between two jobs: a safe job that pays $100 per week and a risky job that pays $130 per week. The value of safety to each is $40 per week. Each person evaluates relative income as follows: Having more income than his roommate provides the equivalent of $30 per week worth of satisfaction; having less implies a reduction of $30 per week worth of satisfaction; and earning the same income as his roommate means no change in satisfaction. Will Tom and Al choose optimally between the two jobs?

10. Refer to Problem 9. If Tom and Al could negotiate binding agreements with one another at no cost, which job would each choose? Suppose negotiation is impractical, and that the only way Tom and Al can achieve greater workplace safety is for the government to adopt safety regulations. If enforcement of the regulations costs $25 per week, would Tom and Al favor their adoption?

■ ANSWERS TO IN-CHAPTER EXERCISES ■

14.1 With 50 percent coverage, David would have to pay $150 for each additional day in the hospital, so he would choose to stay for two days.

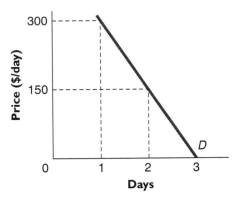

14.2 The optimal stay is still one day. If insurance reimburses $150 per day, then the marginal charge seen by David will be the remaining $150 per day, so he will stay two days. The cost to society of the additional day is $300 and the benefit to David of the extra day is only $225 (the area of the lower shaded figure). The loss in surplus from the additional day's stay is thus $75.

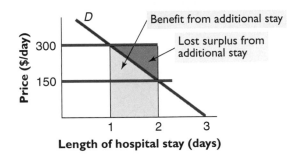

14.3 With a tax of $61 per ton each day, Sludge Oil would adopt process A and Northwest Lumber would adopt process C.

Process (smoke)	A (4 tons/day)	B (3 tons/day)	C (2 tons/day)	D (1 ton/day)	E (0 tons/day)
Cost to Sludge Oil ($/day)	100	200	600	1,300	2,300
Cost to Northwest Lumber ($/day)	300	320	380	480	700

14.4 The payoff matrix would now be as shown below, and the best choice, both individually and collectively, would be the risky job.

		Michael	
		Safe job @ $50/week	Risky job @ $80/week
Don	Safe job @ $50/week	$70 each	$30 for Don $120 for Michael
	Risky job @ $80/week	$120 for Don $30 for Michael	$80 each

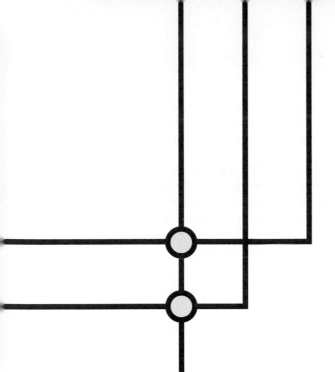

CHAPTER 15

PUBLIC GOODS AND TAX POLICY

■

Government has the power to tax. Unlike a private business, which can get our money only if we voluntarily buy its product, the government can take our money even if we don't want the particular mix of goods and services provided.

Government also has a monopoly on the legitimate use of force. If people break the law, government has the power to restrain them, using force if necessary. It also has the power to deprive lawbreakers of their liberty for extended periods, and, in some places, even to execute them. Government can draft law-abiding citizens into the armed forces and send them into situations in which they must kill others and risk being killed themselves.

These are awesome powers. And although they are often used in the pursuit of noble ends, the historical record abounds with illustrations of their abuse. Voters and politicians of both parties are keenly aware of these abuses. Indeed, contemporary political rhetoric almost invariably entails criticism of bloated, out-of-control government bureaucracy. Even mainstream Democrats—ostensibly the party of activist government in the United States—have conceded the need to curb government's role. For example, as former president Clinton remarked in his 1996 State of the Union Message, "the era of big government is over."

Others advocate even more radical retrenchment. For instance, Harry Browne, the 1996 Libertarian Party presidential candidate, called for abolition of the Internal Revenue Service, the agency responsible for collecting the federal income tax. This step would be tantamount to abolishing the federal government itself, for without tax revenues, there would be no way to pay for public goods and services.

Browne is right, of course, that a sure way to prevent government abuse of power is simply to have no government. But since virtually no society on earth lacks a government, we may suspect that governments, on balance, do more good than harm.

But how big, exactly, should government be? What goods and services should it provide? How should it raise the revenue to pay for them? What other powers should it have to constrain the behavior of its citizens? And how should the various powers we assign to government be apportioned among local, state, and federal levels? Our goal in this chapter will be to employ the principles of microeconomics in an attempt to answer these pragmatic questions.

GOVERNMENT PROVISION OF PUBLIC GOODS

public good a good or service that, to at least some degree, is both nonrival and nonexcludable

One of the primary tasks of government is to provide what economists call **public goods,** such as national defense and the criminal justice system.

PUBLIC GOODS VERSUS PRIVATE GOODS

nonrival good a good whose consumption by one person does not diminish its availability for others

Public goods are those goods or services that are, in varying degrees, **nonrival** and **nonexcludable.** A nonrival good is one whose consumption by one person does not diminish its availability for others. For example, if the military prevents a hostile nation from invading your city, your enjoyment of that protection does not diminish its value to your neighbors. A good is nonexcludable if it is difficult to exclude nonpayers from consuming it. For instance, even if your neighbors don't pay their share of the cost of maintaining an army, they will still enjoy its protection.

nonexcludable good a good that is difficult, or costly, to exclude nonpayers from consuming

Another example of a nonrival and nonexcludable good is an over-the-air broadcast of the *David Letterman Show.* The fact that you tune in one evening does not make the program any less available to others, and once the broadcast has been beamed out over the airwaves, it is difficult to prevent anyone from tuning in. Similarly, if the City of New York puts on a fireworks display in New York harbor to celebrate a special occasion, it cannot charge admission, because the harbor may be viewed from so many different locations in the city. And the fact that additional persons view the display does not in any way diminish its value to other potential viewers.

In contrast, the typical private good is diminished one-for-one by any individual's consumption of it. For instance, when you eat a cheeseburger, it is no longer available for anyone else. Moreover, people can be easily prevented from consuming cheeseburgers they don't pay for.

> ### EXERCISE 15.1
>
> **Which of the following, if any, is nonrival?**
>
> **a. The web site of the Bureau of Labor Statistics at 3 A.M.**
>
> **b. The World Cup Soccer championship game watched in person.**
>
> **c. The World Cup Soccer championship game watched on television.**

pure public good a good or service that, to a high degree, is both nonrival and nonexcludable

Goods that are both highly nonexcludable and nonrival are often called **pure public goods.** Two reasons favor government provision of such goods. First, for-profit private companies would have obvious difficulty recovering their cost of production. Many people might be willing to pay enough to cover the cost of producing the good, but if it is nonexcludable, the company cannot easily charge for it (an example of the free-rider problem discussed in Chapter 12). And second, if the marginal cost of serving additional users is zero once the good has been produced, then charging for the good would be inefficient, even if there were some practical way to do so. This inefficiency often characterizes the provision of **collective goods**—nonrival goods for which it is possible to exclude nonpayers. Pay-per-view cable television is an example. People who don't pay to get HBO don't get to watch *The Sopranos,* a restriction that excludes many viewers who would have benefited from watching. Since the marginal cost to society of their tuning in is literally zero, excluding these viewers is wasteful.

A **pure private good** is one from which nonpayers can easily be excluded and for which one person's consumption creates a one-for-one reduction in the good's availability for others. The theory of perfectly competitive supply developed in Chapter 6 applies to pure private goods, of which basic agricultural products are perhaps the best examples. A **pure commons good** is a rival good that is also nonexcludable, so-called because goods with this combination of properties almost always result in a tragedy of the commons (see Chapter 11). Fish in ocean waters are an example.

The classification scheme defined by the nonrival and nonexcludable properties is summarized in Table 15.1. The columns of the table indicate the extent to which one person's consumption of a good fails to diminish its availability for others. Goods in the right column are nonrival, and those in the left column are not. The rows of the table indicate the difficulty of excluding nonpayers from consuming the good. Goods in the top row are nonexcludable, those in the bottom row, excludable. Private goods (lower-left cell) are rival and excludable. Public goods (upper-right cell) are nonrival and nonexcludable. The two hybrid categories are commons goods (upper-left cell), which are rival but nonexcludable, and collective goods (lower-right cell), which are excludable but nonrival.

collective good a good or service that, to at least some degree, is nonrival but excludable

pure private good one for which nonpayers can easily be excluded and for which each unit consumed by one person means one less unit available for others

pure commons good one for which nonpayers cannot easily be excluded and for which each unit consumed by one person means one less unit available for others

TABLE 15.1
Private, Public, and Hybrid Goods

		Nonrival	
		Low	High
Nonexcludable	High	Commons good (fish in the ocean)	Public good (national defense)
	Low	Private good (wheat)	Collective good (pay-per-view TV)

Collective goods are provided sometimes by government, sometimes by private companies. Most pure public goods are provided by government, but even private companies can sometimes find profitable ways of producing goods that are both nonrival *and* nonexcludable. An example is broadcast radio and television, which covers its costs by selling airtime to advertisers.

The mere fact that a good is a pure public good does not necessarily mean that government ought to provide it. On the contrary, the only public goods the government should even *consider* providing are those whose benefits exceed their costs. The cost of a public good is simply the sum of all explicit and implicit costs incurred to provide it. The benefit of a public good is measured by asking how much people would be willing to pay for it. Although that sounds similar to the way we measure the benefit of a private good, an important distinction exists. The benefit of an additional unit of a private good, such as a cheeseburger, is the highest sum that any individual buyer would be willing to pay for it. In contrast, the benefit of an additional unit of a public good, such as an additional broadcast episode of *Sesame Street,* is the sum of the reservation prices of all people who will watch that episode.

Even if the amount that all beneficiaries of a public good would be willing to pay exceeds its cost, government provision of that good makes sense only if there is no other less costly way of providing it. For example, whereas city governments often pay for fireworks displays, they almost invariably hire private companies to put on these events. Finally, if the benefit of a public good does not exceed its cost, we are better off without it.

PAYING FOR PUBLIC GOODS

Not everyone benefits equally from the provision of a given public good. For example, some people find fireworks displays highly entertaining, but others simply don't care about them, and still others actively dislike them. Ideally, it might seem that the most equitable method of financing a given public good would be to tax people in proportion to their willingness to pay for the good. To illustrate this approach, suppose Jones values a public good at $100, Smith values the same good at $200, and the cost of the good is $240. Jones would then be taxed $80, and Smith would be taxed $160. The good would be provided, and each taxpayer in this example would reap a surplus equal to 25 percent of his tax payment: $20 for Jones, $40 for Smith.

In practice, however, government officials usually lack the information they would need to tax people in proportion to their willingness to pay for specific public goods. (Think about it: If an IRS agent asked you how much you would be willing to pay to have a new freeway and you knew you would be taxed in proportion to the amount you responded, what would you say?) Examples 15.1 to 15.3 illustrate some of the problems that arise in financing public goods and suggests possible solutions to these problems.

EXAMPLE 15.1

Will Prentice and Wilson buy a water filter?

Prentice and Wilson own adjacent summer cottages along an isolated stretch of shoreline on Cayuga Lake. Because of a recent invasion of zebra mussels, each must add chlorine to his water intake valve each week to prevent it from becoming clogged by the tiny mollusks. A manufacturer has introduced a new filtration device that eliminates the nuisance of weekly chlorination. The cost of the device, which has the capacity to serve both houses, is $1,000. Both owners feel equally strongly about having the filter. But because Wilson earns twice as much as Prentice, Wilson is willing to pay up to $800 to have the filter, whereas its value to Prentice, a retired schoolteacher, is only $400. Would either person be willing to purchase the device individually? Is it efficient for them to share its purchase?

Neither will purchase the filter individually because each has a reservation price that is below its selling price. But because the two together value the filter at $1,200, sharing its use would be socially efficient. If they were to do so, total economic surplus would be $200 higher than if they did not buy the filter.

Since sharing the filter is the efficient outcome, we might expect that Prentice and Wilson would quickly reach agreement to purchase it. Unfortunately, however, the joint purchase and sharing of facilities is often easier proposed than accomplished. One hurdle is that people must incur costs merely to get together to discuss joint purchases. With only two people involved, those costs might not be significant. But if hundreds or thousands of people were involved, communication costs could be prohibitive.

With large numbers of people, the free-rider problem also emerges (see Chapter 12). After all, everyone knows that the project will either succeed or fail independently of any one person's contribution to it. Everyone thus has an incentive to withhold contributions—or get a free ride—in the hope that others will give.

Finally, even when only a few people are involved, reaching agreement on a fair sharing of the total expense may be difficult. For example, Prentice and Wilson might be reluctant to disclose their true reservation prices to one another for the same reason that you might be reluctant to disclose your reservation price for a public good to an IRS agent.

These practical concerns may lead us to empower government to buy public goods on our behalf. But as Example 15.2 makes clear, this approach does not eliminate the need to reach political agreement on how public purchases are to be financed.

Will government buy the water filter if there is an "equal tax" rule?

Suppose Prentice and Wilson from Example 15.1 could ask the government to help broker the water filter purchase. And suppose that the government's tax policy must follow a "nondiscrimination" rule that prohibits charging any citizen more for a public good than it charges his or her neighbor. Another rule is that public goods can be provided only if a majority of citizens approve of them. Will a government bound by these rules provide the filter that Prentice and Wilson want?

A tax that collects the same amount from every citizen is called a **head tax.** If the government must rely on a head tax, it must raise $500 from Prentice and $500 from Wilson. But since the device is worth only $400 to Prentice, he will vote against the project, thus denying it a majority. So a democratic government cannot provide the water filter if it must rely on a head tax.

A head tax is an example of a **regressive tax,** one for which the proportion of a taxpayer's income that is paid in taxes declines as the taxpayer's income rises.

The point illustrated by Example 15.2 is not confined to the specific public good considered. It applies whenever taxpayers place significantly different valuations on public goods, as will almost always happen whenever people earn significantly different incomes. An equal-tax rule under these circumstances will almost invariably rule out the provision of many worthwhile public goods.

As Example 15.3 suggests, one solution to this problem is to allow taxes to vary by income.

EXAMPLE 15.2

head tax a tax that collects the same amount from every taxpayer

regressive tax a tax under which the proportion of income paid in taxes declines as income rises

EXAMPLE 15.3

proportional income tax one under which all taxpayers pay the same proportion of their incomes in taxes

Will the government buy the filter if there is a proportional tax on income?

Suppose that Prentice proposes that the government raise revenue by imposing a proportional tax on income to finance the provision of the water filter described in Example 15.1. Will Wilson, who earns twice as much as Prentice, support this proposal?

A **proportional income tax** is one under which all taxpayers pay the same percentage of their incomes in taxes. Under such a tax, Wilson would support Prentice's proposal, because if he didn't, each would fail to enjoy a public good whose benefit exceeds his share of its cost. Under the proportional tax on income, Prentice would contribute $333 toward the $1,000 purchase price of the filter and Wilson would contribute $667. The government would buy the filter, resulting in additional surpluses of $67 for Prentice and $133 for Wilson.

The following example makes the point that just as equal contributions are often a poor way to pay for public goods, they are also often a poor way to share expenses within the household.

ECONOMIC NATURALIST 15.1

Why don't most married couples contribute equally to joint purchases?

Suppose Hillary earns $2,000,000 per year while her husband Bill earns only $20,000. Given her income, Hillary as an individual would want to spend much more than Bill would on housing, travel, entertainment, education for their children, and the many other items they consume jointly. What will happen if the couple adopts a rule that each must contribute an equal amount toward the purchase of such items?

This rule would constrain the couple to live in a small house, take only inexpensive vacations, and skimp on entertainment, dining out, and their children's education. It is therefore easy to see why Hillary might find it attractive to pay considerably more than 50 percent for jointly consumed goods, because doing so would enable *both* of them to consume in the manner their combined income permits.

Public goods and jointly consumed private goods are different from individually consumed private goods in the following important way: *Different individuals are free to consume whatever quantity and quality of most private goods they choose to buy, but jointly consumed goods must be provided in the same quantity and quality for all persons.*

As in the case of private goods, people's willingness to pay for public goods is generally an increasing function of income. Wealthy individuals tend to assign greater value to public goods than low-income people do, not because the wealthy have different tastes but because they have more money. A head tax would result in high-income persons getting smaller amounts of public goods than they want. By increasing the total economic surplus available for all to share, a tax system that assigns a larger share of the tax burden to people with higher incomes makes possible a better outcome for both rich and poor alike. Indeed, virtually all industrialized nations have tax systems that are at least mildly **progressive**, which means that the proportion of income paid in taxes actually rises with a family's income.

Progressive taxation and even proportional taxation have often been criticized as being unfair to the wealthy, who are forced to pay more than others for public goods that all consume in common. The irony in this charge, however, is that exclusive reliance on head taxes, or even proportional taxes, would curtail the provision of public goods and services that are of greatest value to high-income families. Studies have shown, for example, that the income elasticity of demand for public goods such as parks and recreation facilities, clean air and water, public safety, uncongested roads, and aesthetically pleasing public spaces

progressive tax one in which the proportion of income paid in taxes rises as income rises is substantially greater than 1. Failure to rely on progressive taxation would result in gross underprovision of such public goods and services.

 RECAP   **PUBLIC GOODS**

A public good is both nonrival and nonexcludable. Private firms typically cannot recover the costs of producing such goods because they cannot exclude nonpayers from consuming them. Nor would charging for a public good promote efficiency, since one person's consumption of the good does not diminish its availability for others.

Both obstacles can be overcome by creating a government with the power to levy taxes. Even high-income citizens often favor progressive taxes, because proportional or regressive taxes may generate insufficient revenue to pay for the public goods those taxpayers favor.

THE OPTIMAL QUANTITY OF A PUBLIC GOOD

In the examples considered thus far, the question was whether to provide a particular public good and, if so, how to pay for it. In practice, we often confront additional questions about what level and quality of a public good to provide.

Standard cost-benefit logic also applies to these questions. For example, New York City should add another rocket to a fireworks display if and only if the amount that citizens would collectively be willing to pay to see the rocket is at least as great as its cost.

THE DEMAND CURVE FOR A PUBLIC GOOD

To calculate the socially optimal quantity of a public good, we must first construct the demand curve for that public good. The process for doing so differs in an important way from the one we use to generate the market demand curve for a private good.

For a private good, all buyers face the same price and each chooses the quantity he or she wishes to purchase at that price. Recall that to construct the demand curve for a private good from the demand curves for individual consumers, we place the individual demand curves side by side and add them horizontally. That is, for each of a series of fixed prices, we add the resulting quantities demanded on the individual demand curves. In Figure 15.1, for example, we add the individual demand curves for a private good, D_1 and D_2 [parts (a) and (b)], horizontally to obtain the market demand curve for the good D [part (c)].

FIGURE 15.1

Generating the Market Demand Curve for a Private Good.

To construct the market demand curve for a private good (c), we add the individual demand curves (a) and (b) horizontally.

For a public good, all buyers necessarily consume the same quantity, although each may differ in terms of willingness to pay for additional units of the good. Constructing the demand curve for a public good thus entails not horizontal summation of the individual demand curves but vertical summation. That is, for each of a series of quantity values, we must add the prices that individuals are willing to pay for an additional unit of the good. The curves D_1 and D_2 in Figure 15.2(c) and (b) show individual demand curves for a public good by two different people. At each quantity, these curves tell how much the individual would be willing to pay for an additional unit of the public good. If we add D_1 and D_2 vertically, we obtain the total demand curve D for the public good [part (a)].

FIGURE 15.2

Generating the Demand Curve for a Public Good.
To construct the demand curve for a public good (a), we add the individual demand curves (c) and (b) vertically.

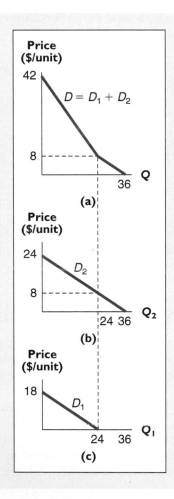

EXERCISE 15.2

Bill and Tom are the only demanders of a public good. If Bill's demand curve is $P_B = 6 - 0.5Q$ and Tom's is $P_T = 12 - Q$, construct the demand curve for this public good.

In Example 15.4, we see how the demand curve for a public good might be used in conjunction with information about costs to determine the optimal level of parkland in a city.

EXAMPLE 15.4

What is the optimal quantity of urban parkland?

The city government of a new planned community must decide how much parkland to provide. The marginal cost curve and the public demand curve for urban parkland are as shown in Figure 15.3. Why is the marginal cost curve upward-sloping and the demand curve downward-sloping? Given these curves, what is the optimal quantity of parkland?

The marginal cost schedule for urban parkland is upward-sloping because of the low-hanging-fruit principle: The city acquires the cheapest parcels of land first, and only then turns to more expensive parcels. Likewise, the marginal willingness-to-pay curve is downward-sloping because of the law of diminishing marginal utility. Just as people are generally willing to pay less for their fifth hot dog than for their first, they are also willing to pay less for the 101st acre of parkland than for the 100th acre. Given these curves, A^* is the optimal quantity of parkland. For any quantity less than A^*, the benefit of additional parkland exceeds its cost, which means that total economic surplus can be made larger by expanding the amount of parkland. For example, at A_0, the community would be willing to pay $200,000 for an additional acre of urban parkland, but its cost is only $80,000. Similarly, for any quantity of parkland in excess of A^*, the community would gain more than it would lose by selling off some parkland.

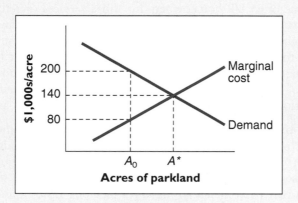

FIGURE 15.3
The Optimal Quantity of Parkland.
The optimal number of acres of urban parkland is A^*, the quantity at which the public's willingness to pay for additional parkland is equal to the marginal cost of parkland.

PRIVATE PROVISION OF PUBLIC GOODS

One advantage of using the government to provide public goods is that once a tax collection agency has been established to finance a single public good, it can be expanded at relatively low cost to generate revenue for additional public goods. Another advantage is that because government has the power to tax, it can summarily assign responsibility for the cost of a public good without endless haggling over who bears what share of the burden. And in the case of goods for which nonpayers cannot be excluded, the government may be the only feasible provider.

But exclusive reliance on government also entails disadvantages. Most fundamentally, the government's one-size-fits-all approach invariably requires many people to pay for public goods they don't want, while others end up having to do without public goods they want desperately. For example, many people vehemently oppose the provision of *any* sex education in the public schools, while others fervently believe that far more such instruction should be provided than is currently offered in most current public school curriculums. In addition, mandatory taxation strikes many people as coercive, even if they approve of the particular public goods being provided.

It is no surprise, then, that governments are not the exclusive providers of public goods in any society. Indeed, many public goods are routinely provided through private channels. The challenge, in each case, is to devise a scheme for raising the required revenues. Here are some methods that seem to work.

Funding by donation In 2001 Americans gave more than $200 billion to private charities, many of which provide public goods to their communities. People also volunteer their time on behalf of organizations that provide public goods. When you paint your house, mow your lawn, or plant a flower garden, you are enhancing the quality of life in your neighborhood, and in that sense you are voluntarily providing a public good to your neighbors.

Development of new means to exclude nonpayers New electronic technology makes it possible to exclude nonpayers from many goods that in the past could not be thus restricted. For instance, broadcast television stations now have the ability to scramble their signals, making them available only to those consumers who purchase descrambling devices.

Private contracting More than 8 million Americans now live in gated private communities—private homeowners' associations that wall off contiguous properties and provide various services to residents. Many of these associations provide security services, schools, and fire protection and in other ways function much like ordinary local governments. Recognizing that individual incentives may not be strong enough to assure socially optimal levels of maintenance and landscaping, these associations often bill homeowners for those services directly. Many of the rules imposed by these associations are even more restrictive than those imposed by local governments, a distinction that is defended on the grounds that people are always free to choose some other neighborhood if they don't like the rules of any particular homeowners' association. Many people would be reluctant to tolerate a municipal ordinance that prevents people from painting their houses purple, yet such restrictions are common in the bylaws of homeowners' associations.

Sale of by-products Many public goods are financed by the sale of rights or services that are generated as by-products of the public goods. For instance, as noted earlier, radio and television programming is a public good that is paid for in many cases by the sale of advertising messages. Internet services are also underwritten in part by commercial messages that pop up or appear in the headers or margins of web pages.

Given the quintessentially voluntary nature of privately provided public goods, it might seem that reliance on private provision might be preferred whenever it proved feasible. But as the following example makes clear, private provision often entails problems of its own.

ECONOMIC NATURALIST 15.2

Why do television networks favor Jerry Springer over *Masterpiece Theater*?

In a given time slot, a television network faces the alternative of broadcasting either the *Jerry Springer Show* or *Masterpiece Theater*. If it chooses *Springer,* it will win 20 percent of the viewing audience, but only 18 percent if it chooses *Masterpiece Theater*. Suppose those who would choose *Springer* would collectively be willing to pay $10 million for the right to see that program, while those who choose *Masterpiece Theater* would be willing to pay $30 million. And suppose, finally, that the time slot is to be financed by a detergent company. Which program will the network choose? Which program would be socially optimal?

A detergent maker cares primarily about the number of people who will see its advertisements and will thus choose the program that will attract the largest audience—here, the *Springer Show*. The fact that those who prefer *Masterpiece Theater* would be willing to pay a lot more to see it is of little concern to the sponsor. But to identify the optimal result from society's point of view, we must take this difference into account. Because the people who prefer *Masterpiece Theater* could pay the *Springer* viewers more than enough to compensate them for relinquishing the time slot, *Masterpiece Theater* is the efficient outcome. But unless its supporters happen to buy more soap in total than the *Springer* viewers, the latter will prevail. In short, reliance on advertising and other indirect mechanisms for financing public goods provides no assurance that the goods chosen will maximize economic surplus.

Of course, the fact that the programs that best suit advertisers' needs may not be socially optimal does not mean that government decisions would necessarily be better. One can imagine, for example, a cultural affairs ministry that would choose television programming that would be "good for us" but that few of us would want to watch.

One way to avoid the inefficiency that arises when advertisers choose programming is to employ pay-per-view methods of paying for television programming. These methods allow viewers to register not just which programs they prefer but also the strength of their preferences, as measured by how much they are willing to pay.

But although pay-per-view TV is more likely to select the programs the public most values, it is also less efficient than broadcast TV in one important respect. As noted earlier, charging each household a fee for viewing discourages some households from tuning in. And since the marginal social cost of serving an additional household is exactly zero, limiting the audience in this way is inefficient. Which of the two inefficiencies is more important—free TV's inefficiency in choosing among programs or pay TV's inefficiency in excluding potential beneficiaries—is an empirical question.

In any event, the mix between private and public provision of public goods and services differs substantially from society to society and from arena to arena within any given society. These differences depend on the nature of available technologies for delivering and paying for public goods, and also on people's preferences.

Why do detergent companies care more about audience size than about how much people would be willing to pay to see the programs they sponsor?

By how much is economic surplus reduced by a pay-per-view charge?

EXAMPLE 15.5

If *Mystery Theater* is shown on pay-per-view television at 10 P.M. on Thursdays, the demand curve for each episode is given by $P = 20 - Q$, where P is the price per household in dollars and Q is the number of households who choose to watch the program (in millions). If the regulated pay-per-view charge is $10 per household, by how much would economic surplus rise if the same episode were shown instead on "free" broadcast public TV?

With a fee of $10 per episode, 10 million households will watch (see Figure 15.4). But if the same episode were shown instead on broadcast public TV, 20 million households would watch. The additional economic surplus reaped by the extra 10 million households is the area of the blue triangle, which is $50 million. The marginal cost of permitting these additional households to watch the episode is zero, so the total gain in surplus is $50 million.

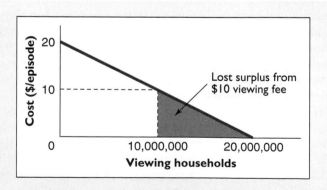

FIGURE 15.4
The Loss in Surplus from a Pay-per-View Fee.
Twice as many households would watch the program if its price were zero instead of $10. The additional economic surplus is the area of the blue triangle, or $50 million.

In general, charging a positive price for a good whose marginal cost is zero will result in a loss in surplus. As we saw in Chapter 7, the size of the loss that results when price is set above marginal cost depends on the price elasticity of demand. When demand is more elastic, the loss in surplus is greater. Exercise 15.3 provides an opportunity to see that principle at work.

EXERCISE 15.3

How would your answer to Example 15.5 have been different if the demand curve had been given instead by $P = 15 - 2Q$?

> **RECAP**   **THE OPTIMAL QUANTITY OF A PUBLIC GOOD**
>
> Because the quantity of a public good must be the same for every consumer, the total demand curve for a public good is constructed by adding individual demand curves vertically. Optimal production of a public good occurs at the quantity for which the demand curve intersects the marginal cost curve for the public good.
>
> Government need not always be the best way to provide public goods. Such goods can be provided by private organizations that rely on charitable contributions or the sale of by-products. Private for-profit companies can also become providers when new technologies such as pay-per-view television convert public goods into collective goods.

ADDITIONAL FUNCTIONS OF GOVERNMENT

The provision of public goods is not the only rationale for the existence of government. Government also creates and enforces the rules without which the efficient production of private goods would not be possible.

EXTERNALITIES AND PROPERTY RIGHTS

As we saw in Chapter 11, for example, externalities often stand in the way of socially optimal resource allocation in private activities. We saw, too, that optimal allocations are unlikely to result whenever property rights are poorly defined (for example, the tragedy of the commons). These observations suggest the existence of two additional important roles for government: the regulation of activities that generate externalities and the definition and enforcement of property rights.

These rationales for government action explain why most governments regulate activities that generate pollution, subsidize education (on the grounds that an educated public creates positive externalities), control access to fishing waters and public timber lands, and enforce zoning laws. Most laws, in fact, represent attempts to define property rights or to control externalities. The law requiring motorists to drive on the right, for example, is an attempt to prevent the activities of one motorist from causing harm to others.

Proponents of minimalist government often object that the government unjustly curtails our freedom when it uses zoning laws to limit the size of the houses we build or imposes fines on motorists who violate highway speed limits. Yet the justification for such regulations is precisely the same as for the laws that prohibit your fist from occupying the same physical space as your neighbor's nose. You are free to swing your fists as you please, provided you cause no harm to others. But if your fist strikes your neighbor's nose, you become a violator of the law and subject to punishment. If the proponents of minimalist government approve of restricting behavior in this way, why do they disapprove of other attempts to discourage behaviors that cause harm to others?

Perhaps their fear is that because externalities are so pervasive, governments that were empowered to regulate them might quickly get out of control. This is by no means an idle fear, and we emphasize that the mere fact that an externality exists does not necessarily mean that the best outcome is for the government to regulate it. As we will see in the next section, regulation entails costs of its own. The ultimate question is therefore a practical one: Will government regulation of the externality in question do more good than harm? Slogans about being free to live without government interference provide little help in answering such questions.

LOCAL, STATE, OR FEDERAL?

Framers of the American Constitution were deeply skeptical of centralized government power. In drafting the Constitution, therefore, they explicitly tried to limit the powers of the federal government as much as possible, delegating most important powers to the states, who in turn delegated many of their powers to governments at the local level.

That the dangers of remote, centralized government ranked high among founding fathers' concerns is no surprise. After all, fresh in their memories was the autocratic treatment received by the American colonies at the hands of the monarchy in England. The founding fathers recognized that government will be more responsive the shorter the distance between officeholders and the voters who elect them.

Another obvious advantage of giving as much authority to local governments as possible is that different communities often have markedly different preferences about how much to spend on public goods, and even on what kinds of public goods to provide. When such decisions are made at the local level, people can shop for a community whose voters' preferences largely coincide with their own. Those who like high levels of public goods and services can band together and authorize high taxes to pay for them. Others who place less value on public services can choose communities in which both services and taxes are lower.

Why, given the many attractions of decisions made at the local level, did the founding fathers create federal and state governments at all? One reason is economies of scale in defense. For a country to survive politically, it must be able to deter aggression by hostile governments. A country consisting only of, say, Concord, New Hampshire, would be ill-equipped to do that. Large, well-equipped armies and navies cost a lot of money, and countries without sufficient population simply cannot afford them.

Defense, however, is not the only reason to empower governments beyond the local or state level. The problem of pollution, for example, is difficult to solve when the various sources of pollution are not subject to regulatory control by a single government. Much of the acid rain experienced in Canada, for instance, is the result of sulfur dioxide emissions from industrial sources in the upper midwest of the United States. These emissions are beyond the reach of Canadian environmental regulations. In many instances, as with the discharge of greenhouse gases, not even a coalition of all the governments in North, Central, and South America would have power to take effective action. Carbon dioxide emitted anywhere on the planet disperses to uniform concentrations around the globe in a matter of months.

The choice between different levels of government, then, often confronts us with difficult trade-offs. Ceding the power of taxation to a federal government often entails painful compromises for voters in individual states. But the loss of political autonomy is an even less attractive option. Similarly, nations are understandably reluctant to cede any of their sovereign powers to a higher authority, but failure to take such steps may entail unacceptable environmental costs in the long run.

> **RECAP** **ADDITIONAL FUNCTIONS OF GOVERNMENT**
>
> Government creates economic surplus not only by providing public goods but also by regulating activities that generate externalities and by defining and enforcing property rights. These rationales explain why most governments regulate pollution, subsidize education, control access to fishing waters and public timber lands, and enforce zoning laws.
>
> Although the framers of the Constitution disliked centralized government power, they recognized that some government functions are not best performed at the local or even state level. Economies of scale argue for provision of defense at the national level. Externalities that transcend local boundaries provide an additional rationale for national or even international government.

SOURCES OF INEFFICIENCY IN THE POLITICAL PROCESS

In most countries, expenditures on public goods, tax policy, and laws regulating behavior are determined in large part by the votes of democratically elected representatives. This process is far from perfect. (Winston Churchill called democracy "the worst form of government, except for any other.") Inefficiencies often arise in the public sphere not because of incompetent or ignorant legislators but because of structural incentive problems.

PORK BARREL LEGISLATION

The following example, drawn not from the public sector but from everyday private life, illustrates one of the important incentive gaps.

Why does check-splitting make the total restaurant bill higher?

ECONOMIC NATURALIST 15.3

Sven Torvaldsen and nine friends are having dinner at la Maison de la Casa House, a four-star restaurant in Minneapolis. To simplify the task of paying for their meal, they have agreed in advance to split the cost of their meal equally, with each paying one-tenth of the total check. Having cleared the entree dishes, the waiter arrives with the dessert menu, on which Sven's two favorite items are pumpkin bread pudding ($10) and chocolate mousse ($6). Sven's reservation prices for these items are $4 and $3, respectively. Will he order dessert, and, if so, which one? Would he order dessert if he were dining by himself?

When Sven and his friends split the total check equally, Sven's payment goes up by one-tenth of the menu price of any dessert he orders. Thus the prices— to him—of the bread pudding and chocolate mousse are $1 and 60 cents, respectively. Because he gets $4 − $1 = $3 of consumer surplus from the bread pudding and only $3 − $0.60 = $2.40 from the chocolate mousse, he will order the bread pudding. If Sven were dining alone, however, his bill would increase dollar for dollar with the menu price of any dessert he ordered. And since the menu prices exceed his corresponding reservation prices, he would not order dessert at all.

The irony, of course, is that if Sven's nine friends have the same preferences regarding dessert, each will order bread pudding and each person's share of the total bill will rise not by $1 but by the full $10. Compared to the alternative of no one having dessert, each diner suffers a $6 loss in consumer surplus. Still, it made sense for each to order bread pudding, since failure to do so would have reduced each diner's bill by only $1.

| EXERCISE 15.4

In the preceding example, would Sven have ordered dessert if there had been only 5 people splitting the check instead of 10?

Alert readers will have noticed the similarity between the problem posed in the preceding example and the one posed in Economic Naturalist 11.7, in which identical twins had a single milkshake to share with two straws. The same incentive problem leads to the inefficient outcome in both cases.

The following example illustrates how the very same incentive problem rears its head in the legislative process.

Why do legislators often support one another's pork barrel spending programs?

Pork barrel programs are government programs that benefit local areas but are of questionable value from a national perspective. Why do voters seem to support legislators who initiate such projects even when the total effect of all such projects on local tax bills far exceeds the local benefits?

Consider a voter in a congressional district that contains one one-hundredth of the country's taxpayers. Suppose that voter's representative is able to deliver a public project that generates benefits of $100 million for the district but that costs the federal government $150 million. Since the district's share of the tax bill for the project will be only $150 million/100 = $1.5 million, residents of the district are $98.5 million better off with the project than without it. And that explains why so many voters favor legislators with a successful record of "bringing home the bacon."

But why would legislator A support such a project in legislator B's home district? After all, B's project will cause A's constituents' taxes to rise—albeit by a small amount—yet they will get no direct benefit from the project. The answer is that if A does not support B's project, then B will not support A's. The practice whereby legislators support one another's pet projects is known as **logrolling.** This practice creates a bias toward excessive spending, much like the bias created when a dinner check is split equally.

ECONOMIC NATURALIST 15.4

pork barrel spending a public expenditure that is larger than the total benefit it creates but that is favored by a legislator because his or her constituents benefit from the expenditure by more than their share of the resulting extra taxes

logrolling the practice whereby legislators support one another's legislative proposals

RENT-SEEKING

A related source of inefficiency in the public sphere occurs because the gains from government projects are often concentrated in the hands of a few beneficiaries, while the costs are spread among many. This means that beneficiaries often have a powerful incentive to organize and lobby in favor of public projects. Individual taxpayers, by contrast, have little at stake in any public project and therefore have little incentive to incur the cost of mobilizing themselves in opposition.

Suppose, for example, that a price support bill for sugar will raise the price of sugar by 10 cents per pound and that the average American family currently consumes 100 pounds of sugar per year. How will this legislation affect the average family's consumption of sugar? Recall from Chapter 5 that a good, such as salt or sugar, whose share in most family budgets is small is likely to have a low price elasticity of demand. Hence each family's sugar consumption will decline only slightly as a result of the 10-cent price hike. The resulting increase in each family's annual expenditures on sugar—slightly less than $10—is scarcely a noticeable burden, and surely not enough to induce many people to complain to their representatives. The same legislation, however, will raise sugar industry revenues by nearly $1 billion annually. With a sum that large at stake, it is certain that the industry will lobby vigorously in its favor.

Why don't citizens vote against those legislators who support such bills? One reason is the problem of rational ignorance, discussed in Chapter 12. Most voters have no idea that a price support bill for sugar and other special-interest bills even exist, much less how individual legislators vote on them. If all voters became well-informed about such bills, the resulting increase in the quality of legislation might well be sufficient to compensate each voter for the cost of becoming informed. But because of the free-rider problem, each voter knows that the outcome of votes in Congress will not be much affected by whether he becomes well-informed.

Still other sources of inefficiency arise even in the case of projects whose benefits exceed their costs. Several years ago, for example, the federal government announced its decision to build a $25 billion high-energy physics research facility (the "superconducting supercollider"), which ignited an intense competition among more than 20 states vying to be chosen as the site for this facility. Hundreds of millions of dollars was spent on proposal preparation, consultants' fees, and various other lobbying activities. Such investments are known as **rent-seeking,** and they tend to be inefficient for the same reason that investments by contestants in other positional arms races are inefficient (see Chapter 11).

rent-seeking the socially unproductive efforts of people or firms to win a prize

Efforts devoted to rent-seeking are socially unproductive because of the simple incentive problem illustrated in Example 15.6.

EXAMPLE 15.6

Why would anyone pay $50 for a $20 bill?

Suppose a $20 bill is to be auctioned off to the highest bidder. The rules of this particular auction require an initial bid of at least 50 cents, and succeeding bids must exceed the previous high bid by at least 50 cents. When the bidding ceases, both the highest bidder and the second-highest bidder must give the amounts they bid to the auctioneer. The highest bidder then receives the $20, and the second-highest bidder gets nothing. For example, if the highest bid is $11 and the second-highest bid is $10.50, the winner earns a net payment of $20 − $11 = $9, and the runner-up loses $10.50. How high will the winning bid be, on average?

Auctions like this one have been extensively studied in the laboratory. And although subjects in these experiments have ranged from business executives to college undergraduates, the pattern of bidding is almost always the same. Following the opening bid, offers proceed quickly to $10, or half the amount being auctioned. A pause then occurs as the subjects appear to digest the fact that with the next bid the sum of the two highest bids will exceed $20, thus taking the auctioneer off the hook. At this point, the second-highest bidder, whose bid stands at $9.50, invariably offers $10.50, apparently preferring a shot at winning $9.50 to a sure loss of $9.50.

In most cases, all but the top two bidders drop out at this point, and the top two quickly escalate their bids. As the bidding approaches $20, a second pause occurs, this time as the bidders appear to recognize that even the highest bidder is likely to come out behind. The second-highest bidder, at $19.50, is understandably reluctant to offer $20.50. But consider the alternative. If he drops out, he will lose $19.50 for sure. But if he offers $20.50 and wins, he will lose only 50 cents. So as long as he thinks there is even a small chance that the other bidder will drop out, it makes sense to continue. Once the $20 threshold has been crossed, the pace of the bidding quickens again, and from then on it is a war of nerves between the two remaining bidders. It is common for the bidding to reach $50 before someone finally yields in frustration.

One might be tempted to think that any intelligent, well-informed person would know better than to become involved in an auction whose incentives so strongly favor costly escalation. But many of the subjects in these auctions have been experienced business professionals; many others have had formal training in the theory of games and strategic interaction. For example, the psychologist Max Bazerman reports that during a recent 10-year period he earned more than $17,000 by auctioning $20 bills to his MBA students at Northwestern University's Kellogg Graduate School of Management, which is consistently among the top-rated MBA programs in the world. In the course of almost 200 of his auctions, the top two bids never totaled less than $39, and in one instance they totaled $407.

As Example 15.7 shows, the incentives that confront participants in the $20 bill auction are strikingly similar to those that confront companies that are vying for lucrative government contracts.

How much will cellular phone companies bid for an exclusive license?

EXAMPLE 15.7

The State of Wyoming has announced its intention to grant an exclusive license to provide cellular phone services within its borders. Two firms have met the deadline for applying for this license. The franchise lasts for exactly one year, during which time the franchisee can expect to make an economic profit of $20 million. The state legislature will choose the applicant that spends the most money lobbying legislators. If the applicants cannot collude, how much will each spend on lobbying?

If both spend the same, each will have a 50-50 chance at the $20 million prize, which means an expected profit of $10 million minus the amount spent lobbying. If the lobbyists could collude, each would agree to spend the same small, token amount on lobbying. But in the absence of a binding agreement, each will be strongly tempted to try to outspend the other. Once each firm's spending reaches $10 million, each will have an expected profit of zero (a 50-50 chance to earn $20 million, minus the $10 million spent on lobbying).

Further bidding would guarantee an expected loss. And yet, if one firm spent $10,000,001 while the other stayed at $10 million, the first firm would get the franchise for sure and earn an economic profit of $9,999,999. The other firm would have an economic loss of $10 million. Rather than face a sure loss of $10 million, it may be tempted to bid $10,000,002. But then, of course, its rival would face a similar incentive to respond to that bid. No matter where the escalation stops, it is sure to dissipate much of the gains that could have been had from the project. And perhaps, as in the $20 bill auction, the total amount dissipated will be even more than the value of the franchise itself.

From the individual perspective, it is easy to see why firms might lobby in this fashion for a chance to win government benefits. From society's perspective, however, this activity is almost purely wasteful. Lobbyists are typically intelligent, well-educated, and socially skilled. The opportunity cost of their time is high. If they were not lobbying government officials on behalf of their clients, they could be producing other goods or services of value. Governments can discourage such waste by selecting contractors not according to the amount they spend lobbying but on the basis of the price they promise to charge for their services. Society will be more successful the more its institutions encourage citizens to pursue activities that create wealth rather than activities that merely transfer existing wealth from one person or company to another.

STARVE THE GOVERNMENT?

The Nobel laureate Milton Friedman has said that no bureaucrat spends taxpayers' money as carefully as those taxpayers themselves would have. And indeed, there can be little doubt that many government expenditures are wasteful. Beyond the fact that logrolling often results in pork barrel programs that would not satisfy the cost-benefit test, we must worry that government employees may not always face strong incentives to get the most for what they spend. The Pentagon, for example, once purchased a coffeemaker for $7,600 and on another occasion paid $600 for a toilet seat. Such expenditures may have been aberrations, but there seems little doubt that private contractors often deliver comparable services at substantially lower costs than their public counterparts.

In their understandable outrage over government waste, many critics have urged major cutbacks in the volume of public goods and services. These critics reason that if we let the government spend more money, there will be more waste. This is true, of course, but only in the trivial sense that there would be more of *everything* the government does—good and bad—if public spending were higher.

One of our most extensive experiences with the consequences of major reductions in government spending comes from the Proposition 13 movement in California. This movement began with the passage of State Proposition 13 in 1978, which mandated large reductions in property taxes. As Californians have belatedly recognized, this remedy for government waste is like trying to starve a tapeworm by not eating. Fasting does harm the tapeworm, sure enough, but it harms the host even more. Residents of the Golden State, who once proudly sent their children to the nation's best schools, are now sending them to some of its worst.

The physician treats an infected patient by prescribing drugs that are toxic to the parasite but not to the host. A similar strategy should guide our attack on government waste. For example, we might consider the adoption of campaign-finance reform laws that would prevent legislators from accepting campaign contributions from the tobacco industry and other special interests whose government subsidies they support.

The question, then, isn't whether bureaucrats know best how to spend our money. Rather, it's "How much of our money do *we* want to spend on public services?" Although we must remain vigilant against government waste, we must also remember that many public services deliver good value for our money.

 RECAP **SOURCES OF INEFFICIENCY IN THE POLITICAL PROCESS**

Government does much to help the economy function more efficiently, but it can also be a source of waste. For example, legislators may support pork barrel projects, which do not satisfy the cost-benefit criterion but which benefit constituents by more than their share of the extra taxes required to pay for the projects.

Rent-seeking, a second important source of inefficiency, occurs when individuals or firms use real resources in an effort to win favors from the government. Voters often fail to discipline legislators who abet rent-seeking, because the free-rider problem gives rise to rational ignorance on the part of many voters.

Concern about government waste has led many to conclude that the best government is necessarily the smallest one. The solution favored by these critics is to starve government by reducing the amount of money it can collect in taxes. Yet starving the government reduces one kind of waste only to increase another by curtailing public services whose benefit exceeds their cost.

WHAT SHOULD WE TAX?

Although the primary purpose of the tax system is to generate the revenue needed to fund public goods and other government expenditures, taxes also have many other consequences, some intended, others not. For example, taxes alter the relative costs and benefits of engaging in different activities. They also affect the distribution of real purchasing power in the economy. The best tax system is one that raises the needed revenues while at the same time having the most beneficial, or least deleterious, side effects.

On the first criterion, the federal tax system has not performed particularly well. Although the federal budget began to show a modest surplus in the late 1990s, until then it had been in continuous deficit since 1969, during which time the federal government had to borrow trillions of dollars to pay its bills. And now, early in the twenty-first century, the federal budget is again in deficit.

The fact that governments and private corporations borrow money in the same capital market explains the phenomenon economists call **crowding out.** When government increases its demand in the market for borrowed funds, interest rates rise, causing firms to cancel some of their planned investment projects. When the government fails to raise enough revenue from taxes to cover the amount it spends on public goods and services, it thus diverts funds from investments that would have helped the economy to grow.

What about the effect of taxes on incentives? As discussed in Chapter 7, taxes will hold production and consumption below socially optimal levels in markets in which the private costs and benefits coincide exactly with all relevant social costs and benefits. Suppose, for example, that the long-run private marginal cost of producing cars is $20,000 per unit and that the demand curve for cars is as shown in Figure 15.5. The equilibrium quantity and price will be 6 million per year and $20,000, respectively. If no externalities accompany the production or consumption of cars, these will be the socially optimal levels for quantity and price. But if we now add a tax of $2,000 per car, the new equilibrium price and quantity will be $22,000 and 4 million, respectively. The loss in economic surplus will be equal to the area of the blue triangle ($2 billion per year), which is the cumulative sum of the differences between what excluded buyers would have been willing to pay for extra cars and the marginal cost of producing those cars.

Economists who write for the popular press have long focused on the loss in surplus caused by taxes like the one shown in Figure 15.5. These economists argue that the economy would perform better if taxes were lower and total government expenditures were smaller.

But arguments for that claim are far from compelling. As discussed in Chapter 7, for example, even if a tax in a market like the one shown in Figure 15.5 did produce a loss in surplus for participants in that market, it might nonetheless be justified if it led to an even larger gain in surplus from the public expenditures it financed. We also saw in Chapter 7 that the deadweight loss from taxing a good (or activity) will be smaller the smaller is the elasticity of demand or supply for the good. This principle suggests that deadweight losses could be minimized by concentrating taxes on goods with highly inelastic supply or demand curves.

crowding out government borrowing leads to higher interest rates, causing private firms to cancel planned investment projects

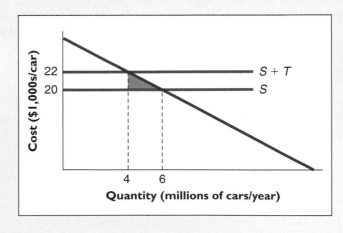

FIGURE 15.5
The Loss in Surplus from a Tax on Cars.
If the supply and demand curves for cars embody all relevant cost benefits of producing and consuming cars, then placing a tax on cars will lead to underproduction of them and a corresponding reduction in economic surplus.

Another difficulty with the argument that taxes harm the economy is more fundamental—namely, that taxes need not cause any loss in surplus at all, even in the markets in which they are directly applied. Suppose, for example, that in the market for cars considered earlier, private marginal cost is again $20,000 but that the production and use of cars now generates air pollution and congestion, negative externalities that sum to $2,000 per car each year. The socially optimal quantity of cars would then be not 6 million per year but only 4 million (see Figure 15.5). Without a tax on cars, the market would reach equilibrium at a price of $20,000 and a quantity of 6 million per year. But with a tax of $2,000 per car, the equilibrium quantity would shrink to 4 million per year, precisely the socially optimal number. Here, the direct effect of the tax is not only not to reduce total economic surplus but actually to augment it by $2 billion per day.

Could we raise enough tax revenue to run the government if we limited ourselves to taxing only those activities that generate negative externalities? No one knows for sure, but it might be possible, for the list of such activities is a long one.

For instance, when someone enters a congested freeway, he creates additional delays for the motorists already there. Existing technology would enable us to levy road-use taxes that reflect these congestion externalities. Each time fossil fuels are burned, they emit greenhouse gases into the atmosphere, which will accelerate the trend toward global warming. A tax on carbon would increase economic surplus by causing decision makers to take this external cost into account. Taxes on other forms of air and water pollution would have similarly benign effects on resource allocation. Recent experience with refundable taxes on food and beverage containers demonstrates that taxes like these can raise needed revenue while at the same time contributing to a cleaner environment.

■ SUMMARY ■

- Our aim in this chapter was to apply principles of microeconomics to the study of the government's role in modern society. One of government's principal tasks is to provide public goods, such as national defense and the criminal justice system. Such goods are, in varying degrees, nonrival and nonexcludable. The first property describes goods for which one person's consumption does not diminish the amount available for others, while the second refers to the difficulty of preventing nonpayers from consuming certain goods.

- Goods that are both highly nonexcludable and nonrival are often called pure public goods. A collective good—such as pay-per-view cable television—is nonrival but excludable. Commons goods are goods that are rival but nonexcludable.

- Because not everyone benefits equally from the provision of any given public good, charging all taxpayers equal amounts for the provision of public goods will generally not be either feasible or desirable. As in the case of private goods, people's willingness to pay for public goods generally increases with income, and most governments therefore levy higher taxes on the rich than on the poor. Tax systems with this property have been criticized on the grounds that they are unfair to the wealthy, but this criticism ignores the fact that alternative tax schemes generally lead to worse outcomes for both rich and poor alike.

- The criterion for providing the optimal quantity or quality of a public good is to keep increasing quantity or quality as long as the marginal benefit of doing so exceeds the marginal cost. One advantage of using the government to provide public goods is that once a tax collection agency has been established to finance a single public good, it can be expanded at relatively low cost to generate revenue to finance additional public goods. A second advantage is that because government has the power to tax, it can easily assign responsibility for the cost of a public good. And in the case of goods for which nonpayers simply cannot be excluded, the government may be the only feasible provider.

- One disadvantage to exclusive reliance on government for public goods provision is the element of coercion inherent in the tax system, which makes some people pay for public goods they don't want, while others do without public goods they do want. Many public goods are provided through private channels, with the necessary funding provided by donations, sale of by-products, by development of new means to exclude nonpayers, and in many cases by private contract. A loss in surplus results, however, whenever monetary charges are levied for the consumption of a nonrival good.

- In addition to providing public goods, government serves two other important roles: the regulation of activities that generate externalities and the definition and enforcement of property rights. Despite a general view that government is more responsive the shorter the distance between citizens and their elected representatives, factors such as economies of scale in the provision of public goods and externalities with broad reach often dictate the assignment of important functions to state or national governments.

- Although history has shown that democracy is the best form of government, it is far from perfect. For example, practices such as logrolling and rent-seeking, common in most democracies, often result in the adoption of laws and public projects whose costs exceed their benefits.

- To finance public goods and services, governments at all levels must tax. But a tax on any activity not only generates revenue, it also creates an incentive to reduce the activity. If the activity would have been pursued at the optimal level in the absence of a tax, taxing it will result in too little of the activity. This observation has led many critics to denounce all taxes as harmful to the economy. Yet the negative effects of taxes on incentives must be weighed against the benefits of the public goods and services financed by tax revenue. Furthermore, taxes on inelastically supplied or demanded activities may generate only small deadweight losses, while taxes on activities that create negative externalities may actually increase economic efficiency.

▪ KEY TERMS ▪

collective good (375)
crowding out (391)
head tax (377)
logrolling (387)
nonexcludable good (374)

nonrival good (374)
pork barrel spending (387)
progressive tax (378)
proportional income tax (378)
public good (374)

pure commons good (375)
pure private good (375)
pure public good (374)
regressive tax (377)
rent-seeking (388)

▪ REVIEW QUESTIONS ▪

1. a. Which of the following goods are nonrival?
   Apples
   Stephen King novels
   Street lighting on campus
   NPR radio broadcasts
   b. Which of these goods are nonexcludable?

2. Give examples of goods that are, for the most part:
   a. Rival but nonexcludable
   b. Nonrival but excludable
   c. Both nonrival and nonexcludable

3. Why might even a wealthy person prefer a proportional income tax to a head tax?

4. True or false: A tax on an activity that generates negative externalities will improve resource allocation in the private sector and also generate revenue that could be used to pay for useful public goods. Explain.

5. Consider a good that would be provided optimally by private market forces. Why is the direct loss in surplus that would result from a tax on this good an overstatement of the loss in surplus caused by the tax?

▪ PROBLEMS ▪

1. Jack and Jill are the only two residents in a neighborhood, and they would like to hire a security guard. The value of a security guard is $50 per month to Jack and $150 per month to Jill. Irrespective of who pays the guard, the guard will protect the entire neighborhood.
   a. What is the most a guard can charge per month and still be assured of being hired by at least one of them?
   b. Suppose the competitive wage for a security guard is $120 per month. The local government proposes a plan whereby Jack and Jill each pay 50 percent of this monthly fee, and asks them to vote on this plan. Will the plan be voted in? Would economic surplus be higher if the neighborhood had a guard?

2. Refer to Problem 1. Suppose Jack earns $1,000 per month and Jill earns $11,000 per month.
   a. Suggest a proportional tax on income that would be accepted by majority vote and would pay for the security guard.
   b. Suppose instead that Jack proposes a tax scheme under which Jack and Jill would each receive the same net benefit from hiring the guard. How much would Jack and Jill pay now? Would Jill agree to this scheme?
   c. What is the practical problem that prevents ideas like the one in part b from working in real-life situations?

3. The following table shows all the marginal benefits for each voter in a small town whose town council is considering a new swimming pool with capacity for at least three citizens. The cost of the pool would be $18 per week and would not depend on the number of people who actually used it.

Voter	Marginal benefit ($/week)
A	12
B	5
C	2

a. If the pool must be financed by a weekly head tax levied on all voters, will the pool be approved by majority vote? Is this outcome socially efficient? Explain.

b. The town council instead decides to auction a franchise off to a private monopoly to build and maintain the pool. If it cannot find such a firm willing to operate the pool, then the pool project will be scrapped. If all such monopolies are constrained by law to charge a single price to users, will the franchise be sold, and if so, how much will it sell for? Is this outcome socially efficient? Explain.

4. Refer to Problem 3. Suppose now that all such monopolies can perfectly price-discriminate.
   a. Will the franchise be sold, and if so, how much will it sell for? Is this outcome socially efficient? Explain.
   b. The town council decides that, rather than auction off the franchise, it will give it away to the firm that spends the most money lobbying council members. If there are four identical firms in the bidding and they cannot collude, what will happen?

5. Two consumers, Smith and Jones, have the following demand curves for Podunk Public Radio broadcasts of recorded opera on Saturdays:

$$\text{Smith:} \qquad P_S = 12 - Q$$
$$\text{Jones:} \qquad P_J = 12 - 2Q,$$

where P_S and P_J represent marginal willingness to pay values for Smith and Jones, respectively, and Q represents the number of hours of opera broadcast each Saturday.
   a. If Smith and Jones are the only public radio listeners in Podunk, construct the demand curve for opera broadcasts.
   b. If the marginal cost of opera broadcasts is $15 per hour, what is the socially optimal number of hours of broadcast opera?

6. Suppose the demand curves for hour-long episodes of the *Jerry Springer Show* and *Masterpiece Theater* are as shown in the following diagram. A television network is considering whether to add one or both programs to its upcoming fall lineup. The only two time slots remaining are sponsored by Colgate, which is under contract to pay the network 10 cents for each viewer who watches the program, out of which the network would have to cover its production costs of $400,000 per episode. (Viewership can be estimated accurately with telephone surveys.) Any time slot the network does not fill with *Springer* or *Masterpiece Theater* will be filled by infomercials for a weight-loss program, for which the network incurs no production costs and for which it receives a fee of $500,000. Viewers will receive $5 million in economic surplus from watching each installment of the infomercial.

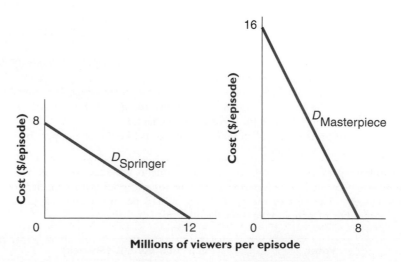

a. How will the network fill the two remaining slots in its fall lineup?
b. Is this outcome socially efficient?

7. Refer to Problem 6. By how much would total economic surplus be higher if each episode of *Masterpiece Theater* were shown on PBS free of charge than if it were shown by a profit-maximizing pay-per-view network?

8. When a TV company chooses a pay-per-view scheme to pay for programming, which of the following statements is true? Explain.
   a. The outcome is socially efficient.
   b. The programs selected will maximize advertising revenue.
   c. The marginal cost to an additional viewer of watching the programs is lower than when advertising is used to finance programming.
   d. The outcome is always more socially efficient than when advertising is used to finance programming.
   e. The variety of programs provided is likely to rise.

9. When a group of people must decide whether to buy a shared public good or service, the free-rider problem frequently occurs because:
   a. People have an incentive to understate how much the facility is really worth to them if they have to pay taxes to finance it.
   b. Each individual's needed contribution is an insignificant amount of the total required.
   c. People have an incentive to overstate how much the facility is worth to them if they don't have to pay taxes to finance it.
   d. People hope that others will value the facility enough to pay for it entirely.
   e. Only one of the above statements is not a reason for the existence of the free-rider problem.

10. The town of Smallsville is considering building a museum. The interest on the money Smallsville will have to borrow to build the museum will be $1,000 per year. Each citizen's marginal benefit from the museum is shown in the following table, and this marginal benefit schedule is public information.
    a. Assuming each citizen voted his or her private interests, would a referendum to build the museum and raise each citizen's annual taxes by $200 pass?
    b. A citizen proposes that the city let a private company build the museum and charge the citizens a lump-sum fee each year to view it as much as they like. Only citizens who paid the fee would be allowed to view the museum. If the private company were allowed to set a single fee, would any company offer to build the museum?
    c. A second citizen proposes allowing the private company to charge different prices to different citizens and auctioning the right to build the museum to the highest bidding company. Again, only the citizens who pay the fee may view the museum. What is the highest bid a private company would make to supply the museum to Smallsville?

Citizen	Marginal benefit from museum ($/year)
Anita	340
Brandon	290
Carlena	240
Dallas	190
Eloise	140

▪ ANSWERS TO IN-CHAPTER EXERCISES ▪

15.1 a. The BLS web site at 3 in the morning has the capacity to serve far more users than it attracts, so an additional user calling up the site does not prevent some other user from doing so. Other web sites, however do not show the nonrival property, at least during certain hours, because they attract more users than their servers can accommodate.
     b. The stadium at the championship game is always full, so anyone who watches the game in person prevents someone else from doing so.
     c. Additional people can watch the game on television without diminishing the availability of the telecast for others.

15.2 To construct the demand curve (a), we first graph Bill's demand curve (c) and Tom's demand curve (b) and then add the two individual demand curves vertically. The equation for the demand curve is $P = 18 - 1.5Q$.

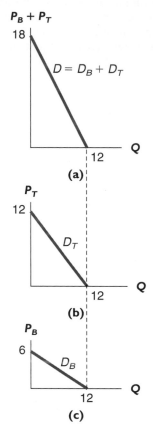

15.3 Whereas elasticity of demand was 1 at a price of $10 on the original demand curve, it is 1.5 on the new demand curve. As a result, the $10 fee now excludes 20 million viewers, and the resulting loss in surplus (again the area of the blue triangle) is now $100 million.

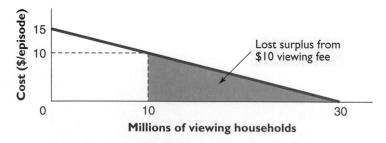

15.4 If Sven orders bread pudding, his share of the bill would now go up by $2 instead of $1. If he orders chocolate mousse, his share of the bill would go up by $1.20 instead of $0.60. So he would still order the bread pudding (surplus = $4 − $2 = $2) rather than the chocolate mousse (surplus = $3 − $1.20 = $1.80).

PART

5

INTERNATIONAL TRADE

■

In Chapter 16 we will address international trade and its effects on the broader economy, showing that if trade is unrestricted, market forces will ensure that countries specialize in producing those goods in which they have a comparative advantage. We will also show that although opening the economy to trade increases economic welfare overall, some groups—such as workers in industries that face competition from foreign producers—may be made worse off, which explains why proposals to expand trade often face political opposition.

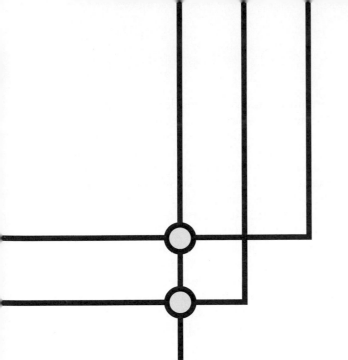

CHAPTER

16

INTERNATIONAL TRADE AND TRADE POLICY

■

On April 13, 1861, Southern troops fired on Fort Sumter in Charleston harbor, initiating the American Civil War. Less than a week later, on April 19, President Lincoln proclaimed a naval blockade of the South. Code-named the Anaconda Plan (after the snake that squeezes its prey to death), the blockade required the Union navy to patrol the Southern coastline, stopping and boarding ships that were attempting to land or depart. The object of the blockade was to prevent the Confederacy from shipping cotton to Europe, where it could be traded for military equipment, clothing, foodstuffs, and other supplies.

Historians are divided on the effectiveness of the Union blockade in choking off Confederate trade. In the early years of the war, the North had too few ships to cover the 3,600-mile Southern coastline, so "running" the blockade was not difficult. But in the latter part of the war the number of Union ships enforcing the blockade increased from about 90 to more than 600, and sailing ships were replaced with faster, more lethal ironclad vessels. Still, private blockade runners—like the fictitious Rhett Butler in Margaret Mitchell's *Gone with the Wind*—attempted to elude the Union navy in small, fast ships. Because the price of raw cotton in Great Britain was between 10 and 20 times what it was in the Confederacy (a differential that indicated disruption in the normal flow of trade), blockade runners enjoyed huge profits when they were successful. But despite their efforts, by 1864 the Southern war effort was seriously hampered by a lack of military equipment and supplies, at least in part as a result of the blockade.

The use of a naval blockade as a weapon of war highlights a paradox in contemporary attitudes toward trade between nations. Presumably, an attempt

He appreciated the economic benefits of trade.

by a foreign power to blockade U.S. ports would today be considered a hostile act that would elicit a strong response from the U.S. government. Yet one often hears politicians and others arguing that trade with other nations is harmful to the United States and should be restricted—in effect, that the United States should blockade its own ports! Despite support from President Clinton and virtually all professional economists, for example, many politicians opposed the 1993 signing of the North American Free Trade Agreement (NAFTA), which was intended to increase U.S. trade with Mexico and Canada, on the grounds that it might cost American jobs. In April 2001, opponents of increased trade demonstrated in Washington, D.C., disrupting meetings of the World Trade Organization, an international body set up to promote trade and enforce trade agreements. So is trade a good thing or not? And if it is, why does it sometimes face determined and even violent opposition?

This chapter addresses international trade and its effects on the broader economy. We will begin by reviewing the idea of *comparative advantage,* which was introduced in Chapter 2. We will show that everyone can enjoy more goods and services if nations specialize in those products in which they have a comparative advantage, and then trade freely among themselves. Furthermore, if trade is unrestricted, market forces will ensure that countries produce those goods in which they have a comparative advantage.

Having shown the potential benefits of trade, we will turn next to the reasons for opposition to trade. Although opening the economy to trade increases economic welfare overall, some groups—such as workers in industries that face competition from foreign producers—may be made worse off. The fact that open trade may hurt some groups creates political pressure to enact measures restricting trade, such as taxes on imported goods (called tariffs) and limits on imports (called quotas). We will analyze the effects of these trade restrictions, along with other ways of responding to concerns about affected industries and workers. From an economic point of view, providing direct assistance to those who are hurt by increased trade is preferable to blocking or restricting trade.

COMPARATIVE ADVANTAGE AS A BASIS FOR TRADE

Chapter 2 began with the story of the Nepalese cook Birkhaman, a remarkable jack-of-all-trades who could do everything, from butchering a goat to fixing an alarm clock. Yet despite his range of skills, Birkhaman, like most Nepalese, was quite poor. The reason for Birkhaman's poverty, as we saw in Chapter 2, was precisely his versatility. Because he did so many different things, he could not hope to become as productive in each separate activity as someone who specialized entirely in that activity.

The alternative to a nation of Birkhamans is a country in which each person specializes in the activity at which he is relatively most efficient, or has a *comparative advantage.* This specialization, combined with trade between producers of different goods and services, allows a society to achieve a higher level of productivity and standard of living than one in which each person is essentially self-sufficient.

This insight, that specialization and trade among individuals can yield impressive gains in productivity, applies equally well to nations. Factors such as climate, natural resources, technology, workers' skills and education, and culture provide countries with comparative advantages in the production of different goods and services. For example, as we saw in Chapter 2, the large number of leading research universities in the United States gives that nation a comparative advantage in the design of technologically sophisticated computer hardware and software. Likewise, the wide international use of the English language endows the United States with a comparative advantage in producing popular films and TV shows.

Similarly, France's climate and topography, together with the accumulated knowledge of generations of vintners, provides that country a comparative advantage in producing fine wines, while Australia's huge expanses of arable land give that country a comparative advantage in producing grain.

The *principle of comparative advantage* tells us that we can all enjoy more goods and services when each country produces according to its comparative advantage, and then trades with other countries. In the next section we explore this fundamental idea in greater detail.

PRODUCTION AND CONSUMPTION POSSIBILITIES AND THE BENEFITS OF TRADE

In this section we will consider how international trade benefits an individual country. To do so, we will contrast the production and consumption opportunities in a **closed economy**—one that does not trade with the rest of the world—with the opportunities in an **open economy**—one that does trade with other economies. Because we will make use of the production possibilities curve, which was introduced in Chapter 2, we will begin by briefly reviewing that concept. We will look first at the PPC for a two-person economy and then at the PPC for a many-person economy. After reviewing the PPC, we will see how a country's production possibilities are related to its citizens' ability to consume in a closed economy versus an open economy.

THE TWO-WORKER PRODUCTION POSSIBILITIES CURVE

Recall that (for a two-good economy) the production possibilities curve (PPC) is a graph that shows the maximum amount of each good that can be produced, at every possible level of production of the other good.[1] To see how the PPC is constructed, let's consider a hypothetical economy, which we'll call Brazil, which has only two workers, Carlos and Maria. Each of these two workers can produce two goods, coffee and computers.

The PPC for a two-worker economy

Two Brazilian workers, Carlos and Maria, can each produce coffee and computers. Carlos can produce either 100 pounds of coffee or 1 computer per week. Maria can produce either 100 pounds of coffee or 2 computers per week. Both Carlos and Maria work 50 weeks per year. Find the production possibilities curve for Brazil.

To construct the PPC for this two-person economy, we ask first how much coffee Brazil could produce if both Carlos and Maria worked full time producing coffee. Between them they can produce 200 pounds of coffee per week, so in 50 weeks they could produce 10,000 pounds of coffee. Thus if we plot coffee production on the vertical axis of the graph of Brazil's PPC, the vertical intercept of the PPC will be 10,000 pounds of coffee per year (point *A* in Figure 16.1). Likewise, if Carlos and Maria produced only computers, between them they could produce 3 computers per week, or 150 computers per year. So the horizontal intercept of Brazil's PPC is 150 computers per year (point *B* in Figure 16.1).

We have found where the Brazilian PPC intersects the two axes of the graph. To find the rest of the PPC, imagine that Carlos and Maria are producing only coffee (point *A* in Figure 16.1), when they decide that they would like to have

Climate and long experience give France a comparative advantage in producing fine wines.

closed economy an economy that does not trade with the rest of the world

open economy an economy that trades with other countries

EXAMPLE 16.1

---

[1]For a many-good economy, the PPC shows the maximum amount of each good that can be produced at any level of production of all the other goods. Focusing on the two-good case allows us to draw the figures on the two-dimensional page. Our conclusions apply to the many-good case, however.

FIGURE 16.1

Production Possibilities Curve for a Two-Worker Economy.

In the portion of the PPC between points *A* and *C*, only Maria is producing computers, so the slope of the PPC in that range reflects Maria's opportunity cost of computers in terms of coffee production forgone. At point *C*, Maria spends all her time on computers and Carlos spends all his time on coffee. Between points *C* and *B*, any additional computers must be produced by Carlos. Thus between points *C* and *B* the slope of the PPC reflects Carlos's opportunity cost of producing computers, in terms of coffee production forgone.

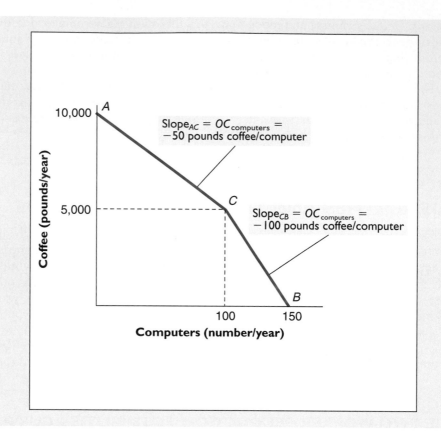

some computers as well. In this situation, which worker should switch from producing coffee to producing computers?

To answer this question, we need to find the one with a *comparative advantage* in producing computers. To do this we must calculate opportunity costs. Carlos can produce either 100 pounds of coffee or 1 computer per week. Because producing a computer leaves him one week less to devote to coffee production, which reduces his coffee output by 100 pounds, Carlos's opportunity cost of producing 1 computer is 100 pounds of coffee. Maria can produce either 100 pounds of coffee or 2 computers per week, so her opportunity cost of producing a computer is 100/2, or 50 pounds of coffee. Because Maria's opportunity cost of producing a computer is lower than Carlos's, she has a comparative advantage in producing computers. By the principle of comparative advantage, Maria should be the one to specialize in computer production. For his part, Carlos has a comparative advantage in producing coffee (see Exercise 16.1), so he should specialize in coffee.

Starting from point *A* in Figure 16.1, where only coffee is produced, we can imagine that Maria begins to produce increasing numbers of computers. The slope of the line emanating from point *A* equals Maria's opportunity cost of producing a computer, $OC_{computers}$, where cost is measured as a negative quantity:

$$\text{Slope} = \text{Maria's } OC_{computers} = \frac{\text{loss in coffee}}{\text{gain in computers}}$$

$$= \frac{-100 \text{ pounds of coffee/week}}{2 \text{ computers/week}} = -50 \text{ pounds of coffee/computer.}$$

As Maria increases the share of her time devoted to computer production, we move down along the straight line from point *A* in Figure 16.1. The slope of the PPC is constant in this region at −50 pounds of coffee per computer, Maria's opportunity cost of computers.

Maria's time is limited to 50 weeks per year, however, so if she keeps increasing her computer production, she will eventually reach a point at which she produces only computers and no coffee. At that point annual production by the two workers taken together will be 100 computers (produced by Maria) and 5,000 pounds of coffee (produced by Carlos, who spends all his time producing coffee). This combination of production is shown at point C on the production possibilities curve.

Once Maria's time is fully devoted to making computers, Brazil can increase its computer production only if Carlos begins to build some computers, too. However, Carlos's opportunity cost, measured as pounds of coffee forgone per computer produced, is greater than Maria's. Hence at point C the slope of the PPC changes, creating a "kink" in the graph. The slope of the PPC to the right of point C is given by

$$\text{Slope} = \text{Carlos's } OC_{\text{computers}} = \frac{\text{loss in coffee}}{\text{gain in computers}}$$

$$= \frac{-100 \text{ pounds of coffee/week}}{1 \text{ computer/week}} = -100 \text{ pounds of coffee/computer.}$$

Note that the slope of the PPC to the right of point C is more negative than the slope to the left of point C, so that the PPC declines more sharply to the right of that point. The fact that the opportunity cost of a computer increases as more computers are produced (the *principle of increasing opportunity cost*) implies the outwardly bowed shape that is characteristic of a production possibilities curve, as shown in Figure 16.1.

EXERCISE 16.1

Example 16.1 showed that Maria has a comparative advantage in producing computers. Show by comparison of opportunity costs that Carlos has a comparative advantage in producing coffee.

THE MANY-WORKER PRODUCTION POSSIBILITIES CURVE

Although the economy considered in Example 16.1 included only two workers, the main ideas apply to economies with more workers. Suppose, for example, that we added a third Brazilian worker, Pedro, whose opportunity cost of producing computers is higher than Maria's but lower than Carlos's. The production possibilities curve for this three-person economy would look something like Figure 16.2. Between points A and C on the PPC shown in Figure 16.2, all computers are produced by Maria, who has the greatest comparative advantage in computer production. Thus the slope of the PPC between points A and C is determined by Maria's opportunity cost, measured as the amount of coffee production forgone for each additional computer produced.

At point C Maria is dedicating all her time to computer production, so someone else must produce any additional computers. Pedro has the next lowest opportunity cost of producing computers, so (following the *principle of increasing opportunity cost*) he begins to produce computers at point C. The slope of the PPC between points C and D is determined by Pedro's opportunity cost, which is greater (more negative) than Maria's opportunity cost. At point D in Figure 16.2, Pedro is producing all the computers he can, so finally Carlos begins to produce computers as well. Thus the slope of the PPC between points D and B reflects Carlos's opportunity cost. Because opportunity cost increases as we move from left to right in the figure, the slope of the PPC becomes more and more negative, leading once again to the outwardly bowed shape.

By similar logic, we can construct a case in which there are many workers, perhaps millions. With many workers, the part of the nation's PPC that is associated with each individual worker becomes very small. As a result, the PPC

FIGURE 16.2

Production Possibilities Curve for a Three-Worker Economy.

The PPC for a three-person economy has two "kinks," at points C and D. Between points A and C only Maria produces computers, and the slope of the PPC represents her opportunity cost of producing computers. At point C Maria is spending all her time making computers, so any additional computers will be produced by Pedro, whose comparative advantage is the next greatest. Between points C and D the slope of the PPC is determined by Pedro's opportunity cost. At point D Pedro is also fully occupied producing computers, so that Carlos must begin producing them if computer production is to increase further. Between points D and B the slope of the PPC reflects Carlos's opportunity cost.

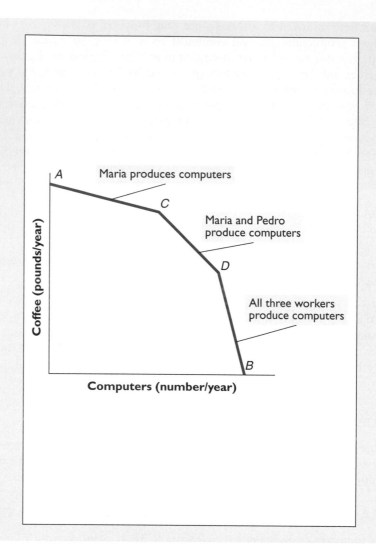

for an economy with many workers has a smoothly bowed shape, as shown in Figure 16.3. With a smoothly curved PPC, the slope at each point still reflects the opportunity cost of producing an additional computer, as illustrated in Figure 16.3. For example, at point C in Figure 16.3, the opportunity cost of producing an extra computer is given by the slope of the line that just touches the PPC at that point. Because computers will be produced first by workers with the greatest comparative advantage (the lowest opportunity cost), the slope of the PPC becomes more and more sharply negative as we read from left to right in the figure.

RECAP **PRODUCTION POSSIBILITIES CURVES**

■ The production possibilities curve (PPC) for a two-good economy is a graph that shows the maximum amount of one good that can be produced at every possible level of production of the other good.

■ The slope of a PPC at any point indicates the opportunity cost, in terms of forgone production of the good on the vertical axis, of increasing production of the good on the horizontal axis by one unit.

■ The more of a good that is already being produced, the greater the opportunity cost of increasing production still further. Thus the slope of the PPC becomes more and more negative as we read from left to right, imparting the characteristic outwardly bowed shape of the curve.

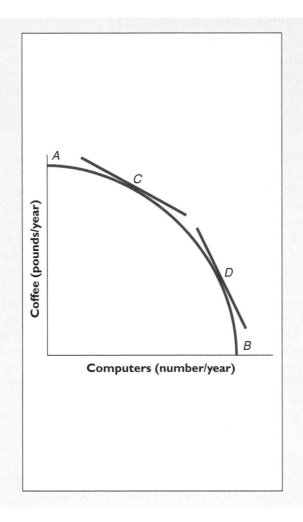

FIGURE 16.3
Production Possibilities Curve for a Many-Worker Economy.
The PPC for a many-worker economy has a smooth, outwardly bowed shape. At each point on the PPC the slope of the curve reflects the opportunity cost, in terms of coffee forgone, of producing an additional computer. For example, the opportunity cost of a computer at point *C* equals the slope of the line that just touches the PPC at that point, and the opportunity cost of a computer at point *D* equals the slope of the line that just touches the PPC there. Because the opportunity cost of producing another computer increases as more computers are produced, the slope of the PPC becomes more and more negative as we read from left to right on the graph.

CONSUMPTION POSSIBILITIES WITH AND WITHOUT INTERNATIONAL TRADE

A country's production possibilities curve shows the quantities of different goods that its economy can produce. However, economic welfare depends most directly not on what a country can *produce,* but on what its citizens can *consume.* The combinations of goods and services that a country's citizens might feasibly consume are called the country's **consumption possibilities.**

The relationship between a country's consumption possibilities and its production possibilities depends on whether the country is open to international trade. In a closed economy with no trade, people can consume only the goods and services produced within their own country. *In a closed economy, then, society's consumption possibilities are identical to its production possibilities.* A situation in which a country is economically self-sufficient, producing everything its citizens consume, is called **autarky.**

The case of an open economy, which trades with the rest of the world, is quite different. In an open economy, people are not restricted to consuming what is produced in their own country, because part of what they produce can be sent abroad in exchange for other goods and services. Indeed, we will see in this section that opening an economy to trade may allow citizens to consume more of everything. Thus *in an open economy, a society's consumption possibilities are typically greater than (and will never be less than) its production possibilities.* We will illustrate this critical point with reference to the two-worker economy studied earlier in the chapter, then briefly consider the more general case of a many-worker economy.

consumption possibilities the combinations of goods and services that a country's citizens might feasibly consume

autarky a situation in which a country is economically self-sufficient

EXAMPLE 16.2   **Brazil's consumption possibilities with trade**

Two Brazilian workers, Carlos and Maria, can produce coffee and computers as described in Example 16.1. Initially the country is closed to trade, and Maria produces only computers, while Carlos produces only coffee. Then the country opens up to trade. World prices are such that 80 pounds of coffee can be traded for 1 computer on the international market and vice versa. How does the opening of Brazil to trade affect Maria's and Carlos's opportunity to consume coffee and computers?

If Maria is producing only computers and Carlos is producing only coffee, then Brazil is at point C on the PPC shown in Figure 16.4 (which is the same as the PPC shown in Figure 16.1). At that point Maria is spending all her time producing 100 computers a year, and Carlos is spending all his time producing 5,000 pounds of coffee a year. If Brazil were closed to trade, Maria and Carlos could obtain more coffee only by producing fewer computers. Specifically, starting at point C on the PPC, they could obtain 50 additional pounds of coffee by giving up 1 computer—by having Maria work 1/2 week less on computers and 1/2 week more producing coffee.

If Brazil opens up to trade, however, then Maria and Carlos can get 80 pounds of coffee in exchange for 1 computer simply by trading computers for coffee on the international market. In other words, they can get an extra 80 pounds of coffee for each computer they give up. To illustrate the degree to which the opportunity to trade benefits Brazil, recall from Example 16.1 that with no trade, Maria's and Carlos's maximum coffee consumption is 10,000 pounds per year (the vertical intercept of the Brazilian PPC). With the opportunity to trade, however, Maria can trade the 100 computers produced at point C for 8,000 pounds of coffee (80 pounds of coffee per computer × 100 computers). Together with the 5,000 pounds of coffee Carlos produces, the coffee obtained through trade raises Brazil's maximum annual coffee consumption from 10,000 to 13,000 pounds per year, as indicated by point F in Figure 16.4. Because trade creates the possibility for Brazil to consume as much as 13,000 pounds of coffee per year, point F is included in Brazil's consumption possibilities, though it would have been unattainable to the Brazilians before the opening up of trade.

FIGURE 16.4
Brazil's Consumption Possibilities with Trade. Without the opportunity to trade, Brazil's consumption possibilities are the same as the Brazilian PPC, represented by line ACB. With the opportunity to trade, however, Brazilians can consume at any point along line FG.

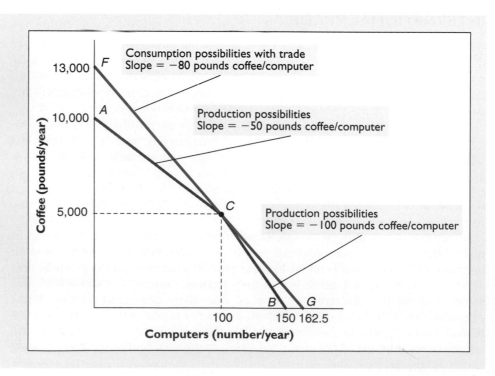

Furthermore, with the opportunity to trade, Maria and Carlos can consume any combination of coffee and computers represented on the straight line between points *F* and *C* in Figure 16.4. This straight line has a slope of −80 pounds of coffee per 1 computer, which is the rate at which the two goods can be exchanged on the international market. So, simply by trading computers for coffee, Maria and Carlos can improve their consumption possibilities at any point except *C*, where their production and consumption possibilities are the same.

Suppose instead that, starting from point *C* on Brazil's PPC, Maria and Carlos decide they want to consume more computers rather than more coffee. With no ability to trade, the opportunity cost of obtaining 1 more computer at point *C* would be 100 pounds of coffee—that is, the amount of coffee that would be lost by having Carlos work 1 more week at producing an extra computer, and hence 1 week fewer at producing coffee. With trade, however, Brazilians can obtain an extra computer at the cost of only 80 pounds of coffee (the price of computers on the international market). In the extreme, if they wanted to consume only computers, the Brazilians could trade the 5,000 pounds of coffee Carlos produces at point *C* for 5,000/80 = 62.5 computers, for a total consumption (with the 100 computers Maria produces) of 162.5 computers. This maximum consumption amount is indicated by point *G* in Figure 16.4. Comparing point *G* with point *B*, we can see that the opportunity to trade increased Brazil's maximum consumption of computers from 150 to 162.5. (Consuming 162.5 computers a year means consuming 325 computers every two years.)

Furthermore, by trading various amounts of coffee for computers, Brazilians can consume any combination of computers and coffee on the straight line between points *C* and *G* in Figure 16.4. Like the segment *FC*, segment *CG* has a slope equal to −80 pounds of coffee per 1 computer, reflecting the rate at which coffee can be traded for computers on the international market. Note that since segments *FC* and *CG* have the same slopes, the line *FG* is a straight line. The line *FG* represents Brazil's consumption possibilities—the combinations of coffee and computers that Carlos and Maria might feasibly consume—when the Brazilian economy is open to trade. By comparing Brazil's consumption possibilities without trade (line *ACB*) and with trade (line *FG*), we can see that Maria and Carlos have a wider range of consumption opportunities when their economy is open.

EXERCISE 16.2

Prior to the opening of trade, suppose that Brazilian residents consumed 80 computers per year. How much coffee were they able to consume each year? Suppose that the Brazilians open up to trade, but they choose to continue to consume 80 computers per year. Now how much coffee can they consume? In answering, use the PPC and consumption possibilities we found in Example 16.2. Does opening to trade make the Brazilians better off?

The same points just made in Example 16.2, which illustrates a two-worker economy, apply in the case of a many-worker economy. Figure 16.5 shows this more general case. With many workers, the PPC (curve *ACB* in the figure) is smoothly bowed. Point *A*, where the PPC intercepts the vertical axis, indicates the maximum amount of coffee the economy can produce, and point *B*, the horizontal intercept of the PPC, shows the maximum number of computers the economy can produce. The intermediate points on the PPC represent alternative combinations of coffee and computers that can be produced. As in the two-worker economy, the slope at each point on the PPC indicates the opportunity cost of producing one additional computer. The more computers that are already being produced, the greater the opportunity cost of increasing computer production still further. Hence the slope of the PPC becomes increasingly negative as we read from left to right.

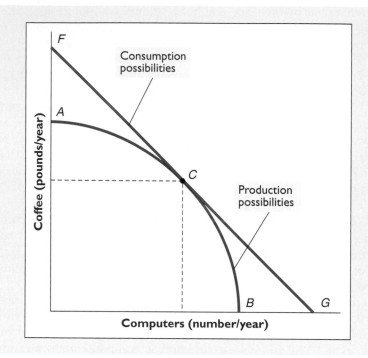

FIGURE 16.5

Consumption Possibilities in a Many-Worker Economy.

The PPC for a many-worker economy is the smooth, outwardly bowed line *ACB*. If the country is open to trade, its consumption possibilities lie on the line *FG*, which just touches the PPC at point *C*. The slope of this line equals the rate at which coffee can be traded for computers at world prices. The country maximizes its consumption possibilities by producing at point *C* and then trading so as to reach its most desired point on line *FG*.

Line *FG* shows the consumption possibilities for this economy if it is open to trade. This line has two key features. First, it is drawn so that it just touches the PPC, at point *C* in Figure 16.5. Second, the slope of line *FG* is determined by the relative prices of coffee and computers on the world market. Specifically, as in the two-worker case (Figure 16.4), the slope of line *FG* tells us how much coffee must be exchanged on world markets to obtain an additional computer.

With access to international trade, Brazil can consume the greatest amount of both coffee and computers by producing at point *C* on the PPC and trading on the international market to obtain the desired combination of coffee and computers on line *FG*. (The exact combination of coffee and computers Brazilians will choose depends on the needs and wants of the population.)

Why should the Brazilians produce at point *C*? At point *C*, and only at that point, the slope of the PPC equals the slope of the consumption possibilities line, *FG*. Hence only at point *C* is the opportunity cost of increasing domestic computer production equal to the opportunity cost of purchasing an extra computer on the world market. If the opportunity cost of producing a computer domestically exceeded the opportunity cost of purchasing a computer on the world market, Brazil would gain by reducing its computer production and importing more computers. Likewise, if the opportunity cost of producing a computer domestically were less than the opportunity cost of purchasing a computer abroad, Brazil would gain by increasing computer production and reducing computer imports. Brazil's best production combination, therefore, is at point *C*, where the domestic and international opportunity costs of acquiring an extra computer, measured in terms of coffee forgone, are equal.

We have already stated the general conclusion that can be drawn from this analysis. Once again, by opening itself up to trade, a country can consume more of *every* good than if it relied solely on its own production (a situation of *autarky*). Graphically, the consumption possibilities line in Figure 16.5 lies above the production possibilities curve, showing that through trade, Brazil can consume combinations of computers and coffee that would not be attainable if its economy were closed to trade.[1]

"The repairs will take awhile. We need a part from Mexico, a part from Brazil and one from Taiwan."

Does "cheap" foreign labor pose a danger to high-wage economies?

Some people argue that high-wage industrialized countries lose by trading with low-wage developing nations. The concern is that the lower average wage that prevails in developing nations will allow those countries to produce most or all goods and services at lower cost. Unable to compete, the industrialized countries will suffer declining wages and rising unemployment. Does "cheap" foreign labor pose a danger to high-wage economies?

The "cheap foreign labor" argument is fallacious because it ignores the principle of comparative advantage and the advantages of specialization. To illustrate the key issues, suppose the United States produces both software and beef. Trade negotiators have proposed to open trade between the United States and a developing nation, Fredonia, which produces the same two products. Real wages are much lower in Fredonia than in the United States. Does this fact imply that Fredonia will undersell the United States in both the software and the beef markets, threatening American workers with the loss of their jobs?

To answer this question, let's first ask *why* wages are lower in Fredonia. As we saw in Chapter 13, real wages are determined by the marginal productivity of labor. Hence, if real wages in Fredonia are radically lower than in the United States, Fredonian workers must be much less productive than U.S. workers. This observation is enough to show why Fredonian producers will not be able to undersell American producers in both industries. Even though Fredonian firms pay lower wages, because of differences in factors such as technology, physical capital, and human capital, a Fredonian worker produces much less output per hour than an American worker. Thus lower Fredonian wages do not necessarily translate into lower production costs.

ECONOMIC NATURALIST 16.1

---

[1]The single point at which consumption possibilities do *not* lie above production possibilities in Figure 16.5 is at point *C*, where production possibilities and consumption possibilities are the same. If Brazilian residents happen to prefer the combination of computers and coffee at point *C* to any other point on *FG*, then they realize no benefit from trade.

Does cheap foreign labor pose a danger to high-wage economies?

Indeed, Fredonia's production costs will tend to be lower than U.S. production costs only in those industries in which Fredonia is *relatively* more productive. Recall the principle of comparative advantage. Suppose that Fredonia is half as productive as the United States in producing beef, but only one-tenth as productive in producing software. In that case, the United States has an absolute advantage in producing both goods, but Fredonia has a comparative advantage in producing beef and the United States has a comparative advantage in producing software. As we have seen in the examples in this chapter, the United States can gain by producing more software and trading the extra software to Fredonians for beef. Fredonia can gain too by trading its beef for software. Far from being hurt by trading with Fredonia, U.S. consumers can have more of both goods through trade.

While the U.S. economy as a whole gains from trade with Fredonia, the United States will have a larger software sector and a smaller beef-producing sector than it would in the absence of trade. That is, some U.S. software will be exported to Fredonia, but some U.S.-produced beef will be replaced by imported Fredonian beef. Hence, although opportunities for workers in the software sector will increase as a result of trade, employment and wages in the beef sector will fall. We will discuss the sectoral impacts of trade in the next section.

RECAP   **CONSUMPTION POSSIBILITIES AND PRODUCTION POSSIBILITIES**

- A country's consumption possibilities are the combinations of goods and services that its citizens might feasibly consume.

- In an economy that is closed to trade, residents can consume only what is produced domestically (a situation of autarky). Hence, in a closed economy, consumption possibilities equal production possibilities.

- The residents of an open economy can trade part of what they produce on international markets. According to the principle of comparative advantage, trade allows everyone to do better than they could otherwise. Thus, in an open economy, consumption possibilities are typically greater than, and will never be less than, production possibilities.

- Graphically, consumption possibilities in an open economy are described by a downward-sloping line that just touches the production possibilities curve (PPC). The slope of this line equals the amount of the good on the vertical axis that must be traded on the international market to obtain one unit of the good on the horizontal axis. A country maximizes its consumption possibilities by producing at the point where the consumption possibilities line just touches the PPC, and then trading so as to reach its most preferred point on the consumption possibilities line.

A SUPPLY AND DEMAND PERSPECTIVE ON TRADE

To this point we have shown that a country can improve its overall consumption possibilities by trading with other countries. In this section we will look more carefully at how international trade affects supply and demand in the markets for specific goods. We will see that when it is costly for workers and firms to change industries, opening up trade with other countries may create groups of winners and losers among producers even as it helps consumers.

Let's see how trade affects the markets for computers and coffee in Brazil. Figure 16.6 shows the supply and demand for computers in that country. As usual, the price is shown on the vertical axis and the quantity on the horizontal axis. For now, think of the price of computers as being measured in terms of coffee rather than in terms of dollars (in other words, we measure the price of computers *relative* to the price of the other good in the economy). As usual, the upward-sloping curve in Figure 16.6 is the supply curve of computers, in this case for computers produced in Brazil; and the downward-sloping curve is the demand curve for computers by Brazilian residents. The supply curve for computers in Brazil reflects the opportunity cost of supplying computers (see Chapter 3). Specifically, at any level of computer production, the relative price at which Brazilian firms are willing to supply an additional computer equals their opportunity cost of doing so. The demand curve, which tells us the number of computers Brazilians will purchase at each relative price, reflects the preferences and buying power of Brazilian consumers.

If the Brazilian economy is closed to international trade, then market equilibrium occurs where the domestic supply and demand curves intersect, at point E in Figure 16.6. The equilibrium price will be p and the equilibrium quantity, q.

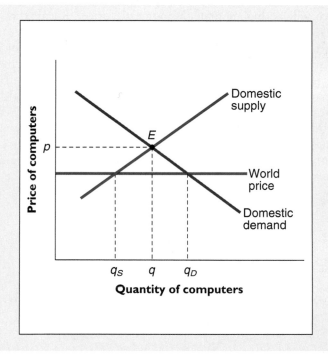

FIGURE 16.6
The Market for Computers in Brazil.
If Brazil is closed to international trade, the equilibrium price and quantity of computers are determined by the intersection of the domestic supply and demand curves at point E. But if Brazil is open to trade, the domestic price of computers must equal the world price. At that price, Brazilians will demand q_D computers, but domestic producers will supply only q_S computers. Thus $q_D - q_S$ computers must be imported from abroad.

If Brazil opens its market to trade, however, the relevant price for computers becomes the **world price** of computers, the price at which computers are traded internationally. The world price for computers is determined by the worldwide supply and demand for computers. If we assume that Brazil's computer market is too small to affect the world price for computers very much, the world price can be treated as fixed, and represented by a horizontal line in the figure. Figure 16.6 shows the world price for computers as being lower than Brazil's closed-economy price.

If Brazilians are free to buy and sell computers on the international market, then the price of computers in Brazil must be the same as the world price. (No one in Brazil will buy a computer at a price above the world price, and no one will sell one at a price below the world price.) Figure 16.6 shows that at the world price, Brazilian consumers and firms demand q_D computers, but Brazilian computer producers will supply only q_S computers. The difference between the two quantities, $q_D - q_S$, is the number of computers that Brazil must import from

world price the price at which a good or service is traded on international markets abroad. Figure 16.6 illustrates a general conclusion: *If the price of a good or service in a closed economy is greater than the world price, and that economy opens itself to trade, the economy will tend to become a net importer of that good or service.*

A different outcome occurs in Brazil's coffee market, shown in Figure 16.7. The price of coffee (measured relative to the price of computers) is shown on the vertical axis, and the quantity of coffee on the horizontal axis. The downward-sloping demand curve in the figure shows how much coffee Brazilian consumers want to buy at each relative price, and the upward-sloping supply curve how much coffee Brazilian producers are willing to supply at each relative price. If Brazil's economy is closed to trade with the rest of the world, then equilibrium in the market for coffee will occur at point *E,* where the domestic demand and supply curves intersect. The quantity produced will be *q* and the price *p.*

Now imagine that Brazil opens its coffee market to international trade. As in the case of computers, if free trade in coffee is permitted, then the prevailing price for coffee in Brazil must be the same as the world price. Unlike the case of computers, however, the world price of coffee as shown in Figure 16.7 is *higher* than the domestic equilibrium price. How do we know that the world price of coffee will be higher than the domestic price? Recall that the price of coffee is measured relative to the price of computers, and vice versa. If the price of computers relative to the price of coffee is higher in Brazil than in the world market, then the price of coffee relative to the price of computers must be lower, as each price is the reciprocal of the other. More generally, as we saw in Chapter 2, when two people or two countries trade with each other, neither can have a comparative advantage in *every* good and service. Thus, in an example with only two goods, if non-Brazilian producers have a comparative advantage in computers, reflected in the lower cost of computers relative to coffee in the world market, then Brazilian producers must have a comparative advantage in coffee. By definition, this comparative advantage implies that the opportunity cost of coffee in terms of computers must be lower in Brazil than in the rest of the world.

FIGURE 16.7
The Market for Coffee in Brazil.
With no international trade, the equilibrium price and quantity of coffee in Brazil are determined by the intersection of the domestic supply and demand curves (point *E*). But if the country opens to trade, the domestic price of coffee must equal the world price. At the higher world price, Brazilians will demand the quantity of coffee q_D, less than the amount supplied by Brazilian producers, q_s. The excess coffee supplied by Brazilian producers, $q_S - q_D$, is exported.

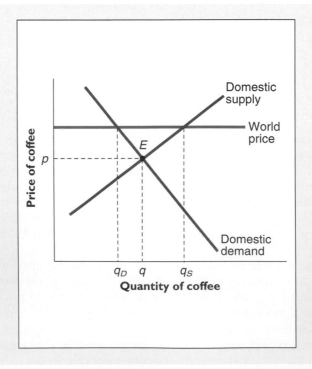

Figure 16.7 shows that at the world price for coffee, Brazilian producers are willing to supply q_S coffee, while Brazilian consumers want to purchase a smaller amount, q_D. The difference between domestic production and domestic consumption, $q_S - q_D$, is exported to the world market. The general conclusion of Figure 16.7 is this: *If the price of a good or service in a closed economy is lower than the world price, and that economy opens itself to trade, the economy will tend to become a net exporter of that good or service.*

These examples illustrate how the market translates comparative advantage into mutually beneficial gains from trade. If trade is unrestricted, then countries with a comparative advantage in a particular good will profit by supplying that good to the world market and using the revenue earned to import goods in which they do not have a comparative advantage. Thus the workings of the free market automatically ensure that goods will be produced where the opportunity cost is lowest, leading to the highest possible consumption possibilities for the world as a whole.

WINNERS AND LOSERS FROM TRADE

If trade is so wonderful, why do politicians so often resist free trade and "globalization"? The reason is that although free trade benefits the economy as a whole, specific groups may not benefit. If groups who are hurt by trade have sufficient political influence, they may be able to persuade politicians to enact policies that restrict the free flow of goods and services across borders.

The supply and demand analyses shown in Figures 16.6 and 16.7 are useful in clarifying who gains and who loses when an economy opens up to trade. Look first at Figure 16.6, which shows the market for computers in Brazil. When Brazil opens its computer market to international competition, Brazilian consumers enjoy a larger quantity of computers at a lower price. Clearly, Brazilian computer users benefit from the free trade in computers. In general, *domestic consumers of imported goods benefit from free trade.* However, Brazilian computer producers will not be so happy about opening their market to international competition. The fall in computer prices to the international level implies that less efficient domestic producers will go out of business, and that those who remain will earn lower profits. Unemployment in the Brazilian computer industry will rise and may persist over time, particularly if displaced computer workers cannot easily move to a new industry.[1] We see that, in general, *domestic producers of imported goods are hurt by free trade.*

Consumers are helped, and producers hurt, when imports increase. The opposite conclusions apply for an increase in exports (see Figure 16.7). In the example of Brazil, an opening of the coffee market raises the domestic price of coffee to the world price and creates the opportunity for Brazil to export coffee. Domestic producers of coffee benefit from the increased market (they can now sell coffee abroad as well as at home) and from the higher price of their product. In short, *domestic producers of exported goods benefit from free trade.* Brazilian coffee drinkers will be less enthusiastic, however, since they must now have to pay the higher world price of coffee, and can therefore consume less. *Thus domestic consumers of exported goods are hurt by free trade.*

Free trade is *efficient* in the sense that it increases the size of the pie available to the economy. Indeed, the efficiency of free trade is an application of the *equilibrium principle:* Markets in equilibrium leave no unexploited opportunities for individuals. Despite the efficiency of free trade, however, some groups may lose from trade, which generates political pressures to block or restrict trade. In the next section we will discuss the major types of policy used to restrict trade.

---

[1]The wages paid to Brazilian computer workers will also fall, reflecting the lower relative price of computers.

RECAP TRADE WINNERS AND LOSERS

Winners

- Consumers of imported goods

- Producers of exported goods

Losers

- Consumers of exported goods

- Producers of imported goods

PROTECTIONIST POLICIES: TARIFFS AND QUOTAS

protectionism the view that free trade is injurious and should be restricted

tariff a tax imposed on an imported good

quota a legal limit on the quantity of a good that may be imported

The view that free trade is injurious and should be restricted is known as **protectionism.** Supporters of this view believe the government should attempt to "protect" domestic markets by raising legal barriers to imports. (Interestingly, protectionists rarely attempt to restrict exports, even though they hurt consumers of the exported good.) Two of the most common types of such barriers are tariffs and quotas. A **tariff** is a tax imposed on an imported good. A **quota** is a legal limit on the quantity of a good that may be imported.

Tariffs

The effects of tariffs and quotas can be explained using supply and demand diagrams. Suppose that Brazilian computer makers, dismayed by the penetration of "their" market by imported computers, persuade their government to impose a tariff—that is, a tax—on every computer imported into the country. Computers produced in Brazil will be exempt from the tax. Figure 16.8 shows the likely effects of this tariff on the domestic Brazilian computer market. The lower of the two horizontal lines in the figure indicates the world price of computers, not including the tariff. The higher of the two lines indicates the price Brazilian consumers will actually pay for imported computers, including the tariff. We refer to the price of computers including the tariff as p_T. The vertical distance between the two lines equals the amount of the tariff that is imposed on each imported computer.

From the point of view of domestic Brazilian producers and consumers, the imposition of the tariff has the same effects as an equivalent increase in the world price of computers. Because the price (including the tariff) of imported computers has risen, Brazilian computer producers will be able to raise the price they charge for their computers to the world price plus tariff, p_T. Thus the price Brazilian consumers must pay—whether their computers are imported or not—equals p_T, represented by the upper horizontal line in Figure 16.8.

The rise in the price of computers created by the tariff affects the quantities of computers supplied and the quantities demanded by Brazilians. Domestic computer producers, facing a higher price for computers, increase their production from q_S to q'_S (see Figure 16.8). Brazilian consumers, also reacting to the higher price, reduce their computer purchases from q_D to q'_D. As a result, the number of imported computers—the difference between domestic purchases and domestic production—falls from $q_D - q_S$ to $q'_D - q'_S$.

Who are the winners and the losers from the tariff, then? Relative to an environment with free trade and no tariff, the winners are the domestic computer producers, who sell more computers and receive a higher price for them. The clearest losers are Brazilian consumers, who must now pay more for their computers. Another winner is the government, which collects revenue from the tariff. The blue area in Figure 16.8 shows the amount of revenue the government collects, equal to the quantity of computer imports after the imposition of the tariff, $q'_D - q'_S$, times the amount of the tariff.

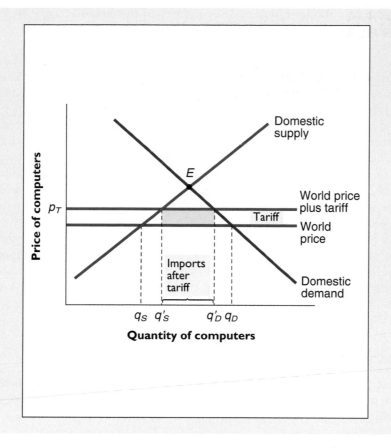

FIGURE 16.8
The Market for Computers after the Imposition of an Import Tariff.
The imposition of a tariff on imported computers raises the price of computers in Brazil to the world price plus tariff, p_T, represented by the upper horizontal line. Domestic production of computers rises from q_S to q'_S, domestic purchases of computers fall from q_D to q'_D, and computer imports fall from $q_D - q_S$ to $q'_D - q'_S$. Brazilian consumers are worse off and Brazilian computer producers are better off. The Brazilian government collects revenue from the tariff equal to the area of the pale blue rectangle.

A tariff on imported computers

EXAMPLE 16.3

Suppose the demand for computers by Brazilian consumers is given by

$$Q^D = 3{,}000 - 0.5P_C,$$

where Q^D is the annual quantity of computers demanded and P_C is the price per computer in dollars. The supply of computers by domestic Brazilian producers is

$$Q^S = 1{,}000 + 0.5P_C,$$

where Q^S is the annual quantity of computers supplied.

  a. Assuming that the Brazilian economy is closed to trade, find the equilibrium price and quantity in the Brazilian computer market.

  b. Assume the economy opens to trade. If the world price of computers is $1,500, find annual Brazilian consumption, production, and imports of computers.

  c. At the request of domestic producers, the Brazilian government imposes a tariff of $300 per imported computer. Find Brazilian consumption, production, and imports of computers after the imposition of the tariff. How much revenue does the tariff raise for the government?

  a. To find the closed-economy price and quantity, we set supply equal to demand:

$$1{,}000 + 0.5P_C = 3{,}000 - 0.5P_C.$$

Solving for P_C gives the equilibrium price, equal to $2,000 per computer. Substituting this equilibrium price into either the supply equation or the demand equation, we find the equilibrium quantity of computers in the Brazilian market, equal to 2,000 computers per year. This equilibrium price and quantity correspond to a point like point E in Figure 16.6.

b. If the economy opens to trade, the domestic price of computers must equal the world price, which is $1,500. At this price, the domestic quantity demanded for computers is $3,000 - 0.5(1,500) = 2,250$ computers per year; the domestic quantity supplied is $1,000 + 0.5(1,500) = 1,750$ computers per year. These quantities correspond to q_D and q_S, respectively, in Figure 16.6. Imports equal the difference between domestic quantities demanded and supplied, or $2,250 - 1,750 = 500$ computers per year.

c. The imposition of a tariff of $300 per computer raises the price from $1,500 (the world price without the tariff) to $1,800. To find Brazilian consumption and production at this price, we set the price equal to $1,800 in the demand and supply equations. Thus the domestic quantity demanded is $3,000 - 0.5(1,800) = 2,100$ computers per year; the domestic quantity supplied is $1,000 + 0.5(1,800) = 1,900$ computers per year. Imports, the difference between the quantity demanded by Brazilians and the quantity supplied by domestic firms, is $2,100 - 1,900 = 200$ computers per year. Thus the tariff has raised the price of computers by $300 and reduced imports by 300 computers per year. The tariff revenue collected by the government is $300/imported computer $\times$ 200 computers/year = $60,000 per year.

EXERCISE 16.3

Repeat parts (b) and (c) of Example 16.3 under the assumption that the world price of computers is $1,200. What happens if the world price is $1,800?

Quotas

An alternative to a tariff is a quota, or legal limit, on the number or value of foreign goods that can be imported. One means of enforcing a quota is to require importers to obtain a license or permit for each good they bring into the country. The government then distributes exactly the same number of permits as the number of goods that may be imported under the quota.

How does the imposition of a quota on, say, computers affect the domestic market for computers? Figure 16.9, which is similar to Figure 16.8, illustrates the effect of a quota on imported computers. As before, assume that at first there are no restrictions on trade. Consumers pay the world price for computers, and $q_D - q_S$ computers are imported. Now suppose once more that domestic computer producers complain to the government about competition from foreign computer makers, and the government agrees to act. However, this time, instead of a tariff, the government imposes a quota on the number of computers that can be imported. For comparability with the tariff analyzed in Figure 16.8, let's assume that the quota permits the same level of imports as entered the country under the tariff: specifically, $q'_D - q'_S$ computers. What effect does this ruling have on the domestic market for computers?

After the imposition of the quota, the quantity of computers supplied to the Brazilian market is the production of domestic firms plus the $q'_D - q'_S$ imported computers allowed under the quota. Figure 16.9 shows the quantity of computers supplied inclusive of the quota. The total supply curve, labeled "Domestic supply plus quota," is the same as the domestic supply curve shifted $q'_D - q'_S$ units to the right. The domestic demand curve is the same as in Figure 16.8. Equilibrium in the domestic market for computers occurs at point F in Figure 16.9, at the intersection of the supply curve including the quota and the domestic demand curve. The figure shows that, relative to the initial situation with free trade, the quota (1) raises the domestic price of computers above the world price, to the level marked p_T in Figure 16.9; (2) reduces domestic purchases of computers from q_D to q'_D;

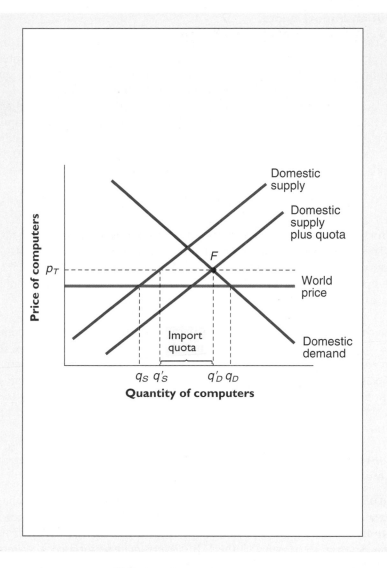

FIGURE 16.9
The Market for Computers after the Imposition of an Import Quota.
The figure shows the effects of the imposition of a quota that permits only $q'_D - q'_S$ computers to be imported. The total supply of computers to the domestic economy equals the domestic economy equals the domestic supply curve shifted to the right by $q'_D - q'_S$ units (the fixed amount of imports). Market equilibrium occurs at point F. The effects of the quota on the domestic market are identical to those of the tariff analyzed in Figure 16.8. The domestic price rises to p_T, domestic production of computers rises from q_S to q'_S, domestic purchases of computers fall from q_D to q'_D, and computer imports fall from $q_D - q_S$ to $q'_D - q'_S$. The quota differs from the tariff in that under a quota system the government collects no revenue.

(3) increases domestic production of computers from q_S to q'_S; and (4) reduces imports to $q'_D - q'_S$, consistent with a quota. Like a tariff, the quota helps domestic producers by increasing their sales and the price they receive for their output, while hurting domestic consumers by forcing them to pay a higher price.

Interestingly, under our assumption that the quota is set to permit the same level of imports as the tariff, the effects on the domestic market of the tariff (Figure 16.8) and the quota (Figure 16.9) are not only similar, they are *equivalent*. Comparing Figures 16.8 and 16.9, you can see that the two policies have identical effects on the domestic price, domestic purchases, domestic production, and imports.

Although the market effects of a tariff and a quota are the same, there is one important difference between the two policies, which is that a tariff generates revenue for the government, whereas a quota does not. With a quota, the revenue that would have gone to the government goes instead to those firms that hold the import licenses. A holder of an import license can purchase a computer at the world price and resell it in the domestic market at price p_T, pocketing the difference. Thus with a tariff the government collects the difference between the world price and the domestic market price of the good; with a quota, private firms or individuals collect that difference. Why then would the government ever impose a quota rather than a tariff? One possibility is that the distribution of import licenses is a means of rewarding the government's political supporters. Sometimes, international political concerns may also play a role (see Economic Naturalist 16.2 for a possible example).

EXAMPLE 16.4

Effects of an import quota

Suppose the supply of and demand for computers in Brazil is as given in Example 16.3, and the government imposes an import quota of 200 computers. Find the equilibrium price in the domestic computer market, as well as the quantities produced by domestic firms and purchased by domestic consumers.

The quantity of computers supplied by domestic Brazilian producers was stated in Example 16.3 to be $1,000 + 0.5P_C$. The quota allows 200 computers per year to be imported. Thus the total quantity of computers supplied, including both domestic production and imports, is $1,000 + 0.5P_C + 200$, or $1,200 + 0.5P_C$. Setting the quantity supplied equal to the quantity demanded, we get

$$1,200 + 0.5P_C = 3,000 - 0.5P_C.$$

Solving for P_C, we find that the price of computers in the domestic Brazilian market is \$1,800. Domestic production of computers is $1,000 + 0.5(1,800) = 1,900$ computers per year, while quantity demanded domestically is $3,000 - 0.5(1,800) = 2,100$ computers per year. The difference between domestic quantity demanded and domestic production, 200 computers per year, is made up by imports.

Note that the domestic price, domestic production, and domestic demand are the same in Examples 16.3 and 16.4. Thus the tariff and the quota have the same effects on the domestic market for computers. The only difference between the two policies is that with a quota, the government does not get the tariff revenue it got in Example 16.3. That revenue goes instead to the holders of import licenses, who can buy computers on the world market at \$1,500 and sell them in the domestic market at \$1,800.

Who benefited from and who was hurt by voluntary export restraints on Japanese automobiles in the 1980s?

ECONOMIC NATURALIST 16.2

After the oil price increases of the 1970s, American consumers began to buy small, fuel-efficient Japanese automobiles in large numbers. Reeling from the new foreign competition, U.S. automobile producers petitioned the U.S. government for assistance. In response, in May 1981 the U.S. government negotiated a system of so-called *voluntary export restraints,* or VERs, with Japan. Under the VER system, each Japanese auto producer would "voluntarily" restrict exports to the United States to an agreed-upon level. VER quotas were changed several times before the system was formally eliminated in 1994. Who benefited from, and who was hurt by, VERs on Japanese automobiles?

Several groups benefited from the VER system. As should be expected, U.S. auto producers saw increased sales and profits when their Japanese competition was reduced. But Japanese automobile producers also profited from the policy, despite the reduction in their U.S. sales. The restrictions on the supply of their automobiles to the U.S. market allowed them to raise their prices in the U.S. market significantly—by several thousand dollars per car by the late 1980s, according to some estimates. From an economic point of view, the VERs functioned like a tariff on Japanese cars, except that the Japanese automobile producers, rather than the U.S. government, got to keep the tariff revenue. A third group that benefited from the VERs was European automobile producers, who saw U.S. demand for their cars rise when Japanese imports declined.

The biggest losers from the VER system were clearly American car buyers, who faced higher prices (particularly for Japanese imports) and reduced selection. During this period dealer discounts on new Japanese cars largely disappeared, and customers often found themselves paying a premium over the list price. Because the economic losses faced by American car buyers exceeded the extra profits received by U.S. automobile producers, the VERs produced a net loss for the U.S. economy that at its greatest was estimated at more than \$3 billion per year.

The U.S. government's choice of a VER system, rather than a tariff or a quota, was somewhat puzzling. If a tariff on Japanese cars had been imposed instead of a VER system, the U.S. government would have collected much of the revenue that went instead to Japanese auto producers. Alternatively, a quota system with import licenses given to U.S. car dealers would have captured some revenue for domestic car dealers rather than Japanese firms. The best explanation for why the U.S. government chose VERs is probably political. U.S. policymakers may have been concerned that the Japanese government would retaliate against U.S. trade restrictions by imposing its own restrictions on U.S. exports. By instituting a system that did minimal financial harm to—or even helped—Japanese auto producers, they may have hoped to avoid retaliation from the Japanese.[1]

Tariffs and quotas are not the only barriers to trade that governments erect. Importers may be subject to unnecessarily complex bureaucratic rules (so-called red tape barriers), and regulations of goods that are nominally intended to promote health and safety sometimes have the side effect, whether intentionally or unintentionally, of restricting trade. One example is European restrictions on imports of genetically modified foods. Although these regulations were motivated in part by concerns about the safety of such foods, they also help to protect Europe's politically powerful farmers from foreign competition.

THE INEFFICIENCY OF PROTECTIONISM

Free trade is efficient because it allows countries to specialize in the production of goods and services in which they have the greatest comparative advantage. Conversely, protectionist policies that limit trade are inefficient—they reduce the total economic pie. (Recall Chapter 3's *efficiency principle,* that efficiency is an important social goal.) Why, then, do governments adopt such policies? The reason is similar to why some city governments impose rent controls (see Chapter 3). Although rent controls reduce economic welfare overall, some people benefit from them—namely, the tenants whose rents are held artificially below market level. Similarly, as we have seen in this section, tariffs and quotas benefit certain groups. Because those who benefit from these restrictions (such as firms facing import competition) are often better organized politically than those who lose from trade barriers (such as consumers in general), lawmakers are sometimes persuaded to enact the restrictions.

Who benefited from "voluntary" export restraints on Japanese cars?

The fact that free trade is efficient suggests an alternative to trade restrictions, however. Because eliminating restrictions on trade increases the overall economic pie, in general the winners from free trade will be able to compensate the losers in such a way that everyone becomes better off. Government programs that assist and retrain workers displaced by import competition are an example of such compensation. Spreading the benefits of free trade—or at least reducing its adverse effects on certain groups—reduces the incentives of those groups to inhibit free trade.

Although we have focused on the winners and losers from trade, not all opposition to free trade is motivated by economic interest. For example, many of the antitrade protesters in Washington, D.C. in 2001 cited environmental concerns. Protecting the environment is an important and laudable goal, but once again the *efficiency principle* suggests that restricting trade is not the most effective means of achieving that goal. Restricting trade lowers world income, reducing the resources available to deal with environmental problems. (High levels of economic development are in fact associated with lower, not higher, amounts of pollution.) Furthermore, much of the income loss arising from barriers to trade is absorbed by poor nations trying to develop their economies. For this reason, leaders of developing countries are among the strongest advocates of free trade.

---

[1] Former president Reagan's autobiography confirms that policymakers were concerned that an alternative method of limiting Japanese imports would provoke the Japanese into taking measures to limit U.S. exports to Japan. See Ronald Reagan, *An American Life,* New York: Simon and Schuster, 1990, p. 274.

ECONOMIC NATURALIST 16.3

What should Lula do about foreign trade?

Running on a political platform that was bitterly critical of globalization's harmful impact on the poor, Luis Inácio da Silva became president of Brazil, Latin America's largest country, on January 1, 2003. Should Lula, as he is popularly known, implement the trade restrictions that many of his constituents so strongly favor?

As we have emphasized, although trade liberalization increases total economic surplus, it provides no guarantee that every group will automatically come out ahead. Many of Lula's constituents might well fare better if tariffs and quotas were implemented to protect the domestic industries in which they toil.

But the efficiency principle tells us that Lula can do even more for his low-income constituents if he does not implement new trade restrictions. Given his strong political mandate, he could instead use the credible threat of such restrictions to persuade the most prosperous Brazilians to fund additional job training and other benefits for Brazil's poor that would be even more valuable to them than new protectionist policies. By making Brazil's economic pie as large as possible, Lula can ensure that rich and poor alike end up with the largest possible slice.

© AP Photo/Eraldo Press

Should Lula implement new protectionist measures in Brazil?

RECAP   A SUPPLY AND DEMAND PERSPECTIVE ON TRADE

- For a closed economy, the domestic supply and demand for a good or service determine the equilibrium price and quantity of that good or service.

- In an open economy, the price of a good or service traded on international markets equals the world price. If the domestic quantity supplied at the world price exceeds the domestic quantity demanded, the difference will be exported to the world market. If the domestic quantity demanded at the world price exceeds the domestic quantity supplied, the difference will be imported.

- Generally, if the price of a good or service in a closed economy is lower than the world price and the economy opens to trade, the country will become a net exporter of that good or service. If the closed-economy price is higher than the world price and the economy opens to trade, the country will tend to become a net importer of the good or service.

- Consumers of imported goods and producers of exported goods benefit from trade, whereas consumers of exported goods and producers of imported goods are hurt by trade. If those groups that are hurt have sufficient political influence, they may persuade the government to enact barriers to trade. The view that free trade is injurious and should be restricted is called protectionism.

- The two most common types of trade barriers are tariffs, or taxes on imported goods, and quotas, legal limits on the quantity that can be imported. A tariff raises the domestic price to the world price plus the tariff. The result is increased domestic production, reduced domestic consumption, and fewer imports. A quota has effects on the domestic market that are similar to those of a quota. The main difference is that under a quota, the government does not collect tariff revenue.

- Trade barriers are inefficient; they reduce the overall size of the economic pie. Thus, in general, the winners from free trade should be able to compensate the losers in such a way that everyone becomes better off. Government programs to help workers displaced by import competition are an example of such compensation.

▪ SUMMARY ▪

- According to the principle of comparative advantage, the best economic outcomes occur when each nation specializes in the goods and services at which it is relatively most productive and then trades with other nations to obtain the goods and services its citizens desire.

- The production possibilities curve (PPC) of a country is a graph that describes the maximum amount of one good that can be produced at every possible level of production of the other good. At any point the slope of a PPC indicates the opportunity cost, in terms of forgone production of the good on the vertical axis, of increasing production of the good on the horizontal axis by one unit. The more of a good that is already being produced, the greater the opportunity cost of increasing production still further. Thus the slope of a PPC becomes more and more negative as we read from left to right. When an economy has many workers, the PPC has a smooth, outwardly bowed shape.

- A country's *consumption possibilities* are the combinations of goods and services that might feasibly be consumed by its citizens. In a *closed economy*—one that does not trade with other countries—the citizens' consumption possibilities are identical to their production possibilities. But in an *open economy*—one that does trade with other countries— consumption possibilities are typically greater than, and never less than, the economy's production possibilities. Graphically, an open economy's consumption possibilities are described by a downward-sloping line that just touches the PPC, whose slope equals the amount of the good on the vertical axis that must be traded to obtain one unit of the good on the horizontal axis. A country achieves its highest consumption possibilities by producing at the point where the consumption possibilities line touches the PPC and then

trading to obtain the most preferred point on the consumption possibilities line.

- In a closed economy, the relative price of a good or service is determined at the intersection of the supply curve of domestic producers and the demand curve of domestic consumers. In an open economy, the relative price of a good or service equals the *world price*—the price determined by supply and demand in the world economy. If the price of a good or service in a closed economy is greater than the world price and the country opens its market to trade, it will become a net importer of that good or service. But if the closed-economy price is below the world price and the country opens itself to trade, it will become a net exporter of that good or service.

- Although free trade is beneficial to the economy as a whole, some groups—such as domestic producers of imported goods—are hurt by free trade. Groups that are hurt by trade may be able to induce the government to impose *protectionist* measures, such as tariffs or quotas. A *tariff* is a tax on an imported good that has the effect of raising the domestic price of the good. A higher domestic price increases domestic supply, reduces domestic demand, and reduces imports of the good. A *quota*, which is a legal limit on the amount of a good that may be imported, has the same effects as a tariff, except that the government collects no tax revenue. (The equivalent amount of revenue goes instead to those firms with the legal authority to import goods.) Because free trade is efficient, the winners from free trade should be able to compensate the losers so that everyone becomes better off. Thus policies to assist those who are harmed by trade, such as assistance and retraining for workers idled by imports, are usually preferable to trade restrictions.

▪ KEY TERMS ▪

autarky (405)
closed economy (401)
consumption possibilities (405)

open economy (401)
protectionism (414)
quota (414)

tariff (414)
world price (411)

▪ REVIEW QUESTIONS ▪

1. Sketch a PPC for a four-worker economy that produces two goods, hot dogs and hamburgers. Give an economic interpretation of the vertical intercept, the horizontal intercept, and the slope of the graph.

2. What is meant by the "consumption possibilities" of a country? How are consumption possibilities related to production possibilities in a closed economy? In an open economy?

3. A small, open economy is equally productive in producing coffee and tea. What will this economy produce if the world price of coffee is twice that of tea? Half that of tea? What will the country produce if the world price of coffee happens to equal the world price of tea?

4. True or false: If a country is more productive in every sector than a neighboring country, then there is no benefit in trading with the neighboring country. Explain.

5. Show graphically the effects of a tariff on imported automobiles on the domestic market for automobiles. Who is hurt by the tariff and why? Who benefits and why?

6. Show graphically the effects of a quota on imported automobiles on the domestic market for automobiles. Who does the quota hurt and who benefits? Explain.

■ PROBLEMS ■

1. An economy has two workers, Anne and Bill. Per day of work, Anne can produce 100 apples or 25 bananas, and Bill can produce 50 apples or 50 bananas. Anne and Bill each work 200 days per year.
   a. Which worker has an absolute advantage in apples? Which has a comparative advantage? Calculate each worker's opportunity cost of producing an additional apple.
   b. Find the maximum number of each type of fruit that can be produced annually in this economy, assuming that none of the other type of fruit is produced. What is the most of each type that can be produced if each worker fully specializes according to his or her comparative advantage?
   c. Draw the PPC for annual production in this economy. Show numerical values for the vertical intercept, the horizontal intercept, and the slopes of each segment of the PPC.

2. A developing economy requires 1,000 hours of work to produce a television set and 10 hours of work to produce a bushel of corn. This economy has available a total of 1,000,000 hours of work per day.
   a. Draw the PPC for daily output of the developing economy. Give numerical values for the PPC's vertical intercept, horizontal intercept, and slope. Relate the slope to the developing country's opportunity cost of producing each good. If this economy does not trade, what are its consumption possibilities?
   b. The developing economy is considering opening trade with a much larger, industrialized economy. The industrialized economy requires 10 hours of work to produce a television set and 1 hour of work to produce a bushel of corn. Show graphically how trading with the industrialized economy affects the developing economy's consumption possibilities. Is opening trade desirable for the developing economy? (*Hint:* When it opens to trade, the developing economy will be fully specialized in one product.)

3. Modifying Example 16.1, suppose that Brazilian worker Carlos can produce either 100 pounds of coffee or 1 computer per week, and a second worker, Maria, can produce either 150 pounds of coffee or 1 computer per week. Both Carlos and Maria work 50 weeks per year.
   a. Find the PPC for Brazil. Give numerical values for the graph's intercepts and slopes. How much of each good is produced if each worker fully specializes according to comparative advantage?
   b. World prices are such that 1 computer trades for 125 pounds of coffee on international markets. If Brazil is open to trade, show Brazil's consumption possibilities graphically. What is the most of each good that Brazilians can consume when the economy is open? Compare to the situation when the economy is closed.
   c. Repeat part b under the assumption that 1 computer trades for 80 pounds of coffee on world markets.

4. Suppose that Carlos and Maria can produce coffee and computers as described in Problem 3. A third worker, Pedro, joins the Brazilian economy. Pedro can produce either 140 pounds of coffee or 1 computer per week. Like the other two workers, Pedro works 50 weeks per year.
   a. Find the PPC for Brazil. Give numerical values of the PPC's intercepts and slopes.
   b. Find Brazil's consumption possibilities if the country is open and 1 computer trades for 125 pounds of coffee on world markets. What is the most of each good that Brazilians can consume when the economy is open? Compare to the situation when the economy is closed.
   c. Repeat part b assuming that 1 computer trades for 200 pounds of coffee on world markets.

5. Suppose that a U.S. worker can produce 1,000 pairs of shoes or 10 industrial robots per year. For simplicity, assume there are no costs other than labor costs and firms earn zero profits. Initially, the U.S. economy is closed. The domestic price of shoes is $30 a pair, so that a U.S. worker can earn $30,000 annually by working in the shoe industry. The domestic price of a robot is $3,000, so that a U.S. worker can also earn $30,000 annually working in the robot industry.

   Now suppose that the U.S. opens trade with the rest of the world. Foreign workers can produce 500 pairs of shoes or 1 robot per year. The world price of shoes after the U.S. opens its markets is $10 a pair, and the world price of robots is $5,000.
   a. What do foreign workers earn annually, in dollars?
   b. When it opens to trade, which good will the United States import and which will it export?
   c. Find the real income of U.S. workers after the opening to trade, measured in (1) the number of pairs of shoes annual worker income will buy and (2) the number of robots annual worker income will buy. Compare to the situation before the opening of trade. Does trading in goods produced by "cheap foreign labor" hurt U.S. workers?
   d. How might your conclusion in part c be modified in the short term, if it is costly for workers to change industries? What policy response might help with this problem?

6. The demand for automobiles in a certain country is given by

$$D = 12,000 - 200P,$$

   where P is the price of a car. Supply by domestic automobile producers is

$$S = 7,000 + 50P.$$

   a. Assuming that the economy is closed, find the equilibrium price and production of automobiles.
   b. The economy opens to trade. The world price of automobiles is 18. Find the domestic quantities demanded and supplied and the quantity of imports or exports. Who will favor the opening of the automobile market to trade, and who will oppose it?
   c. The government imposes a tariff of 1 unit per car. Find the effects on domestic quantities demanded and supplied and on the quantity of imports or exports. Also find the revenue raised by the tariff. Who will favor the imposition of the tariff, and who will oppose it?
   d. Can the government obtain the same results as you found in part c by imposing a quota on automobile imports? Explain.

7. Suppose the domestic demand and supply for automobiles is as given by Problem 6. The world price of automobiles is 16. Foreign car firms have a production cost of 15 per automobile, so they earn a profit of 1 per car.
   a. How many cars will be imported, assuming this country trades freely?
   b. Now suppose foreign car producers are asked "voluntarily" to limit their exports to the home country to half of free trade levels. What will be the equilibrium price of cars in the domestic market if foreign producers comply? Find domestic quantities of cars supplied and demanded.
   c. How will the "voluntary" export restriction affect the profits of foreign car producers?

■ ANSWERS TO IN-CHAPTER EXERCISES ■

16.1 The opportunity cost of producing coffee equals the number of computers given up for each extra pound of coffee produced. Carlos can produce either 100 pounds of coffee or 1 computer per week, so his opportunity cost is given by

$$\frac{\text{Loss in computers}}{\text{Gain in coffee}} = \frac{-1 \text{ computer/week}}{100 \text{ pounds of coffee/week}}$$

$$= -1/100 \text{ computer/pound of coffee.}$$

Maria can produce either 100 pounds of coffee or 2 computers per week, so her opportunity cost is

$$\frac{\text{Loss in computers}}{\text{Gain in coffee}} = \frac{-2 \text{ computers/week}}{100 \text{ pounds of coffee/week}}$$

$$= -1/50 \text{ computer/pound of coffee.}$$

Since each pound of coffee Carlos produces requires the sacrifice of 1/100 of a computer, while each pound of coffee produced by Maria sacrifices 1/50 of a computer, Carlos has the smaller opportunity cost of producing coffee. Thus he has a comparative advantage in producing coffee.

16.2 When the economy is closed, the Brazilians can obtain 80 computers by having Maria work 40 weeks making computers. If Maria works the remaining 10 weeks producing coffee and Carlos works 50 weeks producing coffee, the Brazilians will be able to consume $(10 + 50) \times 100 = 6,000$ pounds of coffee per year.

The world price of computers is 80 pounds of coffee, which is greater than Maria's opportunity cost of producing computers but less than Carlos's opportunity cost. Thus if the economy opens to trade, Maria will specialize in computers and Carlos will specialize in coffee. If Maria produces 100 computers, 80 of which are consumed domestically, 20 computers are available for export. Because a computer is worth 80 pounds of coffee on the world market, the 20 exported computers can be traded for 1,600 pounds of coffee. Carlos still produces 5,000 pounds of coffee. Total coffee consumption in Brazil is thus $1,600 + 5,000 = 6,600$ pounds. Opening to trade has allowed the Brazilians to consume 10 percent more coffee at no sacrifice in computers.

16.3 If the world price of computers is $1,200, domestic demand for computers is $3,000 - 0.5(1,200) = 2,400$ computers. Domestic supply is $1,000 + 0.5(1,200) = 1,600$ computers. The difference between the quantity demanded and the quantity supplied, 800 computers, is imported.

A tariff of $300 raises the domestic price of computers to $1,500. Now domestic demand is $3,000 - 0.5(1,500) = 2,250$, and domestic supply is $1,000 + 0.5(1,500) = 1,750$. The difference, 500 computers, equals imports. Revenue for the government is (300/computer) (500 imported computers) = $150,000.

If the world price of computers is $1,800 and there is no tariff, domestic demand is $3,000 - 0.5(1,800) = 2,100$; domestic supply is $1,000 + 0.5(1,800) = 1,900$; and imports are 200. A tariff of $300 raises the world price to $2,100, which is greater than the domestic price when there is no trade ($2,000). No computers are imported in this case and no tariff revenue is raised.

PART 6

MACROECONOMICS: ISSUES AND DATA

■

Physical scientists study the world at many different scales, ranging from the inner workings of the atom to the vast dimensions of the cosmos. Although the laws of physics are thought to apply at all scales, scientists find that some phenomena are best understood "in the small" and some "in the large." Although the range of scales they must deal with is much more modest than in physics, economists also find it useful to analyze economic behavior at both the small-scale, or "micro" level, and the large-scale, or "macro-" level. This section introduces you to *macroeconomics,* the study of the performance of national economies. Unlike *microeconomics,* which focuses on the behavior of individual households, firms, and markets, macroeconomics takes a bird's-eye view of the economy. So, while a microeconomist might study the determinants of consumer spending on personal computers, macroeconomists analyze the factors that determine aggregate, or total, consumer spending. Experience has shown that, for many issues, the macroeconomic perspective is the more useful.

Chapter 17 begins our discussion of macroeconomics by introducing you to some of the key macroeconomic issues and questions. These include the search for the factors that cause economies to grow, productivity to improve, and living standards to rise over long periods of time. Macroeconomists also study shorter-term fluctuations in the economy (called recessions and expansions), unemployment, inflation, and the economic interdependence among nations, among other topics. Macroeconomic policies—government actions to improve the performance of the economy—are of particular concern to macroeconomists, as the quality of macroeconomic policymaking is a major determinant of a nation's economic health.

To study phenomena like economic growth scientifically, economists must have accurate measurements. Chapters 18 and 19 continue the introduction to macroeconomics by discussing how some key macroeconomic concepts are measured and interpreted. Chapter 18 discusses two important measures of the level of economic activity, the gross domestic product and the unemployment rate. Besides describing how these variables are constructed in practice, this chapter also discusses the issue of how these measures are related to the economic well-being of the typical person. Chapter 19 concerns the measurement of the price level and inflation and includes a discussion of the costs that inflation imposes on the economy. When you have completed Part 6, you will be familiar not only with the major questions that macroeconomists ask but also with some of the most important tools that they use to try to find the answers.

CHAPTER 1

MACROECONOMICS: THE BIRD'S-EYE VIEW OF THE ECONOMY

■

In 1929 the economy of the United States slowed dramatically. Between August of 1929 and the end of 1930, the nation's factories and mines, facing sharp declines in sales, cut their production rates by a remarkable 31 percent. These cutbacks led in turn to mass layoffs: Between 1929 and 1930, the number of people without jobs almost tripled, from about 3 percent of the workforce to nearly 9 percent.[1] Financial markets were equally shaky. The stock market crashed in October 1929, and stocks lost nearly a third of their value in just three weeks.

At first, policymakers and the general public (except for those people who had put their life savings into the stock market) were concerned but not panic-stricken. Americans remembered that the nation had experienced a similar slowdown only eight years earlier, in 1921–1922. That episode had ended quickly, apparently on its own, and the decade that followed (popularly known as the roaring twenties) had been one of unparalleled prosperity. But the fall in production and the rise in unemployment that began in 1929 continued into 1931. In the spring of 1931 the economy seemed to stabilize briefly, and President Herbert Hoover optimistically proclaimed that "prosperity is just around

---

[1]The source for these and most other pre-1960 statistics cited in this chapter is the U.S. Bureau of the Census, *Historical Statistics of the United States: Colonial Times to 1970*, Washington, 1975.

the corner." But in mid-1931 the economy went into an even steeper dive. What historians now call the Great Depression had begun in earnest.

Labor statistics tell the story of the Great Depression from the worker's point of view. Unemployment was extremely high throughout the 1930s, despite government attempts to reduce it through large-scale public employment programs. At the worst point of the Depression, in 1933, one out of every four American workers was unemployed. Joblessness declined gradually to 17 percent of the workforce by 1936 but remained stuck at that level through 1939. Of those lucky enough to have jobs, many were able to work only part-time, while others worked for near-starvation wages.

In some other countries conditions were even worse. In Germany, which had never fully recovered from its defeat in World War I, nearly a third of all workers were without jobs, and many families lost their savings as major banks collapsed. Indeed, the desperate economic situation was a major reason for Adolf Hitler's election as chancellor of Germany in 1933. Introducing extensive government control over the economy, Hitler rearmed the country and ultimately launched what became the most destructive war in history, World War II.

How could such an economic catastrophe have happened? One often-heard hypothesis is that the Great Depression was caused by wild speculation on Wall Street, which provoked the stock market crash. But though stock prices may have been unrealistically high in 1929, there is little evidence to suggest that the fall in stock prices was a major cause of the Depression. A similar crash in October 1987, when stock prices fell a record 23 percent in one day—an event comparable in severity to the crash of October 1929—did not slow the economy significantly. Another reason to doubt that the 1929 stock market crash caused the Great Depression is that, far from being confined to the United States, the Depression was a worldwide event, affecting countries that did not have well-developed stock markets at the time. The more reasonable conclusion is that the onset of the Depression probably caused the stock market crash, rather than the other way round.

Another explanation for the Depression, suggested by some economists in the 1930s, was that free-market economies like those of the United States and Germany are "naturally" unstable, prone to long periods of low production and high unemployment. But this idea too has fallen out of favor, since the period after World War II has generally been one of prosperity and economic growth throughout the industrialized world.

What *did* cause the Great Depression, then? Today most economists who have studied the period blame *poor economic policymaking* both in the United States and in other major industrialized countries. Of course, policymakers did not set out to create an economic catastrophe. Rather, they fell prey to misconceptions of the time about how the economy worked. In other words, the Great Depression, far from being inevitable, *might have been avoided*—if only the state of economic knowledge had been better. From today's perspective, the Great Depression was to economic policymaking what the voyage of the *Titanic* was to ocean navigation.

One of the few benefits of the Great Depression was that it forced economists and policymakers of the 1930s to recognize that there were major gaps in their understanding of how the economy works. This recognition led to the development of a new subfield within economics, called macroeconomics. Recall from Chapter 1 that *macroeconomics* is the study of the performance of national economies and the policies governments use to try to improve that performance.

This chapter will introduce the subject matter and some of the tools of macroeconomics. Although understanding episodes like the Great Depression remains an important concern of macroeconomists, the field has expanded to include the analysis of many other aspects of national economies. Among the issues macroeconomists study are the sources of long-run economic growth and development,

Could better economic policies have prevented the Great Depression?

the causes of high unemployment, and the factors that determine the rate of inflation. Appropriately enough in a world in which economic "globalization" preoccupies businesspeople and policymakers, macroeconomists also study how national economies interact. Since the performance of the national economy has an important bearing on the availability of jobs, the wages workers earn, the prices they pay, and the rates of return they receive on their saving, it's clear that macroeconomics addresses bread-and-butter issues that affect virtually everyone.

In light of the nation's experience during the Great Depression, macroeconomists are particularly concerned with understanding how *macroeconomic policies* work and how they should be applied. **Macroeconomic policies** are government actions designed to affect the performance of the economy as a whole (as opposed to policies intended to affect the performance of the market for a particular good or service, such as sugar or haircuts). The hope is that by understanding more fully how government policies affect the economy, economists can help policymakers do a better job—and avoid serious mistakes, such as those that were made during the Great Depression. On an individual level, educating people about macroeconomic policies and their effects will make for a better-informed citizenry, capable of making well-reasoned decisions in the voting booth.

macroeconomic policies
government actions designed to affect the performance of the economy as a whole

THE MAJOR MACROECONOMIC ISSUES

We defined macroeconomics as the study of the performance of the national economy as well as the policies used to improve that performance. Let's now take a closer look at some of the major economic issues that macroeconomists study.

ECONOMIC GROWTH AND LIVING STANDARDS

Although the wealthy industrialized countries (such as the United States, Canada, Japan, and the countries of western Europe) are certainly not free from poverty, hunger, and homelessness, the typical person in those countries enjoys a standard of living better than at any previous time or place in history. By *standard of living* we mean the degree to which people have access to goods and services that make their lives easier, healthier, safer, and more enjoyable. People with a high living standard enjoy more and better consumer goods: sports utility vehicles, camcorders, cellular phones, and the like. But they also benefit from a longer life expectancy and better general health (the result of high-quality medical care, good nutrition, and good sanitation), from higher literacy rates (the result of greater access to education), from more time and opportunity for cultural enrichment and recreation, from more interesting and fulfilling career options, and from better working conditions. Of course, the *scarcity principle* will always apply—even for the citizen of a rich country, having more of one good thing means having less of another. But higher incomes make these choices much less painful than they would be otherwise. Choosing between a larger apartment and a nicer car is much easier than choosing between feeding your children adequately and sending them to school, the kind of hard choice people in the poorest nations face.

Americans sometimes take their standard of living for granted, or even as a "right." As a Paul Simon lyric proclaims, "God bless our standard of living— let's keep it that way!" But we should realize that the way we live today is radically different from the way people have lived throughout most of history. The current standard of living in the United States is the result of several centuries of sustained *economic growth,* a process of steady increase in the quantity and quality of the goods and services the economy can produce. The basic equation is simple: The more we can produce, the more we can consume. Though not everyone in a society shares equally in the fruits of economic growth, in most cases growth brings an improvement in the average person's standard of living.

To get a sense of the extent of economic growth over time, examine Figure 17.1, which shows how the output of the U.S. economy has increased since 1900. (We discuss the measure of output used here, real gross domestic product, in Chapter 18.) Although output fluctuates at times, the overall trend has been unmistakably upward. Indeed, in 2001 the output of the U.S. economy was more than 25 times what it was in 1900 and more than 5 times its level in 1950. What caused this remarkable economic growth? Can it continue? Should it? These are some of the questions macroeconomists try to answer.

FIGURE 17.1

Output of the U.S. Economy, 1900–2001. The output of the U.S. economy has increased by more than 25 times since 1900 and by more than 5 times since 1950.

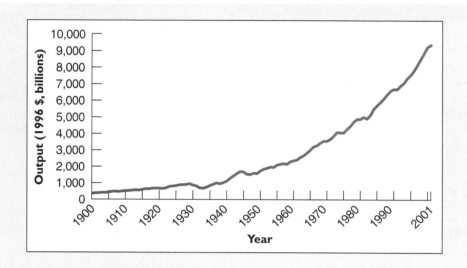

One reason for the growth in U.S. output over the last century has been the rapid growth of the U.S. population, and hence the number of workers available. Because of population growth, increases in *total* output cannot be equated with improvements in the general standard of living. Although increased output means that more goods and services are available, increased population implies that more people are sharing those goods and services. Because the population changes over time, output *per person* is a better indicator of the average living standard than total output.

Figure 17.2 shows output per person in the United States since 1900 (the blue line). Note that the long-term increase in output per person is smaller than the increase in total output shown in Figure 17.1 because of population growth. Nevertheless, the gains made over this long period are still impressive: In 2001 a typical U.S. resident consumed nearly seven times the quantity of goods and services available to a typical resident at the beginning of the century. To put this increase into perspective, according to recent estimates nearly 60 million U.S. households now own two or more automobiles; only about 8 million U.S. households (many of them located in cities, with good access to public transportation) have no car. A remarkable 98 percent of U.S. households own a television—95 percent a color television—and two-thirds subscribe to cable. And as of 2002, nearly 60 percent of adults in the United States were regular users of the Internet.

Nor has the rise in output been reflected entirely in increased availability of consumer goods. For example, as late as 1960, only 41 percent of U.S. adults over age 25 had completed high school, and less than 8 percent had completed four years of college. Today, over 80 percent of the adult population have at least a high school diploma, and about 25 percent have a college degree. Over half the students currently leaving high school will go on to college. Higher incomes, which allow young people to continue their schooling rather than work to support themselves and their families, are a major reason for these increases in educational levels.

Nearly 60 million American households own two or more automobiles.

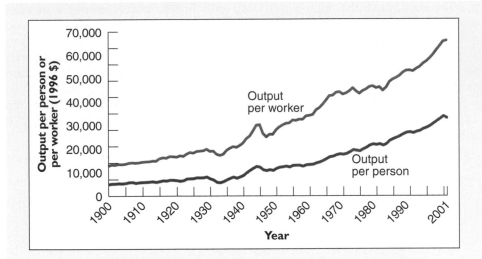

FIGURE 17.2
Output per Person and per Worker in the U.S. Economy, 1900–2001.
The red line shows the output per worker in the U.S. economy since 1900, and the blue line shows output per person. Both have risen substantially. Relative to 1900, output per person today is nearly seven times greater, and output per worker is more than five times greater.

PRODUCTIVITY

While growth in output per person is closely linked to changes in what the typical person can *consume,* macroeconomists are also interested in changes in what the average worker can *produce.* Figure 17.2 shows how output per employed worker (that is, total output divided by the number of people working) has changed since 1900 (red line). The figure shows that in 2001 a U.S. worker could produce more than five times the quantity of goods and services produced by a worker at the beginning of the twentieth century, despite the fact that the workweek is now much shorter than it was 100 years ago.

Economists refer to output per employed worker as **average labor productivity.** As Figure 17.2 shows, average labor productivity and output per person are closely related. This relationship makes sense—as we noted earlier, the more we can produce, the more we can consume. Because of this close link to the average living standard, average labor productivity and the factors that cause it to increase over time are of major concern to macroeconomists.

average labor productivity
output per employed worker

Although the long-term improvement in output per worker is impressive, the *rate* of improvement has slowed somewhat since the 1970s. Between 1950 and 1973 in the United States, output per employed worker increased by 2.1 percent per year. But from 1973 to 1995 the average rate of increase in output per worker was less than 1 percent per year. Since 1995 the pace of productivity growth seems to have picked up again, however, to nearly 2 percent per year. Slowing productivity growth leads to less rapid improvement in living standards, since the supply of goods and services cannot grow as quickly as it does during periods of rapid growth in productivity. Identifying the causes of productivity slowdowns and speedups is thus an important challenge for macroeconomists.

The current standard of living in the United States is not only much higher than in the past but also much higher than in many other nations today. Why have many of the world's countries, including both the developing nations of Asia, Africa, and Latin America and some formerly communist countries of eastern Europe not enjoyed the same rates of economic growth as the industrialized countries? How can the rate of economic growth be improved in these countries? Once again, these are questions of keen interest to macroeconomists.

Productivity and living standards in China and the United States

EXAMPLE 17.1

In 2001 the value of the output of the U.S. economy was about $10,200 billion. In the same year, the estimated value of the output of the People's Republic of China was $1,160 billion (U.S). The populations of the United States and China in 2001 were about 285 million and 1,262 million, respectively, while the number of employed workers in the two countries were approximately 135 million and 710 million.

Find output per person and average labor productivity for the United States and China in 2001. What do the results suggest about comparative living standards in the two countries?

Output per person is simply total output divided by the number of people in an economy, and average labor productivity is output divided by the number of employed workers. Doing the math we get the following results for 2001:

	United States	China
Output per person	$35,790	$ 919
Average labor productivity	$75,556	$1,634

Note that, although the total output of the Chinese economy is more than 11 percent that of the U.S. output, output per person and average labor productivity in China are each only about 2.5 and 2 percent, respectively, of what they are in the United States. Thus, though the Chinese economy may someday rival the U.S. economy in total output, for the time being there remains a large gap in productivity. This gap translates into striking differences in the living standard between the two countries—in access to consumer goods, health care, transportation, education, and other benefits of affluence.

RECESSIONS AND EXPANSIONS

Economies do not always grow steadily; sometimes they go through periods of unusual strength or weakness. A look back at Figure 17.1 shows that although output generally grows over time, it does not always grow smoothly. Particularly striking is the decline in output during the Great Depression of the 1930s, followed by the sharp increase in output during World War II (1941–1945). But the figure shows many more moderate fluctuations in output as well.

Slowdowns in economic growth are called *recessions;* particularly severe economic slowdowns, like the one that began in 1929, are called *depressions.* In the United States, major recessions occurred in 1973–1975 and 1981–1982 (find those recessions in Figure 17.1). More modest downturns occurred in 1990–1991 and 2001. During recessions economic opportunities decline: Jobs are harder to find, people with jobs are less likely to get wage increases, profits are lower, and more companies go out of business. Recessions are particularly hard on economically disadvantaged people, who are most likely to be thrown out of work and have the hardest time finding new jobs.

Sometimes the economy grows unusually quickly. These periods of rapid economic growth are called *expansions,* and particularly strong expansions are called *booms.* During an expansion, jobs are easier to find, more people get raises and promotions, and most businesses thrive.

The alternating cycle of recessions and expansions raises some questions that are central to macroeconomics. What causes these short-term fluctuations in the rate of economic growth? Can government policymakers do anything about them? Should they try?

UNEMPLOYMENT

The *unemployment rate,* the fraction of people who would like to be employed but can't find work, is a key indicator of the state of the labor market. When the unemployment rate is high, work is hard to find, and people who do have jobs typically find it harder to get promotions or wage increases.

Figure 17.3 shows the unemployment rate in the United States since 1900. Unemployment rises during recessions—note the dramatic spike in unemployment during the Great Depression, as well as the increases in unemployment during the 1973–1975 and 1981–1982 recessions. But even in the so-called good times, such as the 1960s and the 1990s, some people are unemployed. Why does unemployment rise so sharply during periods of recession? And why are there always unemployed people, even when the economy is booming?

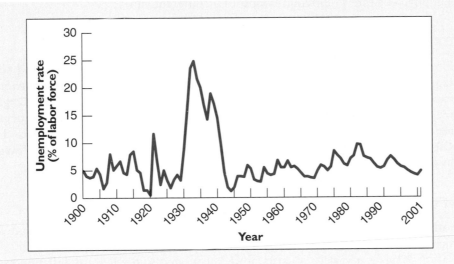

FIGURE 17.3
The U.S. Unemployment Rate, 1900–2001.
The unemployment rate is the percentage of the labor force that is out of work. Unemployment spikes upward during recessions and depressions, but the unemployment rate is always above zero, even in good times.

EXAMPLE 17.2

Increases in unemployment during recessions

Using monthly data on the national civilian unemployment rate, find the increase in the unemployment rate between the onset of recession in November 1973, January 1980, and July 1990 and the peak unemployment rate in the following three years. Compare these increases in unemployment to the increase during the Great Depression.

Unemployment data are collected by the U.S. Bureau of Labor Statistics (BLS) and can be obtained from the BLS home page (http://stats.bls.gov/datahome.htm). Hard copy sources include the *Survey of Current Business,* the *Federal Reserve Bulletin,* and *Economic Indicators.* Monthly data from the BLS home page yield the following comparisons:

Unemployment rate at beginning of recession (%)	Peak unemployment rate (%)	Increase in unemployment rate (%)
4.8 (Nov. 1973)	9.0 (May 1975)	+4.2
6.3 (Jan. 1980)	10.8 (Nov./Dec. 1982)	+4.5
5.5 (July 1990)	7.8 (June 1992)	+2.3

Unemployment increased significantly following the onset of each recession, although the impact of the 1990 recession on the labor market was clearly less serious than that of the 1973 and the 1980 recessions. (Actually, the 1980 recession was a "double dip"—a short recession in 1980, followed by a longer one in 1981–82.) In comparison, during the Great Depression the unemployment rate rose from about 3 percent in 1929 to about 25 percent in 1933, as we mentioned in the introduction to this chapter. Clearly, the 22 percentage point change in the unemployment rate that Americans experienced in the Great Depression dwarfs the effects of these three postwar recessions.

One question of great interest to macroeconomists is why unemployment rates sometimes differ markedly from country to country. For the past two decades unemployment rates in western Europe have more often than not been measured in the "double digits." On average, more than 10 percent of the European workforce has been out of a job during this period, a rate roughly double that in the United States. The high unemployment is particularly puzzling, because during the 1950s and 1960s, European unemployment rates were generally much lower than those in the United States. What explains these differences in the unemployment rate in different countries at different times?

EXERCISE 17.1

Find the most recent unemployment rates for France, Germany, and the United Kingdom, and compare them to the most recent unemployment rate for the United States. A useful source is the home page of the Organization for Economic Cooperation and Development (OECD), an organization of industrialized countries (http://www.oecd.org/). See also the OECD's publication *Main Economic Indicators*. Is unemployment still lower in the United States than in western Europe?

INFLATION

Another important economic statistic is the rate of *inflation*, which is the rate at which prices in general are increasing over time. As we discuss in Chapter 19, inflation imposes a variety of costs on the economy. And when the inflation rate is high, people on fixed incomes, such as pensioners who receive a fixed dollar payment each month, can't keep up with the rising cost of living.

In recent years inflation has been relatively low in the United States, but that has not always been the case (see Figure 17.4 for data on U.S. inflation since 1900). During the 1970s, inflation was a major problem; in fact, many people told poll takers that inflation was "public enemy number one." Why was inflation high in the 1970s, and why is it relatively low today? What difference does it make to the average person?

FIGURE 17.4
The U.S. Inflation Rate, 1900–2001.
The U.S. inflation rate has fluctuated over time. Inflation was high in the 1970s but has been quite low recently.

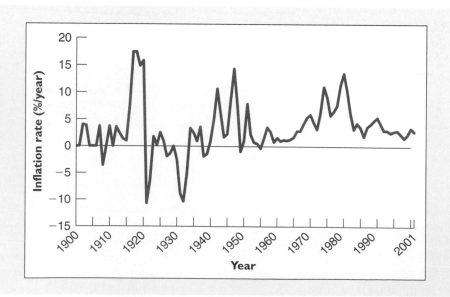

As with unemployment rates, the rate of inflation can differ markedly from country to country. For example, in 2001 the inflation rate was less than 3 percent in the United States, but the nation of Ukraine averaged over 400 percent annual inflation for the whole decade of the 1990s. What accounts for such large differences in inflation rates between countries?

Inflation and unemployment are often linked in policy discussions. One reason for this linkage is the oft-heard argument that unemployment can be reduced only at the cost of higher inflation and that inflation can be reduced only at the cost of higher unemployment. Must the government accept a higher rate of inflation to bring down unemployment, and vice versa?

ECONOMIC INTERDEPENDENCE AMONG NATIONS

National economies do not exist in isolation but are increasingly interdependent. The United States, because of its size and the wide variety of goods and services it produces, is one of the most self-sufficient economies on the planet. Even so, in 1999 the United States exported about 10.8 percent of all the goods and services it produced and imported from abroad 13.3 percent of the goods and services that Americans used.

Sometimes international flows of goods and services become a matter of political and economic concern. For example, congressional representatives of states producing steel or textiles repeatedly complain that low-priced imports of these goods threaten the jobs of their constituents. Ross Perot, the Texas businessman and presidential candidate, predicted such problems when he opposed the adoption of the North American Free Trade Agreement (NAFTA) and similar agreements designed to promote international trade in goods and services. (Perot made famous the phrase "giant sucking sound" to describe what he thought free trade would do to American jobs.) Are free trade agreements, in which countries agree not to tax or otherwise block the international flow of goods and services, a good or bad thing?

"I don't know what the hell happened—one minute I'm at work in Flint, Michigan, then there's a giant sucking sound and suddenly here I am in Mexico."

A related issue is the phenomenon of *trade imbalances,* which occur when the quantity of goods and services that a country sells abroad (its *exports*) differs significantly from the quantity of goods and services its citizens buy from abroad (its *imports*). Figure 17.5 shows U.S. exports and imports (of goods only to allow for a longer data series) since 1900, measured as a percentage of the economy's total output. Prior to the 1970s the United States generally exported more than

FIGURE 17.5

Exports and Imports as a Share of U.S. Output, 1900–2001.

The blue line shows U.S. exports of goods as a percentage of U.S. output. The red line shows U.S. imports of goods relative to U.S. output. For much of its history the United States has exported more than it imported, but over the past two decades imports have greatly outstripped exports.

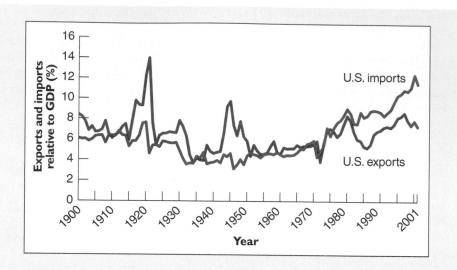

it imported. (Notice the major export booms that occurred after both world wars, when the United States was helping to reconstruct Europe.) Since the 1970s, however, imports to the United States have outstripped exports, creating a situation called a *trade deficit*. Other countries—Japan, for example—export much more than they import. A country such as Japan is said to have a *trade surplus*. What causes trade deficits and surpluses? Are they harmful or helpful?

RECAP **THE MAJOR MACROECONOMIC ISSUES**

- *Economic growth and living standards.* Over the last century the industrialized nations have experienced remarkable economic growth and improvements in living standards. Macroeconomists study the reasons for this extraordinary growth and try to understand why growth rates vary markedly among nations.

- *Productivity.* Average labor productivity, or output per employed worker, is a crucial determinant of living standards. Macroeconomists ask, What causes slowdowns and speedups in the rate of productivity growth?

- *Recessions and expansions.* Economies experience periods of slower growth (recessions) and more rapid growth (expansions). Macroeconomists examine the sources of these fluctuations and the government policies that attempt to moderate them.

- *Unemployment.* The unemployment rate is the fraction of people who would like to be employed but can't find work. Unemployment rises during recessions, but there are always unemployed people even during good times. Macroeconomists study the causes of unemployment, including the reasons why it sometimes differs markedly across countries.

- *Inflation.* The inflation rate is the rate at which prices in general are increasing over time. Questions macroeconomists ask about inflation include, Why does inflation vary over time and across countries? Must a reduction in inflation be accompanied by an increase in unemployment, or vice versa?

- *Economic interdependence among nations.* Modern economies are highly interdependent. Related issues studied by macroeconomists include the desirability of free trade agreements and the causes and effects of trade imbalances.

MACROECONOMIC POLICY

We have seen that macroeconomists are interested in why different countries' economies perform differently and why a particular economy may perform well in some periods and poorly in others. Although many factors contribute to economic performance, government policy is surely among the most important. Understanding the effects of various policies and helping government officials develop better policies are important objectives of macroeconomists.

TYPES OF MACROECONOMIC POLICY

We defined macroeconomic policies as government policies that affect the performance of the economy as a whole, as opposed to the market for a particular good or service. There are three major types of macroeconomic policy: *monetary policy, fiscal policy,* and *structural policy.*

The term **monetary policy** refers to the determination of the nation's money supply. (Cash and coin are the basic forms of money, although as we will see, modern economies have other forms of money as well.) For reasons that we will discuss in later chapters, most economists agree that changes in the money supply affect important macroeconomic variables, including national output, employment, interest rates, inflation, stock prices, and the international value of the dollar. In virtually all countries, monetary policy is controlled by a government institution called the *central bank.* The Federal Reserve System, often called the Fed for short, is the central bank of the United States.

Fiscal policy refers to decisions that determine the government's budget, including the amount and composition of government expenditures and government revenues. The balance between government spending and taxes is a particularly important aspect of fiscal policy. When government officials spend more than they collect in taxes, the government runs a *deficit,* and when they spend less, the government's budget is in *surplus.* As with monetary policy, economists generally agree that fiscal policy can have important effects on the overall performance of the economy. For example, many economists believe that the large deficits run by the federal government during the 1980s were harmful to the nation's economy. Likewise, many would say that the balancing of the federal budget that occurred during the 1990s contributed to the nation's strong economic performance during that decade. Most recently, the federal budget has moved once again into deficit.

monetary policy determination of the nation's money supply

fiscal policy decisions that determine the government's budget, including the amount and composition of government expenditures and government revenues

EXERCISE 17.2

The Congressional Budget Office (CBO) is the government agency that is charged with projecting the federal government's surpluses or deficits. From the CBO's home page (http://www.cbo.gov/), find the most recent value of the federal government's surplus or deficit and the CBO's projected values for the next five years. How do you think these projections are likely to affect congressional deliberations on taxation and government spending?

Finally, the term **structural policy** includes government policies aimed at changing the underlying structure, or institutions, of the nation's economy. Structural policies come in many forms, from minor tinkering to ambitious overhauls of the entire economic system. The move away from government control of the economy and toward a more market-oriented approach in many formerly communist countries, such as Poland, the Czech Republic, and Hungary, is a large-scale example of structural policy. Many developing countries have tried similar structural reforms. Supporters of structural policy hope that, by changing the basic characteristics of the economy or by remaking its institutions, they can stimulate economic growth and improve living standards.

structural policy government policies aimed at changing the underlying structure, or institutions, of the nation's economy

POSITIVE VERSUS NORMATIVE ANALYSES OF MACROECONOMIC POLICY

Macroeconomists are frequently called upon to analyze the effects of a proposed policy. For example, if Congress is debating a tax cut, economists in the Congressional Budget Office or the Treasury may be asked to prepare an analysis of the likely effects of the tax cut on the overall economy, as well as on specific industries, regions, or income groups. An objective analysis aimed at determining only the economic consequences of a particular policy—not whether those consequences are desirable—is called a **positive analysis.** In contrast, a **normative analysis** includes recommendations on whether a particular policy *should* be implemented. While a positive analysis is supposed to be objective and scientific, a normative analysis involves the *values* of the person or organization doing the analysis—conservative, liberal, or middle-of-the-road.

While pundits often joke that economists cannot agree among themselves, the tendency for economists to disagree is exaggerated. When economists do disagree, the controversy often centers on normative judgments (which relate to economists' personal values) rather than on positive analysis (which reflects objective knowledge of the economy). For example, liberal and conservative economists might agree that a particular tax cut would increase the incomes of the relatively wealthy (positive analysis). But they might vehemently disagree on whether the policy *should* be enacted, reflecting their personal views about whether wealthy people deserve a tax break (normative analysis).

The next time you hear or read about a debate over economic issues, try to determine whether the differences between the two positions are primarily *positive* or *normative*. If the debate focuses on the actual effects of the event or policy under discussion, then the disagreement is over positive issues. But if the main question has to do with conflicting personal opinions about the *desirability* of those effects, the debate is normative. The distinction between positive and normative analyses is important, because objective economic research can help to resolve differences over positive issues. When people differ for normative reasons, however, economic analysis is of less use.

positive analysis addresses the economic consequences of a particular event or policy, not whether those consequences are desirable

normative analysis addresses the question of whether a policy *should* be used; normative analysis inevitably involves the values of the person doing the analysis

EXERCISE 17.3

Which of the following statements are positive and which are normative? How can you tell?

a. **A tax increase is likely to lead to lower interest rates.**

b. **Congress should increase taxes to reduce the inappropriately high level of interest rates.**

c. **A tax increase would be acceptable if most of the burden fell on those with incomes over $100,000.**

d. **Higher tariffs (taxes on imports) are needed to protect American jobs.**

e. **An increase in the tariff on imported steel would increase employment of American steelworkers.**

● RECAP   MACROECONOMIC POLICY

Macroeconomic policies affect the performance of the economy as a whole. The three types of macroeconomic policy are monetary policy, fiscal policy, and structural policy. *Monetary policy,* which in the United States is under the control of the Federal Reserve System, refers to the determination of the nation's money supply. *Fiscal policy* involves decisions about the government budget, including its expenditures and tax collections. *Structural policy* refers to government actions to change the underlying structure or institutions of the economy. Structural policy can range from minor tinkering to a major overhaul of the economic system, as with the formerly communist countries that are attempting to convert to market-oriented systems.

The analysis of a proposed policy can be positive or normative. A *positive analysis* addresses the policy's likely economic consequences, but not whether those consequences are desirable. A *normative analysis* addresses the question of whether a proposed policy *should* be used. Debates about normative conclusions inevitably involve personal values and thus generally cannot be resolved by objective economic analysis alone.

AGGREGATION

In Chapter 1 we discussed the difference between macroeconomics, the study of national economies, and microeconomics, the study of individual economic entities, such as households and firms, and the markets for specific goods and services. The main difference between the fields is one of perspective: Macroeconomists take a "bird's-eye view" of the economy, ignoring the fine details to understand how the system works as a whole. Microeconomists work instead at "ground level," studying the economic behavior of individual households, firms, and markets. Both perspectives are useful—indeed essential—to understand what makes an economy work.

Although macroeconomics and microeconomics take different perspectives on the economy, the basic tools of analysis are much the same. In the chapters to come you will see that macroeconomists apply the same core principles as microeconomists in their efforts to understand and predict economic behavior. Even though a national economy is a much bigger entity than a household or even a large firm, the choices and actions of individual decision makers ultimately determine the performance of the economy as a whole. So, for example, to understand saving behavior at the national level, the macroeconomist must first consider what motivates an individual family or household to save. The core principles introduced in Part 1 prove very useful for attacking such questions.

EXERCISE 17.4

Which of the following questions would be studied primarily by macroeconomists? By microeconomists? Explain.

a. Does increased government spending lower the unemployment rate?

b. Does Microsoft Corporation's dominance of the software industry harm consumers?

c. Would a school voucher program improve the quality of education in the United States? (Under a voucher program, parents are given a fixed amount of government aid, which they may use to send their children to any school, public or private.)

d. Should government policymakers aim to reduce inflation still further?

e. Why is the average rate of household saving low in the United States?

f. Does the increase in the number of consumer products being sold over the Internet threaten the profits of conventional retailers?

While macroeconomists use the core principles of economics to understand and predict individual economic decisions, they need a way to relate millions of *aggregation* the adding up of individual economic variables to obtain economywide totals

individual decisions to the behavior of the economy as a whole. One important tool they use to link individual behavior to national economic performance is **aggregation,** the adding up of individual economic variables to obtain economy-wide totals.

For example, macroeconomists don't care whether consumers drink Pepsi or Coke, go to the movie theater or rent videos, drive a convertible or a sports utility vehicle. These individual economic decisions are the province of microeconomics. Instead, macroeconomists add up consumer expenditures on all goods and services during a given period to obtain *aggregate,* or total, consumer expenditure. Similarly, a macroeconomist would not focus on plumbers' wages versus electricians' but would concentrate instead on the average wage of all workers. By focusing on aggregate variables, like total consumer expenditures or the average wage, macroeconomists suppress the mind-boggling details of a complex modern economy to see broad economic trends.

EXAMPLE 17.3   Aggregation (1): A national crime index

To illustrate not only why aggregation is needed but also some of the problems associated with it, consider an issue that is only partly economic: crime. Suppose policymakers want to know whether *in general* the problem of crime in the United States is getting better or worse. How could an analyst obtain a statistical answer to that question?

Police keep detailed records of the crimes reported in their jurisdictions, so in principle a researcher could determine precisely how many purse snatchings occurred last year on New York City subways. But data on the number of crimes of each type in each jurisdiction would produce stacks of computer output. Is there a way to add up, or aggregate, all the crime data to get some sense of the national trend?

Law enforcement agencies such as the FBI use aggregation to obtain national *crime rates,* which are typically expressed as the number of "serious" crimes committed per 100,000 population. For example, the FBI reported that in 2000 some 11.6 million serious crimes (both violent crimes and property crimes) occurred in the United States (http://www.fbi.gov). Dividing the number of crimes by the U.S. population in 2000, which was about 280 million, and multiplying by 100,000 yields the crime rate for 2000, equal to about 4,100 crimes per 100,000 people. This rate represented a substantial drop from the crime rate in 1992, which was nearly 5,700 crimes per 100,000 people. So aggregation (the adding up of many different crimes into a national index) indicates that, in general, serious crime decreased in the United States between 1992 and 2000.

Although aggregation of crime statistics reveals the "big picture," it may obscure important details. The FBI crime index lumps together relatively minor crimes such as petty theft with very serious crimes such as murder and rape. Most people would agree that murder and rape do far more damage than a typical theft, so adding together these two very different types of crimes might give a false picture of crime in the United States. For example, although the U.S. crime rate fell 28 percent between 1992 and 2000, the murder rate fell by more than 40 percent. Since murder is the most serious of crimes, the reduction in crime between 1992 and 2000 was probably more significant than the change in the overall crime rate indicates. The aggregate crime rate glosses over other important details, such as the fact that the most dramatic reductions in crime occurred in urban areas. This loss of detail is a cost of aggregation, the price analysts pay for the ability to look at broad economic or social trends.

EXAMPLE 17.4   Aggregation (2): U.S. exports

The United States exports a wide variety of products and services to many different countries. Kansas farmers sell grain to Russia, Silicon Valley programmers sell software to France, and Hollywood movie studios sell entertainment the world over. Suppose macroeconomists want to compare the total quantities of American-made goods sold to various regions of the world. How could such a comparison be made?

Economists can't add bushels of grain, lines of code, and movie tickets—the units aren't comparable. But they can add the *dollar values* of each—the revenue farmers earned from foreign grain sales, the royalties programmers received for their exported software, and the revenues studios reaped from films shown abroad. By comparing the dollar values of U.S. exports to Europe, Asia, Africa, and other regions in a particular year, economists are able to determine which regions are the biggest customers for American-made goods.

 RECAP **AGGREGATION**

Macroeconomics, the study of national economies, differs from microeconomics, the study of individual economic entities (such as households and firms) and the markets for specific goods and services. Macroeconomists take a "bird's-eye view" of the economy. To study the economy as a whole, macroeconomists make frequent use of aggregation, the adding up of individual economic variables to obtain economywide totals. For example, a macroeconomist is more interested in the determinants of total U.S. exports, as measured by total dollar value, than in the factors that determine the exports of specific goods. A cost of aggregation is that the fine details of the economic situation are often obscured.

STUDYING MACROECONOMICS: A PREVIEW

This chapter introduced many of the key issues of macroeconomics. In the chapters to come we will look at each of these issues in more detail. The next two chapters (Chapters 18 and 19) cover the *measurement* of economic performance, including key variables like the level of economic activity, the extent of unemployment, and the rate of inflation. Obtaining quantitative measurements of the economy, against which theories can be tested, is the crucial first step in answering basic macroeconomic questions like those raised in this chapter.

In Part 7 we will study economic behavior over relatively long periods of time. Chapter 20 examines economic growth and productivity improvement, the fundamental determinants of the average standard of living in the long run. Chapter 21 discusses the long-run determination of employment, unemployment, and wages. In Chapter 22 we study saving and its link to the creation of new capital goods, such as factories and machines. The role played in the economy by money, and its relation to the rate of inflation, is covered in Chapter 23, which also introduces the Federal Reserve, the central bank of the United States, and discusses some of its policy tools. Chapter 24 looks at both domestic and international financial markets and their role in allocating saving to productive uses, in particular their role in promoting international capital flows.

John Maynard Keynes, a celebrated British economist, once wrote that "In the long run, we are all dead." Keynes's statement was intended as an ironic comment on the tendency of economists to downplay short-run economic problems on the grounds that "in the long run," the operation of the free market will always restore economic stability. Keynes, who was particularly active and influential during the Great Depression, correctly viewed the problem of massive unemployment, whether "short run" or not, as the most pressing economic issue of the time.

So why start our study of macroeconomics with the long run? Keynes's comment notwithstanding, long-run economic performance is extremely important, accounting for most of the substantial differences in living standards and economic well-being the world over. Furthermore, studying long-run economic behavior provides important background for understanding short-term fluctuations in the economy.

We turn to those short-term fluctuations in Part 8. Chapter 25 provides background on what happens during recessions and expansions, as well as some historical perspective. Chapter 26 discusses one important source of short-term economic fluctuations, variations in aggregate spending. The chapter also shows how, by influencing aggregate spending, fiscal policy may be able to moderate economic fluctuations. The second major policy tool for stabilizing the economy, monetary policy, is the subject of Chapter 27. Chapter 28 brings inflation into the analysis and discusses the circumstances under which macroeconomic policymakers may face a short-term trade-off between inflation and unemployment.

The international dimension of macroeconomics is the focus of Part 9. (Chapter 16 focused on the issue of international trade and the costs and benefits of unrestricted trade.) Chapter 29 introduces exchange rates between national currencies. We will discuss how exchange rates are determined and how they affect the workings of the economy and macroeconomic policy.

■ SUMMARY ■

- Macroeconomics is the study of the performance of national economies and of the policies governments use to try to improve that performance. Some of the broad issues macroeconomists study are:

  Sources of economic growth and improved living standards
  Trends in *average labor productivity*, or output per employed worker
  Short-term fluctuations in the pace of economic growth (recessions and expansions)
  Causes and cures of unemployment and inflation
  Economic interdependence among nations

- To help explain differences in economic performance among countries, or in economic performance in the same country at different times, macroeconomists study the implementation and effects of macroeconomic policies. *Macroeconomic policies* are government actions designed to affect the performance of the economy as a whole. Macroeconomic policies include *monetary policy* (the

determination of the nation's money supply), *fiscal policy* (relating to decisions about the government's budget), and *structural policy* (aimed at affecting the basic structure and institutions of the economy).

- In studying economic policies, economists apply both *positive analysis* (an objective attempt to determine the consequences of a proposed policy) and *normative analysis* (which addresses whether a particular policy *should* be adopted). Normative analysis involves the values of the person doing the analysis.

- Macroeconomics is distinct from microeconomics, which focuses on the behavior of individual economic entities and specific markets. Macroeconomists make heavy use of *aggregation*, which is the adding up of individual economic variables into economywide totals. Aggregation allows macroeconomists to study the "big picture" of the economy, while ignoring fine details about individual households, firms, and markets.

▪ KEY TERMS ▪

aggregation (440)

average labor productivity (431)

fiscal policy (437)

macroeconomic policies (429)

monetary policy (437)

normative analysis (438)

positive analysis (438)

structural policy (437)

▪ REVIEW QUESTIONS ▪

1. How did the experience of the Great Depression motivate the development of the field of macroeconomics?

2. Generally, how does the standard of living in the United States today compare to the standard of living in other countries? To the standard of living in the United States a century ago?

3. Why is average labor productivity a particularly important economic variable?

4. True or false: Economic growth within a particular country generally proceeds at a constant rate. Explain.

5. True or false: Differences of opinion about economic policy recommendations can always be resolved by objective analysis of the issues. Explain.

6. Baseball statistics, such as batting averages, are calculated and reported for each individual player, for each team, and for the league as a whole. What purposes are served by doing this? Relate to the idea of aggregation in macroeconomics.

7. What type of macroeconomic policy (monetary, fiscal, structural) might include each of the following actions?
   a. A broad government initiative to reduce the country's reliance on agriculture and promote high-technology industries
   b. A reduction in income tax rates
   c. Provision of additional cash to the banking system
   d. An attempt to reduce the government budget deficit by reducing spending
   e. A decision by a developing country to reduce government control of the economy and to become more market-oriented

▪ PROBLEMS ▪

1. Over the next 50 years the Japanese population is expected to decline, while the fraction of the population that is retired is expected to increase sharply. What are the implications of these population changes for total output and average living standards in Japan, assuming that average labor productivity continues to grow? What if average labor productivity stagnates?

2. Is it possible for average living standards to rise during a period in which average labor productivity is falling? Discuss, using a numerical example for illustration.

3. The Bureau of Economic Analysis, or BEA, is a government agency that collects a wide variety of statistics about the U.S. economy. From the BEA's home page (http://www.bea.doc.gov) find data for the most recent year available on U.S. exports and imports of goods and services. Is the United States running a trade surplus or deficit? Calculate the ratio of the surplus or deficit to U.S. exports.

4. Which of the following statements are positive and which are normative?
   a. If the Federal Reserve raises interest rates, demand for housing is likely to fall.
   b. The Federal Reserve should raise interest rates to keep inflation at an acceptably low level.
   c. Stock prices are likely to fall over the next year as the economy slows.
   d. A reduction in the capital gains tax (the tax on profits made in the stock market) would lead to a 10 to 20 percent increase in stock prices.
   e. Congress should not reduce capital gains taxes without also providing tax breaks for lower-income people.

5. Which of the following would be studied by a macroeconomist? By a microeconomist?
   a. The worldwide operations of General Motors
   b. The effect of government subsidies on sugar prices
   c. Factors affecting average wages in the U.S. economy
   d. Inflation in developing countries
   e. The effects of tax cuts on consumer spending

▪ ANSWERS TO IN-CHAPTER EXERCISES ▪

17.1 Your answer will depend upon the current unemployment rate available at the OECD web site.

17.2 Your answer will depend upon the current CBO budget data.

17.3 a. Positive. This is a prediction of the effect of a policy, not a value judgment on whether the policy should be used.

b. Normative. Words like *should* and *inappropriately* express value judgments about the policy.

c. Normative. The statement is about the desirability of certain types of policies, not their likely effects.

d. Normative. The statement is about desirability of a policy.

e. Positive. The statement is a prediction of the likely effects of a policy, not a recommendation on whether the policy should be used.

17.4 a. Macroeconomists. Government spending and the unemployment rate are aggregate concepts pertaining to the national economy.

b. Microeconomists. Microsoft, though large, is an individual firm.

c. Microeconomists. The issue relates to the supply and demand for a specific service, education.

d. Macroeconomists. Inflation is an aggregate, economywide concept.

e. Macroeconomists. Average saving is an aggregate concept.

f. Microeconomists. The focus is on a relatively narrow set of markets and products rather than on the economy as a whole.

MEASURING ECONOMIC ACTIVITY: GDP AND UNEMPLOYMENT

■

"**N**onfarm payrolls grew at a 2 percent rate in the third quarter . . ."

"The Dow Jones stock market index closed up 93 points yesterday in moderate trading . . ."

"Inflation appears subdued as the consumer price index registered an increase of only 0.2 percent last month . . ."

"The unemployment rate last month rose to 6.1 percent, its highest level since . . ."

News reports like these fill the airwaves—some TV and radio stations carry nothing else. In fact, all kinds of people are interested in economic data. The average person hopes to learn something that will be useful in a business decision, a financial investment, or a career move. The professional economist depends on economic data in much the same way that a doctor depends on a patient's vital signs—pulse, blood pressure, and temperature—to make an accurate diagnosis. To understand economic developments and to be able to give useful advice to policymakers, businesspeople, and financial investors, an economist simply must have up-to-date, accurate data. Political leaders and policymakers also need economic data to help them in their decisions and planning.

Interest in measuring the economy, and attempts to do so, date back as far as the mid-seventeenth century, when Sir William Petty (1623–1687) conducted a detailed survey of the land and wealth of Ireland. The British government's purpose in commissioning the survey was to determine the capacity of the Irish people to pay taxes to the Crown. But Petty used the opportunity to measure a variety of social and economic variables and went on to conduct pioneering studies of wealth, production, and population in several other countries. A firm believer in the idea that scientific progress depends first and foremost on accurate measurement, he once interrupted a meeting of the British Royal Society (a distinguished association of scientists, of which Petty was a founding member) to correct a speaker who had used the phrase "considerably bigger." A rule should be passed barring such vague terms, Petty proposed, so that "no word might be used but what marks either number, weight, or measure."[1]

Not until the twentieth century, though, did economic measurement come into its own. World War II was an important catalyst for the development of accurate economic statistics, since its very outcome was thought to depend on the mobilization of economic resources. Two economists, Simon Kuznets in the United States and Richard Stone in the United Kingdom, developed comprehensive systems for measuring a nation's output of goods and services, which were of great help to Allied leaders in their wartime planning. Kuznets and Stone each received a Nobel Prize in economics for their work, which became the basis for the economic accounts used today by almost all the world's countries. The governments of the United States and many other countries now collect and publish a wealth of statistics covering all aspects of their economies.

In this chapter and the next we will discuss how economists measure three basic macroeconomic variables that arise frequently in analyses of the state of the economy: the *gross domestic product,* or *GDP,* the *rate of unemployment,* and the *rate of inflation.* The focus of this chapter is on the first two of these statistics, GDP and the unemployment rate, which both measure the overall level of economic activity in a country.

Measuring economic activity might sound like a straightforward and uncontroversial task, but that is not the case. Indeed, the basic measure of a nation's output of goods and services, the gross domestic product, or GDP, has been criticized on many grounds. Some critics have complained that GDP does not adequately reflect factors such as the effect of economic growth on the environment or the rate of resource depletion. Because of problems like these, they charge, policies based on GDP statistics are likely to be flawed. Unemployment statistics have also been the subject of some controversy. By the end of this chapter you will understand how official measures of output and unemployment are constructed and used and will have gained some insight into these debates over their accuracy. Understanding the strengths and limitations of economic data is the first critical step toward becoming an intelligent user of economic statistics, as well as a necessary background for the economic analysis in the chapters to come.

GROSS DOMESTIC PRODUCT: MEASURING THE NATION'S OUTPUT

Chapter 17 emphasized the link between an economy's output of goods and services and its living standard. We noted that high levels of output per person, and per worker, are typically associated with a high standard of living. But what, exactly, does "output" mean? To study economic growth and productivity scientifically, we need to be more precise about how economists define and measure an economy's output.

The most frequently used measure of an economy's output is called the *gross domestic product,* or *GDP.* GDP is intended to measure how much an economy

---

[1]This story is reported by Charles H. Hull, "Petty's Place in the History of Economic Theory," *Quarterly Journal of Economics,* May 14, 1900, pp. 307–340.

produces in a given period, such as a quarter (three months) or a year. More precisely, **gross domestic product (GDP)** is the market value of the final goods and services produced in a country during a given period. To understand this definition, let's take it apart and examine each of its parts separately. The first key phrase in the definition is "market value."

gross domestic product (GDP)
the market value of the final goods and services produced in a country during a given period

MARKET VALUE

A modern economy produces many different goods and services, from dental floss (a good) to acupuncture (a service). Macroeconomists are not interested in this kind of detail, however; rather, their goal is to understand the behavior of the economy as a whole. For example, a macroeconomist might ask, Has the overall capacity of the economy to produce goods and services increased over time? If so, by how much?

To be able to talk about concepts like the "total output" or "total production"—as opposed to the production of specific items like dental floss—economists need to *aggregate* the quantities of the many different goods and services into a single number. They do so by adding up the *market values* of the different goods and services the economy produces. A simple example will illustrate the process. In the imaginary economy of Orchardia, total production is 4 apples and 6 bananas. To find the total output of Orchardia, we could add the number of apples to the number of bananas and conclude that total output is 10 pieces of fruit. But what if this economy also produced 3 pairs of shoes? There really is no sensible way to add apples and bananas to shoes.

Suppose though that we know that apples sell for $0.25 each, bananas for $0.50 each, and shoes for $20.00 a pair. Then the market value of this economy's production, or its GDP, is equal to

$$(4 \text{ apples} \times \$0.25/\text{apple}) + (6 \text{ bananas} \times \$0.50/\text{banana}) + (3 \text{ pairs of shoes} \times \$20.00/\text{pair}) = \$64.00.$$

Notice that when we calculate total output this way, the more expensive items (the shoes) receive a higher weighting than the cheaper items (the apples and bananas). In general, the amount people are willing to pay for an item is an indication of the economic benefit they expect to receive from it (see Chapter 3). For this reason higher-priced items should count for more in a measure of aggregate output.

Orchardia's GDP

Suppose Orchardia were to produce 3 apples, 3 bananas, and 4 pairs of shoes at the same prices as in the preceding text. What is its GDP now?

Now the Orchardian GDP is equal to

$$(3 \text{ apples} \times \$0.25/\text{apple}) + (3 \text{ bananas} \times \$0.50/\text{banana}) + (4 \text{ pairs of shoes} \times \$20.00/\text{pair}) = \$82.25.$$

EXAMPLE 18.1

Notice that Orchardian GDP is higher in Example 18.1 than in the previous text, even though two of the three goods (apples and bananas) are being produced in smaller quantities than before. The reason is that the good whose production has increased (shoes) is much more valuable than the goods whose production has decreased (apples and bananas).

EXERCISE 18.1

Suppose Orchardia produces the same quantities of the three goods as originally at the same prices (see text preceding Example 18.1). In addition, it produces 5 oranges at $0.30 each. What is the GDP of Orchardia now?

EXERCISE 18.2

Following are data for a recent month on U.S. production of passenger cars and other light vehicles (a category that includes minivans, light trucks, and sports utility vehicles). The data are broken down into two categories: U.S. auto producers (GM, Ford, and Chrysler, now DaimlerChrysler) and foreign-owned plants (such as Honda, Toyota, and BMW). The average selling price is $17,000 for passenger cars and $25,000 for other light vehicles.

	Passenger cars	Other light vehicles
U.S. producers	471,000	714,000
Foreign-owned plants	227,000	63,000

Compare the output of U.S. producers to that of foreign-owned plants in terms of both the total number of vehicles produced and their market values (contribution to GDP). Explain why the two measures give different impressions of the relative importance of production by U.S.-owned and foreign-owned plants.

Market values provide a convenient way to add together, or aggregate, the many different goods and services produced in a modern economy. A drawback of using market values, however, is that not all economically valuable goods and services are bought and sold in markets. For example, the unpaid work of a homemaker, although it is of economic value, is not sold in markets and so isn't counted in GDP. But paid housekeeping and child care services, which are sold in markets, do count. This distinction can create some pitfalls, as Example 18.2 shows.

EXAMPLE 18.2

Women's labor force participation and GDP measurement

The percentage of adult American women working outside the home has increased dramatically in the past four decades, from less than 40 percent in 1960 to about 60 percent today (see Figure 18.1). This trend has led to a substantial increase in the demand for paid day care and housekeeping services, as working wives and mothers require more help at home. How have these changes affected measured GDP?

FIGURE 18.1

Percentages of American Men and Women over Age 16 Working Outside the Home, 1960–2001.
The fraction of American women working outside the home has risen by about 20 percentage points since 1960, while the fraction of men working outside the home has declined slightly.

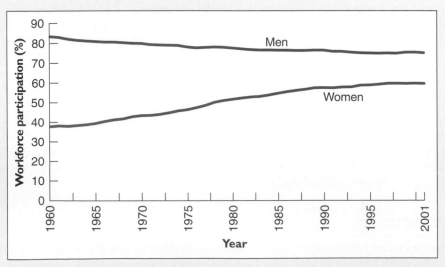

SOURCE: *Economic Report of the President*, February 2002 (http://w3.access.gpo.gov/eop/index.html).

The entry of many women into the labor market has raised measured GDP in two ways. First, the goods and services that women produce in their new jobs have contributed directly to increasing GDP. Second, the fact that paid workers took over previously unpaid housework and child care duties has increased measured GDP by the amount paid to those workers. The first of these two changes represents a genuine increase in economic activity, but the second reflects a transfer of existing economic activities from the unpaid sector to the market sector. Overall, then, the increase in measured GDP associated with increased participation in the labor force by women probably overstates the actual increase in economic activity.

Why has female participation in the labor market increased by so much? What explains the trends illustrated in Figure 18.1?

In a world governed only by economic principles—without social conventions, customs, or traditions—homemaking tasks like cleaning, cooking, and child rearing would be jobs like any other. As such, they would be subject to the principle of comparative advantage: Those people (either men or women) whose comparative advantage lay in performing homemaking tasks would specialize in them, freeing people whose comparative advantage lies elsewhere to work outside the home. In other words, homemaking tasks would be done by those with the lowest opportunity cost in those tasks. In such a world, to see a woman with a medical degree doing housework would be very unusual—her opportunity cost of doing housework would be too high.

But of course we don't live in a world driven only by economic considerations. Traditionally, social custom has severely limited the economic opportunities of women (and in some societies still does). However, social restrictions on women have weakened considerably over the past century, particularly in the industrialized countries, as a result of the increased educational attainment of women, the rise of the feminist movement, and other factors. As traditional social restraints on women have loosened, domestic arrangements have moved in the direction dictated by comparative advantage—to an increasing degree, homemaking tasks are now performed by paid specialists, while the majority of women (and men) work outside the home.

Although homemaking activities are excluded from measured GDP, in a few cases goods and services that are not sold in markets are included in GDP. By far the most important are the goods and services provided by federal, state, and local governments. The protection provided by the army and navy, the transportation convenience of the interstate highway system, and the education provided by the public school system are examples of publicly provided goods and services that are not sold in markets. As market prices for publicly provided goods and services do not exist, economic statisticians add to the GDP the *costs* of providing those goods and services as rough measures of their economic value. For example, to include public education in the GDP, the statisticians add to GDP the salaries of teachers and administrators, the costs of textbooks and supplies, and the like. Similarly, the economic value of the national defense establishment is approximated, for the purposes of measuring GDP, by the *costs* of defense: the pay earned by soldiers and sailors, the costs of acquiring and maintaining weapons, and so on.

With a few exceptions, like publicly provided goods and services, GDP is calculated by adding up market values. However, not all goods and services that have a market value are counted in GDP. As we will see next, GDP includes only those goods and services that are the end products of the production process, called *final goods and services*. Goods and services that are used up in the production process are not counted in GDP.

FINAL GOODS AND SERVICES

Many goods are used in the production process. Before a baker can produce a loaf of bread, grain must be grown and harvested, then the grain must be ground

Why is the female labor force participation rate now more than 50 percent greater than in the 1960s?

final goods or services goods or services consumed by the ultimate user; because they are the end products of the production process, they are counted as part of GDP

intermediate goods or services goods or services used up in the production of final goods and services and therefore not counted as part of GDP

into flour, and, together with other ingredients, baked into bread. Of the three major goods that are produced during this process—the grain, the flour, and the bread—only the bread is used by consumers. Because producing the bread is the ultimate purpose of the process, the bread is called a *final good*. In general, a **final good or service** is the end product of a process, the product or service that consumers actually use. The goods or services produced on the way toward making the final product—here, the grain and the flour—are called **intermediate goods or services.**

Since we are interested in measuring only those items that are of direct economic value, *only final goods and services are included in GDP.* Intermediate goods and services are *not* included. To illustrate, suppose that the grain from the previous example has a market value of $0.50 (the price the milling company paid for the grain). The grain is then ground into flour, which has a market value of $1.20 (the price the baker paid for the flour). Finally, the flour is made into a loaf of fine French bread, worth $2.00 at the local store. In calculating the contribution of these activities to GDP, would we want to add together the values of the grain, the flour, and the bread? No, because the grain and flour are intermediate goods, valuable only because they can be used to make bread. So in this example, the total contribution to GDP is $2.00, the value of the loaf of bread, the final product.

Example 18.3 illustrates the same distinction but this time with a focus on services.

EXAMPLE 18.3

The barber and his assistant

Your barber charges $10 for a haircut. In turn, the barber pays his assistant $2 per haircut in return for sharpening the scissors, sweeping the floor, and other chores. For each haircut given, what is the total contribution of the barber and his assistant, taken together, to GDP?

The answer to this problem is $10, the price, or market value, of the haircut. The haircut is counted in GDP because it is the final service, the one that actually has value to the final user. The services provided by the assistant have value only because they contribute to the production of the haircut; thus they are not counted in GDP.

Example 18.4 illustrates that the same good can be either intermediate or final, depending on how it is used.

EXAMPLE 18.4

A good that can be either intermediate or final

Farmer Brown produces $100 worth of milk. He sells $40 worth of milk to his neighbors and uses the rest to feed his pigs, which he sells to his neighbors for $120. What is Farmer Brown's contribution to the GDP?

The final goods in this example are the $40 worth of milk and the $120 worth of pigs sold to the neighbors. Adding $40 and $120, we get $160, which is Farmer Brown's contribution to the GDP. Note that part of the milk Farmer Brown produced serves as an intermediate good and part as a final good. The $60 worth of milk that is fed to the pigs is an intermediate good, and so it is not counted in GDP. The $40 worth of milk sold to the neighbors is a final good, and so it is counted.

capital good a long-lived good, which is itself produced and used to produce other goods and services

A special type of good that is difficult to classify as intermediate or final is a capital good. A **capital good** is a long-lived good, which is itself produced and used to produce other goods and services. Factories and machines are examples of capital goods. Capital goods do not fit the definition of final goods, since their purpose is to produce other goods. On the other hand, they are not used up during the production process, except over a very long period, so they are not exactly intermediate goods either. For purposes of measuring GDP, economists have agreed to classify newly produced capital goods as final goods. Otherwise, a country that invested in its future by building modern factories and buying new machines would be counted as having a lower GDP than a country that devoted all its resources to producing consumer goods.

We have established the rule that only final goods and services (including newly produced capital goods) are counted in GDP. Intermediate goods and services, which are used up in the production of final goods and services, are not counted. In practice, however, this rule is not easy to apply, because the production process often stretches over several periods. To illustrate, recall the earlier example of the grain that was milled into flour, which in turn was baked into a loaf of French bread. The contribution of the whole process to GDP is $2, the value of the bread (the final product). Suppose, though, that the grain and the flour were produced near the end of the year 2002 and the bread was baked early the next year in 2003. In this case, should we attribute the $2 value of the bread to the GDP for the year 2002 or to the GDP for the year 2003?

Neither choice seems quite right, since part of the bread's production process occurred in each year. Part of the value of the bread should probably be counted in the year 2002 GDP and part in the year 2003 GDP. But how should we make the split? To deal with this problem, economists determine the market value of final goods and services indirectly, by adding up the *value added* by each firm in the production process. The **value added** by any firm equals the market value of its product or service minus the cost of inputs purchased from other firms. As we'll see, summing the value added by all firms (including producers of both intermediate and final goods and services) gives the same answer as simply adding together the value of final goods and services. But the value-added method eliminates the problem of dividing the value of a final good or service between two periods.

value added for any firm, the market value of its product or service minus the cost of inputs purchased from other firms

To illustrate this method, let's revisit the example of the French bread, which is the result of multiple stages of production. We have already determined that the total contribution of this production process to GDP is $2, the value of the bread. Let's show now that we can get the same answer by summing value added. Suppose that the bread is the ultimate product of three corporations: ABC Grain Company, Inc., produces grain; General Flour produces flour; and Hot'n'Fresh Baking produces the bread. If we make the same assumptions as before about the market value of the grain, the flour, and the bread, what is the value added by each of these three companies?

ABC Grain Company produces $0.50 worth of grain, with no inputs from other companies, so ABC's value added is $0.50. General Flour uses $0.50 worth of grain from ABC to produce $1.20 worth of flour. The value added by General Flour is thus the value of its product ($1.20) less the cost of purchased inputs ($0.50), or $0.70. Finally, Hot'n'Fresh Baking buys $1.20 worth of flour from General Flour and uses it to produce $2.00 worth of bread. So the value added by Hot'n'Fresh is $0.80. These calculations are summarized in Table 18.1.

TABLE 18.1
Value Added in Bread Production

Company	Revenues − Cost of purchased inputs = Value added		
ABC Grain	$0.50	$0.00	$0.50
General Flour	$1.20	$0.50	$0.70
Hot'n'Fresh	$2.00	$1.20	$0.80
Total			$2.00

You can see that summing the value added by each company gives the same contribution to GDP, $2.00, as the method based on counting final goods and services only. Basically, the value added by each firm represents the portion of the value of the final good or service that the firm creates in its stage of production. Summing the value added by all firms in the economy yields the total value of final goods and services, or GDP.

You can also see now how the value-added method solves the problem of production processes that bridge two or more periods. Suppose that the grain and flour are produced during the year 2002 but the bread is not baked until 2003. Using the value-added method, the contribution of this production process to the year 2002 GDP is the value added by the grain company plus the value added by the flour company, or $1.20. The contribution of the production process to the year 2003 GDP is the value added by the baker, which is $0.80. Thus part of the value of the final product, the bread, is counted in the GDP for each year, reflecting the fact that part of the production of the bread took place in each year.

EXERCISE 18.3

Amy's card shop receives a shipment of Valentine's Day cards in December 2002. Amy pays the wholesale distributor of the cards a total of $500. In February 2003 she sells the cards for a total of $700. What are the contributions of these transactions to GDP in the years 2002 and 2003?

We have now established that GDP is equal to the market value of final goods and services. Let's look at the last part of the definition, "produced within a country during a given period."

PRODUCED WITHIN A COUNTRY DURING A GIVEN PERIOD

The word *domestic* in the term *gross domestic product* tells us that GDP is a measure of economic activity within a given country. Thus, only production that takes place within the country's borders is counted. For example, the GDP of the United States includes the market value of *all* cars produced within U.S. borders, even if they are made in foreign-owned plants (recall Exercise 18.2). However, cars produced in Mexico by a U.S.-based company like General Motors are *not* counted.

We have seen that GDP is intended to measure the amount of production that occurs during a given period, such as the calendar year. For this reason, only goods and services that are actually produced during a particular year are included in the GDP for that year. Example 18.5 and Exercise 18.4 illustrate.

EXAMPLE 18.5

The sale of a house and GDP

A 20-year-old house is sold to a young family for $200,000. The family pays the real estate agent a 6 percent commission, or $12,000. What is the contribution of this transaction to GDP?

Because the house was not produced during the current year, its value is *not* counted in this year's GDP. (The value of the house was included in the GDP 20 years earlier, the year the house was built.) In general, purchases and sales of existing assets, such as old houses or used cars, do not contribute to the current year's GDP. However, the $12,000 fee paid to the real estate agent represents the market value of the agent's services in helping the family find the house and make the purchase. Since those services were provided during the current year, the agent's fee *is* counted in current-year GDP.

EXERCISE 18.4

Lotta Doe sells 100 shares of stock in Benson Buggywhip for $50 per share. She pays her broker a 2 percent commission for executing the sale. How does Lotta's transaction affect the current-year GDP?

 RECAP   **MEASURING GDP**

Gross domestic product (GDP) equals

the market value

GDP is an aggregate of the market values of the many goods and services produced in the economy.

Goods and services that are not sold in markets, such as unpaid housework, are not counted in GDP. An important exception is goods and services provided by the government, which are included in GDP at the government's cost of providing them.

of final goods and services

Final goods and services (which include capital goods, such as factories and machines) are counted in GDP. Intermediate goods and services, which are used up in the production of final goods and services, are not counted.

In practice, the value of final goods and services is determined by the value-added method. The value added by any firm equals the firm's revenue from selling its product minus the cost of inputs purchased from other firms. Summing the value added by all firms in the production process yields the value of the final good or service.

produced in a country during a given period.

Only goods and services produced within a nation's borders are included in GDP.

Only goods and services produced during the current year (or the portion of the value produced during the current year) are counted as part of the current-year GDP.

THE EXPENDITURE METHOD FOR MEASURING GDP

GDP is a measure of the quantity of goods and services *produced* by an economy. But any good or service that is produced will also be *purchased* and used by some economic agent—a consumer buying Christmas gifts or a firm investing in new machinery, for example. For many purposes, knowing not only how much is produced, but who uses it and how, is important.

Economic statisticians divide the users of the final goods and services that make up the GDP for any given year into four categories: *households, firms, governments,* and the *foreign sector* (that is, foreign purchasers of domestic products). They assume that all the final goods and services that are produced in a country in a given year will be purchased and used by members of one or more of these four groups. Furthermore, the amounts that purchasers spend on various goods and services should be equal to the market values of those goods and services. As a result, GDP can be measured with equal accuracy by either of two methods: (1) adding up the market values of all the final goods and services that are produced domestically, or (2) adding up the total amount spent by each of the four groups on final goods and services and subtracting spending on imported goods and services. The values obtained by the two methods will be the same.

TABLE 18.2
Expenditure Components of U.S. GDP, 2001 (billions of dollars)

Consumption		**6,987.0**
Durable goods	835.9	
Nondurable goods	2,041.3	
Services	4,109.9	
Investment		**1,586.0**
Business fixed investment	1,201.6	
Residential investment	444.8	
Inventory investment	−60.3	
Government purchases		**1,858.0**
Net exports		**−348.9**
Exports	1,034.1	
Imports	1,383.0	
Total: Gross domestic product		**10,082.2**

SOURCE: Bureau of Economic Analysis (http://www.bea.doc).

Corresponding to the four groups of final users are four components of expenditure: consumption, investment, government purchases, and net exports. That is, households consume, firms invest, governments make government purchases, and the foreign sector buys the nation's exports. Table 18.2 gives the dollar values for each of these components for the U.S. economy in 2001. As the table shows, GDP for the United States in 2001 was about $10.1 trillion, roughly $35,400 per person. Detailed definitions of the components of expenditure, and their principal subcomponents, follow. As you read through them, refer to Table 18.2 to get a sense of the relative importance of each type of spending.

consumption expenditure, or consumption spending by households on goods and services, such as food, clothing, and entertainment

Consumption expenditure, or simply **consumption,** is spending by households on goods and services such as food, clothing, and entertainment. Consumption expenditure is subdivided into three subcategories:

- *Consumer durables* are long-lived consumer goods such as cars and furniture. Note that new houses are not treated as consumer durables but as part of investment.

- *Consumer nondurables* are shorter-lived goods like food and clothing.

- *Services,* a large component of consumer spending, include everything from haircuts and taxi rides to legal, financial, and educational services.

investment spending by firms on final goods and services, primarily capital goods and housing

Investment is spending by firms on final goods and services, primarily capital goods and housing. Investment is divided into three subcategories:

- *Business fixed investment* is the purchase by firms of new capital goods such as machinery, factories, and office buildings. (Remember that for the purposes of calculating GDP, long-lived capital goods are treated as final goods rather than as intermediate goods.) Firms buy capital goods to increase their capacity to produce.

- *Residential investment* is construction of new homes and apartment buildings. For GDP accounting purposes, residential investment is treated as an investment by the business sector, which then sells the homes to households.

- *Inventory investment* is the addition of unsold goods to company inventories. In other words, the goods that a firm produces but doesn't sell during the current period are treated, for accounting purposes, as if the firm had bought those goods from itself. (This convention guarantees that production equals expenditure.) Inventory investment can take a negative value, as it did in 2001, if the value of inventories on hand falls over the course of the year.

People often refer to purchases of financial assets, such as stocks or bonds, as "investments." That use of the term is different from the definition we give here. A person who buys a share of a company's stock acquires partial ownership of the *existing* physical and financial assets controlled by the company. A stock purchase does not usually correspond to the creation of *new* physical capital, however, and so is not investment in the sense we are using the term in this chapter. We will generally refer to purchases of financial assets, such as stocks and bonds, as "financial investments," to distinguish them from a firm's investment in new capital goods, such as factories and machines.

Government purchases are purchases by federal, state, and local governments of final goods, such as fighter planes, and services, such as teaching in public schools. Government purchases do *not* include *transfer payments,* which are payments made by the government in return for which no current goods or services are received. Examples of transfer payments (which, again, are *not* included in government purchases) are Social Security benefits, unemployment benefits, pensions paid to government workers, and welfare payments. Interest paid on the government debt is also excluded from government purchases.

Net exports equal exports minus imports.

- *Exports* are domestically produced final goods and services that are sold abroad.

- *Imports* are purchases by domestic buyers of goods and services that were produced abroad. Imports are subtracted from exports to find the net amount of spending on domestically produced goods and services.

government purchases purchases by federal, state, and local governments of final goods and services; government purchases do *not* include *transfer payments,* which are payments made by the government in return for which no current goods or services are received, nor do they include interest paid on the government debt

net exports exports minus imports

A country's net exports reflect the net demand by the rest of the world for its goods and services. Net exports can be negative, since imports can exceed exports in any given year. As Table 18.2 shows, the United States had significantly greater imports than exports in 2001.

The relationship between GDP and expenditures on goods and services can be summarized by an equation. Let

$$Y = \text{gross domestic product, or output}$$
$$C = \text{consumption expenditure}$$
$$I = \text{investment}$$
$$G = \text{government purchases}$$
$$NX = \text{net exports.}$$

Using these symbols, we can write that GDP equals the sum of the four types of expenditure algebraically as

$$Y = C + I + G + NX.$$

EXAMPLE 18.6

Measuring GDP by production and by expenditure

An economy produces 1,000,000 automobiles valued at $15,000 each. Of these, 700,000 are sold to consumers, 200,000 are sold to businesses, 50,000 are sold to the government, and 25,000 are sold abroad. No automobiles are imported. The automobiles left unsold at the end of the year are held in inventory by the auto producers. Find GDP in terms of (a) the market value of production and (b) the components of expenditure. You should get the same answer both ways.

The market value of the production of final goods and services in this economy is 1,000,000 autos times $15,000 per auto, or $15 billion.

To measure GDP in terms of expenditure, we must add spending on consumption, investment, government purchases, and net exports. Consumption is 700,000 autos times $15,000, or $10.5 billion. Government purchases are 50,000 autos times $15,000, or $0.75 billion. Net exports are equal to exports (25,000 autos at $15,000, or $0.375 billion) minus imports (zero), so net exports are $0.375 billion.

But what about investment? Here we must be careful. The 200,000 autos that are sold to businesses, worth $3 billion, count as investment. But notice too that the auto companies produced 1,000,000 automobiles but sold only 975,000 (700,000 + 200,000 + 50,000 + 25,000). Hence 25,000 autos were unsold at the end of the year and were added to the automobile producers' inventories. This addition to producer inventories (25,000 autos at $15,000, or $0.375 billion) counts as inventory investment, which is part of total investment. Thus total investment spending equals the $3 billion worth of autos sold to businesses plus the $0.375 billion in inventory investment, or $3.375 billion.

Recapitulating, in this economy consumption is $10.5 billion, investment (including inventory investment) is $3.375 billion, government purchases equal $0.75 billion, and net exports are $0.375 billion. Summing these four components of expenditure yields $15 billion—the same value for GDP that we got by calculating the market value of production.

EXERCISE 18.5

Extending Example 18.6, suppose that 25,000 of the automobiles purchased by households are imported rather than domestically produced. Domestic production remains at 1,000,000 autos valued at $15,000 each. Once again, find GDP in terms of (a) the market value of production and (b) the components of expenditure.

GDP can be expressed as the sum of expenditures on domestically produced final goods and services. The four types of expenditure that are counted in the GDP, and the economic groups that make each type of expenditure, are as follows:

Who makes the expenditure?	Type of expenditure	Examples
Households	Consumption	Food, clothes, haircuts, new cars
Business firms	Investment	New factories and equipment, new houses, increases in inventory stocks
Governments	Government purchases	New school buildings, new military hardware, salaries of soldiers and government officials
Foreign sector	Net exports, or exports minus imports	Exported manufactured goods, legal or financial services provided by domestic residents to foreigners

GDP AND THE INCOMES OF CAPITAL AND LABOR

The GDP can be thought of equally well as a measure of total production or as a measure of total expenditure—either method of calculating the GDP gives the same final answer. There is yet a third way to think of the GDP, which is as the *incomes of capital and labor.*

Whenever a good or service is produced or sold, the revenue from the sale is distributed to the workers and the owners of the capital involved in the production of the good or service. Thus, except for some technical adjustments that we will ignore, GDP also equals labor income plus capital income. *Labor income* (equal to about 75 percent of GDP) comprises wages, salaries, and the incomes of the self-employed. *Capital income* (about 25 percent of GDP) is made up of payments to owners of physical capital (such as factories, machines, and office buildings) and intangible capital (such as copyrights and patents). The components of capital income include items such as profits earned by businessowners, the rents paid to owners of land or buildings, interest received by bondholders, and the royalties received by the holders of copyrights or patents. Both labor income and capital income are to be understood as measured prior to payment of taxes; ultimately, of course, a portion of both types of income is captured by the government in the form of tax collections.

Figure 18.2 may help you visualize the three equivalent ways of thinking about GDP: the market value of production, the total value of expenditure, and the sum of labor income and capital income. The figure also roughly captures the relative importance of the expenditure and income components. About 65 percent of expenditure is consumption spending, about 20 percent is government purchases, and the rest is investment spending and net exports. (Actually, as Table 18.2 or Figure 17.5 shows, net exports have been negative in recent years, reflecting the U.S. trade deficit.) As we mentioned, labor income is about 75 percent of total income, with capital income making up the rest.

FIGURE 18.2
The Three Faces of GDP.
The GDP can be expressed equally well as (1) the market value of production, (2) total expenditure (consumption, investment, government purchases, net exports), or (3) total income (labor income and capital income).

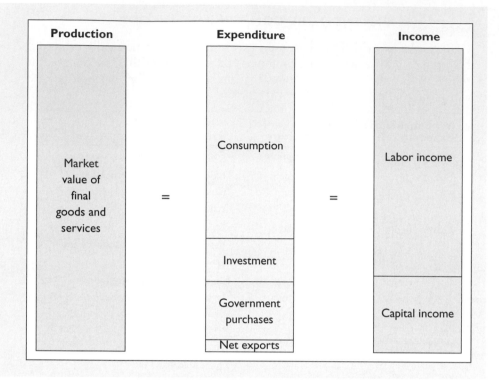

NOMINAL GDP VERSUS REAL GDP

As a measure of the total production of an economy over a given period, such as a particular year, GDP is useful in comparisons of economic activity in different places. For example, GDP data for the year 2002, broken down state by state, could be used to compare aggregate production in New York and California during that year. However, economists are interested in comparing levels of economic activity not only in different *locations* but *over time* as well. For example, a president who is running for reelection on the basis of successful economic policies might want to know by how much output in the U.S. economy had increased during his term.

Using GDP to compare economic activity at two different points in time may give misleading answers, however, as the following example shows. Suppose for the sake of illustration that the economy produces only pizzas and calzones. The prices and quantities of the two goods in the years 2000 and 2004, the beginning and end of the president's term, are shown in Table 18.3. If we calculate GDP in each year as the market value of production, we find that the GDP for 2000 is (10 pizzas × $10/pizza) + (15 calzones × $5/calzone) = $175. The GDP for 2004 is (20 pizzas × $12/pizza) + (30 calzones × $6/calzone) = $420. Comparing the GDP for the year 2004 to the GDP for the year 2000, we might conclude that it is 2.4 times greater ($420/$175).

TABLE 18.3
Prices and Quantities in 2000 and 2004

	Quantity of pizzas	Price of pizzas	Quantity of calzones	Price of calzones
2000	10	$10	15	$5
2004	20	$12	30	$6

But look more closely at the data given in Table 18.3. Can you see what is wrong with this conclusion? The quantities of both pizzas and calzones produced in the year 2004 are exactly twice the quantities produced in the year 2000. If economic activity, as measured by actual production of both goods, exactly doubled over the four years, why do the calculated values of GDP show a greater increase?

The answer, as you also can see from the table, is that prices as well as quantities rose between 2000 and 2004. Because of the increase in prices, the *market value* of production grew more over those four years than the *physical volume* of production. So in this case, GDP is a misleading gauge of economic growth during the president's term, since the physical quantities of the goods and services produced in any given year, not the dollar values, are what determine people's economic well-being. Indeed, if the prices of pizzas and calzones had risen 2.4 times between 2000 and 2004, GDP would have risen 2.4 times as well, with no increase in physical production! In that case, the claim that the economy's (physical) output had more than doubled during the president's term would obviously be wrong.

As this example shows, if we want to use GDP to compare economic activity at different points in time, we need some method of excluding the effects of price changes. In other words, we need to adjust for inflation. To do so, economists use a common set of prices to value quantities produced in different years. The standard approach is to pick a particular year, called the *base year*, and use the prices from that year to calculate the market value of output. When GDP is calculated using the prices from a base year, rather than the current year's prices, it is called **real GDP**, to indicate that it is a measure of real physical production. Real GDP is GDP adjusted for inflation. To distinguish real GDP, in which quantities produced are valued at base-year prices, from GDP valued at current-year prices, economists refer to the latter measure as **nominal GDP**.

real GDP a measure of GDP in which the quantities produced are valued at the prices in a base year rather than at current prices; real GDP measures the actual *physical volume* of production

nominal GDP a measure of GDP in which the quantities produced are valued at current-year prices; nominal GDP measures the *current dollar value* of production

Calculating the change in real GDP over the president's term

EXAMPLE 18.7

Using data from Table 18.3 and assuming that 2000 is the base year, find real GDP for the years 2004 and 2000. By how much did real output grow between 2000 and 2004?

To find real GDP for the year 2004, we must value the quantities produced that year using the prices in the base year, 2000. Using the data in Table 18.3:

Year 2004 real GDP = (year 2004 quantity of pizzas × year 2000 price of pizzas) + (year 2004 quantity of calzones × year 2000 price of calzones)

= (20 × $10) + (30 × $5)

= $350.

The real GDP of this economy in the year 2004 is $350. What is the real GDP for 2000?

By definition, the real GDP for 2000 equals 2000 quantities valued at base-year prices. The base year in this example happens to be 2000, so real GDP for 2000 equals 2000 quantities valued at 2000 prices, which is the same as nominal GDP for 2000. In general, in the base year, real GDP and nominal GDP are the same. We already found nominal GDP for 2000, $175, so that is also the real GDP for 2000.

We can now determine how much real production has actually grown over the four-year period. Since real GDP was $175 in 2000 and $350 in 2004, the physical volume of production doubled between 2000 and 2004. This conclusion makes good sense, since Table 18.3 shows that the production of both pizzas and calzones exactly doubled over the period. By using real GDP, we have eliminated the effects of price changes and obtained a reasonable measure of the actual change in physical production over the four-year span.

Of course, the production of all goods will not necessarily grow in equal proportion, as in Example 18.7. Exercise 18.6 asks you to find real GDP when pizza and calzone production grow at different rates.

EXERCISE 18.6

Suppose production and prices of pizza and calzone in 2000 and 2004 are as follows:

	Quantity of pizzas	Price of pizzas	Quantity of calzones	Price of calzones
2000	10	$10	15	$5
2004	30	$12	30	$6

These data are the same as those in Table 18.3, except that pizza production has tripled rather than doubled between 2000 and 2004. Find real GDP in 2004 and 2000, and calculate the growth in real output over the four-year period. (Continue to assume that 2000 is the base year.)

If you complete Exercise 18.6, you will find that the growth in real GDP between 2000 and 2004 reflects a sort of average of the growth in physical production of pizzas and calzones. Real GDP therefore remains a useful measure of overall physical production, even when the production of different goods and services grows at different rates.

The method of calculating real GDP just described was followed for many decades by the Bureau of Economic Analysis (BEA), the U.S. government agency responsible for GDP statistics. However, in recent years the BEA has adopted a more complicated procedure of determining real GDP, called *chain weighting*. The new procedure makes the official real GDP data less sensitive to the particular base year chosen. However, the chain-weighting and traditional approaches share the basic idea of valuing output in terms of base-year prices, and the results obtained by the two methods are generally similar.

 RECAP **NOMINAL GDP VERSUS REAL GDP**

Real GDP is calculated using the prices of goods and services that prevailed in a base year rather than in the current year. Nominal GDP is calculated using current-year prices. Real GDP is GDP adjusted for inflation; it may be thought of as measuring the physical volume of production. Comparisons of economic activity at different times should always be done using real GDP, not nominal GDP.

REAL GDP IS NOT THE SAME AS ECONOMIC WELL-BEING

Government policymakers pay close attention to real GDP, often behaving as if the greater the GDP, the better. However, real GDP is *not* the same as economic well-being. At best, it is an imperfect measure of economic well-being because, for the most part, it captures only those goods and services that are priced and sold in markets. Many factors that contribute to people's economic well-being are not priced and sold in markets and thus are largely or even entirely omitted from GDP. Maximizing real GDP is not, therefore, always the right goal for government policymakers. Whether or not policies that increase GDP will also make people better off has to be determined on a case-by-case basis.

To understand why an increase in real GDP does not always promote economic well-being, let's look at some factors that are not included in GDP but do affect whether people are better off.

LEISURE TIME

Most Americans (and most people in other industrialized countries as well) work many fewer hours than their great-grandparents did 100 years ago. Early in the twentieth century some industrial workers—steelworkers, for example—worked as many as 12 hours a day, 7 days a week. Today, the 40-hour workweek is typical. Today, Americans also tend to start working later in life (after college or graduate school), and, in many cases, they are able to retire earlier. The increased leisure time available to workers in the United States and other industrialized countries—which allows them to pursue many worthwhile activities, including being with family and friends, participating in sports and hobbies, and pursuing cultural and educational activities—is a major benefit of living in a wealthy society. These extra hours of leisure are not priced in markets, however, and therefore are not reflected in GDP.

Why do people work fewer hours today than their great-grandparents did?

Americans start work later in life, retire earlier, and in many cases work fewer hours per week than people of 50 or 100 years ago.

The *opportunity cost* of working less—retiring earlier, for example, or working fewer hours per week—is the earnings you forgo by not working. If you can make $400 per week at a summer job in a department store, for example, then leaving the job two weeks early to take a trip with some friends has an opportunity cost of $800. The fact that people are working fewer hours today suggests that their opportunity cost of forgone earnings is lower than their grandparents' and great-grandparents' opportunity cost. Why this difference?

Over the past century, rapid economic growth in the United States and other industrialized countries has greatly increased the purchasing power of the average worker's wages (see Chapter 21). In other words, the typical worker today can buy more goods and services with his or her hourly earnings than ever before. This fact would seem to suggest that the opportunity cost of forgone earnings (measured in terms of what those earnings can buy) is greater, not smaller, today than in earlier times. But because the buying power of wages is so much higher today than in the past, Americans can achieve a reasonable standard of living by working fewer hours than they did in the past. Thus, while your grandparents may have had to work long hours to pay the rent or put food on the table, today the extra income from working long hours is more likely to buy relative luxuries, like nicer clothes or a fancier car. Because such discretionary purchases are easier to give up than basic food and shelter, the true opportunity cost of forgone earnings is lower today than it was 50 years ago. As the opportunity cost of leisure has fallen, Americans have chosen to enjoy more of it.

NONMARKET ECONOMIC ACTIVITIES

Not all economically important activities are bought and sold in markets; with a few exceptions, such as government services, nonmarket economic activities are omitted from GDP. We mentioned earlier the example of unpaid housekeeping services. Another example is volunteer services, such as the volunteer fire and rescue squads that serve many small towns. The fact that these unpaid services are left out of GDP does *not* mean that they are unimportant. The problem is that,

ECONOMIC
NATURALIST
18.2

because there are no market prices and quantities for unpaid services, estimating their market values is very difficult.

How far do economists go wrong by leaving nonmarket economic activities out of GDP? The answer depends on the type of economy being studied. Although nonmarket economic activities exist in all economies, they are particularly important in poor economies. For example, in rural villages of developing countries, people commonly trade services with each other or cooperate on various tasks without exchanging any money. Families in these communities also tend to be relatively self-sufficient, growing their own food and providing many of their own basic services (recall the many skills of the Nepalese cook Birkhaman, described in Chapter 2). Because such nonmarket economic activities are not counted in official statistics, GDP data may substantially understate the true amount of economic activity in the poorest countries. In 1999, according to the United Nations,[2] the official GDP per person in Nepal was about $218, an amount that seems impossibly low. Part of the explanation for this figure is that because the Nepalese seldom use formal markets, many economic activities that would ordinarily be included in GDP are excluded from it in Nepal.

Closely related to nonmarket activities is what is called the *underground economy*, which includes transactions that are never reported to government officials and data collectors. The underground economy encompasses both legal and illegal activities, from informal babysitting jobs to organized crime. For instance, some people pay temporary or part-time workers like housecleaners and painters in cash, which allows these workers to avoid paying taxes on their income. Economists who have tried to estimate the value of such services by studying how much cash the public holds have concluded that these sorts of transactions are quite important, even in advanced industrial economies.

ENVIRONMENTAL QUALITY AND RESOURCE DEPLETION

China has recently experienced tremendous growth in real GDP. But in expanding its manufacturing base, it has also suffered a severe decline in air and water quality. Increased pollution certainly detracts from the quality of life, but because air and water quality are not bought and sold in markets, the Chinese GDP does not reflect this downside of their economic growth.

The exploitation of finite natural resources also tends to be overlooked in GDP. When an oil company pumps and sells a barrel of oil, GDP increases by the value of the oil. But the fact that there is one less barrel of oil in the ground, waiting to be pumped sometime in the future, is not reflected in GDP.

A number of efforts have been made to incorporate factors like air quality and resource depletion into a comprehensive measure of GDP. Doing so is difficult, since it often involves placing a dollar value on intangibles, like having a clean river to swim in instead of a dirty one. But the fact that the benefits of environmental quality and resource conservation are hard to measure in dollars and cents does not mean that they are unimportant.

QUALITY OF LIFE

What makes a particular town or city an attractive place in which to live? Some desirable features you might think of are reflected in GDP: spacious, well-constructed homes, good restaurants and stores, a variety of entertainment, and high-quality medical services. However, other indicators of the good life are not sold in markets and so may be omitted from GDP. Examples include a low crime rate, minimal traffic congestion, active civic organizations, and open space. Thus

[2]See p. 446 for *first* footnote.

citizens of a rural area may be justified in opposing the construction of a new shopping center because of its presumed negative effect on the quality of life—even though the new center may increase GDP.

POVERTY AND ECONOMIC INEQUALITY

GDP measures the *total* quantity of goods and services produced and sold in an economy, but it conveys no information about who gets to enjoy those goods and services. Two countries may have identical GDPs but differ radically in the distribution of economic welfare across the population. Suppose, for example, that in one country—call it Equalia—most people have a comfortable middle-class existence; both extreme poverty and extreme wealth are rare. But in another country, Inequalia—which has the same real GDP as Equalia—a few wealthy families control the economy, and the majority of the population lives in poverty. While most people would say that Equalia has a better economic situation overall, that judgment would not be reflected in the GDPs of the two countries, which are the same.

In the United States absolute poverty has been declining. Today, many families whose income is below today's official "poverty line" (in 2001, $17,960 for a family of four) own a television, a car, and in some cases their own home. Some economists have argued that people who are considered poor today live as well as many middle-class people did in the 1950s.

But, though absolute poverty seems to be decreasing in the United States, inequality of income has generally been rising. The chief executive officer of a large U.S. corporation may earn hundreds of times what the typical worker in the same firm receives. Psychologists tell us that people's economic satisfaction depends not only on their absolute economic position—the quantity and quality of food, clothing, and shelter they have—but on what they have compared to what others have. If you own an old, beat-up car but are the only person in your neighborhood to have a car, you may feel privileged. But if everyone else in the neighborhood owns a luxury car, you are likely to be less satisfied. To the extent that such comparisons affect people's well-being, inequality matters as well as absolute poverty. Again, because GDP focuses on total production rather than on the distribution of output, it does not capture the effects of inequality.

BUT GDP IS RELATED TO ECONOMIC WELL-BEING

You might conclude from the list of important factors omitted from the official figures that GDP is useless as a measure of economic welfare. Indeed, numerous critics have made that claim. Clearly, in evaluating the effects of a proposed economic policy, considering only the likely effects on GDP is not sufficient. Planners must also ask whether the policy will affect aspects of economic well-being that are not captured in GDP. Environmental regulations may reduce production of steel, for example, which reduces the GDP. But that fact is not a sufficient basis on which to decide whether such regulations are good or bad. The right way to decide such questions is to apply the *cost-benefit principle* (see Chapter 1). Are the benefits of cleaner air worth more to people than the costs the regulations impose in terms of lost output and lost jobs? If so, then the regulations should be adopted; otherwise, they should not.

Although looking at the effects of a proposed policy on real GDP is not a good enough basis on which to evaluate a policy, real GDP per person *does* tend to be positively associated with many things people value, including a high material standard of living, better health and life expectancies, and better education. We discuss next some of the ways in which a higher real GDP implies greater economic well-being.

AVAILABILITY OF GOODS AND SERVICES

Obviously, citizens of a country with a high GDP are likely to possess more and better goods and services (after all, that is what GDP measures). On average, people in high-GDP countries enjoy larger, better-constructed, and more comfortable homes, higher-quality food and clothing, a greater variety of entertainment and cultural opportunities, better access to transportation and travel, better communications and sanitation, and other advantages. While social commentators may question the value of material consumption—and we agree that riches do not necessarily bring happiness or peace of mind—the majority of people in the world place great importance on achieving material prosperity. Throughout history people have made tremendous sacrifices and taken great risks to secure a higher standard of living for themselves and their families. In fact, to a great extent the United States was built by people who were willing to leave their native lands, often at great personal hardship, in hopes of bettering their economic condition.

HEALTH AND EDUCATION

Beyond an abundance of consumer goods, a high GDP brings other more basic advantages. Table 18.4 shows the differences between rich and poor countries with regard to some important indicators of well-being, including life

TABLE 18.4
GDP and Basic Indicators of Well-Being

Indicator	All developing countries	Least developed countries	Industrialized countries
GDP per person (U.S. dollars)	3,530	1,170	25,860
Life expectancy at birth (years)	64.5	51.7	78.0
Infant mortality rate (per 1,000 live births)	61	100	6
Under-5 mortality rate (per 1,000 live births)	89	159	6
Doctors (per 100,000 people)	78	30	252
Incidence of HIV/AIDS (% in 15–49 age group)	1.3	4.3	0.3
Undernourished people (%)	18	38	Negligible
Primary enrollment rate (as % of age group)	85.7	60.4	99.9
Secondary enrollment rate (as % of age group)	60.4	31.2	96.2
Adult literacy rate (%)	72.9	51.7	98.6

SOURCE: United Nations, *Human Development Report*, 2000–2001, available at http://hdr.undp.org/. All data are for 1999, except doctors per 100,000 people (1992–1995), undernourished people (1996–1998), and enrollment rates (1997). GDP data are adjusted to account for local differences in prices of basic commodities and services (adjusted for purchasing power parity).

expectancy, infant and child mortality rates, number of doctors, measures of nutrition, and educational opportunity. Three groups of countries are compared: (1) developing countries as a group (total population, 4.6 billion); (2) the least developed countries (25 countries with a total population of about 600 million); and (3) the industrialized countries (25 countries, including the United States, Canada, the western European countries, and Japan, with a total population of 850 million). As the first row of Table 18.4 shows, these three groups of countries have radically different levels of GDP per person. Most notably, GDP per person in the industrialized countries is more than 20 times that of the least developed countries.[3]

How do these large differences in GDP relate to other measures of well-being? Table 18.4 shows that on some of the most basic measures of human welfare, the developing countries fare much worse than the industrial countries. A child born in one of the least developed countries has a 10 percent (100/1,000) chance of dying before its first birthday and about a 16 percent (159/1,000) chance of dying before its fifth birthday. The corresponding figures for the industrialized countries are 0.6 percent (6/1,000) and 0.6 percent (6/1,000), respectively. A child born in an industrialized country has a life expectancy of about 78 years, compared to about 52 years for a child born in one of the least developed countries. Superior nutrition, sanitation, and medical services in the richer countries account for these large discrepancies in basic welfare. For treatment of the sick, industrialized countries have about 252 doctors per 100,000 people, compared to 30 doctors per 100,000 people in the least-developed countries. Doctors in the poorest countries, despite their fewer numbers, must contend with much higher rates of illness. For example, the incidence of HIV/AIDS in the least developed countries is 4.3 percent of the population aged 15–49, about 14 times the rate in industrialized countries.

© Bettmann/Corbis

A child born in one of the least developed countries has a 16 percent chance of dying before its fifth birthday.

On another important dimension of human well-being, literacy and education rates, high-GDP countries also have the advantage. As Table 18.4 shows, in the industrialized countries the percentage of adults who can read and write exceeds 98 percent, almost twice the percentage (52 percent) in the poorest developing countries. The percentage of children of primary-school age who are enrolled in school is virtually 100 percent in industrialized countries, compared to about 60 percent in the least developed countries. At the secondary (high school) level the difference is even greater, with about 96 percent of children enrolled in industrialized countries and 31 percent enrolled in the poorest countries. Furthermore, enrollment rates do not capture important differences in the quality of education available in rich and poor countries, as measured by indicators such as the educational backgrounds of teachers and student–teacher ratios. Once again, the average person in an industrialized country seems to be better off than the average person in a poor developing country.

Why do far fewer children complete high school in poor countries than in rich countries?

One possible explanation is that people in poor countries place a lower priority on getting an education than people in rich countries. But immigrants from poor countries often put a heavy emphasis on education—though it may be that people who emigrate from poor countries are unrepresentative of the population as a whole.

An economic naturalist's explanation for the lower schooling rates in poor countries would rely not on cultural differences but on differences in *opportunity*

ECONOMIC NATURALIST 18.3

---

[3]The GDP data in Table 18.4 use U.S. prices to value goods and services in developing nations. Since basic goods and services tend to be cheaper in poor countries, this adjustment significantly increases measured GDP in those countries.

cost. In poor societies, most of which are heavily agricultural, children are an important source of labor. Beyond a certain age, sending children to school imposes a high opportunity cost on the family. Children who are in school are not available to help with planting, harvesting, and other tasks that must be done if the family is to survive. In addition, the cost of books and school supplies imposes a major hardship on poor families. In rich, nonagricultural countries, school-age children have few work opportunities, and their potential earnings are small relative to other sources of family income. The low opportunity cost of sending children to school in rich countries is an important reason for the higher enrollment rates in those countries.

In Chapter 20 we will discuss the costs and benefits of economic growth—which in practice means growth in real GDP per person—in greater depth. In that context we will return to the question of whether a growing real GDP is necessarily equated with greater economic well-being.

◉ RECAP   **REAL GDP AND ECONOMIC WELL-BEING**

Real GDP is at best an imperfect measure of economic well-being. Among the factors affecting well-being omitted from real GDP are the availability of leisure time, nonmarket services such as unpaid homemaking and volunteer services, environmental quality and resource conservation, and quality-of-life indicators such as a low crime rate. The GDP also does not reflect the degree of economic inequality in a country. Because real GDP is not the same as economic well-being, proposed policies should not be evaluated strictly in terms of whether or not they increase the GDP.

Although GDP is not the same as economic well-being, it is positively associated with many things that people value, including a higher material standard of living, better health, longer life expectancies, and higher rates of literacy and educational attainment. This relationship between real GDP and economic well-being has led many people to emigrate from poor nations in search of a better life and has motivated policymakers in developing countries to try to increase their nations' rates of economic growth.

THE UNEMPLOYMENT RATE

In assessing the level of economic activity in a country, economists look at a variety of statistics. Besides real GDP, one statistic that receives a great deal of attention, both from economists and from the general public, is the rate of unemployment. The unemployment rate is a sensitive indicator of conditions in the labor market. When the unemployment rate is low, jobs are secure and relatively easier to find. Low unemployment is often associated with improving wages and working conditions as well, as employers compete to attract and retain workers.

We will discuss labor markets and unemployment in detail in Chapter 21. This chapter will explain how the unemployment rate and some related statistics are defined and measured. It will close with a discussion of the costs of unemployment, both to the unemployed and to the economy as a whole.

MEASURING UNEMPLOYMENT

In the United States, defining and measuring unemployment is the responsibility of the Bureau of Labor Statistics, or BLS. Each month the BLS surveys about

60,000 randomly selected households. Each person in those households who is 16 years or older is placed in one of three categories:

1. *Employed.* A person is employed if he or she worked full-time or part-time (even for a few hours) during the past week or is on vacation or sick leave from a regular job.

2. *Unemployed.* A person is unemployed if he or she did not work during the preceding week but made some effort to find work (for example, by going to a job interview) in the past four weeks.

3. *Out of the labor force.* A person is considered to be out of the labor force if he or she did not work in the past week and did not look for work in the past four weeks. In other words, people who are neither employed nor unemployed (in the sense of looking for work but not being able to find it) are "out of the labor force." Full-time students, unpaid homemakers, retirees, and people unable to work because of disabilities are examples of people who are out of the labor force.

Based on the results of the survey, the BLS estimates how many people in the whole country fit into each of the three categories.

To find the unemployment rate, the BLS must first calculate the size of the *labor force*. The **labor force** is defined as the total number of employed and unemployed people in the economy (the first two categories of respondents to the BLS survey). The **unemployment rate** is then defined as the number of unemployed people divided by the labor force. Notice that people who are out of the labor force (because they are in school, have retired, or are disabled, for example) are not counted as unemployed and thus do not affect the unemployment rate. In general, a high rate of unemployment indicates that the economy is performing poorly.

Another useful statistic is the **participation rate,** or the percentage of the working-age population in the labor force (that is, the percentage that is either employed or looking for work). Figure 18.1 showed participation rates for American women and men since 1960. The participation rate is calculated by dividing the labor force by the working-age (16+) population.

Table 18.5 illustrates the calculation of key labor market statistics, using data based on the BLS survey for July 2002. In that month unemployment was 5.9 percent of the labor force. The participation rate was 66.5 percent; that is, about two out of every three adults had a job or were looking for work. Figure 18.3 shows the U.S. unemployment rate since 1960. Unemployment rates were exceptionally

labor force the total number of employed and unemployed people in the economy

unemployment rate the number of unemployed people divided by the labor force

participation rate the percentage of the working-age population in the labor force (that is, the percentage that is either employed or looking for work)

TABLE 18.5
U.S. Employment Data, July 2002 (in millions)

Employed	134.04
Plus:	
Unemployed	8.35
Equals: Labor force	142.39
Plus:	
Not in labor force	71.63
Equals:	
Working-age (over 16) population	214.02
Unemployment rate = unemployed/labor force = 8.35/142.39 = 5.9%	
Participation rate = labor force/working-age population = 142.39/214.02 = 66.5%	

SOURCE: Bureau of Labor Statistics (http://stats.bls.gov).

FIGURE 18.3

The U.S. Unemployment Rate since 1960.

The unemployment rate— the fraction of the U.S. labor force that is unemployed—was just above 4 percent in the late 1990s, the lowest recorded rate since the latter part of the 1960s. Unemployment rose to about 6 percent in 2002 due to a recession.

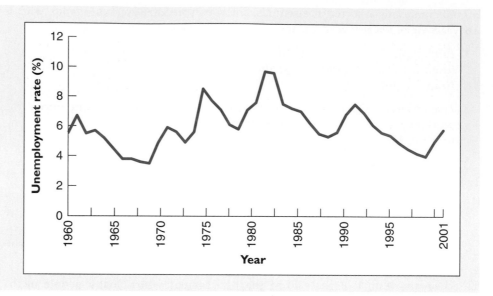

low—just above 4 percent—in the late 1960s and the late 1990s. By this measure, the latter part of the 1990s was an exceptionally good time for American workers. However, unemployment rose in 2001–2002 as the nation fell into recession.

EXERCISE 18.7

Following are July 2002 BLS U.S. employment data for African-Americans.

Employed	14.976 million
Unemployed	1.642 million
Not in the labor force	9.343 million

Find the labor force, the working-age population, the unemployment rate, and the participation rate for African-Americans and compare your results to those in Table 18.5.

THE COSTS OF UNEMPLOYMENT

Unemployment imposes *economic, psychological,* and *social* costs on a nation. From an economic perspective, the main cost of unemployment is the output that is lost because the workforce is not fully utilized. Much of the burden of the reduced output is borne by the unemployed themselves, whose incomes fall when they are not working and whose skills may deteriorate from lack of use. However, society at large also bears part of the economic cost of unemployment. For example, workers who become unemployed are liable to stop paying taxes and start receiving government support payments, such as unemployment benefits. This net drain on the government's budget is a cost to all taxpayers.

The *psychological* costs of unemployment are felt primarily by unemployed workers and their families. Studies show that lengthy periods of unemployment can lead to a loss of self-esteem, feelings of loss of control over one's life, depression, and even suicidal behavior.[4] The unemployed worker's family is likely to feel increased psychological stress, compounded by the economic difficulties created by the loss of income.

[4]For a survey of the literature on the psychological effects of unemployment, see William Darity Jr., and Arthur H. Goldsmith, "Social Psychology, Unemployment and Macroeconomics," *Journal of Economic Perspectives,* 10:121–140, Winter 1996.

The *social* costs of unemployment are a result of the economic and psychological effects. People who have been unemployed for a while tend not only to face severe financial difficulties but also to feel anger, frustration, and despair. Not surprisingly, increases in unemployment tend to be associated with increases in crime, domestic violence, alcoholism, drug abuse, and other social problems. The costs created by these problems are borne not only by the unemployed but by society in general, as more public resources must be spent to counteract these problems—for example, by hiring more police to control crime.

THE DURATION OF UNEMPLOYMENT

In assessing the impact of unemployment on jobless people, economists must know how long individual workers have been without work. Generally, the longer a person has been out of work, the more severe are the economic and psychological costs that person will face. People who are unemployed for only a few weeks, for example, are not likely to suffer a serious reduction in their standard of living, since for a short period they can draw upon their savings and perhaps on government benefits. Nor would we expect someone who is unemployed for only a short time to experience psychological problems such as depression or loss of self-esteem, at least not to the same extent as someone who has been out of work for months or years.

In its surveys, therefore, the BLS asks respondents how long they have been unemployed. A period during which an individual is continuously unemployed is called an **unemployment spell;** it begins when the worker becomes unemployed and ends when the worker either finds a job or leaves the labor force. (Remember, people outside the labor force are not counted as unemployed.) The length of an unemployment spell is called its **duration.** The duration of unemployment rises during recessions, reflecting the greater difficulty of finding work during those periods.

unemployment spell a period during which an individual is continuously unemployed

duration the length of an unemployment spell

At any given time a substantial fraction of unemployed workers has been unemployed for six months or more; we will refer to this group as the *long-term unemployed*. Long-term unemployment creates the highest economic, psychological, and social costs, both for the unemployed themselves and for society as a whole.

Although long-term unemployment is a serious problem, many unemployment spells are quite short. For example, in July 2002, despite a weak labor market, nearly 35 percent of the unemployed had been out of work for just 5 weeks or less, and another 30 percent had been unemployed for 5 to 14 weeks. In other words, only about 35 percent of the unemployed had been without a job for as long as 14 weeks (about 3 months). These statistics are a bit deceptive, however, because short unemployment spells can arise from two very different patterns of labor-market experience. Some people have short unemployment spells that end in their finding a stable long-term job. For the most part, these workers, whom we will refer to as the *short-term unemployed*, do not bear a high cost of unemployment. But other workers have short unemployment spells that typically end either in their withdrawal from the labor force or in a short-term or temporary job that soon leaves the worker unemployed again. Workers whose unemployment spells are broken up by brief periods of employment or withdrawal from the labor force are referred to as the *chronically unemployed*. In terms of the costs of unemployment, the experience of these workers is similar to that of the long-term unemployed.

THE UNEMPLOYMENT RATE VERSUS "TRUE" UNEMPLOYMENT

Like GDP measurement, unemployment measurement has its critics. Most of them argue that the official unemployment rate understates the true extent of unemployment. They point in particular to two groups of people who are not counted among the unemployed: so-called *discouraged workers* and *involuntary part-time workers*.

discouraged workers people who say they would like to have a job but have not made an effort to find one in the past four weeks

Discouraged workers are people who say they would like to have a job but have not made an effort to find one in the past four weeks. Often, discouraged workers tell the survey takers that they have not searched for work because they have tried without success in the past, or because they are convinced that labor-market conditions are such that they will not be able to find a job. Because they have not sought work in the past four weeks, discouraged workers are counted as being out of the labor force rather than unemployed. Some observers have suggested that treating discouraged workers as unemployed would provide a more accurate picture of the labor market.

Involuntary part-time workers are people who say they would like to work full-time but are able to find only part-time work. Because they do have jobs, involuntary part-time workers are counted as employed rather than unemployed. Some economists have suggested that these workers should be counted as partially unemployed.

In response to these criticisms, in recent years the BLS has released special unemployment rates that include estimates of the number of discouraged workers and involuntary part-time workers. In July 2002, when the official unemployment rate was 5.9 percent (see Table 18.5), the BLS calculated that if both discouraged workers and involuntary part-time workers were counted as unemployed, the unemployment rate would have been 9.4 percent. So the problem of discouraged and underemployed workers appears to be fairly significant.

Whether in an official or adjusted version, the unemployment rate is a good overall indicator of labor-market conditions. A high unemployment rate tends to be bad news even for those people who are employed, since raises and promotions are hard to come by in a "slack" labor market. We will discuss the causes and cures of unemployment at some length in Chapter 21 and subsequent chapters.

▪ SUMMARY ▪

- The basic measure of an economy's output is *gross domestic product (GDP)*, the market value of the final goods and services produced in a country during a given period. Expressing output in terms of market values allows economists to aggregate the millions of goods and services produced in a modern economy.

- Only *final goods and services* (which include *capital goods*) are counted in GDP, since they are the only goods and services that directly benefit final users. *Intermediate goods and services*, which are used up in the production of final goods and services, are not counted in GDP, nor are sales of existing assets, such as a 20-year-old house. Summing the value added by each firm in the production process is a useful method of determining the value of final goods and services.

- GDP can also be expressed as the sum of four types of expenditure: *consumption, investment, government purchases,* and *net exports.* These four types of expenditure correspond to the spending of households, firms, the government, and the foreign sector, respectively.

- To compare levels of GDP over time, economists must eliminate the effects of inflation. They do so by measuring the market value of goods and services in terms of the prices in a base year. GDP measured in this way is called *real GDP*, while GDP measured in terms of current-year prices is

called *nominal GDP.* Real GDP should always be used in making comparisons of economic activity over time.

- Real GDP per person is an imperfect measure of economic well-being. With a few exceptions, notably government purchases of goods and services (which are included in GDP at their cost of production), GDP includes only those goods and services sold in markets. It excludes important factors that affect people's well-being, such as the amount of leisure time available to them, the value of unpaid or volunteer services, the quality of the environment, quality of life indicators such as the crime rate, and the degree of economic inequality.

- Real GDP is still a useful indicator of economic well-being, however. Countries with a high real GDP per person not only enjoy high average standards of living; they also tend to have higher life expectancies, low rates of infant and child mortality, and high rates of school enrollment and literacy.

- The unemployment rate, perhaps the best-known indicator of the state of the labor market, is based on surveys conducted by the Bureau of Labor Statistics. The surveys classify all respondents over age 16 as employed, unemployed, or not in the labor force. The *labor force* is the sum of employed and unemployed workers—that is, people who have a job or are looking for one. The *unemployment rate* is calculated as the number of unemployed workers divided by the labor force. The *participation rate* is the percentage of the working-age population that is in the labor force.

- The costs of unemployment include the economic cost of lost output, the psychological costs borne by unemployed workers and their families, and the social costs associated with problems like increased crime and violence. The greatest costs are imposed by long *unemployment spells* (periods of unemployment). Critics of the official unemployment rate argue that it understates "true" unemployment by excluding *discouraged workers* and involuntary part-time workers.

▪ KEY TERMS ▪

capital good (450)
consumption expenditure (454)
discouraged workers (470)
duration (of an unemployment spell) (469)
final goods or services (450)

government purchases (455)
gross domestic product (GDP) (447)
intermediate goods or services (450)
investment (454)
labor force (467)
net exports (455)

nominal GDP (459)
participation rate (467)
real GDP (459)
unemployment rate (467)
unemployment spell (469)
value added (451)

▪ REVIEW QUESTIONS ▪

1. Why do economists use market values when calculating GDP? What is the economic rationale for giving high-value items more weight in GDP than low-value items?

2. A large part of the agricultural sector in developing countries is subsistence farming, in which much of the food that is produced is consumed by the farmer and the farmer's family. Discuss the implications of this fact for the measurement of GDP in poor countries.

3. Give examples of each of the four types of aggregate expenditure. Which of the four represents the largest share of GDP in the United States? Can an expenditure component be negative? Explain.

4. Al's Shoeshine Stand shined 1,000 pairs of shoes last year and 1,200 pairs this year. He charged $4 for a shine last

year and $5 this year. If last year is taken as the base year, find Al's contribution to both nominal GDP and real GDP in both years. Which measure would be better to use if you were trying to measure the change in Al's productivity over the past year? Why?

5. Would you say that real GDP per person is a useful measure of economic well-being? Defend your answer.

6. True or false: A high participation rate in an economy implies a low unemployment rate. Explain.

7. What are the costs of a high unemployment rate? Do you think providing more generous government benefits to the unemployed would increase these costs, reduce these costs, or leave them unchanged? Discuss.

▪ PROBLEMS ▪

1. George and Al, stranded on an island, use clamshells for money. Last year George caught 300 fish and 5 wild boars. Al grew 200 bunches of bananas. In the two-person economy that George and Al set up, fish sell for 1 clamshell each, boars sell for 10 clamshells each, and bananas go for 5 clamshells a bunch. George paid Al a total of 30 clamshells for helping him to dig bait for fishing, and he also purchased five of Al's mature banana trees for 30 clamshells each. What is the GDP of George's and Al's island in terms of clamshells?

2. How would each of the following transactions affect the GDP of the United States?
   a. The U.S. government pays $1 billion in salaries for government workers.
   b. The U.S. government pays $1 billion to Social Security recipients.
   c. The U.S. government pays a U.S. firm $1 billion for newly produced airplane parts.
   d. The U.S. government pays $1 billion in interest to holders of U.S. government bonds.
   e. The U.S. government pays $1 billion to Saudi Arabia for crude oil to add to U.S. official oil reserves.

3. Intelligence Incorporated produces 100 computer chips and sells them for $200 each to Bell Computers. Using the chips and other labor and materials, Bell produces 100 personal computers. Bell sells the computers, bundled with software that Bell licenses from Macrosoft at $50 per computer, to PC Charlie's for $800 each. PC Charlie's sells the computers to the public for $1,000 each. Calculate the total contribution to GDP using the value-added method. Do you get the same answer by summing up the market values of final goods and services?

4. For each of the following transactions, state the effect both on U.S. GDP and on the four components of aggregate expenditure.
   a. Your mother-in-law buys a new car from a U.S. producer.
   b. Your mother-in-law buys a new car imported from Sweden.
   c. Your mother-in-law's car rental business buys a new car from a U.S. producer.
   d. Your mother-in-law's car rental business buys a new car imported from Sweden.
   e. The U.S. government buys a new, domestically produced car for the use of your mother-in-law, who has been appointed the ambassador to Sweden.

5. Here are some data for an economy. Find its GDP. Explain your calculation.

Consumption expenditures	$600
Exports	75
Government purchases of goods and services	200
Construction of new homes and apartments	100
Sales of existing homes and apartments	200
Imports	50
Beginning-of-year inventory stocks	100
End-of-year inventory stocks	125
Business fixed investment	100
Government payments to retirees	100
Household purchases of durable goods	150

6. The nation of Potchatoonie produces hockey pucks, cases of root beer, and back rubs. Here are data on prices and quantities of the three goods in the years 2000 and 2005.

Year	Pucks Quantity	Pucks Price	Root beer Quantity	Root beer Price	Back rubs Quantity	Back rubs Price
2000	100	$5	300	$20	100	$20
2005	125	$7	250	$20	110	$25

Assume that 2000 is the base year. Find nominal GDP and real GDP for both years.

7. The government is considering a policy to reduce air pollution by restricting the use of "dirty" fuels by factories. In deciding whether to implement the policy, how, if at all, should the likely effects of the policy on real GDP be taken into account? Discuss.

8. Here is a report from a not-very-efficient BLS survey taker: "There were 65 people in the houses I visited, 10 of them children under 16 and 10 retired; 25 people had full-time jobs, and 5 had part-time jobs. There were 5 full-time homemakers, 5 full-time students over age 16, and 2 people who were disabled and cannot work. The remaining people did not have jobs but all said they would like one. One of these people had not looked actively for work for 3 months, however."

   Find the labor force, the unemployment rate, and the participation rate implied by the survey taker's report.

9. Ellen is downloading labor market data for the most recent month, but her connection is slow and so far this is all she has been able to get:

Unemployment rate	5.0%
Participation rate	62.5%
Not in the labor force	60 million

Find the labor force, the working-age population, the number of employed workers, and the number of unemployed workers.

10. The towns of Sawyer and Thatcher each have a labor force of 1,200 people. In Sawyer, 100 people were unemployed for the entire year, while the rest of the labor force was employed continuously. In Thatcher every member of the labor force was unemployed for 1 month and employed for 11 months.
    a. What is the average unemployment rate over the year in each of the two towns?
    b. What is the average duration of unemployment spells in each of the two towns?
    c. In which town do you think the costs of unemployment are higher? Explain.

▪ ANSWERS TO IN-CHAPTER EXERCISES ▪

18.1 In the text, GDP was calculated to be $64.00. If in addition Orchardia produces 5 oranges at $0.30 each, GDP is increased by $1.50 to $65.50.

18.2 Plants owned by U.S. companies produced a total of 1,185,000 vehicles, or 4.09 times the 290,000 vehicles produced by foreign-owned plants. In market value terms, with passenger cars valued at $17,000 and other light vehicles at $25,000, plants owned by U.S. companies produced $(471,000 \times \$17,000) + (714,000 \times \$25,000)$, = $25,857,000 worth of vehicles. Foreign-owned plants produced $(227,000 \times \$17,000) + (63,000 \times \$25,000) = \$5,434,000$ worth of vehicles. In market value terms U.S.-owned plants outproduced the foreign-owned plants by a ratio of 4.76 to 1. The U.S. producers have a greater advantage when output is compared in market value terms instead of in terms of number of vehicles because the U.S. companies produce relatively more of the higher-value types of vehicles than the foreign companies do.

18.3 The value added of the wholesale distributor together with the ultimate producers of the cards is $500. Amy's value added—her revenue less her payments to other firms—is $200. Since the cards were produced and purchased by Amy during the year 2002 (we assume), the $500 counts toward year 2001 GDP. The $200 in value added originating in Amy's card shop counts in year 2003 GDP, since Amy actually sold the cards in that year.

18.4 The sale of stock represents a transfer of ownership of part of the assets of Benson Buggywhip, not the production of new goods or services. Hence the stock sale itself does not contribute to GDP. However, the broker's commission of $100 (2 percent of the stock sale proceeds) represents payment for a current service and is counted in GDP.

18.5 As in Example 18.6, the market value of domestic production is 1,000,000 autos times $15,000 per auto, or $15 billion.

Also as in Example 18.6, consumption is $10.5 billion and government purchases are $0.75 billion. However, because 25,000 of the autos that are purchased are imported rather than domestic, the domestic producers have unsold inventories at the end of the year of 50,000 (rather than 25,000 as in Example 18.6). Thus inventory investment is 50,000 autos times $15,000, or $0.75 billion, and total investment (autos purchased by businesses plus inventory investment) is $3.75 billion. Since exports and imports are equal (both are 25,000 autos), net exports (equal to exports minus imports) are zero. Notice that since we subtract imports to get net exports, it is unnecessary also to subtract imports from consumption. Consumption is defined as total purchases by households, not just purchases of domestically produced goods.

Total expenditure is $C + I + G + NX = \$10.5$ billion + $3.75 billion + $0.75 billion + 0 = $15 billion, the same as the market value of production.

18.6 Real GDP in the year 2004 equals the quantities of pizzas and calzones produced in the year 2004, valued at the market prices that prevailed in the base year 2000. So real GDP in 2004 = (30 pizzas × $10/pizza) + (30 calzones × $5/calzone) = $450.

Real GDP in 2000 equals the quantities of pizzas and calzones produced in 2000, valued at 2000 prices, which is $175. Notice that since 2000 is the base year, real GDP and nominal GDP are the same for that year.

The real GDP in the year 2004 is $450/$175, or about 2.6 times what it was in 2000. Hence the expansion of real GDP lies between the threefold increase in pizza production and the doubling in calzone production that occurred between 2000 and 2004.

18.7
$$\text{Labor force} = \text{Employed} + \text{Unemployed}$$
$$= 14.976 \text{ million} + 1.642 \text{ million} = 16.618 \text{ million}$$
$$\text{Working-age population} = \text{Labor force} + \text{Not in labor force}$$
$$= 16.618 \text{ million} + 9.343 \text{ million} = 25.961 \text{ million}$$
$$\text{Unemployment rate} = \frac{\text{Unemployed}}{\text{Labor force}}$$
$$= \frac{1.642 \text{ million}}{16.618 \text{ million}} = 9.9\%$$
$$\text{Participation rate} = \frac{\text{Labor force}}{\text{Working-age population}}$$
$$= \frac{16.618 \text{ million}}{25.961 \text{ million}} = 64.0\%$$

In 2002 African-Americans represented between 10% and 11% of the U.S. labor force and approximately 12% of the working-age population. Note that while the participation rate for African-Americans is similar to that of the overall population the unemployment rate for African-Americans is substantially higher.

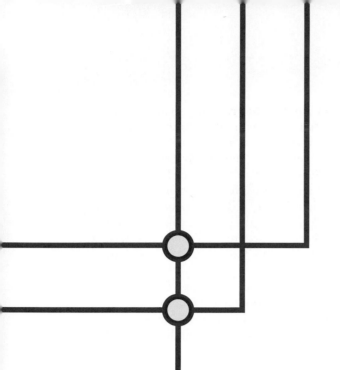

MEASURING THE PRICE LEVEL AND INFLATION

■

There is a story about a Wall Street investor, call her Lotta Doe, who was the first volunteer for an experiment in suspended animation. A team of scientists put Lotta into a deep sleep. Thirty years later she awoke, not having aged a day. Lotta's first action upon awakening was to run to a pay phone to call her broker. When the now-aged broker picked up the phone, Lotta asked how much her portfolio of financial investments, left to grow these 30 years, was now worth. "As of this morning," the broker replied, "your net worth is approximately $100 million."

Lotta was, of course, thrilled with this news. But at that moment the operator's voice broke into the call, and Lotta heard, "Please deposit $5 million for the next 3 minutes."

The story illustrates a simple but very important point, which is that the value of money depends entirely on the prices of the goods and services one wants to buy. A $100 million nest egg is a substantial fortune at the prices prevailing in the United States today, but it is only a pittance if a phone call costs $5 million. Likewise, high and sustained inflation—a rapid and ongoing increase in the prices of most goods and services—can radically reduce the buying power of a given amount of money. Apparently, there had been quite a lot of inflation during the 30 years Lotta Doe was in suspended animation.

Inflation can make a comparison of economic conditions at different points in time quite difficult. We remember being able to buy both a comic book and a chocolate sundae for a quarter. Today the same two items might cost $4 or $5. You might conclude from this fact that kids were much better off in "the good old days," but were they really? Without more information, we can't tell, for though the prices of comic books and sundaes have gone up, so have allowances. The real question is whether young people's spending money has increased as much as or more than the prices of the things they want to buy. If so, then they are no worse off today than we were when we were young and candy bars cost a nickel.

Inflation also creates uncertainty when we try to look into the future, to ask questions such as, "How much should I plan to save for retirement?" The answer to this question depends on how much inflation is likely to occur before one retires (and thus how much heating oil, food, and clothing will cost). Inflation can pose similar problems for policymakers. For example, to plan long-term government spending programs they must estimate how much the government's purchases will cost several years in the future.

An important benefit of studying macroeconomics is learning how to avoid the confusion inflation interjects into comparisons of economic conditions over time or projections for the future. In this chapter, a continuation of our study of the construction and interpretation of economic data, we will see how both prices and inflation are measured and how dollar amounts, such as the price of a comic book, can be "adjusted" to eliminate the effects of inflation. Quantities that are measured in dollars (or other currency units) and then adjusted for inflation are called *real* quantities (recall, for example, the concept of real GDP in Chapter 18). By working with real quantities, economists can avoid the kind of confusion that beset Lotta Doe.

More important than the complications inflation creates for economic measurement are the costs that it imposes on the economy. In this chapter we will see why high inflation can significantly impair an economy's performance, to the extent that economic policymakers claim a low and stable rate of inflation as one of their chief objectives. We will conclude the chapter by showing how inflation is linked to another key economic variable, the rate of interest on financial assets.

THE CONSUMER PRICE INDEX: MEASURING THE PRICE LEVEL

consumer price index (CPI) for any period, measures the cost in that period of a standard basket of goods and services relative to the cost of the same basket of goods and services in a fixed year, called the *base year*

The basic tool economists use to measure the price level and inflation in the U.S. economy is the *consumer price index*, or CPI for short. The CPI is a measure of the "cost of living" during a particular period. Specifically, the **consumer price index (CPI)** for any period measures the cost in that period of a standard set, or basket, of goods and services *relative* to the cost of the same basket of goods and services in a fixed year, called the *base year*.

To illustrate how the CPI is constructed, suppose the government has designated 1995 as the base year. Assume for the sake of simplicity that in 1995 a typical American family's monthly household budget consisted of spending on just three items: rent on a two-bedroom apartment, hamburgers, and movie tickets. In reality, of course, families purchase hundreds of different items each month, but the basic principles of constructing the CPI are the same no matter how many items are included. Suppose too that the family's average monthly expenditures in 1995, the base year, were as shown in Table 19.1.

TABLE 19.1
Monthly Household Budget of the Typical Family in 1995 (Base Year)

Item	Cost (in 1995)
Rent, two-bedroom apartment	$500
Hamburgers (60 at $2.00 each)	120
Movie tickets (10 at $6.00 each)	60
Total expenditure	$680

Now let's fast-forward to the year 2000. Over that period, the prices of various goods and services are likely to have changed; some will have risen and some fallen. Let's suppose that by the year 2000 the rent that our family pays for their two-bedroom apartment has risen to $630. Hamburgers now cost $2.50 each, and the price of movie tickets has risen to $7.00 each. So, in general, prices have been rising.

By how much did the family's cost of living increase between 1995 and 2000? Table 19.2 shows that if the typical family wanted to consume the *same basket of goods and services* in the year 2000 as they did in the year 1995, they would have to spend $850 per month, or $170 more than the $680 per month they spent in 1995. In other words, to live the same way in the year 2000 as they did in the year 1995, the family would have to spend 25 percent more ($170/$680) each month. So, in this example, the cost of living for the typical family rose 25 percent between 1995 and 2000.

TABLE 19.2
Cost of Reproducing the 1995 (Base-Year) Basket of Goods and Services in Year 2000

Item	Cost (in 2000)	Cost (in 1995)
Rent, two-bedroom apartment	$630	$500
Hamburgers (60 at $2.50 each)	150	120
Movie tickets (10 at $7.00 each)	70	60
Total expenditure	$850	$680

The government—actually, the Bureau of Labor Statistics (BLS), the same agency that is responsible for determining the unemployment rate—calculates the official consumer price index (CPI) using essentially the same method. The first step in deriving the CPI is to pick a base year and determine the basket of goods and services that were consumed by the typical family during that year. In practice, the government learns how consumers allocate their spending through a detailed survey, called the Consumer Expenditure Survey, in which randomly selected families record every purchase they make and the price they paid over a given month. (Quite a task!) Let's call the basket of goods and services that results the *base-year basket*. Then, each month BLS employees visit thousands of stores and conduct numerous interviews to determine the current prices of the goods and services in the base-year basket. The CPI in any given year is computed using this formula:

$$\text{CPI} = \frac{\text{Cost of base-year basket of goods and services in current year}}{\text{Cost of base-year basket of goods and services in base year}}.$$

Returning to the example of the typical family that consumes three goods, we can calculate the CPI in the year 2000 as

$$\text{CPI in year 2000} = \frac{\$850}{\$680} = 1.25.$$

In other words, in this example the cost of living in the year 2000 is 25 percent higher than it was in 1995, the base year. Notice that the base-year CPI is always equal to 1.00, since in that year the numerator and the denominator of the CPI formula are the same. The CPI for a given period (such as a month or year) measures the cost of living in that period *relative* to what it was in the base year.

Often news reporters multiply the CPI by 100 to get rid of the decimal point. If we were to do that here, the year 2000 CPI would be expressed as 125 rather than 1.25, and the base-year CPI would be expressed as 100 rather than 1.00. However, some calculations we will do later in the chapter are simplified if the CPI is stated in decimal form, so we will not adopt the convention of multiplying it by 100.

EXAMPLE 19.1

Measuring the typical family's cost of living

Suppose that in addition to the three goods and services the typical family consumed in 1995 they also bought four sweaters at $30 each. In the year 2000 the same sweaters cost $50 each. The prices of the other goods and services in 1995 and 2000 were the same as in Table 19.2. Find the change in the family's cost of living between 1995 and 2000.

In the example in the text, the cost of the base-year (1995) basket was $680. Adding four sweaters at $30 each raises the cost of the base-year basket to $800. What does this same basket (including the four sweaters) cost in 2000? The cost of the apartment, the hamburgers, and the movie tickets is $850, as before. Adding the cost of the four sweaters at $50 each raises the total cost of the basket to $1,050. The CPI equals the cost of the basket in 2000 divided by the cost of the basket in 1995 (the base year), or $1,050/$800 = 1.31. We conclude that the family's cost of living rose 31 percent between 1995 and 2000.

EXERCISE 19.1

Returning to the three-good example in Tables 19.1 and 19.2, find the year 2000 CPI if the rent on the apartment falls from $500 in 1995 to $400 in 2000. The prices for hamburgers and movie tickets in the two years remain the same as in the two tables.

price index a measure of the average price of a given class of goods or services relative to the price of the same goods and services in a base year

The CPI is not itself the price of a specific good or service; it is a *price index*. A **price index** measures the average price of a class of goods or services relative to the price of those same goods or services in a base year. The CPI is an especially well-known price index, one of many economists use to assess economic trends. For example, because manufacturers tend to pass on increases in the prices of raw materials to their customers, economists use indexes of raw materials' prices to try to forecast changes in the prices of manufactured goods. Other indexes are used to study the rate of price change in energy, food, health care, and other major sectors.

EXERCISE 19.2

The consumer price index captures the cost of living for the "typical" or average family. Suppose you were to construct a personal price index to measure changes in your own cost of living over time. In general, how would you go about constructing such an index? Why might changes in your personal price index differ from changes in the CPI?

INFLATION

rate of inflation the annual percentage rate of change in the price level, as measured, for example, by the CPI

The CPI provides a measure of the average *level* of prices relative to prices in the base year. *Inflation,* in contrast, is a measure of how fast the average price level is *changing* over time. The **rate of inflation** is defined as the annual percentage rate of change in the price level, as measured, for example, by the CPI. Suppose, for example, that the CPI has a value of 1.25 in the year 2002 and a value of 1.30 in the year 2003. The rate of inflation between 2002 and 2003 is the percentage increase in the price level, or the increase in the price level (0.05) divided by the initial price level (1.25), which is equal to 4 percent.

Calculating inflation rates: 1972–1976

EXAMPLE 19.2

CPI values for the years 1972 through 1976 are shown below. Find the rates of inflation between 1972 and 1973, 1973 and 1974, 1974 and 1975, and 1975 and 1976.

Year	CPI
1972	0.418
1973	0.444
1974	0.493
1975	0.538
1976	0.569

The inflation rate between 1972 and 1973 is the percentage increase in the price level between those years, or $(0.444 - 0.418)/0.418 = 0.026/0.418 = 0.062 = 6.2$ percent. Do the calculations on your own to confirm that inflation during each of the next three years was 11.0, 9.1, and 5.8 percent, respectively. During the 1970s, inflation rates were much higher than the 2 to 3 percent inflation rates that have prevailed in recent years.

EXERCISE 19.3

Below are CPI values for the years 1929 through 1933. Find the rates of inflation between 1929 and 1930, 1930 and 1931, 1931 and 1932, and 1932 and 1933.

Year	CPI
1929	0.171
1930	0.167
1931	0.152
1932	0.137
1933	0.130

How did inflation rates in the 1930s differ from those of the 1970s?

The results of the calculations for Exercise 19.3 include some examples of *negative* inflation rates. A situation in which the prices of most goods and services are falling over time so that inflation is negative is called **deflation**. The early 1930s was the last time the United States experienced significant deflation. Japan has experienced relatively mild deflation during the past decade.

deflation a situation in which the prices of most goods and services are falling over time so that inflation is negative

ADJUSTING FOR INFLATION

The CPI is an extremely useful tool. Not only does it allow us to measure changes in the cost of living; it can also be used to adjust economic data to eliminate the effects of inflation. In this section we will see how the CPI can be used to convert quantities measured at current dollar values into real terms, a process called *deflating*. We will also see that the CPI can be used to convert real quantities into current-dollar terms, a procedure called *indexing*. Both procedures are useful not only to economists but to anyone who needs to adjust payments, accounting measures, or other economic quantities for the effects of inflation.

DEFLATING A NOMINAL QUANTITY

nominal quantity a quantity that is measured in terms of its current dollar value

An important use of the CPI is to adjust **nominal quantities**—quantities measured at their current dollar values—for the effects of inflation. To illustrate, suppose we know that the typical family in a certain metropolitan area had a total income of $20,000 in 1995 and $22,000 in the year 2000. Was this family economically better off in the year 2000 than in 1995?

Without any more information than this we might be tempted to say yes. After all, their income rose by 10 percent over the five-year period. But prices might also have been rising, as fast or faster than the family's income. Suppose the prices of the goods and services the family consumes rose 25 percent over the same period. Since the family's income rose only 10 percent, we would have to conclude that the family is worse off, in terms of the goods and services they can afford to buy, despite the increase in their *nominal*, or current-dollar, income.

real quantity a quantity that is measured in physical terms—for example, in terms of quantities of goods and services

We can make a more precise comparison of the family's purchasing power in 1995 and 2000 by calculating their incomes in those years in *real* terms. In general, a **real quantity** is one that is measured in physical terms—for example, in terms of quantities of goods and services. To convert a nominal quantity into a real quantity, we must divide the nominal quantity by a price index for the period, as shown in Table 19.3. The calculations in the table show that in *real* or purchasing power terms, the family's income actually *decreased* by $2,400, or 12 percent of their initial real income of $20,000, between 1995 and 2000.

TABLE 19.3
Comparing the Real Values of a Family's Income in 1995 and 2000

Year	Nominal family income	CPI	Real family income = Nominal family income/CPI
1995	$20,000	1.00	$20,000/1.00 = $20,000
2000	$22,000	1.25	$22,000/1.25 = $17,600

deflating (a nominal quantity) the process of dividing a nominal quantity by a price index (such as the CPI) to express the quantity in real terms

The problem for this family is that though their income has been rising in nominal (dollar) terms, it has not kept up with inflation. Dividing a nominal quantity by a price index to express the quantity in real terms is called **deflating** the nominal quantity. (Be careful not to confuse the idea of deflating a nominal quantity with deflation, or negative inflation. The two concepts are different.)

Dividing a nominal quantity by the current value of a price index to measure it in real or purchasing power terms is a very useful tool. It can be used to eliminate the effects of inflation from comparisons of any nominal quantity—workers' wages, health care expenditures, the components of the federal budget—over time. Why does this method work? In general, if you know both how many dollars you have spent on a given item and the item's price, you can figure out how many of the item you bought (by dividing your expenditures by the price). For example, if you spent $100 on hamburgers last month and hamburgers cost $2.50 each, you can determine that you purchased 40 hamburgers. Similarly, if you divide a family's dollar income or expenditures by a price index, which is a measure of the average price of the goods and services they buy, you will obtain a measure of the real quantity of goods and services they purchased. Such real quantities are sometimes referred to as *inflation-adjusted* quantities.

EXAMPLE 19.3

Home run hitters drive Cadillacs

In 1930 the great baseball player Babe Ruth earned a salary of $80,000. When it was pointed out to him that he had earned more than President Hoover, Ruth replied, with some justification, "I had a better year than he did." In 1998 St. Louis Cardinals slugger Mark McGwire earned approximately $8.3 million in the process of breaking both Ruth's and Roger Maris's single-season home run records. Adjusting for inflation, who earned more, Ruth or McGwire?

To answer this question, we need to know that the CPI (using the average of 1982–1984 as the base year) was 0.167 in 1930 and 1.64 in 1998. Dividing Babe Ruth's salary by 0.167, we obtain approximately $479,000, which is Ruth's salary "in 1982–1984 dollars." In other words, to enjoy the same purchasing power during the 1982–1984 period as in 1930, the Babe would have needed a salary of $479,000. Dividing Mark McGwire's 1998 salary by the 1998 CPI, 1.64, yields a salary of $5.06 million in 1982–1984 dollars. We can now compare the salaries of the two power hitters. Although adjusting for inflation brings the two figures closer together (since part of McGwire's higher salary compensates for the increase in prices between 1930 and 1998), in real terms McGwire still earned more than 10 times Ruth's salary. Incidentally, McGwire also earned about 40 times what President Clinton earned.

Clearly, in comparing wages or earnings at two different points in time, we must adjust for changes in the price level. Doing so yields the **real wage**—the wage measured in terms of real purchasing power. The real wage for any given period is calculated by dividing the nominal (dollar) wage by the CPI for that period.

real wage the wage paid to workers measured in terms of real purchasing power; the real wage for any given period is calculated by dividing the nominal (dollar) wage by the CPI for that period

EXERCISE 19.4

In 2001 Barry Bonds of the San Francisco Giants hit 73 home runs, breaking Mark McGwire's record. Bonds earned $10.3 million in 2001. In that year the CPI was 1.78. How did Bonds's real earnings compare to McGwire's?

Real wages of U.S. production workers

EXAMPLE 19.4

Production workers are nonsupervisory workers, such as those who work on factory assembly lines. According to the Bureau of Labor Statistics, http://stats.bls.gov, the average U.S. production worker earned $3.23 per hour in 1970 and $10.01 per hour in 1990. Compare the real wages for this group of workers in these years.

To find the real wage in 1970 and 1990, we need to know that the CPI was 0.388 in 1970 and 1.307 in 1990 (again using the 1982–1984 average as the base period). Dividing $3.23 by 0.388, we find that the real wage in 1970 was $8.32. Dividing $10.01 by 1.307, we find that the real wage in 1990 was only $7.66. In real or purchasing power terms, manufacturing workers' wages fell between 1970 and 1990, despite the fact that the nominal or dollar wage more than tripled.

Figure 19.1 shows nominal wages and real wages for U.S. production workers for the period 1960–2001. Notice the dramatic difference between the two trends.

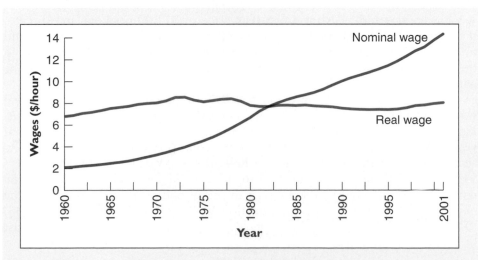

FIGURE 19.1
Nominal and Real Wages for Production Workers, 1960–2001.
Though nominal wages of production workers have risen dramatically since 1960, real wages have stagnated.

Looking only at nominal wages, one might conclude that production-line workers were much better paid in 2001 than in 1960. But once wages are adjusted for inflation, we see that in terms of buying power production-line workers' wages have stagnated since the early 1970s. This example illustrates the crucial importance of adjusting for inflation when comparing dollar values over time.

EXERCISE 19.5

In 1950 the minimum wage prescribed by federal law was $0.75 per hour. In 1997 the minimum wage was raised to $5.15 per hour. How does the real minimum wage in 1950 compare to that of 1997? The CPI was 0.241 in 1950 and 1.61 in 1997.

INDEXING TO MAINTAIN BUYING POWER

The consumer price index can also be used to convert real quantities to nominal quantities. Suppose, for example, that in the year 2000 the government paid certain Social Security recipients $1,000 per month in benefits. Let's assume that Congress would like the buying power of these benefits to remain constant over time so that the recipients' standard of living is unaffected by inflation. To achieve that goal, at what level should Congress set the monthly Social Security benefit in the year 2005?

The nominal, or dollar, benefit Congress should pay in the year 2005 to maintain the purchasing power of retired people depends on how much inflation has taken place between 2000 and 2005. Suppose that the CPI has risen 20 percent between 2000 and 2005. That is, on average the prices of the goods and services consumers buy have risen 20 percent over that period. For Social Security recipients to "keep up" with inflation, their benefit in the year 2005 must be $1,200 per month, or 20 percent more than it was in 2000. In general, to keep purchasing power constant, the dollar benefit must be increased each year by the percentage increase in the CPI.

indexing the practice of increasing a nominal quantity each period by an amount equal to the percentage increase in a specified price index. Indexing prevents the purchasing power of the nominal quantity from being eroded by inflation

The practice of increasing a nominal quantity according to changes in a price index to prevent inflation from eroding purchasing power is called **indexing**. In the case of Social Security, federal law provides for the automatic indexing of benefits. Each year, without any action by Congress, benefits increase by an amount equal to the percentage increase in the CPI. Some labor contracts are indexed as well so that wages are adjusted fully or partially for changes in inflation (see Example 19.5).

EXAMPLE 19.5   **An indexed labor contract**

A labor contract provides for a first-year wage of $12.00 per hour and specifies that the real wage will rise by 2 percent in the second year of the contract and by another 2 percent in the third year. The CPI is 1.00 in the first year, 1.05 in the second year, and 1.10 in the third year. Find the dollar wage that must be paid in the second and third years.

Because the CPI is 1.00 in the first year, both the nominal wage and the real wage are $12.00. Let W_2 stand for the nominal wage in the second year. Deflating by the CPI in the second year, we can express the real wage in the second year as $W_2/1.05$. The contract says that the second-year real wage must be 2 percent higher than the real wage in the first year, so $W_2/1.05 = \$12.00 \times 1.02 = \$12.24$. Multiplying through by 1.05 to solve for W_2, we get $W_2 = \$12.85$, the nominal wage required by the contract in the second year. In the third year the nominal wage W_3 must satisfy the equation $W_3/1.10 = \$12.24 \times 1.02 = \$12.48$. (Why?) Solving this equation for W_3 yields $13.73 as the nominal wage that must be paid in the third year.

EXERCISE 19.6

The minimum wage is not indexed to inflation, but suppose it had been when it was introduced in 1950. What would the nominal minimum wage have been in 1997, the year that Congress raised the minimum wage to $5.15 by legislation? See Exercise 19.5 for the data necessary to answer the question.

Every few years there is a well-publicized battle in Congress over whether the minimum wage should be raised. Why do these heated legislative debates recur so regularly?

ECONOMIC NATURALIST 19.1

Because the minimum wage is not indexed to inflation, its purchasing power falls as prices rise. Congress must therefore raise the nominal minimum wage periodically to keep the real value of the minimum wage from eroding. Ironically, despite the public's impression that Congress has raised the nominal minimum wage steeply over the years, the real minimum wage has fallen about one-third since 1970.

Why doesn't Congress index the minimum wage to the CPI and eliminate the need to reconsider it so often? Evidently, some members of Congress prefer to hold a highly publicized debate on the issue every few years—perhaps because it mobilizes both advocates and opponents of the minimum wage to make campaign donations to those members who represent their views.

 RECAP **METHODS TO ADJUST FOR INFLATION**

Deflating. To correct a nominal quantity, such as a family's dollar income, for changes in the price level, divide it by a price index such as the CPI. This process, called *deflating* the nominal quantity, expresses the nominal quantity in terms of real purchasing power. If nominal quantities from two different years are deflated by a price index with the same base year, the purchasing power of the two deflated quantities can be compared.

Indexing. To ensure that a nominal payment, such as a Social Security benefit, represents a constant level of real purchasing power, increase the nominal quantity each year by a percentage equal to the rate of inflation for that year (a procedure known as *indexing*).

DOES THE CPI MEASURE "TRUE" INFLATION?

You may have concluded that measuring inflation is straightforward, but as with GDP and the unemployment rate, the issue is not free from controversy. Indeed the question of whether U.S. inflation is properly measured has been the subject of serious debates in recent years. Because the CPI is one of the most important U.S. economic statistics, the issue is far from academic. Policymakers pay close attention to the latest inflation numbers when deciding what actions to take. Furthermore, because of the widespread use of indexing, changes in the CPI directly impact the government's budget. For example, if the CPI rises by 3 percent during a given year, by law Social Security benefits—which are a significant part of federal government spending—increase automatically by 3 percent. Many other government payments and private contracts, such as union labor contracts, are indexed to the CPI as well.

When a 1996 report concluded that changes in the CPI are a poor measure of "true" inflation, therefore, a major controversy ensued. The report, prepared by a commission headed by Michael Boskin, formerly the chief economic adviser to President George H. W. Bush, concluded that the official CPI inflation rate *overstates* the true inflation rate by as much as one to two percentage points a year. In other words, if the official CPI inflation rate is reported to be 3 percent, the "true" inflation rate might be 2 percent, or even 1 percent.

If this assessment is in fact correct, the indexing of Social Security and other government benefits to the CPI could be costing the federal government billions of dollars more than necessary every year. In addition, an overstated rate of inflation would lead to an underestimation of the true improvement in living standards over time. If the typical family's nominal income increases by 3 percent per year, and inflation is reported to be 3 percent per year, economists would conclude that American families are experiencing no increase in their real income. But if the "true" inflation rate is really 2 percent per year, then the family's real income is actually rising by 1 percent per year (the 3 percent increase in nominal income minus 2 percent inflation).

The Boskin Commission gave a number of reasons why the official inflation rate, based on the CPI, may overestimate the true rate of inflation. Two are particularly important. First, in practice government statisticians cannot always adjust adequately for changes in the *quality* of goods and services. Suppose a new personal computer has 20 percent more memory, computational speed, and data storage capacity than last year's model. Suppose too for the sake of illustration that its price is 20 percent higher. Has there been inflation in computer prices? Economists would say no; although consumers are paying 20 percent more for a computer, they are getting a 20 percent better machine. The situation is really no different from paying 20 percent more for a pizza that is 20 percent bigger. However, because quality change is difficult to measure precisely and because they have many thousands of goods and services to consider, government statisticians often miss or understate changes in quality. In general, whenever statisticians fail to adjust adequately for improvements in the quality of goods or services, they will tend to overstate inflation. This type of overstatement is called *quality adjustment bias*.

An extreme example of quality adjustment bias can occur whenever a totally new good becomes available. For example, the introduction of the first effective AIDS drugs significantly increased the quality of medical care received by AIDS patients. In practice, however, quality improvements that arise from totally new products are likely to be poorly captured by the CPI, if at all. The problem is that since the new good was not produced in the base year, there is no base-year price with which to compare the current price of the good. Government statisticians use various approaches to correct for this problem, such as comparing the cost of the new drug to the cost of the next-best therapies. But such methods are necessarily imprecise and open to criticism.

The second problem emphasized by the Boskin Commission arises from the fact that the CPI is calculated for a fixed basket of goods and services. This procedure does not allow for the possibility that consumers can switch from products whose prices are rising to those whose prices are stable or falling. Ignoring the fact that consumers can switch from more expensive to less expensive goods leads statisticians to overestimate the true increase in the cost of living.

Suppose, for instance, that people like coffee and tea equally well and in the base year consumed equal amounts of each. But then a frost hits a major coffee-producing nation, causing the price of coffee to double. The increase in coffee prices encourages consumers to forgo coffee and drink tea instead—a switch that doesn't make them much worse off, since they like coffee and tea equally well. However, the CPI, which measures the cost of buying the base-year basket of goods and services, will rise significantly when the price of coffee doubles. This rise in the CPI, which ignores the fact that people can substitute tea for coffee without being made significantly worse off, exaggerates the true increase in the cost of living. This type of overstatement of inflation is called *substitution bias*.

Substitution bias

EXAMPLE 19.6

Suppose the CPI basket for 1995, the base year, is as follows:

Item	Expenditure
Coffee (50 cups at $1/cup)	$ 50.00
Tea (50 cups at $1/cup)	50.00
Scones (100 at $1 each)	100.00
Total	$200.00

Assume that consumers are equally happy to drink coffee or tea with their scones. In 1995, coffee and tea cost the same, and the average person drinks equal amounts of coffee and tea.

In the year 2000, coffee has doubled in price to $2 per cup. Tea remains at $1 per cup, and scones are $1.50 each. What has happened to the cost of living as measured by the CPI? How does this result compare to the true cost of living?

To calculate the value of the CPI for the year 2000, we must first find the cost of consuming the 1995 basket of goods in that year. At year 2000 prices, 50 cups each of coffee and tea and 100 scones cost $(50 \times \$2) + (50 \times \$1) + (100 \times \$1.50) = \$300$. Since consuming the same basket of goods cost $200 in 1995, the base year, the CPI in 2000 is $300/$200, or 1.50. This calculation leads us to conclude that the cost of living has increased 50 percent between 1995 and 2000.

However, we have overlooked the possibility that consumers can substitute a cheaper good (tea) for the more expensive one (coffee). Indeed, since consumers like coffee and tea equally well, when the price of coffee doubles they will shift entirely to tea. Their new consumption basket—100 cups of tea and 100 scones—is just as enjoyable to them as their original basket. If we allow for the substitution of less expensive goods, how much has the cost of living really increased? The cost of 100 cups of tea and 100 scones in the year 2000 is only $250, not $300. From the consumer's point of view, the true cost of living has risen by only $50, or 25 percent. The 50 percent increase in the CPI therefore overstates the increase in the cost of living as the result of substitution bias.

The Boskin Commission's findings have been controversial. While quality adjustment bias and substitution bias undoubtedly distort the measurement of inflation, estimating precisely how much of an overstatement they create is difficult. (If economists knew exactly how big these biases were, they could simply correct the data.) But the Bureau of Labor Statistics (the agency responsible for calculating the CPI) has recently made significant efforts to improve the quality of its data as a result of the Commission's report.

Why is inflation in the health care sector apparently high?

Government statisticians report inflation rates for different categories of goods and services, as well as for the overall consumer basket. According to the official measures, over recent decades the prices of medical services have tended to rise much more rapidly than the prices of other goods and services. Why is inflation in the health care sector apparently high?

Although inflation rates in the health care sector are high, some economists have argued that reported rates greatly overstate the true rate of inflation in that sector. The reason, claim critics, is the quality adjustment bias. Health care is a dynamic sector of the economy, in which ongoing technological change has significantly improved the quality of care. To the extent that official data fail to account for improvements in the quality of medical care, inflation in the health care sector will be overstated.

ECONOMIC
NATURALIST
19.2

Economists Matthew Shapiro and James Wilcox[1] illustrated the problem with the example of changes in the treatment of cataracts, a cloudiness in the lens of the eye that impairs vision. The lens must still be removed surgically, but there have been important improvements in the procedure over the past 30 years. First, surgeons can now replace the defective lens with an artificial one, which improves the patient's vision considerably without contact lenses or thick glasses. Second, the techniques for making and closing the surgical incision have been substantially improved. Besides reducing complications and therefore follow-up visits, the new techniques can be performed in the physician's office, with no hospital stay (older techniques frequently required three nights in the hospital). Thus the new technologies have both improved patient outcomes and reduced the number of hours doctors and nurses spend on the procedure.

Shapiro and Wilcox point out that official measures of health care inflation are based primarily on data such as the doctor's hourly rate or the cost of a night in the hospital. They do not take into account either the reduction in a doctor's time or the shorter hospital stay now needed for procedures such as cataract surgery. Furthermore, Shapiro and Wilcox argue, official measures do not take adequate account of improvements in patient outcomes, such as the improved vision cataract patients now enjoy. Because of the failure to adjust for improvements in the quality of procedures, including increased productivity of medical personnel, official measures may significantly overstate inflation in the health care sector.

THE COSTS OF INFLATION: NOT WHAT YOU THINK

In the late 1970s, when inflation was considerably higher than it is now, the public told poll takers that they viewed it as "public enemy number one"—that is, as the nation's most serious problem. Although U.S. inflation rates have not been very high in recent years, today many Americans remain concerned about inflation or the threat of inflation. Why do people worry so much about inflation? Detailed opinion surveys often find that many people are confused about the meaning of inflation and its economic effects. Before describing the true economic costs of inflation, which are real and serious, let's examine this confusion people experience about inflation and its costs.

price level a measure of the overall level of prices at a particular point in time as measured by a price index such as the CPI

relative price the price of a specific good or service *in comparison to* the prices of other goods and services

We need first to distinguish between the *price level* and the *relative price* of a good or service. The **price level** is a measure of the overall level of prices at a particular point in time as measured by a price index such as the CPI. Recall that the inflation rate is the percentage change in the price level from year to year. In contrast, a **relative price** is the price of a specific good or service *in comparison to* the prices of other goods and services. For example, if the price of oil were to rise by 10 percent while the prices of other goods and services were rising on average by 3 percent, the relative price of oil would increase. But if oil prices rise by 3 percent while other prices rise by 10 percent, the relative price of oil would decrease. That is, oil would become cheaper relative to other goods and services, even though it has not become cheaper in absolute terms.

Public opinion surveys suggest that many people are confused about the distinction between inflation, or an increase in the overall *price level*, and an increase in a specific *relative price*. Suppose that hostilities in the Middle East were to double the price of gas at the pump, leaving other prices unaffected. Appalled by the increase in gasoline prices, people might demand that the government do something about "this inflation." But while the increase in gas prices hurts consumers, is it an example of inflation? Gasoline is only one item in a consumer's budget, one

---

[1]"Mismeasurement in the Consumer Price Index: An Evaluation," in Ben Bernanke and Julio Rotemberg (eds.), NBER *Macroeconomics Annual*, 1996.

of the thousands of goods and services that people buy every day. Thus the increase in the price of gasoline might affect the overall price level, and hence the inflation rate, only slightly. In this example, inflation is not the real problem. What upsets consumers is the change in the *relative price* of oil, particularly compared to the price of labor (wages). By increasing the cost of using a car, the increase in the relative price of oil reduces the income people have left over to spend on other things.

Again, changes in relative prices do *not* necessarily imply a significant amount of inflation. For example, increases in the prices of some goods could well be counterbalanced by decreases in the prices of other goods, in which case the price level and the inflation rate would be largely unaffected. Conversely, inflation can be high without affecting relative prices. Imagine, for example, that all prices in the economy, including wages and salaries, go up exactly 10 percent each year. The inflation rate is 10 percent, but relative prices are not changing. Indeed, because wages (the price of labor) are increasing by 10 percent per year, people's ability to buy goods and services is unaffected by the inflation.

These examples show that changes in the average price level (inflation) and changes in the relative prices of specific goods are two quite different issues. The public's tendency to confuse the two is important, because the remedies for the two problems are different. To counteract changes in relative prices, the government would need to implement policies that affect the supply and demand for specific goods. In the case of an increase in oil prices, for example, the government could try to restore supplies by mediating the peace process in the Middle East. To counteract inflation, however, the government must resort (as we will see) to changes in macroeconomic policies, such as monetary or fiscal policies. If, in confusion, the public forces the government to adopt anti-inflationary policies when the real problem is a relative price change, the economy could actually be hurt by the effort. Here is an example of why economic literacy is important, both to policymakers and the general public.

The price level, relative prices, and inflation

EXAMPLE 19.7

Suppose the value of the CPI is 1.20 in the year 2000, 1.32 in 2001, and 1.40 in 2002. Assume also that the price of oil increases 8 percent between 2000 and 2001 and another 8 percent between 2001 and 2002. What is happening to the price level, the inflation rate, and the relative price of oil?

The price level can be measured by the CPI. Since the CPI is higher in 2001 than in 2000 and higher still in 2002 than in 2001, the price level is rising throughout the period. The inflation rate is the *percentage increase* in the CPI. Since the CPI increases by 10 percent between 2000 and 2001, the inflation rate between those years is 10 percent. However, the CPI increases only about 6 percent between 2001 and 2002 ($1.40/1.32 \approx 1.06$), so the inflation rate decreases to about 6 percent between those years. The decline in the inflation rate implies that although the price level is still rising, it is doing so at a slower pace than the year before.

The price of oil rises 8 percent between 2000 and 2001. But because the general inflation over that period is 10 percent, the relative price of oil—that is, its price *relative to all other goods and services*—falls by about 2 percent (8% − 10% = −2%). Between 2001 and 2002 the price of oil rises by another 8 percent, while the general inflation rate is about 6 percent. Hence the relative price of oil rises between 2001 and 2002 by about 2 percent (8% − 6%).

THE TRUE COSTS OF INFLATION

Having dispelled the common confusion between inflation and relative price changes, we are now free to address the true economic costs of inflation. There are a variety of such costs, each of which tends to reduce the efficiency of the economy. Five of the most important are discussed here.

"SHOE-LEATHER" COSTS

As all shoppers know, cash is convenient. Unlike checks, which are not accepted everywhere, and credit cards, for which a minimum purchase is often required, cash can be used in almost any routine transaction. Businesses, too, find cash convenient to hold. Having plenty of cash on hand facilitates transactions with customers and reduces the need for frequent deposits and withdrawals from the bank.

Inflation raises the cost of holding cash to consumers and businesses. Consider a miser with $10,000 in $20 bills under his mattress. What happens to the buying power of his hoard over time? If inflation is zero so that on average the prices of goods and services are not changing, the buying power of the $10,000 does not change over time. At the end of a year the miser's purchasing power is the same as it was at the beginning of the year. But suppose the inflation rate is 10 percent. In that case, the purchasing power of the miser's hoard will fall by 10 percent each year. After a year, he will have only $9,000 in purchasing power. In general, the higher the rate of inflation, the less people will want to hold cash because of the loss of purchasing power that they will suffer.

Technically, currency is a debt owed by the government to the currency holder. So when currency loses value, the losses to holders of cash are offset by gains to the government, which now owes less in real terms to currency holders. Thus, from the point of view of society as a whole, the loss of purchasing power is not in itself a cost of inflation, because it does not involve wasted resources. (Indeed, no real goods or services were used up when the miser's currency hoard lost part of its value.) However, when faced with inflation, people are not likely to accept a loss in purchasing power but instead will take actions to try to "economize" on their cash holdings. For example, instead of drawing out enough cash for a month the next time they visit the bank, they will draw out only enough to last a week. The inconvenience of visiting the bank more often to minimize one's cash holdings is a real cost of inflation. Similarly, businesses will reduce their cash holdings by sending employees to the bank more frequently, or by installing computerized systems to monitor cash usage. To deal with the increase in bank transactions required by consumers and businesses trying to use less cash, banks will need to hire more employees and expand their operations.

The costs of more frequent trips to the bank, new cash management systems, and expanded employment in banks are real costs. They use up resources, including time and effort, that could be used for other purposes. Traditionally, the costs of economizing on cash have been called *shoe-leather costs*—the idea being that shoe leather is worn out during extra trips to the bank. Shoe-leather costs probably are not a significant problem in the United States today, where inflation is only 2 to 3 percent per year. But in economies with high rates of inflation, they can become quite significant.

EXAMPLE 19.8

Shoe-leather costs at Woodrow's Hardware

Woodrow's Hardware needs $5,000 cash per day for customer transactions. Woodrow has a choice between going to the bank first thing on Monday morning to withdraw $25,000—enough cash for the whole week—or going to the bank first thing every morning for $5,000 each time. Woodrow puts the cost of going to the bank, in terms of inconvenience and lost time, at $4 per trip. Assume that funds left in the bank earn precisely enough interest to keep their purchasing power unaffected by inflation.

If inflation is zero, how often will Woodrow go to the bank? If it is 10 percent? In this example, what are the shoe-leather costs of a 10 percent inflation rate?

If inflation is zero, there is no cost to holding cash. Woodrow will go to the bank only once a week, incurring a shoe-leather cost of $4 per week. But if inflation is 10 percent, Woodrow may need to change his banking habits. If he continues to go to the bank only on Monday mornings, withdrawing $25,000 for the week, what will be Woodrow's average cash holding over the week? At the beginning of each day, his cash holding will be as follows:

Monday	$25,000
Tuesday	20,000
Wednesday	15,000
Thursday	10,000
Friday	5,000

Averaging the holdings on those five days, we can calculate that Woodrow's average cash holding at the beginning of each day is $75,000/5 = $15,000. If inflation is 10 percent a year, over the course of a year the cost to Woodrow of holding an average of $15,000 in cash equals 10 percent of $15,000, or $1,500.

On the other hand, if Woodrow goes to the bank every day, his average cash holding at the beginning of the day will be only $5,000. In that case, his losses from inflation will be $500 (10 percent of $5,000) a year. Will Woodrow start going to the bank every day when inflation reaches 10 percent? The *benefit* of changing his banking behavior is a loss of only $500 per year to inflation, rather than $1,500, or $1,000 saved. The *cost* of going to the bank every day is $4 per trip. Assuming Woodrow's store is open 50 weeks a year, going to the bank 5 days a week instead of 1 day a week adds 200 trips per year, at a total cost of $800. Since the $800 cost is less than the $1,000 benefit, Woodrow will begin going to the bank more often.

To repeat, the shoe-leather costs of a high inflation rate are the extra costs incurred to avoid holding cash. In this example they are the additional $800 per year associated with Woodrow's daily trips to the bank.

"NOISE" IN THE PRICE SYSTEM

In Chapter 3 we described the remarkable economic coordination that is necessary to provide the right amount and the right kinds of food to New Yorkers every day. This feat is not orchestrated by some Food Distribution Ministry staffed by bureaucrats. It is done much better than a Ministry ever could by the workings of free markets, operating without central guidance.

How do free markets transmit the enormous amounts of information necessary to accomplish complex tasks like the provisioning of New York City? The answer, as we saw in Chapter 3, is through the price system. When the owners of French restaurants in Manhattan cannot find sufficient quantities of chanterelles, a particularly rare and desirable mushroom, they bid up its market price. Specialty food suppliers notice the higher price for chanterelles and realize that they can make a profit by supplying more chanterelles to the market. At the same time, price-conscious diners will shift to cheaper, more available mushrooms. The market for chanterelles will reach equilibrium only when there are no more unexploited opportunities for profit, and both suppliers and demanders are satisfied at the market price (the *equilibrium principle*). Multiply this example a million times, and you will gain a sense of how the price system achieves a truly remarkable degree of economic coordination.

When inflation is high, however, the subtle signals that are transmitted through the price system become more difficult to interpret, much in the way that static, or "noise," makes a radio message harder to interpret. In an economy with little or no inflation, the supplier of specialty foodstuffs will immediately recognize the increase in chanterelle prices as a signal to bring more to market. If inflation is high, however, the supplier must ask whether a price increase represents a true increase in the demand for chanterelles or is just a result of the general inflation, which causes all food prices to rise. If the price rise reflects only inflation, the price of chanterelles *relative to other goods and services* has not really

Inflation adds static to the information conveyed by changes in prices.

changed. The supplier therefore should not change the quantity of mushrooms he brings to market.

In an inflationary environment, to discern whether the increase in chanterelle prices is a true signal of increased demand, the supplier needs to know not only the price of chanterelles but also what is happening to the prices of other goods and services. Since this information takes time and effort to collect, the supplier's response to the change in chanterelle prices is likely to be slower and more tentative.

In summary, price changes are the market's way of communicating information to suppliers and demanders. An increase in the price of a good or service, for example, tells demanders to economize on their use of the good or service and suppliers to bring more of it to market. But in the presence of inflation, prices are affected not only by changes in the supply and demand for a product but by changes in the general price level. Inflation creates static, or "noise," in the price system, obscuring the information transmitted by prices and reducing the efficiency of the market system. This reduction in efficiency imposes real economic costs.

DISTORTIONS OF THE TAX SYSTEM

Just as some government expenditures, such as Social Security benefits, are indexed to inflation, many taxes are also indexed. In the United States, people with higher incomes pay a higher *percentage* of their income in taxes. Without indexing, an inflation that raises people's nominal incomes would force them to pay an increasing percentage of their income in taxes, even though their *real* incomes may not have increased. To avoid this phenomenon, which is known as *bracket creep*, Congress has indexed income tax brackets to the CPI. The effect of this indexation is that a family whose nominal income is rising at the same rate as inflation does not have to pay a higher percentage of income in taxes.

Although indexing has solved the problem of bracket creep, many provisions of the tax code have not been indexed, either because of lack of political support or because of the complexity of the task. As a result, inflation can produce unintended changes in the taxes people pay, which in turn may cause them to change their behavior in economically undesirable ways.

To illustrate, an important provision in the business tax code for which inflation poses problems is the *capital depreciation allowance,* which works as follows. Suppose a firm buys a machine for $1,000, expecting it to last for 10 years. Under U.S. tax law, the firm can take one-tenth of the purchase price, or $100, as a deduction from its taxable profits in each of the 10 years. By deducting a fraction of the purchase price from its taxable profits, the firm reduces its taxes. The exact amount of the yearly tax reduction is the tax rate on corporate profits times $100.

The idea behind this provision of the tax code is that the wearing out of the machine is a cost of doing business that should be deducted from the firm's profit. Also, in giving firms a tax break for investing in new machinery, Congress intended to encourage firms to modernize their plants. Yet capital depreciation allowances are not indexed to inflation. Suppose that, at a time when the inflation rate is high, a firm is considering purchasing a $1,000 machine. The managers know that the purchase will allow them to deduct $100 per year from taxable profits for the next 10 years. But that $100 is a fixed amount that is not indexed to inflation. Looking forward, managers will recognize that 5, 6, or 10 years into the future, the real value of the $100 tax deduction will be much lower than at present because of inflation. They will have less incentive to buy the machine and may decide not to make the investment at all. Indeed, many studies have found that a high rate of inflation can significantly reduce the rate at which firms invest in new factories and equipment.

Because the complex U.S. tax code contains hundreds of provisions and tax rates that are not indexed, inflation can seriously distort the incentives provided by the tax system for people to work, save, and invest. The resulting adverse effects on economic efficiency and economic growth represent a real cost of inflation.

UNEXPECTED REDISTRIBUTION OF WEALTH

Yet another concern about inflation is that it may arbitrarily redistribute wealth from one group to another. Consider a group of union workers who signed a contract setting their wages for the next three years. If those wages are not indexed to inflation, then the workers will be vulnerable to upsurges in the price level. Suppose, for example, that inflation is much higher than expected over the three years of the contract. In that case the buying power of the workers' wages—their real wages—will be less than anticipated when they signed the contract.

From society's point of view, is the buying power that workers lose to inflation really "lost"? The answer is no; the loss in their buying power is exactly matched by an unanticipated gain in the employer's buying power, because the real cost of paying the workers is less than anticipated. In other words, the effect of the inflation is not to *destroy* purchasing power but to *redistribute* it, in this case from the workers to the employer. If inflation had been *lower* than expected, the workers would have enjoyed greater purchasing power than they anticipated and the employer would have been the loser.

Another example of the redistribution caused by inflation takes place between borrowers (debtors) and lenders (creditors). Suppose one of the authors of this book wants to buy a house on a lake and borrows $150,000 from the bank to pay for it. Shortly after signing the mortgage agreement, he learns that inflation is likely to be much higher than expected. How should he react to the news? Perhaps as a public-spirited macroeconomist the author should be saddened to hear that inflation is rising, but as a consumer he should be pleased. In real terms, the dollars with which he will repay his loan in the future will be worth much less than expected. The loan officer should be distraught, because the dollars the bank will receive from the author will be worth less, in purchasing power terms, than expected at contract signing. Once again, no real wealth is "lost" to the inflation; rather, the borrower's gain is just offset by the lender's loss. *In general, unexpectedly high inflation rates help borrowers at the expense of lenders,* because borrowers are able to repay their loans in less valuable dollars. Unexpectedly low inflation rates, in contrast, help lenders and hurt borrowers by forcing borrowers to repay in dollars that are worth more than expected when the loan was made.

Although redistributions caused by inflation do not directly destroy wealth, but only transfer it from one group to another, they are still bad for the economy. Our economic system is based on incentives. For it to work well, people must know that if they work hard, save some of their income, and make wise financial investments, they will be rewarded in the long run with greater real wealth and a better standard of living. Some observers have compared a high-inflation economy to a casino, in which wealth is distributed largely by luck—that is, by random fluctuations in the inflation rate. In the long run, a "casino economy" is likely to perform poorly, as its unpredictability discourages people from working and saving. (Why bother if inflation can take away your savings overnight?) Rather, a high-inflation economy encourages people to use up resources in trying to anticipate inflation and protect themselves against it.

INTERFERENCE WITH LONG-RUN PLANNING

The fifth and final cost of inflation we will examine is its tendency to interfere with the long-run planning of households and firms. Many economic decisions take place within a long time horizon. Planning for retirement, for example, may begin when workers are in their twenties or thirties. And firms develop long-run investment and business strategies that look decades into the future.

Clearly, high and erratic inflation can make long-term planning difficult. Suppose, for example, that you want to enjoy a certain standard of living when you retire. How much of your income do you need to save to make your dreams a reality? That depends on what the goods and services you plan to buy will cost 30 or 40 years from now. With high and erratic inflation, even guessing what your chosen lifestyle will cost by the time you retire is extremely difficult. You may end up saving too little and having to compromise on your retirement plans; or you may save too much, sacrificing more than you need to during your working years. Either way, inflation will have proved costly.

In summary, inflation damages the economy in a variety of ways. Some of its effects are difficult to quantify and are therefore controversial. But most economists agree that a low and stable inflation rate is instrumental in maintaining a healthy economy.

 RECAP   **THE TRUE COSTS OF INFLATION**

The public sometimes confuses changes in relative prices (such as the price of oil) with inflation, which is a change in the overall level of prices. This confusion can cause problems, because the remedies for undesired changes in relative prices and for inflation are different.

There are a number of true costs of inflation, which together tend to reduce economic growth and efficiency. These include:

- Shoe-leather costs, or the costs of economizing on cash (for example, by making more frequent trips to the bank or installing a computerized cash management system).

- "Noise" in the price system, which occurs when general inflation makes it difficult for market participants to interpret the information conveyed by prices.

- Distortions of the tax system, for example, when provisions of the tax code are not indexed.

- Unexpected redistributions of wealth, as when higher-than-expected inflation hurts wage earners to the benefit of employers or hurts creditors to the benefit of debtors.

- Interference with long-term planning, arising because people find it difficult to forecast prices over long periods.

HYPERINFLATION

Although there is some disagreement about whether an inflation rate of, say, 5 percent per year imposes important costs on an economy, few economists would question the fact that an inflation rate of 500 percent or 1,000 percent per year disrupts economic performance. A situation in which the inflation rate is extremely high is called **hyperinflation**. Although there is no official threshold above which inflation becomes hyperinflation, inflation rates in the range of 500 to 1,000 percent per year would surely qualify. In the past few decades episodes

hyperinflation a situation in which the inflation rate is extremely high of hyperinflation have occurred in several Latin American countries (including Bolivia, Argentina, and Brazil), in Israel, and in several countries attempting to make the transition from communism to capitalism, including Russia. The United States has never experienced hyperinflation, although the short-lived Confederate States of America suffered severe inflation during the Civil War. Between 1861 and 1865 prices in the Confederacy rose to 92 times their prewar levels.

Hyperinflation greatly magnifies the costs of inflation. For example, shoe-leather costs—a relatively minor consideration in times of low inflation—become quite important during hyperinflation, when people may visit the bank two or three times per day to hold money for as short a time as possible. With prices changing daily or even hourly, markets work quite poorly, slowing economic growth. Massive redistributions of wealth take place, impoverishing many. Not surprisingly, episodes of hyperinflation rarely last more than a few years; they are so disruptive that they quickly lead to public outcry for relief.

How costly is high inflation?

Economic theory suggests that high inflation rates, especially those associated with hyperinflation, reduce economic efficiency and growth. Most economists believe that the economic costs associated with high inflation outweigh the perceived benefits, yet we continue to see episodes of high inflation throughout the world. In reality, how costly are high inflation rates?

Economists Stanley Fischer, Ratna Sahay, and Carlos A. Végh[2] examined the economic performance of 133 market economies over the period 1960–96 and uncovered 45 episodes of high inflation (12-month inflation rates greater than 100%) among 25 different countries. They found that, while uncommon, episodes of high inflation impose significant economic costs on the countries experiencing them. During periods of high inflation, these countries saw real GDP per person fall by an average of 1.6% per year, real consumption per person fall by an average of 1.3% per year, and real investment per person fall by an average of 3.3% per year. During low inflation years these same countries experienced positive growth in each of these variables. In addition, during periods of high inflation, these countries' trade and government budget deficits were larger than during low inflation years.

Falling output and consumption levels caused by high inflation reduce the economic well-being of households and firms, and have a disproportionate effect on poor workers, who are least likely to have their wages indexed to the inflation rate and thus avoid a real loss in purchasing power. As pointed out in the last section, high inflation rates also distort relative prices in the marketplace, leading to a misallocation of resources that can have long-term economic consequences. Falling investment in new capital caused by high inflation, for example, leads not only to a slowdown in current economic activity but also to reduced growth rates of future output. Because of these adverse economic effects, policymakers have an incentive to keep inflation rates low.

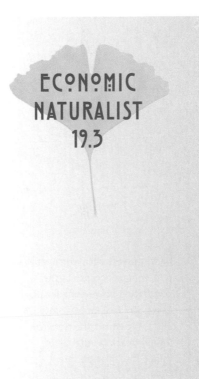

ECONOMIC NATURALIST 19.3

INFLATION AND INTEREST RATES

So far we have focused on the measurement and economic costs of inflation. Another important aspect of inflation is its close relationship to other key macroeconomic variables. For example, economists have long realized that during periods of high inflation interest rates tend to be high as well. We will close this chapter with a look at the relationship between inflation and interest rates, which will provide a useful background in the chapters to come.

---

[2]"Modern Hyper- and High Inflations," *Journal of Economic Literature*, Vol. 11 (September 2002), pp. 837–880.

INFLATION AND THE REAL INTEREST RATE

Earlier in our discussion of the ways in which inflation redistributes wealth, we saw that inflation tends to hurt creditors and help debtors by reducing the value of the dollars with which debts are repaid. The effect of inflation on debtors and creditors can be explained more precisely using an economic concept called the *real interest rate*. An example will illustrate.

Suppose that there are two neighboring countries, Alpha and Beta. In Alpha, whose currency is called the alphan, the inflation rate is zero and is expected to remain at zero. In Beta, where the currency is the betan, the inflation rate is 10 percent and is expected to remain at that level. Bank deposits pay 2 percent annual interest in Alpha and 10 percent annual interest in Beta. In which countries are bank depositors getting a better deal?

You may answer "Beta," since interest rates on deposits are higher in that country. But if you think about the effects of inflation, you will recognize that Alpha, not Beta, offers the better deal to depositors. To see why, think about the change over a year in the real purchasing power of deposits in the two countries. In Alpha, someone who deposits 100 alphans in the bank on January 1 will have 102 alphans on December 31. Because there is no inflation in Alpha, on average prices are the same at the end of the year as they were at the beginning. Thus the 102 alphans the depositor can withdraw represent a 2 percent increase in buying power.

In Beta, the depositor who deposits 100 betans on January 1 will have 110 betans by the end of the year—10 percent more than she started with. But the prices of goods and services in Beta, we have assumed, will also rise by 10 percent. Thus the Beta depositor can afford to buy precisely the same amount of goods and services at the end of the year as she could at the beginning; she gets no increase in buying power. So the Alpha depositor has the better deal, after all.

Economists refer to the annual percentage increase in the *real* purchasing power of a financial asset as the **real interest rate**, or the *real rate of return*, on that asset. In our example, the real purchasing power of deposits rises by 2 percent per year in Alpha and by 0 percent per year in Beta. So the real interest rate on deposits is 2 percent in Alpha and 0 percent in Beta. The real interest rate should be distinguished from the more familiar market interest rate, also called the *nominal interest rate*. The **nominal interest rate** is the annual percentage increase in the nominal, or dollar, value of an asset.

As the example of Alpha and Beta illustrates, we can calculate the real interest rate for any financial asset, from a checking account to a government bond, by subtracting the rate of inflation from the market or nominal interest rate on that asset. So in Alpha, the real interest rate on deposits equals the nominal interest rate (2 percent) minus the inflation rate (0 percent), or 2 percent. Likewise in Beta, the real interest rate equals the nominal interest rate (10 percent) minus the inflation rate (10 percent), or 0 percent.

We can write this definition of the real interest rate in mathematical terms:

$$r = i - \pi,$$

where
r = the real interest rate,
i = the nominal, or market, interest rate,
π = the inflation rate.

real interest rate the annual percentage increase in the purchasing power of a financial asset; the real interest rate on any asset equals the nominal interest rate on that asset minus the inflation rate

nominal interest rate (or market interest rate) the annual percentage increase in the nominal value of a financial asset

EXAMPLE 19.9   **Real interest rates in the 1970s, 1980s, and 1990s**

Following are interest rates on government bonds for selected years in the 1970s, 1980s, and 1990s. In which of these years did the financial investors who bought government bonds get the best deal? The worst deal?

Year	Interest rate (%)	Inflation rate (%)
1970	6.5	5.7
1975	5.8	9.1
1980	11.5	13.5
1985	7.5	3.6
1990	7.5	5.4
1995	5.5	2.8
1999	4.7	2.5

Financial investors and lenders do best when the real (not the nominal) interest rate is high, since the real interest rate measures the increase in their purchasing power. We can calculate the real interest rate for each year by subtracting the inflation rate from the nominal interest rate. The results are 0.8 percent for 1970, −3.3 percent for 1975, −2.0 percent for 1980, 3.9 percent for 1985, 2.1 percent for 1990, 2.7 percent for 1995, and 2.2 percent for 1999. For purchasers of government bonds, the best of these years was 1985, when they enjoyed a real return of 3.9 percent. The worst year was 1975, when their real return was actually negative. In other words, despite receiving 5.8 percent nominal interest, financial investors ended up losing buying power in 1975, as the inflation rate exceeded the interest rate earned by their investments.

Figure 19.2 shows the real interest rate in the United States since 1960 as measured by the nominal interest rate paid on the federal government's debt minus the inflation rate. Note that the real interest rate was negative in the 1970s but reached historically high levels in the mid-1980s.

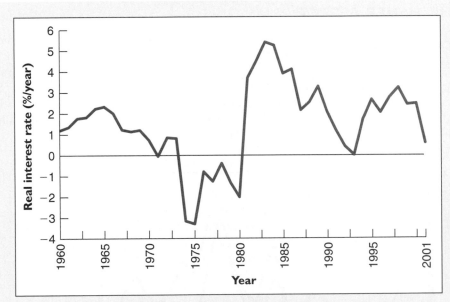

FIGURE 19.2

The Real Interest Rate in the United States, 1960–2001.

The real interest rate is the nominal interest rate—here the interest rate on funds borrowed by the federal government for a term of 3 months—minus the rate of inflation. In the United States, the real interest rate was negative in the 1970s but reached historically high levels in the mid-1980s.

SOURCE: *Economic Report of the President* (http://w3.access.gpo.gov/eop/) and authors' calculations.

EXERCISE 19.7

You have some funds to invest but are unimpressed with the low interest rates your bank offers. You consult a broker, who suggests a bond issued by the government of a small island nation. The broker points out that these bonds pay 25 percent interest—much more than your bank—and

| that the island's government has never failed to repay its debts. What should be your next question?

The concept of the real interest rate helps to explain more precisely why an unexpected surge in inflation is bad for lenders and good for borrowers. For any given nominal interest rate that the lender charges the borrower, the higher the inflation rate, the lower the real interest rate the lender actually receives. So unexpectedly high inflation leaves the lender worse off. Borrowers, on the other hand, are better off when inflation is unexpectedly high, because their real interest rate is lower than anticipated.

Although unexpectedly high inflation hurts lenders and helps borrowers, a high rate of inflation that is *expected* may not redistribute wealth at all, because expected inflation can be built into the nominal interest rate. Suppose, for example, that the lender requires a real interest rate of 2 percent on new loans. If the inflation rate is confidently expected to be zero, the lender can get a 2 percent real interest rate by charging a nominal interest rate of 2 percent. But if the inflation rate is expected to be 10 percent, the lender can still ensure a real interest rate of 2 percent by charging a nominal interest rate of 12 percent. Thus high inflation, if it is *expected,* need not hurt lenders—as long as the lenders can adjust the nominal interest they charge to reflect the expected inflation rate.

| **EXERCISE 19.8**

What is the real rate of return to holding cash? (*Hint:* Does cash pay interest?) Does this real rate of return depend on whether the rate of inflation is correctly anticipated? How does your answer relate to the idea of shoe-leather costs?

THE FISHER EFFECT

Earlier we mentioned the observation that interest rates tend to be high when inflation is high and low when inflation is low. This relationship can be seen in Figure 19.3, which shows both the U.S. inflation rate and a nominal interest rate (the rate at which the government borrows for short periods) from 1960 to the present. Notice that nominal interest rates have tended to be high in periods of high inflation, such as the late 1970s, and relatively low in periods of low inflation, such as the early 1960s and the late 1990s.

FIGURE 19.3
Inflation and Interest Rates in the United States, 1960–2001.
Nominal interest rates tend to be high when inflation is high and low when inflation is low, a phenomenon called the Fisher effect.

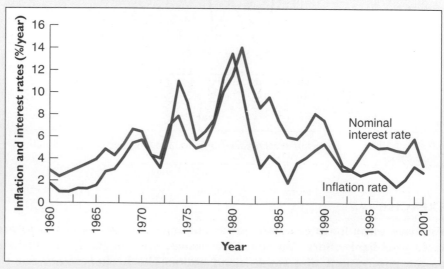

SOURCE: *Economic Report of the President* (http://w3.access.gpo.gov/eop/).

Why do interest rates tend to be high when inflation is high? Our discussion of real interest rates provides the answer. Suppose inflation has recently been high, so borrowers and lenders anticipate that it will be high in the near future. We would expect lenders to raise their nominal interest rate so that their real rate of return will be unaffected. For their part, borrowers are willing to pay higher nominal interest rates when inflation is high, because they understand that the higher nominal interest rate only serves to compensate the lender for the fact that the loan will be repaid in dollars of reduced real value—in real terms, their cost of borrowing is unaffected by an equal increase in the nominal interest rate and the inflation rate. Conversely, when inflation is low, lenders do not need to charge so high a nominal interest rate to ensure a given real return. Thus nominal interest rates will be high when inflation is high and low when inflation is low. This tendency for nominal interest rates to follow inflation rates is called the **Fisher effect**, after the early twentieth-century American economist Irving Fisher, who first pointed out the relationship.

Fisher effect the tendency for nominal interest rates to be high when inflation is high and low when inflation is low

■ SUMMARY ■

- The basic tool for measuring inflation is the *consumer price index,* or CPI. The CPI measures the cost of purchasing a fixed basket of goods and services in any period relative to the cost of the same basket of goods and services in a base year. The *inflation rate* is the annual percentage rate of change in the price level as measured by a *price index* such as the CPI.

- The official U.S. inflation rate, based on the CPI, may overstate the true inflation rate for two reasons: First, it may not adequately reflect improvements in the quality of goods and services. Second, the method of calculating the CPI ignores the fact that consumers can substitute cheaper goods and services for more expensive ones.

- A *nominal quantity* is a quantity that is measured in terms of its current dollar value. Dividing a nominal quantity, such as a family's income or a worker's wage in dollars, by a price index, such as the CPI, expresses that quantity in terms of real purchasing power. This procedure is called *deflating* the nominal quantity. If nominal quantities from two different years are deflated by a common price index, the purchasing power of the two quantities can be compared. To ensure that a nominal payment, such as a Social Security benefit, represents a constant level of real purchasing power, the nominal payment should be increased each year by a percentage equal to the inflation rate. This method of adjusting nominal payments to maintain their purchasing power is called *indexing.*

- The public sometimes confuses increases in the *relative prices* for specific goods or services with inflation, which is an increase in the general price level. Since the remedies for a change in relative prices are different from the remedies for inflation, this confusion can cause problems.

- Inflation imposes a number of true costs on the economy, including "shoe-leather" costs, which are the real resources that are wasted as people try to economize on cash holdings; "noise" in the price system; distortions of the tax system; unexpected redistributions of wealth; and interference with long-run planning. Because of these costs, most economists agree that sustained economic growth is more likely if inflation is low and stable. *Hyperinflation,* a situation in which the inflation rate is extremely high, greatly magnifies the costs of inflation and is highly disruptive to the economy.

- The *real interest rate* is the annual percentage increase in the purchasing power of a financial asset. It is equal to the *nominal,* or *market, interest rate* minus the inflation rate. When inflation is unexpectedly high, the real interest rate is lower than anticipated, which hurts lenders but benefits borrowers. When inflation is unexpectedly low, lenders benefit and borrowers are hurt. To obtain a given real rate of return, lenders must charge a high nominal interest rate when inflation is high and a low nominal interest rate when inflation is low. The tendency for nominal interest rates to be high when inflation is high and low when inflation is low is called the *Fisher effect.*

■ KEY TERMS ■

consumer price index (CPI) (476)
deflating (a nominal quantity) (480)
deflation (479)
Fisher effect (497)
hyperinflation (492)

indexing (482)
nominal interest rate (494)
nominal quantity (480)
price index (478)
price level (486)

rate of inflation (478)
real interest rate (494)
real quantity (480)
real wage (481)
relative price (486)

▪ REVIEW QUESTIONS ▪

1. Explain why changes in the cost of living for any particular individual or family may differ from changes in the official cost-of-living index, the CPI.

2. What is the difference between the *price level* and the *rate of inflation* in an economy?

3. Why is it important to adjust for inflation when comparing nominal quantities (for example, workers' average wages) at different points in time? What is the basic method for adjusting for inflation?

4. Describe how indexation might be used to guarantee that the purchasing power of the wage agreed to in a multiyear labor contract will not be eroded by inflation.

5. Give two reasons why the official inflation rate may understate the "true" rate of inflation. Illustrate by examples.

6. "It's true that unexpected inflation redistributes wealth, from creditors to debtors, for example. But what one side of the bargain loses, the other side gains. So from the perspective of the society as a whole, there is no real cost." Do you agree? Discuss.

7. How does inflation affect the real return on holding cash?

8. True or false: If both the potential lender and the potential borrower correctly anticipate the rate of inflation, inflation will not redistribute wealth from the creditor to the debtor. Explain.

▪ PROBLEMS ▪

1. Government survey takers determine that typical family expenditures each month in the year designated as the base year are as follows:

   20 pizzas at $10 each
   Rent of apartment, $600 per month
   Gasoline and car maintenance, $100
   Phone service (basic service plus 10 long-distance calls), $50

   In the year following the base year, the survey takers determine that pizzas have risen to $11 each, apartment rent is $640, gasoline and maintenance have risen to $120, and phone service has dropped in price to $40.
   a. Find the CPI in the subsequent year and the rate of inflation between the base year and the subsequent year.
   b. The family's nominal income rose by 5 percent between the base year and the subsequent year. Are they worse off or better off in terms of what their income is able to buy?

2. Here are values of the CPI (multiplied by 100) for each year from 1990 to 2001. For each year beginning with 1991, calculate the rate of inflation from the previous year. What happened to inflation rates over the 1990s?

1990	130.7
1991	136.2
1992	140.3
1993	144.5
1994	148.2
1995	152.4
1996	156.9
1997	160.5
1998	163.0
1999	166.6
2000	172.2
2001	177.1

3. According to the U.S. Census Bureau (http://www.census.gov/), nominal income for the typical family of four in the United States (median income) was $24,332 in 1980, $32,777 in 1985, $41,451 in 1990, and $62,228 in 2000. In purchasing power terms, how did family income compare in each of those four years? You will need to know that the CPI (multiplied by 100, 1982–1984 = 100) was 82.4 in 1980, 107.6 in 1985, 130.7 in 1990, and 172.2 in 2000. In general terms, how would your answer be affected if the Boskin Commission's conclusions about the CPI were confirmed?

4. A recent report found that the real entry-level wage for college graduates declined by 8 percent between 1990 and 1997. The nominal entry-level wage in 1997 was $13.65 per hour. Assuming that the findings are correct, what was the nominal entry-level wage in 1990? You will need to use data from Problem 2.

5. Here is a hypothetical income tax schedule, expressed in nominal terms, for the year 2002:

Family income	Taxes due (percent of income)
≤$20,000	10
$20,001–$30,000	12
$30,001–$50,000	15
$50,001–$80,000	20
>$80,000	25

The legislature wants to ensure that families with a given real income are not pushed up into higher tax brackets by inflation. The CPI (times 100) is 175 in 2002 and 185 in 2004. How should the income tax schedule above be adjusted for the year 2004 to meet the legislature's goal?

6. The typical consumer's food basket in the base year 2000 is as follows:

   30 chickens at $3.00 each
   10 hams at $6.00 each
   10 steaks at $8.00 each

A chicken feed shortage causes the price of chickens to rise to $5.00 each in the year 2001. Hams rise to $7.00 each, and the price of steaks is unchanged.
   a. Calculate the change in the "cost-of-eating" index between 2000 and 2001.
   b. Suppose that consumers are completely indifferent between two chickens and one ham. For this example, how large is the substitution bias in the official "cost-of-eating" index?

7. Here are the actual per-gallon prices for unleaded regular gasoline for June of each year between 1978 and 1986, together with the values of the CPIs for those years. For each year from 1979 to 1986, find the CPI inflation rate and the change in the relative price of gasoline, both from the previous year. Would it be fair to say that most of the changes in gas prices during this period were due to general inflation, or were factors specific to the oil market playing a role as well?

Year	Gasoline price ($/gallon)	CPI (1982–1984 = 1.00)
1978	0.663	0.652
1979	0.901	0.726
1980	1.269	0.824
1981	1.391	0.909
1982	1.309	0.965
1983	1.277	0.996
1984	1.229	1.039
1985	1.241	1.076
1986	0.955	1.136

8. Repeat Example 19.8 from the text (shoe-leather costs at Woodrow's Hardware). Calculate shoe-leather costs (relative to the original situation, in which Woodrow goes to the bank once a week) assuming that
   a. Inflation is 5 percent rather than 10 percent.
   b. Inflation is 5 percent and Woodrow's trips to the banks cost $2 each.
   c. Inflation remains at 10 percent and a trip to the bank costs $4, but Woodrow needs $10,000 per day to transact with customers.

9. On January 1, 2000, Albert invested $1,000 at 6 percent interest per year for three years. The CPI on January 1, 2000, stood at 100. On January 1, 2001, the CPI (times 100) was 105, on January 1, 2002, it was 110, and on January 1, 2003, the day Albert's investment matured, the CPI was 118. Find the real rate of interest earned by Albert in each of the three years and his total real return over the three-year period. Assume that interest earnings are reinvested each year and themselves earn interest.

10. Frank is lending $1,000 to Sarah for two years. Frank and Sarah agree that Frank should earn a 2 percent real return per year.
    a. The CPI (times 100) is 100 at the time that Frank makes the loan. It is expected to be 110 in one year and 121 in two years. What nominal rate of interest should Frank charge Sarah?
    b. Suppose Frank and Sarah are unsure about what the CPI will be in two years. Show how Frank and Sarah could index Sarah's annual repayments to ensure that Frank gets an annual 2 percent real rate of return.

11.*The Bureau of Labor Statistics has found that the base-year expenditures of the typical consumer break down as follows:

Food and beverages	17.8%
Housing	42.8%
Apparel and upkeep	6.3%
Transportation	17.2%
Medical care	5.7%
Entertainment	4.4%
Other goods, services	5.8%
Total	100.0%

Suppose that since the base year the prices of food and beverages have increased by 10 percent, the price of housing has increased by 5 percent, and the price of medical care has increased by 10 percent. Other prices are unchanged. Find the CPI for the current year.

■ ANSWERS TO IN-CHAPTER EXERCISES ■

19.1 The cost of the family's basket in 1995 remains at $680, as in Table 19.1. If the rent on their apartment falls to $400 in 2000, the cost of reproducing the 1995 basket of goods and services in 2000 is $620 ($400 for rent + $150 for hamburgers + $70 for movie tickets). The CPI for 2000 is accordingly $620/$680, or 0.912. So in this example, the cost of living fell nearly 9 percent between 1995 and 2000.

19.2 To construct your own personal price index, you would need to determine the basket of goods and services that you personally purchased in the base year. Your personal price index in each period would then be defined as the cost of your personal basket in that period relative to its cost in the base year. To the extent that your mix of purchases differs from that of the typical American consumer, your cost-of-living index will differ from the official CPI. For example, if in the base year you spent a higher share of your budget than the typical American on goods and services that have risen relatively rapidly in price, your personal inflation rate will be higher than the CPI inflation rate.

*Problem marked with an asterisk (*) is more difficult.

19.3 The percentage changes in the CPI in each year from the previous year are as follows:

1930	$-2.3\% = (0.167 - 0.171)/0.171$
1931	-9.0%
1932	-9.9%
1933	-5.1%

Negative inflation is called deflation. The experience of the 1930s, when prices were falling, contrasts sharply with the 1970s, during which prices rose rapidly.

19.4 Bonds's real earnings, in 1982–1987 dollars, were $10.3 million/1.78, or $5.79 million. Bonds earned about 14 percent more than McGwire in real terms.

19.5 The real minimum wage in 1950 is $0.75/0.241, or $3.11 in 1982–1984 dollars. The real minimum wage in 1997 is $5.15/1.61, or $3.20 in 1982–1984 dollars. So the real minimum wage in 1997 is only slightly higher than what it was in 1950.

19.6 The increase in the cost of living between 1950 and 1997 is reflected in the ratio of the 1997 CPI to the 1950 CPI, or 1.61/0.241 = 6.68. That is, the cost of living in 1997 was 6.68 times what it was in 1950. If the minimum wage were indexed to preserve its purchasing power, it would have been 6.68 times higher in 1997 than in 1950, or 6.68 × $0.75 = $5.01. Since the actual minimum wage in 1997 was $5.15, the effect of formal indexation in this case would have been negligible.

19.7 You should be concerned about the real return on your investment, not your nominal return. To calculate your likely real return, you need to know not only the nominal interest paid on the bonds of the island nation but also the prevailing inflation rate in that country. So your next question should be, "What is the rate of inflation in this country likely to be over the period that I am holding these bonds?"

19.8 The real rate of return to cash, as with any asset, is the nominal interest rate less the inflation rate. But cash pays no interest; that is, the nominal interest rate on cash is zero. Therefore, the real rate of return on cash is just minus the inflation rate. In other words, cash loses buying power at a rate equal to the rate of inflation. This rate of return depends on the actual rate of inflation and does not depend on whether the rate of inflation is correctly anticipated.

    If inflation is high so that the real rate of return on cash is very negative, people will take actions to try to reduce their holdings of cash, such as going to the bank more often. The costs associated with trying to reduce holdings of cash are what economists call shoe-leather costs.

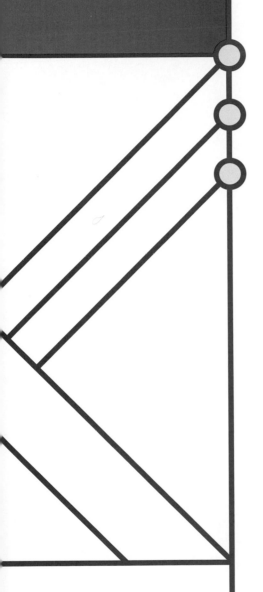

PART

7

THE ECONOMY IN THE LONG RUN

∎

For millennia the great majority of the world's inhabitants eked out a spare existence by tilling the soil. Only a small proportion of the population lived above the level of subsistence, learned to read and write, or traveled more than a few miles from their birthplaces. Large cities grew up, serving as imperial capitals and centers of trade, but the great majority of urban populations lived in dire poverty, subject to malnutrition and disease.

Then, about three centuries ago, a fundamental change occurred. Spurred by technological advances and entrepreneurial innovations, a process of economic growth began. Sustained over many years, this growth in the economy's productive capacity has transformed almost every aspect of how we live—from what we eat and wear to how we work and play. What caused this economic growth? And why have some countries enjoyed substantially greater rates of growth than others? As Nobelist Robert E. Lucas Jr. put it in a classic article on economic development, "The consequences for human welfare involved in questions like these are simply staggering: Once one starts to think about them, it is hard to think about anything else." Although most people would attach less significance to these questions than Lucas did, they are undoubtedly of very great importance.

The subject of Part 7 is the behavior of the economy in the long run, including the factors that cause the economy to grow and develop. Chapter 20 begins by tackling directly the causes and consequences of economic growth. A key conclusion of the chapter is that improvements in average labor productivity are the primary source of rising living standards; hence policies to improve living standards should focus on stimulating productivity. Chapter 21 studies long-term trends in the labor market, analyzing the long-run effects of economic growth on real wages and employment opportunities. As the creation of new capital goods is an important factor underlying rising productivity, Chapter 22 examines the processes of saving and capital formation. Chapter 23 introduces the concept of money and examines its relationship to inflation in the long run. In addition, this chapter introduces the Federal Reserve System and describes how the "Fed" controls the money supply to promote economic stability. Chapter 24 discusses the role of banks, bond markets, and stock markets in allocating saving to productive uses, as well as the role of international capital flows, which facilitate the allocation of saving across countries.

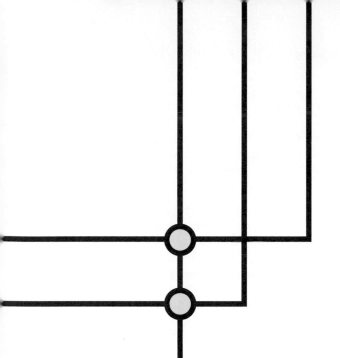

ECONOMIC GROWTH, PRODUCTIVITY, AND LIVING STANDARDS

■

One of us once attended a conference on the effects of economic growth and development on society. A speaker at the conference posed the following question: "Which would you rather be? An ordinary, middle-class American living today, or the richest person in America at the time of George Washington?"

A member of the audience spoke out immediately: "I can answer that question in one word. Dentistry."

The answer drew a laugh, perhaps because it reminded people of George Washington's famous wooden teeth. But it was a good answer. Dentistry in early America—whether the patient was rich or poor—was a primitive affair. Most dentists simply pulled a patient's rotten teeth, with a shot of whiskey for anesthetic.

Other types of medical care were not much better than dentistry. Eighteenth-century doctors had no effective weapons against tuberculosis, typhoid fever, diphtheria, influenza, pneumonia, and other communicable diseases. Such illnesses, now quite treatable, were major killers in Washington's time. Infants and children were particularly susceptible to deadly infectious diseases, especially whooping cough and measles. Even a well-to-do family often lost two or three children to these illnesses. Washington, an unusually large and vigorous

Would you rather be a rich person living in the eighteenth century or a middle-class person living in the twenty-first century?

man, lived to the age of 67, but the average life expectancy during his era was probably not much more than 40 years.

Medical care is not the only aspect of ordinary life that has changed drastically over the past two centuries. Author Stephen Ambrose, in his account of the Lewis and Clark expedition, described the limitations of transportation and communication in early America:

> A critical fact in the world of 1801 was that nothing moved faster than the speed of a horse. No human being, no manufactured item, no bushel of wheat, no side of beef (or any beef on the hoof for that matter), no letter, no information, no idea, order, or instruction of any kind moved faster, and, as far as Jefferson's contemporaries were able to tell, nothing ever would.
>
> And except on a racetrack, no horse moved very fast. Road conditions in the United States ranged from bad to abominable, and there weren't very many of them. The best highway in the country ran from Boston to New York; it took a light stagecoach . . . three full days to make the 175-mile journey. The hundred miles from New York to Philadelphia took two full days.[1]

Today New Yorkers can go to Philadelphia by train in an hour and a half. What would George Washington have thought of that? And how would nineteenth-century pioneers, who crossed the continent by wagon train, have reacted to the idea that their great-grandchildren would be able to have breakfast in New York and lunch the same day in San Francisco?

No doubt you can think of other enormous changes in the way average people live, even over the past few decades. Computer technologies and the Internet have changed the ways people work and study in just a few years, for example. Though these changes are due in large part to scientific advances, such discoveries *by themselves* usually have little effect on most people's lives. New scientific knowledge leads to widespread improvements in living standards only when it is commercially applied. Better understanding of the human immune system, for example, has little impact unless it leads to new therapies or drugs. And a new drug will do little to help unless it is affordable to those who need it.

A tragic illustration of this point is the AIDS epidemic in Africa. Although some new drugs will moderate the effects of the virus that causes AIDS, they are so expensive that they are of little practical value in poverty-stricken African nations grappling with the disease. But even if the drugs were affordable, they would have limited benefit without modern hospitals, trained health professionals, and adequate nutrition and sanitation. In short, most improvements in a nation's living standard are the result not just of scientific and technological advances but of an economic system that makes the benefits of those advances available to the average person.

In this chapter we will explore the sources of economic growth and rising living standards in the modern world. We will begin by reviewing the remarkable economic growth in the industrialized countries, as measured by real GDP per person. Since the mid-nineteenth century (and earlier in some countries), a radical transformation in living standards has occurred in these countries. What explains this transformation? The key to rising living standards is a *continuing increase in average labor productivity,* which depends on several factors, from the skills and motivation workers bring to their jobs to the legal and social environment in which they work. We will analyze each of these factors and discuss its implications for government policies to promote growth. We will also discuss the costs of rapid economic growth and consider whether there may be limits to the amount of economic growth a society can achieve.

[1] Stephen E. Ambrose, *Undaunted Courage: Meriwether Lewis, Thomas Jefferson, and the Opening of the American West,* New York: Touchstone (Simon & Schuster), 1996, p. 52.

THE REMARKABLE RISE IN LIVING STANDARDS: THE RECORD

The advances in health care and transportation mentioned in the beginning of this chapter illustrate only a few of the impressive changes that have taken place in people's material well-being over the past two centuries, particularly in industrialized countries like the United States. To study the factors that affect living standards systematically, however, we must go beyond anecdotes and adopt a specific measure of economic well-being in a particular country and time.

In Chapter 18 we introduced the concept of real GDP as a basic measure of the level of economic activity in a country. Recall that, in essence, real GDP measures the physical volume of goods and services produced within a country's borders during a specific period, such as a quarter or a year. Consequently, real GDP *per person* provides a measure of the quantity of goods and services available to the typical resident of a country at a particular time. Although real GDP per person is certainly not a perfect indicator of economic well-being, as we saw in Chapter 18, it is positively related to a number of pertinent variables, such as life expectancy, infant health, and literacy. Lacking a better alternative, economists have focused on real GDP per person as a key measure of a country's living standard and stage of economic development.

Figure 17.2 showed the remarkable growth in real GDP per person that occurred in the United States between 1900 and 2001. For comparison, Table 20.1 shows real GDP per person in eight major countries in selected years from 1870 to 2000. Figure 20.1 displays the same data graphically for five of the eight countries.

The data in Table 20.1 and Figure 20.1 tell a dramatic story. For example, in the United States (which was already a relatively wealthy industrialized country in 1870), real GDP per person grew more than 11-fold between 1870 and 2000. In Japan, real GDP per person grew more than 25 times over the same period. Underlying these statistics is an amazingly rapid process of economic growth and transformation, through which in just a few generations relatively poor agrarian societies became highly industrialized economies—with average standards of living that could scarcely have been imagined in 1870. As Figure 20.1 shows, a significant part of this growth has occurred since 1950, particularly in Japan.

TABLE 20.1
Real GDP per Person in Selected Countries, 1870–2000 (in 1995 U.S. Dollars)

Country	1870	1913	1950	1979	2000	Annual % change 1870–2000	Annual % change 1950–2000
Australia	5,626	7,385	9,561	18,033	24,708	1.1	1.9
Canada	2,447	5,791	9,362	20,899	26,604	1.8	2.1
France	2,249	4,401	6,049	17,801	22,447	1.8	2.6
Germany	1,205	2,320	5,005	18,014	23,247	2.3	3.1
Italy	2,248	3,167	4,042	13,331	21,930	1.8	3.4
Japan	963	1,825	2,216	16,899	24,772	2.5	4.8
United Kingdom	3,500	5,374	7,832	14,889	21,142	1.4	2.0
United States	2,843	6,745	11,921	22,480	32,629	1.9	2.0

SOURCES: Derived from Angus Maddison, *Phases of Capitalist Development*, Oxford: Oxford University Press, reprinted 1988, Tables A2, B2–B4. Rebased to 1995 and updated to 2000 by the authors using OECD *Quarterly National Accounts*. "Germany" refers to West Germany in 1950 and 1979.

FIGURE 20.1

Real GDP per Person in Five Industrialized Countries, 1870–2000. Economic growth has been especially rapid since the 1950s, particularly in Japan.

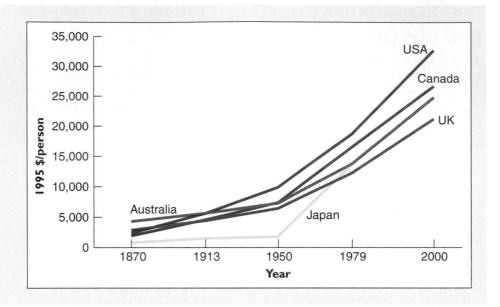

A note of caution is in order. The farther back in time we go, the less precise are historical estimates of real GDP. Most governments did not keep official GDP statistics until after World War II; production records from earlier periods are often incomplete or of questionable accuracy. Comparing economic output over a century or more is also problematic because many goods and services that are produced today were unavailable—indeed, inconceivable—in 1870. How many nineteenth-century horse-drawn wagons, for example, would be the economic equivalent of a BMW 328i automobile or a Boeing 757 jet? Despite the difficulty of making precise comparisons, however, we can say with certainty that the variety, quality, and quantity of available goods and services increased enormously in industrialized countries during the nineteenth and twentieth centuries, a fact reflected in the data on real GDP per capita.

WHY "SMALL" DIFFERENCES IN GROWTH RATES MATTER

The last two columns of Table 20.1 show the annual growth rates of real GDP per person, both for the entire 1870–2000 period and the more recent years, 1950–2000. At first glance these growth rates don't seem to differ much from country to country. For example, for the period 1870–2000, the highest growth rate is 2.5 percent (Japan) and the lowest is 1.1 percent (Australia). But consider the long-run effect of this seemingly "small" difference in annual growth rates. In 1870, in terms of output per person, Australia was by far the richest of the eight countries listed in Table 20.1, with a real GDP per person nearly six times that of Japan. Yet by 2000 Japan had not just caught up to but exceeded Australia. This remarkable change in economic fortunes is the result of the apparently small difference between a 1.1 percent growth rate and a 2.5 percent growth rate, maintained over 130 years.

The fact that what seem to be small differences in growth rates can have large long-run effects results from what is called the *power of compound interest*.

EXAMPLE 20.1

Compound interest (1)

In 1800 your great-great-grandfather deposited $10.00 in a checking account at 4 percent interest. Interest is compounded annually (so that interest paid at the end of each year receives interest itself in later years). Great-Grandpa's will specified that the account be turned over to his most direct descendant (you) in the year 2000. When you withdrew the funds in that year, how much was the account worth?

The account was worth $10.00 in 1800; $10.00 × 1.04 = $10.40 in 1801; $10.00 × 1.04 × 1.04 = $10.00 × (1.04)^2 = $10.82 in 1802; and so on. Since 200 years elapsed between 1800, when the deposit was made, and the year 2000, when the account was closed, the value of the account in the year 2000 was $10.00 × (1.04)^{200}, or $10.00 × 1.04 to the 200th power. Using a calculator, you will find that $10.00 times 1.04 to the 200th power is $25,507.50—a good return for a $10.00 deposit!

Compound interest—an arrangement in which interest is paid not only on the original deposit but on all previously accumulated interest—is distinguished from *simple interest*, in which interest is paid only on the original deposit. If your great-grandfather's account had been deposited at 4 percent simple interest, it would have accumulated only 40 cents each year (4 percent of the original $10.00 deposit), for a total value of $10.00 + 200 × $0.40 = $90.00 after 200 years. The tremendous growth in the value of his account came from the compounding of the interest—hence the phrase "the power of compound interest."

compound interest the payment of interest not only on the original deposit but on all previously accumulated interest

Compound interest (2)

EXAMPLE 20.2

Refer to Example 20.1. What would your great-grandfather's $10.00 deposit have been worth after 200 years if the annual interest rate had been 2 percent? 6 percent?

At 2 percent interest the account would be worth $10.00 in 1800; $10.00 × 1.02 = $10.20 in 1801; $10.00 × (1.02)^2 = $10.40 in 1802; and so on. In the year 2000 the value of the account would be $10.00 × (1.02)^{200}, or $524.85. If the interest rate were 6 percent, after 200 years the account would be worth $10.00 × (1.06)^{200}, or $1,151,259.04. Let's summarize the results of Examples 20.1 and 20.2:

Interest rate (%)	Value of $10 after 200 years
2	$524.85
4	$25,507.50
6	$1,151,259.04

The power of compound interest is that even at relatively low rates of interest, a small sum, compounded over a long enough period, can greatly increase in value. A more subtle point, illustrated by this example, is that small differences in interest rates matter a lot. The difference between a 2 percent and a 4 percent interest rate doesn't seem tremendous, but over a long period of time it implies large differences in the amount of interest accumulated on an account. Likewise, the effect of switching from a 4 percent to a 6 percent interest rate is enormous, as our calculations show.

Economic growth rates are similar to compound interest rates. Just as the value of a bank deposit grows each year at a rate equal to the interest rate, so the size of a nation's economy expands each year at the rate of economic growth. This analogy suggests that even a relatively modest rate of growth in output per person—say, 1 to 2 percent per year—will produce tremendous increases in average living standard over a long period. And relatively small *differences* in growth rates, as in the case of Australia versus Japan, will ultimately produce very different living standards. Over the long run, then, the rate of economic growth is an extremely important variable. Hence, government policy changes or other factors that affect the long-term growth rate even by a small amount will have a major economic impact.

EXERCISE 20.1

Suppose that real GDP per capita in the United States had grown at 2.5 percent per year, as Japan's did, instead of the actual 1.9 percent per year, from 1870 to 2000. How much larger would real GDP per person have been in the United States in 2000?

WHY NATIONS BECOME RICH: THE CRUCIAL ROLE OF AVERAGE LABOR PRODUCTIVITY

What determines a nation's economic growth rate? To get some insight into this vital question, we will find it useful to express real GDP per person as the product of two terms: average labor productivity and the share of the population that is working.

To do this, let Y equal total real output (as measured by real GDP, for example), N equal the number of employed workers, and POP equal the total population. Then real GDP per person can be written as Y/POP; average labor productivity, or output per employed worker, equals Y/N; and the share of the population that is working is N/POP. The relationship between these three variables is

$$\frac{Y}{POP} = \frac{Y}{N} \times \frac{N}{POP},$$

which, as you can see by canceling out N on the right-hand side of the equation, always holds exactly. In words, this basic relationship is

Real GDP per person = Average labor productivity ×
Share of population employed.

This expression for real GDP per person tells us something very basic and intuitive: The quantity of goods and services that each person can consume depends on (1) how much each worker can produce and (2) how many people (as a fraction of the total population) are working. Furthermore, because real GDP per person equals average labor productivity times the share of the population that is employed, real GDP per person can *grow* only to the extent that there is *growth* in worker productivity and/or the fraction of the population that is employed.

Figures 20.2 and 20.3 show the U.S. figures for the three key variables in the relationship above for the period 1960–2000. Figure 20.2 shows both real GDP per person and real GDP per worker (average labor productivity). Figure 20.3 shows the portion of the entire U.S. population (not just the working-age population) that was employed during that period. Once again, we see that the expansion in output per person in the United States has been impressive. Between 1960 and 2000, real GDP per person in the U.S. grew by 160 percent. Thus in 2000, the average American enjoyed about 2 1/2 times as many goods and services as in 1960. Figures 20.2 and 20.3 show that increases in both labor productivity and the share of the population holding a job contributed to this rise in living standard.

Let's look a bit more closely at these two contributing factors, beginning with the share of the population that is employed. As Figure 20.3 shows, between 1960 and 2000 the number of people employed in the United States rose from 36 to 49 percent of the entire population, a remarkable increase. The growing tendency of women to work outside the home (see Economic Naturalist 18.1) was the most important reason for this rise in employment. Another factor leading to higher rates of employment was an increase in the share of the general population that

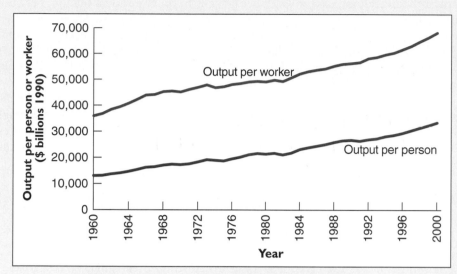

FIGURE 20.2
Real GDP per Person and Average Labor Productivity in the United States, 1960–2000.
Real output per person in the United States grew 160 percent between 1960 and 2000, and real output per worker (average labor productivity) grew by 92 percent.

SOURCE: *Economic Report of the President* (http://w3.access.gpo.gov/eop/).

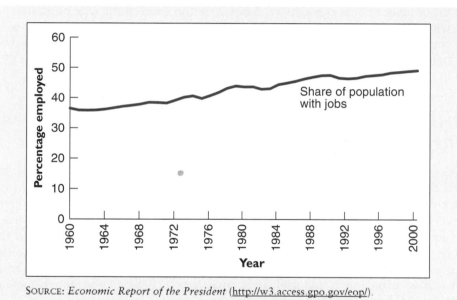

FIGURE 20.3
Share of the U.S. Population Employed, 1960–2000.
The share of the U.S. population holding a job increased from 36 percent in 1960 to 49 percent in 2000.

SOURCE: *Economic Report of the President* (http://w3.access.gpo.gov/eop/).

is of working age (ages 16 to 65). The coming of age of the "baby boom" generation, born in the years after World War II, and to a lesser extent the immigration of young workers from other countries, helped cause this growth in the workforce.

Although the rising share of the U.S. population with jobs contributed significantly to the increase in real GDP per person during the past four decades, this trend almost certainly will not continue in the future. Women's participation in the labor force seems unlikely to continue rising at the same rate as in the past four decades. More important, the baby boom generation, now in its prime years of employment, will begin to reach retirement age around the year 2010. As more and more baby boomers retire, the fraction of the population that is employed will begin to drop, probably significantly. In the long run, then, the improvement in living standards brought about by the rising share of Americans with jobs will likely prove transitory.

What about the other factor that determines output per person, average labor productivity? As Figure 20.2 shows, between 1960 and 2000, average labor productivity in the United States increased by 92 percent, accounting for a sizable share of the overall increase in GDP per person. In other periods, the link between average labor productivity and output per person in the United States has often been even stronger, since in most earlier periods the share of the population holding jobs was more stable than it has been recently. (See Figure 17.2 for the behavior of real GDP per person and average labor productivity in the United States over the period 1900–2000.)

This quick look at recent data supports a more general conclusion. *In the long run, increases in output per person arise primarily from increases in average labor productivity.* In simple terms, the more people can produce, the more they can consume. To understand why economies grow, then, we must understand the reasons for increased labor productivity.

> ⬤ **RECAP** | **ECONOMIC GROWTH AND PRODUCTIVITY**
>
> Real GDP per person, a basic indicator of living standards, has grown dramatically in the industrialized countries. This growth reflects the *power of compound interest:* Even a modest growth rate, if sustained over a long period of time, can lead to large increases in the size of the economy.
>
> Output per person equals average labor productivity times the share of the population that is employed. Since 1960 the share of the U.S. population with jobs has risen significantly, but this variable is likely to decline in coming decades. In the long run, increases in output per person and hence living standards arise primarily from increases in average labor productivity.

THE DETERMINANTS OF AVERAGE LABOR PRODUCTIVITY

What determines the productivity of the average worker in a particular country at a particular time? Popular discussions of this issue often equate worker productivity with the willingness of workers of a given nationality to work hard. Everything else being equal, a culture that promotes hard work certainly tends to increase worker productivity. But intensity of effort alone cannot explain the huge differences in average labor productivity that we observe around the world. For example, average labor productivity in the United States is about 24 times what it is in Indonesia and 100 times what it is in Bangladesh, though there is little doubt that Indonesians and Bangladeshis work very hard.

In this section we will examine six factors that appear to account for the major differences in average labor productivity, both between countries and between generations. Later in the chapter we will discuss how economic policies can influence these factors to spur productivity and growth.

HUMAN CAPITAL

To illustrate the factors that determine average labor productivity, we introduce two prototypical assembly line workers, Lucy and Ethel.

EXAMPLE 20.3   **Lucy and Ethel on the assembly line**

Lucy and Ethel have jobs wrapping chocolate candies and placing them into boxes. Lucy, a novice wrapper, can wrap only 100 candies per hour. Ethel, who has had on-the-job training, can wrap 300 candies per hour. Lucy and Ethel each work 40 hours per week. Find average labor productivity, in terms of candies wrapped per week and candies wrapped per hour, (a) for Lucy, (b) for Ethel, and (c) for Lucy and Ethel as a team.

We have defined average labor productivity in general terms as output per worker. Note, though, that the measurement of average labor productivity depends on the time period that is specified. For example, the data presented in Figure 20.2 tell us how much the average worker produces *in a year*. In this example we are concerned with how much Lucy and Ethel can produce *per hour* of work or *per week* of work. Any one of these ways of measuring labor productivity is equally valid, as long as we are clear about the time unit we are using.

Lucy and Ethel's hourly productivities are given in the problem: Lucy can wrap 100 candies per hour and Ethel can wrap 300. Lucy's weekly productivity is (40 hours/week) × (100 candies wrapped/hour) = 4,000 wrapped candies per week. Ethel's weekly productivity is (40 hours/week) × (300 candies wrapped/hour), or 12,000 candies per week.

Together Lucy and Ethel can wrap 16,000 candies per week. As a team, their average weekly productivity is (16,000 candies wrapped)/(2 weeks of work), or 8,000 candies per week. Their average hourly productivity as a team is (16,000 candies wrapped)/(80 hours of work) = 200 candies per hour. Notice that, taken as a team, the two women's productivity lies midway between their individual productivities.

How productive are these workers?

Ethel is more productive than Lucy because she has had on-the-job training, which has allowed her to develop her candy-wrapping skills to a higher level than Lucy's. Because of her training, Ethel can produce more than Lucy can in a given number of hours.

EXERCISE 20.2

Suppose Ethel attends additional classes in candy wrapping and learns how to wrap 500 candies per hour. Find the output per week and output per hour for Lucy and Ethel, both individually and as a team.

Economists would explain the difference in the two women's performance by saying that Ethel has more human capital than Lucy. *Human capital* comprises the talents, education, training, and skills of workers. Workers with a large stock of human capital are more productive than workers with less training. For example, a secretary who knows how to use a word processing program will be able to type more letters than one who doesn't; an auto mechanic who is familiar with computerized diagnostic equipment will be able to fix engine problems that less well-trained mechanics could not.

Why did West Germany and Japan recover so successfully from the devastation of World War II?

Germany and Japan sustained extensive destruction of their cities and industries during World War II and entered the postwar period impoverished. Yet within 30 years both countries had not only been rebuilt but had become worldwide industrial and economic leaders. What accounts for these "economic miracles"?

Many factors contributed to the economic recovery of West Germany and Japan from World War II, including the substantial aid provided by the United States to Europe under the Marshall Plan and to Japan during the U.S. occupation. Most economists agree, however, that high levels of *human capital* played a crucial role in both countries.

At the end of the war Germany's population was exceptionally well educated, with a large number of highly qualified scientists and engineers. The country also had (and still does today) an extensive apprentice system that provided on-the-job training to young workers. As a result, Germany had a skilled industrial workforce. In addition, the area that became West Germany benefited substantially from an influx of skilled workers from East Germany and the rest of Soviet-controlled

ECONOMIC NATURALIST 20.1

Europe, including 20,000 trained engineers and technicians. Beginning as early as 1949, this concentration of human capital contributed to a major expansion of Germany's technologically sophisticated, highly productive manufacturing sector. By 1960 West Germany was a leading exporter of high-quality manufactured goods, and its citizens enjoyed one of the highest standards of living in Europe.

Japan, which probably sustained greater physical destruction in the war than Germany, also began the postwar period with a skilled and educated labor force. In addition, occupying American forces restructured the Japanese school system and encouraged all Japanese to obtain a good education. Even more so than the Germans, however, the Japanese emphasized on-the-job training. As part of a lifetime employment system, under which workers were expected to stay with the same company their entire career, Japanese firms invested extensively in worker training. The payoff to these investments in human capital was a steady increase in average labor productivity, particularly in manufacturing. By the 1980s Japanese manufactured goods were among the most advanced in the world and Japan's workers among the most skilled.

Although high levels of human capital were instrumental in the rapid economic growth of West Germany and Japan, human capital alone cannot create a high living standard. A case in point is Soviet-dominated East Germany, which had a level of human capital similar to West Germany's after the war but did not enjoy the same economic growth. For reasons we will discuss later in the chapter (see Economic Naturalist 20.3), the communist system imposed by the Soviets utilized East Germany's human capital far less effectively than the economic systems of Japan and West Germany.

Human capital is analogous to physical capital (such as machines and factories) in that it is acquired primarily through the investment of time, energy, and money. For example, to learn how to use a word processing program, a secretary might need to attend a technical school at night. The cost of going to school includes not only the tuition paid but also the *opportunity cost* of the secretary's time spent attending class and studying. The benefit of the schooling is the increase in wages the secretary will earn when the course has been completed. We know by the *cost-benefit principle* that the secretary should learn word processing only if the benefits exceed the costs, including the opportunity costs. In general, then, we would expect to see people acquire additional education and skills when the difference in the wages paid to skilled and unskilled workers is significant.

PHYSICAL CAPITAL

Workers' productivity depends not only on their skills and effort but on the tools they have to work with. Even the most skilled surgeon cannot perform open-heart surgery without sophisticated equipment, and an expert computer programmer is of limited value without a computer. These examples illustrate the importance of *physical capital,* such as factories and machines. More and better capital allows workers to produce more efficiently, as Example 20.4 shows.

EXAMPLE 20.4 **Lucy and Ethel get automated**

Refer to Example 20.3. Lucy and Ethel's boss acquired an electric candy-wrapping machine, which is designed to be operated by one worker. Using this machine, an untrained worker can wrap 500 candies per hour. What are Lucy and Ethel's hourly and weekly outputs now? Will the answer change if the boss gets a second machine? A third?

Suppose for the sake of simplicity that a candy-wrapping machine must be assigned to one worker only. (This assumption rules out sharing arrangements, in which one worker uses the machine on the day shift and another on the night shift.) If the boss buys just one machine, she will assign it to Lucy. (Why? See Exercise 20.3.) Now Lucy will be able to wrap 500 candies per hour, while Ethel can wrap only 300 per hour. Lucy's weekly output will be 20,000 wrapped candies (40 hours × 500 candies wrapped per hour). Ethel's weekly output is still 12,000 wrapped candies (40 hours × 300 candies wrapped per hour). Together they can now wrap 32,000 candies per week, or 16,000 candies per week each. On an hourly basis, average labor productivity for the two women taken together is 32,000 candies wrapped per 80 hours of work, or 400 candies wrapped per hour—twice their average labor productivity before the boss bought the machine.

With two candy-wrapping machines available, both Lucy and Ethel could use a machine. Each could wrap 500 candies per hour, for a total of 40,000 wrapped candies per week. Average labor productivity for both women taken together would be 20,000 wrapped candies per week, or 500 wrapped candies per hour.

What would happen if the boss purchased a third machine? With only two workers, a third machine would be useless: it would add nothing to either total output or average labor productivity.

EXERCISE 20.3

Using the assumptions made in Examples 20.3 and 20.4, explain why the boss should give the single available candy-wrapping machine to Lucy rather than Ethel. (*Hint:* Use *the principle of increasing opportunity cost,* introduced in Chapter 3.)

The candy-wrapping machine is an example of a *capital good,* which was defined in Chapter 18 as a long-lived good, which is itself produced and used to produce other goods and services. Capital goods include machines and equipment (such as computers, earthmovers, or assembly lines) as well as buildings (such as factories or office buildings).

Capital goods like the candy-wrapping machine enhance workers' productivity. Table 20.2 summarizes the results from Examples 20.3 and 20.4. For each number of machines the boss might acquire (column 1), Table 20.2 gives the total weekly output of Lucy and Ethel taken together (column 2), the total number of hours worked by the two women (column 3), and average output per hour (column 4), equal to total weekly output divided by total weekly hours.

Table 20.2 demonstrates two important points about the effect of additional capital on output. First, for a given number of workers, adding more capital generally increases both total output and average labor productivity. For example, adding the first candy-wrapping machine increases weekly output (column 2) by 16,000 candies and average labor productivity (column 4) by 200 candies wrapped per hour.

The second point illustrated by Table 20.2 is that the more capital is already in place, the smaller the benefits of adding extra capital. Notice that the first

TABLE 20.2
Capital, Output, and Productivity in the Candy-Wrapping Factory

(1) Number of machines (capital)	(2) Total number of candies wrapped each week (output)	(3) Total hours worked per week	(4) Candies wrapped per hour worked (productivity)
0	16,000	80	200
1	32,000	80	400
2	40,000	80	500
3	40,000	80	500

machine adds 16,000 candies to total output, but the second machine adds only 8,000. The third machine, which cannot be used since there are only two workers, does not increase output or productivity at all. This result illustrates a general principle of economics, called *diminishing returns to capital*. According to the principle of **diminishing returns to capital,** if the amount of labor and other inputs employed is held constant, then the greater the amount of capital already in use, the less an additional unit of capital adds to production. In the case of the candy-wrapping factory, diminishing returns to capital implies that the first candy-wrapping machine acquired adds more output than the second, which in turn adds more output than the third.

diminishing returns to capital if the amount of labor and other inputs employed is held constant, then the greater the amount of capital already in use, the less an additional unit of capital adds to production

Diminishing returns to capital are a natural consequence of firms' incentive to use each piece of capital as productively as possible. To maximize output, managers will assign the first machine that a firm acquires to the most productive use available, the next machine to the next most productive use, and so on—an illustration of the *principle of increasing opportunity cost,* or *low-hanging-fruit principle* (Chapter 3). When many machines are available, all the highly productive ways of using them already have been exploited. Thus adding yet another machine will not raise output or productivity by very much. If Lucy and Ethel are already operating two candy-wrapping machines, there is little point to buying a third machine, except perhaps as a replacement or spare.

The implications of Table 20.2 can be applied to the question of how to stimulate economic growth. First, increasing the amount of capital available to the workforce will tend to increase output and average labor productivity. The more adequately equipped workers are, the more productive they will be. Second, the degree to which productivity can be increased by an expanding stock of capital is limited. Because of diminishing returns to capital, an economy in which the quantity of capital available to each worker is already very high will not benefit much from further expansion of the capital stock.

Is there empirical evidence that giving workers more capital makes them more productive? Figure 20.4 shows the relationship between average labor productivity (real GDP per worker) and the amount of capital per worker in 15 major countries, including the 8 industrialized countries listed in Table 20.1. The figure shows a strong relationship between the amounts of capital per worker and productivity, consistent with the theory. Note, though, that the relationship between capital and productivity is somewhat weaker for the richest countries. For example, Germany has more capital per worker than the United States, but German workers are less productive than American workers on average. Diminishing returns to capital

FIGURE 20.4
Average Labor Productivity and Capital per Worker in 15 Countries, 1990.
Countries with large amounts of capital per worker also tend to have high average labor productivity, as measured by real GDP per worker.

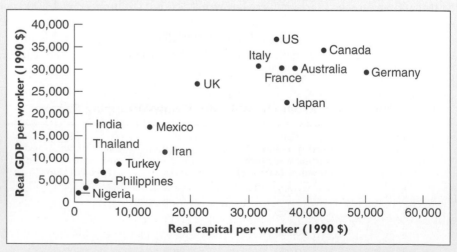

SOURCE: Penn World Tables (www.nber.org). Countries included are those listed in Table 20.1, plus all countries with populations of 40 million or more for which data are available.

may help to explain the weakening of the relationship between capital and productivity at high levels of capital. In addition, Figure 20.4 does not account for many other differences among countries, such as differences in economic systems or government policies. Thus we should not expect to see a perfect relationship between the two variables.

LAND AND OTHER NATURAL RESOURCES

Besides capital goods, other inputs to production help to make workers more productive, among them land, energy, and raw materials. Fertile land is essential to agriculture, and modern manufacturing processes make intensive use of energy and raw materials.

In general, an abundance of natural resources increases the productivity of the workers who use them. For example, a farmer can produce a much larger crop in a land-rich country like the United States or Australia than in a country where the soil is poor or arable land is limited in supply. With the aid of modern farm machinery and great expanses of land, today's American farmers are so productive that even though they constitute less than 3 percent of the population, they provide enough food not only to feed the country but to export to the rest of the world.

Although there are limits to a country's supply of arable land, many other natural resources, such as petroleum and metals, can be obtained through international markets. Because resources can be obtained through trade, countries need not possess large quantities of natural resources within their own borders to achieve economic growth. Indeed, a number of countries have become rich without substantial natural resources of their own, including Japan, Hong Kong, Singapore, and Switzerland. Just as important as possessing natural resources is the ability to use them productively—for example, by means of advanced technologies.

TECHNOLOGY

Besides human capital, physical capital, and natural resources, a country's ability to develop and apply new, more productive technologies will help to determine its productivity. Consider just one industry, transportation. Two centuries ago, as suggested by the quote from Stephen Ambrose in the beginning of the chapter, the horse and wagon were the primary means of transportation—a slow and costly method indeed. But in the nineteenth century, technological advances such as the steam engine supported the expansion of riverborne transportation and the development of a national rail network. In the twentieth century, the invention of the internal combustion engine and the development of aviation, supported by the construction of an extensive infrastructure of roads and airports, have produced increasingly rapid, cheap, and reliable transport. Technological change has clearly been a driving force in the transportation revolution.

New technologies can improve productivity in industries other than the one in which they are introduced. Once farmers could sell their produce only in their local communities, for example. Now the availability of rapid shipping and refrigerated transport allows farmers to sell their products virtually anywhere in the world. With a broader market in which to sell, farmers can specialize in those products best suited to local land and weather conditions. Similarly, factories can obtain their raw materials wherever they are cheapest and most abundant, produce the goods they are most efficient at manufacturing, and sell their products wherever they will fetch the best price. Both these examples illustrate *the principle of comparative advantage,* that overall productivity increases when producers concentrate on those activities at which they are relatively most efficient (see Chapter 3).

Numerous other technological developments led to increased productivity, including advances in communication and medicine and the introduction of computer technology. All indications are that the Internet will have a major impact on the U.S. economy, not just in retailing but in many other sectors. In fact, *most economists would probably agree that new technologies are the single most important source of productivity improvement,* and hence of economic growth in general.

However, economic growth does not automatically follow from breakthroughs in basic science. To make the best use of new knowledge, an economy needs entrepreneurs who can exploit scientific advances commercially, as well as a legal and political environment that encourages the practical application of new knowledge.

EXERCISE 20.4

A new kind of wrapping paper has been invented that makes candy-wrapping quicker and easier. The use of this paper *increases* the number of candies a person can wrap by hand by 200 per hour, and the number of candies a person can wrap by machine by 300 per hour. Using the data from Examples 20.3 and 20.4, construct a table like Table 20.2 that shows how this technological advance affects average labor productivity. Do diminishing returns to capital still hold?

ENTREPRENEURSHIP AND MANAGEMENT

entrepreneurs people who create new economic enterprises

The productivity of workers depends in part on the people who help to decide what to produce and how to produce it: entrepreneurs and managers. **Entrepreneurs** are people who create new economic enterprises. Because of the new products, services, technological processes, and production methods they introduce, entrepreneurs are critical to a dynamic, healthy economy. In the late nineteenth and early twentieth centuries, individuals like Henry Ford and Alfred Sloan (automobiles), Andrew Carnegie (steel), John D. Rockefeller (oil), and J. P. Morgan (finance) played central roles in the development of American industry—and, not incidentally, amassed huge personal fortunes in the process. These people and others like them (including contemporary entrepreneurs like Bill Gates) have been criticized for some of their business practices, in some cases with justification. Clearly, though, they and dozens of other prominent business leaders of the past century have contributed significantly to the growth of the U.S. economy. Henry Ford, for example, developed the idea of mass production, which lowered costs sufficiently to bring automobiles within reach of the average American family. Ford began his business in his garage, a tradition that has been maintained by thousands of innovators ever since.

Entrepreneurship, like any form of creativity, is difficult to teach, although some of the supporting skills, like financial analysis and marketing, can be learned in college or business school. How, then, does a society encourage entrepreneurship? History suggests that the entrepreneurial spirit will always exist; the challenge to society is to channel entrepreneurial energies in economically productive ways. For example, economic policymakers need to ensure that taxation is not so heavy, and regulation not so inflexible, that small businesses—some of which will eventually become big businesses—cannot get off the ground. Sociological factors may play a role as well. Societies in which business and commerce are considered to be beneath the dignity of refined, educated people are less likely to produce successful entrepreneurs (see Economic Naturalist 20.2). In the United States, for the most part, business has been viewed as a respectable activity. Overall, a social and economic milieu that allows entrepreneurship to flourish appears to promote economic growth and rising productivity, perhaps especially so in high-technology eras like our own.

Lucy and Ethel get discovered

A television producer "discovers" Lucy and Ethel working on the production line at the candy factory and makes them stars of their own TV series. The show is a huge success and is seen by millions. How does the producer's discovery of Lucy and Ethel affect their average labor productivity?

Because Lucy and Ethel are so popular, and because television advertising fees are based on the number of people who watch a show, Lucy and Ethel are likely to increase the TV network's revenues by many millions of dollars. This increase in revenues is a measure of Lucy and Ethel's contribution to GDP. Their average labor productivity (in per-hour terms) is their contribution to GDP divided by the number of hours they work on the show. Clearly, Lucy's and Ethel's average labor productivity as TV stars will be many times what it was when they were candy wrappers.

This example illustrates the importance of creative entrepreneurship: If not for the TV producer's entrepreneurial skills, Lucy and Ethel would still be working on the assembly line, where their average labor productivity would be much lower.

EXAMPLE 20.5

Why did medieval China stagnate economically?

The Sung period in China (A.D. 960–1270) was one of considerable technological sophistication; its inventions included paper, waterwheels, water clocks, gunpowder, and possibly the compass. Yet no significant industrialization occurred, and in subsequent centuries Europe saw more economic growth and technological innovation than China. Why did medieval China stagnate economically?

According to research by economist William Baumol,[2] the main impediment to industrialization during the Sung period was a social system that inhibited entrepreneurship. Commerce and industry were considered low-status activities, not fit for an educated person. In addition, the emperor had the right to seize his subjects' property and to take control of their business enterprises—a right that greatly reduced his subjects' incentives to undertake business ventures. The most direct path to status and riches in medieval China was to go through a system of demanding civil service examinations given by the government every three years. The highest scorers on these national examinations were granted lifetime positions in the imperial bureaucracy, where they wielded much power and often became wealthy, in part through corruption. Not surprisingly, medieval China did not develop a dynamic entrepreneurial class, and consequently its scientific and technological advantages did not translate into sustained economic growth. China's experience shows why scientific advances alone cannot guarantee economic growth; to have economic benefits, scientific knowledge must be commercially applied through new products and new, more efficient means of producing goods and services.

ECONOMIC NATURALIST 20.2

Although entrepreneurship may be more glamorous, managers—the people who run businesses on a daily basis—also play an important role in determining average labor productivity. Managerial jobs span a wide range of positions, from the supervisor of the loading dock to the CEO (chief executive officer) at the helm of a *Fortune* 500 company. Managers work to satisfy customers, deal with

---

[2]"Entrepreneurship: Productive, Unproductive, and Destructive," *Journal of Political Economy,* October 1990, pp. 893–921.

suppliers, organize production, obtain financing, assign workers to jobs, and motivate them to work hard and effectively. Such activities enhance labor productivity. For example, in the 1970s and 1980s, Japanese managers introduced new production methods that greatly increased the efficiency of Japanese manufacturing plants. Among them was the *just-in-time* inventory system, in which suppliers deliver production components to the factory just when they are needed, eliminating the need for factories to stockpile components. Japanese managers also pioneered the idea of organizing workers into semi-independent production teams, which allowed workers more flexibility and responsibility than the traditional assembly line. Managers in the United States and other countries studied the Japanese managerial techniques closely and adopted many of them.

THE POLITICAL AND LEGAL ENVIRONMENT

So far we have emphasized the role of the private sector in increasing average labor productivity. But government too has a role to play in fostering improved productivity. One of the key contributions government can make is to provide a *political and legal environment* that encourages people to behave in economically productive ways—to work hard, save and invest wisely, acquire useful information and skills, and provide the goods and services that the public demands.

One specific function of government that appears to be crucial to economic success is the establishment of *well-defined property rights*. Property rights are well defined when the law provides clear rules for determining who owns what resources (through a system of deeds and titles, for example) and how those resources can be used. Imagine living in a society in which a dictator, backed by the military and the police, could take whatever he wanted, and regularly did so. In such a country, what incentive would you have to raise a large crop or to produce other valuable goods and services? Very little, since much of what you produced would likely be taken away from you. Unfortunately, in many countries of the world today, this situation is far from hypothetical.

Political and legal conditions affect the growth of productivity in other ways, as well. Political scientists and economists have documented the fact that *political instability* can be detrimental to economic growth. This finding is reasonable, since entrepreneurs and savers are unlikely to invest their resources in a country whose government is unstable, particularly if the struggle for power involves civil unrest, terrorism, or guerrilla warfare. On the other hand, a political system that promotes the *free and open exchange of ideas* will speed the development of new technologies and products. For example, some economic historians have suggested that the decline of Spain as an economic power was due in part to the advent of the Spanish Inquisition, which permitted no dissent from religious orthodoxy. Because of the Inquisition's persecution of those whose theories about the natural world contradicted Church doctrine, Spanish science and technology languished, and Spain fell behind more tolerant nations like the Netherlands.

EXERCISE 20.5

A Bangladeshi worker who immigrates to America is likely to find that his average labor productivity is much higher in the United States than it was at home. The worker is, of course, the same person he was when he lived in Bangladesh. How can the simple act of moving to the United States increase the worker's productivity? What does your answer say about the incentive to immigrate?

Why did communism fail?

For more than 70 years, from the Russian revolution in 1917 until the collapse of the Soviet Union in 1991, communism was believed by many to pose a major challenge to market-based economic systems. Yet, by the time of the Soviet Union's breakup, the poor economic record of communism had become apparent. Indeed, low living standards in communist countries, compared to those achieved in the West, were a major reason for the popular discontent that brought down the communist system in Europe. Economically speaking, why did communism fail?

The poor growth records of the Soviet Union and other communist countries did not reflect a lack of resources or economic potential. The Soviet Union had a highly educated workforce; a large capital stock; a vast quantity of natural resources, including land and energy; and access to sophisticated technologies. Yet, at the time of its collapse, output per person in the Soviet Union was probably less than one-seventh what it was in the United States.

Most observers would agree that the political and legal environment that established the structure of the communist economic system was a major cause of its ultimate failure. The economic system of the Soviet Union and other communist countries had two main elements: First, the capital stock and other resources were owned by the government rather than by individuals or private corporations. Second, most decisions regarding production and distribution were made and implemented by a government planning agency rather than by individuals and firms interacting through markets. This system performed poorly, we now understand, for several reasons.

One major problem was *the absence of private property rights*. With no ability to acquire a significant amount of private property, Soviet citizens had little incentive to behave in economically productive ways. The owner of an American or Japanese firm is strongly motivated to cut costs and to produce goods that are highly valued by the public, because the owner's income is determined by the firm's profitability. In contrast, the performance of a Soviet firm manager was judged on whether the manager produced the quantities of goods specified by the government's plan—irrespective of the quality of the goods produced or whether consumers wanted them. Soviet managers had little incentive to reduce costs or produce better, more highly valued products, as any extra profits would accrue to the government and not to the manager; nor was there any scope for entrepreneurs to start new businesses. Likewise, workers had little reason to work hard or effectively under the communist system, as pay rates were determined by the government planning agency rather than by the economic value of what the workers produced.

A second major weakness of the communist system was the *absence of free markets*. In centrally planned economies, markets are replaced by detailed government plans that specify what should be produced and how. But, as we saw in the example of New York City's food supply (Chapter 3), the coordination of even relatively basic economic activities can be extremely complex and require a great deal of information, much of which is dispersed among many people. In a market system, changes in prices both convey information about the goods and services people want and provide suppliers the incentives to bring these goods and services to market. Indeed, as we know from the *equilibrium principle,* a market in equilibrium leaves individuals with no unexploited opportunities. Central planners in communist countries proved far less able to deal with this complexity than decentralized markets. As a result, under communism consumers suffered constant shortages and shoddy goods.

After the collapse of communism, many formerly communist countries began the difficult transition to a market-oriented economic system. Changing an entire economic system (the most extreme example of a *structural policy*) is a slow and difficult task, and many countries saw economic conditions worsen at first rather than improve. *Political instability* and the absence of a modern *legal framework,*

ECONOMIC
NATURALIST
20.3

particularly laws applying to commercial transactions, have often hampered the progress of reforms. However, a number of formerly communist countries, including Poland, the Czech Republic, and the former East Germany, have succeeded in implementing Western-style market systems and have begun to achieve significant economic growth.

 RECAP   DETERMINANTS OF AVERAGE LABOR PRODUCTIVITY

Key factors determining average labor productivity in a country include:

■ The skills and training of workers, called *human capital*

■ The quantity and quality of *physical capital*—machines, equipment, and buildings

■ The availability of land and other *natural resources*

■ The sophistication of the *technologies* applied in production

■ The effectiveness of *management* and *entrepreneurship*

■ The broad *social and legal environment*

THE WORLDWIDE PRODUCTIVITY SLOWDOWN—AND RECOVERY?

During the 1950s and 1960s most of the major industrialized countries saw rapid growth in real GDP and average labor productivity. In the 1970s, however, productivity growth began to slow around the world. Slower growth in real GDP and in average living standards followed.

The slowdown in the growth of labor productivity is documented in Table 20.3, which gives data for five major industrialized countries. Note the sharp decline in productivity growth in all eight countries during 1973–1979 compared to 1960–1973. Japan's case was particularly striking: Its productivity growth rate fell from 7.6 percent per year in 1960–1973 to 2.7 percent in 1973–1979. In the United States, annual productivity growth fell from 2.3 percent before 1973 to just 0.6 percent per year during 1973–1979. During the period 1979–2000, productivity growth improved somewhat in the United States and the United Kingdom, but in all five countries, the rate of productivity improvement since 1979 has been much slower than it was prior to 1973.

TABLE 20.3
Average Labor Productivity Growth Rates in Selected Countries, 1960–2000

Country	Percentage growth, annual rates		
	1960–1973	1973–1979	1979–2000
France	4.6	2.3	1.8
Germany	4.0	2.6	2.0
Japan	7.6	2.7	2.0
United Kingdom	2.8	1.3	1.7
United States	2.3	0.6	1.7

SOURCE: Growth rates of real GDP per employed person, Bureau of Labor Statistics and OECD.

The sudden decline in worldwide productivity growth around 1973 is puzzling to economists and policymakers alike. What might have caused it? Some analysts have suggested answers that are specific to the United States, such as the perceived decline in the quality of public education. However, such explanations are not very convincing, since they do not explain why so many other countries had the same problem. In the 1970s and 1980s many economists thought that the fourfold increase in oil prices that followed the Arab–Israeli war (1973) might have caused the slowdown. However, oil prices (relative to the prices of other goods) have long since returned to pre-1973 levels, yet productivity growth has not. Thus oil prices are no longer thought to have played a critical role in the slowdown.

One view of the slowdown in productivity since 1973 is that (at least in part) it is not a real phenomenon but the result of *poor measurement of productivity growth*. According to this argument, many of the productivity improvements that occur in modern services-oriented economies are difficult to capture in economic statistics. For example, the computerization of inventories allows supermarkets to offer customers a wider variety of products, with less chance that a particular product will be out of stock. ATM machines allow people to make banking transactions 24 hours a day, not just when the bank is open. And many medical procedures can be done far more quickly, safely, and painlessly today than just a few years ago (see Economic Naturalist 19.2). In theory, all these improvements in the quality of services should be captured in real GDP, and hence in productivity measures. In reality, accurate measurement of improvements in quality is difficult, as we saw when discussing biases in the CPI in Chapter 19, and some improvements may be missed. If the productivity slowdown is not real but reflects only poor measurement, then economists need not worry about it.

Another explanation, which is not mutually exclusive with the first, has been called the *technological depletion hypothesis*.[3] According to this hypothesis, the high rates of productivity in the 1950s and 1960s reflected an unusual period of "catch-up" after the Depression and the Second World War. Although scientific and technical advances continued to be made during the 1930s and 1940s (many of which arose from military research), depression and war prevented them from being adapted to civilian use. During the 1950s and 1960s, the backlog of technological breakthroughs was applied commercially, producing high rates of productivity growth at first and then a sharp decline in new technological opportunities. Once the catch-up period was over, productivity growth slowed. According to this hypothesis, then, the slowdown in productivity growth since the 1970s reflects a dearth of technological opportunities relative to the immediate postwar period. From this perspective, the 1950s and 1960s were the exception, and the period since the 1970s represents a return to more normal rates of productivity growth.

Although the rate of productivity growth over the past two decades has generally been low, in recent years there have been some hints of a possible recovery in productivity, particularly in the United States. Between 1991 and 2000, U.S. productivity growth averaged nearly 2.3 percent per year, close to the rate achieved prior to 1973. Will this increase in productivity growth be sustained? Optimists argue that the United States is currently leading a new technological revolution, sparked by advances in computers, communications, genetics, and other fields, which will allow productivity to continue to grow indefinitely. Others are more cautious, arguing that the long-run commercial value of the new technologies has yet to be proven. A great deal is riding on which view will turn out to be correct.

---

[3]See, for example, William Nordhaus, "Economic Policy in the Face of Declining Productivity Growth," *European Economic Review*, May/June 1982, pp. 131–158.

THE COSTS OF ECONOMIC GROWTH

Both this chapter and Chapter 18 emphasized the positive effects of economic growth on the average person's living standard. But should societies always strive for the highest possible rate of economic growth? The answer is no. Even if we accept for the moment the idea that increased output per person is always desirable, attaining a higher rate of economic growth does impose costs on society.

What are the costs of increasing economic growth? The most straightforward is the cost of creating new capital. We know that by expanding the capital stock we can increase future productivity and output. But, to increase the capital stock, we must divert resources that could otherwise be used to increase the supply of consumer goods. For example, to add more robot-operated assembly lines, a society must employ more of its skilled technicians in building industrial robots and fewer in designing video games. To build new factories, more carpenters and lumber must be assigned to factory construction and less to finishing basements or renovating family rooms. In short, high rates of investment in new capital require people to tighten their belts, consume less, and save more—a real economic cost.

Should a country undertake a high rate of investment in capital goods at the sacrifice of consumer goods? The answer depends on the extent that people are willing and able to sacrifice consumption today to have a bigger economic pie tomorrow. In a country that is very poor, or is experiencing an economic crisis, people may prefer to keep consumption relatively high and savings and investment relatively low. The midst of a thunderstorm is not the time to be putting something aside for a rainy day! But in a society that is relatively well off, people may be more willing to make sacrifices to achieve higher economic growth in the future.

Consumption sacrificed to capital formation is not the only cost of achieving higher growth. In the United States in the nineteenth and early twentieth centuries, periods of rapid economic growth were often times in which many people worked extremely long hours at dangerous and unpleasant jobs. While those workers helped to build the economy that Americans enjoy today, the costs were great in terms of reduced leisure time and, in some cases, workers' health and safety.

Other costs of growth include the cost of the research and development that is required to improve technology and the costs of acquiring training and skill (human capital). The fact that a higher living standard tomorrow must be purchased at the cost of current sacrifices is an example of the *scarcity principle,* that having more of one good thing usually means having less of another. Because achieving higher economic growth imposes real economic costs, we know from the *cost-benefit principle* that higher growth should be pursued only if the benefits outweigh the costs.

PROMOTING ECONOMIC GROWTH

If a society decides to try to raise its rate of economic growth, what are some of the measures that policymakers might take to achieve this objective? Here is a short list of suggestions, based on our discussion of the factors that contribute to growth in average labor productivity and, hence, output per person.

POLICIES TO INCREASE HUMAN CAPITAL

Because skilled and well-educated workers are more productive than unskilled labor, governments in most countries try to increase the human capital of their citizens by supporting education and training programs. In the United States, government provides public education through high school and grants extensive support to post-secondary schools, including technical schools, colleges, and universities. Publicly

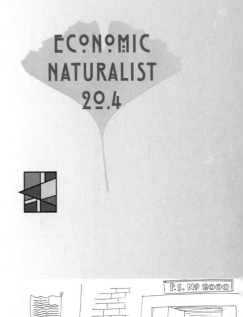

funded early intervention programs like Head Start also attempt to build human capital by helping disadvantaged children prepare for school. To a lesser degree than some other countries, the U.S. government also funds job training for unskilled youths and retraining for workers whose skills have become obsolete.

Why do almost all countries provide free public education?

All industrial countries provide their citizens free public education through high school, and most subsidize college and other post-secondary schools. Why?

Americans are so used to the idea of free public education that this question may seem odd. But why should the government provide free education when it does not provide even more essential goods and services, such as food or medical care, for free, except to the most needy? Furthermore, educational services can be, and indeed commonly are, supplied and demanded on the private market, without the aid of the government.

An important argument for free or at least subsidized education is that the private demand curve for educational services does not include all the social benefits of education. (Recall the *equilibrium principle* of Chapter 3, which states in part that a market in equilibrium may not exploit all gains achievable from collective action.) For example, the democratic political system relies on an educated citizenry to operate effectively—a factor that an individual demander of educational services has little reason to consider. From a narrower economic perspective, we might argue that individuals do not capture the full economic returns from their schooling. For example, people with high human capital, and thus high earnings, pay more taxes—funds that can be used to finance government services and aid the less fortunate. Because of income taxation, the private benefit to acquiring human capital is less than the social benefit, and the demand for education on the private market may be less than optimal from society's viewpoint. Similarly, educated people are more likely than others to contribute to technological development, and hence to general productivity growth, which may benefit many other people besides themselves. Finally, another argument for public support of education is that poor people who would like to invest in human capital may not be able to do so because of insufficient income.

The Nobel laureate Milton Friedman, among many economists, suggested that these arguments may justify government grants, called educational *vouchers,* to help citizens purchase educational services in the private sector, but they do *not* justify the government providing education directly, as through the public school system. Defenders of public education, on the other hand, argue that the government should have some direct control over education in order to set standards and monitor quality. What do you think?

ECONOMIC NATURALIST 20.4

Why do almost all countries provide free public education?

POLICIES THAT PROMOTE SAVING AND INVESTMENT

Average labor productivity increases when workers can utilize a sizable and modern capital stock. To support the creation of new capital, government can encourage high rates of saving and investment in the private sector. Many provisions in the U.S. tax code are designed expressly to stimulate households to save and firms to invest. For example, a household that opens an Individual Retirement Account (IRA) is able to save for retirement without paying taxes on either the funds deposited in the IRA or the interest earned on the account. (However, taxes are due when the funds are withdrawn at retirement.) The intent of IRA legislation is to make saving more financially attractive to American households. Similarly, at various times Congress has instituted an investment tax credit, which reduces the tax bills of firms that invest in new capital. Private-sector saving and investment are discussed in greater detail in Chapter 22.

Government can contribute directly to capital formation through *public investment,* or the creation of government-owned capital. Public investment includes the building of roads, bridges, airports, dams, and, in some countries, energy and communications networks. The construction of the U.S. interstate highway system, begun during the administration of President Eisenhower, is often cited as an example of successful public investment. The interstate system substantially reduced long-haul transportation costs in the United States, improving productivity throughout the economy. Today, the web of computers and communications links we call the Internet is having a similar effect. This project, too, received crucial government funding in its early stages. Many research studies have confirmed that government investment in the *infrastructure,* the public capital that supports private-sector economic activities, can be a significant source of growth.

POLICIES THAT SUPPORT RESEARCH AND DEVELOPMENT

Productivity is enhanced by technological progress, which in turn requires investment in research and development (R&D). In many industries private firms have adequate incentive to conduct research and development activities. There is no need, for example, for the government to finance research for developing a better underarm deodorant. But some types of knowledge, particularly basic scientific knowledge, may have widespread economic benefits that cannot be captured by a single private firm. The developers of the silicon computer chip, for example, were instrumental in creating huge new industries, yet they received only a small portion of the profits flowing from their inventions. Because society in general, rather than the individual inventors, may receive much of the benefit from basic research, government may need to support basic research, as it does through agencies such as the National Science Foundation. The federal government also sponsors a great deal of applied research, particularly in military and space applications. To the extent that national security allows, the government can increase growth by sharing the fruits of such research with the private sector. For example, the Global Positioning System (GPS), which was developed originally for military purposes, is now available in private passenger vehicles, helping drivers find their way.

THE LEGAL AND POLITICAL FRAMEWORK

Although economic growth comes primarily from activities in the private sector, the government plays an essential role in providing the framework within which the private sector can operate productively. We have discussed the importance of secure property rights and a well-functioning legal system, of an economic environment that encourages entrepreneurship, and of political stability and the free and open exchange of ideas. Government policymakers should also consider the potential effects of tax and regulatory policies on activities that increase productivity, such as investment, innovation, and risk taking. Policies that affect the legal and political framework are examples of *structural macroeconomic policies* (see Chapter 17).

THE POOREST COUNTRIES: A SPECIAL CASE?

Radical disparities in living standards exist between the richest and poorest countries of the world (see Table 18.4 for some data). Achieving economic growth in the poorest countries is thus particularly urgent. Are the policy prescriptions of this section relevant to those countries, or are very different types of measures necessary to spur growth in the poorest nations?

To a significant extent, the same factors and policies that promote growth in richer countries apply to the poorest countries as well. Increasing human capital by supporting education and training, increasing rates of saving and investment, investing in public capital and infrastructure, supporting research and development, and encouraging entrepreneurship are all measures that will enhance economic growth in poor countries.

However, to a much greater degree than in richer countries, most poor countries need to improve the legal and political environment that underpins their economies. For example, many developing countries have poorly developed or corrupt legal systems, which discourage entrepreneurship and investment by creating uncertainty about property rights. Taxation and regulation in developing countries are often heavy-handed and administered by inefficient bureaucracies, to the extent that it may take months or years to obtain the approvals needed to start a small business or expand a factory. Regulation is also used to suppress market forces in poor countries; for example, the government, rather than the market, may determine the allocation of bank credit or the prices for agricultural products. Structural policies that aim to ameliorate these problems are important preconditions for generating growth in the poorest countries. But probably most important—and most difficult, for some countries—is establishing political stability and the rule of law. Without political stability, domestic and foreign savers will be reluctant to invest in the country, and economic growth will be difficult if not impossible to achieve.

Can rich countries help poor countries to develop? Historically, richer nations have tried to help by providing financial aid through loans or grants from individual countries (foreign aid) or by loans made by international agencies, such as the World Bank. Experience has shown, however, that financial aid to countries that do not undertake structural reforms, such as reducing excessive regulation or improving the legal system, is of limited value. To make their foreign aid most effective, rich countries should help poor countries achieve political stability and undertake the necessary reforms to the structure of their economies.

ARE THERE LIMITS TO GROWTH?

Earlier in this chapter we saw that even relatively low rates of economic growth, if sustained for a long period, will produce huge increases in the size of the economy. This fact raises the question of whether economic growth can continue indefinitely without depleting natural resources and causing massive damage to the global environment. Does the basic truth that we live in a finite world of finite resources imply that, ultimately, economic growth must come to an end?

The concern that economic growth may not be sustainable is not a new one. An influential 1972 book, *The Limits to Growth*,[4] reported the results of computer simulations that suggested that unless population growth and economic expansion were halted, the world would soon be running out of natural resources, drinkable water, and breathable air. This book, and later works in the same vein, raise some fundamental questions that cannot be done full justice here. However, in some ways its conclusions are misleading.

One problem with the "limits to growth" thesis lies in its underlying concept of economic growth. Those who emphasize the environmental limits on growth assume implicitly that economic growth will always take the form of more of what we have now—more smoky factories, more polluting cars, more fast-food restaurants. If that were indeed the case, then surely there would be limits to the growth the planet can sustain. But growth in real GDP does not necessarily take such a form. Increases in real GDP can also arise from new or higher-quality products. For example, not too long ago tennis rackets were relatively simple items made primarily of wood. Today they are made of newly invented synthetic materials and designed for optimum performance using sophisticated computer simulations. Because these new high-tech tennis rackets are more valued by consumers than the old wooden ones, they increase the real GDP. Likewise, the introduction of new pharmaceuticals has contributed to economic growth, as have the expanded

[4]Donella H. Meadows, Dennis L. Meadows, Jørgen Randers, and William W. Behrens, III, *The Limits to Growth*, New York: New American Library, 1972.

number of TV channels, digital sound, and Internet-based sales. Thus, economic growth need not take the form of more and more of the same old stuff; it can mean newer, better, and perhaps cleaner and more efficient goods and services.

A second problem with the "limits to growth" conclusion is that it overlooks the fact that increased wealth and productivity expand society's capacity to take measures to safeguard the environment. In fact, the most polluted countries in the world are not the richest but those that are in a relatively early stage of industrialization (see Economic Naturalist 20.5). At this stage countries must devote the bulk of their resources to basic needs—food, shelter, health care—and continued industrial expansion. In these countries, clean air and water may be viewed as a luxury rather than a basic need. In more economically developed countries, where the most basic needs are more easily met, extra resources are available to keep the environment clean. Thus continuing economic growth may lead to less, not more, pollution.

A third problem with the pessimistic view of economic growth is that it ignores the power of the market and other social mechanisms to deal with scarcity. During the oil-supply disruptions of the 1970s, newspapers were filled with headlines about the energy crisis and the imminent depletion of world oil supplies. Yet 30 years later, the world's known oil reserves are actually *greater* than they were in the 1970s.

Today's energy situation is so much better than was expected 30 years ago because the market went to work. Reduced oil supplies led to an increase in prices that changed the behavior of both demanders and suppliers. Consumers insulated their homes, purchased more energy-efficient cars and appliances, and switched to alternative sources of energy. Suppliers engaged in a massive hunt for new reserves, opening up major new sources in Latin America, China, and the North Sea. In short, market forces solved the energy crisis.

In general, shortages in any resource will trigger price changes that induce suppliers and demanders to deal with the problem. Simply extrapolating current economic trends into the future ignores the power of the market system to recognize shortages and make the necessary corrections. Government actions spurred by political pressures, such as the allocation of public funds to preserve open space or reduce air pollution, can be expected to supplement market adjustments.

Despite the shortcomings of the "limits to growth" perspective, most economists would agree that not all the problems created by economic growth can be dealt with effectively through the market or the political process. Probably most important, global environmental problems, such as the possibility of global warming or the ongoing destruction of rain forests, are a particular challenge for existing economic and political institutions. Environmental quality is not bought and sold in markets and thus will not automatically reach its optimal level through market processes (recall the *equilibrium principle*). Nor can local or national governments effectively address problems that are global in scope. Unless international mechanisms are established for dealing with global environmental problems, these problems may become worse as economic growth continues.

Why is the air quality so poor in Mexico City?

Developing countries like Mexico, which are neither fully industrialized nor desperately poor, often have severe environmental problems. Why?

One concern about economic growth is that it will cause ever-increasing levels of environmental pollution. Empirical studies show, however, that the relationship between pollution and real GDP per person is more like an inverted U (see Figure 20.5). In other words, as countries move from very low levels of real GDP per person to "middle-income" levels, most measures of pollution tend to worsen, but environmental quality improves as real GDP per person rises even further. One study of the relationship between air quality and real GDP per person found that the level of real GDP per person at which air quality is the worst—indicated by

ECONOMIC NATURALIST 20.5

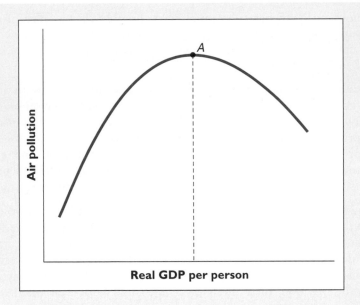

FIGURE 20.5
The Relationship between Air Pollution and Real GDP per Person.
Empirically, air pollution increases with real GDP per person up to a point and then begins to decline. Maximum air pollution (point A) occurs at a level of real GDP per person roughly equal to that of Mexico.

point *A* in Figure 20.5—is roughly equal to the average income level in Mexico.[5] And indeed, the air quality in Mexico City is exceptionally poor, as any visitor to that sprawling metropolis can attest.

That pollution may worsen as a country industrializes is understandable, but why does environmental quality improve when real GDP per person climbs to very high levels? There are a variety of explanations for this phenomenon. Compared to middle-income economies, the richer economies are relatively more concentrated in "clean," high-value services like finance and software production as opposed to pollution-intensive industries like heavy manufacturing. Rich economies are also more likely to have the expertise to develop sophisticated and cost-effective antipollution technologies. But the main reason the richer economies tend to be cleaner is the same reason that the homes of rich people are generally cleaner and in better condition than the homes of the poor. As income rises above the level necessary to fulfill basic needs, more resources remain to dedicate to "luxuries" like a clean environment (the *scarcity principle*). For the rich family, the extra resources will pay for a cleaning service; for the rich country, they will pay for pollution control devices in factories and on automobiles. Indeed, antipollution laws are generally tougher and more strictly enforced in rich countries than in middle-income and poor countries.

 RECAP   **ECONOMIC GROWTH: DEVELOPMENTS AND ISSUES**

- Labor productivity growth slowed throughout the industrialized world in the early 1970s. One possible explanation is that productivity growth has become harder to measure; another is the technological depletion hypothesis, that technological opportunities occur less frequently today than in the immediate postwar period. Some evidence suggests a recent resurgence in productivity growth in the United States.

[5]Gene M. Grossman and Alan B. Krueger, "Environmental Impacts of a North American Free Trade Agreement," in Peter Garber, ed., *The Mexico–U.S. Free Trade Agreement,* Cambridge, MA: MIT Press, 1993. See also Grossman and Krueger, "Economic Growth and the Environment," *Quarterly Journal of Economics,* May 1995, pp. 353–78; and World Bank, *World Development Report: Development and the Environment,* 1992.

■ Economic growth has substantial costs, notably the sacrifice of current consumption that is required to free resources for creating new capital and new technologies. Higher rates of growth should be pursued only if the benefits outweigh the costs.

■ Policies for promoting economic growth include policies to increase human capital (education and training); policies that promote saving and capital formation; policies that support research and development; and the provision of a legal and political framework within which the private sector can operate productively. Deficiencies in the legal and political framework (for example, official corruption or poorly defined property rights) are a special problem for many developing countries.

■ Some have argued that finite resources imply ultimate limits to economic growth. This view overlooks the facts that growth can take the form of better, rather than more, goods and services; that increased wealth frees resources to safeguard the environment; and that political and economic mechanisms exist to address many of the problems associated with growth. However, these mechanisms may not work well when environmental or other problems arising from economic growth are global in scope.

■ SUMMARY ■

- Over the past two centuries the industrialized nations saw enormous improvements in living standards, as reflected in large increases in real GDP per person. Because of the power of *compound interest,* relatively small differences in growth rates, if continued over long periods, can produce large differences in real GDP per person and average living standards. Thus, the rate of long-term economic growth is an economic variable of critical importance.

- Real GDP per person is the product of average labor productivity (real GDP per employed worker) and the share of the population that is employed. Growth in real GDP per person can occur only through growth in average labor productivity, in the share of the population that is working, or both. In the period since 1960, increases in the share of the U.S. population holding a job contributed significantly to rising real GDP per person. But in the past four decades, as in most periods, the main source of the increase in real GDP per person was rising average labor productivity.

- Among the factors that determine labor productivity are the talents, education, training, and skills of workers, or human capital; the quantity and quality of the physical capital that workers use; the availability of land and other natural resources; the application of technology to the production and distribution of goods and services; the effectiveness of *entrepreneurs* and managers; and the broad social and legal environment. Because of *diminishing returns to capital,* beyond a certain point expansion of the capital stock is not the most effective way to increase average labor productivity. Economists generally agree that new technologies are the most important single source of improvements in productivity.

- Since the 1970s the industrial world has experienced a slowdown in productivity growth. Some economists have suggested that the "slowdown" is more the result of an inability to measure increases in the quality of output than of any real economic change. Others have suggested that the exploitation of a backlog of technological opportunities following the Great Depression and World War II led to unusually high growth rates in the 1950s and 1960s, a view called the technological depletion hypothesis. In this view, the slower growth in U.S. productivity since about 1970 in fact reflects a return to a more normal rate of growth. U.S. productivity growth has picked up since about 1991, however, possibly as the result of new technologies.

- Economic growth has costs as well as benefits. Prominent among them is the need to sacrifice current consumption to achieve a high rate of investment in new capital goods; other costs of growing more quickly include extra work effort and the costs of research and development. Thus more economic growth is not necessarily better; whether increased economic growth is desirable depends on whether the benefits of growth outweigh the costs.

- Among the ways in which government can stimulate economic growth are by adopting policies that encourage the creation of human capital; that promote saving and investment, including public investment in infrastructure; that support research and development, particularly in the basic sciences; and that provide a legal and political framework that supports private-sector activities. The poorest countries, with poorly developed legal, tax, and regulatory systems, are often in the greatest need of an improved legal and political framework and increased political stability.

- Are there limits to growth? Arguments that economic growth must be constrained by environmental problems and the limits of natural resources ignore the fact that economic growth can take the form of increasing quality as well as increasing quantity. Indeed, increases in output can provide additional resources for cleaning up the environment. Finally, the market system, together with political processes, can solve many of the problems associated with economic growth. On the other hand, global environmental problems, which can be handled neither by the market nor by individual national governments, have the potential to constrain economic growth.

▪ KEY TERMS ▪

compound interest (509)   diminishing returns to capital (516)   entrepreneurs (518)

▪ REVIEW QUESTIONS ▪

1. What has happened to real GDP per person in the industrialized countries over the past century? What implications does this have for the average person?

2. Why do economists consider growth in average labor productivity to be the key factor in determining long-run living standards?

3. What is *human capital*? Why is it economically important? How is new human capital created?

4. You have employed five workers of varying physical strength to dig a ditch. Workers without shovels have zero productivity in ditchdigging. How should you assign shovels to workers if you don't have enough shovels to go around? How should you assign any additional shovels that you obtain? Using this example, discuss (a) the relationship between the availability of physical capital and average labor productivity and (b) the concept of diminishing returns to capital.

5. Discuss how talented entrepreneurs and effective managers can enhance average labor productivity.

6. What major contributions can the government make to the goal of increasing average labor productivity?

7. What explanations have been offered for the slowdown in productivity growth observed in industrial countries since the early 1970s?

8. Discuss the following statement: "Because the environment is fragile and natural resources are finite, ultimately economic growth must come to an end."

▪ PROBLEMS ▪

1. Richland's real GDP per person is $10,000, and Poorland's real GDP per person is $5,000. However, Richland's real GDP per person is growing at 1 percent per year and Poorland's is growing at 3 percent per year. Compare real GDP per person in the two countries after 10 years and after 20 years. Approximately how many years will it take Poorland to catch up to Richland?

2. Refer to Table 20.3 for growth rates of average labor productivity over the periods 1960–1973, 1973–1979, and 1979–2000. Suppose that growth of average labor productivity in the United States had continued at its 1960–1973 rate until 2000. Proportionally, how much higher would U.S. average labor productivity in 2000 have been, compared to its actual value? (*Note:* You do not need to know the actual values of average labor productivity in any year to solve this problem.) Does your answer shed light on why economists consider the post-1973 productivity slowdown to be an important issue?

3. The "graying of America" will substantially increase the fraction of the population that is retired in the decades to come. To illustrate the implications for U.S. living standards, suppose that over the 40 years following 2000 the share of the population that is working returns to its 1960 level, while average labor productivity increases by as much as it did during 1960–2000. Under this scenario, what would be the net change in real GDP per person between 2000 and 2040? The following data will be useful:

	Average labor productivity	Share of population employed
1960	$35,836	36.4%
2000	$66,588	48.9%

4. Here are data for Canada, Germany, and Japan on the ratio of employment to population in 1979 and 2000:

	1979	2000
Canada	0.45	0.46
Germany	0.34	0.33
Japan	0.47	0.51

Using data from Table 20.1, find average labor productivity for each country in 1979 and in 2000. How much of the increase in output per person in each country over the 1979–2000 period is due to increased labor productivity? To increased employment relative to population?

5. Joanne has just completed high school and is trying to determine whether to go to junior college for two years or go directly to work. Her objective is to maximize the savings she will have in the bank five years from now. If she goes directly to work she will earn $20,000 per year for each of the next five years. If she goes to junior college, for each of the next two years she will earn nothing—indeed, she will have to borrow $6,000 each year to cover tuition and books. This loan must be repaid in full three years after graduation. If she graduates from junior college, in each of the subsequent three years her wages will be $38,000 per year. Joanne's total living expenses and taxes, excluding tuition and books, equal $15,000 per year.
   a. Suppose for simplicity that Joanne can borrow and lend at 0 percent interest. On purely economic grounds, should she go to junior college or work?
   b. Does your answer to part a change if she can earn $23,000 per year with only a high school degree?
   c. Does your answer to part a change if Joanne's tuition and books cost $8,000 per year?
   d.* Suppose that the interest rate at which Joanne can borrow and lend is 10 percent per year, but other data are as in part a. Savings are deposited at the end of the year they are earned and receive (compound) interest at the end of each subsequent year. Similarly, the loans are taken out at the end of the year in which they are needed, and interest does not accrue until the end of the subsequent year. Now that the interest rate has risen, should Joanne go to college or go to work?

6. The Good'n'Fresh Grocery Store has two checkout lanes and four employees. Employees are equally skilled, and all are able either to operate a register (checkers) or bag groceries (baggers). The store owner assigns one checker and one bagger to each lane. A lane with a checker and a bagger can check out 40 customers per hour. A lane with a checker only can check out 25 customers per hour.
   a. In terms of customers checked out per hour, what is total output and average labor productivity for the Good'n'Fresh Grocery Store?
   b. The owner adds a third checkout lane and register. Assuming that no employees are added, what is the best way to reallocate the workers to tasks? What is total output and average labor productivity (in terms of customers checked out per hour) now?
   c. Repeat part b for the addition of a fourth checkout lane, and a fifth. Do you observe diminishing returns to capital in this example?

7. Harrison, Carla, and Fred are housepainters. Harrison and Carla can paint 100 square feet per hour using a standard paintbrush, and Fred can paint 80 square feet per hour. Any of the three can paint 200 square feet per hour using a roller.
   a. Assume Harrison, Carla, and Fred have only paintbrushes at their disposal. What is the average labor productivity, in terms of square feet per painter-hour, for the three painters taken as a team? Assume that the three painters always work the same number of hours.
   b. Repeat part a for the cases in which the team has one, two, three, or four rollers available. Are there diminishing returns to capital?
   c. An improvement in paint quality increases the area that can be covered per hour (by either brushes or rollers) by 20 percent. How does this technological improvement

*Problem marked by an asterisk (*) is more difficult.

affect your answers to part b? Are there diminishing returns to capital? Does the technological improvement increase or reduce the economic value of an additional roller?

8. Hester's Hatchery raises fish. At the end of the current season she has 1,000 fish in the hatchery. She can harvest any number of fish that she wishes, selling them to restaurants for $5 apiece. Because big fish make little fish, for every fish that she leaves in the hatchery this year she will have two fish at the end of next year. The price of fish is expected to be $5 each next year as well. Hester relies entirely on income from current fish sales to support herself.
   a. How many fish should Hester harvest if she wants to maximize the growth of her stock of fish from this season to next season?
   b. Do you think maximizing the growth of her fish stock is an economically sound strategy for Hester? Why or why not? Relate to the text discussion on the costs of economic growth.
   c. How many fish should Hester harvest if she wants to maximize her current income? Do you think this is a good strategy?
   d. Explain why Hester is unlikely to harvest either all or none of her fish, but instead will harvest some and leave the rest to reproduce.

9. True or False: For advances in basic science to translate into improvements in standards of living, they must be supported by favorable economic conditions. Discuss, using concrete examples where possible to illustrate your arguments.

10. Write a short essay evaluating the U.S. economy in terms of each of the six determinants of average labor productivity discussed in the text. Are there any areas in which the U.S. is exceptionally strong, relative to other countries? Areas where the U.S. is less strong than some other countries? Illustrate your arguments with numbers from the *Statistical Abstract of the United States* (available online at www.census.gov/statab/www/) and other sources, as appropriate.

■ ANSWERS TO IN-CHAPTER EXERCISES ■

20.1 If the United States had grown at the Japanese rate for the period 1870–2000, real GDP per person in 2000 would have been ($2,843) × ($1.025^{130}$) = $70,450. Actual GDP per person in the United States in 2000 was $32,629, so at the higher rate of growth output per person would have been $70,450/$32,629 = 2.16 times higher.

20.2 As before Lucy can wrap 4,000 candies per week, or 100 candies per hour. Ethel can wrap 500 candies per hour, and working 40 hours weekly she can wrap 20,000 candies per week. Together Lucy and Ethel can wrap 24,000 candies per week. Since they work a total of 80 hours between them, their output per hour as a team is 24,000 candies wrapped per 80 hours = 300 candies wrapped per hour, midway between their hourly productivities as individuals.

20.3 Because Ethel can wrap 300 candies per hour by hand, the benefit of giving Ethel the machine is 500 − 300 = 200 additional candies wrapped per hour. Because Lucy wraps only 100 candies per hour by hand, the benefit of giving Lucy the machine is 400 additional candies wrapped per hour. So the benefit of giving the machine to Lucy is greater than of giving it to Ethel. Equivalently, if the machine goes to Ethel, then Lucy and Ethel between them can wrap 500 + 100 = 600 candies per hour, but if Lucy uses the machine the team can wrap 300 + 500 = 800 candies per hour. So output is increased by letting Lucy use the machine.

20.4 Now, working by hand, Lucy can wrap 300 candies per hour and Ethel can wrap 500 candies per hour. With a machine, either Lucy or Ethel can wrap 800 candies per hour. As in Exercise 20.3, the benefit of giving a machine to Lucy (500 candies per hour) exceeds the benefit of giving a machine to Ethel (300 candies per hour), so if only one machine is available Lucy should use it.

The table analogous to Table 20.2 now looks like this:

Relationship of Capital, Output, and Productivity in the Candy-Wrapping Factory

Number of machines (K)	Candies wrapped per week (Y)	Total hours worked (N)	Average hourly labor productivity (Y/N)
0	32,000	80	400
1	52,000	80	650
2	64,000	80	800
3	64,000	80	800

Comparing this table with Table 20.2, you can see that technological advance has increased labor productivity for any value of K, the number of machines available.

Adding one machine increases output by 20,000 candies wrapped per week, adding the second machine increases output by 12,000 candies wrapped per week, and adding the third machine does not increase output at all (because there is no worker available to use it). So diminishing returns to capital still hold after the technological improvement.

20.5 Although the individual worker is the same person he was in Bangladesh, by coming to the United States he gains the benefit of factors that enhance average labor productivity in this country, relative to his homeland. These include more and better capital to work with, more natural resources per person, more advanced technologies, sophisticated entrepreneurs and managers, and a political-legal environment that is conducive to high productivity. It is not guaranteed that the value of the immigrant's human capital will rise (it may not, for example, if he speaks no English and has no skills applicable to the U.S. economy), but normally it will.

Since increased productivity leads to higher wages and living standards, on economic grounds the Bangladeshi worker has a strong incentive to immigrate to the United States if he is able to do so.

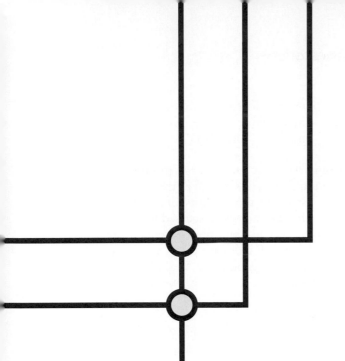

WORKERS, WAGES, AND UNEMPLOYMENT IN THE MODERN ECONOMY

■

A book by *New York Times* columnist Thomas L. Friedman about the changing world economy, *The Lexus and the Olive Tree*,[1] contains a remarkable photograph. Taken in Jerusalem a few years ago, the photo shows an orthodox Jew, Shimon Biton, praying at the Western Wall, one of Judaism's most sacred places. Mr. Biton's devotions are not unusual—indeed thousands of Jews pray at the Wall every day. What *is* unusual about the photograph is that it shows Mr. Biton holding a cell phone up against the Wall. Through the cell phone, a relative of Mr. Biton's in France is fulfilling his religious obligation to pray "at" the Western Wall.

The photograph nicely illustrates the theme of Friedman's book, that one of the most striking features of the modern world is the close juxtaposition of rapid economic and technological change with traditional values and customs. The photograph suggests that Mr. Biton is quite comfortable combining the traditional and the modern, but as Friedman's book emphasizes, not everyone is so comfortable. In many countries, the conflicting pulls of modernization and traditional ways of life have created enormous social conflicts.

[1] New York: Farrar, Straus, & Giroux, 1999.

© AP Photo/Nati Harnik

Economically, Friedman argues, the powerful forces of modernization have widened the gap between the "haves"—those who can take advantage of rapid technological and economic change—and the "have-nots"—those who are unable or unwilling to do so.

In Chapter 20 we examined the remarkable economic growth and increased productivity that have occurred in the industrialized world over the past two centuries. These developments have greatly increased the quantity of goods and services that the economy can produce. But we have not yet discussed how the fruits of economic growth are distributed. Has everyone benefited equally from economic growth and increased productivity? Or as Friedman's thesis would suggest, is the population divided between those who have caught the "train" of economic modernization, enriching themselves in the process, and those who have been left at the station?

To understand how economic growth and change affect different groups, we must turn to the labor market. Except for retirees and others receiving government support, most people rely almost entirely on wages and salaries to pay their bills and put something away for the future. Hence it is in the labor market that most people will see the benefits of the economic growth and increasing productivity. This chapter describes and explains some important trends in the labor markets of industrial countries. Using a supply and demand model of the labor market, we focus first on several important trends in real wages and employment. In the second part of the chapter we turn to the problem of unemployment, especially long-term unemployment. We will see that two key factors contributing to recent trends in wages, employment, and unemployment are the *globalization* of the economy, as reflected in the increasing importance of international trade, and ongoing *technological change*. By the end of the chapter, you will better understand the connection between these macroeconomic developments and the economic fortunes of workers and their families.

FIVE IMPORTANT LABOR MARKET TRENDS

In recent decades, at least five trends have characterized the labor markets of the industrialized world. We divide these trends into two groups: those affecting real wages and those affecting employment and unemployment.

TRENDS IN REAL WAGES

1. Over the twentieth century, all industrial countries have enjoyed substantial growth in real wages.

In the United States in 2000, the average worker's yearly earnings could command nearly twice as many goods and services as in 1960 and about four times as much as in 1929, just prior to the Great Depression. Similar trends have prevailed in other industrialized countries.

2. Since the early 1970s, however, the rate of real wage growth has slowed.

Though the post–World War II period has seen impressive increases in real wages, the fastest rates of increase occurred during the 1960s and early 1970s. In the 13 years between 1960 to 1973 the buying power of workers' incomes rose at a rate of 2.57 percent per year, a strong rate of increase. But from 1973 to 1996, real yearly earnings grew at only 0.93 percent per year. The good news is that, from 1996 to 2001, real earnings grew at 2.75 percent per year, despite a recession in 2001. However, annual earnings growth for the whole 1973–2001 period, at 1.15 percent per year, remained well below what was achieved prior to 1973.

3. Furthermore, recent decades have brought a pronounced increase in wage inequality in the United States.

A growing gap in real wages between skilled and unskilled workers has been of particular concern. Indeed, the real wages of the least-skilled, least-educated workers have actually *declined* since the early 1970s, by as much as 25 to 30 percent according to some studies. At the same time, the best-educated, highest-skilled workers have enjoyed continuing gains in real wages. Data for a recent year showed that, in the United States, the typical worker with a master's degree earned twice the income of a high school graduate and four times the income of a worker with fewer than nine years of schooling. Many observers worry that the United States is developing a "two-tier" labor market: plenty of good jobs at good wages for the well-educated and highly skilled, but less and less opportunity for those without schooling or skills.

Outside the United States, particularly in western Europe, the trend toward wage inequality has been much less pronounced. But, as we will see, employment trends in Europe have not been as encouraging as in the United States. Let's turn now to the trends in employment and unemployment.

TRENDS IN EMPLOYMENT AND UNEMPLOYMENT

4. In the United States, the number of people with jobs has grown substantially in recent decades.

In 1970, about 57 percent of the over-16 population in the United States had jobs. By 2000, total U.S. employment exceeded 135 million people, more than 64 percent of the over-16 population. Between 1980 and 2000, the U.S. economy created more than 35 million new jobs—an increase in total employment of 36 percent—while the over-16 population grew only 25 percent. Similar job growth has *not* occurred in most other industrialized countries, however. In particular:

5. Western European countries have been suffering high rates of unemployment for almost two decades.

In France, for example, an average of 10.9 percent of the workforce was unemployed over the period 1990–2001, compared to just 5.5 percent in the United States. Figure 21.9, page 558, shows recent unemployment rates in four western European countries. Consistent with the high rates of unemployment, rates of job creation in western Europe have been exceptionally weak.

Given the trend toward increasing wage inequality in the United States and the persistence of high unemployment in Europe, we may conclude that a significant fraction of the industrial world's labor force has not been sharing in the recent economic growth and prosperity. Whereas in the United States the problem takes the form of low and falling real wages for unskilled workers, in Europe work is often simply unavailable for the unskilled and sometimes even for the skilled.

What explains these trends in employment and wages? In the remainder of the chapter we will show that a supply and demand analysis of the labor market can help to explain these important developments.

> **RECAP** | **IMPORTANT LABOR MARKET TRENDS**
>
> 1. Over a long period, average real wages have risen substantially both in the United States and in other industrialized countries.
>
> 2. Despite the long-term upward trend in real wages, real wage growth has slowed significantly in the United States since the early 1970s.
>
> 3. In the United States wage inequality has increased dramatically in recent decades. The real wages of most unskilled workers have actually declined, while the real wages of skilled and educated workers have continued to rise.
>
> 4. Employment has grown substantially—indeed, much faster than the working-age population—in the United States in recent decades.
>
> 5. Since about 1980 western European nations have experienced very high rates of unemployment and low rates of job creation.

SUPPLY AND DEMAND IN THE LABOR MARKET

In Chapter 3 we saw how supply and demand analysis can be used to determine equilibrium prices and quantities for individual goods and services. The same approach is equally useful for studying labor market conditions. In the market for labor, the "price" is the wage paid to workers in exchange for their services. The wage is expressed per unit of time, for example, per hour or per year. The "quantity" is the amount of labor firms use, which in this book we will generally measure by number of workers employed. Alternatively, we could state the quantity of labor in terms of the number of hours worked; the choice of units is a matter of convenience.

Who are the demanders and suppliers in the labor market? Firms and other employers demand labor in order to produce goods and services. Virtually all of us supply labor during some phase of our lives. Whenever people work for pay, they are supplying labor services at a price equal to the wage they receive. In this chapter, we will discuss both the supply of and demand for labor, with an emphasis on the demand side of the labor market. Changes in the demand for labor turn out to be key in explaining the aggregate trends in wages and employment described in the preceding section.

The labor market is studied by microeconomists as well as macroeconomists, and both use the tools of supply and demand. However, microeconomists focus on issues such as the determination of wages for specific types of jobs or workers. In this chapter we take the macroeconomic approach and examine factors that affect aggregate, or economywide, trends in employment and wages.

WAGES AND THE DEMAND FOR LABOR

Let's start by thinking about what determines the number of workers employers want to hire at any given wage, that is, the demand for labor. As we will see, the demand for labor depends both on the productivity of labor and the price that the market sets on workers' output. The more productive workers are, or the more valuable the goods and services they produce, the greater the number of workers an employer will want to hire at any given wage.

Table 21.1 shows the relationship between output and the number of workers employed at the Banana Computer Company (BCC), which builds and sells computers. Column 1 of the table shows some different possibilities for the number of technicians BCC could employ in its plant. Column 2 shows how many computers the company can produce each year, depending on the number of

TABLE 21.1
Production and Marginal Product for Banana Computers

(1) Number of workers	(2) Computers produced per year	(3) Marginal product	(4) Value of marginal product (at $3,000/computer)
0	0		
		25	$75,000
1	25		
		23	69,000
2	48		
		21	63,000
3	69		
		19	57,000
4	88		
		17	51,000
5	105		
		15	45,000
6	120		
		13	39,000
7	133		
		11	33,000
8	144		

workers employed. The more workers, the greater the number of computers BCC can produce. For the sake of simplicity, we will assume that the plant, equipment, and materials the workers use to build computers are fixed quantities.

Column 3 of Table 21.1 shows the *marginal product* of each worker, the extra production that is gained by adding one more worker. Note that each additional worker adds less to total production than the previous worker did. The tendency for marginal product to decline as more and more workers are added is called *diminishing returns to labor*. The principle of **diminishing returns to labor** states that if the amount of capital and other inputs in use is held constant, then the greater the quantity of labor already employed, the less each additional worker adds to production.

The principle of diminishing returns to labor is analogous to the principle of diminishing returns to capital discussed in Chapter 20. The economic basis for these principles is the same—that is, the *principle of increasing opportunity cost,* also known as the *low-hanging-fruit principle.* As we saw in Chapter 20, a firm's managers want to use their available inputs in the most productive way possible. Hence an employer who has one worker will assign that worker to the most productive job. If she hires a second worker, she will assign that worker to the second most productive job. The third worker will be given the third most productive job available, and so on. The greater the number of workers already employed, the lower the marginal product of adding another worker, as shown in Table 21.1.

If BCC computers sell for $3,000 each, then column 4 of Table 21.1 shows the *value of the marginal product* of each worker. The value of a worker's marginal product is the amount of extra revenue that the worker generates for the firm. Specifically, the value of the marginal product of each BCC worker is that worker's marginal product, stated in terms of the number of additional computers produced, multiplied by the price of output, here $3,000 per computer. We now have all the information necessary to find BCC's demand for workers.

BCC's demand for labor

Suppose that the going wage for computer technicians is $60,000 per year. BCC managers know that this is the wage being offered by all their competitors, so they cannot hire qualified workers for less. How many technicians will BCC hire? What would the answer be if the wage were $50,000 per year?

diminishing returns to labor if the amount of capital and other inputs in use is held constant, then the greater the quantity of labor already employed, the less each additional worker adds to production

EXAMPLE 21.1

BCC will hire an extra worker if and only if the value of that worker's marginal product (which equals the extra revenue the worker creates for the firm) exceeds the wage BCC must pay. The going wage for computer technicians, which BCC takes as given, is $60,000 per year. Table 21.1 shows that the value of the marginal product of the first, second, and third workers each exceeds $60,000. Hiring these workers will be profitable for BCC because the extra revenue each generates exceeds the wage that BCC must pay. However, the fourth worker's marginal product is worth only $57,000. If BCC's managers hired a fourth worker, they would be paying $60,000 in extra wages for additional output that is worth only $57,000. Since hiring the fourth worker is a money-losing proposition, BCC will hire only three workers. Thus the quantity of labor BCC demands when the going wage is $60,000 per year is three technicians.

If the market wage for computer technicians were $50,000 per year instead of $60,000, the fourth technician would be worth hiring, since the value of his marginal product, $57,000, would be $7,000 more than his wages. The fifth technician would also be worth hiring, since the fifth worker's marginal product is worth $51,000—$1,000 more than the going wage. The value of the marginal product of a sixth technician, however, is only $45,000, so hiring a sixth worker would not be profitable. When wages are $50,000 per year then, BCC's labor demand is five technicians.

EXERCISE 21.1

How many workers will BCC hire if the going wage for technicians is $35,000 per year?

The lower the wage a firm must pay, the more workers it will hire. Thus the demand for labor is like the demand for other goods or services in that the quantity demanded rises as the price (in this case, the wage) falls. Figure 21.1 shows a hypothetical labor demand curve for a firm or industry, with the wage on the vertical axis and employment on the horizontal axis. All else being equal, the higher the wage, the fewer workers a firm or industry will demand.

In our example thus far we have discussed how labor demand depends on the *nominal,* or dollar, wage and the *nominal* price of workers' output. Equivalently, we could have expressed the wage and the price of output in *real* terms, that is, measured relative to the average price of goods and services. The wage measured relative to the general price level is the *real wage;* as we saw in Chapter 19, the real wage expresses the wage in terms of its purchasing power. The price of a specific good or service measured relative to the general price level is

FIGURE 21.1
The Demand Curve for Labor.
The demand curve for labor is downward-sloping. The higher the wage, the fewer workers employers will hire.

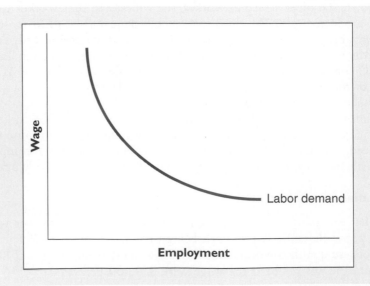

called the *relative price* of that good or service. Because our main interest is in real rather than nominal wages, from this point on we will analyze the demand for labor in terms of the real wage and the relative price of workers' output, rather than in terms of nominal variables.

SHIFTS IN THE DEMAND FOR LABOR

The number of workers that BCC will employ at any given real wage depends on the value of their marginal product, as shown in column 4 of Table 21.1. Changes in the economy that increase the value of workers' marginal product will increase the value of extra workers to BCC, and thus BCC's demand for labor at any given real wage. In other words, any factor that raises the value of the marginal product of BCC's workers will shift BCC's labor demand curve to the right.

Two main factors could increase BCC's labor demand: (1) an increase in the relative price of the company's output (computers) and (2) an increase in the productivity of BCC's workers. Example 21.2 illustrates the first of these possibilities; Example 21.3, the second.

The relative price of computers and BCC's demand for labor   **EXAMPLE 21.2**

Suppose an increase in the demand for BCC's computers raises the relative price of its computers to $5,000 each. How many technicians will BCC hire now, if the real wage is $60,000 per year? If the real wage is $50,000?

The effect of the increase in computer prices is shown in Table 21.2. Columns 1 to 3 of the table are the same as in Table 21.1. The number of computers a given number of technicians can build (column 2) has not changed; hence, the marginal product of particular technicians (column 3) is the same. But because computers can now be sold for $5,000 each instead of $3,000, the *value* of each worker's marginal product has increased by two-thirds (compare column 4 of Table 21.2 with column 4 of Table 21.1).

How does the increase in the relative price of computers affect BCC's demand for labor? Recall from Example 21.1 that when the price of computers was $3,000 and the going wage for technicians was $60,000, BCC's demand for labor was three workers. But now, with computers selling for $5,000 each, the value of the marginal product of each of the first seven workers exceeds $60,000 (Table 21.2).

TABLE 21.2
Production and Marginal Product for Banana Computers after an Increase in Computer Prices

(1) Number of workers	(2) Computers produced per year	(3) Marginal product	(4) Value of marginal product ($5,000/computer)
0	0		
		25	$125,000
1	25		
		23	115,000
2	48		
		21	105,000
3	69		
		19	95,000
4	88		
		17	85,000
5	105		
		15	75,000
6	120		
		13	65,000
7	133		
		11	55,000
8	144		

So if the real wage of computer technicians is still $60,000, BCC would increase its demand from three workers to seven.

Suppose instead that the going real wage for technicians is $50,000. In Example 21.1, when the price of computers was $3,000 and the wage was $50,000, BCC demanded five workers. But if computers sell for $5,000, we can see from column 4 of Table 21.2 that the value of the marginal product of even the eighth worker exceeds the wage of $50,000. So if the real wage is $50,000, the increase in computer prices raises BCC's demand for labor from five workers to eight.

EXERCISE 21.2

How many workers will BCC hire if the going real wage for technicians is $100,000 per year and the relative price of computers is $5,000? Compare your answer to the demand for technicians at a wage of $100,000 when the price of computers is $3,000.

The general conclusion to be drawn from Example 21.2 is that *an increase in the relative price of workers' output increases the demand for labor,* shifting the labor demand curve to the right, as shown in Figure 21.2. A higher relative price for workers' output makes workers more valuable, leading employers to demand more workers at any given real wage.

FIGURE 21.2

A Higher Relative Price of Output Increases the Demand for Labor.

An increase in the relative price of workers' output increases the value of their marginal product, shifting the labor demand curve to the right.

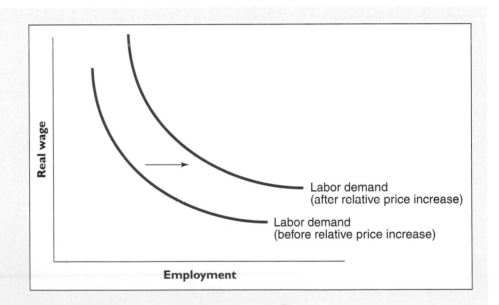

The second factor that affects the demand for labor is worker productivity. Since an increase in productivity increases the value of a worker's marginal product, it also increases the demand for labor, as Example 21.3 shows.

EXAMPLE 21.3   **Worker productivity and BCC's demand for labor**

Suppose BCC adopts a new technology that reduces the number of components to be assembled, permitting each technician to build 50 percent more machines per year. Assume that the relative price of computers is $3,000 per machine. How many technicians will BCC hire if the real wage is $60,000 per year?

Table 21.3 shows workers' marginal products and the value of their marginal products after the 50 percent increase in productivity, assuming that computers sell for $3,000 each.

Before the productivity increase, BCC would have demanded three workers at a wage of $60,000 (Table 21.1). After the productivity increase, however,

TABLE 21.3
Production and Marginal Product for Banana Computers after an Increase in Worker Productivity

(1) Number of workers	(2) Computers produced per year	(3) Marginal product	(4) Value of marginal product ($3,000/computer)
0	0		
		37.5	$112,500
1	37.5		
		34.5	103,500
2	72		
		31.5	94,500
3	103.5		
		28.5	85,500
4	132		
		25.5	76,500
5	157.5		
		22.5	67,500
6	180		
		19.5	58,500
7	199.5		
		16.5	49,500
8	216		

the value of the marginal product of the first six workers exceeds $60,000 (see Table 21.3, column 4). So at a wage of $60,000, BCC's demand for labor increases from three workers to six.

EXERCISE 21.3

How many workers will BCC hire after the 50 percent increase in productivity if the going real wage for technicians is $50,000 per year? Compare this figure to the demand for workers at a $50,000 wage before the increase in productivity.

In general, an increase in worker productivity increases the demand for labor, shifting the labor demand curve to the right, as in Figure 21.3.

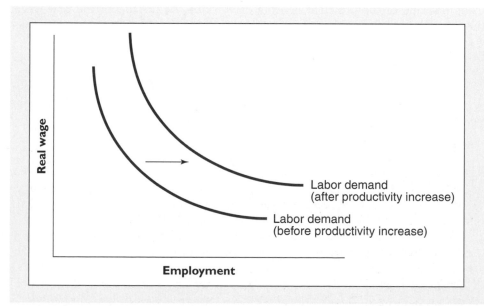

FIGURE 21.3
Higher Productivity Increases the Demand for Labor.
An increase in productivity raises workers' marginal product and—assuming no change in the price of output—the value of their marginal product. Since a productivity increase raises the value of marginal product, employers will hire more workers at any given real wage, shifting the labor demand curve to the right.

THE SUPPLY OF LABOR

We have discussed the demand for labor by employers; to complete the story we need to consider the supply of labor. The suppliers of labor are workers and potential workers. At any given real wage, potential suppliers of labor must decide if they are willing to work. The total number of people who are willing to work at each real wage is the supply of labor.

EXAMPLE 21.4

Will you clean your neighbor's basement or go to the beach?

You were planning to go to the beach today, but your neighbor asks you to clean out his basement. You like the beach a lot more than fighting cobwebs. Do you take the job?

Unless you are motivated primarily by neighborliness, your answer to this job offer would probably be "It depends on how much my neighbor will pay." You probably would not be willing to take the job for $10 or $20, unless you have a severe and immediate need for cash. But if your neighbor were wealthy and eccentric enough to offer you $500 (to take an extreme example), you would very likely say yes. Somewhere between $20 and the unrealistic figure of $500 is the minimum payment you would be willing to accept to tackle the dirty basement. This minimum payment, the *reservation price* you set for your labor, is the compensation level that leaves you just indifferent between working and not working.

In economic terms, deciding whether to work at any given wage is a straightforward application of the *cost-benefit principle*. The cost to you of cleaning out the basement is the opportunity cost of your time (you would rather be surfing) plus the cost you place on having to work in unpleasant conditions. You can measure this total cost in dollars simply by asking yourself, "What is the minimum amount of money I would take to clean out the basement instead of going to the beach?" The minimum payment that you would accept is the same as your reservation price. The benefit of taking the job is measured by the pay you receive, which will go toward that new DVD player you want. You should take the job only if the promised pay (the benefit of working) exceeds your reservation price (the cost of working).

In this example, your willingness to supply labor is greater the higher the wage. In general, the same is true for the population as a whole. Certainly people work for many reasons, including personal satisfaction, the opportunity to develop skills and talents, and the chance to socialize with coworkers. Still, for most people, income is one of the principal benefits of working, so the higher the real wage, the more willing they are to sacrifice other possible uses of their time. The fact

FIGURE 21.4
The Supply of Labor.
The labor supply curve is upward-sloping because, in general, the higher the real wage, the more people are willing to work.

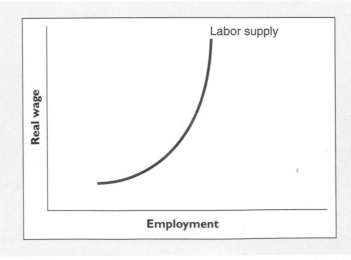

that people are more willing to work when the wage they are offered is higher is captured in the upward slope of the supply curve of labor (see Figure 21.4).

EXERCISE 21.4

You want to make a career in broadcasting. The local radio station is offering an unpaid summer internship that would give you valuable experience. Your alternative to the internship is to earn $3,000 working in a car wash. How would you decide which job to take? Would a decision to take the internship contradict the conclusion that the labor supply curve is upward-sloping?

Might accepting a job that pays no salary ever be a good career move?

SHIFTS IN THE SUPPLY OF LABOR

Any factor that affects the quantity of labor offered at a given real wage will shift the labor supply curve. At the macroeconomic level, the most important factor affecting the supply of labor is the size of the working-age population, which is influenced by factors such as the domestic birthrate, immigration and emigration rates, and the ages at which people normally first enter the workforce and retire. All else being equal, an increase in the working-age population raises the quantity of labor supplied at each real wage, shifting the labor supply curve to the right. Changes in the percentage of people of working age who seek employment—for example, as a result of social changes that encourage women to work outside the home—can also affect the supply of labor.

Now that we have discussed both the demand for and supply of labor, we are ready to apply supply and demand analysis to real-world labor markets. But first, try your hand at using supply and demand analysis to answer the following question.

EXERCISE 21.5

Labor unions typically favor tough restrictions on immigration, while employers tend to favor more liberal rules. Why? (*Hint:* How is an influx of potential workers likely to affect real wages?)

 RECAP   **SUPPLY AND DEMAND IN THE LABOR MARKET**

The demand for labor The extra production gained by adding one more worker is the *marginal product* of that worker. The *value of the marginal product* of a worker is that worker's marginal product times the relative price of the firm's output. A firm will employ a worker only if the worker's value of marginal product, which is the same as the extra revenue the worker generates for the firm, exceeds the real wage that the firm must pay. The lower the real wage, the more workers the firm will find it profitable to employ. Thus the labor demand curve, like most demand curves, is downward-sloping.

For a given real wage, any change that increases the value of workers' marginal products will increase the demand for labor and shift the labor demand curve to the right. Examples of factors that increase labor demand are an increase in the relative price of workers' output and an increase in productivity.

The supply of labor An individual is willing to supply labor if the real wage that is offered is greater than the opportunity cost of the individual's time. Generally, the higher the real wage, the more people are willing to work. Thus the labor supply curve, like most supply curves, is upward-sloping.

For a given real wage, any factor that increases the number of people available and willing to work increases the supply of labor and shifts the labor supply curve to the right. Examples of facts that increase labor supply include an increase in the working-age population or an increase in the share of the working-age population seeking employment.

EXPLAINING THE TRENDS IN REAL WAGES AND EMPLOYMENT

We are now ready to analyze the important trends in real wages and employment discussed earlier in the chapter. We will do so in a series of Economic Naturalist boxes.

Why have real wages increased by so much in the industrialized countries?

ECONOMIC NATURALIST 21.1

As we discussed, real annual earnings in the United States have quadrupled since 1929, and other industrialized countries have experienced similar gains. These increases have greatly improved the standard of living of workers in these countries. Why have real wages increased by so much in the United States and other industrialized countries?

The large increase in real wages results from the sustained growth in productivity experienced by the industrialized countries during the twentieth century. (Figure 17.2, page 431, shows the growth of output per worker in the United States since 1900.) As illustrated by Figure 21.5, increased productivity raises the demand for labor, increasing employment and the real wage.

Of the factors contributing to productivity growth in the industrialized countries, two of the most important were (1) the dramatic technological progress that occurred during the twentieth century and (2) large increases in capital stocks, which provided workers with more and better tools with which to work. Labor supply increased during the century as well, of course (not shown in the diagram). However, the increases in labor demand, driven by rapidly expanding productivity, have been so great as to overwhelm the depressing effect on real wages of increased labor supply.

FIGURE 21.5
An Increase in Productivity Raises the Real Wage.
An increase in productivity raises the demand for labor, shifting the labor demand curve from D to D'. The real wage rises from w to w', and employment rises from N to N'.

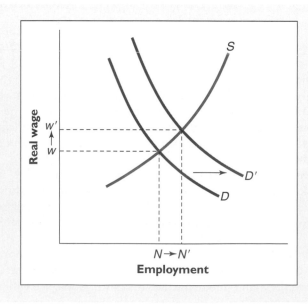

Since the 1970s, real wage growth in the United States has slowed, while employment has expanded rapidly. What accounts for these trends?

With the exception of the period since the late 1990s, rates of real wage growth after 1973 in the United States have been significantly lower than in previous decades. But over much of the recent period the economy has created new jobs at a record rate. What accounts for these trends?

Let's begin with the slowdown in real wage growth since the early 1970s. Supply and demand analysis tells us that a slowdown in real wage growth must result from slower growth in the demand for labor, more rapid growth in the supply of labor, or both. On the demand side, recall from Chapter 20 that since the early 1970s the United States and other industrialized nations have experienced a slowdown in productivity growth. Thus, one possible explanation for the slowdown in the growth of real wages since the early 1970s is the decline in the pace of productivity gains.

Some evidence for a relationship between productivity and real wages is given in Table 21.4, which shows the average annual growth rates in labor productivity and real annual earnings for the 1960s, 1970s, 1980s, and 1990s. You can see that the growth in productivity decade by decade corresponds closely to the growth in real earnings. Particularly striking is the rapid growth of both productivity and wages during the 1960s. Since the 1970s, growth in both productivity and real wages has been significantly slower, although some improvement is apparent in the 1990s.

ECONOMIC NATURALIST 21.2

TABLE 21.4
Growth Rates in Productivity and Real Earnings

	Annual Growth Rate (%)	
	Productivity	Real Earnings
1960–1970	2.33	2.89
1970–1980	0.84	0.79
1980–1990	1.38	1.15
1990–2000	1.89	1.92

SOURCE: *Economic Report of the President*, 2002 (w3.access.gpo.gov/eop). Productivity is real GDP divided by civilian employment; real earnings equal total compensation of employees divided by civilian employment and deflated by the GDP deflator.

While the effects of the slowdown in productivity on the demand for labor are an important reason for declining real wage growth, they can't be the whole story. We know this because, with labor supply held constant, slower growth in labor demand would lead to reduced rates of employment growth, as well as reduced growth in real wages. But job growth in the United States has been rapid in recent decades. Large increases in employment in the face of slow growth of labor demand can be explained only by simultaneous increases in the supply of labor (see Exercise 21.6).

Labor supply in the United States does appear to have grown rapidly recently. As we saw in Chapter 18, for example, increased participation in the labor market by women has increased the U.S. supply of labor since the mid-1970s. Other factors, including the coming of age of the baby boomers and high rates of immigration, also help to explain the increase in the supply of labor. The combination of slower growth in labor demand (the result of the productivity slowdown) and accelerated growth in labor supply (the result of increased participation by women in the workforce, together with other factors) helps to explain why real wage growth has been sluggish for many years in the United States, even as employment has grown rapidly.

What about the future? As we saw in Chapter 20, labor supply growth is likely to slow as the baby boomers retire and the percentage of women in the labor force stabilizes. Productivity has recently grown more quickly, reflecting the benefits of new technologies, among other factors (Chapter 20). So there seems a good chance that the more rapid increases in real wages that began around 1996 will continue in years to come.

EXERCISE 21.6

According to Economic Naturalist 21.2, relatively weak growth in productivity and relatively strong growth in labor supply after about 1973 can explain (1) the slowdown in real wage growth and (2) the more rapid expansion in employment after about 1973. Show this point graphically by drawing two supply and demand diagrams of the labor market, one corresponding to the period 1960–1972 and the other to 1973–1996. Assuming that productivity growth was strong but labor supply growth was modest during 1960–1972, show that we would expect to see rapid real wage growth but only moderate growth in employment in that period. Now apply the same analysis to 1973–1996, assuming that productivity growth is weaker but labor supply growth stronger than in 1960–1972. What do you predict for growth in the real wage and employment in 1973–1996 relative to the earlier period? What could account for increased real wage growth since 1996?

INCREASING WAGE INEQUALITY: THE EFFECTS OF GLOBALIZATION

Another important trend in U.S. labor markets is increasing inequality in wages, especially the tendency for the wages of the less-skilled and less-educated to fall further and further behind those of better-trained workers. We next discuss two reasons for this increasing inequality: (1) globalization and (2) technological change.

Why has the gap between the wages of skilled and unskilled workers widened in recent years? (1) Globalization

In recent years the real wages of more highly skilled and educated workers have continued to rise, while the real wages of less-skilled workers have stagnated or even declined. Does the "globalization" of the world economy have anything to do with this trend?

Many commentators have blamed the increasing divergence between the wages of skilled and unskilled workers on the phenomenon of "globalization." This popular term refers to the fact that to an increasing extent, the markets for many goods and services are becoming international, rather than national or local in scope. While Americans have long been able to buy products from all over the world, the ease with which goods and services can cross borders is increasing rapidly. In part this trend is the result of international trade agreements, such as the North American Free Trade Agreement (NAFTA), which reduced taxes on goods and services traded among Canada, the United States, and Mexico. However, technological advances such as the Internet have also promoted globalization. A recent TV commercial showed a small auto parts manufacturer in Texas bidding over the Internet for a contract from a Japanese auto firm.

The main economic benefit of globalization is increased specialization and the efficiency that it brings. Instead of each country trying to produce everything its citizens consume, each can concentrate on producing those goods and services at which it is relatively most efficient. As implied by the *principle of comparative advantage* (Chapter 2), the result is that consumers of all countries enjoy a greater variety of goods and services, of better quality and at lower prices, than they would without international trade.

ECONOMIC NATURALIST 21.3

The effects of globalization on the *labor* market are mixed, however, which explains why many politicians opposed free trade agreements. Expanded trade means that consumers stop buying certain goods and services from domestic producers and switch to foreign-made products. Consumers would not make this switch unless the foreign products were better, cheaper, or both, so expanded trade clearly makes them better off. But the workers and firm owners in the domestic industries that lose business may well suffer from the increase in foreign competition.

The effects of increasing trade on the labor market can be analyzed using Figure 21.6. The figure contrasts the supply and demand for labor in two different industries, (a) textiles and (b) computer software. Imagine that, initially, there is little or no international trade in these two goods. Without trade, the demand for workers in each industry is indicated by the curves marked D_{textiles} and D_{software}, respectively. Wages and employment in each industry are determined by the intersection of the demand curves and the labor supply curves in each industry. As we have drawn the figure, initially, the real wage is the same in both industries, equal to w. Employment is N_{textiles} in textiles and N_{software} in software.

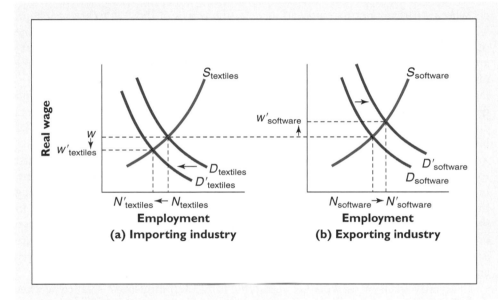

FIGURE 21.6
The Effect of Globalization on the Demand for Workers in Two Industries.
Initially, real wages in the two industries are equal at w. After an increase in trade, (a) demand for workers in the importing industry (textiles) declines, lowering real wages and employment, while (b) demand for workers in the exporting industry (software) increases, raising real wages and employment in that industry.

What will happen when this economy is opened up to trade, perhaps because of a free trade agreement? Under the agreement, countries will begin to produce for export those goods or services at which they are relatively more efficient and to import goods or services that they are relatively less efficient at producing. Suppose the country in this example is relatively more efficient at producing software than manufacturing textiles. With the opening of trade, the country gains new foreign markets for its software and begins to produce for export as well as for domestic use. Meanwhile, because the country is relatively less efficient at producing textiles, consumers begin to purchase foreign-made textiles, which are cheaper or of higher quality, instead of the domestic product. In short, software becomes an exporting industry and textiles an importing industry.

These changes in the demand for domestic products are translated into changes in the demand for labor. The opening of export markets increases the demand for domestic software, raising its relative price. The higher price for domestic software, in turn, raises the value of the marginal products of software workers, shifting the labor demand curve in the software industry to the right, from D_{software} to D'_{software} in Figure 21.6(b). Wages in the software industry rise, from w to w'_{software}, and employment in the industry rises as well. In the textile industry the opposite happens. Demand for domestic textiles falls as consumers switch to imports. The relative price of domestic textiles falls with demand, reducing the value of the marginal product of textile workers and hence the demand for their labor, to $D'_{textiles}$ in Figure 21.6(a). Employment in the textile industry falls, and the real wage falls as well, from w to $w'_{textiles}$.

In sum, Figure 21.6 shows how globalization can contribute to increasing wage inequality. Initially, we assumed that software workers and textile workers received the same wage. However, the opening up of trade raised the wages of workers in the "winning" industry (software) and lowered the wages of workers in the "losing" industry (textiles), increasing inequality.

In practice, the tendency of trade to increase wage inequality may be even worse than depicted in the example, because the great majority of the world's workers, particularly those in developing countries, have relatively low skill levels. Thus, when industrialized countries like the United States open up trade with developing countries, the domestic industries that are likely to face the toughest international competition are those that use mostly low-skilled labor. Conversely, the industries that are likely to do the best in international competition are those that employ mostly skilled workers. Thus increased trade may lower the wages of those workers who are already poorly paid and increase the wages of those who are well paid.

The fact that increasing trade may exacerbate wage inequality explains some of the political resistance to globalization, but in general it does not justify attempts to reverse the trend. Increasing trade and specialization is a major source of improvement in living standards, both in the United States and abroad, so trying to stop the process is counterproductive. Indeed, the economic forces behind globalization—primarily, the desire of consumers for better and cheaper products and of producers for new markets—are so powerful that the process would be hard to stop even if government officials were determined to do so.

Rather than trying to stop globalization, helping the labor market to adjust to the effects of globalization is probably a better course. To a certain extent, indeed, the economy will adjust on its own. Figure 21.6 showed that, following the opening to trade, real wages and employment fall in (a) textiles and rise in (b) software. At that point, wages and job opportunities are much more attractive in the software industry than in textiles. Will this situation persist? Clearly, there is a strong incentive for workers who are able to do so to leave the textile industry and seek employment in the software industry.

worker mobility the movement of workers between jobs, firms, and industries

The movement of workers between jobs, firms, and industries is called **worker mobility.** In our example, worker mobility will tend to reduce labor supply in textiles and increase it in software, as workers move from the contracting industry to the growing one. This process will reverse some of the increase in wage inequality by raising wages in textiles and lowering them in software. It will also shift workers from a less competitive sector to a more competitive sector. To some extent, then, the labor market can adjust on its own to the effects of globalization.

Of course, there are many barriers to a textile worker becoming a software engineer. So there may also be a need for *transition aid* to workers in the affected sectors. Ideally, such aid helps workers train for and find new jobs. If that is not possible or desirable—say, because a worker is nearing retirement—transition aid can take the form of government payments to help the worker maintain his or her standard of living. Because trade and specialization increase the total economic pie, the "winners" from globalization can afford the taxes necessary to finance aid and still enjoy a net benefit from increased trade.

INCREASING WAGE INEQUALITY: TECHNOLOGICAL CHANGE

A second source of increasing wage inequality is ongoing technological change that favors more highly skilled or educated workers. Economic Naturalist 21.4 examines the effect of technological change on the labor market.

Why has the gap between the wages of less-skilled and higher-skilled workers widened in recent years? (2) Technological change

How has the pattern of technological change contributed to increasing inequality of wages?

As we have seen, new scientific knowledge and the technological advances associated with it are a major source of improved productivity and economic growth. Increases in worker productivity are in turn a driving force behind wage increases and higher average living standards. In the long run and on average, technological progress is undoubtedly the worker's friend.

This sweeping statement is not true at all times and in all places, however. Whether a particular technological development is good for a particular worker depends on the effect of that innovation on the worker's value of marginal product and, hence, on his or her wage. For example, at one time the ability to add numbers rapidly and accurately was a valuable skill; a clerk with that skill could expect advancement and higher wages. However, the invention and mass production of the electronic calculator has rendered human calculating skills less valuable, to the detriment of those who have that skill.

History is replete with examples of workers who opposed new technologies out of fear that their skills would become less valuable. In England in the early nineteenth century, rioting workmen destroyed newly introduced labor-saving machinery. The name of the workers' reputed leader, Ned Ludd, has been preserved in the term *Luddite,* meaning a person who is opposed to the introduction of new technologies. The same theme appears in American folk history in the tale of John Henry, the mighty pile-driving man who died in an attempt to show that a human could tunnel into a rock face more quickly than a steam-powered machine.

How do these observations bear on wage inequality? According to some economists, many recent technological advances have taken the form of **skill-biased technological change,** that is, technological change that affects the marginal product of higher-skilled workers differently from that of lower-skilled workers. Specifically, technological developments in recent decades appear to have favored more-skilled and educated workers. Developments in automobile production are a case in point. The advent of mass production techniques in the 1920s provided highly paid work for several generations of relatively low-skilled autoworkers. But in recent years automobile production, like the automobiles themselves, has become considerably more sophisticated. The simplest production jobs have been taken over by robots and computer-controlled machinery, which require skilled operatives who know how to use and maintain the new equipment. Consumer demands for luxury features and customized options has also raised the automakers' demand for highly skilled craftsmen. Thus, in general, the skill requirements for jobs in automobile production have risen. Similarly, few office workers today can escape the need to use computer applications, such as word processing and spreadsheets. And in many places, elementary school teachers are expected to know how to set up a web page or use the Internet.

Figure 21.7 illustrates the effects of technological change that favors skilled workers. Figure 21.7(a) shows the market for unskilled workers; Figure 21.7(b) shows the market for skilled workers. The demand curves labeled $D_{unskilled}$ and $D_{skilled}$ show the demand for each type of worker before a skill-biased technical change. Wages and employment for each type of worker are determined by the intersection of the demand and supply curves in each market. Figure 21.7 shows that, even before the technological change, unskilled workers received lower real wages than skilled workers ($w_{unskilled} < w_{skilled}$), reflecting the lower marginal products of the unskilled.

Now suppose that a new technology—computer-controlled machinery, for example—is introduced. This technological change is biased toward skilled workers, which means that it raises their marginal productivity relative to unskilled workers. We will assume in this example that the new technology also lowers the marginal productivity of unskilled workers, perhaps because they are unable to use

skill-biased technological change technological change that affects the marginal products of higher-skilled workers differently from those of lower-skilled workers

Unimpressed by new technology

FIGURE 21.7

The Effect of Skill-Biased Technological Change on Wage Inequality.

The figure shows the effects of a skill-biased technological change that increases the marginal product of skilled workers and reduces the marginal product of unskilled workers. The resulting increase in the demand for skilled workers raises their wages (b), while the decline in demand for unskilled workers reduces their wages (a). Wage inequality increases.

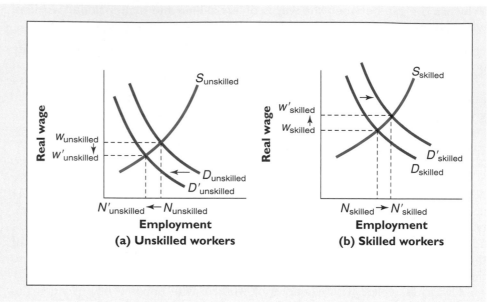

the new technology, but all that is necessary for our conclusions is that they benefit less than skilled workers. Figure 21.7 shows the effect of this change in marginal products. In part (b) the increase in the marginal productivity of skilled workers raises the demand for those workers; the demand curve shifts rightward to $D'_{skilled}$. Accordingly, the real wages and employment of skilled workers also rise. In contrast, because they have been made less productive by the technological change, the demand for unskilled workers shifts leftward to $D'_{unskilled}$ [Figure 21.7(a)]. Lower demand for unskilled workers reduces their real wages and employment.

In summary, this analysis supports the conclusion that technological change that is biased in favor of skilled workers will tend to increase the wage gap between the skilled and unskilled. Empirical studies have confirmed the role of skill-biased technological change in recent increases in wage inequality.

Because new technologies that favor skilled workers increase wage inequality, should government regulators act to block them? As in the case of globalization, most economists would argue against trying to block new technologies, since technological advances are necessary for economic growth and improved living standards. If the Luddites had somehow succeeded in preventing the introduction of labor-saving machinery in Great Britain, economic growth and development over the past few centuries might have been greatly reduced.

The remedies for the problem of wage inequalities caused by technological change are similar to those for wage inequalities caused by globalization. First among them is worker mobility. As the pay differential between skilled and unskilled work increases, unskilled workers will have a stronger incentive to acquire education and skills, to everyone's benefit. A second remedy is transition aid. Government policymakers should consider programs that will help workers to retrain if they are able, or provide income support if they are not.

 RECAP   **EXPLAINING THE TRENDS IN REAL WAGES AND EMPLOYMENT**

The long-term increase in real wages enjoyed by workers in industrial countries results primarily from large productivity gains, which have raised the demand for labor. Technological progress and an expanded and modernized capital stock are two important reasons for these long-term increases in productivity.

The slowdown in real wage growth that began in the 1970s resulted in part from the slowdown in productivity growth (and, hence, the slower growth in labor demand) that occurred at about the same time. Increased labor supply, arising from such factors as the increased participation of women and the coming of age of the baby boom generation, depressed real wages further while also expanding employment. In the latter part of the 1990s, resurgence in productivity growth was accompanied by an increase in real wage growth.

Both globalization and skill-biased technological change contribute to wage inequality. Globalization raises the wages of workers in exporting industries by raising the demand for those workers, while reducing the wages of workers in importing industries. Technological change that favors more-skilled workers increases the demand for such workers, and hence their wages, relative to the wages of less-skilled workers.

Attempting to block either globalization or technological change is not the best response to the problem of wage inequality. To some extent, worker mobility (movement of workers from low-wage to high-wage industries) will offset the inequality created by these forces. Where mobility is not practical, transition aid—government assistance to workers whose employment prospects have worsened—may be the best solution.

UNEMPLOYMENT

The concept of the unemployment rate was introduced in Chapter 18. To review, government survey takers classify adults as employed (holding a job), unemployed (not holding a job, but looking for one), or not in the labor force (not holding a job and not looking for one—retirees, for example). The labor force consists of the employed and the unemployed. The unemployment rate is the percentage of the labor force that is unemployed.

Unemployment rates differ markedly from country to country. In the United States, unemployment rates reached historic lows in 2000—slightly above 4 percent of the labor force—although U.S. rates rose to 6 percent in the 2001 recession. (Figure 18.3, page 468, shows the U.S. unemployment rate since 1960.) In Canada and many western European countries, unemployment rates for many years have been two to three times the U.S. rate. In Europe, unemployment is exceptionally high among young people. Supposedly, high school guidance counselors in Britain once gave high school seniors a pamphlet titled "Leaving School: How to Apply for Unemployment Benefits."

As we saw in Chapter 18, a high unemployment rate has serious economic, psychological, and social costs. Understanding the causes of unemployment and finding ways to reduce it are therefore major concerns of macroeconomists. In the remainder of this chapter we discuss the causes and costs of three types of unemployment, and we will also consider some features of labor markets that may exacerbate the problem.

TYPES OF UNEMPLOYMENT AND THEIR COSTS

Economists have found it useful to think of unemployment as being of three broad types: *frictional* unemployment, *structural* unemployment, and *cyclical* unemployment. Each type of unemployment has different causes and imposes different economic and social costs.

Frictional Unemployment

The function of the labor market is to match available jobs with available workers. If all jobs and workers were the same, or if the set of jobs and workers were static and unchanging, this matching process would be quick and easy. But the real world is more complicated. In practice, both jobs and workers are highly *heterogeneous.* Jobs differ in their location, in the skills they require, in their working conditions and hours, and in many other ways. Workers differ in their career aspirations, their skills and experience, their preferred working hours, their willingness to travel, and so on.

The real labor market is also *dynamic,* or constantly changing and evolving. On the demand side of the labor market, technological advances, globalization, and changing consumer tastes spur the creation of new products, new firms, and even new industries, while outmoded products, firms, and industries disappear. Thus CD players have replaced record players, and word processors have replaced typewriters. As a result of this upheaval, new jobs are constantly being created, while some old jobs cease to be viable. The workforce in a modern economy is equally dynamic. People move, gain new skills, leave the labor force for a time to rear children or go back to school, and even change careers.

Because the labor market is heterogeneous and dynamic, the process of matching jobs with workers often takes time. For example, a software engineer who loses or quits her job in Silicon Valley may take weeks or even months to find an appropriate new job. In her search she will probably consider alternative areas of software development or even totally new challenges. She may also want to think about different regions of the country in which software companies are located, such as North Carolina's Research Triangle or New York City's Silicon Alley. During the period in which she is searching for a new job, she is counted as unemployed.

frictional unemployment the short-term unemployment associated with the process of matching workers with jobs

Short-term unemployment that is associated with the process of matching workers with jobs is called **frictional unemployment.** The *costs* of frictional unemployment are low and may even be negative; that is, frictional unemployment may be economically beneficial. First, frictional unemployment is short-term, so its psychological effects and direct economic losses are minimal. Second, to the extent that the search process leads to a better match between worker and job, a period of frictional unemployment is actually productive, in the sense that it leads to higher output over the long run. Indeed, a certain amount of frictional unemployment seems essential to the smooth functioning of a rapidly changing, dynamic economy.

Structural Unemployment

structural unemployment the long-term and chronic unemployment that exists even when the economy is producing at a normal rate

A second major type of unemployment is **structural unemployment,** or the long-term and chronic unemployment that exists even when the economy is producing at a normal rate. Several factors contribute to structural unemployment. First, a *lack of skills, language barriers,* or *discrimination* keeps some workers from finding stable, long-term jobs. Migrant farmworkers and unskilled construction workers who find short-term or temporary jobs from time to time, but never stay in one job for very long, fit the definition of chronically unemployed.

Second, economic changes sometimes create a *long-term mismatch* between the skills some workers have and the available jobs. The U.S. steel industry, for example, has declined over the years, while the computer industry has grown rapidly. Ideally, steelworkers who lose their jobs would be able to find new jobs in computer firms (worker mobility), so their unemployment would only be frictional in nature. In practice, of course, many ex-steelworkers lack the education, ability, or interest necessary to work in the computer industry. Since their skills are no longer in demand, these workers may drift into chronic or long-term unemployment.

Finally, structural unemployment can result from *structural features of the labor market* that act as barriers to employment. Examples of such barriers include unions and minimum wage laws, both of which may keep wages above their market-clearing level, creating unemployment. We will discuss some of these structural features shortly.

"The one single thought that sustains me is that the fundamentals are good."

The *costs* of structural unemployment are much higher than those of frictional unemployment. Because structurally unemployed workers do little productive work over long periods, their idleness causes substantial economic losses both to the unemployed workers and to society. Structurally unemployed workers also lose out on the opportunity to develop new skills on the job, and their existing skills wither from disuse. Long spells of unemployment are also much more difficult for workers to handle psychologically than the relatively brief spells associated with frictional unemployment.

Cyclical Unemployment

The third type of unemployment occurs during periods of recession (that is, periods of unusually low production) and is called **cyclical unemployment.** The sharp peaks in unemployment shown in Figure 18.3 reflect the cyclical unemployment that occurs during recessions. Increases in cyclical unemployment, although they are relatively short-lived, are associated with significant declines in real GDP and are therefore quite costly economically. We will study cyclical unemployment in more detail later in the chapters dealing with booms and recessions.

cyclical unemployment the extra unemployment that occurs during periods of recession

In principle, frictional, structural, and cyclical unemployment add up to the total unemployment rate. In practice, sharp distinctions often cannot be made between the different categories, so any breakdown of the total unemployment rate into the three types of unemployment is necessarily subjective and approximate.

IMPEDIMENTS TO FULL EMPLOYMENT

In discussing structural unemployment, we mentioned that structural features of the labor market may contribute to long-term and chronic unemployment. Let's discuss a few of those features.

Minimum Wage Laws[2]

The federal government and most states have minimum wage laws, which prescribe the lowest hourly wage that employers may pay to workers. Basic supply and demand analysis shows that if the minimum wage law has any effect at all, it must raise the unemployment rate. Figure 21.8 shows why. The figure shows the demand and supply curves for low-skilled workers, to whom the minimum wage is most relevant. The market-clearing real wage, at which the quantity of labor demanded equals the quantity of labor supplied, is w, and the corresponding level of employment of low-skilled workers is N. Now suppose there is a legal minimum wage w_{min} that exceeds the market-clearing wage w, as shown in Figure 21.8. At the minimum wage, the number of people who want jobs, N_B, exceeds the number of workers that employers are willing to hire, N_A. The result is unemployment in the amount $N_B - N_A$, also equal to the length of the line segment AB in the figure. If there were no minimum wage, this unemployment would not exist, since the labor market would clear at wage w.

FIGURE 21.8

A Legal Minimum Wage May Create Unemployment.

If the minimum wage w_{min} exceeds the market-clearing wage w for low-skilled workers, it will create unemployment equal to the difference between the number of people who want to work at the minimum wage, N_B, and the number of people that employers are willing to hire, N_A.

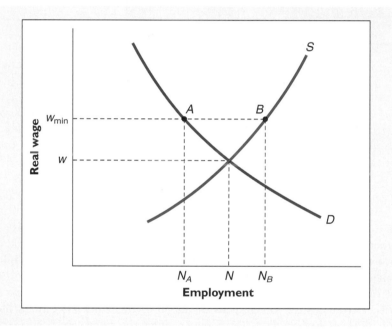

If minimum wages create unemployment, why are they politically popular? A minimum wage creates two classes of workers: those who are lucky enough to find jobs at the minimum wage and those who are shut out because the minimum wage exceeds the market-clearing wage. Workers who do find jobs at the minimum wage will earn more than they would have otherwise, because the minimum wage is higher than the market-clearing wage. If the minimum wage were put to a vote, the number of workers who benefit from the legislation, and who could thus be expected to support it, might well exceed the number of workers who are hurt by it. In creating groups of "winners" and "losers," minimum wage legislation resembles rent control legislation (see Chapter 3). But like rent controls, minimum wages create economic inefficiency. Thus other methods of attacking poverty, such as direct grants to the working poor, might prove more effective.

Labor Unions

Labor unions are organizations that negotiate with employers on behalf of workers. Among the issues that unions negotiate, which are embodied in the contracts they draw up with employers, are the wages workers earn, rules for hiring and firing, the duties of different types of workers, working hours and conditions, and procedures for resolving disputes between workers and employers. Unions

[2]Minimum wages are also discussed in Chapter 13.

gain negotiating power by their power to call a strike—that is, to refuse work until a contract agreement has been reached.

Through the threat of a strike, a union can usually get employers to agree to a wage that is higher than the market-clearing wage. Thus Figure 21.8 could represent conditions in a unionized industry if w_{min} is interpreted as the union wage instead of the legal minimum wage. As in the case of a minimum wage, a union wage that is higher than the market-clearing wage leads to unemployment, in the amount $N_B - N_A$ in Figure 21.8. Furthermore, a high union wage creates a trade-off similar to the one created by a minimum wage. Those workers who are lucky enough to get jobs as union members will be paid more than they would be otherwise. Unfortunately, their gain comes at the expense of other workers who are unemployed as a result of the artificially high union wage.

Are labor unions good for the economy? That is a controversial, emotionally charged question. Early in the twentieth century, some employers who faced little local competition for workers—coal-mining companies in Appalachia, for example—exploited their advantage by forcing workers to toil long hours in dangerous conditions for low pay. Through bitter and sometimes bloody confrontations with these companies, labor organizations succeeded in eliminating many of the worst abuses. Unions also point with pride to their historic political role in supporting progressive labor legislation, such as laws that banned child labor. Finally, union leaders often claim to increase productivity and promote democracy in the workplace by giving workers some voice in the operations of the firm.

Opponents of unions, while acknowledging that these organizations may have played a positive role in the past, question their value in a modern economy. Today, more and more workers are professionals or semiprofessionals, rather than production workers, so they can move relatively easily from firm to firm. Indeed, many labor markets have become national or even international, so today's workers have numerous potential employers. Thus the forces of competition—the fact that employers must persuade talented workers to work for them—should provide adequate protection for workers. Indeed, opponents would argue that unions are becoming increasingly self-defeating, since firms that must pay artificially high union wages and abide by inflexible work rules will not be able to compete in a global economy. The ultimate effect of such handicaps will be the failure of unionized firms and the loss of union jobs. Indeed, unions are in decline in the United States and now represent less than 15 percent of the workforce—a large fraction of which are government workers, such as public school teachers and the police.

Unemployment Insurance

Another structural feature of the labor market that may increase the unemployment rate is the availability of *unemployment insurance,* or government transfer payments to unemployed workers. Unemployment insurance provides an important social benefit in that it helps the unemployed to maintain a decent standard of living while they are looking for a job. But because its availability allows the unemployed to search longer or less intensively for a job, it may lengthen the average amount of time the typical unemployed worker is without a job.

Most economists would argue that unemployment insurance should be generous enough to provide basic support to the unemployed but not so generous as to remove the incentive to actively seek work. Thus, unemployment insurance should last for only a limited time, and its benefits should not be as high as the income a worker receives when working.

Other Government Regulations

Besides minimum wage legislation, many other government regulations bear on the labor market. They include *health and safety regulations,* which establish the safety standards employers must follow, and rules that prohibit racial or gender-based discrimination in hiring. Many of these regulations are beneficial (see

Chapter 13 for further discussion). In some cases, however, the costs of complying with regulations may exceed the benefits they provide. Further, to the extent that regulations increase employer costs and reduce productivity, they depress the demand for labor, lowering real wages and contributing to unemployment. For maximum economic efficiency, legislators should use the *cost-benefit criterion* when deciding what regulations to impose on the labor market.

The points raised in this section can help us to understand one of the important labor market trends discussed earlier in the chapter, namely, the persistence of high unemployment in western Europe.

**ECONOMIC
NATURALIST
21.5**

Why are unemployment rates so high in western Europe?

For more than two decades, unemployment has been exceptionally high in the major countries of western Europe, as Figure 21.9 shows. In 1999, for example, the unemployment rate was 9 percent in Germany and greater than 11 percent in France and Italy, compared with a U.S. unemployment rate that was just above 4 percent. In the 1950s, 1960s, and 1970s, western Europe consistently enjoyed very low unemployment rates. Why has European unemployment been so stubbornly high for the past two decades?

One explanation for the high unemployment in major western European countries is the existence of structural "rigidities" in their labor markets. Relative to the United States, European labor markets are highly regulated. European governments set rules in matters ranging from the number of weeks of vacation workers must receive to the reasons for which a worker can be dismissed. Minimum wages in Europe are high, and unemployment benefits are much more generous than in the United States. European unions are also far more powerful than those in the United States; their wage agreements are often extended by law to all firms in the industry, whether or not they are unionized. This lack of flexibility in labor markets—which some observers refer to as *Eurosclerosis*—causes higher frictional and structural unemployment.

FIGURE 21.9
Unemployment Rates in Western Europe, 1980–2001.
In the major western European countries, unemployment rates have been high for more than two decades.

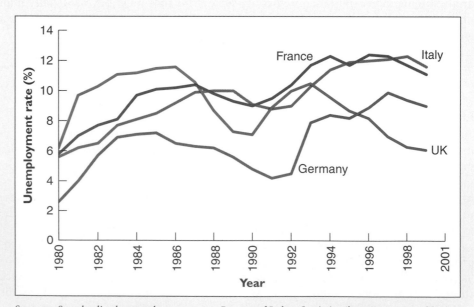

SOURCE: Standardized unemployment rates, Bureau of Labor Statistics (http://www.stats.bls.gov).

If European labor markets are so dysfunctional, why has serious European unemployment emerged only in the past two decades? One explanation turns on the increasing pace of *globalization* and *skill-biased technological change*. As we saw, these two factors decrease the demand for less-skilled labor relative to the demand for skilled labor. In the United States, falling demand has depressed the wages of the less skilled, increasing wage inequality. But in western Europe, high minimum wages, union contracts, generous unemployment insurance, and other factors may have created a floor for the wage that firms could pay or that workers would accept. As the marginal productivity of the less skilled dropped below that floor, firms no longer found it profitable to employ those workers, swelling the ranks of the unemployed. Thus the combination of labor market rigidity and the declining marginal productivity of low-skilled workers may be responsible for the European unemployment problem.

Evidence for the idea that inflexible labor markets have contributed to European unemployment comes from the United Kingdom, where the government of Prime Minister Margaret Thatcher instituted a series of reforms beginning in the early 1980s. Britain has since largely deregulated its labor market so that it functions much more like that in the United States. Figure 21.9 shows that unemployment in Britain has gradually declined and is now lower than in other western European countries. Labor market reforms like those in Britain are examples of *structural policies*.

RECAP   UNEMPLOYMENT

Economists distinguish among three broad types of unemployment. *Frictional unemployment* is the short-term unemployment that is associated with the process of matching workers with jobs. *Structural unemployment* is the long-term or chronic unemployment that occurs even when the economy is producing at a normal rate. *Cyclical unemployment* is the extra unemployment that occurs during periods of recession. Frictional unemployment may be economically beneficial, as improved matching of workers and jobs may increase output in the long run. Structural and cyclical unemployment impose heavy economic costs on workers and society, as well as psychological costs on workers and their families.

Structural features of the labor market may cause structural unemployment. Examples of such features are legal minimum wages or union contracts that set wages above market-clearing levels, unemployment insurance, which allows unemployed workers to search longer or less intensively for a job, and government regulations that impose extra costs on employers. Regulation of the labor market is not necessarily undesirable, but it should be subject to the cost-benefit criterion. Heavy labor market regulation and high unionization rates in western Europe help to explain the persistence of high unemployment rates in those countries.

▪ SUMMARY ▪

- For the average person, the most tangible result of economic growth and increasing productivity is the availability of "good jobs at good wages." Over the long run the U.S. economy has for the most part delivered on this promise, as both real wages and employment have grown strongly. But while growth in employment has recently been rapid, two worrisome trends dog the U.S. labor market: a slowdown since the early 1970s in the growth of real wages and increasing wage inequality. Western Europe has experienced less wage inequality but significantly higher rates of unemployment than the United States.

- Trends in real wages and employment can be studied using a supply and demand model of the labor market. The pro-

ductivity of labor and the relative price of workers' output determine the demand for labor. Employers will hire workers only as long as the value of the marginal product of the last worker hired equals or exceeds the wage the firm must pay. Because of *diminishing returns to labor*, the more workers a firm employs, the less additional product will be obtained by adding yet another worker. The lower the going wage, the more workers will be hired; that is, the demand for labor curve slopes downward. Economic changes that increase the value of labor's marginal product, such as an increase in the relative price of workers' output or an increase in productivity, shift the labor demand curve to the right. Conversely, changes that reduce the value of labor's marginal product shift the labor demand curve to the left.

- The supply curve for labor shows the number of people willing to work at any given real wage. Since more people will work at a higher real wage, the supply curve is upward-sloping. An increase in the working-age population, or a social change that promotes labor market participation (like increased acceptance of women in the labor force) will raise labor supply and shift the labor supply curve to the right.

- Improvements in productivity, which raise the demand for labor, account for the bulk of the increase in U.S. real wages over the last century. The slowdown in real wage growth that has occurred in recent decades is the result of slower growth in labor demand, which was caused in turn by a slowdown in the rate of productivity improvement, and of more rapid growth in labor supply. Rapid growth in labor supply, caused by such factors as immigration and increased labor force participation by women, has also contributed to the continued expansion of employment. Recently, there has been some improvement in the rate of growth of productivity and real wages.

- Two reasons for the increasing wage inequality in the United States are economic globalization and *skill-biased technological change*. Both have increased the demand for, and hence the real wages of, relatively skilled and educated workers. Attempting to block globalization and technological change is counterproductive, however, since both factors are essential to economic growth and increased productivity. To some extent, the movement of workers from lower-paying to higher-paying jobs or industries (*worker mobility*) will counteract the trend toward wage inequality. A policy of providing transition aid and training for workers with obsolete skills is a more useful response to the problem.

- There are three broad types of unemployment: frictional, structural, and cyclical. *Frictional unemployment* is the short-term unemployment associated with the process of matching workers with jobs in a dynamic, heterogeneous labor market. *Structural unemployment* is the long-term and chronic unemployment that exists even when the economy is producing at a normal rate. It arises from a variety of factors, including language barriers, discrimination, structural features of the labor market, lack of skills, or long-term mismatches between the skills workers have and the available jobs. *Cyclical unemployment* is the extra unemployment that occurs during periods of recession. The costs of frictional unemployment are low, as it tends to be brief and to create more productive matches between workers and jobs. But structural unemployment, which is often long term, and cyclical unemployment, which is associated with significant reductions in real GDP, are relatively more costly.

- Structural features of the labor market that may contribute to unemployment include minimum wage laws, which discourage firms from hiring low-skilled workers; labor unions, which can set wages above market-clearing levels; unemployment insurance, which reduces the incentives of the unemployed to find work quickly; and other government regulations, which—although possibly conferring benefits—increase the costs of employing workers. The labor market "rigidity" created by government regulations and union contracts is more of a problem in western Europe than in the United States, which may account for Europe's high unemployment rates.

■ KEY TERMS ■

cyclical unemployment (555)
diminishing returns to labor (539)

frictional unemployment (554)
skill-biased technological change (551)

structural unemployment (554)
worker mobility (550)

■ REVIEW QUESTIONS ■

1. List and discuss the five important labor market trends given in the first section of the chapter. How do these trends either support or qualify the proposition that increasing labor productivity leads to higher standards of living?

2. Alice is very skilled at fixing manual typewriters. Would you expect her high productivity to result in a high real wage for her? Why or why not?

3. Acme Corporation is considering hiring Jane Smith. Based on her other opportunities in the job market, Jane has told Acme that she will work for them for $40,000 per year. How should Acme determine whether to employ her?

4. Why have real wages risen by so much in the United States in the past century? Why did real wage growth

slow for 25 years beginning in the early 1970s? What has been happening to real wages recently?

5. What are two major factors contributing to increased inequality in wages? Briefly, why do these factors raise wage inequality? Contrast possible policy responses to increasing inequality in terms of their effects on economic efficiency.

6. List three types of unemployment and their causes. Which of these types is economically and socially the least costly? Explain.

7. Describe some of the structural features of European labor markets that have helped to keep European unemployment rates high. If these structural features create unemployment, why don't European governments just eliminate them?

▪ PROBLEMS ▪

1. Data on the average earnings of people of different education levels are available from the Bureau of the Census (try online at www.census.gov/population/socdemo/education/tableA-3.txt). Using these data prepare a table showing the earnings of college graduates relative to high school graduates and of college graduates relative to those with less than a high school degree. Show the data for the latest year available, for every fifth year going back to the earliest data available. What are the trends in relative earnings?

2. Production data for Bob's Bicycle Factory are as follows:

Number of workers	Bikes assembled/day
1	10
2	18
3	24
4	28
5	30

   Other than wages, Bob has costs of $100 (for parts and so on) for each bike assembled.
   a. Bikes sell for $130 each. Find the marginal product and the value of the marginal product for each worker (don't forget about Bob's cost of parts).
   b. Make a table showing Bob's demand curve for labor.
   c. Repeat part b for the case in which bikes sell for $140 each.
   d. Repeat part b for the case in which worker productivity increases by 50 percent. Bikes sell for $130 each.

3. The marginal product of a worker in a lightbulb factory equals $30 - N$ bulbs per hour, where N is the total number of workers employed. Lightbulbs sell for $2 each, and there are no costs to producing them other than labor costs.
   a. The going hourly wage for factory workers is $20 per hour. How many workers should the factory manager hire? What if the wage is $30 per hour?
   b. Graph the factory's demand for labor.
   c. Repeat part b for the case in which lightbulbs sell for $3 each.
   d. Suppose the supply of factory workers in the town in which the lightbulb factory is located is 20 workers (in other words, the labor supply curve is vertical at 20 workers). What will be the equilibrium real wage for factory workers in the town if lightbulbs sell for $2 each? If they sell for $3 each?

4. How would each of the following likely affect the real wage and employment of unskilled workers on an automobile plant assembly line?
   a. Demand for the type of car made by the plant increases.
   b. A sharp increase in the price of gas causes many commuters to switch to mass transit.
   c. Because of alternative opportunities, people become less willing to do factory work.
   d. The plant management introduces new assembly line methods that increase the number of cars unskilled workers can produce per hour while reducing defects.
   e. Robots are introduced to do most basic assembly line tasks.
   f. The workers unionize.

5. How would each of the following factors be likely to affect the economywide supply of labor?
   a. The mandatory retirement age is increased.
   b. Increased productivity causes real wages to rise.
   c. War preparations lead to the institution of a national draft, and many young people are called up.
   d. More people decide to have children (consider both short-run and long-run effects).
   e. Social Security benefits are made more generous.

6. Either skilled or unskilled workers can be used to produce a small toy. The marginal product of skilled workers, measured in terms of toys produced per day, equals $200 - N^s$, where N^s is the number of skilled workers employed. Similarly, the marginal product of unskilled workers is $100 - N^u$, where N^u is the number of unskilled workers employed. The toys sell for $3 each.

   a. Assume that there are 100 skilled workers and 50 unskilled workers available (and the labor supply curves for each group are vertical). In dollars, what will be the equilibrium wage for each type of worker? (*Hint:* What are the marginal products and the values of marginal product for each type of worker when all workers are employed?)

   b. Electronic equipment is introduced that increases the marginal product of skilled workers (who can use the equipment) to $300 - N^s$. The marginal products of unskilled workers are unaffected. Now what are the equilibrium wages for the two groups?

   c. Suppose that unskilled workers find it worthwhile to acquire skills when the wage differential between skilled and unskilled workers is $300 per day or greater. Following the introduction of the electronic equipment, how many unskilled workers will become skilled? (*Hint:* How many workers would have to shift from the unskilled to the skilled category to make the equilibrium difference in wages precisely equal to $300 per day?) What are equilibrium wages for skilled and unskilled workers after some unskilled workers acquire training?

7. An economy with no foreign trade produces sweaters and dresses. There are 14 workers in the sweater industry and 26 workers in the dress industry. The marginal product of workers in the sweater industry, measured in sweaters produced per day, is $20 - NS$, where NS is the number of workers employed in the sweater industry. The marginal product of workers in the dress industry, measured in dresses produced per day, is $30 - ND$, where ND is the number of workers employed in the dress industry.

   a. Initially, sweaters sell for $40 apiece and dresses are $60 apiece. Find the equilibrium wage in each industry.

   b. The economy opens up to trade. Foreign demand for domestically produced sweaters is strong, raising the price of sweaters to $50 each. But foreign competition reduces demand for domestically produced dresses so that they now sell for $50 each. Assuming that workers cannot move between industries, what are wages in each industry now? Who has been hurt and who has been helped by the opening up to trade?

   c. Now suppose that workers can move freely from one industry to the other, and will always move to the industry that pays the higher wage. In the long run, how many of the 40 workers in the economy will be in each industry? What wages will they receive? In the long run, are domestic workers hurt or helped by the opening up to foreign trade? Assume that sweaters and dresses continue to sell for $50.

8. For each of the following scenarios, state whether the unemployment is frictional, structural, or cyclical. Justify your answer.

   a. Ted lost his job when the steel mill closed down. He lacks the skills to work in another industry and so has been unemployed over a year.

   b. Alice was laid off from her job at the auto plant because the recession reduced the demand for cars. She expects to get her job back when the economy picks up.

   c. Lance is an unskilled worker who works for local moving companies during their busy seasons. The rest of the year he is unemployed.

   d. Gwen had a job as a clerk but quit when her husband was transferred to another state. She looked for a month before finding a new job that she liked.

   e. Tao looked for a job for six weeks after finishing college. He turned down a couple of offers because they didn't let him use the skills he had acquired in college, but now he has a job in the area that he trained for.

   f. Karen, a software engineer, lost her job when the start-up company she was working for went bankrupt. She interviewed at five companies before accepting a new job in another firm in the same industry.

9. The demand for and supply of labor in a certain industry are given by the equations

$$N^d = 400 - 2w$$
$$N^s = 240 + 2w$$

where N^d is the number of workers employers want to hire, N^s is the number of people willing to work, and both labor demand and labor supply depend on the real wage w, which is measured in dollars per day.

a. Find employment and the real wage in labor market equilibrium.

b. Suppose the minimum wage is $50 per day. Find employment and unemployment. Is anyone made better off by the minimum wage? Worse off? In answering the last part of the question, consider not only workers but employers and other people in the society, such as consumers and taxpayers.

c. Repeat part b except now assume that a union contract requires that workers be paid $60 per day.

d. Repeat part b but, instead of a minimum wage, suppose there is an unemployment benefit that pays $50 per day. Workers are indifferent between earning a wage of $50 per day and remaining unemployed and collecting the benefit.

e. Repeat part b, assuming that the minimum wage is $50 per day. However, assume that the cost of complying with government regulations on workplace safety reduces labor demand to $N^d = 360 - 2w$.

10. The *Economic Report of the President* (ERP), put out annually by the President's Council of Economic Advisers, is available in the library or online (w3.access.gpo.gov/eop). ERP includes both useful articles on recent economic developments and a statistical section that provides historical data on many macro variables.

From the ERP or some other source, find data for the nonrecession year 2000 on the percentage of the unemployed who were out of work less than 5 weeks, between 5 and 14 weeks, and over 26 weeks. What do these data suggest about the relative importance of frictional and structural unemployment in the economy when the economy is not in recession?

Compare the data you found for the most recent year to similar data for the recession years 1981–1982, 1990–1991, and 2001. How do recessions change the proportion of unemployment that is short term and long term?

▪ ANSWERS TO IN-CHAPTER EXERCISES ▪

21.1 The value of the marginal product of the seventh worker is $39,000, and the value of the marginal product of the eighth worker is $33,000. So the seventh but not the eighth worker is profitable to hire at a wage of $35,000.

21.2 With the computer price at $5,000, it is profitable to hire three workers at a wage of $100,000, since the third worker's value of marginal product ($105,000) exceeds $100,000 but the fourth worker's value of marginal product ($95,000) is less than $100,000. At a computer price of $3,000, we can refer to Table 21.1 to find that not even the first worker has a value of marginal product as high as $100,000, so at that computer price BCC will hire no workers. In short, at a wage of $100,000, the increase in the computer price raises the demand for technicians from zero to three.

21.3 The seventh but not the eighth worker's value of marginal product exceeds $50,000 (Table 21.3), so it is profitable to hire seven workers if the going wage is $50,000. From Table 21.1, before the increase in productivity, the first five workers have values of marginal product greater than $50,000, so the demand for labor at a given wage of $50,000 is five workers. Thus the increase in productivity raises the quantity of labor demanded at a wage of $50,000 from five workers to seven workers.

21.4 Even though you are receiving no pay, the valuable experience you gain as an intern is likely to raise the pay you will be able to earn in the future, so it is an investment in human capital. You also find working in the radio station more enjoyable than working in a car wash, presumably. To decide which job to take, you should ask yourself, "Taking into account both the likely increase in my future earnings and my greater enjoyment from working in the radio station, would I be willing to pay $3,000 to work in the radio station rather than in the car wash?" If the answer is yes, then you should work in the radio station, otherwise you should go to the car wash.

A decision to work in the radio station does not contradict the idea of an upward-sloping labor supply curve, if we are willing to think of the total compensation for that job as including not just cash wages but such factors as the value of the training that you receive. Your labor supply curve is still upward-sloping in the sense that the greater the value you place on the internship experience, the more likely you are to accept the job.

21.5 Immigration to a country raises labor supply—indeed, the search for work is one of the most powerful factors drawing immigrants in the first place. As shown in the accompanying figure, an increase in labor supply will tend to lower the wages that employers have to pay (from w to w'), while raising overall employment (from N to N'). Because of its tendency to reduce real wages, labor unions generally oppose large-scale immigration, while employers support it.

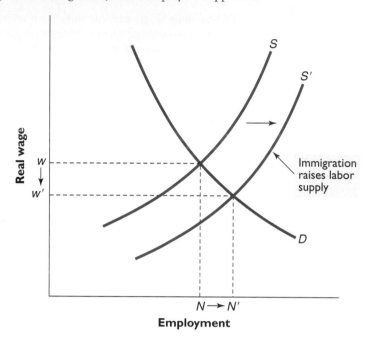

Although the figure shows the overall, or aggregate, supply of labor in the economy, the specific effects of immigration on wages depend on the skills and occupations of the immigrants. Current U.S. immigration policy makes the reunification of families the main reason for admitting immigrants, and for the most part immigrants are not screened by their education or skills. The U.S. also has a good deal of illegal immigration, made up largely of people looking for economic opportunity. These two factors create a tendency for new immigrants to the United States to be relatively low-skilled. Since immigration tends to increase the supply of unskilled labor by relatively more, it depresses wages of domestic low-skilled workers more than it does the wages of domestic high-skilled workers. Some economists, such as George Borjas of Harvard University, have argued that low-skilled immigration is another important factor reducing the wages of less-skilled workers relative to workers with greater skills and education. Borjas argues that the United States should adopt the approach used by Canada and give preference to potential immigrants with relatively higher levels of skills and education.

21.6 Part (a) of the accompanying figure shows the labor market in 1960–1972; part (b) shows the labor market in 1973–1996. For comparability, we set the initial labor supply (S) and demand (D) curves the same in both parts, implying the same initial values of the real wage (w) and employment (N). In part (a) we show the effects of a large increase in labor demand (from D to D'), the result of rapid productivity growth, and a relatively small increase in labor supply (from S to S'). The real wage rises to w' and employment rises to N'. In part (b) we observe the effects of a somewhat smaller increase in labor demand (from D to D'') and a larger increase in labor supply (from S to S''). Part (b), corresponding to the 1973–1996 period, shows a smaller increase in the real wage and a larger increase in employment than part (a), corresponding to 1960–1972. These results are consistent with actual developments in the U.S. labor market over these two periods. Since 1996, more rapid productivity growth, which raises labor demand more quickly, accounts for faster growth in real wages.

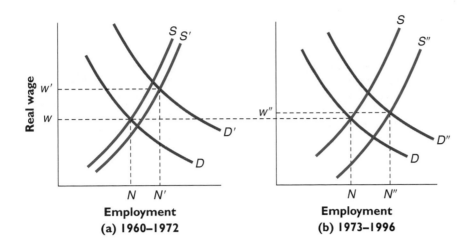

Employment
(a) 1960–1972

Employment
(b) 1973–1996

CHAPTER

22

SAVING AND CAPITAL FORMATION

■

O n your mother's or father's knee you probably heard the fable of the ant and the grasshopper. All summer the ant worked hard laying up food for the winter. The grasshopper mocked the ant's efforts and contented himself with basking in the sunshine, ignoring the ant's earnest warnings. When winter came the ant was well-fed, while the grasshopper starved. Moral: When times are good, the wise put aside something for the future.

Of course, there is also the modern ending to the fable, in which the grasshopper breaks his leg by tripping over the anthill, sues the ant for negligence, and ends up living comfortably on the ant's savings. (Nobody knows what happened to the ant.) Moral: Saving is risky; live for today.

The pitfalls of modern life notwithstanding, saving is important, both to individuals and to nations. People need to save to provide for their retirement and for other future needs, such as their children's education or a new home. An individual's or a family's savings can also provide a crucial buffer in the event of an economic emergency, such as the loss of a job or unexpected medical bills. At the national level, the production of new capital goods—factories, equipment, and housing—is an important factor promoting economic growth and higher living standards. As we will see in this chapter, the resources necessary to produce new capital come primarily from a nation's collective saving.

Because adequate saving is so important both to ensuring families' financial security and creating new capital goods, many people have expressed concern about the low saving rate of American households. Figure 22.1 shows the U.S. household saving rate (the percentage of after-tax household income that is saved) since 1960. Never very high by international standards, the U.S.

household saving rate declined sharply in the mid-1980s and fell again in the mid-1990s, reaching 2.3 percent of household disposable income in 2001.

FIGURE 22.1

Household Saving Rate in the United States, 1960–2001.

The U.S. household saving rate, declining since the mid-1980s, fell to 2.3 percent in 2001.

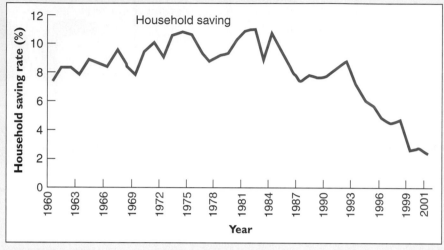

SOURCE: Bureau of Economic Analysis (http://www.bea.gov/).

What was the significance of this precipitous decline? Alarmists saw the data as evidence of "grasshopperish" behavior, and a threat to Americans' future prosperity. The reality, as we will see, is more complex. Many American families do save very little, a choice that is a likely to exact a toll on their economic well-being in the long run. On the other hand, household saving is only one part of the total saving of the U.S. economy, as businesses and governments also save. In fact, the total saving of the U.S. economy, called *national saving,* has not declined significantly in recent years. Thus, if the United States is suffering a "savings shortfall," it is much less severe than might be suggested by the figures on household saving only.

In this chapter we will look at saving and its links to the formation of new capital. We begin by defining the concepts of saving and wealth and exploring the connection between them. We will consider why people choose to save, rather than spending all their income. We then turn to national saving—the collective saving of households, businesses, and government. Because national saving determines the capacity of an economy to create new capital, it is the more important measure of saving from a macroeconomic perspective.

We next discuss capital formation. Most decisions to invest in new capital are made by firms. As we will see, a firm's decision to invest is in many respects analogous to its decision about whether to increase employment; firms will choose to expand their capital stocks when the benefits of doing so exceed the costs. We end the chapter by showing how national saving and capital formation are related, using a supply and demand approach.

SAVING AND WEALTH

saving current income minus spending on current needs

In general, the **saving** of an economic unit—whether a household, a business, a university, or a nation—may be defined as its *current income* minus its *spending on current needs.* For example, if Consuelo earns $300 per week, spends $280 weekly on living expenses such as rent, food, clothes, and entertainment, and deposits the remaining $20 in the bank, her saving is $20 per week. The **saving rate** of any economic unit is its saving divided by its income. Since Consuelo saves $20 of her weekly income of $300, her saving rate is $20/$300, or 6.7 percent.

saving rate saving divided by income

The saving of an economic unit is closely related to its **wealth,** or the value of its assets minus its liabilities. **Assets** are anything of value that one *owns,* either *financial* or *real.* Examples of financial assets that you or your family might own include cash, a checking account, stocks, and bonds. Examples of real assets include a home or other real estate, jewelry, consumer durables like cars, and valuable collectibles. **Liabilities,** on the other hand, are the debts one *owes.* Examples of liabilities are credit card balances, student loans, and mortgages.

wealth the value of *assets* minus *liabilities*

assets anything of value that one *owns*

liabilities the debts one *owes*

Accountants list the assets and liabilities of a family, a firm, a university, or any other economic unit on a *balance sheet.* Comparing the values of the assets and liabilities helps them to determine the economic unit's wealth, also called its *net worth.*

Consuelo constructs her balance sheet

EXAMPLE 22.1

To take stock of her financial position, Consuelo lists her assets and liabilities on a balance sheet. The result is shown in Table 22.1. What is Consuelo's wealth?

TABLE 22.1
Consuelo's Balance Sheet

Assets		Liabilities	
Cash	$ 80	Student loan	$3,000
Checking account	1,200	Credit card balance	250
Shares of stock	1,000		
Car (market value)	3,500		
Furniture (market value)	500		
Total	**$6,280**		**$3,250**
		Net worth	**$3,030**

Consuelo's financial assets are the cash in her wallet, the balance in her checking account, and the current value of some shares of stock her parents gave her. Together her financial assets are worth $2,280. She also lists $4,000 in real assets, the sum of the market values of her car and her furniture. Consuelo's total assets, both financial and real, come to $6,280. Her liabilities are the student loan she owes the bank and the balance due on her credit card, which total $3,250. Consuelo's wealth, or net worth, then, is the value of her assets ($6,280) minus the value of her liabilities ($3,250), or $3,030.

EXERCISE 22.1

What would Consuelo's net worth be if her student loan were for $6,500 rather than $3,000? Construct a new balance sheet for her.

Saving and wealth are related, because saving contributes to wealth. To understand this relationship better, we must distinguish between *stocks* and *flows.*

STOCKS AND FLOWS

Saving is an example of a **flow,** a measure that is defined *per unit of time.* For example, Consuelo's saving is $20 *per week.* Wealth, in contrast, is a **stock,** a measure that is defined *at a point in time.* Consuelo's wealth of $3,030, for example, is her wealth on a particular date—say, January 1, 2003.

flow a measure that is defined *per unit of time*

To visualize the difference between stocks and flows, think of water running into a bathtub. The amount of water in the bathtub at any specific moment—for

stock a measure that is defined *at a point in time*

The flow of saving increases the stock of wealth in the same way that the flow of water through the faucet increases the amount of water in the tub.

example, 40 gallons at 7:15 P.M.—is a stock, because it is measured at a specific point in time. The rate at which the water flows into the tub—for example, 2 gallons per minute—is a flow, because it is measured per unit of time. In many cases, a flow is the *rate of change* in a stock: If we know that there are 40 gallons of water in the tub at 7:15 P.M., for example, and that water is flowing in at 2 gallons per minute, we can easily determine that the stock of water will be changing at the rate of 2 gallons per minute and will equal 42 gallons at 7:16 P.M., 44 gallons at 7:17 P.M., and so on, until the bathtub overflows.

EXERCISE 22.2

Continuing the example of the bathtub: If there are 40 gallons of water in the tub at 7:15 P.M. and water is being *drained* at the rate of 3 gallons per minute, what will be the stock and flow at 7:16 P.M.? At 7:17 P.M.? Does the flow still equal the rate of change in the stock?

The relationship between saving (a flow) and wealth (a stock) is similar to the relationship between the flow of water into a bathtub and the stock of water in the tub in that the *flow* of saving causes the *stock* of wealth to change at the same rate. Indeed, as Example 22.2 illustrates, every dollar that a person saves adds a dollar to his or her wealth.

EXAMPLE 22.2

The link between saving and wealth

Consuelo saves $20 per week. How does this saving affect her wealth? Does the change in her wealth depend on whether Consuelo uses her saving to accumulate assets or to pay down her liabilities?

Consuelo could use the $20 she saved this week to increase her assets—for example, by adding the $20 to her checking account—or to reduce her liabilities—for example, by paying down her credit card balance. Suppose she adds the $20 to her checking account, increasing her assets by $20. Since her liabilities are unchanged, her wealth also increases by $20, to $3,050 (see Table 22.1).

If Consuelo decides to use the $20 she saved this week to pay down her credit card balance, she reduces it from $250 to $230. That action would reduce her liabilities by $20, leaving her assets unchanged. Since wealth equals assets minus liabilities, reducing her liabilities by $20 increases her wealth by $20, to $3,050. Thus, saving $20 per week raises Consuelo's stock of wealth by $20 a week, regardless of whether she uses her saving to increase her assets or reduce her liabilities.

The close relationship between saving and wealth explains why saving is so important to an economy. Higher rates of saving today lead to faster accumulation of wealth, and the wealthier a nation is, the higher its standard of living. Thus a high rate of saving today contributes to an improved standard of living in the future.

CAPITAL GAINS AND LOSSES

Though saving increases wealth, it is not the only factor that determines wealth. Wealth can also change because of changes in the values of the real or financial assets one owns. Suppose Consuelo's shares of stock rise in value, from $1,000 to $1,500. This increase in the value of Consuelo's stock raises her total assets by $500 without affecting her liabilities. As a result, Consuelo's wealth rises by $500, from $3,030 to $3,530 (see Table 22.2).

Changes in the value of existing assets are called **capital gains** when an asset's value increases and **capital losses** when an asset's value decreases. Just as capital gains increase wealth, capital losses decrease wealth. Capital gains and losses are not counted as part of saving, however. Instead, the change in a person's wealth

capital gains increases in the value of existing assets

capital losses decreases in the values of existing assets

TABLE 22.2
Consuelo's Balance Sheet after an Increase in the Value of Her Stocks

Assets		Liabilities	
Cash	$ 80	Student loan	$3,000
Checking account	1,200	Credit card balance	250
Shares of stock	1,500		
Car (market value)	3,500		
Furniture (market value)	500		
Total	**$6,780**		**$3,250**
		Net worth	**$3,530**

during any period equals the saving done during the period plus capital gains or minus capital losses during that period. In terms of an equation,

Change in wealth = Saving + Capital gains − Capital losses.

EXERCISE 22.3

How would each of the following actions or events affect Consuelo's *saving* and her *wealth*?

a. **Consuelo deposits $20 in the bank at the end of the week as usual. She also charges $50 on her credit card, raising her credit card balance to $300.**

b. **Consuelo uses $300 from her checking account to pay off her credit card bill.**

c. **Consuelo's old car is recognized as a classic. Its market value rises from $3,500 to $4,000.**

d. **Consuelo's furniture is damaged and as a result falls in value from $500 to $200.**

Capital gains and losses can have a major effect on one's overall wealth, as Economic Naturalist 22.1 illustrates.

The bull market and household wealth

On the whole, Americans felt very prosperous during the 1990s: Measures of household wealth during this period showed enormous gains. Yet, as Figure 22.1 shows, saving by U.S. households was quite low throughout those years. How did American households increase their wealth in the 1990s while saving very little?

During the 1990s an increasing number of Americans acquired stocks, either directly through purchases or indirectly through their pension and retirement funds. At the same time, stock prices rose at record rates (see Figure 22.2). The strongly rising "bull market," which increased the prices of most stocks, enabled many Americans to enjoy significant capital gains and increased wealth without saving much, if anything. Indeed, some economists argued that the low household saving rate of the 1990s is partially *explained* by the bull market; because capital gains increased household wealth by so much, many people saw no need to save.

The stock market peaked in early 2000 and stock prices fell quite sharply over the following two years. It is interesting that U.S. households did not choose

ECONOMIC NATURALIST 22.1

to save more in 2000–2001 (Figure 22.1), despite the decline in their stock market wealth. One explanation is that an even larger component of household wealth—the value of privately owned homes—rose significantly in 2000–2001, partly offsetting the effect of the decline in stock values on household wealth.

FIGURE 22.2

The Bull Market of the 1990s.

Stock prices rose sharply during the 1990s, greatly increasing the wealth of households that held stocks. This figure shows the Standard & Poor's 500 index of stock prices, divided by the CPI to correct for inflation, for the period 1960–2001. Stock prices peaked in 2000 and fell sharply into 2002.

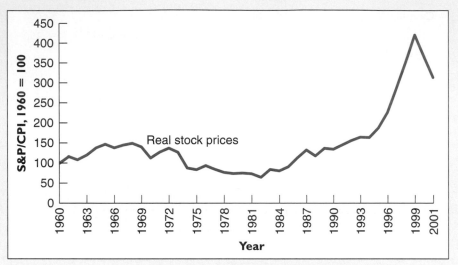

SOURCE: Economic Report of the President (http://w3.access.gpo.gov/eop/)

We have seen how saving is related to the accumulation of wealth. To understand why people choose to save, however, we need to examine their motives for saving.

⬤ **RECAP**   **SAVING AND WEALTH**

In general, *saving* is current income minus spending on current needs. *Wealth* is the value of assets—anything of value that one owns—minus liabilities—the debts one owes. Saving is measured per unit of time (for example, dollars per week) and thus is a *flow*. Wealth is measured at a point in time and thus is a *stock*. In the same way the flow of water through the faucet increases the stock of water in a bathtub, the flow of saving increases the stock of wealth.

Wealth can also be increased by *capital gains* (increases in the value of existing assets) or reduced by *capital losses* (decreases in asset values). The capital gains afforded stockholders by the bull market of the 1990s allowed many families to increase their wealth significantly while doing very little saving.

WHY DO PEOPLE SAVE?

Why do people save part of their income instead of spending everything they earn? Economists have identified at least three broad reasons for saving. First, people save to meet certain long-term objectives, such as a comfortable retirement. By putting away part of their income during their working years, they can live better after retirement than they would if they had to rely solely on Social Security and their company pensions. Other long-term objectives might include college tuition for one's children and the purchase of a new home or car. Since many of these needs occur at fairly predictable stages in one's life, economists call this type of saving **life-cycle saving.**

A second reason to save is to protect oneself and family against unexpected setbacks—the loss of a job, for example, or a costly health problem. Personal

life-cycle saving saving to meet long-term objectives, such as retirement, college attendance, or the purchase of a home financial advisors typically suggest that families maintain an emergency reserve (a "rainy-day fund") equal to three to six months' worth of income. Saving for protection against potential emergencies is called **precautionary saving.**

precautionary saving saving for protection against unexpected setbacks, such as the loss of a job or a medical emergency

"Fortunately, you have the life savings of a man three times your age."

A third reason to save is to accumulate an estate to leave to one's heirs, usually one's children but possibly a favorite charity or other worthy cause. Saving for the purpose of leaving an inheritance, or bequest, is called **bequest saving.** Bequest saving is done primarily by people at the higher end of the income ladder. But because these people control a large share of the nation's wealth, bequest saving is an important part of overall saving.

bequest saving saving done for the purpose of leaving an inheritance

To be sure, people usually do not mentally separate their saving into these three categories; rather, all three reasons for saving motivate most savers to varying degrees. The Economic Naturalist 22.2 shows how the three reasons for saving can explain the high rate of household saving in Japan.

Why do Japanese households save so much?

Japanese households save about 20 percent of their income, an unusually high rate. Although cultural factors are often cited as a reason for their propensity to save, the high saving rate is a relatively recent phenomenon; the Japanese were not especially big savers prior to World War II. Why do the Japanese save so much, then?

Among the reasons for saving we discussed, *life-cycle* reasons are clearly important in Japan. The Japanese have long life expectancies, and many retire relatively early. With a long period of retirement to finance, Japanese families must save a great deal during their working years. Second, even though the Japanese real estate market crashed at the beginning of the 1990s, land and housing prices remain extremely high in Japan compared to other countries. In addition, down payment requirements are typically quite high. Young people must therefore save a great deal, or borrow their parents' savings, to buy their first homes in Japan.

ECONOMIC NATURALIST 22.2

Studies have also found that *bequest saving* is important in Japan. Many older people live with their children after retirement. In return for support and attention during their later years, parents feel they must provide substantial inheritances for their children.

Precautionary saving is probably lower in Japan than in some other countries, however. Although Japan's recent economic troubles have reduced the practice of *lifetime employment,* Japanese firms still make extensive use of the system, which essentially guarantees a job for life to workers who join a firm after graduating from college. This type of job security, coupled with Japan's traditionally low unemployment rate, reduces the need for precautionary saving.

Although most people are usually motivated to save for at least one of the three reasons we have discussed, the amount they choose to save may depend on the economic environment. One economic variable that is quite significant in saving decisions is the real interest rate.

SAVING AND THE REAL INTEREST RATE

Most people don't save by putting cash in a mattress. Instead, they make financial investments that they hope will provide a good return on their saving. For example, a checking account may pay interest on the account balance. More sophisticated financial investments, such as government bonds or shares of stock in a corporation (see Chapter 24), also pay returns in the form of interest payments, dividends, or capital gains. High returns are desirable, of course, because the higher the return, the faster one's savings will grow.

The rate of return that is most relevant to saving decisions is the *real interest rate,* denoted r. Recall from Chapter 19 that the real interest rate is the rate at which the real purchasing power of a financial asset increases over time. The real interest rate equals the market, or nominal, interest rate (i) minus the inflation rate (π).

The real interest rate is relevant to savers because it is the "reward" for saving. Suppose you are thinking of increasing your saving by $1,000 this year, which you can do if you give up your habit of eating out once a week. If the real interest rate is 5 percent, then in a year your extra saving will give you extra purchasing power of $1,050, measured in today's dollars. But if the real interest rate were 10 percent, your sacrifice of $1,000 this year would be rewarded by $1,100 in purchasing power next year. Obviously, all else being equal, you would be more willing to save today if you knew the reward next year would be greater. In either case the *cost* of the extra saving—giving up your weekly night out—is the same. But the *benefit* of the extra saving, in terms of increased purchasing power next year, is higher if the real interest rate is 10 percent rather than 5 percent.

EXAMPLE 22.3

By how much does a high savings rate enhance a family's future living standard?

The Spends and the Thrifts are similar families, except that the Spends save 5 percent of their income each year and the Thrifts save 20 percent. The two families began to save in 1980 and plan to continue to save until their respective breadwinners retire in the year 2015. Both families earn $40,000 a year in real terms in the labor market, and both put their savings in a mutual fund that has yielded a real return of 8 percent per year, a return they expect to continue into the future. Compare the amount that the two families consume in each year from 1980 to 2015, and compare the families' wealth at retirement.

In the first year, 1980, the Spends saved $2,000 (5 percent of their $40,000 income) and consumed $38,000 (95 percent of $40,000). The Thrifts saved $8,000 in 1980 (20 percent of $40,000) and hence consumed only $32,000 in that year, $6,000 less than the Spends. In 1981, the Thrifts' income was $40,640, the extra $640 representing the 8 percent return on their $8,000 savings. The Spends saw their income grow by only $160 (8 percent of their savings of $2,000) in 1981. With an income of $40,640, the Thrifts consumed $32,512 in 1981 (80 percent of $40,640) compared to $38,152 (95 percent of $40,160) for the Spends. The consumption gap between the two families, which started out at $6,000, thus fell to $5,640 after one year.

Because of the more rapid increase in the Thrifts' wealth and hence interest income, each year the Thrifts' income grew faster than the Spends'; each year the Thrifts continued to save 20 percent of their higher incomes compared to only 5 percent for the Spends. Figure 22.3 shows the paths followed by the consumption spending of the two families. You can see that the Thrifts' con-

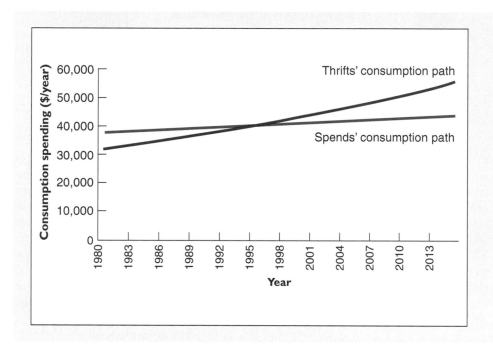

FIGURE 22.3
Consumption Trajectories of the Thrifts and the Spends.
The figure shows consumption spending in each year by two families, the Thrifts and the Spends. Because the Thrifts save more than the Spends, their annual consumption spending rises relatively more quickly. By the time of retirement in the year 2015, the Thrifts are both consuming significantly more each year than the Spends and also have a retirement nest egg that is five times larger.

sumption, though starting at a lower level, grows relatively more quickly. By 1995 the Thrifts had overtaken the Spends, and from that point onward, the amount by which the Thrifts outspent the Spends grew with each passing year. Even though the Spends continued to consume 95 percent of their income each year, their income grew so slowly that by 2000, they were consuming nearly $3,000 a year less than the Thrifts ($41,158 a year versus $43,957). And by the time the two families retire, in 2015, the Thrifts will be consuming more than $12,000 per year more than the Spends ($55,774 versus $43,698). Even more striking is the difference between the retirement nest eggs of the two families. Whereas the Spends will enter retirement with total accumulated savings of just over $77,000, the Thrifts will have more than $385,000, five times as much.

These dramatic differences depend in part on the assumption that the real rate of return is 8 percent—lower than the actual return to mutual funds since 1980 but still a relatively high rate of return from a historical perspective. On the other hand, the Spend family in our example actually saves more than typical U.S. households, many of which carry $5,000 or more in credit card debt at high rates of interest and have no significant savings at all. The point of the example, which remains valid under alternative assumptions about the real interest rate and saving rates, is that, because of the power of compound interest, a high rate of saving pays off handsomely in the long run.

"Someday, son, all this will be mine."

While a higher real interest rate increases the reward for saving, which tends to strengthen people's willingness to save, another force counteracts that extra incentive. Recall that a major reason for saving is to attain specific goals: a comfortable retirement, a college education, or a first home. If the goal is a specific amount—say, $25,000 for a down payment on a home—then a higher rate of return means that households can save *less* and still reach their goal, because funds that are put aside will grow more quickly. For example, to accumulate $25,000 at the end of five years, at a 5 percent interest rate a person would have to save about $4,309 per year. At a 10 percent interest rate, reaching the $25,000 goal would require saving only about $3,723 per year. To the extent that people are *target savers* who save to reach a specific goal, higher interest rates actually decrease the amount they need to save.

In sum, a higher real interest rate has both positive and negative effects on saving—a positive effect because it increases the reward for saving and a negative effect because it reduces the amount people need to save each year to reach a given target. Empirical evidence suggests that, in practice, higher real interest rates lead to modest increases in saving.

SAVING, SELF-CONTROL, AND DEMONSTRATION EFFECTS

The reasons for saving we just discussed are based on the notion that people are rational decision makers who will choose their saving rates to maximize their welfare over the long run. Yet many psychologists, and some economists, have argued instead that people's saving behavior is based as much on psychological as on economic factors. For example, psychologists stress that many people lack the *self-control* to do what they know is in their own best interest. People smoke or eat greasy food, despite the known long-term health risks. Similarly, they may have good intentions about saving but lack the self-control to put aside as much as they ought to each month.

One way to strengthen self-control is to remove temptations from the immediate environment. A person who is trying to quit smoking will make a point of not having cigarettes in the house, and a person with a weight problem will avoid going to a bakery. Similarly, a person who is not saving enough might arrange to use a payroll savings plan, through which a predetermined amount is deducted from each paycheck and set aside in a special account from which withdrawals are not permitted until retirement. Making saving automatic and withdrawals difficult eliminates the temptation to spend all of current earnings or squander accumulated savings. Payroll savings plans have helped many people to increase the amount that they save for retirement or other purposes.

An implication of the self-control hypothesis is that consumer credit arrangements that make borrowing and spending easier may reduce the amount that people save. For example, in recent years banks have encouraged people to borrow against the *equity* in their homes, that is, the value of the home less the value of the outstanding mortgage. Such financial innovations, by increasing the temptation to spend, may have reduced the household saving rate. The increased availability of credit cards with high borrowing limits is another temptation.

Downward pressure on the saving rate may also occur when additional spending by some consumers stimulates additional spending by others. Such *demonstration effects* arise when people use the spending of others as a yardstick by which to measure the adequacy of their own living standards. For example, a family in an upper-middle-class American suburb in which the average house has 3,000 square feet of living space might regard a 1,500-square-foot house as being uncomfortably small—too cramped, for example, to entertain friends in the manner to which community members have become accustomed. In contrast, a similar family living in a low-income neighborhood might find the very same house luxuriously large.

The implication of demonstration effects for saving is that families who live among others who consume more than they do may be strongly motivated to increase their own consumption spending. When satisfaction depends in part on *relative* living standards, an upward spiral may result in which household spending is higher, and saving lower, than would be best for either the individual families involved or for the economy as a whole.

Why do U.S. households save so little?

Household saving in the United States, which has always been comparatively low, has fallen even further in the past decade (Figure 22.1). Surveys show that a significant fraction of American households live from paycheck to paycheck with very little saving. Why do U.S. households save so little?

Economists do not agree on the reasons for low household saving in the United States, although many hypotheses have been suggested.

One possible reason for low saving is the availability of generous government assistance to the elderly. From a *life-cycle* perspective, an important motivation for saving is to provide for retirement. In general, the U.S. government provides a less comprehensive "social safety net" than other industrialized countries; that is, it offers relatively fewer programs to assist people in need. To the extent that the U.S. government does provide income support, however, it is heavily concentrated on the older segment of the population. Together the Social Security and Medicare programs, both of which are designed primarily to assist retired people, constitute a major share of the federal government's expenditures. These programs have been very successful; indeed they have virtually wiped out poverty among the elderly. To the extent that Americans believe that the government will ensure them an adequate living standard in retirement, however, their incentive to save for the future is reduced.

Another important life-cycle objective is buying a home. We have seen that the Japanese must save a great deal to purchase a home because of high house prices and down payment requirements. The same is true in many other countries. But in the United States, with its highly developed financial system, people can buy homes with down payments of 10 percent or even 5 percent of the purchase price. The ready availability of mortgages with low down payments reduces the need to save for the purchase of a home.

What about *precautionary saving*? Unlike Japan and Europe, which had to rebuild after World War II, the United States has not known sustained economic hardship since the Great Depression of the 1930s (which fewer and fewer

ECONOMIC NATURALIST 22.3

Americans are alive to remember). Perhaps the nation's prosperous past has led Americans to be more confident about the future and hence less inclined to save for economic emergencies than other people, even though the United States does not offer the level of employment security found in Japan or in Europe.

U.S. household saving is not only low by international standards, it is declining. The good performance of the stock market in the 1990s along with continuing increases in the prices of family homes probably help to explain this savings decline (see Economic Naturalist 22.1). As long as Americans enjoy capital gains, they see their wealth increase almost without effort, and their incentive to save is reduced.

Psychological factors may also explain Americans' saving behavior. For example, unlike in most countries, U.S. homeowners can easily borrow against their home equity. This ability, made possible by the highly developed U.S. financial markets, may exacerbate *self-control* problems by increasing the temptation to spend. Finally, *demonstration effects* may have depressed saving in recent decades. Chapter 21 discussed the phenomenon of increasing wage inequality, which has improved the relative position of more skilled and educated workers. Increased spending by households at the top of the earnings scale on houses, cars, and other consumption goods may have led those just below them to spend more as well, and so on. Middle-class families that were once content with medium-priced cars may now feel they need Volvos and BMWs to keep up with community standards. To the extent that demonstration effects lead families to spend beyond their means, they reduce their saving rate.

RECAP   **WHY DO PEOPLE SAVE?**

Motivations for saving include saving to meet long-term objectives, such as retirement (*life-cycle saving*), saving for emergencies (*precautionary saving*), and saving to leave an inheritance or bequest (*bequest saving*). The amount that people save also depends on macroeconomic factors, such as the real interest rate. A higher real interest rate stimulates saving by increasing the reward for saving, but it can also depress saving by making it easier for savers to reach a specific savings target. On net, a higher real interest rate appears to lead to modest increases in saving.

Psychological factors may also affect saving rates. If people have *self-control* problems, then financial arrangements (such as automatic payroll deductions) that make it more difficult to spend will increase their saving. People's saving decisions may also be influenced by *demonstration effects*, as when people feel compelled to spend at the same rate as their neighbors, even though they may not be able to afford to do so.

NATIONAL SAVING AND ITS COMPONENTS

Thus far we have been examining the concepts of saving and wealth from the individual's perspective. But macroeconomists are interested primarily in saving and wealth for the country as a whole. In this section we will study *national saving*, or the aggregate saving of the economy. National saving includes the saving of business firms and the government as well as that of households. Later in the chapter we will examine the close link between national saving and the rate of capital formation in an economy.

THE MEASUREMENT OF NATIONAL SAVING

To define the saving rate of a country as a whole, we will start with a basic accounting identity that was introduced in Chapter 18. According to this identity, for the economy as a whole, production (or income) must equal total expenditure. In symbols, the identity is

$$Y = C + I + G + NX,$$

where Y stands for either production or aggregate income (which must be equal), C equals consumption expenditure, I equals investment spending, G equals government purchases of goods and services, and NX equals net exports.

For now, let's assume that net exports *(NX)* is equal to zero, which would be the case if a country did not trade at all with other countries or if its exports and imports were always balanced. (We also discuss the foreign sector in Chapter 16.) With net exports set at zero, the condition that output equals expenditure becomes

$$Y = C + I + G.$$

To determine how much saving is done by the nation as a whole, we can apply the general definition of saving. As for any other economic unit, a nation's saving equals its *current income* less its *spending on current needs*. The current income of the country as a whole is its GDP, or Y, that is, the value of the final goods and services produced within the country's borders during the year.

Identifying the part of total expenditure that corresponds to the nation's spending on current needs is more difficult than identifying the nation's income. The component of aggregate spending that is easiest to classify is investment spending I. We know that investment spending—the acquisition of new factories, equipment, and other capital goods, as well as residential construction—is done to expand the economy's future productive capacity or provide more housing for the future, not to satisfy current needs. So investment spending clearly is *not* part of spending on current needs.

Deciding how much of consumption spending by households, C, and government purchases of goods and services, G, should be counted as spending on current needs is less straightforward. Certainly most consumption spending by households—on food, clothing, utilities, entertainment, and so on—is for current needs. But consumption spending also includes purchases of long-lived *consumer durables,* such as cars, furniture, and appliances. Consumer durables are only partially used up during the current year; they may continue to provide service, in fact, for years after their purchase. So household spending on consumer durables is a combination of spending on current needs and spending on future needs.

As with consumption spending, most government purchases of goods and services are intended to provide for current needs. However, like household purchases, a portion of government purchases is devoted to the acquisition or construction of long-lived capital goods, such as roads, bridges, schools, government buildings, and military hardware. And like consumer durables, these forms of *public capital* are only partially used up during the current year; most will provide useful services far into the future. So, like consumption spending, government purchases are in fact a mixture of spending on current needs and spending on future needs.

Although in reality not all spending by households and the government is for current needs, in practice, determining precisely how much of such spending is for current needs and how much is for future needs is extremely difficult. For this reason, for a long time U.S. government statistics have treated *all* of both consumption expenditures (C) and government purchases (G) as spending on current needs.[1] For simplicity's sake, in this book we will follow the same practice. But keep in mind that because consumption spending and government purchases

---

[1]Recently, however, the official data have begun to distinguish investment in public capital from the rest of government purchases.

do in fact include some spending for future rather than current needs, treating all of C and G as spending on current needs will understate the true amount of national saving.

If we treat all consumption spending and government purchases as spending on current needs, then the nation's saving is its income Y less its spending on current needs, $C + G$. So we can define **national saving** S as

national saving the saving of the entire economy, equal to GDP less consumption expenditures and government purchases of goods and services, or $Y - C - G$

$$S = Y - C - G. \tag{22.1}$$

Figure 22.4 shows the U.S. national saving rate (national saving as a percentage of GDP) for the years 1960 through 2001. Since 1960 the U.S. national saving rate has fluctuated between 12 and 18 percent. Like household saving, national saving declined somewhat over time, though by comparing Figures 22.4 and 22.1 you can see that the decline in national saving has been far more modest. Furthermore, unlike household saving, national saving recovered in the latter 1990s. As we will see next, the reason for these differences between the behavior of national saving and household saving is that saving done by business firms and, more recently, by the government has been substantial.

FIGURE 22.4
U.S. National Saving Rate, 1960–2001.
Since 1960, U.S. national saving has fluctuated between 12 and 18 percent of GDP.

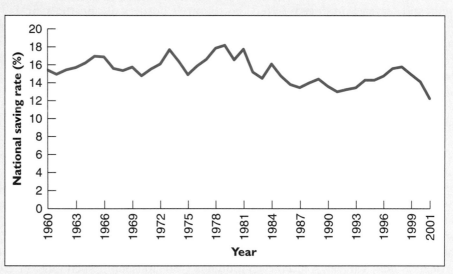

SOURCE: Bureau of Economic Analysis (http://www.bea.gov/)

PRIVATE AND PUBLIC COMPONENTS OF NATIONAL SAVING

To understand national saving better, we will divide it into two major components: private saving, which is saving done by households and businesses, and public saving, which is saving done by the government.

To see how national saving breaks down into public and private saving, we work with the definition of national saving, $S = Y - C - G$. To distinguish private-sector income from public-sector income, we must expand this equation to incorporate taxes as well as payments made by the government to the private sector. Government payments to the private sector include both *transfers* and *interest* paid to individuals and institutions who hold government bonds. **Transfer payments** are payments the government makes to the public for which it receives no current goods or services in return. Social Security benefits, welfare payments, farm support payments, and pensions to government workers are transfer payments.

transfer payments payments the government makes to the public for which it receives no current goods or services in return

Let T stand for taxes paid by the private sector to the government *less* transfer payments and interest payments made by the government to the private sector.

Since T equals private-sector tax payments minus the various benefits and interest payments the private sector receives from the government, we can think of T as net taxes. If we add and then subtract T from the definition of national saving, $S = Y - C - G$, we get

$$S = Y - C - G + T - T.$$

Rearranging this equation and grouping terms, we obtain

$$S = (Y - T - C) + (T - G). \tag{22.2}$$

This equation splits national saving S into two parts, *private saving*, or $Y - T - C$, and *public saving*, $T - G$.

   Private saving, $Y - T - C$, is the saving of the private sector of the economy. Why is $Y - T - C$ a reasonable definition of private saving? Remember that saving equals current income minus spending on current needs. The income of the private (nongovernmental) sector of the economy is the economy's total income Y less net taxes paid to the government, T. The private sector's spending on current needs is its consumption expenditures C. So private-sector saving, equal to private-sector income less spending on current needs, is $Y - T - C$. Letting $S_{private}$ stand for private saving, we can write the definition of private saving as

$$S_{private} = Y - T - C.$$

   Private saving can be further broken down into saving done by households and business firms. *Household saving*, also called personal saving, is saving done by families and individuals. Household saving corresponds to the familiar image of families putting aside part of their incomes each month, and it is the focus of much attention in the news media. But businesses are important savers as well— indeed business saving makes up the bulk of private saving in the United States. Businesses use the revenues from their sales to pay workers' salaries and other operating costs, to pay taxes, and to provide dividends to their shareholders. The funds remaining after these payments have been made are equal to *business saving*. A business firm's savings are available for the purchase of new capital equipment or the expansion of its operations. Alternatively, a business can put its savings in the bank for future use.

   Public saving, $T - G$, is the saving of the government sector, including state and local governments as well as the federal government. Net taxes T are the income of the government. Government purchases G represent the government's spending on current needs (remember that, for the sake of simplicity, we are ignoring the investment portion of government purchases). Thus $T - G$ fits our definition of saving, in this case by the public sector. Letting S_{public} stand for public saving, we can write out the definition of public saving as

$$S_{public} = T - G.$$

   Using Equation 22.2 and the definitions of private and public saving, we can rewrite national saving as

$$S = S_{private} + S_{public}. \tag{22.3}$$

This equation confirms that national saving is the sum of private saving and public saving. Since private saving can be broken down in turn into household and business saving, we see that national saving is made up of the saving of three groups: households, businesses, and the government.

private saving the saving of the private sector of the economy is equal to the after-tax income of the private sector minus consumption expenditures $(Y - T - C)$; private saving can be further broken down into household saving and business saving

public saving the saving of the government sector is equal to net tax payments minus government purchases $(T - G)$

PUBLIC SAVING AND THE GOVERNMENT BUDGET

Although the idea that households and businesses can save is familiar to most people, the fact that the government can also save is less widely understood. Public saving is closely linked to the government's decisions about spending and taxing. Governments finance the bulk of their spending by taxing the private sector. If taxes and spending in a given year are equal, the government is said to have a *balanced budget*. If in any given year the government's spending exceeds its tax collections, the difference is called the **government budget deficit.** If the government runs a deficit, it must make up the difference by borrowing from the public through issuance of government bonds. Algebraically, the government budget deficit can be written as $G - T$, or government purchases minus net tax collections.

government budget deficit the excess of government spending over tax collections ($G - T$)

In some years the government may spend less than it collects in taxes. The excess of tax collections over government spending is called the **government budget surplus.** When a government has a surplus, it uses the extra funds to pay down its outstanding debt to the public. Algebraically, the government budget surplus may be written as $T - G$, or net tax collections less government purchases.

government budget surplus the excess of government tax collections over government spending ($T - G$); the government budget surplus equals public saving

If the algebraic expression for the government budget surplus, $T - G$, looks familiar, that is because it is also the definition of public saving, as we saw earlier. Thus, *public saving is identical to the government budget surplus.* In other words, when the government collects more in taxes than it spends, public saving will be positive. When the government spends more than it collects in taxes so that it runs a deficit, public saving will be negative.

Example 22.4 illustrates the relationships among public saving, the government budget surplus, and national saving.

EXAMPLE 22.4

Government saving

Following are data on U.S. government revenues and expenditures for 2000, in billions of dollars. Find (a) the federal government's budget surplus or deficit, (b) the budget surplus or deficit of state and local governments, and (c) the contribution of the government sector to national saving.

Federal government:	
Receipts	2,046.8
Expenditures	1,828.3
State and local governments:	
Receipts	1,222.6
Expenditures	1,189.8
SOURCE: Economic Report of the President (http://w3.access.gpo.gov/eop/)	

The federal government's receipts minus its expenditures were 2,046.8 − 1,828.3 = 218.5, so the federal government ran a budget surplus of $218.5 billion in 2000. State and local government receipts minus expenditures were 1,222.6 − 1,189.8 = 32.8, so state and local governments ran a collective budget surplus of $32.8 billion. The budget surplus of the entire government sector—that is, the federal surplus plus the state and local surplus—was 218.5 + 32.8 = 251.3, or $251.3 billion. So the contribution of the government sector to U.S. national saving in 2000 was $251.3 billion.

EXERCISE 22.4

Continuing Example 22.4, here are the analogous data on government revenues and expenditures for 1995, in billions of dollars. Again, find (a) the federal government's budget surplus or deficit, (b) the budget surplus or deficit of state and local governments, and (c) the contribution of the government sector to national saving.

Federal government:	
Receipts	1,460.3
Expenditures	1,634.7
State and local governments:	
Receipts	997.7
Expenditures	886.0

If you did Exercise 22.4 correctly, you found that the government sector's contribution to national saving in 1995 was *negative*. The reason is that the federal, state, and local governments taken together ran a budget deficit in that year, reducing national saving by the amount of the budget deficit.

Figure 22.4 showed the U.S. national saving rate since 1960. Figure 22.5 shows the behavior since 1960 of the three components of national saving: household saving, business saving, and public saving, each measured as a percentage of GDP. Note that business saving played a major role in national saving during these years, while the role of household saving was relatively modest. As we saw in Figure 22.1, household saving has been declining since the mid-1980s.

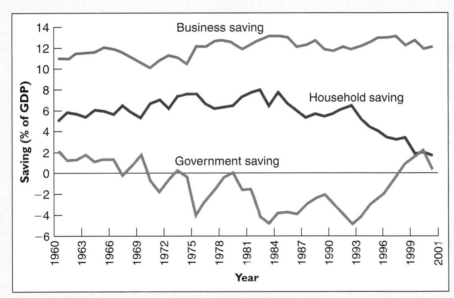

FIGURE 22.5

The Three Components of National Saving, 1960–2001.

Of the three components of national saving, business saving is the most important. In the last decade increased government saving has offset a decline in household saving, although government saving has also fallen since 2001.

SOURCE: Bureau of Economic Analysis (http://www.bea.gov/)

The contribution of public saving has varied considerably over time. Until about 1970, the federal, state, and local governments typically ran a combined surplus, making a positive contribution to national saving. But by the late 1970s, public saving had turned negative, reflecting large budget deficits, particularly at the federal level. For the next two decades, the government was a net drain on national saving. During the late 1990s, however, government budgets moved closer to balance, though deficits are now projected at the federal level for a number of years. The improvement in government saving during the 1990s offset to some extent the decline in household saving.

IS LOW HOUSEHOLD SAVING A PROBLEM?

Figure 22.1 showed that saving by U.S. households, never high by international standards, fell substantially during the 1990s. This decline in the household saving rate received much attention from the news media. Is the United States' low household saving rate as much of a problem as the press suggests?

From a macroeconomic perspective, the problem posed by low household saving has probably been overstated. The key fact often overlooked in media reports is that national saving, not household saving, determines the capacity of an economy to invest in new capital goods and to achieve continued improvement in living standards. Although household saving is low, saving by business firms has been significant. Furthermore, public saving has increased recently, as government budgets moved from deficit toward surplus. Overall, U.S. national saving has been reasonably stable, despite the sharp decline in the household saving rate shown in Figure 22.1. Although U.S. national saving is somewhat low compared to that of other industrialized countries, it has been sufficient to allow the United States to become one of the world's most productive economies.

From a microeconomic perspective, however, the low household saving rate does signal a problem, which is the large and growing inequality in wealth among U.S. households. Saving patterns tend to increase this inequality, since the economically better-off households tend not only to save more but, as businessowners or shareholders, are also the ultimate beneficiaries of the saving done by businesses. Thus the wealth of these households, including both personal assets and the value of the businesses, is great. In contrast, lower-income families, many of whom save very little and do not own a business or shares in a corporation, have very little wealth—in many cases, their life savings are less than $5,000. These households have little protection against setbacks such as chronic illness or job loss and must rely almost entirely on government support programs such as Social Security to fund their retirement. For this group, the low household saving rate is definitely a concern.

 RECAP   **NATIONAL SAVING AND ITS COMPONENTS**

National saving, the saving of the nation as a whole, is defined by $S = Y - C - G$, where Y is GDP, C is consumption spending, and G is government purchases of goods and services. National saving is the sum of public saving and private saving: $S = S_{\text{private}} + S_{\text{public}}$.

Private saving, the saving of the private sector, is defined by $S_{\text{private}} = Y - T - C$, where T is net tax payments. Private saving can be broken down further into household saving and business saving.

Public saving, the saving of the government, is defined by $S_{\text{public}} = T - G$. Public saving equals the government budget surplus, $T - G$. When the government budget is in surplus, government saving is positive; when the government budget is in deficit, public saving is negative.

INVESTMENT AND CAPITAL FORMATION

From the point of view of the economy as a whole, the importance of national saving is that it provides the funds needed for investment. Investment—the creation of new capital goods and housing—is critical to increasing average labor productivity and improving standards of living.

What factors determine whether and how much firms choose to invest? Firms acquire new capital goods for the same reason they hire new workers: They expect that doing so will be profitable. We saw in Chapter 21 that the profitability of employing an extra worker depends primarily on two factors: the cost of employing the worker and the value of the worker's marginal product. In the same way, firms' willingness to acquire new factories and machines depends on the expected *cost* of using them and the expected *benefit,* equal to the value of the marginal product that they will provide.

Should Larry buy a riding lawn mower?

EXAMPLE 22.5

Larry is thinking of going into the lawn care business. He can buy a $4,000 riding mower by taking out a loan at 6 percent annual interest. With this mower and his own labor Larry can net $6,000 per summer, after deduction of costs such as gasoline and maintenance. Of the $6,000 net revenues, 20 percent must be paid to the government in taxes. Assume that Larry could earn $4,400 after taxes by working in an alternative job. Assume also that the lawn mower can always be resold for its original purchase price of $4,000. Should Larry buy the lawn mower?

To decide whether to invest in the capital good (the lawn mower), Larry should compare the financial benefits and costs. With the mower he can earn revenue of $6,000, net of gasoline and maintenance costs. However, 20 percent of that, or $1,200, must be paid in taxes, leaving Larry with $4,800. Larry could earn $4,400 after taxes by working at an alternative job, so the financial benefit to Larry of buying the mower is the difference between $4,800 and $4,400, or $400; $400 is the value of the marginal product of the lawn mower.

Since the mower does not lose value over time and since gasoline and maintenance costs have already been deducted, the only remaining cost Larry should take into account is the interest on the loan for the mower. Larry must pay 6 percent interest on $4,000, or $240 per year. Since this financial cost is less than the financial benefit of $400, the value of the mower's marginal product, Larry should buy the mower.

Larry's decision might change if the costs and benefits of his investment in the mower change, as Example 22.6 shows.

Should Larry buy a riding lawn mower? (continued)

EXAMPLE 22.6

With all other assumptions the same as in Example 22.5, decide whether Larry should buy the mower:

a. If the interest rate is 12 percent rather than 6 percent.

b. If the purchase price of the mower is $7,000 rather than $4,000.

c. If the tax rate on Larry's net revenues is 25 percent rather than 20 percent.

d. If the mower is less efficient than Larry originally thought so that his net revenues will be $5,500 rather than $6,000.

In each case, Larry must compare the financial costs and benefits of buying the mower.

a. If the interest rate is 12 percent, then the interest cost will be 12 percent of $4,000, or $480, which exceeds the value of the mower's marginal product ($400). Larry should not buy the mower.

b. If the cost of the mower is $7,000, then Larry must borrow $7,000 instead of $4,000. At 6 percent interest, his interest cost will be $420—too high to justify the purchase, since the value of the mower's marginal product is $400.

c. If the tax rate on net revenues is 25 percent, then Larry must pay 25 percent of his $6,000 net revenues, or $1,500, in taxes. After taxes, his revenues from mowing will be $4,500, which is only $100 more than he could make working at an alternative job. Furthermore, the $100 will not cover the $240 in interest that Larry would have to pay. So again, Larry should not buy the mower.

d. If the mower is less efficient than originally expected so that Larry can earn net revenues of only $5,500, Larry will be left with only $4,400 after taxes—the same amount he could earn by working at another job. So in this case, the value of the mower's marginal product is zero. At any interest rate greater than zero, Larry should not buy the mower.

EXERCISE 22.5

Repeat Example 22.5, but assume that, over the course of the year, wear and tear reduces the resale value of the lawn mower from $4,000 to $3,800. Should Larry buy the mower?

The examples involving Larry and the lawn mower illustrate the main factors firms must consider when deciding whether to invest in new capital goods. On the cost side, two important factors are the *price of capital goods* and the *real interest rate*. Clearly, the more expensive new capital goods are, the more reluctant firms will be to invest in them. Buying the mower was profitable for Larry when its price was $4,000, but not when its price was $7,000.

Why is the real interest rate an important factor in investment decisions? The most straightforward case is when a firm has to borrow (as Larry did) to purchase its new capital. The real interest rate then determines the real cost to the firm of paying back its debt. Since financing costs are a major part of the total cost of owning and operating a piece of capital, much as mortgage payments are a major part of the cost of owning a home, increases in the real interest rate make the purchase of capital goods less attractive to firms, all else being equal.

Even if a firm does not need to borrow to buy new capital—say, because it has accumulated enough profits to buy the capital outright—the real interest rate remains an important determinant of the desirability of an investment. If a firm does not use its profits to acquire new capital, most likely it will use those profits to acquire financial assets such as bonds, which will earn the firm the real rate of interest. If the firm uses its profits to buy capital rather than to purchase a bond, it forgoes the opportunity to earn the real rate of interest on its funds. Thus the real rate of interest measures the *opportunity cost* of a capital investment. Since an increase in the real interest rate raises the opportunity cost of investing in new capital, it lowers the willingness of firms to invest, even if they do not literally need to borrow to finance new machines or equipment.

On the benefit side, the key factor in determining business investment is the *value of the marginal product* of the new capital, which should be calculated net of both operating and maintenance expenses and taxes paid on the revenues the capital generates. The value of the marginal product is affected by several factors. For example, a technological advance that allows a piece of capital to produce more goods and services would increase the value of its marginal product, as would lower taxes on the revenues produced by the new capital. An increase in the relative price of the good or service that the capital is used to produce will also increase the value of the marginal product and, hence, the desirability of the investment. For example, if the going price for lawn-mowing services were to rise, then all else being equal, investing in the mower would become more profitable for Larry.

Why has investment in computers increased so much in recent decades?

Since about 1980, investment in new computer systems by U.S. firms has risen sharply (see Figure 22.6). Purchases of new computers and software by firms now exceed 2.5 percent of GDP and amount to about 15 percent of all private non-residential investment. Why has investment in computers increased so much?

Investment in computers has increased by much more than other types of investment. Hence, the factors that affect all types of investment (such as the real interest rate and the tax rate) are not likely to be responsible for the boom. The two main causes of increased investment in computers appear to be the declining price of computing power and the increase in the value of the marginal product of computers. In recent years, the price of computing power has fallen at a precipitous rate. An industry rule of thumb is that the amount of computing power that is obtainable at a given price doubles every 18 months. As the price of computing power falls, an investment in computers becomes more and more likely to pass the *cost-benefit* test.

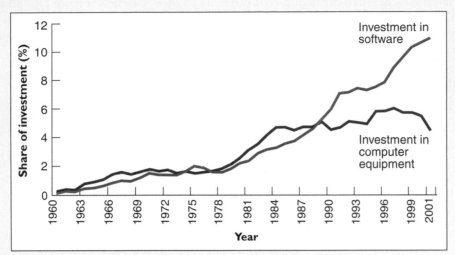

FIGURE 22.6
Investment in Computers and Software, 1960–2001.
Investment in computer equipment and software since 1960 shown as a percentage of private nonresidential investment. Computer-related investments by U.S. firms have risen significantly since about 1980, but investment in computer equipment dropped sharply in 2000 and 2001.

SOURCE: Bureau of Economic Analysis (http://www.bea.gov/).

On the benefit side, for some years after the beginning of the computer boom economists were unable to associate the technology with significant productivity gains. Defenders of investment in computer systems argued that the improvements in goods and services computers create are particularly hard to measure. How does one quantify the value to consumers of 24-hour-a-day access to cash or of the ability to make airline reservations on line? Critics responded that the expected benefits of the computer revolution may have proved illusory because of problems such as user-unfriendly software and poor technical training. However, U.S. productivity has increased noticeably in recent years (see Chapter 20), and many people are now crediting the improvement to investment in computers and computer-related technologies like the Internet. As more firms become convinced that computers do add significantly to productivity and profits, the boom in computer investment can be expected to continue.

RECAP   FACTORS THAT AFFECT INVESTMENT

Any of the following factors will increase the willingness of firms to invest in new capital:

1. A decline in the price of new capital goods

2. A decline in the real interest rate

3. Technological improvement that raises the marginal product of capital

4. Lower taxes on the revenues generated by capital

5. A higher relative price for the firm's output

SAVING, INVESTMENT, AND FINANCIAL MARKETS

Saving and investment are determined by different forces. Ultimately, though, in an economy without international borrowing and lending, national saving must equal investment. The supply of savings (by households, firms, and the government) and the demand for savings (by firms that want to purchase or construct new capital) are equalized through the workings of *financial markets*. Figure 22.7 illustrates this process. Quantities of national saving and investment are measured on the horizontal axis; the real interest rate is shown on the vertical axis. As we will see, in the market for saving, the real interest rate functions as the "price."

FIGURE 22.7
The Supply of and Demand for Savings.
Savings are supplied by households, firms, and the government and demanded by borrowers wishing to invest in new capital goods. The supply of saving (S) increases with the real interest rate, and the demand for saving by investors (I) decreases with the real interest rate. In financial market equilibrium, the real interest rate takes the value that equates the quantity of saving supplied and demanded.

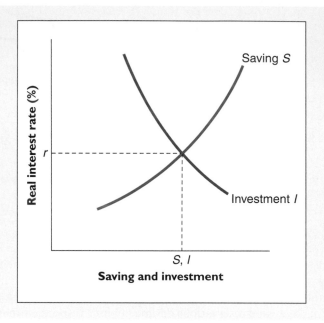

In the figure the supply of savings is shown by the upward-sloping curve marked *S*. This curve shows the quantity of national saving that households, firms, and the government are willing to supply at each value of the real interest rate. The saving curve is upward-sloping because empirical evidence suggests that increases in the real interest rate stimulate saving. The demand for saving is given by the downward-sloping curve marked *I*. This curve shows the quantity of investment in new capital that firms would choose and hence the amount they would need to borrow in financial markets, at each value of the real interest rate. Because higher real interest rates raise the cost of borrowing and reduce firms' willingness to invest, the demand for saving curve is downward-sloping.

Putting aside the possibility of borrowing from foreigners (discussed in Chapter 16), a country can invest only those resources that its savers make available. In equilibrium, then, desired investment (the demand for savings) and desired national saving (the supply of savings) must be equal. As Figure 22.7 suggests, desired saving is equated with desired investment through adjustments in the real interest rate, which functions as the "price" of saving. The movements of the real interest rate clear the market for savings in much the same way that the price of apples clears the market for apples. In Figure 22.7, the real interest rate that clears the market for saving is *r*, the real interest rate that corresponds to the intersection of the supply and demand curves.

The forces that push the real interest rate toward its equilibrium level are similar to the forces that lead to equilibrium in any other supply and demand situation. Suppose, for example, that the real interest rate exceeded *r*. At a higher real interest rate, savers would provide more funds than firms would want to invest. As lenders (savers) competed among themselves to attract borrowers (investors), the real interest rate would be bid down. The real interest rate would fall until it equaled *r*, the only interest rate at which both borrowers and lenders are satisfied, and no opportunities are left unexploited in the financial market (recall Chapter 3's *equilibrium principle*). What would happen if the real interest rate were *lower* than *r*?

Changes in factors *other than the real interest rate* that affect the supply of or demand for saving will shift the curves, leading to a new equilibrium in the financial market. Changes in the real interest rate cannot shift the supply or demand curves, just as a change in the price of apples cannot shift the supply or demand for apples, because the effects of the real interest rate on savings are already incorporated in the slopes of the curves. A few examples will illustrate the use of the supply and demand model of financial markets.

The effects of new technology

EXAMPLE 22.7

Exciting new technologies have been introduced in recent years, ranging from the Internet to new applications of genetics. A number of these technologies appear to have great commercial potential. How does the introduction of new technologies affect saving, investment, and the real interest rate?

The introduction of any new technology with the potential for commercial application creates profit opportunities for those who can bring the fruits of the technology to the public. In economists' language, the technical breakthrough raises the marginal product of new capital. Figure 22.8 shows the effects of a technological breakthrough, with a resulting increase in the marginal product of capital. At any given real interest rate, an increase in the marginal product of capital makes firms more eager to invest. Thus, the advent of the new technology causes the demand for saving to shift upward and to the right, from *I* to *I'*.

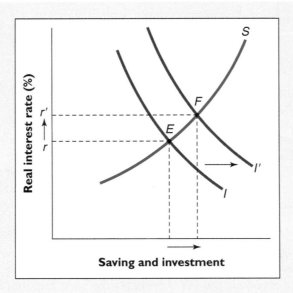

FIGURE 22.8
The Effects of a New Technology on National Saving and Investment.
A technological breakthrough raises the marginal product of new capital goods, increasing desired investment and the demand for savings. The real interest rate rises, as do national saving and investment.

At the new equilibrium point *F*, investment and national saving are higher than before, as is the real interest rate, which rises from *r* to *r'*. The rise in the real interest rate reflects the increased demand for funds by investors as they race to apply the new technologies. Because of the incentive of higher real returns, saving increases as well. Indeed, the real interest rate in the United States was relatively high in the late 1990s (Figure 19.2), as was the rate of investment, reflecting the opportunities created by new technologies.

Example 22.8 examines the effect of changing fiscal policies on the market for saving.

An increase in the government budget deficit

EXAMPLE 22.8

Suppose the government increases its spending without raising taxes, thereby increasing its budget deficit (or reducing its budget surplus). How will this decision affect national saving, investment, and the real interest rate?

National saving includes both private saving (saving by households and businesses) and public saving, which is equivalent to the government budget surplus. An increase in the government budget deficit (or a decline in the surplus) reduces public saving. Assuming that private saving does not change, the reduction in public saving will reduce national saving as well.

Figure 22.9 shows the effect of the increased government budget deficit on the market for saving and investment. At any real interest rate, a larger deficit

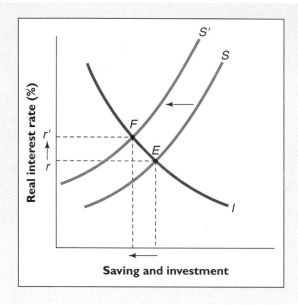

FIGURE 22.9

The Effects of an Increase in the Government Budget Deficit on National Saving and Investment.

An increase in the government budget deficit reduces the supply of saving, raising the real interest rate and lowering investment. The tendency of increased government deficits to reduce investment in new capital is called *crowding out*.

reduces national saving, causing the saving curve to shift to the left, from S to S'. At the new equilibrium point F, the real interest rate is higher at r', and both national saving and investment are lower. In economic terms, the government has dipped further into the pool of private savings to borrow the funds to finance its budget deficit. The government's extra borrowing forces investors to compete for a smaller quantity of available saving, driving up the real interest rate. The higher real interest rate makes investment less attractive, assuring that investment will decrease along with national saving.

crowding out the tendency of increased government deficits to reduce investment spending

The tendency of government budget deficits to reduce investment spending is called **crowding out**. Reduced investment spending implies slower capital formation, and thus lower economic growth, as we saw in Chapter 20. This adverse effect of budget deficits on economic growth is probably the most important cost of deficits, and a major reason why economists advise governments to minimize their deficits.

EXERCISE 22.6

Suppose the general public becomes more "grasshopper-like" and less "ant-like" in their saving decisions, becoming less concerned about saving for the future. How will the change in public attitudes affect the country's rate of capital formation and economic growth?

At the national level, high savings rates lead to greater investment in new capital goods and thus higher standards of living. At the individual or family level, a high saving rate promotes the accumulation of wealth and the achievement of economic security. In this chapter we have studied some of the factors that underlie saving and investment decisions. The next two chapters will look more closely at how savers hold their wealth and at how the financial system allocates the pool of available savings to the most productive investment projects.

▪ SUMMARY ▪

- In general, *saving* equals current income minus spending on current needs; the *saving rate* is the percentage of income that is saved. *Wealth,* or net worth, equals the market value of assets (real or financial items of value) minus liabilities (debts). Saving is a *flow,* being measured in dollars per unit of time; wealth is a *stock,* measured in dollars at a point in time. As the amount of water in a bathtub changes according to the rate at which water flows in, the stock of wealth increases at the saving rate. Wealth also increases if the value of existing assets rises (*capital gains*) and decreases if the value of existing assets falls (*capital losses*).

- Individuals and households save for a variety of reasons, including *life-cycle* objectives, as saving for retirement or a new home; the need to be prepared for an emergency (*precautionary saving*); and the desire to leave an inheritance (*bequest saving*). The amount people save is also affected by the real interest rate, which is the "reward" for saving. Evidence suggests that higher real interest rates lead to modest increases in saving. Saving can also be affected by psychological factors, such as the degree of self-control and the desire to consume at the level of one's neighbors (demonstration effects).

- The saving of an entire country is *national saving S*. National saving is defined by $S = Y - C - G$, where Y represents total output or income, C equals consumption spending, and G equals government purchases of goods and services. National saving can be broken up into private saving, or $Y - T - C$, and public saving, or $T - G$, where T stands for taxes paid to the government less transfer payments and interest paid by the government to the private sector. Private saving can be further broken down into household saving and business saving. In the United States, the bulk of private saving is done by businesses.

- Public saving is equivalent to the government budget surplus, $T - G$; if the government runs a budget deficit, then public saving is negative. The U.S. national saving rate is low relative to other industrialized countries, but it is higher and more stable than U.S. household saving.

- Investment is the purchase or construction of new capital goods, including housing. Firms will invest in new capital goods if the benefits of doing so outweigh the costs. Two factors that determine the cost of investment are the price of new capital goods and the real interest rate. The higher the real interest rate, the more expensive it is to borrow, and the less likely firms are to invest. The benefit of investment is the value of the marginal product of new capital, which depends on factors such as the productivity of new capital goods, the taxes levied on the revenues they generate, and the relative price of the firm's output.

- In the absence of international borrowing or lending, the supply of and demand for national saving must be equal. The supply of national saving depends on the saving decisions of households and businesses and the fiscal policies of the government (which determine public saving). The demand for saving is the amount business firms want to invest in new capital. The real interest rate, which is the "price" of borrowed funds, changes to equate the supply of and demand for national saving. Factors that affect the supply of or demand for saving will change saving, investment, and the equilibrium real interest rate. For example, an increase in the government budget deficit will reduce national saving and investment and raise the equilibrium real interest rate. The tendency of government budget deficits to reduce investment is called *crowding out*.

▪ KEY TERMS ▪

assets (569)
bequest saving (573)
capital gains (570)
capital losses (570)
crowding out (590)
flow (569)
government budget deficit (582)

government budget surplus (582)
liabilities (569)
life-cycle saving (572)
national saving (580)
precautionary saving (573)
private saving (581)

public saving (581)
saving (568)
saving rate (568)
stock (569)
transfer payments (580)
wealth (569)

▪ REVIEW QUESTIONS ▪

1. Explain the relationship between saving and wealth, using the concepts of flows and stocks. Is saving the only means by which wealth can increase? Explain.

2. Give three basic motivations for saving. Illustrate each with an example. What other factors would psychologists cite as being possibly important for saving?

3. Define *national saving*, relating your definition to the general concept of saving. Why does the standard U.S.

definition of national saving potentially understate the true amount of saving being done in the economy?

4. Household saving rates in the U.S. are very low. Is this fact a problem for the U.S. economy? Why or why not?

5. Why do increases in real interest rates reduce the quantity of saving demanded? (*Hint:* Who are the "demanders" of saving?)

6. Name one factor that could increase the supply of saving and one that could increase the demand for saving. Show the effects of each on saving, investment, and the real interest rate.

▪ PROBLEMS ▪

---

1. a. Corey has a mountain bike worth $300, a credit card debt of $150, $200 in cash, a Sandy Koufax baseball card worth $400, $1,200 in a checking account, and an electric bill due for $250. Construct Corey's balance sheet and calculate his net worth. For each remaining part, explain how the event affects Corey's assets, liabilities, and wealth.
    b. Corey goes to a baseball card convention and finds out that his baseball card is a worthless forgery.
    c. Corey uses $150 from his paycheck to pay off his credit card balance. The remainder of his earnings is spent.
    d. Corey writes a $150 check on his checking account to pay off his credit card balance. Of the events in the previous three parts, which, if any, corresponds to saving on Corey's part?

2. State whether each of the following is a stock or a flow, and explain.
    a. The gross domestic product
    b. National saving
    c. The value of the U.S. housing stock on January 1, 2003
    d. The amount of U.S. currency in circulation as of this morning
    e. The government budget deficit
    f. The quantity of outstanding government debt on January 1, 2003

3. Ellie and Vince are a married couple, both with college degrees and jobs. How would you expect each of the following events to affect the amount they save each month? Explain your answers in terms of the basic motivations for saving.
    a. Ellie learns she is pregnant.
    b. Vince reads in the paper about possible layoffs in his industry.
    c. Vince had hoped that his parents would lend financial assistance toward the couple's planned purchase of a house, but he learns that they can't afford it.
    d. Ellie announces that she would like to go to law school in the next few years.
    e. A boom in the stock market greatly increases the value of the couple's retirement funds.
    f. Vince and Ellie agree that they would like to leave a substantial amount to local charities in their wills.

4. Individual Retirement Accounts, or IRAs, were established by the U.S. government to encourage saving. An individual who deposits part of current earnings in an IRA does not have to pay income taxes on the earnings deposited, nor are any income taxes charged on the interest earned by the funds in the IRA. However, when the funds are withdrawn from the IRA, the full amount withdrawn is treated as income and is taxed at the individual's current income tax rate. In contrast, an individual depositing in a non-IRA account has to pay income taxes on the funds deposited and on interest earned in each year but does not have to pay taxes on withdrawals from the account. Another feature of IRAs which is different from a standard saving account is that funds deposited in an IRA cannot be withdrawn prior to retirement, except upon payment of a substantial penalty.
    a. Greg, who is five years from retirement, receives a $10,000 bonus at work. He is trying to decide whether to save this extra income in an IRA account or in a regular savings account. Both accounts earn 5 percent nominal interest, and Greg is in the 30 percent tax bracket in every year (including his retirement year). Compare the amounts that Greg will have in five years under each of the two saving strategies, net of all taxes. Is the IRA a good deal for Greg?
    b. Would you expect the availability of IRAs to increase the amount that households save? Discuss in light of (1) the response of saving to changes in the real interest rate and (2) psychological theories of saving.

5. In each part that follows, use the economic data given to find national saving, private saving, public saving, and the national saving rate.

a. Household saving = 200   Business saving = 400
Government purchases of goods and services = 100
Government transfers and interest payments = 100
Tax collections = 150   GDP = 2,200
b. GDP = 6,000   Tax collections = 1,200
Government transfers and interest payments = 400
Consumption expenditures = 4,500
Government budget surplus = 100
c. Consumption expenditures = 4,000   Investment = 1,000
Government purchases = 1,000   Net exports = 0
Tax collections = 1,500
Government transfers and interest payments = 500

6. Obtain a recent copy of the *Survey of Current Business*, published by the Bureau of Economic Analysis, in the library or on line at www.bea.doc.gov/bea/pubs.htm. In the national data portion of the *Survey*, find nominal data on GDP, consumption, government purchases of goods and services, total government expenditures, and total government receipts for the most recent complete year available (see Tables 1.1 and 3.1). Calculate national saving, private saving, public saving, and the national saving rate. How does the government's contribution to national saving in the most recent period compare to 1999 (see Example 22.4 in the text)?

7. Ellie and Vince are trying to decide whether to purchase a new home. The house they want is priced at $200,000. Annual expenses such as maintenance, taxes, and insurance equal 4 percent of the home's value. If properly maintained, the house's real value is not expected to change. The real interest rate in the economy is 6 percent, and Ellie and Vince can qualify to borrow the full amount of the purchase price (for simplicity, assume no down payment) at that rate. Ignore the fact that mortgage interest payments are tax-deductible in the United States.
a. Ellie and Vince would be willing to pay $1,500 monthly rent to live in a house of the same quality as the one they are thinking about purchasing. Should they buy the house?
b. Does the answer to part a change if they are willing to pay $2,000 monthly rent?
c. Does the answer to part a change if the real interest rate is 4 percent instead of 6 percent?
d. Does the answer to part a change if the developer offers to sell Ellie and Vince the house for $150,000?
e. Why do home-building companies dislike high interest rates?

8. The builder of a new movie theater complex is trying to decide how many screens she wants. Below are her estimates of the number of patrons the complex will attract each year, depending on the number of screens available.

Number of screens	Total number of patrons
1	40,000
2	75,000
3	105,000
4	130,000
5	150,000

After paying the movie distributors and meeting all other noninterest expenses, the owner expects to net $2.00 per ticket sold. Construction costs are $1,000,000 per screen.
a. Make a table showing the value of marginal product for each screen from the first through the fifth. What property is illustrated by the behavior of marginal products?
b. How many screens will be built if the real interest rate is 5.5 percent?
c. If the real interest rate is 7.5 percent?
d. If the real interest rate is 10 percent?
e. If the real interest rate is 5.5 percent, how far would construction costs have to fall before the builder would be willing to build a five-screen complex?

9. For each of the following scenarios, use supply and demand analysis to predict the resulting changes in the real interest rate, national saving, and investment. Show all your diagrams.
   a. The legislature passes a 10 percent investment tax credit. Under this program, for every $100 that a firm spends on new capital equipment, it receives an extra $10 in tax refunds from the government.
   b. A reduction in military spending moves the government's budget from deficit into surplus.
   c. A new generation of computer-controlled machines becomes available. These machines produce manufactured goods much more quickly and with fewer defects.
   d. The government raises its tax on corporate profits. Other tax changes are also made, such that the government's deficit remains unchanged.
   e. Concerns about job security raise precautionary saving.
   f. New environmental regulations increase firms' costs of operating capital.

■ ANSWERS TO IN-CHAPTER EXERCISES ■

22.1 If Consuelo's student loan were for $6,500 instead of $3,000, her liabilities would be $6,750 (the student loan plus the credit card balance) instead of $3,250. The value of her assets, $6,280, is unchanged. In this case Consuelo's wealth is negative, since assets of $6,280 less liabilities of $6,750 equals −$470. Negative wealth or net worth means one owes more than one owns.

22.2 If water is being drained from the tub, the flow is negative, equal to −3 gallons per minute. There are 37 gallons in the tub at 7:16 P.M. and 34 gallons at 7:17 P.M. The rate of change of the stock is −3 gallons per minute, which is the same as the flow.

22.3 a. Consuelo has set aside her usual $20, but she has also incurred a new liability of $50. So her net saving for the week is *minus* $30. Since her assets (her checking account) have increased by $20 but her liabilities (her credit card balance) have increased by $50, her wealth has also declined by $30.
   b. In paying off her credit card bill, Consuelo reduces her assets by $300 by drawing down her checking account and reduces her liabilities by the same amount by reducing her credit card balance to zero. Thus there is no change in her wealth. There is also no change in her saving (note that Consuelo's income and spending on current needs have not changed).
   c. The increase in the value of Consuelo's car raises her assets by $500. So her wealth also rises by $500. Changes in the value of existing assets are not treated as part of saving, however, so her saving is unchanged.
   d. The decline in the value of Consuelo's furniture is a capital loss of $300. Her assets and wealth fall by $300. Her saving is unchanged.

22.4 The federal government had expenditures greater than receipts, so it ran a deficit. The federal deficit equaled expenditures of 1,634.7 minus revenues of 1,460.3, or $174.4 billion. Equivalently, the federal budget surplus was *minus* $174.4 billion. State and local governments had a surplus, equal to receipts of 997.7 minus expenditures of 886.0, or $111.7 billion. The entire government sector ran a deficit of $62.7 billion, as the federal deficit of 174.4 outweighed the state and local surplus of 111.7. (You can also find this answer by adding federal to state and local expenditures and comparing this number to the sum of federal and state-local receipts.) The government sector's contribution to national saving in 1995 was negative, equal to −$62.7 billion.

22.5 The loss of value of $200 over the year is another financial cost of owning the mower, which Larry should take into account in making his decision. His total cost is now $240 in interest costs plus $200 in anticipated loss of value of the mower (known as depreciation), or $440. This exceeds the value of marginal product, $400, and so now Larry should not buy the mower.

22.6 Household saving is part of national saving. A decline in household saving, and hence national saving, at any given real interest rate shifts the saving supply curve to the left. The results are as in Figure 22.9. The real interest rate rises and the equilibrium values of national saving and investment fall. Lower investment is the same as a lower rate of capital formation, which would be expected to slow economic growth.

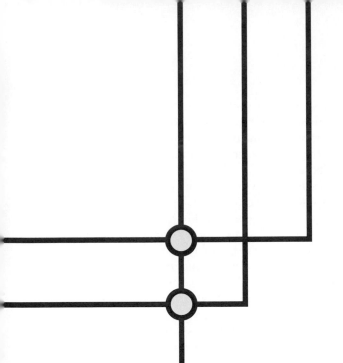

MONEY, PRICES, AND THE FEDERAL RESERVE

■

The Aztec people, who dominated central Mexico until the coming of the Spanish in the sixteenth century, are perhaps best remembered today for their elaborate ceremonies that culminated in human sacrifice. But the Aztec Empire also had a sophisticated economic system, which included active trade not only in a wide variety of agricultural goods—such as corn, tomatoes, and peanuts—but also in manufactured items, including jewelry, sandals, cloaks, baskets, alcohol, and weapons. Slaves and captives—some designated for sacrifice—were also bought and sold. Trade was carried out in local markets, notably in the Aztec capital city, located where Mexico City now stands, and over long distances, as far north as present-day Arizona, for example.[1]

Despite ample supplies of gold, the Aztecs did not use metallic coins to carry out their market transactions, as most European peoples did. Instead, they often used chocolate or, more specifically, cacao "beans" (the seeds of the cacao plant). Prices of goods or services were quoted in cacao beans, in much the same way that today we quote prices in terms of dollars. Cacao beans could also be used to purchase goods, to pay for a service, or to make change—for example, to balance a transaction when a good of greater value was traded for one of lesser value. For larger items, prices were quoted in terms of bags of approximately 24,000 cacao beans, although large purchases might actually be paid for with something easier to carry than bags of cacao beans, such as woven cloaks.

[1]See Jack Weatherford, *The History of Money: From Sandstone to Cyberspace,* New York: Crown Publishers, 1997, for a discussion of the use of money in many economies from the ancients to the present day.

money any asset that can be used in making purchases

Cacao beans were, for the Aztecs, a form of money. In everyday language, people use the word *money* to mean "income" or "wealth," as in "That job pays good money" or "I wish I had as much money as she does." Economists, however, give a much more specific meaning to the term. To the economist, **money** is any asset that can be used in making purchases.

Common examples of money in the modern world are currency and coin. A checking account balance represents another asset that can be used in making payments (as when you write a check to pay for your weekly groceries) and so is also counted as money. In contrast, shares of stock, for example, cannot be used directly in most transactions. Stock must first be sold—that is, converted into cash or a checking account deposit—before further transactions, such as buying your groceries, can be made.

Historically, a wide variety of objects have been used as money, including not only cacao beans but also gold and silver coins, shells, beads, feathers, and, on the Island of Yap, large, immovable boulders. Prior to the use of metallic coins, by far the most common form of money was the cowrie, a type of shell found in the South Pacific. Cowries were used as money in some parts of Africa until very recently, being officially accepted for payment of taxes in Uganda until the beginning of the twentieth century. Today money can be virtually intangible, as in the case of your checking account balance, which exists only in the form of an entry in your bank's computer.

In this chapter we discuss the role of money in modern economies: why it is important, how it is measured, how it is created. Money plays a major role in everyday economic transactions but, as we will see, it is also quite important at the macro level. For example, as we mentioned in Chapter 17, one of the three main types of macroeconomic policy, monetary policy, relates primarily to decisions about how much money should be allowed to circulate in the economy. In the United States, monetary policy is made by the Federal Reserve, the nation's central bank. Because the Federal Reserve, or Fed, determines the nation's money supply, this chapter also introduces the Fed and discusses some of the policy tools at its disposal. Finally, the chapter discusses the important relationship between the amount of money in circulation and the rate of inflation in an economy.

MONEY AND ITS USES

medium of exchange an asset used in purchasing goods and services

barter the direct trade of goods or services for other goods or services

Why do people use money? Money has three principal uses: a *medium of exchange*, a *unit of account*, and a *store of value*.

Money serves as a **medium of exchange** when it is used to purchase goods and services, as when you pay cash for a newspaper or write a check to cover your utilities bill. This is perhaps money's most crucial function. Think about how complicated daily life would become if there were no money. Without money, all economic transactions would have to be in the form of **barter**, which is the direct trade of goods or services for other goods or services.

Barter is highly inefficient because it requires that each party to a trade has something that the other party wants, a so-called double coincidence of wants. For example, under a barter system, a musician could get her dinner only by finding someone willing to trade food for a musical performance. Finding such a match of needs, where each party happens to want exactly what the other person has to offer, would be difficult to do on a regular basis. In a world with money, the musician's problem is considerably simpler. First, she must find someone who is willing to pay money for her musical performance. Then, with the money received, she can purchase the food and other goods and services that she needs. In a society that uses money, it is not necessary that the person who wants to hear music and the person willing to provide food to the musician be one and the same. In other words, there need not be a double coincidence of wants for trades of goods and services to take place.

In a world without money, she could eat only by finding someone willing to trade food for a musical performance.

By eliminating the problem of having to find a double coincidence of wants in order to trade, the use of money in a society permits individuals to specialize in producing particular goods or services, as opposed to having every family or village produce most of what it needs. Specialization greatly increases economic efficiency and material standards of living, as we discussed in Chapter 2 (*the principle of comparative advantage*). This usefulness of money in making transactions explains why savers hold money, even though money generally pays a low rate of return. Cash, for example, pays no interest at all, and the balances in checking accounts usually pay a lower rate of interest than could be obtained in alternative financial investments.

Money's second function is as a *unit of account*. As a **unit of account**, money is the basic yardstick for measuring economic value. In the United States virtually all prices—including the price of labor (wages) and the prices of financial assets, such as shares of General Motors stock—are expressed in dollars. Expressing economic values in a common unit of account allows for easy comparisons. For example, grain can be measured in bushels and coal in tons, but to judge whether 20 bushels of grain is economically more or less valuable than a ton of coal, we express both values in dollar terms. The use of money as a unit of account is closely related to its use as a medium of exchange; because money is used to buy and sell things, it makes sense to express prices of all kinds in money terms.

unit of account a basic measure of economic value

As a **store of value,** its third function, money is a way of holding wealth. For example, the miser who stuffs cash in his mattress or buries gold coins under the old oak tree at midnight is holding wealth in money form. Likewise, if you regularly keep a balance in your checking account, you are holding part of your wealth in the form of money. Although money is usually the primary medium of exchange or unit of account in an economy, it is not the only store of value. There are numerous other ways of holding wealth, such as owning stocks, bonds, or real estate.

store of value an asset that serves as a means of holding wealth

For most people, money is not a particularly good way to hold wealth, apart from its usefulness as a medium of exchange. Unlike government bonds and other types of financial assets, most forms of money pay no interest, and there is always the risk of cash being lost or stolen. However, cash has the advantage of being anonymous and difficult to trace, making it an attractive store of value for smugglers, drug dealers, and others who want their assets to stay out of the view of the Internal Revenue Service.

Private money: Ithaca Hours and LETS

Since money is such a useful tool, why is money usually issued only by governments? Are there examples of privately issued money?

ECONOMIC NATURALIST 23.1

Money is usually issued by the government, not private individuals, but in part this reflects legal restrictions on private money issuance. Where the law allows, private moneys do sometimes emerge.[2] For example, privately issued currencies circulate in more than 30 U.S. communities. In Ithaca, New York, a private currency known as "Ithaca Hours" has circulated since 1991. Instituted by town resident Paul Glover, each Ithaca Hour is equivalent to $10, the average hourly wage of workers in the county. The bills, printed with specially developed inks to prevent counterfeiting, honor local people and the environment. An estimated 1,600 individuals and businesses have earned and spent Hours. Founder Paul Glover argues that the use of Hours, which can't be spent elsewhere, induces people to do more of their shopping in the local economy.

A more high-tech form of private money is associated with computerized trading systems called LETS, for local electronic trading system. These are quite popular in Australia, New Zealand, and Great Britain (the United States has

[2]Barbara A. Good, "Private Money: Everything Old Is New Again," Federal Reserve Bank of Cleveland, *Economic Commentary,* April 1, 1998.

about 10 of them). Participants in a LETS post a list of goods and services they would like to buy or sell. When transactions are made, the appropriate number of "computer credits" is subtracted from the buyer's account and added to the seller's account. People are allowed to have negative balances in their accounts, so participants have to trust other members not to abuse the system by buying many goods and services and then quitting. LETS credits exist in the computer only and are never in the form of paper or metal. In this respect LETS may foreshadow the electronic monetary systems of the future.

What do Ithaca Hours and LETS credits have in common? By functioning as a medium of exchange, each facilitates trade within a community.

MEASURING MONEY

How much money, defined as financial assets usable for making purchases, is there in the U.S. economy at any given time? This question is not simple to answer because in practice it is not easy to draw a clear distinction between those assets that should be counted as money and those that should not. Dollar bills are certainly a form of money, and a van Gogh painting certainly is not. However, brokerage firms now offer accounts that allow their owners to combine financial investments in stocks and bonds with check-writing and credit card privileges. Should the balances in these accounts, or some part of them, be counted as money? It is difficult to tell.

Economists skirt the problem of deciding what is and isn't money by using several alternative definitions of money, which vary in how broadly the concept of money is defined. A relatively "narrow" definition of the amount of money in the U.S. economy is called M1. **M1** is the sum of currency outstanding and balances held in checking accounts. A broader measure of money, called **M2**, includes all the assets in M1 plus some additional assets that are usable in making payments, but at greater cost or inconvenience than currency or checks. Table 23.1 lists the components of M1 and M2 and also gives the amount of

M1 sum of currency outstanding and balances held in checking accounts

M2 All the assets in M1 plus some additional assets that are usable in making payments but at greater cost or inconvenience than currency or checks

TABLE 23.1
Components of M1 and M2, July 2002

M1		1,197.8
Currency	615.1	
Demand deposits	303.8	
Other checkable deposits	270.3	
Travelers' checks	8.6	
M2		5,641.2
M1	1,197.8	
Savings deposits	2,552.8	
Small-denomination time deposits	920.8	
Money market mutual funds	969.8	

NOTES: Billions of dollars, adjusted for seasonal variations. In M1, currency refers to cash and coin. Demand deposits are non-interest-bearing checking accounts, and "other checkable deposits" includes checking accounts that bear interest. M2 includes all the components of M1, balances in savings accounts, "small-denomination" (under $100,000) deposits held at banks for a fixed term, and money market mutual funds (MMMFs). MMMFs are organizations that sell shares, use the proceeds to buy safe assets (like government bonds), and often allow their shareholders some check-writing privileges.

SOURCE: Federal Reserve Bank of St. Louis, FRED database, www.stls.frb.org/research/aggreg.html, or Federal Reserve release H.6.

each type of asset outstanding as of July 2002. For most purposes, however, it is sufficient to think of money as the sum of currency outstanding and balances in checking accounts, or M1.

> **RECAP**   **MONEY AND ITS USES**
>
> *Money* is any asset that can be used in making purchases, such as currency or a checking account. Money serves as a *medium of exchange* when it is used to purchase goods and services. The use of money as a medium of exchange eliminates the need for *barter* and the difficulties of finding a "double coincidence of wants." Money also serves as a *unit of account* and a *store of value.*
>
> In practice, two basic measures of money are M1 and M2. M1, a more narrow measure, is made up primarily of currency and balances held in checking accounts. The broader measure, M2, includes all the assets in M1 plus some additional assets usable in making payments.

COMMERCIAL BANKS AND THE CREATION OF MONEY

What determines the amount of money in the economy? If the economy's supply of money consisted entirely of currency, the answer would be simple: The supply of money would just be equal to the value of the currency created and circulated by the government. However, as we have seen, in modern economies the money supply consists not only of currency but also of deposit balances held by the public in commercial, that is, private, banks. The determination of the money supply in a modern economy thus depends in part on the behavior of commercial banks and their depositors.

To see how the existence of commercial banks affects the money supply, we will use the example of a fictional country, the Republic of Gorgonzola. Initially, we assume, Gorgonzola has no commercial banking system. To make trading easier and eliminate the need for barter, the government directs the central bank of Gorgonzola to put into circulation a million identical paper notes, called guilders. The central bank prints the guilders and distributes them to the populace. At this point the Gorgonzolan money supply is a million guilders.

However, the citizens of Gorgonzola are unhappy with a money supply made up entirely of paper guilders, since the notes may be lost or stolen. In response to the demand for safekeeping of money, some Gorgonzolan entrepreneurs set up a system of commercial banks. At first, these banks are only storage vaults where people can deposit their guilders. When people need to make a payment they can either physically withdraw their guilders or, more conveniently, write a check on their account. Checks give the banks permission to transfer guilders from the account of the person paying by check to the account of the person to whom the check is made out. With a system of payments based on checks the paper guilders need never leave the banking system, although they flow from one bank to another as a depositor of one bank makes a payment to a depositor in another bank. Deposits do not pay interest in this economy; indeed, the banks can make a profit only by charging depositors fees in exchange for safeguarding their cash.

Let's suppose for now that people prefer bank deposits to cash and so deposit all of their guilders with the commercial banks. With all guilders in the vaults of banks, the balance sheet of all of Gorgonzola's commercial banks taken together is as shown in Table 23.2.

The *assets* of the commercial banking system in Gorgonzola are the paper guilders sitting in the vaults of all the individual banks. The banking system's *liabilities* are the deposits of the banks' customers, since checking account balances represent money owed by the banks to the depositors.

TABLE 23.2
Consolidated Balance Sheet of Gorgonzolan Commercial Banks (Initial)

Assets		Liabilities	
Currency	1,000,000 guilders	Deposits	1,000,000 guilders

bank reserves cash or similar assets held by commercial banks for the purpose of meeting depositor withdrawals and payments

100 percent reserve banking a situation in which banks' reserves equal 100 percent of their deposits

Cash or similar assets held by banks are called **bank reserves.** In this example, bank reserves, for all the banks taken together, equal 1,000,000 guilders—the currency listed on the asset side of the consolidated balance sheet. Banks hold reserves to meet depositors' demands for cash withdrawals or to pay checks drawn on their depositors' accounts. In this example, the bank reserves of 1,000,000 guilders equal 100 percent of banks' deposits, which are also 1,000,000 guilders. A situation in which bank reserves equal 100 percent of bank deposits is called **100 percent reserve banking.**

Bank reserves are held by banks in their vaults, rather than circulated among the public, and thus are *not* counted as part of the money supply. However, bank deposit balances, which can be used in making transactions, *are* counted as money. So, after the introduction of "safekeeper" banks in Gorgonzola, the money supply, equal to the value of bank deposits, is 1,000,000 guilders, which is the same as it was prior to the introduction of banks.

After a while, to continue the story, the commercial bankers of Gorgonzola begin to realize that keeping 100 percent reserves against deposits is not necessary. True, a few guilders flow in and out of the typical bank as depositors receive payments or write checks, but for the most part the stacks of paper guilders just sit there in the vaults, untouched and unused. It occurs to the bankers that they can meet the random inflow and outflow of guilders to their banks with reserves that are less than 100 percent of their deposits. After some observation, the bankers conclude that keeping reserves equal to only 10 percent of deposits is enough to meet the random ebb and flow of withdrawals and payments from their individual banks. The remaining 90 percent of deposits, the bankers realize, can be lent out to borrowers to earn interest.

So the bankers decide to keep reserves equal to 100,000 guilders, or 10 percent of their deposits. The other 900,000 guilders they lend out at interest to Gorgonzolan cheese producers who want to use the money to make improvements to their farms. After the loans are made, the balance sheet of all of Gorgonzola's commercial banks taken together has changed, as shown in Table 23.3.

TABLE 23.3
Consolidated Balance Sheet of Gorgonzolan Commercial Banks after One Round of Loans

Assets		Liabilities	
Currency (= reserves)	100,000 guilders	Deposits	1,000,000 guilders
Loans to farmers	900,000 guilders		

reserve-deposit ratio bank reserves divided by deposits

fractional-reserve banking system a banking system in which bank reserves are less than deposits so that the reserve-deposit ratio is less than 100 percent

After the loans are made, the banks' reserves of 100,000 guilders no longer equal 100 percent of the banks' deposits of 1,000,000 guilders. Instead, the **reserve-deposit ratio,** which is bank reserves divided by deposits, is now equal to 100,000/1,000,000, or 10 percent. A banking system in which banks hold fewer reserves than deposits so that the reserve-deposit ratio is less than 100 percent is called a **fractional-reserve banking system.**

Notice that 900,000 guilders have flowed out of the banking system (as loans to farmers) and are now in the hands of the public. But we have assumed that private citizens prefer bank deposits to cash for making transactions. So ultimately people will redeposit the 900,000 guilders in the banking system. After these deposits are made, the consolidated balance sheet of the commercial banks is as in Table 23.4.

TABLE 23.4

Consolidated Balance Sheet of Gorgonzolan Commercial Banks after Guilders Are Redeposited

Assets		Liabilities	
Currency (= reserves)	1,000,000 guilders	Deposits	1,900,000 guilders
Loans to farmers	900,000 guilders		

Notice that bank deposits, and hence the economy's money supply, now equal 1,900,000 guilders. In effect, the existence of the commercial banking system has permitted the creation of new money. These deposits, which are liabilities of the banks, are balanced by assets of 1,000,000 guilders in reserves and 900,000 guilders in loans owed to the banks.

The story does not end here. On examining their balance sheets, the bankers are surprised to see that they once again have "too many" reserves. With deposits of 1,900,000 guilders and a 10 percent reserve-deposit ratio, they need only 190,000 guilders in reserves. But they have 1,000,000 guilders in reserves—810,000 too many. Since lending out their excess guilders is always more profitable than leaving them in the vault, the bankers proceed to make another 810,000 guilders in loans. Eventually these loaned-out guilders are redeposited in the banking system, after which the consolidated balance sheet of the banks is as shown in Table 23.5.

TABLE 23.5

Consolidated Balance Sheet of Gorgonzolan Commercial Banks after Two Rounds of Loans and Redeposits

Assets		Liabilities	
Currency (= reserves)	1,000,000 guilders	Deposits	2,710,000 guilders
Loans to farmers	1,710,000 guilders		

Now the money supply has increased to 2,710,000 guilders, equal to the value of bank deposits. Despite the expansion of loans and deposits, however, the bankers find that their reserves of 1,000,000 guilders *still* exceed the desired level of 10 percent of deposits, which are 2,710,000 guilders. And so yet another round of lending will take place.

EXERCISE 23.1

Determine what the balance sheet of the banking system of Gorgonzola will look like after a third round of lending to farmers and redeposits of guilders into the commercial banking system. What is the money supply at that point?

The process of expansion of loans and deposits will only end when reserves equal 10 percent of bank deposits, because as long as reserves exceed 10 percent of deposits the banks will find it profitable to lend out the extra reserves. Since reserves at the end of every round equal 1,000,000 guilders, for the reserve-deposit ratio to equal 10 percent, total deposits must equal 10,000,000 guilders. Further, since the balance sheet must balance, with assets equal to liabilities, we know as well that at the end of the process loans to cheese producers must equal 9,000,000 guilders. If loans equal 9,000,000 guilders, then bank assets, the sum of loans and reserves (1,000,000 guilders), will equal 10,000,000 guilders, which is the same as bank liabilities (bank deposits). The final consolidated balance sheet is as shown in Table 23.6.

TABLE 23.6
Final Consolidated Balance Sheet of Gorgonzolan Commercial Banks

Assets		Liabilities	
Currency (= reserves)	1,000,000 guilders	Deposits	10,000,000 guilders
Loans to farmers	9,000,000 guilders		

The money supply, which is equal to total deposits, is 10,000,000 guilders at the end of the process. We see that the existence of a fractional-reserve banking system has multiplied the money supply by a factor of 10, relative to the economy with no banks or the economy with 100 percent reserve banking. Put another way, with a 10 percent reserve-deposit ratio, each guilder deposited in the banking system can "support" 10 guilders worth of deposits.

To find the money supply in this example more directly, we observe that deposits will expand through additional rounds of lending as long as the ratio of bank reserves to bank deposits exceeds the reserve-deposit ratio desired by banks. When the actual ratio of bank reserves to deposits equals the desired reserve-deposit ratio, the expansion stops. So ultimately, deposits in the banking system satisfy the following relationship:

$$\frac{\text{Bank reserves}}{\text{Bank deposits}} = \text{Desired reserve-deposit ratio.}$$

This equation can be rewritten to solve for bank deposits:

$$\text{Bank deposits} = \frac{\text{Bank reserves}}{\text{Desired reserve-deposit ratio}}. \tag{23.1}$$

In Gorgonzola, since all the currency in the economy flows into the banking system, bank reserves equal 1,000,000 guilders. The reserve-deposit ratio desired by banks is 0.10. Therefore, using Equation 23.1, we find that bank deposits equal (1,000,000 guilders)/0.10, or 10 million guilders, the same answer we found in the consolidated balance sheet of the banks, Table 23.6.

EXERCISE 23.2

Find deposits and the money supply in Gorgonzola if the banks' desired reserve-deposit ratio is 5 percent rather than 10 percent. What if the total amount of currency circulated by the central bank is 2,000,000 guilders and the desired reserve-deposit ratio remains at 10 percent?

THE MONEY SUPPLY WITH BOTH CURRENCY AND DEPOSITS

In the example of Gorgonzola we assumed that all money is held in the form of deposits in banks. In reality, of course, people keep only part of their money holdings in the form of bank accounts and hold the rest in the form of currency. Fortunately, allowing for the fact that people hold both currency and bank deposits does not greatly complicate the determination of the money supply, as Example 23.1 shows.

The money supply with both currency and deposits

EXAMPLE 23.1

Suppose that the citizens of Gorgonzola choose to hold a total of 500,000 guilders in the form of currency and to deposit the rest of their money in banks. Banks keep reserves equal to 10 percent of deposits. What is the money supply in Gorgonzola?

The money supply is the sum of currency in the hands of the public and bank deposits. Currency in hands of the public is given as 500,000 guilders. What is the quantity of bank deposits? Since 500,000 of the 1,000,000 guilders issued by the central bank are being used by the public in the form of currency, only the remaining 500,000 guilders is available to serve as bank reserves. We know that deposits equals bank reserves divided by the reserve-deposit ratio, so deposits are 500,000 guilders/0.10 = 5,000,000 guilders. The total money supply is the sum of currency in the hands of the public (500,000 guilders) and bank deposits (5,000,000 guilders), or 5,500,000 guilders.

We can write a general relationship that captures the reasoning of Example 23.1. First, let's write out the fact that the money supply equals currency plus bank deposits:

$$\text{Money supply} = \text{Currency held by the public} + \text{Bank deposits.}$$

We also know that bank deposits equal bank reserves divided by the reserve-deposit ratio that is desired by commercial banks (Equation 23.1). Using that relationship to substitute for bank deposits in the expression for the money supply, we get

$$\text{Money supply} = \text{Currency held by public} + \frac{\text{Bank reserves}}{\text{Desired reserve-deposit ratio}}. \quad (23.2)$$

We can use Equation 23.2 to confirm our answer to Example 23.1. In that example, currency held by the public is 500,000 guilders, bank reserves are 500,000 guilders, and the desired reserve-deposit ratio is 0.10. Plugging these values into Equation 23.2, we get that the money supply equals 500,000 + 500,000/0.10 = 5,500,000, the same answer we found before.

The money supply at Christmas

EXAMPLE 23.2

During the Christmas season people choose to hold unusually large amounts of currency for shopping. With no action by the central bank, how would this change in currency holding affect the national money supply?

To illustrate with a numerical example, suppose that initially bank reserves are 500, the amount of currency held by the public is 500, and the desired reserve-deposit ratio in the banking system is 0.2. Inserting these values into Equation 23.2, we find that the money supply equals 500 + 500/0.2 = 3,000.

Now suppose that because of Christmas shopping needs, the public increases its currency holdings to 600 by withdrawing 100 from commercial banks. These withdrawals reduce bank reserves to 400. Using Equation 23.2 we find now that the money supply is 600 + 400/0.2 = 2,600. So the public's increased holdings of currency have caused the money supply to drop, from 3,000 to 2,600. The reason for the drop is that with a reserve-deposit ratio of 20 percent, every dollar in the vaults of banks can "support" $5 of deposits and hence $5 of money supply. However, the same dollar in the hands of the public becomes $1 of currency, contributing only $1 to the total money supply. So when the public withdraws cash from the banks, the overall money supply declines. (We will see in the next section, however, that in practice the central bank has means to offset the impact of the public's actions on the money supply.)

RECAP   COMMERCIAL BANKS AND THE CREATION OF MONEY

Part of the money supply consists of deposits in private commercial banks. Hence the behavior of commercial banks and their depositors help to determine the money supply.

Cash or similar assets held by banks are called *bank reserves*. In modern economies, banks' reserves are less than their deposits, a situation called *fractional-reserve banking*. The ratio of bank reserves to deposits is called the *reserve-deposit ratio;* in a fractional-reserve banking system, this ratio is less than 1.

The portion of deposits not held as reserves can be lent out by the banks to earn interest. Banks will continue to make loans and accept deposits as long as the reserve-deposit ratio exceeds its desired level. This process stops only when the actual and desired reserve-deposit ratios are equal. At that point, total bank deposits equal bank reserves divided by the desired reserve-deposit ratio, and the money supply equals the currency held by the public plus bank deposits (see Equation 23.2).

THE FEDERAL RESERVE SYSTEM

Federal Reserve System (or Fed) the central bank of the United States

For participants in financial markets and the average citizen as well, one of the most important branches of the government is the **Federal Reserve System,** often called the **Fed.** The Fed is the *central bank* of the United States. Like central banks in other countries, the Fed has two main responsibilities.

First, it is responsible for monetary policy, which means that the Fed determines how much money circulates in the economy. As we will see in later chapters, changes in the supply of money can affect many important macroeconomic variables, including interest rates, inflation, unemployment, and exchange rates. Because of its ability to affect key variables, particularly financial variables such as interest rates, financial market participants pay close attention to Fed actions and announcements. As a necessary first step in understanding how Fed policies have the effects that they do, in this chapter we will focus on the basic question of how the Fed affects the supply of money, leaving for later the explanation of why changes in the money supply affect the economy.

Second, along with other government agencies, the Federal Reserve bears important responsibility for the oversight and regulation of financial markets. The Fed also plays a major role during periods of crisis in financial markets. To lay the groundwork for discussing how the Fed carries out its responsibilities, we first briefly review the history and structure of the Federal Reserve System.

THE HISTORY AND STRUCTURE OF THE FEDERAL RESERVE SYSTEM

The Federal Reserve System was created by the Federal Reserve Act, passed by Congress in 1913, and began operations in 1914. Like all central banks, the Fed is a government agency. Unlike commercial banks, which are private businesses whose principal objective is making a profit, central banks like the Fed focus on promoting public goals such as economic growth, low inflation, and the smooth operation of financial markets.

"I'm sorry, sir, but I don't believe you know us well enough to call us the Fed."

The Federal Reserve Act established a system of 12 regional Federal Reserve banks, each associated with a geographical area called a Federal Reserve district. Congress hoped that the establishment of Federal Reserve banks around the country would ensure that different regions were represented in the national policy-making process. In fact, the regional Feds regularly assess economic conditions in their districts and report this information to policymakers in Washington. Regional Federal Reserve banks also provide various services, such as check-clearing services, to the commercial banks in their district.

At the national level, the leadership of the Federal Reserve System is provided by its **Board of Governors.** The Board of Governors, together with a large professional staff, is located in Washington, D.C. The Board consists of seven governors, who are appointed by the president of the United States to 14-year terms. The terms are staggered so that one governor comes up for reappointment every other year. The president also appoints one of these Board members to serve as chairman of the Board of Governors for a term of four years. The Fed chairman, along with the secretary of the Treasury, is probably one of the two most powerful economic policymakers in the United States government, after the president. Recent chairmen, such as Paul Volcker and Alan Greenspan, have been highly regarded and influential.

Decisions about monetary policy are made by a 12-member committee called the **Federal Open Market Committee** (or **FOMC**). The FOMC consists of the seven Fed governors, the president of the Federal Reserve Bank of New York, and four of the presidents of the other regional Federal Reserve banks, who serve on a rotating basis. The FOMC meets approximately eight times a year to review the state of the economy and to determine monetary policy.

Board of Governors the leadership of the Fed, consisting of seven governors appointed by the president to staggered 14-year terms

Federal Open Market Committee (or FOMC) the committee that makes decisions concerning monetary policy

CONTROLLING THE MONEY SUPPLY: OPEN-MARKET OPERATIONS

The Fed's primary responsibility is making monetary policy, which involves decisions about the appropriate size of the nation's money supply. As we saw in the previous section, central banks in general, and the Fed in particular, do not control the money supply directly. However, they can control the money supply indirectly by changing the supply of reserves held by commercial banks.

The Fed has several ways of affecting the supply of bank reserves. By far the most important of these are *open-market operations*. Suppose that the Fed wants to increase bank reserves, with the ultimate goal of increasing bank deposits and the money supply. To accomplish this the Fed buys financial assets, usually government bonds, from the public. To simplify the actual procedure a bit, think of the Fed as paying for the bonds it acquires with newly printed money. Assuming that the public is already holding all the currency that it wants, they will deposit the cash they receive as payment for their bonds in commercial banks. Thus, the reserves of the commercial banking system will increase by an amount equal to the value of the bonds purchased by the Fed. The increase in bank reserves will lead in turn, through the process of lending and redeposit of funds described in the previous section, to an expansion of bank deposits and the money supply, as summarized by Equation 23.2. The Fed's purchase of government bonds from the public, with the result that bank reserves and the money supply are increased, is called an **open-market purchase.**

open-market purchase the purchase of government bonds from the public by the Fed for the purpose of increasing the supply of bank reserves and the money supply

To reduce bank reserves and hence the money supply, the Fed reverses the procedure. It sells some of the government bonds that it holds (acquired in previous open-market purchases) to the public. Assume that the public pays for the bonds by writing checks on their accounts in commercial banks. Then, when the Fed presents the checks to the commercial banks for payment, reserves equal in value to the government bonds sold by the Fed are transferred from the commercial banks to the Fed. The Fed retires these reserves from circulation, lowering the supply of bank reserves and, hence, the overall money supply. The sale of government bonds by the Fed to the public for the purpose of reducing bank reserves and hence the money supply is called an **open-market sale.** Open-market purchases and sales together are called **open-market operations.** Open-market operations are the most convenient and flexible tool that the Federal Reserve has for affecting the money supply and are employed on a regular basis.

open-market sale the sale by the Fed of government bonds to the public for the purpose of reducing bank reserves and the money supply

open-market operations open-market purchases and open-market sales

EXAMPLE 23.3   ### Increasing the money supply by open-market operations

In a particular economy, currency held by the public is 1,000 shekels, bank reserves are 200 shekels, and the desired reserve-deposit ratio is 0.2. What is the money supply? How is the money supply affected if the central bank prints 100 shekels and uses this new currency to buy government bonds from the public? Assume that the public does not wish to change the amount of currency it holds.

As bank reserves are 200 shekels and the reserve-deposit ratio is 0.2, bank deposits must equal 200 shekels/0.2, or 1,000 shekels. The money supply, equal to the sum of currency held by the public and bank deposits, is therefore 2,000 shekels, a result you can confirm using Equation 23.2.

The open-market purchase puts 100 more shekels into the hands of the public. We assume that the public continues to want to hold 1,000 shekels in currency, so they will deposit the additional 100 shekels in the commercial banking system, raising bank reserves from 200 to 300 shekels. As the desired reserve-deposit ratio is 0.2, multiple rounds of lending and redeposit will eventually raise the level of bank deposits to 300 shekels/0.2, or 1,500 shekels. The money supply, equal to 1,000 shekels held by the public plus bank deposits of 1,500 shekels, equals 2,500 shekels. So the open-market purchase of 100 shekels, by raising bank reserves by 100 shekels, has increased the money supply by 500 shekels. Again, you can confirm this result using Equation 23.2.

EXERCISE 23.3

Continuing Example 23.3, suppose that instead of an open-market purchase of 100 shekels the central bank conducts an open-market sale of 50 shekels' worth of government bonds. What happens to bank reserves, bank deposits, and the money supply?

CONTROLLING THE MONEY SUPPLY: DISCOUNT WINDOW LENDING

A second means by which the Fed can affect bank reserves and thus the money supply is by what is called *discount window lending*. When individual commercial banks are short of reserves, they may choose to borrow reserves from the Fed. For historical reasons, lending of reserves by the Federal Reserve to commercial banks is called **discount window lending**. The interest rate that the Fed charges commercial banks that borrow reserves is called the **discount rate**. Loans of reserves by the Fed directly increase the quantity of reserves in the banking system, leading ultimately to increases in bank deposits and the money supply.

discount window lending the lending of reserves by the Federal Reserve to commercial banks

discount rate the interest rate that the Fed charges commercial banks to borrow reserves

CONTROLLING THE MONEY SUPPLY: CHANGING RESERVE REQUIREMENTS

As Equation 23.2 shows, the economy's money supply depends on three factors: the amount of currency the public chooses to hold, the supply of bank reserves, and the reserve-deposit ratio maintained by commercial banks. For given quantities of currency held by the public and of reserves held by the banks, an increase in the reserve-deposit ratio reduces the money supply, as you can see from Equation 23.2. A higher reserve-deposit ratio implies that banks lend out a smaller share of their deposits in each of the rounds of lending and redeposit described earlier, limiting the overall expansion of loans and deposits.

Within a certain range, commercial banks are free to set the reserve-deposit ratio they want to maintain. However, Congress granted the Fed the power to set minimum values of the reserve-deposit ratio for commercial banks. The legally required values of the reserve-deposit ratio set by the Fed are called **reserve requirements.**

Changes in reserve requirements can be used to affect the money supply, although the Fed does not usually use them in this way. For example, suppose that commercial banks are maintaining a 3 percent reserve-deposit ratio, and the Fed wants to contract the money supply. By raising required reserves to, say, 5 percent of deposits, the Fed could force commercial banks to raise their reserve-deposit ratio, at least until it reached 5 percent. As you can see from Equation 23.2, an increase in the reserve-deposit ratio lowers deposits and the money supply. Similarly, a reduction in required reserves by the Fed might allow at least some banks to lower their ratio of reserves to deposits. A decline in the economywide reserve-deposit ratio would in turn cause the money supply to rise.

reserve requirements set by the Fed, the minimum values of the ratio of bank reserves to bank deposits that commercial banks are allowed to maintain

THE FED'S ROLE IN STABILIZING FINANCIAL MARKETS: BANKING PANICS

Besides controlling the money supply, the Fed also has the responsibility (together with other government agencies) of ensuring that financial markets operate smoothly. Indeed, the creation of the Fed in 1913 was prompted by a series of financial market crises that disrupted both the markets themselves and the U.S. economy as a whole. The hope of the Congress was that the Fed would be able to eliminate or at least control such crises.

banking panic an episode in which depositors, spurred by news or rumors of the imminent bankruptcy of one or more banks, rush to withdraw their deposits from the banking system

Historically, in the United States, *banking panics* were perhaps the most disruptive type of recurrent financial crisis. In a **banking panic,** news or rumors of the imminent bankruptcy of one or more banks leads bank depositors to rush to withdraw their funds. Next, we will discuss banking panics and the Fed's attempts to control them.

Why do banking panics occur? An important factor that helps make banking panics possible is the existence of fractional-reserve banking. In a fractional-reserve banking system, like that of the United States and all other industrialized countries, bank reserves are less than deposits, which means that banks do not keep enough cash on hand to pay off their depositors if they were all to decide to withdraw their deposits. Normally this is not a problem, as only a small percentage of depositors attempt to withdraw their funds on any given day. But if a rumor circulates that one or more banks are in financial trouble and may go bankrupt, depositors may panic, lining up to demand their money. Since bank reserves are less than deposits, a sufficiently severe panic could lead even financially healthy banks to run out of cash, forcing them into bankruptcy and closure.

The Federal Reserve was established in response to a particularly severe banking panic that occurred in 1907. The Fed was equipped with two principal tools to try to prevent or moderate banking panics. First, the Fed was given the power to supervise and regulate banks. It was hoped that the public would have greater confidence in banks, and thus be less prone to panic, if people knew that the Fed was keeping a close watch on bankers' activities. Second, the Fed was allowed to make loans to banks through the discount window, discussed earlier. The idea was that, during a panic, banks could borrow cash from the Fed with which to pay off depositors, avoiding the need to close.

No banking panics occurred between 1914, when the Fed was established, and 1930. However, between 1930 and 1933 the United States experienced the worst and most protracted series of banking panics in its history. Economic historians agree that much of the blame for this panic should be placed on the Fed, which neither appreciated the severity of the problem nor acted aggressively enough to contain it.

ECONOMIC NATURALIST 23.2

The banking panics of 1930–1933 and the money supply

The worst banking panics ever experienced in the United States occurred during the early stages of the Great Depression, between 1930 and 1933. During this period approximately one-third of the banks in the United States were forced to close. This near-collapse of the banking system was probably an important reason that the Depression was so severe. With many fewer banks in operation it was very difficult for small businesses and consumers during the early 1930s to obtain credit. Another important effect of the banking panics was to greatly reduce the nation's money supply. Why should banking panics reduce the national money supply?

During a banking panic people are afraid to keep deposits in a bank because of the risk that the bank will go bankrupt and their money will be lost (this was prior to the introduction of federal deposit insurance, discussed below). During the 1930–1933 period, many bank depositors withdrew their money from banks, holding currency instead. These withdrawals reduced bank reserves. Each extra dollar of currency held by the public adds $1 to the money supply; but each extra dollar of bank reserves translates into several dollars of money supply, because in a fractional-reserve banking system each dollar of reserves can "support" several dollars in bank deposits. Thus the public's withdrawals from banks, which increased currency holdings by the public but reduced bank reserves by an equal amount, led to a net decrease in the total money supply (currency plus deposits).

In addition, fearing banking panics and the associated withdrawals by depositors, banks increased their reserve-deposit ratios, which reduced the quantity of deposits that could be supported by any given level of bank reserves. This change in reserve-deposit ratios also tended to reduce the money supply.

Data on currency holdings by the public, the reserve-deposit ratio, bank reserves, and the money supply for selected dates are shown in Table 23.7. Notice the increase over the period in the amount of currency held by the public and in the reserve-deposit ratio, as well as the decline in bank reserves after 1930. The last column shows that the U.S. money supply dropped by about one-third between December 1929 and December 1933.

TABLE 23.7
Key U.S. Monetary Statistics, 1929–1933

	Currency held by public	Reserve-deposit ratio	Bank reserves	Money supply
December 1929	3.85	0.075	3.15	45.9
December 1930	3.79	0.082	3.31	44.1
December 1931	4.59	0.095	3.11	37.3
December 1932	4.82	0.109	3.18	34.0
December 1933	4.85	0.133	3.45	30.8

NOTE: Data on currency, the monetary base, and the money supply are in billions of dollars.

SOURCE: Milton Friedman and Anna J. Schwartz, *A Monetary History of the United States, 1863–1960*, Princeton, N.J.: Princeton University Press, 1963, Table A-1.

Using Equation 23.2, we can see that increases in currency holdings by the public and increases in the reserve-deposit ratio both tend to reduce the money supply. These effects were so powerful in 1930–1933 that the nation's money supply, shown in the fourth column of Table 23.7, dropped precipitously, even though currency holdings and bank reserves, taken separately, actually rose during the period.

EXERCISE 23.4

Using the data from Table 23.7, confirm that the relationship between the money supply and its determinants is consistent with Equation 23.2. Would the money supply have fallen in 1931–1933 if the public had stopped withdrawing deposits after December 1930 so that currency held by the public had remained at its December 1930 level?

EXERCISE 23.5

According to Table 23.7, the U.S. money supply fell from $44.1 billion to $37.3 billion over the course of 1931. The Fed did use open-market purchases during 1931 to replenish bank reserves in the face of depositor withdrawals. Find (a) the quantity of reserves that the Fed injected into the economy in 1931, and (b) the quantity of reserves the Fed would have had to add to the economy to keep the money supply unchanged from 1930, assuming that public currency holdings and reserve-deposit ratios for each year remained as reported in the table. Why has the Fed been criticized for being too timid in 1931?

When the Fed failed to stop the banking panics of the 1930s, policymakers decided to look at other strategies for controlling panics. In 1934 Congress instituted a system of deposit insurance. Under a system of **deposit insurance**, the government guarantees depositors—specifically, under current rules, those with deposits of less than $100,000—that they will get their money back even if the bank goes bankrupt. Deposit insurance eliminates the incentive for people to withdraw their deposits when rumors circulate that the bank is in financial trouble,

deposit insurance a system under which the government guarantees that depositors will not lose any money even if their bank goes bankrupt which nips panics in the bud. Indeed, since deposit insurance was instituted, the United States has had no significant banking panics.

Unfortunately, deposit insurance is not a perfect solution to the problem of banking panics. An important drawback is that when deposit insurance is in force, depositors know they are protected no matter what happens to their bank, and they become completely unconcerned about whether their bank is making prudent loans. This situation can lead to reckless behavior by banks or other insured intermediaries. For example, during the 1980s many savings and loan associations in the United States went bankrupt, in part because of reckless lending and financial investments. Like banks, savings and loans have deposit insurance, so the U.S. government had to pay savings and loans depositors the full value of their deposits. This action ultimately cost U.S. taxpayers hundreds of billions of dollars.

MONEY AND PRICES

From a macroeconomic perspective, a major reason that control of the supply of money is important is that, *in the long run, the amount of money circulating in an economy and the general level of prices are closely linked.* Indeed, it is virtually unheard of for a country to experience high, sustained inflation without a comparably rapid growth in the amount of money held by its citizens. The economist Milton Friedman summarized the inflation–money relationship by saying, "Inflation is always and everywhere a monetary phenomenon." We will see in Part 8 that, over short periods, inflation can arise from sources other than an increase in the supply of money. But over a longer period, and particularly for more severe inflations, Friedman's dictum is certainly correct: The rate of inflation and the rate of growth of the money supply are closely related.

The existence of a close link between money supply and prices should make intuitive sense. Imagine a situation in which the available supply of goods and services is approximately fixed. Then the more cash (say, dollars) that people hold, the more they will be able to bid up the prices of the fixed supply of goods and services. Thus a large money supply relative to the supply of goods and services (too much money chasing too few goods) tends to result in high prices. Likewise, a rapidly *growing* supply of money will lead to quickly *rising* prices—that is, inflation.

VELOCITY

velocity a measure of the speed at which money circulates, or, equivalently, the value of transactions completed in a period of time divided by the stock of money required to make those transactions; numerically, $V = (P \times Y)/M$, where V is velocity, $P \times Y$ is nominal GDP, and M is the money supply whose velocity is being measured

To explore the relationship of money growth and inflation in a bit more detail, it is useful to introduce the concept of *velocity*. In economics, **velocity** is a measure of the speed at which money circulates. For example, a given dollar bill might pass from your hand to the grocer's when you buy a quart of milk. The same dollar may then pass from the grocer to his supplier, from the supplier to the dairy farmer who produced the milk, from the farmer to the feed supply store owner, and so on. The more quickly money circulates from one person to the next, the higher its velocity. More formally, velocity is defined as the value of transactions completed in a period of time divided by the stock of money required to make those transactions. The higher this ratio, the faster the "typical" dollar is circulating.

As a practical matter, we usually do not have precise measures of the total value of transactions taking place in an economy; so, as an approximation, economists often measure the total value of transactions in a given period by nominal GDP for that period. A numerical value of velocity can then be obtained from the following formula:

$$\text{Velocity} = \frac{\text{Value of transactions}}{\text{Money stock}}$$

$$= \frac{\text{Nominal GDP}}{\text{Money stock}}.$$

Let V stand for velocity and let M stand for the particular money stock being considered (for example, M1 or M2). Nominal GDP (a measure of the total value of transactions) equals the price level P times real GDP Y. Using this notation, we can write the definition of velocity as

$$V = \frac{P \times Y}{M} \tag{23.3}$$

The velocity of money in the U.S. economy

EXAMPLE 23.4

In the United States in 2001, M1 was \$1,177.9 billion, M2 was \$5,449.1 billion, and nominal GDP was \$10,082.2 billion. Find the velocity of M1 and of M2 for that year.

Using Equation 23.3, velocity for M1 is given by

$$V = \frac{\$10,082.2 \text{ billion}}{\$1,177.9 \text{ billion}} = 8.56.$$

Similarly, velocity for M2 was

$$V = \frac{\$10,082.2 \text{ billion}}{\$5,449.1 \text{ billion}} = 1.85.$$

You can see that the velocity of M1 is higher than that of M2. This makes sense: Because the components of M1, such as cash and checking accounts, are used more frequently for transactions, each dollar of M1 "turns over" more often than the average dollar of M2.

A variety of factors determine velocity. A leading example is advances in payment technologies, such as the introduction of credit cards and debit cards or the creation of networks of automatic teller machines (ATMs). These new technologies and payment methods have allowed people to carry out their daily business while holding less cash, and thus have tended to increase velocity over time.

MONEY AND INFLATION IN THE LONG RUN

We can use the definition of velocity to see how money and prices are related in the long run. First, rewrite the definition of velocity, Equation 23.3, by multiplying both sides of the equation by the money stock M. This yields

$$M \times V = P \times Y. \tag{23.4}$$

Equation 23.4, a famous relationship in economics, is called for historical reasons the *quantity equation*. The **quantity equation** states that money times velocity equals nominal GDP. Because the quantity equation is simply a rewriting of the definition of velocity, Equation 23.3, it always holds exactly.

The quantity equation is historically important because late nineteenth and early twentieth-century monetary economists, such as Yale's Irving Fisher, used this relationship to theorize about the relationship between money and prices. We can do the same thing here. To keep things simple, imagine that velocity V is determined by current payments technologies and thus is approximately constant over the period we are considering. Likewise, suppose that real output Y is approximately constant. If we use a bar over a variable to indicate that the variable is constant, we can rewrite the quantity equation as

quantity equation money times velocity equals nominal GDP; $M \times V = P \times Y$

$$M \times \overline{V} = P \times \overline{Y}, \tag{23.5}$$

where we are treating $\overline{V}$ and $\overline{Y}$ as fixed numbers.

Now look at Equation 23.5 and imagine that for some reason the Federal Reserve increases the money supply M by 10 percent. Because $\overline{V}$ and $\overline{Y}$ are assumed to be fixed, Equation 23.5 can continue to hold only if the price level P also rises by 10 percent. That is, according to the quantity equation, a 10 percent increase in the money supply M should cause a 10 percent increase in the price level P, that is, an inflation of 10 percent.

The intuition behind this conclusion is the one we mentioned at the beginning of this section. If the quantity of goods and services Y is approximately constant (and assuming also that velocity V is also constant), an increase in the supply of money will lead people to bid up the prices of the available goods and services. Thus high rates of money growth will tend to be associated with high rates of inflation. Figure 23.1 shows this relationship for 10 countries in Latin America during the period 1995–2001. You can see that countries with higher rates of money growth tend also to have higher rates of inflation. The relationship between money growth and inflation is not exact, in part because—contrary to the simplifying assumption we made earlier—velocity and output are not constant but vary over time.

If high rates of money growth lead to inflation, why do countries allow their money supplies to rise quickly? Usually, rapid rates of money growth are the result of large government budget deficits. Particularly in developing countries or countries suffering from war or political instability, governments sometimes find that they cannot raise sufficient taxes or borrow enough from the public to cover their expenditures. In this situation the government's only recourse may be to print new money and use this money to pay its bills. If the resulting increase in the amount of money in circulation is large enough, the result will be inflation.

FIGURE 23.1

Inflation and Money Growth in Latin America, 1995–2001.

Latin American countries with higher rates of growth in their money supplies also tended to have higher rates of inflation between 1995 and 2001. (The data for Argentina and Uruguay end in 2000 and the data for Ecuador end in 1997. In 1997 Ecuador abandoned its currency, the sucre, and began using U.S. dollars instead.)

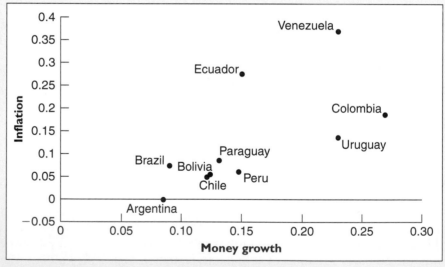

SOURCE: International Monetary Fund, International Financial Statistics

---

⬤ RECAP   **MONEY AND PRICES**

A high rate of money growth generally leads to inflation. The larger the amount of money in circulation, the higher the public will bid up the prices of available goods and services.

Velocity measures the speed at which money circulates; equivalently, it is the value of transactions completed in a period of time divided by the stock of money required to make those transactions. A numerical value for velocity can be obtained from the equation $V = (P \times Y) / M$, where V is velocity, $P \times Y$

is nominal GDP (a measure of the total value of transactions), and M is the money supply.

The *quantity equation* states that money times velocity equals nominal GDP, or, in symbols, $M \times V = P \times Y$. The quantity equation is a restatement of the definition of velocity and thus always holds. If velocity and output are approximately constant, the quantity equation implies that a given percentage increase in the money supply leads to the same percentage increase in the price level. In other words, the rate of growth of the money supply equals the rate of inflation.

▪ SUMMARY ▪

- *Money* is any asset that can be used in making purchases, such as currency and checking account balances. Money has three main functions: It is a *medium of exchange,* which means that it can be used in transactions. It is a *unit of account,* in that economic values are typically measured in units of money (e.g., dollars). And it is a *store of value,* a means by which people can hold wealth. In practice it is difficult to measure the money supply, since many assets have some moneylike features. A relatively narrow measure of money is M1, which includes currency and checking accounts. A broader measure of money, M2, includes all the assets in M1 plus additional assets that are somewhat less convenient to use in transactions than those included in M1.

- Because bank deposits are part of the money supply, the behavior of commercial banks and of bank depositors affects the amount of money in the economy. A key factor is the *reserve-deposit ratio* chosen by banks. *Bank reserves* are cash or similar assets held by commercial banks, for the purpose of meeting depositor withdrawals and payments. The reserve-deposit ratio is bank reserves divided by deposits in banks. A banking system in which all deposits are held as reserves practices *100 percent reserve banking.* Modern banking systems have reserve-deposit ratios less than 100 percent, and are called *fractional-reserve banking systems.*

- Commercial banks create money through multiple rounds of lending and accepting deposits. This process of lending and increasing deposits comes to an end when banks' reserve-deposit ratios equal their desired levels. At that point, bank deposits equal bank reserves divided by the desired reserve-deposit ratio. The money supply equals currency held by the public plus deposits in the banking system.

- The central bank of the United States is called the *Federal Reserve System,* or the Fed for short. The Fed's two main responsibilities are making monetary policy, which means determining how much money will circulate in the economy, and overseeing and regulating financial markets, especially banks. Created in 1914, the Fed is headed by a *Board of Governors* made up of seven governors appointed by the president. One of these seven governors is appointed chairman. The *Federal Open Market Committee,* which meets about eight times a year to determine monetary policy, is made up of the seven governors and five of the presidents of the regional Federal Reserve banks.

- The Fed can affect the money supply indirectly through its control of the supply of bank reserves. The Fed has two ways to change bank reserves: through *open-market operations,* in which the Fed buys or sells government securities in exchange for currency held by banks or the public, or through *discount window lending,* which is the Fed's lending of reserves to commercial banks. In addition the Fed can affect the money supply by changing legal *reserve requirements,* which influences banks' reserve-deposit ratios and hence deposits.

- One of the original purposes of the Federal Reserve was to help eliminate or control banking panics. A *banking panic* is an episode in which depositors, spurred by news or rumors of the imminent bankruptcy of one or more banks, rush to withdraw their deposits from the banking system. Because banks do not keep enough reserves on hand to pay off all depositors, even a financially healthy bank can run out of cash during a panic and be forced to close. The Federal Reserve failed to contain banking panics during the Great Depression, which led to sharp declines in the money supply. The adoption of a system of *deposit insurance* in the United States eliminated banking panics. A disadvantage of deposit insurance is that if banks or other insured intermediaries make bad loans or financial investments, the taxpayers may be responsible for covering the losses.

- In the long run, the rate of growth of the money supply and the rate of inflation are closely linked because a larger amount of money in circulation allows people to bid up the prices of existing goods and services. *Velocity* measures the speed at which money circulates; equivalently, it is the value of transactions completed in a period of time, divided by the stock of money required to make those transactions. Velocity is defined by the equation $V = (P \times Y) / M$, where V is velocity, $P \times Y$ is nominal GDP (a measure of the total value of transactions), and M is the money supply. The definition of velocity can be rewritten as the *quantity equation,* $M \times V = P \times Y$. The quantity equation shows that, if velocity and output are constant, a given percentage increase in the money supply will lead to the same percentage increase in the price level.

▪ KEY TERMS ▪

bank reserves (600)
banking panic (608)
barter (596)
Board of Governors of the Federal
  Reserve System (605)
deposit insurance (609)
discount rate (607)
discount window lending (607)
Federal Open Market Committee
  (FOMC) (605)

Federal Reserve System (the
  Fed) (604)
fractional-reserve banking system
  (600)
M1 (598)
M2 (598)
medium of exchange (596)
money (596)
100 percent reserve banking (600)

open-market operations (606)
open-market purchase (606)
open-market sale (606)
quantity equation (611)
reserve-deposit ratio (600)
reserve requirements (607)
store of value (597)
unit of account (597)
velocity (610)

▪ REVIEW QUESTIONS ▪

1. What is *money?* Why do people hold money even though it pays a lower return than other financial assets?

2. Suppose that the public switches from doing most of its shopping with currency to using checks instead. If the Fed takes no action, what will happen to the national money supply? Explain.

3. The Fed wants to reduce the U.S. money supply. Describe the various actions it might take, and explain how each action would accomplish the Fed's objective.

4. What is a *banking panic?* Prior to the introduction of deposit insurance, why might even a bank that had made sound loans have reason to fear a panic?

5. Define *velocity.* How has the introduction of new payments technologies, such as ATM machines, affected velocity? Explain.

6. Use the quantity equation to explain why money growth and inflation tend to be closely linked.

▪ PROBLEMS ▪

1. During World War II, an Allied soldier named Robert Radford spent several years in a large German prisoner-of-war camp. At times more than 50,000 prisoners were held in the camp, with some freedom to move about within the compound. Radford later wrote an account of his experiences. He described how an economy developed in the camp, in which prisoners traded food, clothing, and other items. Services, such as barbering, were also exchanged. Lacking paper money, the prisoners began to use cigarettes (provided monthly by the Red Cross) as money. Prices were quoted, and payments made, using cigarettes.
   a. In Radford's POW camp, how did cigarettes fulfill the three functions of money?
   b. Why do you think the prisoners used cigarettes as money, as opposed to other items of value such as squares of chocolate or pairs of boots?
   c. Do you think a nonsmoking prisoner would have been willing to accept cigarettes in exchange for a good or service in Radford's camp? Why or why not?

2. Obtain recent data on M1, M2, and their components. (For an online source, see Table 23.1). By what percentage have the two monetary aggregates grown over the past year? Which components of the two aggregates have grown the most quickly?

3. Redo the example of Gorgonzola in the text (see Tables 23.2 to 23.6), assuming that (a) initially, the Gorgonzolan central bank puts 5,000,000 guilders into circulation, and (b) commercial banks desire to hold reserves of 20 percent of deposits. As in the text, assume that the public holds no currency. Show the consolidated balance sheets of Gorgonzolan commercial banks after the initial deposits (compare to Table 23.2), after one round of loans (compare to Table 23.3), after the first redeposit of guilders (compare to Table 23.4), and after two rounds of loans and redeposits (Table 23.5). What are the final values of bank reserves, loans, deposits, and the money supply?

4. a. Bank reserves are 100, the public holds 200 in currency, and the desired reserve-deposit ratio is 0.25. Find deposits and the money supply.

b. The money supply is 500, and currency held by the public equals bank reserves. The desired reserve-deposit ratio is 0.25. Find currency held by the public and bank reserves.

c. The money supply is 1,250, of which 250 is currency held by the public. Bank reserves are 100. Find the desired reserve-deposit ratio.

5. When a central bank increases bank reserves by $1, the money supply rises by more than $1. The amount of extra money created when the central bank increases bank reserves by $1 is called the *money multiplier.*

a. Explain why the money multiplier is generally greater than 1. In what special case would it equal 1?

b. The initial money supply is $1,000, of which $500 is currency held by the public. The desired reserve-deposit ratio is 0.2. Find the increase in money supply associated with increases in bank reserves of $1, $5, and $10. What is the money multiplier in this economy?

c. Find a general rule for calculating the money multiplier.

d. Suppose the Fed wanted to reduce the money multiplier, perhaps because it believes that change would give it more precise control over the money supply. What action could the Fed take to achieve its goal?

6. Refer to Table 23.7. Suppose that the Fed had decided to set the U.S. money supply in December 1932 and in December 1933 at the same value as in December 1930. Assuming that the values of currency held by the public and the reserve-deposit ratio had remained as given in the table, by how much more should the Fed have increased bank reserves at each of those dates to accomplish that objective?

7. Real GDP is $8 trillion, nominal GDP is $10 trillion, M1 is $2 trillion, and M2 is $5 trillion.

a. Find velocity for M1 and for M2.

b. Show that the quantity equation holds for both M1 and M2.

8. You are given the following data for 2004 and 2005:

	2004	2005
Money supply	1,000	1,050
Velocity	8.0	8.0
Real GDP	12,000	12,000

a. Find the price level for 2004 and 2005. What is the rate of inflation between the two years?

b. What is the rate of inflation between 2004 and 2005 if the money supply in 2005 is 1,100 instead of 1050?

c. What is the rate of inflation between 2004 and 2005 if the money supply in 2005 is 1,100 and output in 2005 is 12,600?

▪ ANSWERS TO IN-CHAPTER EXERCISES ▪

23.1 Table 23.5 shows the balance sheet of banks after two rounds of lending and redeposits. At that point deposits are 2,710,000 guilders and reserves are 1,000,000 guilders. Since banks have a desired reserve-deposit ratio of 10 percent, they will keep 271,000 guilders (10 percent of deposits) as reserves and lend out the remaining 729,000 guilders. Loans to farmers are now 2,439,000 guilders. Eventually the 729,000 guilders lent to the farmers will be redeposited into the banks, giving the banks deposits of 3,439,000 guilders and reserves of 1,000,000 guilders. The balance sheet is as shown in the accompanying table.

Assets		Liabilities	
Currency (= reserves)	1,000,000 guilders	Deposits	3,439,000 guilders
Loans to farmers	2,439,000 guilders		

Notice that assets equal liabilities. The money supply equals deposits, or 3,439,000 guilders. Currency held in the banks as reserves does not count in the money supply.

23.2 Because the public holds no currency, the money supply equals bank deposits, which in turn equal bank reserves divided by the reserve-deposit ratio (Equation 23.1). If bank reserves are 1,000,000 and the reserve-deposit ratio is 0.05, then deposits equal 1,000,000/0.05 = 20,000,000 guilders, which is also the money supply. If bank reserves are 2,000,000 guilders and the reserve-deposit ratio is 0.10, then the money supply and deposits are again equal to 20,000,000 guilders, or 2,000,000/0.10.

23.3 If the central bank sells 50 shekels of government bonds in exchange for currency, the immediate effect is to reduce the amount of currency in the hands of the public by 50 shekels. To restore their currency holding to the desired level of 1,000 shekels, the public will withdraw 50 shekels from commercial banks, reducing bank reserves from 200 shekels to 150 shekels. The desired reserve-deposit ratio is 0.2, so ultimately deposits must equal 150 shekels in reserves divided by 0.2, or 750 shekels. (Note that to contract deposits, the commercial banks will have to "call in" loans, reducing their loans outstanding.) The money supply equals 1,000 shekels in currency held by the public plus 750 shekels in deposits, or 1,750 shekels. Thus the open-market purchase has reduced the money supply from 2,000 to 1,750 shekels.

23.4 Verify directly for each date in Table 23.7 that

$$\text{Money supply} = \text{Currency} + \frac{\text{Bank reserves}}{\text{Desired reserve-deposit ratio}}.$$

For example, for December 1929 we can check that 45.9 = 3.85 + 3.15/0.075.

Suppose that the currency held by the public in December 1933 had been 3.79, as in December 1930, rather than 4.85, and that the difference (4.85 − 3.79 = 1.06) had been left in the banks. Then bank reserves in December 1933 would have been 3.45 + 1.06 = 4.51, and the money supply would have been 3.79 + 4.51/0.133 = 37.7. So the money supply would still have fallen between 1930 and 1933 if people had not increased their holdings of currency, but only by about half as much.

23.5 Over the course of 1931, currency holdings by the public rose by $0.80 billion but bank reserves fell overall by only $0.20 billion. Thus the Fed must have replaced $0.60 billion of lost reserves during the year through open-market purchases or discount window lending.

Currency holdings at the end of 1931 were $4.59 billion. To have kept the money supply at the December 1930 value of $44.1 billion, the Fed would have had to ensure that bank deposits equaled $44.1 billion − $4.59 billion, or $39.51 billion. As the reserve-deposit ratio in 1931 was 0.095, this would have required bank reserves of 0.095 × $39.51 billion, or $3.75 billion, compared to the actual value in December 1931 of $3.11 billion. Thus, to keep the money supply from falling, the Fed would have had to increase bank reserves by $0.64 billion more than it did. The Fed has been criticized for increasing bank reserves by only about half what was needed to keep the money supply from falling.

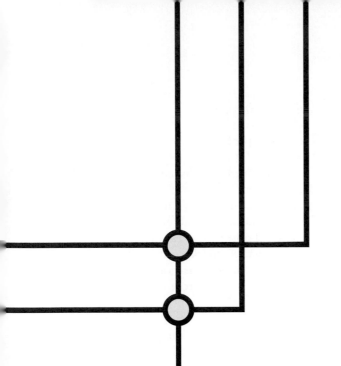

FINANCIAL MARKETS AND INTERNATIONAL CAPITAL FLOWS

■

A recent television ad for an online trading company showed an office worker, call him Ed, sitting in front of his computer. Instead of working, Ed is checking the prices of the stocks he bought over the Internet. Suddenly his eyes widen, as on the computer screen a graph shows the price of his stock shooting up like a rocket. With a whoop Ed heads down to his boss's office, delivers a few well-chosen insults, and quits his job. Unfortunately, when Ed returns to his desk to pack up his belongings, the computer screen shows that the price of his stock has fallen as quickly as it rose. The last we hear of Ed are his futile attempts to convince his boss that he was only kidding.

Ed's story is not a bad metaphor for the behavior of U.S. financial markets in the years around the turn of the millennium. The 1990s were a boom period in the United States, with strong economic growth, record low unemployment rates, and almost nonexistent inflation. This prosperity was mirrored in the spectacular performance of the stock market. In 1999 the Dow Jones index, a popular measure of stock prices, broke 10,000 and then 11,000 for the first time—almost triple the value of the index five years earlier. Prices of stocks of start-up companies, particularly high-technology and Internet companies, rose to stunning levels, making billionaires of some entrepreneurs still in their twenties. Nor were the benefits of rising stock prices confined to the very rich or the very nerdy. Stock ownership among the general population—including both

Would investors have spent $5.3 billion to build the Shoreham Nuclear Power Plant if they had known that regulators would never certify it as safe enough to operate?

direct ownership of stocks and indirect ownership through mutual funds and pension plans—reached record levels. The stock market boom, however, was not sustained. High-tech companies did not produce the profits that their investors had hoped for, and stock prices began to drop. Many start-up companies saw their stock become nearly worthless, and the values of even established companies fell by one-third or more.

During periods such as the 1990s, people often begin to think of the stock market as a place to gamble and, maybe, to strike it rich. Some people do get rich playing the market, and some people, like Ed and many real-life investors in stocks in recent years, lose everything. But the stock market, as well as other financial markets, plays a crucial role in the economy that is not shared by the gambling establishments in Las Vegas or Atlantic City. That role is to ensure that national saving is devoted to the most productive uses.

In Chapter 22 we discussed the importance of national saving. Under most circumstances, a high rate of national saving permits a high rate of capital formation, which both economic logic and experience predict will tend to increase labor productivity and living standards. However, creating new capital does not *guarantee* a richer and more productive economy. History is full of examples of "white elephants," capital projects in which millions, and even billions, of dollars were invested with little economic benefit: nuclear power plants that were never opened, massive dams whose main effect was to divert water supplies and disrupt the local agriculture, new technologies that just didn't work as planned.

A healthy economy not only saves adequately but also invests those savings in a productive way. In market economies, like that of the United States, channeling society's savings into the best possible capital investments is the role of the financial system: banks, stock markets, bond markets, and other financial markets and institutions. For this reason, many economists have argued that the development of well-functioning financial markets is a crucial precursor to sustained economic growth. In the first part of this chapter we discuss some major financial markets and institutions and their role in directing saving to productive uses.

Many of the people who purchased stock in U.S. companies during the roller-coaster years of the late 1990s and early 2000s were foreigners, looking to the United States for investment opportunities. More broadly, in the modern world saving often flows across national boundaries, as savers purchase financial assets in countries other than their own and borrowers look abroad for sources of financing. Flows of funds between lenders and borrowers located in different countries are referred to as *international capital flows*. We discuss the international dimension of saving and capital formation in the second part of the chapter. As we will see, for many countries, including the United States, foreign savings provide an important supplement to domestic savings as a means of financing the formation of new capital.

THE FINANCIAL SYSTEM AND THE ALLOCATION OF SAVING TO PRODUCTIVE USES

We have emphasized the importance of high rates of saving and capital formation for economic growth and increased productivity. High rates of saving and investment by themselves are not sufficient, however. A case in point is the former Soviet Union, which had very high rates of saving and investment but often used its resources very inefficiently, for example, by constructing massive but poorly designed factories that produced inferior goods at high cost. A successful economy not only saves but also uses its savings wisely by applying these limited funds to the investment projects that seem likely to be the most productive.

In the Soviet Union, a centralized bureaucracy made decisions about the allocation of saving to alternative uses. Because the bureaucrats in Moscow had relatively poor information and because they allowed themselves to be influenced by noneconomic considerations such as political favoritism, they often made poor decisions. In a market economy like that of the United States, in contrast, savings are allocated by means of a decentralized, market-oriented financial system. The U.S. financial system consists both of financial institutions, like banks, and financial markets, such as bond markets and stock markets.

The financial system of countries like the United States improves the allocation of savings in at least two distinct ways. First, the financial system provides *information* to savers about which of the many possible uses of their funds are likely to prove most productive and hence pay the highest return. By evaluating the potential productivity of alternative capital investments, the financial system helps to direct savings to its best uses. Second, financial markets help savers to *share the risks* of individual investment projects. Sharing of risks protects individual savers from bearing excessive risk, while at the same time making it possible to direct savings to projects, such as the development of new technologies, which are risky but potentially very productive as well.

In this section we briefly discuss three key components of the financial system: the banking system, the bond market, and the stock market. In doing so we elaborate on the role of the financial system as a whole in providing information about investment projects and in helping savers to share the risks of lending.

THE BANKING SYSTEM

The banking system consists of commercial banks, of which there are thousands in the United States. Commercial banks are privately owned firms that accept deposits from individuals and businesses and use those deposits to make loans. Banks are the most important example of a class of institutions called **financial intermediaries**, firms that extend credit to borrowers using funds raised from savers. Other examples of financial intermediaries are savings and loan associations and credit unions.

financial intermediaries firms that extend credit to borrowers using funds raised from savers

Why are financial intermediaries such as banks, which "stand between" savers and investors, necessary? Why don't individual savers just lend directly to borrowers who want to invest in new capital projects? The main reason is that, through specialization, banks and other intermediaries develop a *comparative advantage* in evaluating the quality of borrowers—the information-gathering function that we referred to a moment ago. Most savers, particularly small savers, do not have the time or the knowledge to determine for themselves which borrowers are likely to use the funds they receive most productively. In contrast, banks and other intermediaries have gained expertise in performing the information-gathering activities necessary for profitable lending, including checking out the borrower's background, determining whether the borrower's business plans make sense, and monitoring the borrower's activities during the life of the loan. Because banks specialize in evaluating potential borrowers, they can perform this function at a much lower cost, and with better results, than individual savers could on their own. Banks also reduce the costs of gathering information about potential borrowers by pooling the savings of many individuals to make large loans. Each large loan needs to be evaluated only once, by the bank, rather than separately by each of the hundreds of individuals whose savings may be pooled to make the loan.

Banks help savers by eliminating their need to gather information about potential borrowers and by directing their savings toward higher-return, more productive investments. Banks help borrowers as well, by providing access to credit that might otherwise not be available. Unlike a *Fortune* 500 corporation, which typically has many ways to raise funds, a small business that wants to buy a copier or remodel its offices will have few options other than going to a bank. Because the bank's lending officer has developed expertise in evaluating small-business loans, and may even have an ongoing business relationship with the

*"O.K., folks, let's move along. I'm sure you've all seen
someone qualify for a loan before."*

small-business owner, the bank will be able to gather the information it needs to
make the loan at a reasonable cost. Likewise, consumers who want to borrow to
finish a basement or add a room to a house will find few good alternatives to a
bank. In sum, banks' expertise at gathering information about alternative lending opportunities allows them to bring together small savers, looking for good
uses for their funds, and small borrowers with worthwhile investment projects.

In addition to being able to earn a return on their savings, a second reason
that people hold bank deposits is to make it easier to make payments. Most bank
deposits allow the holder to write a check against them or draw on them using
a debit card or ATM card. For many transactions, paying by check or debit card
is more convenient than using cash. For example, it is safer to send a check
through the mail than to send cash, and paying by check gives you a record of
the transaction, whereas a cash payment does not. We discussed the role of banks
in the creation of money in the previous chapter.

How has the banking crisis in Japan affected the Japanese economy?

**ECONOMIC
NATURALIST
24.1**

During the 1980s, real estate and stock prices soared in Japan. Japanese banks
made many loans to real estate developers, and the banks themselves acquired
stock in corporations. (Unlike in the United States, in Japan it is legal for commercial banks to own stock.) However, in the early 1990s land prices plummeted
in Japan, leading many bank borrowers to default on their loans. Stock prices
also came down sharply, reducing the value of banks' shareholdings. The net result
was that most Japanese banks fell into severe financial trouble, with many large
banks near bankruptcy. What has been the effect of this crisis, which has lasted
more than a decade, on the Japanese economy?

Relative to the United States, which has more developed stock and bond markets, Japan has traditionally relied very heavily on banks to allocate its savings.
Thus, when the severe financial problems of the banks prevented them from

operating normally, many borrowers found it unusually difficult to obtain credit—a situation known as a "credit crunch." Smaller borrowers, such as small- and medium-sized businesses, had been particularly dependent on banks for credit and thus suffered disproportionately.

The Japanese economy, after many years of robust growth, suffered a severe recession throughout the 1990s. Many factors contributed to this sharp slowdown. However, the virtual breakdown of the banking system certainly did not help the situation, as credit shortages interfered with smaller firms' ability to make capital investments and, in some cases, to purchase raw materials and pay workers. The Japanese government recognized the problem but has responded very slowly, in large part out of reluctance to bear the high costs of returning the banks to a healthy financial condition. Meanwhile, the Japanese economy has continued to perform poorly.

BONDS AND STOCKS

Large and well-established corporations that wish to obtain funds for investment will sometimes go to banks. Unlike the typical small borrower, however, a larger firm usually has alternative ways of raising funds, notably through the corporate bond market and the stock market. We first discuss some of the mechanics of bonds and stocks, then return to the role of bond and stock markets in allocating saving.

Bonds A bond is a legal promise to repay a debt, usually including both the **principal amount,** which is the amount originally lent, and regular interest payments. The promised interest rate when a bond is issued is called the **coupon rate.** The regular interest payments made to the bondholder are called coupon payments. The **coupon payment** of a bond that pays interest annually equals the coupon rate times the principal amount of the bond. For example, if the principal amount of a bond is $1,000,000 and its coupon rate is 5 percent, then the annual coupon payment made to the holder of the bond is (0.05)($1,000,000), or $50,000.

bond a legal promise to repay a debt, usually including both the principal amount and regular interest payments

principal amount the amount originally lent

coupon rate the interest rate promised when a bond is issued

coupon payments regular interest payments made to the bondholder

Corporations and governments frequently raise funds by issuing bonds and selling them to savers. The coupon rate that a newly issued bond has to promise in order to be attractive to savers depends on a number of factors, including the bond's term, its credit risk, and its tax treatment. The *term* of a bond is the length of time before the debt it represents is fully repaid, a period that can range from 30 days to 30 years or more. Generally lenders will demand a higher interest rate to lend for a longer term. *Credit risk* is the risk that the borrower will go bankrupt and thus not repay the loan. A borrower that is viewed as risky will have to pay a higher interest rate to compensate lenders for taking the chance of losing all or part of their financial investment. For example, so-called high-yield bonds, less formally known as "junk bonds," are bonds issued by firms judged to be risky by credit-rating agencies; these bonds pay higher interest rates than bonds issued by companies thought to be less risky.

Bonds also differ in their *tax treatment.* For example, interest paid on bonds issued by local governments, called municipal bonds, is exempt from federal taxes, whereas interest on other types of bonds is treated as taxable income. Because of this tax advantage, lenders are willing to accepting a lower interest rate on municipal bonds.

Bondholders are not required to hold bonds until *maturity,* the time at which they are supposed to be repaid by the issuer, but are always free to sell their bonds in the *bond market,* an organized market run by professional bond traders. The market value of a particular bond at any given point in time is called the *price* of the bond. As it turns out, there is a close relationship between the price of a bond at a given point of time and the interest rate prevailing in financial markets at that time, illustrated by Example 24.1.

EXAMPLE 24.1

Bond prices and interest rates

On January 1, 2003, Tanya purchases a newly issued, two-year government bond with a principal amount of $1,000. The coupon rate on the bond is 5 percent, paid annually. Hence Tanya, or whoever owns the bond at the time, will receive a coupon payment of $50 (5 percent of $1,000) on January 1, 2004, and $1,050 (a $50 coupon payment plus repayment of the original $1,000 lent) on January 1, 2005.

On January 1, 2004, after receiving her first year's coupon payment, Tanya decides to sell her bond to raise the funds to take a vacation. She offers her bond for sale in the bond market. How much can she expect to get for her "used" bond if the prevailing interest rate in the bond market is 6 percent? If the prevailing interest rate is 4 percent?

As we mentioned, the price of a "used" bond at any point in time depends on the prevailing interest rate. Suppose first that, on January 1, 2004, when Tanya takes her bond to the bond market, the prevailing interest rate on newly issued one-year bonds is 6 percent. Would another saver be willing to pay Tanya the full $1,000 principal amount of her bond? No, because the purchaser of Tanya's bond will receive $1,050 in one year, when the bond matures; whereas if he uses his $1,000 to buy a new one-year bond paying 6 percent interest, he will receive $1,060 ($1,000 principal repayment plus $60 interest) in one year. So Tanya's bond is not worth $1,000 to another saver.

How much would another saver be willing to pay for Tanya's bond? Since newly issued one-year bonds pay a 6 percent return, he will buy Tanya's bond only at a price that allows him to earn at least that return. As the holder of Tanya's bond will receive $1,050 ($1,000 principal plus $50 interest) in one year, the price for her bond that allows the purchaser to earn a 6 percent return must satisfy the equation

$$\text{Bond price} \times 1.06 = \$1{,}050.$$

Solving the equation for the bond price, we find that Tanya's bond will sell for $1,050/1.06, or just under $991. To check this result, note that in one year the purchaser of the bond will receive $1,050, or $59 more than he paid. His rate of return is $59/$991, or 6 percent, as expected.

What if the prevailing interest rate had been 4 percent rather than 6 percent? Then the price of Tanya's bond would satisfy the relationship bond price × 1.04 = $1,050, implying that the price of her bond would be $1,050/1.04, or almost $1,010.

What happens if the interest rate when Tanya wants to sell is 5 percent, the same as it was when she originally bought the bond? You should show that in this case the bond would sell at its face value of $1,000.

This example illustrates a general principle, that *bond prices and interest rates are inversely related*. When the interest rate being paid on newly issued bonds rises, the price financial investors are willing to pay for existing bonds falls, and vice versa.

EXERCISE 24.1

Three-year government bonds are issued at a face value (principal amount) of 100 and a coupon rate of 7 percent, interest payable at the end of each year. One year prior to the maturation of these bonds, a newspaper headline reads, "Bad Economic News Causes Prices of Bonds to Plunge," and the story reveals that these three-year bonds have fallen in price to 96. What has happened to interest rates? What is the one-year interest rate at the time of the newspaper story?

Issuing bonds is one means by which a corporation or a government can obtain funds from savers. Another important way of raising funds, but one restricted to corporations, is by issuing stock to the public.

Stocks   A share of **stock** (or *equity*) is a claim to partial ownership of a firm. For example, if a corporation has 1 million shares of stock outstanding, owner-ship of one share is equivalent to ownership of one-millionth of the company. Stockholders receive returns on their financial investment in two forms. First, stockholders receive a regular payment called a **dividend** for each share of stock they own. Dividends are determined by the firm's management and usually depend on the firm's recent profits. Second, stockholders receive returns in the form of *capital gains* when the price of their stock increases (we discussed capital gains and losses in Chapter 22).

> **stock (or equity)** a claim to partial ownership of a firm

> **dividend** a regular payment received by stockholders for each share that they own

Prices of stocks are determined through trading on a stock exchange, such as the New York Stock Exchange. A stock's price rises and falls as the demand for the stock changes. Demand for stocks in turn depends on factors such as news about the prospects of the company. For example, the stock price of a pharma-ceutical company that announces the discovery of an important new drug is likely to rise on the announcement, even if actual production and marketing of the drug is some time away, because financial investors expect the company to become more profitable in the future. Example 24.2 illustrates numerically some key fac-tors that affect stock prices.

How much should you pay for a share of FortuneCookie.com?

EXAMPLE 24.2

You have the opportunity to buy shares in a new company called For-tuneCookie.com, which plans to sell gourmet fortune cookies over the Internet. Your stockbroker estimates that the company will pay $1.00 per share in divi-dends a year from now, and that in a year the market price of the company will be $80.00 per share. Assuming that you accept your broker's estimates as accu-rate, what is the most that you should be willing to pay today per share of For-tuneCookie.com? How does your answer change if you expect a $5.00 dividend? If you expect a $1.00 dividend but an $84.00 stock price in one year?

Based on your broker's estimates, you conclude that in one year each share of FortuneCookie.com you own will be worth $81.00 in your pocket—the $1.00 dividend plus the $80.00 you could get by reselling the stock. Finding the max-imum price you would pay for the stock today therefore boils down to asking how much would you invest today to have $81.00 a year from today. Answer-ing this question in turn requires one more piece of information, which is the expected rate of return that you require in order to be willing to buy stock in this company.

How would you determine your required rate of return to hold stock in For-tuneCookie.com? For the moment, let's imagine that you are not too worried about the potential riskiness of the stock, either because you think that it is a "sure thing" or because you are a devil-may-care type who is not bothered by risk. In that case, your required rate of return to hold FortuneCookie.com should be about the same as you can get on other financial investments, such as gov-ernment bonds. The available return on other financial investments gives the *opportunity cost* of your funds. So, for example, if the interest rate currently being offered by government bonds is 6 percent, you should be willing to accept a 6 percent return to hold FortuneCookie.com as well. In that case, the maximum price you would pay today for a share of FortuneCookie satisfies the equation

$$\text{Stock price} \times 1.06 = \$81.00.$$

This equation defines the stock price you should be willing to pay if you are will-ing to accept a 6 percent return over the next year. Solving this equation yields stock price = $81.00/1.06 = $76.42. If you buy FortuneCookie.com for $76.42, then your return over the year will be ($81.00 − $76.42)/$76.42 = $4.58/$71.42 = 6 percent, which is the rate of return you required to buy the stock.

If instead the dividend is expected to be $5.00, then the total benefit of holding the stock in one year, equal to the expected dividend plus the expected price, is $5.00 + $80.00, or $85.00. Assuming again that you are willing to accept a 6 percent return to hold FortuneCookie.com, the price you are willing to pay for the stock today satisfies the relationship stock price × 1.06 = $85.00. Solving this equation for the stock price yields stock price = $85.00/1.06 = $80.19. Comparing with the previous case we see that a higher expected dividend in the future increases the value of the stock today. That's why good news about the future prospects of a company—such as the announcement by a pharmaceutical company that it has discovered a useful new drug—affects its stock price immediately.

If the expected future price of the stock is $84.00, with the dividend at $1.00, then the value of holding the stock in one year is once again $85.00, and the calculation is the same as the previous one. Again, the price you should be willing to pay for the stock is $80.19.

These examples show that an increase in the future dividend or in the future expected stock price raises the stock price today, whereas an increase in the return a saver requires to hold the stock lowers today's stock price. Since we expect required returns in the stock market to be closely tied to market interest rates, this last result implies that increases in interest rates tend to depress stock prices as well as bond prices.

Our examples also took the future stock price as given. But what determines the future stock price? Just as today's stock price depends on the dividend shareholders expect to receive this year and the stock price a year from now, the stock price a year from now depends on the dividend expected for next year and the stock price two years from now, and so on. Ultimately, then, today's stock price is affected not only by the dividend expected this year but future dividends as well. A company's ability to pay dividends depends on its earnings. Thus, as we noted in the example of the pharmaceutical company that announces the discovery of a new drug, news about future earnings—even earnings quite far in the future—is likely to affect a company's stock price immediately.

> ### EXERCISE 24.2
>
> **As in Example 24.2, you expect a share of FortuneCookie.com to be worth $80.00 per share in one year, and also to pay a dividend of $1.00 in one year. What should you be willing to pay for the stock today if the prevailing interest rate, equal to your required rate of return, is 4 percent? What if the interest rate is 8 percent? In general, how would you expect stock prices to react if economic news arrives that implies that interest rates will rise in the very near future?**

In Example 24.2 we assumed that you were willing to accept a return of 6 percent to hold FortuneCookie.com, the same return that you could get on a government bond. However, financial investments in the stock market are quite risky in that returns to holding stocks can be highly variable and unpredictable. For example, although you expect a share of FortuneCookie.com to be worth $80.00 in one year, you also realize that there is a chance it might sell as low as $50.00 or as high as $110.00 per share. Most financial investors dislike risk and unpredictability and thus have a higher required rate of return for holding risky assets like stocks than for holding relatively safe assets like government bonds. The difference between the required rate of return to hold risky assets and the rate of return on safe assets, like government bonds, is called the **risk premium**. Example 24.3 illustrates the effect of financial investors' dislike of risk on stock prices.

risk premium the rate of return that financial investors require to hold risky assets minus the rate of return on safe assets

Riskiness and stock prices

EXAMPLE 24.3

Continuing Example 24.2, suppose that FortuneCookie.com is expected to pay a $1.00 dividend and have a market price of $80.00 per share in one year. The interest rate on government bonds is 6 percent per year. However, to be willing to hold a risky asset like a share of FortuneCookie.com, you require an expected return four percentage points higher than the rate paid by safe assets like government bonds (a risk premium of 4 percent). Hence you require a 10 percent expected return to hold FortuneCookie.com. What is the most you would be willing to pay for the stock now? What do you conclude about the relationship between perceived riskiness and stock prices?

As a share of FortuneCookie.com is expected to pay $81.00 in one year and the required return is 10 percent, we have stock price × 1.10 = $81.00. Solving for the stock price, we find the price to be $81.00/1.10 = $73.64, less than the price of $76.42 we found when there was no risk premium and the required rate of return was 6 percent (Example 24.2). We conclude that financial investors' dislike of risk, and the resulting risk premium, lowers the prices of risky assets like stocks.

RECAP   **FACTORS AFFECTING STOCK PRICES**

1. An increase in expected future dividends or in the expected future market price of a stock raises the current price of the stock.

2. An increase in interest rates, implying an increase in the required rate of return to hold stocks, lowers the current price of stocks.

3. An increase in perceived riskiness, as reflected in an increase in the risk premium, lowers the current price of stocks.

BOND MARKETS, STOCK MARKETS, AND THE ALLOCATION OF SAVINGS

Like banks, bond markets and stock markets provide a means of channeling funds from savers to borrowers with productive investment opportunities. For example, a corporation that is planning a capital investment but does not want to borrow from a bank has two other options: It can issue new bonds, to be sold to savers in the bond market, or it can issue new shares in itself, which are then sold in the stock market. The proceeds from the sales of new bonds or stocks are then available to the firm to finance its capital investment.

How do stock and bond markets help to ensure that available savings are devoted to the most productive uses? As we mentioned earlier, two important functions served by these markets are gathering information about prospective borrowers and helping savers to share the risks of lending.

The informational role of bond and stock markets Savers and their financial advisors know that to get the highest possible returns on their financial investments, they must find the potential borrowers with the most profitable opportunities. This knowledge provides a powerful incentive to scrutinize potential borrowers carefully.

For example, companies considering a new issue of stocks or bonds know that their recent performance and plans for the future will be carefully studied by professional analysts on Wall Street and other financial investors. If the analysts and other potential purchasers have doubts about the future profitability of the firm, they will offer a relatively low price for the newly issued shares or they will demand a high interest rate on newly issued bonds. Knowing this, a company will be reluctant to go to the bond or stock market for financing unless its management is confident that it can convince financial investors that the firm's planned use of the funds will be profitable. Thus the ongoing search by savers and their financial advisors for high returns leads the bond and stock markets to direct funds to the uses that appear most likely to be productive.

Risk sharing and diversification   Many highly promising investment projects are also quite risky. The successful development of a new drug to lower cholesterol could create billions of dollars in profits for a drug company, for example; but if the drug turns out to be less effective than some others on the market, none of the development costs will be recouped. An individual who lent his or her life savings to help finance the development of the anticholesterol drug might enjoy a handsome return but also takes the chance of losing everything. Savers are generally reluctant to take large risks, so without some means of reducing the risk faced by each saver it might be very hard for the company to find the funds to develop the new drug.

Bond and stock markets help reduce risk by giving savers a means to *diversify* their financial investments. **Diversification** is the practice of spreading one's wealth over a variety of different financial investments to reduce overall risk. The idea of diversification follows from the adage that "you shouldn't put all your eggs in one basket." Rather than putting all of his or her savings in one very risky project, a financial investor will find it much safer to allocate a small amount of savings to each of a large number of stocks and bonds. That way, if some financial assets fall in value, there is a good chance that others will rise in value, with gains offsetting losses. Example 24.4 illustrates the benefits of diversification.

diversification the practice of spreading of one's wealth over a variety of different financial investments to reduce overall risk

EXAMPLE 24.4

The benefits of diversification

Vikram has $1,000 to invest and is considering two stocks, the Smith Umbrella Company and the Jones Suntan Lotion Company. The price of Smith Umbrella stock will rise by 10 percent if it rains but will remain unchanged if the weather is sunny. The price of Jones Suntan stock is expected to rise by 10 percent if it is sunny but will remain unchanged if there is rain. The chance of rain is 50 percent, and the chance of sunshine is 50 percent. How should Vikram invest his $1,000?

If Vikram were to invest all his $1,000 in Smith Umbrella, he has a 50 percent chance of earning a 10 percent return, in the event that it rains, and a 50 percent chance of earning zero, if the weather is sunny. His average return is 50 percent times 10 percent plus 50 percent times zero, or 5 percent. Similarly, an investment in Jones Suntan yields 10 percent return half the time, when it's sunny, and 0 percent return the other half the time, when it rains, for an average return of 5 percent.

Although Vikram can earn an *average* return of 5 percent in either stock, investing in only one stock or the other is quite risky, since the actual return he receives varies widely depending on whether there is rain or shine. Can Vikram *guarantee* himself a 5 percent return, avoiding the uncertainty and risk? Yes, all he has to do is put $500 into each of the two stocks. If it rains, he will earn $50 on his Smith Umbrella stock and nothing on his Jones Suntan. If it's sunny, he will earn nothing on Smith Umbrella but $50 on Jones Suntan. Rain or shine, he is guaranteed to earn $50—a 5 percent return—without risk.

The existence of bond markets and stock markets make it easy for savers to diversify by putting a small amount of their savings into each of a wide variety of different financial assets, each of which represents a share of a particular company or investment project. From society's point of view, diversification makes it possible for risky but worthwhile projects to obtain funding, without individual savers having to bear too much risk.

For the typical person, a particularly convenient way to diversify is to buy bonds and stocks indirectly through mutual funds. A **mutual fund** is a financial intermediary that sells shares in itself to the public, then uses the funds raised to buy a wide variety of financial assets. Holding shares in a mutual fund thus

mutual fund a financial intermediary that sells shares in itself to the public, then uses the funds raised to buy a wide variety of financial assets amounts to owning a little bit of many different financial assets, which helps to achieve diversification. The advantage of mutual funds is that it is usually less costly and time consuming to buy shares in one or two mutual funds than to buy many different stocks and bonds directly. Over the past decade mutual funds have become increasingly popular in the United States.

Why did the U.S. stock market rise sharply in the 1990s, then fall in the new millennium?

ECONOMIC
NATURALIST
24.2

Stock prices soared during the 1990s in the United States. The Standard & Poor's 500 index, which summarizes the stock price performance of 500 major companies, rose 60 percent between 1990 and 1995, then more than doubled between 1995 and 2000. However, in the first two years of the new millennium this index lost nearly half its value. Why did the U.S. stock market boom in the 1990s and bust in the 2000s?

The prices of stocks depend on their purchasers' expectations about future dividends and stock prices and on the rate of return required by potential stockholders. The required rate of return in turn equals the interest rate on safe assets plus the risk premium. In principle, a rise in stock prices could be the result of increased optimism about future dividends, a fall in the required return, or some combination.

Probably both factors contributed to the boom in stock prices in the 1990s. Dividends grew rapidly in the 1990s, reflecting the strong overall performance of the U.S. economy. Encouraged by the promise of new technologies, many financial investors expected future dividends to be even higher.

There is also evidence that the risk premium that people required to hold stocks fell during the 1990s, thereby lowering the total required return and raising stock prices. One possible explanation for a decline in the risk premium in the 1990s is increased diversification. During that decade the number and variety of mutual funds available increased markedly. Millions of Americans invested in these funds, including many who had never owned stock before or had owned stock in only a few companies. This increase in diversification for the typical stock market investor may have lowered the perceived risk of holding stocks, which in turn reduced the risk premium and raised stock prices.

After 2000 both of these favorable factors reversed. The growth in dividends was disappointing to stockholders, in large part because many high-tech firms did not prove as profitable as had been hoped. An additional blow was a series of corporate accounting scandals in 2002, in which it became known that some large firms had taken illegal or unethical actions to make their profits seem larger than in fact they were. A number of factors, including a recession, a major terrorist attack, and the accounting scandals, also increased stockholders' concerns about the riskiness of stocks, so that the risk premium they required to hold stocks rose from its 1990s lows. The combination of lower expected dividends and a higher premium for risk sent stock prices sharply downward.

INTERNATIONAL CAPITAL FLOWS

Our discussion thus far has focused on financial markets operating within a given country, such as the United States. However, economic opportunities are not necessarily restricted by national boundaries. The most productive use of a U.S. citizen's savings might be located far from U.S. soil, in helping to build a factory in Thailand or starting a small business in Poland. Likewise, the best way for a Brazilian saver to diversify her assets and reduce her risks could be to hold bonds and stocks from a number of different countries. Over time, extensive financial markets have developed to permit cross-border borrowing and lending. Financial markets in which borrowers and lenders are residents of different countries are called *international* financial markets.

International financial markets differ from domestic financial markets in at least one important respect: Unlike a domestic financial transaction, an international financial transaction is subject to the laws and regulations of at least two countries, the country that is home to the lender and the country that is home to the borrower. Thus the size and vitality of international financial markets depend on the degree of political and economic cooperation among countries. For example, during the relatively peaceful decades of the late nineteenth and early twentieth centuries, international financial markets were remarkably highly developed. Great Britain, at the time the world's dominant economic power, was a major international lender, dispatching its savings for use around the globe. However, during the turbulent years 1914–1945, two world wars and the Great Depression substantially reduced both international finance and international trade in goods and services. The extent of international finance and trade returned to the levels achieved in the late nineteenth century only in the 1980s.

In thinking about international financial markets, it is useful to understand that lending is economically equivalent to acquiring a real or financial asset, and borrowing is economically equivalent to selling a real or financial asset. For example, savers lend to companies by purchasing stocks or bonds, which are financial assets for the lender and financial liabilities for the borrowing firms. Similarly, lending to a government is accomplished in practice by acquiring a government bond—a financial asset for the lender, and a financial liability for the borrower, in this case the government. Savers can also provide funds by acquiring real assets such as land; if I purchase a parcel of land from you, though I am not making a loan in the usual sense, I am providing you with funds that you can use for consuming or investing. In lieu of interest or dividends from a bond or a stock, I receive the rental value of the land that I purchased.

international capital flows purchases or sales of real and financial assets across international borders

Purchases or sales of real and financial assets across international borders (which are economically equivalent to lending and borrowing across international borders) are known as **international capital flows.** From the perspective of a particular country, say the United States, purchases of domestic (U.S.) assets by foreigners are called **capital inflows;** purchases of foreign assets by domestic (U.S.) households and firms are called **capital outflows.** To remember these terms, it may help to keep in mind that capital inflows represent funds "flowing in" to the country (foreign savers buying domestic assets), while capital outflows are funds "flowing out" of the country (domestic savers buying foreign assets). The difference between the two flows is expressed as *net capital inflows*—capital inflows minus capital outflows—or *net capital outflows*—capital outflows minus capital inflows. Note that capital inflows and outflows are *not* counted as exports or imports, because they refer to the purchase of existing real and financial assets rather than currently produced goods and services.

capital inflows purchases of domestic assets by foreign households and firms

capital outflows purchases of foreign assets by domestic households and firms

From a macroeconomic perspective, international capital flows play two important roles. First, they allow countries whose productive investment opportunities are greater than domestic savings to fill in the gap by borrowing from abroad. Second, they allow countries to run trade imbalances—situations in which the country's exports of goods and services do not equal its imports of goods and services. The rest of this chapter discusses these key roles. We begin by analyzing the important link between international capital flows and trade imbalances.

CAPITAL FLOWS AND THE BALANCE OF TRADE

trade balance (or net exports) the value of a country's exports less the value of its imports in a particular period (quarter or year)

In Chapter 18 we introduced the term *net exports (NX),* the value of a country's exports less the value of its imports. An equivalent term for the value of a country's exports less the value of its imports is the **trade balance.** Because exports need not equal imports in each quarter or year, the trade balance (or net exports) need not always equal zero. If the trade balance is positive in a particular period so that the value of exports exceeds the value of imports, a country is said to have a **trade surplus** for that period equal to the value of its exports minus the value of its imports. If the trade balance is negative, with imports greater than exports, the country is said to have a **trade deficit** equal to the value of its imports minus the value of its exports.

Figure 24.1 shows the components of the U.S. trade balance since 1960 (see Figure 17.5 for data extending back to 1900). The blue line represents U.S. exports as a percentage of GDP; the red line, U.S. imports as a percentage of GDP. When exports exceed imports, the vertical distance between the two lines gives the U.S. trade surplus as a percentage of GDP. When imports exceed exports, the vertical distance between the two lines represents the U.S. trade deficit. Figure 24.1 shows first that international trade has become an increasingly important part of the U.S. economy in the past several decades. In 1960, only 4.8 percent of U.S. GDP was exported, and the value of imports equaled 4.3 percent of U.S. GDP. In 2001, by comparison, 10.3 percent of U.S. production was sold abroad, and imports amounted to 13.7 percent of U.S. GDP. Second, the figure shows that since the late 1970s the United States has consistently run trade deficits, frequently equal to 2 percent or more of GDP. Why has the U.S. trade balance been in deficit for so long? We will answer that question later in this section.

trade surplus when exports exceed imports, the difference between the value of a country's exports and the value of its imports in a given period

trade deficit when imports exceed exports, the difference between the value of a country's imports and the value of its exports in a given period

FIGURE 24.1
The U.S. Trade Balance, 1960–2001.
This figure shows U.S. exports and imports as a percentage of GDP. Since the late 1970s the United States has run a trade deficit, with imports exceeding exports.

SOURCE: Bureau of Economic Analysis (www.bea.gov).

The trade balance represents the difference between the value of goods and services exported by a country and the value of goods and services imported by the country. Net capital inflows represent the difference between purchases of domestic assets by foreigners and purchases of foreign assets by domestic residents. There is a precise and very important link between these two imbalances, which is that in any given period, *the trade balance and net capital inflows sum to zero*. For future reference, let's write this relationship as an equation:

$$NX + KI = 0. \qquad (24.1)$$

where NX is the trade balance (the same as net exports) and we use KI to stand for net capital inflows. The relationship given by Equation 24.1 is an identity, meaning that it is true by definition.

To see why Equation 24.1 holds, consider what happens when (for example) a U.S. resident purchases an imported good, say a Japanese automobile priced at $20,000. Suppose the U.S. buyer pays by check so that the Japanese car manufacturer now holds $20,000 in an account in a U.S. bank. What will the Japanese manufacturer do with this $20,000? Basically, there are two possibilities.

First, the Japanese company may use the $20,000 to buy U.S.-produced goods and services, such as U.S.-manufactured car parts or Hawaiian vacations for its executives. In this case, the United States has $20,000 in exports to balance the $20,000 automobile import. Because exports equal imports, the U.S. trade balance is unaffected by these transactions (for these transactions, NX = 0). And because no assets are bought or sold, there are no capital inflows or outflows ($KI = 0$). So under this scenario, the condition that the trade balance plus net capital inflows equals zero, as stated in Equation 24.1, is satisfied.

Alternatively, the Japanese car producer might use the $20,000 to acquire U.S. assets, such as a U.S. Treasury bond or some land adjacent to its plant in Tennessee. In this case, the United States compiles a trade deficit of $20,000, because the $20,000 car import is not offset by an export ($NX = -\$20,000$). But there is a corresponding capital inflow of $20,000, reflecting the purchase of a U.S. asset by the Japanese ($KI = \$20,000$). So once again the trade balance and net capital inflows sum to zero, and Equation 24.1 is satisfied.[1]

In fact, there is a third possibility, which is that the Japanese car company might swap its dollars to some other party outside the United States. For example, the company might trade its dollars to another Japanese firm or individual in exchange for Japanese yen. However, the acquirer of the dollars would then have the same two options as the car company—to buy U.S. goods and services or acquire U.S. assets—so that the equality of net capital inflows and the trade deficit would continue to hold.

EXERCISE 24.3

A U.S. saver purchases a $20,000 Japanese government bond. Explain why Equation 24.1 is satisfied no matter what the Japanese government does with the $20,000 it receives for its bond.

THE DETERMINANTS OF INTERNATIONAL CAPITAL FLOWS

Capital inflows, recall, are purchases of domestic assets by foreigners, while capital outflows are purchases of foreign assets by domestic residents. For example, capital inflows into the United States include foreign purchases of items such as the stocks and bonds of U.S. companies, U.S. government bonds, and real assets such as land or buildings owned by U.S. residents. Why would foreigners want to acquire U.S. assets, and, conversely, why would Americans want to acquire assets abroad?

The basic factors that determine the attractiveness of any asset, either domestic or foreign, are *return* and *risk*. Financial investors seek high real returns; thus, with other factors (such as the degree of risk and the returns available abroad) held constant, a higher real interest rate in the home country promotes capital inflows by making domestic assets more attractive to foreigners. By the same token, a higher real interest rate in the home country reduces capital outflows by inducing domestic residents to invest their savings at home. Thus, all else being equal, a higher real interest rate at home leads to net capital inflows. Conversely, a low real interest rate at home tends to create net capital outflows, as financial investors look abroad for better opportunities. Figure 24.2 shows the relationship between a country's net capital inflows and the real rate of interest prevailing in that country. When the domestic real interest rate is high, net capital inflows are positive (foreign purchases of domestic assets exceed domestic purchases of foreign assets). But when the real interest rate is low, net capital inflows are negative (that is, the country experiences net capital outflows).

The effect of risk on capital flows is the opposite of the effect of the real interest rate. For a given real interest rate, an increase in the riskiness of domestic assets reduces net capital inflows, as foreigners become less willing to buy the home country's assets, and domestic savers become more inclined to buy foreign assets. For

---

[1] If the Japanese company simply left the $20,000 in the U.S. bank, it would still count as a capital inflow, since the deposit would still be a U.S. asset acquired by foreigners.

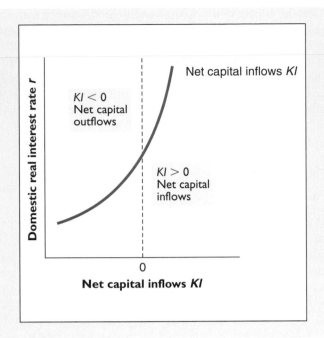

FIGURE 24.2
Net Capital Inflows and the Real Interest Rate.
Holding constant the degree of risk and the real returns available abroad, a high real interest rate in the home country will induce foreigners to buy domestic assets, increasing capital inflows. A high real rate in the home country also reduces the incentive for domestic savers to buy foreign assets, reducing capital outflows. Thus, all else being equal, the higher the domestic real interest rate r, the higher will be net capital inflows KI.

example, political instability, which increases the risk of investing in a country, tends to reduce net capital inflows. Figure 24.3 shows the effect of an increase in risk on capital flows: At each value of the domestic real interest rate, an increase in risk reduces net capital inflows, shifting the capital inflows curve to the left.

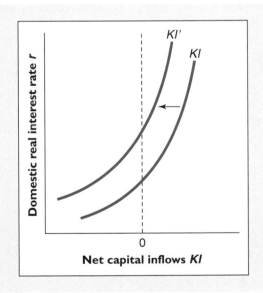

FIGURE 24.3
An Increase in Risk Reduces Net Capital Inflows.
An increase in the riskiness of domestic assets, arising, for example, from an increase in political instability, reduces the willingness of foreign and domestic savers to hold domestic assets. The supply of capital inflows declines at each value of the domestic real interest rate, shifting the KI curve to the left.

EXERCISE 24.4

For given real interest rate and riskiness in the home country, how would you expect net capital inflows to be affected by an increase in real interest rates abroad? Show your answer graphically.

SAVING, INVESTMENT, AND CAPITAL INFLOWS

International capital flows have a close relationship to domestic saving and investment. As we will see next, capital inflows augment the domestic saving pool, increasing the funds available for investment in physical capital, while capital outflows reduce the amount of saving available for investment. Thus capital inflows can help to promote economic growth within a country, and capital outflows to restrain it.

To derive the relationship among capital inflows, saving, and investment, recall from Chapter 18 that total output or income Y must always equal the sum of the four components of expenditure: consumption (C), investment (I), government purchases (G), and net exports (NX). Writing out this identity, we have

$$Y = C + I + G + NX.$$

Next, we subtract $C + G + NX$ from both sides of the identity to obtain

$$Y - C - G - NX = I.$$

In Chapter 22 we saw that national saving S is equal to $Y - C - G$. Furthermore, Equation 24.1 above states that the trade balance plus capital inflows equals zero, or $NX + KI = 0$, which implies that $KI = -NX$. If we substitute S for $Y - C - G$ and KI for $-NX$ in the above equation, we find that

$$S + KI = I. \tag{24.2}$$

Equation 24.2, a key result, says that the sum of national saving S and capital inflows from abroad KI must equal domestic investment in new capital goods, I. In other words, in an open economy, the pool of saving available for domestic investment includes not only national saving (the saving of the domestic private and public sectors) but funds from savers abroad as well.

Chapter 22 introduced the saving-investment diagram, which shows that in a closed economy, the supply of saving must equal the demand for saving. A similar diagram applies to an open economy, except that the supply of saving in an open economy includes net capital inflows as well as domestic saving. Figure 24.4

FIGURE 24.4

The Saving-Investment Diagram for an Open Economy.

The total supply of savings in an open economy is the sum of national saving S and net capital inflows KI. The supply of domestic saving S is shown for comparison. Because a low real interest rate prompts capital outflows $(KI < 0)$, at low values of the domestic interest rate the total supply of saving $S + KI$ is smaller than national saving S. The domestic demand for saving for purposes of capital investment is shown by the curve labeled I. The equilibrium real interest rate r^* sets the total supply of saving, including capital inflows, equal to the domestic demand for saving.

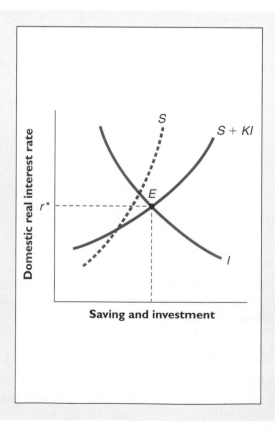

shows the open-economy version of the saving-investment diagram. The domestic real interest rate is shown on the vertical axis and saving and investment flows on the horizontal axis. As in a closed economy, the downward-sloping curve I shows the demand for funds by firms that want to make capital investments. The solid upward-sloping curve, marked $S + KI$, shows the total supply of saving, including *both* domestic saving S and net capital inflows from abroad KI. Also shown, for comparison, is the supply of domestic saving, marked S. You can see that for higher values of the domestic real interest rate, net capital inflows are positive, so the $S + KI$ curve falls to the right of the curve S showing domestic saving only. But at low enough values of the real interest rate r, the economy sustains net capital outflows, as savers look abroad for higher returns on their financial investments. Thus, at low values of the domestic real interest rate, the net supply of savings is lower than it would be in a closed economy, and the $S + KI$ curve falls to the left of the domestic supply of saving curve S. As Figure 24.4 shows, the equilibrium real interest rate in an open economy, r^*, is the level that sets the total amount of saving supplied (including capital inflows from abroad) equal to the amount of saving demanded for purposes of domestic capital investment.

Figure 24.4 also indicates how net capital inflows can benefit an economy. A country that attracts significant amounts of foreign capital flows will have a larger pool of total saving and hence both a lower real interest rate and a higher rate of investment in new capital than it otherwise would. The United States and Canada both benefited from large inflows of capital in the early stages of their economic development, as do many developing countries today. Because capital inflows tend to react very sensitively to risk, an implication is that countries that are politically stable and safeguard the rights of foreign investors will attract more foreign capital and thus grow more quickly than countries without those characteristics.

Although capital inflows are generally beneficial to the countries that receive them, they are not costless. Countries that finance domestic capital formation primarily by capital inflows face the prospect of paying interest and dividends to the foreign financial investors from whom they have borrowed. A number of developing countries have experienced *debt crises,* arising because the domestic investments they made with foreign funds turned out poorly, leaving them insufficient income to pay what they owed their foreign creditors. An advantage to financing domestic capital formation primarily with domestic saving is that the returns from the country's capital investments accrue to domestic savers rather than flowing abroad.

Why did the Argentine economy collapse in 2001–2002?

Argentina, with a wealth of natural resources and an educated population, has long been among the most prosperous economies of Latin America. However, in 2001–2002 the country faced a severe economic crisis. Political dissatisfaction reached so high a level that Argentines rioted in the streets of Buenos Aires, and the country had five different presidents within a span of a few months. Why did the Argentine economy collapse in 2001–2002?

Because Argentina is a developing economy with extensive human and natural resources, investments in new capital goods in that country could potentially be very profitable. However, Argentina's national saving rate is among the lowest in Latin America. To make up the difference between the demand for investment (new capital goods) and the domestic supply of saving, Argentina borrowed extensively from abroad, that is, capital inflows to Argentina were large. These capital inflows helped Argentina to invest more and grow more quickly than it otherwise might have (see Figure 24.4, which shows how capital inflows KI augment the available pool of domestic saving S). However, the rapid capital inflows also implied that, over time, Argentina was building up a large debt to foreigners. Foreigners remained willing to lend to Argentina so long as they expected to earn good returns on their loans.

ECONOMIC
NATURALIST
24.3

Unfortunately, in the late 1990s the situation in Argentina took a turn for the worse. In 1998, following a three-year growth boom, the Argentine economy slowed considerably. Moreover, partly as a result of the slowing economy, which reduced tax receipts and raised the public's demands for government services, the government budgetary situation worsened. The central government of Argentina, which had a budget surplus of over 2 percent of GDP in 1993, began to run large deficits. Free-spending provincial and city governments ran deficits of their own, which exacerbated the nation's fiscal problem.

The increased government budget deficits reduced Argentina's national saving, increasing the need to borrow abroad. But at the same time that Argentina's borrowing needs were rising, foreign lenders began to worry that the country—with its slowing economy, high debt burden, and worsening government budget deficits—was a much riskier location for investment than they had thought. Increased risk reduces the supply of capital inflows (see Figure 24.3) and thus also reduces the total pool of saving available; the result is a higher domestic interest rate, lower domestic investment, and hence a weakening economy. As the economy continued to weaken, and government budgets worsened, foreign lenders became so pessimistic about Argentina that they would lend only at very high interest rates, if at all. Ultimately Argentina was unable to repay even the interest on its foreign debt and was forced to default (refuse to pay). At that point the country became essentially unable to borrow abroad at any price. Investment in Argentina collapsed and real interest rates soared. As of this writing, Argentina is negotiating with public agencies, such as the International Monetary Fund, to try to obtain loans to help rebuild its economy.

THE SAVING RATE AND THE TRADE DEFICIT

We have seen that a country's exports and imports do not necessarily balance in each period. Indeed, the United States has run a trade deficit, with its imports exceeding exports, for many years. What causes trade deficits? Stories in the media sometimes claim that trade deficits occur because a country produces inferior goods that no one wants to buy or because other countries impose unfair trade restrictions on imports. Despite the popularity of these explanations, however, there is little support for them in either economic theory or evidence. For example, the United States has a large trade deficit with China, but no one would claim U.S. goods are generally inferior to Chinese goods. And many developing countries have significant trade deficits even though they, rather than their trading partners, tend to impose the more stringent restrictions on trade.

Economists argue that, rather than the quality of a country's exports or the existence of unfair trade restrictions, *a low rate of national saving is the primary cause of trade deficits.*

To see the link between national saving and the trade deficit, recall the identity $Y = C + I + G + NX$. Subtracting $C + I + G$ from both sides of this equation and rearranging, we get $Y - C - G - I = NX$. Finally, recognizing that national saving S equals $Y - C - G$, we can rewrite the relationship as

$$S - I = NX. \qquad (24.3)$$

Equation 24.3 can also be derived directly from Equations 24.1 and 24.2. According to Equation 24.3, if we hold domestic investment (I) constant, a high rate of national saving S implies a high level of net exports NX, while a low level of national saving implies a low level of net exports. Furthermore, if a country's national saving is less than its investment, or $S < I$, then Equation 24.3 implies that net exports NX will be negative. That is, the country will have a trade deficit. The conclusion from Equation 24.3 is that, holding domestic investment constant, low national saving tends to be associated with a trade deficit ($NX < 0$), and high national saving is associated with a trade surplus ($NX > 0$).

Why does a low rate of national saving tend to be associated with a trade deficit? A country with a low national saving rate is one in which households and the government have high spending rates, relative to domestic income and production. Since part of the spending of households and the government is devoted to imported goods, we would expect a low-saving, high-spending economy to have a high volume of imports. Furthermore, a low-saving economy consumes a large proportion of its domestic production, reducing the quantity of goods and services available for export. With high imports and low exports, a low-saving economy will experience a trade deficit.

A country with a trade deficit must also be receiving capital inflows, as we have seen. (Equation 24.1 tells us that if a trade deficit exists so that $NX < 0$, then it must be true that $KI > 0$—net capital inflows are positive.) Is a low national saving rate also consistent with the existence of net capital inflows? The answer is yes. A country with a low national saving rate will not have sufficient savings of its own to finance domestic investment. Thus there likely will be many good investment opportunities in the country available to foreign savers, leading to capital inflows. Equivalently, a shortage of domestic saving will tend to drive up the domestic real interest rate, which attracts capital flows from abroad.

We conclude that a low rate of national saving tends to create a trade deficit, as well as to promote the capital inflows that must accompany a trade deficit. Economic Naturalist 24.4 illustrates this effect for the case of the United States.

Why is the U.S. trade deficit so large?

As shown by Figure 24.1, U.S. trade was more or less in balance until the mid-1970s. Since the late 1970s, however, the United States has run large trade deficits, particularly in the mid-1980s and since the latter part of the 1990s. Indeed, in 2001 the trade deficit equaled 3.5 percent of U.S. GDP. Why is the U.S. trade deficit so large?

Figure 24.5 shows national saving, investment, and the trade balance for the United States from 1960 to 2001 (all measured relative to GDP). Note that the trade balance has been negative since the late 1970s, indicating a trade deficit. Note also that trade deficits correspond to periods in which investment exceeds national saving, as required by Equation 24.3.

U.S. national saving and investment were roughly in balance in the 1960s and early 1970s, and hence the U.S. trade balance was close to zero during that period.

ECONOMIC NATURALIST 24.4

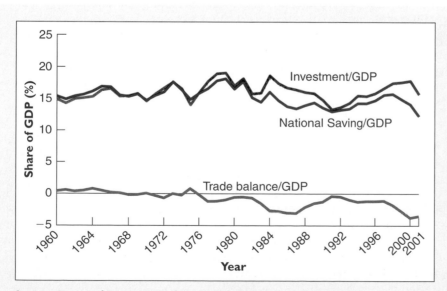

FIGURE 24.5
National Saving, Investment, and the Trade Balance in the United States, 1960–2001.
Since the 1970s U.S. national saving has fallen below domestic investment, implying a significant trade deficit.

SOURCE: Bureau of Economic Analysis (www.bea.gov).

However, U.S. national saving fell sharply during the late 1970s and 1980s. One factor that contributed to the decline in national saving was the large government deficits of the era (see Chapter 22). Because investment did not decline as much as saving, the U.S. trade deficit ballooned in the 1980s, coming under control only when investment fell during the recession of 1990–1991. Saving and investment both recovered during the 1990s, but in the latter part of the 1990s national saving dropped again. This time the federal government was not at fault, since its budget showed a healthy surplus. Rather, the fall in national saving reflected a decline in private saving, the result of a powerful upsurge in consumption spending. Much of the increase in consumption spending was for imported goods and services, which pushed the trade deficit to record levels.

Is the U.S. trade deficit a problem? The trade deficit implies that the United States is relying heavily on foreign savings to finance its domestic capital formation (net capital inflows). These foreign loans must ultimately be repaid with interest. If the foreign savings are well invested and the U.S. economy grows, repayment will not pose a problem. However, if economic growth in the United States slackens, repaying the foreign lenders will impose an economic burden in the future.

"But we're not just talking about buying a car—we're talking about confronting this country's trade deficit with Japan."

RECAP **INTERNATIONAL CAPITAL FLOWS AND THE BALANCE OF TRADE**

■ Purchases or sales of assets across borders are called international capital flows. If a person, firm, or government in (say) the United States borrows from abroad, we say that there is a capital inflow into the United States. In this case, foreign savers are acquiring U.S. assets. If a person, firm, or government in the United States lends to someone abroad, thereby acquiring a foreign asset, we say that there has been a capital outflow from the United States to the foreign country. Net capital inflows to a given country equal capital inflows minus outflows.

■ If a country imports more goods and services than it exports, it must borrow abroad to cover the difference. Likewise, a country that exports more than it imports will lend the difference to foreigners. Thus, as a matter of accounting, the trade balance NX and net capital inflows KI must sum to zero in every period.

- The funds available for domestic investment in new capital goods equal the sum of domestic saving and net capital inflows from abroad. The higher the return and the lower the risk of investing in the domestic country, the greater will be the capital inflows from abroad. Capital inflows benefit an economy by providing more funds for capital investment, but they can become a burden if the returns from investing in new capital goods are insufficient to pay back the foreign lenders.

- An important cause of a trade deficit is a low national saving rate. A country that saves little and spends a lot will tend to import a greater quantity of goods and services than it is able to export. At the same time, the country's low saving rate implies a need for more foreign borrowing to finance domestic investment spending.

To this point in the book we have discussed a variety of issues relating to the long-run performance of the economy, including economic growth, the sources of increasing productivity and improved living standards, the determination of real wages, and the determinants of saving and capital formation. Beginning with the next chapter we will take a more short-run perspective, examining first the causes of recessions and booms in the economy and then turning to policy measures that can be used to affect these fluctuations.

■ SUMMARY ■

- Besides balancing saving and investment in the aggregate, financial markets and institutions play the important role of allocating saving to the most productive investment projects. The financial system improves the allocation of saving in two ways: First, it provides information to savers about which of the many possible uses of their funds are likely to prove must productive, and hence pay the highest return. For example, *financial intermediaries* such as banks develop expertise in evaluating prospective borrowers, making it unnecessary for small savers to do that on their own. Similarly, stock and bond analysts evaluate the business prospects of a company issuing shares of stock or bonds, which determines the price the stock will sell for or the interest rate the company will have to offer on its bond. Second, financial markets help savers share the risks of lending by permitting them to *diversify* their financial investments. Individual savers often hold stocks through *mutual funds,* a type of financial intermediary that reduces risk by holding many different financial assets. By reducing the risk faced by any one saver, financial markets allow risky but potentially very productive projects to be funded.

- Corporations that do not wish to borrow from banks can obtain finance by issuing bonds or stocks. A *bond* is a legal promise to repay a debt, including both the *principal amount* and regular interest payments. The prices of existing bonds decline when interest rates rise. A share of *stock* is a claim to partial ownership of a firm. The price of a stock depends positively on the *dividend* the stock is expected to pay and on the expected future price of the stock and negatively on the rate of return required by financial investors to hold the stock. The required rate of return in turn is the sum of the return on safe assets and the additional return required to compensate financial investors for the riskiness of stocks, called the *risk premium.*

- The *trade balance,* or net exports, is the value of a country's exports less the value of its imports in a particular period. Exports need not equal imports in each period. If exports exceed imports, the difference is called a *trade surplus,* and if imports exceed exports, the difference is called a *trade deficit.* Trade takes place in assets as well as goods and services. Purchases of domestic assets (real or financial) by foreigners are called *capital inflows,* and purchases of foreign assets by domestic savers are called *capital outflows.* Because imports that are not financed by sales of exports must be financed by sales of assets, the trade balance and net capital inflows sum to zero.

- The higher the real interest rate in a country, and the lower the risk of investing there, the higher its capital inflows. The availability of capital inflows expands a country's pool of saving, allowing for more domestic investment and increased growth. A drawback to using capital inflows to finance domestic capital formation is that the returns to capital (interest and dividends) accrue to foreign financial investors rather than domestic residents.

- A low rate of national saving is the primary cause of trade deficits. A low-saving, high-spending country is likely to import more than a high-saving country. It also consumes more of its domestic production, leaving less for export. Finally, a low-saving country is likely to have a high real interest rate, which attracts net capital inflows. Because the sum of the trade balance and capital inflows is zero, a high level of net capital inflows is consistent with a large trade deficit.

▪ KEY TERMS ▪

bond (621)
capital inflows (628)
capital outflows (628)
coupon payments (621)
coupon rate (621)
diversification (626)

dividend (623)
financial intermediaries (619)
international capital flows (628)
mutual fund (626)
principal amount (621)

risk premium (624)
stock (or equity) (623)
trade balance (628)
trade deficit (629)
trade surplus (629)

▪ REVIEW QUESTIONS ▪

1. Give two ways that the financial system helps to improve the allocation of savings. Illustrate with examples.

2. Arjay plans to sell a bond that matures in one year and has a principal value of $1,000. Can he expect to receive $1,000 in the bond market for the bond? Explain.

3. Suppose you are much less concerned about risk than the typical person. Are stocks a good financial investment for you? Why or why not?

4. Stock prices surge but the prices of government bonds remain stable. What can you infer from the behavior of bond prices about the possible causes of the increase in stock values?

5. From the point of view of a given country, say, Spain, give an example of a capital inflow and a capital outflow.

6. How are capital inflows or outflows related to domestic investment in new capital goods?

7. Explain with examples why, in any period, a country's net capital inflows equal its trade deficit.

8. How would increased political instability in a country likely affect capital inflows, the domestic real interest rate, and investment in new capital goods? Show graphically.

▪ PROBLEMS ▪

1. Simon purchases a bond, newly issued by the Amalgamated Corporation, for $1,000. The bond pays $60 to its holder at the end of the first and second years and pays $1,060 upon its maturity at the end of the third year.
   a. What are the principal amount, the term, the coupon rate, and the coupon payment for Simon's bond?
   b. After receiving the second coupon payment (at the end of the second year), Simon decides to sell his bond in the bond market. What price can he expect for his bond if the one-year interest rate at that time is 3 percent? 8 percent? 10 percent?
   c. Can you think of a reason that the price of Simon's bond after two years might fall below $1,000, even though the market interest rate equals the coupon rate?

2. Shares in Brothers Grimm, Inc., manufacturers of gingerbread houses, are expected to pay a dividend of $5.00 in one year and to sell for $100 per share at that time. How much should you be willing to pay today per share of Grimm:
   a. If the safe rate of interest is 5 percent and you believe that investing in Grimm carries no risk?
   b. If the safe rate of interest is 10 percent and you believe that investing in Grimm carries no risk?
   c. If the safe rate of interest is 5 percent but your risk premium is 3 percent?
   d. Repeat parts a to c, assuming that Grimm is not expected to pay a dividend but the expected price is unchanged.

3. Your financial investments consist of U.S. government bonds maturing in ten years and shares in a start-up company doing research in pharmaceuticals. How would you expect each of the following news items to affect the value of your assets? Explain.
   a. Interest rates on newly issued government bonds rise.

b. Inflation is forecasted to be much lower than previously expected (*Hint:* Recall the Fisher effect from Chapter 5.) Assume for simplicity that this information does *not* affect your forecast of the dollar value of the pharmaceutical company's future dividends and stock price.

In parts c to f, interest rates on newly issued government bonds are assumed to remain unchanged.

c. Large swings in the stock market increase financial investors' concerns about market risk.

d. The start-up company whose stock you own announces the development of a valuable new drug. However, the drug will not come to market for at least five years.

e. The pharmaceutical company announces that it will not pay a dividend next year.

f. The federal government announces a system of price controls on prescription drugs.

4. You have $1,000 to invest and are considering buying some combination of the shares of two companies, DonkeyInc and ElephantInc. Shares of DonkeyInc will pay a 10 percent return if the Democrats are elected, an event you believe to have a 40 percent probability; otherwise the shares pay a zero return. Shares of ElephantInc will pay 8 percent if the Republicans are elected (a 60 percent probability), zero otherwise. Either the Democrats or the Republicans will be elected.

a. If your only concern is maximizing your average expected return, with no regard for risk, how should you invest your $1,000?

b. What is your expected return if you invest $500 in each stock? (*Hint:* Consider what your return will be if the Democrats win and if the Republicans win, then weight each outcome by the probability that event occurs.)

c. The strategy of investing $500 in each stock does *not* give the highest possible average expected return. Why might you choose it anyway?

d. Devise an investment strategy that guarantees at least a 4.4 percent return, no matter which party wins.

e. Devise an investment strategy that is riskless, that is, one in which the return on your $1,000 does not depend at all on which party wins.

5. From the web site of the Bureau of Economic Analysis, www.bea.gov, find data on the components of nominal GDP for the most recent quarter available and for the previous two complete years. Find net exports, national saving (which can be derived from the relationship $S = Y - C - G$), and gross private domestic investment for the period, and verify that they satisfy the relationship $S - I = NX$. How has the U.S. trade balance changed over the past two years as a percentage of GDP? Are the changes attributable to changes in the national saving rate, the rate of investment, or both?

6. How do each of the following transactions affect (1) the trade surplus or deficit and (2) capital inflows or outflows for the United States? Show that in each case the identity that the trade balance plus net capital inflows equals zero applies.

a. A U.S. exporter sells software to Israel. She uses the Israeli shekels received to buy stock in an Israeli company.

b. A Mexican firm uses proceeds from its sale of oil to the United States to buy U.S. government debt.

c. A Mexican firm uses proceeds from its sale of oil to the United States to buy oil drilling equipment from a U.S. firm.

d. A Mexican firm receives U.S. dollars from selling oil to the United States. A French firm accepts the dollars as payment for drilling equipment. The French firm uses the dollars to buy U.S. government debt.

e. A British financial investor writes a check on his bank account in New York to purchase shares of General Motors stock (GM is a U.S. company).

7. Use a diagram like Figure 24.4 (solid lines only) to show the effects of each of the following on the real interest rate and capital investment of a country that is a net borrower from abroad.

a. Investment opportunities in the country improve owing to new technologies.

b. The government budget deficit rises.

c. Domestic citizens decide to save more.

d. Foreign investors believe that the riskiness of lending to the country has increased.

8. A country's domestic supply of saving, domestic demand for saving for purposes of capital formation, and supply of net capital inflows are given by the following equations:

$$S = 1,500 + 2,000r,$$
$$I = 2,000 - 4,000r,$$
$$KI = -100 + 6,000r.$$

a. Assuming that the market for saving and investment is in equilibrium, find national saving, capital inflows, domestic investment, and the real interest rate.
b. Repeat part a, assuming that desired national saving declines by 120 at each value of the real interest rate. What effect does a reduction in domestic saving have on capital inflows?
c. Concern about the economy's macroeconomic policies causes capital inflows to fall sharply so that now $KI = -700 + 6,000r$. Repeat part a. What does a reduction in capital inflows do to domestic investment and the real interest rate?

■ ANSWERS TO IN-CHAPTER EXERCISES ■

24.1 Since bond prices fell, interest rates must have risen. To find the interest rate, note that bond investors are willing to pay only 96 today for a bond that will pay back 107 (a coupon payment of 7 plus the principal amount of 100) in one year. To find the one-year return, divide 107 by 96 to get 1.115. Thus the interest rate must have risen to 11.5 percent.

24.2 The share of stock will be worth $81.00 in one year—the sum of its expected future price and the expected dividend. At an interest rate of 4 percent, its value today is $81.00/1.04 = $77.88. At an interest rate of 8 percent, the stock's current value is $81.00/1.08 = $75.00. Recall from Example 24.2 that when the interest rate is 6 percent, the value of a share of FortuneCookie.com is $76.42. Since higher interest rates imply lower stock values, news that interest rates are about to rise should cause the stock market to fall.

24.3 The purchase of the Japanese bond is a capital outflow for the United States, or $KI = -\$20,000$. The Japanese government now holds $20,000. What will it do with these funds? There are basically three possibilities. First, it might use the funds to purchase U.S. goods and services (military equipment, for example). In that case the U.S. trade balance equals +$20,000, and the sum of the trade balance and capital inflows is zero. Second, the Japanese government might acquire U.S. assets, for example, deposits in U.S. banks. In that case a capital inflow to the United States of $20,000 offsets the original capital outflow. Both the trade balance and net capital outflows individually are zero, and so their sum is zero.

Finally, the Japanese government might use the $20,000 to purchase non-U.S. goods, services, or assets—oil from Saudi Arabia, for example. But then the non-U.S. recipient of the $20,000 is holding the funds, and it has the same options that the Japanese government did. Eventually, the funds will be used to purchase U.S. goods, services, or assets, satisfying Equation 24.1. Indeed, even if the recipient holds onto the funds (in cash, or as a U.S. bank deposit), they would still count as a capital inflow to the United States, as U.S. dollars or accounts in a U.S. bank are U.S. assets acquired by foreigners.

24.4 An increase in the real interest rate abroad increases the relative attractiveness of foreign financial investments to both foreign and domestic savers. Net capital inflows to the home country will fall at each level of the domestic real interest rate. The supply curve of net capital inflows shifts left, as in Figure 24.3.

PART

8

THE ECONOMY IN THE SHORT RUN

■

A sign in Redwood City, California, boasts that the Bay Area town has the world's best climate. Redwood City's mean annual temperature and rainfall are similar to that of many other U.S. cities, so on what basis do Redwood City's boosters make their claim? The weather in Redwood City is attractive to many people because it varies so little over the year, being almost equally comfortable and temperate in winter and in summer. A city with the same average yearly temperature as Redwood City, but where the winters are freezing and the summers unbearably hot, would not be nearly so pleasant a place to live.

An analogous idea applies to the performance of the economy. As we saw, over a period of decades or more, the economy's average rate of growth is the crucial determinant of average living standards. But short-term fluctuations of the economy's growth rate around its long-run average matter for economic welfare as well. In particular, periods of slow or negative economic growth, known as *recessions,* may create significant economic hardship and dissatisfaction. In Part 8 we will explore the causes of short-term fluctuations in key economic variables, including output, unemployment, and inflation, and we will discuss the options available to government policymakers for stabilizing the economy.

Chapter 25 provides some necessary background for our study of short-term fluctuations by describing their key characteristics and reviewing the historical record of fluctuations in the U.S. economy. In Chapters 26 through 28 we develop a framework for the analysis of short-term fluctuations and the alternative policy responses. Chapter 26 shows how fluctuations in spending, or *aggregate demand,* may lead to short-run fluctuations in output and employment. That chapter also explains how changes in fiscal policy—policies relating to government spending and taxation—can be used to stabilize spending and output. Chapter 27 focuses on monetary policy, a second tool for stabilizing output and employment. Finally, Chapter 28 incorporates inflation into the analysis, discussing both the sources of inflation and the policies that can be used to control it.

SHORT-TERM ECONOMIC FLUCTUATIONS: AN INTRODUCTION

■

I n early 1991, following the defeat of Iraq in the Gulf War by the United States and its allies, polls showed that 90 percent of the American public approved of the job George H. W. Bush was doing as president. The Gulf War victory followed a number of other popular developments in the foreign policy sphere, including the ouster of the corrupt leader General Manuel Noriega from Panama in December 1989; improved relations with China; apparent progress in Middle East peace talks; and the end of apartheid in South Africa. The collapse of the Soviet Union in December 1991—a stunning event that signaled the end of the Cold War—also occurred during Bush's term. Yet despite these political pluses, in the months following the Gulf War Bush's sky-high approval rating declined sharply. According to one poll, by the time of the Republican national convention in the summer of 1992, only 29 percent of the public approved of Bush's performance. Although the president's ratings improved during the campaign, Bush and his running mate, Dan Quayle, lost the 1992 general election to Bill Clinton and Al Gore, receiving only 39 million of the 104 million votes cast. A third-party candidate, Ross Perot, received nearly 20 million votes.

What caused this turnaround in (the first) President Bush's political fortunes? Despite his high marks from voters in foreign policy, the president's domestic economic policies were widely viewed as ineffective. Bush received much criticism for breaking his campaign pledge not to raise taxes. More important, the economy weakened significantly in 1990–1991, then recovered only slowly. Although inflation was low, by mid-1992 unemployment had reached 7.8 percent of the labor force—2.5 percentage points higher than in the first year of Bush's term, and the highest level since 1984. A sign in Democratic candidate Bill Clinton's campaign headquarters summarized Clinton's strategy for winning the White House: "It's the economy, stupid." Clinton realized the importance of the nation's economic problems and pounded away at the Republican administration's inability to pull the country out of the doldrums. Clinton's focus on the economy was the key to his election.

Clinton's ability to parlay criticism of economic conditions into electoral success is not unusual in U.S. political history. Weakness in the economy played a decisive role in helping Franklin D. Roosevelt to beat Herbert Hoover in 1932, John F. Kennedy to best Richard Nixon in 1960, and Ronald Reagan to defeat Jimmy Carter in 1980. (And in an echo of his father's experience, President George W. Bush found the political popularity he enjoyed after ousting the Taliban from Afghanistan in 2001 eroded by an economic downturn and a slow subsequent recovery.) On the other hand, strong economic conditions have often helped incumbent presidents (or the incumbent's party) to retain office, including Nixon in 1972, Reagan in 1984, and Clinton in 1996. Indeed, a number of empirical studies have suggested that economic performance in the year preceding the election is among the most important determinants of whether an incumbent president is likely to win reelection.

In Part 7 we discussed the factors that determine long-run economic growth. Over the broad sweep of history, those factors determine the economic success of a society. Indeed, over a span of 30, 50, or 100 years, relatively small differences in the rate of economic growth can have an enormous effect on the average person's standard of living. But even though the economic "climate" (long-run economic conditions) is the ultimate determinant of living standards, changes in the economic "weather" (short-run fluctuations in economic conditions) are also important. A good long-run growth record is not much consolation to a worker who has lost her job due to a recession. The bearing that short-term macroeconomic performance has on election results is one indicator of the importance the average person attaches to it.

In this part of the book we study short-term fluctuations in economic activity, commonly known as *recessions* and *expansions*. We will start, in this chapter, with some background on the history and characteristics of these economic ups and downs. However, the main focus of this part is the *causes* of short-term fluctuations, as well as the available *policy responses*. Because the analysis of short-term economic fluctuations can become complex and even controversial, we will proceed in a step-by-step fashion. In Chapter 26 we will introduce a basic—and oversimplified—model of booms and recessions, which we will refer to as the *basic Keynesian model* in honor of its principal originator, the British economist John Maynard Keynes. The basic Keynesian model focuses on the components of aggregate spending, such as consumption spending by households and investment spending by firms, and the effects of changes in spending on total real GDP.

Though this model is a useful starting point, it does not address some key issues. First, and perhaps most important, the basic Keynesian model has little to say about the determinants of inflation. Second, because it focuses on the very short run, this model does not give adequate attention to the economy's own natural tendency to eliminate deviations from full employment over the longer run. Because the basic Keynesian model does not take into account the "self-correcting" tendencies of the economy, it tends to overstate the need for government intervention to offset fluctuations. In Chapters 27 and 28 we will add new features to the model to make it more realistic. By the end of this part, we will have discussed the major causes of short-term economic fluctuations, as well as the options policymakers have in responding to them.

Herbert Hoover
© Bettmann/Corbis

Jimmy Carter
© Bettmann/Corbis

George Bush
© Wally McNamee/Corbis

Victims of recession.

RECESSIONS AND EXPANSIONS

As background to the study of short-term economic fluctuations, let's review the historical record of the fluctuations in the U. S. economy. Figure 25.1 shows the path of real GDP in the United States since 1920. (Figure 17.1, page 430, provides an even longer data series.) As you can see, the growth path of real GDP is not always smooth; the bumps and wiggles correspond to short periods of faster or slower growth.

A period in which the economy is growing at a rate significantly below normal is called a **recession** or a *contraction*. An extremely severe or protracted recession is called a **depression**. You should be able to pick out the Great Depression in Figure 25.1, particularly the sharp initial decline between 1929 and 1933. But you can also see that the U.S. economy was volatile in the mid-1970s and the early 1980s, with serious recessions in 1973–1975 and 1981–1982. A moderate recession (but not moderate enough for the first President Bush) occurred in 1990–1991. The most recent recession began in March 2001, exactly 10 years after the end of the 1990–1991 recession, which was declared over as of March 1991. This 10-year period without a recession was the longest such period in U.S. history.

recession (or contraction) a period in which the economy is growing at a rate significantly below normal

depression a particularly severe or protracted recession

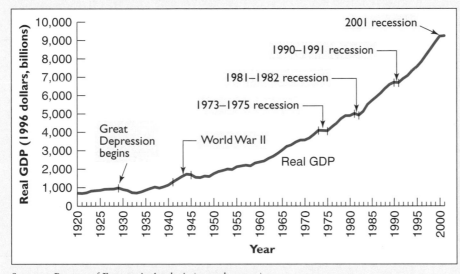

FIGURE 25.1

Fluctuations in U.S. Real GDP, 1920–2001.
Real GDP does not grow smoothly but has speedups (expansions or booms) and slowdowns (recessions or depressions). Note the contraction from 1929 to 1933 (the first phase of the Great Depression), the boom in 1941–1945 (World War II), and the recessions of 1973–1975, 1981–1982, 1990–1991, and 2001.

SOURCE: Bureau of Economic Analysis (www.bea.gov).

A more informal definition of a recession, often cited by reporters, is a period during which real GDP falls for at least two consecutive quarters. This definition is not a bad rule of thumb, as real GDP usually does fall during recessions. However, many economists would argue that periods in which real GDP growth is well below normal, though not actually negative, should be counted as recessions. Another problem with relying on GDP figures for dating recessions is that GDP data can be substantially revised, sometimes years after the fact. In practice, when trying to determine whether a recession is in progress, economists look at a variety of economic data, not just GDP.

Table 25.1 lists the beginning and ending dates of U.S. recessions since 1929, as well as the *duration* (length, in months) of each. The table also gives the highest unemployment rate recorded during each recession and the percentage change in real GDP. (Ignore the last column of the table for now.) The beginning of a recession is called the **peak,** because it represents the high point of economic activity prior to a downturn. The end of a recession, which marks the low point of economic activity prior to a recovery, is called the **trough.** The dates of peaks and troughs reported in Table 25.1 were determined by the National Bureau of Economic Research (NBER), a nonprofit organization of economists that has been a major source of research on short-term economic fluctuations since its founding

peak the beginning of a recession, the high point of economic activity prior to a downturn

trough the end of a recession, the low point of economic activity prior to a recovery in 1920 (see Economic Naturalist 25.1). The NBER is not a government agency, but it is usually treated by the news media and the government as the "official" arbiter of the dates of peaks and troughs.

"Please stand by for a series of tones. The first indicates the official end of the recession, the second indicates prosperity, and the third the return of the recession."

TABLE 25.1
U.S. Recessions since 1929

Peak date (beginning)	Trough date (end)	Duration (months)	Highest unemployment rate (%)	Change in real GDP (%)	Duration of subsequent expansion (months)
Aug. 1929	Mar. 1933	43	24.9	−28.8	50
May 1937	June 1938	13	19.0	−5.5	80
Feb. 1945	Oct. 1945	8	3.9	−8.5	37
Nov. 1948	Oct. 1949	11	5.9	−1.4	45
July 1953	May 1954	10	5.5	−1.2	39
Aug. 1957	Apr. 1958	8	6.8	−1.7	24
Apr. 1960	Feb. 1961	10	6.7	2.3	106
Dec. 1969	Nov. 1970	11	5.9	0.1	36
Nov. 1973	Mar. 1975	16	8.5	−1.1	58
Jan. 1980	July 1980	6	7.6	−0.3	12
July 1981	Nov. 1982	16	9.7	−2.1	92
July 1990	Mar. 1991	8	7.5	−0.9	120
Mar. 2001	Dec. 2001*	9*	6.0*	0.2*	

*Unofficial, based on authors' estimate at time of publication.

SOURCES: Peak and trough dates, National Bureau of Economic Research; unemployment and real GDP, *Historical Statistics of the United States* and *Economic Report of the President*.

NOTES: Unemployment rate is the annual rate. Peak and trough dates from the National Bureau of Economic Research. Unemployment and real GDP data from *Historical Statistics of the United States* and the *Economic Report of the President*. Dates and figures with asterisks are unofficial and represent the authors' best guesses as of the time of publication. Unemployment rate is the annual rate for the trough year or the subsequent year, whichever is higher. Change in annual real GDP is measured from the peak year to the trough year, except that the entry for the 1945 recession is the 1945–1946 change in real GDP, the entry for the 1980 recession is the 1979–1980 change, and the estimated entry for 2001 is the 2000–2001 change.

Table 25.1 shows that since 1929, by far the longest and most severe recession in the United States was the 43-month economic collapse that began in August 1929 and lasted until March 1933, initiating what became known as the Great Depression. Between 1933 and 1937 the economy grew fairly rapidly, so technically the period was not a recession, although unemployment remained very high at close to 20 percent of the workforce. In 1937–1938 the nation was hit by another significant recession. Full economic recovery from the Depression did not come until U.S. entry into World War II at the end of 1941. The economy boomed from 1941 to 1945 (see Figure 25.1), reflecting the enormous wartime production of military equipment and supplies.

In sharp contrast to 1930s, U.S. recessions since World War II have generally been short—between 6 and 16 months, from peak to trough. As Table 25.1 shows, the two most severe postwar recessions, 1973–1975 and 1981–1982, lasted just 16 months. And, though unemployment rates during those two recessions were quite high by today's standards, they were low compared to the Great Depression. Since 1982 the U.S. economy has experienced only two relatively mild recessions, in 1990–1991 and in 2001. Although recent recessions have not been among the worst that Americans have experienced, they warn us to guard against overconfidence. Prosperity and economic stability can never be guaranteed.

The opposite of a recession is an **expansion**—a period in which the economy is growing at a rate that is significantly *above* normal. A particularly strong and protracted expansion is called a **boom**. In the United States, strong expansions occurred during 1933–1937, 1961–1969, 1982–1990, and 1991–2001, with exceptionally strong growth during 1995–2000 (see Figure 25.1). On average, expansions have been much longer than recessions. The final column of Table 25.1 shows the duration, in months, of U.S. expansions since 1929. As you can see in the table, the 1961–1969 expansion lasted 106 months; the 1982–1990 expansion, 92 months. The longest expansion of all began in March 1991, at the trough of the 1990–1991 recession. This expansion lasted 120 months, a full 10 years, until a new recession began in March 2001.

expansion a period in which the economy is growing at a rate significantly above normal

boom a particularly strong and protracted expansion

Calling the 2001 recession

The Business Cycle Dating Committee of the National Bureau of Economic Research determined that a recession, the first in 10 years, began in March 2001. What led the committee to choose that date?

As of the beginning of 2001, there had been no "official" recession in the United States since the one that began in July 1990 and ended in March 1991. As mentioned above, this 10-year period without a recession was the longest expansion in U.S. history. However, the economy weakened considerably during the latter part of 2000 and in the spring and summer of 2001. A further blow was the terrorist attacks of September 11, 2001, which caused the loss of many jobs both in the affected areas and (because people became afraid to travel) in industries such as airlines and hotels. Because of the increased likelihood that a recession had begun, the six economists who form the Business Cycle Dating Committee—the group within the National Bureau of Economic Research that actually determines recession dates—found themselves called upon for the first time in a decade.

The determination of whether and when a recession has begun involves intensive statistical analysis, mixed in with a significant amount of human judgment. The Business Cycle Dating Committee typically relies heavily on a small set of statistical indicators that measure the overall strength of the economy. The committee prefers indicators that are available monthly, because they are available quickly and may provide relatively precise information about the timing of peaks and troughs. Four of the most important indicators used by the committee are

ECONOMIC NATURALIST 25.1

- Industrial production, which measures the output of factories and mines.

- Total sales in manufacturing, wholesale trade, and retail trade.

- Nonfarm employment (the number of people at work outside of agriculture).

- Real after-tax income received by households, excluding transfers like Social Security payments.

Each of these indicators measures a different aspect of the economy. Because their movements tend to coincide with the overall movements in the economy, they are called *coincident indicators*.

Normally the coincident indicators move more or less together; during the 2001 recession they did not. Industrial production and sales in the manufacturing sector began to decline as early as September 2000. This early weakness in manufacturing reflected slow sales of information technology (computers, software, communications devices, and the like) following the collapse of the "dot-com bubble" in the stock market during 2000. (The values of high-tech stocks fell by two-thirds or more during the year.) However, the weakness in manufacturing was not immediately reflected in the economy as a whole, as both employment and personal income grew strongly in the fall of 2000. Employment did not start to decline until around March 2001, and real personal income continued to grow into the fall of 2001.

The failure of the coincident indicators to move closely together made the committee's job difficult. The committee ultimately chose the date of the peak, or beginning of the recession, to be March 2001, the month in which nonfarm employment began to decline. A rationale for their choice is that recessions are supposed to reflect declines in the entire economy, not just a few specific sectors. It might be argued that the decline in nonfarm employment in March 2001 (which counts people at work in the entire economy, outside of agriculture) was the first clear indication that the slowdown which had begun in the high-tech sector had spread to the broader economy.

EXERCISE 25.1

Update Table 25.1 using the National Bureau of Economic Research website (go to http://www.nber.org and click on *business cycle dates*). According to the NBER, is the U.S. economy currently in recession or expansion? How much time has elapsed since the last peak or trough? Explore the NBER website to find additional useful information about current conditions in the U.S. economy.

SOME FACTS ABOUT SHORT-TERM ECONOMIC FLUCTUATIONS

Although Figure 25.1 and Table 25.1 show only twentieth-century data, periods of expansion and recession have been a feature of industrial economies since at least the late eighteenth century. Karl Marx and Friedrich Engels referred to these fluctuations, which they called "commercial crises," in their Communist Manifesto of 1848. In the United States, economists have been studying short-term fluctuations for at least a century. The traditional term for these fluctuations is *business cycles,* and they are still often referred to as *cyclical fluctuations.* Neither term is accurate though; as Figure 25.1 shows, economic fluctuations are not "cyclical" at all in the sense that they recur at predictable intervals, but instead are *irregular in their length and severity.* This irregularity makes the dates of peaks and troughs extremely hard to predict, despite the fact that professional forecasters have devoted a great deal of effort and brainpower to the task.

Expansions and recessions usually are not limited to a few industries or regions but, as noted in Economic Naturalist 25.1, are *felt throughout the economy.* Indeed, the largest fluctuations may have a *global impact.* For instance, the Great Depression of the 1930s affected nearly all the world's economies, and the 1973–1975 and 1981–1982 recessions were also widely felt outside the United States. When

Recessions are very difficult to forecast.

East Asia suffered a major slowdown in the late 1990s, the effects of that slowdown spilled over into many other regions (although not so much the United States).

Even a relatively moderate recession, like the one that occurred in 2001, can have global effects. Figure 25.2, which shows growth rates of real GDP over the period 1999–2002 for Canada, Germany, Japan, the United Kingdom, and the United States, illustrates this point. You can see that—except for Japan, which has performed poorly since the early 1990s—all the countries experienced relatively strong growth in 1999 and 2000. The 2001 recession lowered growth rates in all of the countries, with some recovery apparent in early 2002.

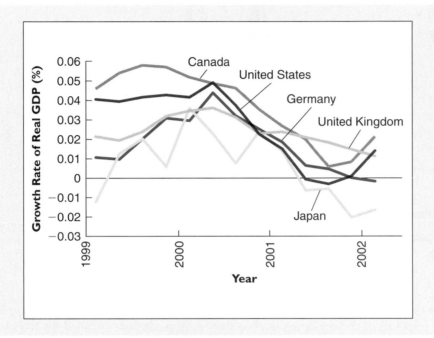

FIGURE 25.2
Real GDP Growth in Five Major Countries, 1999–2002.
Quarterly growth rates (measured as the change in real GDP over the past four quarters) for five major industrialized countries show that all the countries except Japan enjoyed rapid GDP growth in 1999 and 2000. (Japan has been growing slowly for more than a decade.) The 2001 recession was reflected in falling growth rates in all of the major countries, with some recovery apparent in 2002.

Unemployment is a key indicator of short-term economic fluctuations. The unemployment rate typically rises sharply during recessions and recovers (although more slowly) during expansions. Figure 18.3 on page 468 shows the U.S. unemployment rate since 1960. You should be able to identify the recessions that began in 1960, 1969, 1973, 1981, 1990, and 2001 by noting the sharp peaks in the unemployment rate in those years. Recall from Chapter 21 that the part of unemployment that is associated with recessions is called *cyclical unemployment*. Beyond this increase in unemployment, labor market conditions generally worsen during recessions. For example, during recessions real wages grow more slowly, workers are less likely to receive promotions or bonuses, and new entrants to the labor force (such as college graduates) have a much tougher time finding attractive jobs.

Generally, industries that produce *durable goods*, such as cars, houses, and capital equipment, are more affected than others by recessions and booms. In contrast, industries that provide *services* and *nondurable goods* like food are much less sensitive to short-term fluctuations. Thus an automobile worker or a construction worker is far more likely to lose his or her job in a recession than is a barber or a baker.

Like unemployment, *inflation* follows a typical pattern in recessions and expansions, though it is not so sharply defined. Figure 25.3 shows the U.S. inflation rate since 1960; in the figure, periods of recession are indicated by shaded vertical bars. As you can see, recessions tend to be followed soon after by a decline in the rate of inflation. For example, the recession of 1981–1982 was followed by a sharp reduction in inflation. Furthermore, many—though not all—postwar recessions have been preceded by increases in inflation, as Figure 25.3 shows. The behavior of inflation during expansions and recessions will be discussed more fully in Chapter 28.

Unemployment among construction workers rises substantially during recessions.

FIGURE 25.3
U.S. Inflation, 1960–2001.
U.S. inflation since 1960 is measured by the change in the CPI, and periods of recession are indicated by the shaded vertical bars. Note that inflation declined following the recessions of 1960–1961, 1969–1970, 1973–1975, 1981–1982, and 1990–1991 and rose prior to many of those recessions.

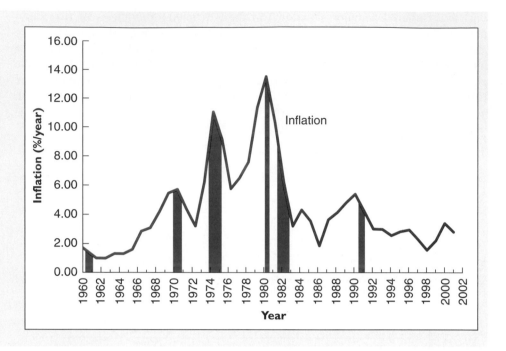

RECAP   **RECESSIONS, BOOMS, AND THEIR CHARACTERISTICS**

■ A recession is a period in which output is growing more slowly than normal. An expansion, or boom, is a period in which output is growing more quickly than normal.

■ The beginning of a recession is called the peak, and its end (which corresponds to the beginning of the subsequent expansion) is called the trough.

■ The sharpest recession in the history of the United States was the initial phase of the Great Depression in 1929–1933. Severe recessions also occurred in 1973–1975 and 1981–1982. Two relatively mild recessions occurred in 1990–1991 and 2001.

■ Short-term economic fluctuations (recessions and expansions) are irregular in length and severity, and thus are difficult to predict.

■ Expansions and recessions have widespread (and sometimes global) impacts, affecting most regions and industries.

■ Unemployment rises sharply during a recession and falls, usually more slowly, during an expansion.

■ Durable goods industries are more affected by expansions and recessions than other industries. Services and nondurable goods industries are less sensitive to ups and downs in the economy.

■ Recessions tend to be followed by a decline in inflation and are often preceded by an increase in inflation.

OUTPUT GAPS AND CYCLICAL UNEMPLOYMENT

If policymakers are to respond appropriately to recessions and expansions, and economists are to study them, knowing whether a particular economic fluctuation is "big" or "small" is essential. Intuitively, a "big" recession or expansion is one in which output and the unemployment rate deviate significantly from their normal or trend levels. In this section we will attempt to be more precise about this idea by introducing the concept of the *output gap*, which measures how far output is from its normal level at a particular time. We will also revisit the idea of *cyclical unemployment,* or the deviation of unemployment from its normal level. Finally, we will examine how these two concepts are related.

POTENTIAL OUTPUT AND THE OUTPUT GAP

The concept of potential output is a useful starting point for thinking about the measurement of expansions and recessions. **Potential output,** also called *potential GDP* or *full-employment output,* is the amount of output (real GDP) that an economy can produce when using its resources, such as capital and labor, at normal rates.[1] Potential output is not a fixed number but grows over time, reflecting increases in both the amounts of available capital and labor and their productivity. We discussed the sources of growth in potential output (the economy's productive capacity) in Chapter 20. We will use the symbol Y^* to signify the economy's potential output at a given point in time.

Why does a nation's output sometimes grow quickly and sometimes slowly, as shown for the United States in Figure 25.1? Logically, there are two possibilities: First, changes in the rate of output growth may reflect *changes in the rate at which the country's potential output is increasing.* For example, unfavorable weather conditions, such as a severe drought, would reduce the rate of potential output growth in an agricultural economy, and a decline in the rate of technological innovation might reduce the rate of potential output growth in an industrial economy. Under the assumption that the country is using its resources at normal rates, so that actual output equals potential output, a significant slowdown in potential output growth would tend to result in recession. Similarly, new technologies, increased capital investment, or a surge in immigration that swells the labor force could produce unusually brisk growth in potential output, and hence an economic boom.

Undoubtedly, changes in the rate of growth of potential output are part of the explanation for expansions and recessions. In the United States, for example, the economic boom of the second half of the 1990s was propelled in part by new information technologies, such as the Internet. And the severe slowdown in Japan during the decade of the 1990s reflected in part a reduction in the growth of potential output, arising from factors such as slower growth in the Japanese labor force and capital stock. When changes in the rate of GDP growth reflect changes in the growth rate of potential output, the appropriate policy responses are those discussed in Chapter 20. In particular, when a recession results from slowing growth in potential output, the government's best response is to try to promote saving, investment, technological innovation, human capital formation, and other activities that support growth.

A second possible explanation for short-term economic fluctuations is that *actual output does not always equal potential output.* For example, potential output may be growing normally, but for some reason the economy's capital and labor resources may not be fully utilized, so that actual output is significantly below the level of potential output. This low level of output, resulting from underutilization of economic resources, would generally be interpreted as a recession. Alternatively, capital and labor may be working much harder than normal—firms may put workers on overtime, for example—so that actual output expands beyond potential output, creating a boom.

At any point in time, the difference between potential output and actual output is called the **output gap.** Recalling that Y^* is the symbol for potential output

potential output, Y^* (or potential GDP or full-employment output) the amount of output (real GDP) that an economy can produce when using its resources, such as capital and labor, at normal rates

output gap, $Y^* - Y$ the difference between the economy's potential output and its actual output at a point in time

---

[1] The term "potential output" is slightly misleading, in that *potential* output is not the same as *maximum* output. Because capital and labor can be utilized at greater-than-normal rates, at least for a time, a country's actual output can exceed its potential output.

recessionary gap a positive output gap, which occurs when potential output exceeds actual output ($Y^* > Y$)

expansionary gap a negative output gap, which occurs when actual output is higher than potential output ($Y > Y^*$)

and that Y stands for actual output (real GDP), we can express the output gap as $Y^* - Y$. A positive output gap—when actual output is below potential, and resources are not being fully utilized—is called a **recessionary gap**. A negative output gap—when actual output is above potential, and resources are being utilized at above-normal rates—is referred to as an **expansionary gap**.

Policymakers generally view both recessionary gaps and expansionary gaps as problems. It is not difficult to see why a recessionary gap is bad news for the economy: When there is a recessionary gap, capital and labor resources are not being fully utilized, and output and employment are below normal levels. This is the sort of situation that poses problems for politicians' reelection prospects, as discussed in this chapter's introduction. An expansionary gap is considered a problem by policymakers for a more subtle reason: What's wrong, after all, with having higher output and employment than normal? A prolonged expansionary gap is problematic because, when faced with a demand for their products that significantly exceeds their normal capacity, firms tend to raise prices. Thus an expansionary gap typically results in increased inflation, which reduces the efficiency of the economy in the longer run. (We discuss the genesis of inflation in more detail in Chapter 28.)

"Ed, this is Art Simbley over at Hollis, Bingham, Cotter & Krone. What did you get for thirty-four across, 'Persian fairy,' four letters?"

Thus, whenever an output gap exists, whether it is recessionary or expansionary, policymakers have an incentive to try to eliminate the gap by returning actual output to potential. In the next three chapters we will discuss both how output gaps arise and the tools that policymakers have for *stabilizing* the economy—that is, bringing actual output into line with potential output.

THE NATURAL RATE OF UNEMPLOYMENT AND CYCLICAL UNEMPLOYMENT

Whether recessions arise because of slower growth in potential output or because actual output falls below potential, they bring bad times. In either case output falls (or at least grows more slowly), implying reduced living standards. Recessionary output gaps are particularly frustrating for policymakers, however, because they imply that the economy has the *capacity* to produce more, but for some reason available resources are not being fully utilized. Recessionary gaps are *inefficient* in that they unnecessarily reduce the total economic pie, making the typical person worse off.

An important indicator of the low utilization of resources during recessions is the unemployment rate. In general, a *high* unemployment rate means that labor resources are not being fully utilized, so that output has fallen below potential (a recessionary gap). By the same logic, an unusually *low* unemployment rate suggests that labor is being utilized at a rate greater than normal, so that actual output exceeds potential output (an expansionary gap).

To better understand the relationship between the output gap and unemployment, recall from Chapter 21 the three broad types of unemployment: frictional unemployment, structural unemployment, and cyclical unemployment. *Frictional unemployment* is the short-term unemployment that is associated with the matching of workers and jobs. Some amount of frictional unemployment is necessary for the labor market to function efficiently in a dynamic, changing economy. *Structural unemployment* is the long-term and chronic unemployment that occurs even when the economy is producing at its normal rate. Structural unemployment often results when workers' skills are outmoded and do not meet the needs of employers—so, for example, steelworkers may become structurally unemployed as the steel industry goes into a long-term decline, unless those workers can retrain to find jobs in growing industries. Finally, *cyclical unemployment* is the extra unemployment that occurs during periods of recession. Unlike cyclical unemployment, which is present only during recessions, frictional unemployment and structural unemployment are always present in the labor market, even when the economy is operating normally. Economists call the part of the total unemployment rate that is attributable to frictional and structural unemployment the **natural rate of unemployment.** Put another way, the natural rate of unemployment is the unemployment rate that prevails when cyclical unemployment is zero, so that the economy has neither a recessionary nor an expansionary output gap. We will denote the natural rate of unemployment as u^*.

Cyclical unemployment, which is the difference between the total unemployment rate and the natural rate, can thus be expressed as $u - u^*$, where u is the actual unemployment rate and u^* denotes the natural rate of unemployment. In a recession, the actual unemployment rate u exceeds the natural unemployment rate u^*, so cyclical unemployment, $u - u^*$, is positive. When the economy experiences an expansionary gap, in contrast, the actual unemployment rate is lower than the natural rate, so that cyclical unemployment is negative. Negative cyclical unemployment corresponds to a situation in which labor is being used more intensively than normal, so that actual unemployment has dipped below its usual frictional and structural levels.

natural rate of unemployment, u^* the part of the total unemployment rate that is attributable to frictional and structural unemployment; equivalently, the unemployment rate that prevails when cyclical unemployment is zero, so that the economy has neither a recessionary nor an expansionary output gap

Why has the natural rate of unemployment in the United States apparently declined?

According to the Congressional Budget Office, which regularly estimates the natural rate of unemployment in the United States, the natural rate has fallen steadily since about 1979, from 6.3 percent of the labor force to about 5.2 percent.[2] Some economists, noting that unemployment remained close to 4 percent for several years around the turn of the millennium, have argued for an even lower natural rate, perhaps 4.5 percent or lower. Why is the U.S. natural rate of unemployment apparently so much lower today than it was 20 years ago?

ECONOMIC NATURALIST 25.2

[2]Congressional Budget Office, *Economic and Budget Outlook: Fiscal Years 2001–2010*, Table F-1, available online at http://www.cbo.gov/.

The natural rate of unemployment may have fallen because of reduced frictional unemployment, reduced structural unemployment, or both. A variety of ideas have been advanced to explain declines in both types of unemployment. One promising suggestion is based on the changing age structure of the U.S. labor force.[3] The average age of U.S. workers is rising, reflecting the aging of the baby boom generation. Indeed, over the past 20 years the share of the labor force aged 16–24 has fallen from about 25 percent to about 16 percent. Since young workers are more prone to unemployment than older workers, the aging of the labor force may help to explain the overall decline in unemployment.

Why are young workers more likely to be unemployed? Compared to teenagers and workers in their twenties, older workers are much more likely to hold long-term, stable jobs. In contrast, younger workers tend to hold short-term jobs, perhaps because they are not ready to commit to a particular career, or because their time in the labor market is interrupted by schooling or military service. Because they change jobs more often, younger workers are more prone than others to frictional unemployment. They also have fewer skills, on average, than older workers, so they may experience more structural unemployment. As workers age and gain experience, however, their risk of unemployment declines.

Another possible explanation for the declining natural rate of unemployment is that labor markets have become more efficient at matching workers with jobs, thereby reducing both frictional and structural unemployment. For example, agencies that arrange temporary help have become much more commonplace in the United States in recent years. Although the placements these agencies make are intended to be temporary, they often become permanent when an employer and worker discover that a particularly good match has been made. Online job services, which allow workers to search for jobs nationally and even internationally, are also becoming increasingly important. By reducing the time people must spend in unemployment and by creating more lasting matches between workers and jobs, temporary help agencies, online job services, and similar innovations may have reduced the natural rate of unemployment.[4]

OKUN'S LAW

Okun's law each extra percentage point of cyclical unemployment is associated with about a 2 percentage point increase in the output gap, measured in relation to potential output

What is the relationship between an output gap and the amount of cyclical unemployment in the economy? We have already observed that by definition, cyclical unemployment is positive when the economy has a recessionary gap, negative when there is an expansionary gap, and zero when there is no output gap. A more quantitative relationship between cyclical unemployment and the output gap is given by a rule of thumb called *Okun's law*, after Arthur Okun, one of President Kennedy's chief economic advisers. According to **Okun's law**, each extra percentage point of cyclical unemployment is associated with about a 2 percentage point increase in the output gap, measured in relation to potential output.[5] So, for example, if cyclical unemployment increases from 1 percent to 2 percent of the labor force, the recessionary gap will increase from 2 percent to 4 percent of potential GDP. Example 25.1 illustrates further.

---

[3]See Robert Shimer, "Why Is the U.S. Unemployment Rate So Much Lower?" in B. Bernanke and J. Rotemberg, eds., *NBER Macroeconomics Annual*, 1998.

[4]For a detailed analysis of factors affecting the natural rate, see Lawrence Katz and Alan Krueger, "The High-Pressure U.S. Labor Market of the 1990s," *Brookings Papers on Economic Activity*, 1:1–88, 1999.

[5]This relationship between unemployment and output has weakened over time. When Arthur Okun first formulated his law in the 1960s, he suggested that each extra percentage point of unemployment was associated with about a 3 percentage point increase in the output gap.

Okun's law and the output gap in the U.S. economy

EXAMPLE 25.1

Following are the actual unemployment rate, the natural unemployment rate, and potential GDP (in billions of dollars) for the U.S. economy in three selected years. Using Okun's law, estimate the output gap in each year, in billions of dollars.

Year	u	u*	Y*
1982	9.7%	6.1%	3,433
1991	6.8	5.8	6,093
1998	4.5	5.2	8,563

SOURCES: Unemployment rate, *Economic Report of the President*. Natural unemployment rate and potential GDP, Congressional Budget Office.

In 1982 cyclical unemployment, $u - u^*$, was 9.7% − 6.1%, or 3.6 percent of the labor force. According to Okun's law, the output gap for that year would be twice that percentage, or 7.2 percent of potential output. Since potential output in 1982 was $3,433 billion, the value of the output gap for that year was 7.2% × $3,433 billion, or $247 billion.

In 1991 cyclical unemployment was 6.8% − 5.8%, or 1.0 percent of the labor force. According to Okun's law, the output gap for 1991 would be twice 1.0 percent, or 2.0 percent of potential GDP. Since potential GDP in 1991 was $6,093 billion, the output gap in that year should have been 2.0% × $6,093, or $122 billion.

Both 1982 and 1991 were recession years, so the output gaps were recessionary gaps. In contrast, 1998 was a year of expansion, in which unemployment was below the natural rate and the economy experienced an expansionary gap. Cyclical unemployment in 1998 was 4.5% − 5.2%, or −0.7 percent. The output gap in 1998 should therefore have been about −1.4 percent of the potential GDP of $8,563 billion, or −$120 billion. In other words, in 1998 actual GDP was about $120 billion greater than potential GDP.

EXERCISE 25.2

In the first half of 2002 the U.S. unemployment rate averaged about 6 percent. Assuming that the natural rate is 5.2 percent, by what percentage amount did actual GDP differ from potential GDP in the first six months of 2002?

The output losses sustained in recessions, calculated according to Okun's law, can be quite significant. In Example 25.1 we found the U.S. output gap in 1982 to be $247 billion. The U.S. population in 1982 was about 230 million. Hence the output loss per person in that year equaled the total output gap of $247 billion divided by 230 million people, or about $1,074—about $4,300 for a family of four. Adjusting for inflation between 1982 and 2001, the equivalent cost in terms of 2001 dollars would have been about $7,100 for a family of four. This calculation implies that output gaps and cyclical unemployment may have significant costs—a conclusion that justifies the concern that the public and policymakers have about recessions.

Why did the Federal Reserve take measures to slow down the economy in 1999 and 2000?

As noted in Chapters 17 and 23, monetary policy decisions of the Federal Reserve—actions that change the level of the nation's money supply—affect the performance of the U.S. economy. Why did the Federal Reserve take measures to slow down the economy in 1999 and 2000?

Throughout the 1990s cyclical unemployment in the U.S. fell dramatically, becoming negative sometime in 1997, according to Congressional Budget Office

ECONOMIC
NATURALIST
25.3

estimates. Okun's law indicates that growing negative cyclical unemployment rates signal an increasing expansionary gap (illustrated in Example 25.1), and with it an increased risk of future inflation.

In 1997 and 1998 the Federal Reserve argued that the inflationary pressures typically caused by rapidly expanding output and falling unemployment rates were being offset by productivity gains and international competition, leaving inflation rates lower than expected. Because inflation remained low during this period—despite a small but growing expansionary gap—the Federal Reserve did little to eliminate the gap.

However, as the actual unemployment rate continued to fall throughout 1999 and early 2000 the expansionary gap continued to widen, causing the Federal Reserve to grow increasingly concerned about the growing imbalance between actual and potential GDP and the threat of increasing inflation. In response, the Federal Reserve took actions in 1999 and 2000 to slow the growth of output and bring actual and potential output closer into alignment (we will give more details about how the Fed can do this in Chapters 27 and 28). The Fed's actions helped to "promote overall balance in the economy"[6] and restrain inflation throughout 2000. By early 2001, however, the U.S. economy stalled and fell into recession (a topic analyzed in Economic Naturalist 26.2), leading the Federal Reserve to reverse course and take policy measures aimed at eliminating the growing *recessionary* gap.

 RECAP   **OUTPUT GAPS, CYCLICAL UNEMPLOYMENT, AND OKUN'S LAW**

Potential output is the amount of output (real GDP) that an economy can produce when using its resources, such as capital and labor, at normal rates. The output gap, $Y^* - Y$, is the difference between potential output Y^* and actual output Y. When actual output is below potential, the resulting output gap is called a recessionary gap. When actual output is above potential, the difference is called an expansionary gap. A recessionary gap reflects a waste of resources, while an expansionary gap threatens to ignite inflation; hence policymakers have an incentive to try to eliminate both types of output gaps.

The natural rate of unemployment u^* is the sum of the frictional and structural unemployment rates. It is the rate of unemployment that is observed when the economy is operating at a normal level, with no output gap.

Cyclical unemployment, $u - u^*$, is the difference between the actual unemployment rate u and the natural rate of unemployment u^*. Cyclical unemployment is positive when there is a recessionary gap, negative when there is an expansionary gap, and zero when there is no output gap.

Okun's law relates cyclical unemployment and the output gap. According to this rule of thumb, each percentage point increase in cyclical unemployment is associated with about a 2 percentage point increase in the output gap, measured in relation to potential output.

WHY DO SHORT-TERM FLUCTUATIONS OCCUR? A PREVIEW AND A PARABLE

What causes periods of recession and expansion? In the preceding section we discussed two possible reasons for slowdowns and speedups in real GDP growth. First, growth in potential output itself may slow down or speed up, reflecting

---

[6]Testimony of Chairman Alan Greenspan, *The Federal Reserve's semiannual report on the economy and monetary policy,* Committee on Banking and Financial Services, U.S. House of Representatives February 17, 2000. Available online: http://www.federalreserve.gov/boarddocs/hh/2000/February/Testimony.htm

changes in the growth rates of available capital and labor and in the pace of technological progress. Second, even if potential output is growing normally, actual output may be higher or lower than potential output—that is, expansionary or recessionary output gaps may develop. Earlier in this book we discussed some of the reasons that growth in potential output can vary, and the options that policymakers have for stimulating growth in potential output. But we have not yet addressed the question of how output gaps can arise or what policymakers should do in response. The causes and cures of output gaps will be a major topic of the next three chapters. Here is a brief preview of the main conclusions of those chapters:

1. In a world in which prices adjusted immediately to balance the quantities supplied and demanded for all goods and services, output gaps would not exist. However, for many goods and services, the assumption that prices will adjust immediately is not realistic. Instead, many firms adjust the prices of their output only periodically. In particular, rather than changing prices with every variation in demand, firms tend to adjust to changes in demand in the short run by varying the quantity of output they produce and sell. This type of behavior is known as "meeting the demand" at a preset price.

2. Because in the short run firms tend to meet the demand for their output at preset prices, changes in the amount that customers decide to spend will affect output. When total spending is low for some reason, output may fall below potential output; conversely, when spending is high output may rise above potential output. In other words, *changes in economywide spending are the primary cause of output gaps*. Thus government policies can help to eliminate output gaps by influencing total spending. For example, the government can affect total spending directly simply by changing its own level of purchases.

3. Although firms tend to meet demand in the short run, they will not be willing to do so indefinitely. If customer demand continues to differ from potential output, firms will eventually adjust their prices to eliminate output gaps. If demand exceeds potential output (an expansionary gap), firms will raise their prices aggressively, spurring inflation. If demand falls below potential output (a recessionary gap), firms will raise their prices less aggressively or even cut prices, reducing inflation.

4. Over the longer run, price changes by firms eliminate any output gap and bring production back into line with the economy's potential output. Thus the economy is "self-correcting" in the sense that it operates to eliminate output gaps over time. Because of this self-correcting tendency, in the long run actual output equals potential output, so that output is determined by the economy's productive capacity rather than by the rate of spending. In the long run, total spending influences only the rate of inflation.

These ideas will become clearer as we proceed through the next chapters. Before plunging into the details of the analysis, though, let's consider an example that illustrates the links between spending and output in the short and long run.

Al's ice cream store produces gourmet ice cream on the premises and sells it directly to the public. What determines the amount of ice cream that Al produces on a daily basis? The productive capacity, or potential output, of the shop is one important factor. Specifically, Al's potential output of ice cream depends on the amount of capital (number of ice cream makers) and labor (number of workers) that he employs, and on the productivity of that capital and labor. Although Al's potential output usually changes rather slowly, on occasion it can fluctuate significantly—for example, if an ice cream maker breaks down or Al contracts the flu.

The main source of day-to-day variations in Al's ice cream production, however, is not changes in potential output but fluctuations in the demand for ice cream by the public. Some of these fluctuations in spending occur predictably over the course of the day (more demand in the afternoon than in the morning, for example), the week (more demand on weekends), or the year (more demand in the summer). Other changes in demand are less regular—more demand on a hot day than a cool one, or when a parade is passing by the store. Some changes in demand are hard for Al to interpret: For example, a surge in demand for rocky road ice cream on one particular Tuesday could reflect a permanent change in consumer tastes, or it might just be a random, one-time event.

How should Al react to these ebbs and flows in the demand for ice cream? The basic supply-and-demand model that we introduced in Chapter 3, if applied to the market for ice cream, would predict that the price of ice cream should change with every change in the demand for ice cream. For example, prices should rise just after the movie theater next door to Al's shop lets out on Friday night, and they should fall on unusually cold, blustery days, when most people would prefer a hot cider to an ice cream cone. Indeed, taken literally, the supply and demand model of Chapter 3 predicts that ice cream prices should change almost moment to moment. Imagine Al standing in front of his shop like an auctioneer, calling out prices in an effort to determine how many people are willing to buy at each price!

Of course, we do not expect to see this behavior by an ice cream store owner. Price setting by auction does in fact occur in some markets, such as the market for grain or the stock market, but it is not the normal procedure in most retail markets, such as the market for ice cream. Why this difference? The basic reason is that sometimes the economic benefits of hiring an auctioneer and setting up an auction exceed the costs of doing so, and sometimes they do not. In the market for grain, for example, many buyers and sellers gather together in the same place at the same time to trade large volumes of standardized goods (bushels of grain). In that kind of situation, an auction is an efficient way to determine prices and balance the quantities supplied and demanded. In an ice cream store, by contrast, customers come in by twos and threes at random times throughout the day. Some want shakes, some cones, and some sodas. With small numbers of customers and a low sales volume at any given time, the costs involved in selling ice cream by auction are much greater than the benefits of allowing prices to vary with demand.

So how does Al the ice cream store manager deal with changes in the demand for ice cream? Observation suggests that he begins by setting prices based on the best information he has about the demand for his product and the costs of production. Perhaps he prints up a menu or makes a sign announcing the prices. Then, over a period of time, he will keep his prices fixed and serve as many customers as want to buy (up to the point where he runs out of ice cream or room in the store at these prices). This behavior is what we call "meeting the demand" at preset prices, and it implies that *in the short run,* the amount of ice cream Al produces and sells is determined by the demand for his products.

However, *in the long run* the situation is quite different. Suppose, for example, that Al's ice cream earns a citywide reputation for its freshness and flavor. Day after day Al observes long lines in his store. His ice cream maker is overtaxed, as are his employees and his table space. There can no longer be any doubt that at current prices, the quantity of ice cream the public wants to consume exceeds what Al is able and willing to supply on a normal basis (his potential output). Expanding the store is an attractive possibility, but not one (we assume) that is immediately feasible. What will Al do?

Certainly one thing Al can do is raise his prices. At higher prices, Al will earn higher profits. Moreover, raising ice cream prices will bring the quantity of ice cream demanded closer to Al's normal production capacity—his potential output. Indeed, when the price of Al's ice cream finally rises to its equilibrium level, the shop's actual output will equal its potential output. Thus, over the long run, ice cream prices adjust to their equilibrium level, and the amount that is sold is determined by potential output.

This example illustrates in a simple way the links between spending and output—except, of course, that we must think of this story as applying to the whole economy, not to a single business. The key point is that there is an important difference between the short run and the long run. In the short run, producers often choose not to change their prices, but rather to meet the demand at preset prices. Because output is determined by demand, in the short run total spending plays a central role in determining the level of economic activity. Thus Al's ice cream store enjoys a boom on an unusually hot day, when the demand for ice cream is strong, while an unseasonably cold day brings an ice cream recession. But in the long run, prices adjust to their market-clearing levels, and output equals potential output. Thus the quantities of inputs and the productivity with which they are used are the primary determinants of economic activity in the long run, as we saw in Chapter 20. Although total spending affects output in the short run, in the long run its main effects are on prices.

Why did the Coca-Cola Company test a vending machine that "knows" when the weather is hot?

According to the *New York Times* (October 28, 1999, p. C1), the Coca-Cola Company has quietly tested a soda vending machine that includes a temperature sensor. Why would Coca-Cola want a vending machine that "knows" when the weather is hot?

When the weather is hot, the demand for refreshing soft drinks rises, increasing their market-clearing price. To take advantage of this variation in consumer demand, the vending machines that Coca-Cola tested were equipped with a computer chip that gave them the capability to raise soda prices automatically when the temperature climbs. The company's chairman and chief executive, M. Douglas Ivester, described in an interview how the desire for a cold drink increases during a sports championship final held in the summer heat. "So it is fair that it should be more expensive," Mr. Ivester was quoted as saying. "The machine will simply make this process automatic." Company officials suggested numerous other ways in which vending machine prices could be made dependent on demand. For example, machines could be programmed to reduce prices during off-peak hours or at low-traffic machines.

In traditional vending machines, cold drinks are priced in a way analogous to the way Al prices his ice cream: A price is set, and demand is met at the preset price, until the machine runs of soda. The weather-sensitive vending machine illustrates how technology may change pricing practices in the future. Indeed, increased computing power and access to the Internet have already allowed some firms, such as airline companies, to change prices almost continuously in response to variations in demand. Conceivably, the practice of meeting demand at a preset price may someday be obsolete.

On the other hand, Coca-Cola's experiments with "smart" vending machines also illustrate the barriers to fully flexible pricing in practice. First, the new vending machines are more costly than the standard model. In deciding whether to use them, the company must decide whether the extra profits from variable pricing justify the extra cost of the machines. Second, in early tests many consumers reacted negatively to the new machines, complaining that they take unfair advantage of thirsty customers. In practice, customer complaints and concerns about "fairness" make companies less willing to vary prices sensitively with changing demand.

ECONOMIC NATURALIST 25.4

■ SUMMARY ■

- Real GDP does not grow smoothly. Periods in which the economy is growing at a rate significantly below normal are called *recessions;* periods in which the economy is growing at a rate significantly above normal are called *expansions.* A severe or protracted recession, like the long decline that occurred between 1929 and 1933, is called a *depression,* while a particularly strong expansion is called a *boom.*

- The beginning of a recession is called the *peak,* because it represents the high point of economic activity prior to a downturn. The end of a recession, which marks the low point of economic activity prior to a recovery, is called the *trough.* Since World War II, U.S. recessions have been much shorter on average than booms, lasting between 6 and 16 months. The longest boom period in U.S. history began with the end of the 1990–1991 recession in March 1991, ending exactly 10 years later in March 2001 when a new recession began.

- Short-term economic fluctuations are irregular in length and severity, and are thus hard to forecast. Expansions and recessions are typically felt throughout the economy and may even be global in scope. Unemployment rises sharply during recessions, while inflation tends to fall during or shortly after a recession. Durable goods industries tend to be particularly sensitive to recessions and booms, whereas services and nondurable goods industries are less sensitive.

- *Potential output,* also called potential GDP or full-employment output, is the amount of output (real GDP) that an economy can produce when it is using its resources, such as capital and labor, at normal rates. The difference between potential output and actual output is the *output*

gap. When output is below potential, the gap is called a *recessionary gap;* when output is above potential, the difference is called an *expansionary gap.* Recessions can occur either because potential output is growing unusually slowly or because actual output is below potential. Because recessionary gaps represent wasted resources and expansionary gaps threaten to create inflation, policymakers have an incentive to try to eliminate both types of gap.

- The *natural rate of unemployment* is the part of the total unemployment rate that is attributable to frictional and structural unemployment. Equivalently, the natural rate of unemployment is the rate of unemployment that exists when the output gap is zero. Cyclical unemployment, the part of unemployment that is associated with recessions and expansions, equals the total unemployment rate less the natural unemployment rate. Cyclical unemployment is related to the output gap by *Okun's law,* which states that each extra percentage point of cyclical unemployment is associated with about a 2 percentage point increase in the output gap, measured in relation to potential output.

- In the next several chapters our study of recessions and expansions will focus on the role of economywide spending. If firms adjust prices only periodically, and in the meantime produce enough output to meet demand, then fluctuations in spending will lead to fluctuations in output over the short run. During that short-run period, government policies that influence aggregate spending may help to eliminate output gaps. In the long run, however, firms' price changes will eliminate output gaps—that is, the economy will "self-correct"—and total spending will influence only the rate of inflation.

■ KEY TERMS ■

boom (647)
depression (645)
expansion (647)
expansionary gap (652)
natural rate of unemployment,
   u^* (653)

Okun's law (654)
output gap, $Y^* - Y$ (651)
peak (645)
potential output, Y^* (or potential
   GDP or full-employment output)
   (651)

recession (or contraction) (645)
recessionary gap (652)
trough (645)

■ REVIEW QUESTIONS ■

1. Define *recession* and *expansion.* What are the beginning and ending points of a recession called? In the postwar United States, which have been longer on average, recessions or expansions?

2. Why is the traditional term *business cycles* a misnomer? How does your answer relate to the ease or difficulty of forecasting peaks and troughs?

3. Which firm is likely to see its profits reduced the most in a recession: an automobile producer, a manufacturer of boots and shoes, or a janitorial service? Which is likely to see its profits reduced the least? Explain.

4. How is each of the following likely to be affected by a recession: the natural unemployment rate, the cyclical unemployment rate, the inflation rate, the poll ratings of the president?

5. Define *potential output*. Is it possible for an economy to produce an amount greater than potential output? Explain.

6. True or false: All recessions are the result of output gaps. Explain.

7. True or false: When output equals potential output, the unemployment rate is zero. Explain.

8. If the natural rate of unemployment is 5 percent, what is the total rate of unemployment if output is 2 percent below potential output? What if output is 2 percent above potential output?

▪ PROBLEMS ▪

1. Using Table 25.1, find the average duration, the minimum duration, and the maximum duration of expansions in the United States since 1929. Are expansions getting longer or shorter on average over time? Is there any tendency for long expansions to be followed by long recessions?

2. From the homepage of the Bureau of Economic Analysis (http://www.bea.gov/bea/dn1.htm) obtain quarterly data for U.S. real GDP for 2001 and 2002. Did the 2001 recession satisfy the informal criterion that a recession must have two consecutive quarters of negative GDP growth?

3. Given below are data on real GDP and potential GDP for the United States for the years 1988–1993, in billions of 1992 dollars. For each year calculate the output gap as a percentage of potential GDP, and state whether the gap is a recessionary gap or an expansionary gap. Also calculate the year-to-year growth rates of real GDP. Can you identify the recession that occurred during this period?

Year	Real GDP	Potential GDP
1988	5,844	5,788
1989	6,056	5,943
1990	6,172	6,102
1991	6,075	6,265
1992	6,214	6,432
1993	6,360	6,604

SOURCE: International Monetary Fund.

4. From the homepage of the Bureau of Labor Statistics (http://stats.bls.gov/), obtain the most recent available data on the unemployment rate for workers aged 16–19 and workers aged 20 or over. How do they differ? What are some of the reasons for the difference? How does this difference relate to the decline in the overall natural rate of unemployment since 1980?

5. Using Okun's law, fill in the four pieces of missing data in the table below. The data are hypothetical.

Year	Real GDP	Potential GDP	Natural unemployment rate (%)	Actual unemployment rate (%)
2001	7,840	8,000	(a)	6
2002	8,100	(b)	5	5
2003	(c)	8,200	4.5	4
2004	8,415	8,250	5	(d)

■ ANSWERS TO IN-CHAPTER EXERCISES ■

25.1 Answers will vary, depending on when the data is obtained.

25.2 The actual unemployment rate in the first half of 2002 exceeded the natural rate by 0.8 percent, so by Okun's law actual output fell below potential output by $2 \times 0.8\% = 1.6\%$ of potential output (a recessionary gap).

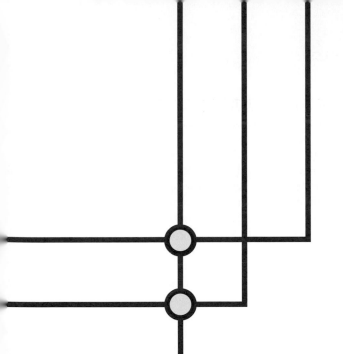

SPENDING AND OUTPUT IN THE SHORT RUN

■

When one of the authors of this book was a small boy, he used to spend some time every summer with his grandparents, who lived a few hours from his home. A favorite activity of his during these visits was to spend a summer evening on the front porch with his grandmother, listening to her stories. For some reason Grandma's recounting of her own life was particularly fascinating to her grandson.

Grandma had spent the early years of her marriage in New England, during the worst part of the Great Depression. In one of her reminiscences she remarked that at that time, in the mid-1930s, it had been a satisfaction to her to be able to buy her children a new pair of shoes every year. In the small town where she and her family lived, many children had to wear their shoes until they fell apart, and a few unlucky boys and girls went to school barefoot. Her grandson thought this was scandalous: "Why didn't their parents just buy them new shoes?" he demanded.

"They couldn't," said Grandma. "They didn't have the money. Most of the fathers had lost their jobs because of the Depression."

"What kind of jobs did they have?"

"They worked in the shoe factories, which had to close down."

"Why did the factories close down?"

"Because," Grandma explained, "nobody had any money to buy shoes."

The grandson was only six or seven years old at the time, but even he could see that there was something badly wrong with Grandma's logic. On the one side were boarded-up shoe factories and shoe workers with no jobs; on the other, children without shoes. Why couldn't the shoe factories just open and produce the shoes the children so badly needed? He made his point quite firmly, but Grandma just shrugged and said it didn't work that way.

The story of the closed-down shoe factories illustrates in a microcosm the cost to society of a recessionary gap. In an economy with a recessionary gap, available resources, which could in principle be used to produce valuable goods and services, are instead allowed to lie fallow. This waste of resources lowers the economy's output and economic welfare, compared to its potential.

Grandma's account also suggests how such an unfortunate situation might come about. Suppose factory owners and other producers, being reluctant to accumulate unsold goods on their shelves, produce just enough output to satisfy the demand for their products. And suppose that, for some reason, the public's willingness or ability to spend declines. If spending declines, factories will respond by cutting their production (because they don't want to produce goods they can't sell) and by laying off workers who are no longer needed. And because the workers who are laid off will lose most of their income—a particularly serious loss in the 1930s, in the days before government-sponsored unemployment insurance was common—they must reduce their own spending. As their spending declines, factories will reduce their production again, laying off more workers, who in turn reduce their spending—and so on, in a vicious circle. In this scenario, the problem is not a lack of productive capacity—the factories have not lost their ability to produce—but rather *insufficient spending* to support the normal level of production.

The idea that a decline in aggregate spending may cause output to fall below potential output was one of the key insights of John Maynard Keynes, a highly influential British economist of the first half of the twentieth century. Box 26.1

© Bettmann/Corbis

BOX 26.1: JOHN MAYNARD KEYNES AND THE KEYNESIAN REVOLUTION

John Maynard Keynes (1883–1946), perhaps the most influential economist of the twentieth century, was a remarkable individual who combined a brilliant career as an economic theorist with an active life in diplomacy, finance, journalism, and the arts. Keynes (pronouced "canes") first came to prominence at the end of World War I when he attended the Versailles peace conference as a representative of the British Treasury. He was appalled by the shortsightedness of the diplomats at the conference, particularly their insistence that the defeated Germans make huge compensatory payments (called reparations) to the victorious nations. In his widely read book *The Economic Consequences of the Peace* (1919), Keynes argued that the reparations imposed on Germany were impossibly large, and that attempts to extract the payments would prevent Germany's economic recovery and perhaps lead to another war. Unfortunately for the world, he turned out to be right.

In the period between the two world wars, Keynes held a professorship at Cambridge, where his father had taught economics. Keynes's early writings had been on mathematics and logic, but after his experience in Versailles he began to work primarily on economics, producing several well-regarded books. He developed an imposing intellectual reputation, editing Great Britain's leading scholarly journal in economics, writing articles for newspapers and magazines, advising the government, and playing a major role in the political and economic debates of the day. On the side, Keynes made fortunes both for himself and for King's College (a part of Cambridge University) by speculating in international currencies and commodities. He was also an active member of the Bloomsbury Group, a circle of leading artists, performers, and writers that included E. M. Forster and Virginia Woolf. In 1925 Keynes married the glamorous Russian ballerina Lydia Lopokova. Theirs was by all accounts a very successful marriage, and Keynes devoted significant energies to managing his wife's career and promoting the arts in Britain.

Like other economists of the time, Keynes struggled to understand the Great Depression that gripped the world in the 1930s. His work on the problem led to the publication in 1936 of *The General Theory of Employment, Interest, and Money*. In the *General Theory*, Keynes tried to explain how economies can remain at low levels of output and employment for protracted periods. He stressed a number of factors, most notably that aggregate spending may be too low to permit full employment during such periods. Keynes recommended increases in government spending as the most effective way to increase aggregate spending and restore full employment.

The *General Theory* is a difficult book, reflecting Keynes's own struggle to understand the complex causes of the Depression. In retrospect, some of the *General Theory*'s arguments seem unclear or even inconsistent. Yet the book is full of fertile ideas, many of which had a worldwide impact and eventually led to what has been called the *Keynesian revolution*. Over the years many economists have added to or modified Keynes's conception, to the point that Keynes himself, were he alive today, probably would not recognize much of what is now called Keynesian economics. But the ideas that insufficient aggregate spending can lead to recession and that government policies can help to restore full employment are still critical to Keynesian theory.

In 1937 a heart attack curtailed Keynes's activities, but he remained an important figure on the world scene. In 1944 he led the British delegation to the international conference in Bretton Woods, New Hampshire, which established the key elements of the postwar international monetary and financial system, including the International Monetary Fund and the World Bank. Keynes died in 1946.

gives a brief account of Keynes's life and ideas. The goal of this chapter is to present a theory, or model, of how recessions and expansions may arise from fluctuations in aggregate spending, along the lines first suggested by Keynes. This model, which we call the *basic Keynesian model*, is also known as the *Keynesian cross*, after the diagram that is used to illustrate the theory. In the body of the chapter we will emphasize a numerical and graphical approach to the basic Keynesian model. The appendix to this chapter provides a more general algebraic analysis.

We will begin with a brief discussion of the key assumptions of the basic Keynesian model. We will then turn to the important concept of total, or aggregate, *planned spending* in the economy. We will show how, in the short run, the rate of aggregate spending helps to determine the level of output, which can be greater than or less than potential output. In other words, depending on the level of spending, the economy may develop an output gap. "Too little" spending leads to a recessionary output gap, while "too much" creates an expansionary output gap.

An implication of the basic Keynesian model is that government policies that affect the level of spending can be used to reduce or eliminate output gaps. Policies used in this way are called *stabilization policies*. Keynes himself argued for the active use of fiscal policy—policy relating to government spending and taxes—to eliminate output gaps and stabilize the economy. In the latter part of this chapter we will show why Keynes thought fiscal policy could help to stabilize the economy, and we will discuss the usefulness of fiscal policy as a stabilization tool.

As we mentioned in Chapter 25, the basic Keynesian model is not a complete or entirely realistic model of the economy, since it applies only to the relatively short period during which firms do not adjust their prices but instead meet the demand forthcoming at preset prices. Furthermore, by treating prices as fixed, the basic Keynesian model presented in this chapter does not address the determination of inflation. Nevertheless, this model is an essential building block of leading current theories of short-run economic fluctuations and stabilization policies.

In subsequent chapters we will extend the basic Keynesian model to incorporate inflation and other important features of the economy.

THE KEYNESIAN MODEL'S CRUCIAL ASSUMPTION: FIRMS MEET DEMAND AT PRESET PRICES

The basic Keynesian model is built on a key assumption, highlighted in Box 26.2. This assumption is that firms do not continuously change their prices as supply and demand conditions change; rather, over short periods, firms tend to keep their prices fixed and *meet the demand* that is forthcoming at those prices. As we will see, the assumption that firms vary their production in order to meet demand at preset prices implies that fluctuations in spending will have powerful effects on the nation's real GDP.

BOX 26.2: KEY ASSUMPTION OF THE BASIC KEYNESIAN MODEL

In the short run, firms meet the demand for their products at preset prices.

Firms do not respond to every change in the demand for their products by changing their prices. Instead, they typically set a price for some period, then *meet the demand* at that price. By "meeting the demand," we mean that firms produce just enough to satisfy their customers at the prices that have been set.

The assumption that over short periods of time, firms meet the demand for their products at preset prices is generally realistic. Think of the stores where you shop. The price of a pair of jeans does not fluctuate from moment to moment according to the number of customers who enter the store or the latest news about the price of denim. Instead, the store posts a price and sells jeans to any customer who wants to buy at that price, at least until the store runs out of stock. Similarly, the corner pizza restaurant may leave the price of its large pie unchanged for months or longer, allowing its pizza production to be determined by the number of customers who want to buy at the preset price.

menu costs the costs of changing prices

Firms do not normally change their prices frequently because doing so would be costly. Economists refer to the costs of changing prices as **menu costs**. In the case of the pizza restaurant, the menu cost is literally just that—the cost of printing up a new menu when prices change. Similarly, the clothing store faces the cost of remarking all its merchandise if the manager changes prices. But menu costs may also include other kinds of costs—for example, the cost of doing a market survey to determine what price to charge and the cost of informing customers about price changes. Economic Naturalist 26.1 discusses how technology may affect menu costs in the future.

Menu costs will not prevent firms from changing their prices indefinitely. As we saw in the case of Al's ice cream store (see Chapter 25), too great an imbalance between demand and supply, as reflected by a difference between sales and potential output, will eventually lead firms to change their prices. If no one is buying jeans, for example, at some point the clothing store will mark down its jeans prices. Or if the pizza restaurant becomes the local hot spot, with a line of customers stretching out the door, eventually the manager will raise the price of a large pie. Like many other economic decisions, the decision to change prices reflects a cost-benefit comparison: Prices should be changed if the benefit of doing so—the fact that sales will be brought more nearly in line with the firm's normal production capacity—outweighs the menu costs associated with making the change. As we have stressed, the basic Keynesian model developed in this chapter ignores the fact that prices will eventually adjust, and should therefore be interpreted as applying to the short run.

Will new technologies eliminate menu costs?

Thanks to new technologies, changing prices and informing customers about price changes is becoming increasingly less costly. Will technology eliminate menu costs as a factor in price setting?

Keynesian theory is based on the assumption that costs of changing prices, which economists refer to as menu costs, are sufficiently large to prevent firms from adjusting prices immediately in response to changing market conditions. However, in many industries, new technologies have eliminated or greatly reduced the direct costs of changing prices. For example, the use of bar codes to identify individual products, together with scanner technologies, allows a grocery store manager to change prices with just a few keystrokes, without having to change the price label on each can of soup or loaf of bread. Airlines use sophisticated computer software to implement complex pricing strategies, under which two travelers on the same flight to Milwaukee may pay very different fares, depending on whether they are business or vacation travelers and on how far in advance their flights were booked. Online retailers, such as booksellers, have the ability to vary their prices by type of customer and even by individual customer, while other Internet-based companies, such as Ebay and Priceline, allow for negotiation over the price of each individual purchase. As described in Economic Naturalist 25.4, the Coca-Cola company experimented with a vending machine that automatically varied the price of a soft drink according to the outdoor temperature, charging more when the weather is hot.

Will these reductions in the direct costs of changing prices make the Keynesian theory, which assumes that firms meet demand at preset prices, less relevant to the real world? This is certainly a possibility that macroeconomists must take into account. However, it is unlikely that new technologies will completely eliminate the costs of changing prices anytime soon. Gathering the information about market conditions needed to set the profit-maximizing price—including the prices charged by competitors, the costs of producing the good or service, and the likely demand for the product—will remain costly for firms. Another cost of changing prices is the use of valuable managerial time and attention needed to make informed pricing decisions. A more subtle cost of changing prices—particularly raising prices—is that doing so may lead regular customers to rethink their choice of suppliers and decide to search for a better deal elsewhere.

ECONOMIC NATURALIST 26.1

"You thought we would offer lower fares? How insensitive."

PLANNED AGGREGATE EXPENDITURE

In the Keynesian theory discussed in this chapter, output at each point in time is determined by the amount that people throughout the economy want to spend—what we will refer to as *planned aggregate expenditure*. Specifically, **planned aggregate expenditure (PAE)** is total planned spending on final goods and services.

The four components of spending on final goods and services were introduced in Chapter 18:

1. *Consumer expenditure,* or simply *consumption* (C), is spending by households on final goods and services. Examples of consumer expenditure are spending on food, clothes, and entertainment and on consumer durable goods like automobiles and furniture.

2. *Investment* (I) is spending by firms on new capital goods, such as office buildings, factories, and equipment. Spending on new houses and apartment buildings (residential investment) and increases in inventories (inventory investment) are also included in investment.[1]

planned aggregate expenditure (PAE)
total planned spending on final goods and services

---

[1]In everyday conversations, people often use the term "investment" to mean *financial* investment, for example, the purchase of stocks or bonds. As we discussed earlier, we use "investment" here to mean spending on new capital goods, such as factories, housing, and equipment, which is not the same as financial investment. This distinction is important to keep in mind.

3. *Government purchases* (G) is spending by governments (federal, state, and local) on goods and services. Examples of government purchases include new schools and hospitals, military hardware, equipment for the space program, and the services of government employees, such as soldiers, police, and government office workers. Recall from Chapter 18 that *transfer payments,* such as social security benefits and unemployment insurance, and interest on the government debt are *not* included in government purchases. Transfer payments and interest contribute to aggregate expenditure only at the point when they are spent by their recipients (for example, when a recipient of a Social Security check uses the funds to buy food, clothing, or other consumption goods).

4. *Net exports* (NX) equals exports minus imports. Exports are sales of domestically produced goods and services to foreigners; imports are purchases by domestic residents of goods and services produced abroad. Net exports represents the net demand for domestic goods by foreigners.

Together these four types of spending—by households, firms, the government, and the rest of the world—sum to total, or aggregate, spending.

PLANNED SPENDING VERSUS ACTUAL SPENDING

In the Keynesian model, output is determined by planned aggregate expenditure, or planned spending for short. Could *planned* spending ever differ from *actual* spending? The answer is yes. The most important case is that of a firm that sells either less or more of its product than expected. As was noted in Chapter 18, additions to the stocks of goods sitting in a firm's warehouse are treated in official government statistics as inventory investment by the firm. In effect, government statisticians assume that the firm buys its unsold output from itself; they then count those purchases as part of the firm's investment spending.[2]

Suppose, then, that a firm's actual sales are less than expected, so that part of what it had planned to sell remains in the warehouse. In this case, the firm's actual investment, including the unexpected increases in its inventory, is greater than its planned investment, which did not include the added inventory. Suppose we agree to let I^p equal the firm's planned investment, including planned inventory investment. A firm that sells less of its output than planned, and therefore adds more to its inventory than planned, will find that its actual investment (including unplanned inventory investment) exceeds its planned investment, so that $I > I^p$.

What about a firm that sells more of its output than expected? In that case, the firm will add less to its inventory than it planned, so actual investment will be less than planned investment, or $I < I^p$. Example 26.1 gives a numerical illustration.

EXAMPLE 26.1

Actual and planned investment

The Fly-by-Night Kite Company produces $5,000,000 worth of kites during the year. It expects sales of $4,800,000 for the year, leaving $200,000 worth of kites to be stored in the warehouse for future sale. During the year, Fly-by-Night adds $1,000,000 in new production equipment as part of an expansion plan. Find Fly-by-Night's actual investment I and its planned investment I^p if actual kite sales turn out to be $4,600,000. What if sales are $4,800,000? What if they are $5,000,000?

Fly-by-Night's planned investment I^p equals its purchases of new production equipment ($1,000,000) plus its planned additions to inventory ($200,000), for a total of $1,200,000 in planned investment. The company's planned investment does not depend on how much it actually sells.

[2]For the purposes of measuring GDP, treating unsold output as being purchased by its producer has the advantage of ensuring that actual production and actual expenditure are equal.

If Fly-by-Night sells only $4,600,000 worth of kites, it will add $400,000 in kites to its inventory instead of the $200,000 worth originally planned. In this case, actual investment equals the $1,000,000 in new equipment plus the $400,000 in inventory investment, so $I = $1,400,000. We see that when the firm sells less output than planned, actual investment exceeds planned investment ($I > I^p$).

If Fly-by-Night has $4,800,000 in sales, then it will add $200,000 in kites to inventory, just as planned. In this case, actual and planned investment are the same:

$$I = I^p = $1,200,000.$$

Finally, if Fly-by-Night sells $5,000,000 worth of kites, it will have no output to add to inventory. Its inventory investment will be zero, and its total actual investment (including the new equipment) will equal $1,000,000, which is less than its planned investment of $1,200,000 ($I < I^p$).

Because firms that are meeting the demand for their product or service at pre-set prices cannot control how much they sell, their actual investment (including inventory investment) may well differ from their planned investment. However, for households, the government, and foreign purchasers, we may reasonably assume that actual spending and planned spending are the same. Thus, from now on we will assume that, for consumption, government purchases, and net exports, actual spending equals planned spending.

With these assumptions, we can define planned aggregate expenditure by the following equation:

$$PAE = C + I^p + G + NX. \tag{26.1}$$

Equation 26.1 says that planned aggregate expenditure is the sum of planned spending by households, firms, governments, and foreigners. We use a superscript p to distinguish planned investment spending by firms, I^p, from actual investment spending, I. However, because planned spending equals actual spending for households, the government, and foreigners, we do not need to use superscripts for consumption, government purchases, or net exports.

HEY BIG SPENDER! CONSUMER SPENDING AND THE ECONOMY

The largest component of planned aggregate expenditure—nearly two-thirds of total spending—is consumption spending, denoted C. As already mentioned, consumer spending includes household purchases of goods, such as groceries and clothing; services, such as health care, concerts, and college tuition; and consumer durables, such as cars, furniture, and home computers. Thus consumers' willingness to spend affects sales and profitability in a wide range of industries. (Households' purchases of new homes are classified as investment, rather than consumption; but home purchases represent another channel through which household decisions affect total spending.)

What determines how much people plan to spend on consumer goods and services in a given period? While many factors are relevant, a particularly important determinant of the amount people plan to consume is their after-tax, or *disposable*, income. All else being equal, households and individuals with higher disposable incomes will consume more than those with lower disposable incomes. Keynes himself stressed the importance of disposable income in determining household consumption decisions, claiming a "psychological law" that people would tie their spending closely to their incomes.

Recall from Chapter 22 that the disposable income of the private sector is the total production of the economy, Y, less net taxes (taxes minus transfers), or T. So we can assume that consumption spending (C) increases as disposable income ($Y - T$) increases. As already mentioned, other factors may also affect consumption, such as the real interest rate, also discussed in Chapter 22. For now we will ignore those other factors, returning to some of them later.

A general equation that captures the link between consumption and the private sector's disposable income is

$$C = \overline{C} + c(Y - T). \tag{26.2}$$

consumption function the
relationship between
consumption spending and its
determinants, in particular,
disposable (after-tax) income.

This equation, which we will dissect in a moment, is known as the *consumption function*. The **consumption function** relates consumption spending to its determinants, in particular, disposable (after-tax) income.

Let's look at the consumption function, Equation 26.2, more carefully. The right side of the equation contains two terms, $\overline{C}$ and $c(Y - T)$. The first term, $\overline{C}$, is a constant term in the equation that is intended to capture factors *other than disposable income* that affect consumption. For example, suppose consumers were to become more optimistic about the future, so that they desire to consume more and save less at any given level of their current disposable incomes. An increase in desired consumption at any given level of disposable income would be represented in the consumption function as an increase in the term $\overline{C}$.

We can imagine other factors that may affect the term $\overline{C}$ in the consumption function. Suppose, for example, that there is a boom in the stock market or a sharp increase in home prices, making consumers feel wealthier and hence more inclined to spend, for a given level of current disposable income. This effect could be captured by assuming that $\overline{C}$ increases. Likewise, a fall in home prices or stock prices that made consumers feel poorer and less inclined to spend would be represented by a decrease in $\overline{C}$. Economists refer to the effect of changes in asset prices on households' wealth and hence their consumption spending as the **wealth effect** of changes in asset prices.

wealth effect the tendency of
changes in asset prices to affect
households' wealth and thus
their spending on consumption
goods

What effect did the 2000–2002 decline in U.S. stock market values have on consumption spending?

From March 2000 to October 2002, the U.S. stock market suffered a 49 percent drop in value as measured by the Standard and Poor's 500 stock index, a widely referenced benchmark of U.S. stock performance. What effect did this decline in U.S. stock market values have on consumption spending?

According to MIT economist James Poterba, U.S. households owned roughly 13.3 trillion dollars of corporate stock in 2000.[3] If households' stock market holdings reflect those of the Standard and Poor's stock index, the 49 percent drop in the value of the stock market wiped out approximately 6.5 trillion dollars of household wealth in two years. According to economic models based on historical experience, a dollar's decrease in household wealth reduces consumer spending by 3 to 7 cents per year, so the reduction in stock market wealth had the potential to reduce overall consumer spending by 195 billion to 455 billion dollars, a drop of approximately 3 percent to 7 percent. Yet, real consumption spending continued to rise from 2000 through 2002. Why did this happen?

Despite the start of a recession in March 2001, overall consumption spending remained strong during 2000–2002 for a variety of reasons. Housing prices rose dramatically during this period, increasing consumers' housing wealth and offsetting their decline in stock-related wealth. In addition, as Economic Naturalist 25.1 points out, consumers' real after-tax income continued to grow into

[3]"The Stock Market and the Consumer," *Hoover Institution Weekly Essays*, November 6, 2000. Online: www-hoover.stanford.edu/pubaffairs/we/current/poterba_1100.html.

the fall of 2001, helping to maintain strong consumer spending despite the drop in the stock market. Finally, throughout 2001 and into early 2002, the Federal Reserve significantly reduced interest rates (how the Federal Reserve does this will be discussed in Chapter 27). A reduction in interest rates helps to promote consumer spending, especially on "big-ticket" items such as automobiles, by reducing consumers' borrowing costs. Overall, while the drop in stock market values clearly had a negative effect on consumer wealth, other offsetting factors helped to keep the 2000–2002 stock market decline from dampening consumption spending during this period.

The second term on the right side of Equation 26.2, $c(Y - T)$, reflects the effect of disposable income, $Y - T$, on consumption. The parameter c, a fixed number, is called the *marginal propensity to consume*. The **marginal propensity to consume (MPC)** is the amount by which consumption rises when current disposable income rises by one dollar. Presumably, if people receive an extra dollar of income, they will consume part of the dollar and save the rest. In other words, their consumption will increase, but by less than the full dollar of extra income. Thus it is realistic to assume that the marginal propensity to consume is greater than 0 (an increase in income leads to an increase in consumption) but less than 1 (the increase in consumption will be less than the full increase in income). Mathematically, we can summarize these assumptions as $0 < c < 1$.

> ***marginal propensity to consume (MPC),*** or *c* the amount by which consumption rises when disposable income rises by one dollar. We assume that $0 < c < 1$

Figure 26.1 shows a hypothetical consumption function, with consumption spending (C) on the vertical axis and disposable income ($Y - T$) on the horizontal axis. The intercept of the consumption function on the vertical axis equals exogenous consumption $\overline{C}$, and the slope of the consumption function equals the marginal propensity to consume, c.

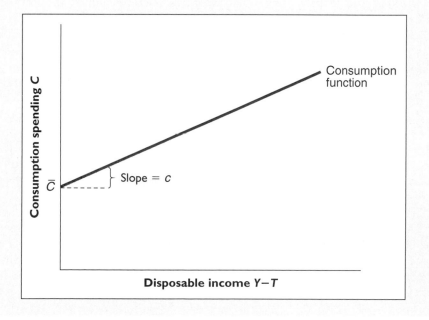

FIGURE 26.1
A Consumption Function.
The consumption function relates households' consumption spending, *C*, to disposable income, *Y − T*. The vertical intercept of this consumption function is the exogenous component of consumption, *C̄*, and the slope of the line equals the marginal propensity to consume, *c*.

To see how this consumption function fits reality, compare Figure 26.1 to Figure 26.2, which shows the relationship between aggregate real consumption expenditures and real disposable income in the United States for the period 1960–2001. Figure 26.2, a type of diagram called a *scatter plot*, shows aggregate real consumption on the vertical axis and aggregate real disposable income on the horizontal axis. Each point on the graph corresponds to a year between 1960 and 2001 (selected years are indicated in the figure). The position of each point is determined by the combination of consumption and disposable income associated with that year. As you can see, there is indeed a close relationship

FIGURE 26.2
The U.S. Consumption Function, 1960–2001.
Each point on this figure represents a combination of aggregate real consumption and aggregate real disposable income for a specific year between 1960 and 2001. Note the strong positive relationship between consumption and disposable income.

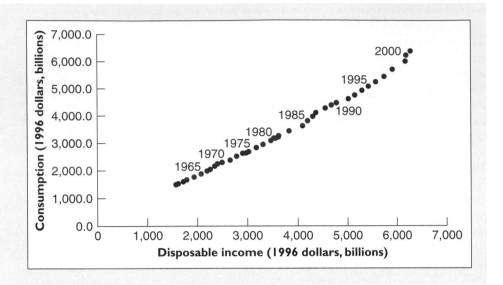

between aggregate consumption and disposable income: Higher disposable income implies higher consumption.

PLANNED AGGREGATE EXPENDITURE AND OUTPUT

Thinking back to Grandma's reminiscences, recall that an important element of her story involved the links among production, income, and spending. As the shoe factories in Grandma's town reduced production, the incomes of both factory workers and factory owners fell. Workers' incomes fell as the number of hours of work per week were reduced (a common practice during the Depression), as workers were laid off, or as wages were cut. Factory owners' income fell as profits declined. Reduced incomes, in turn, forced both workers and factory owners to curtail their spending—which led to still lower production and further reductions in income. This vicious circle led the economy further and further into recession.

The logic of Grandma's story has two key elements: (1) declines in production (which imply declines in the income received by producers) lead to reduced spending; and (2) reductions in spending lead to declines in production and income. In this section we look at the first part of the story, the effects of production and income on spending. We return later in this chapter to the effects of spending on production and income.

Why do changes in production and income affect planned aggregate spending? The consumption function, which relates consumption to disposable income, is the basic source of this relationship. Because consumption spending C is a large part of planned aggregate spending, and because consumption depends on output Y, aggregate spending as a whole depends on output. Example 26.2 illustrates this relationship numerically.

EXAMPLE 26.2

Linking planned aggregate expenditure to output

In a particular economy, the consumption function is

$$C = 620 + 0.8(Y - T),$$

so that the intercept term in the consumption function $\bar{C}$, equals 620, and the marginal propensity to consume c equals 0.8. Also, suppose that we are given that planned investment spending $I^p = 220$, government purchases $G = 300$, net exports $NX = 20$, and taxes $T = 250$.

Write a numerical equation linking planned aggregate expenditure *PAE* to output *Y*. How does planned spending change when output and hence income change?

Recall the definition of planned aggregate expenditure, Equation 26.1:

$$PAE = C + I^P + G + NX$$

To find a numerical equation for planned aggregate expenditure, we need to find numerical expressions for each of its four components. The first component of spending, consumption, is defined by the consumption function, $C = 620 + 0.8 (Y - T)$. Since taxes $T = 250$, we can substitute for *T* to write the consumption function as $C = 620 + 0.8(Y - 250)$. Now plug this expression for *C* into the definition of planned aggregate expenditure above to get

$$PAE = [620 + 0.8(Y - 250)] + I^P + G + NX,$$

where we have just replaced *C* by its value as determined by the consumption function. Similarly, we can substitute the given numerical values of planned investment I^P, government purchases *G*, and net exports *NX* into the definition of planned aggregate expenditure to get

$$PAE = [620 + 0.8(Y - 250)] + 220 + 300 + 20.$$

To simplify this equation, first note that $0.8(Y - 250) = 0.8Y - 200$, then add all the terms that don't depend on output *Y*. The result is

$$PAE = (620 - 200 + 220 + 300 + 20) + 0.8Y$$
$$= 960 + 0.8Y.$$

The final expression shows the relationship between planned aggregate expenditure and output in this numerical example. Note that, according to this equation, a $1 increase in *Y* leads to an increase in *PAE* of (0.8) ($1), or 80 cents. The reason for this is that the marginal propensity to consume, *c*, in this example is 0.8. Hence a $1 increase in income raises consumption spending by 80 cents. Since consumption is a component of total planned spending, total spending rises by 80 cents as well.

The solution to Example 26.2 illustrates a general point: Planned aggregate expenditure can be divided into two parts, a part that depends on output (*Y*) and a part that is independent of output. The portion of planned aggregate expenditure that is independent of output is called **autonomous expenditure.** In Example 26.2, autonomous expenditure is the constant term in the equation for planned aggregate expenditure, or 960. This portion of planned spending, being a fixed number, does not vary when output varies. By contrast, the portion of planned aggregate expenditure that depends on output (*Y*) is called **induced expenditure.** In Example 26.2, induced expenditure equals 0.8*Y*, the second term in the expression for planned aggregate expenditure. Note that the numerical value of induced expenditure depends, by definition, on the numerical value taken by output. Autonomous expenditure and induced expenditure together equal planned aggregate expenditure.

autonomous expenditure the portion of planned aggregate expenditure that is independent of output

induced expenditure the portion of planned aggregate expenditure that depends on output *Y*

RECAP   **PLANNED AGGREGATE EXPENDITURE**

Planned aggregate expenditure (*PAE*) is total planned spending on final goods and services. The four components of planned spending are consumer expenditure (*C*), planned investment (I^P), government purchases (*G*), and net exports (*NX*). Planned investment differs from actual investment when firms' sales are different from what they expected, so that additions to inventory (a component of investment) are different from what firms anticipated.

The largest component of aggregate expenditure is consumer expenditure, or simply consumption. Consumption depends on disposable, or after-tax, income, according to a relationship known as the consumption function, stated algebraically as $C = \overline{C} + c(Y - T)$.

The constant term in the consumption function, $\overline{C}$, captures factors other than disposable income that affect consumer spending. For example, an increase in housing or stock prices that makes households wealthier and thus more willing to spend—an effect called the wealth effect—could be captured by an increase in $\overline{C}$. The slope of the consumption function equals the marginal propensity to consume, c, where $0 < c < 1$. This is the amount by which consumption rises when disposable income rises by one dollar.

Increases in output Y, which imply equal increases in income, cause consumption to rise. As consumption is part of planned aggregate expenditure, planned spending depends on output as well. The portion of planned aggregate expenditure that depends on output is called induced expenditure. The portion of planned aggregate expenditure that is independent of output is autonomous expenditure.

SHORT-RUN EQUILIBRIUM OUTPUT

Now that we have defined planned aggregate expenditure and seen how it is related to output, the next task is to see how output itself is determined. Recall the assumption of the basic Keynesian model: In the short run, producers leave prices at preset levels and simply meet the demand that is forthcoming at those prices. In other words, during the short-run period in which prices are preset, firms produce an amount that is equal to planned aggregate expenditure. Accordingly, we define **short-run equilibrium output** as the level of output at which output Y equals planned aggregate expenditure PAE:

short-run equilibrium output
the level of output at which output Y equals planned aggregate expenditure PAE; short-run equilibrium output is the level of output that prevails during the period in which prices are predetermined

$$Y = PAE. \tag{26.3}$$

Short-run equilibrium output is the level of output that prevails during the period in which prices are predetermined.

We can find the short-run equilibrium output for the economy described in Example 26.2 using Table 26.1. Column 1 of the table gives some possible values for short-run equilibrium output. To find the correct value, we must compare

TABLE 26.1
Numerical Determination of Short-Run Equilibrium Output

(1) Output Y	(2) Planned aggregate expenditure $PAE = 960 + 0.8Y$	(3) $Y - PAE$	(4) $Y = PAE?$
4,000	4,160	−160	No
4,200	4,320	−120	No
4,400	4,480	−80	No
4,600	4,640	−40	No
4,800	4,800	0	**Yes**
5,000	4,960	40	No
5,200	5,120	80	No

each to the value of planned aggregate expenditure at that output level. Column 2 shows the value of planned aggregate expenditure corresponding to the values of short-run equilibrium output in column 1. Recall that in Example 26.2, planned spending is determined by the equation

$$PAE = 960 + 0.8Y.$$

Because consumption rises with output, total planned spending (which includes consumption) rises also. But if you compare columns 1 and 2, you will see that when output rises by 200, planned spending rises by only 160. That is because the marginal propensity to consume in this economy is 0.8, so that each dollar in added income raises consumption and planned spending by 80 cents.

Again, short-run equilibrium output is the level of output at which $Y = PAE$, or, equivalently, $Y - PAE$, = 0. Looking at Table 26.1, we can see there is only one level of output that satisfies that condition, $Y = 4,800$. At that level, output and planned aggregate expenditure are precisely equal, so that producers are just meeting the demand for their goods and services.

In this economy, what would happen if output differed from its equilibrium value of 4,800? Suppose, for example, that output were 4,000. Looking at the second column of Table 26.1, you can see that when output is 4,000, planned aggregate expenditure equals 960 + 0.8(4,000), or 4,160. Thus if output is 4,000, firms are not producing enough to meet the demand. They will find that as sales exceed the amounts they are producing, their inventories of finished goods are being depleted by 160 per year, and that actual investment (including inventory investment) is less than planned investment. Under the assumption that firms are committed to meeting their customers' demand, firms will respond by expanding their production.

Would expanding production to 4,160, the level of planned spending firms faced when output was 4,000, be enough? The answer is no, because of induced expenditure. That is, as firms expand their output, aggregate income (wages and profits) rises with it, which in turn leads to higher levels of consumption. Indeed, if output expands to 4,160, planned spending will increase as well, to 960 + 0.8(4,160), or 4,288. So an output level of 4,160 will still be insufficient to meet demand. As Table 26.1 shows, output will not be sufficient to meet planned aggregate expenditure until it expands to its short-run equilibrium value of 4,800.

What if output were initially greater than its equilibrium value—say, 5,000? From Table 26.1 we can see that when output equals 5,000, planned spending equals only 4,960—less than what firms are producing. So at an output level of 5,000, firms will not sell all they produce, and they will find that their merchandise is piling up on store shelves and in warehouses (actual investment, including inventory investment, is greater than planned investment). In response, firms will cut their production runs. As Table 26.1 shows, they will have to reduce production to its equilibrium value of 4,800 before output just matches planned spending.

EXERCISE 26.1

Construct a table like Table 26.1 for an economy like the one we have been working with, assuming that the consumption function is $C = 820 + 0.7(Y - T)$ and that $I^P = 600$, $G = 600$, $NX = 200$, and $T = 600$.

What is short-run equilibrium output in this economy? (*Hint:* Try using values for output above 5,000.)

Short-run equilibrium output can also be determined graphically, as Example 26.3 shows.

EXAMPLE 26.3

Finding short-run equilibrium output (graphical approach)

Using a graphical approach, find short-run equilibrium output for the economy described in Example 26.2.

Figure 26.3 shows the graphical determination of short-run equilibrium output for the economy described in Example 26.2. Output Y is plotted on the horizontal axis and planned aggregate expenditure PAE on the vertical axis. The figure contains two lines, one of which is a 45° line extending from the origin. In general, a 45° line from the origin includes the points at which the variable on the vertical axis equals the variable on the horizontal axis. Hence, in this case, the 45° line represents the equation $Y = PAE$. Since short-run equilibrium output must satisfy the equation $Y = PAE$, the combination of output and spending that satisfies this condition must lie somewhere on the 45° line in Figure 26.3.

FIGURE 26.3

Determination of Short-Run Equilibrium Output (Keynesian Cross).

The 45° line represents the short-run equilibrium condition $Y = PAE$. The line $PAE = 960 + 0.8Y$, referred to as the expenditure line, shows the relationship of planned aggregate expenditure to output. Short-run equilibrium output (4,800) is determined at the intersection of the two lines, point E. This type of diagram is known as a Keynesian cross.

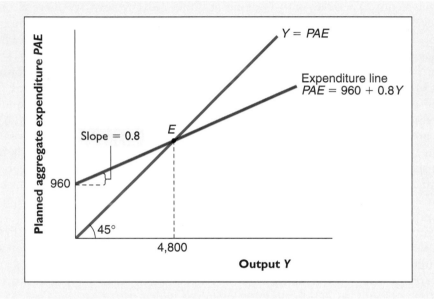

The second line in Figure 26.3, less steep than the 45° line, shows the relationship between planned aggregate expenditure PAE and output Y. Because it summarizes how planned spending depends on output, we will call this line the *expenditure line*. In this example, we know that the relationship between planned aggregate expenditure and output (the equation for the expenditure line) is

$$PAE = 960 + 0.8Y.$$

According to this equation, when $Y = 0$, the value of PAE is 960. Thus 960 is the intercept of the expenditure line, as shown in Figure 26.3. Notice that *the intercept of the expenditure line equals autonomous expenditure,* a result that will always hold. The slope of the line relating aggregate demand to output is 0.8, the value of the coefficient of output in the equation $PAE = 960 + 0.8Y$. Where does the number 0.8 come from? (*Hint:* What determines by how much aggregate spending increases when output rises by a dollar?)

Only one point in Figure 26.3 is consistent with *both* the definition of short-run equilibrium output, $Y = PAE$, and the given relationship between planned spending and output, $PAE = 960 + 0.8Y$. That point is the intersection of the two lines, point E. At point E, short-run equilibrium output equals 4,800, which is the same value that we obtained using Table 26.1 and by a direct numerical solution. At points to the right of E, output exceeds planned aggregate expenditure. Hence, to the right of point E, firms will be producing more than they can sell, which will lead them to reduce their rate of production. By contrast, to the left of point E, planned aggregate spending exceeds output. In that region, firms will not be producing enough to meet demand, and they will tend to increase their production. Only at point E, where output equals 4,800, will firms be producing enough to just satisfy planned spending on goods and services.

The diagram in Figure 26.3 is often called the *Keynesian cross*, after its characteristic shape. The Keynesian cross shows graphically how short-run equilibrium output is determined in a world in which producers meet demand at predetermined prices.

Use a Keynesian cross diagram to show graphically the determination of short-run equilibrium output for the economy described in Exercise 26.1. What are the intercept and the slope of the expenditure line?

PLANNED SPENDING AND THE OUTPUT GAP

We are now ready to use the basic Keynesian model to show how insufficient spending can lead to a recession. To illustrate the effects of spending changes on output, we will continue to work with the economy introduced in Example 26.2. We have shown that in this economy, short-run equilibrium output equals 4,800. Let's now make the additional assumption that potential output in this economy also equals 4,800, or $Y^* = 4,800$, so that initially there is no output gap. Starting from this position of full employment, Example 26.4 shows how a fall in planned aggregate expenditure can lead to a recession.

A fall in planned spending leads to a recession

For the economy introduced in Example 26.2, we have found that short-run equilibrium output Y equals 4,800. Assume also that potential output Y^* equals 4,800, so that the output gap $Y^* - Y$ equals zero.

Suppose, though, that consumers become more pessimistic about the future, so that they begin to spend less at every level of current disposable income. We can capture this change by assuming that $\overline{C}$, the constant term in the consumption function, falls to a lower level. To be specific, suppose that $\overline{C}$ falls by 10 units, which in turn implies a decline in autonomous expenditure of 10 units. What is the effect of this reduction in planned spending on the economy?

We can see the effects of the decline in consumer spending on the economy using the Keynesian cross diagram. Figure 26.4 shows the original short-run

EXAMPLE 26.4

FIGURE 26.4

A Decline in Planned Spending Leads to a Recession.

A decline in consumers' willingness to spend at any current level of disposable income reduces planned autonomous expenditure and shifts the expenditure line down. The short-run equilibrium point drops from E to F, reducing output and opening up a recessionary gap.

equilibrium point of the model (E), at the intersection of the 45° line, along which $Y = PAE$, and the original expenditure line, representing the equation $PAE = 960 + 0.8Y$. As before, the initial value of short-run equilibrium output is 4,800, which we have now assumed also corresponds to potential output Y^*. But what happens if $\overline{C}$ declines by 10, reducing autonomous expenditure by 10 as well?

Originally, autonomous expenditure in this economy was 960, so a decline of 10 units causes it to fall to 950. Instead of the economy's planned spending being described by the equation $PAE = 960 + 0.8Y$, as initially, it is now given by $PAE = 950 + 0.8Y$. What does this change imply for the graph in Figure 26.4? Since the intercept of the expenditure line (equal to autonomous expenditure) has decreased from 960 to 950, the effect of the decline in consumer spending will be to shift the expenditure line down in parallel fashion, by 10 units. Figure 26.4 indicates this downward shift in the expenditure line. The new short-run equilibrium point is at point F, where the new, lower expenditure line intersects the 45° line.

Point F is to the left of the original equilibrium point E, so we can see that output and spending have fallen from their initial levels. Since output at point F is lower than potential output, 4,800, we see that the fall in consumer spending has resulted in a recessionary gap in the economy. More generally, starting from a situation of full employment (where output equals potential output), any decline in autonomous expenditure leads to a recession.

Numerically, how large is the recessionary gap in Figure 26.4? To answer this question, we can use Table 26.2, which is in the same form as Table 26.1. The key difference is that in Table 26.2 planned aggregate expenditure is given by $PAE = 950 + 0.8Y$, rather than by $PAE = 960 + 0.8Y$, as in Table 26.1.

TABLE 26.2
**Determination of Short-Run Equilibrium Output
after a Fall in Spending**

(1) Output Y	(2) Planned aggregate expenditure $PAE = 950 + 0.8Y$	(3) Y − PAE	(4) Y = PAE?
4,600	4,630	−30	No
4,650	4,670	−20	No
4,700	4,710	−10	No
4,750	4,750	0	**Yes**
4,800	4,790	10	No
4,850	4,830	20	No
4,900	4,870	30	No
4,950	4,910	40	No
5,000	4,950	50	No

As in Table 26.1, the first column of the table shows alternative possible values of output Y, and the second column shows the levels of planned aggregate expenditure PAE implied by each value of output in the first column. Notice that 4,800, the value of short-run equilibrium output found in Table 26.1, is no longer an equilibrium; when output is 4,800, planned spending is 4,790, so output and planned spending are not equal. As the table shows, following the decline in planned aggregate expenditure, short-run equilibrium output is 4,750, the only value of output for which $Y = PAE$. Thus a drop of 10 units in autonomous expenditure has led to a 50-unit decline in short-run equilibrium output. If full-employment output is 4,800, then the recessionary gap shown in Figure 26.4 is 4,800 − 4,750 = 50 units.

EXERCISE 26.3

In the economy described in Example 26.4, we found a recessionary gap of 50, relative to potential output of 4,800. Suppose that in this economy, the natural rate of unemployment u^* is 5 percent. What will the actual unemployment rate be after the recessionary gap appears? (*Hint*: Recall Okun's law from Chapter 25.)

Example 26.4 showed that a decline in autonomous expenditure, arising from a decreased willingness of consumers to spend, causes short-run equilibrium output to fall and opens up a recessionary gap. The same conclusion applies to declines in autonomous expenditure arising from other sources. Suppose, for example, that firms become disillusioned with new technologies and cut back their planned investment in new equipment. In terms of the model, this reluctance of firms to invest can be interpreted as a decline in planned investment spending I^p. Under our assumption that planned investment spending is given and does not depend on output, planned investment is part of autonomous expenditure. So a decline in planned investment spending depresses autonomous expenditure and output, in precisely the same way that a decline in the autonomous part of consumption spending does. Similar conclusions apply to declines in other components of autonomous expenditure, such as government purchases and net exports, as we will see in later applications.

EXERCISE 26.4

Repeat the analysis of Example 26.4, except assume that consumers become *more* rather than less confident about the future. As a result, $\bar{C}$ rises by 10 units, which in turn raises autonomous expenditure by 10 units. Show graphically that this increase in consumers' willingness to spend leads to an expansionary output gap. Find the numerical value of the expansionary output gap.

"These are hard times for retailers, so we should show them our support in every way we can."

ECONOMIC NATURALIST 26.3

What caused the 1990–1991 recession?

As we saw in Chapter 25, the 1990–1991 recession came at the wrong time for the first President Bush, ultimately costing him the election. What caused the output of the U.S. economy to fall below its potential during that period?

Two factors have received a substantial part of the blame for the 1990–1991 recession, one being a *decline in consumer confidence*. Organizations such as the Conference Board and the Survey Research Center of the University of Michigan perform regular consumer surveys, in which people are asked their views about the future of the economy in general and their own fortunes in particular. Consumer responses are then summarized in measures of "consumer confidence." A high level of confidence implies that people are optimistic about both their own economic futures and the future of the economy in general. Economists have found that when consumers are optimistic, they are more likely to spend, particularly on big-ticket items such as cars and vacations. Hence, when consumer confidence took its sharpest-ever plunge following Iraq's invasion of Kuwait and the associated spike in oil prices in August 1990, economists and policymakers winced. As Americans became increasingly concerned both about U.S. energy security and the possibility of a ground war in the Middle East, planned aggregate expenditure and hence output fell, as analyzed by Example 26.4.

The second factor in the 1990–1991 recession, a *credit crunch*, arose from problems in the U.S. banking system. During the 1980s, many U.S. banks had made large real estate loans, taking undeveloped land or commercial real estate as collateral. When land and other real estate prices fell sharply in the late 1980s, banks suffered serious losses. Some regions of the country, such as New England, were hit especially hard. Many financially distressed banks either had no new funds to lend or were not permitted to lend by government regulators. This decline in the supply of credit from banks made credit costlier and more difficult to obtain for many borrowers, especially small and medium-sized firms. Without access to credit, these firms could not make capital investments, further reducing planned spending and output. In terms of the model presented in this chapter, a decline in planned investment spending brought about by a credit crunch can be thought of as a fall in planned investment spending I^p. Like the decline in $\overline{C}$ illustrated in Example 26.4, a fall in I^p reduces planned expenditure and hence short-run equilibrium output.

ECONOMIC NATURALIST 26.4

Why was the deep Japanese recession of the 1990s bad news for the rest of East Asia?

During the 1990s Japan suffered a prolonged economic slump, still ongoing as of this writing. Japan's economic problems were a major concern not only of the Japanese but of policymakers in other East Asian countries, such as Thailand and Singapore. Why did East Asian policymakers worry about the effects of the Japanese slump on their own economies?

Although the economies of Japan and its East Asian neighbors are intertwined in many ways, one of the most important links is through trade. Much of the economic success of East Asia has been based on the development of export industries, and over the years Japan has been the most important customer for East Asian goods. When the economy slumped in the 1990s, Japanese households and firms reduced their purchases of imported goods sharply. This fall in demand dealt a major blow to the export industries of other East Asian countries.

Not just the owners and workers of export industries were affected, though; as wages and profits in export industries fell, so did domestic spending in the East Asian nations. The declines in domestic spending reduced sales at home as well as abroad, further weakening the East Asian economies. In terms of the model, the decline in exports to Japan reduced net exports *NX*, and thus autonomous expenditure, in East Asian countries. The fall in autonomous expenditure led to a recessionary gap, much like that shown in Figure 26.4.

Japan is not the only country whose economic ups and downs have had a major impact on its trading partners. Because the United States is the most important trading partner of both Canada and Mexico, the U.S. recession that began in 2001 (see Economic Naturalist 26.5) led to declining exports and recessions in Canada and Mexico as well. East Asia, which exports high-tech goods to the United States, was also hurt by the U.S recession, with GDP in countries such as Singapore dropping sharply.

What caused the 2001 recession in the United States?

According to the National Bureau of Economic Research, a recession began in the United States in March 2001—the first U.S. recession in 10 years (see Economic Naturalist 25.1 for a discussion of the NBER's "call"). What caused the 2001 recession in the United States?

Consumer spending is nearly two-thirds of aggregate expenditure, so it should not be surprising that most recessions involve significant reductions in spending by households. In this respect, the 2001 recession in the United States was quite unusual, as consumer spending remained fairly strong throughout most of the downturn (see Economic Naturalist 26.2). Instead, this recession can be attributed primarily to a steep drop in investment spending by firms.

Why did investment expenditures fall? The period between 1995 and 2000 had been one of high rates of investment and rapid growth in the U.S. economy, fueled in large part by optimism about new technologies such as the Internet, fiber optics, and genetic engineering. However, by mid-2000 it was becoming apparent that some of the new technologies would not be as profitable as had been hoped. The prices of shares in high-tech companies fell sharply during the year and corporations cut back their investments in computers, software, telecommunications equipment, and the like. Although at first the decline was concentrated in the high-tech sector, the slowdown spread to other parts of the economy. Total employment peaked and began to decline in March 2001.

An additional shock occurred on September 11, 2001, when terrorist attacks destroyed the World Trade Center in New York City and inflicted heavy damage on the Pentagon in Washington, D.C. People became afraid to travel, and the demand for air travel, hotel rooms, and tourist services plummeted, worsening the downturn. However, consumers regained confidence surprisingly quickly—for example, spurred by generous rebates, they purchased a record number of automobiles during October. Increased government spending on security and defense also raised planned aggregate expenditure by the end of the year. The U.S. economy rebounded sharply in the first quarter of 2002.

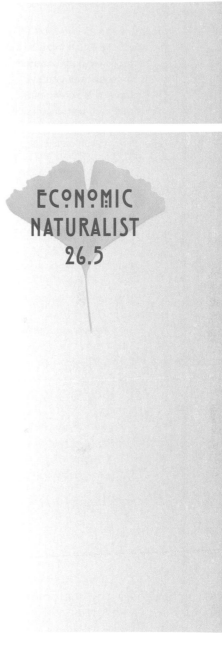

ECONOMIC NATURALIST 26.5

THE MULTIPLIER

In Example 26.4, earlier in the chapter, we analyzed a case in which the initial decline in consumer spending (as measured by the fall in $\overline{C}$) was only 10 units, and yet short-run equilibrium output fell by 50 units. Why did a relatively modest initial decline in consumer spending lead to a much larger fall in output?

The reason the impact on output was greater than the initial change in spending is the "vicious circle" effect suggested by Grandma's reminiscences about the Great Depression. Specifically, a fall in consumer spending not only reduces the sales of consumer goods directly; it also reduces the incomes of workers and owners in the industries that produce consumer goods. As their incomes fall, these workers and capital owners reduce their spending, which reduces the output and incomes of *other* producers in the economy. And these reductions in income lead to still further cuts in spending. Ultimately, these successive rounds of declines in spending and income may lead to a decrease in planned aggregate expenditure and output that is significantly greater than the change in spending that started the process.

income-expenditure multiplier
the effect of a 1-unit increase in autonomous expenditure on short-run equilibrium output; for example, a multiplier of 5 means that a 10-unit decrease in autonomous expenditure reduces short-run equilibrium output by 50 units

The effect on short-run equilibrium output of a 1-unit increase in autonomous expenditure is called the **income-expenditure multiplier**, or the *multiplier* for short. In the economy of Example 26.4 the multiplier is 5. That is, each 1-unit change in autonomous expenditure leads to a 5-unit change in short-run equilibrium output in the same direction (or, as we saw in Example 26.4, a 10-unit change in autonomous expenditure leads to a 50-unit change in short-run equilibrium output). The idea that a change in spending may lead to a significantly larger change in short-run equilibrium output is a key feature of the basic Keynesian model.

What determines how large the multiplier will be? An important factor is the marginal propensity to consume (MPC) out of disposable income c. If the MPC is large, then falls in income will cause people to reduce their spending sharply, and the multiplier effect will then also be large. If the marginal propensity to consume is small, then people will not reduce spending so much when income falls, and the multiplier will also be small. Appendix B to this chapter provides more details on the multiplier in the basic Keynesian model, including a formula that allows us to calculate the value of the multiplier under specific assumptions about the economy.

> ### RECAP FINDING SHORT-RUN EQUILIBRIUM OUTPUT
>
> Short-run equilibrium output is the level of output at which output equals planned aggregate expenditure, or, in symbols, $Y = PAE$. For a specific sample economy, short-run equilibrium output can be solved for numerically, as in Table 26.1, or graphically.
>
> The graphical solution is based on a diagram called the Keynesian cross. The Keynesian cross diagram includes two lines: a 45° line that represents the condition $Y = PAE$, and the expenditure line, which shows the relationship of planned aggregate expenditure to output. Short-run equilibrium output is determined at the intersection of the two lines. If short-run equilibrium output differs from potential output, an output gap exists.
>
> Increases in autonomous expenditure shift the expenditure line upward, increasing short-run equilibrium output; decreases in autonomous expenditure shift the expenditure line downward, leading to declines in short-run equilibrium output. Decreases in autonomous expenditure that drive actual output below potential output are a source of recessions.
>
> Generally, a one-unit change in autonomous expenditure leads to a larger change in short-run equilibrium output, reflecting the working of the income-expenditure multiplier. The multiplier arises because a given initial increase in spending raises the incomes of producers, which leads them to spend more, raising the incomes and spending of other producers, and so on.

STABILIZING PLANNED SPENDING: THE ROLE OF FISCAL POLICY

stabilization policies
government policies that are used to affect planned aggregate expenditure, with the objective of eliminating output gaps

expansionary policies
government policy actions intended to increase planned spending and output

According to the basic Keynesian model, inadequate spending is an important cause of recessions. To fight recessions—at least, those caused by insufficient demand rather than slow growth of potential output—policymakers must find ways to stimulate planned spending. Policies that are used to affect planned aggregate expenditure, with the objective of eliminating output gaps, are called **stabilization policies.** Policy actions intended to increase planned spending and output are called **expansionary policies**; expansionary policy actions are normally taken when the economy is in recession. It is also possible, as we have seen, for the economy to be "overheated," with output greater than potential output (an expansionary gap). The risk of an expansionary gap, as we will see in more detail later, is that it may lead to an increase in inflation. To offset an expansionary gap, policymakers will try to reduce spending and output. **Contractionary policies** are policy actions intended to reduced planned spending and output.

contractionary policies government policy actions designed to reduce planned spending and output

The two major tools of stabilization policy are *monetary policy* and *fiscal policy*. Recall that monetary policy refers to decisions about the size of the money supply, whereas fiscal policy refers to decisions about the government's budget—how much the government spends and how much tax revenue it collects. In the remainder of this chapter we will focus on how fiscal policy can be used to influence spending in the basic Keynesian model, as well as on some practical issues that arise in the use of fiscal policy in the real world. Monetary policy will be discussed in Chapters 27 and 28.

GOVERNMENT PURCHASES AND PLANNED SPENDING

Decisions about government spending represent one of the two main components of fiscal policy, the other being decisions about taxes and transfer payments. As was mentioned earlier (see Box 26.1), Keynes himself felt that changes in government purchases were probably the most effective tool for reducing or eliminating output gaps. His basic argument was straightforward: Government purchases of goods and services, being a component of planned aggregate expenditure, directly affect total spending. If output gaps are caused by too much or too little total spending, then the government can help to guide the economy toward full employment by changing its own level of spending. Keynes's views seemed to be vindicated by the events of the 1930s, notably the fact that the Depression did not finally end until governments greatly increased their military spending in the latter part of the decade.

Example 26.5 shows how increased government purchases of goods and services can help to eliminate a recessionary gap. (The effects of government spending on transfer programs, such as unemployment benefits, are a bit different. We will return to that case shortly.)

An increase in the government's purchases eliminates a recessionary gap

EXAMPLE 26.5

In Example 26.4, we found that a drop of 10 units in consumer spending creates a recessionary gap of 50 units. How can the government eliminate the output gap and restore full employment by changing its purchases of goods and services G?

In Example 26.4, we found that planned aggregate expenditure was given by the equation $PAE = 960 + 0.8Y$, so that autonomous expenditure equaled 960. The 10-unit drop in $\overline{C}$ implied a 10-unit drop in autonomous expenditure, to 950. Because the multiplier in that sample economy equaled 5, this 10-unit decline in autonomous expenditure resulted in turn in a 50-unit decline in short-run equilibrium output.

To offset the effects of the consumption decline, the government would have to restore autonomous expenditure to its original value, 960. Under our assumption that government purchases are simply given and do not depend on output, government purchases are part of autonomous expenditure, and changes in government purchases change autonomous expenditure one-for-one. Thus, to increase autonomous expenditure from 950 to 960, the government should simply increase its purchases by 10 units (for example, by increasing spending on military defense or road construction). According to the basic Keynesian model, this increase in government purchases should return autonomous expenditure and hence output to their original levels.

The effect of the increase in government purchases is shown graphically in Figure 26.5. After the 10-unit decline in the autonomous component of consumption

FIGURE 26.5

An Increase in Government Purchases Eliminates a Recessionary Gap.

After a 10-unit decline in the autonomous part of consumer spending $\overline{C}$, the economy is at point F, with a recessionary gap of 50 (see Figure 26.4). A 10-unit increase in government purchases raises autonomous expenditure by 10 units, shifting the expenditure line back to its original position and raising the equilibrium point from F to E. At point E, where output equals potential output ($Y = Y^* = 4,800$), the output gap has been eliminated.

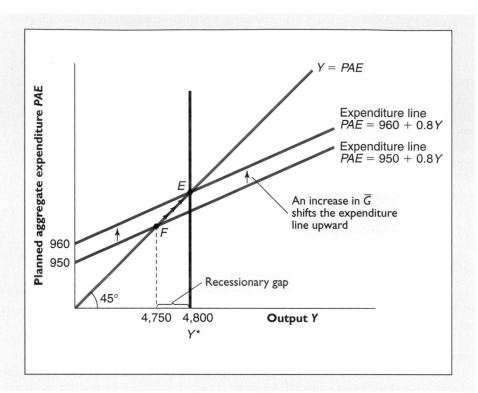

spending $\overline{C}$, the economy is at point F, with a 50-unit recessionary gap. A 10-unit increase in government purchases raises autonomous expenditure by 10 units, raising the intercept of the expenditure line by 10 units and causing the expenditure line to shift upward in parallel fashion. The economy returns to point E, where short-run equilibrium output equals potential output ($Y = Y^* = 4,800$) and the output gap has been eliminated.

EXERCISE 26.5

In Exercise 26.4, you considered the case in which consumers become more rather than less confident, leading to an expansionary output gap. Discuss how a change in government purchases could be used to eliminate this output gap. Show your analysis graphically.

To this point we have been considering the effect of fiscal policy on a hypothetical economy. Economic Naturalists 26.6 and 26.7 illustrate the application of fiscal policy in real economies.

Why is Japan building roads nobody wants to use?

A few years ago Japanese officials decided to build a 160-mile-long toll road on the northern island of Hokkaido. Thus far the costs of the road have been about $60 million per mile. Very few drivers use the road, largely because an existing highway that runs parallel to the new toll road is free. Officials tried to attract drivers by offering prizes and running promotional contests. Though the campaign succeeded in increasing the average number of cars on the road to 862 per day, the route is still the least used highway in Japan (*The New York Times*, November 25, 1999, p. A1). Why is Japan building roads nobody wants to use?

As noted in Economic Naturalist 26.4, Japan spent the 1990s in a deep slump. In response, the Japanese government periodically initiated large spending programs to try to stimulate the economy. Indeed, during the 1990s the Japanese government spent more than $1 trillion on public works projects. More than $10 billion was

ECONOMIC NATURALIST 26.6

spent on the Tokyo subway system alone, an amount so far over budget that subway tokens will have to cost an estimated $9.50 each if the investment is ever to be recouped. (Even more frustrating to passengers, the subway does not run in a complete circle, requiring them to make inconvenient transfers to traverse the city.) Other examples of government spending programs include the construction of multimillion-dollar concert halls in small towns, elaborate tunnels where simple roads would have been adequate, and the digging up and relaying of cobblestone sidewalks. Despite all this spending, the Japanese slump has dragged on.

The basic Keynesian model implies that increases in government spending such as those undertaken in Japan should help to increase output and employment. Japanese public works projects do appear to have stimulated the economy, though not enough to pull Japan out of recession. Why has Japan's fiscal policy proved inadequate to the task? Some critics have argued that the Japanese government was unconscionably slow in initiating the fiscal expansion, and that when spending was finally increased, it was simply not enough, relative to the size of the Japanese economy and the depth of the recession. Another possibility, which lies outside the basic Keynesian model, is that the wasteful nature of much of the government spending demoralized Japanese consumers, who realized that as taxpayers they would at some point be responsible for the costs incurred in building roads nobody wants to use. Reduced consumer confidence implies reduced consumption spending, which may to some extent have offset the stimulus from government spending. Very possibly, more productive investments of Japanese public funds would have had a greater impact on aggregate expenditure (by avoiding the fall in consumer confidence); certainly, they would have had a greater long-term benefit in terms of increasing the potential output of the economy.

Does military spending stimulate the economy?

An antiwar poster from the 1960s bore the message "War is good business. Invest your son." War itself poses too many economic and human costs to be good business, but military spending could be a different matter. According to the basic Keynesian model, increases in planned aggregate expenditure resulting from stepped-up government purchases may help bring an economy out of a recession or depression. Does military spending stimulate aggregate demand? Figure 26.6 shows U.S. military spending as a share of GDP from 1940 to 2001. The shaded areas in the figure correspond to periods of recession as shown in Table 25.1.

ECONOMIC NATURALIST 26.7

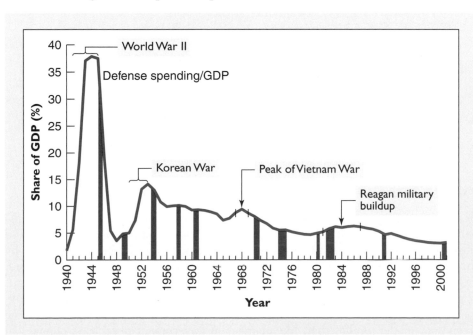

FIGURE 26.6

U.S. Military Expenditures as a Share of GDP, 1940–2001.

Military expenditures as a share of GDP rose during World War II, the Korean War, the Vietnam War, and the Reagan military buildup of the early 1980s. Increased military spending is generally associated with an expanding economy and declining unemployment. The shaded areas indicate periods of recession.

Note the spike that occurred during World War II (1941–1945), when military spending reached nearly 38 percent of U.S. GDP, as well as the surge during the Korean War (1950–1953). Smaller increases in military spending relative to GDP occurred at the peak of the Vietnam War in 1967–1969 and during the Reagan military buildup of the 1980s.

Figure 26.6 provides some support for the idea that expanded military spending tends to promote growth in aggregate demand. The clearest case is the World War II era, during which massive military spending helped the U.S. economy to recover from the Great Depression. The U.S. unemployment rate fell from 17.2 percent of the workforce in 1939 (when defense spending was less than 2 percent of GDP) to 1.2 percent in 1944 (when defense spending was greater than 37 percent of GDP). Two brief recessions, in 1945 and 1948–1949, followed the end of the war and the sharp decline in military spending. At the time, though, many people feared that the war's end would bring a resumption of the Great Depression, so the relative mildness of the two postwar recessions was something of a relief.

Increases in defense spending during the post–World War II period were also associated with economic expansions. The Korean War of 1950–1953 occurred simultaneously with a strong expansion, during which the unemployment rate dropped from 5.9 percent in 1949 to 2.9 percent in 1953. A recession began in 1954, the year after the armistice was signed, though military spending had not yet declined much. Economic expansions also occurred during the Vietnam-era military buildup in the 1960s and the Reagan buildup of the 1980s. Finally, on a smaller scale, increased government spending for military purposes and homeland security probably contributed to the relative mildness of the U.S. recession that began in 2001. These episodes support the idea that increases in government purchases—in this case, of weapons, other military supplies, and the services of military personnel—can help to stimulate the economy.

"Your majesty, my voyage will not only forge a new route to the spices of the East but also create over three thousand new jobs."

TAXES, TRANSFERS, AND AGGREGATE SPENDING

Besides making decisions about government purchases of goods and services, fiscal policymakers also determine the level and types of taxes to be collected and transfer payments to be made. (Transfer payments, recall, are payments made by the government to the public, for which no current goods or services are received. Examples of transfer payments are unemployment insurance benefits, Social Security benefits, and income support payments to farmers. Once again, transfer payments are *not* included in government purchases of goods and services.) The basic Keynesian model implies that, like changes in government purchases, changes in the level of taxes or transfers can be used to affect planned aggregate expenditure and thus eliminate output gaps.

Unlike changes in government purchases, however, changes in taxes or transfers do not affect planned spending directly. Instead they work indirectly, by changing disposable income in the private sector. For example, either a tax cut or an increase in government transfer payments increases disposable income, equal to $Y - T$. According to the consumption function, when disposable income rises, households should spend more. Thus a tax cut or increase in transfers should increase planned aggregate expenditure. Likewise, an increase in taxes or a cut in transfers, by lowering households' disposable income, will tend to lower planned spending. Example 26.6 illustrates the effects of a tax cut on spending and output.

Using a tax cut to close a recessionary gap

EXAMPLE 26.6

In Example 26.4, we found that in our hypothetical economy, an initial drop in consumer spending of 10 units creates a recessionary gap of 50 units. Example 26.5 showed that this recessionary gap could be eliminated by a 10-unit increase in government purchases. Suppose that, instead of increasing government purchases, fiscal policymakers decided to stimulate consumer spending by changing the level of tax collections. By how much should they change taxes to eliminate the output gap?

A common first guess at the answer to this problem is that policymakers should cut taxes by 10, but that guess is not correct. Let's see why.

The source of the recessionary gap in Example 26.4 is the reduction that households made in their consumption spending by 10 units at each level of output Y—that is, the constant term $\overline{C}$ in the consumption function is assumed to have fallen 10 units. To eliminate this recessionary gap, the change in taxes must induce households to increase their consumption spending by 10 units at each output level. However, if taxes T are cut by 10 units, raising disposable income $Y - T$ by 10 units, consumption at each level of output Y will increase by only 8 units.

Why? The reason is that the marginal propensity to consume out of disposable income in our example is 0.8, so that consumption spending increases by only 0.8 times the amount of the tax cut. (The rest of the tax cut is saved.) An increase in autonomous expenditure of 8 units is not enough to return output to its full-employment level, in this example.

To raise consumption spending by 10 units, fiscal policymakers must instead cut taxes by 12.5 units. Because $0.8(12.5) = 10$, a tax cut of 12.5 will spur households to increase their consumption by 10 units at each level of output. That increase will just offset the 10-unit decrease in $\overline{C}$ in this example, restoring the economy to full employment.

Note that since T refers to *net taxes,* or taxes less transfers, the same result could be obtained by increasing transfer payments by 12.5 units. Because households spend 0.8 times any increase in transfer payments they receive, this policy would also raise consumption spending by 10 units at any level of output.

Graphically, the effect of the tax cut is identical to the effect of the increase in government purchases, shown in Figure 26.5. Because it leads to a 10-unit increase in consumption at any level of output, the tax cut shifts the expenditure line up by 10 units. Equilibrium is attained at point E in Figure 26.5, where output again equals potential output.

EXERCISE 26.6

In a particular economy, a 20-unit increase in planned investment moved the economy from an initial situation with no output gap to a situation with an expansionary gap. Describe two ways in which fiscal policy could be used to offset this expansionary gap. Assume the marginal propensity to consume equals 0.5.

Why did the federal government send out millions of $300 and $600 checks to households in 2001?

On May 25, 2001, Congress passed the Economic Growth and Tax Relief Reconciliation Act (EGTRRA) of 2001, which President George W. Bush signed on June 7. The EGTRRA made significant cuts in income tax rates and also provided for one-time tax rebate checks of up to $300 for individual taxpayers and up to $600 for married taxpayers filing a joint return. Millions of families received these checks in August and September of 2001, with payments totaling about $38 billion. Why did the federal government send out these checks?

Although the 2001 recession was not officially "declared" until November 2001 (when the National Bureau of Economic Research announced that the recession had begun in March), there was clear evidence by the spring of 2001 that the economy was slowing. Congress and the president hoped that by sending tax rebate checks to households, they could stimulate spending and perhaps avoid recession. In retrospect, the timing of the tax rebate was quite good, since the economy and consumer confidence were further buffeted by the terrorist attacks on New York City and Washington on September 11, 2001.

Did the tax rebates have their intended effect of stimulating consumer spending? It is difficult to know with any certainty, since we do not know how much households would have spent if they had not received these extra funds. A University of Michigan survey conducted in August, September, and October 2001 found that only 22 percent of households anticipated spending most of their rebates.[4] If this number is accurate, it would suggest the rebates had a relatively small effect on planned spending. On the other hand, consumer spending held up remarkably well during the last quarter of 2001 and into 2002, assisting the economy's recovery substantially. Most economists would agree that fiscal policy generally—including not only the tax rebates, but also significantly increased spending for the military and for domestic security following September 11—was an important reason that the 2001 recession was relatively short and mild.

 RECAP **FISCAL POLICY AND PLANNED SPENDING**

Fiscal policy includes two general tools for affecting total spending and eliminating output gaps: (1) changes in government purchases and (2) changes in taxes or transfer payments. An increase in government purchases increases autonomous expenditure by an equal amount. A reduction in taxes or an

---

[4]Matthew D. Shapiro and Joel Slemrod, *Consumer Response to Tax Rebates,* National Bureau of Economic Research Working Paper 8672, December 2001.

increase in transfer payments increases autonomous expenditure by an amount equal to the marginal propensity to consume times the reduction in taxes or increase in transfers. The ultimate effect of a fiscal policy change on short-run equilibrium output equals the change in autonomous expenditure times the multiplier. Accordingly, if the economy is in recession, an increase in government purchases, a cut in taxes, or an increase in transfers can be used to stimulate spending and eliminate the recessionary gap.

FISCAL POLICY AS A STABILIZATION TOOL: THREE QUALIFICATIONS

The basic Keynesian model might lead you to think that precise use of fiscal policy can eliminate output gaps. But as is often the case, the real world is more complicated than economic models suggest. We close the chapter with three qualifications about the use of fiscal policy as a stabilization tool.

FISCAL POLICY AND THE SUPPLY SIDE

We have focused so far on the use of fiscal policy to affect planned aggregate expenditure. However, most economists would agree that *fiscal policy may affect potential output as well as planned aggregate expenditure.* On the spending side, for example, investments in public capital, such as roads, airports, and schools, can play a major role in the growth of potential output, as we discussed in Chapter 20. On the other side of the ledger, tax and transfer programs may well affect the incentives, and thus the economic behavior, of households and firms. For example, a high tax rate on interest income may reduce the willingness of people to save for the future, while a tax break on new investment may encourage firms to increase their rate of capital formation. Such changes in saving or investment will in turn affect potential output. Many other examples could be given of how taxes and transfers affect economic behavior and thus possibly affect potential output as well.

Some critics of the Keynesian theory have gone so far as to argue that the *only* effects of fiscal policy that matter are effects on potential output. This was essentially the view of the so-called *supply-siders,* a group of economists and journalists whose influence reached a high point during the first Reagan term (1981–1985). Supply-siders focused on the need for tax cuts, arguing that lower tax rates would lead people to work harder (because they would be allowed to keep a larger share of their earnings), to save more, and to be more willing to innovate and take risks. Through their arguments that lower taxes would substantially increase potential output, with no significant effect on planned spending, the supply-siders provided crucial support for the large tax cuts that took place under the Reagan administration. Supply-sider ideas also were used to support the long-term income tax cut passed under President George W. Bush in 2001.

A more balanced view is that fiscal policy affects *both* planned spending *and* potential output. Thus, in making fiscal policy, government officials should take into account not only the need to stabilize planned aggregate expenditure but also the likely effects of government spending, taxes, and transfers on the economy's productive capacity.

THE PROBLEM OF DEFICITS

A second consideration for fiscal policymakers thinking about stabilization policies is *the need to avoid large and persistent budget deficits.* Recall from Chapter 22 that the government's budget deficit is the excess of government spending over tax collections. Sustained government deficits can be harmful because they reduce national saving, which in turn reduces investment in new capital goods—an important source of long-run economic growth. The need to keep deficits under control may make increasing spending or cutting taxes to fight a slowdown a less attractive option, both economically and politically. For example, Japan has substantially increased government spending over the past decade in its attempts to stimulate its lagging economy (see Economic Naturalist 26.6). The Japanese government's budget deficit has in the process become so large that the Japanese prime minister ruled out additional fiscal stimulus until the deficit can be brought under better control.

THE RELATIVE INFLEXIBILITY OF FISCAL POLICY

The third qualification about the use of fiscal policy is that *fiscal policy is not always flexible enough to be useful for stabilization.* Our examples have implicitly assumed that the government can change spending or taxes relatively quickly in order to eliminate output gaps. In reality, changes in government spending or taxes must usually go through a lengthy legislative process, which reduces the ability of fiscal policy to respond in a timely way to economic conditions. For example, budget and tax changes proposed by the president must typically be submitted to Congress 18 months or more before they go into effect. Another factor that limits the flexibility of fiscal policy is that fiscal policymakers have many other objectives besides stabilizing aggregate spending, from ensuring an adequate national defense to providing income support to the poor. What happens if, say, the need to strengthen the national defense requires an increase in government spending, but the need to contain planned aggregate expenditure requires a decrease in government spending? Such conflicts can be difficult to resolve through the political process.

This lack of flexibility means that fiscal policy is less useful for stabilizing spending than the basic Keynesian model suggests. Nevertheless, most economists view fiscal policy as an important stabilizing force, for two reasons. The first is the presence of **automatic stabilizers**, provisions in the law that imply *automatic* increases in government spending or decreases in taxes when real output declines. For example, some government spending is earmarked as "recession aid"; it flows to communities automatically when the unemployment rate reaches a certain level. Taxes and transfer payments also respond automatically to output gaps: When GDP declines, income tax collections fall (because households' taxable incomes fall) while unemployment insurance payments and welfare benefits rise—all without any explicit action by Congress. These automatic changes in government spending and tax collections help to increase planned spending during recessions and reduce it during expansions, without the delays inherent in the legislative process.

The second reason that fiscal policy is an important stabilizing force is that although fiscal policy may be difficult to change quickly, it may still be useful for dealing with prolonged episodes of recession. The Great Depression of the 1930s and the Japanese slump of the 1990s are two cases in point. However, because of the relative lack of flexibility of fiscal policy, in modern economies aggregate spending is more usually stabilized through monetary policy. The stabilizing role of monetary policy is the subject of the next chapter.

automatic stabilizers
provisions in the law that imply *automatic* increases in government spending or decreases in taxes when real output declines

---

▪ SUMMARY ▪

- The basic Keynesian model shows how fluctuations in planned aggregate expenditure, or total planned spending, can cause actual output to differ from potential output. Too

little spending leads to a recessionary output gap; too much spending creates an expansionary output gap. This model relies on the crucial assumption that firms do not respond to every change in demand by changing prices. Instead, they typically set a price for some period, then meet the demand forthcoming at that price. Firms do not change prices continually because changing prices entails costs, called *menu costs*.

- *Planned aggregate expenditure* is total planned spending on final goods and services. The four components of total spending are consumption, investment, government purchases, and net exports. Planned and actual consumption, government purchases, and net exports are generally assumed to be the same. Actual investment may differ from planned investment, because firms may sell a greater or lesser amount of their production than they expected. If firms sell less than they expected, for example, they are forced to add more goods to inventory than anticipated. And because additions to inventory are counted as part of investment, in this case actual investment (including inventory investment) is greater than planned investment.

- Consumption is related to disposable, or after-tax, income by a relationship called the *consumption function*. The amount by which desired consumption rises when disposable income rises by one dollar is called the *marginal propensity to consume* (MPC, or c). The marginal propensity to consume is always greater than zero but less than one (that is, $0 < c < 1$).

- An increase in real output raises planned aggregate expenditure, since higher output (and, equivalently, higher income) encourages households to consume more. Planned aggregate expenditure can be broken down into two components, autonomous expenditure and induced expenditure. *Autonomous expenditure* is the portion of planned spending that is independent of output; *induced expenditure* is the portion of spending that depends on output.

- In the period in which prices are fixed, *short-run equilibrium output* is the level of output that just equals planned aggregate expenditure. Short-run equilibrium can be determined numerically by a table which compares alternative values of output and the planned spending implied by each level of output. Short-run equilibrium output can also be determined graphically in a Keynesian cross diagram, drawn with planned aggregate expenditure on the vertical axis and output on the horizontal axis. The Keynesian cross contains two lines: an expenditure line, which relates planned aggregate expenditure to output, and a 45° line,

which represents the condition that short-run equilibrium output equals planned aggregate expenditure. Short-run equilibrium output is determined at the point at which these two lines intersect.

- Changes in autonomous expenditure will lead to changes in short-run equilibrium output. In particular, if the economy is initially at full employment, a fall in autonomous expenditure will create a recessionary gap and a rise in autonomous expenditure will create an expansionary gap. The amount by which a one-unit increase in autonomous expenditure raises short-run equilibrium output is called the *multiplier*. An increase in autonomous expenditure not only raises spending directly; it also raises the incomes of producers, who in turn increase their spending, and so on. Hence the multiplier is greater than 1; that is, a one-dollar increase in autonomous expenditure tends to raise short-run equilibrium output by more than one dollar.

- To eliminate output gaps and restore full employment, the government employs *stabilization policies*. The two major types of stabilization policy are monetary policy and fiscal policy. Stabilization policies work by changing planned aggregate expenditure and hence short-run equilibrium output. For example, an increase in government purchases raises autonomous expenditure directly, so it can be used to reduce or eliminate a recessionary gap. Similarly, a cut in taxes or an increase in transfer payments increases the public's disposable income, raising consumption spending at each level of output by an amount equal to the marginal propensity to consume times the cut in taxes or increase in transfers. Higher consumer spending, in turn, raises short-run equilibrium output.

- Three qualifications must be made to the use of fiscal policy as a stabilization tool. First, fiscal policy may affect potential output as well as aggregate spending. Second, large and persistent government budget deficits reduce national saving and growth; the need to keep deficits under control may limit the use of expansionary fiscal policies. Finally, because changes in fiscal policy must go through a lengthy legislative process, fiscal policy is not always flexible enough to be useful for short-run stabilization. However, *automatic stabilizers*—provisions in the law that imply automatic increases in government spending or reductions in taxes when output declines—can overcome the problem of legislative delays to some extent and contribute to economic stability.

■ KEY TERMS ■

automatic stabilizers (690)
autonomous expenditure (673)
consumption function (670)
contractionary policies (683)
expansionary policies (682)

induced expenditure (673)
income-expenditure multiplier (682)
marginal propensity to consume (MPC), or c (671)
menu costs (666)

planned aggregate expenditure (*PAE*) (667)
short-run equilibrium output (674)
stabilization policies (682)
wealth effect (670)

▪ REVIEW QUESTIONS ▪

1. What is the key assumption of the basic Keynesian model? Explain why this assumption is needed if one is to accept the view that aggregate spending is a driving force behind short-term economic fluctuations.

2. Give an example of a good or service whose price changes very frequently and one whose price changes relatively infrequently. What accounts for the difference?

3. Define *planned aggregate expenditure* and list its components. Why does planned spending change when output changes?

4. Explain how planned spending and actual spending can differ. Illustrate with an example.

5. Sketch a graph of the consumption function, labeling the axes of the graph. Discuss the economic meaning of (a) a movement from left to right along the graph of the consumption function; and (b) a parallel upward shift of the consumption function. Give an example of a factor that could lead to a parallel upward shift of the consumption function.

6. Sketch the Keynesian cross diagram. Explain in words the economic significance of the two lines graphed in the diagram. Given only this diagram, how could you determine autonomous expenditure, induced expenditure, the marginal propensity to consume, and short-run equilibrium output?

7. Using the Keynesian cross diagram, illustrate the two causes of the 1990–1991 recession discussed in Economic Naturalist 26.3.

8. Define the *multiplier*. In economic terms, why is the multiplier greater than 1?

9. The government is considering two alternative policies, one involving increased government purchases of 50 units, the other involving a tax cut of 50 units. Which policy will stimulate planned aggregate expenditure by more? Why?

10. Discuss three reasons why the use of fiscal policy to stabilize the economy is more complicated than suggested by the basic Keynesian model.

▪ PROBLEMS ▪

1. Acme Manufacturing is producing $4,000,000 worth of goods this year and expects to sell its entire production. It is also planning to purchase $1,500,000 in new equipment during the year. At the beginning of the year the company has $500,000 in inventory in its warehouse. Find actual investment and planned investment if
   a. Acme actually sells $3,850,000 worth of goods.
   b. Acme actually sells $4,000,000 worth of goods.
   c. Acme actually sells $4,200,00 worth of goods.

   Assuming that Acme's situation is similar to that of other firms, in which of these three cases is output equal to short-run equilibrium output?

2. Data on before-tax income, taxes paid, and consumption spending for the Simpson family in various years are given below.

Before-tax income ($)	Taxes paid ($)	Consumption spending ($)
25,000	3,000	20,000
27,000	3,500	21,350
28,000	3,700	22,070
30,000	4,000	23,600

   a. Graph the Simpsons' consumption function and find their household's marginal propensity to consume.
   b. How much would you expect the Simpsons to consume if their income was $32,000 and they paid taxes of $5,000?
   c. Homer Simpson wins a lottery prize. As a result, the Simpson family increases its consumption by $1,000 at each level of after-tax income. ("Income" does not include the prize money.) How does this change affect the graph of their consumption function? How does it affect their marginal propensity to consume?

3. An economy is described by the following equations:

$$C = 1,800 + 0.6(Y - T)$$
$$I^P = 900$$
$$G = 1,500$$
$$NX = 100$$
$$T = 1,500$$
$$Y^* = 9,000$$

   a. Find a numerical equation linking planned aggregate expenditure to output.
   b. Find autonomous expenditure and induced expenditure in this economy.

4. For the economy described in Problem 3:
   a. Construct a table like Table 26.1 to find short-run equilibrium output. Consider possible values for short-run equilibrium output ranging from 8,200 to 9,000.
   b. Show the determination of short-run equilibrium output for this economy using the Keynesian cross diagram.
   c. What is the output gap for this economy? If the natural rate of unemployment is 4 percent, what is the actual unemployment rate for this economy (use Okun's law)?

5. For the economy described in Problem 3, find the effect on short-run equilibrium output of
   a. An increase in government purchases from 1,500 to 1,600.
   b. A decrease in tax collections from 1,500 to 1,400 (leaving government purchases at their original value).
   c. A decrease in planned investment spending from 900 to 800.

   Assume each of these changes is a change in autonomous expenditure. Take as given that the multiplier for this economy is 2.5. If you have studied Appendix B in this chapter, show why this is so.

6. An economy is initially at full employment, but a decrease in planned investment spending (a component of autonomous expenditure) pushes the economy into recession. Assume that the MPC of this economy is 0.75 and that the multiplier is 4.
   a. How large is the recessionary gap after the fall in planned investment?
   b. By how much would the government have to change its purchases to restore the economy to full employment?
   c. Alternatively, by how much would the government have to change taxes?
   d.* Suppose that the government's budget is initially in balance, with government spending equal to taxes collected. A balanced-budget law forbids the government from running a deficit. Is there anything that fiscal policymakers could do to restore full employment in this economy, assuming they do not want to violate the balanced-budget law?

7. An economy is described by the following equations:

$$C = 40 + 0.8(Y - T)$$
$$I^P = 70$$
$$G = 120$$
$$NX = 10$$
$$T = 150$$
$$Y^* = 580$$

   The multiplier in this economy is 5.

   a. Find a numerical equation relating planned aggregate expenditure to output.
   b. Construct a table to find the value of short-run equilibrium output. (*Hint:* The economy is fairly close to full employment.)
   c. By how much would government purchases have to change in order to eliminate any output gap? By how much would taxes have to change? Show the effects of these fiscal policy changes in a Keynesian cross diagram.
   d. Repeat part c assuming that $Y^* = 630$.

*Problems marked by an asterisk (*) are more difficult.

8.* For the following economy, find autonomous expenditure, the multiplier, short-run equilibrium output, and the output gap. By how much would autonomous expenditure have to change to eliminate the output gap?

$$C = 3,000 + 0.5(Y - T)$$
$$I^P = 1,500$$
$$G = 2,500$$
$$NX = 200$$
$$T = 2,000$$
$$Y^* = 12,000$$

9.* An economy has zero net exports. Otherwise, it is identical to the economy described in Problem 7.
a. Find short-run equilibrium output.
b. Economic recovery abroad increases the demand for the country's exports; as a result, NX rises to 100. What happens to short-run equilibrium output?
c. Repeat part b, but this time assume that foreign economies are slowing, reducing the demand for the country's exports, so that $NX = -100$. (A negative value of net exports means that exports are less than imports.)
d. How do your results help to explain the tendency of recessions and expansions to spread across countries?

10.* This problem illustrates the workings of automatic stabilizers. Suppose that the components of planned spending in an economy are as described in Appendix A: $C = \overline{C} + c(Y - T)$, $I^P = \overline{I}$, $G = \overline{G}$, and $NX = \overline{NX}$. However, suppose that, realistically, taxes are not fixed but depend on income. Specifically, we assume

$$T = tY,$$

where t is the fraction of income paid in taxes (the tax rate). As we will see in this problem, a tax system of this sort serves as an automatic stabilizer, because taxes collected automatically fall when incomes fall.

a. Find an algebraic expression for short-run equilibrium output in this economy.
b. Find an algebraic expression for the multiplier, that is, the amount that output changes when autonomous expenditure changes by 1 unit. Compare the expression you found to the formula for the multiplier when taxes are fixed. Show that making taxes proportional to income reduces the multiplier.
c. Explain how reducing the size of the multiplier helps to stabilize the economy, holding constant the typical size of fluctuations in the components of autonomous expenditure.
d. Suppose $\overline{C} = 500$, $\overline{I} = 1,500$, $\overline{G} = 2,000$, $\overline{NX} = 0$, $c = 0.8$, and $t = 0.25$. Calculate numerical values for short-run equilibrium output and the multiplier.

■ ANSWERS TO IN-CHAPTER EXERCISES ■

26.1 First we need to find an equation that relates planned aggregate expenditure PAE to output Y. We start with the definition of planned aggregate expenditure and then substitute the numerical values given in the problem:

$$PAE = C + I^P + G + NX$$
$$= [\overline{C} + c(Y - T)] + I^P + G + NX$$
$$= [820 + 0.7(Y - 600)] + 600 + 600 + 200$$
$$= 1,800 + 0.7Y.$$

*Problems marked by an asterisk (*) are more difficult.

Using this relationship we construct a table analogous to Table 26.1. Some trial and error is necessary to find an appropriate range of guesses for output (column 1).

Determination of short-run equilbrium output

(1) Output Y	(2) Planned aggregate expenditure PAE = 1,800 + 0.7Y	(3) Y − PAE	(4) Y = PAE?
5,000	5,300	−300	No
5,200	5,440	−240	No
5,400	5,580	−180	No
5,600	5,720	−120	No
5,800	5,860	−60	No
6,000	6,000	0	**Yes**
6,200	6,140	60	No
6,400	6,280	120	No
6,600	6,420	180	No

Short-run equilibrium output equals 6,000, as that is the only level of output that satisfies the condition $Y = PAE$.

26.2 The graph shows the determination of short-run equilibrium output, $Y = 6,000$. The intercept of the expenditure line is 1,800 and its slope is 0.7. Notice that the intercept equals autonomous expenditure and the slope equals the marginal propensity to consume.

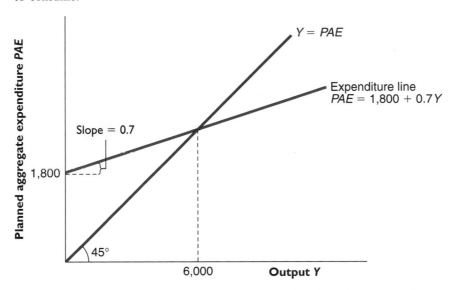

26.3 This problem is an application of Okun's law, introduced in Chapter 25. The recessionary gap in this example is 50/4,800, or about 1.04 percent, of potential output. By Okun's law, cyclical unemployment is one-half the percentage size of the output gap, or 0.52 percent. As the natural rate of unemployment is 5 percent, total unemployment rate after the recessionary gap appears will be approximately 5.52 percent.

26.4 This exercise is just the reverse of Example 26.4. An increase in $\overline{C}$ of 10 units raises autonomous expenditure and hence the intercept of the expenditure line by 10 units. The expenditure line shifts up, in parallel fashion, by 10 units, leading to an increase in output and an expansionary output gap. As output falls by 50 units in Example 26.4, it rises by 50 units, to 4,850, in the case analyzed here. To verify that short-run equilibrium output equals 4,850, note that an increase of 10 units in autonomous expenditure implies that PAE rises from $960 + 0.8Y$ to $970 + 0.8Y$. When $Y = 4,850$, then $PAE = 970 + 0.8(4,850) = 4,850$, so that we have $Y = PAE$.

26.5 In Exercise 26.4 we saw that a 10-unit increase in $\overline{C}$ increases autonomous expenditure and hence the intercept of the expenditure line by 10 units. The expenditure line shifts upward, in parallel fashion, by 10 units, leading to an expansionary output gap. To offset this gap, the government should reduce its purchases by 10 units, returning autonomous expenditure to its original level. The expenditure line shifts back down to its original position, restoring output to its initial full-employment level. The graph is just the reverse of Figure 26.5, with the expenditure line being shifted up by the increase in consumption and down by the offsetting reduction in government purchases.

26.6 The 20-unit increase in planned investment is a 20-unit increase in autonomous expenditure, which will lead to an even greater increase in short-run equilibrium output. To offset the 20-unit increase in autonomous expenditure by means of fiscal policy, the government can reduce its purchases by 20 units. Alternatively, it could raise taxes (or cut transfers) to reduce consumption spending. Since the MPC = 0.5, to reduce consumption spending by 20 units at each level of output, the government will need to increase taxes (or reduce transfers) by 40 units. At each level of output, a 40-unit tax increase will reduce disposable income by 40 units and cause consumers to reduce their spending by $0.5 \times 40 = 20$ units, as needed to eliminate the expansionary output gap.

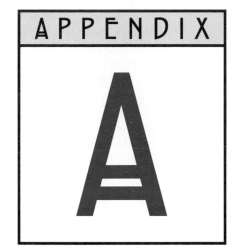

AN ALGEBRAIC SOLUTION OF THE BASIC KEYNESIAN MODEL

■

This chapter has shown how to solve the basic Keynesian model numerically and graphically, using the Keynesian cross diagram. In this appendix we will show how to find a more general algebraic solution for short-run equilibrium output in the basic Keynesian model. This solution has the advantage of showing clearly the links between short-run equilibrium output, the multiplier, and autonomous expenditure. The general method can also be applied when we make changes to the basic Keynesian model, as we will see in following chapters.

The model we will work with is the same one presented in the main part of the chapter. Start with the definition of planned aggregate expenditure, Equation 26.1:

$$PAE = C + I^p + G + NX. \qquad (26.1)$$

Equation 26.1 says that planned aggregate expenditure is the sum of the four types of planned spending: consumption spending by households C; planned investment spending by firms I^p; government purchases G; and net exports purchased by foreigners NX.

The first component of planned aggregate expenditure, consumption spending, is determined by the *consumption function*, Equation 26.2:

$$C = \overline{C} + c(Y - T). \qquad (26.2)$$

The consumption function says that consumption spending increases when disposable (after-tax) income $Y - T$ increases. Each dollar increase in disposable income raises consumption spending by c dollars, where c, known as the *marginal propensity to consume,* is a number between 0 and 1. Other factors affecting consumption spending are captured by the term $\overline{C}$. For example, a boom in the stock market that leads consumers to spend more at each level of disposable income (a *wealth effect*) would be represented as an increase in $\overline{C}$.

As in the body of the chapter, we assume that planned investment, government purchases, net exports, and net tax collections are simply given numbers. A variable whose value is fixed and given from outside the model is called an *exogenous* variable; so, in other words, we are assuming that planned investment, government purchases, net exports, and net tax collections are exogenous variables. Using an overbar to denote the given value of an exogenous variable, we can write this assumption as

$$I^p = \overline{I} \qquad \text{Planned investment,}$$
$$G = \overline{G} \qquad \text{Government purchases,}$$
$$NX = \overline{NX} \qquad \text{Net exports,}$$
$$T = \overline{T} \qquad \text{Net taxes (taxes less transfers).}$$

So, for example, $\overline{I}$ is the given value of planned investment spending, as determined outside the model. In our examples we will set $\overline{I}$ and the other exogenous variables equal to some particular number.

Our goal is to solve algebraically for *short-run equilibrium output,* the level of output that prevails during the period in which prices are predetermined. The first step is to relate planned aggregate expenditure *PAE* to output Y. Starting with the definition of planned aggregate expenditure (Equation 26.1), use the consumption function (Equation 26.2) to substitute for consumption spending C and replace I^p, G, NX, and T with their exogenous values. With these substitutions, planned aggregate expenditure can be written as

$$PAE = [\overline{C} - c(Y - \overline{T})] + \overline{I} + \overline{G} + \overline{NX}.$$

Rearranging this equation to separate the terms that do and do not depend on output Y, we get

$$PAE = [\overline{C} - c\overline{T} + \overline{I} + \overline{G} + \overline{NX}] + cY. \qquad (26A.1)$$

Equation 26A.1 is an important equation, because it shows the relationship between planned aggregate expenditure *PAE* and output Y. The bracketed term on the right side of the equation represents *autonomous expenditure,* the part of planned spending that does not depend on output. The term cY represents *induced expenditure,* the part of planned spending that does depend on output. Equation 26A.1 is also the equation that describes the *expenditure line* in the Keynesian cross diagram; it shows that the intercept of the expenditure line equals autonomous expenditure and the slope of the expenditure line equals the marginal propensity to consume.

We can illustrate how Equation 26A.1 works numerically by using Example 26.2 in the text. That example assumed the following numerical values: $\overline{C} = 620$, $\overline{I} = 220$, $\overline{G} = 300$, $\overline{NX} = 20$, $\overline{T} = 250$, and $c = 0.8$. Plugging these values into Equation 26A.1 and simplifying, we get

$$PAE = 960 + 0.8Y,$$

which is the same answer we found in Example 26.2. Autonomous expenditure in this example equals 960, and induced expenditure equals $0.8Y$.

The second step in solving for short-run equilibrium output begins with the definition of short-run equilibrium output (Equation 26.3):

$$Y = PAE.$$

Remember that short-run equilibrium output is the value of output at which output equals planned aggregate expenditure. Using Equation 26A.1 to substitute for PAE in the definition of short-run equilibrium output, we get

$$Y = [\overline{C} - c\overline{T} + \overline{I} + \overline{G} + \overline{NX}] + cY.$$

The value of Y that solves this equation is the value of short-run equilibrium output. To solve for Y, group all terms involving Y on the left side of the equation:

$$Y - cY = [\overline{C} - c\overline{T} + \overline{I} + \overline{G} + \overline{NX}]$$

or

$$Y(1 - c) = [\overline{C} - c\overline{T} + \overline{I} + \overline{G} + \overline{NX}].$$

Dividing both sides of the equation by $(1 - c)$ gives

$$Y = \left(\frac{1}{1 - c}\right)[\overline{C} - c\overline{T} + \overline{I} + \overline{G} + \overline{NX}]. \tag{26A.2}$$

Equation 26A.2 gives short-run equilibrium output for our model economy in terms of the exogenous values $\overline{C}, \overline{I}, \overline{G}, \overline{NX}$, and $\overline{T}$ and the marginal propensity to consume, c. We can use this formula to solve for short-run equilibrium output in specific numerical examples. For example, suppose that we once again plug in the numerical values assumed in Example 26.2: $\overline{C} = 620$, $\overline{I} = 220$, $\overline{G} = 300$, $\overline{NX} = 20$, $\overline{T} = 250$, and $c = 0.8$. We get

$$Y = \left(\frac{1}{1 - 0.8}\right)[620 - 0.8(250) + 220 + 300 + 20] = \frac{1}{0.2}(960) = 5(960) = 4,800,$$

which is the same answer we found more laboriously using Table 26.1.

EXERCISE 26A.1

Use Equation 26A.2 to find short-run equilibrium output for the economy described in Exercise 26.1 in the text. What are the intercept and the slope of the expenditure line?

Equation 26A.2 shows clearly the relationship between autonomous expenditure and short-run equilibrium output. Autonomous expenditure is the first term on the right side of Equation 13A.1, equal to $\overline{C} - c\overline{T} + \overline{I} + \overline{G} + \overline{NX}$. The equation shows that a one-unit increase in autonomous expenditure increases short-run equilibrium output by $1/(1 - c)$ units. In other words, we can see from Equation 26A.2 that the *multiplier* for this model equals $1/(1 - c)$. Further discussion of the multiplier is given in the second appendix to the chapter.

▪ ANSWERS TO IN-APPENDIX EXERCISE ▪

26A.1 The equation describing short-run equilibrium output is

$$Y = \left(\frac{1}{1 - c}\right)(\overline{C} - c\overline{T} + \overline{I} + \overline{G} + \overline{NX}). \tag{26A.2}$$

Using data from Exercise 26.1, set $\overline{C} = 820$, $c = 0.7$, $\overline{I} = 600$, $\overline{G} = 600$, $\overline{NX} = 200$, and $\overline{T} = 600$. Plugging these values into Equation (26A.2) we get

$$Y = \left(\frac{1}{1 - 0.7}\right)[820 - 0.7(600 + 600 + 600 + 200)] = 3.33 \times 1{,}800 = 6{,}000,$$

which is the same result obtained in Exercise 26.1.

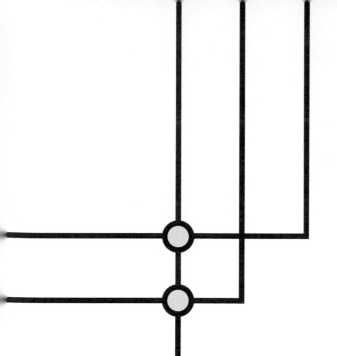

THE MULTIPLIER IN THE BASIC KEYNESIAN MODEL

■

T his appendix builds on Example 26.4 in the text to give a more complete explanation of the *income-expenditure multiplier* in the basic Keynesian model. In Example 26.4, we saw that a drop in autonomous expenditure of 10 units caused a decline in short-run equilibrium output of 50 units, five times as great as the initial change in spending. Hence the multiplier in this example is 5.

To see why this multiplier effect occurs, note that the initial decrease of 10 in consumer spending (more precisely, in the constant term of the consumption function, $\overline{C}$) in Example 26.4 has two effects. First, the fall in consumer spending directly reduces planned aggregate expenditure by 10 units. Second, the fall in spending also reduces by 10 units the incomes of producers (workers and firm owners) of consumer goods. Under the assumption of Example 26.4 that the marginal propensity to consume is 0.8, the producers of consumer goods will therefore reduce *their* consumption spending by 8, or 0.8 times their income loss of 10. This reduction in spending cuts the income of *other* producers by 8 units, leading them to reduce their spending by 6.4, or 0.8 times their income loss of 8. These income reductions of 6.4 lead still other producers to cut their spending by 5.12, or 0.8 times 6.4, and so on. In principle this process continues indefinitely, although after many rounds of spending and income reductions the effects become quite small.

When all these "rounds" of income and spending reductions are added, the *total* effect on planned spending of the initial reduction of 10 in consumer spending is

$$10 + 8 + 6.4 + 5.12 + \cdots.$$

The three dots indicate that the series of reductions continues indefinitely. The total effect of the initial decrease in consumption can also be written as

$$10[1 + 0.8 + (0.8)^2 + (0.8)^3 + \cdots].$$

This expression highlights the fact that the spending that takes place in each round is 0.8 times the spending in the previous round (0.8), because that is the marginal propensity to consume out of the income generated by the previous round of spending.

A useful algebraic relationship, which applies to any number x greater than 0 but less than 1, is

$$1 + x + x^2 + x^3 + \cdots = \frac{1}{1-x}.$$

If we set $x = 0.8$, this formula implies that the total effect of the decline in consumption spending on aggregate demand and output is

$$10 \left(\frac{1}{1-0.8}\right) = 10\left(\frac{1}{0.2}\right) = 10 \times 5 = 50.$$

This answer is consistent with our earlier calculation, which showed that short-run equilibrium output fell by 50 units, from 4,800 to 4,750.

By a similar analysis we can also find a general algebraic expression for the multiplier in the basic Keynesian model. Recalling that c is the marginal propensity to consume out of disposable income, we know that a 1-unit increase in autonomous expenditure raises spending and income by 1 unit in the first round; by $c \times 1 = c$ units in the second round; by $c \times c = c^2$ units in the second round; by $c \times c^2 = c^3$ units in the third round; and so on. Thus the total effect on short-run equilibrium output of a 1-unit increase in autonomous expenditure is given by

$$1 + c + c^2 + c^3 + \cdots.$$

Applying the algebraic formula given above, and recalling that $0 < c < 1$, we can rewrite this expression as $1/(1 - c)$. Thus, in a basic Keynesian model with a marginal propensity to consume of c, the multiplier equals $1/(1 - c)$, the same result found in Appendix A to this chapter. Note that if $c = 0.8$, then $1/(1 - c) = 1/(1 - 0.8) = 5$, which is the same value of the multiplier we found numerically above.

STABILIZING THE ECONOMY: THE ROLE OF THE FED

∎

Financial market participants and commentators go to remarkable lengths to try to predict the actions of the Federal Reserve. For a while, the CNBC financial news program *Squawk Box* reported regularly on what the commentators called the Greenspan Briefcase Indicator. The idea was to spot Fed chairman Alan Greenspan on his way to meet with the Federal Open Market Committee, the group that determines U.S. monetary policy. If Greenspan's briefcase was packed full, presumably with macroeconomic data and analyses, the guess was that the Fed planned to change interest rates. A slim briefcase meant no change in rates was likely.

"It was right 17 out of the first 20 times," the program's anchor Mark Haines noted, "but it has a built-in self-destruct mechanism, because Greenspan packs his [own] briefcase. He can make it wrong or right. He has never publicly acknowledged the indicator, but we have reason to believe that he knows about it. We have to consider the fact that he wants us to stop doing it because the last two times the briefcase has been wrong, and that's disturbing."[1]

The Briefcase Indicator is but one example of the close public scrutiny that the chairman of the Federal Reserve and other monetary policymakers face. Every speech, every congressional testimony, every interview from a member of the Board of Governors is closely analyzed for clues about the future course of monetary policy. In self-defense, Greenspan and other policymakers have become masters of the carefully worded but often ambiguous public statement

---

[1]Robert H. Frank, "Safety in Numbers," *New York Times Magazine*, November 28, 1999, p. 35.

calculated to leave the "Fed-watchers" guessing. The reason for the intense public interest in the Federal Reserve's decisions about monetary policy—and especially the level of interest rates—is that those decisions have important implications both for financial markets and for the economy in general.

In this chapter we examine the workings of monetary policy, one of the two major types of *stabilization policy.* (The other type, fiscal policy, was discussed in Chapter 26.) As we saw in Chapter 26, stabilization policies are government policies that are meant to influence planned aggregate expenditure, with the goal of eliminating output gaps. Both types of stabilization policy, monetary and fiscal, are important and have been useful at various times. However, monetary policy, which can be changed quickly by a decision of the Federal Reserve's Federal Open Market Committee (FOMC), is more flexible and responsive than fiscal policy, which can be changed only by legislative action by Congress. Under normal circumstances, therefore, monetary policy is used more actively than fiscal policy to help stabilize the economy.

We will begin this chapter by discussing how the Fed uses its ability to control the money supply to influence the level of interest rates. We then turn to the economic effects of changes in interest rates. Building on our analysis of the basic Keynesian model in Chapter 26, we will see that, in the short run, monetary policy works by affecting planned spending and thus short-run equilibrium output. We will defer discussion of the other major effect of monetary policy actions, changes in the rate of inflation. The effects of monetary policy on inflation are addressed in Chapter 28.

THE FEDERAL RESERVE AND INTEREST RATES

When we introduced the Federal Reserve System in Chapter 23, we focused on the Fed's tools for controlling the *money supply,* that is, the quantity of currency and checking accounts held by the public. Determining the nation's money supply is the primary task of monetary policymakers. But if you follow the economic news regularly, you may find the idea that the Fed's job is to control the money supply a bit foreign, because the news media nearly always focus on the Fed's decisions about *interest rates.* Indeed, the announcement the Fed makes after each meeting of the Federal Open Market Committee nearly always concerns its plan for a particular short-term interest rate, called the *federal funds rate* (more on the federal funds rate later).

Actually, there is no contradiction between the two ways of looking at monetary policy—as control of the money supply or as the setting of interest rates. As we will see in this section, controlling the money supply and controlling the nominal interest rate are two sides of the same coin: Any value of the money supply chosen by the Fed implies a specific setting for the nominal interest rate, and vice versa. The reason for this close connection is that the nominal interest rate is effectively the "price" of money (or, more accurately, its opportunity cost). So, by controlling the quantity of money supplied to the economy, the Fed also controls the "price" of money (the nominal interest rate).

To better understand how the Fed determines interest rates, we will look first at the market for money, beginning with the demand side of that market. We will see that given the demand for money by the public, the Fed can control interest rates by changing the amount of money it supplies. Later we will show how the Fed uses control of interest rates to influence planned spending and the state of the economy.

THE DEMAND FOR MONEY

Recall from Chapter 23 that *money* refers to the set of assets, such as cash and checking accounts, that are usable in transactions. Money is also a store of value, like stocks, bonds, or real estate—in other words, a type of financial asset. As a financial asset, money is a way of holding wealth.

Anyone who has some wealth must determine the *form* in which he or she wishes to hold that wealth. For example, if Louis has wealth of $10,000, he could if he wished hold all $10,000 in cash. Or he could hold $5,000 of his wealth in the form of cash and $5,000 in government bonds. Or he could hold $1,000 in cash, $2,000 in a checking account, $2,000 in government bonds, and $5,000 in rare stamps. Indeed, there are thousands of different real and financial assets to choose from, all of which can be held in different amounts and combinations, so Louis's choices are virtually infinite. The decision about the forms in which to hold one's wealth is called the **portfolio allocation decision.**

What determines the particular mix of assets that Louis or another wealth holder will choose? All else being equal, people generally prefer to hold assets that they expect to pay a high *return* and do not carry too much *risk*. They may also try to reduce the overall risk they face through *diversification*—that is, by owning a variety of different assets.[2] Many people own some real assets, such as a car or a home, because they provide services (transportation or shelter) and often a financial return (an increase in value, as when the price of a home rises in a strong real estate market).

Here we do not need to analyze the entire portfolio allocation decision, but only one part of it—namely, the decision about how much of one's wealth to hold in the form of *money* (cash and checking accounts). The amount of wealth an individual chooses to hold in the form of money is that individual's **demand for money.** So if Louis decided to hold his entire $10,000 in the form of cash, his demand for money would be $10,000. But if he were to hold $1,000 in cash, $2,000 in a checking account, $2,000 in government bonds, and $5,000 in rare stamps, his demand for money would be only $3,000—that is, $1,000 in cash plus the $2,000 in his checking account.

portfolio allocation decision the decision about the forms in which to hold one's wealth

demand for money the amount of wealth an individual chooses to hold in the form of money

Consuelo's demand for money

EXAMPLE 27.1

Example 22.1 presented the balance sheet of an individual named Consuelo (see Table 22.1). What is her demand for money? If Consuelo wanted to increase her money holdings by $100, how could she do so? What if she wanted to reduce her money holdings by $100?

Looking back at Table 22.1, p. 569, we see that Consuelo's balance sheet shows five different asset types: cash, a checking account, shares of stock, a car, and furniture. Of these assets, the first two (the cash and the checking account) are forms of money. As shown in Table 22.1, Consuelo's money holdings consist of $80 in cash and $1,200 in her checking account. Thus Consuelo's demand for money—the amount of wealth she chooses to hold in the form of money—is $1,280.

There are many different ways in which Consuelo could increase her money holdings, or demand for money, by $100. She could sell $100 worth of stock and deposit the proceeds in the bank. That action would leave the total value of her assets and her wealth unchanged (because the decrease in her stockholdings would be offset by the increase in her checking account) but would increase her money holdings by $100. Another possibility would be to take a $100 cash advance on her credit card. That action would increase both her money holdings and her assets by $100 but would also increase her liabilities—specifically, her credit card balance—by $100. Once again, her total wealth would not change, though her money holdings would increase.

To reduce her money holdings, Consuelo need only use some of her cash or checking account balance to acquire a nonmoney asset or pay down a liability.

[2]Chapter 24 discusses risk, return, and diversification in more detail.

For example, if she were to buy an additional $100 of stock by writing a check against her bank account, her money holdings would decline by $100. Similarly, writing a check to reduce her credit card balance by $100 would reduce her money holdings by $100. You can confirm that though her money holdings decline, in neither case does Consuelo's total wealth change.

How much money should an individual (or household) choose to hold? Application of the *cost-benefit principle* tells us that an individual should increase his or her money holdings only so long as the benefit of doing so exceeds the cost. As we saw in Chapter 23, the principal *benefit* of holding money is its usefulness in carrying out transactions. Consuelo's shares of stock, her car, and her furniture are all valuable assets, but she cannot use them to buy groceries or pay her rent. She can make routine payments using cash or her checking account, however. Because of its usefulness in daily transactions, Consuelo will almost certainly want to hold some of her wealth in the form of money. Furthermore, if Consuelo is a high-income individual, she will probably choose to hold more money than someone with a lower income would, because she is likely to spend more and carry out more transactions that the low-income person.

Consuelo's benefit from holding money is also affected by the technological and financial sophistication of the society she lives in. For example, in the United States, developments such as credit cards, debit cards, and ATM machines have generally reduced the amount of money people need to carry out routine transactions, decreasing the public's demand for money at given levels of income. In the United States in 1960, for example, money holdings in the form of cash and checking account balances (the monetary aggregate M1) were about 28 percent of GDP. By 2002 that ratio had fallen to 11 percent of GDP.

Although money is an extremely useful asset, there is also a cost to holding money—more precisely, an opportunity cost—which arises from the fact that most forms of money pay little or no interest. Cash pays zero interest, and most checking accounts pay either no interest or very low rates. For the sake of simplicity, we will just assume that *the nominal interest rate on money is zero*. In contrast, most alternative assets, such as bonds or stocks, pay a positive nominal return. A bond, for example, pays a fixed amount of interest each period to the holder, while stocks pay dividends and may also increase in value (capital gains).

The cost of holding money arises because, in order to hold an extra dollar of wealth in the form of money, a person must reduce by one dollar the amount of wealth held in the form of higher-yielding assets, such as bonds or stocks. The *opportunity cost* of holding money is measured by the interest rate that could have been earned if the person had chosen to hold interest-bearing assets instead of money. All else being equal, the higher the nominal interest rate, the higher the opportunity cost of holding money, and hence the less money people will choose to hold.

We have been talking about the demand for money by individuals, but businesses also hold money to carry out transactions with customers and to pay workers and suppliers. The same general factors that determine individuals' money demand also affect the demand for money by businesses. That is, in choosing how much money to hold, a business, like an individual, will compare the benefits of holding money for use in transactions with the opportunity cost of holding a non-interest-bearing asset. Although we will not differentiate between the money held by individuals and the money held by businesses in discussing money demand, you should be aware that in the U.S. economy, businesses hold a significant portion—more than half—of the total money stock. Example 27.2 illustrates the determination of money demand by a businessowner.

Innovations such as ATM machines have reduced the amount of money that people need to hold for routine transactions.

© Aaron Haupt/Stock Boston

How much money should Kim's restaurants hold?

EXAMPLE 27.2

Kim owns several successful restaurants. Her accountant informs her that on the typical day her restaurants are holding a total of $50,000 in cash on the premises. The accountant points out that if Kim's restaurants reduced their cash holdings, Kim could use the extra cash to purchase interest-bearing government bonds.

The accountant proposes two methods of reducing the amount of cash Kim's restaurants hold. First, she could increase the frequency of cash pickups by her armored car service. The extra service would cost $500 annually but would allow Kim's restaurants to reduce their average cash holding to $40,000. Second, in addition to the extra pickups, Kim could employ a computerized cash management service to help her keep closer tabs on the inflows and outflows of cash at her restaurants. The service costs $700 a year, but the accountant estimates that, together with more frequent pickups, the more efficient cash management provided by the service could help Kim reduce average cash holdings at her restaurants to $30,000.

The interest rate on government bonds is 6 percent. How much money should Kim's restaurants hold? What if the interest rate on government bonds is 8 percent?

Kim's restaurants need to hold cash to carry out their normal business, but holding cash also has an opportunity cost, which is the interest those funds could be earning if they were held in the form of government bonds instead of zero-interest cash. As the interest rate on government bonds is 6 percent, each $10,000 by which Kim can reduce her restaurants' money holdings yields an annual benefit of $600 (6 percent of $10,000).

If Kim increases the frequency of pickups by her armored car service, reducing the restaurants' average money holdings from $50,000 to $40,000, the benefit will be the additional $600 in interest income that Kim will earn. The cost is the $500 charged by the armored car company. Since the benefit exceeds the cost, Kim should purchase the extra service and reduce the average cash holdings at her restaurants to $40,000.

Should Kim go a step further and employ the cash management service as well? Doing so would reduce average cash holdings at the restaurants from $40,000 to $30,000, which has a benefit in terms of extra interest income of $600 per year. However, this benefit is less than the cost of the cash management service, which is $700 per year. So Kim should *not* employ the cash management service and instead should maintain average cash holdings in her restaurants of $40,000.

If the interest rate on government bonds rises to 8 percent, then the benefit of each $10,000 reduction in average money holdings is $800 per year (8 percent of $10,000) in extra interest income. In this case the benefit of employing the cash management service, $800, exceeds the cost of doing so, which is $700. So Kim should employ the service, reducing the average cash holdings of her business to $30,000. The example shows that a higher nominal interest rate on alternative assets reduces the quantity of money demanded.

EXERCISE 27.1

The interest rate on government bonds falls from 6 percent to 4 percent. How much cash should Kim's restaurants hold now?

MACROECONOMIC FACTORS THAT AFFECT THE DEMAND FOR MONEY

In any household or business the demand for money will depend on a variety of individual circumstances. For example, a high-volume retail business that serves thousands of customers each day will probably choose to have more money on hand than a legal firm that bills clients and pays employees monthly. But while individuals and businesses vary considerably in the amount of money they choose to hold, three macroeconomic factors affect the demand for money quite broadly: the nominal interest rate, real output, and the price level. As we see next, the nominal interest rate affects the cost of holding money throughout the economy, while real output and the price level affect the benefits of money.

- *The nominal interest rate (i).* We have seen that the interest rate paid on alternatives to money, such as government bonds, determines the opportunity cost of holding money. The higher the prevailing nominal interest rate, the greater the opportunity cost of holding money, and hence the less money individuals and businesses will demand.

What do we mean by *the* nominal interest rate? As we have discussed, there are thousands of different assets, each with its own interest rate (rate of return). So can we really talk about *the* nominal interest rate? The answer is that, while there are many different assets, each with its own corresponding interest rate, the rates on those assets tend to rise and fall together. This is to be expected, because if the interest rates on some assets were to rise sharply while the rates on other assets declined, financial investors would flock to the assets paying high rates and refuse to buy the assets paying low rates. So, although there are many different interest rates in practice, speaking of the general level of interest rates usually does make sense. In this book, when we talk about *the* nominal interest rate, what we have in mind is some average measure of interest rates. This simplification is one more application of the macroeconomic concept of *aggregation,* introduced in Chapter 17.

The nominal interest rate is a macroeconomic factor that affects the cost of holding money. A macroeconomic factor that affects the *benefit* of holding money is

- *Real income or output (Y).* An increase in aggregate real income or output—as measured, for example, by real GDP—raises the quantity of goods and services that people and businesses want to buy and sell. When the economy enters a boom, for example, people do more shopping and stores have more customers. To accommodate the increase in transactions, both individuals and businesses need to hold more money. Thus higher real output raises the demand for money.

A second macroeconomic factor affecting the benefit of holding money is

- *The price level (P).* The higher the prices of goods and services, the more dollars (or yen, or euros) are needed to make a given set of transactions. Thus a higher price level is associated with a higher demand for money.

Today, when a couple of teenagers go out for a movie and snacks on Saturday night, they need probably five times as much cash as their parents did 25 years ago. Because the prices of movie tickets and popcorn have risen steeply over 25 years, more money (that is, more dollars) is needed to pay for a Saturday night date than in the past. By the way, the fact that prices are higher today does *not* imply that people are worse off today than in the past, because nominal wages and salaries have also risen substantially. In general, however, higher prices do imply that people need to keep a greater number of dollars available, in cash or in a checking account.

THE MONEY DEMAND CURVE

For the purposes of monetary policymaking, economists are most interested in the aggregate, or economywide, demand for money. The interaction of the aggregate demand for money, determined by the public, and the supply of money,

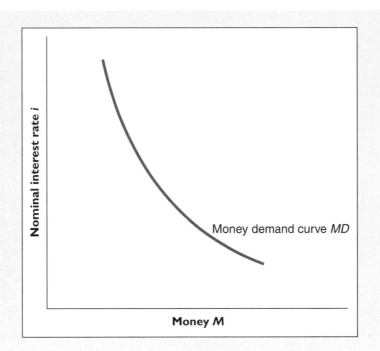

FIGURE 27.1
**The Money Demand
Curve.**
The money demand curve
relates the economywide
demand for money to the
nominal interest rate.
Because an increase in the
nominal interest rate raises
the opportunity cost of
holding money, the money
demand curve slopes down.

which is set by the Fed, determines the nominal interest rate that prevails in the economy.

The economywide demand for money can be represented graphically by the *money demand curve* (see Figure 27.1). The **money demand curve** relates the aggregate quantity of money demanded M to the nominal interest rate i. The quantity of money demanded M is a nominal quantity, measured in dollars (or yen, or euros, depending on the country). Because an increase in the nominal interest rate increases the opportunity cost of holding money, which reduces the quantity of money demanded, the money demand curve slopes down.

If we think of the nominal interest rate as the "price" (more precisely, the opportunity cost) of money and the amount of money people want to hold as the "quantity," the money demand curve is analogous to the demand curve for a good or service. As with a standard demand curve, the fact that a higher price of money leads people to demand less of it is captured in the downward slope of the demand curve. Furthermore, as in a standard demand curve, changes in factors other than the price of money (the nominal interest rate) can cause the demand curve for money to shift. For a given nominal interest rate, any change that makes people want to hold more money will shift the money demand curve to the right, and any change that makes people want to hold less money will shift the money demand curve to the left. We have already identified two macroeconomic factors other than the nominal interest rate that affect the economywide demand for money: real output and the price level. Because an increase in either of these variables increases the demand for money, it shifts the money demand curve rightward, as shown in Figure 27.2. Similarly, a fall in real output or the general price level reduces money demand, shifting the money demand curve leftward.

The money demand curve may also shift in response to other changes that affect the cost or benefit of holding money, such as the technological and financial advances we mentioned earlier. For example, the introduction of ATM machines reduced the amount of money people choose to hold and thus shifted the economywide money demand curve to the left. Economic Naturalist 27.1 describes another potential source of shifts in the demand for money, holdings of U.S. dollars by foreigners.

money demand curve Shows the relationship between the aggregate quantity of money demanded M and the nominal interest rate i; because an increase in the nominal interest rate increases the opportunity cost of holding money, which reduces the quantity of money demanded, the money demand curve slopes down

FIGURE 27.2

A Shift in the Money Demand Curve.

At a given nominal interest rate, any change that makes people want to hold more money—such as an increase in the general price level or in real GDP—will shift the money demand curve to the right.

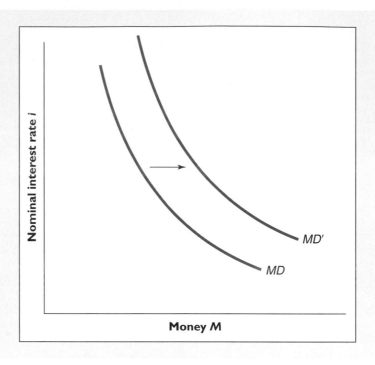

ECONOMIC NATURALIST 27.1

Why does the average Argentine hold more U.S. dollars than the average U.S. citizen?

Estimates are that the value of U.S. dollars circulating in Argentina exceeds $1,000 per person, which is higher than the per capita dollar holdings in the United States. A number of other countries, including those that once belonged to the former Soviet Union, also hold large quantities of dollars. In all, as much as $300 billion in U.S. currency—more than half the total amount issued—may be circulating outside the borders of the United States. Why do Argentines and other non-U.S. residents hold so many dollars?

U.S. residents and businesses hold dollars primarily for transactions purposes, rather than as a store of value. As a store of value, interest-bearing bonds and dividend-paying stocks are a better choice for Americans than zero-interest money. But this is not necessarily the case for the citizens of other countries, particularly nations that are economically or politically unstable. Argentina, for example, endured many years of high and erratic inflation in the 1970s and 1980s, which sharply eroded the value of financial investments denominated in Argentine pesos. Lacking better alternatives, many Argentines began saving in the form of U.S. currency—dollar bills hidden in the mattress or plastered into the wall—which they correctly believed to be more stable in value than peso-denominated assets.

Argentina's use of dollars became officially recognized in 1990. In that year the country instituted a new monetary system, called a currency board, under which U.S. dollars and Argentine pesos by law traded freely one for one. Under the currency board system, Argentines became accustomed to carrying U.S. dollars in their wallets for transactions purposes, along with pesos. However, in 2001 Argentina's monetary problems returned with a vengeance, as the currency board system broke down, the peso plummeted in value relative to the dollar, and inflation returned. The Argentine demand for dollars is thus likely only to increase in the next few years.

The countries formed as a result of the breakup of the Soviet Union have endured not only high inflation, but political instability and uncertainty as well. In a politically volatile environment, citizens face the risk that their savings, including their bank deposits, will be confiscated or heavily taxed by the government.

Often they conclude that a hidden cache of U.S. dollars—an estimated $1 million in 100-dollar bills can be stored in a suitcase—is the safest way to hold wealth.

In practice, changes in the foreign demand for U.S. dollars are an important source of fluctuation in the U.S. money demand curve. For example, large quantities of U.S. dollars flowed abroad during the Gulf War of 1990–1991, reflecting concerns among residents of the Middle East about regional instability. This increase in the demand for dollars shifted the U.S. money demand curve substantially to the right, as in Figure 27.2. Because policymakers at the Federal Reserve are concerned primarily with the number of dollars circulating in the U.S. economy, rather than in the world as a whole, they pay close attention to these international flows of greenbacks.

RECAP   MONEY DEMAND

For the economy as a whole, the demand for money is the amount of wealth that individuals, households, and businesses choose to hold in the form of money. The opportunity cost of holding money is measured by the nominal interest rate i, which is the return that could be earned on alternative assets such as bonds. The benefit of holding money is its usefulness in transactions.

Increases in real GDP (Y) or the price level (P) raise the nominal volume of transactions and thus the economywide demand for money. The demand for money is also affected by technological and financial innovations, such as the introduction of ATM machines, that affect the costs or benefits of holding money.

The money demand curve relates the economywide demand for money to the nominal interest rate. Because an increase in the nominal interest rate raises the opportunity cost of holding money, the money demand curve slopes downward.

Changes in factors other than the nominal interest rate that affect the demand for money can shift the money demand curve. For example, increases in real GDP or the price level raise the demand for money, shifting the money demand curve to the right, whereas decreases shift the money demand curve to the left.

THE SUPPLY OF MONEY AND MONEY MARKET EQUILIBRIUM

Where there is demand, can supply be far behind? As we have seen, the *supply of money* is controlled by the central bank—in the United States, the Federal Reserve, or Fed. The Fed's primary tool for controlling the money supply is *open-market operations*. For example, to increase the money supply, the Fed can use newly created money to buy government bonds from the public (an open-market purchase), which puts the new money into circulation.

Figure 27.3 shows the demand for and the supply of money in a single diagram. The nominal interest rate is on the vertical axis, and the nominal quantity of money (in dollars) is on the horizontal axis. As we have seen, because a higher nominal interest rate increases the opportunity cost of holding money, the money demand curve slopes downward. And because the Fed fixes the supply of money, we have drawn the *money supply curve* as a vertical line that intercepts the horizontal axis at the quantity of money chosen by the Fed, denoted M.

As in standard supply and demand analysis, equilibrium in the market for money occurs at the intersection of the supply and demand curves, shown as point E in Figure 27.3. The equilibrium amount of money in circulation, M, is simply the amount of money the Fed chooses to supply. The equilibrium nominal

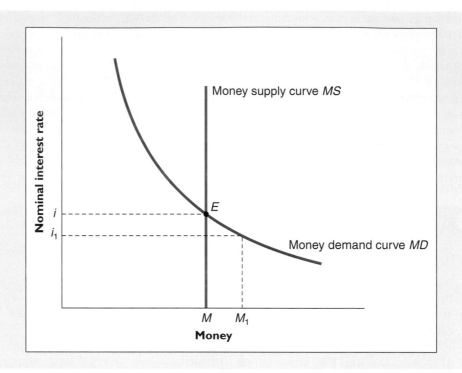

FIGURE 27.3

Equilibrium in the Market for Money.

Equilibrium in the market for money occurs at point *E*, where the demand for money by the public equals the amount of money supplied by the Federal Reserve. The equilibrium nominal interest rate, which equates the supply of and demand for money, is *i*.

interest rate *i* is the interest rate at which the quantity of money demanded by the public, as determined by the money demand curve, equals the fixed supply of money made available by the Fed.

To understand how the market for money reaches equilibrium, it may be helpful to recall the relationship between interest rates and the market price of bonds that was introduced in Chapter 24 (see Example 24.1). As we saw in the earlier chapter, the prices of existing bonds are *inversely related* to the current interest rate. Higher interest rates imply lower bond prices, and lower interest rates imply higher bond prices. With this relationship between interest rates and bond prices in mind, let's ask what happens if, say, the nominal interest rate is initially below the equilibrium level in the market for money—for example, at a value such as i_1 in Figure 27.3. At that interest rate the public's demand for money is M_1, which is greater than the actual amount of money in circulation, equal to *M*. How will the public—households and firms—react if the amount of money they hold is less than they would like? To increase their holdings of money, people will try to sell some of the interest-bearing assets they hold, such as bonds. But if everyone is trying to sell bonds and there are no willing buyers, then all the attempt to reduce bond holdings will achieve is to drive down the price of bonds, in the same way that a glut of apples will drive down the price of apples.

A fall in the price of bonds, however, is equivalent to an increase in interest rates. Thus the public's collective attempt to increase its money holdings by selling bonds and other interest-bearing assets, which has the effect of lowering bond prices, also implies higher market interest rates. As interest rates rise, the quantity of money demanded by the public will decline (represented by a right-to-left movement along the money demand curve), as will the desire to sell bonds. Only when the interest rate reaches its equilibrium value, *i* in Figure 27.3, will people be content to hold the quantities of money and other assets that are actually available in the economy.

EXERCISE 27.2

Describe the adjustment process in the market for money if the nominal interest rate is initially above rather than below its equilibrium value. What happens to the price of bonds as the money market adjusts toward equilibrium?

HOW THE FED CONTROLS THE NOMINAL INTEREST RATE

We began this section by noting that the public and the press usually talk about Fed policy in terms of decisions about the nominal interest rate rather than the money supply. Indeed, Fed policymakers themselves usually describe their plans in terms of a target value for the interest rate. We now have the necessary background to understand how the Fed translates the ability to determine the economy's money supply into control of the nominal interest rate.

Figure 27.3 showed that the nominal interest rate is determined by equilibrium in the market for money. Let's suppose that for some reason the Fed decides to lower the interest rate. As we will see, to lower the interest rate the Fed must increase the supply of money, which can be accomplished by using newly created money to purchase government bonds from the public (an open-market purchase).

Figure 27.4 shows the effects of such an increase in the money supply by the Fed. If the initial money supply is M, then equilibrium in the money market occurs at point E in the figure, and the equilibrium nominal interest rate is i. Now suppose the Fed, by means of open-market purchases of bonds, increases the money supply to M'. This increase in the money supply shifts the vertical money supply curve to the right, which shifts the equilibrium in the money market from point E to point F (see Figure 27.4). Note that at point F the equilibrium nominal interest rate has declined, from i to i'. The nominal interest rate must decline if the public is to be persuaded to hold the extra money that has been injected into the economy.

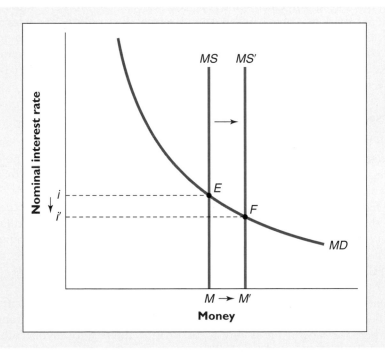

FIGURE 27.4
The Fed Lowers the Nominal Interest Rate.
The Fed can lower the equilibrium nominal interest rate by increasing the supply of money. For the given money demand curve, an increase in the money supply from M to M' shifts the equilibrium point in the money market from E to F, lowering the equilibrium nominal interest rate from i to i'.

To understand what happens in financial markets when the Fed expands the money supply, recall once again the inverse relationship between interest rates and the price of bonds. To increase the money supply, the Fed must buy government bonds from the public. However, if households and firms are initially satisfied with their asset holdings, they will be willing to sell bonds only at a price that is higher than the initial price. That is, the Fed's bond purchases will drive up the price of bonds in the open market. But we know that higher bond prices imply lower interest rates. Thus the Fed's bond purchases lower the prevailing nominal interest rate.

A similar scenario unfolds if the Fed decides to raise interest rates. To raise interest rates, the Fed must *reduce* the money supply. Reduction of the money supply is accomplished by an open-market sale—the sale of government bonds to the public in exchange for money. (The Fed keeps a large inventory of government bonds, acquired through previous open-market purchases, for use in open-market operations.) But in the attempt to sell bonds on the open market, the Fed will drive down the price of bonds. Given the inverse relationship between the price of bonds and the interest rate, the fall in bond prices is equivalent to a rise in the interest rate. In terms of money demand and money supply, the higher interest rate is necessary to persuade the public to hold less money.

As Figures 27.3 and 27.4 illustrate, control of the interest rate is not separate from control of the money supply. If Fed officials choose to set the nominal interest rate at a particular level, they can do so only by setting the money supply at a level consistent with the target interest rate. The Fed *cannot* set the interest rate and the money supply independently, since for any given money demand curve, a particular interest rate implies a particular size of the money supply, and vice versa.

Since monetary policy actions can be expressed in terms of either the interest rate or the money supply, why does the Fed (and almost every other central bank) choose to communicate its policy decisions to the public in terms of a target nominal interest rate rather than a target money supply? One reason, as we will see shortly, is that the main effects of monetary policy on both the economy and financial markets are exerted through interest rates. Consequently, the interest rate is often the best summary of the overall impact of the Fed's actions. Another reason for focusing on interest rates is that they are more familiar to the public than the money supply. Finally, interest rates can be monitored continuously in the financial markets, which makes the effects of Fed policies on interest rates easy to observe. By contrast, measuring the amount of money in the economy requires collecting data on bank deposits, with the consequence that several weeks may pass before policymakers and the public know precisely how Fed actions have affected the money supply.

What's so important about the federal funds rate?

Although thousands of interest rates and other financial data are easily available, the interest rate that is perhaps most closely watched by the public, politicians, the media, and the financial markets is the *federal funds rate*. What is the federal funds rate, and why is it so important?

The **federal funds rate** is the interest rate commercial banks charge each other for very short-term (usually overnight) loans. For example, a bank that has insufficient reserves to meet its legal reserve requirements (see Chapter 23) might borrow reserves for a few days from a bank that has extra reserves. Despite its name, the federal funds rate is not an official government interest rate and is not connected to the federal government.

Because the market for loans between commercial banks is tiny compared to some other financial markets, such as the market for government bonds, one might expect the federal funds rate to be of little interest to anyone other than the managers of commercial banks. But enormous attention is paid to this interest rate, because over most of the past 40 years, the Fed has expressed its policies in terms of a target value for it. Indeed, at the close of every meeting of the Federal Open Market Committee, the Fed announces whether the federal funds rate will be increased, decreased, or left unchanged. The Fed may also indicate the likely direction of future changes in the federal funds rate. Thus more than any other financial variable, changes in the federal funds rate indicate the Fed's plans for monetary policy.

Why does the Fed choose to focus on this particular nominal interest rate over all others? As we saw in Chapter 23, in practice the Fed affects the money supply through its control of bank reserves. Because open-market operations directly affect the supply of bank reserves, the Fed's control over the federal funds rate is particularly tight. However, if Fed officials chose to do so, they could probably signal their intended policies just as effectively in terms of another short-term nominal interest rate, such as the rate on short-term government debt.

Figure 27.5 shows the behavior of the federal funds rate since 1970. As you can see, the Fed has allowed this interest rate to vary considerably in response to economic conditions. Later in the chapter we will consider two specific episodes in which the Fed changed the federal funds rate in response to an economic slowdown.

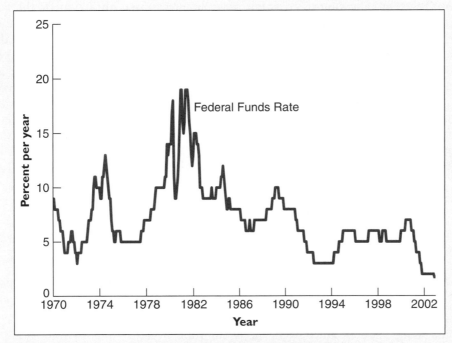

FIGURE 27.5
The Federal Funds Rate, 1970–2002.
The federal funds rate is the interest rate commercial banks charge each other for short-term loans. It is closely watched because the Fed expresses its policies in terms of a target value for the federal funds rate. The Fed has allowed the federal funds rate to vary considerably in response to economic conditions.

SOURCE: Federal Reserve Bank of St. Louis (http://www.stls.frb.org/fred/).

CAN THE FED CONTROL THE REAL INTEREST RATE?

Through its control of the money supply the Fed can control the economy's *nominal* interest rate. But many important economic decisions, such as the decisions to save and invest, depend on the *real* interest rate. To affect those decisions, the Fed must exert some control over the real interest rate.

Most economists believe that the Fed can control the real interest rate, at least for some period. To see why, recall the definition of the real interest rate from Chapter 19:

$$r = i - \pi.$$

The real interest rate r equals the nominal interest rate i minus the rate of inflation π. As we have seen, the Fed can control the nominal interest rate quite precisely through its ability to determine the money supply. Furthermore, inflation appears to change relatively slowly in response to changes in policy or economic conditions, for reasons we will discuss in the next chapter. Because inflation tends to adjust slowly, actions by the Fed to change the nominal interest rate generally lead the real interest rate to change by about the same amount.

The idea that the Fed can set the real interest rate appears to contradict the analysis in Chapter 22, which concluded that the real interest rate is determined by the condition that national saving must equal investment in new capital goods.

This apparent contradiction is rooted in a difference in the time frame being considered. Because inflation does not adjust quickly, the Fed can control the real interest rate over the short run. In the long run, however—that is, over periods of several years or more—the inflation rate and other economic variables will adjust, and the balance of saving and investment will determine the real interest rate. Thus the Fed's ability to influence consumption and investment spending through its control of the real interest rate is strongest in the short run.

In discussing the Fed's control over interest rates, we should also return to a point mentioned earlier in this chapter: In reality, not just one but many thousands of interest rates are seen in the economy. Because interest rates tend to move together (allowing us to speak of *the* interest rate), an action by the Fed to change the federal funds rate generally causes other interest rates to change in the same direction. However, the tendency of other interest rates (such as the long-term government bond rate or the rate on bonds issued by corporations) to move in the same direction as the federal funds rate is only a tendency, not an exact relationship. In practice, then, the Fed's control of other interest rates may be somewhat less precise than its control of the federal funds rate—a fact that complicates the Fed's policymaking.

RECAP **THE FEDERAL RESERVE AND INTEREST RATES**

In the market for money, the money demand curve slopes downward, reflecting the fact that a higher nominal interest rate increases the opportunity cost of holding money and thus reduces the amount of money people want to hold. The money supply curve is vertical at the quantity of money that the Fed chooses to supply. The equilibrium nominal interest rate i is the interest rate at which the quantity of money demanded by the public equals the fixed supply of money made available by the Fed.

The Federal Reserve controls the nominal interest rate by changing the supply of money. An open-market purchase of government bonds increases the money supply and lowers the equilibrium nominal interest rate. Conversely, an open-market sale of bonds reduces the money supply and increases the nominal interest rate. The Fed can prevent changes in the demand for money from affecting the nominal interest rate by adjusting the quantity of money supplied appropriately. The Fed typically expresses its policy intentions in terms of a target for a specific nominal interest rate, the federal funds rate.

Because inflation is slow to adjust, in the short run the Fed can control the real interest rate (equal to the nominal interest rate minus the inflation rate) as well as the nominal interest rate. In the long run, however, the real interest rate is determined by the balance of saving and investment.

THE EFFECTS OF FEDERAL RESERVE ACTIONS ON THE ECONOMY

Now that we have seen how the Fed can influence interest rates (both nominal and real), we can consider how monetary policy can be used to eliminate output gaps and stabilize the economy. The basic idea is relatively straightforward. As we will see in this section, planned aggregate expenditure is affected by the level of real interest rate prevailing in the economy. Specifically, a lower real interest rate encourages higher planned spending by households and firms, while a higher real interest rate reduces spending. By adjusting the real interest rate, the Fed can move planned spending in the desired direction. Under the assumption of the basic Keynesian model that firms produce just enough goods and services to meet the demand for their output, the Fed's stabilization of planned spending leads to stabilization of aggregate output and employment as well. In this section we will first explain how planned aggregate expenditure is related to the real interest rate. Then we will show how the Fed can use changes in the real interest rate to fight a recession or inflation.

PLANNED AGGREGATE EXPENDITURE AND THE REAL INTEREST RATE

In Chapter 26 we saw how planned spending is affected by changes in real output Y. Changes in output affect the private sector's disposable income $(Y - T)$, which in turn influences consumption spending—a relationship captured by the consumption function.

A second variable that has potentially important effects on aggregate expenditure is the real interest rate r. In Chapter 24, in our discussion of saving and investment, we saw that the real interest rate influences the behavior of both households and firms.

For households, the effect of a higher real interest rate is to increase the reward for saving, which leads households to save more.[3] At a given level of income, households can save more only if they consume less. Thus, saying that a higher real interest rate *increases* saving is the same as saying that a higher real interest rate *reduces* consumption spending at each level of income. The idea that higher real interest rates reduce household spending makes intuitive sense. Think, for example, about people's willingness to buy consumer durables, such as automobiles or furniture. Purchases of consumer durables, which are part of consumption spending, are often financed by borrowing from a bank, credit union, or finance company. When the real interest rate rises, the monthly finance charges associated with the purchase of a car or a piano are higher, and people become less willing or able to make the purchase. Thus a higher real interest rate reduces people's willingness to spend on consumer goods, holding constant disposable income and other factors that affect consumption.

Besides reducing consumption spending, a higher real interest rate also discourages firms from making capital investments. As in the case of a consumer thinking of buying a car or a piano, when a rise in the real interest rate increases financing costs, firms may reconsider their plans to invest. For example, upgrading a computer system may be profitable for a manufacturing firm when the cost of the system can be financed by borrowing at a real interest rate of 3 percent. However, if the real interest rate rises to 6 percent, doubling the cost of funds to the firm, the same upgrade may not be profitable and the firm may choose not to invest. We should also remember that residential investment—the building of houses and apartment buildings—is also part of investment spending. Higher interest rates, in the form of higher mortgage rates, certainly discourage this kind of investment spending as well.

The conclusion is that, at any given level of output, *both consumption spending and planned investment spending decline when the real interest rate increases*. Conversely, a fall in the real interest rate tends to stimulate consumption and investment spending by reducing financing costs. Example 27.3 is a numerical illustration of how planned aggregate expenditure can be related to the real interest rate and output.

When the real interest rate rises, financing a new car becomes more expensive and fewer cars are purchased.

[3]Because a higher real interest rate also reduces the amount households must put aside to reach a given savings target, the net effect of a higher real interest rate on saving is theoretically ambiguous. However, empirical evidence suggests that higher real interest rates have a modest positive effect on saving.

EXAMPLE 27.3   **Planned aggregate expenditure and the real interest rate**

In a certain economy, the components of planned spending are given by

$$C = 640 + 0.8(Y - T) - 400r,$$
$$I^P = 250 - 600r,$$
$$G = 300,$$
$$NX = 20,$$
$$T = 250.$$

Find the relationship of planned aggregate expenditure to the real interest rate r and output Y in this economy. Find autonomous expenditure and induced expenditure.

This example is similar to Example 26.2, except that now the real interest rate r is allowed to affect both consumption and planned investment. For example, the final term in the equation describing consumption, $-400r$, implies that a 1 percent (0.01) increase in the real interest rate, from 4 percent to 5 percent, for example, reduces consumption spending by $400(0.01) = 4$ units. Similarly, the final term in the equation for planned investment tells us that in this example, a 1 percent increase in the real interest rate lowers planned investment by $600(0.01) = 6$ units. Thus the overall effect of a 1 percent increase in the real interest rate is to lower planned aggregate expenditure by 10 units, the sum of the effects on consumption and investment. As in the earlier examples, disposable income $(Y - T)$ is assumed to affect consumption spending through a marginal propensity to consume of 0.8 (see the first equation), and government purchases G, net exports NX, and taxes T are assumed to be fixed numbers.

To find a numerical equation that describes the relationship of planned aggregate expenditure (PAE) to output, we can begin as in Chapter 26 with the general definition of planned aggregate expenditure:

$$PAE = C + I^P + G + NX.$$

Substituting for the four components of expenditure, using the equations describing each type of spending, we get

$$PAE = [640 + 0.8(Y - 250) - 400r] + [250 - 600r] + 300 + 20.$$

The first term in brackets on the right side of this equation is the expression for consumption, using the fact that taxes $T = 250$; the second bracketed term is planned investment; and the last two terms correspond to the given numerical values of government purchases and net exports. If we simplify this equation and group together the terms that do not depend on output Y and the terms that do depend on output, we get

$$PAE = [(640 - 0.8 \times 250 - 400r) + (250 - 600r) + 300 + 20] + 0.8Y,$$

or, simplifying further,

$$PAE = [1,010 - 1,000r] + 0.8Y. \tag{27.1}$$

In Equation 27.1, the term in brackets is *autonomous expenditure,* the portion of planned aggregate expenditure that does not depend on output. *Notice that in this example autonomous expenditure depends on the real interest rate r.* Induced expenditure, the portion of planned aggregate expenditure that does depend on output, equals $0.8Y$ in this example.

The real interest rate and short-run equilibrium output

EXAMPLE 27.4

In the economy described in Example 27.3, the real interest rate r is set by the Fed to equal 0.05 (5 percent). Find short-run equilibrium output.

We found in Example 27.3 that, in this economy, planned aggregate expenditure is given by Equation 27.1. We are given that the Fed sets the real interest rate at 5 percent. Setting $r = 0.05$ in Equation 27.1 gives

$$PAE = [1,010 - 1,000 \times (0.05)] + 0.8Y.$$

Simplifying, we get

$$PAE = 960 + 0.8Y.$$

So, when the real interest rate is 5 percent, autonomous expenditure is 960 and induced expenditure is $0.8Y$. Short-run equilibrium output is the level of output that equals planned aggregate spending. To find short-run equilibrium output, we could now apply the tabular method used in Chapter 26, comparing alternative values of output with the planned aggregate expenditure at that level of output. Short-run equilibrium output would be determined as the value of output such that output just equals spending, or

$$Y = PAE.$$

However, conveniently, when we compare this example with Example 26.2 in the last chapter, we see that the equation for planned aggregate expenditure, $PAE = 960 + 0.8Y$, is identical to what we found there. Thus Table 26.1, which we used to solve Example 26.2, applies to this example as well, and we get the same answer for short-run equilibrium output, which is $Y = 4,800$.

Short-run equilibrium output can also be found graphically, using the Keynesian cross diagram from Chapter 26. Again, since the equation for planned aggregate output is the same as in Example 26.2, Figure 26.3 applies equally well here.

EXERCISE 27.3

For the economy described in Example 27.4, suppose the Fed sets the real interest rate at 3 percent rather than at 5 percent. Find short-run equilibrium output. (*Hint:* Consider values between 4,500 and 5,500.)

THE FED FIGHTS A RECESSION

We have seen that the Fed can control the real interest rate, and that the real interest rate in turn affects planned spending and short-run equilibrium output. Putting these two results together, we can see how Fed actions may help to stabilize the economy.

Suppose the economy faces a recessionary gap—a situation in which real output is below potential output, and planned spending is "too low." To fight a recessionary gap, the Fed should reduce the real interest rate, stimulating consumption and investment spending. According to the theory we have developed, this increase in planned spending will cause output to rise, restoring the economy to full employment. Example 27.5 illustrates this point by extending Example 27.4.

The Fed fights a recession

EXAMPLE 27.5

For the economy described in Example 27.4, suppose potential output Y^* equals 5,000. As before, the Fed has set the real interest rate equal to 5 percent. At that real interest rate, what is the output gap? What should the Fed do to eliminate the output gap and restore full employment? You are given that the multiplier in this economy is 5.

In Example 27.4 we showed that with the real interest rate at 5 percent, short-run equilibrium output for this economy is 4,800. Potential output is 5,000, so the output gap $(Y - Y^*)$ equals $5,000 - 4,800 = 200$. Because actual output is below potential, this economy faces a recessionary gap.

To fight the recession, the Fed should lower the real interest rate, raising aggregate expenditure until output reaches 5,000, the full-employment level. That is, the Fed's objective is to increase output by 200. Because the multiplier equals 5, to increase output by 200 the Fed must increase autonomous expenditure by $200/5 = 40$ units. By how much should the Fed reduce the real interest rate to increase autonomous expenditure by 40 units? Autonomous expenditure in this economy is $[1,010 - 1,000r]$, as you can see from Equation 27.1, so that each percentage point reduction in r increases autonomous expenditure by $1,000 \times (0.01) = 10$ units. To increase autonomous expenditure by 40, then, the Fed should lower the real interest rate by 4 percentage points, from 5 percent to 1 percent.

In summary, to eliminate the recessionary gap of 200, the Fed should lower the real interest rate from 5 percent to 1 percent. Notice that the Fed's decrease in the real interest rate increases short-run equilibrium output, as economic logic suggests.

The Fed's recession-fighting policy is shown graphically in Figure 27.6. The reduction in the real interest rate raises planned spending at each level of output, shifting the expenditure line upward. When the real interest rate equals 1 percent, the expenditure line intersects the $Y = PAE$ line at $Y = 5,000$, so that output and potential output are equal. A reduction in interest rates by the Fed, made with the intention of reducing a recessionary gap in this way, is an example of an *expansionary* monetary policy—or, less formally, a *monetary easing*.

FIGURE 27.6

The Fed Fights a Recession.

When the real interest rate is 5 percent, the expenditure line intersects the $Y = PAE$ line at point E. At that point output is 4,800, below the economy's potential output of 5,000 (a recessionary gap of 200). If the Fed reduces the real interest rate to 1 percent, stimulating consumption and investment spending, the expenditure line will shift upward. At the new point of intersection F, output will equal potential output at 5,000.

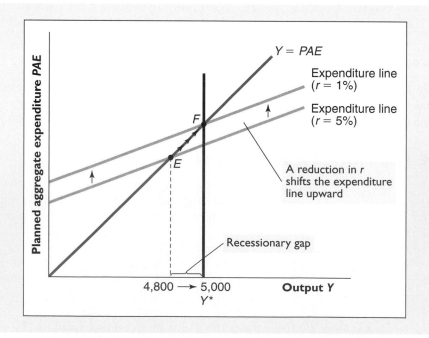

EXERCISE 27.4

Continuing Example 27.5, suppose that potential output is 4,850 rather than 5,000. By how much should the Fed cut the real interest rate to restore full employment? You may take as given that the multiplier is 5.

Why did the Fed cut the federal funds rate 23 times between 1989 and 1992?

The federal funds rate fell sharply between 1989 and 1992 (see Figure 27.5). At its peak in March 1989, the federal funds rate was 9.9 percent; by December 1992 it had fallen to 2.9 percent. During this period the Federal Reserve announced reductions in the target federal funds rate on 23 separate occasions. Why did the Fed cut the federal funds rate so much in this period?

The U.S. economy went into recession in the summer of 1991, about the time Iraq invaded Kuwait. In an attempt to stimulate the economy, the Fed cut the federal funds rate numerous times. By March 1991, the trough of the recession, this key interest rate stood at 6.1 percent—almost 4 percentage points below its value two years earlier. Despite the Fed's actions, however, the economy recovered only slowly. Although the recession ended in March 1991, the unemployment rate continued to climb. The media dubbed the weak expansion a "jobless recovery."

The unusually slow recovery from the 1990–1991 recession puzzled economists as well as the media. Alan Greenspan, the chairman of the Fed, suggested that financial problems such as the credit crunch in the banking sector (see Economic Naturalist 26.3) were creating "financial headwinds" that held back economic growth. The Fed reacted to the sluggish performance of the economy by continuing to cut the federal funds rate, which reached 2.9 percent in December 1992 and remained around 3 percent until the spring of 1994. The Fed's policy appears ultimately to have been successful. Economic growth eventually picked up and the unemployment rate began to fall, reaching record lows by the end of the 1990s. Indeed, the expansion that began in March 1991 ultimately became the longest in U.S. history.

ECONOMIC NATURALIST 27.3

How did the Fed respond to recession and the terror attacks in 2001?

The U.S. economy began slowing in the fall of 2000, with investment in high-tech equipment falling particularly sharply (see Economic Naturalist 26.5). According to the National Bureau of Economic Research, a recession began in March 2001. To make matters worse, on September 11, 2001, terrorist attacks on New York City and Washington shocked the nation and led to serious problems in the travel and financial industries, among others. How did the Federal Reserve react to these events?

The Fed first began to respond to growing evidence of an economic slowdown at the end of the year 2000. At the time the federal funds rate stood at about 6.5 percent (see Figure 27.5). The Fed's most dramatic move was a surprise cut of 0.5 percentage points in the funds rate in January 2001, between regularly scheduled meetings of the Federal Open Market Committee. Further rate cuts followed, and by July the funds rate was below 4 percent. By summer's end, however, there was still considerable uncertainty about the likely severity of the economic slowdown.

The picture changed suddenly on September 11, 2001, when the terror attacks on the World Trade Center and the Pentagon killed more than 3,000 people. The terrorist attacks imposed great economic as well as human costs. The physical damage in lower Manhattan was in the billions of dollars, and many offices and businesses in the area had to close. The Fed, in its role as supervisor of the financial system, worked hard to assist in the restoration of normal operations in the financial district of New York City. (The Federal Reserve Bank of New York, which actually conducts open-market operations, is only a block from the site of the World Trade Center.) The Fed also tried to ease financial conditions by temporarily lowering the federal funds rate to as low as 1.25 percent, in the week following the attack.

In the weeks and months following September 11, the Fed turned its attention from the direct impact of the attack to the possible indirect effects on the

ECONOMIC NATURALIST 27.4

U.S. economy. The Fed was worried that consumers, nervous about the future, would severely cut back their spending; together with the ongoing weakness in investment, a fall in consumption spending could sharply worsen the recession. To stimulate spending, the Fed continued to cut the federal funds rate. By January 2002, the funds rate was at 1.75 percent, nearly 5 percentage points lower than a year earlier. The Fed kept the interest rate at that low level until November 2002, when it lowered the federal funds rate another .5 percentage point, to 1.25 percent.

As of this writing, a (weak) recovery from the recession that began in 2001 appears to be under way. A variety of factors have helped the economy, including expansionary fiscal policy (see Economic Naturalist 26.8). Most economists agree that expansionary actions by the Fed also played a constructive role in reducing the economic impact of the recession and the September 11 attacks.

THE FED FIGHTS INFLATION

To this point we have focused on the problem of stabilizing output, without considering inflation. In the next chapter we will see how ongoing inflation can be incorporated into our analysis. For now we will simply note that one important cause of inflation is an expansionary output gap—a situation in which planned spending, and hence actual output, exceeds potential output. When an expansionary gap exists, firms find that the demand for their output exceeds their normal rate of production. Although firms may be content to meet this excess demand at previously determined prices for some time, if the high demand persists, they will ultimately raise their prices, spurring inflation.

Because an expansionary gap tends to lead to inflation, the Fed moves to eliminate expansionary gaps as well as recessionary gaps. The procedure for getting rid of an expansionary gap—a situation in which output is "too high" relative to potential output—is the reverse of that for fighting a recessionary gap, a situation in which output is "too low." As we have seen, the cure for a recessionary gap is to reduce the real interest rate, an action that stimulates planned spending and increases output. The cure for an expansionary gap is to *raise* the real interest rate, which reduces consumption and planned investment by raising the cost of borrowing. The resulting fall in planned spending leads in turn to a decline in output and to a reduction in inflationary pressures.

EXAMPLE 27.6

The Fed fights inflation

For the economy studied in Examples 27.4 and 27.5, assume that potential output is 4,600 rather than 5,000. At the initial real interest rate of 5 percent, short-run equilibrium output is 4,800, so this economy has an expansionary gap of 200. How should the Fed change the real interest rate to eliminate this gap?

In Example 27.5 we were told that the multiplier in this economy is 5. Hence, to reduce total output by 200, the Fed needs to reduce autonomous expenditure by $200/5 = 40$ units. From Equation 27.1, we know that autonomous expenditure in this economy is $[1,010 - 1,000r]$, so that each percentage point (0.01) increase in the real interest rate lowers autonomous expenditure by 10 units ($1,000 \times 0.01$). We conclude that to eliminate the inflationary gap, the Fed should raise the real interest rate by 4 percentage points (0.04), from 5 percent to 9 percent. The higher real interest rate will reduce planned aggregate expenditure and output to the level of potential output, 4,600, eliminating inflationary pressures.

The effects of the Fed's inflation-fighting policy are shown in Figure 27.7. With the real interest rate at 5 percent, the expenditure line intersects the

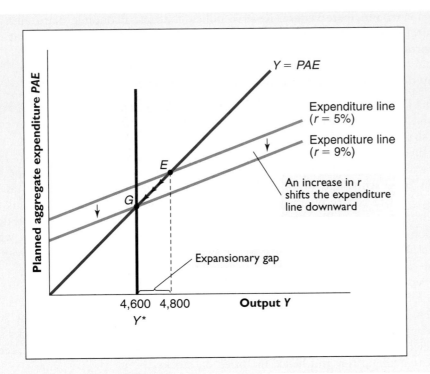

FIGURE 27.7
The Fed Fights Inflation.
When the real interest rate
is 5 percent, the expenditure
line intersects the $Y = PAE$,
or 45°, line at point E, where
short-run equilibrium output
equals 4,800. If potential
output is 4,600, an
expansionary output gap of
200 exists. If the Fed raises
the real interest rate to
9 percent, reducing planned
aggregate expenditure, the
expenditure line shifts
downward. At the new
intersection point G, actual
output equals potential
output at 4,600, and the
expansionary gap is eliminated.

$Y = PAE$ line at point E in the figure, where output equals 4,800. To reduce planned spending and output, the Fed raises the real interest rate to 9 percent. The higher real interest rate slows consumption and investment spending, moving the expenditure line downward. At the new equilibrium point G, actual output equals potential output at 4,600. The Fed's raising the real interest rate—a contractionary policy action—has thus eliminated the expansionary output gap, and with it, the threat of inflation.

"Personally, I liked this roller coaster a lot better before the Federal Reserve Board got hold of it."

The Fed's interest rate policies affect the economy as a whole, but they have a particularly important effect on financial markets. The introduction to this chapter noted the tremendous lengths financial market participants will go to in an attempt to anticipate Federal Reserve policy changes. Economic Naturalist 27.5 illustrates the type of information financial investors look for, and why it is so important to them.

Why does news of inflation hurt the stock market?

Financial market participants watch data on inflation extremely closely. A report that inflation is increasing or is higher than expected often causes stock prices to fall sharply. Why does bad news about inflation hurt the stock market?

Investors in the financial markets worry about inflation because of its likely impact on Federal Reserve policy. Financial investors understand that the Fed, when faced with signs of an expansionary gap, is likely to raise interest rates in an attempt to reduce planned spending and "cool down" the economy. This type of contractionary policy action hurts stock prices in two ways. First, it slows down economic activity, reducing the expected sales and profits of companies whose shares are traded in the stock market. Lower profits, in turn, reduce the dividends those firms are likely to pay their shareholders.

Second, higher real interest rates reduce the value of stocks by increasing the required return for holding stocks. We saw in Chapter 24 that an increase in the return financial investors require in order to hold stocks lowers current stock prices. Intuitively, if interest rates rise, interest-bearing alternatives to stocks such as newly issued government bonds will become more attractive to investors, reducing the demand for, and hence the price of, stocks.

ECONOMIC NATURALIST 27.5

"Interest rates gyrated wildly today, on rumors that the Federal Reserve Board would be replaced by the cast of 'Saturday Night Live.'"

Should the Federal Reserve respond to changes in stock prices?

ECONOMIC NATURALIST 27.6

Many credit the Federal Reserve and its chairman, Alan Greenspan, for effective monetary policymaking that set the stage for sustained economic growth and rising asset prices throughout the 1990s, in particular the second half of the decade. Between January 1995 and March 2000 the S&P 500 stock market index rose from a value of 459 to 1,527, a phenomenal 233 percent increase in just over five years, as the U.S. economy enjoyed a record-long business cycle expansion. Indeed, the stock market's strong, sustained rise helped to fuel additional consumer spending, which in turn promoted further economic expansion.

However, as stock prices fell sharply in the two years after their March 2000 peak, some people questioned whether the Federal Reserve should have preemptively raised interest rates to constrain investors' "irrational exuberance."[4] Overly optimistic investor sentiment led to a speculative run-up in stock prices that eventually burst in 2000 as investors began to realize that firms' earnings could not support the stock prices that were being paid. Earlier intervention by the Federal Reserve, critics argued, would have slowed down the dramatic increase in stock prices and therefore could have prevented the resulting stock market "crash" and the resulting loss of consumer wealth. As this chapter makes clear, the Federal Reserve's primary focus is on reducing output gaps and keeping inflation low. Should the Fed also respond to changing stock prices when it makes decisions about monetary policy?

At a symposium in August 2002, Alan Greenspan defended the Fed's monetary policymaking performance in the late 1990s, pointing out that it is very difficult to identify asset bubbles—surges in prices of assets to unsustainable levels— "until after the fact—that is, when its bursting confirm(s) its existence."[5] Even if such a speculative bubble could be identified, Greenspan noted, the Federal Reserve could have done little—short of "inducing a substantial contraction in economic activity"—to prevent investors' speculation from driving up stock prices. Indeed, Greenspan claimed, "the notion that a well-timed incremental tightening could have been calibrated to prevent the late 1990s bubble is almost surely an illusion." Rather, the Federal Reserve was focusing as early as 1999 on policies that would "mitigate the fallout when it occurs and, hopefully, ease the transition to the next expansion."[6]

Greenspan's remarks strongly suggest that in the absence of macroeconomic models that provide a comprehensive understanding of how dramatic movements in stock prices develop in the economy, the Federal Reserve should maintain its policymaking focus on reducing output gaps and keeping inflation low. Current research on the appropriate role of stock prices in the formulation of monetary policy is mixed: some researchers have come to the conclusion that changes in stock prices should affect monetary policy only to the extent that those changes affect future inflationary expectations, while others find strong support for including stock prices in the Fed's monetary policy decisions. Until economic research provides a definitive answer to this important question, the Fed will continue to monitor stock market conditions, but focus its monetary policymaking attention on the economic effects of changes in stock prices on inflation, spending, and output, rather than the stock prices themselves.

THE FED'S POLICY REACTION FUNCTION

The Fed attempts to stabilize the economy by manipulating the real interest rate. When the economy faces a recessionary gap, the Fed reduces the real interest rate in order to stimulate spending. When an expansionary gap exists, so that inflation threatens to become a problem, the Fed restrains spending by raising the real interest rate. Economists sometimes find it convenient to summarize the behavior of the Fed in terms of a *policy reaction function*. In general, a **policy reaction function** describes how the action a policymaker takes depends on the state of the economy. Here, the policymaker's action is the Fed's choice of the real interest rate, and the state of the economy is given by factors such as the output gap or the inflation rate. Economic Naturalist 27.7 describes one attempt to quantify the Fed's policy reaction function.

policy reaction function describes how the action a policymaker takes depends on the state of the economy

---

[4]Fed Chairman Alan Greenspan mentioned the possibility of "irrational exuberance" driving investor behavior in a December 5, 1996, speech, which is available online at http://www.federalreserve.gov/boarddocs/speeches/1996/19961205.htm.

[5]The text of Greenspan's speech is available online at http://www.federalreserve.gov/boarddocs/speeches/2002/20020830/default.htm.

[6]*The Federal Reserve's Semiannual Report on Monetary Policy*, testimony of Chairman Alan Greenspan before the Committee on Banking and Financial Services, U.S. House of Representatives July 22, 1999. Available online at: http://www.federalreserve.gov/boarddocs/hh/1999/July/Testimony.htm.

What is the Taylor rule?

In 1993 economist John Taylor proposed a "rule," now known as the Taylor rule, to describe the behavior of the Fed.[7] What is the Taylor rule? Does the Fed always follow it?

The rule Taylor proposed is not a rule in any legal sense but is instead an attempt to describe the Fed's behavior in terms of a quantitative policy reaction function. Taylor's "rule" can be written as

$$r = 0.01 - 0.5(\frac{Y^* - Y}{Y^*}) + 0.5\pi$$

where r is the real interest rate set by the Fed, expressed as a decimal (for example, 5% = 0.05); $Y^* - Y$ is the current output gap (the difference between potential and actual output); $(Y^* - Y)/Y^*$ is the output gap relative to potential output; and π is the inflation rate, expressed as a decimal (for example, a 2 percent inflation rate is expressed as 0.02). According to the Taylor rule, the Fed responds to both output gaps and the rate of inflation. For example, the formula implies that if a recessionary gap equal to a fraction 0.01 of potential output develops, the Fed will reduce the real interest rate by 0.5 percentage points (that is, 0.005). Similarly, if inflation rises by 1 percentage point (0.01), according to the Taylor rule the Fed will increase the real interest rate by 0.5 percentage points (0.005). Taylor has shown that his rule does in fact describe the behavior of the Fed under Chairman Alan Greenspan reasonably accurately. Thus the Taylor rule is a real-world example of a policy reaction function.

Although the Taylor rule has worked well as a description of the Fed's behavior, we reiterate that it is not a rule in any legal sense. The Fed is perfectly free to deviate from it and does so when circumstances warrant. Still, the Taylor rule provides a useful benchmark for assessing, and predicting, the Fed's actions.

EXERCISE 27.5

This exercise asks you to apply the Taylor rule. Suppose inflation is 3 percent and the output gap is zero. According to the Taylor rule, at what value should the Fed set the real interest rate? The nominal interest rate? Suppose the Fed were to receive new information showing that there is a 1 percent recessionary gap (inflation is still 3 percent). According to the Taylor rule, how should the Fed change the real interest rate, if at all?

Notice that according to the Taylor rule, the Fed responds to two variables—the output gap and inflation. In principle, any number of economic variables, from stock prices to the value of the dollar in terms of the Japanese yen, could affect Fed policy and thus appear in the policy reaction function. For the sake of simplicity, in applying the policy reaction function idea in the next chapter, we will assume that the Fed's choice of the real interest rate depends on only one variable—the rate of inflation. This simplification will not change our main results in any significant way. Furthermore, as we will see, having the Fed react only to inflation captures the most important aspect of Fed behavior—namely, its tendency to raise the real interest rate when the economy is "overheating" (experiencing an expansionary gap) and to reduce it when the economy is sluggish (experiencing a recessionary gap).

Table 27.1 describes an example of a policy reaction function according to which the Fed reacts only to inflation. According to the policy reaction function given in the table, the higher the rate of inflation, the higher the real interest rate

[7]John Taylor, "Discretion versus Policy Rules in Practice," *Carnegie-Rochester Conference Series on Public Policy*, 1963, pp. 195–227.

TABLE 27.1
A Policy Reaction Function for the Fed

Rate of inflation, π	Real interest rate set by Fed, r
0.00 (= 0%)	0.02 (= 2%)
0.01	0.03
0.02	0.04
0.03	0.05
0.04	0.06

set by the Fed. This relationship is consistent with the idea that the Fed responds to an expansionary gap (which threatens to lead to increased inflation) by raising the real interest rate. Figure 27.8 is a graph of this policy reaction function. The vertical axis of the graph shows the real interest rate chosen by the Fed; the horizontal axis shows the rate of inflation. The upward slope of the policy reaction function captures the idea that the Fed reacts to increases in inflation by raising the real interest rate.

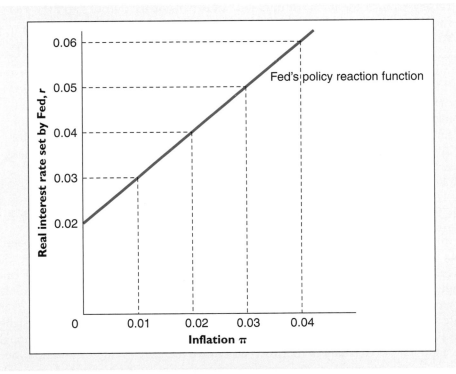

FIGURE 27.8
An Example of a Fed Policy Reaction Function.
This hypothetical example of a policy reaction function for the Fed shows the real interest rate the Fed sets in response to any given value of the inflation rate. The upward slope captures the idea that the Fed raises the real interest rate when inflation rises. The numerical values in the figure are from Table 27.1.

How does the Fed determine its policy reaction function? In practice the process is a complex one, involving a combination of statistical analysis of the economy and human judgment. However, two useful insights into the process can be drawn even from the simplified policy reaction function shown in Table 27.1 and Figure 27.8. First, as we mentioned earlier in the chapter, though the Fed controls the real interest rate in the short run, in the long run the real interest rate is determined by the balance of saving and investment. To illustrate the implication of this fact for the Fed's choice of policy reaction function, suppose that the Fed estimates the long-run value of the real interest rate (as determined by the supply and demand for saving) to be 4 percent, or 0.04. By examining Table 27.1, we can see that the Fed's policy reaction function implies a long-run value of the real interest rate of 4 percent only if the inflation rate in the long run is 2 percent. Thus the Fed's choice of this policy reaction function makes sense only if the Fed's long-run target rate of inflation is 2 percent. We conclude that one important determinant of the Fed's policy reaction function is the policymakers' objective for inflation.

Second, the Fed's policy reaction function contains information not only about the central bank's long-run inflation target but also about how aggressively the Fed plans to pursue that target. To illustrate, suppose the Fed's policy reaction function was very flat, implying that the Fed changes the real interest rate rather modestly in response to increases or decreases in inflation. In this case we would conclude that the Fed does not intend to be very aggressive in its attempts to offset movements in inflation away from the target level. In contrast, if the reaction function slopes steeply upward, so that a given change in inflation elicits a large adjustment of the real interest rate by the Fed, we would say that the Fed plans to be quite aggressive in responding to changes in inflation.

> **RECAP** **MONETARY POLICY AND THE ECONOMY**
>
> An increase in the real interest rate reduces both consumption spending and planned investment spending. Through its control of the real interest rate, the Fed is thus able to influence planned spending and short-run equilibrium output. To fight a recession (a recessionary output gap), the Fed should lower the real interest rate, stimulating planned spending and output. Conversely, to fight the threat of inflation (an expansionary output gap), the Fed should raise the real interest rate, reducing planned spending and output.
>
> The Fed's policy reaction function relates its policy action (specifically, its setting of the real interest rate) to the state of the economy. For the sake of simplicity, we consider a policy reaction function in which the real interest rate set by the Fed depends only on the rate of inflation. Because the Fed raises the real interest rate when inflation rises, in order to restrain spending, the Fed's policy reaction is upward-sloping. The Fed's policy reaction function contains information about the central bank's long-run target for inflation and the aggressiveness with which it intends to pursue that target.

MONETARY POLICYMAKING: ART OR SCIENCE?

In this chapter we analyzed the basic economics underlying real-world monetary policy. As part of the analysis we worked through some examples showing the calculation of the real interest rate that is needed to restore output to its full-employment level. While those examples are useful in understanding how monetary policy works—as with our analysis of fiscal policy in Chapter 26—they overstate the precision of monetary policymaking. The real-world economy is highly complex, and our knowledge of its workings is imperfect. For example, though we assumed in our analysis that the Fed knows the exact value of potential output, in reality potential output can be estimated only approximately. As a result, at any given time the Fed has only a rough idea of the size of the output gap. Similarly, Fed policymakers have only an approximate idea of the effect of a given change in the real interest rate on planned spending, or the length of time before that effect will occur. Because of these uncertainties, the Fed tends to proceed cautiously. Fed policymakers avoid large changes in interest rates and rarely raise or lower the federal funds rate more than one-half of a percentage point (from 5.50 percent to 5.00 percent, for example) at any one time. Indeed, the typical change in the interest rate is one-quarter of a percentage point.

Is monetary policymaking an art or a science, then? In practice it appears to be both. Scientific analyses, such as the development of detailed statistical models of the economy, have proved useful in making monetary policy. But human judgment based on long experience—what has been called the "art" of monetary policy—plays a crucial role in successful policymaking and is likely to continue to do so.

▪ SUMMARY ▪

- Monetary policy is one of two types of stabilization policy, the other being fiscal policy. Although the Federal Reserve operates by controlling the money supply, the media's attention nearly always focuses on the Fed's decisions about interest rates, not the money supply. There is no contradiction between these two ways of looking at monetary policy, however, as the Fed's ability to control the money supply is the source of its ability to control interest rates.

- The nominal interest rate is determined in the market for money, which has both a demand side and a supply side. For the economy as a whole, the *demand for money* is the amount of wealth households and businesses choose to hold in the form of money (such as cash or checking accounts). The demand for money is determined by a comparison of cost and benefits. The opportunity cost of holding money, which pays either zero interest or very low interest, is the interest that could have been earned by holding interest-bearing assets instead of money. Because the nominal interest rate measures the opportunity cost of holding a dollar in the form of money, an increase in the nominal interest rate reduces the quantity of money demanded. The benefit of money is its usefulness in carrying out transactions. All else being equal, an increase in the volume of transactions increases the demand for money. At the macroeconomic level, an increase in the price level or in real GDP increases the dollar volume of transactions, and thus the demand for money.

- The *money demand curve* relates the aggregate quantity of money demanded to the nominal interest rate. Because an increase in the nominal interest rate increases the opportunity cost of holding money, which reduces the quantity of money demanded, the money demand curve slopes down. Factors other than the nominal interest rate that affect the demand for money will shift the demand curve to the right or left. For example, an increase in the price level or real GDP increases the demand for money, shifting the money demand curve to the right.

- The Federal Reserve determines the supply of money through the use of open-market operations. The supply curve for money is vertical at the value of the money supply set by the Fed. Money market equilibrium occurs at the nominal interest rate at which money demand equals the money supply. The Fed can reduce the nominal interest rate by increasing the money supply (shifting the money supply curve to the right) or increase the nominal interest rate by reducing the money supply (shifting the money supply curve to the left). The nominal interest rate that the Fed targets most closely is the *federal funds rate*, which is the rate commercial banks charge each other for very short-term loans.

- In the short run, the Fed can control the real interest rate as well as the nominal interest rate. Recall that the real interest rate equals the nominal interest rate minus the inflation rate. Because the inflation rate adjusts relatively slowly, the Fed can change the real interest rate by changing the nominal interest rate. In the long run, the real interest rate is determined by the balance of saving and investment (Chapter 22).

- The Federal Reserve's actions affect the economy because changes in the real interest rate affect planned spending. For example, an increase in the real interest rate raises the cost of borrowing, reducing consumption and planned investment. Thus, by increasing the real interest rate, the Fed can reduce planned spending and short-run equilibrium output. Conversely, by reducing the real interest rate, the Fed can stimulate planned aggregate expenditure and thereby raise short-run equilibrium output. The Fed's ultimate objective is to eliminate output gaps. To eliminate a recessionary output gap, the Fed will lower the real interest rate. To eliminate an expansionary output gap the Fed will raise the real interest rate.

- A *policy reaction function* describes how the action a policymaker takes depends on the state of the economy. For example, a policy reaction function for the Fed could specify the real interest rate set by the Fed for each value of inflation.

- In practice, the Fed's information about the level of potential output and the size and speed of the effects of its actions is imprecise. Thus monetary policymaking is as much an art as a science.

▪ KEY TERMS ▪

demand for money (705)　　　　money demand curve (709)　　　　portfolio allocation decision (705)
federal funds rate (714)　　　　policy reaction function (725)

▪ REVIEW QUESTIONS ▪

1. What is the *demand for money*? How does the demand for money depend on the nominal interest rate? On the price level? On income? Explain in terms of the costs and benefits of holding money.

2. Show graphically how the Fed controls the nominal interest rate. Can the Fed control the real interest rate?

3. What effect does an open-market purchase of bonds by the Fed have on nominal interest rates? Discuss in terms

of (a) the effect of the purchase on bond prices and (b) the effect of the purchase on the supply of money.

4. You hear a news report that employment growth is lower than expected. How do you expect that report to affect market interest rates? Explain. (*Hint:* Assume that Fed policymakers have access to the same data that you do.)

5. Why does the real interest rate affect planned aggregate expenditure? Give examples.

6. The Fed faces a recessionary gap. How would you expect it to respond? Explain step by step how its policy change is likely to affect the economy.

7. The Fed decides to take a *contractionary* policy action. What would you expect to happen to the nominal interest rate, the real interest rate, and the money supply? Under what circumstances would this type of policy action most likely be appropriate?

8. Define *policy reaction function*. Sketch a policy reaction function relating the Fed's setting of the real interest rate to inflation.

9. Discuss why the analysis of this chapter overstates the precision with which monetary policy can be used to eliminate output gaps.

■ PROBLEMS ■

1. During the heavy Christmas shopping season, sales of retail stores, online sales firms, and other merchants rise significantly.
   a. What would you expect to happen to the money demand curve during the Christmas season? Show graphically.
   b. If the Fed took no action, what would happen to nominal interest rates around Christmas?
   c. In fact, nominal interest rates do not change significantly in the fourth quarter of the year, due to deliberate Fed policy. Explain and show graphically how the Fed can ensure that nominal interest rates remain stable around Christmas.

2. The following table shows Uma's estimated annual benefits of holding different amounts of money:

Average money holdings ($)	Total benefit ($)
500	35
600	47
700	57
800	65
900	71
1,000	75
1,100	77
1,200	77

   a. How much money will Uma hold on average if the nominal interest rate is 9 percent? 5 percent? 3 percent? Assume that she wants her money holding to be a multiple of $100. (*Hint:* Make a table comparing the extra benefit of each additional $100 in money holdings with the opportunity cost, in terms of forgone interest, of additional money holdings.)
   b. Graph Uma's money demand curve for interest rates between 1 percent and 12 percent.

3. How would you expect each of the following to affect the economywide demand for money? Explain.
   a. Competition among brokers forces down the commission charge for selling holdings of bonds or stocks.
   b. Grocery stores begin to accept credit cards in payment.
   c. Financial investors become concerned about increasing riskiness of stocks.
   d. Online banking allows customers to check balances and transfer funds between checking and mutual fund investments 24 hours a day.
   e. The economy enters a boom period.
   f. Political instability increases in developing nations.

4. Suppose the economywide demand for money is given by $P(0.2Y - 25,000i)$. The price level P equals 3.0, and real output Y equals 10,000. At what value should the Fed set the nominal money supply if
   a. It wants to set the nominal interest rate at 4 percent?
   b. It wants to set the nominal interest rate at 6 percent?

5. An economy is described by the following equations:

$$C = 2,600 + 0.8(Y - T) - 10,000r,$$
$$I^P = 2,000 - 10,000r,$$
$$G = 1,800,$$
$$NX = 0,$$
$$T = 3,000.$$

   The real interest rate, expressed as a decimal, is 0.10 (that is, 10 percent). Find a numerical equation relating planned aggregate expenditure to output. Using a table or other method, solve for short-run equilibrium output. Show your result graphically using the Keynesian cross diagram.

6. For the economy described in Problem 5 above:
   a. Potential output Y^* equals 12,000. What real interest rate should the Fed set to bring the economy to full employment? You may take as given that the multiplier for this economy is 5.
   b. Repeat part a for the case in which potential output $Y^* = 9,000$.
   c.* Show that the real interest rate you found in part a sets national saving at potential output, defined as $Y^* - C - G$, equal to planned investment, I^P. This result shows that the real interest rate must be consistent with equilibrium in the market for saving when the economy is at full employment.

7.* Here is another set of equations describing an economy:

$$C = 14,400 + 0.5(Y - T) - 40,000r,$$
$$I^P = 8,000 - 20,000r,$$
$$G = 7,000,$$
$$NX = -1,800,$$
$$T = 8,000,$$
$$Y^* = 40,000.$$

   a. Find a numerical equation relating planned aggregate expenditure to output and to the real interest rate.
   b. At what value should the Fed set the real interest rate to eliminate any output gap? (*Hint*: Set output Y equal to the value of potential output given above in the equation you found in part a. Then solve for the real interest rate that also sets planned aggregate expenditure equal to potential output.)

8. Supposing that the Fed follows the Taylor rule (the Economic Naturalist 27.7), find the real interest rate and the nominal interest rate that the Fed will set in each of the following situations:
   a. Inflation of 4 percent and an expansionary gap equal to 1 percent of potential output.
   b. Inflation of 2 percent and a recessionary gap equal to 2 percent of potential output.
   c. Inflation of 6 percent and no output gap.
   d. Inflation of 2 percent and a recessionary gap of 5 percent. (Can the Fed set a negative real interest rate? If so, how?)

9. In mid-2002, with inflation at 2 percent, some economists estimated the size of the recessionary gap to be about 2 percent of potential output. At that time, the Fed was holding the (nominal) federal funds rate at 1.75 percent. How does the Fed's setting of the federal funds rate compare with what would be predicted by the Taylor rule?

*Problems marked with an asterisk (*) are more difficult.

10. By law, the Federal Reserve must report twice each year to Congress about monetary policy and the state of the economy. When the Monetary Policy Report is presented, it is customary for the Fed chairman to testify before Congress, to update legislators on the economic situation.

Obtain a copy of the most recent Monetary Policy Report from the Fed's web page http://www.federalreserve.gov/ (click "Monetary Policy" and follow the links). In the period covered by the testimony, did monetary policy ease, tighten, or remain neutral? What principal developments in the economy led the Fed to take the actions that it did?

▪ ANSWERS TO IN-CHAPTER EXERCISES ▪

27.1 At 4 percent interest, the benefit of each $10,000 reduction in cash holdings is $400 per year (4% × $10,000). In this case the cost of the extra armored car service, $500 a year, exceeds the benefit of reducing cash holdings by $10,000. Kim's restaurants should therefore continue to hold $50,000 in cash. Comparing this result with Example 27.2, you can see that the demand for money by Kim's restaurants is lower, the higher the nominal interest rate.

27.2 If the nominal interest rate is above its equilibrium value, then people are holding more money than they would like. To bring their money holdings down, they will use some of their money to buy interest-bearing assets such as bonds.

If everyone is trying to buy bonds, however, the price of bonds will be bid up. An increase in bond prices is equivalent to a fall in market interest rates. As interest rates fall, people will be willing to hold more money. Eventually interest rates will fall enough that people are content to hold the amount of money supplied by the Fed, and the money market will be in equilibrium.

27.3 If $r = 0.03$, then consumption is $C = 640 + 0.8(Y - 250) - 400(0.03) = 428 + 0.8Y$, and planned investment is $I^P = 250 - 600(0.03) = 232$. Planned aggregate expenditure is given by

$$PAE = C + I^P + G + NX$$
$$= (428 + 0.8Y) + 232 + 300 + 20$$
$$= 980 + 0.8Y.$$

To find short-run equilibrium output, we can construct a table analogous to Table 27.1. As usual, some trial and error is necessary to find an appropriate range of guesses for output (column 1).

Determination of short-run equilibrium output

(1) Output Y	(2) Planned aggregate expenditure PAE = 980 + 0.8Y	(3) Y − PAE	(4) Y = PAE?
4,500	4,580	−80	No
4,600	4,660	−60	No
4,700	4,740	−40	No
4,800	4,820	−20	No
4,900	4,900	0	**Yes**
5,000	4,980	20	No
5,100	5,060	40	No
5,200	5,140	60	No
5,300	5,220	80	No
5,400	5,300	100	No
5,500	5,380	120	No

Short-run equilibrium output equals 4,900, as that is the only level of output that satisfies the condition $Y = PAE$.

The answer can be obtained more quickly by simply setting $Y = PAE$ and solving for short-run equilibrium output Y. Remembering that $PAE = 980 + 0.8Y$ and substitution for PAE, we get

$$Y = 980 + 0.8Y$$
$$Y(1 - 0.8) = 980$$
$$Y = 5 \times 980 = 4,900.$$

So lowering the real interest rate from 5 percent to 3 percent increases short-run equilibrium output from 4,800 (as found in Example 27.4) to 4,900.

If you have read Appendix 26B on the multiplier, there is yet another way to find the answer. Using Appendix 26B we can determine that the multiplier in this model is 5, since $1/(1 - c) = 1/(1 - 0.8) = 5$. Each percentage point reduction in the real interest rate increases consumption by 4 units and planned investment by 6 units, for a total impact on planned spending of 10 units per percentage point reduction. Reducing the real interest rate by 2 percentage points, from 5 percent to 3 percent, thus increases autonomous expenditure by 20 units. Because the multiplier is 5, an increase of 20 in autonomous expenditure raises short-run equilibrium output by $20 \times 5 = 100$ units, from the value of 4,800 we found in Example 27.4 to the new value of 4,900.

27.4   When the real interest rate is 5 percent, output is 4,800. Each percentage point reduction in the real interest rate increases autonomous expenditure by 10 units. Since the multiplier in this model is 5, to raise output by 50 units the real interest rate should be cut by 1 percentage point, from 5 percent to 4 percent. Increasing output by 50 units, to 4,850, eliminates the output gap.

27.5   If $\pi = 0.03$ and the output gap is zero, we can plug these values into the Taylor rule to obtain

$$r = 0.01 - 0.5(0) + 0.5(0.03) = 0.025 = 2.5\%.$$

So the real interest rate implied by the Taylor rule when inflation is 3 percent and the output gap is zero is 2.5 percent. The nominal interest rate equals the real rate plus the inflation rate, or $2.5\% + 3\% = 5.5\%$.

If there is a recessionary gap of 1 percent of potential output, the Taylor rule formula becomes

$$r = 0.01 - 0.5(0.01) + 0.5(0.03) = 0.02 = 2\%.$$

The nominal interest rate implied by the Taylor rule in this case is the 2 percent real rate plus the 3 percent inflation rate, or 5 percent. So the Taylor rule has the Fed lowering the interest rate when the economy goes into recession, which is both sensible and realistic.

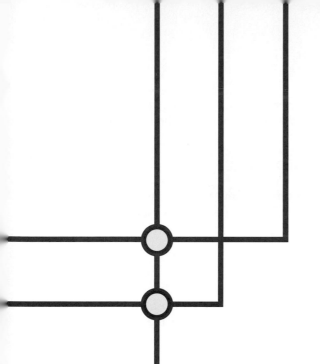

MONETARY POLICY IN THE BASIC KEYNESIAN MODEL

■

This appendix extends the algebraic analysis of the basic Keynesian model that was presented in Appendix 26A to include the role of monetary policy. The main difference from Appendix 26A is that in this analysis the real interest rate is allowed to affect planned spending. We will not describe the supply and demand for money algebraically but will simply assume that the Fed can set the real interest rate r at any level it chooses.

The real interest rate affects consumption and planned investment. To capture these effects, we will modify the equations for those two components of spending as follows:

$$C = \overline{C} + c(Y - T) - ar,$$
$$I^P = \overline{I} - br.$$

The first equation is the consumption function with an additional term, equal to $-ar$. Think of a as a fixed number, greater than zero, that measures the strength of the interest rate effect on consumption. Thus the term $-ar$ captures the idea that when the real interest rate r rises, consumption declines by a times the increase in the interest rate. Likewise, the second equation adds the term $-br$ to the equation for planned investment spending. The parameter b is a fixed positive number that measures how strongly changes in the real interest rate affect planned investment; for example, if the real interest rate r rises, planned investment is assumed to decline by b times the increase in the real interest rate. We continue to assume that government purchases, taxes, and net exports are exogenous variables, so that $G = \overline{G}$, $T = \overline{T}$, and $NX = \overline{NX}$.

To solve for short-run equilibrium output, we start as usual by finding the relationship of planned aggregate expenditure to output. The definition of planned aggregate expenditure is

$$PAE = C + I^P + G + NX.$$

Substituting the modified equations for consumption and planned investment into this definition, along with the exogenous values of government spending, net exports, and taxes, we get

$$PAE = [\overline{C} + c(Y - \overline{T}) - ar] + [\overline{I} - br] + \overline{G} + \overline{NX}.$$

The first term in brackets on the right side describes the behavior of consumption, and the second bracketed term describes planned investment. Rearranging this equation in order to group together terms that depend on the real interest rate and terms that depend on output, we find

$$PAE = [\overline{C} - c\overline{T} + \overline{I} + \overline{G} + \overline{NX}] - (a + b)r + cY.$$

This equation is similar to Equation 26A.1, in the first appendix to Chapter 26, except that it has an extra term, $-(a + b)r$, on the right side. This extra term captures the idea that an increase in the real interest rate reduces consumption and planned investment, lowering planned spending. Notice that the term $-(a + b)r$ is part of autonomous expenditure, since it does not depend on output. Since autonomous expenditure determines the intercept of the expenditure line in the Keynesian cross diagram, changes in the real interest rate will shift the expenditure line up (if the real interest rate decreases) or down (if the real interest rate increases).

To find short-run equilibrium output, we uses the definition of short-run equilibrium output to set $Y = PAE$ and solve for Y:

$$Y = PAE$$
$$= [\overline{C} - c\overline{T} + \overline{I} + \overline{G} + \overline{NX}] - (a + b)r + cY$$
$$Y(1 - c) = [\overline{C} - c\overline{T} + \overline{I} + \overline{G} + \overline{NX}] - (a + b)r$$
$$Y = \left(\frac{1}{1 - c}\right)[(\overline{C} - c\overline{T} + \overline{I} + \overline{G} + \overline{NX}) - (a + b)r]. \quad (27A.1)$$

Equation 27A.1 shows that short-run equilibrium output once again equals the multiplier, $1/(1 - c)$, times autonomous expenditure, $\overline{C} - c\overline{T} + \overline{I} + \overline{G} + \overline{NX} - (a + b)r$. Autonomous expenditure in turn depends on the real interest rate r. The equation also shows that the impact of a change in the real interest rate on short-run equilibrium output depends on two factors: (1) the effect of a change in the real interest rate on consumption and planned investment, which depends on the magnitude of $(a + b)$; and (2) the size of the multiplier, $1/(1 - c)$, which relates changes in autonomous expenditure to changes in short-run equilibrium output. The larger the effect of the real interest rate on planned spending, and the larger the multiplier, the more powerful will be the effect of a given change in the real interest rate on short-run equilibrium output.

To check Equation 27A.1, we can use it to resolve Example 27.4 (see page 719). In that example we are given $\overline{C} = 640, \overline{I} = 250, \overline{G} = 300, \overline{NX} = 20, \overline{T} = 250$, $c = 0.8$, $a = 400$, and $b = 600$. The real interest rate set by the Fed is 5 percent, or 0.05. Substituting these values into Equation 27A.1 and solving, we obtain

$$Y = \left(\frac{1}{1 - 0.8}\right)[640 - 0.8 \times 250 + 250 + 300 + 20 - (400 + 600) \times 0.05]$$
$$= 5 \times 960 = 4,800$$

This is the same result we found in Example 27.4.

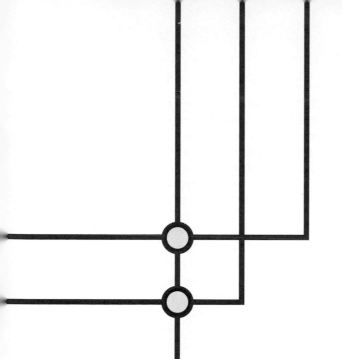

CHAPTER 28

INFLATION AND AGGREGATE SUPPLY

■

On October 6, 1979, the Federal Open Market Committee, the policymaking committee of the Federal Reserve, held a highly unusual—and unusually secretive—Saturday meeting. Fed chairman Paul Volcker may have called the Saturday meeting because he knew the financial markets would be closed and thus would not be able to respond to any "leaks" to the press about the discussions. Or perhaps he hoped that the visit of Pope John Paul II to Washington on the same day would distract the news media from goings-on at the Fed. However unnoticed this meeting may have been at the time, in retrospect it marked a turning point in postwar U.S. economic history.

When Volcker called the October 6 meeting, he had been chairman of the Fed for only six weeks. Six feet eight inches tall with a booming bass voice, and a chain-smoker of cheap cigars, Volcker had a reputation for financial conservatism and personal toughness. Partly for those qualities, President Carter had appointed Volcker to head the Federal Reserve in August 1979. Carter needed a tough Fed chairman to restore confidence in both the economy and the government's economic policies. The U.S. economy faced many problems, including a doubling of oil prices following the overthrow of the Shah of Iran and a worrisome slowdown in productivity growth. But in the minds of the public, the biggest economic worry was an inflation rate that seemed to be out of control. In the second half of 1979, the annual rate of increase in consumer prices had reached 13 percent; by the spring of 1980 the inflation rate had risen to nearly 16 percent. Volcker's assignment: to bring inflation under control and stabilize the U.S. economy.

Paul Volcker faced a tough assignment.

Volcker knew that getting rid of inflation would not be easy, and he warned his colleagues that a "shock treatment" might be necessary. His plan was couched in technical details, but in essence he proposed to reduce the rate of growth of the money supply sharply. Everyone in the room knew that slowing the growth of the money supply would cause interest rates to rise and aggregate spending to fall. Inflation might be brought down, but at what cost in terms of recession, lost output, and lost jobs? And how would the financial markets, which were already shaky, react to the new approach?

Officials in the room stirred nervously as Volcker spoke about the necessity of the move. Finally a vote was called. Every hand went up.

What happened next? We'll return to this story before the chapter ends, but first we need to introduce the basic framework for understanding inflation and the policies used to control it. In the previous two chapters we made the assumption that firms are willing to meet the demand for their products at preset prices. When firms simply produce what is demanded, the level of planned aggregate expenditure determines the nation's real GDP. If the resulting level of short-run equilibrium output is lower than potential output, a recessionary output gap develops, and if the resulting level of output exceeds potential output, the economy experiences an expansionary gap. As we saw in Chapters 26 and 27, policymakers can attempt to eliminate output gaps by taking actions that affect the level of autonomous expenditure, such as changing the level of government spending or taxes (fiscal policy) or using the Fed's control of the money supply to change the real interest rate (monetary policy).

The basic Keynesian model is useful for understanding the role of spending in the short-run determination of output, but it is too simplified to provide a fully realistic description of the economy. The main shortcoming of the basic Keynesian model is that it does not explain the behavior of *inflation*. Although firms may meet demand at preset prices for a time, as assumed in the basic Keynesian model, prices do *not* remain fixed indefinitely. Indeed, sometimes they may rise quite rapidly—the phenomenon of high inflation—imposing significant costs on the economy in the process. In this chapter we will extend the basic Keynesian model to allow for ongoing inflation. As we will show, the extended model can be conveniently represented by a new diagram, called the *aggregate demand–aggregate supply diagram*. Using this extended analysis, we will be able to show how macroeconomic policies affect inflation as well as output, illustrating in the process the difficult trade-offs policymakers sometimes face. We will emphasize numerical and graphical analysis of output and inflation in the body of the chapter. The appendix at the end of the chapter presents an algebraic treatment.

INFLATION, SPENDING, AND OUTPUT: THE AGGREGATE DEMAND CURVE

aggregate demand (AD) curve shows the relationship between short-run equilibrium output Y and the rate of inflation π; the name of the curve reflects the fact that short-run equilibrium output is determined by, and equals, total planned spending in the economy; increases in inflation reduce planned spending and short-run equilibrium output, so the aggregate demand curve is downward-sloping

To begin incorporating inflation into the model, our first step is to introduce a new relationship, called the *aggregate demand curve*, which is shown graphically in Figure 28.1. The **aggregate demand (AD) curve** shows the relationship between short-run equilibrium output Y and the rate of inflation, denoted π. The name of the curve reflects the fact that, as we have seen, short-run equilibrium output is determined by total planned spending, or demand, in the economy. Indeed, by definition, short-run equilibrium output *equals* planned aggregate expenditure, so that we could just as well say that the AD curve shows the relationship between inflation and spending.[1]

[1]It is important to distinguish the aggregate demand curve from the expenditure line, introduced as part of the Keynesian cross diagram in Chapter 26. The upward-sloping expenditure line shows the relationship between planned aggregate expenditure and output. Again, the aggregate demand (AD) curve shows the relationship between short-run equilibrium output (which equals planned spending) and inflation.

We will see shortly that, all else being equal, *an increase in the rate of inflation tends to reduce short-run equilibrium output*. Therefore, in a diagram showing inflation π on the vertical axis and output Y on the horizontal axis (Figure 28.1), the aggregate demand curve is downward-sloping.[2] Note that we refer to the *AD* "curve," even though the relationship is drawn as a straight line in Figure 28.1. In general, the *AD* curve can be either straight or curving.

Why does higher inflation lead to a lower level of planned spending and short-run equilibrium output? As we will see next, one important reason is the Fed's response to increases in inflation.

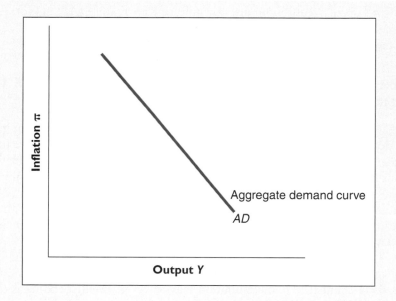

FIGURE 28.1

The Aggregate Demand Curve.

The aggregate demand curve *AD* shows the relationship between short-run equilibrium output *Y* and the rate of inflation π. Because short-run equilibrium output equals planned spending, the *AD* curve also shows the relationship between inflation and planned spending. The downward slope of the *AD* curve implies that an increase in inflation reduces short-run equilibrium output.

INFLATION, THE FED, AND THE *AD* CURVE

One of the primary responsibilities of the Fed, or any central bank, is to maintain a low and stable rate of inflation. For example, in recent years the Fed has tried to keep inflation in the United States in the range of 2 to 3 percent. By keeping inflation low, the central bank tries to avoid the costs high inflation imposes on the economy.

What can the Fed do to keep inflation low and stable? As we have already mentioned, one situation that is likely to lead to increased inflation is an expansionary output gap, in which short-run equilibrium output exceeds potential output. When output is above potential output, firms must produce at above-normal capacity to meet the demands of their customers. Like Al's ice cream store, described in Chapter 25, firms may be willing to do this for a time. But eventually they will adjust to the high level of demand by raising prices, contributing to inflation. To control inflation, then, the Fed needs to dampen planned spending and output when they threaten to exceed potential output.

How can the Fed avoid a situation of economic "overheating," in which spending and output exceed potential output? As we saw in the previous chapter, the Fed can act to reduce autonomous expenditure, and hence short-run equilibrium output, by raising the real interest rate. This behavior by the Fed is a key

---

[2]Economists sometimes define the aggregate demand curve as the relationship between aggregate demand and the *price level*, rather than inflation, which is the *rate of change* of the price level. The definition used here both simplifies the analysis and yields results more consistent with real-world data. For a comparison of the two approaches, see David Romer, "Keynesian Macroeconomics without the LM Curve," *Journal of Economic Perspectives*, Spring 2000, pp. 149–170. The graphical analysis used in this chapter follows closely the approach recommended by Romer.

factor that underlies the link between inflation and output that is summarized by the aggregate demand curve. When inflation is high, the Fed responds by raising the real interest rate (as implied by the Fed's *policy reaction function,* introduced in Chapter 27). The increase in the real interest rate reduces consumption and investment spending (autonomous expenditure) and hence reduces short-run equilibrium output. Because higher inflation leads, through the Fed's actions, to a reduction in output, the aggregate demand (*AD*) curve is downward-sloping, as Figure 28.1 shows. We can summarize this chain of reasoning symbolically as follows:

$$\pi \uparrow \Rightarrow r \uparrow \Rightarrow \text{autonomous expenditure} \downarrow \Rightarrow Y \downarrow \qquad (AD \text{ curve})$$

where, recall, π is inflation, r is the real interest rate, and Y is output.

OTHER REASONS FOR THE DOWNWARD SLOPE OF THE *AD* CURVE

Although we focus here on the behavior of the Fed as the source of the *AD* curve's downward slope, there are other channels through which higher inflation reduces planned spending and thus short-run equilibrium output. Hence the downward slope of the *AD* curve does not depend on the Fed behaving in the particular way just described.

One additional reason for the downward slope of the *AD* curve is the effect of inflation on the *real value of money* held by households and businesses. At high levels of inflation, the purchasing power of money held by the public declines rapidly. This reduction in the public's real wealth may cause households to restrain consumption spending, reducing short-run equilibrium output.

A second channel by which inflation may affect planned spending is through *distributional effects.* Studies have found that people who are less well off are often hurt more by inflation than wealthier people are. For example, retirees on fixed incomes and workers receiving the minimum wage (which is set in dollar terms) lose buying power when prices are rising rapidly. Less affluent people are also likely to be relatively unsophisticated in making financial investments and hence less able than wealthier citizens to protect their savings against inflation.

People at the lower end of the income distribution tend to spend a greater percentage of their disposable income than do wealthier individuals. Thus, if a burst of inflation redistributes resources from relatively high-spending, less affluent households toward relatively high-saving, more affluent households, overall spending may decline.

A third connection between inflation and aggregate demand arises because higher rates of inflation generate *uncertainty* for households and businesses. When inflation is high, people become less certain about what things will cost in the future, and uncertainty makes planning more difficult. In an uncertain economic environment, both households and firms may become more cautious, reducing their spending as a result.

A final link between inflation and total spending operates through the *prices of domestic goods and services sold abroad.* As we will see in Chapter 29, the foreign price of domestic goods depends in part on the rate at which the domestic currency, such as the dollar, exchanges for foreign currencies, such as the British pound. However, for constant rates of exchange between currencies, a rise in domestic inflation causes the prices of domestic goods in foreign markets to rise more quickly. As domestic goods become relatively more expensive to prospective foreign purchasers, export sales decline. Net exports are part of aggregate expenditure, and so once more we find that increased inflation is likely to reduce spending. All these factors contribute to the downward slope of the *AD* curve, together with the behavior of the Fed.

SHIFTS OF THE AGGREGATE DEMAND CURVE

The downward slope of the aggregate demand, or *AD*, curve shown in Figure 28.1 reflects the fact that *all other factors held constant*, a higher level of inflation will lead to lower planned spending and thus lower short-run equilibrium output. Again, a principal reason higher inflation reduces planned spending and output is that the Fed tends to react to increases in inflation by raising the real interest rate, which in turn reduces consumption and planned investment, two important components of planned aggregate expenditure.

However, even if inflation is held constant, various factors can affect planned spending and short-run equilibrium output. Graphically, as we will see in this section, these factors will cause the *AD* curve to shift. Specifically, for a given level of inflation, if there is a change in the economy that *increases* short-run equilibrium output, the *AD* curve will shift to the *right*. If, on the other hand, the change *reduces* short-run equilibrium output at each level of inflation, the *AD* curve will shift to the *left*. We will focus on two sorts of changes in the economy that shift the aggregate demand curve: (1) changes in spending caused by factors other than output or interest rates, which we will refer to as *exogenous* changes in spending; and (2) changes in the Fed's monetary policy, as reflected in a shift in the Fed's policy reaction function.

Changes in Spending

We have seen that planned aggregate expenditure depends both on output (through the consumption function) and on the real interest rate (which affects both consumption and planned investment). However, many factors other than output or the real interest rate can affect planned spending. For example, at given levels of output and the real interest rate, fiscal policy affects the level of government purchases, and changes in consumer confidence can affect consumption spending. Likewise, new technological opportunities may lead firms to increase their planned investment, and an increased willingness of foreigners to purchases domestic goods will raise net exports. We will refer to changes in planned spending unrelated to changes in output or the real interest rate as *exogenous* changes in spending.

For a given inflation rate (and thus for a given real interest rate set by the Fed), an exogenous increase in spending raises short-run equilibrium output, for the reasons we have discussed in the past two chapters. Because it increases output at each level of inflation, *an exogenous increase in spending shifts the AD curve to the right*. This result is illustrated graphically in Figure 28.2. Imagine,

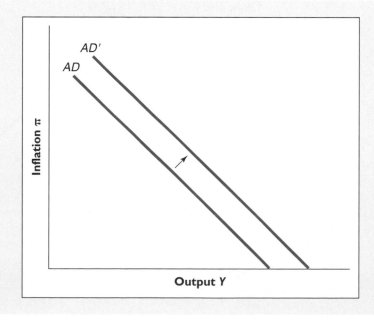

FIGURE 28.2

Effect of an Increase in Exogenous Spending.

The *AD* curve is seen both *before* (*AD*) and *after* (*AD'*) an increase in exogenous spending—specifically, an increase in consumption spending resulting from a rise in the stock market. If the inflation rate and the real interest rate set by the Fed are held constant, an increase in exogenous spending raises short-run equilibrium output. As a result, the *AD* curve will shift to the right, from *AD* to *AD'*.

for example, that a rise in the stock market makes consumers more willing to spend (the wealth effect). Then, for each level of inflation, aggregate spending and short-run equilibrium output will be higher, a change which is shown as a shift of the *AD* curve to the right, from *AD* to *AD'*.

Similarly, at a given inflation rate, an exogenous decline in spending—for example, a fall in government purchases resulting from a more restrictive fiscal policy—causes short-run equilibrium output to fall. We conclude that *an exogenous decrease in spending shifts the AD curve to the left*.

> ## EXERCISE 28.1
>
> **Determine how the following events will affect the *AD* curve:**
>
> **a. Due to widespread concerns about future weakness in the economy, businesses reduce their spending on new capital.**
>
> **b. The federal government reduces income taxes.**

Changes in the Fed's Policy Reaction Function

Recall that the Fed's policy reaction function describes how the Fed sets the real interest rate at each level of inflation. This relationship is built into the *AD* curve—indeed, it accounts in part for the curve's downward slope. As long as the Fed sets the real interest rate according to an unchanged reaction function, its adjustments in the real rate will not cause the *AD* curve to shift. Under normal circumstances the Fed generally follows a stable policy reaction function.

However, on occasion the Fed may choose to be significantly "tighter" or "easier" than normal for a given rate of inflation. For example, if inflation is high and has stubbornly refused to decrease, the Fed might choose a tighter monetary policy, setting the real interest rate higher than normal at each given rate of inflation. This change of policy can be interpreted as an upward shift in the Fed's policy reaction function, as shown in Figure 28.3(a). A decision by the Fed to become

FIGURE 28.3
A Shift in the Fed's Policy Reaction Function.

If inflation has remained too high for an extended period, the Fed may choose a "tighter" monetary policy, by setting the real interest rate at a higher level than usual for each given rate of inflation. Graphically, this change corresponds to an upward movement in the Fed's policy reaction function (a). This change to a tighter monetary policy shifts the *AD* curve to the left (b). If a protracted recession led the Fed to decide to set a lower real interest rate at each level of inflation, the Fed's policy reaction function would shift downward and the *AD* curve would shift to the right.

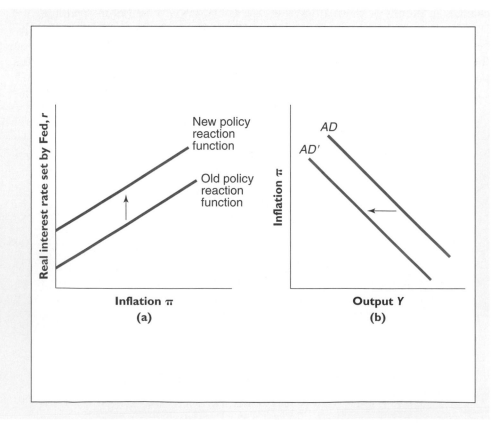

more "hawkish" about inflation—that is, to set the real interest rate at a higher level for each given rate of inflation—reduces planned expenditure and thus short-run equilibrium output at each rate of inflation. Thus an upward shift of the Fed's policy reaction function leads the *AD* curve to shift to the left [Figure 28.3(b)]. Later in the chapter we will interpret Chairman Volcker's attack on inflation in 1979 as precisely such a policy shift.

Similarly, if the nation is experiencing an unusually severe and protracted recession, the Fed may choose to change its policies and set the real interest rate lower than normal, given the rate of inflation. This change in policy can be interpreted as a downward shift of the Fed's policy reaction function. Given the rate of inflation, a lower-than-normal setting of the real interest rate will lead to higher levels of expenditure and short-run equilibrium output. Therefore, a downward shift of the Fed's policy reaction function causes the *AD* curve to shift to the right.

EXERCISE 28.2

Explain why a shift in monetary policy like that shown in Figure 28.3 can be interpreted as a decline in the Fed's long-run "target" for the inflation rate. (*Hint:* In the long run, the real interest rate set by the Fed must be consistent with the real interest rate determined in the market for saving and investment.)

SHIFTS OF THE *AD* CURVE VERSUS MOVEMENTS ALONG THE *AD* CURVE

Let's end this section by reviewing and summarizing the important distinction between *movements along* the *AD* curve and *shifts* of the *AD* curve.

The downward slope of the *AD* curve captures the inverse relationship between inflation, on the one hand, and short-run equilibrium output, on the other. As we have seen, a rise in the inflation rate leads the Fed to raise the real interest rate, according to its policy reaction function. The higher real interest rate, in turn, depresses planned spending and hence lowers short-run equilibrium output. The downward slope of the *AD* curve embodies this relationship among inflation, spending, and output. Hence changes in the inflation rate, and the resulting changes in the real interest rate and short-run equilibrium output, are represented by *movements along* the *AD* curve. In particular, as long as the Fed sets the real interest rate in accordance with a fixed policy reaction function, changes in the real interest rate will *not* shift the *AD* curve.

However, any factor that changes the short-run equilibrium level of output *at a given level of inflation* will *shift* the *AD* curve—to the right if short-run equilibrium output increases, or to the left if short-run equilibrium output decreases. We have identified two factors that can shift the *AD* curve: exogenous changes in spending (that is, changes in spending unrelated to output or the real interest rate) and changes in the Fed's policy reaction function. An exogenous increase in spending or a downward shift of the Fed's policy reaction function increases short-run equilibrium output at every level of inflation, hence shifting the *AD* curve to the right. An exogenous decline in spending or an upward shift in the Fed's policy reaction function decreases short-run equilibrium output at every level of inflation, shifting the *AD* curve to the left.

EXERCISE 28.3

What is the difference, if any, between the following?

a. An upward shift in the Fed's policy reaction function

b. **A response by the Fed to higher inflation, for a given policy reaction function.**

How does each scenario affect the *AD* curve?

> **RECAP** **THE AGGREGATE DEMAND (*AD*) CURVE**
>
> ■ The *AD* curve shows the relationship between short-run equilibrium output and inflation. Higher inflation leads the Fed to raise the real interest rate, which reduces autonomous expenditure and thus short-run equilibrium output. Therefore, the *AD* curve slopes downward.
>
> ■ The *AD* curve may also slope downward because (1) higher inflation reduces the real value of money held by the public, reducing wealth and spending; (2) inflation redistributes resources from less affluent people, who spend a high percentage of their disposable income, to more affluent people, who spend a smaller percentage of disposable income; (3) higher inflation creates greater uncertainty in planning for households and firms, reducing their spending; and (4) for a constant rate of exchange between the dollar and other currencies, rising prices of domestic goods and services reduce foreign sales and hence net exports (a component of aggregate spending).
>
> ■ An exogenous increase in spending raises short-run equilibrium output at each value of inflation, and so shifts the *AD* curve to the right. Conversely, an exogenous decrease in spending shifts the *AD* curve to the left.
>
> ■ A change to an easier monetary policy, as reflected by a downward shift in the Fed's policy reaction function, shifts the *AD* curve to the right. A change to a tighter, more anti-inflationary monetary policy, as reflected by an upward shift in the Fed's policy reaction function, shifts the *AD* curve to the left.
>
> ■ Assuming no change in the Fed's reaction function, changes in inflation correspond to movements *along* the *AD* curve; they do not *shift* the *AD* curve.

INFLATION AND AGGREGATE SUPPLY

Thus far in this chapter we have focused on how changes in inflation affect spending and short-run equilibrium output, a relationship captured by the *AD* curve. But we have not yet discussed how inflation itself is determined. In the rest of the chapter we will examine the main factors that determine the inflation rate in modern industrial economies, as well as the options that policymakers have to control inflation. In doing so we will introduce a useful diagram for analyzing the behavior of output and inflation, called the *aggregate demand–aggregate supply diagram*.

Physicists have noted that a body will tend to keep moving at a constant speed and direction unless it is acted upon by some outside force—a tendency they refer to as *inertia*. Applying this concept to economics, many observers have noted that inflation seems to be inertial, in the sense that it tends to remain roughly constant as long as the economy is at full employment and there are no external shocks to the price level. In the first part of this section we will discuss why inflation behaves in this way.

However, just as a physical object will change speed if it is acted on by outside forces, so various economic forces can change the rate of inflation. Later in this section we will discuss three factors that can cause the inflation rate to change. The first is the presence of an *output gap*: Inflation tends to rise when there is an expansionary output gap and to fall when there is a recessionary output gap. The second factor that can affect the inflation rate is a shock that directly affects prices, which we will refer to as an *inflation shock*. A large increase in the price of imported oil, for example, raises the price of gasoline, heating oil, and other fuels, as well as of goods made with oil or services using oil. Finally, the third factor that directly affects the inflation rate is a *shock to potential output,* or a sharp change in the level of potential output—a natural disaster that destroyed a significant portion of a country's factories and businesses is one extreme example. Together, inflationary shocks and shocks to potential output are known as *aggregate supply shocks*.

INFLATION INERTIA

In low-inflation industrial economies like that of the United States today, inflation tends to change relatively slowly from year to year, a phenomenon that is sometimes referred to as *inflation inertia*. If the rate of inflation in one year is 2 percent, it may be 3 percent or even 4 percent in the next year. But unless the nation experiences very unusual economic conditions, inflation is unlikely to rise to 6 percent or 8 percent or fall to −2 percent in the following year. This relatively sluggish behavior contrasts sharply with the behavior of economic variables such as stock or commodity prices, which can change rapidly from day to day. For example, oil prices might well rise by 20 percent over the course of a year and then fall 20 percent over the next year. Yet since about 1992, the U.S. inflation rate has generally remained in the range of 2–3 percent per year.

Why does inflation tend to adjust relatively slowly in modern industrial economies? To answer this question, we must consider two closely related factors that play an important role in determining the inflation rate: the behavior of the public's *inflation expectations* and the existence of *long-term wage and price contracts*.

First, consider the public's expectations about inflation. In negotiating future wages and prices, both buyers and sellers take into account the rate of inflation they expect to prevail in the next few years. As a result, today's *expectations* of future inflation may help to determine the future inflation rate. Suppose, for example, that office worker Fred and his boss Colleen agree that Fred's performance this past year justifies an increase of 2 percent in his real wage for next year. What *nominal*, or dollar, wage increase should they agree on? If Fred believes that inflation is likely to be 3 percent over the next year, he will ask for a 5 percent increase in his nominal wage to obtain a 2 percent increase in his real wage. If Colleen agrees that inflation is likely to be 3 percent, she should be willing to go along with a 5 percent nominal increase, knowing that it implies only a 2 percent increase in Fred's real wage. Thus the rate at which Fred and Colleen *expect* prices to rise affects the rate at which at least one price—Fred's nominal wage—*actually* rises.

A similar dynamic affects the contracts for production inputs other than labor. For example, if Colleen is negotiating with her office supply company, the prices she will agree to pay for next year's deliveries of copy paper and staples will depend on what she expects the inflation rate to be. If Colleen anticipates that the price of office supplies will not change relative to the prices of other goods and services, and that the general inflation rate will be 3 percent, then she should be willing to agree to a 3 percent increase in the price of office supplies. On the other hand, if she expects the general inflation rate to be 6 percent, then she will agree to pay 6 percent more for copy paper and staples next year, knowing that a nominal increase of 6 percent implies no change in the price of office supplies relative to other goods and services.

Economywide, then, the higher the expected rate of inflation, the more nominal wages and the cost of other inputs will tend to rise. But if wages and other costs of production grow rapidly in response to expected inflation, firms will have to raise their prices rapidly as well in order to cover their costs. Thus a high rate of expected inflation tends to lead to a high rate of actual inflation. Similarly, if expected inflation is low, leading wages and other costs to rise relatively slowly, actual inflation should be low as well.

> ### EXERCISE 28.4
>
> **Assume that employers and workers agree that real wages should rise by 2 percent next year.**
>
> a. **If inflation is expected to be 2 percent next year, what will happen to nominal wages next year?**
>
> b. **If inflation is expected to be 4 percent next year, rather than 2 percent, what will happen to nominal wages next year?**
>
> c. **Use your answers from parts a and b to explain how an increase in expected inflation will tend to affect the following year's actual rate of inflation.**

The conclusion that actual inflation is partially determined by expected inflation raises the question of what determines inflation expectations. To a great extent, people's expectations are influenced by their recent experience. If inflation has been low and stable for some time, people are likely to expect it to continue to be low. But if inflation has recently been high, people will expect it to continue to be high. If inflation has been unpredictable, alternating between low and high levels, the public's expectations will likewise tend to be volatile, rising or falling with news or rumors about economic conditions or economic policy.

Figure 28.4 illustrates schematically how low and stable inflation may tend to be self-perpetuating. As the figure shows, if inflation has been low for some time, people will continue to expect low inflation. Increases in nominal wages and other production costs will thus tend to be small. If firms raise prices only by enough to cover costs, then actual inflation will be low, as expected. This low actual rate will in turn promote low expected inflation, perpetuating the "virtuous circle." The same logic applies in reverse in an economy with high inflation: A persistently high inflation rate leads the public to expect high inflation, resulting in higher increases in nominal wages and other production costs. This in turn contributes to a high rate of actual inflation, and so on in a vicious circle. This role of inflation expectations in the determination of wage and price increases helps to explain why inflation often seems to adjust slowly.

FIGURE 28.4
A Virtuous Circle of Low Inflation and Low Expected Inflation.
Low inflation leads people to expect low inflation in the future. As a result, they agree to accept small increases in wages and in the prices of the goods and services they supply, which keeps inflation—and expected inflation—low. In a similar way, high inflation leads people to expect high inflation, which in turn tends to produce high inflation.

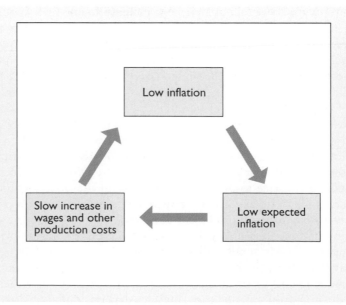

The role of inflation expectations in the slow adjustment of inflation is strengthened by a second key element, the existence of *long-term wage and price contracts*. Union wage contracts, for example, often extend for three years into the future.

Likewise, contracts that set the prices manufacturing firms pay for parts and raw materials often cover several years. Long-term contracts serve to "build in" wage and price increases that depend on inflation expectations at the time the contracts were signed. For example, a union negotiating in a high-inflation environment is much more likely to demand a rapid increase in nominal wages over the life of the contract than would a union in an economy in which prices are stable.

To summarize, in the absence of external shocks, inflation tends to remain relatively stable over time—at least in low-inflation industrial economies like that of the United States. In other words, inflation is *inertial* (or as some people put it, "sticky"). Inflation tends to be inertial for two main reasons. The first is the behavior of people's expectations of inflation. A low inflation rate leads people to expect low inflation in the future, which results in reduced pressure for wage and price increases. Similarly, a high inflation rate leads people to expect high inflation in the future, resulting in more rapid increases in wages and prices. Second, the effects of expectations are reinforced by the existence of long-term wage and price contracts, which is the second reason inflation tends to be stable over time. Long-term contracts tend to build in the effects of people's inflation expectations.

Although the rate of inflation tends to be inertial, it does of course change over time. We next discuss a key factor causing the inflation rate to change.

EXERCISE 28.5

Based on Figure 28.4, discuss why the Federal Reserve has a strong incentive to maintain a low inflation rate in the economy.

THE OUTPUT GAP AND INFLATION

An important factor influencing the rate of inflation is the output gap, or the difference between potential output and actual output ($Y^* - Y$). We have seen that, in the short run, firms will meet the demand for their output at previously determined prices. For example, Al's ice cream shop will serve ice cream to any customer who comes into the shop at the prices posted behind the counter. The level of output that is determined by the demand at preset prices is called short-run equilibrium output.

At a particular time the level of short-run equilibrium output may happen to equal the economy's long-run productive capacity, or potential output. But that is not necessarily the case. Output may exceed potential output, giving rise to an expansionary gap, or it may fall short of potential output, producing a recessionary gap. Let's consider what happens to inflation in each of these three possible cases: no output gap, an expansionary gap, and a recessionary gap.

If actual output equals potential output, then by definition there is no output gap. When the output gap is zero, firms are satisfied, in the sense that their sales equal their normal production rates. As a result, firms have no incentive either to reduce or increase their prices *relative* to the prices of other goods and services. However, the fact that firms are satisfied with their sales does *not* imply that inflation—the rate of change in the overall price level—is zero.

To see why, let's go back to the idea of inflation inertia. Suppose that inflation has recently been steady at 3 percent per year, so that the public has come to expect an inflation rate of 3 percent per year. If the public's inflation expectations are reflected in the wage and price increases agreed to in long-term contracts, then firms will find their labor and materials costs are rising at 3 percent per year. To cover their costs, firms will need to raise their prices by 3 percent per year. Note that if all firms are raising their prices by 3 percent per year, the *relative* prices of various goods and services in the economy—say, the price of ice cream relative to the price of a taxi ride—will not change. Nevertheless, the economywide rate of inflation equals 3 percent, the same as in previous years. We conclude that, *if the output gap is zero, the rate of inflation will tend to remain the same.*

Suppose instead that an expansionary gap exists, so that most firms' sales exceed their normal production rates. As we might expect in situations in which the quantity demanded exceeds the quantity firms desire to supply, firms will ultimately respond by trying to increase their relative prices. To do so, they will increase their prices by *more* than the increase in their costs. If all firms behave this way, then the general price level will begin to rise more rapidly than before. Thus, *when an expansionary gap exists, the rate of inflation will tend to increase.*

Finally, if a recessionary gap exists, firms will be selling an amount less than their capacity to produce, and they will have an incentive to cut their relative prices so they can sell more. In this case, firms will raise their prices less than needed to cover fully their increases in costs, as determined by the existing inflation rate. As a result, *when a recessionary gap exists, the rate of inflation will tend to decrease.* These important results are summarized in Box 28.1.

BOX 28.1: THE OUTPUT GAP AND INFLATION

Relationship of output to potential output		Behavior of inflation
1. No output gap $Y = Y^*$	$\rightarrow$	Inflation remains unchanged
2. Expansionary gap $Y > Y^*$	$\rightarrow$	Inflation rises $\pi \uparrow$
3. Recessionary gap $Y < Y^*$	$\rightarrow$	Inflation falls $\pi \downarrow$

EXAMPLE 28.1

Spending changes and inflation

In Chapters 26 and 27 we saw that changes in spending can create expansionary or recessionary gaps. Therefore, based on the discussion above, we can conclude that changes in spending also lead to changes in the rate of inflation. If the economy is currently operating at potential output, what effect will a fall in consumer confidence that makes consumers less willing to spend at each level of disposable income have on the rate of inflation in the economy?

A decrease in exogenous consumption spending, *C,* for a given level of inflation, output, and real interest rates, reduces aggregate expenditures and short-run equilibrium output. If the economy was originally operating at potential output, the reduction in consumption will cause a recessionary gap, since actual output, *Y,* will now be less than potential output, Y^*. As indicated above, when $Y < Y^*$, the rate of inflation will tend to fall because firms' sales fall short of normal production rates, leading them to slow down the rate at which they increase their prices.

EXERCISE 28.6

Suppose that firms become optimistic about the future and decide to increase their investment in new capital. What effect will this have on the rate of inflation, assuming that the economy is currently operating at potential output?

THE AGGREGATE DEMAND–AGGREGATE SUPPLY DIAGRAM

The adjustment of inflation in response to an output gap can be shown conveniently in a diagram. Figure 28.5, drawn with inflation π on the vertical axis and

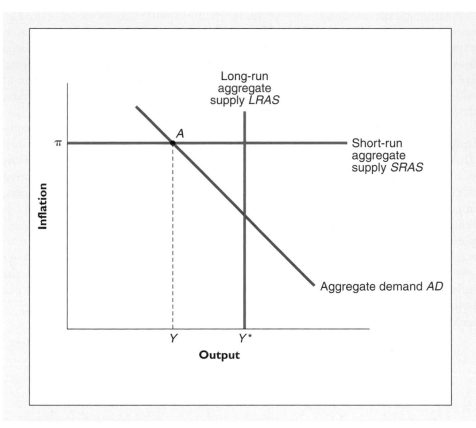

FIGURE 28.5
The Aggregate Demand–Aggregate Supply (AD-AS) Diagram.
This diagram has three elements: the *AD* curve, which shows how short-run equilibrium output depends on inflation; the long-run aggregate supply (*LRAS*) line, which marks the economy's potential output *Y**; and the short-run aggregate supply (*SRAS*) line, which shows the current value of inflation *π*. Short-run equilibrium output, which is equal to *Y* here, is determined by the intersection of the *AD* curve and the *SRAS* line (point *A*). Because actual output *Y* is less than potential output *Y**, this economy has a recessionary gap.

real output *Y* on the horizontal axis, is an example of an *aggregate demand–aggregate supply diagram,* or *AD-AS diagram* for short. The diagram has three elements, one of which is the downward-sloping *AD* curve, introduced earlier in the chapter. Recall that the *AD* curve shows how planned aggregate spending, and hence short-run equilibrium output, depends on the inflation rate. The second element is a vertical line marking the economy's potential output *Y**. Because potential output represents the economy's long-run productive capacity, we will refer to this vertical line as the **long-run aggregate supply line,** or *LRAS* line. The third element in Figure 28.5, and a new one, is the *short-run aggregate supply line,* labeled *SRAS* in the diagram. The **short-run aggregate supply (*SRAS*) line** is a horizontal line that shows the current rate of inflation in the economy, which in the figure is labeled *π*. We can think of the current rate of inflation as having been determined by past expectations of inflation and past pricing decisions. The short-run aggregate supply line is horizontal because, in the short run, producers supply whatever output is demanded at preset prices.

The *AD-AS* diagram can be used to determine the level of output prevailing at any particular time. As we have seen, the inflation rate at any moment is given directly by the position of the *SRAS* line—for example, current inflation equals *π* in Figure 28.5. To find the current level of output, recall that the *AD* curve shows the level of short-run equilibrium output at any given rate of inflation. Since the inflation rate in this economy is *π*, we can infer from Figure 28.5 that short-run equilibrium output must equal *Y,* which corresponds to the intersection of the *AD* curve and the *SRAS* line (point *A* in the figure). Notice that in Figure 28.5, short-run equilibrium output *Y* is smaller than potential output *Y**, so there is a recessionary gap in this economy.

The intersection of the *AD* curve and the *SRAS* line (point *A* in Figure 28.5) is referred to as the point of *short-run equilibrium* in this economy. When the economy is in **short-run equilibrium,** inflation equals the value determined by past expectations and past pricing decisions, and output equals the level of short-run equilibrium output that is consistent with that inflation rate.

long-run aggregate supply (LRAS) line a vertical line showing the economy's potential output *Y**

short-run aggregate supply (SRAS) line a horizontal line showing the current rate of inflation, as determined by past expectations and pricing decisions

short-run equilibrium a situation in which inflation equals the value determined by past expectations and pricing decisions and output equals the level of short-run equilibrium output that is consistent with that inflation rate; graphically, short-run equilibrium occurs at the intersection of the *AD* curve and the *SRAS* line

Although the economy may be in short-run equilibrium at point *A* in Figure 28.5, it will not remain there. The reason is that at point *A*, the economy is experiencing a recessionary gap (output is less than potential output, as indicated by the *LRAS* line). As we have just seen, when a recessionary gap exists, firms are not selling as much as they would like to and so they slow down the rate at which they increase their prices. Eventually, the low level of aggregate demand that is associated with a recessionary gap causes the inflation rate to fall.

The adjustment of inflation in response to a recessionary gap is shown graphically in Figure 28.6. As inflation declines, the *SRAS* line moves downward, from *SRAS* to *SRAS'*. Because of inflation inertia (caused by the slow adjustment of the public's inflation expectations and the existence of long-term contracts), inflation adjusts downward only gradually. However, as long as a recessionary gap exists, inflation will continue to fall, and the *SRAS* line will move downward until it intersects the *AD* curve at point *B* in the figure. At that point, actual output equals potential output and the recessionary gap has been eliminated. Because there is no further pressure on inflation at point *B*, the inflation rate stabilizes at the lower level. A situation like that represented by point *B* in Figure 28.6, in which the inflation rate is stable and actual output equals potential output, is referred to as **long-run equilibrium** of the economy. Long-run equilibrium occurs when the *AD* curve, the *SRAS* line, and the *LRAS* line all intersect at a single point.

long-run equilibrium a situation in which actual output equals potential output and the inflation rate is stable; graphically, long-run equilibrium occurs when the *AD* curve, the *SRAS* line, and the *LRAS* line all intersect at a single point

FIGURE 28.6
The Adjustment of Inflation When a Recessionary Gap Exists.
At the initial short-run equilibrium point *A*, a recessionary gap exists, which puts downward pressure on inflation. As inflation gradually falls, the *SRAS* line moves downward until it reaches *SRAS'*, and actual output equals potential output (point *B*). Once the recessionary gap has been eliminated, inflation stabilizes at π^*, and the economy settles into long-run equilibrium at the intersection of *AD*, *LRAS*, and *SRAS'* (point *B*).

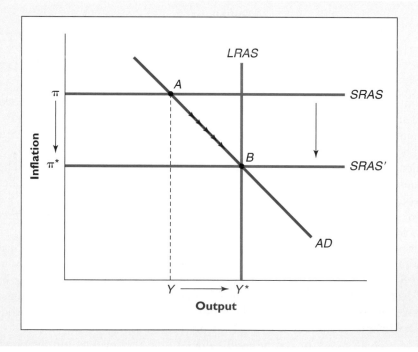

Figure 28.6 illustrates the important point that when a recessionary gap exists, inflation will tend to fall. It also shows that as inflation declines, short-run equilibrium output rises, increasing gradually from *Y* to *Y** as the short-run equilibrium point moves down the *AD* curve. The source of this increase in output is the behavior of the Federal Reserve, which lowers the real interest rate as inflation falls, stimulating aggregate demand. Falling inflation stimulates spending and output in other ways, such as by reducing uncertainty.[3] As output rises, cyclical unemployment, which by Okun's law is proportional to the output gap, also declines. This process of falling inflation, falling real interest rates, rising output, and falling unemployment continues until the economy reaches full employment at point *B* in Figure 28.6, the economy's long-run equilibrium point.

[3]Our explanation for the downward slope of the *AD* curve, earlier in the chapter, described some of these other factors.

What happens if instead of a recessionary gap, the economy has an expansionary gap, with output greater than potential output? An expansionary gap would cause the rate of inflation to *rise,* as firms respond to high demand by raising their prices more rapidly than their costs are rising. In graphical terms, an expansionary gap would cause the *SRAS* line to move upward over time. Inflation and the *SRAS* line would continue to rise until the economy reached long-run equilibrium, with actual output equal to potential output. This process is illustrated in Figure 28.7. Initially, the economy is in short-run equilibrium at point *A,* where $Y > Y^*$ (an expansionary gap). The expansionary gap causes inflation to rise over time; graphically, the short-run aggregate supply line moves upward, from *SRAS* to *SRAS'.* As the *SRAS* line rises, short-run equilibrium output falls—the result of the Fed's tendency to increase the real interest rate when inflation rises. Eventually the *SRAS* line intersects the *AD* curve *LRAS* and line at point *B,* where the economy reaches long-run equilibrium, with no output gap and stable inflation.

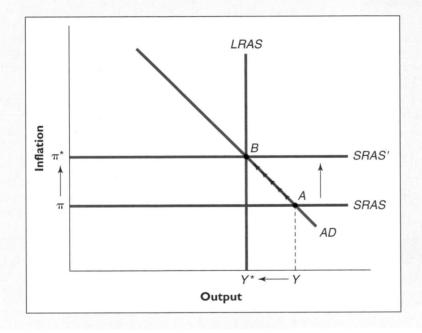

FIGURE 28.7
The Adjustment of Inflation When an Expansionary Gap Exists.
At the initial short-run equilibrium point A, an expansionary gap exists. Inflation rises gradually (the SRAS line moves upward) and output falls. The process continues until the economy reaches long-run equilibrium at point B, where inflation stabilizes and the output gap is eliminated.

THE SELF-CORRECTING ECONOMY

Our analysis of Figures 28.6 and 28.7 makes an important general point: The economy tends to be *self-correcting* in the long run. In other words, given enough time, output gaps tend to disappear without changes in monetary or fiscal policy (other than the change in the real interest rate embodied in the Fed's policy reaction function). Expansionary output gaps are eliminated by rising inflation, while recessionary output gaps are eliminated by falling inflation. This result contrasts sharply with the basic Keynesian model, which does not include a self-correcting mechanism. The difference in results is explained by the fact that the basic Keynesian model concentrates on the short-run period, during which prices do not adjust, and does not take into account the changes in prices and inflation that occur over a longer period.

Does the economy's tendency to self-correct imply that aggressive monetary and fiscal policies are not needed to stabilize output? The answer to this question depends crucially on the *speed* with which the self-correction process takes place. If self-correction takes place very slowly, so that actual output differs from potential for protracted periods, then active use of monetary and fiscal policy can help to stabilize output. But if self-correction is rapid, then active stabilization policies are probably not justified in most cases, given the lags and uncertainties that are involved in policymaking in practice. Indeed, if the economy returns to full employment quickly, then attempts by policymakers to stabilize spending and output may end up doing more harm than good, for example, by causing actual output to "overshoot" potential output.

The speed with which a particular economy corrects itself depends on a variety of factors, including the prevalence of long-term contracts and the efficiency and flexibility of product and labor markets. (For a case study, see the comparison of U.S. and European labor markets in Chapter 21.) However, a reasonable conclusion is that the greater the initial output gap, the longer the economy's process of self-correction will take. This observation suggests that stabilization policies should not be used actively to try to eliminate relatively small output gaps, but that they may be quite useful in remedying large gaps—for example, when the unemployment rate is exceptionally high.

> **RECAP**   **AD-AS AND THE SELF-CORRECTING ECONOMY**
>
> The economy is in short-run equilibrium when inflation equals the value determined by past expectations and pricing decisions, and output equals the level of short-run equilibrium output that is consistent with that inflation rate. Graphically, short-run equilibrium occurs at the intersection of the *AD* curve and the *SRAS* line.
>
> The economy is in long-run equilibrium when actual output equals potential output (there is no output gap) and the inflation rate is stable. Graphically, long-run equilibrium occurs when the *AD* curve, the *SRAS* line, and the *LRAS* line intersect at a common point.
>
> Inflation adjusts gradually to bring the economy into long-run equilibrium (a phenomenon called the economy's self-correcting tendency). Inflation rises to eliminate an expansionary gap and falls to eliminate a recessionary gap. Graphically, the *SRAS* line moves up or down as needed to bring the economy into long-run equilibrium.
>
> The more rapid the self-correction process, the less need for active stabilization policies to eliminate output gaps. In practice, policymakers' attempts to eliminate output gaps are more likely to be helpful when the output gap is large than when it is small.

SOURCES OF INFLATION

We have seen that inflation can rise or fall in response to an output gap. But what creates the output gaps that give rise to changes in inflation? And are there factors besides output gaps that can affect the inflation rate? In this section we use the *AD-AS* diagram to explore the ultimate sources of inflation. We first discuss how excessive growth in aggregate spending can spur inflation, then turn to factors operating through the supply side of the economy.

EXCESSIVE AGGREGATE SPENDING

One important source of inflation in practice is excessive aggregate spending—or, in more colloquial terms, "too much spending chasing too few goods." Example 28.2 illustrates.

EXAMPLE 28.2   **Military buildups and inflation**

Wars and military buildups are sometimes associated with increased inflation. Explain why, using the *AD-AS* diagram. Can the Fed do anything to prevent the increase in inflation caused by a military buildup?

Wars and military buildups are potentially inflationary because increased spending on military hardware raises total demand relative to the economy's productive capacity. In the face of rising sales, firms increase their prices more quickly, raising the inflation rate.

The two panels of Figure 28.8 illustrate this process. Looking first at Figure 28.8(a), suppose that the economy is initially in long-run equilibrium at point *A*, where the aggregate demand curve *AD* intersects both the short-run and long-run aggregate supply lines, *SRAS* and *LRAS*, respectively. Point *A* is a long-run equilibrium point, with output equal to potential output and stable inflation. Now suppose that the government decides to spend more on armaments. Increased military spending is an increase in government purchases *G*, an exogenous increase in spending. We saw earlier that, for a given level of inflation, an exogenous increase in spending raises short-run equilibrium output, shifting the *AD* curve to the right. Figure 28.8(a) shows the aggregate demand curve shifting rightward, from *AD* to *AD'*, as the result of increased military expenditure. The economy moves to a new, short-run equilibrium at point *B*, where *AD'* intersects *SRAS*. Note that at point *B* actual output has risen above potential, to $Y > Y^*$, creating an expansionary gap. Because inflation is inertial and does not change in the short run, the immediate effect of the increase in government purchases is only to increase output, just as we saw in the Keynesian cross analysis of Chapter 26.

The process doesn't stop there, however, because inflation will not remain the same indefinitely. At point *B* an expansionary gap exists, so inflation will gradually begin to increase. Figure 28.8(b) shows this increase in inflation as a shift of the *SRAS* line from its initial position to a higher level, *SRAS'*. When inflation has risen to π', enough to eliminate the output gap (point *C*), the economy is back in long-run equilibrium. We see now that the increase in output created by the military buildup was only temporary. In the long run, actual output has returned to the level of potential output, but at a higher rate of inflation.

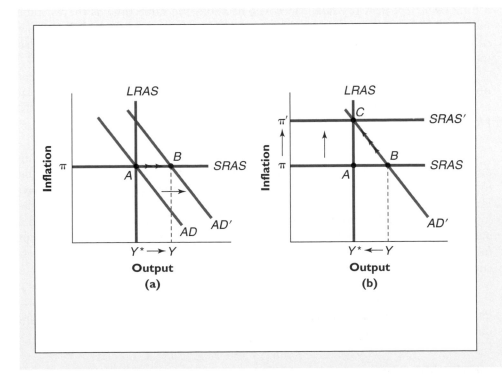

FIGURE 28.8
War and Military Buildup as a Source of Inflation.
(a) An increase in military spending shifts the *AD* curve to the right, from *AD* to *AD'*. At the new short-run equilibrium point *B*, actual output has risen above potential output *Y**, creating an expansionary gap. (b) This gap leads to rising inflation, shown as an upward movement of the *SRAS* line, from *SRAS* to *SRAS'*. At the new long-run equilibrium point *C*, actual output has fallen back to the level of potential output, but at π' inflation is higher than it was originally.

Does the Fed have the power to prevent the increased inflation that is induced by a rise in military spending? The answer is yes. We saw earlier that a decision by the Fed to set a higher real interest rate at any given level of inflation—an upward shift in the policy reaction function—will shift the *AD* curve to the left. So if the Fed aggressively tightens monetary policy (shifts its reaction function) as the military buildup proceeds, it can reverse the rightward shift of the *AD* curve caused by increased government spending. Offsetting the rightward shift of the *AD* curve in turn avoids the development of an expansionary gap, with its inflationary consequences. The Fed's policy works because the higher real interest rate it sets at each level of inflation acts to reduce consumption and investment spending. The reduction in private spending offsets the increase in demand by the government, eliminating—or at least moderating—the inflationary impact of the military purchases.

We should not conclude, by the way, that avoiding the inflationary consequences of a military buildup makes the buildup costless to society. As we have just noted, inflation can be avoided only if consumption and investment are reduced by a policy of higher real interest rates. Effectively, the private sector must give up some resources so that more of the nation's output can be devoted to military purposes. This reduction in resources reduces both current living standards (by reducing consumption) and future living standards (by reducing investment).

ECONOMIC NATURALIST 28.1

How did inflation get started in the United States in the 1960s?

In the United States from 1959 through 1963, inflation hovered around 1 percent per year. Beginning in 1964, however, inflation began to rise, reaching nearly 6 percent in 1970. Why did inflation become a problem in the United States in the 1960s?

Increases in government spending, plus the failure of the Federal Reserve to act to contain inflation, appear to explain most of the increase in inflation during the 1960s. On the fiscal side, military expenditures increased dramatically in the latter part of the decade, as the war in Vietnam escalated. Defense spending rose from $50.6 billion, or about 7.4 percent of GDP, in 1965 to $81.9 billion, or 9.4 percent of GDP, in 1968, and it remained at a high level for some years. To appreciate the size of this military buildup relative to the size of the economy, note that the *increase* in military spending alone between 1965 and 1968 was about 2 percent of GDP. In contrast, in 2001 the *total* U.S. defense budget was a little over 3 percent of GDP. Moreover, at about the same time as the wartime military buildup, government spending on social programs—reflecting the impact of President Lyndon Johnson's Great Society and War on Poverty initiatives—also increased dramatically.

These government-induced increases in total spending contributed to an economic boom. Indeed the 1961–1969 economic expansion was the longest in history at the time, being surpassed only recently by the long expansion of the 1990s. However, an expansionary gap developed and eventually inflation began to rise, as would have been predicted by the analysis in Example 28.2.

An interesting contrast exists between these effects of the 1960s military buildup and those of the 1980s buildup under President Reagan, which did not lead to an increase in inflation. One important difference between the two eras was the behavior of the Federal Reserve. As we saw in Example 28.2, the Fed can offset the inflationary impact of increased government spending by fighting inflation more aggressively (shifting its policy reaction function upward). Except for a brief attempt in 1966, the Federal Reserve generally did not try actively to offset inflationary pressures during the 1960s. That failure may have been simply a miscalculation, or it may have reflected a reluctance to take the politically unpopular step of slowing the economy during a period of great political turmoil. But in the early 1980s, under Paul Volcker, the Federal Reserve acted vigorously to contain inflation. As a result, inflation actually declined in the 1980s, despite the military buildup.

EXERCISE 28.7

In Example 28.1 we found that a decline in consumer spending tends to reduce the rate of inflation. Using the *AD-AS* diagram, illustrate the short-run and long-run effects of a fall in consumer spending on inflation. How does the decline in spending affect output in the short run and in the long run?

"I told you the Fed should have tightened."

Whereas output gaps cause gradual changes in inflation, on occasion an economic shock can cause a relatively rapid increase or decrease in inflation. Such jolts to prices, which we call *inflation shocks,* are the subject of the next section.

INFLATION SHOCKS

In late 1973, at the time of the Yom Kippur War between Israel and a coalition of Arab nations, the Organization of Petroleum-Exporting Countries (OPEC) dramatically cut its supplies of crude oil to the industrialized nations, quadrupling world oil prices. The sharp increase in oil prices was quickly transferred to the price of gasoline, heating oil, and goods and services that were heavily dependent on oil, such as air travel. The effects of the oil price increase, together with agricultural shortages that increased the price of food, contributed to a significant rise in the overall U.S. inflation rate in 1974.[4]

The increase in inflation in 1974 is an example of what is referred to as an *inflation shock.* An **inflation shock** is a sudden change in the normal behavior of inflation, unrelated to the nation's output gap. An inflation shock that causes an increase in inflation, like the large rise in oil prices in 1973, is called an *adverse* inflation shock. An inflation shock that reduces inflation, such as the sharp decline in oil prices that occurred in 1986, is called a *favorable* inflation shock. Economic Naturalist 28.2 gives more details on the economic effects of inflation shocks.

Why did inflation escalate in the United States in the 1970s?

Having risen in the second half of the 1960s, inflation continued to rise in the 1970s. Already at 6.2 percent in 1973, inflation jumped to 11.0 percent in 1974. After subsiding from 1974 to 1978, it began to rise again in 1979, to 11.4 percent, and reached 13.5 percent in 1980. Why did inflation increase so much in the 1970s?

We have already described the quadrupling of oil prices in late 1973 and the sharp increases in agricultural prices at about the same time, which together constituted an adverse inflation shock. A second inflation shock occurred in 1979,

OPEC's 1974 cutback in oil production created long lines, rising prices, and frayed tempers at the gas pump.

inflation shock a sudden change in the normal behavior of inflation, unrelated to the nation's output gap

ECONOMIC NATURALIST 28.2

[4]In Chapter 19 we distinguished between relative price changes (changes in the prices of individual goods) and inflation (changes in the overall price level). In the 1973–1974 episode changes in the prices of individual categories of goods, such as energy and food, were sufficiently large and pervasive that the overall price level was significantly affected. Thus these relative price changes carried an inflationary impact as well.

when the turmoil of the Iranian Revolution restricted the flow of oil from the Middle East and doubled oil prices yet again.

Figure 28.9 shows the effects of an adverse inflation shock on a hypothetical economy. Before the inflation shock occurs, the economy is in long-run equilibrium at point A, at the intersection of AD, LRAS, and SRAS. At point A actual output is equal to potential output Y*, and the inflation rate is stable at π. However, an adverse inflation shock directly increases inflation, so that the SRAS line shifts rapidly upward to SRAS'. A new short-run equilibrium is established at point B, where SRAS' intersects the aggregate demand curve AD. In the wake of the inflation shock, inflation rises to π' and output falls, from Y* to Y'. Thus an inflation shock creates the worst possible scenario: higher inflation coupled with a recessionary gap. The combination of inflation and recession has been referred to as *stagflation*, or stagnation plus inflation. The U.S. economy experienced a stagflation in 1973–1975, after the first oil shock, and again in 1980, after the second oil shock.

FIGURE 28.9

The Effects of an Adverse Inflation Shock.

Starting from long-run equilibrium at point A, an adverse inflation shock directly raises current inflation, causing the SRAS line to shift upward to SRAS'. At the new short-run equilibrium, point B, inflation has risen to π' and output has fallen to Y', creating a recessionary gap. If the Fed does nothing, eventually the economy will return to point A, restoring the original inflation rate but suffering a long recession in the process. The Fed could ease monetary policy by shifting down its policy reaction function, shifting the AD curve to AD' and restoring full employment more quickly at point C. The cost of this strategy is that inflation remains at its higher level.

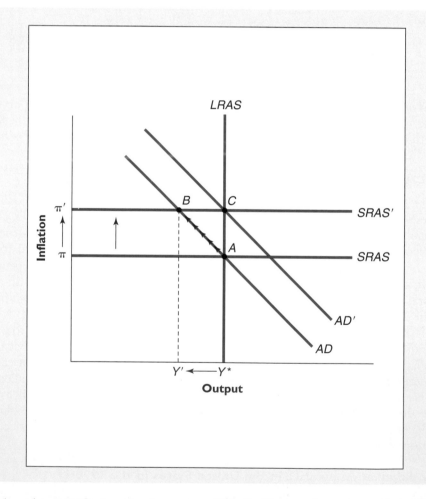

An adverse inflation shock poses a difficult dilemma for macroeconomic policymakers. To see why, suppose monetary and fiscal policies were left unchanged following an inflationary shock. In that case, inflation would eventually abate and return to its original level. Graphically, the economy would reach its short-run equilibrium at point B in Figure 28.9 soon after the inflation shock. However, because of the recessionary gap that exists at point B, eventually inflation would begin to drift downward, until finally the recessionary gap is eliminated. Graphically, this decline in inflation would be represented by a downward movement of the SRAS line, from SRAS' back to SRAS. Inflation would stop declining only when long-run equilibrium is restored, at point A in the figure, where inflation is at its original level of π and output equals potential output.

However, although a "do-nothing" policy approach would ultimately eliminate both the output gap and the surge in inflation, it would also put the economy through a deep and protracted recession, as actual output remains below potential output until the inflation adjustment process is completed. To avoid such an economically and politically costly outcome, policymakers might opt to eliminate the recessionary gap more quickly. By aggressively easing monetary policy (more precisely, by shifting down its policy reaction function), for example, the Fed could shift the AD curve to the right, from AD to AD', taking the economy to a new long-run equilibrium, point C in Figure 28.9. This expansionary policy would help to restore output to the full-employment level more quickly, but as the figure shows, it would also allow inflation to stabilize at the new, higher level.

In sum, inflation shocks pose a true dilemma for policymakers. If they leave their policies unchanged—a "steady-as-she-goes" approach—inflation will eventually subside, but the nation may experience a lengthy and severe recession. If instead they act aggressively to expand aggregate spending, the recession will end more quickly, but inflation will stabilize at a higher level. In the 1970s, though U.S. policymakers tried to strike a balance between stabilizing output and containing inflation, the combination of recession and increased inflation hobbled the economy.

In Chapter 23 we discussed the long-run relationship between inflation and money growth. The example of an inflation shock shows that inflation does not always originate from excessive money growth; it can arise from a variety of factors. However, our analysis also shows that, in the absence of monetary easing, inflation that arises from factors such as inflation shocks will eventually die away. By contrast, *sustained* inflation requires that monetary policy remain easy, that is, policymakers allow the money supply to rise rapidly. In this respect, our analysis of this chapter is consistent with the earlier long-run analysis, which concluded that sustained inflation is possible only if monetary policy is sufficiently expansionary.

EXERCISE 28.8

Inflation shocks can also be beneficial for the economy, such as when oil prices declined in the late 1990s. What effect would a decrease in oil prices have on output and inflation?

SHOCKS TO POTENTIAL OUTPUT

In analyzing the effects of increased oil prices on the U.S. economy in the 1970s, we assumed that potential output was unchanged in the wake of the shock. However, the sharp rise in oil prices during that period probably affected the economy's potential output as well. As oil prices rose, for example, many companies retired less energy-efficient equipment or scrapped older "gas-guzzling" vehicles. A smaller capital stock implies lower potential output.

If the increases in oil prices did reduce potential output, their inflationary impact would have been compounded. Figure 28.10 illustrates the effects on the economy of a sudden decline in potential output. For the sake of simplicity, the figure includes only the effects of the reduction in potential output, and not the direct effect of the inflation shock. (Problem 7 at the end of the chapter asks you to combine the two effects.)

Suppose once again that the economy is in long-run equilibrium at point A. Then potential output falls unexpectedly, from Y^* to $Y^{*\prime}$, shifting the long-run aggregate supply line leftward from $LRAS$ to $LRAS'$. After this decline in potential output, is the economy still in long-run equilibrium at point A? The answer is no, because output now exceeds potential output at that point. In other words,

FIGURE 28.10

The Effects of a Shock to Potential Output.
The economy is in long-run equilibrium at point *A* when a decline in potential output, from *Y** to *Y*'*, creates an expansionary gap. Inflation rises, and the short-run aggregate supply line shifts upward from *SRAS* to *SRAS'*. A new long-run equilibrium is reached at point *B*, where actual output equals the new, lower level of potential output, *Y*'*, and inflation has risen to *π'*. Because it is the result of a fall in potential output, the decline in output is permanent.

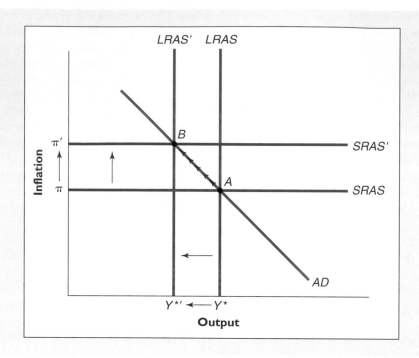

aggregate supply shock either an inflation shock or a shock to potential output; adverse aggregate supply shocks of both types reduce output and increase inflation

an expansionary gap has developed. This gap reflects the fact that although planned spending has not changed, the capacity of firms to supply goods and services has been reduced.

As we have seen, an expansionary gap leads to rising inflation. In Figure 28.10, increasing inflation is represented by an upward movement of the *SRAS* line. Eventually the short-run aggregate supply line reaches *SRAS'*, and the economy reaches a new long-run equilibrium at point *B*. (Why is point *B* a long-run, and not just a short-run equilibrium?) At that point output has fallen to the new, lower level of potential output, *Y*'*, and inflation has risen to *π'*.

Sharp changes in potential output and inflation shocks are both referred to as **aggregate supply shocks.** As we have seen, an adverse aggregate supply shock of either type leads to lower output and higher inflation, and therefore poses a difficult challenge for policymakers. A difference between the two types of aggregate supply shocks is that the output losses associated with an adverse inflation shock are temporary (because the economy self-corrects and will ultimately return to its initial level of potential output), but those associated with a fall in potential output are permanent (output remains lower even after the economy has reached a new long-run equilibrium).

Why was the United States able to experience rapid growth and low inflation in the latter part of the 1990s?

ECONOMIC NATURALIST 28.3

The second half of the 1990s was a boom period in the U.S. economy. As Table 28.1 shows, real GDP growth during the 1995–2000 period was 4 percent per year, significantly higher than the average growth rate over the previous decade; and unemployment averaged only 4.6 percent, also significantly better than the prior decade. Despite this rapid economic growth, inflation during 1995–2000 was contained, averaging only 2.4 percent per year. Why was the United States able to enjoy both rapid growth and low inflation in the latter 1990s?

During the latter part of the 1990s the U.S. economy benefited from a positive shock to potential output. An important source of the faster-than-usual expansion of potential output was impressive technological advance, particularly in computers and software, as well as the application of these advances in areas ranging from automobile production to retail inventory management. One of the most prominent developments, the rapid growth of the Internet, not only made it possible for consumers to shop or find information online but also helped companies to improve their efficiency, for example, by improving coordination between manufacturers and their suppliers. These advances were reflected in more rapid productivity growth; as Table 28.1 shows, average annual growth of output per hour worked accelerated from 1.4 percent during the 1985–1995 period to a remarkable 2.5 percent during 1995–2000.

Graphically, the effects of a positive shock to potential output are just the reverse of those seen in Figure 28.10, which shows the effects of an adverse shock. A positive shock to potential output causes the *LRAS* line to shift right, leading in the short run to a recessionary gap (output is lower than the new, higher level of potential output). Inflation declines, reflected in a downward movement of the *SRAS* line. In the new, long-run equilibrium, output is higher and inflation lower than initially. These results are consistent with the U.S. experience of the latter part of the 1990s.

TABLE 28.1
U.S. Macroeconomic Data, Annual Averages, 1985–2000

Years	% Growth in real GDP	Unemployment rate (%)	Inflation rate (%)	Productivity growth (%)
1985–1995	2.8	6.3	3.5	1.4
1995–2000	4.0	4.6	2.4	2.5

SOURCE: *Economic Report of the President*, various tables. Real GDP is measured in 1996 dollars. The unemployment rate is the average civilian unemployment rate for the period. Inflation is measured by the CPI. Productivity is measured by output per hour of work, nonfarm business sector.

EXERCISE 28.9

What if productivity hadn't increased in the late 1990s? How would the economy have been different in 2000?

 RECAP **SOURCES OF INFLATION**

Inflation may result from excessive spending, which creates an expansionary output gap and puts upward pressure on inflation. An example is a military buildup, which raises government purchases. Monetary policy or fiscal policy can be used to offset excessive spending, preventing higher inflation from emerging.

Inflation may also arise from an aggregate supply shock, either an inflation shock or a shock to potential output. An inflation shock is a sudden change in the normal behavior of inflation, unrelated to the nation's output gap. An example of an inflation shock is a run-up in energy and food prices large enough to raise the overall price level. An inflation shock creates stagflation, a combination of recession and higher inflation.

Stagflation poses a difficult dilemma for policymakers. If they take no action, eventually inflation will subside and output will recover, but in the interim the economy may suffer a protracted period of recession. If they use monetary or fiscal policy to increase aggregate demand, they will shorten the recession but will also lock in the higher level of inflation.

A shock to potential output is a sharp change in potential output. Like an adverse inflation shock, an adverse shock to potential output results in both higher inflation and lower output. Because lower potential output implies that productive capacity has fallen, however, output does not recover following a shock to potential output, as it eventually does following an inflation shock.

CONTROLLING INFLATION

High or even moderate rates of inflation can impose significant costs to the economy. Indeed, over the past several decades a consensus has developed among economists and policymakers that low and stable inflation is important and perhaps necessary for sustained economic growth. What, then, should policymakers do if the inflation rate is too high? As Example 28.3 will show, inflation can be slowed by policies that shift the aggregate demand curve leftward. Unfortunately, although they produce long-term gains in productivity and economic growth, such policies are likely to impose significant short-run costs in the form of lost output and increased unemployment.

EXAMPLE 28.3

The effects of anti-inflationary monetary policy

Suppose that, although the economy is at full employment, the inflation rate is 10 percent—too high to be consistent with economic efficiency and long-term economic growth. The Fed decides to tighten monetary policy to reduce the inflation rate to 3 percent. What will happen to output, unemployment, and inflation in the short run? Over the long run?

The economic effects of a monetary tightening are very different in the short and long run. Figure 28.11(a) shows the short-run effect. Initially, the economy is in long-run equilibrium at point *A*, where actual output equals potential output. But at point *A* the inflation rate, 10 percent, is high, as indicated by the aggregate supply line, *SRAS*.

To bring inflation down to 3 percent, what can policymakers do? To get "tough" on inflation, the Fed must set the real interest rate at a level higher than normal, given the rate of inflation. In other words, the Fed must shift its policy reaction function upward, as in Figure 28.3(a). At a constant rate of inflation, an increase in the real interest rate set by the Fed will reduce consumption and investment spending, lowering aggregate demand at every inflation rate. As we saw earlier in the chapter, this monetary tightening by the Fed causes the *AD* curve to shift leftward, from *AD* to *AD'* in Figure 28.11(a).

After the Fed's action, the *AD'* curve and the *SRAS* line intersect at point *B* in Figure 28.11(a), the new short-run equilibrium point. At point *B* actual output has fallen to *Y*, which is less than potential output *Y**. In other words, the Fed's action has allowed a recessionary gap to develop, one result of which will be that unemployment will exceed the natural rate. At point *B*, however, the inflation rate has not changed, remaining at 10 percent. We conclude that in the short run, a monetary tightening pushes the economy into recession but has little or no effect on the inflation rate, because of inflation inertia.

The short-run effects of the anti-inflationary shift in monetary policy—lower output, higher unemployment, and little or no reduction of inflation—are to say the least not very encouraging, and they explain why such policy shifts are often highly unpopular in their early stages. Fortunately, however, we have not reached the end of the story, because the economy will not remain at point *B* indefinitely. The reason is that the existence of a recessionary gap at that point eventually causes inflation to decline, as firms become more reluctant to raise their prices in the face of weak demand.

Graphically, the eventual decline in inflation that results from a recessionary gap is represented by the downward movement of the short-run aggregate supply line, from *SRAS* to *SRAS'* in Figure 28.11(b). Inflation will continue to fall until the economy returns to long-run equilibrium at point *C*. At that point, actual output has returned to potential, and the inflation rate has stabilized at 3 percent. So we see that a tight monetary policy inflicts short-term pain (a decline in output, high unemployment, and a high real interest rate) to achieve a long-term gain (a permanent reduction in inflation). Incidentally, the result that an upward

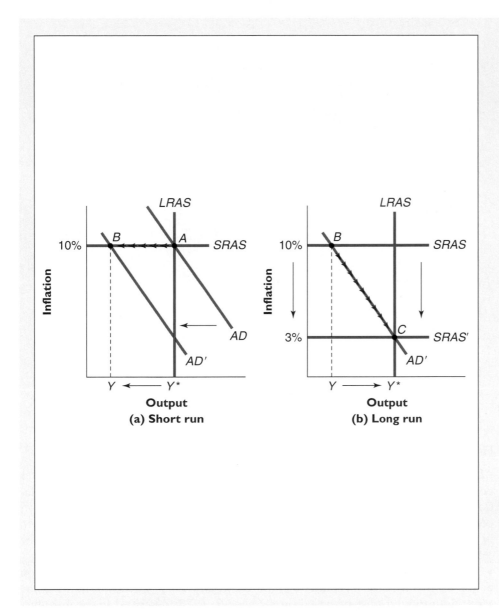

FIGURE 28.11
Short-Run and Long-Run Effects of an Anti-inflationary Monetary Policy.
(a) Initially the economy is in long-run equilibrium at point A, with actual output equal to potential and the inflation rate at 10 percent. If an anti-inflationary policy shift by the Fed shifts the AD curve to the left, from AD to AD', the economy will reach a new short-run equilibrium at point B, at the intersection of AD' and SRAS. As short-run equilibrium output falls to Y, a recessionary gap opens up. The inflation rate does not change in the short run. (b) Following the tightening of monetary policy, a recessionary gap exists at point B, which eventually causes inflation to decline. The short-run aggregate supply line moves downward, from SRAS to SRAS'. Long-run equilibrium is restored at point C. In the long run, real output returns to potential and inflation stabilizes at a lower level (3 percent in this figure).

shift in the monetary policy reaction function leads to a permanently lower rate of inflation suggests a useful alternative way to think about such shifts: An upward shift in the Fed's reaction function is equivalent to a decline in its long-term target for inflation (see Exercise 28.2). Similarly, a downward shift in the Fed's reaction function could be interpreted as an increase in the Fed's long-term inflation target.

Economic Naturalist 28.4 discusses the real-life episode of Fed tightening with which we began this chapter.

EXERCISE 28.10

Show the typical time paths of output, inflation, and the real interest rate when the Fed employs an anti-inflationary monetary policy. Draw a separate graph for each variable, showing time on the horizontal axis. Be sure to distinguish the short run from the long run. Specific numerical values are not necessary.

"I don't <u>like</u> 6 per-cent unemployment, either. But I can live with it."

ECONOMIC
NATURALIST
28.4

How was inflation conquered in the 1980s?

After reaching double-digit levels in the late 1970s, inflation in the United States declined sharply in the 1980s. After peaking at 13.5 percent in 1980, the inflation rate fell all the way to 3.2 percent in 1983, and it remained in the 2–5 percent range for the rest of the decade. In the 1990s inflation fell even lower, in the 2–3 percent range in most years. How was inflation conquered in the 1980s?

The person who was most directly responsible for the conquest of inflation in the 1980s was the Federal Reserve's chairman, Paul Volcker. Following the secret Saturday meeting he called on October 6, 1979 (described in the introduction to this chapter), the Federal Open Market Committee agreed to adopt a strongly anti-inflationary monetary policy. The results of this policy change on the U.S. economy are shown in Table 28.2, which includes selected macroeconomic data for the period 1978–1985.

The data in Table 28.2 fit our analysis of anti-inflationary monetary policy quite well. First, as our model predicts, in the short run the Fed's sharp tightening of monetary policy led to a recession. In fact, two recessions followed the Fed's action in 1979, a short one in 1980 and a deeper one in 1981–1982. Note that growth in real GDP was negative in 1980 and 1982, and the unemployment rate rose significantly, peaking at 9.7 percent in 1982. Nominal and real interest rates also rose, a direct effect of the shift in monetary policy. Inflation, however, did not respond much during the period 1979–1981. All these results are consistent with the short-run analysis in Figure 28.11.

By 1983, however, the situation had changed markedly. The economy had recovered, with strong growth in real GDP in 1983–1985 (see Table 28.2). In 1984 the unemployment rate, which tends to lag the recovery, began to decline. Interest rates remained relatively high, perhaps reflecting other factors besides monetary policy. Most significantly, inflation fell in 1982–1983 and stabilized at a much lower level. Inflation has remained low in the United States ever since.

TABLE 28.2
U.S. Macroeconomic Data, 1978–1985

Year	Growth in real GDP %	Unemployment rate (%)	Inflation rate (%)	Nominal interest rate (%)	Real interest rate (%)
1978	5.5	6.1	7.6	8.3	0.7
1979	3.2	5.8	11.4	9.7	−1.7
1980	−0.2	7.1	13.5	11.6	−1.9
1981	2.5	7.6	10.3	14.4	4.1
1982	−2.0	9.7	6.2	12.9	6.7
1983	4.3	9.6	3.2	10.5	7.3
1984	7.3	7.5	4.3	11.9	7.6
1985	3.8	7.2	3.6	9.6	6.0

SOURCE: *Economic Report of the President,* various tables. Real GDP is measured in 1996 dollars. Inflation is measured by the CPI. The nominal interest rate is the average annual value of the three-month Treasury bill rate. The real interest rate equals the nominal interest rate minus the inflation rate.

A substantial reduction in the rate of inflation, like the one the Fed engineered in the 1980s, is called a **disinflation.** But again, disinflation comes at the cost of a large recessionary gap and high unemployment like that experienced by the United States in the early 1980s. Is this cost worth bearing? This question is not an easy one to answer, because the costs of inflation are difficult to measure. Policymakers around the world appear to agree on the necessity of containing inflation, however, as many countries fought to bring their own inflation rates down to 2 percent or less in the 1980s and 1990s. Canada and Great Britain are among the many industrial countries that have borne the costs of sharp reductions in inflation.

disinflation a substantial reduction in the rate of inflation

Can the costs of disinflation be reduced? Unfortunately, no one has found a pain-free method of lowering the inflation rate. Accordingly, in recent years central banks around the world have striven to keep inflation at manageable levels, to avoid the costs of disinflation. In the United States, under Chairman Alan Greenspan, the Federal Reserve has followed a strategy of *preemptive strikes,* raising interest rates at the first sign that inflation might soon begin to creep upward. This strategy appears to have been successful in keeping inflation low and avoiding the need for costly disinflation. Other countries—Canada, Great Britain, Sweden, Mexico, Brazil, Chile, Israel, and many others—have announced explicit numerical *targets* for the long-run inflation rate, usually in the range of 1–3 percent per year. The philosophy behind inflation targets is the same as that behind the Fed's preemptive approach to inflation: If inflation can be kept low, the economy can enjoy the resulting long-term benefits without having to incur the short-term costs of disinflationary policies like the ones followed by Chairman Volcker.

Can inflation be too low?

As the last section points out, the Federal Reserve is normally focused on keeping inflation from rising too fast, but by late 2002, some Fed policymakers began to worry that inflation might actually be too low. Why?

Minutes of the Federal Reserve's September 24, 2002, Federal Open Market Committee meeting, where Federal Reserve policymakers determine future monetary policy actions, indicate that committee members were concerned that continuing

ECONOMIC
NATURALIST
28.5

weakness in the U.S. economy was likely to lead to "quite low and perhaps declining inflation" well into 2003.[5] With prices of consumer goods rising only about 1.5 percent from September 2001 to September 2002, members noted that "further sizable disinflation that resulted in a nominal inflation rate near zero could create problems for the implementation of monetary policy through conventional means in the event of an adverse shock to the economy."

The potential for future monetary policymaking problems was raised by the combination of low inflation rates, low interest rates, and the possibility of further economic weakness. During 2001 and 2002 the Federal Reserve reduced its target for the federal funds rate to 1.75 percent, the lowest levels in four decades, in an attempt to provide economic stimulus to an economy slowly emerging from recession. With an inflation rate of 1.5 percent, the resulting real rate of interest—the difference between the nominal interest rate and the inflation rate—was nearly zero percent by September 2002.

Why did this create a potential problem for the Federal Reserve? With inflation rates already low and possibly falling, if the Fed was forced in the future to further stimulate aggregate spending in response to a negative economywide spending shock—a real possibility given the concerns about a U.S. military confrontation with Iraq—it might need to reduce the real rate of interest below zero percent. As pointed out in Chapter 27, business and consumer spending respond to real interest rates, not nominal interest rates. However, in a period of declining inflation, the Federal Reserve needs to reduce nominal interest rates by more than the fall in inflation to reduce the real rate of interest. With the federal funds rate already at historic lows, Fed officials were worried that they would not be able to lower nominal interest rates enough to reduce real interest rates further. In particular, if the inflation rate fell to zero percent, the Fed would not be able to generate a negative real federal funds rate, thereby limiting the Fed's ability to conduct expansionary monetary policy to offset a recessionary gap. Indeed, partly as a preemptive measure to prevent further economic weakening and declines in inflation, the Fed acted at its next meeting, in November 2002, to cut the federal funds rate to 1.25 percent.

However, Fed officials at the time also noted that, even if the federal funds rate were to be reduced all the way to zero percent, the Fed would still have a variety of options available to stimulate aggregate spending in the U.S. economy. For example, the Federal Reserve could buy long-term U.S. Treasury bonds, reducing long-term interest rates, in an effort to spur investment spending. As pointed out in Chapter 27, the Fed's monetary actions typically focus on the federal funds rate, a very short-term interest rate that may or may not move in concert with long-term interest rates that particularly influence mortgage lending. In addition, the Federal Reserve could increase its discount window lending to banks to promote increased consumer and business lending, intervene in foreign exchange markets to reduce the value of the dollar in an attempt to stimulate net exports, or finance a federal government tax cut by buying additional bonds, the modern-day equivalent of printing money.

All of these "nontraditional" Fed policy actions have the effect of injecting more money into the economy, leading to increased aggregate spending and higher inflation rates over time. By using these monetary policy tools the Fed could, if necessary, generate negative real interest rates by inducing higher inflation, even if the federal funds rate is at zero percent. Thus, while low inflation rates, coupled with low interest rates, make monetary policymaking more complicated, interest rates can't ever really be "too low" to eliminate the Fed's ability to stimulate the economy.

---

[5]Minutes from the Federal Reserve's September 2002 FOMC meeting are available online at http://www.federalreserve.gov/fomc/minutes/20020924.htm.

RECAP **CONTROLLING INFLATION**

Inflation can be controlled by policies that shift the aggregate demand curve leftward, such as a move to a "tighter" monetary policy (an upward shift in the monetary policy reaction function). In the short run, the effects of an anti-inflationary monetary policy are felt largely on output, so that a disinflation (a substantial reduction in inflation) may create a significant recessionary gap. According to the theory, in the long run output should return to potential and inflation should decline. These predictions appear to have been borne out during the Volcker disinflation of the early 1980s.

■ SUMMARY ■

- This chapter extended the basic Keynesian model to include inflation. First, we showed how planned spending and short-run equilibrium output are related to inflation, a relationship that is summarized by the aggregate demand curve. Second, we discussed how inflation itself is determined. In the short run, inflation is determined by past expectations and pricing decisions, but in the longer run inflation adjusts as needed to eliminate output gaps.

- The *aggregate demand (AD) curve* shows the relationship between short-run equilibrium output and inflation. Because short-run equilibrium output is equal to planned spending, the aggregate demand curve also relates spending to inflation. Increases in inflation reduce planned spending and short-run equilibrium output, so the aggregate demand curve is downward-sloping.

- The inverse relationship of inflation and short-run equilibrium output is the result, in large part, of the behavior of the Federal Reserve. To keep inflation low and stable, the Fed reacts to rising inflation by increasing the real interest rate. A higher real interest rate reduces consumption and planned investment, lowering planned aggregate expenditure and hence short-run equilibrium output. Other reasons that the aggregate demand curve slopes downward include the effects of inflation on the real value of money, distributional effects (inflation redistributes wealth from the poor, who save relatively little, to the more affluent, who save more), uncertainty created by inflation, and the impact of inflation on foreign sales of domestic goods.

- For any given value of inflation, an exogenous increase in spending (that is, an increase in spending at given levels of output and the real interest rate) raises short-run equilibrium output, shifting the aggregate demand (AD) curve to the right. Likewise, an exogenous decline in spending shifts the AD curve to the left. The AD curve can also be shifted by a change in the Fed's policy reaction function. If the Fed gets "tougher," shifting up its reaction function and thus choosing a higher real interest rate at each level of inflation, the aggregate demand curve will shift to the left. If the Fed gets "easier," shifting down its reaction function and thus

setting a lower real interest rate at each level of inflation, the AD curve will shift to the right.

- In low-inflation industrial economies like the United States today, inflation tends to be inertial, or slow to adjust to changes in the economy. This inertial behavior reflects the fact that inflation depends in part on people's expectations of future inflation, which in turn depend on their recent experience with inflation. Long-term wage and price contracts tend to "build in" the effects of people's expectations for multiyear periods. In the aggregate demand–aggregate supply diagram, the *short-run aggregate supply (SRAS) line* is a horizontal line that shows the current rate of inflation, as determined by past expectations and pricing decisions.

- Although inflation is inertial, it does change over time in response to output gaps. An expansionary gap tends to raise the inflation rate, because firms raise their prices more quickly when they are facing demand that exceeds their normal productive capacity. A recessionary gap tends to reduce the inflation rate, as firms become more reluctant to raise their prices.

- The economy is in *short-run equilibrium* when the inflation rate equals the value determined by past expectations and pricing decisions, and output equals the level of short-run equilibrium output that is consistent with that inflation rate. Graphically, short-run equilibrium occurs at the intersection of the AD curve and the SRAS line. If an output gap exists, however, the inflation rate will adjust to eliminate the gap. Graphically, the SRAS line moves upward or downward as needed to restore output to its full-employment level. When the inflation rate is stable and actual output equals potential output, the economy is in *long-run equilibrium*. Graphically, long-run equilibrium corresponds to the common intersection point of the AD curve, the SRAS line, and the long-run aggregate supply (LRAS) line, a vertical line that marks the economy's potential output.

- Because the economy tends to move toward long-run equilibrium on its own through the adjustment of the inflation rate, it is said to be self-correcting. The more rapid the self-correction process, the smaller the need for active stabilization policies to eliminate output gaps. In practice, the larger the output gap, the more useful such policies are.

- One source of inflation is excessive spending, which leads to expansionary output gaps. Aggregate supply shocks are another source of inflation. *Aggregate supply shocks* include both *inflation shocks*—sudden changes in the normal behavior of inflation, created, for example, by a rise in the price of imported oil—and shocks to potential output. Adverse supply shocks both lower output and increase inflation, creating a difficult dilemma for policymakers.

- To reduce inflation, policymakers must shift the aggregate demand curve to the left, usually through a shift in monetary policy toward greater "tightness." In the short run, the main effects of an anti-inflationary policy may be reduced output and higher unemployment, as the economy experiences a recessionary gap. These short-run costs of *disinflation* must be balanced against the long-run benefits of a lower rate of inflation. Over time, output and employment will return to normal levels and inflation declines. The disinflation engineered by the Fed under Chairman Paul Volcker in the early 1980s followed this pattern.

▪ KEY TERMS ▪

aggregate demand (*AD*) curve (738)
aggregate supply shock (758)
disinflation (763)
inflation shock (755)

long-run aggregate supply (*LRAS*)
line (749)
long-run equilibrium (750)

short-run aggregate supply (*SRAS*)
line (749)
short-run equilibrium (749)

▪ REVIEW QUESTIONS ▪

1. What two variables are related by the aggregate demand (*AD*) curve? Explain how the behavior of the Fed helps to determine the slope of this curve. List and discuss two other factors that lead the curve to have the slope that it does.

2. State how each of the following affects the *AD* curve and explain:
   a. An increase in government purchases.
   b. A cut in taxes.
   c. A decline in planned investment spending by firms.
   d. A decision by the Fed to lower the real interest rate at each level of inflation.

3. Why does the overall rate of inflation tend to adjust more slowly than prices of commodities, such as oil or grain?

4. Discuss the relationship between output gaps and inflation. How is this relationship captured in the aggregate demand–aggregate supply diagram?

5. Sketch an aggregate demand–aggregate supply diagram depicting an economy away from long-run equi-

librium. Indicate the economy's short-run equilibrium point. Discuss how the economy reaches long-run equilibrium over a period of time. Illustrate the process in your diagram.

6. True or false: The economy's self-correcting tendency makes active use of stabilization policy unnecessary. Explain.

7. What factors led to increased inflation in the United States in the 1960s and 1970s?

8. Why does an adverse inflation shock pose a particularly difficult dilemma for policymakers?

9. How does a tight monetary policy, like that conducted by the Volcker Fed in the early 1980s, affect output, inflation, and the real interest rate in the short run? In the long run?

10. Most central banks place great value on keeping inflation low and stable. Why do they view this objective as so important?

▪ PROBLEMS ▪

1. We saw in Chapter 27 that short-run equilibrium output falls when the Fed raises the real interest rate. Suppose the relationship between short-run equilibrium output Y and the real interest rate r set by the Fed is given by

$$Y = 1,000 - 1,000r.$$

Suppose also that the Fed's reaction function is the one shown in Table 27.1 and reproduced in the appendix to this chapter. For whole-number inflation rates between

0 and 4 percent, find the real interest rate by the Fed and the resulting short-run equilibrium output. Graph the aggregate demand curve numerically.

2. For the economy in Problem 1, suppose that potential output $Y^* = 960$. From the policy reaction function in Table 27.1, what can you infer about the Fed's objective for the inflation rate in the long term?

3. An economy's aggregate demand curve (the relationship between short-run equilibrium output and inflation) is described by the equation

$$Y = 13,000 - 20,000\pi.$$

Initially, the inflation rate is 4 percent, or $\pi = 0.04$. Potential output Y^* equals 12,000.
a. Find inflation and output in short-run equilibrium.
b. Find inflation and output in long-run equilibrium.

Show your work.

4. This problem asks you to trace out the adjustment of inflation when the economy starts with an output gap. Suppose that the economy's aggregate demand curve is

$$Y = 1,000 - 1,000\pi,$$

where Y is short-run equilibrium output and π is the inflation rate, measured as a decimal. Potential output Y^* equals 950, and the initial inflation rate is 10 percent ($\pi = 0.10$).
a. Find output and inflation for this economy in short-run equilibrium and in long-run equilibrium.
b. Suppose that, each quarter, inflation adjusts according to the following rule:

This quarter's inflation = Last quarter's inflation $- 0.0004(Y^* - Y)$.

Starting from the initial value of 10 percent for inflation, find the value of inflation for each of the next five quarters. Does inflation come close to its long-run value?

5. For each of the following, use an *AD-AS* diagram to show the short-run and long-run effects on output and inflation. Assume the economy starts in long-run equilibrium.
a. An increase in consumer confidence that leads to higher consumption spending.
b. A reduction in taxes.
c. An easing of monetary policy by the Fed (a downward shift in the policy reaction function).
d. A sharp drop in oil prices.
e. A war that raises government purchases.

6. Suppose that the government cuts taxes in response to a recessionary gap, but because of legislative delays the tax cut is not put in place for 18 months. Using an *AD-AS* diagram and assuming that the government's objective is to stabilize output and inflation, show how this policy action might actually prove to be counterproductive.

7. Suppose that a permanent increase in oil prices both creates an inflationary shock and reduces potential output. Use an *AD-AS* diagram to show the effects of the oil price increase on output and inflation in the short run and the long run, assuming that there is no policy response. What happens if the Fed responds to the oil price increase by tightening monetary policy?

8. An economy is initially in recession. Using the *AD-AS* diagram, show the process of adjustment
a. If the Fed responds by easing monetary policy (moving its reaction function down).
b. If the Fed takes no action.

What are the costs and benefits of each approach, in terms of output loss and inflation?

9.* Planned aggregate expenditure in Lotusland depends on real GDP and the real interest rate according to the following equation:

$$PAE = 3,000 + 0.8Y - 2,000r.$$

The Bank of Lotusland, the central bank, has announced that it will set the real interest rate according to the following policy reaction function:

Rate of inflation, π	Real interest rate, r
0.0	0.02
0.01	0.03
0.02	0.04
0.03	0.05
0.04	0.06

For the rates of inflation given, find autonomous expenditure and short-run equilibrium output in Lotusland. Graph the AD curve.

10.* An economy is described by the following equations:

$$C = 1,600 + 0.6(Y - T) - 2,000r,$$
$$I^P = 2,500 - 1,000r,$$
$$G = \overline{G} = 2,000,$$
$$NX = \overline{NX} = 50,$$
$$T = T = 2,000.$$

Suppose also that the central bank's policy reaction function is the same as in Problem 9 above.
a. Find an equation relating planned spending to output and the real interest rate.
b. Construct a table showing the relationship between short-run equilibrium output and inflation, for inflation rates between 0 and 4 percent. Using this table, graph the AD curve for the economy.
c. Repeat parts a and b, assuming that government purchases have increased to 2,100. How does an increase in government purchases affect the AD curve?

11.* For the economy described in Problem 10, suppose that the central bank's policy reaction function is as follows:

Rate of inflation, π	Real interest rate, r
0.0	0.04
0.01	0.045
0.02	0.05
0.03	0.055
0.04	0.06

a. Construct a table showing the relationship between short-run equilibrium output and the inflation rate for values of inflation between zero and 4 percent. Graph the aggregate demand curve of the economy.
b. Suppose that the central bank decides to lower the real interest rate by 0.5 percentage point at each value of inflation. Repeat part a. How does this change in monetary policy affect the aggregate demand curve?

*Problems marked with an asterisk (*) are more difficult.

▪ ANSWERS TO IN-CHAPTER EXERCISES ▪

28.1 a. At the current level of inflation, output, and real interest rate, an exogenous reduction in business spending on new capital will reduce planned investment, causing a decline in overall aggregate expenditures (*AE*), and a reduction in short-run equilibrium output. Because output has fallen for a given level of inflation, the decrease in business spending leads to a leftward shift in the *AD* curve.

   b. At the current level of inflation, output, and real interest rate, a reduction in federal income taxes increases consumers' disposable income ($Y-T$), which leads to an exogenous increase in consumption at all income levels, as illustrated in Chapter 26. The upward shift in the consumption function increases overall aggregate expenditures (*AE*) and leads to an increase in short-run equilibrium output. Because output has increased for a given level of inflation, the reduction in income taxes leads to a rightward shift in the *AD* curve.

28.2 In the long run, the real interest rate set by the Fed must be consistent with the real interest rate determined in the market for saving and investment. To find the Fed's long-run inflation target, take as given the real interest rate determined in the long run by the market for saving and investment and read off the corresponding inflation rate from the Fed's policy reaction function. As the accompanying figure illustrates, a tightening of Fed policy (an upward shift of the policy reaction function) implies that, for any given long-run real interest rate, the Fed's inflation target must be lower.

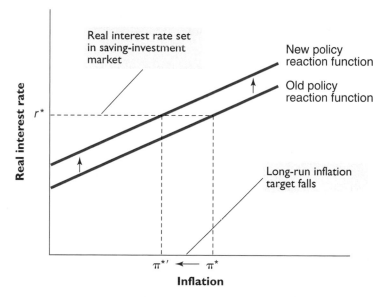

28.3 a. An upward shift in the Fed's policy reaction function means that the Federal Reserve is raising the real interest rate associated with a given level of inflation. An increase in the real interest rate causes both consumption and planned investment spending to fall, reducing overall aggregate expenditures and short-run equilibrium output. Thus, a shift in the Fed's policy reaction function causes the output level to fall for a given level of inflation, resulting in a leftward shift in the *AD* curve.

   b. The Federal Reserve's policy reaction function illustrates that the Federal Reserve responds to rising inflation rates by raising the real interest rate (a move *along* the policy reaction function), which causes a reduction in overall aggregate expenditures and short-run equilibrium output. However, in this case the Fed's response to higher inflation causes a *move along* a given *AD* curve.

   Note that while the two actions appear to be similar, there is a key difference. In the first case the Fed is changing its policy rule for a *given inflation rate,* while in the second case the Fed is responding to a *changing inflation rate.* Changes in aggregate spending for a given inflation rate shift the *AD* curve, while changes in aggregate spending resulting from Fed policy responses to a rise or fall in inflation lead to moves along a given *AD* curve.

28.4   a. If inflation is expected to be two percent next year and workers are expecting a two percent increase in their real wages, then they will expect, and ask for, a four percent increase in their nominal wages.

     b. If inflation is expected to be four percent next year, rather than two percent, workers will expect, and ask for, a six percent increase in their nominal wages.

     c. If wage costs rise, firms will need to increase the prices of their goods and services to cover their increased costs, leading to an increase in inflation. In part b, when expected inflation was four percent, firms will be faced with larger increases in nominal wages than in part a, when expected inflation was only two percent. Thus, we can expect firms to raise prices by more when expected inflation is four percent than when expected inflation is two percent. From this example, we can conclude that increased inflationary expectations lead to higher inflation.

28.5 If the inflation rate is high, the economy will tend to stay in this high-inflation state due to expectations of high inflation and the existence of long-term wage and price contracts, while if the inflation rate is low, the economy will likewise tend to stay in this low-inflation state for similar reasons. However, since high inflation rates impose economic costs on society, as pointed out in Chapter 19, the Federal Reserve has an incentive to avoid the high-inflation state by keeping inflation low, which helps to maintain people's expectations of low inflation and leads to lower future inflation rates—perpetuating the "virtuous circle" illustrated in Figure 28.4.

28.6 An increase in spending on new capital by firms for a given level of inflation, output, and real interest rate increases aggregate expenditures and short-run equilibrium output. Since the economy was originally operating at potential output, the increase in investment spending will lead to an expansionary gap; actual output, Y, will now be greater than potential output, Y^*. When $Y > Y^*$, the rate of inflation will tend to rise.

28.7 The effects will be the opposite of those illustrated in Figure 28.8. Beginning in a long-run equilibrium with output equal to potential output and stable inflation (that is, where the aggregate demand (AD) curve intersects both the short-run and long-run aggregate supply lines ($SRAS$ and $LRAS$, respectively)), the fall in consumption spending will initially lead to a leftward shift in the AD curve and the economy moves to a new, lower, short-run equilibrium output level at the same inflation rate. The shift in AD creates a recessionary gap, since Y is now less than Y^*. The immediate effect of the decrease in consumption spending is only to reduce output. However, over time inflation will fall because of the recessionary gap. As inflation falls the $SRAS$ line will shift downward. The Federal Reserve responds to the fall in inflation by reducing real interest rates, leading to an increase in aggregate expenditure and output, a move down along the new AD curve. When inflation has fallen enough (and real interest rates have fallen enough) to eliminate the output gap the economy will be back in long-run equilibrium where output equals potential output but the inflation rate will be lower than before the fall in consumption spending.

28.8 A decrease in oil prices is an example of a "beneficial" inflation shock and the economic effects of such a shock are the reverse of those illustrated in Figure 28.9. In this case, starting from a long-run equilibrium where output equals potential output, a beneficial inflation shock reduces current inflation, causing the $SRAS$ line to shift downward. The downward shift in the $SRAS$ curve leads to a short-run equilibrium with lower inflation and higher output, creating an expansionary gap. If the Fed does nothing, eventually the $SRAS$ will begin to shift upward and the economy will return to its original inflation and output levels. However, the Fed may instead choose to tighten its monetary policy by shifting up its policy reaction function, raising the current real interest rate, shifting the AD curve to the left and restoring equilibrium at potential GDP, but at the new, lower inflation rate.

28.9 If productivity growth hadn't increased in the last half of the 1990s the $LRAS$ would not have shifted as far to the right as it actually did. As a consequence, the average inflation rate would not have fallen as much as illustrated in Table 28.1 and average real GDP growth would have been smaller. Similarly, if productivity growth slows in the future from its actual 1995–2000 rate, we can expect higher inflation and lower GDP growth than we otherwise would have experienced.

28.10

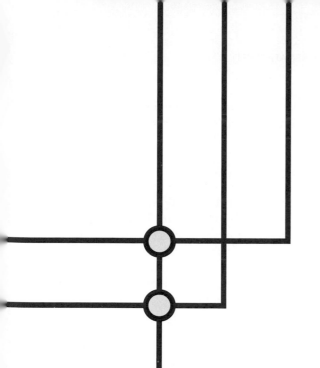

THE ALGEBRA OF AGGREGATE DEMAND AND AGGREGATE SUPPLY

■

In this appendix we will derive the aggregate demand curve algebraically. Then we will show how together aggregate demand and aggregate supply determine the short-run and long-run equilibrium points of the economy.

THE AGGREGATE DEMAND CURVE

In the appendix to Chapter 27, Equation 27A.1 showed that short-run equilibrium output depends on both exogenous components of expenditure and the real interest rate:

$$Y = \left(\frac{1}{1-c}\right)[\overline{C} - c\overline{T} + \overline{I} + \overline{G} + \overline{NX} - (a+b)r], \qquad (27A.1)$$

where $1/(1-c)$ is the multiplier, $\overline{C} - c\overline{T} + \overline{I} + \overline{G} + \overline{NX}$ is the exogenous component of planned spending, the term in brackets is autonomous expenditure, and a and b are positive numbers that measure the effect of changes in the real interest rate on consumption and planned investment, respectively.

The aggregate demand curve incorporates the behavior of the Fed, as described by its policy reaction function. According to its policy reaction function, when inflation rises, the Fed raises the real interest rate. Thus the Fed's policy reaction function can be written as an equation relating the real interest rate r to inflation π:

$$r = \bar{r} + g\pi, \tag{28A.1}$$

where $\bar{r}$ and g are positive constants chosen by Fed officials. This equation states that when inflation π rises by 1 percentage point—say from 2 to 3 percent per year—the Fed responds by raising the real interest rate by g percentage points. So, for example, if $g = 0.5$, an increase in inflation from 2 to 3 percent would lead the Fed to raise the real interest rate by 0.5 percent. The intercept term $\bar{r}$ tells us at what level the Fed would set the real interest rate if inflation happened to be zero (so that the term $g\pi$ dropped out of the equation).

Equations 27A.1 and 28A.1 together allow us to derive the aggregate demand curve. We can think of the curve as being derived in two steps: First, for any given value of inflation π, use the policy reaction function, Equation 28A.1, to find the real interest rate by the Fed. Second, for that real interest rate, use Equation 27A.1 to find short-run equilibrium output Y. The relationship between inflation and short-run equilibrium output derived in these two steps is the aggregate demand curve.

Alternatively, we can combine the equation for short-run equilibrium output with the equation for the policy reaction function by substituting the right-hand side of Equation 28A.1 for the real interest rate r in Equation 27A.1:

$$Y = \left(\frac{1}{1 - c}\right)[\bar{C} - c\bar{T} + \bar{I} + \bar{G} + \bar{NX} - (a + b)(\bar{r} + g\pi)]. \tag{28A.2}$$

This equation, which is the general algebraic expression for the AD curve, summarizes the link between inflation and short-run equilibrium output, as shown graphically in Figure 28.1. Note that Equation 28A.2 implies that an increase in inflation π reduces short-run equilibrium output Y, so that the AD curve is downward-sloping.

For a numerical illustration, we can use the parameter values from Example 27.3. For the economy studied in Example 27.3, we assumed that $\bar{C} = 640$, $\bar{T} = 250$, $\bar{I} = 250$, $\bar{G} = 300$, $\bar{NX} = 20$, $c = 0.8$, $a = 400$, and $b = 600$. To derive the aggregate demand curve, we also need values for the Fed's policy reaction function; for illustration, we use the policy reaction function shown in Table 27.1, reproduced here for convenience.

TABLE 27.1
A Policy Reaction Function for the Fed

Rate of inflation, π	Real interest rate set by Fed, r
0.00 (= 0%)	0.02 (= 2%)
0.01	0.03
0.02	0.04
0.03	0.05
0.04	0.06

Table 27.1 relates the Fed's choice of the real interest rate to the inflation rate. To derive the aggregate demand curve, it will be useful to express the policy reaction function in the form of an equation like Equation 28A.1. To do this, note that when inflation π equals zero, the real interest rate r equals 2 percent. Therefore, the constant term in the Fed's policy reaction function $\bar{r}$ equals 2 percent,

or 0.02. Second, Table 27.1 shows that the real interest rate rises one point for each point that inflation rises; therefore the slope g of the reaction function equals 1.0. So the Fed's policy reaction function can be expressed as

$$r = 0.02 + \pi,$$

which is Equation 28A.1 with $\bar{r} = 0.02$ and $g = 1$.

Substituting these numerical values into Equation 28A.2 and simplifying, we get the following numerical equation for the AD curve:

$$Y = 5[640 - 0.8(250) + 250 + 300 + 20 - (400 + 600)(0.02 + \pi)] \quad \text{(28A.3)}$$
$$Y = 4{,}950 - 5{,}000\pi \quad \text{(28A.4)}$$

Note that in this equation, higher values of inflation imply lower values of short-run equilibrium output, so the aggregate demand curve is downward-sloping. To check this equation, suppose that inflation is 3 percent, so that the Fed sets the real interest rate at 5 percent (see Table 27.1). Setting $\pi = 0.03$ in Equation 28A.4 yields $Y = 4{,}800$. This is consistent with the answer we found in Example 27.4, where we showed for the same economy that when $r = 0.05$ (the value of the real interest rate set by the Fed when $\pi = 0.03$), then short-run equilibrium output $Y = 4{,}800$.

SHIFTS OF THE AGGREGATE DEMAND CURVE

Recall that exogenous changes in spending or in the Fed's policy reaction function will shift the AD curve (see pages 741–743). These results follow from Equation 28A.2. First, the equation shows that for a given rate of inflation π, an increase in exogenous spending, $\bar{C} - c\bar{T} + \bar{I} + \bar{G} + \overline{NX}$, will raise short-run equilibrium output Y. Thus an increase in exogenous spending shifts the AD curve to the right; conversely, a decrease in exogenous spending shifts the AD curve to the left.

A shift in the Fed's policy reaction can be captured by a change in the intercept term $\bar{r}$ in Equation 28A.1. For example, suppose the Fed tightens monetary policy by setting the real interest rate 1 percent higher than before at every level of inflation. Such a change is equivalent to raising the intercept term $\bar{r}$ in the policy reaction function by 0.01. If you look at Equation 28A.2, you will see that with the level of inflation held constant, an increase in $\bar{r}$ reduces short-run equilibrium output. Thus a tightening of monetary policy (an upward movement in the monetary policy reaction function) shifts the AD curve to the left. Conversely, an easing of monetary policy (represented by a decline in $\bar{r}$ or a downward shift in the policy reaction function) shifts the AD curve to the right.

EXERCISE 28A.1

a. For the economy described above, find an algebraic equation for the AD curve after an exogenous increase in spending (say, in planned investment) of 10 units.

b. For the economy described above, find an algebraic equation for the AD curve after a tightening of monetary policy which involves setting the real interest rate 1 percent higher at each level of inflation.

SHORT-RUN EQUILIBRIUM

Recall that in short-run equilibrium, inflation is equal to its previously determined value, and the $SRAS$ line is horizontal at that value. At that level of inflation, the level of output in short-run equilibrium is given by the aggregate demand curve,

Equation 28A.2. For instance, in the economy described, suppose the current value of inflation is 5 percent. The value of short-run equilibrium output is therefore

$$Y = 4{,}950 - 5{,}000\pi = 4{,}950 - 5{,}000(0.05)$$
$$= 4{,}700.$$

LONG-RUN EQUILIBRIUM

In long-run equilibrium, actual output Y equals potential output Y^*. Thus, in long-run equilibrium, the inflation rate can be obtained from the equation for the AD curve by substituting Y^* for Y. To illustrate, let's write the equation for the AD curve in this sample economy, Equation 28A.4, once again:

$$Y = 4{,}950 - 5{,}000\pi.$$

Suppose, in addition, that potential output $Y^* = 4{,}900$. Substituting this value for Y in the aggregate demand equation yields

$$4{,}900 = 4{,}950 - 5{,}000\pi.$$

Solving for the inflation rate π we get

$$\pi = 0.01 = 1\%.$$

When this economy is in long-run equilibrium, then, the inflation rate will be 1 percent. If we start from the value of inflation in short-run equilibrium, 5 percent, we can see that the short-run aggregate supply line must shift downward until inflation reaches 1 percent before long-run equilibrium can be achieved.

■ ANSWERS TO IN-APPENDIX EXERCISES ■

28A.1 The algebraic solutions for the AD curves in each case, obtained by substituting the numerical values into the formula, are given below.
a. $Y = 5{,}000 - 5{,}000\pi.$
b. $Y = 4{,}900 - 5{,}000\pi.$

9

THE INTERNATIONAL ECONOMY

■

One of the defining economic trends of recent decades is the "globalization" of national economies. Since the mid-1980s, the value of international trade has increased at nearly twice the rate of world GDP, and the volume of international financial transactions has expanded at many times that rate. From a long-run perspective, the rapidly increasing integration of national economies we see today is not unprecedented: Before World War I, Great Britain was the center of an international economic system that was in many ways nearly as "globalized" as our own, with extensive international trade and lending. But even the most far-seeing nineteenth-century merchant or banker would be astonished by the sense of *immediacy* that recent revolutionary changes in communications and transportation have imparted to international economic relations. For example, teleconferencing and the Internet now permit people on opposite sides of the globe to conduct "face-to-face" business negotiations and transactions.

We introduced international dimensions of the economy at several points in this book already (for example, in our discussion of comparative advantage and trade in Chapter 2 and our analysis of the labor market effects of globalization in Chapter 21). Chapter 16 continued our analysis of international trade, considering both the broad benefits of trade and the reasons why we sometimes see attempts to block or reduce trade. In Part 5 we will look at the international economy in greater detail. Chapter 29 focuses on a particularly important variable in international economics, the *exchange rate*. The exchange rate plays a key role in determining patterns of trade. Furthermore, as we will see, the type of exchange rate system a country adopts has important implications for the effectiveness of its macroeconomic policies.

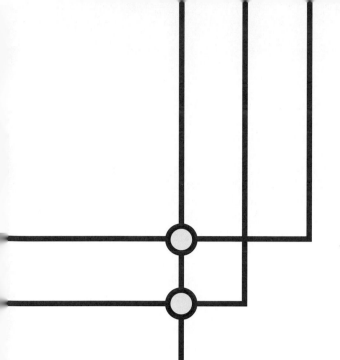

CHAPTER

29

EXCHANGE RATES
AND THE OPEN ECONOMY

■

T wo Americans visiting London were commiserating over their problems understanding English currency. "Pounds, shillings, tuppence, thruppence, bob, and quid, it's driving me crazy," said the first American. "This morning it took me 20 minutes to figure out how much to pay the taxi driver."

The second American was more upbeat. "Actually," he said, "since I adopted my new system, I haven't had any problems at all."

The first American looked interested. "What's your new system?"

"Well," replied the second, "now, whenever I take a taxi, I just give the driver all the English money I have. And would you believe it, I have got the fare exactly right every time!"

Dealing with unfamiliar currencies—and translating the value of foreign money into dollars—is a problem every international traveler faces. The traveler's problem is complicated by the fact that *exchange rates*—the rates at which one country's money trades for another—may change unpredictably. Thus the number of British pounds, Russian rubles, Japanese yen, or Australian dollars that a U.S. dollar can buy may vary over time, sometimes quite a lot.

The economic consequences of variable exchange rates are much broader than their impact on travel and tourism, however. For example, the competitiveness of U.S. exports depends in part on the prices of U.S. goods in terms of foreign currencies, which in turn depend on the exchange rate between the U.S. dollar and those currencies. Likewise, the prices Americans pay for imported goods depend in part on the value of the dollar relative to the currencies of the countries that produce those goods. Exchange rates also affect the value of financial investments made across national borders. For countries that are heavily dependent on trade and international capital flows—the majority of the world's nations—fluctuations in the exchange rate may have a significant economic impact.

This chapter discusses exchange rates and the role they play in open economies. We will start by distinguishing between the *nominal exchange rate*—the rate at which one national currency trades for another—and the *real exchange rate*—the rate at which one country's goods trade for another's. We will show how exchange rates affect the prices of exports and imports, and thus the pattern of trade.

Next we will turn to the question of how exchange rates are determined. Exchange rates may be divided into two broad categories, flexible and fixed. The value of a *flexible* exchange rate is determined freely in the market for national currencies, known as the *foreign exchange market*. Flexible exchange rates vary continually with changes in the supply of and demand for national currencies. In contrast, the value of a *fixed* exchange rate is set by the government at a constant level. Because most large industrial countries, including the United States, have a flexible exchange rate, we will focus on that case first. We will see that a country's monetary policy plays a particularly important role in determining the exchange rate. Furthermore, in an open economy with a flexible exchange rate, the exchange rate becomes a tool of monetary policy, in much the same way as the real interest rate.

Although most large industrial countries have a flexible exchange rate, many small and developing economies fix their exchange rates, so we will consider the case of fixed exchange rates as well. We will explain first how a country's government (usually, its central bank) goes about maintaining a fixed exchange rate at the officially determined level. Though fixing the exchange rate generally reduces day-to-day fluctuations in the value of a nation's currency, we will see that, at times, a fixed exchange rate can become severely unstable, with potentially serious economic consequences. We will close the chapter by discussing the relative merits of fixed and flexible exchange rates.

EXCHANGE RATES

The economic benefits of trade between nations in goods, services, and assets are similar to the benefits of trade within a nation. In both cases, trade in goods and services permits greater specialization and efficiency, whereas trade in assets allows financial investors to earn higher returns while providing funds for worthwhile capital projects. However, there is a difference between the two cases, which is that trade in goods, services, and assets *within* a nation normally involves a single currency—dollars, yen, pesos, or whatever the country's official form of money happens to be—whereas trade *between* nations usually involves dealing in different currencies. So, for example, if an American resident wants to purchase an automobile manufactured in South Korea, she (or more likely, the automobile dealer) must first trade dollars for the Korean currency, called the won. The Korean car manufacturer is then paid in won. Similarly, an Argentine who wants to purchase shares in a U.S. company (a U.S. financial asset) must first trade his Argentine pesos for dollars and then use the dollars to purchase the shares.

NOMINAL EXCHANGE RATES

Because international transactions generally require that one currency be traded for another, the relative values of different currencies are an important factor in international economic relations. The rate at which two currencies can be traded for each other is called the **nominal exchange rate,** or more simply the *exchange rate,* between the two currencies. For example, if one U.S. dollar can be exchanged for 110 Japanese yen, the nominal exchange rate between the U.S. and Japanese currencies is 110 yen per dollar. Each country has many nominal exchange rates, one corresponding to each currency against which its own currency is traded. Thus the dollar's value can be quoted in terms of English pounds, Swedish kroner, Israeli shekels, Russian rubles, or dozens of other currencies. Table 29.1 gives exchange rates between the dollar and six other important currencies as of the close of business in New York City on September 4, 2002.

nominal exchange rate the rate at which two currencies can be traded for each other

TABLE 29.1
Nominal Exchange Rates for the U.S. Dollar

Country	Foreign currency/dollar	Dollar/foreign currency
United Kingdom (pound)	0.6393	1.5643
Canada (Canadian dollar)	1.5674	0.6380
Mexico (peso)	9.9850	0.1002
Japan (yen)	118.0000	0.00848
Switzerland (Swiss franc)	1.4760	0.6775
South Korea (won)	1,190.1000	0.00084

SOURCE: *The Wall Street Journal,* September 5, 2002.

As Table 29.1 shows, exchange rates can be expressed either as the amount of foreign currency needed to purchase one dollar (left column) or as the number of dollars needed to purchase one unit of the foreign currency (right column). These two ways of expressing the exchange rate are equivalent: Each is the reciprocal of the other. For example, on September 4, 2002, the U.S.–Canadian exchange rate could have been expressed either as 1.5674 Canadian dollars per U.S. dollar or as 0.6380 U.S. dollars per Canadian dollar, where 0.6380 = 1/1.5674.

Nominal exchange rates

Based on Table 29.1, find the exchange rate between the British and Canadian currencies. Express the exchange rate in both Canadian dollars per pound and pounds per Canadian dollar.

From Table 29.1, we see that 0.6393 British pounds will buy a U.S. dollar, and that 1.5674 Canadian dollars will buy a U.S. dollar. Therefore 0.6393 British pounds and 1.5674 Canadian dollars are equal in value:

$$0.6393 \text{ pounds} = 1.5674 \text{ Canadian dollars.}$$

Dividing both sides of this equation by 1.5674, we get

$$0.4079 \text{ pounds} = 1 \text{ Canadian dollar.}$$

In other words, the British–Canadian exchange rate can be expressed as 0.4079 pounds per Canadian dollar. Alternatively, the exchange rate can be expressed as 1/0.4079 = 2.45 Canadian dollars per pound.

EXAMPLE 29.1

EXERCISE 29.1

From the business section of the newspaper or an online source (try the Federal Reserve Bank of St. Louis FRED database, http://research.

stlouisfed.org/fred/data/exchange.html), find recent quotations of the value of the U.S. dollar against the British pound, the Canadian dollar, and the Japanese yen. Based on these data find the exchange rate (a) between the pound and the Canadian dollar and (b) between the Canadian dollar and the yen. Express the exchange rates you derive in two ways (e.g., both as pounds per Canadian dollar and as Canadian dollars per pound).

Figure 29.1 shows the nominal exchange rate for the U.S. dollar for 1973 to 2002. Rather than showing the value of the dollar relative to that of an individual foreign currency, such as the Japanese yen or the British pound, the figure expresses the value of the dollar as an average of its values against other major currencies. This average value of the dollar is measured relative to a base value of 100 in 1973. So, for example, a value of 120 for the dollar in a particular year implies that the dollar was 20 percent more valuable in that year, relative to other major currencies, than it was in 1973.

You can see from Figure 29.1 that the dollar's value has fluctuated over time, sometimes increasing (as in the period 1980–1985) and sometimes decreasing (as in 1985–1987). An increase in the value of a currency relative to other currencies is known as an **appreciation;** a decline in the value of a currency relative to other currencies is called a **depreciation.** So we can say that the dollar appreciated in 1980–1985 and depreciated in 1985–1987. We will discuss the reasons a currency may appreciate or depreciate later in this chapter.

In this chapter we will use the symbol e to stand for a country's nominal exchange rate. Although the exchange rate can be expressed either as foreign currency units per unit of domestic currency, or vice versa, as we saw in Table 29.1, let's agree to define e as *the number of units of the foreign currency that the domestic currency will buy.* For example, if we treat the United States as the "home" or "domestic" country and Japan as the "foreign" country, e will be defined as the number of Japanese yen that one dollar will buy. Defining the nominal exchange rate this way implies that an *increase* in e corresponds to an *appreciation,* or a strengthening, of the home currency, while a *decrease* in e implies a *depreciation,* or weakening, of the home currency.

appreciation an increase in the value of a currency relative to other currencies

depreciation a decrease in the value of a currency relative to other currencies

FIGURE 29.1
The U.S. Nominal Exchange Rate, 1973–2002.
This figure expresses the value of the dollar from 1973 to 2002 as an average of its values against other major currencies, relative to a base value of 100 in 1973.

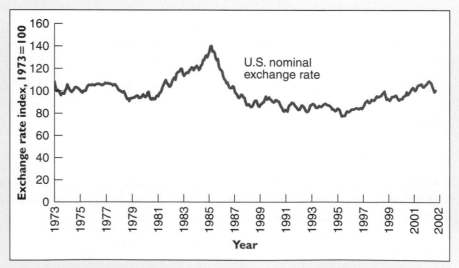

SOURCE: Federal Reserve Bank of St. Louis, FRED database (http://research.stlouisfed.org/fred/data/exchange.html).

"On the foreign-exchange markets today, the dollar fell against all major currencies and the doughnut."

FLEXIBLE VERSUS FIXED EXCHANGE RATES

As we saw in Figure 29.1, the exchange rate between the U.S. dollar and other currencies isn't constant but varies continually. Indeed, changes in the value of the dollar occur daily, hourly, even minute by minute. Such fluctuations in the value of a currency are normal for countries like the United States, which have a *flexible* or *floating exchange rate*. The value of a **flexible exchange rate** is not officially fixed but varies according to the supply and demand for the currency in the **foreign exchange market**—the market on which currencies of various nations are traded for one another. We will discuss the factors that determine the supply and demand for currencies shortly.

Some countries do not allow their currency values to vary with market conditions but instead maintain a *fixed exchange rate*. The value of a **fixed exchange rate** is set by official government policy. (A government that establishes a fixed exchange rate typically determines the exchange rate's value independently, but sometimes exchange rates are set according to an agreement among a number of governments.) Some countries fix their exchange rates in terms of the U.S. dollar (Argentina, for example), but there are other possibilities. Some French-speaking African countries have traditionally fixed the value of their currencies in terms of the French franc. Under the gold standard, which many countries used until its collapse during the Great Depression, currency values were fixed in terms of ounces of gold. In the next part of the chapter we will focus on flexible exchange rates, but we will return later to the case of fixed rates. We will also discuss the costs and benefits of each type of exchange rate.

THE REAL EXCHANGE RATE

The nominal exchange rate tells us the price of the domestic currency in terms of a foreign currency. As we will see in this section, the *real exchange rate* tells us the price of the average domestic *good or service* in terms of the average foreign *good or service*. We will also see that a country's real exchange rate has important implications for its ability to sell its exports abroad.

To provide background for discussing the real exchange rate, imagine you are in charge of purchasing for a U.S. corporation that is planning to acquire a large number of new computers. The company's computer specialist has identified two models, one Japanese-made and one U.S.-made, that meet the necessary

flexible exchange rate an exchange rate whose value is not officially fixed but varies according to the supply and demand for the currency in the foreign exchange market

foreign exchange market the market on which currencies of various nations are traded for one another

fixed exchange rate an exchange rate whose value is set by official government policy specifications. Since the two models are essentially equivalent, the company will buy the one with the lower price. However, since the computers are priced in the currencies of the countries of manufacture, the price comparison is not so straightforward. Your mission—should you decide to accept it—is to determine which of the two models is cheaper.

To complete your assignment you will need two pieces of information: the nominal exchange rate between the dollar and the yen and the prices of the two models in terms of the currencies of their countries of manufacture. Example 29.2 shows how you can use this information to determine which model is cheaper.

EXAMPLE 29.2

Comparing prices expressed in different currencies

A U.S.-made computer costs $2,400, and a similar Japanese-made computer costs 242,000 yen. If the nominal exchange rate is 110 yen per dollar, which computer is the better buy?

To make this price comparison, we must measure the prices of both computers in terms of the same currency. To make the comparison in dollars, we first convert the Japanese computer's price into dollars. The price in terms of Japanese yen is ¥242,000 (the symbol ¥ means "yen"), and we are told that ¥110 = $1. To find the dollar price of the computer, then, we observe that for any good or service,

$$\text{Price in yen} = \text{Price in dollars} \times \text{Value of dollar in terms of yen.}$$

Note that the value of a dollar in terms of yen is just the yen–dollar exchange rate. Making this substitution and solving, we get

$$\text{Price in dollars} = \frac{\text{Price in yen}}{\text{Yen–dollar exchange rate}}$$
$$= \frac{¥242,000}{¥110/\$1} = \$2,200.$$

Notice that the yen symbol appears in both the numerator and the denominator of the ratio, so it cancels out. Our conclusion is that the Japanese computer is cheaper than the U.S. computer at $2,200, or $200 less than the price of the U.S. computer, $2,400. The Japanese computer is the better deal.

EXERCISE 29.2

Continuing Example 29.2, compare the prices of the Japanese and American computers by expressing both prices in terms of yen.

In Example 29.2, the fact that the Japanese computer was cheaper implied that your firm would choose it over the U.S.-made computer. In general, a country's ability to compete in international markets depends in part on the prices of its goods and services *relative* to the prices of foreign goods and services, when the prices are measured in a common currency. In the hypothetical example of the Japanese and U.S. computers, the price of the domestic (U.S.) good relative to the price of the foreign (Japanese) good is $2,400/$2,200, or 1.09. So the U.S. computer is 9 percent more expensive than the Japanese computer, putting the U.S. product at a competitive disadvantage.

More generally, economists ask whether *on average* the goods and services produced by a particular country are expensive relative to the goods and services produced by other countries. This question can be answered by the country's *real exchange rate*. Specifically, a country's **real exchange rate** is the price of the average domestic good or service *relative* to the price of the average foreign good or service, when prices are expressed in terms of a common currency.

real exchange rate the price of the average domestic good or service *relative* to the price of the average foreign good or service, when prices are expressed in terms of a common currency

To obtain a formula for the real exchange rate, recall that e equals the nominal exchange rate (the number of units of foreign currency per dollar) and that P equals the domestic price level, as measured, for example, by the consumer price index. We will use P as a measure of the price of the "average" domestic good or service. Similarly, let P^f equal the foreign price level. We will use P^f as the measure of the price of the "average" foreign good or service.

The real exchange rate equals the price of the average domestic good or service relative to the price of the average foreign good or service. It would not be correct, however, to define the real exchange rate as the ratio P/P^f, because the two price levels are expressed in different currencies. As we saw in Example 29.2, to convert foreign prices into dollars, we must divide the foreign price by the exchange rate. By this rule, the price in dollars of the average foreign good or service equals P^f/e. Now we can write the real exchange rate as

$$\text{Real exchange rate} = \frac{\text{Price of domestic good}}{\text{Price of foreign good, in dollars}}$$

$$= \frac{P}{P^f/e}.$$

To simplify this expression, multiply the numerator and denominator by e to get

$$\text{Real exchange rate} = \frac{eP}{P^f}, \tag{29.1}$$

which is the formula for the real exchange rate.

To check this formula, let's use it to re-solve the computer example, Example 29.2. (For this exercise, we imagine that computers are the only good produced by the United States and Japan, so the real exchange rate becomes just the price of U.S. computers relative to Japanese computers.) In that example, the nominal exchange rate e was ¥110/\$1, the domestic price P (of a computer) was \$2,400, and the foreign price P^f was ¥242,000. Applying Equation 29.1, we get

$$\text{Real exchange rate (for computers)} = \frac{(¥110/\$1) \times \$2,400}{¥242,000}$$

$$= \frac{¥264,000}{¥242,000}$$

$$= 1.09,$$

which is the same answer we got earlier.

The real exchange rate, an overall measure of the cost of domestic goods relative to foreign goods, is an important economic variable. As Example 29.2 suggests, when the real exchange rate is high, domestic goods are on average more expensive than foreign goods (when priced in the same currency). A high real exchange rate implies that domestic producers will have difficulty exporting to other countries (domestic goods will be "overpriced"), while foreign goods will sell well in the home country (because imported goods are cheap relative to goods produced at home). Since a high real exchange rate tends to reduce exports and increase imports, we conclude that *net exports will tend to be low when the real exchange rate is high.* Conversely, if the real exchange rate is low, then the home country will find it easier to export (because its goods are priced below those of foreign competitors), while domestic residents will buy fewer imports (because imports are expensive relative to domestic goods). *Thus net exports will tend to be high when the real exchange rate is low.*

Equation 29.1 also shows that the real exchange rate tends to move in the same direction as the nominal exchange rate e (since e appears in the numerator of the formula for the real exchange rate). To the extent that real and nominal exchange rates move in the same direction, we can conclude that net exports will be hurt by a high nominal exchange rate and helped by a low nominal exchange rate.

Does a strong currency imply a strong economy?

ECONOMIC NATURALIST 29.1

Politicians and the public sometimes take pride in the fact that their national currency is "strong," meaning that its value in terms of other currencies is high or rising. Likewise, policymakers sometimes view a depreciating ("weak") currency as a sign of economic failure. Does a strong currency necessarily imply a strong economy?

Contrary to popular impression, there is no simple connection between the strength of a country's currency and the strength of its economy. For example, Figure 29.1 shows that the value of the U.S. dollar relative to other major currencies was greater in the year 1973 than in the year 2000, though U.S. economic performance was considerably better in 2000 than in 1973, a period of deep recession and rising inflation. Indeed, the one period shown in Figure 29.1 during which the dollar rose markedly in value, 1980–1985, was a time of recession and high unemployment in the United States.

One reason a strong currency does not necessarily imply a strong economy is that an appreciating currency (an increase in e) tends to raise the real exchange rate (equal to eP/P^f), which may hurt a country's net exports. For example, if the dollar strengthens against the yen (that is, if a dollar buys more yen than before), Japanese goods will become cheaper in terms of dollars. The result may be that Americans prefer to buy Japanese goods rather than goods produced at home. Likewise, a stronger dollar implies that each yen buys fewer dollars, so exported U.S. goods become more expensive to Japanese consumers. As U.S. goods become more expensive in terms of yen, the willingness of Japanese consumers to buy U.S. exports declines. A strong dollar may therefore imply lower sales and profits for U.S. industries that export, as well as for U.S. industries (like automobile manufacturers) that compete with foreign firms for the domestic U.S. market.

RECAP EXCHANGE RATES

- The nominal exchange rate between two currencies is the rate at which the currencies can be traded for each other. More precisely, the nominal exchange rate e for any given country is the number of units of foreign currency that can be bought for one unit of the domestic currency.

- An appreciation is an increase in the value of a currency relative to other currencies (a rise in e); a depreciation is a decline in a currency's value (a fall in e).

- An exchange rate can be either flexible—meaning that it varies freely according to supply and demand for the currency in the foreign exchange market—or fixed, meaning that its value is established by official government policy.

- The real exchange rate is the price of the average domestic good or service relative to the price of the average foreign good or service, when prices are expressed in terms of a common currency. A useful formula for the real exchange rate is eP/P^f, where e is the nominal exchange rate, P is the domestic price level, and P^f is the foreign price level.

- An increase in the real exchange rate implies that domestic goods are becoming more expensive relative to foreign goods, which tends to reduce exports and stimulate imports. Conversely, a decline in the real exchange rate tends to increase net exports.

THE DETERMINATION OF THE EXCHANGE RATE

Countries that have flexible exchange rates, such as the United States, see the international values of their currencies change continually. What determines the value of the nominal exchange rate at any point in time? In this section we will try to answer this basic economic question. Again, our focus for the moment is on flexible exchange rates, whose values are determined by the foreign exchange market. Later in the chapter we discuss the case of fixed exchange rates.

A SIMPLE THEORY OF EXCHANGE RATES: PURCHASING POWER PARITY (PPP)

The most basic theory of how nominal exchange rates are determined is called *purchasing power parity,* or PPP. To understand this theory, we must first discuss a fundamental economic concept, called *the law of one price.* The **law of one price** states that if transportation costs are relatively small, the price of an internationally traded commodity must be the same in all locations. For example, if transportation costs are not too large, the price of a bushel of wheat ought to be the same in Bombay, India, and Sydney, Australia. Suppose that were not the case—that the price of wheat in Sydney were only half the price in Bombay. In that case grain merchants would have a strong incentive to buy wheat in Sydney and ship it to Bombay, where it could be sold at double the price of purchase. As wheat left Sydney, reducing the local supply, the price of wheat in Sydney would rise, while the inflow of wheat into Bombay would reduce the price in Bombay. According to the *equilibrium principle* (Chapter 3), the international market for wheat would return to equilibrium only when unexploited opportunities to profit had been eliminated—specifically, only when the prices of wheat in Sydney and in Bombay became equal or nearly equal (with the difference being less than the cost of transporting wheat from Australia to India).

> **law of one price** if transportation costs are relatively small, the price of an internationally traded commodity must be the same in all locations

If the law of one price were to hold for all goods and services (which is not a realistic assumption, as we will see shortly), then the value of the nominal exchange rate would be determined as Example 29.3 illustrates.

How many Indian rupees equal one Australian dollar? (1)

EXAMPLE 29.3

Suppose that a bushel of grain costs 5 Australian dollars in Sydney and 150 rupees in Bombay. If the law of one price holds for grain, what is the nominal exchange rate between Australia and India?

Because the market value of a bushel of grain must be the same in both locations, we know that the Australian price of wheat must equal the Indian price of wheat, so that

$$5 \text{ Australian dollars} = 150 \text{ Indian rupees.}$$

Dividing by 5, we get

$$1 \text{ Australian dollar} = 30 \text{ Indian rupees.}$$

Thus the nominal exchange rate between Australia and India should be 30 rupees per Australian dollar.

EXERCISE 29.3

The price of gold is $300 per ounce in New York and 2,500 kronor per ounce in Stockholm, Sweden. If the law of one price holds for gold, what is the nominal exchange rate between the U.S. dollar and the Swedish krona?

purchasing power parity (PPP) the theory that nominal exchange rates are determined as necessary for the law of one price to hold

Example 29.3 and Exercise 29.3 illustrate the application of the purchasing power parity theory. According to the **purchasing power parity (PPP)** theory, nominal exchange rates are determined as necessary for the law of one price to hold.

A particularly useful prediction of the PPP theory is that in the long run, the *currencies of countries that experience significant inflation will tend to depreciate.* To see why, we will extend the analysis in Example 29.3.

EXAMPLE 29.4

How many Indian rupees equal one Australian dollar? (2)

Suppose India experiences significant inflation so that the price of a bushel of grain in Bombay rises from 150 to 300 rupees. Australia has no inflation, so the price of grain in Sydney remains unchanged at 5 Australian dollars. If the law of one price holds for grain, what will happen to the nominal exchange rate between Australia and India?

As in Example 29.3, we know that the market value of a bushel of grain must be the same in both locations. Therefore,

$$5 \text{ Australian dollars} = 300 \text{ rupees.}$$

Equivalently,

$$1 \text{ Australian dollar} = 60 \text{ rupees.}$$

The nominal exchange rate is now 60 rupees per Australian dollar. Before India's inflation, the nominal exchange rate was 30 rupees per Australian dollar (Example 29.3). So in this example, inflation has caused the rupee to depreciate against the Australian dollar. Conversely, Australia, with no inflation, has seen its currency appreciate against the rupee.

This link between inflation and depreciation makes economic sense. Inflation implies that a nation's currency is losing purchasing power in the domestic market. Analogously, exchange rate depreciation implies that the nation's currency is losing purchasing power in international markets.

Figure 29.2 shows annual rates of inflation and nominal exchange rate depreciation for the 10 largest South American countries from 1995 to 2001. Inflation is measured as the annual rate of change in the country's consumer price index; depreciation is measured relative to the U.S. dollar. As you can see, inflation varied greatly among South American countries during the period. For example, Argentina's inflation rate was essentially the same as that of the United States, while Venezuela had inflation of 37 percent per year and Ecuador's inflation was 45 percent per year.

Figure 29.2 shows that, as the PPP theory implies, countries with higher inflation during the 1995–2001 period tended to experience the most rapid depreciation of their currencies.

SHORTCOMINGS OF THE PPP THEORY

Empirical studies have found that the PPP theory is useful for predicting changes in nominal exchange rates over the relatively long run. In particular, this theory helps to explain the tendency of countries with high inflation to experience depreciation of their exchange rates, as shown in Figure 29.2. However, the theory is less successful in predicting short-run movements in exchange rates.

A particularly dramatic failure of the PPP theory occurred in the United States in the early 1980s. As Figure 29.1 indicates, between 1980 and 1985 the value of the U.S. dollar rose nearly 50 percent relative to the currencies of U.S. trading partners. This strong appreciation was followed by an even more rapid depreciation during 1986 and 1987. PPP theory could explain this roller-coaster behavior

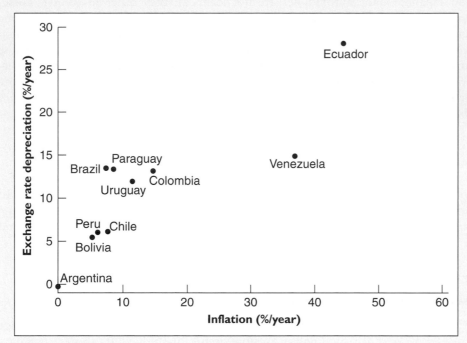

SOURCE: International Monetary Fund, *International Financial Statistics*, and authors' calculations.

FIGURE 29.2
Inflation and Currency Depreciation in South America, 1995–2001.
The annual rates of inflation and nominal exchange-rate depreciation (relative to the U.S. dollar) in 10 South American countries varied considerably during 1995–2001. High inflation was associated with rapid depreciation of the nominal exchange rate.

only if inflation were far lower in the United States than in U.S. trading partners from 1980 to 1985, and far higher from 1986 to 1987. In fact, inflation was similar in the United States and its trading partners throughout both periods.

Why does the PPP theory work less well in the short run than the long run? Recall that this theory relies on the law of one price, which says that the price of an internationally traded commodity must be the same in all locations. The law of one price works well for goods such as grain or gold, which are standardized commodities that are traded widely. However, *not all goods and services are traded internationally*, and *not all goods are standardized commodities*.

Many goods and services are not traded internationally, because the assumption underlying the law of one price—that transportation costs are relatively small—does not hold for them. For example, for Indians to export haircuts to Australia, they would need to transport an Indian barber to Australia every time a Sydney resident desired a trim. Because transportation costs prevent haircuts from being traded internationally, the law of one price does not apply to them. Thus, even if the price of haircuts in Australia were double the price of haircuts in India, market forces would not necessarily force prices toward equality in the short run. (Over the long run, some Indian barbers might emigrate to Australia.) Other examples of nontraded goods and services are agricultural land, buildings, heavy construction materials (whose value is low relative to their transportation costs), and highly perishable foods. In addition, some products use nontraded goods and services as inputs: A McDonald's hamburger served in Moscow has both a tradable component (frozen hamburger patties) and a nontradable component (the labor of counter workers). In general, the greater the share of nontraded goods and services in a nation's output, the less precisely the PPP theory will apply to the country's exchange rate.[1]

The second reason the law of one price and the PPP theory sometimes fail to apply is that not all internationally traded goods and services are perfectly standardized commodities, like grain or gold. For example, U.S.–made automobiles

---

[1]Trade barriers, such as tariffs and quotas, also increase the costs associated with shipping goods from one country to another. Thus trade barriers reduce the applicability of the law of one price in much the same way that physical transportation costs do.

and Japanese-made automobiles are not identical; they differ in styling, horse-power, reliability, and other features. As a result, some people strongly prefer one nation's cars to the other's. Thus if Japanese cars cost 10 percent more than American cars, U.S. automobile exports will not necessarily flood the Japanese market, since many Japanese will still prefer Japanese-made cars even at a 10 percent premium. Of course, there are limits to how far prices can diverge before people will switch to the cheaper product. But the law of one price, and hence the PPP theory, will not apply exactly to nonstandardized goods.

To summarize, the PPP theory works reasonably well as an explanation of exchange rate behavior over the long run, but not in the short run. Because transportation costs limit international trade in many goods and services, and because not all goods that are traded are standardized commodities, the law of one price (on which the PPP theory is based) works only imperfectly in the short run. To understand the short-run movements of exchange rates we need to incorporate some additional factors. In the next section we will study a supply and demand framework for the determination of exchange rates.

THE DETERMINATION OF THE EXCHANGE RATE: A SUPPLY AND DEMAND ANALYSIS

Although the PPP theory helps to explain the long-run behavior of the exchange rate, supply and demand analysis is more useful for studying its short-run behavior. As we will see, dollars are demanded in the foreign exchange market by foreigners who seek to purchase U.S. goods and assets and are supplied by U.S. residents who need foreign currencies to buy foreign goods and assets. The equilibrium exchange rate is the value of the dollar that equates the number of dollars supplied and demanded in the foreign exchange market. In this section we will discuss the factors that affect the supply and demand for dollars, and thus the U.S. exchange rate.

One note before we proceed: In Chapter 27 we described how the supply of money by the Fed and the demand for money by the public help to determine the nominal interest rate. However, the supply and demand for money in the domestic economy, as presented in Chapter 27, are *not* equivalent to the supply and demand for dollars in the foreign exchange market. As mentioned, the foreign exchange market is the market in which the currencies of various nations are traded for one another. The supply of dollars to the foreign exchange market is *not* the same as the money supply set by the Fed; rather, it is the number of dollars U.S. households and firms offer to trade for other currencies. Likewise, the demand for dollars in the foreign exchange market is *not* the same as the domestic demand for money, but the number of dollars holders of foreign currencies seek to buy. To understand the distinction, it may help to keep in mind that while the Fed determines the total supply of dollars in the U.S. economy, a dollar does not "count" as having been supplied to the foreign exchange market until some holder of dollars, such as a household or firm, tries to trade it for a foreign currency.

The Supply of Dollars

Anyone who holds dollars, from an international bank to a Russian citizen whose dollars are buried in the backyard, is a potential supplier of dollars to the foreign exchange market. In practice, however, the principal suppliers of dollars to the foreign exchange market are U.S. households and firms. Why would a U.S. household or firm want to supply dollars in exchange for foreign currency? There are two major reasons. First, a U.S. household or firm may need foreign currency *to purchase foreign goods or services*. For example, a U.S. automobile importer may need yen to purchase Japanese cars, or an American tourist may need yen to make purchases in Tokyo. Second, a U.S. household or firm may need foreign currency *to purchase foreign assets.* For example, an American mutual fund may wish to acquire stocks issued by Japanese companies, or an individual U.S. saver may want to purchase Japanese government bonds. Because Japanese assets are priced in yen, the U.S. household or firm will need to trade dollars for yen to acquire these assets.

The supply of dollars to the foreign exchange market is illustrated in Figure 29.3. We will focus on the market in which dollars are traded for Japanese yen, but bear in mind that similar markets exist for every other pair of traded currencies. The vertical axis of the figure shows the U.S.–Japanese exchange rate as measured by the number of yen that can be purchased with each dollar. The horizontal axis shows the number of dollars being traded in the yen–dollar market.

Note that the supply curve for dollars is upward-sloping. In other words, the more yen each dollar can buy, the more dollars people are willing to supply to the foreign exchange market. Why? At given prices for Japanese goods, services, and assets, the more yen a dollar can buy, the cheaper those goods, services, and assets will be in dollar terms. For example, if a video game costs 5,000 yen in Japan, and a dollar can buy 100 yen, the dollar price of the video game will be $50. However, if a dollar can buy 200 yen, then the dollar price of the same video game will be $25. Assuming that lower dollar prices will induce Americans to increase their expenditures on Japanese goods, services, and assets, a higher yen–dollar exchange rate will increase the supply of dollars to the foreign exchange market. Thus the supply curve for dollars is upward-sloping.

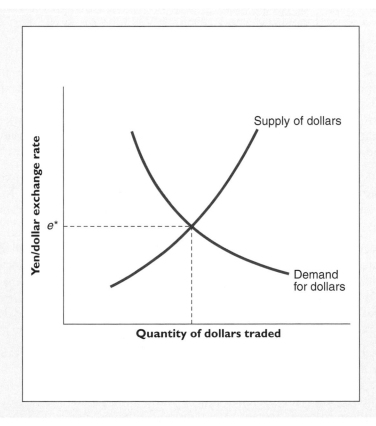

FIGURE 29.3
The Supply and Demand for Dollars in the Yen–Dollar Market.
The supply of dollars to the foreign exchange market is upward-sloping, because an increase in the number of yen offered for each dollar makes Japanese goods, services, and assets more attractive to U.S. buyers. Similarly, the demand for dollars is downward-sloping, because holders of yen will be less willing to buy dollars the more expensive they are in terms of yen. The equilibrium exchange rate e*, also called the *fundamental value of the exchange rate,* equates the quantities of dollars supplied and demanded.

The Demand for Dollars

In the yen–dollar foreign exchange market, demanders of dollars are those who wish to acquire dollars in exchange for yen. Most demanders of dollars in the yen–dollar market are Japanese households and firms, although anyone who happens to hold yen is free to trade them for dollars. Why demand dollars? The reasons for acquiring dollars are analogous to those for acquiring yen. First, households and firms that hold yen will demand dollars *so that they can purchase U.S. goods and services.* For example, a Japanese firm that wants to license U.S.-produced software needs dollars to pay the required fees, and a Japanese student studying in an American university must pay tuition in dollars. The firm or the student can acquire the necessary dollars only by offering yen in exchange. Second, households and firms demand dollars *in order to purchase U.S. assets.* The purchase of Hawaiian real estate by a Japanese company or the acquisition of Microsoft stock by a Japanese pension fund are two examples.

The demand for dollars is represented by the downward-sloping curve in Figure 29.3. The curve slopes downward because the more yen a Japanese citizen must pay to acquire a dollar, the less attractive U.S. goods, services, and assets will be. Hence the demand for dollars will be low when dollars are expensive in terms of yen and high when dollars are cheap in terms of yen.

The Equilibrium Value of the Dollar

As mentioned earlier, the United States maintains a flexible, or floating, exchange rate, which means that the value of the dollar is determined by the forces of supply and demand in the foreign exchange market. In Figure 29.3 the equilibrium value of the dollar is e^*, the yen–dollar exchange rate at which the quantity of dollars supplied equals the quantity of dollars demanded. The equilibrium value of the exchange rate is also called the **fundamental value of the exchange rate.** In general, the equilibrium value of the dollar is not constant but changes with shifts in the supply of and demand for dollars in the foreign exchange market.

fundamental value of the exchange rate (or equilibrium exchange rate) the exchange rate that equates the quantities of the currency supplied and demanded in the foreign exchange market

CHANGES IN THE SUPPLY OF DOLLARS

Recall that people supply dollars to the yen–dollar foreign exchange market in order to purchase Japanese goods, services, and assets. Factors that affect the desire of U.S. households and firms to acquire Japanese goods, services, and assets will therefore affect the supply of dollars to the foreign exchange market. Some factors that will *increase* the supply of dollars, shifting the supply curve for dollars to the right, include:

- An increased preference for Japanese goods. For example, suppose that Japanese firms produce some popular new consumer electronics. To acquire the yen needed to buy these goods, American importers will increase their supply of dollars to the foreign exchange market.

- An increase in U.S. real GDP. An increase in U.S. real GDP will raise the incomes of Americans, allowing them to consume more goods and services (recall the consumption function, introduced in Chapter 26). Some part of this increase in consumption will take the form of goods imported from Japan. To buy more Japanese goods, Americans will supply more dollars to acquire the necessary yen.

- An increase in the real interest rate on Japanese assets. Recall that U.S. households and firms acquire yen in order to purchase Japanese assets as well as goods and services. Other factors, such as risk, held constant, the higher the real interest rate paid by Japanese assets, the more Japanese assets Americans will choose to hold. To purchase additional Japanese assets, U.S. households and firms will supply more dollars to the foreign exchange market.

Conversely, reduced demand for Japanese goods, a lower U.S. GDP, or a lower real interest rate on Japanese assets will *reduce* the number of yen Americans need, in turn reducing their supply of dollars to the foreign exchange market and shifting the supply curve for dollars to the left. Of course, any shift in the supply curve for dollars will affect the equilibrium exchange rate, as Example 29.5 shows.

Supplying dollars, demanding yen.

Video games, the yen, and the dollar

EXAMPLE 29.5

Suppose Japanese firms come to dominate the video game market, with games that are more exciting and realistic than those produced in the United States. All else being equal, how will this change affect the relative value of the yen and the dollar?

The increased quality of Japanese video games will increase the demand for the games in the United States. To acquire the yen necessary to buy more Japanese video games, U.S. importers will supply more dollars to the foreign exchange market. As Figure 29.4 shows, the increased supply of dollars will reduce the value of the dollar. In other words, a dollar will buy fewer yen than it did before. At the same time, the yen will increase in value: A given number of yen will buy more dollars than it did before.

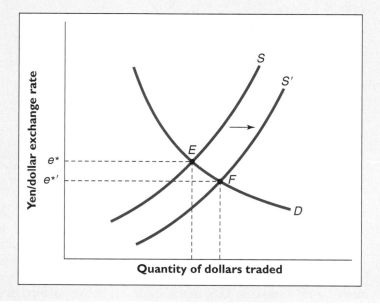

FIGURE 29.4

An Increase in the Supply of Dollars Lowers the Value of the Dollar.
Increased U.S. demand for Japanese video games forces Americans to supply more dollars to the foreign exchange market to acquire the yen they need to buy the games. The supply curve for dollars shifts from S to S', lowering the value of the dollar in terms of yen. The fundamental value of the exchange rate falls from e^* to $e^{*'}$.

EXERCISE 29.4

The U.S. goes into a recession, and real GDP falls. All else equal, how is this economic weakness likely to affect the value of the dollar?

CHANGES IN THE DEMAND FOR DOLLARS

The factors that can cause a change in the demand for dollars in the foreign exchange market, and thus a shift of the dollar demand curve, are analogous to the factors that affect the supply of dollars. Factors that will *increase* the demand for dollars include:

- An increased preference for U.S. goods. For example, Japanese airlines might find that U.S.-built aircraft are superior to others, and decide to expand the number of American-made planes in their fleets. To buy the American planes, Japanese airlines would demand more dollars on the foreign exchange market.

- An increase in real GDP abroad, which implies higher incomes abroad, and thus more demand for imports from the United States.

- An increase in the real interest rate on U.S. assets, which would make those assets more attractive to foreign savers. To acquire U.S. assets, Japanese savers would demand more dollars.

MONETARY POLICY AND THE EXCHANGE RATE

Of the many factors that could influence a country's exchange rate, among the most important is the monetary policy of the country's central bank. As we will see, monetary policy affects the exchange rate primarily through its effect on the real interest rate.

FIGURE 29.5
A Tightening of Monetary Policy Strengthens the Dollar.
Tighter monetary policy in the United States raises the domestic real interest rate, increasing the demand for U.S. assets by foreign savers. An increased demand for U.S. assets in turn increases the demand for dollars. The demand curve shifts from D to D', leading the exchange rate to appreciate from e^* to $e^{*'}$.

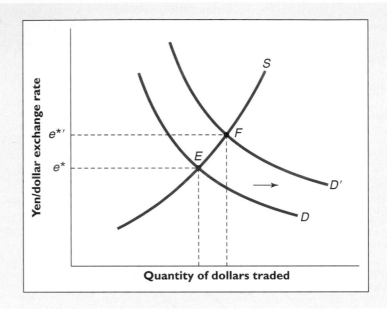

Suppose the Fed is concerned about inflation and tightens U.S. monetary policy in response. The effects of this policy change on the value of the dollar are shown in Figure 29.5. Before the policy change, the equilibrium value of the exchange rate is e^*, at the intersection of supply curve S and the demand curve D (point E in the figure). The tightening of monetary policy raises the domestic U.S. real interest rate r, making U.S. assets more attractive to foreign financial investors. The increased willingness of foreign investors to buy U.S. assets increases the demand for dollars, shifting the demand curve rightward from D to D' and the equilibrium point from E to F. As a result of this increase in demand, the equilibrium value of the dollar rises from e^* to $e^{*'}$.

In short, a tightening of monetary policy by the Fed raises the demand for dollars, causing the dollar to appreciate. By similar logic, an easing of monetary policy, which reduces the real interest rate, would weaken the demand for the dollar, causing it to depreciate.

Why did the dollar appreciate nearly 50 percent in the first half of the 1980s?

ECONOMIC NATURALIST 29.2

Figure 29.1 showed the strong appreciation of the U. S. dollar in 1980–1985, followed by a sharp depreciation in 1986–1987. We saw earlier that the PPP theory cannot explain this roller-coaster behavior. What *can* explain it?

Tight monetary policy, and the associated high real interest rate, were important causes of the dollar's remarkable appreciation during 1980–1985. As we saw in Economic Naturalist 28.4, U.S. inflation peaked at 13.5 percent in 1980. Under the leadership of Chairman Paul Volcker, the Fed responded to the surge in inflation by raising the real interest rate sharply in hopes of reducing aggregate demand and inflationary pressures. As a result, the real interest rate in the United States rose from negative values in 1979 and 1980 to more than 7 percent in 1983 and 1984 (see Table 28.2). Attracted by these high real returns, foreign savers rushed to buy U.S. assets, driving the value of the dollar up significantly.

The Fed's attempt to bring down inflation was successful. By the middle of the 1980s the Fed was able to ease U.S. monetary policy. The resulting decline in the real interest rate reduced the demand for U.S. assets, and thus for dollars, at which point the dollar fell back almost to its 1980 level.

THE EXCHANGE RATE AS A TOOL OF MONETARY POLICY

In a closed economy, monetary policy affects aggregate demand solely through the real interest rate. For example, by raising the real interest rate, a tight monetary policy reduces consumption and investment spending. We will see next that in an open economy with a flexible exchange rate, the exchange rate serves as another channel for monetary policy, one that reinforces the effects of the real interest rate.

To illustrate, suppose that policymakers are concerned about inflation and decide to restrain aggregate demand. To do so, they increase the real interest rate, reducing consumption and investment spending. But, as Figure 29.5 shows, the higher real interest rate also increases the demand for dollars, causing the dollar to appreciate. The stronger dollar, in turn, further reduces aggregate demand. Why? As we saw in discussing the real exchange rate, a stronger dollar reduces the cost of imported goods, increasing imports. It also makes U.S. exports more costly to foreign buyers, which tends to reduce exports. Recall that net exports—or exports minus imports—is one of the four components of aggregate demand. Thus, by reducing exports and increasing imports, a stronger dollar (more precisely, a higher real exchange rate) reduces aggregate demand.

In sum, when the exchange rate is flexible, a tighter monetary policy reduces net exports (through a stronger dollar) as well as consumption and investment spending (through a higher real interest rate). Conversely, an easier monetary policy weakens the dollar and stimulates net exports, reinforcing the effect of the lower real interest rate on consumption and investment spending. Thus, relative to the case of a closed economy we studied earlier, *monetary policy is more effective in an open economy with a flexible exchange rate.*

The tightening of monetary policy under Fed Chairman Volcker in the early 1980s illustrates the effect of monetary policy on net exports (the trade balance). As we saw in Economic Naturalist 29.2, Volcker's tight-money policies were a major reason for the 50 percent appreciation of the dollar during 1980–1985. In 1980 and 1981, the United States enjoyed a trade surplus, with exports that modestly exceeded imports. Largely in response to a stronger dollar, the U.S. trade balance fell into deficit after 1981. By the end of 1985 the U.S. trade deficit was about 3 percent of GDP, a substantial shift in less than half a decade.

RECAP   **DETERMINING THE EXCHANGE RATE**

- The most basic theory of nominal exchange rate determination, purchasing power parity (PPP), is based on the law of one price. The law of one price states that if transportation costs are relatively small, the price of an internationally traded commodity must be the same in all locations. According to the PPP theory, the nominal exchange rate between two currencies can be found by setting the price of a traded commodity in one currency equal to the price of the same commodity expressed in the second currency.

- A useful prediction of the PPP theory is that the currencies of countries that experience significant inflation will tend to depreciate over the long run. However, the PPP theory does not work well in the short run. The fact that many goods and services are nontraded, and that not all traded goods are standardized, reduces the applicability of the law of one price, and hence of the PPP theory.

- Supply and demand analysis is a useful tool for studying the short-run determination of the exchange rate. U.S. households and firms supply dollars to the foreign exchange market to acquire foreign currencies, which they need to purchase foreign goods, services, and assets. Foreigners demand dollars in the foreign exchange market to purchase U.S. goods, services, and assets. The equilibrium exchange rate, also called the fundamental value of the exchange rate, equates the quantities of dollars supplied and demanded in the foreign exchange market.

- An increased preference for foreign goods, an increase in U.S. real GDP, or an increase in the real interest rate on foreign assets will increase the supply of dollars on the foreign exchange market, lowering the value of the dollar. An increased preference for U.S. goods by foreigners, an increase in real GDP abroad, or an increase in the real interest rate on U.S. assets will increase the demand for dollars, raising the value of the dollar.

- A tight monetary policy raises the real interest rate, increasing the demand for dollars and strengthening the dollar. A stronger dollar reinforces the effects of tight monetary policy on aggregate spending by reducing net exports, a component of aggregate demand. Conversely, an easy monetary policy lowers the real interest rate, weakening the dollar.

FIXED EXCHANGE RATES

So far we have focused on the case of flexible exchange rates, the relevant case for most large industrial countries like the United States. However, the alternative approach, fixing the exchange rate, has been quite important historically and is still used in many countries, especially small or developing nations. In this section we will see how our conclusions change when the nominal exchange rate is fixed rather than flexible. One important difference is that when a country maintains a fixed exchange rate, its ability to use monetary policy as a stabilization tool is greatly reduced.

HOW TO FIX AN EXCHANGE RATE

In contrast to a flexible exchange rate, whose value is determined solely by supply and demand in the foreign exchange market, the value of a fixed exchange rate is determined by the government (in practice, usually the finance ministry or treasury department, with the cooperation of the central bank). Today, the value of a fixed exchange rate is usually set in terms of a major currency (for instance, Argentina pegs its currency one-for-one to the dollar), or relative to a "basket" of currencies, typically those of the country's trading partners. Historically, currency values were often fixed in terms of gold or other precious metals, but in recent years precious metals have rarely if ever been used for that purpose.

Once an exchange rate has been fixed, the government usually attempts to keep it unchanged for some time.[2] However, sometimes economic circumstances force the government to change the value of the exchange rate. A reduction in the official value of a currency is called a **devaluation;** an increase in the official

devaluation a reduction in the official value of a currency (in a fixed exchange rate system)

[2]There are exceptions to this statement. Some countries employ a *crawling peg* system, under which the exchange rate is fixed at a value that changes in a preannounced way over time. For example, the government may announce that the value of the fixed exchange rate will fall 2 percent each year. Other countries use a *target zone* system, in which the exchange rate is allowed to deviate by a small amount from its fixed value. To focus on the key issues, we will assume that the exchange rate is fixed at a single value for a protracted period.

value is called a **revaluation**. The devaluation of a fixed exchange rate is analogous to the depreciation of a flexible exchange rate; both involve a reduction in the currency's value. Conversely, a revaluation is analogous to an appreciation.

The supply and demand diagram we used to study flexible exchange rates can be adapted to analyze fixed exchange rates. Let's consider the case of a country called Latinia, whose currency is called the peso. Figure 29.6 shows the supply and demand for the Latinian peso in the foreign exchange market. Pesos are *supplied* to the foreign exchange market by Latinian households and firms who want to acquire foreign currencies to purchase foreign goods and assets. Pesos are *demanded* by holders of foreign currencies who need pesos to purchase Latinian goods and assets. Figure 29.6 shows that the quantities of pesos supplied and demanded in the foreign exchange market are equal when a peso equals 0.1 dollars (10 pesos to the dollar). Hence 0.1 dollars per peso is the *fundamental value* of the peso. If Latinia had a flexible-exchange-rate system, the peso would trade at 10 pesos to the dollar in the foreign exchange market.

But let's suppose that Latinia has a fixed exchange rate and that the government has decreed the value of the Latinian peso to be 8 pesos to the dollar, or 0.125 dollars per peso. This official value of the peso, 0.125 dollars, is indicated by the solid horizontal line in Figure 29.6. Notice that it is greater than the fundamental value, corresponding to the intersection of the supply and demand curves. When the officially fixed value of an exchange rate is greater than its fundamental value, the exchange rate is said to be **overvalued**. The official value of an exchange rate can also be lower than its fundamental value, in which case the exchange rate is said to be **undervalued**.

In this example, Latinia's commitment to hold the peso at 8 to the dollar is inconsistent with the fundamental value of 10 to the dollar, as determined by supply and demand in the foreign exchange market (the Latinian peso is overvalued). How could the Latinian government deal with this inconsistency? There are several possibilities. First, Latinia could simply devalue its currency, from 0.125 dollars per peso to 0.10 dollars per peso, which would bring the peso's official value into line with its fundamental value. As we will see, devaluation is often the ultimate result of an overvaluation of a currency. However, a country with a fixed exchange rate will be reluctant to change the official value of its exchange rate every time the fundamental value changes. If a country must continuously adjust its exchange rate to market conditions, it might as well switch to a flexible exchange rate.

revaluation an increase in the official value of a currency (in a fixed-exchange-rate system)

overvalued exchange rate an exchange rate that has an officially fixed value greater than its fundamental value

undervalued exchange rate an exchange rate that has an officially fixed value less than its fundamental value

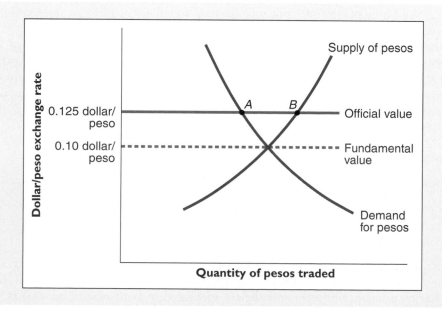

FIGURE 29.6
An Overvalued Exchange Rate.
The peso's official value (0.125 dollars) is shown as greater than its fundamental value (0.10 dollars), as determined by supply and demand in the foreign exchange market. Thus the peso is overvalued. To maintain the fixed value, the government must purchase pesos in the quantity *AB* each period.

As a second alternative, Latinia could try to maintain its overvalued exchange rate by restricting international transactions. Imposing quotas on imports and prohibiting domestic households and firms from acquiring foreign assets would effectively reduce the supply of pesos to the foreign exchange market, raising the fundamental value of the currency. An even more extreme action would be to prohibit Latinians from exchanging the peso for other currencies without government approval, a policy that would effectively allow the government to determine directly the supply of pesos to the foreign exchange market. Such measures might help to maintain the official value of the peso. However, restrictions on trade and capital flows are extremely costly to the economy, because they reduce the gains from specialization and trade and deny domestic households and firms access to foreign capital markets. Thus, a policy of restricting international transactions to maintain a fixed exchange rate is likely to do more harm than good.

The third and most widely used approach to maintaining an overvalued exchange rate is for the government to become a demander of its own currency in the foreign exchange market. Figure 29.6 shows that at the official exchange rate of 0.125 dollars per peso, the private sector supply of pesos (point *B*) exceeds the private sector demand for pesos (point *A*). To keep the peso from falling below its official value, in each period the Latinian government could purchase a quantity of pesos in the foreign exchange market equal to the length of the line segment *AB* in Figure 29.6. If the government followed this strategy, then at the official exchange rate of 0.125 dollars per peso, the total demand for pesos (private demand at point *A* plus government demand *AB*) would equal the private supply of pesos (point *B*). This situation is analogous to government attempts to keep the price of a commodity, like grain or milk, above its market level. To maintain an official price of grain that is above the market-clearing price, the government must stand ready to purchase the excess supply of grain forthcoming at the official price. In the same way, to keep the "price" of its currency above the market-clearing level, the government must buy the excess pesos supplied at the official price.

international reserves foreign currency assets held by a government for the purpose of purchasing the domestic currency in the foreign exchange market

balance-of-payments deficit the net decline in a country's stock of international reserves over a year

balance-of-payments surplus the net increase in a country's stock of international reserves over a year

To be able to purchase its own currency and maintain an overvalued exchange rate, the government (usually the central bank) must hold foreign currency assets, called **international reserves,** or simply *reserves.* For example, the Latinian central bank may hold dollar deposits in U.S. banks or U.S. government debt, which it can trade for pesos in the foreign exchange market as needed. In the situation shown in Figure 29.6, to keep the peso at its official value, in each period the Latinian central bank will have to spend an amount of international reserves equal to the length of the line segment *AB*.

Because a country with an overvalued exchange rate must use part of its reserves to support the value of its currency in each period, over time its available reserves will decline. The net decline in a country's stock of international reserves over a year is called its **balance-of-payments deficit.** Conversely, if a country experiences a net increase in its international reserves over the year, the increase is called its **balance-of-payments surplus.**

EXAMPLE 29.6

Latinia's balance-of-payments deficit

The demand for and supply of Latinian pesos in the foreign exchange market are

$$\text{Demand} = 25{,}000 - 50{,}000e,$$
$$\text{Supply} = 17{,}600 + 24{,}000e,$$

where the Latinian exchange rate *e* is measured in dollars per peso. Officially, the value of the peso is 0.125 dollars. Find the fundamental value of the peso and the Latinian balance-of-payments deficit, measured in both pesos and dollars.

To find the fundamental value of the peso, equate the demand and supply for pesos:

$$25,000 - 50,000e = 17,600 + 24,000e.$$

Solving for e, we get

$$7,400 = 74,000e$$
$$e = 0.10.$$

So the fundamental value of the exchange rate is 0.10 dollars per peso, as in Figure 29.6.

At the official exchange rate, 0.125 dollars per peso, the demand for pesos is $25,000 - 50,000(0.125) = 18,750$, and the supply of pesos is $17,600 + 24,000(0.125) = 20,600$. Thus the quantity of pesos supplied to the foreign exchange market exceeds the quantity of pesos demanded by $20,600 - 18,750 = 1,850$ pesos. To maintain the fixed rate, the Latinian government must purchase 1,850 pesos per period, which is the Latinian balance-of-payments deficit. Since pesos are purchased at the official rate of 8 pesos to the dollar, the balance-of-payments deficit in dollars is $(1,850 \text{ pesos}) \times (0.125 \text{ dollars/peso}) = \$(1,850/8) = \$231.25$.

EXERCISE 29.5

Repeat Example 29.6 under the assumption that the fixed value of the peso is 0.15 dollars per peso. What do you conclude about the relationship between the degree of currency overvaluation and the resulting balance-of-payments deficit?

Although a government can maintain an overvalued exchange rate for a time by offering to buy back its own currency at the official price, there is a limit to this strategy, since no government's stock of international reserves is infinite. Eventually the government will run out of reserves, and the fixed exchange rate will collapse. As we will see next, the collapse of a fixed exchange rate can be quite sudden and dramatic.

EXERCISE 29.6

Diagram a case in which a fixed exchange rate is *undervalued* rather than overvalued. Show that, to maintain the fixed exchange rate, the central bank must use domestic currency to purchase foreign currency in the foreign exchange market. With an undervalued exchange rate, is the country's central bank in danger of running out of international reserves? (*Hint:* Keep in mind that a central bank is always free to print more of its own currency.)

SPECULATIVE ATTACKS

A government's attempt to maintain an overvalued exchange rate can be ended quickly and unexpectedly by the onset of a *speculative attack*. A **speculative attack** involves massive selling of domestic currency assets by both domestic and foreign financial investors. For example, in a speculative attack on the Latinian peso, financial investors would attempt to get rid of any financial assets—stocks, bonds, deposits in banks—denominated in pesos. A speculative attack is most likely to occur when financial investors fear that an overvalued currency will soon be devalued, since in a devaluation, financial assets denominated in the domestic currency suddenly become worth much less in terms of other currencies. Ironically,

speculative attack a massive selling of domestic currency assets by financial investors speculative attacks, which are usually prompted by *fear* of devaluation, may turn out to be the *cause* of devaluation. Thus a speculative attack may actually be a self-fulfilling prophecy.

The effects of a speculative attack on the market for pesos are shown in Figure 29.7. At first, the situation is the same as in Figure 29.6: The supply and demand for Latinian pesos are indicated by the curves marked *S* and *D*, implying a fundamental value of the peso of 0.10 dollars per peso. As before, the official value of the peso is 0.125 dollars per peso—greater than the fundamental value—so the peso is overvalued. To maintain the fixed value of the peso, each period the Latinian central bank must use its international reserves to buy back pesos, in the amount corresponding to the line segment *AB* in the figure.

Suppose, though, that financial investors fear that Latinia may soon devalue its currency, perhaps because the central bank's reserves are getting low. If the peso were to be devalued from its official value of 8 pesos to the dollar to its fundamental value of 10 pesos per dollar, then a 1 million peso investment, worth $125,000 at the fixed exchange rate, would suddenly be worth only $100,000. To try to avoid these losses, financial investors will sell their peso-denominated assets and offer pesos on the foreign exchange market. The resulting flood of pesos into the market will shift the supply curve of pesos to the right, from *S* to *S′* in Figure 29.7.

This speculative attack creates a serious problem for the Latinian central bank. Prior to the attack, maintaining the value of the peso required the central bank to spend each period an amount of international reserves corresponding to the line segment *AB*. Now suddenly the central bank must spend a larger quantity of reserves, equal to the distance *AC* in Figure 29.7, to maintain the fixed

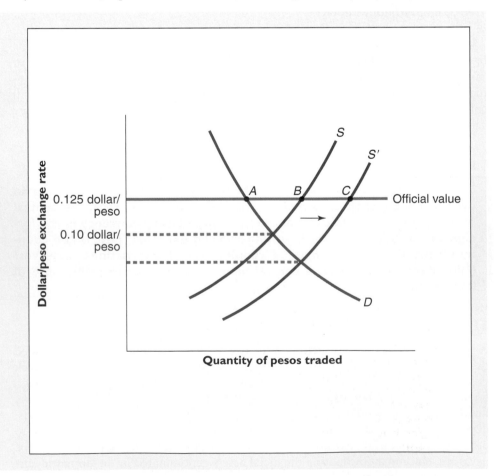

FIGURE 29.7
A Speculative Attack on the Peso.
Initially, the peso is overvalued at 0.125 dollars per peso. To maintain the official rate, the central bank must buy pesos in the amount *AB* each period. Fearful of possible devaluation, financial investors launch a speculative attack, selling peso-denominated assets and supplying pesos to the foreign exchange market. As a result, the supply of pesos shifts from *S* to *S′*, lowering the fundamental value of the currency still further and forcing the central bank to buy pesos in the amount *AC* to maintain the official exchange rate. This more rapid loss of reserves may lead the central bank to devalue the peso, confirming financial investors' fears.

exchange rate. These extra reserves are needed to purchase the pesos being sold by panicky financial investors. In practice, such speculative attacks often force a devaluation by reducing the central bank's reserves to the point where further defense of the fixed exchange rate is considered hopeless. Thus a speculative attack ignited by fears of devaluation may actually end up producing the very devaluation that was feared.

Can a speculative attack occur under flexible exchange rates?

The last section described the self-fulfilling nature of speculative attacks in a fixed-exchange rate system: fears of a currency devaluation often lead to actual currency devaluation. Can a speculative attack occur in a flexible exchange rate system?

As noted earlier, a speculative attack on a currency involves large-scale selling of a country's domestic currency assets by both domestic and foreign financial investors based on fears of a future decline in the value of the country's currency. The economic effects of a speculative attack are illustrated in Figure 29.7: an increase in the supply of the domestic currency that lowers the fundamental value of the currency, often dramatically. Brazil experienced just this sort of deterioration in the value of its currency, the real (pronounced ray-al'), during 2002, in anticipation of a presidential victory by Brazilian Worker's Party candidate, Luis Inacio da Silva, who goes by the nickname "Lula." Investors were concerned that da Silva would break from the economic policies of outgoing president Fernando Henrique Cardoso, who helped to stabilize Brazil's economy, South America's largest, since his first presidential election in 1994.

In the early 1990s, just prior to Mr. Cardoso's election, high inflation stunted Brazil's economic performance and reduced foreign investment, weakening future economic growth prospects. Inflation averaged over 20 percent per month since the late 1980s and reached a monthly rate of nearly 50 percent (over 10,000 percent per year!) by June 1994, when newly elected president Cardoso instituted a bold economic plan that included the creation of a new currency—the real—that was directly linked to the value of the U.S. dollar. Immediately the inflation rate dropped to less than 10 percent per month, and by 1997 the *annual* inflation rate was in the single digits. However, by 1998, increasing Brazilian budget and current-account deficits led to a speculative attack that led to a dramatic devaluation of the real in January 1999 and an uncoupling of the real from the U.S. dollar. Since 1999 the Brazilian currency has been allowed to fluctuate freely but has remained relatively stable, along with the Brazilian economy: inflation remains in the single digits, poverty has been reduced, and a variety of social indicators have improved. Progress has come with a cost, however: rising government debt to pay for Cardoso's social programs.

Concerns about the growing government debt and the increasing popularity of opposition party candidate da Silva led to another round of downward pressure on the real during 2002 as investors began to sell off financial assets denominated in reals. Investors were concerned that da Silva, if elected president, would be unwilling to make the tough government spending and taxing decisions that would be necessary to stabilize the government's debt, raising concerns of a government default, higher inflation, and even further downward pressure on the real. As a result, by the end of September the real had reached record lows and inflation was on the rise.

However, following da Silva's landslide election victory in early October, pledges that he would continue Cardoso's fight against inflation and promote fiscal policy discipline, along with a new international loan package from the International Monetary Fund, helped to calm currency and financial markets, sparking hopes for continued economic growth with low inflation, rising currency values, and falling interest rates. Whether da Silva will be able to avoid further downward pressure on the real will depend upon investors' confidence that he will carry out his presidential pledges.

ECONOMIC
NATURALIST
29.3

MONETARY POLICY AND THE FIXED EXCHANGE RATE

We have seen that there is no really satisfactory way of maintaining a fixed exchange rate above its fundamental value for an extended period. A central bank can maintain an overvalued exchange rate for a time by using international reserves to buy up the excess supply of its currency in the foreign exchange market. But a country's international reserves are limited and may eventually be exhausted by the attempt to keep the exchange rate artificially high. Moreover, speculative attacks often hasten the collapse of an overvalued exchange rate.

An alternative to trying to maintain an overvalued exchange rate is to take actions that increase the fundamental value of the exchange rate. If the exchange rate's fundamental value can be raised enough to equal its official value, then the overvaluation problem will be eliminated. The most effective way to change the exchange rate's fundamental value is through monetary policy. As we saw earlier in the chapter, a tight monetary policy that raises the real interest rate will increase the demand for the domestic currency, as domestic assets become more attractive to foreign financial investors. Increased demand for the currency will in turn raise its fundamental value.

The use of monetary policy to support a fixed exchange rate is shown in Figure 29.8. At first, the demand and supply of the Latinian peso in the foreign exchange market are given by the curves *D* and *S,* so the fundamental value of the peso equals 0.10 dollars per peso—less than the official value of 0.125 dollars per peso. Just as before, the peso is overvalued. This time, however, the Latinian central bank uses monetary policy to eliminate the overvaluation problem. To do so, the central bank increases the domestic real interest rate, making Latinian assets more attractive to foreign financial investors and raising the demand for pesos from *D* to *D'*. After this increase in the demand for pesos, the fundamental value of the peso equals the officially fixed value, as can be seen in

FIGURE 29.8
A Tightening of Monetary Policy Eliminates an Overvaluation.
With the demand for the peso given by *D* and the supply given by *S,* equilibrium occurs at point *E* and the fundamental value of the peso equals 0.10 dollars per peso—below the official value of 0.125 dollars per peso. The overvaluation of the peso can be eliminated by tighter monetary policy, which raises the domestic real interest rate, making domestic assets more attractive to foreign financial investors. The resulting increase in demand for the peso, from *D* to *D'*, raises the peso's fundamental value to 0.125 dollars per peso, the official value. The peso is no longer overvalued.

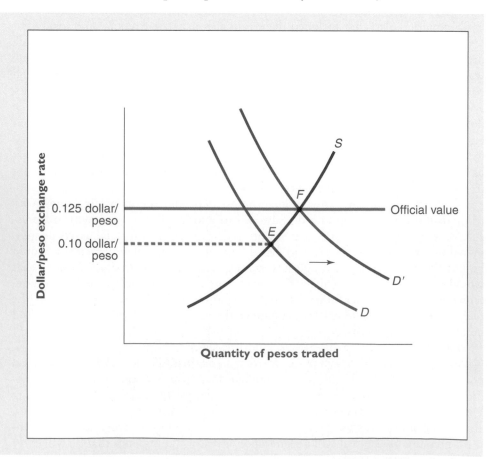

Figure 29.8. Because the peso is no longer overvalued, it can be maintained at its fixed value without loss of international reserves or fear of speculative attack. Conversely, an easing of monetary policy (a lower real interest rate) could be used to remedy an undervaluation, in which the official exchange rate is below the fundamental value.

Although monetary policy can be used to keep the fundamental value of the exchange rate equal to the official value, using monetary policy in this way has some drawbacks. In particular, *if monetary policy is used to set the fundamental value of the exchange rate equal to the official value, it is no longer available for stabilizing the domestic economy*. Suppose, for example, that the Latinian economy were suffering a recession due to insufficient aggregate demand at the same time that its exchange rate is overvalued. The Latinian central bank could lower the real interest rate to increase spending and output, or it could raise the real interest rate to eliminate overvaluation of the exchange rate, *but it cannot do both*. Hence, if Latinian officials decide to maintain the fixed exchange rate, they must give up any hope of fighting the recession using monetary policy. The fact that a fixed exchange rate limits or eliminates the use of monetary policy for the purpose of stabilizing aggregate demand is one of the most important features of a fixed-exchange-rate system.

The conflict monetary policymakers face, between stabilizing the exchange rate and stabilizing the domestic economy, is most severe when the exchange rate is under a speculative attack. A speculative attack lowers the fundamental value of the exchange rate still further, by increasing the supply of the currency in the foreign exchange market (see Figure 29.7). To stop a speculative attack, the central bank must raise the fundamental value of the currency a great deal, which requires a large increase in the real interest rate. (In a famous episode in 1992, the Swedish central bank responded to an attack on its currency by raising the short-term interest rate to 500 percent!) However, because the increase in the real interest rate that is necessary to stop a speculative attack reduces aggregate demand, it can cause a severe economic slowdown. Economic Naturalist 29.4 describes a real-world example of this phenomenon.

"It's just a flesh wound. I got it defending the dollar."

What were the causes and consequences of the East Asian crisis of 1997–1998?

During the past three decades the countries of East Asia have enjoyed impressive economic growth and stability. But the "East Asian miracle" seemed to end in 1997, when a wave of speculative attacks hit the region's currencies. Thailand, which had kept a constant value for its currency in terms of the U.S. dollar for more than a decade, was the first to come under attack, but the crisis spread to other countries, including South Korea, Indonesia, and Malaysia. Each of these countries was ultimately forced to devalue its currency. What caused this crisis, and what were its consequences?

Because of the impressive economic record of the East Asian countries, the speculative attacks on their currencies were unexpected by most policymakers, economists, and financial investors. With the benefit of hindsight, however, we can identify some problems in the East Asian economies that contributed to the crisis. Perhaps the most serious problems concerned their banking systems. In the decade prior to the crisis, East Asian banks received large inflows of capital from foreign financial investors hoping to profit from the East Asian miracle. Those inflows would have been a boon if they had been well invested, but unfortunately, many bankers used the funds to make loans to family members, friends, or the politically well-connected—a phenomenon that became known as *crony capitalism*. The results were poor returns on investment and defaults by many borrowers. Ultimately, foreign investors realized that the returns to investing in East Asia would be much lower than expected. When they began to sell off their assets, the process snowballed into a full-fledged speculative attack on the East Asian currencies.

Despite assistance by international lenders such as the International Monetary Fund (see Box 29.1), the effects of the speculative attacks on the East Asian economies were severe. The prices of assets such as stocks and land plummeted, and there were banking panics in several nations. (See Chapter 23 for a discussion of banking panics.) In an attempt to raise the fundamental values of their exchange rates and stave off additional devaluation, several of the countries increased their real interest rates sharply. However, the rise in real interest rates depressed aggregate demand, contributing to sharp declines in output and rising unemployment.

Fortunately, by 1999 most East Asian economies had begun to recover. Still, the crisis impressed the potential dangers of fixed exchange rates quite sharply in the minds of policymakers in developing countries. Another lesson from the crisis is that banking regulations need to be structured so as to promote economically sound lending rather than crony capitalism.

BOX 29.1: THE INTERNATIONAL MONETARY FUND

The International Monetary Fund (IMF) was established after World War II. An international agency, the IMF is controlled by a 24-member Executive Board. Eight Executive Board members represent individual countries (China, France, Germany, Japan, Russia, Saudi Arabia, the United Kingdom, and the United States); the other 16 members each represent a group of countries. A managing director oversees the IMF's operations and its approximately 2,600 employees.

The original purpose of the IMF was to help manage the system of fixed exchange rates, called the Bretton Woods system, put in place after the war. Under Bretton Woods, the IMF's principal role was to lend international reserves to member countries who needed them so that those countries could maintain their exchange rates at the official values. However, by 1973 the United States, the United Kingdom, Germany, and most other industrial nations had abandoned fixed exchange rates for flexible rates, leaving the IMF to find a new mission. Since 1973 the IMF has been involved primarily in lending to developing countries. It lent heavily to Mexico when that country experienced speculative attacks in 1994, and it made loans to East Asian countries during the 1997–1998 crisis. Other countries that received large IMF loans in recent years include Russia and Brazil.

The IMF's performance in recent crises has been controversial. Many observers credit the IMF with helping Mexico, the East Asian nations, and others to recover quickly from the effects of speculative attacks and contend that the IMF plays a vital role in maintaining international economic stability. However, some critics have charged that the IMF has required recipients of its loans to follow economic policies—such as tight monetary policies and fiscal cutbacks—that have turned out to be ill-advised. Others have claimed that the IMF's loans help foreign financial investors and the richest people in the countries receiving loans, rather than the average person. (The IMF has been severely embarrassed by reports that much of the nearly $5 billion it lent to Russia in 1998 has disappeared into the bank accounts of unscrupulous citizens, including gangsters.)

The IMF has also come into conflict with the World Bank, a separate international institution that was set up at about the same time as the IMF. The World Bank, whose mission is to provide long-term loans to help poor nations develop their economies, has complained that IMF interventions in poor countries interfered with World Bank programs and objectives. In 2000, a report commissioned by the U.S. Congress recommended reducing the IMF's powers (as well as, incidentally, those of the World Bank). The debate over the IMF's proper role will no doubt continue.

How did policy mistakes contribute to the Great Depression?

Chapter 17 introduced the study of macroeconomics with the claim that policy mistakes played a major role in causing the Great Depression. Now that we are close to completing our study of macroeconomics, we can be more specific about that claim. How did policy mistakes contribute to the Great Depression?

Many policy mistakes (as well as a great deal of bad luck) contributed to the severity of the Depression. For example, U.S. policymakers, in an attempt to protect domestic industries, imposed the infamous Hawley-Smoot tariff in 1930. Other countries quickly retaliated with their own tariffs, leading to the virtual collapse of international trade.

However, the most serious mistakes by far were in the realm of monetary policy.[3] As we saw in Chapter 23, the U.S. money supply contracted by one-third between 1929 and 1933 (Table 23.7). Associated with this unprecedented decline in the money supply were sharply falling output and prices and surging unemployment.

At least three separate policy errors were responsible for the collapse of the U.S. money supply between 1929 and 1933. First, the Federal Reserve tightened monetary policy significantly in 1928 and 1929, despite the absence of inflation. Fed officials took this action primarily in an attempt to "rein in" the booming stock market, which they feared was rising too quickly. Their "success" in dampening stock market speculation was more than they bargained for, however, as rising interest rates and a slowing economy contributed to a crash in stock prices that began in October 1929.

The second critical policy error was allowing thousands of U.S. banks to fail during the banking panics of 1930 to 1933. Apparently officials believed that the failures would eliminate only the weakest banks, strengthening the banking system

ECONOMIC NATURALIST 29.5

[3]A classic 1963 book by Milton Friedman and Anna Schwartz, *A Monetary History of the United States: 1867–1960* (Princeton University Press), was the first to provide detailed support for the view that poor monetary policy helped to cause the Depression.

overall. However, the banking panics sharply reduced bank deposits and the overall money supply, for reasons discussed in Economic Naturalist 23.2.

The third policy error, related to the subject of this chapter, arose from the U.S. government's exchange rate policies. When the Depression began, the United States, like most other major countries, was on the gold standard, with the value of the dollar officially set in terms of gold.[4] By establishing a fixed value for the dollar, the United States effectively created a fixed exchange rate between the dollar and other currencies whose values were set in terms of gold. As the Depression worsened, Fed officials were urged by Congress to ease monetary policy to stop the fall in output and prices. However, as we saw earlier, under a fixed exchange rate monetary policy cannot be used to stabilize the domestic economy. Specifically, policymakers of the early 1930s feared that if they eased monetary policy, foreign financial investors might perceive the dollar to be overvalued and launch a speculative attack, forcing a devaluation of the dollar or even the abandonment of the gold standard altogether. The Fed therefore made no serious attempt to arrest the collapse of the money supply.

With hindsight, we can see that the Fed's decision to put a higher priority on remaining on the gold standard than on stimulating the economy was a major error. Indeed, countries that abandoned the gold standard in favor of a floating exchange rate, such as Great Britain and Sweden, or which had never been on the gold standard (Spain and China), were able to increase their money supplies and to recover much more quickly from the Depression than the United States did. The Fed evidently believed, erroneously as it turned out, that stability of the exchange rate would somehow translate into overall economic stability.

Upon taking office in March 1933, Franklin D. Roosevelt reversed several of these policy errors. He took active measures to restore the health of the banking system, and he suspended the gold standard. The money supply stopped falling and began to grow rapidly. Output, prices, and stock prices recovered rapidly during 1933 to 1937, although unemployment remained high. However, ultimate recovery from the Depression was interrupted by another recession in 1937–1938.

RECAP   FIXED EXCHANGE RATES

- The value of a fixed exchange rate is set by the government. The official value of a fixed exchange rate may differ from its fundamental value, as determined by supply and demand in the foreign exchange market. An exchange rate whose officially fixed value exceeds its fundamental value is overvalued; an exchange rate whose officially fixed value is below its fundamental value is undervalued.

- For an overvalued exchange rate, the quantity of the currency supplied to the foreign exchange market at the official exchange rate exceeds the quantity demanded. The government can maintain an overvalued exchange rate for a time by using its international reserves (foreign currency assets) to purchase the excess supply of its currency. The net decline in a country's stock of international reserves during the year is its balance-of-payments deficit.

- Because a country's international reserves are limited, it cannot maintain an overvalued exchange rate indefinitely. Moreover, if financial investors fear an impending devaluation of the exchange rate, they may launch a speculative attack, selling domestic currency assets and supplying large amounts of the country's currency to the foreign exchange market—an

[4]The value of the dollar in 1929 was such that the price of 1 ounce of gold was fixed at $20.67.

action that exhausts the country's reserves even more quickly. Because rapid loss of reserves may force a devaluation, financial investors' fear of devaluation may prove a self-fulfilling prophecy.

■ A tight monetary policy, which increases the real interest rate, raises the demand for the currency and hence its fundamental value. By raising a currency's fundamental value to its official value, tight monetary policies can eliminate the problem of overvaluation and stabilize the exchange rate. However, if monetary policy is used to set the fundamental value of the exchange rate, it is no longer available for stabilizing the domestic economy.

SHOULD EXCHANGE RATES BE FIXED OR FLEXIBLE?

Should countries adopt fixed or flexible exchange rates? In briefly comparing the two systems, we will focus on two major issues: (1) the effects of the exchange rate system on monetary policy and (2) the effects of the exchange rate system on trade and economic integration.

On the issue of monetary policy, we have seen that the type of exchange rate a country has strongly affects the central bank's ability to use monetary policy to stabilize the economy. A flexible exchange rate actually strengthens the impact of monetary policy on aggregate demand. But a fixed exchange rate prevents policymakers from using monetary policy to stabilize the economy, because they must instead use it to keep the exchange rate's fundamental value at its official value (or else risk speculative attack).

In large economies like that of the United States, giving up the power to stabilize the domestic economy via monetary policy makes little sense. Thus large economies should nearly always employ a flexible exchange rate. However, in small economies, giving up this power may have some benefits. An interesting case is that of Argentina, which for the period 1991–2001 maintained a one-to-one exchange rate between its peso and the U.S. dollar. Although prior to 1991 Argentina had suffered periods of hyperinflation, while the peso was pegged to the dollar Argentina's inflation rate essentially equaled that of the United States (see Figure 29.2). By tying its currency to the dollar and giving up the freedom to set its monetary policy, Argentina attempted to commit itself to avoiding the inflationary policies of the past, and instead placed itself under the "umbrella" of the Federal Reserve. Unfortunately, early in 2002 investors' fears that Argentina would not be able to repay its international debts led to a speculative attack on the Argentine peso. The fixed exchange rate collapsed, the peso depreciated, and Argentina experienced an economic crisis. The lesson is that a fixed exchange rate alone cannot stop inflation in a small economy, if other policies are not sound as well. Large fiscal deficits, which were financed by foreign borrowing, ultimately pushed Argentina into crisis.

The second important issue is the effect of the exchange rate on trade and economic integration. Proponents of fixed exchange rates argue that fixed rates promote international trade and cross-border economic cooperation by reducing uncertainty about future exchange rates. For example, a firm that is considering building up its export business knows that its potential profits will depend on the future value of its own country's currency relative to the currencies of the countries to which it exports. Under a flexible-exchange-rate regime, the value of the home currency fluctuates with changes in supply and demand and is therefore difficult to predict far in advance. Such uncertainty may make the firm reluctant to expand its export business. Supporters of fixed exchange rates argue that if the exchange rate is officially fixed, uncertainty about the future exchange rate is reduced or eliminated.

One problem with this argument, which has been underscored by episodes like the East Asian crisis and the Argentine crisis, is that fixed exchange rates are not guaranteed to remain fixed forever. Although they do not fluctuate from day to day as flexible rates do, a speculative attack on a fixed exchange rate may lead suddenly and unpredictably to a large devaluation. Thus a firm that is trying to forecast the exchange rate 10 years into the future may face as much uncertainty if the exchange rate is fixed as if it is flexible.

The potential instability of fixed exchange rates caused by speculative attacks has led some countries to try a more radical solution to the problem of uncertainty about exchange rates: the adoption of a common currency. Economic Naturalist 29.6 describes an important instance of this strategy.

ECONOMIC NATURALIST 29.6

Why have 11 European countries adopted a common currency?

Effective January 1, 1999, eleven western European nations, including France, Germany, and Italy, adopted a common currency, called the euro. In several stages the euro replaced the French franc, the German mark, the Italian lira, and other national currencies. The process was completed in early 2002 when the old currencies were completely eliminated and replaced by euros. Why have these nations adopted a common currency?

For some decades the nations of western Europe have worked to increase economic cooperation and trade among themselves. European leaders recognized that a unified and integrated European economy would be more productive and perhaps more competitive with the U.S. economy than a fragmented one. As part of this effort, these countries established fixed exchange rates under the auspices of a system called the European Monetary System (EMS). Unfortunately, the EMS did not prove stable. Numerous devaluations of the various currencies occurred, and in 1992 severe speculative attacks forced several nations, including Great Britain, to abandon the fixed-exchange-rate system.

In December 1991, in Maastricht in the Netherlands, the member countries of the European Community (EC) adopted a treaty popularly known as the Maastricht Treaty. One of the major provisions of the treaty, which took effect in November 1993, was that member countries would strive to adopt a common currency. This common currency, known as the euro, was formally adopted on January 1, 1999. The advent of the euro means that Europeans will no longer have to change currencies when trading with other European countries, much as Americans from different states can trade with each other without worrying that a "New York dollar" will change in value relative to a "California dollar." The euro should help to promote European trade and cooperation while eliminating the problem of speculative attacks on the currencies of individual countries.

Because western Europe now has a single currency, it also must have a common monetary policy. The EC members agreed that European monetary policy would be put under the control of a new European Central Bank (ECB), a multinational institution located in Frankfurt, Germany. The ECB has in effect become "Europe's Fed." One potential problem with having a single monetary policy for 11 different countries is that different countries may face different economic conditions, so a single monetary policy cannot respond to all of them. What will the ECB do, for example, if Italy is suffering from a recession (which requires an easing of monetary policy) while Germany is worried about inflation (which requires a tightening)? Whether the requirement of a single monetary policy will create conflicts of interest among the member nations of the European Community remains to be seen.

■ SUMMARY ■

- The *nominal exchange rate* between two currencies is the rate at which the currencies can be traded for each other. A rise in the value of a currency relative to other currencies is called an *appreciation;* a decline in the value of a currency is called a *depreciation.*

- Exchange rates can be flexible or fixed. The value of a *flexible exchange rate* is determined by the supply and demand for the currency in the *foreign exchange market,* the market on which currencies of various nations are traded for one another. The government sets the value of a *fixed exchange rate.*

- The *real exchange rate* is the price of the average domestic good or service *relative* to the price of the average foreign good or service, when prices are expressed in terms of a common currency. An increase in the real exchange rate implies that domestic goods and services are becoming more expensive relative to foreign goods and services, which tends to reduce exports and increase imports. Conversely, a decline in the real exchange rate tends to increase net exports.

- A basic theory of nominal exchange rate determination, the *purchasing power parity* (PPP) theory, is based on the law of one price. The *law of one price* states that if transportation costs are relatively small, the price of an internationally traded commodity must be the same in all locations. According to the PPP theory, we can find the nominal exchange rate between two currencies by setting the price of a commodity in one of the currencies equal to the price of the commodity in the second currency. The PPP theory correctly predicts that the currencies of countries that experience significant inflation will tend to depreciate in the long run. However, the fact that many goods and services are not traded internationally, and that not all traded goods are standardized, makes the PPP theory less useful for explaining short-run changes in exchange rates.

- Supply and demand analysis is a useful tool for studying the determination of exchange rates in the short run. The equilibrium exchange rate, also called the *fundamental value of the exchange rate,* equates the quantities of the currency supplied and demanded in the foreign exchange market. A currency is supplied by domestic residents who wish to acquire foreign currencies to purchase foreign goods, services, and assets. An increased preference for foreign goods, an increase in the domestic GDP, or an increase in the real interest rate on foreign assets will all increase the supply of a currency on the foreign exchange market and thus lower its value. A currency is demanded by foreigners who wish to purchase domestic goods, services, and assets. An increased preference for domestic goods by foreigners, an increase in real GDP abroad, or an increase in the domestic real interest rate will all increase the demand for the currency on the foreign exchange market and thus increase its value.

- If the exchange rate is flexible, a tight monetary policy (by raising the real interest rate) increases the demand for the currency and causes it to appreciate. The stronger currency reinforces the effects of the tight monetary policy on aggregate demand by reducing net exports. Conversely, easy monetary policy lowers the real interest rate and weakens the currency, which in turn stimulates net exports.

- The value of a fixed exchange rate is officially established by the government. A fixed exchange rate whose official value exceeds its fundamental value in the foreign exchange market is said to be *overvalued.* An exchange rate whose official value is below its fundamental value is *undervalued.* A reduction in the official value of a fixed exchange rate is called a *devaluation;* an increase in its official value is called a *revaluation.*

- For an overvalued exchange rate, the quantity of the currency supplied at the official exchange rate exceeds the quantity demanded. To maintain the official rate, the country's central bank must use its *international reserves* (foreign currency assets) to purchase the excess supply of its currency in the foreign exchange market. Because a country's international reserves are limited, it cannot maintain an overvalued exchange rate indefinitely. Moreover, if financial investors fear an impending devaluation of the exchange rate, they may launch a *speculative attack,* selling their domestic currency assets and supplying large quantities of the currency to the foreign exchange market. Because speculative attacks cause a country's central bank to spend its international reserves even more quickly, they often force a devaluation.

- A tight monetary policy, by raising the fundamental value of the exchange rate, can eliminate the problem of overvaluation. However, if monetary policy is used to set the fundamental value of the exchange rate equal to the official value, it is no longer available for stabilizing the domestic economy. Thus under fixed exchange rates, monetary policy has little or no power to affect domestic output and employment.

- Because a fixed exchange rate implies that monetary policy can no longer be used for domestic stabilization, most large countries employ a flexible exchange rate. A fixed exchange rate may benefit a small country by forcing its central bank to follow the monetary policies of the country to which it has tied its rate. Advocates of fixed exchange rates argue that they increase trade and economic integration by making the exchange rate more predictable. However, the threat of speculative attacks greatly reduces the long-term predictability of a fixed exchange rate.

▪ KEY TERMS ▪

appreciation (782)
balance-of-payments deficit (798)
balance-of-payment surplus (798)
depreciation (782)
devaluation (796)
fixed exchange rate (783)
flexible exchange rate (783)

foreign exchange market (783)
fundamental value of the exchange rate (792)
international reserves (798)
law of one price (787)
nominal exchange rate (781)

overvalued exchange rate (797)
purchasing power parity (PPP) (788)
real exchange rate (784)
revaluation (797)
speculative attack (799)
undervalued exchange rate (797)

▪ REVIEW QUESTIONS ▪

1. Japanese yen trade at 110 yen per dollar and Mexico pesos trade at 10 pesos per dollar. What is the nominal exchange rate between the yen and the peso? Express in two ways.

2. Define *nominal exchange rate* and *real exchange rate*. How are the two concepts related? Which type of exchange rate most directly affects a country's ability to export its goods and services?

3. Would you expect the law of one price to apply to crude oil? To fresh milk? To taxi rides? To compact discs produced in different countries by local recording artists? Explain your answer in each case.

4. Why do U.S. households and firms supply dollars to the foreign exchange market? Why do foreigners demand dollars in the foreign exchange market?

5. Under a flexible exchange rate, how does an easing of monetary policy (a lower real interest rate) affect the value of the exchange rate? Does this change in the exchange rate tend to weaken or strengthen the effect of the monetary ease on output and employment? Explain.

6. Define *overvalued exchange rate*. Discuss four ways in which government policymakers can respond to an overvaluation. What are the drawbacks of each approach?

7. Use a supply and demand diagram to illustrate the effects of a speculative attack on an overvalued exchange rate. Why do speculative attacks often result in a devaluation?

8. Contrast fixed and flexible exchange rates in terms of how they affect (a) the ability of monetary policy to stabilize domestic output and (b) the predictability of future exchange rates.

▪ PROBLEMS ▪

1. Using the data in Table 29.1, find the nominal exchange rate between the Mexican peso and the Japanese yen. Express in two ways. How do your answers change if the peso appreciates by 10 percent against the dollar while the value of the yen against the dollar remains unchanged?

2. A British-made automobile is priced at £20,000 (20,000 British pounds). A comparable U.S.–made car costs $26,000. One pound trades for $1.50 in the foreign exchange market. Find the real exchange rate for automobiles from the perspective of the United States and from the perspective of Great Britain. Which country's cars are more competitively priced?

3. Between last year and this year, the CPI in Blueland rose from 100 to 110 and the CPI in Redland rose from 100 to 105. Blueland's currency unit, the blue, was worth $1 (U.S.) last year and is worth 90 cents (U.S.) this year. Redland's currency unit, the red, was worth 50 cents (U.S.) last year and is worth 45 cents (U.S.) this year.

   Find the percentage change from last year to this year in Blueland's *nominal* exchange rate with Redland and in Blueland's *real* exchange rate with Redland. (Treat Blueland as the home country.) Relative to Redland, do you expect Blueland's exports to be helped or hurt by these changes in exchange rates?

4. The demand for U.S.-made cars in Japan is given by

   Japanese demand = 10,000 − 0.001(Price of U.S. cars in yen).

Similarly, the demand for Japanese-made cars in the United States is

U.S. demand = 30,000 − 0.2(Price of Japanese cars in dollars).

The domestic price of a U.S.-made car is $20,000, and the domestic price of a Japanese-made car is ¥2,500,000. From the perspective of the United States, find the real exchange rate in terms of cars and net exports of cars to Japan, if:

a. The nominal exchange rate is 100 yen per dollar.

b. The nominal exchange rate is 125 yen per dollar.

How does an appreciation of the dollar affect U.S. net exports of automobiles (considering only the Japanese market)?

5. a. Gold is $350 per ounce in the United States and 2,800 pesos per ounce in Mexico. What nominal exchange rate between U.S. dollars and Mexican pesos is implied by the PPP theory?

  b. Mexico experiences inflation so that the price of gold rises to 4,200 pesos per ounce. Gold remains $350 per ounce in the United States. According to the PPP theory, what happens to the exchange rate? What general principle does this example illustrate?

  c. Gold is $350 per ounce in the United States and 4,200 pesos per ounce in Mexico. Crude oil (excluding taxes and transportation costs) is $30 per barrel in the United States. According to the PPP theory, what should a barrel of crude oil cost in Mexico?

  d. Gold is $350 per ounce in the United States. The exchange rate between the United States and Canada is 0.70 U.S. dollars per Canadian dollar. How much does an ounce of gold cost in Canada?

6. How would each of the following be likely to affect the value of the dollar, all else being equal? Explain.

  a. U.S. stocks are perceived as having become much riskier financial investments.

  b. European computer firms switch from U.S.-produced software to software produced in India, Israel, and other nations.

  c. As East Asian economies recover, international financial investors become aware of many new, high-return investment opportunities in the region.

  d. The U.S. government imposes a large tariff on imported automobiles.

  e. The Federal Reserve reports that it is less concerned about inflation and more concerned about an impending recession in the United States.

  f. U.S. consumers increase their spending on imported goods.

7. The demand for and supply of shekels in the foreign exchange market are

$$\text{Demand} = 30,000 - 8,000e,$$
$$\text{Supply} = 25,000 + 12,000e,$$

where the nominal exchange rate is expressed as U.S. dollars per shekel.

  a. What is the fundamental value of the shekel?

  b. The shekel is fixed at 0.30 U.S. dollars. Is the shekel overvalued, undervalued, or neither? Find the balance-of-payments deficit or surplus in both shekels and dollars. What happens to the country's international reserves over time?

  c. Repeat part b for the case in which the shekel is fixed at 0.20 U.S. dollars.

8. The annual demand for and supply of shekels in the foreign exchange market is as given in Problem 7. The shekel is fixed at 0.30 dollars per shekel. The country's international reserves are $600. Foreign financial investors hold checking accounts in the country in the amount of 5,000 shekels.

  a. Suppose that foreign financial investors do not fear a devaluation of the shekel, and thus do not convert their shekel checking accounts into dollars. Can the shekel be maintained at its fixed value of 0.30 U.S. dollars for the next year?

  b. Now suppose that foreign financial investors come to expect a possible devaluation of the shekel to 0.25 U.S. dollars. Why should this possibility worry them?

  c. In response to their concern about devaluation, foreign financial investors withdraw all funds from their checking accounts and attempt to convert those shekels into dollars. What happens?

  d. Discuss why the foreign investors' forecast of devaluation can be considered a "self-fulfilling prophecy."

9. Eastland's currency is called the eastmark, and Westland's currency is called the westmark. In the market in which eastmarks and westmarks are traded for each other, the supply of and demand for eastmarks are given by

$$\text{Demand} = 25{,}000 - 5{,}000e - 50{,}000(r_E - r_W),$$
$$\text{Supply} = 18{,}500 + 8{,}000e - 50{,}000(r_E - r_W).$$

The nominal exchange rate e is measured as westmarks per eastmark, and r_E and r_W are the real interest rates prevailing in Eastland and Westland, respectively.

a. Explain why it makes economic sense for the two real interest rates to appear in the demand and supply equations in the way they do.

b. Initially, $r_E = r_W = 0.10$, or 10 percent. Find the fundamental value of the eastmark.

c. The Westlandian central bank grows concerned about inflation and raises Westland's real interest rate to 12 percent. What happens to the fundamental value of the eastmark?

d. Assume that the exchange rate is flexible and that Eastland does not change its real interest rate following the increase in Westland's real interest rate. Is the action of the Westlandian central bank likely to increase or reduce aggregate demand in Eastland? Discuss.

e. Now suppose that the exchange rate is fixed at the value you found in part b. After the action by the Westlandian central bank, what will the Eastlandian central bank have to do to keep its exchange rate from being overvalued? What effect will this action have on the Eastlandian economy?

f. In the context of this example, discuss the effect of fixed exchange rates on the ability of a country to run an independent monetary policy.

■ ANSWERS TO IN-CHAPTER EXERCISES ■

29.1 Answers will vary, depending on when the data are obtained.

29.2 The dollar price of the U.S. computer is $2,400, and each dollar is equal to 110 yen. Therefore the yen price of the U.S. computer is (110 yen/dollar) × ($2,400), or 264,000 yen. The price of the Japanese computer is 242,000 yen. Thus the conclusion that the Japanese model is cheaper does not depend on the currency in which the comparison is made.

29.3 Since the law of one price holds for gold, its price per ounce must be the same in New York and Stockholm:

$$\$300 = 2{,}500 \text{ kronor.}$$

Dividing both sides by 300, we get

$$\$1 = 8.33 \text{ kronor.}$$

So the exchange rate is 8.33 kronor per dollar.

29.4 A decline in U.S. GDP reduces consumer incomes and hence imports. As Americans are purchasing fewer imports, they supply fewer dollars to the foreign exchange market, so the supply curve for dollars shifts to the left. Reduced supply raises the equilibrium value of the dollar.

29.5 At a fixed value for the peso of 0.15 dollars, the demand for the peso equals $25{,}000 - 50{,}000(0.15) = 17{,}500$. The supply of the peso equals $17{,}600 + 24{,}000(0.15) = 21{,}200$. The quantity supplied at the official rate exceeds the quantity demanded by 3,700. Latinia will have to purchase 3,700 pesos each period, so its balance-of-payments deficit will equal 3,700 pesos, or $3{,}700 \times 0.15 = 555$ dollars. This balance-of-payments deficit is larger than we found in Example 29.6. We conclude that the greater the degree of overvaluation, the larger the country's balance-of-payments deficit is likely to be.

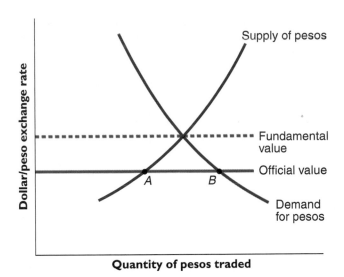

Quantity of pesos traded

29.6 The figure shows a situation in which the official value of the currency is *below* the fundamental value, as determined by the supply of and demand for the currency in the foreign exchange market, so the currency is undervalued. At the official value of the exchange rate, the quantity demanded of the domestic currency (point *B*) exceeds the quantity supplied (point *A*). To maintain the official value, the central bank must supply domestic currency to the foreign exchange market each period in the amount *AB*. In contrast to the case of an overvalued exchange rate, here the central bank is providing its own currency to the foreign exchange market and receiving foreign currencies in return.

Then central bank can print as much of its own currency as it likes, and so with an undervalued currency there is no danger of running out of international reserves. Indeed, the central bank's stock of international reserves increases in the amount *AB* each period, as it receives foreign currencies in exchange for the domestic currency it supplies.

GLOSSARY

A

Absolute advantage. One person has an absolute advantage over another if he or she takes fewer hours to perform a task than the other person.

Accounting profit. The difference between a firm's total revenue and its explicit costs.

Adverse selection. The pattern in which insurance tends to be purchased disproportionately by those who are most costly for companies to insure.

Aggregate demand (*AD*). Total planned spending on final goods and services.

Aggregate demand (*AD*) curve. Shows the relationship between aggregate demand and inflation; because short-run equilibrium output equals aggregate demand, the aggregate demand curve also shows the relationship between short-run equilibrium output and inflation; increases in inflation reduce aggregate demand and short-run equilibrium output, so the aggregate demand curve is downward-sloping.

Aggregate supply shock. Either an inflation shock or a shock to potential output; adverse aggregate supply shocks of both types reduce output and increase inflation.

Aggregation. The adding up of individual economic variables to obtain economywide totals.

Allocative function of price. Changes in prices direct resources away from overcrowded markets and toward markets that are underserved.

Appreciation. An increase in the value of a currency relative to other currencies.

Assets. Anything of value that one owns.

Asymmetric information. Situations in which buyers and sellers are not equally well informed about the characteristics of goods and services for sale in the marketplace.

Attainable point. Any combination of goods that can be produced using currently available resources.

Autarky. A situation in which a country is economically self-sufficient.

Automatic stabilizers. Provisions in the law that imply automatic increases in government spending or decreases in taxes when real output declines.

Autonomous expenditure. The portion of planned aggregate expenditure that is independent of output.

Average benefit. Total benefit of undertaking *n* units of an activity divided by *n*.

Average cost. Total cost of undertaking *n* units of an activity divided by *n*.

Average labor productivity. Output per employed worker.

Average total cost (ATC). Total cost divided by total output.

Average variable cost (AVC). Variable cost divided by total output.

B

Balance-of-payments deficit. The net decline in a country's stock of international reserves over a year.

Balance-of-payments surplus. The net increase in a country's stock of international reserves over a year.

Bank reserves. Cash or similar assets held by commercial banks for the purpose of meeting depositor withdrawals and payments.

Banking panic. An episode in which depositors, spurred by news or rumors of the imminent bankruptcy of one or more banks, rush to withdraw their deposits from the banking system.

Barrier to entry. Any force that prevents firms from entering a new market.

Barter. The direct trade of goods or services for other goods or services.

Basic elements of a game. The players, the strategies available to each player, and the payoffs each player receives for each possible combination of strategies.

Bequest saving. Saving done for the purpose of leaving an inheritance.

Better-than-fair gamble. A gamble whose expected value is positive.

Board of Governors. The leadership of the Fed, consisting of seven governors appointed by the President to staggered 14-year terms.

Bond. A legal promise to repay a debt, usually including both the principal amount and regular interest payments.

Boom. A particularly strong and protracted expansion.

Breakeven income level. Under a negative income tax, the level of before-tax income at which a family's tax liability exactly offsets its initial tax credit.

Buyer's reservation price. The largest dollar amount the buyer would be willing to pay for a good.

Buyer's surplus. The difference between the buyer's reservation price and the price he or she actually pays.

C

Capital gains. Increases in the value of existing assets.

Capital good. A long-lived good, which is itself produced and used to produce other goods and services.

Capital inflows. Purchases of domestic assets by foreign households and firms.

Capital losses. Decreases in the value of existing assets.

Capital outflows. Purchases of foreign assets by domestic households and firms.

Cartel. A coalition of firms that agrees to restrict output for the purpose of earning an economic profit.

Cash on the table. Economic metaphor for unexploited gain from exchange.

Change in demand. A shift of the entire demand curve.

Change in supply. A shift of the entire supply curve.

Change in the quantity demanded. A movement along the demand curve that occurs in response to a change in price.

Change in the quantity supplied. A movement along the supply curve that occurs in response to a change in price.

Closed economy. An economy that does not trade with the rest of the world.

Coase theorem. If at no cost people can negotiate the purchase and sale of the right to perform activities that cause externalities, they can always arrive at efficient solutions to the problems caused by externalities.

Collective good. A good or service that, to at least some degree, is nonrival but excludable.

Commitment device. A way of changing incentives so as to make otherwise empty threats or promises credible.

Commitment problem. A situation in which people cannot achieve their goals because of an inability to make credible threats or promises.

Comparative advantage. One person has a comparative advantage over another if his or her opportunity cost of performing a task is lower than the other person's opportunity cost.

Compensating wage differential. A difference in the wage rate—negative or positive—that reflects the attractiveness of a job's working conditions.

Complements. Two goods are complements in consumption if an increase in the price of one causes a leftward shift in the demand curve for the other.

Compound interest. The payment of interest not only on the original deposit but on all previously accumulated interest.

Constant (or parameter). A quantity that is fixed in value.

Constant returns to scale. A production process is said to have constant returns to scale if, when all inputs are changed by a given proportion, output changes by the same proportion.

Consumer price index (CPI). For any period, measures the cost in that period of a standard basket of goods and services relative to the cost of the same basket of goods and services in a fixed year, called the *base year*.

Consumer surplus. The economic surplus gained by the buyers of a product as measured by the cumulative difference between their respective reservation prices and the price they actually paid.

Consumption expenditure. Spending by households on goods and services, such as food, clothing, and entertainment.

Consumption function. The relationship between consumption spending and its determinants, such as disposable (after-tax) income.

Consumption possibilities. The combination of goods and services that a country's citizens might feasibly consume.

Contraction. *See* Recession.

Contractionary monetary policy. An increase in interest rates by the Fed, made with the intention of reducing an expansionary gap; also known as *monetary tightening*.

Contractionary policies. Government policy actions designed to reduce planned spending and output.

Cost-plus regulation. A method of regulation under which the regulated firm is permitted to charge a price equal to its explicit costs of production plus a markup to cover the opportunity cost of resources provided by the firm's owners.

Costly-to-fake principle. To communicate information credibly to a potential rival, a signal must be costly or difficult to fake.

Coupon payments. Regular interest payments made to the bondholder.

Coupon rate. The interest rate promised when a bond is issued.

Credible promise. A promise to take an action that is in the promiser's interest to keep.

Credible threat. A threat to take an action that is in the threatener's interest to carry out.

Cross-price elasticity of demand. The percentage by which the quantity demanded of the first good changes in response to a 1 percent change in the price of the second.

Crowding out. Government borrowing that leads private firms to cancel planned investment projects because of higher interest rates.

Customer discrimination. The willingness of consumers to pay more for a product produced by members of a favored group, even if the quality of the product is unaffected.

Cyclical unemployment. The extra unemployment that occurs during periods of recession.

D

Deadweight loss. The deadweight loss caused by a policy is the reduction in economic surplus that results from adoption of that policy.

Decision tree (or game tree). A diagram that describes the possible moves in a game in sequence and lists the payoffs that correspond to each possible combination of moves.

Deflating (a nominal quantity). The process of dividing a nominal quantity by a price index (such as the CPI) to express the quantity in real terms.

Deflation. A situation in which the prices of most goods and services are falling over time so that inflation is negative.

Demand curve. A curve or schedule showing the total quantity of a good that buyers wish to buy at each price.

Demand for money. The amount of wealth an individual or firm chooses to hold in the form of money.

Dependent variable. A variable in an equation whose value is determined by the value taken by another variable in the equation.

Deposit insurance. A system under which the government guarantees that depositors will not lose any money even if their bank goes bankrupt.

Depreciation. A decrease in the value of a currency relative to other currencies.

Depression. A particularly severe or protracted recession.

Devaluation. A reduction in the official value of a currency (in a fixed-exchange-rate system).

Diminishing returns to capital. If the amount of labor and other inputs employed is held constant, then the greater the amount of capital already in use, the less an additional unit of capital adds to production.

Diminishing returns to labor. If the amount of capital and other inputs in use is held constant, then the greater the quantity of labor already employed, the less each additional worker adds to production.

Disappearing political discourse. The theory that people who support a position may remain silent, because speaking out would create a risk of being misunderstood.

Discount rate. The interest rate that the Fed charges commercial banks to borrow reserves.

Discount window lending. The lending of reserves by the Federal Reserve to commercial banks.

Discouraged workers. People who say they would like to have a job but have not made an effort to find one in the past four weeks.

Disinflation. A substantial reduction in the rate of inflation.

Diversification. The practice of spreading one's wealth over a variety of different financial investments to reduce overall risk.

Dividend. A regular payment received by stockholders for each share that they own.

Dominant strategy. One that yields a higher payoff no matter what the other players in a game choose.

Dominated strategy. Any other strategy available to a player who has a dominant strategy.

Duration. The length of an unemployment spell.

E

Earned-income tax credit (EITC). A policy under which low-income workers receive credits on their federal income tax.

Economic loss. An economic profit that is less than zero.

Economic profit. The difference between a firm's total revenue and the sum of its explicit and implicit costs; also called *excess profit*.

Economic rent. That part of the payment for a factor of production that exceeds the owner's reservation price, the price below which the owner would not supply the factor.

Economic surplus. The economic surplus from taking any action is the benefit of taking the action minus its cost.

Economics. The study of how people make choices under conditions of scarcity and of the results of those choices for society.

Efficiency or economic efficiency. Condition that occurs when all goods and services are produced and consumed at their respective socially optimal levels.

Efficient (or Pareto-efficient). A situation is efficient if no change is possible that will help some people without harming others.

Efficient markets hypothesis. The theory that the current price of stock in a corporation reflects all relevant information about its current and future earnings prospects.

Efficient point. Any combination of goods for which currently available resources do not allow an increase in the production of one good without a reduction in the production of the other.

Efficient quantity. The efficient quantity of any good is the quantity that maximizes the economic surplus that results from producing and consuming the good.

Elastic. The demand for a good is elastic with respect to price if its price elasticity of demand is greater than 1.

Employer discrimination. An arbitrary preference by an employer for one group of workers over another.

Entrepreneurs. People who create new economic enterprises.

Equation. A mathematical expression that describes the relationship between two or more variables.

Equilibrium. A stable, balanced, or unchanging situation in which all forces at work within a system are canceled by others.

Equilibrium exchange rate. *See* **Fundamental value of the exchange rate.**

Equilibrium price and equilibrium quantity. The price and quantity of a good at the intersection of the supply and demand curves for the good.

Excess demand (or shortage). The difference between the quantity supplied and the quantity demanded when the price of a good lies below the equilibrium price; buyers are dissatisfied when there is excess demand.

Excess supply (or surplus). The difference between the quantity supplied and the quantity demanded when the price of a good exceeds the equilibrium price; sellers are dissatisfied when there is excess supply.

Expansion. A period in which the economy is growing at a rate significantly above normal.

Expansionary gap. A negative output gap, which occurs when actual output is higher than potential output.

Expansionary monetary policy. A reduction in interest rates by the Fed, made with the intention of reducing a recessionary gap; also known as *monetary easing*.

Expansionary policies. Government policy actions intended to increase planned spending and output.

Expected value of a gamble. The sum of the possible outcomes of the gamble multiplied by their respective probabilities.

Explicit costs. The actual payments a firm makes to its factors of production and other suppliers.

External benefit (or positive externality). A benefit of an activity received by people other than those who pursue the activity.

External cost (or negative externality). A cost of an activity that falls on people other than those who pursue the activity.

Externality. An external cost or benefit of an activity.

F

Factor of production. An input used in the production of a good or service.

Fair gamble. A gamble whose expected value is zero.

Federal funds rate. The interest rate that commercial banks charge each other for very short-term (usually overnight) loans; because the Fed frequently sets its policy in the form of a target for the federal funds rate, this rate is closely watched in financial markets.

Federal Open Market Committee (or FOMC). The committee that makes decisions concerning monetary policy.

Federal Reserve System (or Fed). The central bank of the United States; also called the *Fed*.

Final goods or services. Goods or services consumed by the ultimate user; because they are the end products of the production process, they are counted as part of GDP.

Financial intermediaries. Firms that extend credit to borrowers using funds raised from savers.

First-dollar insurance coverage. Insurance that pays all expenses generated by the insured activity.

Fiscal policy. Decisions that determine the government's budget, including the amount and composition of government expenditures and government revenues.

Fisher effect. The tendency for nominal interest rates to be high when inflation is high and low when inflation is low.

Fixed cost. A cost that does not vary with the level of an activity.

Fixed exchange rate. An exchange rate whose value is set by official government policy.

Fixed factor of production. An input whose quantity cannot be altered in the short run.

Flexible exchange rate. An exchange rate whose value is not officially fixed but varies according to the supply and demand for the currency in the foreign exchange market.

Flow. A measure that is defined per unit of time.

Foreign exchange market. The market on which currencies of various nations are traded for one another.

Fractional-reserve banking system. A banking system in which bank reserves are less than deposits so that the reserve-deposit ratio is less than 100 percent.

Free-rider problem. An incentive problem in which too little of a good or service is produced because nonpayers cannot be excluded from using it.

Frictional unemployment. The short-term unemployment associated with the process of matching workers with jobs.

Fundamental value of the exchange rate (or equilibrium exchange rate). The exchange rate that equates the quantities of the currency supplied and demanded in the foreign exchange market.

G

Game tree. *See* Decision tree.

Government budget deficit. The excess of government spending over tax collections $(G - T)$.

Government budget surplus. The excess of government tax collections over government spending $(T - G)$; the government budget surplus equals public saving.

Government purchases. Purchases by federal, state, and local governments of final goods and services; government purchases do *not* include *transfer payments,* which are payments made by the government in return for which no current goods or services are received, nor do they include interest paid on the government debt.

Gross domestic product (GDP). The market value of the final goods and services produced in a country during a given period.

H

Head tax. A tax that collects the same amount from every taxpayer.

Health maintenance organization (HMO). A group of physicians that provides health services to individuals and families for a fixed annual fee.

Human capital. An amalgam of factors such as education, training, experience, intelligence, energy, work habits, trustworthiness, initiative, and others that affect the value of a worker's marginal product.

Human capital theory. A theory of pay determination that says a worker's wage will be proportional to his or her stock of human capital.

Hurdle method of price discrimination. The practice by which a seller offers a discount to all buyers who overcome some obstacle.

Hyperinflation. A situation in which the inflation rate is extremely high.

I

Imperfectly competitive firm. A firm that has at least some control over the market price of its product.

Implicit costs. All the firm's opportunity costs of the resources supplied by the firm's owners.

Income effect. The change in the quantity demanded of a good that results because a change in the price of a good changes the buyer's purchasing power.

Income elasticity of demand. The percentage by which a good's quantity demanded changes in response to a 1 percent change in income.

Income-expenditure multiplier. The effect of a one-unit increase in autonomous aggregate demand on short-run equilibrium output.

Increasing returns to scale. A production process is said to have increasing returns to scale if, when all inputs are changed by a given proportion, output changes by more than that proportion; also called *economies of scale.*

Independent variable. A variable in an equation whose value determines the value taken by another variable in the equation.

Indexing. The practice of increasing a nominal quantity each period by an amount equal to the percentage increase in a specified price index. Indexing prevents the purchasing power of the nominal quantity from being eroded by inflation.

Induced aggregate demand. The portion of aggregate demand that is determined within the model.

Induced expenditure. The portion of planned aggregate expenditure that depends on output Y.

Inefficient point. Any combination of goods for which currently available resources enable an increase in the production of one good without a reduction in the production of the other.

Inelastic. The demand for a good is inelastic with respect to price if its price elasticity of demand is less than 1.

Inferior good. A good whose demand curve shifts leftward when the incomes of buyers increase.

Inflation shock. A sudden change in the normal behavior of inflation, unrelated to the nation's output gap.

In-kind transfer. A payment made not in the form of cash but in the form of a good or service.

Intermediate goods or services. Goods or services used up in the production of final goods and services and therefore not counted as part of GDP.

International capital flows. Purchases or sales of real and financial assets across international borders.

International reserves. Foreign currency assets held by a government for the purpose of purchasing the domestic currency in the foreign exchange market.

Investment. Spending by firms on final goods and services, primarily capital goods and housing.

Invisible hand theory. A theory stating that the actions of independent, self-interested buyers and sellers will often result in the most efficient allocation of resources.

L

Labor force. The total number of employed and unemployed people in the economy.

Labor union. A group of workers who bargain collectively with employers for better wages and working conditions.

Law of diminishing marginal utility. The tendency for the additional utility gained from consuming an additional unit of a good to diminish as consumption increases beyond some point.

Law of diminishing returns. A property of the relationship between the amount of a good or service produced and the amount of a variable factor required to produce it; the law says that when some factors of production are fixed, increased production of the good eventually requires ever larger increases in the variable factor.

Law of one price. If transportation costs are relatively small, the price of an internationally traded commodity must be the same in all locations.

Lemons model. George Akerlof's explanation of how asymmetric information tends to reduce the average quality of goods offered for sale.

Liabilities. The debts one owes.

Life-cycle saving. Saving to meet long-term objectives, such as retirement, college attendance, or the purchase of a home.

Logrolling. The practice whereby legislators support one another's legislative proposals.

Long run. A period of time of sufficient length that all the firm's factors of production are variable.

Long-run aggregate supply (*LRAS*) line. A vertical line showing the economy's potential output Y^*.

Long-run equilibrium. A situation in which actual output equals potential output and the inflation rate is stable; graphically, long-run equilibrium occurs when the *AD* curve, the *SRAS* line, and the *LRAS* line all intersect at a single point.

M

M1. Sum of currency outstanding and balances held in checking accounts.

M2. All the assets in M1 plus some additional assets that are usable in making payments but at greater cost or inconvenience than currency or checks.

Macroeconomic policies. Government actions designed to affect the performance of the economy as a whole.

Macroeconomics. The study of the performance of national economies and the policies that governments use to try to improve that performance.

Marginal benefit. The marginal benefit of an activity is the increase in total benefit that results from carrying out one additional unit of the activity.

Marginal cost. The marginal cost of an activity is the increase in total cost that results from carrying out one additional unit of the activity.

Marginal labor cost. The amount by which a monopsonist's total wage bill goes up if it hires an extra worker.

Marginal product of labor (*MP*). The additional output a firm gets by employing one additional unit of labor.

Marginal propensity to consume (*MPC*). The amount by which consumption rises when disposable income rises by \$1; we assume that $0 < MPC < 1$.

Marginal revenue. The change in a firm's total revenue that results from a one-unit change in output.

Marginal utility. The additional utility gained from consuming an additional unit of a good.

Market. The market for any good consists of all buyers or sellers of that good.

Market equilibrium. Occurs when all buyers and sellers are satisfied with their respective quantities at the market price.

Market power. A firm's ability to raise the price of a good without losing all its sales.

Means-tested. A benefit program is means-tested if its benefit level declines as the recipient earns additional income.

Medium of exchange. An asset used in purchasing goods and services.

Menu costs. The costs of changing prices.

Microeconomics. The study of individual choice under scarcity and its implications for the behavior of prices and quantities in individual markets.

Monetary policy. Determination of the nation's money supply.

Money. Any asset that can be used in making purchases.

Money demand curve. Shows the relationship between the aggregate quantity of money demanded M and the nominal interest rate i; because an increase in the nominal interest rate increases the opportunity cost of holding money, which reduces the quantity of money demanded, the money demand curve slopes down.

Monopolistically competitive firm. One of a large number of firms that produce slightly differentiated products that are reasonably close substitutes for one another.

Monopsony. A market with only a single buyer.

Moral hazard. The tendency of people to expend less effort protecting those goods that are insured against theft or damage.

Multiplier. *See* **Income-expenditure multiplier.**

Mutual fund. A financial intermediary that sells shares in itself to the public, then uses the funds raised to buy a wide variety of financial assets.

N

Nash equilibrium. Any combination of strategies in which each player's strategy is his or her best choice, given the other players' strategies.

National saving. The saving of the entire economy, equal to GDP less consumption expenditures and government purchases of goods and services, or $Y - C - G$.

Natural monopoly. A monopoly that results from economies of scale (increasing returns to scale).

Natural rate of unemployment, u^*. The part of the total unemployment rate that is attributable to frictional and structural unemployment; equivalently, the unemployment rate that prevails when cyclical unemployment is zero, so the economy has neither a recessionary nor an expansionary output gap.

Negative externality. *See* **External cost.**

Negative income tax. A system under which the government would grant every citizen a cash payment each year, financed by an additional tax on earned income.

Net exports. Exports minus imports.

Nominal exchange rate. The rate at which two currencies can be traded for each other.

Nominal GDP. A measure of GDP in which the quantities produced are valued at current-year prices; nominal GDP measures the *current dollar value* of production.

Nominal interest rate. The annual percentage increase in the nominal value of a financial asset; also known as the *market interest rate*.

Nominal price. Absolute price of a good in dollar terms.

Nominal quantity. A quantity that is measured in terms of its current dollar value.

Nonexcludable good. A good that is difficult, or costly, to exclude nonpayers from consuming.

Nonrival good. A good whose consumption by one person does not diminish its availability for others.

Normal good. A good whose demand curve shifts rightward when the incomes of buyers increase.

Normal profit. The opportunity cost of the resources supplied by the firm's owners; Normal profit = Accounting profit − Economic profit.

Normative analysis. Addresses the question of whether a policy *should* be used; normative analysis inevitably involves the values of the person doing the analysis.

O

Okun's law. States that each extra percentage point of cyclical unemployment is associated with about a 2 percentage point increase in the output gap, measured in relation to potential output.

Oligopolist. A firm that produces a product for which only a few rival firms produce close substitutes.

100 percent reserve banking. A situation in which banks' reserves equal 100 percent of their deposits.

Open economy. An economy that trades with other countries.

Open-market operations. Open-market purchases and open-market sales.

Open-market purchase. The purchase of government bonds from the public by the Fed for the purpose of increasing the supply of bank reserves and the money supply.

Open-market sale. The sale by the Fed of government bonds to the public for the purpose of reducing bank reserves and the money supply.

Opportunity cost. The opportunity cost of an activity is the value of the next-best alternative that must be forgone to undertake the activity.

Optimal combination of goods. The affordable combination that yields the highest total utility.

Output gap, $Y^* - Y$. The difference between the economy's potential output and its actual output at a point in time.

Overvalued exchange rate. An exchange rate that has an officially fixed value greater than its fundamental value.

P

Parameter. *See* **Constant.**

Pareto-efficient. *See* **Efficient.**

Participation rate. The percentage of the working-age population in the labor force (that is, the percentage that is either employed or looking for work).

Payoff matrix. A table that describes the payoffs in a game for each possible combination of strategies.

Peak. The beginning of a recession, the high point of economic activity prior to a downturn.

Perfect hurdle. One that completely segregates buyers whose reservation prices lie above some threshold from others whose reservation prices lie below it, imposing no cost on those who jump the hurdle.

Perfectly competitive market. A market in which no individual supplier has significant influence on the market price of the product.

Perfectly discriminating monopolist. A firm that charges each buyer exactly his or her reservation price.

Perfectly elastic demand. The demand for a good is perfectly elastic with respect to price if its price elasticity of demand is infinite.

Perfectly elastic supply curve. A supply curve whose elasticity with respect to price is infinite.

Perfectly inelastic demand. The demand for a good is perfectly inelastic with respect to price if its price elasticity of demand is zero.

Perfectly inelastic supply curve. A supply curve whose elasticity with respect to price is zero.

Personal Responsibility Act. The 1996 federal law that transferred responsibility for welfare programs from the federal level to the state level and placed a five-year lifetime limit on payment of AFDC benefits to any given recipient.

Planned aggregate expenditure (*PAE*). Total planned spending on goods and services.

Policy reaction function. Describes how the action a policymaker takes depends on the state of the economy.

Pork barrel spending. A public expenditure that is larger than the total benefit it creates but that is favored by a legislator because his or her constituents benefit from the expenditure by more than their share of the resulting extra taxes.

Portfolio allocation decision. The decision about the forms in which to hold one's wealth.

Positional arms control agreement. An agreement in which contestants attempt to limit mutually offsetting investments in performance enhancement.

Positional arms race. A series of mutually offsetting investments in performance enhancement that is stimulated by a positional externality.

Positional externality. Occurs when an increase in one person's performance reduces the expected reward of another's in situations in which reward depends on relative performance.

Positive analysis. Addresses the economic consequences of a particular event or policy, not whether those consequences are desirable.

Positive externality. *See* **External benefit.**

Potential output, Y^*. The amount of output (real GDP) that an economy can produce when using its resources, such as capital and labor, at normal rates; also known as *potential GDP* or *full-employment output*.

Poverty threshold. The level of income below which the federal government classifies a family as poor.

Precautionary saving. Saving for protection against unexpected setbacks, such as the loss of a job or a medical emergency.

Present value. When the annual interest rate is r, the present value (*PV*) of a payment M to be received T years from now is the amount that would have to be deposited today at an annual interest rate r to generate a balance of M after T years: $PV = M/(1 + r)^T$.

Price ceiling. A maximum allowable price, specified by law.

Price discrimination. The practice of charging different buyers different prices for essentially the same good or service.

Price elasticity of demand. The percentage change in the quantity demanded of a good or service that results from a 1 percent change in its price.

Price elasticity of supply. The percentage change in the quantity supplied that will occur in response to a 1 percent change in the price of a good or service.

Price floor. A law or regulation that guarantees that suppliers will receive at least a specified amount for their product.

Price index. A measure of the average price of a given class of goods or services relative to the price of the same goods and services in a base year.

Price level. A measure of the overall level of prices at a particular point in time as measured by a price index such as the CPI.

Price setter. A firm with at least some latitude to set its own price.

Price taker. A firm that has no influence over the price at which it sells its product.

Principal amount. The amount originally lent.

Prisoner's dilemma. A game in which each player has a dominant strategy, and when each plays it, the resulting payoffs are smaller than if each had played a dominated strategy.

Private saving. The saving of the private sector of the economy is equal to the after-tax income of the private sector minus consumption expenditures $(Y - T - C)$; private saving can be further broken down into household saving and business saving.

Producer surplus. The economic surplus gained by the sellers of a product as measured by the cumulative difference between the price received and their respective reservation prices.

Production possibilities curve. A graph that describes the maximum amount of one good that can be produced for every possible level of production of the other good.

Profit. The total revenue a firm receives from the sale of its product minus all costs—explicit and implicit—incurred in producing it.

Profit-maximizing firm. A firm whose primary goal is to maximize the difference between its total revenues and total costs.

Profitable firm. A firm whose total revenue exceeds its total cost.

Progressive tax. One in which the proportion of income paid in taxes rises as income rises.

Proportional income tax. One under which all taxpayers pay the same proportion of their incomes in taxes.

Protectionism. The view that free trade is injurious and should be restricted.

Public good. A good or service that, to at least some degree, is both nonrival and nonexcludable.

Public saving. The saving of the government sector is equal to net tax payments minus government purchases $(T - G)$.

Purchasing power parity (PPP). The theory that nominal exchange rates are determined as necessary for the law of one price to hold.

Pure commons good. One for which nonpayers cannot easily be excluded and for which each unit consumed by one person means one less unit available for others.

Pure monopoly. The only supplier of a unique product with no close substitutes.

Pure private good. One for which nonpayers can easily be excluded and for which each unit consumed by one person means one less unit available for others.

Pure public good. A good or service that, to a high degree, is both nonrival and nonexcludable.

Q

Quantity equation. Money times velocity equals nominal GDP: $M \times V = P \times Y$.

Quota. A legal limit on the quantity of a good that may be imported.

R

Rate of inflation. The annual percentage rate of change in the price level, as measured, for example, by the CPI.

Rational person. Someone with well-defined goals who tries to fulfill those goals as best he or she can.

Rationing function of price. Changes in prices that distribute scarce goods to those consumers who value them most highly.

Real exchange rate. The price of the average domestic good or service *relative* to the price of the average foreign good or service, when prices are expressed in terms of a common currency.

Real GDP. A measure of GDP in which the quantities produced are valued at the prices in a base year rather than at current prices; real GDP measures the actual *physical volume* of production.

Real interest rate. The annual percentage increase in the purchasing power of a financial asset; the real interest rate on any asset equals the nominal interest rate on that asset minus the inflation rate.

Real price. Dollar price of a good relative to the average dollar price of all other goods and services.

Real quantity. A quantity that is measured in physical terms—for example, in terms of quantities of goods and services.

Real wage. The wage paid to workers measured in terms of real purchasing power; the real wage for any given period is calculated by dividing the nominal (dollar) wage by the CPI for that period.

Recession (or contraction). A period in which the economy is growing at a rate significantly below normal.

Recessionary gap. A positive output gap, which occurs when potential output exceeds actual output $(Y^* > Y)$.

Regressive tax. A tax under which the proportion of income paid in taxes declines as income rises.

Relative price. The price of a specific good or service *in comparison to* the prices of other goods and services.

Rent-seeking. The socially unproductive efforts of people or firms to win a prize.

Repeated prisoner's dilemma. A standard prisoner's dilemma that confronts the same players repeatedly.

Reservation price. The highest price someone is willing to pay to obtain any good or service, or the lowest payment someone would accept for giving up a good or performing a service.

Reserve requirements. Set by the Fed, the minimum values of the ratio of bank reserves to bank deposits that commercial banks are allowed to maintain.

Reserve-deposit ratio. Bank reserves divided by deposits.

Revaluation. An increase in the official value of a currency (in a fixed-exchange-rate system).**Risk-averse person.** Someone who would refuse any fair gamble.

Risk premium. The rate of return that financial investors require to hold risky assets minus the rate of return on safe assets.**Run.** *See* Slope.

Risk-averse person. Someone who would refuse any fair gamble.

Risk-neutral person. Someone who would accept any gamble that is fair or better.

Run. *See* **Slope.**

S

Saving. Current income minus spending on current needs.

Saving rate. Saving divided by income.

Seller's reservation price. The smallest dollar amount for which a seller would be willing to sell an additional unit, generally equal to marginal cost.

Seller's surplus. The difference between the price received by the seller and his or her reservation price.

Short run. A period of time sufficiently short that at least some of the firm's factors of production are fixed.

Short-run aggregate supply (*SRAS*) line. A horizontal line showing the current rate of inflation, as determined by past expectations and pricing decisions.

Short-run equilibrium. A situation in which inflation equals the value determined by past expectations and pricing decisions, and output equals the level of short-run equilibrium output that is consistent with that inflation rate; graphically, short-run equilibrium occurs at the intersection of the *AD* curve and the *SRAS* line.

Short-run equilibrium output. The level of output at which output *Y* equals aggregate demand *AD*; the level of output that prevails during the period in which prices are predetermined.

Shortage. *See* **Excess demand.**

Skill-biased technological change. Technological change that affects the marginal products of higher-skilled workers differently from those of lower-skilled workers.

Slope. In a straight line, the ratio of the vertical distance the straight line travels between any two points (*rise*) to the corresponding horizontal distance (*run*).

Socially optimal quantity. The quantity of a good that results in the maximum possible economic surplus from producing and consuming the good.

Speculative attack. A massive selling of domestic currency assets by financial investors.

Stabilization policies. Government policies that are used to affect aggregate demand, with the objective of eliminating output gaps.

Statistical discrimination. The practice of making judgments about the quality of people, goods, or services based on the characteristics of the groups to which they belong.

Stock. A measure that is defined *at a point in time*.

Stock (or equity). A claim to partial ownership of a firm.

Store of value. An asset that serves as a means of holding wealth.

Structural policy. Government policies aimed at changing the underlying structure, or institutions, of the nation's economy.

Structural unemployment. The long-term and chronic unemployment that exists even when the economy is producing at a normal rate.

Substitutes. Two goods are substitutes in consumption if an increase in the price of one causes a rightward shift in the demand curve for the other.

Substitution effect. The change in the quantity demanded of a good that results because buyers switch to or from substitutes when the price of the good changes.

Sunk cost. A cost that is beyond recovery at the moment a decision must be made.

Supply curve. A curve or schedule showing the total quantity of a good that sellers wish to sell at each price.

Surplus. *See* **Excess supply.**

T

Tariff. A tax imposed on an imported good.

Time value of money. The fact that a given dollar amount today is equivalent to a larger dollar amount in the future, because the money can be invested in an interest-bearing account in the meantime.

Tit-for-tat. A strategy for the repeated prisoner's dilemma in which players cooperate on the first move, then mimic their partner's last move on each successive move.

Total cost. The sum of all payments made to the firm's fixed and variable factors of production.

Total economic surplus. The sum of all the individual economic surpluses gained by buyers and sellers who participate in the market.

Total expenditure = Total revenue. The dollar amount consumers spend on a product is equal to the dollar amount sellers receive.

Total revenue. *See* **Total expenditure.**

Total surplus. The difference between the buyer's reservation price and the seller's reservation price.

Trade balance (or net exports). The value of a country's exports less the value of its imports in a particular period (quarter or year).

Trade deficit. When imports exceed exports, the difference between the value of a country's imports and the value of its exports in a given period.

Trade surplus. When exports exceed imports, the difference between the value of a country's exports and the value of its imports in a given period.

Tragedy of the commons. The tendency for a resource that has no price to be used until its marginal benefit falls to zero.

Transfer payments. Payments the government makes to the public for which it receives no current goods or services in return.

Trough. The end of a recession, the low point of economic activity prior to a recovery.

U

Ultimatum bargaining game. One in which the first player has the power to confront the second player with a take-it-or-leave-it offer.

Unattainable point. Any combination of goods that cannot be produced using currently available resources.

Undervalued exchange rate. An exchange rate that has an officially fixed value less than its fundamental value.

Unemployment rate. The number of unemployed people divided by the labor force.

Unemployment spell. A period during which an individual is continuously unemployed.

Unit elastic. The demand for a good is unit elastic with respect to price if its price elasticity of demand is equal to 1.

Unit of account. A basic measure of economic value.

Utilitarianism. A moral theory in which the right course of action is the one that results in the highest total utility.

V

Value added. For any firm, the market value of its product or service minus the cost of inputs purchased from other firms.

Value of marginal product of labor. The dollar value of the additional output a firm gets by employing one additional unit of labor.

Variable. A quantity that is free to take a range of different values.

Variable cost. A cost that varies with the level of an activity.

Variable factor of production. An input whose quantity can be altered in the short run.

Velocity. A measure of the speed at which money circulates, or equivalently, the value of a transaction completed in a period of time divided by the stock of money required to make those transactions; numerically, $V = (P \times Y)/M$, where V is velocity, $P \times Y$ is nominal GDP, and M is the money supply whose velocity is being measured.

Vertical intercept. The value taken by the dependent variable when the independent variable equals zero.

W

Wealth. The value of assets minus liabilities.

Wealth effect. The tendency of changes in asset prices to affect households' wealth and thus their spending on consumer goods.

Winner-take-all labor market. One in which small differences in human capital translate into large differences in pay.

Worker mobility. The movement of workers between jobs, firms, and industries.

Workers' compensation. A government insurance system that provides benefits to workers who are injured on the job.

World price. The price at which a good or service is traded on international markets.